Dear Professor Hodge,

(Ezekiel 33:11) "I have no pleasure in the death of the wicked; but that the wicked turn from his way, and live."

Take care,

Andy Bostom

ADVANCE PRAISE FOR *THE LEGACY OF ISLAMIC ANTISEMITISM*

"Dr. Andrew Bostom has written and edited the definitive book on Muslim antisemitism. Bostom demolishes, once and for all, the myth that Muslim antisemitism is a twentieth-century European import, conclusively demonstrating that its grim history is as old as Islam itself. This is a priceless, indispensable, and authoritative resource that is being made available when it is most needed."

—Richard L. Rubenstein, President Emeritus, University of Bridgeport; Lawton Distinguished Professor of Religion Emeritus, Florida State University; and author of *After Auschwitz*, *The Cunning of History*, and *Jihad and Genocide: The Nuclear Dimension* (forthcoming)

"It has long been a staple of anti-Israel propaganda that Muslims have never had anything against Judaism or Jews but only against Zionism and Zionists. Andrew Bostom debunks this spurious claim by exposing a deep and pervasive anti-Jewish bigotry dating to Islam's earliest days, and indeed to the Muslim Prophet Muhammad himself. Small wonder that some of the hoariest and most bizarre themes of European antisemitism should have struck a responsive chord when they made their way into the Islamic and Arab worlds over the course of the centuries, turning them into the most prolific producers of antisemitic ideas and attitudes in today's world."

—Efraim Karsh, Head of Mediterranean Studies, University of London, and author of *Empires of the Sand: The Struggle for Mastery in the Middle East 1789–1923* and *Islamic Imperialism: A History*

"Andrew Bostom has performed a rare and welcome service with the publication of *The Legacy of Islamic Antisemitism*. He has patiently assembled an enormous body of primary sources that documents the brutal Jew-hatred that has characterized much of Islamic culture from its earliest days. The book's importance goes far beyond the historical record, for it shows convincingly that the fledgling movement—and widespread Western hopes—to reform Islam, and imbue it with anything approaching true toleration, faces enormous obstacles."

—Dr. Michael Ledeen, author of *Universal Fascism* and *The Iranian Time Bomb*, and resident scholar at the American Enterprise Institute

"For years scholars focused almost exclusively on the roots of Christian and secular antisemitism to understand the animosity targeted toward Jews in Western civilization during more than two millennia. But there's a parallel tradition, one far more explosive today: Islamic antisemitism and anti-Zionism. It's crucial that we don't shy away from analyzing its misconceptions, its history and strategics. Andrew Bostom offers a wide-ranging sampler of readings to start the task, from the Qur'an itself and the early biographers of Muhammad to the premodern theologians and jurists, and onward to the major articulators of discontent in the modern era. His eye-opening anthology should become an essential resource."

—Ilan Stavans, Lewis-Sebring Professor in Latin American and Latino Culture and Five-College 40th Anniversary Professor, Amherst College, and author of *The Disappearance: A Novella and Stories* and editor of *The Schocken Book of Modern Sephardic Literature* and *The Scroll and the Cross: 1,000 Years of Jewish-Hispanic Literature*

"Andrew Bostom's new book, *The Legacy of Islamic Antisemitism*, demolishes the fashionable but dangerous myth that there was no antisemitism in the Muslim world until the Middle East became 'infected' with it by Nazi propaganda in the 1930s. As in his earlier work, *The Legacy of Jihad*, Dr. Bostom has rendered an invaluable service to those who are interested in understanding the historical realities of Islam, free from the distortions of political correctness. Both books should be mandatory reading for those who wish to grasp the enormous challenge that Islam poses to the free and open societies of the West."

—Lee Harris, author of *Civilization and Its Enemies: The Next Stage of History* and *The Suicide of Reason: Radical Islam's Challenge to the West*

"Andrew Bostom's brilliant and extensive research and documentation put an end to the myth of Muslim tolerance of Jews often expressed when we say, 'We don't hate Jews, we hate Israel.' The question now is, are we going to face uncomfortable truths and end our denial or continue the unspeakable hatred?"

—Nonie Darwish, author of *Now They Call Me Infidel*

"*The Legacy of Islamic Antisemitism* is the most comprehensive analysis of the anti-Jewish hatred that has been entrenched in Islamic culture and politics since the advent of Islam under Muhammad. This book is a must read for anyone who wants to understand what underlies the incessant Muslim animus against Jews and the Jewish State of Israel, in particular."

—Brigitte Gabriel, author of *Because They Hate*

The Legacy of
Islamic Antisemitism

The Legacy of Islamic Antisemitism

From Sacred Texts to Solemn History

Edited by Andrew G. Bostom

Foreword by Ibn Warraq

Prometheus Books

59 John Glenn Drive
Amherst, New York 14228–2119

Published 2008 by Prometheus Books

Inquiries should be addressed to
Prometheus Books
59 John Glenn Drive
Amherst, New York 14228–2119
VOICE: 716–691–0133, ext. 210
FAX: 716–691–0137
WWW.PROMETHEUSBOOKS.COM

12 11 10 09 08   5 4 3 2 1

Library of Congress Cataloging-in-Publication Data

The legacy of Islamic antisemitism : from sacred texts to solemn history / edited by Andrew G. Bostom / foreword by Ibn Warraq.
    p. cm.
Includes bibliographical references and indexes.
ISBN 978-1-59102-554-2 (hardcover : alk. paper)
  1. Jews in the Koran. 2. Jews in the Hadith. 3. Antisemitism—Islamic countries. 4. Islam—Relations—Judaism. 5. Judaism—Relations—Islam.

BP134.J4 L45 2007
297.2/82—dc22
                                                                    2007038274

Every attempt has been made to trace accurate ownership of copyrighted material in this book. Errors and omissions will be corrected in subsequent editions, provided that notification is sent to the publishers.

Printed in the United States of America on acid-free paper

Contents

Acknowledgments

Only the boundless patience and great personal sacrifice of my best friend and beloved wife, Leah, allowed me to complete this book. I am also indebted to the guidance, support, and inspiration I received from mentors and dear friends, most notably: Ibn Warraq, Alyssa Lappen, Diana West, Bat Ye'or, David Littman, Hugh Fitzgerald, Robert Spencer, Hillel Stavis, Jerry Gordon, Rachel Ehrenfeld, and Charles Jacobs. Gifted translators made invaluable contributions to this compendium: Dr. Michael Schub, Rivkah Fishman, Susan Emanuel, Michael J. Miller, Colin Meade, "UL," and Martine Chauvet. Sanity-sparing technical assistance with the manuscript was provided by Alyssa Lappen (double duty!), Diann Sullivan, and Allie Marshall.

The book is dedicated to my beautiful, rapidly growing children, Esther and Yonah, and my mother, Rifka.

Introductory Quotes

The nation of Ishmael . . . persecute us severely and devise ways to harm us and to debase us. . . . None has matched it in debasing and humiliating us. None has been able to reduce us as they have. We have done as our sages of blessed memory instructed us, bearing the lies and absurdities of Ishmael. We listen, but remain silent. . . . In spite of all this, we are not spared from the ferocity of their wickedness, and their outbursts at any time. On the contrary, the more we suffer and choose to conciliate them, the more they choose to act belligerently toward us.

—Maimonides, *Epistle to the Jews of Yemen* (1172)

[T]he Jews are said never to pass under the triumphal arch of Titus in Rome. But if they were to react in a similar way to the many bitter memories they have of their treatment in Muslim countries, I dare not guess where they would find a route not closed by like prohibitions.

—Abbe Goddard, *Le Maroc* (1858)

"The Koran, of course became a mine of anti-Jewish passages. The hadith did not lag behind. Popular preachers used and embellished such material."

—Moshe Perlmann, introduction to Samau'al al-Maghribi's *Ifham al-Yahud* (*Silencing the Jews*) (1964)

And humiliation and wretchedness were stamped upon them and they were visited with wrath from Allah. That was because they disbelieved in Allah's revelations and slew the prophets wrongfully. That was for their disobedience and transgression.

—Qur'an 2:61

[A]bout His words "and humiliation and wretchedness were stamped upon them," 'These are the Jews of the Children of Israel.' I said: 'Are they the Copts of Egypt?' He said: "What have the Copts of Egypt to do with this? No, by God, they are not; but they are the Jews, the Children of Israel." . . . By "and slew the prophets wrongfully," He means that they used to kill the Messengers of God without God's leave, denying their messages and rejecting their prophethood.

—Tabari (d. 923), great early Muslim historian and Qur'anic commentator on verse 2:61, above

Love of the Prophet requires hatred of the Jews.

—al-Maghili, prominent theologian in Morocco, late fifteenth century, from a verse he composed

Whenever a Jew is killed, it is for the benefit of Islam.

—Sirhindi, important Indian Sufi theologian of the early seventeenth century

[The] Koran describes the Jews with their own particular degenerate characteristics, i.e. killing the prophets of Allah, corrupting His words by putting them in the wrong places, consuming the people's wealth frivolously, refusal to distance themselves from the evil they do, and other ugly characteristics caused by their deep-rooted lasciviousness . . . only a minority of the Jews keep their word. . . . [A]ll Jews are not the same. The good ones become Muslims, the bad ones do not.

—Muhammad Sayyid Tantawi, grand imam of Al-Azhar University, Cairo, 1996–present, from his *Banu Isra'il fi al-Qur'an wa al-Sunna* (*Jews in the Koran and the Traditions*) (1986)

Read history and you will understand that the Jews of yesterday are the evil fathers of the Jews of today, who are evil offspring, infidels, distorters of [others'] words, calf-worshippers, prophet-murderers, prophecy-deniers . . . the scum of the human race whom Allah cursed and turned into apes and pigs. . . . These are the Jews, an ongoing continuum of deceit, obstinacy, licentiousness, evil, and corruption.

—Abd Al-Rahman Al-Sudayyis, imam and preacher at the Al-Haraam mosque—the most important mosque in Mecca—April 19, 2002

Up to the very first day that I immigrated to America, I used to believe that Jewish people were not human creatures, that they had different features, different voices than the human race. Unfortunately this is the way I was raised.

—Wafa Sultan, March 13, 2006

I have a confession to make. If you are Jewish. . . . I used to hate you. I hated you because I thought you were responsible for the war which took my father from me for so long. . . . When we had no water, I thought you closed the tap. . . . If my mother was unkind to me, I knew you were definitely behind it. If and when I failed an exam, I knew it was your fault. You are by nature evil, you had evil powers and you used them to evil ends. Learning to hate you was easy. Unlearning it was difficult.

—Ayaan Hirsi Ali, May 4, 2006

A Note on the Cover Art*

The cover art is a reproduction of Alfred Dehodencq's *Execution d'une juive au Maroc* (Execution of a Moroccan Jewess) painted in 1860. Dehodencq was a French painter (b. April 23, 1822, in Paris; d. January 2, 1882, in Paris), known for his images of Spanish and Arab life, purportedly influenced by a "youthful obsession with the romantic writings of Byron and Chateaubriand."[1] Preferring color as a means of expression, Dehodencq's palette has been described as "rich, often gaudy," and his handling "robust and sketchlike."[2] Dramatic scenes of violence, despotism, and fanaticism dominate his portrayals of Morocco.

Dehodencq's *Execution of a Moroccan Jewess* is based upon the actual execution of a Jewess from Tangier, Morocco—Sol Hachuel—believed to have occurred in 1834.[3] Falsely accused of having become a Muslim, upon adamantly and steadfastly maintaining her Jewish faith ("A Jewess I was born, a Jewess I wish to die),"[4] the seventeen-year-old Sol[5] was beheaded publicly for this contrived "apostasy" from Islam.

A detailed near-contemporary account of Sol Hachuel's heroic martyrdom—based on eyewitness interviews[6]—was published in 1837 by Eugenio Maria Romero. The following is a summary of Romero's narrative.[7]

The younger of two children of Chaim and Simcha Hachuel, Sol was described as a beautiful young woman.[8] Her father was a merchant of very modest means, but also a highly educated man who conducted Talmudic study groups in the Hachuel household. Through these community gatherings, Sol acquired enough Jewish religious instruction to develop an unyielding confidence in her own Judaic beliefs. Typical of families that were not prosperous, Sol's mother kept house, leaving her daughter practically to herself. Sol developed a friendship with a Muslim woman, Tahra de Mesoodi. Apparently Tahra entertained the pious Muslim hope—a particularly important impetus under the code of Maliki Islamic law predominant in Morocco—to convert infidels to Islam.[9] Romero elaborates:

> It being a precept of the Alcoran [Qur'an], the Arabs consider the conversion of a heretic (for such they deem all those of a different faith) to their belief as a most meritorious act; they hesitate not at the means they employ to make such conquests, when opportunities offer. The artful friend, when in conversation with the young Jewess, but as if undesignedly, never failed to boast of the excellence of her religion, the benefits it offered to its professors, and the esteem those who embraced it acquired from all true believers; but the amiable and innocent Sol,[10] of a different disposition to her wily neighbor, listened to her only with pity, for firmly fixed in her belief, and an enthusiast of the laws in which she had been born, she attributed to excess of religious zeal, the constant eulogiums that the Mooress bestowed on the dogmas of her faith.[11]

Based solely on Tahra's denunciation of Sol to the Basha Arbi Esudio—which included the false claim of Sol's conversion to (and subsequent reversion from) Islam, an allegation punishable by death (for apostasy) under Islamic law—the Basha had Sol brought before him.[12] Romero includes the following note regarding the court of Tangier:

> The Governors of Tangier, when administering justice, sit at their doors, accompanied by their Secretaries. The soldiers, charged with the police and execution of their orders, are about the same place with drawn swords and sticks; the accused is placed kneeling before the Governor; in this mode, justice is executed.

Sol told the Basha forthrightly she had never intended to convert to Islam:

> You have been deceived, Sir. . . . I never pronounced such words: she [Tahra] proposed it [conversion] to me, but I did not consent.[13]

Then, in the first of three iterations, Sol pronounced the memorable line that became her epitaph: "A Jewess I was born, a Jewess I wish to die."[14]

The Basha Arbi Esudio attempts to assure Sol's conversion to Islam by enticement and coercion. He offered her protection from parental interference, wealth (in the forms of silk and gold), and "happiness," but to no avail. Arbi Esudio then threatened the obstinate Sol for having adopted Islam and "reverted" to Judaism:

> I will load you with chains. . . . I will have you torn piece-meal by wild beasts, you shall not see the light of day, you shall perish of hunger, and experience the rigor of my vengeance and indignation, in having provoked the anger of the Prophet.[15]

Sol replied:

> I will patiently bear the weight of your chains; I will give my limbs to be torn piece-meal by wild beasts; I will renounce for ever the light of day: I will perish of hunger: and when all the evils of life are

---

*Cover art reproduced from the original painting in Musée d'Art d'Histoire du Judaïsme, Paris.

accumulated on me by your orders, I will smile at your indignation, and the anger of your Prophet: since neither he, nor you have been able to overcome a weak female! It is clear that Heaven is not to auspicious to making proselytes to your faith.[16]

A further enraged Arbi Esudio then declared:

Atrocious blasphemer! . . . you have profaned the name I revere; you are unworthy of my consideration; I will bury you in a secret dungeon, and smile when I see you drink of the cup of bitterness. Convey this Jewess to prison! . . . Let her feel the effect of my vengeance, by being placed in the darkest cell![17]

Dispatched to a lightless dungeon, Sol was detained incommunicado, with an iron collar around her neck and chains on both her hands and feet. Bribery alone secured her modest favors from the jailers.[18] Her utterly distraught parents, acting in a manner that became customary for Moroccan Jews, devoid of political rights and security, appealed to a European diplomat to obtain Sol's release.[19] Don Jose Rico,[20] the Spanish vice consul, made a vigorous but ultimately unsuccessful effort to free Sol.

The Basha ordered Sol to be sent to Fez (the imperial capital) to allow the sultan to decide her fate. Arbi Esudio also required that her hapless parents pay forty dollars for Sol's transport to Fez, as well as the fee for her execution.[21] Romero's account of these events includes the following details:

The Governor [Basha] summoned [Chaim] Hachuel before him and communicated the mandate of the Emperor; at the same time telling him that his daughter would depart for the Court on the following morning, and that within two hours he must bring him forty dollars for the expense of the journey. . . . The trembling and afflicted parent bewailed this sentence as the height of his misfortune, but the ferocious tyrant showed not the least compassion; he declared the impossibility of procuring the money in so short a period; the order was repeated, and he was told that if it was brought a single minute beyond the time, he should receive 500 blows of the bastinado.

The unhappy Hebrew resigned himself to fulfill, as best he could, the command of the Governor; but on his knees entreated that, since the departure of his unfortunate daughter could not be avoided, he might be permitted to accompany her. "I prohibit under pain of death," answered the proud Arab, "that neither you nor any of your family, nor any Jew travel within ten leagues of this impious girl." Having pronounced this in a most haughty tone, he ordered from his presence the afflicted father.[22]

Romero also notes:

[I]f a person is condemned to the bastinado, after having received it, he has to pay the executioner whatever he chooses to demand for inflicting it.[23]

Fortunately the impoverished Chaim Hachuel received forty dollars from Don Jose Rico, thus avoiding the brutal punishment of five hundred blows of the bastinado for nonpayment. Serels observes in his 1991 analysis, "A Jew at this time had to pay even for his own death."[24]

Romero subsequently describes how Sol was bound and transported by mule to Fez:

The most obdurate heart would have felt moved at so unfeeling an act. Sol was suddenly seated on the mule; her feet fettered, and tied with a strong cord which fastened round her hands, hurting her delicate flesh, a thousand turns and twists around her body fastened by the same rope to the trappings of the beast.[25]

In Fez, the sultan decided to have the Cadi[26] prosecute and judge Sol. The Cadi summoned the Chachamim (Jewish sages), who (in conjunction with a concerted effort by the Jewish community) attempted to spare her life.[27] Informed by the Cadi that Sol would be beheaded if she did not profess Islam, and that the overall Jewish community might be endangered, the Chachamim tried to persuade Sol to convert. Sol rejected their advice and accepted her martyrdom. Romero recounts the Cadi's reaction, having overheard the discussions between the Chachamim and Sol:

[H]e dispatched them. Immediately he went to his desk, took out the papers containing the cause of the Jewess, wrote on it her contumacy, referring to her repeated blasphemy of the Prophet and his dogmas, and condemned her to be publicly beheaded.[28]

Having refused even a pretense of conversion, Sol was condemned by the Sultan to beheading in a public square in Fez. Sol prayed and fasted as the day of her execution approached. Masses of Arabs congregated on the day of her execution held in the Soco (major market) of Fez, on market day.[29] Romero contrasts the anticipatory emotions of the Muslims, Jews, and Sol herself:

The Moors, whose religious fanaticism is indescribable, prepared, with their accustomed joy, to witness the horrid scene. The Jews of the city . . . were moved with the deepest sorrow; but they could do nothing to avert it [the execution]; they could only assemble, and be prepared to act according to circumstances. . . . The troubled Sol spent the whole day in prayer and meditation; she refused food; and anxiously awaited the moment that would terminate her miserable existence.[30]

On the day of her beheading, Sol was dragged to the execution site, where the executioner brandished his sword two or three times over her head. Sol was allowed to wash her hands and recite the Shema prayer, as she requested.[31] Apparently, the sultan had instructed that the executioners wound Sol (which was done), in the hope of her last-minute conversion to Islam. However, upon seeing her own blood, Sol professed her innocence and denounced her persecutors. With that utterance, she was beheaded. Impressed by the courage and sincerity of this Tangierian Jewess, Fez's Jewish community paid to have not only her corpse and head, but also the bloodstained earth, retrieved for burial, consistent with Jewish law. Sol Hachuel was buried, wrapped in linen cloth, in the Jewish cemetery of Fez, and subsequently bestowed the appellation Hasadiqua—the saintly.[32]

Romero provides additional details that capture all these elements of the final execution day narrative: the fanaticism of the Muslim masses, the conduct of the executioners and their heroic victim, and the reaction of the Jewish community:

Compassion, mildness, grief, and every sentiment that could move the heart, were depicted on the countenance of the lovely victim; but pity is a feeling little known in Fez: the streets were crowded with Moors of all ages and sexes, who made the air resound with their discordant cries. "Here comes," said they, "she who blasphemed the Prophet—death! death! to the impious wretch!"[33]

These men [the executioners], hardened by cruelty, gave the order to march [Sol] to [her] death; they tied a strong rope round her neck, and commenced dragging her as if she were a beast.[34]

[Sol] then raising her streaming eyes to heaven, she repeated with the utmost devotion, the Shema, which having concluded; kneeling and casting her eyes to the ground, she said to the executioner—"I have finished, dispose of my life!"[35]

One of the executioners seizing the arms of the victim, bound them tightly behind her; then brandishing his scimitar in the air, holding her beautiful tresses, he slightly wounded her; in an instant, her bosom and clothes were covered with blood—"There is yet time," said he, "to become Mahometan, and save your life!" But turning toward him, she said, "Do not make me linger—behead me at once—for dying as I do, innocent of any crime, the God of Abraham will avenge my death!" These were her last words—the executioner raised his arm—it fell—the scimitar separated the head from the trunk—in an instant, the most constant of her sex, fell a bleeding, lifeless corpse—she ceased to exist.—Horrid spectacle![36]

The Jews had engaged some Moors to take up the corpse, and gather the earth that was spotted with her innocent blood, the moment the execution was over. They faithfully performed the charge, wrapping her mortal remains in a fine linen cloth, [and] delivered it to the Jews assembled in their cemetery, where they were digging a deep grave for her, adjoining to one in which reposed the ashes of a Sage of great reputation. The same day the Jewish martyr was interred amidst the tears and sobs of a numerous concourse of people who attended her obsequies.[37]

Sol Hachuel's martyrdom illustrates, starkly, the plight of Moroccan Jews—lower-caste, noncitizen *dhimmi* pariahs subject to the sacralized discrimination of Islamic law. Leon Godard's 1860 travelogue, *Description et histoire du Maroc*, characterized the prevailing mid-nineteenth-century conditions for Moroccan Jewry (noting their status as being "somewhat better" in Tangier).[38]

[I]in the cities, the Jews live in separate quarters surrounded by high walls called the *Mellah*, or the salted earth, dry and cursed. They are locked in from sundown to sunrise and on Holidays, all day. They pay the Moorish guards who protect them by guarding the door of this Ghetto, rarely cleaned, where foul-smelling trash accumulates and where a strange population swarms. It is divided by Synagogues and ruled by the rabbis who have great authority. They are the ones who allocate the capitation tax that the government sets for each Mellah, and who make sure the poor are helped using the common goods. They have eight days to pay the tax; after that, and without warning the Mellah can be pillaged. They have to give gifts to the Emperor at the four Muslim holidays and when there is a happy event like a birth or a marriage, they have to entertain the imperial family.

According to the laws, the Jews cannot cultivate earth,—own land or houses outside the Mellah,—use buildings as security,—ride a horse in front of a town or even in the country other than on a saddle for a mule,—or hit a Muslim, even to defend themselves except in their own house if it has been violated,—be a witness in front of a Court or speak in front of tribunals. If allowed to speak in front of a tribunal, they have to be squatting in front of the judge. They cannot raise a bid for food in a Muslim market,—or walk in some streets, in front of Mosques or Koubas, without holding their slippers in their hands,—or get married without the permission of the Sultan. . . .

They have to dress only in black or dark color,—wear a black hat different than the turban and not to tie with more than one knot the black scarf holding their headgear,—place to the right the opening of their *Yallah* or black or blue coat, so that the left arm is not free and the hood falls on the same side,—keep the black hat always visible, trying not to pull down the hood,—run to carry their dead to the cemetery, and be careful not to encounter a Muslim funeral.[39]

David Littman compiled and translated primary source documents from the Alliance Israélite Universelle's Moroccan archives covering the period between 1903 and 1912, some seventy to eighty years after the execution of Sol Hachuel.[40] Repeated eyewitness accounts depict graphically what Littman aptly characterizes as "the humiliation, misery and exposure to physical violence which was still the lot of the ordinary Moroccan Jew in the first decade of the twentieth century."[41] A confirmatory official report presented by Jacob H. Schiff to US Secretary of State Elihu Root in November 1905, entitled "Jewish Restrictions in Morocco, Especially in the Interior," stated bluntly, in the accompanying enclosure, "which restrictions, when read by an American, appear most grotesque."[42] Finally, Serels provides this summary analysis of Moroccan Jewish behaviors in dealing with their oppressed status under Muslim rule, all of which are displayed in the tragic narrative of Hasadiqua, Sol Hachuel:

The Jews had four responses to their lack of political rights and security. First, bribery; second, prayer and fasting; third, appeal for foreign intervention and protection; fourth, silent resignation to the consequences.[43]

NOTES

1. Jane Munro, "Dehodencq, Alfred," Grove Art Online, http://www.groveart.com/shared/views/article.html/section =art.021845. Bibliographic sources for this online entry: G. Seailles, *Alfred Dehodencq: L'Homme et l'artiste* (Paris, 1910); V. Plat, "Alfred Dehodencq, 1822–1882" (PhD diss., Ecole Louvre, Paris, 1977).

2. Munro, "Dehodencq, Alfred."

3. Eugenio Maria Romero, *El martirio de joven Hachuel o la heroina Hebrea* (Gibraltar: Imprinta Militar, 1837) published as an anonymous English translation, *Jewish Heroine of the Nineteenth Century: A Tale Founded on Fact* (London, 1839); Isidore Loeb, "A Jewish Woman Martyred in Morocco" (1834), *Archives Israelite*, part 1, 41, no. 22 (May 27, 1880): 181–82; part 2, 41, no. 23: 187–88; part 3, 41, no. 24: 196–97, English translation by Michael J. Miller; J. E. Budgett

Meakin, "The Jews of Morocco," *Jewish Quarterly Review* 4, no. 3 (April 1892): 376; Romero, Loeb, and Meakin concur on the date of 1834 for Sol's execution, while J. J. Benjamin's *Eight Years in Asia and Africa, From 1846 to 1855* (Hanover, 1863), p. 321, claims the execution took place in 1831. M. Mitchell Serels, in his *A History of the Jews of Tangier in the Nineteenth and Twentieth Centuries* (New York: Sepher-Hermon Press, 1991), p. 187n11, notes additional sources suggesting her execution may have occurred as early as 1830.

4. Romero, *Jewish Heroine of the Nineteenth Century*, p. 19.

5. Elaborating on the same sources discussed by Serels in note 3 above, Sol's reported age at the time of her execution varies from thirteen to seventeen years old.

6. Romero, *Jewish Heroine of the Nineteenth Century*, p. v:

A casual accident brought to my notice, a fact worthy to be handed down to posterity. Enthusiastically I addressed myself to an eye-witness of the scene, and my heart being ever open to misfortune, I was desirous of offering humble tribute to virtue and heroism. The emotion caused by the recital of the sufferings of the youthful Hachuel, led me to cross the sea and visit the burning clime where her blood was shed. There speaking with ocular witnesses of the sad scene, I saw bitter tears flow from the eyes of her respectable parents.

7. Ibid.; also Loeb, "A Jewish Woman Martyred in Morocco" (1834).

8. The mid-nineteenth-century chronicle of M. Leon Godard, *Description et histoire du Maroc* (Paris, 1860), p. 18, contains this reference to the pulchritude of Moroccan Jewesses from the perspective of European observers:

But the European artists who paid some attention to Moroccan Jewish women are tempted to say, with the officers of Holpherne: "How can we despise the Hebrew people when their women are so beautiful: *Quis condemnat populum Hebraeorum qui tám decoras mulieres habent?*" A sensualist can admire the radiance of their complexion, the regularity of their features, the fire of a dark eye and all the beauty of the Jewish characteristics in their purity.

9. Andrew Chouraqui, *La Condition Juridique de L'Israelite Marocain* (Paris: Alliance Israélite Universelle, 1950), p. 53.

10. Romero, *Jewish Heroine of the Nineteenth Century*, pp. 10–11.

11. Romero's anonymous English translator calls Sol "Phoebe," a direct translation of her Spanish name. Serels, *A History of the Jews of Tangier*, p. 187n14.

12. Romero, *Jewish Heroine of the Nineteenth Century*, p. 17. And according to Maliki jurisprudence (and Islamic law in general), the sultan was Allah's representative. The Basha, in turn, represented the sultan within the larger towns. The ruler of the smaller towns, tribes, and douars (Arabian "tent villages"), was the Kaid. The Kaid and the Basha had the right to judge civil, commercial, or criminal matters. A Qur'anic judge or Cadi was appointed by the sultan to adjudicate personal status matters. Chouraqui, *La Condition Juridique de L'Israelite Marocain*, pp. 117–19.

13. Romero, *Jewish Heroine of the Nineteenth Century*, pp. 18–19.

14. Ibid., p. 19.

15. Ibid., p. 29.

16. Ibid.

17. Ibid., pp. 29–30.

18. Ibid., p. 44.

19. Ibid., p. 45.

20. Serels, in *A History of the Jews of Tangier*, p. 188n31, maintains that diplomatic sources do not list a Don Jose Rico as vice consul in Tangier, and suggests that the title may be honorific.

21. Romero, *Jewish Heroine of the Nineteenth Century*, pp. 45–49.

22. Ibid., pp. 46–47.

23. Ibid., p. 46.

24. Serels, *A History of the Jews of Tangier*, p. 9.

25. Romero, *Jewish Heroine of the Nineteenth Century*, p. 53.

26. Ibid., p. 7. See note 12, above.

27. Ibid., pp. 82–83.

28. Ibid., p. 83.

29. Ibid., pp. 87–92.

30. Ibid., p. 86.

31. "Hear, O Israel! The Lord or God, the Lord is One," Deut. 6:4.

32. Serels, *A History of the Jews of Tangier*, p. 10.

33. *Jewish Heroine of the Nineteenth Century*, pp. 89–90.

34. Ibid., p. 89.

35. Ibid., p. 91.

36. Ibid., p. 92.

37. Ibid., pp. 92–93.

38. Serels explains that Tangier's history of European occupation and colonization in the fifteenth through seventeenth centuries had, in the eyes of the Moroccan sultans, "already defiled" the city, so it was decided to confine the foreign embassies to Tangier, rather than allow these non-Muslims into the imperial capital of Fez (*A History of the Jews of Tangier*, pp. 1–2). Regardless, Meakin (c. 1892) confirmed that Jews were not confined to a mellah (walled and locked ghetto) in Tangier, due, he believed, to the "advantages afforded by the presence of so many foreigners," which conferred upon the Jews a "comparative immunity from the indignities inflicted further inland." See "The Jews of Morocco," p. 378.

39. Leon Godard, *Description et histoire du Maroc*, pp. 16–17.

40. David G. Littman, "Jews under Muslim Rule—II: Morocco 1903–1912," *Wiener Library Bulletin* 29 (1976): 3–19.

41. Ibid., p. 4.

42. "Jewish Restrictions in Morocco, Especially in the Interior," report to Secretary of State Elihu presented by Jacob H. Schiff, November 21, 1905, from *The American Jewish Yearbook* (Philadelphia, 1906), pp. 94–98.

43. Serels, *A History of the Jews of Tangier*, p. 10.

Editor's Note on the Text

Below I have provided a brief list of some of the most prominent spelling variants that are used given the range of translated languages, translators, and eras from which the materials derive, regardless of original language.

Readers may also wish to reference the indices if they have additional questions.

A´isha, Ā'isha, Aïscha, Aisha, A'isha, Āyi<u>sh</u>ah, Aysha

Cadi, cadi, Qadi, qadi,

Caid, caid, caïd, Qaid, qaid, Kaid, kaid

Banu, Banū, Benou

Banu, Banū, Beni, or Benou Qurayza, or Qurayzah

dimmi, *dimmi*, dimmī, *dimmī*, dhimmi, *dhimmi*, *dhimmī*, *dhimmī*

Hijaz or Hijāz

jizya, jizyah

Muhammad, Mohammed, Mahomet

Sabbath or sabbath

Foreword by Ibn Warraq

Is Islamic antisemitism only a modern phenomenon? What of the so-called Golden Age of Islamic tolerance, above all as depicted in Islamic Spain? Here the willingness to accept the clichés of the Romantics is palpable. And for those whom we expect to have done their own research, and not merely to accept and pass on, these clichés so often disappoint.

Consider the case of Amartya Sen, a celebrated economist and winner of the Nobel Prize. Sen has, in recent years, written on subjects outside his normal area of research. Unfortunately, he seems not to have bothered to check his history, something that would have been easy given the resources available to him.

Here is how Amartya Sen treats, for example, the Myth of Maimonides. Amartya Sen tells us twice in his book *Identity and Violence* that when "the Jewish Philosopher Maimonides was forced to emigrate from an intolerant Europe in the twelfth century, he found a tolerant refuge in the Arab world."[1] I do not know how to characterize this misinterpretation of history—"willful," "grotesque," "dishonest," or "typical"? It is certainly an indication that in the present intellectual climate one can denigrate Europe any way one wishes, to the point of distorting history, without, evidently, any one of the distinguished scholars who blurbed the book raising an eyebrow. Ironically, the one reviewer who did object to Sen's "potted history," which "is tailored for interfaith dialogues," was Fouad Ajami in the *Washington Post*.[2] Ajami reminded Sen that

> this will not do as history. Maimonides, born in 1135, did not flee "Europe" for the "Arab world": He fled his native Córdoba in Spain, which was then in the grip of religious-political terror, choking under the yoke of a Berber Muslim dynasty, the Almohads, that was to snuff out all that remained of the culture of conviviencia and made the life of Spain's Jews (and of the free spirits among its Muslims) utter hell. Maimonides and his family fled the fire of the Muslim city-states in the Iberian Peninsula to Morocco and then to Jerusalem. There was darkness and terror in Morocco as well, and Jerusalem was equally inhospitable in the time of the Crusader Kingdom. Deliverance came only in Cairo—the exception, not the rule, its social peace maintained by the enlightened Saladin.

Moses Maimonides (1135–1204), Jewish rabbi, physician, and philosopher, was fleeing the Muslims, the intolerant Almohads who conquered Cordoba in 1148. The Almohads persecuted the Jews, and offered them the choice of conversion to Islam, death, or exile. Maimonides' family and other Jews chose exile. But this did not bring any peace to the Jews who had to be on the move constantly to avoid the all-conquering Almohads. After a brief sojourn in Morocco and the Holy Land, Maimonides settled in Fostat, Egypt, where he was physician to the Grand Vizier Alfadhil, and possibly Saladin, the Kurdish sultan.

Maimonides' *The Epistle to the Jews of Yemen*[3] was written in about 1172 in reply to inquiries by Jacob ben Netan'el al-Fayyūmi, the then head of the Jewish community in Yemen. The Jews of Yemen were passing through a crisis, as they were being forced to convert to Islam, a campaign launched in about 1165 by 'Abd-al-Nabī ibn Mahdi. Maimonides provided them with guidance and with what encouragement he could. The Epistle to the Jews of Yemen gives a clear view of what Maimonides thought of Muhammad the Prophet, "the Madman," as he calls him, and of Islam generally. This is what Maimonides writes:

> You write that the rebel leader in Yemen decreed compulsory apostasy for the Jews by forcing the Jewish inhabitants of all the places he had subdued to desert the Jewish religion just as the Berbers had compelled them to do in Maghreb [i.e., Islamic West]. Verily, this news has broken our backs and has astounded and dumbfounded the whole of our community. And rightly so. For these are evil tidings, "and whosoever heareth of them, both his ears tingle" (1 Samuel 3:11). Indeed our hearts are weakened, our minds are confused, and the powers of the body wasted because of the dire misfortunes which brought religious persecutions upon us from the two ends of the world, the East and the West, "so that the enemies were in the midst of Israel, some on this side, and some on that side" (Joshua 8:22).

Maimonides points out that persistent persecutions of the Jews by the Muslims amounts to forced conversion:

> [T]he continuous persecutions will cause many to drift away from our faith, to have misgivings, or to go astray, because they witnessed our feebleness, and noted the triumph of our adversaries and their dominion over us . . .

He continues: "After him arose the Madman who emulated his precursor since he paved the way for him. But he added the further objective of procuring rule and submission, and he invented his well known religion." Many medieval Jewish writers commonly referred to Muhammad as *ha-meshugga'*, Madman—the Hebrew term, as Norman Stillman notes, being "pregnant with connotations."[4]

21

Maimonides points to one of the reasons for Muslim hatred of Jews:

> Inasmuch as the Muslims could not find a single proof in the entire Bible nor a reference or possible allusion to their prophet which they could utilize, they were compelled to accuse us saying, "You have altered the text of the Torah, and expunged every trace of the name of Mohammed therefrom." They could find nothing stronger than this ignominious argument.

He notes the depth of Muslim hatred for the Jews, but he also remarks on the Jewish tendency of denial, a feature that he insists will hasten their destruction:

> Remember, my co-religionists, that on account of the vast number of our sins, God has hurled us in the midst of this people, the Arabs, who have persecuted us severely, and passed baneful and discriminatory legislation against us, as Scripture has forewarned us, 'Our enemies themselves shall judge us' (Deuteronomy 32:31). *Never did a nation molest, degrade, debase and hate us as much as they . . . .* Although we were dishonored by them beyond human endurance, and had to put with their fabrications, yet we behaved like him who is depicted by the inspired writer, "But I am as a deaf man, I hear not, and I am as a dumb man that openeth not his mouth" (Psalms 38:14). Similarly our sages instructed us to bear the prevarications and preposterousness of Ishmael in silence. They found a cryptic allusion for this attitude in the names of his sons "Mishma, Dumah, and Massa" (Genesis 25:14), which was interpreted to mean, "Listen, be silent, and endure" (Targum Pseudo-Jonathan, ad locum). We have acquiesced, both old and young, to inure ourselves to humiliation, as Isaiah instructed us "I gave my back to the smiters, and my cheeks to them that plucked off the hair" (50:6). All this notwithstanding, we do not escape this continued maltreatment which well nigh crushes us. No matter how much we suffer and elect to remain at peace with them, they stir up strife and sedition, as David predicted, "I am all peace, but when I speak, they are for war" (Psalms 120:7). If, therefore, we start trouble and claim power from them absurdly and preposterously we certainly give ourselves up to destruction.

During the last fifteen years, certain Western scholars have tried to argue that, first, Islamic antisemitism—that is, hatred of Jews—is only a recent phenomenon learned from the Nazis during and after the 1940s and, second, that Jews lived safely under Muslim rule for centuries, especially during the Golden Age of Muslim Spain. Both assertions are unsupported by the evidence. Islam 1, that is, the Islam of the texts, as found in the Qur'an and hadith (the sayings and deeds of the Prophet and his companions) and in the sira (the biography of Muhammad, which obviously overlaps with the hadith), and Islam 2—that is, the Islam developed or elaborated from those texts early on by the Qur'anic commentators and jurisconsults, and then set in stone more than a millennium ago—and even Islam 3, in the sense of Islamic civilization—that is, what Muslims actually did historically—have all been deeply antisemitic. That is, all have been anti-infidel, so that Christians too are regarded with disdain and contempt and hatred, but the Jews have been served, or been seen to have merited, a special animus.

ISLAM 1: QUR'AN, MUHAMMAD, HADITH, AND SUNNA

Muhammad set the example for antisemitism. The oldest extant biography of Muhammad, that by Ibn Ishaq as transmitted by Ibn Hisham, is replete with the Prophet's evident hatred of Jews. He had individual Jews assassinated if he felt they had somehow insulted or disobeyed him. When Muhammad gave the command "Kill any Jew that falls into your power,"[5] one of his followers, Ibn Mas'ud, assassinated Ibn Sunayna, a Jewish merchant. Other followers of Muhammad were happy to obey similar orders from their leader: "Our attack upon God's enemy cast terror among the Jews, and there was no Jew in Medina who did not fear for his life."[6] Other Jews killed included Sallam ibn Abu'l-Huqayq,[7] Ka'b b.al-Ashraf,[8] and al-Yusayr.[9] The Jewish tribe Banu Qurayza, consisting of between six hundred and eight hundred men, was exterminated,[10] while the Jewish tribe of Banu'l-Nadir was attacked. Those who remained alive were banished.[11]

Here are two additional examples of Muhammad's attitude to Jews; first from Ibn Sa'd's sira:

> Then occurred the "sariyyah" [raid] of Salim Ibn Umayr al-Amri against Abu Afak, the Jew, in [the month of] Shawwal in the beginning of the twentieth month from the hijrah [immigration from Mecca to Medina in 622 AD], of the Apostle of Allah. Abu Afak, was from Banu Amr Ibn Awf, and was an old man who had attained the age of one hundred and twenty years. He was a Jew, and used to instigate the people against the Apostle of Allah, and composed (satirical) verses [about Muhammad].
>
> Salim Ibn Umayr, who was one of the great weepers and who had participated in Badr, said, "I take a vow that I shall either kill Abu Afak or die before him." He waited for an opportunity until a hot night came, and Abu Afak slept in an open place. Salim Ibn Umayr knew it, so he placed the sword on his liver and pressed it till it reached his bed. The enemy of Allah screamed and the people

who were his followers, rushed to him, took him to his house and interred him.[12]

The second example comes from al-Bukhari's canonical hadith collection:

> Bani An-Nadir and Bani Quraiza fought, so the Prophet [Muhammad] exiled Bani An-Nadir and allowed Bani Quraiza to remain at their places. He then killed their men and distributed their women, children and property among the Muslims, but some of them came to the Prophet and he granted them safety, and they embraced Islam. He exiled all the Jews from Medina. They were the Jews of Bani Qainuqa', the tribe of 'Abdullah bin Salam and the Jews of Bani Haritha and all the other Jews of Medina.[13]

Muhammad's intolerance of other religions is well attested: "I was told that the last injunction the apostle [Muhammad] gave [before his death] was in his words 'Let not two religions be left in the Arabian peninsula'";[14] or, as Abu Dawoud put it, "The Apostle of Allah said, 'I will certainly expel the Jews and the Christians from Arabia.'"[15]

After September 11, 2001, many Muslims and apologists of Islam glibly came out with the following Qur'anic quote to show that Islam and the Qur'an disapproved of violence and killing: "Whoever killed a human being shall be looked upon as though he had killed all mankind" (Qur'an 5:32). Unfortunately, these wonderful-sounding words, which come from a preexisting Jewish text (*Mishnah*, IV Division),[16] are quoted out of context. For the very next verse offers quite a different meaning from that of 5:32:

> That was why We laid it down for the Israelites that whoever killed a human being, except as a punishment for murder or other villainy in the land, shall be looked upon as though he had killed all mankind; and that whoever saved a human life shall be regarded as though he had saved all mankind. Our apostles brought them veritable proofs: yet it was not long before many of them committed great evils in the land. Those that make war against God and His apostle and spread disorder shall be put to death or crucified or have their hands and feet cut off on alternate sides, or be banished from the country. (Qur'an 5:33)

The supposedly noble sentiments of the first verse, taken from a Jewish source, are entirely undercut by the second verse, which becomes a murderous menacing by Muhammad of the Jews. Far from abjuring violence, these verses aggressively insist that any who oppose the Prophet will be killed, or crucified, mutilated, and banished.

As for the intolerance against Jews and Christians, and their inferior status as *dhimmis*, we have:

> Fight against such of those to whom the Scriptures were given as believe neither in God nor the Last Day, who do not forbid what God and His apostle have forbidden, and do not embrace the true faith, until they pay tribute out of hand and are utterly subdued.
>
> The Jews say Ezra is the son of God, while the Christians say the Messiah is the son of God. Such are their assertions, by which they imitate the infidels of old. God confound them! How perverse they are!
>
> They make of their clerics and their monks, and of the Messiah, the son of Mary, Lords besides God; though they were ordered to serve one God only. There is no god but Him. Exalted be He above those whom they deify besides Him! . . .
>
> It is He who has sent forth His apostle with guidance and the true Faith to make it triumphant over all religions, however much the idolaters may dislike it.
>
> O you who believe! Lo! many of the Jewish rabbis and the Christian monks devour the wealth of mankind wantonly and debar men from the way of Allah; they who hoard up gold and silver and spend it not in the way of Allah, unto them give tidings of painful doom. (Qur'an 9:29–35)

The moral of all the above is clear: Islam is the only true religion, Jews and Christians are devious, money grubbing, are not to be trusted, and even have to pay a tax in the most humiliating way:

> Wretchedness and baseness were stamped upon them [that is, the Jews], and they were visited with wrath from Allah. That was because they disbelieved in Allah's revelations and slew the prophets wrongfully. That was for their disobedience and transgression. (Qur'an 2:61)

Have you not seen those who have received a portion of the Scripture? They purchase error, and they want you to go astray from the path. But Allah knows best who your enemies are, and it is sufficient to have Allah as a friend. It is sufficient to have Allah as a helper. Some of the Jews pervert words from their meanings, and say, "We hear and we disobey," and "Hear without hearing," and "Heed us!" twisting with their tongues and slandering religion. If they had said, "We have heard and obey," or "Hear and observe us" it would have been better for them and more upright. But Allah had cursed them for their disbelief, so they believe not, except for a few. (Qur'an 4:44–46)

And for the evildoing of the Jews, We have forbidden them some good things that were previously permitted them, and because of their barring many from Allah's way. And for their taking usury that was prohibited for them, and because of their consuming people's wealth under false pretense. We have prepared for the unbelievers among them a painful punishment. (Qur'an 4:160–61)[17]

ISLAM 2: QUR'ANIC COMMENTATORS

Baydawi (d. c. 1316), in *Anwaar al-Tanziil Wa-Asraar al-Ta'wiil*, provided this gloss on Qur'an 2:61:

"[H]umiliation and wretchedness" covered them like a dome, or stuck to them like wet clay to a wall—a metaphor for their denial of the bounty. The Jews are mostly humiliated and wretched either of their own accord, or out of coercion of the fear of having their *jizya* doubled. . . . Either they became deserving of His wrath [or] . . . the affliction of "humiliation and wretchedness" and the deserving wrath which preceded this.[18]

Ibn Kathir (d. 1373) emphasized the Jews' eternal humiliation in accord with Qur'an 2:61:

This ayah indicates that the Children of Israel were plagued with humiliation, and this will continue, meaning it will never cease. They will continue to suffer humiliation at the hands of all who interact with them, along with the disgrace that they feel inwardly.[19]

ISLAM 3: ISLAMIC CIVILIZATION

Here are examples of the persecution of Jews in Islamic lands: the massacre of more than six thousand Jews in Fez (Morocco) in 1033; of the hundreds of Jews killed between 1010 and 1013 near Cordoba, and other parts of Muslim Spain; and the massacre of the entire Jewish community of roughly four thousand in Granada during the Muslim riots of 1066. Referring to the latter massacre, Robert Wistrich writes: "This was a disaster, as serious as that which overtook the Rhineland Jews thirty years later during the First Crusade, yet it has rarely received much scholarly attention." Wistrich continues:

In Kairouan [Tunisia] the Jews were persecuted and forced to leave in 1016, returning later only to be expelled again. In Tunis in 1145 they were forced to convert or to leave, and during the following decade there were fierce anti-Jewish persecutions throughout the country. A similar pattern of events occurred in Morocco after the massacre of Jews in Marrakesh in 1232. Indeed, in the Islamic world from Spain to the Arabian peninsula the looting and

killing of Jews, along with punitive taxation, confinement to ghettos, the enforced wearing of distinguishing marks on clothes (an innovation in which Islam preceded medieval Christendom), and other humiliations were rife.[20]

Fouad Ajami, in his review of Sen's book, spoke of "the culture of conviviencia," what others have called the Golden Age of Tolerance in Spain before it was destroyed by the intolerance of the Almohads. Unfortunately, the "Golden Age" also turns out to be a myth—invented, ironically, by the Jews themselves. The myth may well have originated as early as the twelfth century, when Abraham Ibn Daud in his *Sefer ha-Qabbalah* contrasted an idealized period of tolerance of the salons of Toledo to the contemporary barbarism of the Berber dynasty. But the myth took a firm grip on the imagination of the Jews in the nineteenth century thanks to the bibliographer Moritz Steinschneider and the historian Heinrich Graetz, and perhaps the influence of Benjamin Disraeli's novel *Coningsby*, published in 1844. Here is a passage from the novel, giving a romantic picture of Muslim Spain:

. . . that fair and unrivaled civilization in which the children of Ishmael rewarded the children of Israel with equal rights and privileges with themselves. During these halcyon centuries, it is difficult to distinguish the followers of Moses from the votary of Mohammed. Both alike built palaces, gardens and fountains; filled equally the highest offices of state, competed in an extensive and enlightened commerce, rivaled each other in renowned universities.[21]

Ever since the seventeenth and eighteenth centuries, Western intellectuals from Pierre Bayle to Voltaire and Montesquieu had used the putative tolerance of Islam with which to belabor Christianity and her relative intolerance. Against a background of a rise in the pseudo-scientific racism of the nineteenth century, Jane Gerber has observed that Jewish historians looked to Islam "for support, seeking real or imagined allies and models of tolerance in the East. The cult of a powerful, dazzling and brilliant Andalusia in the midst of an ignorant and intolerant Europe formed an important component in these contemporary intellectual currents."[22] But Gerber concludes her sober assessment of the Golden Age myth with these reflections:

The aristocratic bearing of a select class of courtiers and poets, however, should not blind us to the reality that this tightly knit circle of leaders and aspirants to power was neither the whole of Spanish Jewish history nor of Spanish Jewish society. Their gilded moments of the tenth and eleventh century are but a brief chapter in a longer saga. No doubt,

Ibn Daud's polemic provided consolation and inspiration to a crisis-ridden twelfth century elite, just as the golden age imagery could comfort dejected exiles after 1492. It suited the needs of nineteenth century advocates of Jewish emancipation in Europe or the twentieth century contestants in the ongoing debate over Palestine. . . . The history of the Jews in Muslim lands, especially Muslim Spain, needs to be studied on its own terms, without myth or countermyth.[23]

And that is exactly what Andrew Bostom has done: provide a history of the Jews in Muslim lands, without myth. Bostom provides the necessary corrective to the idealized portraits of the golden age or the absolute tolerance of Ottoman Turkey. Patiently and methodically, he shows the real situation of Jews against a background of the institution of *dhimmitude*, which relentlessly persecuted all non-Muslims and reduced their lives to a misery, further punctuated with massacres and pogroms, all grimly recorded by him. Bostom also takes into account the discoveries of the Cairo Geniza, which forced even the great historian Shlomo Dov Goitein (d. 1985) to revise his ideas about the situation of Jews in Islamic lands. While the West has recognized its own shameful part in the slave trade and antisemitic persecution, and has taken steps to make amends where possible, the Islamic lands remain in constant denial. Until Islamic countries acknowledge the realities of anti-Jewish persecution in their history, there is no hope of combating the continuing hatred of Jews in modern times, from Morocco to Indonesia.

NOTES

1. Amartya Sen, *Identity and Violence: The Illusion of Destiny* (New York: W. W. Norton, 2006), p. 66, and also at p. 16: "distinguished Jewish philosopher fled an intolerant Europe."

2. Fouad Ajami, "Enemies, a Love Story: A Nobel Laureate Argues That Civilizations Are Not Clashing," *Washington Post*, April 2, 2006.

3. Moses Maimonides, *Moses Maimonides' Epistle to Yemen: The Arabic Original and the Three Hebrew Versions,* edited from manuscripts with introduction and notes by Abraham S. Halkin, and an English translation by Boaz Cohen (New York: American Academy for Jewish Research, 1952).

4. Norman Stillman, *The Jews of Arab Lands. A History and Source Book* (Philadelphia: Jewish Publication Society of America, 1979) pp. 236, 236n8. Salo W. Baron, from his essay "The Historical Outlooks of Maimonides," *Proceedings of the American Academy for Jewish Research, 1934–1935*, vol. 6, p. 82, concurs regarding this common reference to Muhammad as a madman:

Following an apparently prevalent usage he [Maimonides] calls the founder of Islam a "madman," with both religious and political aspirations, who failed to formulate any new religious idea, but merely restated well-known concepts.

Nevertheless, Muhammad, Baron observes,

. . . attracted a large following and inflicted many wrongs upon the Jews, being himself responsible for the massacre of 24,000. Following his example the Muslims of the subsequent generations oppressed the Jews and debased them even more harshly than any other nation. This statement is an obvious reflection of Maimuni's earlier experiences in Spain and Morocco.

5. Ibn Ishaq, *The Life of Muhammad*, trans. A. Guillaume (New York: Oxford University Press, 2001), p. 369.

6. Ibid., p. 368.

7. Ibid., pp. 482–83.

8. Ibid., pp. 364–69.

9. Ibid., pp. 665–66.

10. Ibid., pp. 461–69.

11. Ibid., pp. 437–45.

12. Ibn Sa'd, *Kitab al Tabaqat,* trans. S. M. Haq, 2 vols. (New Delhi), 1:32.

13. *Sahih Al-Bukhari*, trans. M. Muhsin Khan (New Delhi: Kitab Bhavan, 1987), vol. 5, bk. 59: Book of al-Maghazi (Raids), hadith 362, p. 241.

14. Ishaq, *The Life of Muhammad*, p. 689.

15. Abu Dawood, *Sunan*, 3 vols. (New Delhi: Kitab Bhavan, 1997), vol. 2, hadith 3024, p. 861.

16. *Mishnah*, trans. Jacob Neusner (New Haven, CT: Yale University Press, 1988), The Fourth Division: The Order of Damages, Sanhedrin 4:5.J.: "Therefore man was created alone, (1) to teach you that whoever destroys a single Israelite soul is deemed by Scripture as if he had destroyed a whole world" (p. 591).

17. Here are some more quotes from the Koran:

Fight against such of those who have been given the Scripture [Jews and Christians] as believe not in Allah nor the Last Day, and forbid not that which Allah has forbidden by His Messenger, and follow not the religion of truth, until they pay the tribute [poll-tax] readily, and are utterly subdued. The Jews say, "Ezra is the son of Allah," and the Christians say, " The Messiah is the son of Allah." Those are the words of their mouths, conforming to the words of the unbelievers before them. Allah attack them! How perverse they are! They have taken their rabbis and their monks as lords besides Allah, and so too the Messiah son of Mary, though they were commanded to serve but one God. There is no God but He. Allah is exalted above that which they deify beside Him. (Qur'an 9:29–31)

O you who believe! Lo! many of the [Jewish] rabbis and the [Christian] monks devour the wealth of mankind wantonly and debar [men] from the way of Allah. They who hoard up gold and silver and spend it not in the way of Allah, unto them give tidings of a painful doom. (Qur'an 9:34)

Why do not the rabbis and the priests forbid their evil-speaking and devouring of illicit gain? Verily evil is their handiwork. The Jews say, "Allah's hands are fettered." Their hands are fettered, and they are cursed for what they have said! On the contrary, His hands are spread open. He bestows as He wills. That which has been revealed to you from your Lord will surely increase the arrogance and unbelief of many among them. We have cast enmity and hatred among them until the Day of Resurrection. Every time they light the fire of war, Allah extinguishes it. They hasten to spread corruption throughout the earth, but Allah does not love corrupters! (Qur'an 5:63–64)

We made a covenant with the Israelites and sent forth apostles among them. But whenever an apostle came to them with a message that did not suit their fancies, some they accused of lying and others they put to death. They thought no harm would follow: they were blind and deaf. God is ever watching their actions. (Qur'an 5:70–71)

Indeed, you will surely find that the most vehement of men in enmity to those who believe are the Jews and the polytheists. (Qur'an 5:82)

O you who believe! Take not the Jews and the Christians for friends. They are friends one to another. He among you who takes them for friends is one of them. (Qur'an 5:51)

O you who believe! Choose not for friends such of those who received the Scripture [Jews and Christians] before you, and of the disbelievers, as make jest and sport of your religion. But keep your duty to Allah of you are true believers. (Qur'an 5:57)

Say: O, People of the Scripture [Jews and Christians]! Do you blame us for aught else than that we believe in Allah and that which is revealed unto us and that which was revealed aforetime, and because most of you are evil-doers? (Qur'an 5:59)

Among them [Jews and Christians] there are people who are moderate, but many of them are of evil conduct. (Qur'an 5:66)

He brought down from their strongholds those who had supported them from among the People of the Book [Jews of Bani Qurayza] and cast terror into their hearts, so that some you killed and others you took captive. (Qur'an 33:26)

Say: "Shall I tell you who will receive a worse reward from God? Those whom [i.e., Jews] God has cursed and with whom He has been angry, transforming them into apes and swine, and those who serve the devil. Worse is the plight of these, and they have strayed farther from the right path." (Qur'an 5:60)

18. Baydawi, H. O. *Commentaius in Coranum. Anwaar al-Tanziil Wa-Asraar al-Ta'wiil*, ed. H. O. Fleischer (1846–48; reprint, Osnabrück: 1968), p. 63. English translation by Michael Schub.

More quotes from Baydawi:

"[B]ecause they disbelieved and killed the prophets unjustly" by reason of their disbelief in miracles, e.g. the splitting of the sea, the clouds giving shade, and the sending of the manna and quails, and splitting of the rock into twelve fountains or, disbelief in the revealed books, e.g. the Gospel, Qur'an, the verse of stoning, and the Torah verse in which Muhammad is depicted; and their killing of the prophets like Shay`aa [Isaiah], Zakariyyaa, Yahyaa, et al., all killed unjustly because they considered that of these prophets nothing was to be believed and thus they deserved to be killed.

In addition [God] accuses them of following fantasy and love of this world, as he demonstrates in His saying [line 14] "this if for their transgression and sin," i.e., rebelliousness, contrariness, and hostility brought them into disbelief in the signs, and killing the prophets. Venal sins lead to serious sins, just as small bits of obedience lead to larger ones. . . . God repeated this proof of what is *inveterate* [in the Jews], which is the reason for their unbelief and murder, and which is the cause of their committing sins and transgressing the bounds God set.

19. Ibn Kathir, *Tafsir Ibn Kathir* (Riyadh: 2000), vol. 1, pp. 245–46.

Al-Hassan commented, "Allah humiliated them under the feet of the Muslims, who appeared at a time when the Majus (Zoroastrians) were taking the jizya from the Jews." Also, Abu Al-'Aliyah, Ar-Rabi bin Anas and As-Suddi said that "misery" used in that ayah means "poverty." 'Atiyah Al-'Awfi said that "misery" means, "paying the tilth (tax)." In addition, Ad-Dahhak commented on Allah's statement, "and they drew on themselves the wrath of Allah," "They deserved Allah's anger." Also, Ibn

Jarir said that, "and they drew on themselves the wrath of Allah" means, "They went back with the wrath." Similarly, Allah said, "Verily, I intend to let you draw my sin on yourself as well as yours" (Qur'an 5:29) meaning, "You will end up carrying my and your mistakes instead of me." Thus the meaning of the ayah becomes, "They went back carrying Allah's anger: Allah's wrath descended upon them; they deserved Allah's anger."

Allah's statement, "That was because they used to disbelieve in the Ayat (proofs, evidence, etc.) of Allah and killed the Prophets wrongfully," means "This is what We rewarded the Children of Israel with: humiliation and misery." Allah's anger that descended on the Children of Israel was a part of the humiliation they earned, because of their defiance of the truth, disbelief in Allah's Law, i.e., the Prophets and their following. The Children of Israel rejected the Messengers even killing them. Surely there is no form of disbelief worse than disbelieving in Allah's ayat and murdering the Prophets of Allah.

20. Robert Wistrich, *Antisemitism—The Longest Hatred* (New York: Schocken Books, 1991), p. 196

21. Benjamin Disraeli, *Coningsby*, bk. 4, chap. 10, quoted in Bernard Lewis, *Islam in History* (New York: 1973), p. 317n15.

22. Jane Gerber, "Towards an Understanding of the Term 'The Golden Age' as an Historical Reality," in *The Heritage of the Jews of Spain*, ed. Aviva Doron (Tel Aviv: Levinsky College of Education Publishing House, 1994), p. 16.

23. Ibid., pp. 21–22.

PART I

❖❖❖

Islamic Antisemitism—
Jew Hatred in Islam

CHAPTER 1

A Survey of Its Theological-Juridical Origins and Historical Manifestations

ANDREW G. BOSTOM

INTRODUCTION

Robert Wistrich[1] has emphasized the problematic nature of the term "antisemitism," derived from a group of cognate "Semitic" (i.e., stemming from the biblical Shem, one of Noah's three sons) languages—Hebrew, Aramaic, Arabic, Babylonian, Assyrian, and Ethiopic—and applied, inappropriately, to a pseudoscientific racial designation by the German journalist Wilhelm Marr in the 1870s. Regardless, for the past century, as Wistrich notes,

> the illogical term "antisemitism" . . . [w]hich never really meant hatred of "Semites" (for example, Arabs [emphasis added]) at all, but rather hatred of Jews, has come to be accepted in general usage as denoting all forms of hostility towards Jews and Judaism throughout history.[2]

Bernard Lewis debunked a common apologetic argument, which exploits the limitations of the term antisemitism—and asserts that Arabs somehow are incapable of antisemitism:

> The argument is sometimes put forward that the Arabs cannot be antisemitic because they themselves are Semites. Such a statement is self-evidently absurd, and the argument that supports it is doubly flawed. First the term "Semite" has no meaning as applied to groups as heterogeneous as the Arabs or the Jews, and indeed it could be argued that the use of such terms is in itself a sign of racism and certainly of ignorance or bad faith. Second, antisemitism has never anywhere been concerned with anyone but Jews, and it is therefore available to Arabs as to other people as an option should they choose it.[3]

But perhaps the strongest evidence that antisemitism was never meant to be directed at Arabs (or Muslims, or any non-Jews) comes from the perpetrators of genocidal antisemitic violence, the Nazis.[4] During a November 1942 press conference, a Berlin foreign ministry spokesman, as reported in the *New York Times*, took "great pains" to assure Arabs that Nazi antisemitic policies were directed at Jews, *exclusively*. The spokesman elaborated:

> The difference between Germany's attitude toward Jews and Arabs has been clearly shown in the exchange of letters between the former Prime Minister of Iraq, Rashid Ali, and the German Institute for Racial Problems. We have never said the Arabs were inferior as a race. On the contrary, we have always pointed out the glorious historic past of the Arab people.[5]

Moreover, in the specific context of the Arab Muslim world during the High Middle Ages (c. 950–1250 CE), S. D. Goitein's seminal analyses of the Geniza documentary record employed the term antisemitism

> in order to differentiate animosity against Jews from the discrimination practiced by Islam against non-Muslims in general. Our scrutiny of the Geniza material has proved the existence of "antisemitism" in the time and the area considered here.[6]

Goitein cites as concrete proof of his assertion that a unique strain of Islamic Jew hatred was extant at this time (i.e., up to a millennium ago)—exploding the common assumption of its absence[7]—the fact that letters from the Cairo Geniza material

> have a special word for it and, most significantly, one not found in the Bible or in Talmudic literature (nor registered in any Hebrew dictionary), but one much used and obviously coined in the Geniza period. It is *sin'ūth*, "hatred," a Jew-baiter being called *sōnē*, "a hater."[8]

Incidents of such Muslim Jew hatred documented by Goitein in the Geniza come from northern Syria (Salamiyya and al-Mar'arra), Morocco (Fez), and Egypt (Alexandria), with references to the latter being particularly frequent.[9] The dubious reputation of al-Mar'arra as a hub of Muslim antisemitism is confirmed in a letter congratulating a Jewish merchant upon escaping from the town unharmed:

> The first thing that God the exalted has done with you and with all Israel, of which you are the crown, is that he saved you from Mar'arra, despite the *sin'ūth* [hatred] of the Muslim inhabitants . . .[10]

A business letter written by a son in Fez, Morocco, to his father in Almeria, Spain (around 1100 CE), notes,

> Antisemitism in this country is such that, in comparison with it, life in Almeria is salvation. May God in his mercy grant me a safe departure.[11]

Regarding some of the multiple Geniza references to antisemitism in Alexandria, Egypt, Goitein observes at length:

> Around the middle of the eleventh century we already read about "the oppression by bandits and rulers of the city." At approximately the same time a merchant, known to us from many letters as a sober and steady person, writes that despite urgent business, he has been unable to leave the house for the bazaar for three days, for the terror was great and if anyone wanted to take advantage of the absence of the head of the family he could do so unpunished. At the turn of the century there was a threat that the ancient practice of turning the estates of foreigners who died in Egypt over to the juridical authorities of their respective communities would be discontinued. A writer discussing this matter emphasizes that "the people of Alexandria" are not like those of Cairo. If they were allowed to lay their hands on Jewish property, nothing would remain of it. In the same period a Jewish scholar traveling to Alexandria stops over for a week in al-Fuwaa (the terminal of the waterway connecting that city with the Nile), asking his brother in the capital to secure for him a letter of recommendation to the Muslim chief judge of Alexandria, "for you know only too well the antisemitism of the population of that city."

An occurrence characteristic of this situation is vividly described in a Geniza letter. A Jewish notable bearing the title "the elder (or head) of the congregations," namely, of the Palestinian and Babylonian congregations of Alexandria, was falsely accused of having had an affair with a girl of dubious reputation in a caravanserai. When the girl denied it, the accusers, members of the secret police, urged her to tell the qadi that the Jew had taken her by force and then paid her; otherwise she would be lead on a donkey through the town and burned. Soon a crowd of about a thousand people gathered and dragged the notable before the qadi. The latter examined the would-be witnesses one by one separately, and found out that their testimony was false. "However," the letter continues, "the secret police forced the qadi to give judgment against his own conviction, and now *sin'ūth* has been let loose in an unprecedented manner. Kindly send a letter to the qadi so that his heart will be strengthened in his favorable attitude toward the Jews, as it had been before. Otherwise, they will perish; for antisemitism is continually taking on new forms and everyone in the town has become a police inspector over the Jews in the worst way of *sin'ūth*." The letter concludes with the request that the addressee assist the . . . Jewish community, using either his influential position or money to get the notable out of prison.

The precarious situation facing the Jews of Alexandria from time to time found their expression also in official documents. A memorandum by the Jewish community of that city addressed to the Nagid Samuel b. Hanaya (1140–1159) described the state of lawlessness to which it was exposed because of the high-handed and fraudulent practices of the officials of the poll tax. Even the honor of the women was not safe from the impudence of those oppressors.[12]

Despite all of the following—clear historical evidence of specific Islamic antisemitism, from the Geniza record of the High Middle Ages (including the coinage of a unique Hebrew word to characterize such Muslim Jew hatred, i.e., *sin'ūth*), published in full by Goitein as of 1971;[13] important studies of foundational Muslim sources detailing the sacralized rationale for Islam's anti-Jewish bigotry, including Hartwig Hirschfeld's mid-1880s essay series on Muhammad's subjugation of the Jews of Medina;[14] George Vajda's elegant, comprehensive 1937 analysis[15] focusing primarily on the hadith (the putative words and deeds of the Muslim Prophet Muhammad, as recorded by pious transmitters); and, much more recently, Haggai Ben-Shammai's concise 1988 study[16] of key examples of Jew hatred in the Qur'an and Qur'anic exegesis—conventional academic (and journalistic) wisdom continues to assert that Muslim Jew hatred is entirely a twentieth-century phenomenon, a mere by-product of the advent of the Zionist movement and the protracted Arab-Israeli conflict over the lands comprising the original 1922 mandate for historical Palestine (i.e., modern Israel, Jordan, Judea, Samaria, and Gaza). Such thinking also contends that this strain of Jew hatred is a loose amalgam of recycled medieval Christian Judeophobic motifs, calumnies from the Czarist Russia "Protocols of the Elders of Zion," and standard Nazi propaganda. A prototypical assessment of this ilk was written by the journalist Lawrence Wright in his widely acclaimed investigative account of the events leading to the cataclysmic acts of jihad terrorism on September 11, 2001.

> Until the end of World War II . . . Jews lived safely —although submissively—under Muslim rule for 1,200 years, enjoying full religious freedom; but in the 1930s, Nazi propaganda on Arabic-language shortwave radio, coupled with slanders by Christian missionaries in the region, infected the area with this ancient Western prejudice [antisemitism]. After the war, Cairo became a sanctuary for Nazis, who advised the military and the government. The rise of the Islamist movement coincided with the decline of fascism, but they overlapped in Egypt, and the germ passed into a new carrier. [17]

Wright's statement was not accompanied by documentation—this *was* the accepted wisdom after all. And in its essence, Wright's views are entirely consistent with those of the more elaborate prevailing scholarly analyses summarized quite accurately by Esther Webman in 1994:

> Antisemitism did not exist in the traditional Islamic world. . . . Antisemitism is, in fact, a relatively new phenomenon in the Arab world, gaining ground particularly since the eruption of the Arab-Israeli conflict in the mid-twentieth century. Nazi-style anti-Semitic books and publications have been produced openly. For example, there are at least nine different Arabic translations of the "Protocols of the Elders of Zion," which was translated into Arabic for the first time in the 1920s. . . . The development of European-style antisemitism in the Arab countries is related to three major factors: first, penetration during the nineteenth and twentieth centuries of a variety of European ideologies and concepts into the Arab world, among them antisemitism; second, the collapse of traditional political systems and of the loyalties and practices associated with them, giving way to the emergence of nationalistic government structures less tolerant in their treatment of religious, ethnic, and ideological minorities; and third, and most crucial, the development of the conflict over the domination of Palestine, beginning with Jewish resettlement in the late nineteenth century, followed by the establishment of the State of Israel and the ensuing Arab-Israeli conflict. . . . Themes borrowed from European Christendom were adapted by incorporating references in them. [18]

But this very flawed construct ignores primary, uniquely Islamic components of Muslim Jew hatred, both past and present. Indeed, for the Muslim masses, basic Islamic education in the Qur'an, hadith, and sira (earliest Muslim biographies of Muhammad) may create an immutable superstructure of Jew hatred on to which non-Muslim sources of Jew hatred are easily grafted.

The uncomfortable examination of Islamic doctrines and history is required in order to understand the enduring phenomenon of Muslim Jew hatred, which dates back to the origins of Islam. We can no longer view Muslim Jew hatred as a "borrowed phenomenon," seen exclusively, or even primarily, through the prism of Nazism and the Holocaust, the tragic legacy of Judeophobic Christian traditions, or "The Protocols of the Elders of Zion" from Czarist Russia. For example, Muhammad Sayyid Tantawi wrote these words in his seven-hundred-page treatise rationalizing Muslim Jew hatred, *Banu Isra'il fi al-Qur'an wa al-Sunna* (*Jews in the Qur'an and the Traditions*), originally published in the 1960s, and then reissued in 1986:

> [The] Qur'an describes the Jews with their own particular degenerate characteristics, i.e. killing the prophets of Allah, corrupting His words by putting them in the wrong places, consuming the people's wealth frivolously, refusal to distance themselves from the evil they do, and other ugly characteristics caused by their deep-rooted lasciviousness . . . only a minority of the Jews keep their word. . . . [A]ll Jews are not the same. The good ones become Muslims, the bad ones do not. (Qur'an 3:113) [19]

Tantawi was apparently rewarded for this scholarly effort by being named Grand Imam of Al-Azhar University in 1996, a position he still holds. These are the expressed, "carefully researched" views on Jews held by the nearest Muslim equivalent to a pope—the head of the most prestigious center of Muslim learning in Sunni Islam, Sunnis representing some 85 percent of the world's Muslims. And Sheikh Tantawi has not mollified such hate-mongering beliefs since becoming the Grand Imam of Al-Azhar as his statements on the Jews as "enemies of Allah, descendants of apes and pigs," [20] the legitimacy of homicide bombing of Jews, [21] or "dialogue" with Jews (just below), make clear. [22]

> . . . anyone who avoids meeting with the enemies in order to counter their dubious claims and stick fingers into their eyes, is a coward. My stance stems from Allah's book [the Qur'an], more than one-third of which deals with the Jews. . . . [I] wrote a dissertation dealing with them [the Jews], all their false claims and their punishment by Allah. I still believe in everything written in that dissertation. [i.e., from above, in *Banu Isra'il fi al-Qur'an wa al-Sunna*]

Tantawi's case illustrates the prevalence and depth of sacralized, "normative" Jew hatred in the contemporary

Muslim world. Even if all non-Muslim Judeophobic themes were to disappear miraculously overnight from the Islamic world, the living legacy of anti-Jewish hatred, and violence rooted in Islam's sacred texts— Qur'an, hadith, and sira—would remain intact. The assessment and understanding of Islamic antisemitism must begin with an unapologetic analysis of the anti-Jewish motifs contained in these foundational texts of Islam.

Antisemitism in the Qur'an

Composed in Arabic, and divided into chapters (suras) and verses (ayah; plural, ayat), the Qur'an contains some 80,000 words, 6,200 to 6,240 verses, and 114 suras, arranged from longest to shortest in length. Irrespective of chronology, i.e., when they were putatively revealed to the Muslim prophet Muhammad, the longer suras appear first in the actual arrangement of the Qur'an.[23] Theodore Nöldeke (d. 1930), whose seminal 1860 *Geschichte des Qorans* remains a vital tool for Qur'anic research, elaborated on the "revelation process," as understood by Muslims, in 1891:

> To the faith of the Muslims . . . the Koran is the word of God, and such also is the claim which the book itself advances. . . . The rationale for the revelation is explained in the Koran itself as follows:— In heaven is the original text ("the mother of the book," [sura] xliii. [verse] 3; "a concealed book," lv.77; "a well-guarded tablet," lxxxv.22). By a process of sending down (*tanzil*), one piece after another was communicated to the Prophet. The mediator was an angel, who is called sometimes the "Spirit" (xxxvi.193), sometimes the "holy Spirit" (xvi.104), and at a later time "Gabriel" (ii.91). This angel dictates the revelation to the Prophet, who repeats it after him, and afterward proclaims it to the world (lxxxvii.6, etc.). . . . It is an explicit statement of the Koran that the sacred book was revealed ("sent down") by God, not all at once, but piecemeal and gradually (xxv.34). This is evident from the actual composition of the book, and is confirmed by Muslim tradition. That is to say, Muhammad issued his revelation in flyleaves of greater or less extent. A single piece of this kind was called either, like the entire collection, *qur'an*, i.e., "reading," or rather "recitation;" or *kitab*, "writing;" or *sura*, which is the late-Hebrew *shura*, and means literally "series." The last became, in the lifetime of Muhammad, the regular designation of the individual sections as distinguished from the whole collection; and accordingly it is the name given to the separate chapters of the Koran.[24]

And to this day, for the Muslim masses, as Ibn Warraq notes,

> . . . the Koran remains the infallible word of God, the immediate word of God sent down, through the intermediary of a "spirit" or "holy spirit" or Gabriel, to Muhammad in perfect, pure Arabic; and every thing contained therein is eternal and uncreated. The original text is in heaven. . . . The angel dictated the revelation to the Prophet, who repeated it after him, and then revealed it to the world. Modern Muslims also claim that these revelations have been preserved exactly as revealed to Muhammad, without any change, addition, or loss whatsoever . . . the Koran remains for all Muslims, and not just "fundamentalists" the uncreated word of God Himself. It is valid for all times and places; its ideals are, according to all Muslims, absolutely true and beyond any criticism.[25]

The Qur'anic depiction of the Jews—their traits as thus characterized being deemed both infallible and timeless—has been summarized in elegant, complementary discussions by Haggai Ben-Shammai,[26] and Saul S. Friedman.[27] Ben-Shammai focuses on two key examples of Jew hatred in the Qur'an (and Qur'anic exegesis)— the "curse against the Jews" (in sura 2, verse 61), and Qur'anic verses (most notably, sura 5, verse 82) rationalizing why Jews were to be held in greater contempt than Christians.[28] Friedman's presentation is a remarkably compendious synthesis of anti-Jewish motifs developed in the Qur'an—Jews as misguided souls designated to suffer a "lighter punishment" in the corporeal world, but ultimately consigned to the hellfire if they fail to accept the "true faith" of Islam.[29]

Ben-Shammai[30] highlights the centrality of the Jews' "abasement and humiliation," and being "laden with God's anger" in the corpus of Muslim exegetic literature on Qur'an 2:61, including the hadith and Qur'anic commentaries. Despite the literal reference of 2:61 to the Israelites in the wilderness during their exodus from Egypt, he notes,[31]

> to all of the Muslim exegetes, without exception, it was absolutely clear that the reference was to the Jews of their day. The Arabic word translated as "pitched upon them" also means, literally, that the "abasement and poverty" were decreed for them forever. The "abasement" is the payment of the poll tax [jizya][32] and the humiliating ceremony involved. As for the "poverty," this insured their remaining impoverished forever. There are traditions which attribute this interpretation to Muhammad himself.[33]

The terrifying rage decreed upon the Jews forever is connected in the hadith and exegeses to Qur'an 1:7, where Muslims ask Allah to guide them rightly, not in the path of those who provoke and must bear His wrath. This verse is in turn linked to Qur'anic verses 5:60 and 5:78, which describe the Jews' transformation into apes and swine (5:60), having been "cursed by the tongue of David, and Jesus, Mary's son" (5:78).[34]

Ben-Shammai explains the primary reason for this "fearful decree," which resulted in the Jews being "so terribly cursed":

[F]rom time immemorial the Jews rejected God's signs, the wonders performed by the prophets. They did not accept the prophecy of Jesus whom the Koran counts among the prophets. But this is all part of the Jews' nature: they are by their very nature deceitful and treacherous.[35]

Although the Jews initially longed for Muhammad to triumph over the pagan Arabs, "Would that Allah send this prophet of whom our Book says that his coming is assured" (according to a tradition cited by Ben-Shammai),[36] realizing that Muhammad was not one of them, Ben-Shammai observes, quoting from Qur'an 5:64,

they then denied him out of jealousy of the Arabs, though they knew in truth he is the prophet. Furthermore, this Jewish trait brought them to grave heresy. They thought that they would succeed not only in leading humankind astray but also in fooling God . . . (5:64). "The Jews have said, God's hand is tied. . . . As often as they light a fire for war, God will extinguish it." Exegetes cite traditions which prove that the Jews always hated the true prophets and put them to death. Therefore they always failed in their wars and their Temple was destroyed time and again.[37]

Ben-Shammai's analysis[38] of Qur'an 5:82 ("Thou wilt surely find the most hostile of men to the believers are the Jews and the idolaters; and thou wilt surely find the nearest of them in love to the believers are those who say 'We are Christians'; that, because some of them are priests and monks, and they wax not proud"), links this verse to Qur'an 3:54–56,[39] and in turn to the tradition, "The Christians are to be above the Jews until the day of Judgment, for there is no land where the Christians are not above the Jews, neither in the east nor the west. The Jews are degraded in all the lands."

He emphasizes that in the traditions,

the Christians have a clear priority over the Jews. If we posit that the early tradition reflects the historical development of early Islam and that the political, economic, and social reality was apt to produce this preference, there is no doubt that these traditions reflect this reality.[40]

Both classical and modern Qur'anic exegeses by seminal Muslim commentators uphold Ben-Shammai's interpre-

tation of the anti-Jewish motifs featured in Qur'an 2:61 and 5:82. The great Muslim historian and Qur'anic exegete Tabari (d. 923), for example, interpreted the Qur'anic curse upon the Jews in 2:61 as follows:

"[A]basement and poverty were imposed and laid down upon them," as when someone says "the imam imposed the poll tax (*jizya*) on free non-Muslim subjects," or "The man imposed land tax on his slave," meaning thereby that he obliged him [to pay] it, or, "The commander imposed a sortie on his troops," meaning he made it their duty.

God commanded His believing servants *not* to give them [i.e., the non-Muslim people of the scripture] security—as long as they continued to disbelieve in Him and His Messenger—unless they paid the poll tax to them; God said: "Fight those who believe not in God and the Last Day and do not forbid what God and His Messenger have forbidden—such men as practice not the religion of truth [Islam], being of those who have been given the Book [Bible]—until they pay the poll tax, being humble." (Qur'an 9:29)

Ibn Zaid said about His words "and abasement and poverty were imposed upon them," "These are the Jews of the Children of Israel." I said: "Are they the Copts of Egypt?" He said: "What have the Copts of Egypt to do with this? No, by God, they are not; but they are the Jews, the Children of Israel."

By "and slain the prophets unrightfully" He means that they used to kill the Messengers of God without God's leave, denying their messages and rejecting their prophethood.[41]

Tabari's own related commentary on the posture to be assumed by a tributary during *jizya* collection (derived from Qur'an 9:29) underscores the deliberately humiliating character of this Qur'anic poll tax:

The dhimmis' [non-Muslim tributary's] posture during the collection of the *jizya*—[lowering themselves] by walking on their hands, . . . reluctantly.[42]

Baydawi (d. c. 1316), in his important Qur'anic exegesis *Anwaar al-Tanziil Wa-Asraar al-Ta'wiil*, provided this analysis of Qur'an 2:61:

"[H]umiliation and wretchedness" covered them like a dome, or stuck to them like wet clay to a wall—a metaphor for their denial of the bounty. The Jews are mostly humiliated and wretched either of their own accord, or out of coercion of the fear of having their *jizya* doubled. . . . Either they became deserving of His wrath [or] . . . the affliction of "humiliation and wretchedness" and the deserving wrath which preceded this.

"[B]ecause they disbelieved and killed the prophets unjustly" by reason of their disbelief in miracles, e.g. the splitting of the sea, the clouds giving shade, and the sending of the manna and quails, and splitting of the rock into twelve fountains or, disbelief in the revealed books, e.g. the Gospel, Qur'an, the verse of stoning, and the Torah verse in which Muhammad is depicted; and their killing of the prophets like Shay'aa [Isaiah], Zakariyyaa, Yahyaa, et al., all killed unjustly because they considered that of these prophets nothing was to be believed and thus they deserved to be killed.

In addition [God] accuses them of following fantasy and love of this world, as he demonstrates in His saying [line 14] "this if for their transgression and sin" i.e. rebelliousness, contrariness, and hostility brought them into disbelief in the signs, and killing the prophets. Venal sins lead to serious sins, just as small bits of obedience lead to larger ones. . . . God repeated this proof of what is *inveterate* [in the Jews], which is the reason for their unbelief and murder, and which is the cause of their committing sins and transgressing the bounds God set.[43]

Ibn Kathir (d. 1373), another prominent Qur'anic commentator, emphasized the Jews' eternal humiliation in accord with Qur'an 2:61:

This ayah indicates that the Children of Israel were plagued with humiliation, and this will continue, meaning it will never cease. They will continue to suffer humiliation at the hands of all who interact with them, along with the disgrace that they feel inwardly.

Al-Hassan commented, "Allah humiliated them under the feet of the Muslims, who appeared at a time when the Majus (Zoroastrians) were taking the jizya from the Jews. Also, Abu Al-'Aliyah, Ar-Rabi bin Anas and As-Suddi said that "misery" used in that ayah means "poverty." 'Atiyah Al-'Awfi said that "misery" means, "paying the tilth (tax)." In addition, Ad-Dahhak commented on Allah's statement, "and they drew on themselves the wrath of Allah," 'They deserved Allah's anger'. Also, Ibn Jarir said that, "and they drew on themselves the wrath of Allah" means, "They went back with the wrath." Similarly, Allah said, "Verily, I intend to let you draw my sin on yourself as well as yours" (Qur'an 5:29) meaning, "You will end up carrying my and your mistakes instead of me." Thus the meaning of the ayah becomes, "They went back carrying Allah's anger: Allah's wrath descended upon them; they deserved Allah's anger."

Allah's statement, "That was because they used to disbelieve in the Ayat (proofs, evidence, etc.) of Allah and killed the Prophets wrongfully," means "This is what We rewarded the Children of Israel with: humiliation and misery." Allah's anger that descended on the Children of Israel was a part of the humiliation they earned, because of their defiance of the truth, disbelief in Allah's Law, i.e., the Prophets and their following. The Children of Israel rejected the Messengers even killing them. Surely there is no form of disbelief worse than disbelieving in Allah's ayat and murdering the Prophets of Allah.[44]

The prolific modern Qur'anic commentator Sayyid Qutb (d. 1966), in contrast to the classical exegeses cited above, focuses initially on the plight of the Jews in biblical Egypt:

Moses is telling them to go back to Egypt and resume their servile, humble, humdrum life where they can have their cucumber, lentils, garlic, and onion. They would not, it seems, be strong enough for the great and noble task God had called on them to undertake. . . . I favor this second meaning because it reminds the Israelites of their misery and humiliation in Egypt. . . . "Ignominy and humiliation stamped upon them [the Jews] and they incurred the wrath of God" (Verse 61). Historically, this came later as a result of their disbelief in God's revelations, their killing of some of the prophets, and their general disobedience. These developments occurred several generations after Moses, but "ignominy and humiliation" are mentioned here because they fit the context of their condescension and insolence. Moses reminded them of the suffering and distress they had undergone in Egypt and of God's kindness in delivering them from the Pharoah.[45]

However, largely consistent with the classical commentaries on Qur'an 2:61 of Tabari, Baydawi, and Ibn Kathir, which emphasize (especially Baydawi and Ibn Kathir) the "inveterate" nature of the Jews, Qutb ultimately concludes:

No other nation has shown more intransigence and obstinacy than the Jews. They viciously and mercilessly killed and mutilated a number of prophets and messengers. They have over the centuries displayed the most extreme attitudes towards God, and towards their own religion and people. Nevertheless they have always boasted of their virtue and made the implausible claims of being the most rightly-guided nation, the chosen people of God and the only people that shall be saved. Such claims are totally refuted by the Qur'an.[46]

Finally, Sayyid Abul A'la Mawdudi (d. 1979), one of the most widely read and influential Muslim scholars of the twentieth century,[46] wrote the following commentary on Qur'an 2:61 in what is considered his "magnum opus" (completed in 1973), the *Tafhim al Qur'an* (*Towards Understanding the Qur'an*):[47]

> The Israelites recorded their crimes in detail in their own history.... The same hostility to Prophets is evident from the life of Jesus.... This is a shameful chapter in the record of the Jewish nation, to which the Qur'an refers here in passing. It is evident that when a nation chooses its most notoriously criminal and wicked people for positions of leadership, and its righteous and holy men for gaol [jail] and the scaffold, God has no alternative but to lay His curse and damnation on that nation.[48]

The Qur'an, as discussed by Ben-Shammai,[49] also maintains in sura 5, verse 82, that the Jews harbored a singular hatred of the Muslims, which distinguished them in this regard, from the Christians:

> Thou wilt find the most vehement of mankind in hostility to those who believe (to be) the Jews and the idolaters. And thou wilt find the nearest of them in affection to those who believe (to be) those who say: Lo! We are Christians. That is because there are among them priests and monks, and because they are not proud.

The classical Qur'anic commentaries of Tabari, Zamakashari (d. 1143), Baydawi, and Ibn Kathir on Qur'an 5:82 demonstrate a uniformity of opinion on the confirmed animus of the Jews toward the Muslims, which is repeatedly linked to the curse of Qur'an 2:61.

Tabari:

> In my [Tabari's] opinion, [the Christians] are not like the Jews who always scheme in order to murder the emissaries and the prophets, and who oppose God in his positive and negative commandments, and who corrupt His scripture which He revealed in His books.[50]

Zamakshari:

> Here God portrays the Jews as being unyielding and as acknowledging the truth only grudgingly.... On account of their vehement enmity against the believers, God places the Jews together with the idolaters; indeed, going even further, he shows them to be at the head, since they are mentioned before the idolaters. God does the same in his words: "And thou shalt find them (the Jews) the eagerest of men for life—even more so than the idolaters. Each of them wishes he could be given a life of a thousand years; but the grant of life would

not save him from chastisement—for God sees well all that they do!" (sura 2:96/90). The Jews are surely like this, and even worse! From the Prophet (the following is related): "If a Muslim is alone with two Jews, they will try to kill him.".... The Jews focused their hostility to the Muslims in the most overt and intense manner ...[51]

Baydawi:

> [B]ecause of [the Jews'] intense obstinacy, multi-faceted disbelief, and their addiction to following their whims, their adherence to the blind following of their tradition, their distancing themselves from the truth, and their unrelenting denial of, and hostility toward, the prophets ... [the Christians] ... easiness to deal with, the softness of their hearts, their dismissal of gain in this world, and their serious concern with learning and good deeds ... their acceptance of the truth as soon as they understand it; or, because of their humility as opposed to the arrogance of the Jews.[52]

Ibn Kathir:

> Allah said, "Verily you will find the strongest among men in enmity to the believers the Jews and those who commit Shirk [i.e., the polytheists, or idolators]." This describes the Jews, since their disbelief is that of rebellion, defiance, opposing the truth, belittling other people, and degrading the scholars. This is why the Jews—may Allah's continued curses descend on them until the Day of Resurrection—killed many of their Prophets and tried to kill the Messenger of Allah several times, as well as performing magic spells against him and poisoning him. They also incited their likes among the polytheists against the Prophet.[53]

Once again, Qutb's extensive modern exegesis on Qur'an 5:82 simply confirms the views of these classical commentators on the inveterate hatred of the Jews for the true, primordial faith of Islam (and its votaries, i.e., the Muslims). Extending the collective judgments of Tabari, Zamakshari, Baydawi, and Ibn Kathir to reflect, logically, on historical events as a continuum, from the time of Muhammad, through the twentieth century, Qutb maintains,

> What is noteworthy about the phrasing of this statement [Qur'an 5:82] is the fact that the Jews are mentioned ahead of the idolaters in being most hostile to the believers, and their hostility is open and easily recognized by anyone who cares to pay attention.... By mentioning the Jews first in this instance, when it would be thought they would be less than the idolators in their hostility to the believers as they have

revealed Scriptures of their own, makes the ordering particularly significant. Because of the way it is phrased, the statement directs attention to the fact that the Scriptures have not changed the Jews and that they are just the same as the unbelievers in their ardent hostility towards the believers. This is the least that can be said, although it is possible that the statement means that in their hostility to the believers, the Jews took the lead, their animosity greater than that of the idolators.

When we look at the history of Islam ever since its very early days until the present moment, we have no doubt that the hostility of the Jews to the believers has always been more fierce, determined and longer lasting than the hostility of the idolators and unbelievers. From the very first moment the Muslim state was established in Madinah, the Jews adopted a hostile attitude towards it. They schemed against the Muslim community from the outset of its very existence. Qur'anic references to this hostility and scheming are sufficient to give a good idea of the unabating war the Jews have waged against Islam and its Messenger (peace be upon him), and the Muslim community throughout history. Indeed, this war has not abated for a single moment throughout fourteen centuries. It continues to rage throughout the world even today.

The war that the Jews have launched against Islam has been much longer lasting and wider in spectrum than that launched against it by pagans and unbelievers both in old and modern times, although the latter has also been ferocious. The fight with the Arabian idolators in the early days of Islam did not last more than 20 years. Of similar duration was the battle against the Persian Empire. In modern times, we see that the war launched against Islam by paganism in India is and has been manifestly ferocious, but it does not equal the ferocity of the Zionist war against Islam. . . . The only battle against Islam which is comparable to that of the Jews in respect of its duration was that of the Crusades . . .[54]

Qutb, not surprisingly, concludes:

We remind ourselves of this history in order to appreciate God's purpose in mentioning the Jews ahead of the idolators in the ranking of those who are hostile to Islam. . . . Theirs is a wicked nature which is full of hatred for Islam, its Prophet and its followers. Hence, God warns His Messenger and the believers against its designs. This wicked and most vile nature could only be defeated in past history by Islam and its followers when they truly followed Islamic principles. Our modern world will not be saved from this wicked nature except by Islam, and only when its people implement Islam completely in their lives.[55]

Ben-Shammai, arguing for prolonged historical continuity, "As has been stated, this tradition (i.e., of more intense Muslim-Jewish hatred) has remained alive to this very day,"[56] refers to the travelogue accounts of Edward William Lane, which record Lane's observations of Egyptian society, written in 1835.[57] But Ben-Shammai fails to discuss a remarkable essay by the polymath Arabic writer al-Jahiz (d. 869),[58] composed a millennium earlier, which bolsters his argument by illustrating the anti-Jewish attitudes prevalent within an important early Islamic society. Al-Jahiz's essay—an anti-Christian polemic believed to have been commissioned by the Abbasid caliph al-Mutawakkil (d. 861), who inaugurated a literary campaign against the Christians[59]—explores the reasons why the Muslim masses prefer the Christians to the Jews. This empirical preference (although decried by the author)[60] is acknowledged by al-Jahiz from the outset:

I shall begin to enumerate the causes which made the Christians more liked by the masses than the Magians [Zoroastrians], and made men consider them more sincere than the Jews, more endeared, less treacherous, less unbelieving, and less deserving of punishment. For all this there are manifold and evident causes.[61]

Al-Jahiz offers two primary explanations for this abiding hostility of the Muslim rank and file toward the Jews. First was the "rancorous" relationship between the early Muslim community, exiles from Mecca, and their Jewish neighbors in Medina:

When the [Muslim] Emigrants [from Mecca] became the neighbors of the Jews [in Medina] . . . the Jews began to envy the Muslims the blessings of their new faith,[62] and the union which resulted after dissension. They proceeded to undermine the belief of our [i.e., the Muslim] masses, and to lead them astray. They aided our enemies and those envious of us. From mere misleading speech and stinging words they plunged into an open declaration of enmity, so that the Muslims mobilized their forces, exerting themselves morally and materially to banish the Jews and destroy them. Their strife became long-drawn and widespread, so that it worked itself up into a rage, and created yet greater animosity and more intensified rancor. The Christians, however, because of their remoteness from Mecca and Medina, did not have to put up with religious controversies, and did not have occasion to stir up trouble, and be involved in war. That was the first cause of our dislike of the Jews, and our partiality toward the Christians.[63]

However, al-Jahiz then identifies as "the most potent cause" of this particular animus toward the Jews, Qur'an 5:82, and its interpretation by the contemporary (i.e., mid-ninth-century) Muslim masses.[64] It is also worth noting that al-Jahiz (described as a "skeptic," who harbored "indifferent views toward religion in general")[64a] included these sociological observations that reveal the interface between Islamic religious and indigenous (*and indigenous ethnic/racial discriminatory attitudes toward*) Jews expressed a millennium before any secular Western European antisemitic ideologies would be exported to the Muslim Near East:

> Our people [the Muslims] observing thus the occupations of the Jews and the Christians concluded that the religion of the Jews must compare unfavorably as do their professions, and that their unbelief must be the foulest of all, since they are the filthiest of all nations. Why the Christians, ugly as they are, are physically less repulsive than the Jews may be explained by the fact that the Jews, by not intermarrying, have intensified the offensiveness of their features. Exotic elements have not mingled with them; neither have males of alien races had intercourse with their women, nor have their men cohabited with females of a foreign stock. The Jewish race therefore has been denied high mental qualities, sound physique, and superior lactation. The same results obtain when horses, camels, donkeys, and pigeons are inbred.[64b]

Al-Jahiz's contention that the Muslims harbored greater enmity toward the Jews than the Christians is supported by the independent observations of another Arab author active during the beginning of the ninth century in Iraq, the Sufi theologian al-Harith al-Muhasibi (d. 857).[64c] He maintained that because the Jews stubbornly denied Muhammad's truth, they were "in the eyes of the Muslims worse than the Christians."[64d]

One thousand years later, Lane's testimony on the difference between the attitude of Egyptian Muslims toward the Jews and the Christians again highlights the influence of Qur'an 5:82:

> They [the Jews] are held in the utmost contempt and abhorrence by the Muslims in general, and they are said to bear a more inveterate hatred than any other people to the Muslims and the Muslim religion. It is said, in the Koran [quoting 5:82] "Thou shalt surely find the most violent of all men to those who have believed to be the Jews . . . "[65]

Lane further notes:

> It is a common saying among the Muslims in this country, "Such one hates me with the hate of the Jews." We cannot wonder, then, that the Jews are

detested far more than are the Christians. Not long ago, they used often to be jostled in the streets of Cairo, and sometimes beaten for merely passing on the right hand of a Muslim. At present, they are less oppressed: but still they scarcely ever dare to utter a word of abuse when reviled or beaten unjustly by the meanest Arab or Turk; for many a Jew has been put to death upon a false and malicious accusation of uttering disrespectful words against the Koran or the Prophet. It is common to hear an Arab abuse his jaded ass, and, after applying to him various opprobrious epithets, end by calling the beast a Jew.[66]

Ben-Shammai's discussion also omits a series of subsequent nineteenth-century accounts that validate and expand upon Lane's narrative. For example, the French surgeon A. B. Clot, who resided in Egypt from 1825 to 1848 and served Muhammad Ali as a medical adviser, earning the honorific title "Bey," made these confirmatory observations written in 1840, five years after Lane's travelogue first appeared in 1835:

> The Israelite race is the one that the Muslims hate the most. They think that the Jews hate Islam more than any other nation. . . . Speaking of a fierce enemy, the Muslims say: "He hates me the way the Jews hate us." During the past century, the Israelites were often put to death because they were accused rightly or wrongly to have said something disrespectful about the Koran.[67]

And three decades later, such hateful attitudes, directed at the Jews specifically, persisted among Egyptian Muslims, as recorded in 1873 by Moritz Lüttke:

> The Muslim hates no other religion as he hates that of the Jews . . . even now that all forms of political oppression have ceased, at a time when such great tolerance is shown to the Christian population, the Arabs still bear the same contemptuous hatred of the Jews. It is a commonplace occurrence, for example, for two Arabs reviling each other to call each other Ibn Yahūdī (or "son of a Jew") as the supreme insult. . . . It should be mentioned that in these cases, they pronounce the word Yahūdī in a violent and contemptuous tone that would be hard to reproduce.[68]

Jacob Landau's modern analysis of Egyptian Jewry in the nineteenth century elucidates the predictable outcome of these bigoted archetypes "constantly repeated in various forms"—the escalation from rhetorical to physical violence against Jews:

> [I]t is interesting to note that even the *fallāhīn*, the Egyptian peasantry (almost all of them Muslim), certainly did not know many Jews at close quarters,

but nevertheless would revile them. The enmity some Muslims felt for the Jews incited them to violence, persecution, and physical assault, as in 1882. . . . Hostility was not necessarily the result of envy, for many Jews were poverty-stricken and even destitute and were sometimes forced to apply for financial assistance to their co-religionists abroad.[69]

Saul S. Friedman—in contrast to Ben-Shammai's detailed but narrow focus—weaves together a much fuller array of anti-Jewish Qur'anic motifs in his very concise and logical presentation.[70] The Qur'an acknowledges that Allah assisted the Israelites' passage across the Red Sea (Qur'an 10:90) and resettled them in a sanctified land (Qur'an 10:93). He further granted them Scriptures, while bestowing upon them wisdom and prophethood (Qur'an 45:16) without evil motives (Qur'an 11:110). Those Jews who fathomed the revelation of the true book (i.e., the Qur'an) would enjoy the blessings of paradise (Qur'an 27:76–81). However, as Friedman observes:

Unfortunately, these were few, because Jews had wronged themselves (Qur'an 16:118) by losing faith (Qur'an 7:168) and breaking the covenant (Qur'an 5:13). Sounding much like an ante-Nicean polemic, the Qur'an contends that the Jews are a nation that has "passed away" (Qur'an 2:134, 2:141). Twice God sent his instruments (the Assyrians [or Babylonians?] and Romans)[71] to punish this perverse people (Qur'an 17:4–5), and their dispersal over the face of the earth (Qur'an 34:7; 59:3) is proof of his rejection (Qur'an 7:168). For the arrogant Jews who still claim to be His chosen people, the Qur'an instructs, "Say: 'You of Jewry, if you assert that you are the friends of God, apart from other men, then do you long for death, if you speak truly" (Qur'an 62:6).[72]

Friedman then enumerates key examples of the "impressive indictment of the Jews' sins" contained within the Qur'an:

Apart from breaking the convenant, "they denied the revelations of Allah and killed their prophets unjustly" (Qur'an 4:155). Abuse of prophets is a consistent theme. In the Sura of the Cow [i.e., sura 2], Jews are asked, "Why did you kill the prophets of Allah if you are true believers?" (Qur'an 2:91). Jews are chastised for plotting against Jesus (Qur'an 3:55 and 4:157). Instead of revering Muhammad, whom they ridicule as Ra'ina (the evil one) (Qur'an 2:104; 4:46), these "perverse" creatures say Ezra is the messiah and they worship rabbis who defraud men of their possessions (Qur'an 9:30).[73]

Referenced passingly in Qur'an 59:1 as unbelievers and hypocrites, Friedman notes how the Jews are "especially vilified" in the suras held by Muslims to be later, or Medinan, revelations.[74]

In a long diatribe in the Sura of the Cow, where they are typified as an "envious" people (Qur'an 2:109) whose hearts are "hard as rock" (Qur'an 2:74), Jews are accused of confounding the truth (Qur'an 2:42), deliberately perverting scripture (Qur'an 2:75), and telling lies (Qur'an 2:78). Illiterate, senseless people of little faith (Qur'an 2:89), they engage in vague and wishful fancies (Qur'an 2:111). Shame and misery have been stamped on them for their transgressions (Qur'an 2:62),[75] which include usury (Qur'an 2:275), breaking the Sabbath (Qur'an 2:65), sorcery (Qur'an 2:102), hedonism (Qur'an 2:95),[75a] and idol worship (Qur'an 2:53).[75b]

Qur'an 4:51 again mentions the Jews' idol worship, in connection with "false gods," and, as Friedman notes, this accusation is then linked to a long series of other "iniquities" for which the Jews are faulted.[76]

[T]heir lack of faith, taking words out of context, disobedience and distortion (Qur'an 4:45),[77] their "monstrous falsehoods" (Qur'an 4:156), usury, and cheating (Qur'an 4:160).[78] The charge of cheating is prominently featured in Imran [sura 3] where most Jews are accused of being "evildoers" (Qur'an 3:111)[78a] who, deceived by their own lies (Qur'an 3:24), try to "debar believers from the path of Allah and seek to make it crooked" (Qur'an 3:99). Jews mislead (Qur'an 3:69), confound the truth (Qur'an 3:71), twist tongues (Qur'an 3:79),[78b] and say, "We are not bound to keep faith with Gentiles" (Qur'an 3:75). Believers are advised by the Sura of The Table [sura 5] not to take these clannish people as their friends (Qur'an 5:51). "The most implacable of men in their enmity to the faithful" (Qur'an 5:82), Jews are blind and deaf to the truth (Qur'an 5:71). What they have not forgotten, they have perverted.

All these charges build to a denouement (as if part of a theological indictment, conviction, and sentencing process) in Qur'anic verses 58:14–19, which state:

Do you see those that have befriended a people [the Jews] with whom Allah is angry?

They belong neither to you nor to them. They knowingly swear to falsehoods.

Allah has prepared for them a grievous scourge. Evil indeed is that which they have done.

They use their faith as a disguise and debar others from the path of Allah. A shameful scourge awaits them.

Neither their wealth nor their children shall in the least protect them from Allah. They are the heirs of Hell and there they shall abide forever.

On the day when Allah restores them all to life, they will swear to Him as they now swear to you, thinking that their oaths will help them. Surely they are liars all.

Satan has gained possession of them and caused them to forget Allah's warning. They are the confederates of Satan; Satan's confederates assuredly will be lost.[79]

Friedman's discussion concludes with an elaboration of the "ultimate sin" committed by the Jews, and their appropriate punishment.[80]

[T]hey are among the devil's minions (Qur'an 4:60). Cursed by God, their faces will be obliterated (Qur'an 4:47). If they do not accept the true faith, on the day of judgment, they will be made into apes (Qur'an 2:65, and 7:166) and burn in the hellfire (Qur'an 4:55). As it is written in the Sura of the Proof [i.e., sura 98], "The unbelievers among the People of the Book and the pagans shall burn forever in the fire of Hell. They are the vilest of all creatures" (Qur'an 98:7).[81]

Ben-Shammai and Friedman illustrate anti-Jewish motifs in the Qur'an either broadly (Friedman),[82] or in a more focused way (Ben Shammai).[83] Ronald Nettler's 1990 analysis confirms Ben Shammai's conclusions:

The main portrayal of the Jews in the Qur'an is that of rejectors of Allah's truth and persecutors of his prophets. This meant, of course, that the Jews were mortal enemies of Islam. From this motif were derived other, subsidiary themes. Here the Jews were portrayed as possessors of a tarnished truth (which they themselves tarnished) who, for the most part, could not recognize in Muhammad's revelation the most perfect version of their own. They ought to have welcomed and acknowledged this new doctrine of completion and fulfillment. Instead they denied and rejected it. Rather than put their full weight behind Muhammad's people they chose to oppose him, sometimes even aiding his enemies. Yet it was the Jews, from Islam's point of view who, more than anyone else, were obliged to give such acknowledgment. It is hardly surprising then, that the Qur'an in one well-known condemnation [Qur'an 5:82] of the Jews described them as "the most hostile in intent toward the believers" along with the pagans. This already encapsulated, in essence, the Qur'anic view of the Jews.[84]

Nettler further illustrates how such Qur'anic archetypes of Jews were amplified in the hadith, sira, and early Islamic theological and historical literature, which complement the Qur'an as foundational sources of Islamic beliefs. These core texts—summarized elegantly by Nett-

tler—assert that the Jews caused Muhammad's agonizing death by poisoning,[85] and maintain that it was a renegade Jew (Abd Allah b. Saba)[86] who fomented the nearly cataclysmic civil strife over the succession of the "Rightly Guided Caliphs," and was also responsible for the Shi'ite heresy and resultant Shi'a sectarianism:

Such a stubborn denial of truth—part of the "eternal" Jewish nature, as early Islam conceived it—impelled the Jews to act with conspiratorial malevolence toward Muhammad and his new tradition. Hence the various motifs of Jewish perfidy in early Islamic theoretical and historical literature. The Jews' role as allies of Muhammad's various opponents was, for example, a commonplace in the hadith, sira, and historical literature. One of the most extreme forms of Jewish perfidiousness alleged in the Islamic sources was the portrayal of the Jews as the killers of Muhammad. In keeping with the Qur'anic portrayal of the Jews as persecutors and even killers of their own prophets, this idea brought the story up to date, as it were, in a sort of *denouement* of the long drama of Jewish attacks on the prophets and prophecy. The archetypal logic of the tale was flawless: in Islamic terms, this was the final Jewish assault on the apex of prophetic religion. . . . [R]ecounted . . . in the standard story of Muhammad's painful and protracted death from poisoning by a Jewish woman.

Another early archetype of Jewish perfidy and destructiveness toward Islam was the story of Abd Allah b. Saba, the man held responsible, in the main Sunni historiographical accounts, for the first serious internal rebellion suffered by Islam. Culminating in the assassination of Islam's third caliph, Uthman, this rebellion was traditionally perceived as the first, and fateful, breach in Muslim unity; the breach that adumbrated the subsequent period of harsh internal strife and dangerous disunity which marked the permanent loss of Islam's political innocence. Described in the sources as an uprising in which the putative Jew, and alleged founder of the heterodox Shi'ite sect, Abd Allah b. Saba, played the key role, the portrayal of this major Islamic catastrophe exuded resonances of Jewish and Jewish-inspired heterodox elements conspiring to wreck the political stability and security of Islam; indeed wreck Islam itself.[87]

Syrian President Bashar al-Assad, in a speech welcoming Pope John Paul II to Damascus on May 5, 2001, demonstrated how the "flawlessly updated" Islamic motif of Jews as prophet killers and torturers is used to vilify both Jews and the Jewish State of Israel:

We notice them [i.e., the Jews] aggressing against Muslim and Christian Holy Sites in Palestine, violating the sanctity of the Holy Mosque (Al-Aqsa), of the church of Sepulcher in Jerusalem and of the Church of Nativity in Bethlehem. *They [i.e., the Jews] try to kill all the principles of divine faiths with the same mentality of betraying Jesus Christ and torturing Him, and in the same way that they tried to commit treachery against Prophet Mohammad (peace be upon Him).*[87a]

Ben-Shammai, Nettler, and Friedman omit from their discussions, however, any comprehensive analysis of Qur'an 9:29: "Fight against such of those who have been given the Scripture as believe not in Allah nor the Last Day, and forbid not that which Allah hath forbidden by His messenger, and follow not the Religion of Truth, until they pay the tribute readily, being brought low." The injunctions delineated in this verse clearly do not apply to Jews alone, including Christians and perhaps Zoroastrians, as well. Yet Qur'an 9:29 and the modes of subjugation it mandates for the Jews (and those other of "Scriptured" faiths)—via peaceful or violently imposed submission—provide the framework for implementing the myriad dictates of the Qur'an, including its antisemitic injunctions, under Shari'a, the sacralized Islamic jural order.

Ibn Kathir's fourteenth-century commentary[88] expresses the classical Muslim orthodoxy on Qur'an 9:29—the verse that links the unique Islamic institution of jihad war, integrally, to the imposition of the pact of submission (or *dhimma*) upon the vanquished "Scriptured" (or *dhimmi*) peoples, primarily Jews and Christians:

[W]hen the People of the Scriptures disbelieved in Muhammad, they had no beneficial faith in any Messenger or what the Messengers brought. Rather they followed their religions because this conformed with their ideas, lusts, and the ways of their forefathers, not because they are Allah's laws and religion. Had they been true believers in their religions, that faith would have directed them to believe in Muhammad because all Prophets gave the good news of Muhammad's advent and commanded them to obey and follow him. Yet when he was sent, they disbelieved in him, even though he is the mightiest of all Messengers. Therefore, they do not follow the religion of earlier Prophets because these religions came from Allah, but because these suit their desires and lusts. Therefore, their claimed faith in an earlier Prophet will not benefit them because they disbelieved in the master, the mightiest, the last and most perfect of all Prophets. Hence Allah's statement "Fight against those who believe not in Allah, nor in the Last Day, nor forbid that which has been forbidden by Allah and His Messenger, and those who acknowledge not the religion of truth among the People of the Scripture."

This honorable Ayah was revealed with the order

to fight the People of the Book, after the pagans were defeated, the people entered Allah's region in large numbers, and the Arabian Peninsula was secured under the Muslims' control. Allah commanded His Messenger to fight the People of the Scriptures, Jews and Christians. . . . Allah said, "until they pay the Jizya," if they do not choose to embrace Islam, "with willing submission," in defeat and subservience, "and feel themselves subdued," disgraced, humiliated and belittled. Therefore, Muslims are not allowed to honor the people of Dhimma or elevate them above Muslims, for they are miserable, disgraced, and humiliated.

Moreover, forcing Jews in particular to pay the Qur'anic poll tax "tribute," "readily," while "being brought low," is consistent with their overall humiliation and abasement in accord with Qur'an 2:61 and its directly related verses.

Mawdudi's commentary provides the twentieth-century confirmation of this orthodox view of Qur'an 9:29, expressed in a modern idiom:

The Jews and Christians have corrupted their faith since they have distorted certain basic components of that [true] belief [i.e., Islam]. . . . The People of the Book do not follow the Law revealed by God through His Messenger.

The purpose for which the Muslims are required to fight is not as one might think to compel the unbelievers into embracing Islam. Rather their purpose is to put an end to the sovereignty and supremacy of the unbelievers so that the latter are unable to rule over men. The authority to rule should only be vested in those who follow the true faith; unbelievers who do not follow this true faith should live in a state of subordination. . . . Jizyah symbolizes the submission of the unbelievers to the suzerainty of Islam. To pay the jizyah of their own hands "humbled" refers to payment in a state of submission. "Humbled" also reinforces the idea that the believers, rather than the unbelievers, should be the rulers in performance of their duty as God's vicegerents.

Some nineteenth-century Muslim writers and their followers in our own times never seem to tire of their apologies for jizyah. But God's religion does not require that apologetic explanations be made on its behalf. The simple fact is that according to Islam, non-Muslims have been granted the freedom to stay outside the Islamic fold and to cling to their false, man-made ways if they so wish. They have, however, absolutely no right to seize the reigns of power in any part of God's earth nor to direct the collective affairs of human beings according to their own misconceived doctrines. For if they are given such an opportunity, corruption and mischief will ensue. In such a situation the believers would be under an obligation to do their utmost to dislodge them from political power and to make them live in subservience to the Islamic way of life.

One of the advantages of jizyah is that it reminds the Dhimmis every year that because they do not embrace Islam . . . they have to pay a price—jizyah—for clinging to their errors.[89]

Earlier, in relation to Qur'an 5:82, a few brief examples were provided[90] illustrating the historical continuity (from ninth-century Baghdad/Iraq to nineteenth-century Egypt) of the hateful attitudes toward Jews this specific verse (5:82) engendered among the Muslim masses, as chronicled by contemporary observers, both Muslim and non-Muslim. Having now presented a full spectrum of the major anti-Jewish motifs in the Qur'an, additional illustrations demonstrating their persistent influence on Muslim attitudes (and resultant behaviors) toward Jews can be provided. Four themes will be considered: (1) the Jews being associated with Satan and consigned to hell (Qur'an 4:60, 4:55, 58:14–19, and 98:6), (2) the imposition of the Qur'anic poll tax (*jizya*; Qur'an 9:29) on Jews, specifically; (3) the related enforcement of the Qur'anic (2:61) "curse" upon the Jews for killing the prophets, and other transgressions against Allah's will, meriting their permanent humiliation and abasement; and, last in connection to this curse, (4) the Jews' transformation into apes/swine as punishment (Qur'an 2:65, 5:60, and 7:166).

Formal decrees (or modern pronouncements) and opinions from Muslim rulers, jurisconsults, and theologians—past and present—have repeatedly associated non-Muslim *dhimmis* in general, or Jews specifically, with Satan, and the torments of being consigned deservedly to Hell. The Abbasid caliph al-Mutawakkil in an anti-dhimmi decree dated 850, according to Tabari's account, ". . . commanded that wooden images of devils[91] be nailed to the doors of their homes to distinguish them from the homes of Muslims."[92] Ibn Abdun, a Muslim jurist from Seville, Spain, invoked Qur'an 58:19 in a section of his treatise (dated 1100) on *dhimmi* servitudes that discussed the appropriate dress of *dhimmis* and how Muslims should "greet" them:

You must not allow any . . . Jew or Christian to wear the attire of great men, doctors of law, or the wealthy. On the contrary, they must be objects of contempt and disgust; they are not entitled to a greeting of peace ["Peace upon you!" (*as-salam alaykum!*)]. In effect [quoting 58:19] "Satan has gained the mastery over them, and caused them to forget God's Remembrance. Those are Satan's party; why, Satan's party, surely, they are the losers!" They must wear a distinctive, ignominious sign.[93]

A September 2002 review of Friday sermons from Saudi Arabian mosques indicates that these motifs remain vibrant in popular modern Islamic religious teaching. At a mosque in Mecca, Sheikh Adnan Ahmed Siyami stated,

[Islam] believes that only Islam and the "Camp of Kufur [unbelief]" exist, and that there is no way to reach Paradise and to be delivered from Hell except by walking in the path of our Prophet Muhammad and joining Islam. Any other way leads to Hell.[94]

Sheikh Muhammad Saleh Al-Munajjid, another contemporary Saudi cleric, referred to the Jews, explicitly in his related discussion during a sermon delivered at a mosque in Al-Damam:

The Jews are the helpers of Satan. The Jews are the cause of the misery of the human race, together with the infidels and the other polytheists. Satan leads them to Hell and to a miserable fate.

The common expressions and practices of ordinary Muslims demonstrate how such associations of the Jews with Satan and hell have long been imbibed by the masses. Solomon b. Jeroham, the authoritative Karaite Jewish exegete who lived in Jerusalem during the mid-tenth century,[95] confirmed that the hateful doctrine regarding salutation (and humiliation), illustrated (above) by Ibn Abdun's treatise,[96] was actually practiced by Muslims in their encounters with Jews. Solomon included the following observation in his 955–956 commentary on the Book of Lamentations:

What can you say about people [Muslims] who curse you when you greet them, and when you do not greet them humiliate you and offend you?[97]

Sir John Drummond-Hay (1816–1893) was a British diplomat and fluent linguist with an extensive knowledge about Morocco, having lived with his father (Consul-General Edward Drummond-Hay) in Tangier from the age of sixteen, and served as a trusted personal adviser to three generations of Moroccan sultans. Writing in 1844, Sir John noted the belief among Muslims of the North African Maghreb (especially Morocco) that

. . . if a Muhammadan walks on a Jewish grave he gives relief to the infidel in it, who is in torture, and that for this reason he should keep away from the grave.[98]

Indeed the notion that Jews are condemned, rightfully, to such eternal torment after death is made clear by Muhammad, as recorded in the canonical hadith collections of Bukhari and Muslim:

Narrated Aisha: Once Allah's Apostle passed by the (grave of) a Jewess, whose relatives were weeping over her. He said, "They are weeping over her and she is being tortured in her grave."[99]

Narrated Abi Ayub: Once the Prophet went out after Sunset and heard a dreadful voice, and said, "The Jews are being punished in their graves."[100]

Tudor Parfitt's 1996 analysis of the twentieth-century exodus of Yemen's Jews,[101] leading to the liquidation of their ancient community, observed that Jews figured prominently in Yemeni proverbs and expressions, including this common reference to hellfire:

It used to be the case after saying "It's hot today" to comment "Ah! A Jew must have perished"—an allusion to the Jew burning in Hell.

The *jizya* collection ritual, consistent with Qur'an 9:29, fulfills the prescribed debasement of Jews and other *dhimmis*. Al-Suyuti (d. 1505), author (along with his mentor) of a seminal Qur'anic commentary (*Tafsir al-Jalalyn*), made these recommendations regarding *jizya* collection:

[J]izya is part of land and slaves . . . is incumbent upon the People of the Book . . . on people who allow wine [Jews and Christians] and pig-meat [Christians]. . . . [Saaghiruuna means] submissively . . . [it means] by coercion . . . ['an yadin means] directly, not trusting the trickery of an intermediary . . . by force . . . without resistance . . . in an unpraiseworthy manner . . . while you stand and [the dhimmi] sits with the whip in front of you [you take] the money while he has dirt on his head.[102]

Al-Maghili (d. 1504), a contemporary of Al-Suyuti and an important North African theologian whose writings on the *dhimmis* influenced both the Muslim masses of his day and the followers through the nineteenth and early twentieth centuries, insisted that affronts be inflicted upon the *dhimmis*, especially Jews, when collecting the *jizya*:

On the day for tax collecting, they should be assembled in a public place, like the *souk*. They should present themselves there, standing up at the lowest, vilest place. The auxiliaries of the Law should stand above them, striking a menacing pose, so that appears to their eyes and to the eyes of the others that our purpose is to debase them by pretending to take their belongings. They will realize that we do them a favor [again] by accepting the *jizya* from them and letting them go [their way]. Then they shall be brought one by one [before the official responsible] for collecting the tax. While paying,

the *dhimmi* will receive a slap and will be pushed back in such fashion that he will think that he has escaped the sword thanks to this [insult]. This is how the friends of the Lord in the first and last generations act toward their miscreant enemies, for power belongs to God, to His Apostle and to the Believers.[103]

The enduring legacy of Al-Maghili's teachings is evident in two remarkable accounts of the humiliating conditions under which the *jizya* was still being collected from Moroccan Jews in the modern era. An Italian Jew traveling in Morocco in 1894 reported the following:

The kaid Uwida and the kadi Mawlay Mustafa had mounted their tent today near the Mellah [Jewish ghetto] gate and had summoned the Jews in order to collect from them the poll tax [*jizya*] which they are obliged to pay the sultan. They had me summoned also. I first inquired whether those who were European-protected subjects had to pay this tax. Having learned that a great many of them had already paid it, I wished to do likewise. After having remitted the amount of the tax to the two officials, I received from the kadi's guard two blows in the back of the neck. Addressing the kadi and the kaid, I said 'Know that I am an Italian protected subject.' Whereupon the kadi said to his guard: 'Remove the kerchief covering his head and strike him strongly; he can then go and complain wherever he wants.' The guards hastily obeyed and struck me once again more violently. This public mistreatment of a European-protected subject demonstrates to all the Arabs that they can, with impunity, mistreat the Jews.[104]

And in a letter from January 30, 1911, by Avram Elmaleh, head of the Fez boys' school, to the president of the Alliance Israélite Universelle in Paris, we learn the degrading conditions imposed upon the rabbinical leaders of the Moroccan Jewish community in connection with "community business" (i.e., payment of the *jizya*), even into the second decade of the twentieth century:

I have the honor to acknowledge receipt of your letter No. 1283 of 30 January, enclosing a letter from Rabbi Vidal Sarfaty. The rabbi asks you to intervene with Si Mohamed el Mokri, the Moroccan Minister of Foreign Affairs, at present in Paris, for the abolition of the degrading custom imposed on Jews, not to enter Dar el Maghzen except barefoot. Unfortunately, the facts given in Rabbi Vidal's letter are correct. Jews must take off their shoes at the gate of Dar-Maghzen. Quite apart from the humiliation involved in this measure, it is an intolerable suffering for our co-religionists to be obliged to stand many hours barefoot on the earth of the Palace courtyard, which is either cold and damp or white-hot from the summer sun. Rabbi Vidal, a regular visitor to the Dar-Maghzen in connection with community business or on behalf of individuals, has often returned ill from a rather too long sojourn in front of the offices. It is my opinion that it would be impossible to obtain an order from the Sultan to allow Jews to enter the Palace with their shoes on. It is a concession which his pride would not permit, and one quite contrary to the Muslim conception of the relative positions of the Jews and themselves.[105]

Only when Morocco became a French protectorate was there effective abolition of such Shari'a-based practices, affording Jews, as Stillman observes, "far greater security and opportunity" than had existed in the "chaotic and violent days" prior to its (1912) establishment.[106] However, even a quarter century after the establishment of a French protectorate in Tunisia (May 1881), as described by Jacques Chalom (in 1908), rural Tunisian Jews were still required to pay the *jizya* (termed *majba* in Tunisia).[107] Moreover, Jews in Yemen and Afghanistan continued to pay the *jizya* until the liquidation of their communities after Israel was established in 1948.[108]

Although Yemen's twentieth century rulers (Imam Yahya and his son Ahmad) dispensed with public ceremonial degradation, the deliberately threatening and humiliating atmospherics of *jizya* collection persisted. Aviva Klein-Franke describes the collection process:

> The Imam [Yahya, and later his son Ahmad] would nominate a respectable Jew to collect the Poll Tax. The nominated was called *Ma'mūr*, Sheikh or *ʿĀqil*. . . . He was ordered to prepare a list of all the Jewish males in his community who had reached the age of thirteen years for the purpose of collecting the Djizya . . . The *ʿUqqāl* [assistants to the *Ma'mūr*] also had to mention those Jews who had emigrated. As we have seen, the Imam confiscated the property of anyone who left the Yemen. Jews were not allowed to sell their property before leaving the country—everything would be forfeited to the Imam by his [Imam Yahya's] decree of 1920.

> Before the *ʿUqqāl* collected the money, a street crier went through the Jewish quarter, proclaiming that the Imam expected everyone to pay the Djizya without delay. Failure to do so meant that a soldier, *Baqaa*, might be billeted on those in default until such time as they paid. . . . Usually the Jews paid without any objection . . . they could send a written appeal to the Imam. If a Jew still refused to pay the Djizya, the Imam would accept no further excuses and would send his soldiers to the recalcitrant Jew

until he was willing to pay. This meant soldiers might stay in his household for a few days. The Jew had to house them and do everything to satisfy their needs, otherwise soldiers would complain to the Imam that they had not been treated well, and that they had been insulted as Muslims. Not only would such an arrangement cost the person much more than the Djizya he owed, he could even end up in prison.[109]

According to a 1950 report, the Jews of Afghanistan were subjected to governmental anti-Jewish bias, and the religious zeal of local Muslim populations, right until their final exodus (typically escaping to India and thence to Israel). This ongoing discrimination included their public humiliation during collection of the *jizya*:

> [T]he Jews in Afghanistan are still subject to all the forms of discrimination which rigorous adherence to the Koran [9:29] requires. They have to pay the jizyah poll-tax imposed upon infidels, and the payment is accompanied by humiliating ceremonies.[110]

The degrading *jizya* collection ritual was a salient feature of broader anti-*dhimmi* regulations codified into Islamic law, consistent with Qur'an 9:29. The "contract of the *jizya*," "*dhimma*," or "system of dhimmitude" encompassed other obligatory and recommended regulations for the conquered non-Muslim *dhimmi* peoples, including Jews, such as:[111] the prohibition of arms for the vanquished non-Muslims (*dhimmis*) and of church bells; restrictions concerning the building and restoration of churches, synagogues, and temples; inequality between Muslims and non-Muslims with regard to taxes and penal law; the refusal of *dhimmi* testimony by Muslim courts;[112] a requirement that Jews and other non-Muslims wear special clothes; and the overall humiliation and abasement of non-Muslims. It is important to note that these regulations and attitudes were institutionalized as permanent features of the sacred Islamic law, or Shari'a. The writings of the much-lionized Sufi theologian and jurist al-Ghazali (d. 1111; the famous theologian, philosopher, and paragon of mystical Sufism, who, as noted by the renowned scholar W. M. Watt, has been "acclaimed in both the East and West as the greatest Muslim after Muhammad")[113] highlight how the institution of *dhimmitude* was simply a normative and prominent feature of the Shari'a:

> [T]he *dhimmi* is obliged not to mention Allah or His Apostle. . . . Jews, Christians, and Majians must pay the *jizya* [poll tax on non-Muslims] . . . on offering up the *jizya*, the *dhimmi* must hang his head while the official takes hold of his beard and hits [the *dhimmi*] on the protruberant bone beneath his ear [i.e., the mandible]. . . . They are not permitted to ostentatiously display their wine or church

bells . . . their houses may not be higher than the Muslim's, no matter how low that is. The *dhimmi* may not ride an elegant horse or mule; he may ride a donkey only if the saddle[-work] is of wood. He may not walk on the good part of the road. They [the *dhimmis*] have to wear [an identifying] patch [on their clothing], even women, and even in the [public] baths . . . [*dhimmis*] must hold their tongue.[114]

Two particularly humiliating "vocations" were imposed upon Jews by their Muslim overlords in Yemen and Morocco, where Jews formed the only substantive non-Muslim *dhimmi* populations. Yemenite Jews had to remove human feces and other waste matter (urine that failed to evaporate, etc.) from Muslim areas, initially in Sanaa and later in other communities such as Shibam, Yarim, and Dhamar.[114a] Decrees requiring this obligation were issued in the late eighteenth or early nineteenth century and reintroduced in 1913.[114b] Yehuda Nini reproduces an 1874 letter written by a Yemenite Jew to the Alliance Israélite in Paris, lamenting the practice:

[I]t is 86 years since our forefathers suffered the cruel decree and great shame to the nation of Israel from the east to sundown . . . for in the days of our fathers, 86 years ago, there arose a judge known as *Qadi*, and said unto the king and his ministers who lived in that time that the Lord, Blessed be He, had only created the Jews out of love of the other nations, to do their work and be enslaved by them at their will, and to do the most contemptible and lowly of tasks. And of them all . . . the greatest contamination of all, to clear their privies and streets and pathways of the filthy dung and the great filth in that place and to collect all that is left of the dung, may your Honor pardon the expression.[114c]

Moroccan Jews were confined to ghettos in the major cities such as Fez (since the thirteenth century) called *mellahs* (salty earth), which derives from the fact it was here that they were forced to salt the decapitated heads of executed rebels for public exposition.[114d] This brutally imposed humiliating practice—which could be enforced even on the Jewish Sabbath—persisted through the late nineteenth century, as described by Eliezer Bashan:

In the 1870s, Jews were forced to salt the decapitated heads of rebels on the Sabbath. For example, Berber tribes frequently revolted against Sultan Muhammad XVIII. In order to force them to accept his authority, he would engage in punitive military campaigns. Among the tribes were the Musa, located south of Marrakesh. In 1872, the Sultan succeeded in quelling their revolt and forty-eight of their captives were condemned to death. In October 1872, on the order of the Sultan, they were dis-patched to Rabat for beheading. Their decapitated heads were to be exposed on the gates of the town for three days. Since the heads were to be sent to Fez, Jewish ritual slaughterers (Hebrew, *shohetim*) were forced to salt them and hang them for exposure on the Sabbath. Despite threats by the governor of Rabat, the Jews refused to do so. He then ordered soldiers to enter the homes of those who refused and drag them outside. After they were flogged, the Jews complied and performed the task and the heads of the rebels were exposed in public.[114e]

Various anti-*dhimmi* regulations became integral to the permanent "humiliation and wretchedness" prescribed for the Jews, specifically, by the Qur'anic curse of 2:61. Breaches of this regulatory pact (or *dhimma*) by Jews—whether real or perceived—could have disastrous consequences, including fully sanctioned jihad violence directed at them.[115] For example, the poet Abu Ishaq al-Elbiri is believed to have helped incite the Muslim masses in 1066 against the Jewish vizier of Granada, Joseph Ibn Naghrela, with a vitriolic anti-Jewish ode emphasizing how the *dhimma* had been violated. Abu Ishaq wrote:

Bring them down to their place and Return them to the most abject station. They used to roam around us in tatters Covered with contempt, humiliation, and scorn. They used to rummage amongst the dungheaps for a bit of a filthy rag to serve as a shroud for a man to be buried in. . . . Do not consider that killing them is treachery. Nay, it would be treachery to leave them scoffing. [The translator then summarizes: "The Jews have broken their covenant (i.e., overstepped their station, with reference to the Covenant of Umar) and compunction would be out of place."][116]

A contemporary chronicle written by sultan 'Abd Allah (who became Sultan of Granada in 1073) confirms that a breach in the system of *dhimmitude* precipitated the outburst of anti-Jewish violence by the Muslims of Granada:

Both the common people and the nobles were disgusted by the cunning of the Jews, the notorious changes they had brought in the order of things, and the positions they occupied in violation of their pact [i.e., the *dhimma*]. Allah decreed their destruction on Saturday 10 Safar 459 (December 31, 1066). . . . The Jew [Joseph Ibn Naghrela] fled into the interior of the palace, but the mob pursued him there, seized him, and killed him. They then put every Jew in the city to the sword and took vast quantities of their property.[117]

The pogrom by Granada's Muslims resulted in the assassination of Joseph Ibn Naghrela and the massacre of some three thousand to four thousand Granadan Jews, along with the pillage of the Jewish community.[118] This figure equals or exceeds the number of Jews reportedly killed by the Crusaders during their pillage of the Rhineland some thirty years later at the outset of the First Crusade.[119]

The Mongol conquest of Baghdad in 1258 under Hulagu Khan (d. 1265) destroyed Muslim suzerainty and the domination of Islam as a state religion, rendering it "a religion among all others."[120] Mongol rule thus eliminated the system of *dhimmitude*, and, in contrast to Islamic chauvinism, writes Walter Fischel,

the principle of tolerance for all faiths, maintained by the Il Khans [Mongol rulers], (depriving) the [Islamic] concept of the "Protected People" the ahl adh-Dhimma [*dhimmi* system] . . . of its former importance; with it fell the extremely varied professional restrictions into which it had expanded, . . . primarily those regarding the admission of Jews and Christians to government posts.[121]

The thirteenth-century Christian chronicler Bar Hebraeus recorded this telling observation:

With the Mongols there is neither slave nor free man, neither believer nor pagan, neither Christian nor Jew; but they regard all men as belonging to one and the same stock.[122]

And the Iraqi Ghazi b. al-Wasiti (fl. 1292), author of a contemporary Muslim treatise on the *dhimmis*, noted:

A firman of the Il Khan [Hulagu] had appeared to the effect that everyone should have the right to profane his faith openly and his religious connection; and that the members of one religious body should not oppose those of another.[123]

Fischel concludes:

For Christians and Jews, the two groups chiefly affected by the ahl adh-Dhimma policy, current until then, this change in constitutional and religious principles implied a considerable amelioration of their position; whereas for the Muslims it meant they had sunk to a depth hitherto unknown in their history.[124]

The brief rise and calamitous fall of Sa'd ad-Daula—which mirrored the experience of his Jewish co-religionists—took place during this Mongol epoch. Sa'd ad-Daula was a Jewish physician who successfully reformed the Mongol revenue and taxation system for Iraq. In recognition of these services, he was appointed by the Mongol emperor Arghun (who reigned from 1284 to 1291) to the position of administrative vizier (in 1289) over Arghun's empire. According to Bar Hebraeus,

The king of kings [Arghun] ordered that Sa'd ad-Daula, the Jew, hitherto the Governor of Baghdad, should be appointed Chief of the administrative officials . . . throughout all provinces of the Empire.[125]

Despite being a successful and responsible administrator (which even the Muslim sources confirm),[126] the appointment of a Jew as the vizier of a heathen ruler over a predominantly Muslim region predictably aroused the wrath of the Muslim masses. This reaction was expressed through and exacerbated by "all kinds of [Muslim] diatribes, satirical poems, and libels."[127] Ibn al-Fuwati (d. 1323), a contemporary Muslim historian from Baghdad, recorded this particularly revealing example that emphasized traditional anti-Jewish motifs from the Qur'an:

In the year 689/1291 a document was prepared which contained libels against Sa'd ad-Daula, together with verses from the Qur'an and the history of the prophets, that stated the Jews to be a people whom Allah hath debased.[128]

Another contemporary Muslim source, the chronicler and poet Wassaf,[129] according to Fischel, "empties the vials of hatred on the Jew Sa'd ad-Daula and brings the most implausible accusations against him."[130] These accusations included the claims that Sa'd had advised Arghun to cut down trees in Baghdad (dating from the days of the conquered Muslim Abbasid dynasty) and build a fleet to attack Mecca and convert the cuboidal Ka'ba (the holiest place and structure in Islam) to a heathen temple.[131] Wassaf's account also quotes satirical verses to demonstrate the extent of public dissatisfaction with what he terms "Jewish Domination," adding to the existing line, "Turn Jews, for heaven itself hath turned a Jew," his own:

Yet wait and ye shall hear their torments cry
And see them fall and perish presently.[132]

When Arghun took ill, influential Mongol dukes inimical to Sa'd ad-Daula for purely political reasons shifted the "blame" for Arghun's terminal illness to the Jewish physician-vizier. Sa'd and his supporters were arrested and a large number of them executed (1291).[133] Sa'd ad-Daula's murder precipitated a broad attack on Jewry throughout the Il Khan Empire, beginning in the Baghdad Jewish ghetto, where, according to Bar Hebraeus and Wassaf, despite Jewish resistance,

when the report of the murder of the Jew was heard, the Arabs armed themselves and went to the quarter of the Jews, because the Jews were all living together in quarter[134] ... in Baghdad more than a hundred of the noble and wealthy Jews were slain, and their property plundered.[135]

Wassaf and Ibn al-Fuwati further reveal that such attacks spread well beyond Baghdad:

> Throughout the lands of Islam, the Jewish people were oppressed and their goods plundered . . . there was no town left in Iraq in which the Jews were not served with that which had happened to them in Baghdad, until a part of them embraced Islam, although they later turned back again.[136]

Bar Hebraeus was moved to depict the calamity for the Jews in these poignant words:

> The trials and wrath which were stirred up against the Jews at this time neither tongue can utter nor the pen write down.[137]

Walter Fischel concludes that "a tremendous wave of suffering and persecution must have overwhelmed the entire Jewry of Iraq and Persia," while noting "[t]he Muslims, however, gave expression to their joy at the end of Jewish domination in many verses filled with enmity against the Jews."[138] One such celebratory verse, by the poet Zaynu'd-Din Ali b. Sa'id, reiterated antisemitic Qur'anic motifs of the Jews as "wretched dupes of error and despair," "foulest race," "hatefulest," dispatched to "hell" in "molten torments," doomed "without reprieve," and leaving behind "How many did they leave!"—gardens and fountains (Qur'an 44:25).[139]

> Throughout the lands they're shamed and desolate.
> God hath dispersed their dominant accord,
> And they are melted by the burnished sword.
>
> Grim captains made them drink Death's cup of ill,
> Until their skulls the blood-bathed streets did fill,
> And from their dwellings seized the wealth
>   they'd gained,
> And their well-guarded women's rooms profaned.
> O wretched dupes of error and despair,
> At length the trap hath caught you in its snare!
>
> O foulest race who e'er on earth did thrive
> And hatefulest of those who still survive
>
> God sped the soul of him who was their chief
> To hell, whose mirk [murk] is despair and grief.
> In molten torments they were prisoned,
> In trailing chains they to their doom were led.
> Take warning from this doom without reprieve;
> Recite the verse [44:25]:[140] "How many did they
>   leave!"

The Jewish vizier in Fez, Morocco, from 1464–1465, Haroun ben Battas, and his co-religionist community became victims of the same stereotyped anti-*dhimmi* and anti-Jewish Muslim prejudices displayed earlier in Granada (1066) and Baghdad (1290–1291).[141] A contemporary travelogue by the Egyptian author and merchant 'Abd el-Basit, who was studying in Tlemcen at the time, gives the following account of the rationale for Haroun's appointment to vizier by Sultan 'Abd el-Haq ben Abu Said:

> 'Abd el-Haq kept him [the Jew, Haroun] very close to him, and made him his confidant, until the whole kingdom was given into his hand. He trusted him because he thought it impossible that the Jew (as a non-Muslim) would exceed his authority, as 'Abd el-Haq understood it.[142]

'Abd el-Basit's narrative maintains that Haroun used his position to enhance the fortunes of the Jewish elites ("In his days the Jews of Fez and its districts became great; they were influential and important . . . "), and, in additional clear violations of the *dhimma*, rode a mount ("In the presence of his master, he rode horses marked with the vizerial seal") and carried a sword with a Qur'anic inscription ("And that Jew wore a sword on an iron belt engraved with the verse *al-kursi* [2:255]").[143]

Haroun's tragic fate—and that of the Jewish community of Fez—were sealed by the following course of events. The preacher of Fez's main mosque (the Kairouanian mosque), Sayyidi Abu 'Abdallah Muhammad, was already well known for his anti-Jewish diatribes. Upon learning of Haroun's comportment and the alleged insult of a sharif (tribal protector)[144] by one of Haroun's deputies, he incited the local Muslim population with cries of jihad, as described by 'Abd el-Basit:

> He and the Muslims were greatly vexed because of the Jews, their influence and their control over the Muslims. In his sermon on Friday at the Great Jami of Fez, named Jami' al-Qarawiyyin, he always preached about the Jews and also dared to incite the people: perhaps they would rise up because of this for Allah's sake and revolt. And the matter became known, and he became famous because of this. And when the insult to the *sharifa* occurred, he dedicated his soul to Allah, left his house and loudly proclaimed in the streets and alleys of Fez: He who will not go forth for the sake of Allah has no *muruwwa* [Bedouin chivalry] and no religion! And he went on to shout: Jihad, Jihad! He also ordered others to issue this call in the streets of Fez, and the people heard it, and presently revolted with him. They were joined by the great multitude from "all the low places" [Qur'an 22:27] in Fez.[145]

The aroused Muslim throng sought religious sanction from one of Fez's most esteemed sharifs. However, he refused to support their rebellion without receiving a (consensus) fatwa from the 'Ulema (clerical authorities), since the sultan was directly implicated. In their appeal to the esteemed chief mufti of Fez, Abu 'Abd Allah Muhammad al-Qauri, the Muslims, led by Sayyidi Abu 'Abdallah Muhammad, argued that the Jews had violated the *dhimma*. The chief mufti claimed he could not support their revolt because he was fearful of the sultan and his coterie. But the inflamed crowd ultimately compelled the chief mufti to countenance their actions after threatening the mufti's reputation—and his very life. Under duress, the chief mufti issued a fatwa making it licit to attack the Jews and revolt against the sultan. Thereupon, the Muslim rabble attacked the Jewish quarter in Fez, slaughtering its inhabitants. 'Abd el-Basit's account describes these events approvingly:

[T]hey [the Muslim rabble] took him [Sayyidi Abu 'Abdallah Muhammad] and began to stream to the house of the sheriff Muhmammad ibn 'Imran, who was mazwar (in charge) of the shurafa in Fez. . . . But he, in spite of his status, personal authority and great energy, when the preacher [Sayyidi Abu 'Abdallah Muhammad] came in to him and tried to stir him up (against the Jews), did not respond, contending that it was improper for him to revolt while there were theologians in Fez who had not yet been asked for an opinion in the matter. They (the crowd) hastened to the theologians and assembled them, including the greatest of them at that time, the scholar and *mufti*. . . . Abu 'Abd Allah Muhammad al-Qauri. He and the other assembled persons were brought to the house of the sayyid the sherif. The preacher [Sayyidi Abu 'Abdallah Muhammad] hastened to say to them: "Go forth with us to the Jihad; fight for the renewal of Islam!" The crowd repeated his words and said: "If you will not fight together with us, you will be the first whom we shall fight; for you, *shurafa* and theologians, are content to be ruled by Jews." Then they shouted again: "Jihad, Jihad!" meaning to incite them nearby. They demanded of al-Qauri that he give a theological opinion, but he refused to do so, claiming that he was afraid of the authorities. They continued to prod him, after preparing a written question on the incident and on what that Jew [Haroun] and the Jews had done, saying that it constituted a violation of the Covenant [*dhimma*], and even more than that. They drew their swords and called out to al-Qauri: "We, too, have authority and power. We have risen up for Allah's sake and pledged our lives. This is the question which we ask you to answer according to the law of Allah, blessed be he. If you will not do so, we shall let the world do without you, for you are a theologian who does not act in conformity with his theology."

They added other things in the same vein. And they gave him no rest until he wrote with his own hand a permit to kill the Jews, and another permit to revolt . . . even against the sultan. When he had finished writing, they hastened to the *hara* (the Jewish quarter) and wielded their swords against the Jews, killing as many of them as Allah wanted them to kill; they did not omit even one until they killed the last, so as to clear the quarter of them. This was a glorious day in Fez and a great slaughter. A numerous Jewish community was killed on that day. Afterwards they [the Muslim rabble] turned to the palace of the government, devastated it and killed the Jew who was in it, namely the deputy of the vizier.[146]

Shortly afterward, the same fate was suffered by Haroun and the sultan. And in turn, the Jews of smaller communities outside Fez were also massacred, as noted again with satisfaction by 'Abd el-Basit:

Thereafter the people of the cities distant from Fez learnt of these events. They rose up against the Jews of the cities and did to them what the people of Fez had done to their Jews. The Jews were thus befallen by a calamity the like of which had never occurred before;[147] as many of them as Allah—blessed be he—decreed were killed.[148]

The Hebrew chronicles *Kisseh ha-Melakhim*[149] and *Yahas Fes* ("Only twenty heads of family and a small number of women and children escaped death")[150] confirm that few Jews survived this Muslim jihad in Fez. Jane Gerber's discussion of the 1465 Fez pogrom concludes with an understated assessment:

[T]he rise to prominence of a Jewish vizier or emissary should *not* [emphasis in original] be construed as evidence of Jewish security or acceptance in a given historical period. As Haroun's demise so dramatically illustrates, the rise of a Jew to an important governmental post was symptomatic of the complete alienation of the Marinids [ruling Moroccan Muslim dynasty] from their subjects rather than of Jewish acceptance on the basis of equality.[151]

Within a quarter century (c. 1490), anti-Jewish agitation by one of the most prominent sheikhs of the era, al-Maghili (d. 1504–1505), precipitated the wholesale slaughter of Jews in the southern Moroccan oasis of Touat.[152] Al-Maghili's determination of the Jews' status was summarized concisely by his sixteenth-century biographer, Ibn 'Askar (d. 1578).[153]

He held the view that the Jews—may God curse them—had no bond [of protection (*dhimma*)], since they had broken it by their association with men of authority among the Muslims, [an action] which went contrary to the humiliation and abasement (*al-dhull wa'l-saghar*) stipulated in the payment of *jizya*, and that the breaking of this pact by some of them redounded upon all of them. He declared it licit to spill their blood, and plunder their property and announced that dealing with them was more important than dealing with any other [category] of unbelievers.[154]

Al-Maghili's own writings emphasized that the Jews of Touat made their tribute payments irregularly, and in varying amounts. He argued that such payments were tantamount to bribery and not valid *jizya*, remitted annually during a deliberately humiliating public ceremony.[155] Al-Maghili further insisted that the Jews had no right to maintain their synagogue in neighboring Tamantit (i.e., where the Jews of Touat's synagogue was located). He claimed the synagogue was constructed illegally on Muslim land, and its continued existence violated the Qur'anic principle of the Jews' deserved abasement and humiliation.[156]

Hunwick has provided a succinct elucidation of al-Maghili's legal arguments. He also acknowledges that al-Maghili's treatise on the *dhimmis* (i.e., Jews) read like an "inflammatory sermon." And when al-Maghili preached these views to the Muslim masses, he fomented violence against the Jews:

Any Muslim who befriended a Jew or came to his defense, or opposed the destruction of the synagogue was to be considered an unbeliever. *Dhimmis* must be kept in a permanent state of abasement (*saghar*). This is why *jizya* must be paid in a public ceremony in which the *dhimmi* at the moment of payment is given a tap on the neck and pushed forward to show him he has thus escaped the sword. This abasement is more important than the sum paid. No religious edifice may be erected by a *dhimmi* in the land of Islam and if any governor gave permission for one, this permission must be revoked and the building torn down. This is because the manifestation of the *dhimmi's* religion in the form of a building is a contradiction of the concept of abasement. The same argument applies to the association of *dhimmis* with sultans, viziers, judges and other persons in authority. This is a "flouting of the laws of Islam," since it is a negation of the abasement which is stipulated for the continued dwelling of a dhimmi in the lands of Islam. The situation he is condemning here is not only that which he would claim was current in Touat, but also by implication that which obtained in Fez, Tlemcen, and other North African cities.

The bulk of the populace, poor and ignorant, could be aroused to violence against the Jewish community by making these "outsiders" the scapegoat for all their ills. It only needed a preacher who could appeal to the masses by an appeal for the defense of "religion" to spark off a wave of looting and killing. Al-Maghili, by his preaching, his polemical prose and his verse diatribes was just such a catalyst.[157]

Al-Maghili recounted stridently antisemitic "vignettes" portraying Jewish malevolence such as these anecdotes about Jewesses preparing bread for Muslim consumption:

A person told me that he saw a Jewess mixing bread flour for a Muslim. He observed that she was picking her nose with her hand and continuing to mix the flour without washing her hand. A second person also told me that he saw another Jewess mixing bread flour for a Muslim. He saw her picking lice from her head and killing them with her nails and continuing mixing the flour without washing her hands. There are many stories of this nature. None can suspect the credibility of [stories such as] these and worse than these, except one who is blind to reality. Do you not see what Allah the Most High has said?[158]

But al-Maghili's anti-Jewish views are perhaps best encapsulated in a verse diatribe he composed:

Love of the Prophet requires hatred of the Jews. Regret what has passed and do not do it again. The one who is intimate with the enemies of the Prophet [i.e., the Jews], when he goes to the grave and on the day of Resurrection will be directed to the burning fire. Who will there be to rescue him when the Fire approaches the face with which he pleased the Jews?[158a]

He added,

They [the Jews] are indeed the most hostile people against us and against our beloved Prophet . . . they criticize our religion, mock our prayers and insult our master and savior Muhammad.[158b]

H. I. Gwarzo observes:

He [al-Maghili] was not so much concerned about the Jews, who although numerous, were still a minority. They would be at his mercy as long as he had the support of the public.

He succeeded in showing the masses that the issue was of either loving the Prophet or loving the Jews; Muslims must choose one of the two—they should choose between going to Paradise or going to Hell. The choice of the masses was obvious—they must certainly love the Prophet rather than the Jews; they would certainly prefer Paradise to Hell.

His following became great and he succeeded in creating ferment in the territories.[159]

Mobilizing this popular support, al-Maghili led a pogrom during which the Jews of Touat were massacred, and their synagogue in neighboring Tamantit destroyed. It was indeed "a short step from considering the Jews 'enemies of the Prophet' to considering them enemies of the *umma* [Muslim community] at large."[159a]

The twentieth-century flowering of the Zionist movement and subsequent creation of Israel—a sovereign state, administered by Jews liberated from the system of *dhimmitude*, adjacent to the very cradle of Arab Islam—has been accompanied, not surprisingly, by an outpouring of traditional Islamic antisemitism. Raphael Israeli observes that this "unbearable challenge" to the sacralized Islamic order has created a "vicious circle" of Islamic antisemitism and anti-Zionism:

The ingathering of the Jews into modern Israel constitutes from this traditional Muslim viewpoint, which is still upheld by Muslim scholars of the Holy Law, and probably by many of their Muslim constituencies, an unbearable challenge to the authority of the Muslim faith.

Jews were debased and humiliated in the first place; Zionism is marked by the derogatory traits that are characteristic of Jews; and in turn Zionism and Israel further debase the Jews by their inherent inhuman attitudes. Israeli politics, society and culture are all imbued with the evils that the Jews have transmitted from one generation to another . . . so the vicious cycle is complete.[160]

Even the pejorative image of "violent" Jews as the "new Mongols"—coined in the early 1980s by a burgeoning Islamic fundamentalist movement[161]—evokes an ironic historical association uncomfortable for Muslims: the fact that the Mongol emperor Hulagu—(as noted earlier)[162] also overturned the system of *dhimmitude* after his armies captured Baghdad in 1258, destroying the Abbasid caliphate.

The past five decades—including a period before "the 1967 Shock" and Israel's "demeaning of the abode of Islam" (Dar al Islam)[163]—have witnessed ceaseless calls by Islamic religious, political, and intellectual leaders—for a forcible return to the permanent state of "wretchedness and humiliation" enjoined for the Jews in Qur'an 2:61 and 3:112. Writing in 1962, Ahmad Yusuf Ahmad warned that, despite assistance from Western powers,

[T]hey will not on any account be able to exempt them [the Jews] from the divine injunction and decree that they shall have no rest or permanency or tranquility, they will be chastised with degradation and poverty and be visited by the wrath of God.[164]

Two years later, Abdullah al-Tall further dismissed the Jews' attempts at self-reliance in the face of Allah's unavoidable decree:

Despite all their efforts to appear as possessors of power and the capacity to resist, the word of God is supreme and the Qur'an records the views of heaven, the will of the heaven and its verdict.[165]

The Fourth Conference of the Academy of Islamic Research convened in Cairo in the fall of 1968 to discuss the theological significance of the Middle East conflict. Sheikh Hassan Ma'moun, the grand imam of Al-Azhar University, in his inaugural address to the conference, acknowledged that the "bitterness" of the 1967 Arab defeat by Israel

was further intensified by the fact that the unexpected event occurred before a roguish Zionism whose adherents had been destined to dispersion by the Deity. [Quoting Qur'an 2:61] "And humiliation and wretchedness were stamped upon them and they were visited with wrath from God."[166]

The lengthiest single conference paper (all of which were compiled in a 935-page tome),[167] a 158-page analysis by Muhammad El Sayyed Huscin al-Dahabi entitled "Israelite Narratives in Exegesis and Tradition," invoked a Qur'anic commentary by Tabari to sanction the Jews' permanent abasement:

Then he [Tabari] added, They killed their Prophet. Thereupon, God smote them with humiliation and took away kingship from them. Thus, they became the most lowly and degraded amongst nations, having to pay tribute and yielding to the authority of foreign kings. In such a plight will they ever remain.[168]

And four years later (April 25, 1972), in a speech celebrating the birthday of the Muslim Prophet Muhammad, Egyptian president Anwar el-Sadat warned, "[T]hey [the Jews] shall return and be as the Qur'an said of them 'condemned to humiliation and misery'"[169]—a year before Egypt's surprise attack during Yom Kippur started the 1973 war with Israel.

The "return" being invoked in all these pronouncements is a return to the Islamic Shari'a-based system of *dhimmitude* for Jews, and a dissolution of the sovereign state of Israel. Although written in the pseudosecular[170] language of Arab nationalism, the 1968 Palestine Liberation Organization charter's call for Jews to live "under the aegis of an Arab state in the framework of Arab society,"[171] has been termed aptly "the Palestinian Dhimma."[172] Indeed, the theological-juridical antecedent of this Palestinian Dhimma dates back to 1920: a formal request by Musa Kazem el-Husseini (then president of the Arab Palestinian Congress) to British high commissioner Herbert Samuels to restore the Shari'a,[173] which had only been fully abrogated two years earlier, when Britain ended four centuries of Ottoman Muslim rule of Palestine. Moreover, in recent years, this goal has been reaffirmed openly by official Palestinian Authority clerics. For example, Sheikh Muhammad Ibrahim Al-Madhi, during a Friday sermon broadcast live on June 6, 2001, on Palestinian Authority Television from the Sheik 'Ijlin Mosque in Gaza, stated:

> We welcome, as we did in the past, any Jew who wants to live in this land as a Dhimmi, just as the Jews have lived in our countries, as Dhimmis, and have earned appreciation, and some of them have even reached the positions of counselor or minister here and there. We welcome the Jews to live as Dhimmis, but the rule in this land and in all the Muslim countries must be the rule of Allah.[174]

Subsequently, during an interview by *Wall Street Journal* reporter Karby Legget (published in the December 23, 2005, edition of the *Wall Street Journal*, p. A1), Hassam El-Masalmeh, who then headed the Hamas contingent at the municipal council of Bethlehem, confirmed his organization's plan to reinstitute the *jizya*. El-Masalmeh stated:

> We in Hamas intend to implement this tax (i.e., the *jizya*) someday. We say it openly—we welcome everyone to Palestine but only if they agree to live under our rules.

All of historical Palestine—modern Israel (within the 1949 armistice borders), Gaza, Judea, Samaria, and modern Jordan—whose pre-Islamic inhabitants—Jews, Samaritans, and Christians—were conquered by jihad in the fourth decade of the seventh century[175]—is considered "*fay* territory,"[176] a permanent part of the Dar al Islam, where Islamic law must forever prevail. Israel, governed by "usurper" infidel Jews on such "*fay* territory"—no longer an appropriately subjugated *dhimmi* (Qur'an 9:29) people living, additionally, as per Qur'an 2:61, in "wretchedness and humiliation"—must be destroyed in a collective jihad by the entire Muslim community.

Accordingly, there have been unceasing cries for jihad in historical Palestine during the modern era, in the 1920s and 1930s by Hajj Amin El Husseini[177] and Izz Al-Din al Qassam,[178] by Yasser Arafat throughout his forty years as leader of Fatah and the Palestine Liberation Organization,[179] and presently under Hamas.[180]

Hamas's foundational covenant,[181] whose motto states (in Article 8) "Allah is its goal, the Prophet its model to be followed, the Koran its constitution, Jihad its way, and death for the sake of Allah its loftiest desire," reiterates (in Article 11) that all of historical Palestine is a permanent Islamic religious endowment (*waqf*): "In this respect, it is like any other land that the Muslims have conquered by force, because the Muslims consecrated it at the time of the conquest as religious endowment for all generations of Muslims until the Day of Resurrection." The Hamas Covenant also (in Article 13) rejects "so-called peace solutions," and insists (in Article 15) upon waging an annihilationist jihad to eradicate Israel, even invoking the apocalyptic hadith (in Article 7) from the canonical collections of Bukhari and Muslim:

> The hour of judgment shall not come until the Muslims fight the Jews and kill them, so that the Jews hide behind trees and stones, and each tree and stone will say: "Oh Muslim, oh servant of Allah, there is a Jew behind me, come and kill him," except for the Gharqad tree, for it is the tree of the Jews.[182]

Throughout Arafat's tenure as the major Palestinian Arab leader, and now under the Hamas government, efforts to destroy Israel and replace it with an Arab Muslim Shari'a-based entity were integrated into the larger Islamic *umma*'s jihad against the Jewish state, as declared repeatedly in official conference pronouncements from various clerical or political organizations of the Muslim (both Arab and non-Arab) nations and in the individual statements of influential Muslim religious leaders. Concrete examples spanning the years from 1968 to 2006 are provided below:

> From the Fourth Conference of the Academy of Islamic Research, Cairo, 1968 presentation by Sheikh Hassan Khalid, Mufti of the Republic of Lebanon—
>
> Your honorable conference has been an Arab, Islamic and patriotic necessity in view of the present circumstances in which the Arabs and Muslims face the most serious difficulties. All Muslims expect you to expound Allah's decree concerning the Palestine cause, to proclaim that decree, in all clarity, throughout the Arab and Muslim world. We do not think this decree absolves any Muslim or Arab from *Jihad* (Holy War) which has now become a duty incumbent upon the Arabs and Muslims to liberate the land, preserve honor, retaliate for [lost] dignity, restore the Aqsa Mosque, the church of Resurrection, and to purge the birthplace of prophecy, the seat of revelation, the meeting-place of Prophets, the starting-point of Isra [Muhammad's "night journey"], and the scenes of the holy spirit, from the hands of Zionism—the enemy of man, of truth, of justice, and the enemy of Allah. . . . The well-balanced judgment frankly expressed with firm conviction is the first stop on the road of victory. The hoped-for judgment is that of Muslim Scholars who draw their conclusions from the Book of Allah, and the Sunna of His prophet. May Allah guard your meeting, and guide your steps! May your decisive word rise to the

occasion and enlighten the Arab and Muslim world, so that it may be a battle-cry, urging millions of Muslims and Arabs on to the field of Jihad, which will lead us to the place that once was ours. . . . Muslims who are distant from the battle-field of Palestine, such as the Algerians, the Moroccans, all the Africans, Saudi Arabia people, Yemeni people, the Indians, Iraqi people, the Russians, and the Europeans are indeed sinful if they do not hasten to offer all possible means to achieve success and gain victory in the Islamic battle against their enemies and the enemies of their religion. Particularly, this battle is not a mere combat between two parties but it is a battle between two religions (namely, it is a religious battle). Zionism in fact represents a very perilous cancer, aiming at domineering the Arab countries and the whole Islamic world.[183]

From the Mecca Islamic Summit Conference, 1981—

The undertaking by all Islamic countries of psychological mobilization through their various official, semi-official, and popular mass media, of their people for Jihad to liberate Al-Quds. . . . Ensuring military coordination among the front-line states and the Palestine Liberation Organization, on the one hand, and the Islamic States on the other, to ensure full utilization of the potentialities of the Islamic States in the service of the military effort; and setting up a military office in the Islamic Secretariat to be responsible for such coordination, in agreement with the Committee on Al-Quds. . . .

Resolution No.2/3.P (IS) on the Cause of Palestine and the Middle East: Considering that the Liberation of Al-Quds and its restoration to Arab sovereignty, as well as the liberation of the holy places from Zionist occupation, are a pre-requisite to the Jihad that all Islamic States must wage, each according to its means. . . .

Resolution No.5/3-P (IS)—Declaration of Holy Jihad:

Taking these facts into consideration, the Kings, Emirs, and Presidents of Islamic States, meeting at this Conference and in this holy land, studied this situation and concluded that it could no longer be tolerated that the forthcoming stage should be devoted to effective action to vindicate right and deter wrong-doing; and have unanimously.

Decided: To declare holy Jihad, as the duty of every Muslim, man or woman, ordained by the Shariah and glorious traditions of Islam; To call upon all Muslims, living inside or outside Islamic countries, to discharge this duty by contributing each according to his capacity in the case of Allah Almighty, Islamic brotherhood, and righteousness; To specify that Islamic states, in declaring Holy Jihad to save Al-Quds al-Sharif, in support of the

Palestinian people, and to secure withdrawal from the occupied Arab territories, wish to explain to the world that Holy Jihad is an Islamic concept which may not be misinterpreted or misconstrued, and that the practical measures to put into effect would be in accordance with that concept and by incessant consultations among Islamic states.[184]

From the 2003 Putrajaya Islamic Summit speech by former Malaysian Prime Minister Dr. Mahathir Mohammad—

To begin with, the governments of all the Muslim countries can close ranks and have a common stand . . . on Palestine. . . . We need guns and rockets, bombs and warplanes, tanks and warships. . . . We may want to re-create the first century of the Hijrah, the way of life in those times, in order to practice what we think to be the true Islamic way of life. 1.3 billion Muslims cannot be defeated by a few million Jews. There must be a way. And we can only find a way if we stop to think, to assess our weaknesses and our strength, to plan, to strategize and then to counter-attack. As Muslims, we must seek guidance from the Al-Quran and the Sunnah of the Prophet. Surely the 23 years' struggle of the Prophet can provide us with some guidance as to what we can and should do.[185]

Sheikh Yusuf al-Qaradawi, the immensely popular Spiritual Leader of the Muslim Brotherhood, and Head of the European Fatwah Council, during one of his widely viewed Qatar TV sermons, February 25, 2006—

All the school of Islamic jurisprudence—the Sunni, the Shiite . . . and all the ancient and modern schools of jurisprudence—agree that any invader, who occupies even an inch of land of the Muslims, must face resistance. The Muslims of that country must carry out the resistance, and the rest of the Muslims must help them. If the people of that country are incapable or reluctant, we must fight to defend the land of Islam, even if the local [Muslims] give it up.

They must not allow anyone to take a single piece of land away from Islam. That is what we are fighting the Jews for. We are fighting them. . . . Our religion commands us. . . . We are fighting in the name of religion, in the name of Islam, which makes this Jihad an individual duty, in which the entire nation takes part, and whoever is killed in this [jihad] is a martyr. This is why I ruled that martyrdom operations are permitted, because he commits martyrdom for the sake of Allah, and sacrifices his soul for the sake of Allah. We do not disassociate Islam from the war. On the contrary, disassociating Islam from the war is the reason for our defeat. We are fighting in the name of Islam.[186]

Perhaps the most striking Qur'anic motifs for the Jews' debasement are the references to their transformation into apes (Qur'an 2:65 and 7:166), or apes and swine (Qur'an 5:60). Setting aside the casuistry of Muslim exegetic discussions over whether this transformation was physical or metaphorical[187] (i.e., reflecting the Jews moral depravity, even Satan worship),[188] and the alleged "immediate cause"—Sabbath breaking—ultimately these verses are but another manifestation, albeit dramatic, of what Ibn Kathir terms "the eternal humiliation placed upon the Jews" (referring to 7:166–67),[189] including, adds Suyuti (referring to 5:60), damnation to hellfire.[190]

Just prior to orchestrating the mass execution of the adult males from the besieged Medinan Jewish tribe the Banu Qurayza (and distributing their women, children, and possessions as "booty" for the Muslims),[190a] Muhammad, according to his earliest Muslim biographer, Ibn Ishaq (d. 767–770), addressed these Jews with menacing, hateful derision: "You brothers of monkeys, has God disgraced you and brought His vengeance upon you?"[190b] (Another early Muslim biographer of Muhammad, Ibn Sa'd [d. 845], reports that Muhammad stated, "brothers of monkeys and pigs, fear me, fear me!")[190c] Many subsequent historical examples from diverse Islamic societies during a continuum of more than eleven hundred years—the ninth century through the present—demonstrate that this Qur'anic motif has been employed against Jews as an outward sign of their physical humiliation, and, more significantly, in polemical incitement against Jews, or odes celebrating their having been disgraced and slaughtered.

A fatwa written by the ninth-century jurist from Kairouan, Ifiqiyya (modern Tunisia), Qadi [Shari'a judge] Ahmed b. Talib (d. 889),

compelled the dhimmis to wear upon the shoulder a patch of white cloth (riqa') that bore the image of an ape (for Jews) . . . and to nail onto their doors a board bearing the sign of a monkey.[191]

He further ordered,

A Jew who dresses like the Muslims and fails to wear the clothing that distinguishes him from them will be incarcerated, beaten, and paraded ignominiously through the places inhabited by the Jews and the Christians as an example.[192]

Abu Ishaq's verse of condemnation against the vizier Joseph b. Samuel Naghrela and the Granadan Jewish community, which helped incite the 1066 Granada pogrom, with its massacre of some three thousand to four thousand Jews, contains the following line.[193]

Many a pious Muslim is in awe of the vilest infidel ape.[194]

Moshe Perlmann, in his analysis of the Muslim anti-Jewish polemic of eleventh-century Granada, notes,

[Abu Ishaq] Elbīrī used the epithet "ape" (qird) profusely when referring to Jews. Such indeed was the parlance.[195]

Perlmann then cites the related Qur'anic passages (i.e., 2:65, 5:60, and 7:166) upon which such "nomenclature" was based.[196]

Anti-Jewish riots and massacres by Muslims accompanied the 1291 death of Jewish physician-vizier Sa'd ad-Daula in Baghdad, the plundering and killing of Jews extending throughout Iraq (and possibly into Persia).[197] These events, which marked the collapse of a transient Jewish ascendancy (afforded by the ruling Mongols' abrogation of the system of dhimmitude),[198] were celebrated in an ode by the Muslim preacher Zaynu'd-Din 'Ali b. Said.[199] His verse opens with a debasing reference to the Jews as apes:

His name we praise who rules the firmament.
These apish Jews are done away and shent [ruined or destroyed].[200]

The bitter anti-Jewish sentiments of the theologian Al-Mahgili (d. 1504–1505) were expressed in both his writing and his preaching.[201] Referring to the Jews as "brothers of apes" (consistent with Zamakshari's classical Qur'anic commentary on verse 5:60),[202] who incessantly blasphemed the Prophet Muhammad and whose entire conduct demonstrated their hatred of Muslims, Al-Maghili posed the rhetorical question: What should be done about them?[203] He "answered" this question by fomenting a Muslim pogrom (in c. 1490) against the Jews of Touat, which plundered and killed them en masse, and destroyed their synagogue in neighboring Tamantit.[204]

Apart from being used to incite or extol mass violence against Jews, the degrading Qur'anic references to Jews as apes and pigs were more commonly employed in daily life to reflect chronic attitudes Muslims felt toward Jews. A mid-nineteenth-century eyewitness account from Jerusalem by the missionary Gregory Wortabet (published in 1856) captures these routine sentiments (which Wortabet also attributes to the canonical hadith about Muhammad's poisoning):

The Jew is still an object of scorn, and nowhere is the name of "Yahoodi (Jew)" more looked down upon than here in the city of his fathers. One day, as I was passing the Damascus gate, I saw an Arab hurrying on his donkey amid imprecations such as the following: "Emshi ya Ibn-el-Yahoodi (Walk, thou son of a Jew)! Yulaan abuk ya Ibn-el-Yahoodi (Cursed be thy father, thou son of a Jew)!"
    I need not give any more illustrations of the

manner in which the man went on. The reader will observe, that the man did not curse the donkey, but the Jew, the father of the donkey. Walking up to him, I said, "Why do you curse the Jew? What harm has he done you?"

"*El Yahoodi khanzeer* (the Jew is a hog)!" answered the man.

"How do you make that out?" I said. "Is not the Jew as good as you or I?"

"Ogh!" ejaculated the man, his eyes twinkling with fierce rage, and his brow knitting.

By this time he was getting out of my hearing. I was pursuing my walk, when he turned round, and said, "*El Yahoodi khanzeer! Khanzeer el Yahoodi!* (The Jew is a hog! A hog is a Jew!)"

Now I must tell the reader, that, in the Mahomedan vocabulary, there is no word lower than a hog, that animal being in their estimation the most defiled of animals; and good Mahomedans are prohibited by the Koran from eating it. The Jew, in their estimation, is the vilest of the human family, and is the object of their pious hatred, perhaps from the recollection that a Jewess of Khaibar first undermined the health of the prophet by infusing poison into his food.[205] Hence a hog and a Jew are esteemed alike in the eye of a Moslem, both being the lowest of their kind; and now the reader will better understand the meaning of the man's words, "*El Yahoodi khanzeer!*"[206]

Tudor Parfitt notes two less overtly degrading variations on these themes, which persisted at least through the latter half of the twentieth century in Yemen:

[I]f someone behaves badly while eating—either taking more than they can eat, or throwing food around, the response is likely to be "O Jew!" or "Pig." Monkeys are customarily called *Said* or *Salim*—both common Jewish names. . . . *Salim* particularly is viewed by Muslims as being the most typical Jewish name of all. If you do not happen to know a Jew's name you call him *Salim*.[207]

At present, the invocation of Qur'an inspired references to the Jews as apes and pigs—conveyed through print, audio, video, and Internet venues—pervades Arab Muslim religious and political discourse.[208] A small representative sampling from 2001 and 2002 follows:

Sheikh Ibrahim Mahdi, an official Palestinian Authority cleric, from a sermon at the Sheikh 'Ijlin Mosque in Gaza, April 3, 2001—"There is no choice but to direct all our pressures against the Jews, the infidels, the people cursed by the Qur'an. Allah referred to them as, apes, pigs, worshippers of the [golden] calf and of satan."[209]

Egyptian Sheikh Atiyyah Saqr, former chairman of the Religious Rulings Commission at the Al-Azhar University in Egypt issued a fatwa, which was made public in Germany on April 15, 2002, entitled *Reincarnation of the Souls of the Children of Israel in the Bodies of Apes and Pigs*. The crux of his "modern" interpretation of Qur'an 5:60 is that the Jews punishment was—"Allah incarnated their souls in the bodies of apes and pigs, and turned them into humiliated ones, or in other words—outcasts, wretched and despised ones."[210]

From an article published by the columnist Dr. Muhammad bin Sa'ad al-Shwey'ir in the Saudi daily *al-Jazirah*, June 7, 2002—"Allah decreed that the Jews be humiliated, He cursed them and turned them into apes and pigs. Whenever they ignite the fire of war, Allah extinguishes it. They disseminate corruption over the face of the world, they fight the believers [i.e., the Muslims] only from within fortified villages or from behind walls."[211]

Saudi Sheikh Abd Al-Rahman Al-Sudayyis, imam and preacher at the Al-Haram Mosque, which includes the cuboidal Ka'ba, the most important shrine in Islam, from an April 2002 sermon—"Read history and you will understand that the Jews of yesterday are the evil fathers of the Jews of today, who are evil offspring, infidels, distorters of [God's] words, calf-worshippers, prophet-murderers, prophecy-deniers . . . the scum of the human race whom Allah cursed and turned into apes and pigs. . . . These are the Jews, an ongoing continuum of deceit, obstinacy, licentiousness, evil, and corruption."[212]

Even young children are inculcated with these beliefs and coached to repeat them for additional public consumption.[213] A May 2002 broadcast on the Saudi satellite television station Iqraa, which claims on its Web site "to highlight aspects of Arab Islamic culture that inspire admiration . . . to highlight the true, tolerant image of Islam and refute the accusations directed against it," featured an interview of a three-and-a-half-year-old "real Muslim girl" about Jews, on *The Muslim Women's Magazine* program. When the little girl was asked whether she liked Jews, she replied, "No." Asked why not, she replied that Jews were "apes and pigs." The moderator then asked, "Who said this?" And the child answered, "Our God." "Where did He say this?" asked the moderator. "In the Qur'an," this three-and-a-half-year-old girl replied. At the close of the interview, the moderator stated approvingly: "No [parents] could wish for Allah to give them a more believing girl than she. . . . May Allah bless her and both her father and mother."

Given the murderous historical legacy of Muslim societies that invoked these Qur'anic motifs (i.e., in Granada, Baghdad, and Touat, Morocco), as described earlier, Menachem Milson's contemporary warning is not overstated:

> This insult should not be dismissed as mere vulgar invective, nor should the belief that Jews were transmogrified into apes, pigs or other creatures be seen merely as a sign of primitive magical thinking. Repeated reference to Jews as despised beasts dehumanizes them and provides justification for their destruction.[214]

Apropos of Milson's concern, Sudanese dictator Omar al-Bashir repeated these dehumanizing Qur'anic motifs when he issued a vitriolic call for jihad against Israel during a speech delivered at the headquarters of the ruling Islamic party in Khartoum, broadcast live by Radio Monte Carlo on April 5, 2002:

> Let us prepare ourselves for the decisive battle against the Jews, those apes, pigs, and worshippers of calves. This should be a decisive battle.... There will be no peace with the Jews.... This battle is the battle, and this jihad is the jihad.[215]

Following the murderous acts of jihad terrorism committed on September 11, 2001, Ibn Warraq highlighted the tragic irony of many apologists quoting selectively from Qur'an 5:32—"whoso slays a soul ... shall be as if he had slain mankind altogether; and whoso gives life to a soul, shall be as if he has given life to mankind altogether"—attempting to demonstrate that the Qur'ran disapproved of violence and killing. Here is the entire verse (5:32), quoted in full context, with the intimately related verse, Qur'an 5:33:

> (5:32) Therefore We prescribed for the Children of Israel that whoso slays a soul not to retaliate for a soul slain, nor for corruption done in the land, shall be as if he had slain mankind altogether; and whoso gives life to a soul, shall be as if he has given life to mankind altogether. Our Messengers have already come to them with the clear signs; then many of them thereafter commit excesses in the earth. (5:33) This is the recompense of those who fight against God and His Messenger, and hasten about the earth, to do corruption there: they shall be slaughtered, or crucified, or their hands and feet shall alternately be struck off; or they shall be banished from the land. That is a degradation for them in this world; and in the world to come awaits them a mighty chastisement.
>
> [For direct comparison see, Mishna, Sanhedrin, IV, 5, "Thus was created a single man, to teach us that every person who loses a single soul, it shall be written about him as if he has lost the entire world, and every person who sustains a single soul, it shall be written about him as if he has sustained the entire world."]

As Warraq noted, with regard to Qur'an 5:32–33,[216]

> The supposedly noble sentiments are in fact a warning to Jews. "Behave, or else" is the message. Far from abjuring violence, these verses aggressively point out that anyone opposing the Prophet will be killed, crucified, mutilated, and banished.[217]

After reiterating the Qur'an's major accusations against the "inveterate" Jews, and their eternal punishments— Jews falsifying their scriptures, and holding false doctrines (such as Ezra being the son of God [Qur'an 9:30], which in fact Jews never proclaimed),[218] so they must be compelled to return to the true religion, Islam; Jews harboring an intense hatred of all genuine Muslims and being punished for their sins (especially the curse of Qur'an 2:61), or even by transformation into apes and swine (Qur'an 2:65, 5:60, and 7:166)—Warraq concluded with this measured observation:

> The attitude enjoined upon the Muslims toward Jews can only be described as antisemitic, and it certainly was not conducive to better understanding, tolerance, or coexistence.[219]

ANTISEMITISM IN THE HADITH AND EARLY MUSLIM BIOGRAPHIES OF MUHAMMAD

The Hadith

Hadith, which means "story" ("narrative"), refers to any report of what the Muslim Prophet Muhammad said or did, or his tacit assent to something said or done in his presence.[220] (Hadith is also used as the technical term for the "science" of such "Traditions.") As a result of a lengthy process that continued for centuries after Muhammad's death (in 632), the hadith emerged for Muslims as second in authority to the Qur'an itself.[221] Sunna, which means "path," refers to a normative custom of Muhammad or of the early Islamic community.[222] The hadith "justify and confirm" the Sunna.[223] Henri Lammens highlights the importance of the Sunna (and, by extension, the hadith):

> As early as the first century A.H. [the seventh century] the following aphorism was pronounced: "The Sunna can dispense with the Qur'an, but not the Qur'an with the Sunna." Proceeding to still further lengths, some Muslims assert that "in controversial matters, the Sunna overrules the authority of the Qur'an, but not vice versa" ... all admit the Sunna completes and explains it [the Qur'an].[224]

The hadith compiled by al-Bukhari (d. 870) and Muslim b. al-Hajjaj (d. 875) are considered, respectively, to be the most important authoritative collections. The titles *Sahih* ("sound") and *Jami*, indicating their comprehensiveness, signify the high esteem in which they are held.[225] James Robson summarizes their comprehensive content:

> In addition to giving information about religious duties, law and everyday practice, they contain a considerable amount of biographical and other material. Nothing is too unimportant to form a valid topic for tradition. Guidance is given even on the most intimate matters of personal life. The compilers of Tradition seem to have had a keen desire to leave nothing to chance, so guidance is to be found on almost every conceivable subject.[226]

Four other compilations, called *Sunan* works, indicating that they are limited to matters of religious and social practice and law, also became authoritative. Abu Dawud (d. 888), al-Tirmidhi (d. 892), Ibn Maja (d. 896), and al-Nasi (d. 915) compiled these works. By the beginning of the twelfth century, Ibn Maja's collection became the last of these compilations of hadith to be recognized as "canonical."[227]

Despite appearances of rigor in the methods employed to assemble the various canonical hadith collections,[228] the meticulous studies of Ignaz Goldziher[229] and Joseph Schacht[230] (and others) demonstrate that while the hadith reflect theological-juridical "tendencies" during Islam's formative early centuries, they are useless as a source of objective historical information. Schacht argued for abandoning the "one-sided traditional sham-castle" based upon

> the gratuitous assumptions that there existed originally an authentic core of information going back to the time of the Prophet, that spurious and tendentious additions were made to every succeeding generation, that many of these were eliminated by the criticism of *isnads* ["chains" of pious Muslim transmitters] as practiced by the Muhammadan scholars, that other spurious traditions escaped rejection, but that the genuine core was not completely overlaid by later accretions.[231]

Alternatively, Schacht, a legal scholar, urged that these deconstructed "materials" be re-evaluated in their real context, i.e., the evolution of Islamic law, especially during the time of al-Shafi'i (d. 820; after whom the Shafi'ite school of Islamic jurisprudence was named).[232] Sixty years earlier Goldziher had suggested more broadly that, although ahistorical, the hadith reflected important aspects of social and religious development during the first two centuries after the advent of Islam.

> In the absence of authentic evidence it would indeed be rash to attempt to express the most tentative opinion as to which parts of the hadith are the oldest original material, or even as to which of them date back to the generations immediately following the Prophet's death. Closer acquaintance with the vast stock of hadiths induces skeptical caution rather than optimistic trust regarding the material brought together in the carefully compiled collections.
>
> The hadith will not serve as a document for the history of the infancy of Islam, but rather as a reflection of the tendencies which appeared in the community during the maturer stages of its development . . . the greater part of it [the hadith, reflecting] the religious . . . and social development of Islam during the first two centuries.[233]

The conception of Goldziher provides a useful framework for an examination of the anti-Jewish motifs in the hadith.

Georges Vajda's 1937 essay "Juifs et Musulmans selon Le Hadit" (Jews and Muslims according to the Hadith)[234]—a magisterial seventy-page analysis—remains the definitive study of Jews and their relations with Muhammad and Muslims, as depicted in the hadith. Vajda, in light of the scholarship of Goldziher (especially) on the inadequacy of the canonical hadith as "history," chose not to limit himself to these six collections:

> As soon as one renounces using the hadiths as absolutely sure and trustworthy documentation, it is evidently vain to try to take account of the value judgments that Muslim criticism emits regarding any isolated tradition, any collection, or the individual credibility of any traditionalist. Therefore I have been very wide-ranging in making use of documents and the "six books," as well as of the *Musnad* by Ahmed ibn Hanbal and the *Muwatta* by Mālik, not forgetting the commentaries to which I was able to have access, Kastalāni on Buhārī, Nawawi on Muslim, and Zurkāni on the *Muwatta*. Ibn Sa'd's *Tabakāt* and Tabarī's *Tafsīr* have also been consulted. It would no doubt have been possible and even desirable to prolong this promenade through the vast fields of the *hadith*.[235]

The remainder of this discussion of antisemitism in the hadith relies upon the themes developed by Vajda, amplified with excerpts from the canonical hadith, and other Traditions, themselves.

Both anti-*dhimmi* and specific anti-Jewish motifs figure prominently in Vajda's detailed assessment. He begins by emphasizing Goldziher's prior "discovery" of the animating principle prescribed for Muslims with regard to the customs of non-Muslims: *khalifuhum*, which means "do not do like them."[236] Vajda illustrates this attitude with regard to basic grooming and dress:

> Leaving his apartments, the prophet found old men *Ansar* whose beards were white. He told them: "Assembly of Ansār, dye yourselves red or yellow and do the contrary of the people of the Book." We

told him: "Apostle of Allah, the people of the Book wear the *sirwāl* (pantaloons) and do not wear the *izār*." The prophet says "Wear the *sirwāl* and wear the *izār*, and do the contrary of the people of the Book." We told him "The people of the Book wear ankle-boots (huff) and do not wear sandals (*na'l*)." He says: "Wear ankle-boots and wear sandals, and do the contrary of the people of the Book." We told him: "The people of the Book trim their beards and grow their mustaches." He says: "Trim the mustache and grow the beard, and do the contrary of the people of the Book."

". . . grow your beard, remove your mustaches, alter your white hair and do not resemble Jews or Christians."

The prophet also forbids as a Jewish custom the *qaza* (partial removal of the hair).

Also branded was the use of false hair/hairpieces/wigs. According to a tradition reported in several compilations (Sa'id b. al-Musayyab and Humayd b. 'Abdalrahmān), during the last *khuTba* that he pronounced in Medina, the caliph Mu'awiya I showed the faithful a toupée of false hair, saying "I never saw that done except among the Jews, the prophet had called it 'falseness' (*zūr*)"; or in another version: "people of Medina, where are your wise men? I heard the prophet, who prohibited doing the like and said: 'the children of Israel perished when their women took [false hair].'"

Almost always it is recommended to dye the hair in contrast to the Jews (or to Jews and Christians).[237]

Even sanctioned Muslim practices of onanism/masturbation and bestiality (as Vajda notes, "on which the hadiths cited by Tabari [d. 923] give such exact, if repellant details"),[238] in particular with slaves whom the Muslims wished to avoid impregnating, became a source of friction vis-à-vis the Jews.

The Jews protested against this procedure [*coitus interruptus* with slaves]. Here is what a tradition of Abū Sa'īd al-Hudrī relates: someone comes to find the prophet and tells him: "I have a slave with whom I interrupt coitus, for I do not want her to conceive, but I want what men want. But the Jews claim that *coitus interruptus* is an attenuated case of the exposure of newborn girls." The prophet replied: "The Jews have lied. If Allah wants to create it, you are not capable of preventing [the child from being conceived]."

The same Companion found himself implicated in an analogous incident after the expedition of al'Muraysi in year 5 [after the Hijra, i.e., 622]. The partial restraint of the Muslims, permitting them the

satisfaction of their concupiscence without compromising the hope for ransoming the captives, was approved by the prophet, with the same motive as in the preceding hadith. But when Abū Sa'īd wanted to sell a young girl from the booty, a Jew observed at the market that she was certainly pregnant by him; the Muslim assured him that he had practiced '*azl*, to which the Jew replied that it was an attenuated form of coitus. Informed of this discussion, the prophet could only denounce the lies of the Jews.

The frankly reproving attitude of the Jews toward the sexual dissipation of the Arabs may be illustrated by many Talmudic texts. They found conjugal relations during the day repugnant, at least unless they were invisible. The indecencies committed in the course of the act implied physical infirmities for any child: muteness, deafness, blindness, paralysis. Onanism was severely reproved.[239]

The customs to be observed at funerals, the matters of burial plots and tombs and, more decidedly, Muhammad's view of the fate of buried Jews, also illustrate anti-Jewish animus:

Another tradition ('Bāda b. al'Sāmit) recounts that in following funerals, the prophet had the habit of standing until the dead person was put in his tomb. One day a *haber* [rabbi] passed and told him that the Jews did likewise, at which Mohammed invited those attending to sit down so as not to do as the Jews.

Still, in another opinion, "one should not go with slow steps with the coffin like the Jews do." 'Imrān b. al-Husayn (died 52) ordered when dying: "when after my death you take me outside, go quickly and do not walk slowly like the Jews and the Christians."

A hadith that was widespread relates that during his agony the prophet cursed the Jews and Christians who had taken the tombs of their prophets as sites of worship.

When the prophet was taken by an attack, he threw a *hamīsa* (a sort of robe) over his face; when he came around, we lifted him while he said: 'May God curse the Jews and the Christians, they have taken the tombs of their prophets for sites of worship' (Aysha adds: 'he put them on guard [Muslims] against similar practices'). Elsewhere, one finds this curse without the tale that frames it, Ab 'Bayda relates it as the prophet's last recommendation, at the same time as the order to expel the Jews from the Arabian peninsula.

"Aisha (the wife of the Prophet) Once Allah's Apostle passed by (the grave of) a Jewess whose relatives were weeping over her. He said, 'They are weeping over her and she is being tortured in her grave.'"

"'Amra daughter of 'Abd al Rahman narrated that she heard (from) 'A'isha and made a mention to her about 'Abdullah b. 'Umar as saying: 'The dead is punished because of the lamentation of the living.' Upon this 'A'isha said: 'May Allah have mercy upon the father of 'Abd al-Rahman (Ibn 'Umar). He did not tell a lie, but he forgot or made a mistake. The Messenger of Allah (may peace be upon him) happened to pass by a (dead) Jewess who was being lamented. Upon this he said: 'They weep over her and she is being punished in the grave.'"[240]

Moreover, public lamentation over the dead became forbidden to the Jews (and Christians).[241]

The hadith further condemn certain physical gestures for being specific to Jews:

A hadith disapproves of Muslims who salute each other by making a sign with their fingers like the Jews, or with the hand like the Christians. Aisha did not like her protégé Masrūq to put his hands on his hips for, she said, only the Jews do that.

Raising the hands in prayer is a Jewish gesture.

One should not sway (nawadān) while praying, as the Jews do.[242]

The hadith also portray the Jews' hatred and jealousy of Muhammad. Vajda observes that according to the hadith,

the Jews knew very well that it was Mohammed who should accomplish the prediction of their books. If, then, they did not follow him, this was not out of ignorance but out of jealousy and national particularism.[243]

He then provides two examples of this recurring motif:

The apostle of Allah entered the Bayt al-Midrās and said: "Send me the wisest person among you." They said: "It is Abdallāh b. Sriyā." The apostle of Allah remained alone with him and adjured him by his religion, by the blessings that God had showered [on the Jews] by nourishing them with manna and [salwaa] quail and protecting them by clouds [to answer him]: "Do you know that I am the apostle of Allah?" He answered: "By God, yes, and of course these people [the Jews] know what I know and that your description is clearly found in the Torah, but they are envious of you." [The prophet:] "What prevents you yourself?" He answered: "I feel repugnant at doing otherwise than my people, but perhaps they will follow you and convert to Islam, and then I will convert [also]."

A Jew said to his comrade: "Let us go find the prophet to ask him about this verse (Koran 17:101):

'We brought Moses nine signs.'" His comrade says: "Do not say *prophet* in speaking of him, for if he heard this, he would have four eyes." They ask him and he tells them: "You would not associate anything with God, you would not commit larceny, you would not fornicate, you would not kill the soul that God has forbidden, except through justice, you would not practice magic, you would not lend at usury, you would not deliver the innocent to the men invested with authority to be put to death, you would not slander an honest women [*var.* you would not desert the army on campaign] and on you, Jews, it is especially imposed to not violate the Sabbath." He embraced his hands and his feet, saying: "We confess that you are a prophet." He said: "And what prevents you from following me?" They replied: "David prayed that [prophecy?] never quit his descendants and so we fear that the Jews would kill us if we converted to Islam."[244]

Despite being convinced of the authenticity of Muhammad's divine mission, as Vajda notes, the hadith accusation that the Jews did not become votaries of Islam due to pride in their birth and appetite for domination became a recurrent theme in later Muslim polemics.[245]

Striking evidence of Jewish perfidy in the hadith is illustrated by their continual, surreptitious cursing of the Muslims while ostensibly offering proper greetings:

"A Jew greeted the apostle of Allah by saying *al-sām 'alayka* (May poison be on you, for may peace be upon you). [The prophet said:] 'Bring him to me.' He told him: 'Did you say *al-sām 'alayka?*' 'Yes.' The apostle of Allah said: 'When the people of the Book greet use, say *wa'alayka.*'"

A slightly more developed version: "When the prophet was sitting amid his companions, here comes a Jew who greets them. The prophet had him come back and asked him: 'What did you say?' 'I said *al-sām 'alayka.*' The prophet concluded: 'When an individual of people of the Book greets you, say *and to you*, meaning *what you have said.*'"

A slightly dramatized tale: "A Jew passed by the prophet and his companions, greeted them, and the prophet's companions returned the greeting. The prophet declared: 'He said *al-sām 'alaykum.*' They apprehended the Jew, brought him back, and he admitted it. The prophet said: 'Render back to them what they said.'"

Another version features 'Omar with his habitual violence: "An individual of the people of the Book arrived and greeted the prophet by saying *al-sām 'alaykumi*. Then 'Omar said: 'Apostle of Allah, should I cut off his head?' He answered: 'No. When they greet you, say *wa'alaykum.*'"

Elsewhere, the scene is embellished by Aysha's intervention: "The Jews came to find the prophet and told him *al-sām 'alayka*. The prophet replied [to them]: '*Al-sām 'alaykum.*' Then Aysha cried: '*Al-sām 'alaykum*, brothers of monkeys and pigs and the curse of Allah and his anger!' The prophet said: 'Gently.' She replied: 'Apostle of Allah, did you not hear what they said?' The prophet: 'Did you not hear what I replied to them? [Know] Aysha [that] gentleness ornaments everything, but everything is spoiled if one suppresses it.'"[246]

Vajda offers these explanations for why the hadith are so richly endowed with (and "pleased to raise") examples attesting to Jewish perfidy:

It is impossible for a real incident to be the basis of this group of anecdotes, which are mutually irreconcilable. But it is also probable that they were born of the desire to legitimate a governing arrangement whose practical application must have suffered some difficulties in conquered countries, where even the most elementary relations were daily making the new masters confront a significant non-Muslim population.

This important series of hadiths illustrates so vividly the insolence and crudeness of Jews that later, when the jurists (*fukahā*; especially Western ones) decreed pitiless sanctions against whoever insulted or mocked the prophet, it was wondered why Mohammed had not dealt severely with the Jews who saluted him with *al-sām 'alaykum*. The cadi/judge 'Iyād replied: "especially [he used] diplomacy so as not to scare minds away at the start of Islam by rigorous measures; in addition, the incriminating words of the Jews had not been pronounced distinctly enough to constitute a public outrage."[247]

Another commonplace charge in the hadith is that Jews altered their sacred texts, deleting Muhammad's name and precise description. Vajda includes these two vivid examples:

This was transmitted in the name of 'Abdallāh b. Mas'ūd: "Allah sent his prophet to have someone entered into paradise. He entered into the synagogue [al-kanīsa] [where] a Jew was just in the course of reading [them] the Torah. When they [the Jews] arrived at the description of the prophet, they stopped. But in a corner of the synagogue was a sick person. The prophet said: 'Why did you stop?' The sick person replied: 'They arrived at the description of the prophet, which is why they stopped.' Then the sick person dragged himself up to the book of the Torah, grabbed it and read until he came to the description of the prophet and of his community and he said: 'Here is your description and the description of your community. I confess that there is no other God but Allah and that you are the apostle of Allah.' Then he rendered up his soul."

Another version of the same story is found in Ibn Sa'd. The prophet accompanied by Abu Bakr and 'Omar passed beside a Jew who was reading in a book of the Torah for one of his sick parents. The prophet adjured the Jew to tell him if his description was found in the Torah. When he shook his head no, the sick person contradicted him, pronounced profession of Muslim faith, and expired. The prophet himself recited the prayer at his burial and wrapped him in his winding sheet.[248]

However, the prime example of the Jews' illegitimate alteration of the Torah cited in the hadith "with most self-satisfaction" concerns the prescribed punishment for adultery. As per the hadith, a controversy arose between the Jews and Muslims over legislation concerning adultery. The narrative emphasizes the Jews perfidy and overt disrespect for their own revealed scriptures. Vajda examines several of these hadith:

The Jews brought to the prophet an adulterous couple and claimed that their book prescribed punishing them by blackening their faces so as to cover them with shame. Mohammed told them: "You are lying, [the punishment ordered] for this crime is lapidation; so bring the Torah and recite it if you are telling the truth" (Cf. Koran 3:93, which in context relates to the alimentary prohibitions of the Jews). The one-eyed reader of the Jews named Ibn Sūriyā started to read; arriving at a certain passage, he covered it with his hand. Mohammed invited him to lift it; when he lifted it, it shone. So, the Jews admitted that lapidation was indeed prescribed in the Torah, but then kept this law hidden. The prophet had the guilty ones stoned.

[Sahih] Muslim gives this story with several *isnād* [chains of transmission]. In the first hadith, the punishment indicated by the Jews is a little more exactly described: "We blacken their faces, we place them on a mounting, their faces turned toward each other, and we make them take a tour of the town." The reader is anonymous [Some fellow] (*fatā*); it is 'Abdallāh b. Salām who engages the prophet in ordering the reader to raise his mind, under which is found the verse about lapidation. One of the versions gathered by Abū Dāwūd situates the scene in the *Bayt al-Midrās* (house of study); another specifies that the guilty ones received a hundred lashes with a tarred cord.

Another variant in [Sahih] Muslim and in Ibn Māja highlights the perfidy of the Jews even more, as well as the little respect they have for their revealed book. "They passed by the prophet with a flagellated Jew with a blackened face. He called them and asked them: 'Is that the punishment for adultery that you find in your book?' 'Yes.' He fetches one of their wise men and adjures him by the God who revealed the Torah to Moses to tell him if this is really the punishment for adultery [ordered] in their book. The latter answered; 'No, if you had not adjured me in this fashion I would not have told you.' We found [that the punishment for adultery is] lapidation, but this sin was widespread among our great and when we seized great personages, we let them off, but to the weak we applied the punishment. [Finally] we said to ourselves: "Let us agree on a punishment that we will apply to the great as to the weak." We then instituted the blackening of the face and flagellation instead of lapidation.' The apostle of Allah cried: 'God, I am the first who has revived your order after they killed it off.' On which came the revelation of Koran 5:41, ['O Messenger! Let not them grieve thee who vie one with another in the race to disbelief, of such as say with their mouths: "We believe, but their hearts believe not, and of the Jews: listeners for the sake of falsehood, listeners on behalf of other folk who come not unto thee, changing words from their context and saying: If this be given unto you, receive it, but if this be not given unto you, then beware! He whom Allah doometh unto sin, thou (by thine efforts) wilt avail him naught against Allah. Those are they for whom the Will of Allah is that He cleanse not their hearts. Theirs in the world will be ignominy, and in the Hereafter an awful doom'].[249]

Bearing in mind that the Qur'an itself prescribes flagellation for adultery (i.e., Qur'an 24:2: "The adulterer and the adulteress, scourge ye each one of them [with] a hundred stripes"), if confirmed by four eyewitnesses, Vajda summarizes the ironies in alleging Jewish perfidy with regard to the stoning of adulterers:

The prophet reproaches the Jews for having substituted a rule they had themselves invented for God's own law concerning adultery. He applies this law to a Jew, and if one believes the traditions (which are no more or less worthy of credit than any others), he applied it, as did [Caliph] 'Omar, to the Muslims too. Nevertheless, the "lapidation verse" has not been accepted in the Koran's canonic text, which replaces it, in the most recent passages relating to adultery, precisely with the flagellation whose practice by the Jews is regarded as an arbitrary alteration of the primitive revelation. Unless one rejects *en bloc* the traditions relating to the *rajm* [lapidation = stoning] as

forged for the sole purpose of shaming the Jews as falsifiers of their revelation and to glorify Mohammed, who saw clearly through their criminal actions, it is necessary to regard the procedure censured by the prophet as having been really used in the ghettos (*juiveries*) of *Hijāz*. But in that case, the effective legislation of the Koran concerning the punishment of adultery, definitively consecrated by surah 24 [verse 2], derives in a direct line from Jewish practice, consecrated by Mohammed.[250]

Another series of hadith elaborate on Qur'an 3:93 ("All food was lawful unto the Children of Israel, save that which Israel forbade himself, [in days] before the Torah was revealed. Say: Produce the Torah and read it [unto us] if ye are truthful"), and associated Qur'anic exegeses, which accuse the Jews of misrepresenting their alimentary prohibitions, most notably camel's flesh, as in fact described in the Torah (Leviticus 11:4: "Nevertheless these shall ye not eat of them that chew the cud, or of them that divide the hoof: as the camel, because he cheweth the cud, but divideth not the hoof; he is unclean unto you"). Vajda notes, for example, that the classical Qur'anic commentator Tabari

gathered a great number of interpretations of this verse. According to Suddī, Jacob [the biblical patriarch] suffered in the night from sciatica; he made the vow never to eat any nerve if God would deliver him from this malady. The Jews claim to follow their ancestor but they are lying, for it is God who imposed on them alimentary restrictions, on account of their sins. According to Dahhāk the verse means to say that neither before nor after the revelation did God forbid anything to the Jews, except that for the reason that we know, Jacob made the vow to abstain from consuming nerves. Ibn 'Abbās explains: any food was permitted to the children of Israel before the revelation of the Torah, but Jacob forswore nerves, and his children imitated him, without the interdiction being in the Torah. Tabarī lingers over this exegesis, not without modifying it. Before the revelation of the Torah, nothing was forbidden to the children of Israel, but Jacob, suffering from sciatica, forswore nerves, etc. Then, in revealing the Torah, God prohibited certain foods to the Jews.[251]

Additional hadith cited by Vajda present matters with a slight variation—Jacob's prohibition on camel's flesh and milk is self-imposed:

'Abdallāh b. Katīr (and others): Jacob, suffering from sciatica, renounces by a vow, so as to get better, his preferred food: flesh and milk of the camel. According to Hasan, the Jews falsely pretended that the interdiction by Jacob of camel flesh is found in the Torah, whereas in fact it is prior to the revelation and is not in the Torah at all; this is also the opinion of Ibn Abbās. The latter doctor reconciles the two series of traditions by teaching that Jacob forbid himself both the nerves and flesh of camels. He had consumed meat not cleaned of the sciatic nerve and fell ill and swore never to eat it again.[252]

As Vajda further indicates, Tabari subscribes to this latter interpretation because

the Jews still prohibit nerves [in general] and the flesh of the camel [in particular]. He then cites, under the name of Ibn 'Abbās, the question the Jews put to Mohammed that we have seen. Mohammed invites the Jews to bring the Torah and read it so as to make manifest their falsehood; God has never forbid these things. It is a proof of the authenticity of Mohammed's mission that he, an 'ummī [i.e., a/the prophet] has unmasked the lie of Jewish doctors that most of their co-religionists had not perceived.[253]

Vajda's concluding analysis summarized the evolution of this anti-Jewish polemical theme, which ignores Leviticus (11:4):

Let us try to retrace the evolution of this polemic theme, whose elements we have just analyzed. The familiar narration of Genesis (Jacob's struggle with the angel in Genesis 32:25–33) closes with the remark: "This is why the children of Israel do not eat the sciatic nerve." So this is a custom that was never raised, within the Pentateuch, to the rank of a positive interdiction. The Biblical motif is unknown or ignored by Muslim tradition. The Koran speaks, without being precise, of a prohibition voluntarily assumed by Israel. Tradition designates as the object of the interdiction either the sciatic nerve (with a motive alien to Jewish sources) or else the meat and milk of the camel. These two indications are reconciled, but the tendency (supported indeed by the remainder of the Koranic verse) that is everywhere subsidiary, is to demonstrate that the interdiction is not revealed and hence is expressly willed by God (or else, according to some who are still in conformity with the thinking of the Koran on this point, imposed after the fact on Jews on account of their sins). It is due to Jacob's private initiative, something followed by his descendants, but it does not oblige the Muslims by any means to do so.

The Muslim polemic does not want to admit that this interdiction is written in the Torah, for that would put the national dish of the Arabs on the same footing as pork, for example.[254]

Other traditions attribute evil spells to the Jews. Vajda provides two examples of this motif, the latter not being consistently clear as to its "magical origins" in the various iterations:

The biography of the prophet recounts that he had a spell cast upon him by the Jew Labīd b.al-al'A'sam. The charm was broken when, thanks to the intervention of Jibril (or Jibril and Mikā'il, or two anonymous personages), who indicated the place where Labīd had hidden the hair of the prophet, which he had taken and braided into magic knots and introduced into the male flower of the palm tree.

Another case is much less clear. Ibn 'Omar recounts that when he went to Khaybar to attend the division of the crop between Jews and the treasurer of Egypt, in conformity with the pact in force, the Jews bewitched him so well that his right hand froze at the fist. It was after this event that 'Omar expelled them from Khaybar.

Bukhārī's version leaves out the bewitching; 'Abdallāh b.'Omar was the victim of a nocturnal assault when he went to Khaybar to inspect a property he owned. According to a tradition from Wākidī, the Jews were expelled for having incited slaves to assassinate their masters. Finally, a tradition recorded by Ibn Sa'd reports that 'Omar expelled the Jews of Khaybar because at that time the Muslims already had enough manpower to cultivate their palm groves without turning to tenant farmers. Consequently it is difficult to admit the historicity or at the very least the magic origin of the accident of Ibn 'Omar. This story had to have been invented so as to lay the responsibility for the expulsion of the Jews of Khaybar on themselves.[255]

And after the Muslims initially conquered the Jewish farming oasis of Khaybar, one of the vanquished Jewesses reportedly served Muhammad poisoned mutton (or goat), which resulted, ultimately, in his protracted, agonizing death:

Anas reported that a Jewess came to Allah's Messenger (may peace be upon him) with poisoned mutton and he took of that what had been brought to him (Allah's Messenger). (When the effects of this poison were felt by him) he called for her and asked her about that, whereupon she said: I had determined to kill you. Thereupon he said: Allah will never give you the power to do it. He (the narrator) said that they (the Companion's of the Holy Prophet) said: Should we not kill her? Thereupon he said: No. He (Anas) said: I felt (the effects of this poison) on the uvula of Allah's Messenger. [Sahih Muslim bk. 026, no. 5430]

Narrated Anas bin Malik: A Jewess brought a poisoned (cooked) sheep for the Prophet who ate from it. She was brought to the Prophet and he was asked, "Shall we kill her?" He said, "No." I continued to see the effect of the poison on the palate of the mouth of Allah's Apostle. [Sahih Bukhari vol. 3, bk. 47, no. 786]

Ibn Sa'd's biography, however, maintains that the offending Jewess gave Muhammad poisoned goat, and insists that she was not spared:

She [a Khaybar Jewess, Zaynab Bint al-Harith] poisoned the goat putting more poison in the forelegs. . . . The Apostle of Allah took the foreleg, a piece of which he put into his mouth. . . . The Apostle of Allah sent for Zaynab Bint al-Harith [and] . . . handed her over to [those] who put her to death. . . . The Apostle of Allah lived after this three years, till in consequence of his pain he passed away. During his illness he used to say: I did not cease to find the effect of the poisoned morsel I took at Khaybar.[256]

Vajda's research further demonstrates how Muslim eschatology highlights the Jews supreme hostility toward Islam. Jews are described as adherents of the Dajjâl—the Muslim equivalent of the Antichrist—and as per another tradition, the Dajjâl is in fact Jewish. At his appearance, other traditions state that the Dajjâl will be accompanied by seventy thousand Jews from Isfahan wrapped in their robes and armed with polished sabers, their heads covered with a sort of veil. When the Dajjâl is defeated, his Jewish companions will be slaughtered—everything will deliver them up except for the so-called gharkad tree. Thus, according to a canonical hadith (*Sahih Muslim*, book 40, number 6985), if a Jew seeks refuge under a tree or a stone, these objects will be able to speak to tell a Muslim: "There is a Jew behind me; come and kill him!"[257] Another hadith variant, which takes place in Jerusalem, is described by James Robson.

[M]ost of the Arabs will be in Jerusalem when Jesus [i.e., Isa,[258] the Muslim Jesus] will descend. The *imam* will give place to him, but Jesus will tell him to lead the prayers. Afterwards, Jesus will order the door to be opened, and the Dajjal will be seen there with 70,000 armed Jews. The Dajjal will begin to melt, but Jesus will pursue and catch him and kill him at the east gate of Ludd. God will rout the Jews who will find that even the places where they shelter will shout out where they are hiding.[259]

Vajda emphasizes how the notion of jihad "ransom" extends even into Islamic eschatology:

Not only are the Jews vanquished in the eschatological war, but they will serve as ransom for the Mus-

lims in the fires of hell. The sins of certain Muslims will weigh on them like mountains, but on the day of resurrection, these sins will be lifted and laid upon the Jews.[260]

And in the corporeal world, Vajda observes, "distrust must reign" in Muslims' relations with Jews, because

the Jews . . . are rebels to the solicitations of Islam and keep their religious traditions in a way liable to lead Muslims into error. Even when Islam knowingly borrows from Judaism, these borrowings are presented as amendments of the corresponding Jewish customs, unless they expressly forge traditions that aim to efface the true origin of the rite in question, by transposing it either into Arab paganism or into "Israelite" or pre-Israelite antiquity . . . especially beware of asking them for information of a religious kind.[260a]

But it is the Jews' stubborn malevolence, Vajda further notes, that is their defining worldly characteristic:

Jews are represented in the darkest colors [i.e., in the hadith]. Convinced by the clear testimony of their books that Mohammed was the true prophet, they refused to convert, out of envy, jealousy and national particularism, even out of private interest. They have falsified their sacred books and do not apply the laws of God; nevertheless, they pursued Mohammed with their raillery and their oaths, and harassed him with questions, an enterprise that turned to their own confusion and merely corroborated the authenticity of the supernatural science of the prophet. From words they moved to action: sorcery, poisoning, assassination held no scruples for them.[261]

Vajda concludes that these archetypes, in turn, justify Muslim animus toward the Jews, and the admonition to at best "subject [the Jews] to Muslim domination," as *dhimmis*, treated "with contempt," under certain "humiliating arrangements."[262] Subsequent regional surveys across time (including the documents section) will provide copious evidence of the chronic anti-Jewish animus—sanctioned by the hadith—which was an indelible feature of the *dhimmi* condition for Jews.

One particularly tragic fate befell the Jews of Yemen based on rigid adherence to a motif in the hadith (and sira). Imam al-Mahdi, a pious seventeenth-century Yemenite ruler, acted upon the well-known statement from the canonical hadith, attributed to a death bed wish of Muhammad himself, as recorded by Umar (the second Rightly Guided Caliph): "Two religions shall not remain together in the peninsula of the Arabs."[262a] In his fanatic zeal for Islam, al-Mahdi wished to fulfill the mandate of this hadith in Yemen as well. Thus al-Mahdi, in

1679–1680, ordered the entire Jewish population of Yemen—men, women, and children—exiled to the plain of Tihama, known for its salty water and soil, and generally unfavorable climate.[262b] A twentieth-century German tourist described Tihama as follows:

Tihama is a dreadful place because of its terrible heat. Temperatures of fifty degrees centigrade in the shade last for several days. The Bedouins, who are used to a variety of climatic conditions, do not dare to cross the coastal strip between the Red Sea and the mountains of Yemen before sunset . . . the meager waters of the inner Tihama are salty and not potable, at least as far as Europeans are concerned. Therefore, for example, the drinking water for the port city Hudayda must be carried on the backs of donkeys from mountains as far as eighty miles away. The climate of Tihama is the most harmful to one's health in the entire Arabian peninsula. Harsh cases of malaria which gradually destroy the health of its inhabitants are a common occurrence. Even the Italian physicians in Hudayda are not able to do much against it.[262c]

In addition to the expulsion, there was destruction of synagogues, desecration of the Torah scrolls, and inducement for conversion to Islam. *Only one quarter of those thousands of Jews expelled returned to their homes; the rest perished*, dying primarily from exposure, due to the intense heat, lack of potable water, and the resultant spread of epidemic disease. *Of the major Yemenite Jewish community in San'a, for example, which had numbered about ten thousand, only about one-tenth—one thousand—survived this catastrophic exile.*[262d]

Brief modern examples, presented below, illustrate the ongoing relevance of two Jewish archetypes from the hadith as sources of Islamic antisemitism.

The Qur'anic curse (verse 2:61, repeated in 3:112) upon the Jews for (primarily) rejecting—even slaying—Allah's prophets is updated with perfect archetypal logic in the canonical hadith allegation of Muhammad's poisoning by a Khaybar Jewess, which culminates in his painful and protracted death. Eliz Sanasarian provides a striking contemporary (1980s) example from Iran that affirmed this hadith account as objective, factual history during the examination of young adult candidates for national teacher training programs. Sanasarian notes,

[T]he subject became one of the questions in the ideological test for the Teachers' Training College where students were given a multiple-choice question in order to identify the instigator of the martyrdom of the Prophet Muhammad, the "correct" answer being "a Jewess."[263]

The 1988 Hamas charter, in section 7,[264] quotes from the apocalyptic canonical hadith ("The hour of judgment shall not come until the Muslims fight the Jews and kill them, so that the Jews hide behind trees and stones, and each tree and stone will say: 'Oh Muslim, oh servant of Allah, there is a Jew behind me, come and kill him,' except for the Gharqad tree, for it is the tree of the Jews."), detailing one account of the Jews' annihilation. And a British television investigation broadcast on January 11, 2007, revealed that this eschatological theme was part of a video sermon during which a sheikh (Feiz) could be seen "imitating the noise of a pig when referring to Jewish people [consistent with Qur'an 5:60], who he says will be killed (in a mass extermination) on the 'day of judgment.'" A DVD format recording of this sermon was sold at the London Central Mosque, "one of London's most established mosques," in Regent's Park.[265] Such contemporary eschatological antisemitism began to be popularized two decades ago when the Egyptian writer Sayyid Ayyub started publishing works in Arabic maintaining that the Dajjâl was already active on earth, and that he was Jewish.[265a] Ayyub's view was reiterated more recently by an Indian Muslim writer, Mohamad Yasin Owadally,[265b] who is convinced that "the Jews are waiting impatiently for the coming of Dajjal, their beloved king,"[265c] because:

Zionists in their bloodthirsty lust for power are not satisfied with Palestine. In their arrogance, they openly admit that they want all Syria . . . Lebanon . . . Jordan . . . Iraq . . . Iskenderun [fromer Alexandretta, in southwestern Turkey] . . . the Sinai . . . the Delta area of Egypt and the Upper Hejaz and Najd. . . . They even want the holy Medinah. . . . Their main aim is to exterminate Islam.[265d]

The Early Muslim Biographies of Muhammad (Sira, Sirat)

Sira, which can mean "epistle," "pamphlet," or "manifesto," also means "biography," "the life and times of." The most widely used names for the traditional early Muslim accounts of Muhammad's life and background are "the sīra," "sīrat rasūl allāh," or "sīra al-Cnabawiyya."[266] Ibn Ishaq of Medina (d. 767–770)[267] composed the earliest full-length biography of Muhammad, *Sīrat Rasūl Allāh* (*Biography of the Prophet of Allah*),[268] nearly 150 years after the Muslim prophet's death. However, as Raven has observed, "[T]here has hardly been any written standard text by Ishaq himself . . . we depend upon his transmitters,"[269] most notably Ibn Hisham's (d. 834) selections from Ishaq's work.[270] The combined efforts of Ibn Ishaq and Ibn Hisham produced a biography that placed Muhammad in the tradition of the earlier prophets, with Ibn Hisham (perhaps) focusing the perspective on ancient Arabia.[271] Two other important early Muslim biographies of Muhammad were composed by al-Wakidi

(d. 822),[272] and his student and secretary, Ibn Sa'd (d. 845).[273] The accounts by al-Wakidi (Kitāb al-Maghāzī) and Ibn Sa'd (Kitāb al-Tabakāt al-kabīr) concentrate on the life and times of Muhammad, only,[274] in particular the many battles, razzias (raids), and even political assassinations he led or sanctioned.[275]

Michael Cook's assessment of the sīra,[276] including Ishaq's foundational biography (which according to A. Guillaume, author of an authoritative modern English translation of *Sīrat Rasūl Allāh*,[277] ". . . had no serious rival . . . "), recalls the intractable limitations discussed earlier with regard to the hadith as sources of objective history. On the one hand, Cook observes, there is a prevalent view[278]

that the chains are genuine and the authorities are authors. Thus we can simply extend back the kind of reconstruction that works for the biographies of Ibn Ishaq's day. For example, he and his contemporaries make frequent reference to Zuhri (d. 742), a major figure of the previous generation. An energetic researcher could then collect all the quotations relating to the life of Muhammad that are given on Zuhri's authority, and hope to emerge with something like a reconstruction of his work. It would of course have to be conceded that the further back we go, the more blurred our reconstructions are likely to become. But this is a small price to pay for the overall assurance of the reliability of our sources. If these sources preserve for us a literature that reaches back to the contemporaries of Muhammad, and if they preserve the testimony of numerous independent witnesses, then there is little room for the skeptic in the study of Muhammad's life.[279]

Yet Cook also makes clear that

false ascription was rife among the eighth-century scholars, and that in any case Ibn Ishaq and his contemporaries were drawing on an oral tradition. Neither of these propositions is as arbitrary as it sounds. We have reason to believe that numerous traditions on questions of dogma and law were provided with spurious chains of authorities by those who put them in circulation; and at the same time we have much evidence of controversy in the eighth century as to whether it was permissible to reduce oral tradition to writing. The implications of this view for the reliability of our sources are clearly rather negative. If we cannot trust the chains of authorities, we can no longer claim to know that we have before us the separately transmitted accounts of independent witnesses; and if knowledge of the life of Muhammad was transmitted orally for a century before it was reduced to writing, then the chances are that the material will have undergone considerable alteration in the process.[280]

Disregarding their validity as sources for the historical advent of Islam, what matters ultimately is the lasting impact of the pious Muslim narrative as recorded in the sīra on Islamic doctrine and Muslim behavior. Robert Spencer's 2006 biography of Muhammad elucidates this point:

[I]t is less important to know what really happened in Muhammad's life than what Muslims have generally accepted as having happened, for the latter still forms the foundation of Muslim belief, practice, and law.[281]

Ibn Ishaq's biography chronicles the evolution of Muhammad's teaching and behaviors that accompanied the *hijra*, or migration, to Medina from Mecca in 622. Initially,

[t]he apostle had not been given permission to fight, or allowed to shed blood. . . . He had simply been ordered to call men to God and endure insult and forgive the ignorant. The Quraysh had persecuted his followers, seducing some from their religion, and exiling others from their country. They had to choose whether to give up their religion, be maltreated at home, or to flee the country, some to Abyssinia [Ethiopia], others to Medina.[282]

Then, after being "wronged" and "badly treated," Muhammad and his followers were enjoined to fight in self-defense:

When Quraysh became insolent toward God and rejected his gracious purpose, accused his Prophet of lying, and ill-treated and exiled those who served Him and proclaimed His unity, believed in his prophet, and held fast to His religion, He gave permission to His apostle to fight and to protect himself against those who wronged them and treated them badly. The first verse which was sent down on this subject from what I have heard from 'Urwa b. al-Zubayr and other learned persons was: [Qur'an 22:39–41] "Permission is given to those who fight because they have been wronged. God is well able to help them,—those who have been driven out of their houses without right only because they said God is our Lord. Had not God used some men to keep back others, cloisters and churches and oratories and mosques wherein the name of God is constantly mentioned would have been destroyed. Assuredly God will help those who help Him. God is Almighty. Those who if we make them strong in the land will establish prayer, pay the poor tax, enjoin kindness, and forbid iniquity. To God belongs the end of matters." The meaning is: "I have allowed them to fight only because they have been unjustly treated while their sole offense against men has been that they worship God. When they are in the ascendant they will establish prayer, pay the poor tax, enjoin kindness, and forbid iniquity, i.e., the prophet and his companions, all of them."[283]

Spencer emphasizes that the phrase "When they are in the ascendant" refers to the establishment of a ruling Islamic community or state wherein Muslims will perform regularly prescribed prayer, pay the *zakat* ("poor tax"), and institute the Shari'a (Islamic law).[284]

But the revelation process continues: Ibn Ishaq tellingly quotes Qur'an 2:193, sanctioning aggressive warfare—a doctrine that was ultimately elaborated into the uniquely Islamic institution of jihad.

> Then God sent down to him: "Fight them so that there be no more seduction [i.e., to idolatry; modern translations state "persecution," or "oppression"], i.e., until no believer is seduced from his religion. And the religion is God's, i.e., until God alone is worshipped."[285]

Such was the mind-set when, according to Ibn Ishaq,[286]

> the apostle commanded his companions, the emigrants of his people and those Muslims who were with him in Mecca, to emigrate and to link up with their brethren the Anṣār.[287]

At the time of Muhammad's arrival in Medina (622), several Jewish tribes, most important the Banu Qaynuqa, Banu Nadir, and Banu Qurayza, inhabited the city.[288] Muslim sources described Medina (Yathrib) as having been a Jewish city founded by a Palestinian diaspora population that had survived the revolt against the Romans. Distinct from the nomadic Arab tribes, the Jews of the north Arabian Peninsula were highly productive oasis farmers. These Jews were eventually joined by itinerant Arab tribes from southern Arabia who settled adjacent to them and transitioned to a sedentary existence.[289] The pagan Arab inhabitants of Medina in 622 were composed of two clans, the Aws and Khazraj (sometimes referred to collectively as Banu Qayla).[290] Bitter and sanguinary rivalries and divisions—the Jewish B. Nadir and B. Quraysh tribes siding with the Aws; the Jewish B. Qaynuqa with the Khazraj—had taken their toll on all these Medinan tribes. Soon after Muhammad reached Medina in September of 622, he purportedly created a federation consisting of the Medinan tribes and his followers from Mecca, based upon an agreement known as the Constitution of Medina. Ibn Ishaq describes this putative document as follows:

> The apostle wrote a document concerning the emigrants and the helpers in which he made a friendly agreement with the Jews and established them in their religion and their property, and stated the reciprocal obligations.[291]

Thorough analyses by modern scholars indicate that this constitution was part of Muhammad's design to neutralize the Jews and establish a hegemonic order, which is in fact what occurred. The assessments of Julius Wellhausen (1889), A. J. Wensinck (1908), and Moshe Gil (1974), which concur on this critical argument, are presented chronologically.

Julius Wellhausen:

> I doubt that there was indeed a written agreement of which both parties had a copy. The Jews never referred to their document. The Banū Qurayza claimed that there was no agreement between them and Muhammad. Their leader Ka'b ibn Asad, did not tear up a document, rather a shoelace, to demonstrate symbolically the breach with the Medinans. In any case, there cannot have been a general agreement with the Jews, but only special arrangements with individual clans, for the Jews were no political unit, rather each of their clans formed a confederation with the neighboring Arab clan. As far as I am concerned, Muhammad left the existing relations of individual Jewish clans with the families or clans of the ansār and incorporated them in the ummah. This was all he did. Muhammad had no direct relationship with the Jews but only by way of the ansār. It was only they who had obligations towards the Jews, and had to honor them. Muhammad's obligations derived from this, and it was only because of consideration for the ansār that he did not declare them fair game. . . . In spite of what has been said, I do not doubt the authenticity of the constitution as transmitted by Ibn Isḥāq. But it did not represent an agreement with the Jews.
>
> [Islamic] Tradition has a simple explanation why Muhammad's relation with the Jews was so little affected by the agreement: Every hostile act of Muhammad was precipitated by the Jews and justified by planned or accomplished treachery, even though they had no intention openly to break the agreement. Muhammad himself supplies the interpretation in Koran 8:55–58: "Lo! the worst of beasts in Allah's sight are the ungrateful who will not believe. [8:55]; Those of them with whom thou madest a treaty, and then at every opportunity they break their treaty, and they keep not duty (to Allah). [8:56]; If thou comest on them in the war, deal with them so as to strike fear in those who are behind them, that haply they may remember. [8:57]; And if thou fearest treachery from any folk, then throw back to them (their treaty) fairly. Lo! Allah loveth not the treacherous. [8:58]"[292]

We, however, will find that it was Muhammad who committed the perfidy. He gladly used every chance to punish the Jews, and contrived to create reasons if there were none.[293]

A. J. Wensinck:

The constitution was no treaty concluded between muhājirūn, anṣār, and the Jews. It was an edict defining the relation of the three parties; above them was Allah, i.e., Muhammad. It was evidence of his great authority that, after a short stay in Medina, he, the stranger could lay down the law for all segments of the population.

In religious matters the break with the Jews was irreconcilable. Muhammad did not express his annoyance over this. For the time being, he needed the Jews and included them in the ummah. His first plan failed; he had come to Medina hoping the town would soon be a religious unity as a theocratic monarchy under his leadership. If the Jews would have recognized him, this hope might have been realized. . . . But the Jews showed no such inclination. What to do? They could not be attacked openly because Muhammad's position was still insufficiently established. All he could do was to use them in his plans, or in any case, neutralize them.

When he realized that in the long run a common basis was impossible, he looked for an alternative which he found in the dogma of the religion of Abraham. The proclamation of this dogma coincided with the break with the Jews. Therefore, the constitution must have been written in the middle of the year 2 A.H. [year 2 after the hijra of 622; year 1 starts July 16, 622, and year 2 on July 5, 623] because the *terminus ad quem* [goal or finishing point] for dating the document is the battle of Badr in Ramadān 2 A.H. Quite clearly, it is unthinkable that after the battle of Badr Muhammad should have promised the Jews help against internal or external enemies, freedom of worship, or declared the territory of Yathrib [Medina] inviolable ground since he was on the point of attacking Banū Qaynuqāʿ. The battle of Badr gave Muhammad the opportunity to repeal all concessions made to the Jews. This victory was a success which increased his authority among Banū Qaylah [i.e., the Aws and Khazraj, or anṣār] and allowed him to act with far greater confidence. From then on he felt he could do without the Jews; consequently he did not wait long to express his exasperation.[294]

Moshe Gil:

The document is better understood as an act of preparation for war, and not as its result. Through his alliance with the Arab tribes of Medina the Prophet gained enough strength to achieve a gradual anti-Jewish policy, despite the reluctance of his Medinese allies, who had formerly been those of the Jews. . . . It is therefore an obvious alibi that Muslim sources have developed a tradition about a treaty between Muhammad and the Jews, be it this document or a lost one, as presumed by some modern scholars. Elsewhere, it is declared in complete sincerity that Muhammad, without invoking any treaty, simply asked the B. Qaynuqāʿ before taking action against them, to accept Islam.[295] One of the *hulafāʾ* [allies, confederates] ʿUbāda b. al-Sāmit of the clan B. ʿAwf declares that he takes as *walīs* [ruler] God and His Prophet, and renounces (*abraʾu*) the *hilf* [oath, sworn alliance] with B. Qaynuqāʿ. ʿUbāda also says further to ʿAbdallah b. Ubayy: *Taghayyarat al qulūbu wa-maḥāʾl-islāmuʾl-ʿuhūda* ("The disposition of the hearts has changed and Islam has cancelled [any] treaties"). Usayd b. Hudyr, when reminded by the B. Qurayza about the fact that they are *mawālī* [clients, feudal tenants] of his tribe, the Aws, answers: "There is no *ʿahd ill* [contractual obligation] between us." The document therefore, was not a covenant with the Jews. On the contrary, it was a formal statement of intent to disengage the Arab clans of Medina from the Jewish neighbors they had been allied with up to that time.[296]

Hartwig Hirschfeld's detailed analysis of Muhammad's interactions with the Jews includes this opening summary of the "mutual disappointment" that characterized their relationship, and the predictably disastrous results for the Jews:

The Jews, for their part, were singularly disappointed in their expectations. The way in which Muhammad understood revelation, his ignorance and his clumsiness in religious questions in no way encouraged them to greet him as their Messiah. He tried at first to win them over to his teachings by sweetness and persuasion; they replied by posing once again the questions that they had already asked him; his answers, filled with gross errors, provoked their laughter and mockery. From this, of course, resulted a deep hostility between Muhammad and the Jews, whose only crime was to pass a severe judgment on the enterprise of this Arab who styled himself "God's prophet" and to find his conduct ridiculous, his knowledge false, and his regulations thoughtless. This judgment, which was well founded, was nevertheless politically incorrect [*une faute politique*], and the consequences thereof inevitably would prove to be disastrous for a minority that lacked direction or cohesion.[297]

During his attempts at proselytization, Muhammad's ignorance of Jewish doctrine was ridiculed by rabbis and Jewish poets.[298] Ibn Ishaq accuses them of "hostility . . . , envy, hatred, and malice because God ha[d] chosen his apostle from the Arabs,"[299] consistent with the Muslim traditionalists perspective:

> It was the Jewish rabbis who used to annoy the apostle with questions and introduce confusion, so as to confound the truth with falsity. The Quran used to come down in reference to these questions of theirs, though some of the questions about what was allowed and forbidden came from the Muslims themselves.[300]

In essence, Ibn Ishaq concedes, these Jews—especially the rabbis—made queries of Muhammad:

> These were the Jewish rabbis, the rancorous opponents of the apostle and his companions, the men who asked questions, and stirred up trouble against Islam to try to extinguish it.[301]

Ibn Ishaq records[302] one fortuitous conversion of a Jew to Islam—the rabbi 'Abdallah b. Salam, whose example was followed by several members of the B. Qaynuqa tribe.[303] However, as Hirschfeld observes,

> These conversions, . . . were still exceptional cases, and Islam had few initiates among the Jews. The followers of Mohammed were almost all uneducated, rough-hewn Arabs, ignorant even of the very principles of the religion that they had embraced. As for the Jews, they responded to the prophet's advances with jesting. That is when Mohammed began to replace persuasion with violence; those who were not sincere in the Moslem beliefs, whether Jews or Arabs, were beaten and driven from the mosques. Abu Bakr [the first "rightly Guided Caliph," d. 634] himself, who was usually so prudent and moderate, made his way into the Jewish school and rained blows upon the rabbi Finhās. To reward him for this exploit, Mohammed favored him with a revelation. (Qur'an 3:177–81, 186)[304]

Ibn Ishaq's description of Abu Bakr's outburst includes these details:

> Abu Bakr went into a Jewish school and found a good many men gathered round a certain Finhās, one of their learned rabbis, and another rabbi called Ashya'. Abu Bakr called on the former to fear God and become a Muslim because he knew that Muhammad was the apostle of God who had brought the truth from Him and that they would find it written in the Torah and the Gospel. Finhās replied: "We are not poor compared to Allah but He is poor compared to us. We do not humble ourselves to Him as He humbles Himself to us; we are independent of Him while He needs us. Were He

independent of us He would not ask us to lend Him our money as your master pretends, prohibiting you to take interest and allowing us to. Had He been independent of us He would not have given us interest."

> Abu Bakr was enraged and hit Finhās hard in the face, saying, "Were it not for the treaty between us I would cut off your head, you enemy of Allah!" Finhās immediately went to the apostle and said, "Look, Muhammad, at what your companion has done." The apostle asked Abu Bakr what had impelled him to do such a thing and he answered: "The enemy of Allah spoke blasphemy. He alleged that Allah was poor and that they were rich and I was so angry that I hit his face." Finhās contradicted this and denied that he had said it, so Allah sent down refuting him and confirming what Abu Bakr had said: "Allah has heard the speech of those who say: 'Allah is poor and we are rich.' We shall write what they say and their killing the prophets wrongfully and we shall say, Taste the punishment of burning." [Qur'an 3:181]

> And there came down concerning Abu Bakr and the anger that he felt: "And you will certainly hear from those who received the book before you and from the polytheists much wrong but if you persevere and fear God that is of the steadfastness of things." [Qur'an 3:186]

> Then He said concerning what Finhās and the other rabbis with him said: "And when God laid a charge upon those who had received the book: You are to make it clear to men and not to conceal it, they cast it behind their backs and sold it for a small price. Wretched is the exchange! Think not that those who rejoice in what they have done and want to be praised for what they have not done—think not that they will escape the punishment: theirs will be a painful punishment." [Qur'an 3:187] He means Finhās and Ashya' and the rabbis like them who rejoice in what they enjoy of worldly things by making error attractive to men and wish to be praised for what they have not done so that men will say they are learned when they are nothing of the kind, not bringing them to truth and guidance and wanting men to say that they have so done.[305]

At about the same time, Muhammad is said to have written a letter to the Jews of Khaybar (then mostly belonging to the B. Nadir tribe), attempting to convert them to Islam. This appeal was to no avail,[306] as were others, despite Muhammad's proselytizing zeal.[307] The Jew's stubborn refusal to convert to Islam decisively altered the trajectory of Muhammad's religious thinking, as characterized by Hirschfeld.[308]

> The resistance that the Jews put up to all attempts at converting them changed in a singular manner the

direction of Muhammad's religious thinking. Until then he had adopted Jewish ceremonies for his new religion; he had been turning toward Jerusalem to pray and had used the same method as the Jews of calling the faithful together to prayer . . . finally, he had the faithful summoned from the top of a tower by a man's voice. Then he commanded the Muslims to turn toward Mecca while they prayed. This sudden change, to his way of thinking, had a twofold purpose: to show the Jews that he was making himself independent of their laws, and to flatter the national self-esteem of the Arabs. Although he responded weakly to the Jews who were astonished at this change, there is nevertheless no doubt about his real sentiment.

It was around that time that Muhammad inaugurated a new system of propaganda to recruit followers and to put an end to opposition against his teachings: he used force. Upon learning that a caravan of Quraysh was about to get under way, he instructed a certain number of his friends to position themselves in ambush so as to attack the travelers. One of the Quraysh was killed, two others were taken captive, while the fourth fled. This incident took place during the holy month of the Arabs, in which it was forbidden to engage in battle. Muhammad, who had even shared with the murderers in the spoils from his enemies, justified his conduct and that of his friends by means of a new revelation. [Qur'an 2:217][309] The Jews vehemently scoffed at this *modus operandi* of the prophet, who of course resolved that he would take revenge on his adversaries as soon as circumstances would allow.

The Battle of Badr—during which the Muslims, aided by Allah and a thousand angels, killed forty-nine Meccans, took an equal number prisoner, and acquired considerable booty—established the power of nascent Islam.[310] Afterward, Muhammad launched a campaign of political assassinations of Jewish (or presumptively Jewish) poets and leaders.[311] These assassinations were followed by the siege, expropriation, and expulsion of the Medinan Jewish tribes B. Qaynuqa and B. Nadir, and the subsequent massacre of the Jewish men of the B. Qurayza, whose wives, children, and possessions were then seized as booty by the Muslims.[312]

Asma, daughter of Marwan, wrote satirical verses against Muhammad, so he ordered her assassination.[313] Hirschfeld writes that Muslim traditionalists (such as al-Wakidi) "justify this murder by saying that this woman was Jewish and defiled the mosques."[314] The following is William Muir's description of Asma's assassination and its aftermath, according to the sira:

The first blood shed at Medina with the countenance of Mahomet was that of a woman. Asma, daughter of Marwan, belonged to a disaffected tribe, the Bani [Aws], and to a family which had not yet thrown off their ancestral faith. She made no secret of her dislike to Islam; and being a poetess, compsed some couplets, after the battle of Bedr [Badr], on the folly of her fellow citizens in receiving and trusting one who had slain the chief men amongst his own people. The verses spread from mouth to mouth (for such was one of the few means possessed by the Arabs of giving expression to public opinion), and at least reached the ears of the Mussulmans. They were offended; and Omeir, a blind man of the same tribe (and according to some a former husband of Asma) vowed that he would kill the author. It was but a few days after the return of Mahomet from Bedr, that this man, in the dead of night, crept into the apartment where, surrounded by her little ones, Asma lay asleep. Feeling stealthily with his hand, he removed her infant from her breast, and plunged his sword into her bosom with such force that it passed through her back. Next morning, being present in the Mosque at prayers, Mahomet, who was aware of the bloody design, said to Omeir: "Hast thou slain the daughter of Marwan?" "Yes," he answered; "but tell me is there any cause of apprehension for what I have done?" "None," said Mahomet; "a couple of goats will not knock their heads together for it." Then turning to the people assembled in the Mosque, he said: "If ye desire to see a man that hath assisted the Lord and his Prophet, look ye here!" "What!" Omar exclaimed, "the blind Omeir!" "Nay," replied the Prophet, "call him not blind; rather call him *Omeir the Seeing*."

As the assassin returned to his home in Upper Medina, he passed the sons of Asma burying their mother; they accused him of the murder, which without compunction he avowed, and added that if they dared to repeat such things as she had uttered, he would slay the whole clan of them. The bloody threat had the desired effect. Those of the family who had secretly espoused the cause of Mahomet, now succumbed before the fierce determination and growing influence of the Prophet's followers. Indeed, as Sprenger[315] remarks, the only course by which they could now preserve their honor without entering on a hopeless blood-feud, was the adoption of Islam.[316]

Soon afterward, another (Jewish) poet who dared to write verses critical of Muhammad, Abu 'Afak, reportedly a centenarian, was assassinated on Muhammad's order while he slept. Muir provides these details:

Many weeks did not elapse before another foul murder was committed by the express command of Mahomet. Abu Afak belonged to the Bani Amr (whose doubtful loyalty is marked by the message sent to them by Mahomet on his march to Bedr); he had embraced Judaism, but still lived with his tribe in Upper Medina. Though (as is said) above a hundred years of age he was active in his opposition to the new religion. He, too, composed some stinging and disloyal verses which annoyed the Mussulmans. The Prophet signified his wish for his assassination by saying: "Who will rid me of this pestilent fellow?" A convert from amongst the Bani Amr watched his opportunity, and falling unawares upon the aged man, as he slept in the court-yard outside his house, dispatched him with his sword. The death shriek of the Jew drew the neighbors to the spot; but though they vowed vengeance against the murderer, he escaped unrecognized.[317]

Attempting to exploit the fear aroused by these assassinations,[318] Muhammad admonished the Jews of Medina (specifically, the B. Qaynuqa) one more time to convert to Islam. Ibn Ishaq records this threatening appeal, and the associated Qur'anic revelation (3:12–13):

The apostle assembled them in their market and addressed them as follows: "O Jews, beware lest God bring upon you the vengeance that He brought upon Quraysh and become Muslims. You know that I am a prophet who has been sent—you will find that in your scriptures and God's covenant with you." They replied, "O Muhammad, you seem to think that we are your people. Do not deceive yourself because you encountered a people with no knowledge of war and got the better of them; for by God if we fight you, you will find that we are real men!"

A freedman of the family of Zayd b. Thabit from Sa'id b. Jubayr or from 'Ikrima from Ibn 'Abbas told me that the latter said the following verses came down about them: "Say to those who disbelieve: you will be vanquished and gathered to Hell, an evil resting place. You have already had a sign in the two forces which met, i.e. the apostle's companions at Badr and the Quraysh. "One force fought in the way of God; the other, disbelievers, thought they saw double their own force with their very eyes. God strengthens with His help whom He will. Verily in that is an example for the discerning."[319]

Once the B. Qaynuqa defied this threat, the outcome was predictable. Muir recounts the events leading to their subjugation and expulsion from Medina:

An incident soon occurred which afforded the pretext for an attack. An Arab girl married to a convert of Medina, went to a goldsmith's shop in the marketplace of the Cainucaa [B. Qaynuqa], and, while waiting for some ornaments, sat down. A silly neighbor, unperceived, pinned the lower hem of her skirt behind to the upper dress. When she arose, the awkward exposure excited laughter, and she screamed with shame. A Mussulman, being apprised of the affront, slew the offending Jew; the brethren of the Jew, in their turn fell upon the Mussulman and killed him. The family of the murdered Mussulman appealed to the converts of Medina, who espoused their cause. Though bound by a friendly treaty, Mahomet made no attempt to compose the quarrel, nor any demand that the guilty should be singled out and brought to justice. Without further communication, he marshaled his followers, and, placing the great white banner in the hands of Hamza, marched forth to attack the offending tribe. Their settlement was sufficiently fortified to resist assault. It was therefore invested, and a strict blockade maintained. This happened within one month from the Battle of Bedr.

The Bani Cainucaa were besieged closely by Mahomet for fifteen days. They had expected that Abdallah ibn Obey and the Bani Khazraj, with whom they had long been in close bonds of defensive alliance, would have interfered on their behalf; but no one dared to stir. At last, despairing of the looked-for aid, they surrendered at discretion. As, one by one, they issued from the stronghold, their hands were tied behind their backs, and preparations made for execution. But Abdallah, fallen as he was from his high estate, could not endure to see his faithful allies massacred in cold blood. Approaching Mahomet, he begged for mercy to be shown them; but Mahomet turned his face away. Abdallah persisted in his suit, and seizing the Prophet by the side, as he stood armed in his coat of mail, reiterated the petition. "Let me alone!" cried Mahomet; but Abdallah did not relax his hold. The marks of anger mantled in the Prophet's face, and again he exclaimed loudly: "Wretch, let me go!" "Nay!" said Abdallah, "I will not let thee go until thou hast compassion on my friends; 300 soldiers armed in mail, and 400 unequipped—they defended me on the fields of Hadaick and Boath from every foe. Wilt thou cut them down in one day, O Mahomet? As for me, I am one that verily feareth the vicissitudes of fortune." Abdallah was yet too strong for Mahomet with safety to neglect the appeal so urgently preferred. "Let them go!" the Prophet said, reluctantly; "God curse them, and God curse him also!" So Mahomet released them from death, and commanded that they should be sent into exile. They were lead forth some distance by Obada, one of the Khazrajite "leaders"; thence they proceeded to the Jewish settlement of Wadi al Cora, and, there being assisted with carriage, reached Adzraat, a territory on the confines of Syria.

The spoil consisted mainly of armor and gold-smiths' tools, for that was the chief occupation of the tribe: they possessed no agricultural property, nor any fields. Mahomet took his choice of arms—three bows, three swords, and two coats of mail. The royal fifth was then set aside, and the remainder distributed amongst the army.[320]

Muhammad's ultimate political goals vis-à-vis the Jews were becoming quite apparent:

The Jews might now see clearly the designs of Mahomet. It was no petty question of an affronted female. Blood had no doubt been shed in the quarrel; but it was shed equally on both sides. And had there not been a deadly enmity, and a predetermination to root out the Israelites, the difference might easily have been composed. Moreover Mahomet was bound by treaty to deal justly and amicably with the tribe: the murderer alone was "liable to retaliation." Indeed, of such minor importance was the quarrel, that some biographers do not mention it at all, but justify the attack by a divine revelation of Jewish treachery. The violent proceedings of Mahomet widened also to some extent the breach between his followers and the disaffected citizens. Abdallah thus upbraided Obada (they were both principals in the confederacy with the Bani Cainucaa) for the part he had taken in abandoning their allies, and aiding in their exile: "What! Art thou free from the oath with which we ratified their alliance? Hast thou forgotten how they stood by us, and shed for us their blood, on such and such a field?"—and he began enumerating the engagements in which they had fought together. Obada cut him short with the decisive answer: "Hearts have changed. Islam hath blotted all treaties out."[321]

The expulsion of the B. Qaynuqa made the remaining Jewish tribes of Medina more vulnerable. Following a series of caravan raids (of varied success), and an interlude of calm,[322] Muhammad began a renewed campaign of assassinations starting with the murder of Ka'b b. al 'Ashraf, the son of a Jewess from the B. Nadir. Ibn Warraq summarizes the events surrounding this assassination:

He [Ka'b] had gone to Mecca after the battle of Badr and had composed poems in praise of the dead, trying to stir up the Meccans to avenge their heroes of Badr. Rather foolishly he returned to Medina, where Muhammad prayed aloud, "O Lord, deliver me from the son of Ashraf, in whatsoever way it seems good to you, because of his open sedition and his verses." But the Banu Nadir were powerful enough to protect Ka'b, and the Muslims who volunteered to murder him explained to the Prophet

that only by cunning could they hope to accomplish their task. The conspirators met in Muhammad's house, and as they emerged at night, the Prophet gave them his full blessings. Pretending to be Ka'b's friends, the Muslims lured him out into the night and, in a suitable spot near a waterfall, murdered him. They threw Ka'b's head at the Prophet's feet. Muhammad praised their good work in the cause of God.[323]

Ibn Ishaq records these telling words of one of the conspirators:

Our attack upon God's enemy cast terror among the Jews, and there was no Jew in Medina who did not fear for his life.[324]

Indeed this fear was well founded, as on the very morning after Ka'b's murder, Muhammad encouraged the Muslims to slay Jews indiscriminately, according to Ibn Ishaq:

The apostle said, "Kill any Jew that falls into your power." Thereupon Muhayyisa b. Mas'ud leapt upon Ibn Sunayna, a Jewish merchant with whom they had social and business relations, and killed him. Huwayyisa was not a Muslim at the time though he was the elder brother. When Muhayyisa killed him Huwayyisa began to beat him, saying, "You enemy of God, did you kill him when much of the fat on your belly comes from his wealth?" Muhayyisa answered, "Had the one who ordered me to kill him ordered me to kill you I would have cut your head off." He said that this was the beginning of Huwayyisa's acceptance of Islam. The other replied, "By God, if Muhammad had ordered you to kill me would you have killed me?" He said, "Yes, by God, had he ordered me to cut off your head I would have done so." He exclaimed, "By God, a religion which can bring you to this is marvellous!" and he became a Muslim.[325]

Not surprisingly, as Muir notes,

The Jews were now in extreme alarm. None ventured abroad. Every family lived in fear of a night attack; every individual dreaded the fate of Kab and Ibn Sanin . . . the Jews thenceforward lived (as well they might) in a state of depression and disquietude.[326]

Clearly these murders, particularly of Ka'b, were a prelude to a general attack on the B. Nadir. But this enterprise was delayed by the Muslims' defeat at Uhud (AH 3; 625 CE), a setback to Muhammad's power and prestige.[327] Hirschfeld characterizes his inevitable course of action:

In order to restore his military glory and avenge their insults—the mere memory of which roused his indignation—the prophet resolved to have done with the Jews. Furthermore he felt encouraged by the calm and indifference with which they had witnessed the expulsion of the Banu Qaynuqa and the murder of Ka'b.[328]

The alleged pretext for Muhammad's campaign against the B. Nadir, and the results of the Muslims' attack, are summarized by Hirschfeld, as follows:

A Muslim had killed two members of the Banu Amir tribe. Muhammad, accompanied by Abu Bakr, Umar and Ali, went to the Banu Nadir and asked them to join with him in apologizing for that double murder. His friends waited for him at the entrance to his dwelling; they saw him return in great haste. Muhammad told them that a divine revelation warned him that the Jew 'Amr b. Jiḥāsh (b. Ka'b), refusing to obey the orders of Sallam b. Mishkam, was planning to throw a rock down on him from the height of his citadel so as to kill him. This accusation was certainly false and only served as a pretext to attack the Banu Nadir, whose destruction had been decided long ago. Muhammad laid siege to the citadels of his enemies and, contrary to all customs, gave orders to burn and cut down the palm trees at Boeira. Abdallah b. Ubayy urged those who were under siege not to persist, and he promised to intercede in their favor with the prophet. The latter agreed to allow the Banu Nadir to come out of their fortresses, unarmed, and he permitted each group of three persons to take with them a camel's load of their belongings. The Banu Nadir accepted these conditions, loaded their beasts, carrying off the wooden materials of which their houses were built, and withdrew, to the sound of music, to the North, where they settled, partly in Khaybar, partly in Adzraât in Syria. Among those who decided to stay in Khaybar were the brother and the sons of Kinana Rabi b. Abu'l-Huqayq and the rabbi Huyayy. Two Banu Nadir, Yāmīn b. 'Umayr and Abou Sad b. Wahb, embraced Islam in order to save their fortune and remain in Medina. The lands and houses of the emigrants were divided up among the Muslims.[329]

Hirschfeld concludes that the forced emigration of the B. Nadir resulted from a lack of "energy, resolve, and unity," compounded by a fearful awareness that "they would not be able to continue living in a land where betrayal and murder prevailed, and where their adversaries would surely increase in numbers and strength over time."[330] Muhammad, in contrast, was well aware of the bounty of the exiled B. Nadir, whose lands and possessions became Muslim booty, celebrated in Qur'an

59:1–10, and subsequently codified into Islamic law (as "*fay* territory," etc.).[331] Ibn Ishaq emphasizes how this "Sura of Exile" (sura 59)

came down in which is recorded how God wreaked His vengeance on them [the Jews] and gave His apostle power over them and how He dealt with them. God said: "He it is who turned out those who disbelieved of the scripture people from their homes to the first exile. You did not think that they would go out and they thought that their forts would protect them from God. But God came upon them from a direction they had not reckoned and He cast terror into their hearts so that they destroyed their houses with their own hands and the hands of the believers." That refers to their destroying their houses to extract the lintels of the doors when they carried them away. "So consider this, you who have understanding. Had not God prescribed deportation against them," which was vengeance from God, "He would have punished them in this world," i.e., with the sword, "and in the next world there would be the punishment of hell" as well. "The palm-trees which you cut down or left standing upon their roots." Lina means other than the best kind of dates. "It was by God's permission," i.e., they were cut down by God's order; it was not destruction but was vengeance from God, "and to humble evildoers." "The spoil which God gave the apostle from them," i.e., from B. al-Nadir. "You did not urge on your cavalry or riding camels for the sake of it, but God gives His apostle power over whom He wills and God is Almighty," i.e., it was peculiar to him. "The spoil which God gave the apostle from the people of the towns belongs to God and His apostle." What the Muslims gallop against with horses and camels and what is captured by force of arms belongs to God and the apostle. "And is for the next of kin and orphans and the poor and the wayfarer so that it should not circulate among your rich men; and what the apostle gives you take and abstain from what he forbids you." He says this is another division between Muslims concerning what is taken in war according to what God prescribed to him.

Then God said, "Have you seen those who are disaffected," meaning 'Abdullah b. Ubayy and his companions and those who are like-minded "who say to their brothers of the scripture people who disbelieve," i.e., the B. Al-Nadir, up to the words "like those who a short time before them tasted the misery of their acts and had a painful punishment," i.e., the B. Qaynuqa. Then as far as the words "Like Satan when he said to man Disbelieve," and when man disbelieved he said, "I am quit of you. I fear Allah the Lord of the worlds and the punishment of both is that they will be in hell everlastingly. That is the reward of the evildoers."[332]

The last remaining Jewish tribe in Medina was Banu Qurayza. During the Battle of the Trench (627), when the Meccans and their allies had besieged Medina, B. Qurayza contributed to the city's defense but on the whole remained neutral.[333] After a fortuitous storm helped break the siege, the loyalty of the B. Qurayza was questioned, and Muhammad, inspired by another divine revelation, moved against them.[334] When Muhammad approached the fortifications of the B. Qurayza, according to Ibn Ishaq, he declared, "You brothers of apes, has God disgraced you and brought his vengeance upon you?"[335]

A consensus Muslim account of the subsequent events that led to the massacre of the B. Qurayza has been compiled by M. J. Kister.[336] Twice the Qurayza made offers to surrender and depart from their stronghold, leaving behind their land and property. Initially they requested to take one camel load of possessions per person, but when Muhammad refused this request the Qurayza asked to be allowed to depart without any property, taking with them only their families. However, Muhammad insisted that the Qurayza surrender unconditionally and subject themselves to his judgment. Compelled to surrender, the Qurayza were lead to Medina. The men, with their hands pinioned behind their backs, were put in a court, while the women and children were said to have been put into a separate court. A third (and final) appeal for leniency for the Qurayza was made to Muhammad by their tribal allies, the Aws. Muhammad again declined, and instead he appointed as arbiter Sa'd Mu'ad from the Aws, who soon rendered his concise verdict: The men were to be put to death, the women and children sold into slavery, the spoils divided among the Muslims.

Muhammad ratified the judgment, stating that Sa'd's decree was a decree of Allah pronounced from above the Seven Heavens. Thus some six hundred to nine hundred men from the Qurayza were led on Muhammad's order to the market of Medina. Trenches were dug and the men were beheaded, and their decapitated corpses buried in the trenches while Muhammad watched in attendance. Male youths who had not reached puberty were spared. Women and children were sold into slavery, a number of them being distributed as gifts among Muhammad's companions. According to Ibn Ishaq, Muhammad chose one of the Qurayza women (Rayhana) for himself. Qurayza property and other possessions (including weapons) were also divided up as additional "booty" among the Muslims. The following details have been chronicled consistently by Muslim sources: The arbiter (Sa'd Mu'ad) was appointed by Muhammad himself, Muhammad observed in person the horrific executions, Muhammad claimed as a wife a woman (Rayhana) previously married to one of the slaughtered Qurayza tribesmen, the substantial material benefits (i.e., property, receipts from the sale of the enslaved) that accrued to the Muslims as a result of the massacre, the extinction of the Qurayza.

Abu Yusuf (d. 798), the prominent Hanafi jurist who advised Abbasid caliph Harun al-Rashid (d. 809), made the following observations about the Qurayza massacre in his writings on jihad:

> Whenever the Muslims besiege an enemy stronghold, establish a treaty with the besieged who agree to surrender on certain conditions that will be decided by a delegate, and this man decides that their soldiers are to be executed and their women and children taken prisoner, this decision is lawful. This was the decision of *Sa'ad b. Mu'ad in connection with the Banu Qurayza* . . . it is up to the imam to decide what treatment is to be meted out to them and he will choose that which is preferable for religion and for Islam. If he esteems that the execution of the fighting men and the enslavement of their women and children is better for Islam and its followers, then he will act thus, *emulating the example of Sa'ad b. Mu'ad.*[337]

Al-Mawardi (d. 1072), another eminent Muslim jurist from Baghdad, characterized the slaughter of the Qurayza as a religious duty incumbent on Muhammad. Kister quotes al-Mawardi as follows: "[I]t was not permitted (for Muhammad) to forgive (in a case of) God's injunction incumbent upon them; he could only forgive (transgressions) in matters concerning his own person."[338] The notion that this slaughter was sanctioned by God as revealed to Muhammad was, according to Kister, reflective of " . . . the current (as of 1986) Sunni view about the slaughter of the Banu Qurayza."[339]

W. H. T. Gairdner, also relying exclusively upon Muslim sources characterizing the slaughter of the Qurayza, highlights the pivotal role that Muhammad himself played in orchestrating the overall events:

> The umpire who gave the fatal decision (Sa'ad) was extravagantly praised by Muhammad. Yet his action was wholly and admittedly due to his lust for personal vengeance on a tribe which had occasioned him a painful wound. In the agony of its treatment he cried out—"O God, let not my soul go forth ere thou has cooled my eye from the Bani Quraiza." *This* was the arbiter to whose word the fate of that tribe was given over. His sentiments were well-known to Muhammad, who appointed him. It is perfectly clear from that that their slaughter had been decreed. What makes it clearer still is the assertion of another biographer that Muhammad had refused to treat with the Bani Quraiza at all until they had "come down to receive the judgment of the Apostle of God." Accordingly "they came down"; in other words put themselves in his power. And only then was the arbitration of Sa'ad proposed and accepted—but not accepted until it had been forced on him by Muhammad; for Sa'ad first declined and

tried to make Muhammad take the responsibility, but was told "*qad amarak Allahu takhuma fihim*" "Allah has commanded you to give sentence in their case." From every point of view therefore the evidence is simply crushing that Muhammad was the ultimate author of this massacre.[340]

In the immediate aftermath of the massacre, the Muslims benefited substantially from the Qurayza's assets, which they seized as booty. The land and property acquired helped the Muslims gain their economic independence. The military strength of the Muslim community of Medina grew due to the weapons obtained and the fact that captured women and children taken as slaves were sold for horses and more weapons, facilitating enlargement of the Muslim armed forces for further conquests. Conversely, the Jewish tribe of the Qurayza ceased to exist.

Muhammad prepared for his campaign against Khaybar—a farming oasis and the last Jewish stronghold in northern Arabia, where survivors (most notably, the B. Nadir) of the Muslims' earlier attacks on Medinan Jewry had also sought refuge—by two further political assassinations. Hirschfeld describes these murders of prominent Khaybar Jews:

Abu Rafi Sallam b. Abu'l-Huqayq was in Khaybar. Muhammad, who feared that he might cause him difficulties, sent murderers after him. Five men from the tribe of the Khazraj traveled to Khaybar, slipped into Sallam's dwelling at night and closed the doors. Sallam was on the upper floor; his wife went down and asked the men what they wanted. They replied that they had come to buy some wheat, entered the chamber where Sallam was in bed, and stabbed him. At the cries of the victim's wife, some Jews came running with torches, but the murderers had managed to escape. After the death of Sallam, the chieftain of the Jews of Khaybar was Al-Yoseir b. Rizâm. Since the latter was one of those who had incited the Ghatafan to attack the prophet, Muhammad sent against him a band of assassins headed by the poet Abdallâh b. Rawâha, which included the murderers of Abu Rafi Sallam. Their plan failed, but they managed to persuade Al-Yoseir that Muhammad was summoning him to appoint him to an important position. Seduced by that promise, he left for Medina, accompanied by several friends. Along the way, the men who had been sent by Muhammad attacked those who had trusted their words and killed them.[341]

Ibn Ishaq's account of Abu Rafi Sallam b. Abu'l-Huqayq's assassination spares none of the gruesome details:

When they [the Muslim assassins] got to Khaybar they went to Sallam's house by night, having locked every door in the settlement on the inhabitants. Now he was in an upper chamber of his to which a ladder led up. They mounted this until they came to the door and asked to be allowed to come in. His wife came out and asked who they were and they told her that they were Arabs in search of supplies. She told them that their man was here and that they could come in. When we entered we bolted the door of the room on her and ourselves fearing lest something should come between us and him. His wife shrieked and warned him of us, so we ran at him with our swords as he was on his bed. The only thing that guided us in the darkness of the night was his whiteness like an Egyptian blanket. When his wife shrieked one of our number would lift his sword against her; then he would remember the apostle's ban on killing women and withdraw his hand; but for that we would have made an end of her that night. When we had smitten him with our swords 'Abdullah b. Unays bore down with his sword into his belly until it went right through him, as he was saying "Qat ñ qatnī" i.e., "It's enough."

We [the Muslim assassins] went out. Now 'Abdullah b. 'Atik had poor sight, and fell from the ladder and sprained his arm severely, so we carried him until we brought him to one of their water channels and went into it. The people lit lamps and went in search of us in all directions until, despairing of finding us, they returned to their master and gathered round him as he was dying. We asked each other how we could know that the enemy of God was dead, and one of us volunteered to go and see; so off he went and mingled with the people. He said, "I found his wife and some Jews gathered round him. She had a lamp in her hand and was peering into his face and saying to them 'By God, I certainly heard the voice of 'Abdullah b. 'Atik. Then I decided I must be wrong and thought 'How can Ibn 'Atik be in this country?'" Then she turned towards him, looking into his face, and said, "By the God of the Jews he is dead!" Never have I heard sweeter words than those.

Then he came to us and told us the news, and we picked up our companion and took him to the apostle and told him that we had killed God's enemy. We disputed before him as to who had killed him, each of us laying claim to the deed. The apostle demanded to see our swords and when he looked at them he said, "It is the sword of 'Abdullah b. Unays that killed him; I can see traces of food on it."[341a]

The brutal, sanguinary assaults by the Muslims that ensued shortly afterward resulted in the complete subjugation of the Jews of Khaybar (and, by extension, Fadak), as summarized by Hirschfeld:

These murders were the prelude to a general attack against the Israelites of Khaybar. Muhammad, at the head of 1,400 foot soldiers and 300 horsemen, marched against that city and arrived during the night. In the morning the Israelites, going out to the fields as usual, noticed armed Muslims everywhere.

Little by little all the forts fell into the hands of the Muslims, with the exception of Wâtih and Solâlim. A great number of Jews were taken prisoner, among them Kinana b. Ar-Rabi b. Abu'l-Huqayq and his fiancée, Safiyya, daughter of Huyayy. Safiyya was very beautiful, and Muhammad wanted to take her as his wife; he summoned her fiancé Kinana, and under the pretext of making him tell where he had hidden the treasures of the Banu Nadir that had been entrusted to his protection, he subjected him to atrocious tortures, put him to death, and then married Safiyya. All the combatants who were captured with weapons in hand were killed; almost nine hundred died in this way.

The two other forts that were still putting up resistance surrendered shortly after to the Muslims. The soldiers' lives were spared, but they had to hand over all their treasures to Muhammad and abandon their lands to the victors. However, since they were better farmers than the Muslims, they could continue to cultivate these lands, on the condition that they would deliver half of the harvest to their masters and leave the countryside as soon as Muhammad demanded it. The Jews of Fadak, whose chieftain was named Youschah b. Noun, and those of Teimâ and Wâdi-l-Kôrâ, terrified by the defeat of the inhabitants of Khaybar, likewise submitted to Muhammad.[341b]

Ibn Ishaq chronicled the torture-murder of Kinana b. Ar-Rabi b. Abu'l-Huqayq, on Muhammad's orders, as follows:

When he [Muhammad] asked him [Kinana] about the rest [of the treasure] he refused to produce it, so the apostle gave orders to al-Zubayr b. al-'Awwam, "Torture him until you extract what he has," so he kindled a fire with flint and steel on his chest until he was nearly dead. Then the apostle delivered him to Muhammad b. Maslama and he struck off his head, in revenge for his brother Mahmud.[342]

Following the conquest of Khaybar, the hadith and sira accounts refer to an event that updates with impeccable logic the Qur'anic curse upon the Jews (2:61) for having wrongfully slain Allah's earlier prophets—a Khaybar Jewess is accused of serving Muhammad poisoned mutton (or goat), leading ultimately to his protracted and painful death.[343] Ibn Sa'd's sira (*Kitab Al-Tabaqat Al-Kabir*) focuses on the Jewish conspiracy behind this poisoning, while insisting adamantly that the Khaybar Jewess perpetrator was put to death:

The Jews discussed about poisons and became united in one poison. She [a Khaybar Jewess, Zaynab Bint al-Harith] poisoned the goat putting more poison in the forelegs. . . . The Apostle of Allah took the foreleg, a piece of which he put into his mouth. . . . The Apostle of Allah sent for Zaynab Bint al-Harith [and] . . . handed her over to the heirs of Bishr Ibn al-Barra [who the Jewess had also poisoned, leading to his rapid death] who put her to death. *This is the approved version* [emphasis added]. . . . The Apostle of Allah lived after this three years, till in consequence of his pain he passed away. During his illness he used to say: I did not cease to find the effect of the poisoned morsel I took at Khaybar.[344]

The political rationale for Muhammad's campaign against Khaybar has been discussed by Hirschfeld and D. S. Margoliouth. Hirschfeld, in his review of Leone Caetani's *Annali dell Islam*, agrees with the latter's assessment:

The author [Caetani] is undoubtedly right in saying that the reasons given by the Muslim traditionalists are worthless, as Muhammad's real motive was a purely political one, an additional motive being the opportunity which it gave of employing a number of followers unskilled in work but eager for spoil.[345]

Hirschfeld then adds, based upon his own research of the documentary record:

The expedition against Khaybar was a distinct breach of faith, as two years previously Muhammad had given the Jews of Khaybar and Maqna a charter of liberty which has fortunately been preserved, and traces of which are also to be found in the works of al-Wakidi and al-Baladhuri.[346]

Margoliouth expands upon these arguments, and concludes,

[I]n plundering Meccans he [Muhammad] could plead that he had been driven from his home and possessions: and with the Jewish tribes of Medina he had in each case some outrage, real or pretended, to avenge. But the people of Khaybar, all that distance from Medina, had certainly done him and his followers no wrong: for their leaving unavenged the murder of one[347] of their number by his emissary was no act of aggression. Ali, when told to lead the forces against them, had to enquire for what he was fighting: and was told that he must compel them to adopt the formulae of Islam. Khaybar was attacked because there was booty to be acquired there, and the plea for attacking it was that its inhabitants were not Muslims.[348]

Georges Vajda, in turn, reminds us of the theological animus that motivated Muhammad's political subjugation of the Jews specifically, and became an indelible part of Muslim attitudes toward Jews across space and time:

> The more Mohammed advanced his career in Medina, the more his resentment against Jews grew. This evolution was rather natural since the Jews, not content with disappointing his expectations of seeing them rally unreservedly to his cause, riddled him with sarcasm, cast doubt on the authenticity of his prophetic mission, and lastly had the fault of possessing vast resources in chattels and land, which the prophet could not do without in order to secure his domination in Medina and the execution of vast projects of religious and political conquest.[349]

Muhammad's campaigns against the Jews of northern Arabia (i.e., Medina and Khaybar) may have had both near- and long-term ramifications: the launching of the Great Jihad,[350] which would subject the major Jewish communities of the Near East to Muslim conquest and colonization, and the imposition of Islamic law.

REGIONAL CASE STUDIES OF THE *DHIMMI* CONDITION FOR JEWS: HISTORICAL PALESTINE, MUSLIM SPAIN, OTTOMAN AND REPUBLICAN TURKEY, AND SHI'ITE IRAN

This detailed survey of the Jewish experience of *dhimmitude* was confined to the historical examples of Palestine, Muslim Spain, the Ottoman Empire and Turkish Republic, and Iran, for two primary reasons. First, these diverse geographical and sociopolitical settings illustrate shared realities intrinsic to the implementation of jihad-imposed *dhimmitude*, both "acutely" and as permanent institutions. Second, completely ahistorical conceptions of Muslim Spain and the Ottoman Empire, in particular, persist and continue to distort the overall paradigm of the *dhimmi* condition for Jews.

From Jihad to Dhimmitude:
Historical Palestine as "Prototype"

There is just one historically relevant meaning of jihad, despite an apologetic literature that dates back a century.[351] *Jahada*, the root of the word jihad, appears forty times in the Qur'an, under a variety of grammatical forms. With four exceptions (suras 6:109, 16:40, 24:53, and 35:42), all the other thirty-six usages are variations of the third form of the verb, *jahida*.[352] *Jahida* in the Qur'an and in subsequent Islamic understanding to both Muslim luminaries—from the greatest jurists and scholars of classical Islam (including Abu Yusuf, Averroës, Ibn Khaldun, and Al Ghazzali)[353]—and ordinary people meant and means "he fought, warred or waged war against unbe-

lievers and the like," as described by the seminal Arabic lexicographer E. W. Lane.[354] Thus Lane, who studied both the etymology and usage of the term, observed, "Jihad came to be used by *the Muslims* [emphasis added] to signify wag[ing] war, against unbelievers."[355]

The essential pattern of the jihad war is captured in the great Muslim historian al-Tabari's recording of the recommendation given by Umar b. al-Khattab to the commander of the troops he sent to al-Basrah (636 CE), during the conquest of Iraq. Umar (the second "Rightly Guided Caliph") reportedly said:

> Summon the people to God; those who respond to your call, accept it from them, (This is to say, accept their conversion as genuine and refrain from fighting them) but those who refuse must pay the poll tax out of humiliation and lowliness. (Qur'an 9:29) If they refuse this, it is the sword without leniency. Fear God with regard to what you have been entrusted.[356]

Jihad was pursued century after century, because jihad, which means "to strive in the path of Allah," embodied an ideology and a jurisdiction. Both were formally conceived by Muslim jurisconsults and theologians from the eighth to ninth centuries onward, based on their interpretation of Qur'anic verses (e.g., 2:214–15; 4:76–79; 8:39–42; 9:5–6; 9:29),[356a] and long chapters in the Traditions (especially those recorded by al-Bukhari [d. 869][357] and Muslim [d. 874]).[358] The consensus on the nature of jihad from all four schools of Sunni Islamic jurisprudence (i.e., Maliki, Hanbali, Hanafi, and Shafi'i) and seminal Shi'ite clerics is clear.[359] Ibn Khaldun (d. 1406), jurist (Maliki), renowned philosopher, historian, and sociologist—summarized these consensus opinions from five centuries of prior Muslim jurisprudence with regard to the uniquely Islamic institution of jihad:

> In the Muslim community, the holy war is a religious duty, because of the universalism of the [Muslim] mission and [the obligation to] convert everybody to Islam either by persuasion or by force. . . . The other religious groups did not have a universal mission, and the holy war was not a religious duty for them, save only for purposes of defense. . . . Islam is under obligation to gain power over other nations.[360]

Indeed, even the famous Sufi theologian al-Ghazali (see earlier discussion, and note 114) wrote the following about jihad:

> [O]ne must go on jihad (i.e., warlike razzias or raids) at least once a year . . . one may use a catapult against them [non-Muslims] when they are in a fortress, even if among them are women and children. One may set fire to them and/or drown them. . . . If a person of the

Ahl al-Kitab [People of the Book—Jews and Christians, typically] is enslaved, his marriage is [automatically] revoked. . . . One may cut down their trees. . . . One must destroy their useless books. Jihadists may take as booty whatever they decide . . . they may steal as much food as they need.[361]

Shi'ite jurisprudence was in agreement with the Sunni consensus on the basic nature of jihad war, as reflected in this excerpt from the Jami-i-Abbasi (the popular Persian manual of Shi'a law) written by al-Amili (d. 1622), a distinguished theologian under Shah Abbas I:

Islamic Holy war [jihad] against followers of other religions, such as Jews, is required unless they convert to Islam or pay the poll tax.[362]

Modern analyses by Armand Abel and Bassam Tibi highlight the characteristic features of the uniquely Islamic institution of jihad war, including its sacralized origins and timelessness, sanctioning of attacks against all those not under Islamic suzerainty, and incompatibility with the Western conception of "just war."

Armand Abel (1958):

For the Believer, the Koran presents the obligation to make war "in the way of God." At the time when this text was revealed, it was justified by the need to defend the community at Medina against the attacks of the "polytheists" of Mecca, and by the need to extend and enrich it at the expense of the Judeo-Christians, in particular the Jews of Khaybar. To all people, the book offered conversion as a means of making peace. To the People of the Book, it left the choice between conversion and "redemption," which at first was understood along the lines of the ancient manner in which the Arabs waged war, whereby the captive repurchased his freedom and his life at the cost of humiliation and a ransom. . . . The hadith that shows the Prophet writing "to" Negus, "to" Caesar," "to" Khosroès, in order to invite them to convert, is nothing but the seal of approval placed on this pretense, incorporating it into the totality of tradition that serves as a guide to the Umma. Together with the duty of the "war in the way of God" (or jihad), this universalistic aspiration would lead the Moslems to see the world as being divided fundamentally into two parts. On the one hand there was that part of the world where Islam prevailed, where salvation had been announced, where the religion that ought to reign was practiced; this was the Dar ul Islam. On the other hand, there was the part which still awaited the establishment of the saving religion and which constituted, by definition, the object of the holy war. This was the Dar ul Harb. The latter, in the view of the Moslem jurists, was not populated by people who had a natural right not to practice Islam, but rather by people destined to become Moslems who, through impiousness and rebellion, refused to accept this great benefit. Since they were destined sooner or later to be converted at the approach of the victorious armies of the Prophet's successor, or else killed for their rebelliousness, they were the rebel subjects of the Caliph. Their kings were nothing but odious tyrants who, by opposing the progress of the saving religion together with their armies, were following a Satanic inspiration and rising up against the designs of Providence. And so no respite should be granted them, no truce: perpetual war should be their lot, waged in the course of the winter and summer ghazu [razzias]. If the sovereign of the country thus attacked desired peace, it was possible for him, just like for any other tributary or community, to pay the tribute for himself and for his subjects. Thus the [Byzantine] Empress Irene [d. 803] "purchased peace at the price of her humiliation," according to the formula stated in the dhimma contract itself, by paying 70,000 pounds in gold annually to the Caliph of Baghdad. Many other princes agreed in this way to become tributaries—often after long struggles—and to see their dominions pass from the status of dar al Harb to that of dar al Sulh. In this way, those of their subjects who lived within the boundaries of the territory ruled by the Caliphate were spared the uncertainty of being exposed arbitrarily, without any guarantee, to the military operations of the summer ghazu and the winter ghazu: indeed, anything within the reach of the Moslem armies as they advanced, being property of impious men and rebels, was legitimately considered their booty; their men, seized by armed soldiers, were mercilessly consigned to the lot specified in the Koranic verse about the sword, and their women and children were treated like things.[363]

Bassam Tibi (1996):

The establishment of the new Islamic polity at Medina and the spread of the new religion were accomplished by waging war. The sword became the symbolic image of Islam in the West. In this formative period of classical Islam, Islamic militancy was reinforced by the superiority of Muslims over their enemies. Islamic jurists never dealt with relations with non-Muslims under conditions other than those of "the house of war," except for the temporary cessation of hostilities under a limited truce. . . . At its core, Islam is a religious mission to all humanity. Muslims are religiously obliged to disseminate the Islamic faith throughout the world. "We have sent you forth to all mankind" (Q. 34:28).

If non-Muslims submit to conversion or subjugation, this call (da'wa) can be pursued peacefully. If they do not, Muslims are obliged to wage war against them. In Islam, peace requires that non-Muslims submit to the call of Islam, either by converting or by accepting the status of a religious minority (dhimmi) and paying the imposed poll tax, jizya. World peace, the final stage of the da'wa, is reached only with the conversion or submission of all mankind to Islam. . . . Muslims believe that expansion through war is not aggression but a fulfillment of the Qur'anic command to spread Islam as a way to peace. The resort to force to disseminate Islam is not war (harb), a word that is used only to describe the use of force by non-Muslims. Islamic wars are not hurub (the plural of harb) but rather futuhat, acts of "opening" the world to Islam and expressing Islamic jihad. Relations between dar al-Islam, the home of peace, and dar al-harb, the world of unbelievers, nevertheless take place in a state of war, according to the Qur'an and to the authoritative commentaries of Islamic jurists. Unbelievers who stand in the way, creating obstacles for the da'wa, are blamed for this state of war, for the da'wa can be pursued peacefully if others submit to it. In other words, those who resist Islam cause wars and are responsible for them. Only when Muslim power is weak is "temporary truce" (hudna) allowed (Islamic jurists differ on the definition of "temporary"). The notion of temporary peace introduces a third realm: territories under temporary treaties with Muslim powers (dar al-sulh or at times, dar al-'ahd). . . . The Western distinction between just and unjust wars linked to specific grounds for war is unknown in Islam. Any war against unbelievers, whatever its immediate ground, is morally justified. Only in this sense can one distinguish just and unjust wars in Islamic tradition. When Muslims wage war for the dissemination of Islam, it is a just war (futuhat, literally "opening," in the sense of opening the world, through the use of force, to the call of Islam); when non-Muslims attack Muslims, it is an unjust war ('idwan). The usual Western interpretation of jihad as a "just war" in the Western sense, is therefore a misreading of this Islamic concept. . . . According to the Western just war concept, just wars are limited to a single issue; they are not universal and permanent wars grounded on a religious worldview.[364]

By the time of the classical Muslim historian al-Tabari's death in 923, jihad wars had expanded the Muslim empire from the Iberian Peninsula to the Indian subcontinent. Subsequent Muslim conquests continued in Asia, as well as on Christian eastern European lands. The Christian kingdoms of Armenia, Byzantium, Bulgaria, Serbia, Bosnia, Herzegovina, Croatia, and Albania, in addition to parts of Poland and Hungary, were also conquered and Islamized. Arab Muslim invaders additionally engaged in continuous jihad raids that ravaged and enslaved sub-Saharan African animist populations, extending to the southern Sudan. When the Muslim armies were stopped at the gates of Vienna in 1683, over a millennium of jihad had transpired.[365] These tremendous military successes spawned a triumphalist jihad literature. Muslim historians recorded in detail the number of infidels slain or enslaved, the cities and villages that were pillaged, and the lands, treasure, and movable goods seized. Christian (Coptic, Armenian, Jacobite, Greek, Slav, etc.) as well as Hebrew sources, and even the scant Hindu and Buddhist writings that survived the ravages of the Muslim conquests, independently validate this narrative, and complement the Muslim perspective by providing testimonies of the suffering of the non-Muslim victims of jihad wars.[366]

Jihad Conquests and Early Muslim Rule in Syro-Palestine

Moshe Gil, in his comprehensive *A History of Palestine, 634–1099*, emphasizes the singular centrality that Palestine occupied in the mind of its pre-Islamic Jewish inhabitants, who referred to the land as "al-Sham." Indeed, as Gil observes, the sizable Jewish population in Palestine (which formed a majority of its inhabitants when grouped with the Samaritans) at the dawn of the Arab Muslim conquest were "the direct descendants of the generations of Jews who had lived there since the days of Joshua bin Nun, in other words for some 2000 years."[367] He also explodes the ahistorical thesis of scholars who:

perceive an ethnic motivation behind the [jihad] conquests. They see Arabs everywhere: even the Canaanites and the Philistines were Arabs, according to their theories. This applies to an even greater degree to the population of Palestine and Syria in the seventh century, who were certainly Semites. Thus, according to their claims, the conquering Arab forces in the course of their battles, actually encountered their own people or at least members of their own race who spoke the same language. . . . This is of course a very distorted view: Semitism is not a race and only relates to a sphere of language. The populations met along the route of battle, living in cities or the country side, were not Arabs and did not speak Arabic. We do know of Bedouin tribes at that time who inhabited the borderlands and the southern desert of Palestine, west of the Euphrates (Hira) in the Syrian desert, Palmyra, and elsewhere. But the cultivated inner regions and the cities were inhabited by Jews and Christians who spoke Aramaic. They did not sense any special ties to the Bedouin; if anything it was the contrary. Their proximity and the danger of an invasion from that quarter disturbed their peace of mind and this is amply reflected both in the writings of the Church Fathers and in Talmudic sources.[368]

Gil concludes that views of the jihad conquest of Palestine expressed in the sources from the vanquished, indigenous non-Muslim populations

> reflect the attitude of the towns and villages in Palestine quite accurately; the attitude of a sedentary population, of farmers and craftsmen, toward nomads whose source of income is the camel and who frequently attack the towns, pillage and slaughter the inhabitants, and endanger the lives of the wayfarer. These sources completely contradict the argument . . . to the effect that the villagers and townsmen in Palestine accepted the invasion of those tribes bearing the banner of Islam with open arms of their so-called racial affinity.[369]

Bat Ye'or[370] summarizes the Arab Muslim conquest of Palestine as follows:

> Abu Bakr organized the invasion of Syria [Syro-Palestine] which Muhammad had already envisaged. He gathered tribes from the Hijaz, Najd, and Yemen and advised Abu Ubayda, in charge of operations in the Golan, to plunder the countryside, but due to a lack of adequate weaponry, to refrain from attacking towns. Consequently, the whole Gaza region up to Cesarea was sacked and devastated in the campaign of 634. Four thousand Jewish, Christian, and Samaritan peasants who defended their land were massacred. The villages of the Negev were pillaged by Amr b. al-As, while the Arabs overran the countryside, cut communications, and made roads perilous. Towns such as Jerusalem, Gaza, Jaffa, Cesarea, Nablus, and Beth Shean were isolated and closed their gates. In his sermon on Christmas day 634, the patriarch of Jerusalem, Sophronius, lamented over the impossibility of going on pilgrimage to Bethlehem, as was the custom because the Christians were being forcibly kept in Jerusalem: "not detained by tangible bonds, but chained and nailed by fear of the Saracens," whose "savage, barbarous and bloody sword" kept them locked up in the town. . . . Sophronius, in his sermon on the Day of the Epiphany 636, bewailed the destruction of the churches and monasteries, the sacked towns, the fields laid waste, the villages burned down by the nomads who were overrunning the country.
>
> *Why is there no end to the bloodshed? Why are churches being destroyed and the cross desecrated? The Saracens, "abomination of desolation" foretold by the Prophet (Daniel 12:11),*

> *are passing through lands forbidden to them, plundering cities and destroying fields, burning villages and razing holy monasteries . . . and priding themselves they will conquer the whole world.*[371]

> In a letter the same year to Sergius, the patriarch of Constantinople, he mentions the ravages wrought by the Arabs. Thousands of people perished in 639, victims of the famine and plague that resulted from these destructions.
>
> The countryside [in Syro-Palestine, Iraq, Persia, and Armenia] suffered constant razzias, while those who escaped the sword swelled the contingents of enslaved women and children, shared out among the soldiers after the deduction of the fifth [share of the "booty"] reserved for the caliph.

S. D. Goitein, in referring to Sophronius's descriptions as well as other contemporary sources, adds,

> [W]e learn incidentally that the villages and unwalled cities suffered more than the fortified cities from the sudden invasion by the sons of the desert. This is also evidenced by the ruins of the synagogues at Eshtamo'a in southern Judea.[371a]

Moreover, the Muslim chronicler al-Baladhuri (d. 892 CE) maintained that thirty thousand Samaritans and twenty thousand Jews lived in Caesarea alone just prior to the Arab Muslim conquest; afterward, all evidence of them disappears.[372]

The tenth-century Jacobite chronicler Michael the Syrian wrote that the ongoing Arab razzias and expeditions in Syro-Palestine (as well as in Iraq, Persia, and Armenia) were characterized by repeated and systematic pillage:

> The Taiyaye [Arabs] grew rich, increased and overran [the lands] which they took from the Romans [Byzantines] and which were given over to pillage.[373]

And following the surrender of the city of Damascus, he notes:

> Umar [b. al-Khattab] sent Khalid [b. Walid] with an army to the Aleppo and Antioch region. There, they murdered a large number of people. No one escaped them. Whatever may be said of the evils that Syria suffered, they cannot be recounted because of their great number; for the Yaiyaye [Arabs] were the great rod of God's wrath.[374]

Gil further elaborates on the initial wave of jihad conquests, and details the lasting destruction they wrought:

[A]t the time of the conquest, Palestine was inhabited by Jews and Christians . . . .The Arab tribes were to be found in the border areas, in keeping with arrangements made with the Byzantine rulers . . . one can assume that the local population suffered immensely during the course of the war [i.e., jihad conquests] and it is very likely that many villages were destroyed and uprooted in the frontier regions, and that the lot of these local populations was very bitter indeed. It appears that the period of the conquest was also that of the destruction of the synagogues and churches of the Byzantine era, remnants of which have been unearthed in our own time and are still being discovered. The assumption is based both on what is said in a few Christian sources . . . and on Muslim sources describing 'Umar's [Umar b. al-Khattab] visits to al-Sham. There is no doubt that one of the main purposes of these visits was to establish order and put an end to the devastation and slaughter of the local population. . . . Towns in the western strip and the central strip (the region of the red sand hills and the swamps) in the Sharon, decreased from fifty-eight to seventeen! It is estimated that the erosion of the soil from the western slopes of the Judaean mountains reached—as a result of the agricultural uprooting during the Muslim period—the gigantic extent of 2,000 to 4,000 cubic meters. . . . We find direct evidence of the destruction of agriculture and the desertion of the villages in the fact that the papyri of Nessana are completely discontinued after the year 700. One can assume that at the time the inhabitants abandoned the place, evidently because of the inter-tribal warfare among the Arabs which completely undermined the internal security of the area.[375]

An archaeological analysis by Naphtali Lewis emphasizes that the distress of the inhabitants was exacerbated after the year 700. Conditions became unbearable, due to the general political situation and worsening attitudes toward the *dhimmis*, rendering the Negev a wasteland:

It was precisely at this period in the Caliphate of Abd-al-Malik and his sons (685–743 C.E.) that the Arab state embarked on a new, nationalistic policy. The official records of Islam began to be kept in Arabic . . . and non-Arabs began to be eliminated from government service. With this Arabization of rule came increasing fiscal burdens for the Christians—burdens which they could now no longer escape by conversion to Islam. . . . [This] may well have rendered life impossible for the villagers of the Negev, who had already before . . . had occasion to complain of fiscal oppression. In the period of their prosperity . . . the production of the Negev villages was supplemented by financial assistance

from the Byzantine Emperors, in the form of stipends and emoluments paid the military settlers; in the first half-century of Arab rule, which terminated this positive support but otherwise changed conditions little, life could apparently still be sustained—and where life is even barely bearable people are generally reluctant to leave their homes; but when the government changed its policy and began to make conditions as a result become increasingly difficult, life in the southern desert became impossible and the Negev villages disappeared . . . growing Arab strength . . . drove out the Negev inhabitants; the weakness of central authority in the area would result from the growing depopulation and relapse into nomadism.[376]

Finally, Gil has translated these observations by the tenth-century Karaite commentator Yefet b. 'Ali expressing awareness of the fact that there was great destruction in Palestine and that there were places that remained uninhabited, while there were other places to which people returned and settled:

[T]he places which were completely destroyed so that no memory of them remains, like Samaria . . . and the second . . . are the places which have been destroyed and ruined, but despite this there are guards and people living there, such as Hebron and others.[377]

Gil also captures the stark, unromantic reality of Muslim-ruled Palestine during this era, which included the initial jihad conquest and establishment of Arab Muslim rule, from 634 to 661; Umayyad-Damascene rule, from 661 until 750; Abbasid-Baghdadian rule, from 750 through 878; Turco-Egyptian rule (Tulunids and Ikshidids) from 878 until 970—"interrupted" by Abbasid-Baghdadian rule again, between 905 and 930; nearly two generations of war including numerous participants, the dominant party being the Fatimids, from 970 through 1030; just over forty years of Fatimid-Egyptian rule, between 1030 and 1071; and a generation of (Seljuq) Turkish (or "Turcoman") rule encompassing most of Palestine, from 1071 until 1099.[378]

The Abbasids moved the capital city from Damascus (seat of the Umayyad Empire) to Baghdad, absorbed much of the Syrian and Persian culture as well as Persian methods of governance, and ushered in a putative "Golden Age." Gil and Bat Ye'or offer revealing assessments of this Golden Age *dhimmitude* and its adverse impact on the conquered, indigenous Jews and Christians of Palestine. Under early Abbasid rule (approximately 750–755 CE, perhaps during the reign of Abul Abbas Abdullah al-Saffah), Greek sources report orders demanding the removal of crosses over churches, bans on church services and teaching of the scriptures, the eviction of monks from their monasteries, and excessive taxation.[379] Gil notes that in 772 CE, when Caliph al-Mansur visited Jerusalem,

> he ordered a special mark should be stamped on the hands of the Christians and the Jews. Many Christians fled to Byzantium.[380]

Bat Ye'or elucidates the fiscal oppression inherent in eighth-century Palestine that devastated the *dhimmi* Jewish and Christian peasantry: "Over-taxed and tortured by the tax collectors, the villagers fled into hiding or emigrated into towns."[381] She quotes from a detailed chronicle of an eighth-century monk completed in 774: "The men scattered, they became wanderers everywhere; the fields were laid waste, the countryside pillaged; the people went from one land to another."[382] The Greek chronicler Theophanes (as summarized by Gil) provides a contemporary description of the chaotic events that transpired after the death of the caliph Harun al-Rashid in 809 CE and the ensuing fratricidal war that erupted between the brothers al-Amin and al-Ma'mun, rendering Palestine "the scene of violence, rape, and murder."[383]

Perhaps the clearest outward manifestations of the inferiority and humiliation of the *dhimmis* were the prohibitions regarding their dress "codes," and the demands that distinguishing signs be placed on the entrances of *dhimmi* houses. During the Abbasid caliphates of Harun al-Rashid (786–809) and al-Mutawwakil (847–861), Jews and Christians were required to wear yellow (as patches attached to their garments or hats).[384] Later, to differentiate further between Christians and Jews, the Christians were required to wear blue. In 850, consistent with Qur'anic verses associating them with Satan and hell,[385] al-Mutawwakil decreed that Jews and Christians attach wooden images of devils to the doors of their homes to distinguish them from the homes of Muslims. Bat Ye'or summarizes the oppression of the *dhimmis* throughout the Abbasid Empire under al-Mutawwakil as "a wave of religious persecution, forced conversions, and the elimination of churches and synagogues."[386]

Amitai ben Shephatia, a poet who lived in southern Italy, expressed the anguish felt by Jews over the continued control of their holy city, Jerusalem, by alien elements in a verse composed around the year 900:

> I mention God and groan
> As I see every city built on its mound
> And the city of God utterly downtrodden.[387]

Salomon b. Jeroham ("The Wise"), a major Karaite exegete who flourished in Jerusalem between 940 and 960,[388] and experienced Muslim rule directly, wrote the following in his commentary on Lamentations 1:3 regarding the sufferings of the Jews under Islam.[389]

As for Ishmael, there is no limit to their brutality and harshness. It is from them that [the Psalmist] asks to be rescued when he says [Ps. 120:5–7]: "This is worse than life in Meshech[390] or camping in Kedar.[391] Too long have I lived among people who hate peace, who, when I propose peace, are all for war." What can you say about a people who curse you when you greet them, and when you do not greet them humiliate you and offend you? When you talk to them, they want you to differ with them so that you be considered a sinner. I have learned that the Jews of Samarqand and the region when they say "God is one" [people who hear it], testify that by [saying] so they have become Muslims. Therefore, if they want to remain Jews they can only resort to saying "There are a thousand gods, or ten, or less or more." Then the Muslims say: "You are indeed infidels" and will let them hold their religion. The calamities inflicted upon the Jews (under Islam) are countless.

During the early eleventh-century period of al-Hakim's reign, religious assaults and hostility intensified. As Gil notes,

> [T]he destruction of the churches at the Holy Sepulchre [1009 CE] marked the beginning of a whole series of acts of oppression against the Christian population, which according to reliable sources, extended to coercion to convert to Islam.[392]

Yahya b. Sa'id's description of the events surrounding the destruction of the Churches of the Holy Sepulchre is summarized by Gil:

> They dismantled the Church of the Resurrection to its very foundations, apart from what could not be destroyed or pulled up, and they also destroyed the Golgotha and the Church of St Constantine and all that they contained, as well as the sacred grave stones. They even tried to dig up the graves and wipe out all traces of their existence. Indeed they broke and uprooted most of them. They also laid waste to a convent in the neighborhood. . . . The authorities took all the other property belonging to the Church of the Holy Sepulchre and its pious foundations and all its furnishings and treasures.[393]

Citing both Muslim (al-Quda'i, Ibn Khallikan, and Ibn Al-Athir) and non-Muslim (Bar Hebraeus) sources, Gil also describes the edicts al-Hakim imposed upon the Christians and Jews beginning in August 1011:

> They were ordered to wear black turbans. The Christians had to wear a cross the length of a cubit and weighing five ratls around their necks the Jews were obliged to wear a block of wood of similar

weight . . . they had to wear some distinguishing mark in the bath-houses, and finally al-Hakim decided that there were to be separate bath-houses for their use. . . . Ibn Al-Athir conveys . . . that al-Hakim ordered (after the destruction of the Church of the Resurrection in Jerusalem . . .) that all the churches in the realm be destroyed, and this was done, and that the Jews and Christians were then to accept Islam, or emigrate to Byzantine lands. They were also obliged to wear special distinguishing signs. Many converted. . . . Bar Hebraeus speaks of thousands of churches which were destroyed in the Fatimid kingdom at that time; the decree regarding the wearing of the cross around the neck was also, he says, a means of pressuring the Christians to convert. The wooden block the Jews were obliged to wear, had to be in the shape of a calf, as a reminder of the golden calf.[394]

According to Salo W. Baron, in order to escape al-Hakim's persecutions, many Jews fled the Fatimid kingdom and obtained refuge in the Byzantine Empire under Basil II (r. 976–1025).[394a]

In a separate, focused analysis of the conditions of the *dhimmis* of Jerusalem, Gil concludes that during the early through the mid-eleventh century, the Jews suffered both economically and physically:

> Economic conditions in Jerusalem were rather harsh, and the yeshiva often issued urgent appeals for aid. Besides, there were frequent acts of oppression on the part of the Muslim authorities. Very often special heavy taxes were imposed, which aggravated the already precarious situation of both the yeshiva and the Jewish population of Jerusalem. It must be remembered that taxation in Jerusalem was probably different from that found in other parts of the Muslim world. It seems that Jews there had to pay a comprehensive lump sum for the whole Jewish population of the city, regardless of its numbers. When the population decreased as a result of wars and Bedouin upheavals, the burden on each individual became heavier. In such situations the yeshiva was forced to borrow money, against heavy interest, from wealthy Muslims. When the time of repayment arrived, Jewish notables were in danger of being imprisoned, as the yeshiva was not in a position to accumulate the funds it had to return. In some cases people were actually incarcerated and it took a great deal of effort to collect the funds necessary for their release. An example is the letter written by Abraham, the son and main assistant of Solomon b. Yehuda, head of the yeshiva, to the sons of Mevasser, a family of parnasim of Fustat, asking them to keep their promise to send the aid in time to pay the *kharaj*.[395]

Muslim Turcoman rule of Palestine for the nearly three decades just prior to the Crusades (1071–1099) was characterized by such unrelenting warfare and devastation that an imminent "End of Days" atmosphere was engendered.[396] For example, Gil describes one of Atsiz b. Awaq's jihad campaigns in Syro-Palestine at around 1077 CE:

> Then Atsiz advanced on Jerusalem from Damascus, placed the city under siege, and promised its inhabitants the *aman*; on this basis, the inhabitants opened the gates of the city to him. Atsiz prevailed over Jerusalem, completely ignoring his promise of *aman*, and went on a rampage. He slaughtered 3,000 people there. . . . He also conducted campaigns of annihilation against Ramla, until all its people had fled, and against Gaza, where he murdered the entire population. He likewise massacred people in al-'Arish and elsewhere and wrought endless havoc in Damascus, where only 3,000 of the original 500,000 inhabitants had remained, due to starvation and scarcity. Jaffa, too, was attacked, and its governor . . . fled from the town to Tyre, together with all the city's inhabitants, while the walls of Jaffa were destroyed on Atsiz' orders.[397]

A contemporary Russian chronicle cited by Gil indicates that the Turcomans "destroyed and desolated the cities and the villages from Antioch to Jerusalem. They murdered, took captive, pillaged, set on fire; they destroyed churches and monasteries."[398]

Gil notes that these observations are confirmed by Geniza documents, describing how "the Turcoman occupation denoted terrible calamities, such as the taking captive of the people of Ramla, the cutting off of roads, the obduracy of the commanders, the aura of anxiety and panic, and so on."[399] He continues, "We do not know what Atsiz' attitude was to the Jewish population in 1078, during the cruel suppression of the uprisings and the destruction of towns, but the fact that from this date onwards, we barely find letters from Palestine (apart from Ascalon and Caesarea) in the Geniza documents, speaks for itself."[400]

A contemporary poem by Solomon ha-Kohen b. Joseph, believed to be a descendant of the Geonim, an illustrious family of Palestinian Jewish religious leaders, speaks of destruction and ruin, the burning of harvests, the razing of plantations, the desecration of cemeteries, and acts of violence, slaughter, and plunder:

> They were a strange and cruel people, girt with garments of many colors,/Armed and officered-chiefs among 'the terrible ones'—/And capped with helmets, black and red,/With bow and spear and full quivers;/And they trumpet like elephants, and roar as the roaring ocean,/To terrify, to frighten those who oppose them,/

And they are wicked men and sinners, madmen, not sane,/ And they laid waste the cities, and they were made desolate/And they rejoiced in their hearts, hoping to inherit./

He [God] also remembered what they had done to the people of Jerusalem,/ That they had besieged them twice in two years,/ And burned the heaped corn and destroyed the places,/ And cut down the trees and trampled upon the vineyards,/And surrounded the city upon the high mountains,/And despoiled the graves and threw out the bones,/And built palaces, to protect themselves against the heat,/And erected an altar to slay upon it the abominations;/And the men and the women ride upon the walls, Crying unto the God of gods, to quiet the great anger,/ Standing the whole night, banishing sleep,/While the enemy destroys, evening and morning,/And break down the whole earth, and lay bare the ground,/ And stand on the highways, intending to slay like Cain,/ And cut off the ears, and also the nose,/And rob the garments, leaving them stand naked,/ And also roar like lions, and roar like young lions;/ They do not resemble men, they are like beasts,/ And also harlots and adulterers, and they inflame themselves with males,/ They are bad and wicked and spiteful as Sodomites./ And they impoverished the sons of nobles, and starved the delicately bred./ And all the people of the city went out and cried in the field,/ And covered their lips, silent in their pains,/ And they had no mercy on widows, and pitied not the orphans.[401]

Gil concludes that as a result of the Turcoman jihad,

Palestine was drawn into a whirlpool of anarchy and insecurity, of internal wars among the Turks themselves and between them (generally in collaboration with the Arab tribes) and the Fatimids. Here and there, in one or another area, a delicate state of balance was arrived at for a few years. By and large, however, the Turcoman period, which lasted less than thirty years, was one of slaughter and vandalism, of economic hardship and the uprooting of populations. Terrible suffering, eviction and wandering, was the particular lot of the Jewish population, and chiefly its leadership, the Palestinian yeshiva.[402]

Gil offers this sobering overall assessment from his extensive, copiously documented analysis of the initial period of Muslim rule of Palestine, from 634 to 1099:

These facts do not call for much interpretation; together they simply form a picture of almost unceasing insecurity, of endless rebellions and wars, of upheavals and instability.[403]

Palestinian Jewry under the Mamluks and Ottomans

The brutal nature of the Crusaders' conquest of Palestine, particularly of the major cities, beginning in 1098–1099, has been copiously documented.[404] However, the devastation wrought by both Crusader conquest and rule (through the last decades of the thirteenth century) did not approach—let alone exceed—what transpired during the first four and a half centuries of Muslim jihad conquests, endless internecine struggles for Muslim dominance, and imposition of *dhimmitude*. As Emmanuel Sivan has observed, regarding Crusader dominion,

[P]ractical considerations appear to have outweighed religious fanaticism and, when it came to the peasantry, the "infidel children of the devil" in the villages were spared. It was clear to the Crusaders that they were themselves too few to dispense with the labor of local . . . farmers in cultivating the soil.[405]

Moreover, the testimony of Isaac b. Samuel of Acre (1270–1350), one of the most outstanding Kabbalists of his time, is illuminating. Conversant with Islamic theology and often using Arabic in his exegesis, Isaac nevertheless believed that it was preferable to live under the yoke of Christendom rather than that of Islamdom. Acre was taken from the Crusaders by the Mamluks in 1291 in a very brutal jihad conquest described by Runciman:

Soon the Moslem soldiers penetrated right through the city, slaying everyone, old men, women and children alike. A few lucky citizens who stayed in their houses were taken alive and sold as slaves, but not many were spared. No one could tell the number of those that perished. . . . Some prisoners were freed and returned to Europe after nine or ten years of captivity. . . . Many women and children disappeared for ever into the harems of Mameluk emirs. Owing to the plentiful supply the price of a girl dropped to a drachma a piece in the slave market at Damascus. But the number of Christians that were slain was greater still. . . . As soon as Acre was in his power, the Sultan (al-Ashraf Khalil) set about its systematic destruction. . . . The houses and bazaars were pillaged, then burned; the buildings (of the Orders) and the fortified towers and castles were dismantled; the city walls were left to disintegrate. When the German pilgrim, Ludolf of Suchem passed by some forty years later, only a few peasants lived amongst the ruins of the once splendid capital.[406]

Isaac was at Acre when that town was conquered (by Al-Malik al-Ashraf), and was thrown into prison with many of his co-religionists but he escaped the massacre. Accordingly, in 1305,[407] despite the precept to dwell in the Holy Land, Isaac b. Samuel fled to Italy and thence to Christian Spain, where he wrote:

> The word ziz in Arabic is derogatory, for when they wish to say in that tongue, "Strike him upon the head," "Give him a blow upon the neck," they say zazzhu ('hit him"). . . . Indeed, on account of our sins they strike upon the head the children of Israel who dwell in their lands and they thus extort money from them by force. For they say in their tongue, mal al-yahudi mubah, "it is lawful to take money of the Jews." For, in the eyes of the Muslims, the children of Israel are as open to abuse as an unprotected field. Even in their law and statutes they rule that the testimony of a Muslim is always to be believed against that of a Jew. For this reason our rabbis of blessed memory have said, "Rather beneath the yoke of Edom [Christendom] than that of Ishmael." They plead for mercy before the Holy One, Blessed be He, saying, "Master of the World, either let us live beneath Thy shadow or else beneath that of the children of Edom" (a Talmudic verse).[408]

Following the interlude of Crusader dominion over Palestine (1099–1291), Muslim rule was restored under the Mamluks. C. E. Bosworth characterizes the repercussions for the *dhimmi* Christian and Jewish communities in Egypt and Syro-Palestine due to efforts by the Mamluk Sultans (1250–1516) "to keep alight the spirit of jihad and the feelings of Muslim xenophobia," as follows:

> All through the Mamluk period, Muslim feeling was whipped up by popular preachers, by fatwas against the lawfulness of employing dhimmis in public offices, and by books and tracts from scholars of such eminence as Ibn Taymiyya. Persecutions and massacres mounted, with peaks of violence in such years as 700/1301, 721/1321 and 755/1354; discriminatory laws against dhimmis were revived; efforts were made to reduce the . . . proportion of Copts in official positions; and churches and monasteries were closed or destroyed. It was often only necessary for the state to give a lead and then let popular feeling do the rest. One might in this connection cite the destruction of the Zuhri church in old Cairo in 721/1321, which an-Nasir Nasir ad-Din Muhammad b. Qala'un did not pull down outright, but left high and dry by excavating around it, until a fanatical mob finished off the job by deliberately destroying the church. The tribunals of qadis, whose primary concern was with Muslim heterodoxy, not infrequently dealt in a draconian manner with the back-sliding Christian renegades and some Christians and Jews. From the later Sultanate of Muhammad b. Qala'un

(709–41/1309–40, his third and longest reign), [H. Laoust] dates the real ruin of Coptic Christianity as a force in the mainstream of Egyptian life. Conversions to Islam, always a steady trickle, now became a flood, and even in regions like Upper Egypt, which adjoined the Christian region of Nubia and had long been a Coptic stronghold, became majority Muslim. The Jews were less obvious targets for Muslim wrath, being numerically weaker and unsupported by powerful external nations of the same faith; nevertheless, Muslim historical sources and the Geniza documents . . . have amply shown that the lot of the Jews of Egypt at this time was hard indeed.[409]

Even the recent (1999) apologetic assessement of late fifteenth-century Mamluk Palestine by Donald P. Little, which finds such virtue in the prevailing Shari'a "legal norms and institutions," acknowledges the intensity of Muslim resentment over so-called *dhimmi* prerogatives among both the ulema and masses.[409a] Little also concedes,

> as the contests over holy places, as well as the attempt to enforce compulsory conversion of *dhimmi* orphans to Islam,[409b] prove, the entire Muslim establishment of jurists, scholars, and politicians at the highest level, both in Jerusalem and Cairo, could be quickly *mobilized* to assert Muslim and Mamluk interests.[409c]

Fifty years earlier (1949), Goitein published an analysis of the writings of Ibn 'Ubayya (a fifteenth-century Shafi'ite qadi), which inspired a fanatic Muslim mob (led by the elderly Abu Alazam) to "mobilize" and destroy Jerusalem's only existing synagogue in 1474.[409d]

Jewish access to the Machpelah (Makhpela) cave (near Hebron), believed to contain the tomb of the Patriarchs (over which the conquering Muslims built a mosque),[410] under the Mamluks, and later the Ottomans, reflects prevailing anti-*dhimmi*—and specifically anti-Jewish—attitudes during these combined periods of more than seven centuries of continuous Muslim rule. Prior to 1266 the conditions of such visits were described[411] by the twelfth-century chronicler Benjamin of Tudela.[412] In order to see the putative sepulchers of the Patriarchs contained within the cave, visitors were required to make a payment. Benjamin adds,

> If a Jew gives an additional fee to the keeper of the cave, an iron door which dates from the time of our forefathers opens, and the visitor descends with a lighted candle. He crosses two empty caves, and in the third sees six tombs, on which the names of the three Patriarchs and their wives are inscribed in Hebrew characters. The cave is filled with barrels containing bones of people, which are taken there as to a sacred place. At the end of the field of the

Machpelah stands Abraham's house with a spring in front of it.[413]

However, in 1266 the Mamluk Sultan Baybars, upon visting Hebron, prohibited Jews and Christians entrance to Machpelah.[414] This prohibition would remain in place for Jews through the end of the British Mandate period (1948); ordinary Christians, other than rare exceptions for dignitaries (such as the Prince of Wales in 1862), were also forbidden entry until 1922. Eliezer Bashan summarized the history of this discriminatory prohibition during a period of more than six hundred years, beginning with an anecdote from 1336.[415]

European travelers who visited Hebron before the Ottoman period and during the Ottoman period (1517–1917) and who tried to visit the cave were not allowed in, and they wrote the same applied to the Jews. They were permitted to pray only outside the walls. John Mandeville, for example, who was born in England and pilgrimaged to the Holy Land in 1336, arrived at Hebron and wrote the following: "They suffer no Christian man to enter that place but if it be of special grace of the sultan, for they hold Christian men and Jews as dogs, and they say that they should not enter into so holy a place."

An English gentleman who visited there in 1753 and again ten years later reported Jews were not even allowed to walk in the street leading to the cave. The danger that faces a Christian who approaches the place is described in the following report (published in 1845): "The Moslems guard this tomb with the greatest jealousy, and woe to that Christian who sets foot within its portal."

The vice-consul of France in Basra, who tried to visit there in 1834, requested the Muazzin[416] to let him in, but he was told that he would first be required to embrace Islam. A missionary (H. Bonar) who visited Hebron in 1856 and was prohibited from entering expressed his opinion in the following passage, stressing the different manner and behavior of Jews and Christians: "Muslim fanaticism has shut this cave against the world; nowhere is this fanaticism wilder . . . than in El-Khulil (Hebron). The Jewish Temple had its great court open to all; Christian cathedrals and churches invite all to enter; only Mahomedanism with peculiar exclusiveness closes every gate of its mosque against the stranger."

S. Ehrlich, a Jewish trader from Russia, who wanted to visit this holy place, disguised himself as a Muslim imam, and succeeded in entering the cave in 1833.

The first Christian who was permitted to enter the cave was the Prince of Wales in 1862. He was privileged not only because of his royal personality but because of the political situation after the Crimean War of 1856. Great Britain and the Ottomans enjoyed special relations owing to the resistance of the latter to the expansion of Russia. . . . The Ottoman authorities tried to accustom the Muslim population to a more tolerant attitude to Europeans and Christians, but the fanatic local population and its leaders did not accept the tolerant attitude and continued to impose limitations on regular Christians. Just after the visit of the Prince, a plague began in Hebron, which the Muslims considered a punishment from God because of the desecration of the holy place, and the population was on the verge of a rebellion. Under the British Mandate (1922–1948) Christians were given free access to the building, but not Jews.

Although episodes of violent anarchy diminished during the four centuries of Ottoman suzerainty, the degrading conditions of the indigenous Jews and Christians living under the Shari'a's jurisdiction remained unchanged. For example, Samuel b. Ishaq Uceda, a major Kabbalist from Safed at the end of the sixteenth century, refers in his commentary on *The Lamentations of Jeremiah* to the situation of the Jews in the Land of Israel (Palestine):

"The princess among the provinces, how is she become tributary!" . . . Perhaps this is an allusion to the situation that prevails in our times, for there is no town in the [Ottoman] empire in which the Jews are subjected to such heavy taxes and dues as in the Land of Israel, and particularly in Jerusalem. Were it not for the funds sent by the communities in Exile, no Jew could survive here on account of the numerous taxes, as the prophet said in connection with the "princess of the provinces": "They hunt our steps, that we cannot go into our own streets." . . . The nations humiliate us to such an extent that we are not allowed to walk in the streets. The Jew is obliged to step aside in order to let the Gentile [Muslim] pass first. And if the Jew does not turn aside of his own will, he is forced to do so. This law is particularly enforced in Jerusalem, more so than in other localities. For this reason the text specifies " . . . in our own streets," that is, those of Jerusalem.[417]

A century later Canon Antoine Morison from Bar-le-Duc in France, while traveling in the Levant in 1698, observed that the Jews in Jerusalem are "there in misery and under the most cruel and shameful slavery," and although a large community, they were subjected to extortion.[418] Similar contemporary observations regarding the plight of both Palestinian Jews and Christians were made by the Polish Jew Gedaliah of Siemiatyce (d. 1716), who, braving numerous perils, came to Jerusalem in 1700. These appalling conditions, recorded in his book, *Pray for the Peace of Jerusalem*, forced him to return to Europe in order to raise funds for the Jews of Jerusalem:

> We [Jews] were obliged to give a large sum of money to the Muslim authorities in Jerusalem in order to be allowed to build a new synagogue. Although the old synagogue was small and we only wanted to enlarge it very slightly, it was forbidden under Islamic law to modify the least part. . . . In addition to the expenses in bribes destined to win the favor of the Muslims, each male was obliged to pay an annual poll tax of two pieces of gold to the sultan. The rich man was not obliged to give more, but the poor man could not give less. Every year, generally during the festival of the Passover, an official from Constantinople would arrive in Jerusalem. He who did not have the means to pay the tax was thrown into prison and the Jewish community was obliged to redeem him. The official remained in Jerusalem for about two months and consequently, during that period, the poor people would hide wherever they could, but if ever they were caught, they would be redeemed by community funds. The official sent his soldiers throughout the streets to control the papers of the passers-by, for a certificate was provided to those who had already paid the tax. If anyone was found without his certificate, he had to present himself before the official with the required sum, otherwise he was imprisoned until such time as he could be redeemed.
>
> The Christians are also obliged to pay the poll-tax . . . during the week, the paupers dared not show themselves outside . . . in their wickedness, the [Muslim] soldiers would go to the synagogues, waiting by the doors, requesting the certificate of payment from the congregants who emerged. . . .
>
> No Jew or Christian is allowed to ride a horse, but a donkey is permitted, for [in the eyes of Muslims] Christians and Jews are inferior beings. . . . The Muslims do not allow any member of another faith—unless he converts to their religion—entry to the Temple [Mount] area, for they claim that no other religion is sufficiently pure to enter this holy spot. They never weary of claiming that, although God had originally chosen the people of Israel, He had since abandoned them on account of their iniquity in order to choose the Muslims. . . .
>
> In the Land of Israel, no member of any other religion besides Islam may wear the color green, even if it is a thread [of cotton] like that with which we decorate our prayer shawls. If a Muslim perceives it, that could bring trouble. Similarly, it is not permitted to wear a green or white turban. On the Sabbath, however, we wear white turbans, on the crown of which we place a piece of cloth of another color as a distinguishing mark. The Christians are not allowed to wear a turban, but they wear a hat instead, as is customary in Poland. Moreover, the Muslim law requires that each religious denomination wear its specific garment so that each people may be distinguished from another. This distinction also applies to footwear. Indeed, the Jews wear shoes of a dark blue color, whereas Christians wear red shoes. No one can use green, for this color is worn solely by Muslims. The latter are very hostile toward Jews and inflict upon them vexations in the streets of the city . . . the common folk persecute the Jews, for we are forbidden to defend ourselves against the Turks or the Arabs. If an Arab strikes a Jew, he [the Jew] must appease him but dare not rebuke him, for fear that he may be struck even harder, which they [the Arabs] do without the slightest scruple. This is the way the Oriental Jews react, for they are accustomed to this treatment, whereas the European Jews, who are not yet accustomed to suffer being assaulted by the Arabs, insult them in return.
>
> Even the Christians are subjected to these vexations. If a Jew offends a Muslim, the latter strikes him a brutal blow with his shoe in order to demean him, without anyone's being able to prevent him from doing it. The Christians fall victim to the same treatment and they suffer as much as the Jews, except that the former are very rich by reason of the subsidies that they receive from abroad, and they use this money to bribe the Arabs. As for the Jews, they do not possess much money with which to oil the palms of the Muslims, and consequently they are subject to much greater suffering.[419]

Moshe Maoz maintains that this state of affairs persisted for Jews (and Christians) living under Ottoman rule within (Syro-)Palestine, through at least the 1830s:

> [T]he position of the Jews was in many ways precarious. Like their Christian fellow subjects, the Jews were inferior citizens in the Muslim-Ottoman state which was based on the principle of Muslim superiority. They were regarded as state protégés (dhimmis) and had to pay a special poll tax (jizya) for that protection and as a sign of their inferior status. Their testimony was not accepted in the courts of justice, and in cases of the murder of a Jew or Christian by a Muslim, the latter was usually not condemned to death. In addition, Jews as well as Christians were normally not acceptable for appointments to the highest administrative posts; they were forbidden to carry arms (thus, to serve in the army), to ride horses in towns or to wear Muslim dress. They were also not usually allowed to build or repair places of worship and were often subjected to oppression, extortion and violence by both the local authorities and the Muslim popula-

tion. The Jews in Ottoman Palestine and Syria lived under such ambivalent and precarious conditions for a number of centuries.[420]

Maoz describes the fate of the Jew Hayim Farhi, who became treasury manager and administrative advisor to Ahmad Pasha al Jezzar, vali (governor) of the Pashalik (territory) of Sidon (1775–1804). Subsequently, during the reign of al-Jezzar's successor, Sulyaman Pasha (1804–1818), Farhi was appointed supervisor of income and expenditure, coordinator of the province's accounts with the central treasury, and overall director of administrative functions, accruing considerable power and influence. As Maoz, explains, however,

> Farhi's prominent position in Acre was, however, unique at that time, due to the mild character of Sulayman Pasha "the Just" (al-Adil) who, in addition, owed Hayim his ascendancy to the pashalik. For during the previous reign of Jezzar Pasha, Farhi was no more than an ordinary senior official, and upon falling into disfavor—he was even discharged and arrested, one of his eyes was gouged out and his nose and ears cut.
>
> That the position of Hayim Farhi was very precarious was even more evident under Sulyaman's successor, 'Abdallah Pasha (1819–1831). At the beginning of his rule, Farhi's influence was at its peak and the Pasha was allegedly "unable to do anything without Hayim's consent." But a short time later, in 1820, Farhi was executed and his property confiscated upon 'Abdallah's orders. It is evident that such a case was by no means uncommon as regards Jews or Christians during the period of the Pashas' rule. J. L. Burkhardt, the perceptive Swiss traveler, noted in 1811: " . . . there is scarcely an instance in the modern history of Syria of a Christian or Jew having long enjoyed the power or riches he may have acquired. These persons are always taken off in the last moment of their apparent glory."[421]

The case of the notable Hayim Farhi (and his family) illustrates the tenuous status of the Jewish community in Syro-Palestine:

> The unstable position of the Farhis in Acre and Damascus (in Damascus too the Farhis were occasionally subject to arbitrary treatment) may serve as an illustration of the shaky position of the Jewish communities in Ottoman Palestine and Syria for many years. In certain circumstances—under tolerant rulers such as Sulayman Pasha, and in certain places—such as Aleppo, Jews enjoyed a certain degree of personal safety and religious freedom, and a few of them also acquired economic prosperity as well as social status. These circumstances, however, were rare or limited. Sulayman al-Adil

("The Wise") was unique; more typical rulers were Ahmad al-Jezzar (the Butcher) and 'Abdallah Pasha. They conducted a tyrannical and oppressive regime which affected large sections of the local population, particularly the Jews and Christians.[422]

Maoz makes these additional observations about Aleppo, which was a thoroughfare for international commerce and center of European activities (including consular and business communities), versus outlying areas, comparing the conditions for Jews under consular protection relative to the local population under Ottoman rule:

> A number of Jewish families, mostly foreign proteges who belonged to those communities, were indeed relatively secure and prosperous. But many other local Jews, ordinary Ottoman subjects, were occasionally subject to violence and oppression from various quarters. If that was the case in tolerant Aleppo, in other towns which were imbued with religious intolerance and were distant from Istanbul, the Jewish population was perhaps the most oppressed element.
>
> One of the major sources of their oppression was the local governors, public officials, soldiers and policemen, who maltreated Jews and extorted money from them in various ways. It is true that Muslim townsmen were occasionally oppressed and squeezed by tyrannical rulers and greedy soldiers. But many Muslims were nevertheless able to protect themselves against their oppressors with the help of the influential religious notables, or by placing themselves under the protection of local powerful leaders and military groups. It was also not very infrequent that Muslim masses would revolt against oppressive rulers and expel them from the town, or even kill them. The Jewish population obviously did not dare and was unable to oppose its oppressors; and in places where they managed to acquire protection of influential local notables they had to pay high sums for that protection. Otherwise—and this was another source of their misery—Jews were squeezed by local Muslim notables and molested by Muslim mobs. To quote a Jewish source: "When a Jew walked among them [the Muslims] in the market, one would throw a stone at him in order to kill him, another would pull his beard and a third his ear lock, yet another spit on his face and he became a symbol of abuse."[423]

There were clear improvements in prevailing conditions for Christian dhimmis when Ibrahim Pasha occupied and ruled the Syro-Palestinian provinces from 1830–1841. The Jews, in contrast, experienced much less amelioration of their oppressed status, according to Maoz.[424]

Their position was, no doubt, improved in some respects, in comparison with the past. They were occasionally permitted to repair old synagogues or to erect new ones; Jews were also represented in the new local *majlises* (legislative assemblies) and were officially given equal status before the new civil courts. Muslim notables were strictly ordered not to levy illegal dues and taxes on Jews, while a number of Muslim civilians, as well as some Egyptian soldiers, were severely punished for having maltreated Jews.

It should, however, be noted here that the measures taken to protect the Jews were only partly a result of the government's initiative and good will; they were mainly the consequence of the intervention and pressure from the European consuls. As Jews themselves stated: "Had it not been the consuls' supervision, we would have been destroyed and lost, since the Gentiles wish but to eat the Jews and to accuse them falsely."

Nevertheless neither the consuls nor the authorities were able to prevent all the acts of aggression which were directed against Jews, particularly in small towns . . . in fact, there occurred during the short period of Egyptian rule some of the gravest anti-Jewish outbreaks in the recent history of Palestine and Syria. In Hebron, for example, Jews were massacred [including the rape-murder of five young girls][425] in 1834 by Egyptian soldiers who came to put down a local Muslim rebellion. About the same time Jewish houses and shops in Jerusalem were broken into and looted by local Muslim insurgents, who dominated the town for a long time. Similarly, the Jews of Safed were brutally attacked by Muslim and Druze peasants from the vicinity in 1834 and again in 1837 (after the Safed earthquake).

As Mr. Young, the English Consul in Jerusalem, noted in 1839: "The spirit of toleration towards the Jews is not yet known here to the same extent it is in Europe . . . still a Jew in Jerusalem is not estimated much above a dog."

The Safed pogrom alluded to by Maoz lasted thirty-three days in June/July 1834, and was particularly devastating—many Jews were killed, hundreds wounded, and the town nearly destroyed. Malachi has provided these details based upon eyewitness sources and accounts:

The Arabs slaughtered the Jews who could not flee Safed. Many who hid in caves and graveyards were found out by the vandals and killed in their hiding places. . . . They did not show compassion towards the elderly or the young, children or pregnant women. They burned Torah scrolls and tore holy books, ripped prayer shawls and phylacteries (*tefillin*). . . . The rioters tortured women and chil-

dren in the synagogues and "defiled gentle women on parchment scrolls of the Torah" in front of their husbands and their children. Those who tried to protect their wives and courageously defend their honor were murdered by the bandits.[426]

The prevailing conditions for Jews did not improve in a consistent or substantive manner even after the mid-nineteenth-century treaties imposed by the European powers on the weakened Ottoman Empire included provisions for the Tanzimat reforms. These reforms were designed to end the discriminatory laws of *dhimmitude* for both Jews and Christians, living under the Ottoman Shari'a. European consuls endeavored to maintain compliance with at least two cardinal principles central to any meaningful implementation of these reforms: respect for the life and property of non-Muslims, and the right of Christians and Jews to provide evidence in Islamic courts when a Muslim was a party. Unfortunately, these efforts to replace the concept of Muslim superiority over "infidels," with the principle of equal rights, failed.[426a]

Although Maoz contends the Tanzimat period was accompanied by "markedly better" conditions for Jews, at least "in comparison with the past," he concedes,

It should not be denied that Jews as well as Christians in Palestine and Syria were in that period still far from being equal members in the local political community. Despite the Tanzimat edicts, which promised equality between non-Muslims and Muslims, the dhimmis continued to be actually inferior before the law of the state and its institutions. They had still to pay the poll-tax (jizya)—or from 1855 the bedel (compulsory exemption tax from military service). Their testimony against Muslims was completely discounted in the *mahkama* (Muslim court), and in the various new Ottoman secular courts such testimony was occasionally rejected. Jews and Christians would similarly be discriminated against in cases brought before the *majlises*; even their deputies in these councils were usually disregarded and occasionally maltreated by their Muslim colleagues.[427]

Eyewitness accounts from the time of the first iteration of the reforms (in 1839), almost a decade later (1847), and again two years after the second series of reforms in 1856 (issued at the conclusion of the Crimean War) paint a rather gloomy picture of continued anti-Jewish discrimination in Syro-Palestine. For example, the Scottish clerics A. A. Bonar and R. M. McCheyne, who visited Palestine in 1839 to inquire into the condition of the Jews there, published these observations in their *A Narrative of a Mission of Inquiry to the Jews from the Church of Scotland in 1839*:

There is none of the sacred places over which the Moslem's keep so jealous a watch as the tomb of Abraham . . . travellers in general being forbidden to approach even the door of the Mosque [built by the conquering Muslims over the tomb of Abraham]. . . . The Jews at present are permitted only to look through a hole near the entrance, and to pray with their face toward the grave of Abraham . . . the synagogues of Jerusalem . . . are six in number, all of them small and poorly furnished, and four of them under one roof. . . . The reading desk is little else than an elevated part of the floor, enclosed with a wooden railing. . . . We were much impressed with the melancholy aspect of the Jews in Jerusalem. The meanness of their dress, their pale faces, and timid expression, all seem to betoken great wretchedness. . . . We found all the Jews here [in Safed] living in a state of great alarm . . . the Bedouins were every day threatening an attack to plunder the town. . . . We observed how poorly clad most of the Jews seemed to be, and were told that they had buried under ground all their valuable clothes, their money, and other precious things. It was easy to read their deep anxiety in the very expression of their countenances. . . . And all this in their own land![428]

The Jewish travelouge writer J. J. Binyamin II recorded the following account after his 1847 sojourn in Palestine:

Deep misery and continual oppression are the right words to describe the condition of the Children of Israel in the land of their fathers. . . . They are entirely destitute of every legal protection and every means of safety. Instead of security afforded by law, which is unknown in these countries, they are completely under the orders of the Sheiks and Pashas, men, whose character and feelings inspire but little confidence from the beginning. It is only the European Consuls who frequently take care of the oppressed, and afford them some protection. . . . With unheard of rapacity tax upon tax is levied on them, and with the exception of Jerusalem, the taxes demanded are arbitrary. Whole communities have been impoverished by the exorbitant claims of the Sheiks, who, under the most trifling pretences and without being subject to any control, oppress the Jews with fresh burdens. . . . In the strict sense of the word the Jews are not even masters of their own property. They do not even venture to complain when they are robbed and plundered. . . . Their lives are taken into as little consideration as their property; they are exposed to the caprice of any one; even the smallest pretext, even a harmless discussion, a word dropped in conversation, is enough to cause bloody reprisals. Violence of every kind is of daily occurrence. When, for instance in

the contests of Mahomet Ali with the Sublime Porte, the City of Hebron was besieged by Egyptian troops and taken by storm, the Jews were murdered and plundered, and the survivors scarcely even allowed to retain a few rags to cover themselves. No pen can describe the despair of these unfortunates. The women were treated with brutal cruelty; and even to this day, many are found, who since that time are miserable cripples. With truth can the Lamentations of Jeremiah be employed here. Since that great misfortune up to the present day, the Jews of Hebron languish in the deepest misery, and the present Sheik is unwearied in his endeavors, not to allow their condition to be ameliorated, but on the contrary, he makes it worse. . . . The chief evidence of their miserable condition is the universal poverty which we remarked in Palestine, and which is here truly astounding; for nowhere else in our long journeys, in Europe, Asia and Africa did we observe it among the Jews. It even causes leprosy among the Jews of Palestine, as in former times. Robbed of their means of subsistence from the cultivation of the soil and the pursuit of trade, they exist upon the charity of their brethren in the faith in foreign parts. . . . In a word the state of the Jews in Palestine, physically and mentally, is an unbearable one.[429]

British Jerusalem consul James Finn reported in July and November 1858 that both physical insecurity for Jews in Palestine and their inequality before the law persisted despite the second iteration of Ottoman reforms in 1856:

[July 8, 1858] . . . in consequence of a series of disgusting insults offered to Jews and Jewesses in Hebron, I obtained such orders as I could from the Pasha's agent in this city. . . . Finding these not answered entirely as might be desired, I repaired to the neighborhood of Hebron myself—and found the whole government of that important and turbulent district being administered by a very old Bashi Bozuk officer as the town governor; and a military Boluk Bashi with five starved and ragged Bashi Bozuk men as soldiers—The rural district is left entirely to peasant Sheikhs, with one responsible over the rest. The streets of the town were paraded by fanatic Dervishes—and during my stay there a Jewish house was forcibly entered by night, iron bars of the window broken, and heavy stones thrown by invisible hands at every person approaching the place to afford help. One of the Members of the Council affirmed that they were not obliged to obey orders from the Pasha's deputy—and another declared his right derived from time immemorial in his family, to enter Jewish houses, and take toll or contributions any time without giving account. When others present in the Council exclaimed against this he said—"Well then I will forbear from taking it myself, but things will happen which will compel the Jews to come and kiss my feet to induce me to take their money." On hearing of my arrival in the vicinity he went away to the villages, refusing to obey the summons to Jerusalem, and I believe the Pasha cannot really compel him to come here—he being a privileged member of the Council, and recognized in Constantinople.

[November 11, 1858] And my Hebrew Dragoman [translator] having a case for judgment in the Makhameh [Muslim court] before the new Kadi [judge], although accompanied by my Kawass [constable], and announcing his office, was commanded to stand up humbly and take off his shoes before his case could be heard. He did not however comply—But during the process although the thief had previously confessed to the robbery in presence of Jews, the Kadi would not proceed without the testimony of two Moslems—when the Jewish witnesses were offered, he refused to accept their testimony—and the offensive term adopted towards Jews in former times (more offensive than Giaour for Christians) was used by the Kadi's servants . . . such circumstances exhibit the working of the present Turkish government in Jerusalem.[430]

Tudor Parfitt's comprehensive 1987 study of the Jews of Palestine during the nineteenth century concluded with these summary observations covering the entire period of his analysis, through 1882:

Inside the towns, Jews and other dhimmis were frequently attacked, wounded, and even killed by local Muslims and Turkish soldiers. Such attacks were frequently for trivial reasons: Wilson [in British Foreign Office correspondence] recalled having met a Jew who had been badly wounded by a Turkish soldier for not having instantly dismounted when ordered to give up his donkey to a soldier of the Sultan. Many Jews were killed for less. On occasion the authorities attempted to get some form of redress but this was by no means always the case: the Turkish authorities themselves were sometimes responsible for beating Jews to death for some unproven charge. After one such occasion [British Consul] Young remarked: "I must say I am sorry and surprised that the Governor could have acted so savage a part—for certainly what I have seen of him I should have thought him superior to such wanton inhumanity—but it was a Jew without friends or protection—it serves to show well that it is not without reason that the poor Jew, even in the nineteenth century, lives from day to day in terror of his life."

In fact, it took some time [i.e., at least a decade after the 1839 reforms] before these courts did accept dhimmi testimony in Palestine. The fact that

Jews were represented on the meclis [provincial legal council] did not contribute a great deal to the amelioration of the legal position of the Jews: the Jewish representatives were tolerated grudgingly and were humiliated and intimidated to the point that they were afraid to offer any opposition to the Muslim representatives. In addition the constitution of the meclis was in no sense fairly representative of the population. In Jerusalem in the 1870s the meclis consisted of four Muslims, three Christians and only one Jew—at a time when Jews constituted over half the population of the city. . . . Perhaps even more to the point, the courts were biased against the Jews and even when a case was heard in a properly assembled court where dhimmi testimony was admissible the court would still almost invariably rule against the Jews. It should be noted that a non-dhimmi [e.g., foreign] Jew was still not permitted to appear and witness in either the mahkama [specific Muslim council] or the meclis.[431]

World War I

During World War I in Palestine, between 1915 and 1917, the *New York Times* published a series of reports on Ottoman-inspired and local Arab Muslim–assisted antisemitic persecution that affected Jerusalem and the other major Jewish population centers.[432] For example, by the end of January 1915, seven thousand Palestinian Jewish refugees—men, women, and children—had fled to British-controlled Alexandria, Egypt. Three *New York Times* accounts from January and February 1915 provide these details of the earlier period.

On Jan. 8, Djemal Pasha[433] ordered the destruction of all Jewish colonization documents within a fortnight under penalty of death. . . . In many cases land settled by Jews was handed over to Arabs, and wheat collected by the relief committee in Galilee was confiscated in order to feed the army. The Moslem peasantry are being armed with any weapons discovered in Jewish hands. . . . The United States cruiser Tennessee has been fitted up on the lines of a troop ship for the accommodation of about 1,500 refugees, and is plying regularly between Alexandria and Jaffa. . . . A proclamation issued by the commander of the Fourth [Turkish] Army Corps describes Zionism as a revolutionary anti-Tukish movement which must be stamped out. Accordingly the local governing committees have been dissolved and the sternest measures have been taken to insure that all Jews who remain on their holdings shall be Ottoman subjects. . . . Nearly all the [7,000] Jewish refugees in Alexandria come from Jerusalem and other large towns, among them being over 1,000 young men of the artisan class who refused to become Ottomans.[433a]

By April of 1917, conditions deteriorated further for Palestinian Jewry, which faced threats of annihilation from the Ottoman government. Many Jews were in fact deported, expropriated, and starved, in an ominous parallel to the genocidal deportations of the Armenian *dhimmi* communities throughout Anatolia.[434] Indeed, as related by Yair Auron,

> Fear of the Turkish actions was bound up with alarm that the Turks might do to the Jewish community in Palestine, or at least to the Zionist elements within it, what they had done to the Armenians. This concern was expressed in additional evidence from the early days of the war, from which we can conclude that the Armenian tragedy was known in the Yishuv [Jewish community in Palestine].[435]

A mass expulsion of the Jews of Jerusalem, although ordered twice by Djemal Pasha, was averted only through the efforts of the Ottoman Turks' World War I allies, the German government, which sought to avoid international condemnation.[436] The eight thousand Jews of Jaffa, however, were expelled quite brutally, a cruel fate the Arab Muslims and the Christians of the city did not share. Moreover, these deportations took place months before the small pro-British Nili spy ring of Zionist Jews was discovered by the Turks in October 1917, and its leading figures killed.[437] A report by United States consul Garrels (in Alexandria, Egypt) describing the Jaffa deportation of early April 1917 (published in the June 3, 1917, *New York Times*), included these details of the Jews' plight:

> The orders of evacuation were aimed chiefly at the Jewish population. Even German, Austro-Hungarian, and Bulgarian Jews were ordered to leave the town. Mohammedans and Christians were allowed to remain provided they were holders of individual permits. The Jews who sought the permits were refused. On April 1 the Jews were ordered to leave the country within 48 hours. Those who rode from Jaffa to Petach Tikvah had to pay from 100 to 200 francs instead of the normal fare of 15 to 25 francs. The Turkish drivers practically refused to receive anything but gold, the Turkish paper note being taken as the equivalent of 17.50 piastres for a note of 100 piastres.
>
> Already about a week earlier 300 Jews had been deported in a most cruel manner from Jerusalem. Djemal Pasha openly declared that the joy of the Jews on the approach of the British forces would be short-lived, as he would make them share the fate of the Armenians.
>
> In Jaffa Djemal Pasha cynically assured the Jews that it was for their own good and interests that he drove them out. Those who had not succeeded in leaving on April 1 were graciously accorded permission to remain at Jaffa over the Easter holiday.

> Thus 8000 were evicted from their houses and not allowed to carry off their belongings or provisions. Their houses were looted and pillaged even before the owners had left. A swarm of pillaging Bedouin women, Arabs with donkeys, camels, etc., came like birds of prey and proceeded to carry off valuables and furniture.
>
> The Jewish suburbs have been totally sacked under the paternal eye of the authorities. By way of example two Jews from Yemen were hanged at the entrance of the Jewish suburb of Tel Aviv in order to clearly indicate the fate in store for any Jew who might be so foolish as to oppose the looters. The roads to the Jewish colonies north of Jaffa are lined with thousands of starving Jewish refugees. The most appalling scenes of cruelty and robbery are reported by absolutely reliable eyewitnesses. Dozens of cases are reported of wealthy Jews who were found dead in the sandhills around Tel Aviv. In order to drive off the bands of robbers preying on the refugees on the roads the young men of the Jewish villages organized a body of guards to watch in turn the roads. These guards have been arrested and maltreated by the authorities.
>
> The Mohammedan populations have also left the town recently, but they are allowed to live in the orchards and country houses surrounding Jaffa and are permitted to enter the town daily to look after their property, but not a single Jew has been allowed to return to Jaffa.
>
> The same fate awaits all Jews in Palestine. Djemal Pasha is too cunning to order cold-blooded massacres. His method is to drive the population to starvation and to death by thirst, epidemics, etc., which according to himself, are merely calamities sent by God.[438]

Auron cites a very tenable hypothesis put forth at that time in a journal of the British Zionist movement as to why the looming slaughter of the Jews of Palestine did not occur—the advance of the British army (from immediately adjacent Egypt) and its potential willingness "to hold the military and Turkish authorities directly responsible for a policy of slaughter and destruction of the Jews"—may have averted this disaster.[438a]

From the British Mandate to the Present Era

Ultimately, enforced abrogation of the laws and social practices of *dhimmitude* required the dismantling of the Ottoman Empire, which occurred only during the European Mandate period following World War I. Remarkably, soon afterward (i.e., within two years of the abrogation of the Shari'a!), by 1920, Musa Kazem el-Husseini, former governor of Jaffa during the final years of the Ottoman rule and president of the Arab (primarily Muslim) Palestinian Congress, demanded restoration of the Shari'a in a letter to the British high commissioner, Herbert Samuels:

> No individual or Government has any right to represent the country in legislating laws because the country is better acquainted with its own needs and because laws, as Jurists state, are the reflection of the people's spirit and because [Ottoman] Turkey has drafted such laws as suit our customs. This was done relying upon the Shari'a (Religious Law), in force in Arabic territories, that is engraved in the very hearts of the Arabs and has been assimilated in their customs and that has been applied . . . in the modern [Arab] states. . . . We therefore ask the British government . . . that it should respect these laws [i.e., the Shari'a] . . . that were in force under the Turkish regime.[439]

Subsequently, a strong Arab Muslim irredentist current promulgated the forcible restoration of *dhimmitude* via jihad. Shai Lachman outlines the two parallel processes that accompanied this transition and culminated in the widespread violence of 1936–1939:

> The Muslim-Christian Associations gradually declined and disappeared in the course of the (nineteen) thirties, giving way to new communal formations focusing on the idea of defending Muslim holy places in Palestine and on mobilizing the Arab people for the coming struggle by means of Islamic symbols. Such were the Young Men's Muslim Associations (Jam'iyyat al-shubban al-muslimin), which, towards the end of the twenties began forming on a strictly communal basis and which included in their program pronounced anti-Jewish propaganda.[440]

Two prominent Muslim personalities—Sheikh Izz al-Din al-Qassam and Hajj Amin el-Husseini, the former Mufti of Jerusalem—embodied this trend. And both these leaders relied upon the ideology of jihad, with its virulent anti-infidel (i.e., anti-Jewish, anti-Christian, and anti-Western) incitement, to garner popular support.

Sheikh Izz al-Din al-Qassam (1871 or 1882–1935) was an Al-Azhar-trained cleric who studied under Muhammad Abdu, a well-known Muslim thinker. Al-Qassam was reportedly a participant in anti-British activities during his sojourn in Cairo. Assisted by Ottoman authorities, he later organized an anti-Italian campaign from Syria, that is, "He called the people to jihad," when Italy invaded Libya in 1912. By early 1921 al-Qassam moved to Palestine, settling in Haifa, where he was shortly afterward appointed imam of the al-Istiqlal mosque (January 1922). A persuasive orator and preacher, al-Qassam soon gathered around him a coterie of dedicated followers. Just prior to the 1929 riots and anti-Jewish pogroms, al-Qassam had secured three critically influential positions that allowed him to disseminate his militant ideology—imam, Shari'a Register of the northern (Palestinian) area, and prominent Young Men's Muslim Association member.[441]

Lachman has summarized the main motifs and consequences of al-Qassam's doctrine:

> Al-Qassam's Weltanschauung was wholly rooted in Islam, which constituted the nexus of all his ideas and deeds. Al-Qassam was an orthodox Muslim, whose supreme ideal was to fulfill the precepts of his faith and do the Creator's will, and whose conviction it was that Islam must be defended and its orthodox form preserved. This was to be accomplished by defending Islam internally against infidelity and heresy; and politically against external enemies, namely the West—with which Islam was in political and ideological conflict—and the Zionist enterprise. . . . In his sermons [following his mentor, Muhammad Abdu], he preached for . . . a return to the principles and values of the original . . . faith . . . in the spirit of the Hanbali school of Islamic jurisprudence . . . manifested, inter alia, in a pronounced xenophobic and anti-Jewish militant stance. He preached the preservation of the country's Muslim-Arab character and urged an uncompromising and intensified struggle against the British Mandate and the Jewish National Home in Palestine. Palestine could be freed from the danger of Jewish domination, he believed, not by sporadic protests, demonstrations, or riots which were soon forgotten, but by an organized and methodical armed struggle. In his sermons he often quoted verses from the Qur'an referring to jihad, linking them with topical matters and his own political ideas.
>
> Al-Qassam actually put his preaching into practice. . . . After the 1929 riots, al-Qassam intensified his anti-Jewish agitation. He justified on religious grounds the excesses committed during the riots, and in 1930, even managed to obtain a fatwa from the Mufti of Damascus, Sheikh Badr al-Din al-Taji al-Hasani, authorizing the use of violence against the British and the Jews. He made a practice of reading this fatwa in mosques and in secret meetings with his disciples and followers . . . in the early 1930s [al-Qassam] proceeded to establish a secret association, called "The Black Hand" (al-kaff al-aswad), whose aim was to kill Jews and generally to terrorize the Jewish population in the North.[442]

This description of the clandestine organization al-Qassam formed sounds quite similar to contemporary jihad terrorist groups operating in Judea, Samaria, and Gaza:

> [I]n some ways [it] resembled a dervish order; its members grew their beards wild, called themselves

"sheikhs," and upon initiation to the secret society, took a stringent religious oath before al-Qassam to guard closely its secrets and to devote their lives to the war against the Jews. At meetings held in mosques and secret places around Haifa, al-Qassam would preach to the society's members to prepare themselves for the eventual jihad and self-sacrifice. They were also trained in the use of arms. As one of the Qassamite leaders recalls: " . . . The meetings would commence with religious instruction by the Sheikh, who would then turn to preaching for the jihad. Finally, the [rifle instructor] would take each member of the audience in turn and teach him the handling of the rifle." . . . [I]n the Jenin mountains . . . at nightfall they would go into villages, or would build fires and continue prayer by their light. They imagined themselves as the mujahidun of Muhammad's days and later periods, who consecrated themselves to the Holy War.[443]

Between 1921 and al-Qassam's death in 1935, the mufti of Jerusalem, Hajj Amin el-Husseini, and the sheikh appear to have cooperated, overall, due to their shared goals. Describing their relationship as "quite complex and uneven," Lachman, for example, concludes:

During the (nineteen) twenties, both were on good terms, their understanding probably based on identity of views and mutual esteem. It was then that al-Qassam was appointed imam of the al-Istiqlal mosque and sharia register—appointments which required the Mufti's prior consent and approval and were financed by the awqaf administration. The cooperation may well have increased as a result of the 1929 riots. One source claims that al-Qassam's men took an active part in the bloody riots. . . . Later towards the mid-1930s, there was a falling out between the two men. The reason for this is unknown, but it seems to have been closely related to al-Qassam's independent activity. . . . As long as the terrorist activity was directed only at Jewish targets, the Mufti saw nothing wrong with this. On the contrary, it fell in line with his own anti-Jewish policy; he secretly encouraged it and apparently extended financial aid to al-Qassam and his organization.[444]

Al-Qassam and his devoted followers committed various acts of jihad terror targeting Jewish civilians in northern Palestine from 1931 through 1935. On November 20, 1935, al-Qassam was surrounded by British police in a cave near Jenin [Yabed], and killed along with three of his henchmen. Concealed within the folds of al-Qassam's turban, a talisman was discovered containing the following verses:

O God save me from the terrible armory of the infidel
O God let your religion win and go victorious
O God protect me in my coming adventure.[445]

The slain sheikh and his comrades were lauded as holy warriors for the fatherland, and his funeral procession, departing from Haifa for the Muslim cemetery at Balad al-Shaykh,

became an impressive national demonstration. Shops and schools closed and thousands of persons walked behind the biers, which were draped with flags and national emblems. Sheikh Yunis al-Khatib said: "Dear and sainted friend, I heard you preaching from this lectern, leaning on your sword; now that you have left us you have become, by God, a greater preacher than you ever were in your lifetime." Several policemen were wounded when the mob began stoning the police during the burial ceremony.[446]

In the immediate aftermath of his death,

Virtually overnight, Izz al-Din al-Qassam became the object of a full-fledged cult. The bearded Sheikh's picture appeared in all the Arabic-language papers, accompanied by banner headlines and inflammatory articles; memorial prayers were held in mosques throughout the country. He was proclaimed a martyr who had sacrificed himself for the fatherland, his grave at Balad al-Shaykh became a place of pilgrimage, and his deeds were extolled as an illustrious example to be followed by all. In addition, a countrywide fund-raising campaign was launched in aid of families of the fallen, and leading Arab lawyers volunteered to defend the members of the [surviving] band who were put on trial.[447]

Al-Qassam's followers were at the vanguard of the 1936–1939 Arab revolt, engaging in multiple acts of murderous jihad terror against Palestinian Jews, the British, and Christian Arabs.[448] Anti-Christian leaflets were apparently distributed in Haifa by Qassamite operatives accusing the Christians of secession and treason. Qassamites also murdered Michel Mitri, the Christian president of the Jaffa Arab Worker's Association.[449] Ultimately, the Qassamite movement devolved into an organ of nihilistic violence:

As their strength grew . . . they gradually threw off all sense of responsibility. Qassamite terror was particularly bloodthirsty. From an organization committed to fight the Jews and the British, the Qassamites became one of the most anarchical and destructive forces ever to arise in the Palestinian Arab community. Their campaign of terror and the indiscriminate murders they committed contributed heavily to the rebellion's disintegration from within, and caused the accumulation of a terrible blood debt in the Arab community.[450]

Lachman described the living legacy of al-Qassam and the Qassamites in 1982, his observations being perhaps even more valid at present, given the unfettered jihadism so prevalent among the Palestinian Arab masses and the ascendancy of contemporary terrorist organizations such as Hamas (with its al-Qassam "brigades" and rockets) and Islamic Jihad:

> [T]he Qassamite myth has not died, and continues to be revered to this very day. Sheikh Izz al-Din al-Qassam's deeds and personality are highly extolled by the Palestinian fedayeen organizations, including the most radical leftist and secular ones such as the Popular Front for the Liberation of Palestine (Habash). . . . Publications of the Palestinian organizations describe him as the pioneer of the Palestinian armed struggle (al-Fatah dubs him "the first commander of the Palestinian Revolution"), as a model of personal sacrifice and endeavor . . . and as one who, by his very deeds ignited the torch of the "heroic revolt of 1936-1939." . . . Up to this day, military units named after Sheikh Izz al-Din al-Qassam may be found in almost all Palestinian organizations. Al-Qassam's major contribution to the Palestinian armed struggle was clearly defined by Leila Khaled. "The Popular Front for the Liberation of Palestine," she wrote, "begins where Qassam left off: his generation started the revolution; my generation intends to finish it."[451]

Hajj Amin el-Husseini was appointed mufti of Jerusalem by the British high commissioner, in May 1921, a title he retained, following the Ottoman practice, for the remainder of his life.[452] Throughout his public career, the mufti relied upon traditional Qur'anic anti-Jewish motifs to arouse the Arab street. For example, during the incitement that led to the 1929 Arab revolt in Palestine, he called for combating and slaughtering "the Jews," not merely Zionists. In fact, most of the Jewish victims of the 1929 Arab revolt were Jews from the centuries-old *dhimmi* communities (for example, in Hebron), as opposed to recent settlers identified with the Zionist movement.[453] With the ascent of Nazi Germany in the 1930s and 1940s, the mufti and his coterie intensified their anti-Semitic activities to secure support from Hitler's Germany (and later Bosnian Muslims, as well as the overall Arab Muslim world), for a jihad to annihilate the Jews of Palestine. Following his expulsion from Palestine by the British, the mufti fomented a brutal anti-Jewish pogrom in Baghdad (1941), concurrent with his failed effort to install a pro-Nazi Iraqi government.[454] Escaping to Europe after this unsuccessful coup attempt,

the mufti spent the remainder of World War II in Germany and Italy. From this sanctuary, he provided active support for the Germans by recruiting Bosnian Muslims, in addition to Muslim minorities from the Caucasus, for dedicated Nazi SS units.[455] The mufti's objectives for these recruits—and Muslims in general—were made explicit during his multiple wartime radio broadcasts from Berlin, heard throughout the Arab world: an international campaign of genocide against the Jews. For example, during his March 1, 1944, broadcast he stated, "Kill the Jews wherever you find them. This pleases God, history, and religion."[456]

Hajj Amin made an especially important contribution to the German war effort in Yugoslovia where the Bosnian Muslim SS units he recruited (in particular the Handzar Division) brutally suppressed local Nazi resistance movements. The mufti's pamphlet entitled "Islam and the Jews" was published by the Nazis in Croatian and German for distribution during the war to these Bosnian Muslim SS units.[457] And Jan Wanner has observed,

> His [the mufti's] appeals . . . addressed to the Bosnian Muslims were . . . close in many respects to the argumentation used by contemporary Islamic fundamentalists . . . the Mufti viewed only as a new interpretation of the traditional concept of the Islamic community (*umma*), sharing with Nazism common enemies.[457a]

This hateful propaganda served to incite the slaughter of Jews, and Serb Christians as well. Indeed, the Bosnian Muslim Handzar SS Division was responsible for the destruction of whole Bosnian Jewish and Serbian communities, including the massacre of Jews and Serbs and the deportation of survivors to Auschwitz for extermination. However, these heinous crimes, for which the mufti bears direct responsibility, had only a limited impact on the overall destruction of European Jewry when compared with his nefarious wartime campaign to prevent Jewish emigration from Europe to Palestine. Wanner, in his 1986 analysis of the mufti's collaboration with Nazi Germany during World War II, concluded,

> [T]he darkest aspect of the Mufti's activities in the final stage of the war was undoubtedly his personal share in the extermination of Europe's Jewish population. On May 17, 1943, he wrote a personal letter to Ribbentrop, asking him to prevent the transfer of 4500 Bulgarian Jews, 4000 of them children, to Palestine. In May and June of the same year, he sent a number of letters to the governments of Bulgaria, Italy, Rumania, and Hungary, with the request not to permit even individual Jewish emigration and to allow the transfer of Jews to Poland where, he claimed, they would be "under active supervision." The trials of Eichmann's henchmen,

including Dieter Wislicency who was executed in Bratislava, Czechoslovakia, confirmed that this was not an isolated act by the Mufti.[458]

Invoking the personal support of such prominent Nazis as Heinrich Himmler and Adolf Eichmann,[459] the mufti's relentless hectoring of German, Romanian, and Hungarian government officials caused the cancellation of an estimated 480,000 exit visas that had been granted to Jews (80,000 from Romania and 400,000 from Hungary). As a result, these hapless individuals were deported to Polish concentration camps. A United Nations Assembly document presented in 1947, which contained the mufti's June 28, 1943, letter to the Hungarian foreign minister requesting the deportation of Hungarian Jews to Poland, includes this stark, telling annotation: "As a Sequel to This Request 400,000 Jews Were Subsequently Killed." And according to historian Howard M. Sachar, meetings the mufti held with Hitler in 1941 and 1942 led to an understanding whereby Hitler's forces would invade Palestine with the goal being "not the occupation of the Arab lands, but solely the destruction of Palestin(ian) Jewry."[460] Moreover, in April 2006 the director of the Nazi research center in Ludwigsburg, Klaus-Michael Mallman, and Berlin historian Martin Cueppers revealed that a murderous Einsatzgruppe Egypt, connected to Rommel's Africa Korps, was stationed in Athens awaiting British expulsion from the Levant prior to beginning their planned slaughter of the roughly five hundred thousand Jews in Palestine. This plan was aborted only after Rommel's defeat by Montgomery at El Alamein, Egypt, in October/November 1942.[461]

The mufti escaped to the Middle East after the war to avoid capture and possible prosecution for war crimes. The mufti was unrelenting in his espousal of a virulent Judeophobic hatred as the focal tenet of his ideology in the aftermath of World War II, and the creation of the State of Israel. David Pryce-Jones has elucidated the preeminent status of antisemitism in the mufti's bitter legacy:

These, then, were the images and preconceptions to which Hajj Amin could appeal once he became the leading Palestinian power holder. In memoirs written at the end of his life, when the bankruptcy of these images and preconceptions was starkly visible, he was still speaking of the Jews as " . . . notorious for perfidy and falsification and distortion and cruelty of which the noble Koran provides the strongest testimony against them." His hatred for Jews was instinctive, tribal; he wished to cut them down, declaring to their face, "Nothing but the sword will decide the future of this country." That this came true amid calamity and ruin was Hajj Amin's memorial to posterity. [462]

Pryce-Jones's insights underscore the profound impact of the mufti's personal convictions and hateful messages on the development of Arab and Palestinian political culture in the latter half of the twentieth century to the present. It is undeniable that the mufti's virulent antisemitism continues to influence Arab policy toward Israel. Not surprisingly, Yasser Arafat, beginning at the age of sixteen, worked for the mufti performing terrorist operations. Arafat always characterized the mufti as his primary spiritual and political mentor.

Yasser Arafat orchestrated a relentless campaign of four decades of brutal jihad terrorism against Israel, beginning in the early 1960s,[463] until his recent death, interspersed with a bloody jihad (during the mid-1970s and early 1980s) against the Christians of Lebanon.[464] Chameleonlike, Arafat adopted a thin veneer of so-called secular radicalism, particularly during the late 1960s and 1970s. Sober analysis reveals, however, that shorn of these superficial secular trappings, Arafat's core ideology remained quintessentially Islamic, that is, rooted in jihad, throughout his career as a terrorist leader. This argument is supported by voluminous evidence. Arafat's initial organized acts of jihad terrorism, border raids,[465] mimicked the celebrated ghazi forays of Islam's early jihadists. Historian Charles Emmanuel Dufourcq described this phenomenon as it pertained to Muslim penetration into medieval North Africa, and Europe:

It is not difficult to understand that such expeditions sowed terror. The historian al-Maqqari, who wrote in seventeenth-century Tlemcen in Algeria, explains that the panic created by the Arab horsemen and sailors, at the time of the Muslim expansion in the zones that saw those raids and landings, facilitated the later conquest, if that was decided on: "Allah," he says, "thus instilled such fear among the infidels that they did not dare to go and fight the conquerors; they only approached them as suppliants, to beg for peace."[466]

Upon Khomeini's ascension to power in Iran, Arafat immediately cabled the ayatollah relaying these shared jihadist sentiments (February 13, 1979):

I pray Allah to guide your step along the path of faith and Holy War (Jihad) in Iran, continuing the combat until we arrive at the walls of Jerusalem, where we shall raise the flags of our two revolutions.[467]

And even after the Oslo accords, literally within a week of signing the specific Gaza-Jericho agreements, Arafat issued a brazen pronouncement (at a meeting of South African Muslim leaders) reflecting his unchanged jihadist views:

The jihad will continue and Jerusalem is not for the Palestinian people alone. . . . It is for the entire Muslim umma. You are responsible for Palestine and Jerusalem before me. . . . No, it is not their capital, it is our capital.[468]

During the final decade of his life Arafat reiterated these sentiments on numerous occasions—and acted upon them, orchestrating an escalating campaign of jihad terrorism (most prominently homicide bombing "martyrdom" operations)[469] that led to Israel's Operation Defensive Shield military operations in the West Bank, two days after the Netanya Passover massacre on March 27, 2002.[470]

Moreover, throughout Arafat's tenure as the major Palestinian Arab leader, his efforts to destroy Israel and replace it with an Arab Muslim Shari'a-based entity were integrated into the larger Islamic *umma*'s jihad against the Jewish state, as declared repeatedly in official conference pronouncements from various clerical or political organizations of the Muslim (both Arab and non-Arab) nations.[471]

After more than thirteen centuries of almost uninterrupted jihad in historical Palestine, it is not surprising that a finalized constitution proposed for a Palestinian Arab state declared all aspects of Palestinian state law to be subservient to the Shari'a,[472] in harmony with the popular will (i.e., 79.9 percent of Palestinians want the PA to follow the Shari'a—Islamic religious law—including 68.6 percent who wanted the Shari'a as the *exclusive* code of law, according to data published by the Palestinian Center for Research and Cultural Dialogue, March 3, 2005). Moreover, contemporary Palestinian Authority religious intelligentsia openly support restoration of the oppressive system of *dhimmitude* within a Muslim-dominated Israel as well.[473] An assessment of such anachronistic, discriminatory views was provided by the Catholic archbishop of the Galilee, Butrus Al-Mu'alem, who, in a June 1999 statement, dismissed the notion of modern *dhimmis* submitting to Muslims:

> It is strange to me that there remains such backwardness in our society; while humans have already reached space, the stars, and the moon . . . there are still those who amuse themselves with fossilized notions.[474]

The Hamas contingent at the municipal council of Bethlehem confirmed (as reported by Karby Legget in the December 23, 2005, edition of the *Wall Street Journal*, p. A1) the organizations plan to reinstitute the humiliating *jizya*, and such policies, even their threatened implementation, will likely exacerbate the ongoing Christian exodus from Arab-controlled Judea/Samaria, especially Bethlehem. An early April 2006 Reuters report[475] indicated that one thousand Christians per year were leaving these areas due to Muslim depredations, including assaults on Christians, uprooting their olive trees, and scrawling graffiti that depicts nuns being raped. After Hamas issued a warning to the YMCA of Qalqilya to close its offices and leave town, as reported on April 21, 2006, a Qalqilya Christian leader commented:

The face of the new Hamas government is coming to the forefront now that they finally took over and have a lot more confidence. They want to create a territory free of Christians and Jews.[476]

However, even more ominous is the prospect that Hamas, following a resounding electoral victory in January 2006, will pursue its openly expressed goal of jihad genocide vis-à-vis Israeli Jews. In a Hamas preelection video from December 12, 2005, the jihadist terror organization reiterated that it would not give up its armed struggle until Israel is destroyed entirely.

The Hamas message also celebrated the organization's love of death as being superior to Israel's love of life, while expressing support for those Israeli Arabs who wish to destroy Israel "from within." Hamas eagerly anticipates a day when its flag will fly over not only Jerusalem, but all Israeli cities, including Acre and Haifa. The following are verbatim quotes from this Hamas video:

> We succeeded, with Allah's grace, to raise an ideological generation that loves death like our enemies love life. We will not abandon the way of Jihad and Shahada [Martyrdom] as long as one inch of our holy land is in the hands of the Jews. . . . Congratulations to our people of 1948 [Israeli Arabs] on the liberation of Gaza. You wish to destroy them [the Israelis] from their interior. We will never forget you, and never leave you. A day will come when our flag will fly above all the quarters of our land. Our flag will fly on the minarets of Jerusalem, and the walls of Acre, and the quarters of Haifa.[477]

Hamas leader Mahmoud Zahar stated plainly in early January 2006,

> We are running for the Legislative Council to put an end to the vestiges of Oslo.[478]

And this rhetoric remained consistent in the aftermath of Hamas's electoral landslide. Khaled Mashaal, the head of Hamas, stated on Friday, February 3, 2006, that Hamas would never recognize Israel's right to exist, but *might* be willing to negotiate a "hudna" or long-term ceasefire with the Jewish state.[479] Mashaal's views are entirely consistent with the classical jihad rules on this point. As noted by Antoine Fattal, in his seminal 1958 analysis of Islamic law,

> when Moslems are in a subordinate state, they can negotiate a truce with the Harbis lasting no more than ten years, which they are obliged to revoke unilaterally as soon as they regain the upper hand, following the example of the Prophet after Hudaibiyya.[480]

Interviewed by the Palestinian Authority newspaper *Al-Hayyat al-Jedida*, Mashaal said that Hamas would "never recognize the legitimacy of the Zionist state that was founded on our land."[481]

There have been ceaseless calls for jihad in Palestine during modern times: in the 1920s and 1930s by Hajj Amin el-Husseini and Izz al-Din al-Qassam, by Yasser Arafat throughout his forty years as leader of Fatah and the PLO, and now under Hamas. Hamas's foundational covenant calls for an annihilationist jihad to eradicate Israel. It states, "There is no solution to the Palestinian problem except by jihad."[482] Iranian Revolutionary Guard officers have been assisting Hamas commanders in arming and training a new jihadist army called the Murbitun—a name that derives from the pious Almoravid religious warriors—Islamized Berbers whose jihad campaigns ravaged North Africa and Iberia in the eleventh and twelfth centuries.[483] And on April 1, 2006, Palestinian minister of foreign affairs Mahmoud al-Zahar made clear the goal of such jihadists: "Our dream to have our independent state on all historic Palestine . . . will become real one day. I'm certain of this because there is no place for the state of Israel on this land."[484]

During an early December 2006 trip to Iran, Hamas prime minister Ismail Haniyeh, speaking to thousands of students at the University of Tehran, declared: "We will never recognize the Zionist government. We will continue the jihad until Jerusalem is liberated." He also maintained that Iran provides the Palestinians with "strategic depth" in their fight against Israel.[485]

Speaking simultaneously in a Palestinian refugee camp near Damascus, Khaled Mashaal (described alternately as the "political leader" of Hamas and the leader of its Syrian branch) took a slightly different tack, but ultimately arrived at the same final message. Mashaal stated that "if Israel and the U.S. want to end the bloodshed in the region, they must accede to the Palestinians' demands." Specifically, he said, Israel must withdraw to the 1949 armistice lines, release all Palestinian prisoners, accept a "right of return" for Palestinian refugees to within the 1949 armistice borders, and dismantle all so-called settlements. Otherwise, Hamas will wage open war against Israel, Mashaal warned. Although Mashaal maintained that all the Palestinian factions agree that a Palestinian state must be established, without compromise, on the 1949 armistice borders, he added, with candor, "[O]ur long-term goal is the liberation of Palestine [i.e., including that portion within the 1949 armistice borders]. . . . Israel and the U.S. are deluding themselves if they think that we are not capable of doing this."[486]

Bat Ye'or observed in 1985 that jihad remained

the main cause of the Arab-Israeli conflict. Since Israelis are to be regarded, perforce, only as a religious community, their national characteristics—a geographical territory related to a past history, a

system of legislation, a specific language and culture—are consequently denied. The "Arab" character of the Palestinian territory is inherent in the logic of jihad. Having become fay territory by conquest (i.e. "taken from an infidel people"), it must remain within the dar al-Islam. The State of Israel, established on this fay territory, is consequently illegal.[487]

And, she concluded,

Israel represents the successful national liberation of a dhimmi civilization. On a territory formerly Arabized by the jihad and the dhimma, a pre-Islamic language, culture, topographical geography, and national institutions have been restored to life. This reversed the process of centuries in which the cultural, social and political structures of the indigenous population of Palestine were destroyed. In 1974, Abu Iyad, second-in-command to Arafat in the Fatah hierarchy, announced: "We intend to struggle so that our Palestinian homeland does not become a new Andalusia." The comparison of Andalusia to Palestine was not fortuitous since both countries were Arabized, and then de-Arabized by a pre-Arabic culture.[488]

Mythical Andalusia: From Jihad to Dhimmitude in Muslim Spain

Jane Gerber has described how the entire history of the Jewish experience in Muslim Spain, which was characterized by "extremes of creativity and humiliation," the latter including "some of their [the Jews] most demoralized moments in the complex saga of life in dispersion," came to be "garishly packaged as 'The Golden Age.'"[489] She argues that two currents of apologetics—one emanating from nineteenth-century Jewish historians; the other, contemporary Arab historians—have sustained this fictional conception.[490] Regarding the nineteenth-century phenomenon, Gerber observes,

. . . for nineteenth century Jewish historians, apologetics and politics were never far removed from the enterprise of reconstructing the Jewish past. Graetz[491] was merely amplifying the expressed *Wissenschaft* [knowledge, gained by systematic research] apologetic that toleration of the Jews is important to civilization and its progress. The notion of all of Spain as a "golden age" fit perfectly into this ideological mold. The moral and practical message of such apologetics was clear. Could not a mutually beneficial arrangement between the Jews and the host culture once again be effective? History, particularly Sephardic history, in Graetz's view, had shown that the Jews were capable of bringing a strong national force, maintaining their own individuality yet contributing significantly to the nation at large. Could Jewish-Gentile symbiosis take place again—this time in modern Germany?[492]

She then alludes to the "new currency" afforded the mythical golden age image,

as Arab "tolerance" is juxtaposed to Jewish "ingratitude" in the campaign against Israel.[493]

Cairo University professor of medieval history Said Abdel Fattah Ashour's address at the notorious 1968 Fourth Conference of the Academy of Islamic Research[494] in Cairo epitomizes the modern Arab genre of this myth—a grossly distorted apologetic, rife with antisemitic vitriol:

[T]he Jews throughout history received no better or kinder treatment than that of [the] Muslims. The egoism and greed of Jews subjected them to persecution by the Romans in early times and by various peoples of Christian Europe in the Middle Ages. They found in Muslims—as Jewish writers themselves admit—merciful brothers who regarded them as fellow believers and did not allow religious differences [to] affect their treatment or attitude toward them. Spain provides a clear example of the big difference in the treatment of Jews by Muslims and Christians. While Muslims in Andalusia were kind to Jews and allowed them to receive their learning in mosques, Christian rulers who came after Muslim rule in Andalusia burned Jews in masses. Ferdinand and Isabella issued a decree in 1492, expelling all the Jews of Spain in a period of four months, not allowing them to take their money and riches with them. The majority of those expelled Jews went to Islamic Morocco and North Africa where they were welcomed. Muslims' experience with Jews was always bitter and difficult, for the Jews returned sincerity with treachery and kindness with ingratitude.[495]

Gerber concludes her analysis of the origins of the golden age myth in Muslim Spain with this sobering assessment:

The aristocratic bearing of a select class of courtiers and poets . . . should not blind us to the reality that this tightly knit circle of leaders and aspirants to power was neither the whole of Spanish Jewish history nor of Spanish Jewish society. Their gilded moments of the tenth and eleventh century are but a brief chapter in a longer saga.[496]

Indeed the chronic conditions for Jews in Muslim Spain were typical of the overall system of jihad-imposed *dhimmitude*.

The Iberian Peninsula was conquered in 710–716 by Arab tribes originating from northern, central, and southern Arabia. Massive Berber and Arab immigration, and the colonization of the Iberian Peninsula, followed the conquest. Most churches were converted into mosques. Although the conquest had been planned and conducted jointly with a faction of Iberian Christian dissidents, including a bishop, it proceeded as a classical jihad with massive pillages, enslavements, deportations, and killings. Toledo, which had first submitted to the Arabs in 711 or 712, revolted in 713. The town was punished by pillage and all the notables had their throats cut. In 730 the Cerdagne (in Septimania, near Barcelona) was ravaged and a bishop burned alive. In the regions under stable Islamic control, subjugated non-Muslim *dhimmis*—Jews and Christians—like elsewhere in other Islamic lands, were prohibited from building new churches or synagogues, or restoring the old ones. Segregated in special quarters, they had to wear discriminatory clothing. Subjected to heavy taxes, the Christian peasantry formed a servile class exploited by the dominant Arab ruling elites; many abandoned their land and fled to the towns. Harsh reprisals with mutilations and crucifixions would sanction the Mozarab (Christian *dhimmis*) calls for help from the Christian kings. Moreover, if one *dhimmi* harmed a Muslim, the whole community would lose its status of protection, leaving it open to pillage, enslavement, and arbitrary killing.[497]

By the end of the eighth century, the rulers of North Africa and of Andalusia had introduced rigorous Maliki jurisprudence as the predominant school of Muslim law. Thus, as Evariste Lévi-Provençal observed three quarters of a century ago,

The Muslim Andalusian state thus appears from its earliest origins as the defender and champion of a jealous orthodoxy, more and more ossified in a blind respect for a rigid doctrine, suspecting and condemning in advance the least effort of rational speculation.[498]

For example, J. M. Safran discusses an early codification of the rules of the marketplace (where Muslims and non-Muslims would be most likely to interact), written by al-Kinani (d. 901),[498a] a student of the Cordovan jurist Ibn Habib (d. 853), "known as the scholar of Spain *par excellence*,"[498b] who was also one of the most ardent proponents of Maliki doctrine in Muslim Spain:

[T]he problem arises of "the Jew or Christian who is discovered trying to blend with the Muslims by not wearing the *riqā* [cloth patch, which as described earlier (in note 191) might be required to have an emblem of an ape for a Jew, or a pig for a Christian] or zunnār [belt]." Kinani's insistence that Jews and Christians wear the distinguishing piece of cloth or belt required of them is an instance of a legally defined sartorial differentiation being recon-firmed. . . . His insistence may have had as much to do with concerns for ritual purity and food prohibi-tions as for the visible representation of social and political hierarchy, and it reinforced limits of inter-communal relations.[498c]

Charles Emmanuel Dufourcq provides these concrete illustrations of the resulting religious and legal discrimi-nations *dhimmis* suffered, and the accompanying incen-tives for them to convert to Islam:

> A learned Moslem jurist of Hispanic Christian descent who lived around the year 1000, Ahmed ibn Said ibn Hazm (father of the famous mid-eleventh-century author Ibn Hazm) gives glimpses, in sev-eral of his juridical consultations, of how the freedom of the "infidels" was constantly at risk. Non-payment of the head-tax by a dhimmi made him liable to all the Islamic penalties for debtors who did not repay their creditors; the offender could be sold into slavery or even put to death. In addition, non-payment of the head-tax by one or several dhimmis—especially if it was fraudulent—allowed the Moslem authority, at its discretion, to put an end to the autonomy of the community to which the guilty party or parties belonged. Thus, from one day to the next, all the Christians [or Jews] in a city could lose their status as a protected people through the fault of just one of them. Every-thing could be called into question, including their personal liberty. . . . Furthermore, non-payment of the legal tribute was not the only reason for abro-gating the status of the "People of the Book"; another was "public outrage against the Islamic faith," for example, leaving exposed, for Moslems to see, a cross or wine or even pigs.
>
> [B]y converting [to Islam], one would no longer have to be confined to a given district, or be the victim of discriminatory measures or suffer humili-ations. . . . Furthermore, the entire Islamic law tended to favor conversions. When an "infidel" became a Moslem, he immediately benefited from a complete amnesty for all of his earlier crimes, even if he had been sentenced to the death penalty, even if it was for having insulted the Prophet or blasphemed against the Word of God: his conver-sion acquitted him of all his faults, of all his pre-vious sins. A legal opinion given by a *mufti* from al-Andalus in the ninth century is very instructive: a Christian *dhimmi* kidnapped and violated a Moslem woman; when he was arrested and condemned to death, he immediately converted to Islam; he was automatically pardoned, while being constrained to marry the woman and to provide for her a dowry in keeping with her status. The *mufti* who was con-sulted about the affair, perhaps by a brother of the

woman, found that the court decision was perfectly legal, but specified that if that convert did not become a Moslem in good faith and secretly remained a Christian, he should be flogged, slaugh-tered and crucified.[499]

Al-Andalus represented the land of jihad par excellence. Every year (or multiple times within a year as "seasonal" razzias [*ghazwa*]) raiding expeditions were sent to ravage the Christian Spanish kingdoms to the north, the Basque regions, or France and the Rhone Valley, bringing back booty and slaves. Andalusian corsairs attacked and invaded along the Sicilian and Italian coasts, even as far as the Aegean Islands, looting and burning as they went. Many thousands of non-Muslim captives were deported to slavery in Andalusia, where the caliph kept a militia of tens of thousands of Christian slaves, brought from all parts of Christian Europe (the *Saqaliba*), and a harem filled with captured Christian women. Bat Ye'or summarizes these events as follows:

> Breaking out of Arabia and from the conquered regions—Mesopotamia, Syria, Palestine—these successive waves of immigrants settled in Spain and terrorized southern France. Reaching as far as Avignon, they plundered the Rhone valley by repeated razzias. In 793 C.E., the suburbs of Nar-bonne were burned down and its outskirts raided. Calls to *jihad* attracted the fanaticized hordes in the ribats (monastery-fortresses) spanning the Islamo-Spainish frontiers. Towns were pillaged and rural areas devastated. In 981, Zamora and the sur-rounding countryside in the kingdom of Leon suf-fered destruction and the deportation of four thou-sand prisoners. Four years later, Barcelona was destroyed by fire and nearly all its inhabitants mas-sacred or taken prisoner; several years after its con-quest in 987, Coimbra remained desolate; Leon was demolished and its countryside ruined. In 997, San-tiago de Compostela was pillaged and razed to the ground. Three years later, Castille was put to fire and sword by Muslim troops and the population, captured in the course of these campaigns, enslaved and deported. The invasions by the Almoravides and the Almohades (eleventh to thirteenth cen-turies), Berber dynasties from the Maghreb, reacti-vated the *jihad*.[500]

Society was sharply divided along ethnic and religious lines, with the Arab tribes at the top of the hierarchy, fol-lowed by the Berbers, who were never recognized as equals despite their Islamization; lower in the scale came the mullawadun converts, and, at the very bottom, the *dhimmi* Christians and Jews. The Andalusian Maliki jurist Ibn Abdun (d. 1134) offered these telling legal opinions regarding Jews and Christians in Seville around 1100:

No . . . Jew or Christian may be allowed to wear the dress of an aristocrat, nor of a jurist, nor of a wealthy individual; on the contrary they must be detested and avoided. It is forbidden to [greet] them with the [expression], "Peace be upon you." In effect, "Satan has gained possession of them, and caused them to forget God's warning. They are the confederates of Satan's party; Satan's confederates will surely be the losers!" (Qur'an 58:19) A distinctive sign must be imposed upon them in order that they may be recognized and this will be for them a form of disgrace.[501]

Ibn Abdun also forbade the selling of scientific books to *dhimmis* under the pretext that they translated them and attributed them to their co-religionists and bishops. (In fact, plagiarism is difficult to prove, since whole Jewish and Christian libraries were looted and destroyed.) Another prominent Andalusian jurist, Ibn Hazm of Cordoba (d. 1064), wrote that Allah had established the infidels' ownership of their property merely to provide booty for Muslims.[502]

Two major paroxysms of anti-Jewish violence occurred in Muslim Spain during the early and mid-eleventh century.[503] The first took place in Cordoba between 1010 and 1013, part of an extended period of chaotic internecine Muslim struggle at the culmination of Umayyad rule. The Berber Muslim chieftain Sulaiman attacked the Jews of Cordoba (perhaps on April 19, 1013) destroying their dwellings, pillaging their storehouses, and driving them in terror (including Samuel Naghrela)[503a] from the city.[503b] According to Avraham Grossman,

> many hundreds of Jews were killed (mainly in Cordoba), and there are those who think the toll was in the thousands.[503c]

Grossman also notes the relative paucity of scholarly references to these confirmed pogroms:

> This event is almost unmentioned in the literature.[504]

The second catastrophic anti-Jewish outburst transpired five decades later, in 1066 in Granada. These attacks were preceded and accompanied by bitter anti-Jewish propaganda, most notably the polemical writings of Ibn Hazm and a poem by Abu Ishaq directed against the Jewish vizier of Granada, Joseph b. Samuel Naghrela.

Ibn Hazm (d. 1064), the famed theologian, savant, and man of letters, composed three major works on the subject of Jews and Judaism. Moreover, as Perlmann notes,

> Even later, Ibn Hazm felt compelled to resume his polemics against Judaism, and this time directly against Samuel [Naghrela, Joseph's father, who served as vizier prior to his son], for he heard that

the latter had written a pamphlet against the claim of the Koran to divine origin.[505]

His earlier polemical works, written to refute Jews, not to persuade them, characterize the Jewish disputants in harshly negative terms:

> [H]e thought they were trying to explain away difficulties with tricks and lies. "It has happened to us so often in our disputes with their savants. . . . They are prone to lie . . . whenever they want to wiggle out of difficulty in a dispute"; a contemptible trait. The author enjoys thoroughly the confusion, helplessness, defeat of his adversaries when pressed by his unrelenting critique.[506]

Ibn Hazm's hostile attitude toward the Jews sacred texts—which, he claims, they have deliberately and deceitfully altered—is summarized by Perlmann:

> The scriptures of the Jews, then, are mere forgeries, distortions. The Muslim attitude toward the scriptures should be one of absolute rejection. The Muslim accepts only the Koran, and only from the Koran he knows of previous revelations, among them one called Torah and one called Gospel, but he finds that the Torah of the Jews at best presents a text that has been tampered with extensively and has no validity.
>
> Who then produced the present text? Who was the forger? He must have been a liar, a contemptible character, either an ignorant ass or a conscious, purposeful, malicious, arch-misleader; nay, he must have been a coarse atheist, scoffing and mocking at any belief or religious feeling, who viciously mixed truth and falsehood to the detriment of future generations.
>
> Ibn Hazm writes about this author-forger mostly *without* naming him. But in a few passages he names him definitely: Ezra, the Aaronid scribe who flourished sometime before the second destruction.
>
> The Talmud was also compiled by atheists. They bribed Paul and sent him to mislead the early Christians by teaching them to believe in Jesus' divinity. The Jews possibly wanted to corrupt Islam in the same way by fomenting schism by the propaganda of 'Abdallah b. Sabā' [a renegade Yemenite Jew accused of being the first Shi'ite and fomenting the most profound sectarian strife in Islam: the Sunni-Shi'ite split].[507]

As Perlmann further observes, Ibn Hazm attacks the Jews themselves with vehement bluntness:

> Dirty, vile, filthy, stinking are epithets he frequently hurls against the Jews. Everyone who knows them, he contends recognizes that they are the filthiest

people, a villainous breed, false, mean and cowardly. Ps. 103, 15–16 [("his days are as grass, as a flower of the field")] shows an atheist materialist concept, he says, "and indeed the religion of the Jews tends strongly towards that, for there is not in their Torah any mention of the next world, or of reward after death. . . . They combine materialism, plurality in deity, anthropomorphism, and every stupidity in the world."

He judges not by chapter and verse only but by the qualities he ascribes to the Jewish people. Jacob filched the blessing assigned to Esau: "By God, it is the way of the Jews. You will not find among them, with rare exceptions, but a treacherous villain."

"They, both the ancient and the modern, are altogether the worst liars. Though I have encountered many of them, I have never seen among them a truth seeker, except two men only."

"They are the filthiest and vilest of peoples, their unbelief horrid, their ignorance abominable." Among minds, theirs are like the odor of garlic among odors.

What a people, what a lineage! Abraham marries his own sister. Isaac is a thief. Jacob married Leah in error. Reuben fornicates with his father's wife, Judah with his son's. (A slip: Joshua and Rahab). Amram married his aunt, which is against the law, and Moses was born from this union. David commits the crime against Uriah. Absalom defiles his father's wives.

Let them persist in their vain hopes for a glorious future; hopes that are the stock-in-trade of fools. Sometimes their leaders perceive the truth but will be stubborn against reason in blind fidelity to their ancestors, and group feeling, and the desire to perpetuate their worldly position.[508]

But it was Ibn Hazm's later return to anti-Jewish polemical writings—a frontal attack on Samuel Naghrela—that may have contributed more immediately to the 1066 Granadan pogrom. He accuses Samuel of criticizing both the Qur'an and the Muslim prophet:

A man who was filled with hatred towards the Apostle—a man who is, in secret, a materialist, a free-thinker, a Jew—of that most contemptible of religions, the most vile of faiths . . . loosened his tongue . . . and became conceited in his vile soul, as a result of his wealth. His riches, his gold and his silver robbed him of his wretched senses; so he compiled a book in which he set out to demonstrate the alleged contradictions in the Word of God, the Koran.[509]

And Ibn Hazm also condemns the Muslim ruling elites for allowing such a state of affairs to exist:

"It is my firm hope that God will treat those who befriend the Jews and take them into their confidence as He treated the Jews themselves. . . . For whosoever amongst Muslim princes has listened to all this and still continues to befriend the Jews, holding intercourse with them, well deserves to be overtaken by the same humiliation and to suffer in this world the same griefs which God has meted out to the Jews, apart from their chastisement in the next world. Whosoever acts in this manner will be recompensed by suffering along with the Jews themselves, according to God's warning in their Torah, in the Fifth Book (Deuteronomy XXVIII.15–58). . . . On their own evidence, this is God's message, and the chastisement He has apportioned them. . . . Then let any prince upon whom God has bestowed some of His bounty take heed. . . . Let him get away from this filthy, stinking, dirty crew beset with God's anger and malediction, with humiliation and wretchedness, misfortune, filth and dirt, as no other people has ever been. Let him know that the garments in which God has enwrapped them are more obnoxious than war, and more contagious than elephantiasis. May God keep us from rebelling against Him and His decision, from honouring those whom He has humiliated, by raising up those whom He has cast down."[510]

Abu Ishaq's verse also contributed to the anti-Jewish incitement that culminated in the slaughter of Granada's Jews—Joseph b. Samuel Naghrela himself and some three thousand to four thousand others.[511] The poem invoked antisemitic Qur'anic motifs—the "humiliation and abasement (wretchedness)" curse of Qur'an 2:61, including perhaps the most dramatic manifestation of this curse: the Jews (in this case Joseph specifically) as apes, their punishment in verses 2:65, 5:60, and 7:166. It further threatened the Muslim ruling class with mass popular unrest for having permitted Samuel's tenure—in clear violation of the *dhimma*.[512]

Grossman points out how this large-scale massacre has received scant attention by scholars compared, for example, to the ravages of the Crusaders in the Rhineland three decades later, and suggests why this event has been relatively ignored:

The degree of harm done to this important community is not less than that done to the community of Mainz in 1096. Yet what a difference there is in the research literature dealing with the two of them! Though this difference is attributable in great measure to the religious, political, and social foundations of the Crusader's movement of 1096, as well as to the heroic martyrdom of many members of the Ashkenazi communities in those persecutions—two factors which, in the nature of things, claimed the attention of the scholars—there is no doubt that the fact that these scholars were in Europe greatly influenced the character of their research.[513]

The discriminatory policies of the Berber Muslim Almoravids, who arrived in Spain in 1086, and subsequently those of the even more fanaticized Almohad Berber Muslims (who arrived in Spain in 1146–1147) caused a rapid attrition of the pre-Islamic Iberian Christian (Mozarab) communities, nearly extinguishing them. The Almoravid attitude toward the Mozarabs is well reflected by three successive expulsions of the latter to Morocco in 1106, 1126, and 1138. The oppressed Mozarabs sent emissaries to the king of Aragon, Alphonso 1st le Batailleur (1104–1134), asking him to come to their rescue and deliver them from the Almoravids. Following the raid the king of Aragon launched in Andalusia in 1125–1126 in responding to the pleas of Granada's Mozarabs, the latter were deported en masse to Morocco in the fall of 1126.[514]

Although as Hirschberg observes, "[W]e do not know whether the Jews suffered more [from the Almoravid jihad] than the rest of the civilian population,"[515] it is clear the Christian *dhimmis* bore the brunt of Almoravid discriminatory practices in the areas conquered and colonized by these invaders. Jews were apparently spared from the major deportations (accompanied by imprisonments, murders, and church destructions)[516] of their Christian *dhimmi* counterparts, suffering much less serious financial and property losses.[517] Hirschberg, for example, maintains that,

> in 1071 Yusuf ibn Tashfin imposed upon the Jews a *farida* (compulsory levy), which yielded 100,000 dinars, a very considerable sum; this seems to have been a kind of property confiscation.[518]

The jihad depredations of the Almohads (1130–1232) wreaked enormous destruction on both the Jewish and the Christian populations in Spain and North Africa. Hirschberg includes this summary of a contemporary Judeo-Arabic account by Solomon Cohen (which comports with Arab historian Ibn Baydhaq's sequence of events), from January 1148 CE, describing the Muslim Almohad conquests in North Africa and Spain.

> Abd al-Mumin . . . the leader of the Almohads after the death of Muhammad Ibn Tumart[519] the Mahdi . . . captured Tlemcen [in the Maghreb] and killed all those who were in it, including the Jews, except those who embraced Islam. . . . [In Sijilmasa] one hundred and fifty persons were killed for clinging to their [Jewish] faith. . . . All the cities in the Almoravid [dynastic rulers of North Africa and Spain prior to the Almohads] state were conquered by the Almohads. One hundred thousand persons

were killed in Fez on that occasion, and 120,000 in Marrakesh. The Jews in all [Maghreb] localities [conquered] . . . groaned under the heavy yoke of the Almohads; many had been killed, many others converted; none were able to appear in public as Jews. . . . Large areas between Seville and Tortosa [in Spain] had likewise fallen into Almohad hands.[520]

This devastation—massacre, captivity, and forced conversion—was described by the Jewish chronicler Abraham Ibn Daud, and the poet Abraham Ibn Ezra. Suspicious of the sincerity of the Jewish converts to Islam, Muslim "inquisitors,"—antedating their Christian Spanish counterparts by three centuries—removed the children from such families, placing them in the care of Muslim educators.[521] When Sijilmasa (an oasis town southwest of Fez) was conquered by the Almohads in 1146, the Jews were given the option of conversion or death. While 150 Jews chose martyrdom, others converted to Islam, including the *dayyan* (rabbi, or assistant rabbi) Joseph b. Amram (who later reverted to Judaism). The town of Dar'a suffered a similar fate. Abraham Ibn Ezra's moving elegy *Ahah Yarad Al Sefarad* describes the Almohad destruction of both Spanish (Seville, Cordova, Jaen, Almeria) and North African Jewish communities, including Sijilmasa and Dar'a (along with others in Marrakesh, Fez, Tlemcen, Ceuta, and Meknes).[522]

Ibn Aqnin (d. 1220), a renowned philosopher and commentator who was born in Barcelona in 1150, fled the Almohad persecutions with his family, escaping to Fez. Living there as a crypto-Jew, he met Maimonides and recorded his own poignant writings about the sufferings of the Jews under Almohad rule.[523] Ibn Aqnin wrote during the reign of Abu Yusuf al-Mansur (r. 1184–1199), four decades after the onset of the Almohad persecutions in 1140. Thus the Jews forcibly converted to Islam were already third-generation Muslims. Despite this, al-Mansur continued to impose restrictions upon them, which Ibn Aqnin chronicles. From his *Tibb al-nufus* (*Therapy of the Soul*), Ibn Aqnin laments:

> Our hearts are disquieted and our souls are affrighted at every moment that passes, for we have no security or stability. . . . Past persecutions and former decrees were directed against those who remained faithful to the Law of Israel and kept them tenaciously so that they would even die for the sake of Heaven. In the event that they submitted to their demands, [our enemies] would extol and honor them. . . . But in the present persecutions, on the contrary, however much we appear to obey their instructions to embrace their religion and forsake our own, they burden our yoke and render our travail more arduous. . . . Behold the hardships of the apostates of our land who completely abandoned the faith and changed their attire on account of

these persecutions. But their conversion has been of no avail to them whatsoever, for they are subjected to the same vexations as those who have remained faithful to their creed. Indeed, even the conversion of their fathers or grandfathers . . . has been of no advantage to them.

If we were to consider the persecutions that have befallen us in recent years, we would not find anything comparable recorded by our ancestors in their annals. We are made the object of inquisitions; great and small testify against us and judgments are pronounced, the least of which render lawful the spilling of our blood, the confiscation of our property, and the dishonor of our wives. But thanks to the grace of God, who has taken pity on the faithful remnant, their testimonies have proved contradictory, for the nobles pleaded in our favor while the common folk testified against us, and the custom of the land would not allow the testimony of the vulgar to supersede that of the gentry. These measures were renewed repeatedly and God took pity twice and thrice. Then a new decree was issued, more bitter than the first, which annulled our right to inheritance and to the custody of our children, placing them in the hands of the Muslims, fulfilling that which is written, "Thy sons and thy daughters shall be given unto another people" (Deut. 28:32). They intended thereby to dissipate our belongings and make us assimilate with the Muslims. For the [Muslim] custodians are able to dispose of our young children and their belongings as they see fit. If they were given to an individual who feared Allah, then he would endeavor to educate the children in his religion, for one of their principles is that all children are originally born as Muslims and only their parents bring them up as Jews, Christians, or Magians. Thus, if this individual educates them in [what they state is] their original religion [i.e., Islam] and does not leave the children with those [i.e., the Jews] that will abduct them therefrom, he will obtain a considerable reward from Allah. . . .

Then another misfortune and terrible trial fell to our lot, ". . . such as never was since there was a nation *even* to that same time . . ." (Dan. 12:1). We were prohibited to practice commerce, which is our livelihood, for there is no life without the food to sustain our bodies and clothes to protect them from the heat and cold. The latter can only be obtained through trade for this is their source and cause, without which its effect, namely our existence, would disappear. In so doing their design was to weaken our strong and annihilate our weak. . . .

Then they imposed upon us distinctive garments as it was foretold in the Holy Scriptures, "And thou shalt become an astonishment [a repulsion], a proverb, and byword, among all nations whither the Lord shall lead thee" (Deut. 28:37). The word

repulsion signifies "desolation" on account of the scorn of the nations at our state of humiliation, abasement, and contempt. For no other nation can be compared unto us, no matter how persecuted they be. Indeed, our scorn of ourselves is greater than that of the nations toward us. We have become a repulsion and an example so that when they desire to exaggerate a state of contempt or humiliation that has befallen any of them or their fellows they say, "My humiliation was like that of the Jews." Similarly, if they wish to offend or insult their neighbor, after having exhausted all other insults, or if they are in anger against their son or a slave, they will say "O you Jew." Likewise if they want to curse someone in the worst possible manner, they say, "May Allah bless him and grant him peace—make you like them and count you among their number." If they want to describe a distasteful deed or a blemish they say, "Even a Jew, with his detestable ways, would not be content with such a thing." Thus we have become a proverb wherefrom they derive instruction and reproach. . . . A "byword" refers to our outward appearance, which is distinguishable from members of other groups. The Hebrew word is a diminutive meaning *"dishonor,"* for the garments that have been imposed upon us are the vilest, the most degrading, and the most humiliating attire. . . .

As for the decree enforcing the wearing of long sleeves, its purpose was to make us resemble the inferior state of women, who are without strength. They were intended by their length to make us unsightly, whereas their color was to make us loathsome. . . . The ugly bonnets they have placed upon our heads are meant to contradict ". . . and bonnets shalt thou make for them, for glory and for beauty" (Exod. 28:40) (145b). . . . The purpose of these distinctive garments is to differentiate us from among them so that we should be recognized in our dealings with them without any doubt, in order that they might treat us with disparagement and humiliation. . . . Moreover it allows our blood to be spilled with impunity. For whenever we travel on the wayside from town to town, we are waylaid by robbers and brigands and are murdered secretly at night or killed in broad daylight. . . .

Now, the purpose of the persecution of Ishmael, whether they require us to renounce our religion in public or in private is only to annihilate the faith of Israel and consequently one is bound to accept death rather than commit the slightest sin . . . as did the martyrs of Fez, Sijilmasa, and Dar'a.[524]

Ibn Aqnin's observations were confirmed by the contemporary Muslim historian of the Almohads, al-Marrakushi (d. 1224):

Toward the end of his reign [1198], Abu Yusuf [Abu Yusuf Ya'qub al-Mansur, 1184–1198, Almohad ruler of Spain and North Africa] ordered the Jewish inhabitants of the Maghreb to make themselves conspicuous among the rest of the population by assuming a special attire consisting of dark blue garments, the sleeves of which were so wide as to reach to their feet and—instead of a turban—to hang over the ears a cap whose form was so ill-conceived as to be easily mistaken for a pack-saddle. This apparel became the costume of all the Jews of the Maghreb and remained obligatory until the end of the prince's reign and the beginning of that of his son Abu Abd Allah [Abu Muhammad Abd Allah al-Adil, the Just, 1224–1227]. The latter made a concession only after appeals of all kinds had been made by the Jews, who had entreated all those whom they thought might be helpful to intercede on their behalf. Abu Abd Allah obliged them to wear yellow garments and turbans, the very costume they still wear in the present year 621 [1224].[525]

Moreover, al-Marrakushi further acknowledges that in addition to these humiliating impositions on the forced Jewish converts to Islam, they were held in suspicion as crypto-Jews, under threat of slaughter, expropriation, and enslavement:

Abu Yusuf's misgivings as to the sincerity of their conversion to Islam prompted him to take this measure and impose upon them a specific dress. "If I were sure," said he, "that they had really become Muslims, I would let them assimilate through marriage and other means; on the other hand, had I evidence that they had remained infidels I would have them massacred, reduce their children to slavery and confiscate their belongings for the benefit of the believers."[526]

Maimonides, the outstanding philosopher and physician, also experienced the Almohad persecutions, and had to flee Cordoba with his entire family in 1148, temporarily residing in Fez—disguised as a Muslim—before finding asylum in Fatimid Egypt. Despite the fact that Maimonides is frequently referred to as a paragon of Jewish achievement facilitated by the enlightened rule of Andalusia, his own words debunk this utopian view:

You know, my brethren, that on account of our sins God has cast us into the midst of this people, the nation of Ishmael, who persecute us severely, and who devise ways to harm us and to debase us. . . . No nation has ever done more harm to Israel. None has matched it in debasing and humiliating us. None has been able to reduce us as they have. . . . We have borne their imposed degradation, their

lies, and absurdities, which are beyond human power to bear. We have become as in the words of the psalmist, "But I am as a deaf man, I hear not, and I am as a dumb man that opens not his mouth" (Ps. 38:14). We have done as our sages of blessed memory have instructed us, bearing the lies and absurdities of Ishmael. We listen, but remain silent. . . . In spite of all this, we are not spared from the ferocity of their wickedness and their outbursts at any time. On the contrary, the more we suffer and choose to conciliate them, the more they choose to act belligerently toward us. Thus David has depicted our plight: "I am at peace, but when I speak, they are for war!" (Ps. 120:7).[527]

Moreover, fearing the widely prevalent doctrinal fanaticism of the Muslim masses, Maimonides cautioned Jews never to teach Muslims Torah, to avoid being accused by their Muslim interlocutors of blasphemy and punished; in contrast Maimonides had no such reservations about Jews teaching Torah to "the uncircumcised," that is, Christians.

[I]t is permitted to teach the commandments and the explanations according to [rabbinic] law to the Christians, but it is prohibited to do likewise for the Muslims. You know, in effect, that according to their belief this Torah is not from heaven and if you teach them something, they will find it contrary to their tradition, because their practices are confused and their opinions bizarre *mippnei she-ba'uu la-hem debariim be-ma`asiim* [because a mish-mash of various practices and strange, inapplicable statements were received by them]. What [one teaches them] will not convince them of the falseness of their opinions, but they will interpret it according to their erroneous principles and they will oppress us. [F]or this reason . . . they hate all [non-Muslims] who live among them. It would then just be a stumbling block for the Israelites who, because of their sins, are in captivity among them. On the contrary, the uncircumcised [Christians] admit that the text of the Torah, such as we have it, is intact. They interpret it only in an erroneous way and use it for purposes of the allegorical exegesis that is proper to them *Ve-yirmezuu bah ha-remaziim hay-yedu`iim la-hem* [They would exchange secret signs known only to them]. If one informs them about the correct interpretation, there is hope that they will return from their error, and even if they do not, there is not a stumbling block for Israel, for they do not find in their religious law any contradiction with ours.[527a]

Finally, expanding upon Jane Gerber's thesis (on the "garish" myth of a golden age),[528] Richard Fletcher offered a fair assessment of interfaith relationships in Muslim Spain, and his view of additional contemporary currents responsible for obfuscating that history:

The witness of those who lived through the horrors of the Berber conquest, of the Andalusian fitnah in the early eleventh century, of the Almoravid invasion—to mention only a few disruptive episodes—must give it [i.e., the roseate view of Muslim Spain] the lie. The simple and verifiable historical truth is that Moorish Spain was more often a land of turmoil than it was of tranquility. . . . Tolerance? Ask the Jews of Granada who were massacred in 1066, or the Christians who were deported by the Almoravids to Morocco in 1126 (like the Moriscos five centuries later). . . . In the second half of the twentieth century a new agent of obfuscation makes its appearance: the guilt of the liberal conscience, which sees the evils of colonialism—assumed rather than demonstrated—foreshadowed in the Christian conquest of al-Andalus and the persecution of the Moriscos (but not, oddly, in the Moorish conquest and colonization). Stir the mix well together and issue it free to credulous academics and media persons throughout the western world. Then pour it generously over the truth . . . in the cultural conditions that prevail in the west today the past has to be marketed, and to be successfully marketed it has to be attractively packaged. Medieval Spain in a state of nature lacks wide appeal. Self-indulgent fantasies of glamour . . . do wonders for sharpening up its image. But Moorish Spain was not a tolerant and enlightened society even in its most cultivated epoch.[529]

From Andalusia to the Ottoman Empire

The brutal jihad conquests of the Almohads—followed by their discriminatory practices as rulers—resulted in a massive emigration of Jews and forced Jewish converts to Islam from both Almohad-controlled Spain and the North African Maghreb, to the Christian kingdoms of the Iberian Peninsula.[530] During the first half of the thirteenth century, Jaime I of Aragon, in particular, as Mercedes Garcia-Arenal notes,

created a general policy of sheltering Jews in his territories, granting "guidage," safe conduct, and letters of naturalization to all Jews who, by land or sea were able to come and establish themselves in the states of Majorca, Catalonia, and Valencia. Among these documents are preserved the safe-conduct passes granted to two Jewish families from Sijilmasa, dated 1247, Valencia. For some time prior to this, Jewish converts to Islam had been permitted to return to their former religion if they so wished.[531]

Between 1367 and 1417, however, Spanish Jewry, including the descendants of those Jews who had escaped the Muslim Almohad depredations, experienced

an era of "furious persecutions,"[532] including anti-Jewish pogroms, which caused the majority of Spanish Jews to abjure their faith under coercion and convert to Christianity (becoming "Marranos").[533] Subsequently, those Marranos whose conversion was deemed "insincere" would be subjected to the fanaticism of the Spanish Inquisition, officially decreed by the Spanish rulers Ferdinand and Isabella on September 27, 1480.[534] Following the issuance of an "expulsion" decree in 1492— a dozen years after the founding of the Inquisition—until 1499, as Henry Kamen has established, only a minority of Jews left Spain—most decided to convert.[535] Indeed, as Kamen observes,

The "expulsion" decree of 1492 was a decree aimed not at expulsion but at conversion.[536]

Moreover a total of perhaps forty to fifty thousand Jews were expelled between 1492 and 1499, and no more than half of those sought refuge under the suzerainty of Ottoman Muslim rule (debunking the ahistorical notion of an en masse Jewish emigration to the Ottoman Empire). Kamen describes these events as follows:

[E]migration to the Ottoman Empire certainly took place, but slowly and in stages. Many exiles fled from the Mediterranean coast of Spain, but virtually all went only to the neighboring countries; the difficulty of arranging sea transport is sufficient explanation for the limited radius of movement, though the important fact must also be borne in mind that Judaism was tolerated in all the territories concerned, and there was little need to go as far as the Levant.

Thanks to the public toleration of Judaism in neighboring territory (Navarre, Portugal, Provence), little migration from the peninsula took place except among communities which faced the Mediterranean coast, and which therefore were forced to take ship. Possibly over 10,000 Jews left the Mediterranean coast in 1492 and 1493, but many of these were Castilian and not exclusively Aragonese; the figure of 10,000, in any case, is our ceiling for the likely total of all Jews in the crown of Aragon. If we accept the Jewish total for Castile as being around 70,000 persons in 1492, we may allow that over half of these emigrated; but it was an emigration that was in great measure reversed by the high number of returnees, so that the possible final emigration from Castile may not have been much above 30,000 persons. Even allowing for a possible overlap between this figure and that given above for Aragon, the total Spanish emigration looks like being closer to 40,000 or 50,000.[537]

To complete this morose cycle of persecution, the vacuum filled by those Jews expelled from Spain at the end of the fifteenth century and relocated by the Ottomans—for example, in the regions of Salonika and Constantinople (Istanbul) itself—was created when their co-religionist counterparts—the Jews living under Byzantine rule—were subjected to massacre, pillage, enslavement, and deportation by these same Ottoman conquerors during their jihad campaigns of the early to mid-fifteenth century.[538]

Ottoman "Tolerance": Jews under Ottoman Rule—From Jihad to Sürgün to Dhimmitude

Wittek, citing the oldest-known Ottoman source—the versified chronicle of Ahmedi—maintains that the fourteenth-century Ottomans believed they, too, "were a community of Ghazis, of champions of the Mohammedan religion; a community of the Moslem march-warriors, devoted to the struggle with the infidels in their neighborhood."[539]

Sir Paul Rycaut (1629–1700) served as a dragoman (Turkish interpreter) and assistant to the British ambassador (starting in 1665), before being appointed British Consul to Smyrna for eleven years (1667–1678).[540] Rycaut also wrote major historical works on the Ottoman Empire, one of which described the importance attached to the "Office of the Mufti."[540a]

The Mufti (or Shaykh al Islam)[540b] is the principal head of the Mahometan Religion or Oracle of all doubtful questions in the Law, and is a person of great esteem amongst the Turks; his election is solely in the Grand Signor [Sultan], who chooses a man to that Office always famous for his Learning in the Law and eminent for his virtues and strictness of Life; his Authority is so great amongst them, that when he passes judgment or Determination in any point, the Grand Signor himself will in no wise [ways] contradict or oppose it. . . . In matters of State the Sultan demands his opinion, whether it be in Condemnation of any great man to Death, or in making War or Peace, or other important Affairs of the Empire; either to appear the more just and religious, or to incline the People more willingly to Obedience. And this practice is used in business of greatest moment; scarce a Visier [Vizier] is proscribed, or a Pashaw [Pasha] for pretence of crime displaced, or any matter of great alteration or change designed, but the Grand Signor arms himself with the Mufti's Sentence.

Molla Khosrew (d. 1480) was a celebrated writer and Hanafi jurist who was appointed the Ottoman Shaykh-al-Islam by Sultan Mehmed II in 1469.[540c] One of Molla Khosrew's authoritative, widely cited legal works reiterated these classical views on jihad:

[J]ihad is a *fard al-kifaya*, that is, that one must begin the fight against the enemy, even when he

[the enemy] may not have taken the initiative to fight, because the Prophet . . . early on . . . allowed believers to defend themselves, later, however, he ordered them to take the initiative at certain times of the year, that is, at the end of the haram months, saying, "Kill the idolaters wherever you find them . . ." (Q9:5). He finally ordered fighting without limitations, at all times and in all places, saying, "Fight those who do not believe in God, and in the Last Day . . . " (Q9:29); there are also other [similar] verses on the subject. This shows that it is a *fard al-kifaya*.[540d]

The contemporary Turkish scholar of Ottoman history Halil Inalcik has emphasized how this conception of jihad—as formulated by Molla Khosrew and both his predecessors and followers—was a primary motivation for the conquests of the Ottoman Turks:

The ideal of gaza, Holy War, was an important factor in the foundation and development of the Ottoman state. Society in the frontier principalities conformed to a particular cultural pattern imbued with the ideal of continuous Holy War and continuous expansion of the Dar ul Islam—the realms of Islam—until they covered the whole world.[541]

Incited by pious Muslim theologians, these *ghazis* were at the vanguard of (both the earlier Seljuk Turk) and Ottoman jihad conquests. A. E. Vacalopoulos highlights the role of the dervishes during the Ottoman campaigns:

[F]anatical dervishes and other devout Muslim leaders . . . constantly toiled for the dissemination of Islam. They had done so from the very beginning of the Ottoman state and had played an important part in the consolidation and extension of Islam. These dervishes were particularly active in the uninhabited frontier regions of the east. Here they settled down with their families, attracted other settlers, and thus became the virtual founders of whole new villages, whose inhabitants invariably exhibited the same qualities of deep religious fervor. From places such as these, the dervishes or their agents would emerge to take part in new military enterprises for the extension of the Islamic state.[542]

Speros Vryonis has provided this schematic, clinical assessment of the jihad conquest and colonization of Asia Minor by the Seljuks and Ottoman Turks:

The conquest, or should I say the conquests of Asia Minor were in operation over a period of four centuries. Thus the Christian societies of Asia Minor were submitted to extensive periods of intense warfare, incursions, and destructions which undermined the existence of the Christian church. In the first century of Turkish conquests and invasions from the mid-eleventh to the late twelfth century, the sources reveal that some 63 towns and villages were destroyed. The inhabitants of other towns and villages were enslaved and taken off to the Muslim slave markets.[543]

The Islamization of Asia Minor was complemented by parallel and subsequent Ottoman jihad campaigns in the Balkans.[544] As of 1326, yearly razzias by the emirs of Asia Minor targeted southern Thrace, southern Macedonia, and the coastal areas of southern Greece. Around 1360, the Ottomans, under Suleiman (son of Sultan Orchan) and later Sultan Murad I (1359–1389), launched bona fide campaigns of jihad conquest, capturing and occupying a series of cities and towns in Byzantine and Bulgarian Thrace. Following the battle of Cernomen (September 26, 1371), the Ottomans penetrated westward, occupying within fifteen years a large number of towns in western Bulgaria and in Macedonia. Ottoman invasions during this period also occurred in the Peloponnesus [or "Morea," the southern Greek peninsula], central Greece, Epirus, Thessaly, Albania, and Montenegro. By 1388 most of northeast Bulgaria was conquered, and following the battle of Kosovo (1389), Serbia came under Ottoman suzerainty. Bayezid I (1389–1402) undertook devastating campaigns in Bosnia, Hungary, and Wallachia, in addition to turning south and again attacking central Greece and the Peloponnesus. After a hiatus during their struggle against the Mongol invaders, the Ottomans renewed their Balkan offensive in 1421. Successful Ottoman campaigns were waged in the Peloponnesus, Serbia, and Hungary, culminating with the victory at the Second Battle of Kosovo (1448). With the accession to power of Mehmed II, the Ottomans commenced their definitive conquest of the Balkan Peninsula. Constantinople was captured on May 29, 1453, marking the end of the Byzantine Empire. By 1460, the Ottomans had completely vanquished both Serbia and the Peloponnesus. Bosnia and Trebizond fell in 1463, followed by Albania in 1468. With the conquest of Herzegovina in 1483, the Ottomans became rulers of the entire Balkan Peninsula. Angelov, highlighting the later campaigns of Murad II (1421–1451) and Mehmed II (1451–1481), described the impact of the Ottoman jihad on the vanquished Balkan populations:

[T]he conquest of the Balkan Peninsula accomplished by the Turks over the course of about two centuries caused the incalculable ruin of material goods, countless massacres, the enslavement and exile of a great part of the population—in a word, a general and protracted decline of productivity, as was the case with Asia Minor after it was occupied by the same invaders. This decline in productivity is all the more striking when one recalls that in the mid-fourteenth century, as the Ottomans were

gaining a foothold on the peninsula, the States that existed there—Byzantium, Bulgaria and Serbia—had already reached a rather high level of economic and cultural development. . . . The campaigns of Murad II (1421–1451) and especially those of his successor, Mehmed II (1451–1481) in Serbia, Bosnia, Albania and in the Byzantine princedom of the Peloponnesus, were of a particularly devastating character. . . . It [the Peloponnesus] was invaded in 1446 by the armies of Murad II, which destroyed a great number of places and took thousands of prisoners. Twelve years later, during the summer of 1458, the Balkan Peninsula was invaded by an enormous Turkish army under the command of Mehmed II and his first lieutenant Mahmoud Pasha. After a siege that lasted four months, Corinth fell into enemy hands. Its walls were razed, and many places that the sultan considered useless were destroyed. The work by Kritobulos contains an account of the Ottoman campaigns, which clearly shows us the vast destruction caused by the invaders in these regions. Two years later another Turkish army burst into the Peloponnesus. This time Gardiki and several other places were ruined. Finally, in 1464, for the third time, the destructive rage of the invaders was aimed at the Peloponnesus. That was when the Ottomans battled the Venetians and leveled the city of Argos to its foundations.[545]

The Initial Incorporation of the Jews into the Ottoman Empire: From Jihad to **Sürgün**

Joseph Hacker's pioneering scholarship[546] has revealed the origins of another myth—that of a remarkable Ottoman Muslim benevolence toward Jews. Hacker notes that historians since Heinrich Graetz (who, as discussed earlier)[547] also promoted the ahistorical notion of a golden age Muslim-Jewish symbiosis in an ecumenical Muslim Spain.

[D]escribed in idyllic colors the evolution of relations and links between the Jews and Ottomans, and even the happenings of the conquest of Constantinople and the fate of the Jews of the city were not depicted authentically. These approaches affected the understanding of the scholars of the Ottoman Empire who relied on students of Jewish history and upon "their sources." Thus they tended to continue to minimize and swallow up all tensions in those relations and links, and to describe them as idyllic only.[548]

Hacker's research singles out the 1523 book of the Talmudist Eliyah Kapsali, *Seder Eliyah Zuta*, composed in Crete in 1523, and its embellishment by the seventeenth-century Egyptian chronicler Rabbi Yosef Sambari (probably from Alexandria) in his *Divrei Yosef*:

[T]hat became the version accepted by modern historiography of the history of the Jews in the Ottoman Empire, and the sürgün [forced population transfer] phenomenon and all its attendant [discriminatory] features was not considered at all. If the sürgün was mentioned at all in the writings of the [Jewish] scholars of the Empire, it was held to be an insignificant, indecisive episode in the history of the Jews. The relations between Jews and Ottomans were thus felt to be both idyllic and monotonous from their very inception, no distinction being made either between kinds of Jewish populations or between one period and another throughout the fifteenth and sixteenth centuries.

Kapsali conceals all criticism and tries to cover up and obliterate inconvenient facts. . . . This is also apparently the reason for his utterly ignoring the Romaniot [Byzantine] Jews and their fate at the time of the conquest of Constantinople, and of the suffering of the others exiled there after the conquest.[549]

The Jews, like other inhabitants of the Byzantine Empire, suffered heavily from the Ottoman jihad conquests,[550] and policies of colonization and forced population transfer (i.e., the sürgün system).[550a] This also explains the disappearance of several Jewish communities, including Salonika, and their founding anew by Jewish immigrants from Spain.[550b] Moreover, even these Spanish Jewish immigrants could subsequently be subjected to *sürgün* deportations (as were elite families of Spanish Jews settled in Salonika [c. 1508], and then exiled to Rhodes in 1523),[551] with relegation, thereafter, to permanent *sürgün* status.

Hacker emphasizes how the sürgün (the meanings of the root "sür" and the suffix "gün" include *exile, persecution*, and *expulsion*)[552] decrees of obligatory transfer were experienced as a punishment its victims sought to avoid.[553] Those who refused to emigrate once they were ordered to could be put to death,[554] and Hacker describes the lasting impact of being designated *sürgün*—a form of vassalage that restricted movement and social interactions, and resulted in economic penalties, including double taxation:

[I]t is completely evident that departing and settling in the ruined city [i.e., Constantinople] were considered a severe decree. A study of the status and obligations of a person exiled by decree of the authorities shows that from the time the person exiled to a certain region he was forbidden to leave it without permission of the *shubashi* (the chief of police) or some other representative of the authorities. Not only he himself was forbidden to leave the area, his children were likewise forbidden to leave, and he was sometimes forbidden to marry a person who was not, like himself, an exile. Furthermore he was obliged to engage in certain occupations if it

was for this occupation that he had been exiled and was not permitted to change his occupation. Though he enjoyed a partial tax exemption for a given period of time and in most cases a dwelling place, as well, the property (real estate) he had owned in his previous domicile was on occasion taken from him by the authorities—without compensation, and sometimes divided up amongst the military. These limitations on his freedom would continue indefinitely. In fact a person becoming a *sürgün* would assume a special appropriate legal status which differentiated clearly between him and the other residents of the regions in his personal status, in his freedom of movement, and sometimes in his occupation as well. In Istanbul, for example, all new arrivals were first organized in special neighborhoods and in predetermined areas according to their origin, and were not permitted to move to other parts of the city to reside.

When a person was registered by the authorities as a *sürgün*, and when he had been sent to his new place of residence, this sürgün status adhered to him and his offspring until "the end of time." No one was able to free himself of this status, which obligated him—first and foremost—to be a vassal of his place of residence, without the ability to leave it before first having obtained the permission of the authorities. This limitation had decisive effects on the lives both of the individual and the general public. This topic comes up quite a few times in the sources available, both with respect to the individual and regarding the public. Concerning the individual, the subject is mentioned with regard to brides and bridegrooms who were *sürgün*: one of the parties involved considered this to be justification for cancellation of the wedding. People were also unable to leave their place for either the purpose of bearing witness or for a legal session elsewhere. However, the more complex subject which surely left its impression on the lives of these Jews is that of double taxation. The *sürgün*'s status as a vassal to his place of residence was expressed on occasion not so much by virtue of his physical presence in his place of exile as by his registration in the authorities' taxation books. The individual was sometimes permitted to leave the city for a limited or lengthy period of time, on condition that he pay his taxes at the place where he was registered. This arrangement would lead to the community where he actually resided (lived and worked there) demanding that he pay taxes to the authorities and to the community in his place of active residence. And though at first glance, he was exempt from this by Ottoman law (at least insofar as paying taxes to the authorities), the communities refused to concede, for in their opinion the taxes were determined by the tax collectors according to the quantity of the economic activity and the number of people in the community. They claimed that the authorities imposed their taxes on the community without taking into consideration the fact that a person was *sürgün* and paid his taxes elsewhere.

As a result those Romaniot [Byzantine] Jews exiled to Istanbul in the fifteenth century, who asked permission to leave the town for economic activities, had to receive permits for that from the authorities (either the *shubashi* or his assistant, or by agreement of the directors of the *wakf* [Muslim religious endowment, typically plots of land and/or buildings; like a "trust"] to which they paid their taxes, for the money was earmarked for this *wakf* from the very earliest of times, when they were exiled to Istanbul). When they received their permit to leave or when they left without a permit, and operated in another town, the community in which they lived would not agree to give up its portion of the taxes in their new place. Thus, every such person was obliged to pay double taxes. From the available Hebrew sources it would seem that this demand remained valid as late as the seventeenth century; it may even have grown stronger as the Romaniots left town in larger and larger numbers. It was a serious economic obstacle for the descendants of the Romaniots, most of whom were *sürgün*, and for the descendants of those Spanish and Portuguese emigrés who became *sürgün* as a result of one of the sixteenth-century conquests.

From a letter by the scholars of Istanbul written between 1601 and 1605 to assist a Romaniot Jew of Istanbul, we learn that about one hundred and fifty years after they became *sürgün*, this status was still an obstacle for their descendants. And though "individuals became nay and [the authorities] no longer distinguished between Romaniot and Spaniard," the Romaniot congregations responsible for the payment of their members' taxes in Istanbul did not facilitate a person's leaving "unless he guaranteed his congregation by means of a certain guarantor who would pay for him any tax requirement and levy imposed by the crown." This encumbrance of being vassal to a place, or at least this heavy financial obligation to one's previous place of residence, was a burden endured by the vast majority of Romaniots, and it seems that only a few Spanish Jews were encumbered by it. The problem was well known, and suffices to explain somewhat the Romaniot inferiority, whose legal and economic status was inferior to those of the migrants from Europe (even though they were the more ancient population group). This is a surprising situation whereby it was preferable to be a migrant Jew from a foreign land than to be a long-time Jewish resident of the Empire as early as the fifteenth century.

As an external sign of the degree of influence the *sürgün* phenomenon had on the Jews of Istanbul, as late as the eighteenth century, one might consider the fact that the term came to be accepted as a familial name for the Jewish community, though it bore negative connotations.[555]

Hacker records the observations of prominent contemporary Jews forcibly deported from their places of origin to Constantinople (renamed Istanbul) after its brutal jihad conquest in 1453.[556] Twenty to thirty Jewish communities were removed en bloc from Anatolia and the Rumelia (Albania, Macedonia, and Thrace) to Istanbul, including, by 1456, all the Karaite dignitaries previously living in Edirne.[557] He notes,

> The Karaites (too) experienced bitterness and sorrow arising from the new circumstances.[557a]

Writings of Byzantine Jews also address the Ottoman conquest of Constantinople. Laments on the fall of Constantinople and the fate of its community and other communities subjected to the ravages of the fifteenth-century Ottoman jihad campaigns were written during this period by Jews such as Rabbi Ephraim b. Gershon, a doctor and homilist from Veroia (Macedonia, forty miles WSW of Salonika), and Rabbi Michael Balbo of Crete.[558]

Ephraim b. Gershon's "relatively moderate words" describe his own fate and that of the Jewish community of Veroia. He initially fled to Negroponte (under Venetian control) when his community was forcibly exiled to Istanbul. Later he joined his co-religionists in Istanbul expressing his anti-Ottoman feelings during a homily delivered in 1469. Ephraim b. Gershon writes that these *sürgün* Jews suffered not only property and financial losses, but also the abandonment of places to which they were emotionally attached and great damage to their physical health. His 1469 sermon includes the following words.[559]

> All this stems from our enslavement and the sorrow we cause ourselves in our pursuit of a livelihood: we call upon God and He will hear our voices. He will take pity and have mercy on us and redeem us.[560]

According to Hacker, Ephraim saw Islamic (i.e., Ottoman) and Christian (i.e., Venetian, Byzantine) rule over Jews—living "among the Gentiles"—as equivalent:

> Rabbi Ephraim views the Ottoman Empire as the prophet Daniel's fourth kingdom from which Israel will be redeemed when it collapses, and the Jews return to their homeland.
>
> [I]t is clear that after his arrival in Istanbul no change took place in Ephraim ben Gershon's basic approach to the Ottomans. As a Jew living (and

who apparently was also born) under Ottoman rule, he perceived no difference between this regime and a Christian one, with regard to the function and status of these kingdoms in universal history and with regard to their place in the redemption of the Jews from among the Gentiles. At first he preferred to move to a Venetian area; later he returned to the Ottoman sphere of influence and rejoined his brethren in Istanbul, where he spoke in public, hinting at his reservations regarding the regime and the kingdom. Under this Ishmaelite government, just as under other authorities, there prevailed circumstances where the individual would be well advised when "in exile amongst the seven tribes and *asked to pay taxes or to convert*, hand over a portion of your capital in order to be saved. This is the meaning of 'Give a portion to seven,' i.e., to the seven tribes.'"561

Rabbi Michael Balbo of Candia, Crete (b. spring 1411, and still alive December 1480), was a well-known community figure who compiled his own letters in addition to those of others, most of which were written during the second and third quarters of the fifteenth century.562 His observations, as Hacker notes, provide "more severe descriptions" of the fate of these Byzantine Jewish communities.563 One letter apparently originating from Corfu includes this characterization of the political upheavals which accompanied the Ottoman jihad:

At this time the King maker [the Ottoman Sultan] enthroned a king of the Archers [Gen. 21:20, Ishmael] over each town and district; he decreed upon the poor, wandering nation go into exile, and went to gather them up to the daughter of Edom, Constantinople [Lamentations 4:21, as applied to Constantinople], and the Almighty enabled him to succeed [according to Exodus 21:13: "And one who did lie in wait, but God caused to come about."]. Everyone lamented. The robbery [Isa. 51:19–20: "These two have befallen you; who shall lament you? Desolation and ruin, famine and war; how shall I console you? Your sons have been wasted, they lie at the head of all the streets . . ."] and the disaster, the famine and the sword and the forced conversion of children at this time defy comforting. All are affected and desolated by the oppressor [Isa. 51:13], and there is no tranquility [Deut. 32:36].564

The fate of the Jews was not different from that of Christians in either Constantinople itself or other areas conquered by the Ottoman jihad campaigns.565 Large numbers of Jews were killed; others were taken captive, and Jewish children were enslaved, some being forcibly converted to Islam, and brought to *devshirme* (the coercive levies of adolescent non-Muslim male children, almost exclusively Christians, for the Ottoman slave-soldier

Janissary system).566 Extant letters describe the forced exiling of the captive Jews to Istanbul and are filled with anti-Ottoman sentiments. Hacker elucidates the contents of the Corfu letter in the overall context of other contemporary observations from prominent Byzantine Jews, before drawing his own summary conclusions:

This letter paints a picture of Jews severely harmed by the Ottoman wars and conquests in the days of Mehmet II. The description indicates that the Jews of Corfu were well aware of the processes of the Ottoman conquest. The conquest was accompanied by the appointment of governors over the occupied territories by the "Kingmaker," i.e., the Sultan. These Muslim governors were responsible for the stabilization and the development of the conquered region. At the same time, this letter describes the colonizing activities and the transfer of the Jewish population to Istanbul. Whether the letter is describing the conquest of an area previously under Byzantine or Latin control, subsequent to the conquest of Constantinople, or an event during the conquest of Constantinople itself and its consequences, the process is similar. The people view their exile as a catastrophe, and the conquest as manslaughter and loss of property. The picture is one of crisis and distress. This letter also hints at the phenomenon of converting Jewish children to Islam. In fact, this would seem to be the first evidence of the fact that in the heat of the conquest, the fate of Jewish children was the same as that of Christian children: conversion, in order to absorb them into the Janissary army. The induction of Christian children into the Janissary army, known as devshirme, was one of the harsher decrees imposed upon the conquered populace, and various towns that surrendered to the Ottomans without resistance requested, and sometimes received by virtue of this, an exemption from the *sürgün* and from the devshirme. The evidence before us is somewhat vague. Were the conquerors incapable, in the heat of battle, of distinguishing between Christian inhabitants and non-Christians? Or perhaps they had not yet formulated the policy familiar to us from the later periods, in accordance with which they exempted the Jews from devshirme and even forbade them from being drafted into the Janissary army.

From the letter, furthermore, it becomes clear that the person for whom it was compiled had gone into exile to Istanbul, and lost whatever he had owned. When he tried to return and engage in trade, he was taken captive, and now people succeeded in redeeming him from captivity and in rehabilitating him and his family. Another source also discusses the fate of Jews in the unstable period and their captivity at the hands of the Ottomans. In this source, the Ottomans are termed "men of wickedness and deceit, Riphath and Togarmah" (referring to Genesis 10:3), and fear is expressed, lest the captives "be assimilated" into their captors. The personal histories of two of the intellectuals of the period show, too, that they were captives, and it would seem that they were referring to their captivity at the hands of the Ottomans. R[abbi] Mordekhai Comtino tells of his imprisonment in the town of Edirne, whereas R[abbi] Shalom Anabi of Istanbul—who was in contact with R[abbi] Michael Balbo who copied many of his writings—wrote of himself: "Ensnared in the net of captivity," or "who surrounded us so that we were ensnared in the net of captivity."

. . . [I]n Michael Balbo's aforementioned notebook there is a dirge to the fall of Constantinople into Ottoman hands, which was probably written shortly after news of the event had been received. This dirge calls the conquerors "a violent people." "The embroidered great eagle, Riphath and Togarmah" is here depicted as one who destroys, who ruins, who robs and kills Jews. This is a dirge in which R[abbi] Michael Balbo mourns the fate of the Jewish community of Constantinople, and according to his description, this event was a terrible disaster for the Jews, who were robbed and killed by the conquering force, as were the other inhabitants of the city.

The picture painted by the writings of these Romaniots in the Ottoman Empire and in the Latin colonies on its outskirts during the third quarter of the fifteenth century, is one of people who underwent heavy suffering as a result of the processes of conquest and population transfers to Istanbul.[567]

The *sürgün* policy was applied rigorously throughout the reign of Mehmet II—often affecting the lives of Jews—and at least intermittently by his successor, Bayezid II. While it is unknown whether the Jews, specifically, were involved in the population transfers of Bayezid II, the subsequent regimes of Selim I and Süleyman the Magnificent did exile and transfer Jews between regions of the expanding Ottoman Empire in the aftermath of their jihad conquests: from Egypt to Istanbul after Selim I conquered Mamluk Syria and Egypt in 1516–1517; from Salonika to Rhodes following the conquest of Rhodes in 1522 by Süleyman the Magnificent; and after the conquest of Buda(pest) following the battle of Mohacs in 1526 (and the final subjugation of Buda and its environs in 1541), Jews were exiled from this ancient capital of Hungary to locations throughout the Ottoman Empire, including Istanbul, Sofia (Bulgaria), Kavalla (northeast Macedonia), Edirne, and perhaps even Safed.[568]

Upon reviewing the available contemporary evidence regarding the 1517 *sürgün* of Egypt's Jews, especially a letter from the Cairo geniza (by Meir Saragos of Egypt)

written during the first half of the sixteenth century, Hacker concludes,

> The description tells of the limitations and the supervision to which they were subjected and which prevented them from moving their location and accepting appointments to the positions they desired. The limitations of the *sürgün* are very prominent here. Similarly, it is clear that the phenomenon of *sürgün* was common and many were ensnared in its coils. People were responsible for dealing with the affairs of those who became *sürgün*, while the latter attempted to free themselves by attaching themselves to some position—either to avoid going into exile or to leave one place of exile for another, steps which were forbidden to any *sürgün*.[569]

Yitzhak Ibn Farash was originally exiled from Spain to Portugal, and later departed for Salonika, where he settled in 1508. Yitzhak apparently wrote about the 1523 transfer of Jews from Salonika to Rhodes because his son-in-law was one of those designated as *sürgün*. He states,

> From Salonika, Monday the 13th of Av 5283 (1523) there went to Rhodes against their will a hundred and fifty of the richest and the most respected land lords in the country, men, women, and children, at the command of the king [Süleyman the Magnificent] . . . an official coming and taking them off by boat.[570]

While such transfers "of the richest and most respected . . . landlords" accrued obvious advantages to the Ottomans who sought to facilitate the socioeconomic development of new areas of jihad conquest, in this case Rhodes, as Hacker observes,

> The hasty and rapid process of exiling the *sürgün* led to various familial, social, economic and legal complications. . . . These exiles would seem to have been forced to remain in Rhodes, and were unable to leave, but the sources adduced make it evident that people did succeed in escaping from the island even though they were forbidden to do so.[571]

Concerted efforts by the Jews of Safed did succeed ultimately in canceling the decreed *sürgün* deportation of two-thirds of their community to Cyprus, following the island's conquest (under Selim II) by the Ottomans in 1571 (the reprieve being confirmed in January 1579).[572] Yosef Mataron provided a contemporary account of a *sürgün* decree imposed upon his family in conjunction with these events. Yosef's description of his extensive efforts to have this transfer abrogated reflect how oppressive the *sürgün* decrees were considered by Jews. However, despite the success of the Safed community appeals, Hacker notes,

> at the same time, . . . the governor [of Cyprus] succeeded in delaying a boat with 100 Jews on board who had been on their way from Salonika to Safed, and in getting permission to resettle them in Cyprus, despite their desire to go on to Palestine.
>
> During this period various members of the Jewish communities in Salonika, Safed and elsewhere, whose status was questioned, who lost favor with the authorities, or were caught engaging in economic and criminal offenses, were exiled to Cyprus.[573]

Regarding the later *sürgün* deportations (primarily under Selim I and Süleyman the Magnificent), Hacker writes,

> From the various facts exhibited here, it may be deduced that the *sürgün* system remained in force throughout the sixteenth and the beginning of the seventeenth century, and affected to a very considerable degree the lives of the Jews of the [Ottoman] Empire. These facts, which certainly do not reflect every event which actually took place, show that whenever a significant conquest occurred—under Selim I, Süleyman the Magnificent or Selim II—Jews were moved from their homes and, as they were considered a productive element of the population, it was considered good to exploit them for purposes of regional development. Whenever the Jews were living in territory recently conquered, they would be exiled to Istanbul or some other urban area, while on other occasions they were moved from their homes in the Empire in order to resettle and develop new territories.[574]

Three overall conclusions are drawn by Hacker:

(1) Strong anti-Ottoman feelings prevailed among important Byzantine Jewish circles in the first decades after the fall of Constantinople. These feelings were openly expressed by people living under Latin rule and to some extent even in Istanbul.

(2) Mehmed II's policies toward non-Muslims made possible the substantial economic and social development of the Jewish communities in the empire, and especially in the capital—Istanbul. These communities were protected by him against popular hatred, including blood libels. However, this policy was not continued by Bayezid II and there is evidence that under his rule the Jews suffered both forced conversions to Islam, and severe restrictions in their religious life.

(3) The friendly policies of Mehmed on the one hand,

and the good reception by Bayezid II of Spanish Jewry on the other, caused the Jewish writers of the sixteenth century to overlook both the destruction that Byzantine Jewry suffered during the Ottoman jihad conquests and the later outbursts of oppression under both Bayezid II and Selim I.[575]

Hacker illustrates this latter process (3) in his animated discussion of the rather crudely redacted narrative of the sixteenth-century Ottoman hagiographer Eliyah Kapsali:

> [T]hough he [Kapsali] was well aware of the fact that Bayezid II's policies towards the Jews were very different from those of Mehmet II, and that in his day attempts were made to pressure the Jews to adopt Islam and strict decrees were promulgated against the existence of synagogues erected after the Ottoman conquest, he was still careful to describe Bayezid II as the perfect Jew lover and protector. The truth is revealed with his description of Selim [I], Bayezid's heir. Here he saw fit to praise Selim as follows:
>
> > "Now on the third day of the reign of Sultan Selim, the Sultan gave an order and permitted the Jews to reopen the synagogues his father Sultan Bayezid [II], had closed . . . for he was pious . . . and he even restored to Judaism many Jews whom the Turks had forced to convert contrary to their own wishes."

And so not only did he conceal the fate of *sürgün* Jews and disguise them as voluntary migrants who came to settle in the royal capital at the invitation of the King; not only did he obscure the bitter fate of the Jews of conquered Constantinople; he also attempted to cover up as much as possible the zealous policies of Bayezid II against religious minorities—including the Jews—after the expulsion. And all to avoid harming the image of the Sultan and his major work: throwing open the gates of the kingdom before the expelled Jews of Spain and Portugal, guaranteeing their physical security and preparing the conditions for their free economic activity. There is thus in his book not a single hint or even trace of criticism of the Sultans of his generation: Mehmet [Mehmed] II, Bayezid II, and Selim I.[576]

Ottoman Dhimmitude: *The Jewish Experience*

The institutional regulations of *dhimmitude* were applied to all Jews (and the much larger Christian minority populations) under Ottoman suzerainty, regardless of whether or not they were designated, in addition, as *sürgün*. Once again, the influential writings of Mehmed II's leading cleric (Shaykh-al-Islam), Molla Khosrew,[577] elucidate the guiding principles and concrete directives of these theological-juridical regulations—which are entirely consistent with the vast corpus of Sunni Islamic jurisprudence.[578]

Molla Khosrew reiterates these classical views on the *jizya*—a blood ransom poll tax demanded in lieu of being slain and completely dispossessed. The *jizya* was collected regularly (most often annually), in person, and in a manner that confers the subjects' humiliation, due to their willingly imperfect belief, consistent with Qur'an 9:29. Of note also is the specific admonition to Jews.[579]

Jizya is a term that refers to that which is collected of the *dhimmi*, in exchange for their life and belongings . . . [belongings] referring here exclusively to land and non-moveable property [as] nothing else, except the land and the home, remain in the hands of the conquered.

There are two kinds of tribute, or *jizya*: one is agreed upon following surrender; the other is set by the *Imam* if the enemy has been vanquished by Muslims following a battle. The agreed-upon *jizya* is not subject to later negotiations. The only situations that allow the cessation of payment are the following: death, conversion to Islam, the onset of a physical handicap, such as blindness, mutilation, or old age, to such a degree as to no longer allow work. . . . [and] the debt contracted due to the non-payment of the previous year's *jizya* should not expire. . . . The obligation to pay the *jizya* ends with death or with conversion to Islam, because the divine law, [Shari'a] considers such an obligation to be an earthly punishment: it serves the punitive purpose of chasing away evil from the world.

The *jizya* should not be accepted when payment is made through an intermediary, rather, the payer should come in person to pay, and remain standing: he who is collecting should, on the other hand, be sitting. In the *al-hidaya* text, the tax collector is also expected to shake the clothing of the payer, saying "Pay the *jizya*, oh *dhimmi*," further, . . . the tax collector can also say, ***"Oh Jew, enemy of God, pay!"*** [emphasis added] . . . In other texts . . . we read that the *dhimmi* should be hit on the neck[580] at the time of collection.

Also in accord with classical Islamic jurisprudence, Molla Khosrew outlines the typical regulations—regarding religious structures and practice; the prohibition on bearing arms; and distinguishing forms of dress, modes of travel, neighborhoods, and abodes—which complemented the *jizya* collection and formed the basis for the system of *dhimmitude* (in this specific case, the Ottoman version):

Building a synagogue or a church or a [Zoroastrian] Temple of Fire is not allowed. The term synagogue [*kanisa*] indicates a place of worship of the Jews, while church [*bay'a*] indicates a place of worship of the Christians. A place for spiritual retreat is also considered like a church. The prohibition concerns places constructed specifically for the purpose of religious rites, not areas for prayer set up within private homes, and this is applicable within the *dar-al-islam*. In any case, the right to rebuild that which was destroyed is granted, as buildings devoted to worship can be built in a place where such a building had been erected previously. It is not possible, however, to move from the original location, and to build elsewhere, as this would require erecting another building.

It is possible for *dhimmis* to coexist with Muslims, but in specified locations such as a particular neighborhood. In no case should that be on Arab land, because the collaborators may not take those lands as a place of residence, according to the Prophet's *hadith*, which states, *"there may not coexist two religions on Arab land."* The houses of the *dhimmi* must be marked, in order not to violate the terms of the contract [*ahd*] so as to deserve to be put to death.

[T]he *dhimmi* must be distinguishable by his clothing and by his means of transportation, by the way he loads his beast of burden, by his equipment, etc. For these reasons he may not appear riding a horse, *or bearing arms*, and he must always show his *kusfig*. This is a small cord, as thick as a finger, made of wool or animal hair, tied around the belly of the *dhimmi*, but different from a belt [*zunnar*], as the latter is made of silk.

The dhimmi must ride a saddle of the *kakaf* type. The ideal situation would be for them not to ride any animal, but if they should do so out of necessity in a place crowded with Muslims, they should dismount and proceed on foot. Their passageways should be made narrow. *Dhimmi* women, too, must be distinguishable by keeping to pre-established roads and *hammams*.

In any case, they must be kept from exhibiting their sinful practices, such as usury, and their customs, their songs, their dances, all that which is forbidden in any case. . . . Should there be a festival, they should not celebrate by carrying crosses.[581]

The Ottoman system of *dhimmitude*—consistent with all other variants of this Shari'a-based institution—conferred upon Jews (and all *dhimmis*) two basic legal disabilities that denied them both protection and redress when victimized: the prohibition of the right to bear arms and the inadmissibility of *dhimmi* legal evidence when a Muslim was a party.[582] And (as noted earlier) even the series of reforms imposed by European powers (as so-called capitulations) upon the weakening Ottoman Empire during its final eight decades almost continuously (through 1914) failed to rectify these institutionalized legal discriminations in a substantive manner.[583] For example, Dadrian notes that during a December 1876 Ottoman Turkish conference in Constantinople—twenty years after the *second* iteration of the Tanzimat reforms in 1856—the right of non-Muslims to bear arms was rejected as a violation of the Shari'a:

> After summoning and consulting the Ulema, the Islamic doctors of law, the Shaykh-al-Islam, their head, issued a *Fetva* [fatwa], the peremptory final opinion declaring such possession of arms by non-Muslim subjects a violation of the Islamic Sacred Law.[584]

A series of extensive European consular investigations conducted throughout the Ottoman Empire during the latter half of the nineteenth century confirmed the trivial impact of these reforms on the fundamental right of Jews and Christians to present legal evidence in Muslim-administered courts. Their testimony continued to be

> utterly rejected in the lower criminal courts, and only received in the higher courts when corroborated by a Mussulman. . . . A Mussulman's simple allegation, unbacked by evidence, will upset the best founded and most incontrovertible claim.[585]

As a result of this ongoing dual disenfranchisement, the modern Ottomanist Roderick Davison concluded:

> Ottoman equality was not attained in the Tanzimat period [i.e., mid- to late-nineteenth century, 1839–1876], nor yet after the Young Turk revolution of 1908.[586]

Moritz Levy[587] and Ivo Andric[588] have documented the dress codes, transportation and arms prohibitions, and excessive taxation (or bribes and outright extortion) imposed upon the Jewish community of Bosnia under Ottoman rule throughout the seventeenth and eighteenth centuries. These observations recall the contemporary experiences of the Jews in Ottoman Palestine during this same period, as described previously.[589]

From at least 1579, as decreed by Sultan Murad III, through 1714, the Ottoman authorities applied "strict measures" to prevent Jews and Christians from dressing like Muslims. Particular attention was paid to headdress; distinctions in footwear, while less fastidious, were also required, and violations of the footwear prohibitions became a source of bribery extorted by the Muslim constabulary and religious authorities.[590] Jews and Christians were also forbidden to ride horses in towns and their precincts. Levy describes these prohibitions and

cites an example of a bribe required to lift this restriction (transiently) during an early nineteenth-century funeral for a Jew:

> When Christians or Jews set out on a journey, they had to wait until they were outside the town before mounting their horses. Even outside the town, non-Muslims must not be ostentatious or conspicuous. The harness must be cheap and simple. The saddle must not have fittings of silver or any other metal, or have fringes or any other decoration. The reins must be made exclusively of black leather (not red, white or yellow) and be without tassels or other appendages on the horse's head, neck or mane, as was customary among the Turks of Bosnia. There is only one brief mention of these matters in the records, from 1804, which states: 22 groschen [coinage of silver or copper] to the Qadi and Mutessellim, for permission to ride horses at the funeral of (the Shasham David).[591]

Predictably, Jews and Christians could not bear guns, sabers, and other "prestigious weapons."[592] Levy further documents how bribes were required from the Sarajevo Jewish community to allow Jewish women to bathe after menstruation in accord with Mosaic purity laws:

> [T]he Qadi forbade Jewish women from visiting the baths after the second hour before sunset, i.e. at precisely the time when Jewish law prescribes the aforementioned ablutions. In this respect we find in the records: 1767–53 groschen to the Qadi for permission for women to visit the baths [at the appropriate time]. . . . The same point appears in the records for 1769 and 1778.[593]

Moreover, between 1748 and 1802, payments were extorted from Sarajevo's Jews by the Muslim Buljukbaša (i.e., Pasha, who also acted as the public executioner) so that condemned Christians (almost exclusively) would not be hanged at the Jewish ghetto gates, thereby averting another form of public humiliation of the Jewish community.[594] Ivo Andric provides two additional eighteenth-century examples of Sarajevo's Jews as "profitable targets of extortion" by the Muslim ruling elites. The payments Andric documents were required in order for the Jewish community to avoid unpaid, forced labor corvées and be allowed to rebuild a synagogue destroyed by fire.

> The *Pinakes* . . . the account books of the Sarajevo Jews, offer a true picture in many ways of conditions as they were then. The year 1730 saw a disbursement of 720 puli [90 dinar] for the mutesilim, so as to be spared working Saturdays on the fortification [i.e., in corvées; Andric further indicates that Christians were deployed in such corvées on

Sundays]. It was an outlay repeated in the years to come.

. . . In the year 1794 the Jews of Sarajevo won permission through an imperial firman to rebuild their synagogue, which had recently burned down. It hardly need be said that the usual stipulations applied. "No more than any of the confessions are they allowed to enlarge such a structure by so much as a jot or a tittle in the process of re-erecting it." And to the imperial firman were attached the usual formalities—permission of the vizier, permission of the kadi, two separate commissions, and so on. All this took more than two years and cost a tidy sum.[595]

The readiness with which the Jews acceded to such extortions was explained by Levy as follows:

> Acts of violence and extortion by the Pashas against the Jews plunged them into the depths of darkest night. . . . There were many unpleasant run-ins with the authorities from time to time, which, however, were susceptible to settlement by means of money.[596]

Lastly, regarding the brutal enforcement of *dhimmi* dress restrictions in the heart of Istanbul itself, British ambassador James Porter (who served there between 1746 and 1762) recorded two tragic examples from 1758, involving the summary executions of a Jew and an Armenian:

> (*February 3, 1758*) The order against Christians and Jews dress, except in modest Cloaths [clothes], browns, blacks . . . as to caps and boots . . . is most rigorously executed in a Manner unknown before *which alarms much all those who are not Mahometans*, and makes them apprehend the most Rigour; it seems however but natural, when it is considered, that it comes from a self-denying religious Prince [Sultan Mustafa III].
>
> (*June 3, 1758*) This time of Ramazan [Ramadan] is mostly taken up by day in sleep, by Night in eating, so that we have few occurrences of any importance, except what the Grand Seignor [Sultan Mustafa III] himself affords us he is determined to keep his laws, and to have them executed concerning dress has been often repeated, and with it uncommon solemnity, yet as in former Reigns, after some weeks it was seldom attended to, but gradually transgressed, these people whose ruling Passion is directed that way, thought it was forgot, and betook themselves to their old course, *a Jew on his Sabbath was the first victim*, the Grand Seignor going the rounds incognito, met him, and not having the Executioner with him, *without sending him [the Jew] to the Vizir, had him executed, and his throat cut that*

> *moment, the day after an Armenian followed*, he was sent to the Vizir, who attempted to save him, and condemned him to the Galleys, but the Capigilar Cheaia [head of the guards] came to the Porte at night, attended with the executioner, to know what was become of the delinquent, *that first Minister had brought him directly from the Galleys and his head struck off, that he might inform his Master he had anticipated his Orders.*[597]

The messianic career of Shabbetai Zevi (1626–1678)—his rise and ignominious fall in the latter half of the seventeenth century—engendered discord, and ultimately, despondent apathy in the Ottoman Jewish community.[598] The son of a Jewish commercial agent from the port of Izmir (ancient Smyrna; southwest Turkey today), Shabbetai was expelled from his community in 1651 (for pronouncing the name of God publicly), and by 1658 he and his acolytes had begun a campaign of proselytization designed to prepare the Jewish communities of the Ottoman Empire (and beyond) for the looming messianic age. By 1665 Shabbetai declared himself the messiah, inspiring numbers of Jews to abandon their regular occupations in anticipation of the onset of his messianic reign. Alarmed at the ferment within these Jewish communities and the theological-juridical challenge Shabbetai Zevi's mission posed to Ottoman authority, Sultan Muhammad IV had him imprisoned.[599] Shabbetai was converted to Islam under threat of death (or via other coercive means). The contemporary travelogue of Edward Brown (1644–1708) maintains simply that a Kasim Pasha (a physician married to the sultan's sister, who served as Ottoman governor of Budapest from April 1666–May 1667),

> so handled him [Shabbetai], that he was glad to turn Turk.[600]

A more detailed account is provided from another contemporary historical memoir published by Sir Paul Rycaut in 1680:

> That having given public scandal to the Professors of the Mahometan Religion, and done dishonor to his Sovereign Authority, by pretending to withdraw from him so considerable a portion as the land of Palestine, his Treason and Crime could not be expiated without becoming a Mahometan Convert; which if he refused to do, the State was ready at the Gate of the Seraglio to impale him. Shabbetai being now reduced to his last game and extremity, not being in the least doubtful what to do; for to die for what he was assured was false was against Nature, and the death of a mad man: replied with much cheerfulness, that he was contented to turn Turk, and that it was not of force, but of choice, having been a long time desirous of so glorious a profes-

sion, he esteemed himself much honored, that an opportunity to own it first in the presence of the Grand Signor [Sultan].[601]

Shabbetai Zevi's conversion to Islam—the Ottoman authorities were loath to execute him at any rate lest he become a martyr[602]—demoralized and divided the Jewish community. Zeitlin offers this bleak assessment in the aftermath of the messianic fervor aroused by Shabbetai and his followers.

> The messianic movement did not collapse entirely because of the conversion of Shabbetai Zevi to Islam. True, many Jews became despondent and lost their worldly possessions and were disillusioned in their ideals when they saw how they had been deceived. But the adventurer Nathan "the prophet" continued his propaganda tinctured with mysticism. Many of those who had been followers of Shabbetai Zevi accepted Islam and became known as Dönme,[603] a Judeo-Muslim sect.
>
> Those Jews who opposed Shabbetai Zevi before his conversion either were passive or were afraid of being persecuted, but some like Rabbi Jacob Sasportas and Rabbi Jacob Cagiz who did not accept Shabbetai Zevi as the messiah and fought against the movement were persecuted. After the conversion those who were suspected of being adherents of the messianic movement were condemned. Those who were persecuted previously for their disbelief in Shabbetai Zevi now became the persecutors. Some rabbis adopted the role of inquisitors; anyone who did not conform to their point of view was branded a heretic, a follower of the Shabbetai movement, and was persecuted. A reign of suspicion prevailed among the Jewish people who were divided into hostile groups, issuing anathemas against each other.
>
> The rabbis had been greatly venerated during the Middle Ages and the Jews always considered them their spiritual leaders; now the rabbis of the seventeenth century failed them; they did not lead them during this "messianic" movement. They followed the masses. Either through fear or lack of courage they failed to fight this movement as being dangerous and deceptive. Thus the Jews lost their faith in the rabbis and spiritual leaders. The consequences of this movement . . . were tragic in every respect. The price the Jewish people paid for mysticism was tragic.[604]

Perlmann summarized the legacy of the Dönme, the Judeo-Islamic converts, as follows:

> On the whole the Muslims were indifferent to the sect's existence, but from time to time there was a spurt of inquiry, or persecution (e.g., in 1720, 1859, and 1875). Imputing Dönme origin to undesirables is not unknown.[605]

Accounts from European travelers to Ottoman Turkey throughout the eighteenth and nineteenth centuries are quite uniform in their depiction of the prevailing negative Muslim attitudes toward Jews. The objects of hatred and debasement, Jews reacted with servile pusillanimity. Despite the financial success of a small elite (an observation that dates back to the Jews first integration into the Ottoman Empire),[606] the majority of Ottoman Jews lived in penury and attendant squalor.[607] Carsten Niebuhr (1733–1815), the German traveler who reached Constantinople (Istanbul) in February 1767, observed that Turkish Jews were routinely insulted by the local Muslims, who addressed them as

> *Tschefied* ["dirty Jew," colloquially] which is still more opprobrious than *Dsjaur* [giaour; "infidel"].[608]

Charles McFarlane, who visited Istanbul in 1828, wrote that the Jews were "the last and most degraded of the Turkish Rayahs [minorities]."[609] McFarlane contrasted the resulting obsequious attitudes of the Jews in Turkey with those of their European British co-religionists:

> Throughout the Ottoman domains, their pusillanimity is so excessive, that they will flee before the uplifted hand of a child. Yet in England the Jews become bold and expert pugilists, and are as ready to resent an insult as any other of His Majesty's liege subjects. A striking proof of the effects of oppression in one country, and of liberty, and of the protection of equal laws, in the other.[610]

A confirmatory description was provided by Julia Pardhoe in her 1836 eyewitness account of conditions for Istanbul's Jews:

> I never saw the curse denounced against the children of Israel more fully brought to bear than in the East; where it may truly be said that "their hand is against every man, and every man's hand against them."—Where they are considered rather as a link between animals and human beings, then as men possessed of the same attributes, warmed by the same sun, chilled by the same breeze, subject to the same feelings, and impulses, and joys, and sorrows, as their fellow-mortals.
>
> There is a subdued and spiritless expression about the Eastern Jew, of which the comparatively tolerant European can picture to himself no possible idea until he has looked upon it. . . . *It is impossible to express the contemptuous hatred in which the Osmanlis [Ottoman Turks] hold the Jewish people*; and the veriest urchin who may encounter one of the fallen nation on his path, has his meed of insult

to add to the degradation of the outcast and wandering race of Israel. Nor dare the oppressed party revenge himself upon this puny enemy, whom his very name suffices to raise up against him.

I remember, on the occasion of the great festival at Kahaitchana (Kâthane), seeing a Turkish boy of perhaps ten years of age, approach a group of Jewesses, and deliberately fixing upon one whose delicate state of health should have been her protection from insult, gave her so violent a blow as to deprive her of consciousness, and level her to the earth. As I sprang forward to the assistance of this unfortunate, I was held back by a Turk of my acquaintance, a man of rank, and I had hitherto believed, divested of such painful prejudices; who bade me not agitate, or trouble myself on the occasion, as the woman *was only a Jewess!* And of the numbers of Turkish females who stood looking on, not one raised a hand to assist the wretched victim of gratuitous barbarity.[611]

Two decades later (in 1856), the Turcophilic Italian traveler Ubicini, echoing the observation seventy years earlier of Niebuhr[612] that the Ottoman Muslims "despise the Jews, and freely apply to them the epithet *tchîffut* (*çıfıt*; mean, avaricious; colloquially, "dirty Jew"),[613] also recorded these poignant characterizations of the Ottoman Jews plight, which emphasized their resigned degradation (tinged with patient faith in their deliverance) and extreme poverty.[614]

Patient, industrious, and resigned to their fate, they wore without apparent sense of humiliation the colored *beneesh* [*jehoudane*; a cloak with open sleeves] *which the ancient sumptuary* [denoting restrictions, in this case, regarding dress] *laws of the empire enjoined as a mark to distinguish them from the Mussulman*, and took as much pains to withdraw from notice as the Greeks to put themselves forward. United by an indissoluble bond of common faith and common interest, which gathers strength from their *isolation* and *the contempt with which they are regarded*, whilst they appear to be occupied only with their commerce and indifferent to all beyond, secretly cherish the hope of one day regaining possession of Jerusalem, and therefore with patient assiduity continue the uninterrupted series of their annals up to the day marked as the end of the great captivity. This indeed is the central point of their union; this is rather their faith than their hope; and for this reason Jews are seldom found engaged in the cultivation of soil, which for them is always the "land of the stranger, and house of bondage." Here they may have been born—here perhaps they may die: but still they may be called upon to depart at a moment's warning, and, holding themselves, therefore, in readiness for the long

expected signal, they await its arrival with that patient and submissive faith from which oppressed races derive their strength and consolation.

Rarely do we see the Jews of Turkey in any elevated position, or following any of the liberal professions; and such of the nation as are distinguished by their wealth as merchants, or their skill as medical practitioners,[615] or whose science and talents shed luster on their community. Will generally be found to belong to the colonies of European Jews already mentioned. Thus, as we perceive, the Jews are the poorest of all the subjects of the Porte. To form any idea of their poverty it is only necessary to ride, on any day of the week, through the quarter of Balata, where the Jews of the capital chiefly dwell. Few more filthy places can be found; the observer is afflicted by an appearance of misery, resulting not from design, as in the neighboring quarter of the Fanar, but from real poverty: whilst in the street his path is constantly crossed by men in ragged garments, with haggard countenances, wearing an anxious expression. The half-opened windows of the low, damp houses reveal glimpses of women of small stature, thin, wan-looking, and of a livid paleness, wearing no veil, but a coarse linen cloth round the head; and surrounded by a swarm of meager, dropsical, rickety children, the whole forming a sad and depressing spectacle. . . . , Poverty in turn engenders uncleanly habits . . . and the effect is a proportionate mortality. Thus, when the cholera was raging in Constantinople in 1848, the deaths from October to the end of December were 16 percent among the Jews; whilst among the Greeks the ratio was only 7½; among the Armenians 4½; and among the Mussulmans scarcely 4 [percent].

Reports from the Alliance Israélite Universel d[616] during the late nineteenth and early twentieth century reiterate the findings of Ubicini (above) from the mid-nineteenth century. Descriptions of the Jewish communities make repeated references to their "poverty, misery, and distress."[617] Although Istanbul—a city of nearly 1 million in 1900, including a Jewish community of some 50,000—included a small affluent elite of Jews inhabiting comfortable quarters, their living conditions were clearly exceptional:

[T]he two most characteristic Jewish suburbs of the Ottoman capital, Haskoy and Balat, looked like a network of half-ruined hovels and their misery was more hideous than anywhere else. Balat, whose narrow alleys sheltered some ten thousand Jews, had even the dubious distinction of being one of the foulest smelling localities of the Golden Horn [an estuary which divides Istanbul].

[I]t sufficed to wander through a Jewish quarter to be aware of the extent of extreme destitution of its inhabitants. Dark and tortuous alleys, dilapidated houses, cramped and unsanitary living quarters, such was at the end of the nineteenth century the characteristic aspect of most of the [Jewish] ghettoes of Turkey. In certain Anatolian towns, in Izmir [Smyrna] and Aydin for instance, an important part of the Jewish population lived in *cortijos*, vast enclosed yards where dozens of families were herded together. Sometimes these families, each confined to a single small room, comprised ten to fifteen members. . . . For example, one of the numerous rabbis of the city of Aydin lived with his wife, their children, and the family of his married son in a slum of three-by-four meters, with a single room, at once bedroom, kitchen and washroom. . . . The situation was very similar in the *cortijos* of Izmir. And when each Friday the Muslim landlord came with his suitcase to collect the rent, numerous lodgers could but sob and implore for a delay in payment of the debt.

Jewish ghettoes meant misery, but also overpopulation. In the correspondence of the [Alliance] schoolmasters, poverty and proliferation of the species appear practically always together, closely related to each other. It would seem that families of eight, ten, or even fifteen people living under the same roof, were not exceptional, especially in smaller towns, such Silivri [in Thrace], Aydin, or Tire.[618]

Such abject poverty and concomitant malnutrition and overcrowding made the Jewish communities especially vulnerable (as also described earlier by Ubicini) to the epidemics of the era: cholera, smallpox, diptheria, typhoid, and puerperal ("childbed") fever (a postpartum septicemia):

In large cities, such as Izmir or Istanbul, such epidemics were more frequent and more deadly than elsewhere. The "suspect illness" that broke out in Izmir in 1893—the word cholera was carefully avoided—was doomed to remain in the memory of local Jews, like the great plague of 1865, as one of the most terrible calamities that ever struck their community. Neither were small localities immune from danger. The cholera epidemic which broke out in Bursa in 1894 was, it would seem, just as deadly as that of Izmir. In this same city, in November 1900, four to five children died of smallpox every day in the Jewish community.[619]

Not surprisingly, in order to escape these conditions, at the onset of the twentieth century Turkish Jews began emigrating to North and South American, European, and African cities.[620] Thus, according to the *American Jewish Yearbook*,[621] almost eight thousand Jews emigrated from Turkey to the United States between 1899 and 1912.

The Alliance reports further indicate that Jews living in rural eastern Anatolia suffered severely throughout this period due primarily to Muslim Kurdish depredations:

In Diyarbarkir, Urfa, Siverek, Mardin, and several other cities of this region, Kurds continuously attacked Jewish communities, forcing them to pay taxes and contributions in addition to those already exacted by the Turkish authorities. The slightest tendency to resist was immediately suppressed with blood. Jews were crushed with scorn and had to accept all sorts of humiliations. Thus, for instance, when rains were delayed in spring or late in autumn, Kurds went to Jewish graveyards, dug up newly buried corpses, cut off the heads and threw them in the river to appease Heaven's wrath and bring on rain. In spite of the complaints of Jews to Turkish authorities, the perpetrators of such misdeeds remained, as was to be expected, undiscovered.

Toward the end of the nineteenth century, the insecurity of the Kurd[ish] country was so great that Jewish peddlers could no longer venture outside the cities. The communities of the vilayet [province] of Diyarbarkir fell into misery and diminished year after year. Thus, whilst in 1874 the town of Siverek situated on the Urfa road counted about fifty Jewish families, three decades later Joseph Niego, entrusted with a mission in Asia Minor by the Jewish Colonization Association, found only twenty-six households, totaling about 100 persons. Similarly, the 500 Jews who, according to Vital Cuinet, constituted the community of Mardin toward the end of the nineteenth century, were all gone by 1906. At that time, there remained in this town only one Jew, who had the task of guarding the synagogue.[622]

Jews in Modern (Republican) Turkey

Kemal Atatürk (1881–1938) forged the modern Turkish nation and its political institutions in the disastrous aftermath of World War I and the collapse of the Ottoman Empire. Endeavoring to realize his vision of a modern secular state and its new Turkish citizenry, Atatürk

closed religious schools, undermined the dervish orders, Latinized the alphabet to isolate Turks from their rich Ottoman heritage, and invented a new history and "new" language for the new Turkish citizen. Alongside the hat law (outlawing the fez and compelling the wearing of Western hats), legislation stipulated the Turkification of names, spoken language, and education of the ostensibly new citizen.[623]

But the "Turkification" process—an enforced homogeneity—helped render Turkey incapable of upholding one of the cardinal provisions of the 1923 Treaty of Lausanne. This treaty reestablished Turkish sovereignty over almost all the territory comprising the contemporary Turkish Republic and abolished the so-called capitulations, which allowed European powers to intervene on behalf of non-Muslim (almost exclusively Christian) religious minorities in the former Ottoman Empire.[624] In return, Turkey was required to guarantee minority (and overall citizens') rights consistent with modern, progressive standards.[625]

Turkification combined European models of state and nationalism, Ziya Gökalp's theories of inherent racial-cultural qualities,[626] and other components into a rather bizarre amalgam of Turcocentric historical and linguistic doctrines. Vryonis provides this apt characterization:

> The *Türk Tarih Tezi* [Turkish Historical Thesis] thus appropriated the creation of all civilizations (it was taken by other Turkish scholars, in their application, as far as Africa, western Europe, North and South America), for the civilizational genius of the Turks. The key to the whole theory is twofold: the assumption that all brachycephalic or alpine types were and are Turks, and that only brachycephalic types had/have the genius for creation of civilizations. The grotesqueness of the theory is amazing to historian and scholar. Nevertheless, we must remember that it was pretty much a state doctrine for the period of the 1930s when Atatürk was, in effect, the state. Second, it was disseminated through the Turkish educational institutions that were inculcating literacy in a population for the first time on a mass scale, and among which the overwhelming preponderance was illiterate. . . . *Thus cultural and political creativity are inherent in the Turkish genius alone. This is a Turkification of de Gobineau's theory of the racial, and therefore civilizational, superiority of the Aryans. . . . The doctrine is an almost pure form of racism.*

> The *Güneş Dil Teorisi* [the Sun Theory of Language] . . . emphasized the antiquity of the Turkish language and made the bold assertion that it was the source for other languages. . . . This theory made [Turkish the origin] of such other languages as Sumerian, Hittite, Arabic, Persian, Latin, and French, Turkish languages. The *Güneş Dil Teorisi* had a double aspect: linguistic and historical, and the linguistic would have been meaningless to Atatürk and his collaborators without the historical dimension. They were not interested primarily in the linguistic merits of the theory, whatever it might be argued they were, but in what they felt were the historical implications for the Turkish people. Thus, the *Güneş Dil Teorisi* must be understood with the *Türk Tarih Tezi*.[627]

Apologetic rationalizations for these doctrines have even appeared in the West. For example, Bernard Lewis justified such racially based distortions of Turkish and world history on two grounds: the need to develop a national Turkish identity to combat Pan-Turanism, a popular Turcocentric imperialistic movement[628] that sought the creation of a new empire uniting Turkish and Tatar peoples from the Aegean Sea to the Far East; and, to bolster the spirits of the Turks, whose image had been tarnished so scandalously (according to Lewis) in Western (European) writings. Lewis went so far as to draw a moral equivalence between the negative portrayal of Jews and Turks in Western literature, ignoring the rather profound difference between demonizing a small, powerless minority (i.e., Jews) on purely theological and racial grounds, and expressing fear and loathing of the denizens of a large, invading foreign civilization whose self-proclaimed holy warriors (*ghazi*s) had brutally conquered, enslaved, colonized, and ruled the Balkans and much of Eastern Europe, for half a millennium:

> It would be a grave error to deride all this as the whim of an autocrat. Atatürk was too great a man to organize an elaborate campaign of this sort out of mere caprice, or out of simple desire for national self-glorification. One of the reasons for the campaign was the need to provide some comfort for Turkish national self-respect, which had been sadly undermined during the last century or two. First, there was the demoralizing effect of a long period of almost uninterrupted defeat and withdrawal by the Imperial Ottoman forces. Then there was the inevitable reaction to Western prejudice. It is difficult not to sympathize with the frustration of the young Turk, eager for enlightenment, who applied himself to the study of Western languages, to find that in most of them his name is an insult. In the English dictionary the Turk shares with the Jew (and the Welshman) the distinction of having given his name to a term of abuse.[629]

The legacy of Ottoman *dhimmitude*—including the convulsive jihad violence directed at non-Muslim minorities during the final Young Turk regime—was ingrained in the bigoted ideology of Kemalist nationalism. David Brown describes how these attitudes negated the principles embodied by the minority protection clauses in the Lausanne Treaty:

> During the Lausanne Peace negotiations (1922–23), the Turkish delegation had wholeheartedly subscribed to the freedom of non-Muslims in Turkey to maintain their distinct religions and cultures. These rights were enshrined in the minority clauses of the Treaty of Lausanne (articles 37–44). The principle of religious and ethnic toleration, however, went counter to the drive for Turkification and secularization so eagerly pursued by the Governments of Kemal Atatürk and later on by his successor Ismet Inönü. The urge of Turkish nationalism and the cultural and institutional metamorphosis of the Turkish majority

left little room for the religious, ethnic, and linguistic self-assertion of the non-Muslims in Turkey. This was also partly the outcome of Ottoman/Kemalist ideology which drew a clear line between Muslim Turks and the non-Muslim minorities.[630]

Thus on October 19, 1923, less than three months after the signing of the Lausanne Treaty (July 24, 1923), Fevzi Bey, the Turkish minister of public works, declared during a press conference,

> According to the arrangements concluded with the foreign companies, the latter must engage Turkish employees only. This does not mean that they can employ all subjects of the Grand National Assembly of Turkey indiscriminately. They must employ Muslim Turks only. If the foreign companies do not shortly dismiss their Greek, Armenian, and Jewish servants, I shall be compelled to cancel the privileges under which they are authorized to function in Turkey. This decision is irrevocable.[630a]

But that decision clearly contradicted article 39 of the Lausanne Treaty, which guaranteed equal treatment and opportunities for non-Muslim minorities. Neville Henderson, who served as a British high commissioner in Istanbul, noted in an October 23, 1923, memorandum,

> [T]he persistent unofficial pressure brought to bear on foreign companies and institutions to employ Muslims at the expense of non-Muslim Turkish nationals is in flagrant contradiction with the minority clauses of the Lausanne Treaty.[631]

Formal anti-Greek legislation passed by the Turkish parliament beginning in 1932 (law #2007), and subsequently, observes Vryonis,

> barred entry to a large number of professions and trades to the so-called *e tablis* "established ones" or "settlers," a euphemism for Greek citizens of Istanbul who were allowed to remain in the city following the treaty of Lausanne in 1923). A series of some thirty-one laws during the period between the two world wars severely crippled and finally paralyzed the community as a result of these efforts to reduce its political, legal, economic, and cultural presence. The laws against the *e talis*, for example, forbade them from some thirty trades, including those of tailor, itinerant merchant, photographer, carpenter, and doorman, as well as from professions of more "elevated" social and economic status such as medicine, law, insurance, and real estate. Some 10,000 Greek *etablis* were thus deprived of their livelihoods and forced to abandon their homes and businesses in Istanbul and emigrate, penniless, to Greece (at the expense of the Greek state).[632]

During the summer of 1934 a paroxysm of antisemitic violence took place within this general atmosphere of Turkish Muslim xenophobia. Hatice Bayraktar summarizes the events that ravaged the Jewish community of Eastern Thrace:

> The persecutions, euphemistically referred to as the "Thracian events" (*Trakya Olaylari*), started at the end of June 1934 in the district of Çanakkale, a region in northwestern Asia Minor that also included the Gallipoli peninsula and the Dardanelles [i.e., in the Çanakkale Province on the southern (Asiatic) coast of the Dardanelles (or Hellespont). Çanakkale, is also a town and seaport in Turkey. Çanakkale Province is the second province (the first one is Istanbul) in Turkey that has lands on two different continents (Europe and Asia)]. Menacing letters were received, Jews were physically beaten and their shops were boycotted. The wave of antisemitic attacks rapidly spread northward and, within a couple of days, almost all of Turkish Thrace was in an uproar. In the small town of Kriklareli, located close to the Bulgarian frontier, attacks escalated into a pogrom: during the night of July 3–4, the homes of Jewish inhabitants were raided and their properties looted. Thousands of panic-stricken Jews fled to Istanbul. An official statement spoke of 3,000 refugees, comprising about a quarter of the 13,000 Jews in Eastern Thrace and the adjacent Çanakkale district, though the real number may have been even higher. After a delay of several days the Turkish government finally reacted and issued orders to the local authorities to quell the riots and sent military units to the sites of unrest.[633]

According to Bayraktar, the Turkish inspector general of Thrace, Ibrahim Tali Öngören—known as a prominent "Ittihadist"[634] during World War I who had helped organize terrorist squadrons in eastern Anatolia comprised of "brigands"[635]—played a pivotal role in orchestrating the 1934 pogrom. Tali composed a ninety-page report dated June 16, 1934, based on his extensive tour of Thracian towns and villages between May 6 and June 7 of that year. Bayraktar maintains that Tali's report includes repeated references to the Jewish communities he claims to have encountered, casting them in the most negative light:

> Tali explained that Thracian Jewry ruled over the economy of the province, either directly or indirectly by extorting funds from local landowners by means of loans, credit or partnerships. In the section entitled "The Jewish Problem in Thrace," Tali complained about the huge economic losses caused by corrupt officials acting on behalf of Jews.

> Tali's descriptions are surely exaggerated and,

moreover, conform to the most common antisemitic stereotypes. He did not hesitate to attribute negative behaviors and characteristics to the Jews, such as betrayal, hiding one's real intentions, worshipping gold, being obtrusive, hungry for power, and last but not least, disloyal to Turkey.[636]

Tali also asserted (quoting directly from his report):

In Thrace it is absolutely necessary and of crucial importance for Turkish life, the Turkish economy, Turkish security, the Turkish regime and the revolution to abolish Jewry, which comprises a hidden danger for us and wants to lay the groundwork for communism in our country, in collaboration with labor organizations, in the most radical manner.[637]

Bayraktar proposes that these three major factors contributed to the pogrom:[638] concerns about a possible Italian attack, via Thrace or the Dardanelles, which justified forced evacuation of "non-Turkish elements" from strategically sensitive zones; negative stereotypes of Jews held by Turkish Muslims in Thrace (from both traditional Islamic sources and "folklore");[639] and Tali's own virulent antisemitism. She concludes that Tali may simply have carried out Turkish governmental policy on an accelerated time scale.

There can be no doubt that Tali was determined to root out the local "Jewish problem," and the sooner the better. Since he was the highest-ranking representative of the Turkish government in Thrace, equipped with wide-ranging powers over military and civilian forces and experienced in organizing terrorist bands, one is minded to conclude that he himself initiated the expulsion of Jewish inhabitants. This theory fits well with the circumstances already mentioned, such as the fact that rumors about the government's intention to get rid of the Jews only started circulating in mid-June, after Tali's return to Edirne, and that the police, gendarmes and the military ignored criminal acts perpetrated in front of their eyes throughout the whole province and only intervened when orders to do so arrived from the government in Ankara. . . . It is very likely that Tali, being a leading member of the CHF [Cumhuriyet Halk Firkasi, People's Republican Party], at that time the ruling, and sole, political party in Turkey] himself, used local party functionaries to carry out his plans by applying unofficial pressure. Accordingly, both the Greek ambassador and the German embassy attributed the pogrom to the CHF. Furthermore, the Greek consul in Edirne reported a direct link between the incidents and the local People's House, one of hundreds of similar institutions (*Halk Evleri*) throughout Turkey that were used by the CHF for cultural propaganda.

Given its claims of equality for all Turkish citizens—granted, in any case, by the Turkish constitution—and its willingness to punish severely those responsible for the violence, one cannot help wondering why the Turkish government did not dismiss Tali immediately. Irrespective of his role in the pogrom, how could a man like Tali, after having given written evidence of attitudes that clearly contradicted the official line, be left in a powerful position? Surprisingly—or perhaps not—Tali remained in office at least until the beginning of 1935 when he was replaced by a military officer, General Kazim Dirik. . . . It is not only that Tali was not dismissed but also that the return of the Jewish refugees was not really fully supported by the government that strongly argued for the theory that Tali had actually done no more than what the Turkish government expected of him, namely, the removal of non-Turkish elements, regarded as potentially dangerous, from the regions bordering Turkey's European neighbors and also from the Straits; in other words, from those regions seen to be most sensitive from a strategic point of view.

. . . [I]t must have been decided at some point to use unofficial means to get rid of unwanted non-Muslim elements. In Thrace the majority of these were Jews; hence, the expulsion was almost bound to take on the character of an antisemitic pogrom. Because of his own dislike of Jews, Tali almost certainly would have approved of this plan. Traditional and negative stereotypes of Jews held by Muslim Turks in Thrace may also have been contributing factors. . . . Probably at some point, the process of applying unofficial pressure on the Jews, intended to be a slow one, ran out of control and took the form of widespread antisemitic violence. The Turkish government then felt obliged to deny its actual intentions, and to stop the persecutions accordingly.[639a]

Frank Weber has summarized Turkey's unenviable record of treatment of its small Jewish minority during the years leading up to World War II, following the 1934 pogrom against Thracian Jewry:

Ataturk . . . would not permit the immigration into Turkey of central European Jews whose futures were endangered by the rising tide of Hitler's own antisemitism. In some cases, his government contemplated deporting Jews back to central Europe, even though they had been domiciled in Turkey for years. The Turks never carried out these expulsions, but Inonu, when he came to power, absolutely refused to alter Ataturk's restrictions on Jewish immigration. Even when Chaim Weizmann, the Zionist leader, promised that each Jewish immigrant would bring a capital of three thousand pounds sterling, the new president would not change his mind. Instead, he allowed the Turkish press to circulate wild rumors about the Jews, who were accused, among other things, of selling olive oil adulterated with machine oil to simple Turkish consumers. Inonu cited Hitler's antisemitism in support of his own, and announced that one of the goals of his new government would be the elimination of the Jewish middlemen from the Turkish economy.[640]

Turkey's World War II flirtation with Nazi Germany included the signing of a Turco-German "friendship and non-aggression pact" on June 18, 1941.[641] At about the same time, the Turkish government began conscripting all Christian and Jewish males between the ages of eighteen and forty-five into heavy labor battalions (*amele tabulart*). Alexandris notes the hardships incurred, and fears aroused among the minority communities by those discriminatory mobilizations, which were disbanded for unclear reasons by mid-1942:

[T]hese men were sent to special camps in Anatolia each containing about 5000 men. There, the men were instructed to engage themselves in noncombative capacities such as roadbuilding. The concentration of all non-Muslim males in such camps aroused great apprehension in minority circles in Istanbul. Their fears were intensified when reports of harsh conditions and high mortality rate reputed to have prevailed in the camps reached Istanbul. On December 8, 1941, however, those men between ages 38 and 45 were allowed to return to their homes. The rest spent another six months before they were eventually released. It is reasonable to assume that the whole operation was a device engineered to get the minorities out of the strategically sensitive area of Istanbul and the Straits. There is also some evidence to suggest that the Turkish government suspected a number of non-Muslims, almost all Armenians, to be involved in "fifth column" activities against Turkey.[642]

Bernard Wasserstein recounted the horrible fate of 767 Jewish refugees from Romania escaping the Holocaust aboard the *Struma*—a rotting, seventy-five-year-old yacht whose desperate human cargo was denied refuge by Turkey when the vessel stalled at Istanbul:

It was a rough night in the Black Sea on February 24, 1942. Ten kilometers or so from the shore, a 75 year-old, 240-ton converted yacht, carrying 767 Jewish refugees from Romania, exploded, probably after being hit by a torpedo, fired in error by a Soviet submarine. The vessel sank with the loss of all except one of the passengers. The Struma had

left Constanza [Romania] on December 12, 1941, bound for Palestine. But on arrival at Istanbul three days later, her engine broke down and she was unable to proceed. While engineers tried unsuccessfully to restore the ship to seaworthiness, the Turkish and British governments wrangled about the onward passage of the refugees. The Turks refused to allow them to land unless they had guarantees of admission to some other country. The British refused to grant them certificates to enter Palestine. The failure of the two governments to agree culminated in the boat being towed out to sea and abandoned to the waves. . . . The truth, in this instance was at least as discreditable to the Turks, who were in fact, informed of the British concession [whereby teenage children aboard the ship would, after all, be allowed to enter Palestine], but adamantly refused to allow the children to travel overland across Turkey to Palestine. No ship was available to take them, and in the end they drowned with their families when the Struma foundered . . . the only force used in the episode was that applied by between one and two hundred Turkish policemen who overpowered resistance from the debilitated refugees and supervised the towing of the rotten, still engine-less hulk out beyond territorial waters. They then abandoned the passengers to near-certain death.[643]

Wasserstein's broader discussion of Turkey's wartime policies toward Jews concludes "there is little in the Turkish record to boast about," and suggests the "nadir" was reached with the enactment (November 1942) of the capital tax—a brutally discriminatory levy that targeted Jews, Dönmes, and the Christian minorities (Greeks and Armenians) in Turkey.[644]

The government of Şükrü Saraçoğlu on November 12, 1942, passed legislation (law #4305) known as the *varlik vergisi*, or capital tax.[645] On January 12, 1943, an additional regulation (regulation #21/19288)[646] was passed that decreed forced labor for nonpayment of the *varlik vergisi*. Our fundamental source for the conception and implementation of this discriminatory legislation is the memoir of Faik Ökte,[647] who, serving as Istanbul's *defterdar* (director of finances), became the primary administrator of the capital tax. Ökte's memoir is quite candid about the guiding principle of this legislation—conceived initially as "general directions" from Saraçoğlu and the ruling CHF party (*Cumhuriyet Halk Firkasi*, People's Republican Party)] elites: the taxation was to be applied in an entirely discriminatory and punitive manner against the non-Muslim minorities.

Despite admittedly lacking the data to arrive at accurate assessments, Ökte and his colleagues proceeded based on "rough estimates . . . of taxable wealth."[648] Their most concerted efforts—consistent with the spirit and philosophy of the *varlik vergisi*—were directed at segregating the pool of taxpayers along confessional lines. Thus Ökte's thinking and actions—even more so those of his superiors—reflect the persistent legacy of the system of Ottoman *dhimmitude*, energetically reinforced by a modern nationalistic bias, linked indelibly to its historical past. Excerpts from Ökte's memoir reveal the development of his taxation assessment and collection scheme, which was felt to be too accommodating by the Ankara regime. Ankara's subsequent decision to levy discriminatory taxes on the descendants of the late seventeenth-century Sabbatian Jewish converts to Islam (i.e., the Dönmes)—an action Bernard Lewis characterizes as "the misbegotten offspring of German racialism on Ottoman fanaticism"[649]—elicited Ökte's harshest criticism:

I had asked every single local board for lists of all those liable to wealth tax *stressing that there should be separate lists for the Muslim Turks and the non-Muslim Greeks, Armenians, and Jews* [emphasis added]. . . . The assessment was especially careful to separate the Turkish from the Greek, Armenian, and Jewish taxpayers.

While the finance inspectors were busy classifying the tax lists forwarded by the local assessment boards, [Şevket] Adalan [Ökte's colleague] and I searched for a formula to tax those who had hitherto been liable to profits tax and who constituted 80% of the entire taxable population. We finally agreed to divide them into two categories—the Muslim Turks and the non-Muslim Greeks, Armenians, and Jews. Relying on Article 34 of the Profits Tax Law No. 2395, *we managed, while remaining within the letter of the law, to impose a token tax on Muslims and [to] tax minorities at a rate two or three times over that of their Turkish co-citizens* [emphasis added].

But Ankara thought differently. When Şevket Adalan took the tax assessment lists for Istanbul to the capital, the Turkish government, while approving our proposed system of classification (Muslims/non-Muslims) set new tax rates for the Greeks, Armenians, and Jews. *Instead of being two or three times more, as we suggested, non-Muslim taxes were to be five to ten times the amounts levied on Muslim Turks with corresponding estimated wealth* [emphasis added]. . . . What appeared so glaring in the new assessment lists was the difference between the tax rates imposed on Muslim Turks on the one hand and the Greek, Armenian, and Jewish minorities on the other. But the greatest surprise that Adalan brought from Ankara was the order to include private salary earners and peddlers in the Capital Tax. Both my colleagues and I [had] envisaged the Varlik tax as a tax on capital. . . . Such a tax could not have been collected from salary earners who were themselves victims of the inflationary conditions and had already witnessed a dramatic drop in their standard of living. *According to instructions from Ankara, we had the power to exempt sections of the salary-earning group from the tax. As a result Adalan and I agreed to exempt all the Muslim Turkish salary earners and concentrate solely on the non-Muslims. Our suggestion met with the approval of Ankara* [emphasis added].

. . . [O]n the verbal instructions of Ankara, a new class of taxpayers, the Dönme class (D) (of Jewish converts to Islam) was instituted, which was taxed at rates double those for Muslims (M). After a thorough examination of the available data some Dönme Turks were taken out of the lists and placed in the class of extraordinary taxpayers. At a stroke our system began to be permeated by Hitler's hysterical racist attitudes.[650]

The manner of taxing the Dönmes, and also the foreign residents, further emphasizes the anti-Jewish and anti-Greek animus of the *varlik vergisi*.[651] Discriminatory taxation of foreign residents based upon their religious affiliation was barred by preexisting legislation. Moreover, consulates and embassies could intervene (albeit with limited success) on behalf of their citizens. These consular interventions were precluded for non-Turkish Jews and Greeks, who were subjected to the full range of discriminatory taxes, especially as Greece was then under Axis occupation.[652] Indeed, the *varlik vergisi* was met with "expressions of fatherly approval" from Nazi Germany.[653] Alexandris highlights the influence of Nazi racist ideology on a Turkish regime desirous of "currying favor" with Germany:

The influence of racist ideology in Ankara may be illustrated by the imposition of discriminatory taxes on the Dönme Turks. Faik Ökte reveals that past family records were investigated in order to determine which Turks were of Jewish origin. Encouraged by the government's attitude a bitter anti-Dönme campaign was inaugurated in the large urban centers. *These Muslims of Oriental Jewish origin were bitterly denounced in the press for "being worse than Jews, because they pretended to be Turks and wanted to have the best of both worlds"* [emphasis added]. This campaign presented a radical break with past Turkish attitudes. While playing a prominent part in the Young Turk revolution, the Dönme Turks continued to be active in the Kemalist movement. The American educated journalist Ahmet Emin Yalman, a Dönme Turk, was a leading Turkish publicist. So was the author of Le Kemalisme, Tekin Alp (Moise Cohen). Apart from their contribution in the intellectual and professional spheres of Turkish life, the Dönme Turks also distinguished themselves in commerce, filling the vacuum created by the departure of Greek and

Armenian businessmen in 1922–23. Again the official inclusion of Jews from the Axis countries in the non-Muslim category indicated Turkish desire to curry favor with the Germans by following antisemitic policies. In turn the Nazis wholeheartedly approved of the varlik episode.[654]

Financial analyses by Edward Clark[655] and Alexandris[656] demonstrate the grossly discriminatory financial impact of the *varlik vergisi* collections on the non-Muslim minorities. Alexandris summarizes the findings:

[T]he non-Muslim element was assessed at 233,000,000 TL [Turkish lira] (or nearly 52 per cent) while the Muslim share was 122,500,000 (or 29 per cent) and that of the foreigners 79,500,000 (or 19 per cent). The extent that the Turkish government expected the minorities to contribute to the varlik is better illustrated when Turkish population statistics are considered. From a total population of 16,188,767 in 1935, the non-Muslim population of Turkey did not exceed 300,000 persons. Beside Ökte's account, reports from the British Embassy in Turkey provide further conclusive evidence of the harsh and often prohibitive rates of taxation imposed on the minorities. Thus, a survey by British businessmen of some 100 of the largest profit-making enterprises in Istanbul showed that in the case of the Armenian firms the assessments were 232 per cent of the capital, of the Jewish 184 per cent, of the Greek 159 per cent and of the Muslim Turkish 4.9 per cent.[657]

An editorial in the *New York Times* dated September 17, 1943, based upon reports by C. L. Sulzberger from Turkey, quoted nearly identical confiscatory taxation ratios: Greek Orthodox at 156 percent of annual income, 179 percent for Jews, and 232 percent for Armenians—compared to 4.96 percent of annual income for Muslim Turks.[658]

Moreover, the four to five thousand non-Muslims deported to the camps at Aşkale for "defaulting" on this punitive taxation scheme experienced harassment (especially during transport); cramped, filthy living conditions; poor nutrition; and limited access to medical care, as characterized by Alexandris:

[T]here is conclusive evidence to suggest that the *varlik vergisi* victims suffered considerable harassment particularly during their transportation to the internment camps. After visiting an internment camp in the middle of February 1943, the British Colonel Binns described the treatment which was meted out to defaulting taxpayers.

"This morning I visited the barn at Demikarpi where some forty merchants, lawyers, and others have been imprisoned for the last ten days and are being dispatched this evening to Aşkale to join the 32 already there. The room in which they are imprisoned is some fifteen yards in length by eight yards in width. . . . There was not a stick of furniture of any kind with the exception of one stove. The room was full of weeping men, women, and children who had come to say goodbye and to bring deportees odd parcels of food and clothing. A most depressing and wretched picture."

The original upper age-limit of 55 was not respected as fourteen out of the thirty-two deportees sent to Aşkale January 27, 1943 were over the age of 55. Nor were the sick and ailing spared. Amongst those defaulting taxpayers dispatched to the internment camp there was a 70 year old partly paralyzed Jew, Shaban, while another, Behar, aged 65, was handicapped. According to a Greek report, dated May 19, 1943 and based on information smuggled out periodically by the internees, the level of nutrition and cleanliness in the camp was extremely low, while medical assistance was very difficult to obtain and had to be paid for. Conditions in these camps, it was maintained in the report, were responsible for several deaths among the deportees. Thus, a Jewish businessman named Romano died on March 28, after a short illness suffered lying on some straw in a stable at Aşkale. On May 1, Basil Konstantinidis, a Constantinopolitan Greek died at Erzurum from a heart attack after his return from compulsory labor. He, the account concluded, was refused any medical attention. Overall, the human casualties of this sad affair were twenty-one, of which eleven were Greeks. Reflecting on the hardships caused by the varlik affair, Sir Knatchbull-Hugessen asserted that "the treatment and handling of the deportees has been characterized by roughness and inconsiderateness." He then went on to conclude that

". . . there is unfortunately every reason to believe that the conditions under which these unfortunate people have to pass their days and nights are unworthy of a modern civilized country."[659]

Vryonis sees the *varlik vergisi* as a predictable successor to the 1941 labor battalion corvées for minorities, and stresses the harsh, lasting consequences of this discriminatory legislation:

[T]he *varlik vergesi* succeeded the discriminatory legal regime of labor battalions and once more placed the minorities under dire threat of imposed, harsh labor, this time in an even less fortunate geographical and climactic region—Aşkale, in north-eastern Turkey, known as the *Turkish Siberia*—but added to this punishment a destructive financial component.

Ökte not only administered the property evaluation required by the new law, but (despite his feeble claims to the contrary) also enforced the resulting taxation and sanctions with a savage ferocity that sent off thousands to the snowbound camps of Aşkale for default. He further exempted lower-income Muslims from paying their assessments in contrast to his actions regarding their very numerous minority co-citizens, who were shipped off to camps under stringent conditions.

The *varlik vergesi's* levies were to be paid within fifteen days of the law's promulgation, with a grace period of another fifteen days (to be paid off with interest). Those who defaulted were to be sent to Aşkale's camps, where they were to labor for two liras a day (one lira to be applied to the tax debt), with responsibility for their own food, clothing, and medical care (to the degree that it was available). It has been estimated that, at this rate of compensation, many defaulters would have had to work for 250 years to pay off the exorbitant taxes levied. Furthermore, defaulters' property, as well as that of all ascending and descending, was then to be sold off at public auction as necessary to pay off the tax liability. In other words, according to Ökte's memoirs, despite being sent to a labor camp—and thus ostensibly beginning the process of paying off one's "debt"—one still lost one's property (in addition to one's freedom). Servitude was therefore, not a compensation for default but an *additional*, and particularly egregious, punishment. There was to be no appeal against assessments of property value or tax payments. If a defaulter was serving in the Turkish armed forces, he was to finish his military service and then be dispatched to a labor camp.

The recent book by Turkish journalist Ridvan Akar, *Varlik Vergisi Kanunu* [1992], raises the figures of those sent off to the camps to some 4,000–5,000, and places them in the tax bracket of TL 40,000. He attributes the primary motivations for the varlik vergisi to both the Turkish state's desire to destroy the non-Muslim minorities and the influence of Nazi antisemitism.

Lira for lira, the inequity of the law was monstrous and had as its goal the economic and social destruction of Turkey's minorities and their communities.[660]

Writing just prior to World War II (November 1938), D. E. Webster, an unabashed enthusiast for Kemalism, acknowledged some of the more mundane failures of Atatürk's regime to accord "equal and civil rights" to non-Muslim minorities:

Only Muslim Turkish girls are accepted for training in the Red Crescent Nursing School, and only Muslim Turks achieve any standing in the army. Although Christian and Jewish citizens must perform the same service as others, they are assigned to menial tasks. Even young men of the greatest ability fail to pass the examinations for advancement into the officers training school if they be not of the [Islamic] Faith.[661]

This chronic background discrimination was compounded during the World War II years by bitter experiences for the minorities—scapegoating escalated to frank persecution: their conscription in corvées, and then punitive, ruinous taxation leading to their expropriation and deportation to "Turkish Siberia." A memorandum from March 1946 composed by the Jewish Agency for Palestine offered the following somber assessment of Turkey's Jews in the aftermath of World War II, and predicted significant numbers of the community would emigrate given the opportunity:

The Jews—like other minorities—have no share in political life. They are not admitted into the People's [Republican] Party [CHF], which was till the end of 1945 the only party in Turkey. There is hardly a Jew in the civil service or in the numerous economic institutions established by the State (banks, industial enterprises, etc.). When, for example, several years ago the Government acquired the electric corporation of Istanbul from its Belgian owners, it dismissed all Jewish employees with the exception of one or two indispensable experts.

As a result of the operation of the present regime, Jewish communal life is almost completely stifled. The local Jewish communities are allowed to deal only with religious and welfare matters, and administer the few Jewish schools and hospitals left, under the strict supervision of the State. Zionism has been outlawed, not because of any specific opposition to it, but as a result of the all-around ban on independent political activity and on any form of association involving international affiliations. In the latter respect, the Zionist movement has shared the fate of Freemasonry.

In response to current international developments, a tendency towards some measure of democracy set in in recent months. It has found expression in the extension of freedom of the press, the establishment of an "opposition party," and other measures. In this connection, for the first time in the history of the Turkish Republic, two young Jews were admitted to the military (*Harhiye*), while several Jewish clerks were engaged by the State banks. *Undue importance should not be attached to these innovations* [emphasis added]. In January, 1946, a

British newspaper published in Egypt summed up the plight of the minorities in Turkey as follows: "Reports by Greeks, Armenians, and Jews all agree in one respect. These minorities prefer emigration to economic ruin or social humiliation as outcasts" ["The Minority Policy in Turkey," *Egyptian Gazette*, Cairo, January 4, 1946]. Indeed it is hardly surprising that during the war demand for immigration permits from Turkey grew steadily and that the Jewish youth of the country, of whom many are already in Palestine, is imbued with a strong Zionist feeling and determination to settle in Palestine.[662]

Ensuing demographic data confirmed the prediction of this March 1946 memorandum: from 1948 to 1950, almost thirty-one thousand of Turkey's roughly seventy-seven thousand Jews—40 percent—emigrated to the newly created State of Israel. Turkey's Jewish population continued to decline in the 1950s, particularly after the 1955 Istanbul pogrom (discussed below), reaching approximately thirty-two thousand in 1964.[663] At present, it is believed only twenty thousand Jews remain in Turkey.[664]

Already by 1952, Bernard Lewis warned, presciently, about the open reemergence of Islam in Turkey with the 1950 ascent of Menderes's Demokrat Parti, just twelve years after Atatürk's death:

> [T]he deepest Islamic roots of Turkish life and culture are still alive, and the ultimate identity of Turk and Muslim in Turkey is still unchallenged. The resurgence of Islam after a long interval responds to a profound national need. The occasional outburst of the *tarikas* [Sufi orders], far more than the limited restoration of official Islam, show how powerful are the forces stirring beneath the surface. The path that the revival will take is still not clear. If simple reaction has its way, much of the work of the last century will be undone, and Turkey will slip back into the darkness from which she painfully emerged.[665]

M. Hakun Yavuz, whose alternative view is that of a champion of Turkey's re-Islamization,[666] traces the origins of this process to the "ironic ambivalence" of Kemalism's secular ideologues. The Kemalists' harsh suppression of most public manifestations and all political aspirations of Islam promoted a clandestine Islamic identity, which has also reacquired its traditional politicization:

> Even for the secular intellectuals, there always had been an ironic ambivalence surrounding the Islamic component of Turkish identity. For example, one "author" of secular Turkish nationalism, Ali Haydar, viewed Islam as a *sine qua non* for being a Turk; a

non-Muslim, even one whose mother language was Turkish, could not be a real Turk. He categorically said: *"It is impossible to make non-Muslims sincere Turkish citizens. But at least we can make them respect Turks"* [emphasis added]. Haydar's ideas were not exceptional and indicate that, at a fundamental level, Turkish identity, even during the most doctrinaire Republican period, could not elude religion as an important component of its supposedly secular, national identity. . . . Ironically, despite its fierce hostility to religion, Kemalist secular nationalism never was able to disengage itself or its putative nation from its Islamic heritage.

> By removing Islam from the public domain, the Kemalist revolutionaries were seeking to cut off the populace from their own shared language of imagination. This policy succeeded in large urban centers but failed to transform the majority of the populace in the rural areas of Turkey. . . . By seeking to suppress virtually all manifestations of Islam in what was a deeply religious society, the Kemalist elite actually promoted the politicization of a furtive Islamic identity and ensured a struggle between the secular and Muslim groups' control of the state. . . . Ismet Özel, an ex-Marxist convert and the most prominent Islamist intellectual, argued that it was Atatürk's reforms that, ironically Islamicized Turkey by forcing people to internalize and value their religious identity and not simply take it for granted as in the past.

> In addition to the Sufi orders, textually based communities that evolved from them, such as the Nurcus, also helped to internalize and externalize Islamic political identity by redefining the function of the state. Said Nursi called on believers to shield their inner self from the oppressive "reforms" of the Republic. Mehmet Kirkinci, a prominent Nurcu leader of Erzurum, has referred to this process as an internal *hijra* or migration of Muslims. He argues that "the sun of Islam set down in 1925 and dawned in 1950 with the writings of Said, which enlighten the darkness of Kemalism with its light [nur]."[667]

Returning to the Menderes decade (1950–1960), Vryonis summarizes the practical and less salutary effects of this "reawakening" of Turkish Islam, which the Demokrat Party (DP) exploited,

> not only electorally, but also through support of religious schools and the building of mosques. The dervish orders reappeared, and many of their followers actively supported DP candidates in elections. There was also a noticeable increase at prayers in mosques, with the equally noticeable opposition of secularists. US diplomatic reports from Turkey describe the rising sociopolitical importance of Islam at the time. *In fact, the reports*

of American, British, and Greek diplomats all agreed that the violence of September 6–7 [1955; i.e., the Istanbul pogrom] *was also indicative of religious fanaticism: even some Turkish commentators referred to the fact that the Menderes government had exploited this fanaticism in the course of the violence* [emphasis added]. Patriarch Athênagoras in his sorrowful letter to Menderes, referred to the pogrom as "a persecution of the Church and its Christians."[668]

Vryonis's comprehensive reassessment of the 1955 Istanbul pogrom catalogues in painstaking detail the plight of the Greek Orthodox community, which bore the brunt of the savage, devastating violence, and the further ruinous policies put in place in its aftermath.[669] He also notes that "some 500 Jewish stores were destroyed in the 1955 pogrom, and conditions for Istanbul's Jews . . . [became] oppressive."[670] During the decade following the pogrom, Sephardic Jews were forbidden to speak Ladino [Judeo-Spanish], openly antisemitic Turkish newspapers appeared,[671] and a story published on April 5, 1964, in *Tages Nachtrichten*, the large German-language daily from Tel Aviv, Israel, maintained,

> The Turkish authorities are interfering in all internal affairs of the Jewish community, and even the appointment of a Rabbi must be approved by the Turkish government.[672]

Yavuz traces (and celebrates) the triumphal emergence of both Necmettin Erbakan (in 1996) and more recently Recep Tayyip Erdogan (in 2002)—two Turkish prime ministers he identifies as "Islamist"—to the "spirit of Menderes" (1950–1960), which reactivated Islam as the "lexicon from which coding and legitimation took place."[673] Examining the same period, through the 1980s, Jacob Landau assessed the impact of the Islamists' (whom he defined broadly as "those Muslims involved in politics") return "to the mainstream of political life," on attitudes toward Jews:

> Islamic literature and press in Turkey since 1950 indeed displays a progression of animus towards Jews and even more so towards the State of Israel and its guiding ideology, Zionism. In other words, anti-Jewish motifs are increasingly evident in Turkish Islamist pronouncements appearing in the two decades following 1950. These views assumed an inceasingly strident tone, although it is only since the 1970s that they began to display a growing anti-Zionist and anti-Israeli tenor on political and economic grounds.

> [B]y bolstering their anti-Jewish propaganda with frequent quotations from the Koran and Hadith, and

by incorporating into it anti-Zionist and anti-Israel invective, the Turkish Islamists have turned it into a cardinal part of their ideology and have been fostering a villain image which appeared to increase their popular support.[674]

Landau singles out the National Salvation Party and its founder and chairman, Necmettin Erbakan, as the most significant examples of Islamists exploiting systematized anti-Jewish, anti-Zionist bigotry.[675] Erbakan's ascension to deputy prime minister in January 1974, Landau observes, was marked by Pan-Islamic overtures and

> accompanied by increasing verbal violence against Jews, Zionism, and the State of Israel. Erbakan's attacks . . . may well have added to his popularity, whether in Government or Opposition, among the rank-and-file of his own party, too.

> Erbakan and his followers made no secret of these views and moves, many of which were widely reported in the Turkish press. Particularly revealing are the National Salvation Party's organs, especially its daily *Milli Gazete* (The National Newspaper), published in Isatnbul since Januray 12, 1973. *Milli Gazete* has maintained a relentlessly militant Islamic stance, even after the September 12, 1980 military intervention closed down the National Salvation Party along with all other parties—and severely curtailed the public activity of all former political figures, including Erbakan. . . . Indeed, the almost daily attacks on Jews, Zionism, and the State of Israel, *usually labeled the foes of Islam* [emphasis added], have persisted over a dozen years. Thus, every move of Israel or its representatives, in Turkey or abroad, was widely—and hostilely—commented upon as *harmful to Islam*, or at least *helpful to Islam's enemies* [emphasis added].[676]

Landau concluded in his 1988 analysis that the Islamists represented the "most extreme" strain of antisemitism extant in Turkey, and traditional Islamic motifs (i.e., "frequent quotations from the Koran and Hadith") were central to this hatred:

> *Nurtured by early Islam's animus towards Judaism* [emphasis added], Islamist exponents, more than others in Turkey, integrate their invective against Jews, Zionism, and Israel. Their arguments have been taken up by free-lance spokesmen; then by would-be-scholars who attempted to bolster their conclusions by using spurious source materials; lastly by organized groups with a marked Islamist character, which employ anti-Jewish, anti-Zionist and anti-Israel slogans and arguments in their political speeches and press as a means of promoting their own brand of propaganda. In doing so, Islamist bias in Turkey is increasingly directed

against Jews, Zionism, and Israel, simultaneously—in general without attempting to distinguish between the three targets. This combination has proved particularly effective, propaganda-wise, from the Islamists' point of view. It has exploited the general atmosphere in a state and society whose political leadership initiated a cooling-off of relations with Israel, in the last few years; conversely, Islamist propaganda has encouraged this cooling-off and contributed to it in no little degree, by successfully shaping a villain image in which the Jews, Zionism, and Israel were essential components.[677]

Although Landau's important analysis was published in 1988, it only covered events through the early 1980s.[678] The succeeding decades have witnessed two popularly elected Islamist, according to Yavuz, those "whose political philosophy was based on Islam,"[679] prime ministers: Necmettin Erbakan in 1996 and the current Turkish leader, Erdogan, in 2002. Erbakan's antisemitic views were discussed earlier. In 1974 Recep Tayyip Erdogan, then serving as president of the Istanbul Youth Group of the Islamist National Salvation Party (founded by Erbakan), wrote, directed, and played the leading role in a theatrical play entitled *Maskomya*.[679a] Rifat Bali, a Turkish historian, observes that *Maskomya*,

> or in its correct form Mas-kom-Ya, was a theatrical play that was staged everywhere in the 1970s, as part of the "cultural" activities of MSP [National Salvation Party] Youth Branches. The unabbreviated version of Mas-kom-Ya is Mason-Kommunist-Yahudi [Mason-Communist-Jew]. It is known that the play was built on the "evil" nature of these three concepts, and the hatred toward them.[680]

These same decades of ascendancy for the Islamist parties have been marked by a burgeoning antisemitism in the Turkish media,[681] along with murderous Muslim attacks on the two major Istanbul synagogues, Neve Shalom in 1986[682] and Neve Shalom and Beth Israel in 2003.[683] Another attack on the Neve Shalom synagogue in 1992 caused no casualties due to increased security.[684] While the 1986 attack was perpetrated by the Fatah Revolutionary Council, a Palestinian terrorist organization led by Abu Nidal, the 1992 and 2003 attacks were committed by indigenous Turkish Muslim groups.[685] Moreover, all these acts of terrorism targeting Jews occurred against a backdrop of relentless antisemitic propaganda conflating Jews, Zionism, and Israel—spearheaded by Islamist groups emphasizing traditional Islamic motifs of Jew hatred—a campaign that continues unabated.[686] For example, *Milli Gazete*, the daily produced by Erbakan's National Salvation Party since January 1973 and a major Islamist organ, published articles in February and April of 2005 that were toxic amalgams of ahistorical drivel, and virulently antisemitic and anti-*dhimmi* Qur'anic motifs:

(*February 4, 2005*) The Ottomans saved the Jews from the hands of the Christians, who murdered them along with the Muslims in Endulus [Muslim Spain]. When Russia and Hungary persecuted the Jews, again the Ottomans saved them. The Muslim Turks rescued Jews yet again from the hands of Hitler, who was himself a hidden Jew. . . . From the beginning, the Ottomans showed hospitality, seemingly even allotting the best homes to the Jews—along the Bosphorus, in Istanbul's most luxurious area.

And, characteristic of their savage, treacherous [nature], in return they [the Jews] first overthrew the Sultan Abdul Hamid and destroyed the Ottomans; [then], like insects, they ate away at the Ottoman [Empire]; and as if this were not enough, they stabbed the Muslim Turkish soldiers in Palestine in the back.

Judaism is synonymous with treason. . . . They [the Jews] even betrayed God. . . . When God told them to bow their heads while entering Al-Quds [Jerusalem], they entered with their heads up. The prophets sent to them, such as Zachariah and Isaiah, were murdered by the Jews. . . . In fact no amount of pages or lines would be sufficient to explain the Qur'anic chapters and our Lord Prophet's [Muhammad's] words that tell us of the betrayals of the Jews.

(*April 13, 2005*) Some people in this country are mistaken in how they treat Christians and Jews. Such mistakes are harming not only the perpetrators, but also all the young Muslims of this land, and directly, or indirectly, this country.

Heading the list of these mistakes is the respect and reverence shown to Christians and Jews. . . . It is a mistake to include them in the protocol of meetings, to let them speak, to applaud them, to quote their words in the newspapers. . . . It is not just wrong, it is a frighteningly grave mistake.

It is a mistake for so-called professors, writers, thinkers, and famous intellectuals to make "sympathetic" statements about Christians and Jews. Particularly, to say that "they too will go to heaven" is an even bigger mistake. . . . Christians and Jews, who have rejected our Prophet and refuse to recite "Muhammad is the Messenger of God" belong forever in Hell. . . . In the eyes of God, there is only one religion, and that is Islam. . . . There is only one book, and that is the Qur'an. . . . For so-called "dignitaries" to present Christianity and Judaism as "godly religions" is terribly wrong.[687]

The April 2005 edition of the monthly *Aylik*, produced by a Turkish jihadist organization that claimed responsibility for the November 15, 2003, synagogue bombings in Istanbul, contained eighteen pages of antisemitic material. An article written by Cumali Dalkilic, entitled

"Why Antisemitism?" combined traditional Qur'anic antisemitic motifs with Nazi antisemitism and Holocaust denial. Another article's title repeats the very pejorative Turkish Muslim characterization of Jews, which translates as "filthy Jews" (a pejorative term for Jews whose usage was recorded by Niebuhr in 1794 and Ubicini in 1856, based upon their visits to Ottoman Turkey)[688]— "The Cifit's [The Filthy Jews'] Castle"—and also targets the Dönme:

> *"Why Antisemitism?"* . . . declares the Jews the "enemy" of the Turks, of Islam, and of the entire world. Jews are alleged to have a "disgusting nature" and are defined as "the people eternally cursed by God and His prophets, who are not wanted by anyone and thrown out of every place." The article quotes many pages from *Mein Kampf* and shows admiration for Hitler, calling him "a hero," "a true mind," that grasped the meaning of the Jew and the Jewish problem, "a true statesman to whom no other can stand up." The article, which also includes excerpts from the notorious Protocols of the Elders of Zion, ends with Holocaust denial. . . .
>
> *"The Cifit's [Filthy Jews'] Castle"* attacks the Dönme, claiming that they are not "real Muslims" or real "Turks" but "filthy Jews" under cover, and they are responsible for the present secularism in Turkey, as well as for all the wrongdoings in the world. The article also states that "the only barrier before the filthy Jews is the wall of Islam."[689]

Rifat Bali, a Turkish historian, has noted another manifestation of contemporary antisemitism promulgated largely by Islamists: Israel's so-called Kurdish Card (in fact a book with this title has been sold in Turkey for the past several years), which claims Massoud Barzani, leader of the Kurdish Democratic Party, is Jewish, which in turn allegedly supports the theory that Israel wishes to "create a Jewish state from the Nile to the Euphrates . . . [including] the Kurdish area."[690] And Bali made this passionate indictment of Turkey's tolerance of antisemitism, published soon after the November 2003 synagogue bombings:

> In the recent past, some . . . events led Turks, with the help of the media, to face up to some disturbing realities within their society. The spotlight came on, but soon it went off, and the incidents were all but forgotten, either because the agenda changed, or because the investigations dragged on without conclusion. I fear that, similarly, the repugnant reality of antisemitism, which was always present in Turkey and came undeniably to the fore in the [November 15, 2003] synagogue attacks, will also soon be forgotten. . . .
>
> In the aftermath of the violence suffered in Istanbul on Saturday, November 15, Turkish society had the opportunity to confront face to face the antisemitism which is incorporated in the political Islamic movement. However, the political leaders, the media, the intellectual elite, the Israeli government . . . the Chief Rabbi and the secular leaders in his entourage as the representatives of the Turkish-Jewish community, [all] seemed determined to ignore that opportunity. Everyone apparently shared the view of the conservative and nationalist columnist Taha Akyol, who two days after the attack wrote in *Milliyet* [November 17, 2003], ". . . there has never been antisemitism in Turkey in its racist or religious sense."
>
> . . . In recent years, not only in the Islamic sector, but in virtually all ideological variants, we have seen incessant discussions on the topic of Dönmes, "decoding" the names of individuals and "exposing" them as "Jews." Isn't this behavior a provocation to violence for raging fanatics against innocent persons whose ancestors are "presumed" to be Jewish?
>
> . . . The ones responsible for the November 15, 2003 violence are the government, the society, and the political, intellectual, cultural and media elite that turn a blind eye to these facts, and that do not enforce the relevant clauses of Turkish criminal law against such behavior. They shield themselves behind the argument of "freedom of the press," legitimize and elevate antisemitic writers as "enlightened," and refrain from stressing the antisemitic nature of the November 15 attacks, referring to them only as "terrorism."
>
> . . . Every [Turkish] government since 1950 bears the responsibility for the situation we find ourselves in today. This is because they remained silent with regard to the hateful rhetoric against Jews, and took no steps to make the Jews feel like real Turkish citizens.
>
> . . . Also responsible for this situation are the writers of yesteryears' "religious," today's "Islamist" media, and all "opinion makers" who, since the establishment of the State of Israel, have incessantly and untiringly engaged in a rhetoric of hatred against Jews and continue to poison the minds of the future generations. . . .
>
> Prime Minister Recep Tayyip Erdogan and the AKP government must publicly denounce [both] the antisemitic discourse of political Islam, from which he emerged and which he declared later to have abandoned, and those who insist on perpetuating such discourse. *Turkey's Jews are not dhimmis in need of the tolerance and the protection of the Muslim majority. They are citizens of the Republic of Turkey* [emphasis added].[691]

Interviewed for a November 19, 2003, story in the *Christian Science Monitor*, Bali acknowledged the chronic plight of Turkey's small, dwindling Jewish community (echoing concerns documented six decades earlier),[692] which the bombings transiently illuminated—a largely marginalized society, whose shrinking numbers and "other problems" were deliberately downplayed by community leaders:

> The Turkish Jews have not been fully integrated or Turkified, and they have had to limit their expectations. A kid grows up knowing he is never going to become a government minister, so no one tries, and the same goes for positions in the military.[693]

Rifat Bali's observations on Turkish antisemitism and the predicament of the Jewish community following the November 2003 synagogue bombings fit neatly within the context of overarching historical forces elucidated by Vryonis in 2005:

> Greeks, Armenians, and Jews are the principal non-Muslim minorities that remain in Turkey. Their numbers, however, have diminished drastically because of the historical developments that led to the creation of modern Turkey, and the practices, theories, and mentalities that sought to obliterate ethnic identities, first in the crumbling Ottoman state and then in its modern Turkish successor. The Turkish state's record of behavior toward these now tiny ethnic minorities, located primarily in the region around and in Istanbul, has been one of grudging and limited acceptance, heavily vitiated by acts of state terror and repression, aided and abetted by significant portions of the area's dominant Muslim population. Indeed, extremist segments of the latter remain a constant threat to the minorities, carrying out their own more violent acts against their non-Muslim co-citizens, often with the indifference or even active but unspoken complicity of state authorities.[694]

Bernard Lewis compared the poor conditions for Jews in the nineteenth-century Ottoman Empire with their even worse circumstances in Iran. He wrote,

> Compared to the Jews of Iran, the Jews of the Ottoman Empire were living in paradise.[695]

Lewis's comment provides a fitting segue to the next section on the Jewish experience of *dhimmitude* in Shi'ite Iran.

The Dhimmi Condition for Iranian Jewry under Shi'ite Rule, Sixteenth Century to the Present

At the outset of the sixteenth century, the Iran's Safavid rulers formally established Shi'a Islam as the state religion, while permitting a clerical hierarchy nearly unlim-

ited control and influence over all aspects of public life. The profound influence of the Shi'ite clerical elite continued for almost four centuries (although interrupted, between 1722–1795, by a period of Sunni Afghan invasion and dominance),[697] through the later Qajar period (1795–1925), as characterized by E. G. Browne:

> The Mujtahids and Mulla are a great force in Persia and concern themselves with every department of human activity from the minutest detail of personal purification to the largest issues of politics.[698]

These Shi'ite clerics emphasized the notion of the ritual uncleanliness (*najis*) of Jews in particular, but also Christians, Zoroastrians, and others as the cornerstone of interconfessional relationships toward non-Muslims.[699] The impact of this *najis* conception was already apparent to European visitors to Persia during the reign of the first Safavid shah, Ismail I (1502–1524). The Portuguese traveler Tome Pires observed (between 1512 and 1515) that "Sheikh Ismail . . . never spares the life of any Jew,"[700] while another European travelogue notes, "the great hatred (Ismail I) bears against the Jews."[701] During the reign of Shah Tahmasp I (d. 1576), the British merchant and traveler Anthony Jenkinson (a Christian), when finally granted an audience with the shah,

> was required to wear "basmackes" (a kind of overshoes), because being a giaour [infidel], it was thought he would contaminate the imperial precincts . . . when he was dismissed from the Shah's presence, [Jenkinson stated] "after me followed a man with a basanet of sand, sifting all the way that I had gone within the said palace"—as though covering something unclean.[702]

Two examples of the restrictive codes for Jews conceived and applied during the Safavid period (1502–1725) are presented below,[703] in tables 1 and 2. Their persistent application into the Qajar period, which includes the modern era (1795–1925), is confirmed by the observations of the mid-nineteenth-century traveler Israel Joseph Benjamin in Table 3,[703a] and a listing of the 1892 Hamadan edict conditions in Table 4.[703b]

TABLE 1.
BEHAVIOR CODE OF ABUL HASSAN LARI (1622)

1. Houses that are too high (higher than a Muslim's) must be lowered.
2. Jews may not circulate freely among the Believers.
3. In their stores, Jews must sit on low stools, in order they not see the purchaser's face.
4. Jews must wear a specially constructed hat of eleven colors.
5. Around this hat they must sew a yellow ribbon, three meters long.

6. Women must tie many little bells on their sandals.
7. Jewish women must also wear a black chador.
8. When a Jew speaks to a Muslim, he must humbly lower his head.

TABLE 2.
THE JAM'I ABBASI OF AL-AMILI, INSTITUTED BY SHAH ABBAS I (1588–1629) AND ADMINISTERED IN SOME MEASURE UNTIL 1925

1. Jews are not permitted to dress like Muslims.
2. A Jew must exhibit a yellow or red "badge of dishonor" on his chest.
3. A Jew is not permitted to ride on a horse.
4. When riding on an ass, he must hang both legs on one side.
5. He is not entitled to bear arms.
6. On the street and in the market, he must pass stealthily from a corner or from the side.
7. Jewish women are not permitted to cover their faces.
8. The Jew is restricted from establishing boundaries of private property.
9. A Jew who becomes a Muslim, is forbidden to return to Judaism.
10. Upon disclosure of a disagreement between Jew and Muslim, the Jew's argument has no merit.
11. In Muslim cities, the Jew is forbidden to build a synagogue.
12. A Jew is not entitled to have his house built higher than a Muslim's.

TABLE 3.
LISTING BY ISRAEL JOSEPH BENJAMIN (1818–1864) OF THE "OPPRESSIONS" SUFFERED BY PERSIAN JEWS DURING THE MID-NINETEENTH CENTURY

1. Throughout Persia the Jews are obliged to live in a part of town separated from the other inhabitants; for they are considered as unclean creatures, who bring contamination with their intercourse and presence.
2. They have no right to carry on trade in stuff goods.
3. Even in the streets of their own quarter of the town they are not allowed to keep open any shop. They may only sell there spices and drugs, or carry on the trade of a jeweler, in which they have attained great perfection.
4. Under the pretext of their being unclean, they are treated with the greatest severity, and should they enter a street, inhabited by Mussulmans, they are pelted by the boys and mobbed with stones and dirt.
5. For the same reason they are forbidden to go out when it rains; for it is said the rain would wash dirt off them, which would sully the feet of the Mussulmans.
6. If a Jew is recognized as such in the streets, he is subjected to the greatest of insults. The passers-by spit in his face, and sometimes beat him so unmercifully and is obliged to be carried home.
7. If a Persian kills a Jew, and the family of the deceased can bring forward two Mussulmans as witnesses to the fact, the murderer is punished by a fine of 12 tumauns (600 piastres); but if two such witnesses cannot be produced, the crime remains unpunished, even though it has been publicly committed, and is well known.
8. The flesh of the animals slaughtered according to Hebrew custom, but as Trefe declared, must not be sold to any Mussulmans. The slaughterers are compelled to bury the meat, for even the Christians do not venture to buy it, fearing the mockery and insult of the Persians.
9. If a Jew enters a shop to buy anything, he is forbidden to inspect the goods, but must stand at respectful distance and ask the price. Should his hand incautiously touch the goods, he must take them at any price the seller chooses for them.
10. Sometimes the Persians intrude into the dwellings of the Jews and take possession of whatever pleases them. Should the owner make the least opposition in defense of his property, he incurs the danger of atoning for it with his life.
11. Upon the least dispute between a Jew and a Persian, the former is immediately dragged before the Achund [Muslim cleric] and, if the complainant can bring forward two witnesses, the Jew is condemned to pay a heavy fine. If he is too poor to pay this penalty in money, he must pay it in his person. He is stripped to the waist, bound to a stake, and receives forty blows with a stick. Should the sufferer utter the least cry of pain during this proceeding, the blows already given are not counted, and the punishment is begun afresh.
12. In the same manner, the Jewish children, when they get into a quarrel with those of the Mussulmans, are immediately lead before the Achund, and punished with blows.
13. A Jew who travels in Persia is taxed in every inn and every caravanserai he enters. If he hesitates to satisfy any demands that may happen to be made on him, they fall upon him, and maltreat him until he yields to their terms.
14. If, as already mentioned, a Jew shows himself in the street during the three days of Katel (feast of the mourning for the death of the Persian founder of the religion of Ali) he is sure to be murdered.
15. Daily and hourly new suspicions are raised against the Jews, in order to obtain excuses for fresh extortion; the desire of gain is always the chief incitement to fanaticism.

TABLE 4.
CONDITIONS IMPOSED UPON THE JEWS OF HAMADAN, 1892

1. The Jews are forbidden to leave their houses when it rains or snows [to prevent the impurity of the Jews being transmitted to the Shi'ite Muslims].

2. Jewish women are obliged to expose their faces in public [like prostitutes].
3. They must cover themselves with a two-colored izar [an izar is a big piece of material with which Eastern women are obliged to cover themselves when leaving their houses].
4. The men must not wear fine clothes, the only material being permitted them being a blue cotton fabric.
5. They are forbidden to wear matching shoes.
6. Every Jew is obliged to wear a piece of red cloth on his chest.
7. A Jew must never overtake a Muslim on a public street.
8. He is forbidden to talk loudly to a Muslim.
9. A Jewish creditor of a Muslim must claim his debt in a quavering and respectful manner.
10. If a Muslim insults a Jew, the latter must drop his head and remain silent.
11. A Jew who buys meat must wrap and conceal it carefully from Muslims.
12. It is forbidden to build fine edifices.
13. It is forbidden for him to have a house higher than that of his Muslim neighbor.
14. Neither must he use plaster for whitewashing.
15. The entrance of his house must be low.
16. The Jew cannot put on his coat; he must be satisfied to carry it rolled under his arm.
17. It is forbidden for him to cut his beard, or even to trim it slightly with scissors.
18. It is forbidden for Jews to leave the town or enjoy the fresh air of the countryside.
19. It is forbidden for Jewish doctors to ride on horseback [this right was generally forbidden to all non-Muslims, except doctors].
20. A Jew suspected of drinking spirits must not appear in the street; if he does he should be put to death immediately.
21. Weddings must be celebrated in the greatest secrecy.
22. Jews must not consume good fruit.

A letter dated October, 27, 1892, by S. Somekh of the Alliance Israélite Universelle regarding the Hamadan edict, provides this context:

The latter [i.e., the Jews] have a choice between automatic acceptance, conversion to Islam, or their annihilation. Some who live from hand to mouth have consented to these humiliating and cruel conditions through fear, without offering resistance; thirty of the most prominent members of the community were surprised in the telegraph office, where they had gone to telegraph their grievances to Teheran. They were compelled to embrace the Muslim faith to escape from certain death. But the majority is in hiding and does not dare to venture into the streets.[703c]

The latter part of the reign of Shah Abbas I (1588–1629) was marked by progressively increasing measures of anti-Jewish persecution, from the strict imposition of dress regulations to the confiscation (and destruction) of Hebrew books and writings, culminating in the forced conversion of the Jews of Isfahan, the center of Persian Jewry.[704] Walter Fischel elaborates on the exploits of two renegade Jewish converts to Islam, Abul Hasan Lari (of Lar) and Simon Tob Mumin of Isfahan. Lari was instrumental in having the Shi'ite authorities enforce restrictive headdress and badging regulations as visible signs of discrimination and humiliation. Lari succeeded in having these regulations applied to Jews as confirmed by the accounts of European travelers to Iran. For example, Jean de Thevenot (1633–1667) commented that Jews were required

[t]o wear a little square piece of stuff two or three fingers broad . . . it had to be sewn to their labor gown and it matters not what that piece be of, provided that the color be different from that of the clothes to which it is sewed.[705]

And when the British physician John Fryer visited Lar in 1676, he noted that "the Jews are only recognizable by the upper garment marked with a patch of different color."[706]

However the renegade Abul Hasan Lari's "mission" foreshadowed more severe hardships imposed upon the Jews because of *their image as sorcerers and practitioners of black magic*, which was *"as deeply embedded in the minds of the [Muslim] masses as it had been in medieval Europe"* [emphasis added].[707] The consequences of these bigoted superstitions were predictable:

It was therefore easy to arouse their [the Muslim masses] fears and suspicions at the slightest provocation, and to accuse them [the Jews] of possessing cabalistic Hebrew writings, amulets, talismans, *segulot, goralot*, and *refu'ot*, which they [the Jews] were using against the Islamic authorities. Encouraged by another Jewish renegade, Siman Tob Mumin from Isfahan, who denounced his co-religionists to the authorities, the Grand Vizier was quick in ordering the confiscation of all Hebrew cabalistic writings and having them thrown into the river.[708]

These punitive measures in turn forebode additional persecutions, which culminated in the Jews of Isfahan being forcibly converted to Islam toward the end of Abbas I's rule. Moreover, even when Isfahan's Jews allowed living to return to Judaism under Shah Saf'i, they continued to live under the permanent threat posed by the "law of apostasy," till the late nineteenth century.

One of the most dangerous measures which threatened the very existence of the Jewish community in

Isfahan and elsewhere was the so-called "law of apostasy" promulgated at the end of Abbas I's rule and renewed in the reign of Abbas II. According to this law, any Jew or Christian becoming a Muslim could claim the property of his relatives, however distant. This decree, making the transfer of goods and property a reward for those who became apostates from their former religion, became a great threat to the very survival of the Jews. *While the Christian population in Isfahan protested, through the intervention of the Pope, and the Christian powers in Europe, against the injustice of this edict, there did not arise a defender of the rights of Jews in Persia* [emphasis added]. Although the calamity which this law implied was lessened by the small number of Jewish apostates who made use of this inducement, it was a steady threat to the existence of Jewish community life and brought about untold hardship. It was only in the 19th century that leaders of European Jewry such as Sir Moses Montefiore and Adolph Cremieux took up the fight for their brethren in Persia against this discriminatory law. Apart from this legal discrimination, the Jews of Isfahan were particularly singled out for persecution and forced conversion in the seventeenth century. *It is reported that they were forced to profess Islam publicly; that many of their rabbis were executed, and that only under Shah Safi (1629–1642), the successor of Abbas I, were the Jews of Isfahan, after seven years of Marrano life, permitted to return publicly to their Jewish religion* [emphasis added].[709]

After a relatively brief respite under Shah Saf'i (1629–1642), the severe persecutions wrought by his successor, Shah Abbas II (1642–1666), as Fischel explains, nearly extinguished the Iranian Jewish community outright.[710]

Determined to purify the Persian soil from the "uncleanliness" caused by the presence of non-believers (Jews and Christians in Isfahan) a group of fanatical Shi'ites obtained a decree from the young Shah Abbas II in 1656 which gave the Grand Vizier, I'timad ad-Daula, full power to force the Jews to become Muslims. In consequence, a wave of persecution swept over Isfahan and the other Jewish communities, a tragedy which can only be compared with the persecution of the Jews in Spain in the fifteenth century [more appositely, the thirteenth-century Almohad persecutions].

[T]he important eyewitness Jewish chronicles, the *Kitab i Anusi* . . . describe in great detail how the Jews were compelled to abandon their religion, how they were drawn out of their quarters on Friday evening into the hills around the city and, after torture, 350 Jews are said to have been forced to [con-

vert] to Islam. Their synagogues were closed and the Jews were lead to the Mosque, where they had to proclaim publicly the Muslim confession of faith, after which a Mullah, a Shi'a religious leader, instructed the newly-converted Muslims in the Qur'an and Islamic tradition and practice. These newly-converted Muslims had to break with the Jewish past, to allow their daughters to be married to Muslims, and to have their new Muslim names registered in a special *Divan* [council]. To test publicly their complete break with the Jewish tradition, some were even forced to eat a portion of camel meat boiled in milk. After their forced conversion, they were called New Muslims, Jadid al-Islam. They were then, of course, freed from the payment of the poll tax and from wearing a special headgear or badge.

The resistance of the Jews developed the phenomenon of "Marranos," Anusim, and for years they lived a dual religious life by remaining secretly Jews while confessing Islam officially.[711]

Fischel also refers to the fact that contemporary Christian sources "confirm . . . with an astounding and tragic unanimity" the historical details of the Judaeo-Persian chronicle regarding the plight of the Jews of Isfahan (and Persia, more generally).[712] For example, the Armenian chronicler Arakel of Tabriz included a chapter entitled "History of the Hebrews of the City of Isfahan and of all Hebrews in the Territory of the Kings of Persia—The Case of Their Conversion to Islam." Arakel describes the escalating brutality employed to convert the hapless Jewish population to Islam—deportation, deliberately harsh exposure to the elements, starvation, imprisonment, and beatings. According to his account, the forced conversion of a rabbi marked a turning point in this ugly sequence of events.

[A]fter many words and promises, the Hakham's [rabbi's] sentence was pronounced. "If he does not embrace the Muslim faith, his stomach will be split open and he will be paraded through the town attached to a camel;[713] his property and his family would be consigned to pillage." The sentence given, a camel was brought, on which he was seated, the executioners came and bared his stomach, then they beat him with a naked sword, saying that either he apostasized or his stomach would be split open. Fear of death as well as affection for those close to him having led him to weaken, he was made to pronounce his belief in the Muslim faith, and he was incorporated into the religion of Muhammad, which was cause of untold joy to the [Muslim] Persians. . . . Those [Jews following their rabbi's forced conversion] who resisted were kept in prison; then they were brought back to the tribunal two or three times, even more often, and were urged to apostasize. By these actions, all the prisoners were led to the religion of Muhammad; in the space of a month, three hundred and fifty men became Muslims. Ever since then, half the Jews having adopted the religion of the Persians, their nation lost what the Persians gained by their ascendancy over them: they were not even allowed to exist any longer, for every day they were dragged by force before the ehtim al-dawla [ranking Muslim official] and there they were forced to become Persians. The Persians put so much determination into their violence, aimed at conversion, that all Jews living in Isfahan . . . about three hundred families, adopted the religion of Muhammad.[714]

Additional confirmation is provided by eyewitness accounts from Carmelite priests (an enclosed Catholic order founded in the twelfth century by Saint Bertold [d. after 1185] on Mount Carmel, Israel), residing in Isfahan:

The Jews have been forced to become Muhammadans, and in order to 'purify' the city of Isfahan they are obliging all the Armenians who were near the city to go and live outside . . . [February 24, 1657].

I cannot say all, but shall only tell you that the King of Persia has thrown off the mask, and let the venom he has in his heart be seen. He has ordered that all the Jews in his realm should become Muslims, to the number of 100,000 [May 12, 1657].

Everything is done by one of his (Abbas II's) ministers called Itimad-ud-Dauleh, who is very hostile to Catholics and Christians, whom he expelled from Isfahan. Armenians in Julfa and the Hebrews he has forced to become Muslims, and many of the Armenians at the present day are becoming Muslims, especially the sons, in order to inherit their father's property; because they have made an accursed law, by which all Christians who become Muslims inherit everything [August 20, 1660].[715]

Alexander de Rhodes (1591–1660), a Jesuit missionary who spent the final decade of his life in Persia (dying in Isfahan), included a chapter in a book on these experiences entitled "The Jews in Persia Compelled to Become Muhammadans and the Christians Delivered from the Fear of a Like Evil." He describes the plight of the Jews during this time, as follows:

The Jews had spread themselves all over Persia in far greater numbers than might be supposed, and were leading a most peaceable existence without any suspicion of the terrible misfortune which was hanging over their heads. It came as an unexpected blow and threw them into dreadful consternation when, all of a sudden, an edict from the King was

issued and published in every place in Persia commanding them, on pain of death, to abjure the Jewish religion and profess, thenceforth, that of Muhammad.

The terror and consternation recorded in Scripture (Esther iii and iv), which the ancestors of this unhappy nation suffered long ago, when Haman, their cruel enemy, caused the fatal decree obtained from the King against them to be proclaimed throughout this same kingdom, may be taken as a picture of the fear and anguish experienced by these, their descendants, at the first news of this edict.[716]

Muhammad Baqer al-Majlisi (d. 1699), the highest institutionalized clerical officer under both Shah Sulayman (1666–1694) and Shah Husayn (1694–1722), was perhaps the most influential cleric of the Safavid Shi'ite theocracy in Persia. By design, he wrote many works in Persian to disseminate key aspects of the Shi'a ethos among ordinary persons. His treatise, "Lightning Bolts against the Jews," was written in Persian, and, despite its title, was actually an overall guideline to anti-*dhimmi* regulations for all non-Muslims within the Shi'ite theocracy.[717] Al-Majlisi, in this treatise, describes the standard humiliating requisites for non-Muslims living under the Shari'a, first and foremost, the blood ransom *jizya*, a poll tax based on Qur'an 9:29. He then enumerates six other restrictions relating to worship, housing, dress, transportation, and weapons (specifically, to render the *dhimmis* defenseless), before outlining the unique Shi'ite impurity or "najas" regulations. It is these latter najas prohibitions that led anthropology professor Laurence Loeb (who studied and lived within the Jewish community of southern Iran in the early 1970s) to observe that "[f]ear of pollution by Jews led to great excesses and peculiar behavior by Muslims."[718] According to Al-Majlisi,

And, that they should not enter the pool while a Muslim is bathing at the public baths. . . . It is also incumbent upon Muslims that they should not accept from them victuals with which they had come into contact, such as distillates, which cannot be purified. If something can be purified, such as clothes, if they are dry, they can be accepted, they are clean. But if they [the *dhimmis*] had come into contact with those clothes in moisture they should be rinsed with water after being obtained. As for hide, or that which has been made of hide such as shoes and boots, and meat, whose religious cleanliness and lawfulness are conditional on the animal's being slaughtered [according to the *Shari'a*], these may not be taken from them. Similarly, liquids that have been preserved in skins, such as oils, grape syrup, [fruit] juices, myrobalan [an astringent fruit extract used in tanning], and the like, if they have been put in skin containers or water skins, these should [also] not be accepted from them. . . . *It would also be better if the ruler of the Muslims would establish that all infidels could not move out of their homes on days when it rains or snows because they would make Muslims impure* [emphasis added].[718a]

Ignaz Goldziher believed that Shi'ism manifested this greater doctrinal intolerance toward non-Muslims, relative to Sunni Islam, because of the Shi'ites' "literalist" conception of *najis*:

> On examining the legal documents, we find that the Shi'i legal position toward other faiths is much harsher and stiffer than that taken by Sunni Muslims. Their law reveals a heightened intolerance to people of other beliefs. . . . Of the severe rule in the Qur'an (9:28) that "unbelievers are unclean," Sunni Islam has accepted an interpretation that is as good as a repeal. Shi'i law, on the other hand, has maintained the literal sense of the rule; it declares the bodily substance of the unbeliever to be ritually unclean, and lists the touching of an unbeliever among the ten things that produce *najasa*, [najis] ritual impurity.[719]

The enduring nature of the fanatical *najis* regulation prohibiting *dhimmis* from being outdoors during rain and/or snow, is well established. For examples, see item 5 of Benjamin's list of "oppressions" (table 3, above) and item 1 of Hamadan's 1892 anti-Jewish regulations (table 4, above) as well as this account provided by the missionary Napier Malcolm, who lived in the Yezd area at the close of the nineteenth century:

> They [the strict Shi'as] make a distinction between wet and dry; only a few years ago it was dangerous for an Armenian Christian to leave his suburb and go into the bazaars in Isfahan on a wet [rainy] day. "A wet dog is worse than a dry dog."[720]

Moreover, the late Persian Jewish scholar Sarah (Sorour) Soroudi related this family anecdote:

> In his youth, early in the 20th century, my late father was eyewitness to the implementation of this regulation. A group of elder Jewish leaders in Kashan had to approach the head clergy of the town (a Shi'i community from early Islamic times, long before the Safavids, and known for its religious fervor) to discuss a matter of great urgency to the community. It was a rainy day and they had to send a Muslim messenger to ask for special permission to leave the ghetto. Permission granted, they reached the house of the clergy but, because of the rain, they were not allowed to stand even in the

hallway. They remained outside, drenched, and talked to the mullah who stood inside next to the window.
>
> As late as 1923, the Jews of Iran counted this regulation as one of the anti-Jewish restrictions still practiced in the country.[721]

And this disconcerting twentieth-century anecdote from an informant living in Shiraz was recounted by Loeb:

> When I was a boy, I went with my father to the house of a non-Jew on business. When we were on our way, it started to rain. We stopped near a man who had apparently fallen and was bleeding. As we started to help him, a Muslim *akhond* (theologian) stopped and asked me who I was and what I was doing. Upon discovering that I was a Jew, he reached for a stick to hit me for defiling him by being near him in the rain. My father ran to him and begged the *akhond* to hit him instead.[722]

Far worse, the dehumanizing character of these popularized "impurity" regulations appears to have fomented recurring Muslim anti-Jewish violence, including pogroms and forced conversions, throughout the seventeenth, eighteenth, and nineteenth centuries, as opposed to merely unpleasant "odd behaviors" by individual Muslims toward Jews. Indeed, the oppression of Persian Jewry continued unabated, perhaps even intensifying, during both Safavid successors of Shah Abbas II, Shah Sulayman (1666–1694), and Shah Husayn (1694–1722).[723] Fischel highlights the prominent role played by the conception of *najas* in this sustained anti-*dhimmi* persecution:

> Day by day accounts of eyewitnesses establish beyond doubt how the notion of the ritual uncleanliness of the non-Muslims raged wildly all over the country, affecting Christians and Jews alike, and how the times of Shah Abbas II seem to have been revived.[724]

A Chronicle of the Carmelites includes these observations from 1678 and 1702, the 1678 entry recounting a particularly gruesome event:

> As all were apprehensive of a great barrenness of the soil from a protracted drought, a general dearness of corn being already experienced, everyone began to pour out prayers to God, each in the fashion of his own religion to implore the gift and succor of rain. But certain zealots of the Muhammadan faith, anxious as they had been unable to obtain anything from God by the rites and prayers enjoined on their own sect, lest some possibly more fortunate result should happen to be attributed to the votive offerings of another religion, complained to the king that the Jews and the Armenians by the

unbounded license of their tenets had contrived the harm of the Muhammadan faith, and brought to naught the national religious rites with alien sacrileges. So the Shah [Suliaman], not in possession of his wits, admitting as a serious crime what he had heard exaggerated by the pretended sincerity of the false accusers, orders on the tenth day of the month of May (1678) those of the Jews, whose flight could be forestalled, to be seized and, with a hasty sentence of his furious temper, that the abdomens of their principal men should be ripped open—which was at once put into execution. *The bellies of the Rabbi or priest of the Hebrews and of two of their chief men having been slit open, they perished: and their corpses, thrown out into the great royal square, called the Maidan, lay for a week unburied, while for a burial permit a tax of four Tumans was being levied for each. Then for the rest if them (the Jews) fetters and chains were waived on payment of a fine of 600 Tumans (one Tuman is 15 scudi, or piastres). But the Armenians, who were involved with the same accusation and were in peril of being generally slaughtered, having a certain grandee to protect them with the king, obtained pardon by paying some hundreds of Tumans as the price of their remaining unharmed* [emphasis added].

[B]y the arbitrariness of the now reigning Shah Sultan Husain, whom the flattery of certain of his officials in giving him the surname "Din Parwar" [fosterer of the religion], i.e., "zealous promoter of religious law," *has instigated, all races, subjects of his dominions, are obliged to profess the Muhammadan religion* [emphasis added]; after having begun this by the forced circumcision of the Gabrs [Zoroastrians] of the ancient Persian belief, still remaining worshippers of the perpetual fire, who lived in a very populous suburb above Julfa; passing on to wanting to do the same to all the Christians of Julfa, some four or five years back the decree for which would already have been issued had it not been for its execution being prevented by the king's grandmother who is the owner and overlord of Julfa: yielding therefore to such powerful patronage for the time being, they attacked the somewhat more remote villages, little short of a hundred, by exactions of an intolerable grievousness, in order to compel them to find escape from these by having recourse to the immunity of Islam.[725]

The overthrow of the Safavid dynasty was accompanied by an initial period of anarchy and rebellion.[726] A contemporary Jewish chronicler of these struggles, Babai ibn Farhad, lamented, "At a time when the Muhammadans fight amongst each other, how much less safe were the Jews."[727] However,

Only the downfall of the Safavid dynasty, through the successful invasion of the Afghans and the subsequent rise of a new tolerant [Sunni] ruler, Nadir Shah (1734–1747), saved the Jews of Isfahan and the Jews of Persia as a whole from complete annihilation.[728]

The advent of the Qajar dynasty in 1795 marked a return to Shi'ite theocratic orthodoxy. Thus, according to Fischel,

Since the religious and political foundations of the Qajar dynasty were but a continuation of those of the Safavids, the "law of apostasy" and the notion of the ritual uncleanliness of the Jews remained the basis of the attitude toward the Jews.

The Jew being ritually unclean, had to be differentiated from the believer externally in every possible way. This became the decisive factor making the life of the Jews in the 19th century an uninterrupted sequence of persecution and oppression. They could not appear in public, much less perform their religious ceremonies, without being treated with scorn and contempt by the Muslim inhabitants of Persia.[729]

European travelers confirm that the *najis* conception was applied to Jews with fanatical rigidity throughout nineteenth-century Persia. Rabbi David d'Beth Hillel, who traveled in Persia during the reign of Shah Fath Ali (1797–1834), provided these characterizations, based on personal experience:

They (the Shi'ites) do not eat with anyone of another nation, even touching their bread and liquids or fresh fruits; they consider it as defiled and will never eat it. . . . [It is their belief] that all the other nations are unclean, that no one who believes in Mohammad ought to be well acquainted with them and ought not to touch their victuals—and only to be acquainted with them in trade. . . . [Arriving one night at a village near Bashaka] nobody would receive me into their houses for any money I offered them, saying that the house would be defiled by my coming in, because they knew me to be a Jew and the same night was a very cold one and abundance of snow had fallen and it was impossible to sleep in the street. After many supplications, I gave half a rupee to be allowed to sleep in a stable among their cattle.[730]

There are many confirmatory nineteenth-century reports of the strict application of *najas* regulations towards Jews. Table 3 (above) includes Benjamin's listing of mid-nineteenth-century "oppressions" related to *najis*. James Fraser noted that Jews were forbidden from using the public baths,[731] and Henry Stern further described how in the holy Shi'ite city of Qom, the few [Jews] who are allowed to reside here come from Koshan [Kashan, in Isfahan province], Isfahan, and the ostentatious vocation which they pursue is peddling; but as the pious living in the religious atmosphere of so many descendants of the Prophet would be shocked at the idea of touching anything that has passed the hands of a defiled and impure Jew, they have had recourse to a more profitable traffic, the sale of spirituous liquors.[732]

In the late nineteenth century Napier Malcolm reported, "It is more easy to get the Mussulmans to eat food with the Parsis than with the Jews, whose religion ranks higher than Zoroastrianism in the popular regard,"[733] and Reverend Isaac Adams observed, "Christians and Jews are not subject to decapitation as they are considered unclean by the Mohammedans and not sufficiently worthy of this privilege."[734]

Regardless, Soroudi comments,

The impurity of the non-Muslim and his belongings, however, never deterred Shi'ah Muslims from plundering Jewish or Zoroastrian quarters on the smallest pretext or as a result of clerical or official instigation.[735]

Rabbi d'Beth Hillel also described incidences of violent persecutions, including murder and forced conversions, directed at Persian Jews in Urmia and Shiraz:

[From Urmia, 1826] A Mohammedan child being missing, the Persians accused the Jews of having murdered him in order to use his blood for the coming Passover (which was, however, a full five months away). Consequently, they rounded up all the Jews and removed them to prison, with the exception of their chief [Rabbi], he being a very old man and much respected. . . . His children, however, were taken prisoner. One of the Jews was hewn in two in the gate of the town and the others were nearly beaten to death.

[Forced conversions in Shiraz] . . . some years ago a number of Jews turned Mohammedan owing to great oppression from the Mohammedans. They are not, however, connected with them in marriage, but with their own people, and it is the same in many parts of Persia where Jews have become Mohammedan by reason of great oppression.[736]

The missionary Asahel Grant further reported,

During my residence in Ooroomiah [Urmia], a Jew was publicly burned to death in the city by order of the governor, on an allegation of that pretended crime [i.e., a blood libel]! Naphtha was freely poured over him, the torch was applied, and

the miserable man was instantly enveloped in flame![737]

Fischel offers these observations based on the narrative of d'Beth Hillel and additional eyewitness accounts, which describe the rendering of Tabriz, *Judenrein*, and the forced conversion of the Jews of Meshed to Islam:

Due to the persecution of their Moslem neighbors, many once flourishing communities entirely disappeared. Maragha, for example, ceased to be the seat of a Jewish community around 1800, when the Jews were driven out on account of a blood libel. Similarly, Tabriz, where over 50 Jewish families are supposed to have lived, became *Judenrein* towards the end of the 18th century through similar circumstances.

The peak of the forced elimination of Jewish communities occurred under Shah Mahmud (1834–48), during whose rule the Jewish population in Meshed, in eastern Persia, was forcibly converted, an event which not only remained unchallenged by Persian authorities, but also remained unknown and unnoticed by European Jews.[738]

Reverend Joseph Wolff provided this contemporary travelogue account of the mid-nineteenth-century events in Meshed, including the practice of crypto-Judaism:

The occasion was as follows: A poor woman had a sore hand. A Mussulman physician advised her to kill a dog and put her hand in the blood of it. She did so; when suddenly the whole population rose and said that they had done it in derision of their prophet. Thirty-five Jews were killed in a few minutes; the rest, struck with terror, became Mohammedans. They are now more zealous Jews in secret than ever, but call themselves *Anusim*, the Compelled Ones.[739]

And Fischel wrote a modern analysis of the Meshed pogrom and forced conversions in 1949, which highlighted these details:

The [Jewish] woman [see Wolff's account above] hired a Persian boy to catch a dog in the street and then kill it in her courtyard. Following a dispute about payment, the boy ran off in a rage. A rumor that the Jews had killed a dog on the holiest of holy days [the day of mourning for Husain, the grandson of Muhammad] and had even called it Husain to insult the Mohammedans. When this rumor reached the thousands assembled in mourning at the Mosque of the Imam Riza, hundreds of the devout, together with Shaikhs, Mullahs, Sayyids, and other spiritual leaders, rushed to the Jewish quarter. There they plundered, robbed, and burned. Soon the synagogue and the scrolls of the Law stood in flames; many scores of Jews were wounded and some thirty-five were left dead in the streets. The mob would have destroyed the entire Jewish quarter had not a group of priests given their word that the survivors would be converted to Islam. For the remaining Jews the only chance of survival was to recite the Moslem confession of faith. This they did, and on the following day they were officially accepted into Islam. . . . They were now called, "Jadid al-Islam," or "neo-Moslem." With this acceptance of Islam, the convert was immediately freed from all his previous restrictions; he was no longer required to wear a special hat or have his hair dressed in a special way or wear any particular Jewish badge on his clothes, nor was he required to pay the poll-tax (*jizya*). His "uncleanliness" was gone—he was now a Moslem among Moslems. . . . The mosque became the legal meeting place of the Jedidim. There, they were under the supervision of the chief priest, *the Mujtahid, who exercised the dual role of instructor in Mohammedanism and inquisitor for Islam* [emphasis added]. He acted as the official head of the Jews as well as their supreme judicial authority. Demanding the diligent study of the Koran and the traditional books, he forbade ritual slaughtering, circumcision on the 8th day, ordered mixed marriages between Jedidim and Moslems, and was empowered to grant permission for burial. In 1839, then, the Jewish community in Meshed officially ceased to exist. Yet this forced conversion could not extinguish Judaism in the hearts of the Jedidim; the hope that they might one day return to their own religion remained alive in them.[740]

During the nearly fifty-year reign (1848–1896) of Nasr ad-Din Shah, reform efforts to improve the plight of non-Muslims—in particular, Jews—were opposed strenuously and effectively by the Shi'ite clerical hierarchy. Accordingly,

[u]nder Nasr ad-Din Jews continued to suffer, not only in consequence of the deep-rooted hatred against them and the conception of ritual uncleanliness, but also as a result of legal discrimination of a most severe nature. Thus the entire community of Jews was held responsible for crimes and misdemeanors committed by its individual members; the oath of a Jew was not received in a court of justice; a Jew converted to the Muslim religion could claim to be the sole inheritor of family property, to the exclusion of all relatives who had not changed their religion, thereby causing the greatest possible distress to those Jews who preferred death to apostasy. In many towns the Jew was prohibited from keeping a shop in the bazaars, while in addition to the legal taxes the local authorities levied arbitrary exactions on the Jews. Although the Jew had the nominal right of appeal to a superior court of justice he did not exercise that right because of the fear of vengeance of the lower tribunal. The life of a Jew was not protected by law, inasmuch as the murderer of a Jew could purchase immunity by payment of a fine.[741]

Loeb maintains that the Jews were also victimized by tax farming throughout the nineteenth century, which reduced them "to virtual serfdom."[742] C. J. Wills, an English physician who traveled widely in Iran from 1866 to 1881 while working for the Indo-European Telegraph Department, illustrates this abusive practice in a contemporary late nineteenth-century account:

The principle is very simple. The Jews of a province are assessed at a tax of a certain amount. Someone pays this amount to the local governor together with a bribe; and the wretched Jews are immediately placed under his authority for the financial year. It is a simple speculation. If times are good, the farmer of the Jews makes a good profit; if they are bad he gains nothing, or may fail to extract from them as much as he has paid out of pocket—in that case, woe betide them. During the Persian famine the Jews suffered great straits before the receipt of subsidies sent from Europe by their co-religionists. The farmer of the Jewish colony in a great Persian city (of course a Persian Mohammedan) having seized their goods and clothes, proceeded, in the cold of Persian winter, to remove the doors and windows of their hovels and to wantonly burn them. The farmer was losing money, and sought thus to enforce what he considered his rights. No Persian pitied the unfortunates; they were Jews and so beyond the pale of pity. Every street boy raises his hand against the wretched Hebrew; he is beaten and buffeted in the streets, spat upon in the bazaar. The only person he can appeal to is the farmer of the Jews. From him, he will obtain a certain amount of protection if he be actually robbed of money or goods; not from the farmer's sense of justice, but because the complainant, were his wrongs unredressed, might be unable to pay his share of the tax.[743]

Wills also provides these acerbic descriptions of two of the most egregious forms of degradation, both public and private, suffered by the Jews throughout the nineteenth century:

At every public festival—even at the royal salaam [salute], before the King's face—the Jews are collected, and a number of them are flung into the *hauz* or tank, that King and mob may be amused by seeing them crawl out half-drowned and covered with mud. The same kindly ceremony is witnessed whenever a provincial governor holds high festival: there are fireworks and Jews.

When a Jew marries, a rabble of the Mahommedan ruffians of the town invite themselves to the ceremony, and, after a scene of riot and intoxication, not infrequently beat their host and his relations and insult the women of the community; only leaving the Jewish quarter when they have slept off the drink they have swallowed at their unwilling host's expense.[744]

Despite a number of direct, hopeful meetings between the shah and prominent European Jews and Jewish organizations throughout western Europe in 1873, Fischel concludes,

The intervention of European Jewry in favor of their Persian brothers did not bring about the hoped-for improvement and scarcely lessened the persecution and suffering of the Jews after the return of the Shah from Europe.

After his visit to Europe Nasr ad-Din issued a number of decrees and firmans which brought about some social and administrative changes in favor of the Jews, but the government was apparently too weak to prevent the recurrence of public outbreaks against the Jews. Even the law which provided that a Jew who turned Muslim had the right to claim the entire property of his family, although abolished in Teheran in 1883, was still in force in some provinces in the Persian empire as a result of the opposition of the clergy. In 1888, a massacre of the Jews occurred in Isfahan and Shiraz, which brought about intervention and investigation of the British consulate.[745]

The reigns of Muzafar ad-Din Shah (1896–1907, following the assassination of Nasr ad-Din), Shah Muhammad (1907–1909), and Shah Ahmad (1909–1925) included a nascent constitutional movement, which again aroused hopes for the elimination of religious oppression against Persian Jews and other non-Muslims. However,

neither the Jews nor the Armenian Christians or Parsee Zoroastrian minorities were yet permitted to send a deputy of their own group to parliament. At first the Jews were compelled to agree to be represented by a Muslim. . . . Unfortunately, three months after the convening of Parliament Shah Muzafar ad-Din died, and under Shah Muhammad (1907–1909) the constitutional movement very quickly disappointed the high hopes which the liberal elements of the Muslims and the Jews in Persia had entertained. Anti-Jewish riots became common, particularly in Kermanshah in 1909.[746]

Apropos of Fischel's observation, David Littman has provided the full translation of an Alliance Israélite Universelle report of the 1910 Shiraz pogrom, which was precipitated by two false accusations against the Jewish community: desecrating copies of the Qur'an by placing them in cesspools (latrines), and the ritual murder of a child.

(*M. Nataf, October 31, 1910*) *What happened yesterday in the Jewish quarter exceeds, in its horror and barbarity, anything that the most fertile imagination can conceive. In the space of a few hours, in less time than it would take to describe it, 6,000 men, women, children and the elderly were stripped of everything they possessed* [emphasis added].

In relating the dreadful incidents which occurred yesterday, the sequence of events will be followed wherever possible. . . . First a few retrospective details: about three weeks ago, some scavengers were busy cleaning out the cesspools of a Jewish house when they brought to light an old book, a few pages of which were unsoiled and which was recognized as a Koran.

On the first day of the festival of Succoth, some Jews were returning home from synagogue in the morning when they noticed at the entrance of their house a veiled Muslim woman holding a parcel under her arm. As soon as she saw them approaching, she hurriedly threw her parcel into the cesspool . . . then she ran away. The parcel was hastily pulled out. Once again, it was a Koran. It was placed in a safe place and I was informed. This time, I considered it necessary at least to acquaint the high priest of the city, Mirza Ibrahim, with the facts. I was not sure, in effect, that other Korans had not been thrown, likewise as the first ones, into Jewish houses without the knowledge of their inhabitants, and it was prudent for this dignitary to be informed, in case one of these books should be discovered and seized on as a pretext to molest the Jews. Mirza Ibrahim promised me his kindly assistance, should the occasion arise, and advised me to mention the incident as little as possible.

On the eve of the next to last day of the festival, at around 10 o'clock in the evening, the house of the community's two chief rabbis was invaded by a gang of people without authorization. They were accompanied by a bazaar merchant who pretended that one of his children, a girl of four, had disappeared in this afternoon and was indubitably in the Jewish quarter, where she had been confined or killed in order to have her blood. The unfortunate rabbis, terrorized to a degree that may be imagined, swore that they were not aware that a Muslim child had strayed into the Jewish quarter and protested against such a monstrous accusation. The *loutis* ("good for nothings") withdrew after threatening to put the Jewish quarter to fire and sword if the little girl had not been found by noon the next day. On the morrow, I was informed that, on the previous day, the body of a child, assumed to be that of the little Muslim girl, missing six days beforehand, had been found one kilometer away from the city behind an old abandoned palace, one hundred meters from the Jewish cemetery; it was rumored abroad that Jews had killed her and that any Jew who ventured out of the quarter would be well and truly chastised.

I heard these details at the school where I was at the time, and there first perceived the clamor of the crowd, which was gradually gathering in front of the government palace and which, collecting around the body of the alleged little Muslim girl found close to the Jewish cemetery (*it was subsequently established that the body was that of a little Jewish boy buried eight days ago and disinterred, for the requirements of the cause, being completely putrefied and absolutely unrecognizable*) [emphasis added] was accusing the Jews of having committed this heinous crime, for which it demanded vengeance.

Then Cawan-el-Mulk, the temporary governor, having ordered his troopers to disperse the frenzied mob, they headed for the Jewish quarter, where they arrived at the same time as the soldiers sent by Nasr-ed-Dowlet. These latter, as if they were obeying an order, were the first to fling themselves at the Jewish houses, thereby giving the signal to plunder. *The carnage and destruction which then occurred for six to seven hours is beyond the capacity to describe. . . . Not a single one of the Jewish quarter's 260 houses was spared* [emphasis added]. Soldiery, *loutis*, *sayyids* [descendants of the prophet and/or Muslim dignitaries], even women and children, driven and excited, less by religious fanaticism than by a frenetic need to plunder and appropriate the Jews' possessions, engaged in a tremendous rush for the spoils. At one point, about a hundred men from the *Kashgais* tribe, who were in town to sell some livestock, joined the first assailants, thereby completing the work of destruction.

The thieves formed a chain in the street. They passed along the line, carpets, bundles of goods, bales of merchandise . . . , anything, in a word, which was saleable. Anything which didn't have a commercial value or which, on account of its weight or size, could not be carried off was, in a fury of vandalism, destroyed and broken. The doors and windows of the houses were torn off their hinges and carried away or smashed to pieces. The rooms and cellars were literally ploughed up to see whether the substratum wasn't concealing some wealth.

But these fanatics weren't satisfied to rob the Jews of their possessions. They engaged in all sorts of violence against their persons. As soon as their quarter was stormed, the Jews fled in all directions, some to the houses of Muslim friends, others to the British Consulate, on to the terraces, and even into mosques. A few remained to try and defend their property. They paid for it with their lives or a serious injury. Twelve of them were killed in this way in the mêlée. Another fifteen were stabbed or hit with bludgeons or bullets from rifles or revolvers; they are in an alarming condition. A further forty sustained light injuries. An unlucky woman was wearing gold rings in her ears. A soldier ordered her to surrender them. She made haste to comply and had taken off one of the rings and was trying to remove the other when the impatient fanatic found it more expeditious to tear off the ear lobe together with the ring. Another woman was wearing around her neck a big silk braid to which was attached a small silver case containing some amulets. A louti tried to snatch it from her and, seeing that the braid held, cut it with his knife, making at the same time a deep gash in the flesh of the unfortunate Jewess. How many more such atrocious scenes have occurred, of which I have not yet heard!

In short the outcome of yesterday's events is as follows: 12 people dead and about 50 more or less seriously injured, whilst the five to six thousand people comprising Shiraz community now possess nothing in the world but the few tatters they were wearing when their quarter was invaded [emphasis added].

What is striking, and appears strange, about these sad circumstances is the inertia of the local authorities, who seem to have done only one thing— encourage the soldiers, in conjunction with the populace, to attack and plunder the Jewish quarter. . . .

Early this morning, I went to the Jewish quarter. How can I describe the scene of pitiful distress and frightful desolation which I witnessed? The streets, which, 48 hours previously, were full of the bustle of life and the most intense activity, now give the poignant impression of a city in mourning, a place ravaged by some cataclysm, a heart-rending valley of tears. Women, men and old folk are rolling in the dust, beating their chests and demanding justice. Others, plunged into a state of genuine stupor, appear to be unconscious and in the throes of an awful nightmare which won't end.[746a]

Reza Pahlavi's spectacular rise to power in 1925 was accompanied by dramatic reforms, including secularization and Westernization efforts, as well as a revitalization of Iran's pre-Islamic spiritual and cultural heritage. This profound sociopolitical transformation had very positive consequences for Iranian Jewry. Walter Fischel's analysis from the late 1940s (published in 1950), along with Laurence Loeb's complementary insights three decades later, underscore the impact of the Pahlavis' (Reza Shah and Mohammad Reza Shah) reforms:

> In breaking the power of the Shia clergy, which for centuries had stood in the way of progress, he [Reza Shah] shaped a modernized and secularized state, freed almost entirely from the fetters of a once fanatical and powerful clergy. . . . The rebirth of the Persian state and the manifold reforms implied therein tended also to create conditions more favorable to Jews. It enabled them to enjoy, along with the other citizens of Persia, that freedom and liberty which they had long been denied.

> The Pahlavi period . . . has been the most favorable era for Persian Jews since Parthian rule [175 BC to 226 CE] . . . the "Law of Apostasy" was abrogated about 1930. While Reza Shah did prohibit political Zionism and condoned the execution of the popular liberal Jewish reformer Hayyim Effendi, his rule was on the whole, an era of new opportunities for the Persian Jew. Hostile outbreaks against the Jews have been prevented by the government. Jews are no longer legally barred from any profession. They are required to serve in the army and pay the same taxes as Muslims. The elimination of the face-veil removed a source of insult to Jewish women, who had been previously required have their faces covered; now all women are supposed to appear unveiled in public. . . . Secular educations were available to Jewish girls as well as to boys, and, for the first time, Jews could become government-licensed teachers. . . . Since the ascendance of Mohammad Reza Shah (Aryamehr) in 1941, the situation has further improved. . . . Not only has the number of poor been reduced, but a new bourgeoisie is emerging. . . . For the first time Jews are spending their money on cars, carpets, houses, travel, and clothing. Teheran has attracted provincial Jews in large numbers and has become the center of Iranian Jewish life. . . . The Pahlavi era has seen vastly improved communications between Iranian Jewry and the rest of the world. Hundreds of boys and girls attend college and boarding school in the United States and Europe. Israeli emissaries come for periods of two years to teach in the Jewish schools. . . . A small Jewish publication industry has arisen since 1925. . . . Books on Jewish history, Zionism, the Hebrew language and classroom texts have since been published. . . . On March 15, 1950, Iran extended de facto recognition to Israel. Relations with Israel are good and trade is growing.[747]

But Loeb, who finished his anthropological field work in southern Iran during the waning years of Pahlavi rule, concluded on this cautionary, prescient note in 1976, emphasizing the Jews' tenuous status:

> Despite the favorable attitude of the government and the relative prosperity of the Jewish community, all Iranian Jews acknowledge the precarious nature of the present situation. There are still sporadic outbreaks against them because the Muslim clergy constantly berates Jews, inciting the masses who make no effort to hide their animosity towards the Jew. Most Jews express the belief that it is only the personal strength and goodwill of the Shah that protects them: that plus God's intervention! *If either should fail* . . . [emphasis added][748]

The so-called Khomeini revolution, which deposed Mohammad Reza Shah, was in reality a mere return to oppressive Shi'ite theocratic rule, the predominant form of Persian/Iranian governance since 1502. Conditions for all non-Muslim religious minorities, particularly for Bahais and Jews, rapidly deteriorated. David Littman recounts the Jews' immediate plight:

> In the months preceding the Shah's departure on 16 January 1979, the religious minorities . . . were already beginning to feel insecure. . . . Twenty thousand Jews left the country before the triumphant return of the Ayatollah Khomeini on 1 February. . . . On 16 March, the honorary president of the Iranian Jewish community, Habib Elghanian, a wealthy businessman, was arrested and charged by an Islamic revolutionary tribunal with "corruption" and "contacts with Israel and Zionism"; he was shot on 8 May.[749]

And Littman concluded this 1979 essay with the following appeal:

> It is to be hoped that the new regime will not revert to the pre-Pahlavi attitudes of the Shī'a clergy, but will prefer a path of equality for all of its citizens, thus demonstrating in practice the "tolerant" attitude of Islam so frequently proclaimed.[749a]

Littman's essay also alludes to the emigration of 20,000 Iranian Jews just prior to Khomeini's assumption of power. The demographic decline of Iranian Jewry since the creation of Israel has been rather dramatic even including the relatively "halcyon days" before 1978–1979—from nearly 120,000 in 1948 to roughly 70,000 in 1978, and at present barely 20,000.[749b]

The writings and speeches of the most influential religious ideologues of this restored Shi'ite theocracy—including Khomeini himself—make apparent their seamless connection to the oppressive doctrines of their forebears in the Safavid and Qajar dynasties. For example, Sultanhussein Tabandeh, the Iranian Shi'ite leader of the Ne'ematullahi Sultanalishahi Sufi Order, wrote an "Islamic perspective" on the Universal Declaration of Human Rights.[750] According to Professor Eliz Sanasarian's important study of religious minorities in the Islamic Republic, Tabandeh's tract became "the core ideological work upon which the Iranian government . . . based its non-Muslim policy."[751] Tabandeh[752] begins his discussion by lauding as a champion "of the oppressed" Shah Ismail I (1502–1524), the repressive and bigoted founder of the Safavid dynasty who "bore hatred against the Jews and ordered their eyes to be gouged out if they happened to be found in his vicinity."[753] It is critical to understand that Tabandeh's key views on non-Muslims, summarized below, were implemented "almost verbatim in the Islamic Republic of Iran."[754] In essence, Tabandeh simply reaffirms the sacralized inequality of non-Muslims relative to Muslims, under the Shari'a:

Thus if [a] Muslim commits adultery his punishment is 100 lashes, the shaving of his head, and one year of banishment. But if the man is not a Muslim and commits adultery with a Muslim woman his penalty is execution. . . . Similarly if a Muslim deliberately murders another Muslim he falls under the law of retaliation and must by law be put to death by the next of kin. But if a non-Muslim who dies at the hand of a Muslim has by lifelong habit been a non-Muslim, the penalty of death is not valid. Instead the Muslim murderer must pay a fine and be punished with the lash.

Since Islam regards non-Muslims as on a lower level of belief and conviction, if a Muslim kills a non-Muslim . . . then his punishment must not be the retaliatory death, since the faith and conviction he possesses is loftier than that of the man slain. . . . Again, the penalties of a non-Muslim guilty of fornication with a Muslim woman are augmented because, in addition to the crime against morality, social duty and religion, he has committed sacrilege, in that he has disgraced a Muslim and thereby cast scorn upon the Muslims in general, and so must be executed.

Islam and its peoples must be above the infidels, and never permit non-Muslims to acquire lordship over them. Since the marriage of a Muslim woman to an infidel husband (in accordance with the verse quoted: 'Men are guardians for women') means her subordination to an infidel, that fact makes the marriage void, because it does not obey the conditions laid down to make a contract valid. As the Sura ("The Woman to be Examined," [i.e., sura 60, specifically verse 60:10]) says: "Turn them not back to infidels: for they are not lawful unto infidels nor are infidels lawful unto them (i.e., in wedlock)."[755]

And Sanasarian emphasizes the centrality of this notion of Islam's superiority to all other faiths:

[E]ven the so-called moderate elements [in the Islamic Republic] believed in its truth. Mehdi Barzagan, an engineer by training and religiously devout by family line and personal practice, became the prime minister of the Provisional Government in 1979. He believed that man must have one of the monotheistic religions in order to battle selfishness, materialism, and communism. Yet the choice was not a difficult one. [Barzagan stated,] "Among monotheist religions, Zoroastrianism is obsolete, Judaism has bred materialism, and Christianity is dictated by its church. Islam is the only way out." In this line of thinking, there is no recognition of Hinduism, Buddhism, Bahaism, or other religions.[756]

The conception of najas or ritual uncleanliness of the non-Muslim has also been reaffirmed. Ayatollah Khomeini stated explicitly, "Non-Muslims of any religion or creed are *najis*."[757] Khomeini elaborated his views on *najis* and non-Muslims with a specific reference to Jews, as follows:

Eleven things are unclean: urine, excrement, sperm, blood, a dog, a pig, bones, *a non-Muslim man and woman* [emphasis added], wine, beer, perspiration of a camel that eats filth. . . . The whole body of a non-Muslim is unclean, even his hair, his nails, and all the secretions of his body. . . . A child below the age of puberty is unclean if his parents and grandparents are not Muslims; but if he has a Muslim for a forebear, then he is clean. . . . The body, saliva, nasal secretions, and perspiration of a non-Muslim man or woman who converts to Islam automatically become pure. As for the garments, if they were in contact with the sweat of the body before conversion, they will remain unclean. . . . It is not strictly prohibited for a Muslim to work in an establishment run by a Muslim who employs Jews, if the products do not aid Israel in one way or another. However it is shameful [for a Muslim] to be under the orders of a Jewish departmental head.[758]

The Iranian ayatollah Hossein-Ali Montazeri further indicated that a non-Muslim (*kafir*'s) impurity was "a political order from Islam and must be adhered to by the followers of Islam, and the goal [was] to promote general hatred toward those who are outside Muslim circles." This "hatred" was to assure that Muslims would not succumb to corrupt—that is, non-Islamic—thoughts.[759] Sanasarian provides a striking example of the practical impact of this renewed *najis* consciousness:

In the case of the Coca-Cola plant, for example, the owner (an Armenian) fled the country, the factory was confiscated, and Armenian workers were fired. Several years later, the family members were allowed to oversee the daily operations of the plant, and Armenians were allowed to work at the clerical level; however, the production workers remained Muslim. Armenian workers were never rehired on the grounds that non-Muslims should not touch the bottles or their contents, which may be consumed by Muslims.[760]

Khomeini's views were the most influential in shaping the ideology of the revitalized Shi'ite theocracy, and his attitudes toward Jews (both before and after he assumed power) were particularly negative. Khomeini's speeches and writings invoked a panoply of *Judenhass* motifs, including orthodox interpretations of sacralized Muslim texts (for example, describing the destruction of the Banu Qurayza), and the Shi'ite conception of *najas*. More ominously, Khomeini's rhetoric blurred the distinction between Jews and Israelis, reiterated paranoid conspiracy theories about Jews (both within Persia/Iran, and beyond), and endorsed the annihilation of the Jewish State. Sanasarian highlights these disturbing predilections:

> The Jews and Israelis were interchangeable entities who had penetrated all facets of life. Iran was being "trampled upon under Jewish boots." The Jews had conspired to kill the Qajar king Naser al-Din Shah and had a historically grand design to rule through a new monarchy and a new government (the Pahlavi dynasty): "Gentlemen, be frightened. They are such monsters." In a vitriolic attack on Mohammad Reza Shah's celebration of 2500 years of Persian monarchy in 1971, Khomeini declared that Israeli technicians had planned the celebrations and they were behind the exuberant expenses and overspending. Objecting to the sale of oil to Israel, he said: "We should not ignore that the Jews want to take over Islamic countries.". . . In an address to the Syrian foreign minister after the Revolution Khomeini lamented: "If Muslims got together and each poured one bucket of water on Israel, a flood would wash away Israel."[761]

Sanasarian provides one particularly disturbing example of this Islamic state-sanctioned Jew hatred, involving the malevolent indoctrination of young adult candidates for national teacher training programs. Affirming as objective, factual history the hadith account (e.g., Sahih Bukhari, volume 3, book 47, number 786) of Muhammad's supposed poisoning by a Jewish woman from ancient Khaybar, she notes,

> Even worse, the subject became one of the questions in the ideological test for the Teachers' Training College where students were given a multiple-choice question in order to identify the insti-

gator of the martyrdom of the Prophet Muhammad, the "correct" answer being "a Jewess."[762]

Reza Afshari's seminal analysis of human rights in contemporary Iran summarizes the predictable consequences for Jews of the Khomeini revolution:

> As antisemitism found official expression . . . and the anti-Israeli state propaganda became shriller, Iranian Jews felt quite uncertain about their future under the theocracy. Early in 1979, the execution of Habib Elqaniyan, a wealthy, self-made businessman, a symbol of success for many Iranian Jews, hastened emigration. The departure of the chief rabbi for Europe in the summer of 1980 underlined the fact that the hardships that awaited the remaining Jewish Iranians would far surpass those of other protected minorities.[763]

Beyond the well-publicized execution of Habib Elganian in May 1979, an excess of Jews compared to other "recognized religious minorities" were imprisoned, and by 1982 nine more Jews had been executed.[764]

Afshari also captures the crushing psychosocial impact on Iran's remaining Jews of restored Shi'ite theocratic rule—the recrudescence of a fully servile *dhimmi* mentality:

> The Jewish leaders had to go so far as to openly denounce the policies of the State of Israel. It was disquieting to read a news item that reported the Jewish representative in the Majlis criticizing, in carefully chosen words . . . actions of his co-religionists in Israel, especially when upon the conclusion of his remarks the other (Shi'ite) deputies burst into the chant "Death to Israel!" The contemporary state violating the human rights of its citizens left behind a trail of *pathological behaviors* [emphasis added]. . . . Equally baffling, if not placed against the Jewish community's predicament, was the statement by the Jewish leaders concerning the arrests of thirteen Jews charged with espionage for Israel in June 1999. "The Islamic Republic of Iran has demonstrated to the world that it has treated the Jewish community and other religious minorities well; the Iranian Jewish community has enjoyed constitutional rights of citizenship, and the arrest and charges against a number of Iranian Jews has nothing to do with their religion." The bureaucratic side of the state needed such a statement, and the Jewish leaders in Tehran had no choice but to oblige.[765]

The early twentieth-century sociologist and geographer Jovan Cvijic, in his detailed psychosocial analysis of the Serbian and other Christian *dhimmis* under Turkish Muslim rule, described how the fear of recurrent violence accentuated their submission, engendering proto-typical *dhimmi* adaptive behaviors:

> [They became] . . . accustomed to belonging to an inferior, servile class, whose duty it is to make themselves acceptable to the master, to humble themselves before him and to please him. These people become close-mouthed, secretive, cunning; they lose all confidence in others; they grow used to hypocrisy and meanness because these are necessary in order for them to live and to avoid violent punishments.
>
> The direct influence of oppression and violence is manifested in almost all the Christians as feelings of fear and apprehension. Whenever Moslem brigands or evil-doers made their appearance somewhere, entire districts used to live in terror, often for months on end. There are regions where the Christian population has lived under a reign of fear from birth until death. In certain parts of Macedonia, they don't tell you how they fought against the Turks or against the Albanians, but rather about the way that they managed to flee from them, or the ruse that they used to escape them. In Macedonia I heard people say: "Even in our dreams we flee from the Turks and the Albanians." It is true that for about twenty years a certain number of them have regained their composure, but the deep-seated feeling has not changed among the masses of people. Even after the liberation in 1912 one could tell that a large number of Christians had not yet become aware of their new status: fear could still be read on their faces.[766]

Afshari's blunt description of the same phenomenon among contemporary Iranian Jews labels such behaviors a "pathological," if understandable, response to their "predicament." The apotheosis of Iranian Jewish *dhimmitude* is perhaps Parviz Yeshaya. A staunch anti-Zionist, Yeshaya, who until recently headed the Jewish Committee in Tehran, was one of the first Jews to support Ayatollah Khomeini, and has called for the destruction of the state of Israel.[767] And public *dhimmi* behaviors were again evident in the summer of 2006. During the conflagration on the Israeli-Lebanon border—initiated by the Iranian regime's jihadist proxy organization, Hezbollah—Jews from the southern Iranian city of Shiraz were prominently displayed on state-run television participating in a regime-sponsored pro-Hezbollah rally.[768]

Hezbollah's name, "The Party of Allah," derives from Qur'an 5:56—"And whoever takes Allah and His messenger and those who believe for a guardian, then surely *the party of Allah* are they that shall be triumphant." In a public statement issued February 15–16, 1986, Hezbollah stressed its indelible links to Iran and Ayatollah Khomeini ("We obey the orders of one leader wise and just . . . ") and conceived of itself as a "nation" linked to Muslims worldwide by "a strong ideological and political bond, namely Islam." Expressed in the political language of the Qur'an, Hezbollah's ideology encompasses, triumphantly (as per the slogan adorning the party emblem, "The Party of Allah Is Sure to Triumph") at least three major objectives: transforming Lebanon into a Shari'a state, destroying Israel, and establishing regional followed by international Islamic hegemony—that is bringing the region, then the world under Shari'a law:

> [W]e do not constitute an organized party in Lebanon. Nor are we a tight political cadre. We are an *umma* linked to the Muslims of the whole world by the solid doctrinal and religious connection of Islam, whose message God wanted to be fulfilled by the Seal of the Prophets, i.e., Muhammad. This is why whatever touches or strikes Muslims, in Afghanistan, Iraq, the Philippines and everywhere reverberates throughout the Muslim umma of which we are an integral part. Our behavior is dictated to us by legal principles laid down by the light of an overall political conception defined by the leading jurist (*wilayat al-faqih*).
>
> As for our culture, it is based on the Holy Qur'an, the Sunna and the legal rulings of the faqih who is our source of imitation (*marja' al-taqlid*). Our culture is crystal clear. It is not complicated and is accessible to all.
>
> No one can imagine the importance of our military potential as our military apparatus is not separate from our overall social fabric. Each of us is a fighting soldier. And when it becomes necessary to carry out the Holy war (Jihad), each of us takes up his assignment in the fight in accordance with the injunctions of the Law, and that in the framework of the mission carried out under the tutelage of the Commanding Jurist.
>
> . . . [O]ur struggle [against Israel] will end only when this entity is obliterated. We recognize no treaty with it, no cease fire, and no peace agreements, whether separate or consolidated.[769]

Demonizing Israel and Jews—via motifs in the Qur'an, hadith, and sira—Hezbollah views the jihad against the "Zionist entity" as an annihilationist war intrinsic to broader conflicts: the struggle between the Islamic world and the non-Muslim world, and the historical struggle between Islam and Judaism. The most senior clerical authority for Hezbollah, Husayn Fadlallah, has stated, "We find in the Qur'an that the Jews are the most aggressive towards the Muslims . . . because of their aggressive resistance to the unity of the faith." Fadlallah repeatedly refers to anti-Jewish archetypes in the Qur'an, hadith, and sira: the corrupt, treacherous, and aggressive nature of the Jews; their reputation as killers of prophets, who spread corruption on earth; and the notion that the Jews engaged in conspiratorial efforts against the Muslim prophet Muhammad. Fadlallah argues, that ultimately, "[e]ither we destroy Israel or Israel destroys us."[770] Hassan Nasrallah, current secretary general of Hezbollah, and a prote é of Ayatollah Ali Khamenei, presently Iran's highest-ranking political and religious authority (its "Guardian Jurisprudent"), has reiterated these antisemitic views with particular vehemence. Invoking motifs from Islam's foundational texts, Nasrallah has characterized Jews as the "grandsons of apes and pigs," and as "Allah's most cowardly and greedy creatures." He elaborates these themes into an annihilationist animus against all Jews, not merely Israelis:

Anyone who reads the Qur'an and the holy writings of the monotheistic religions sees what they did to the prophets, and what acts of madness and slaughter the Jews carried out throughout history. . . .

Anyone who reads these texts cannot think of coexistence with them, of peace with them, or about accepting their presence, not only in Palestine of 1948 but even in a small village in Palestine, because they are a cancer which is liable to spread again at any moment. . . . There is no solution to the conflict in this region except with the disappearance of Israel.

If we searched the entire world for a person more cowardly, despicable, weak and feeble in psyche, mind, ideology and religion, we would not find anyone like the Jew. Notice, I do not say the Israeli. . . . [I]f they [the Jews] all gather in Israel, it will save us the trouble of going after them worldwide.[771]

Hezbollah is viscerally opposed to Judaism and the existence of Israel, stressing the eternal conflict between the Jews and Islam. Eradicating Israel represents an early stage of Hezbollah's Pan-Islamic ambitions and its jihad against the rest of the non-Muslim world.

Support for Hezbollah—which seeks the destruction of Israel, the Middle East's lone state liberated from the system of *dhimmitude*—abroad is mirrored by contemporary Iran's treatment of its own Jews (and other non-Muslim populations) since 1979. *Dhimmitude* has been formally reimposed, and in the case of Jews, complemented by state-supported antisemitism, irrespective of any given regime's "moderation."

Law professor Ann Mayer's discussion of the Iranian Constitution reveals how this document, subservient to Shari'a norms (Article 4)—in her words, a "Shari'a-based system"—subjects non-Muslim minorities to legalized discriminations.[772] Article 144, for example, effectively excludes non-Muslims from the Iranian military, Mayer notes, "just as *dhimmis* were [excluded] in pre-modern Iran."[773] Article 14 states, in part,

The government of the Islamic Republic of Iran and all Muslims are duty-bound to treat non-Muslims *in conformity with ethical norms and the principles of Islamic justice* [emphasis added] and equity, and to respect their human rights [hoquq-e ensani]. This principle applies to all who refrain from engaging in conspiracy or activity against Islam and the Islamic Republic of Iran.[774]

But the application of "Islamic justice"—Shari'a law—severely limits non-Muslim rights vis-à-vis universal modern standards. Mayer concludes,

Far from granting non-Muslims protections for the rights to which they are entitled under international law, the constitution reinforces the principle that all rights are subject to Shari'a qualifications. In addition, Article 14 provides that the human rights that non-Muslims enjoy, which one may assume will be very limited to begin with, are to be forfeited if the non-Muslims become involved in activity against the Islamic Republic, a vague standard affording a broad range of potential justifications for curbing their rights. It is interesting that this article provides special grounds for depriving non-Muslims of human rights, even though there is already a general provision in Article 26 that enables the government to curb the activities of groups, including "minority religious associations," if they are contrary to the principles of Islam or the Islamic Republic." Article 14 seems to contemplate even more extensive deprivations of human rights than those involved in the curbs placed on the freedom of association by Article 26. Taken together, they betoken a suspicion on the part of the drafters of the constitution that non-Muslims are likely to be disposed to oppose Iran's Islamic Republic. Of course, given the Islamic bias in the system, such opposition would only be natural.[775]

Other discriminatory liabilities implicit in Iran's legal code are exploited fully, worsening the plight of Iran's Jews. These include the imposition of collective punishment on a Jewish community for an individual act, a "contract of silence" regarding anti-Jewish discrimination and persecution, and an unrelenting campaign of virulent antisemitism openly expressed by the Iranian media and religious and political hierarchy. Pooya Dayanim, an Iranian Jewish attorney, recently summarized these phenomena:

This reluctance to criticize, or even the eagerness to support the Islamic Regime, however, is not evidence of informal intimidation of the Jewish Community by government officials, but is also, and more significantly, a result of an obligatory contractual agreement between the minority community and the Islamic Republic. The silence, therefore, of the Iranian Jewish community inside Iran concerning discrimination and persecution is in itself evidence of the dangerous and precarious situation the community finds itself in and which it is unable to denounce without breaking its contractual agreement as a religious minority living in a Muslim land.

This contractual agreement under Shari'a Islamic Law presupposes complete loyalty to the Islamic Regime, in exchange for which the minority community receives second-class, limited privileges in practicing its religion. If the terms of this contract are breached, supposedly even by individual members of the community, the limited privileges of the entire community can be suspended or revoked or the minority community (in this instance the Jewish community) can even face deportation from the country. Under these circumstances the Iranian Jewish Community must avoid any statements that could be interpreted as critical of the regime and forces the government-imposed or government-tolerated leaders of the Iranian Jewish Community to turn in or turn against those individual members of the community who are brave enough to dare to speak out about the true condition of Jews in Iran.

After the arrest of 13 Jews in Shiraz and Isfahan in March of 1999 on trumped up charges of spying for Israel and the United States, the Iranian Jewish Community leaders inside Iran (Parviz Yeshaya, Manouchehr Eliasi and Maurice Motamed) not only did not inform anyone on the outside world about the situation but became enforcers of silence asking Iranian Jewish leaders outside of Iran to remain silent as well. It was only in July of 1999 that the case was revealed to the world in an exclusive interview granted the BBC by an Iranian Jewish leader based in the United States [home to sixty-five thousand Iranian Jews compared to the approximately twenty thousand that still remain in Iran] who feared that the imprisoned Jews faced immediate execution and decided to break his silence and save their lives. However, even during the trial, during which the Iranian Jewish Community knew they had the support of the international media and governments worldwide, statements from the official Iranian Jewish community were very measured, generally limiting themselves to faith that the accused would be treated fairly.

While the Islamic Republic does not guarantee the right of free speech and protest to any of its citizens, the situation, because of the Islamic Law, is considerably worse for the Jews. If an Iranian Muslim criticizes the Islamic Republic, he himself can be punished; if a Jew does it, under the laws of the Islamic Republic his actions may legally affect the well-being of the entire Jewish community. Given, moreover, the suspicion in which Jews are generally held because of actual or perceived connections to Israel, the level of intimidation, especially regarding anyone who could be thought to speak for the community in general is extreme. Iranian Jewish leaders in the United States who have been brave enough to speak out have repeatedly been threatened by Iranian agents that their life and the life of their loved ones are in danger because of their decision to speak out and that they should stay silent.

Ayatollah Khamenei, Iran's supreme leader . . . in March 2001, denied the Holocaust and called the survivors of the death camps " . . . a bunch of hooligans who emigrated to Palestine." On May 18, 2001, in a televised speech, Khamenei directly attacked the Jews, calling Jews the enemies of the prophet Mohammad and threatened the Jews with expulsion and expropriation of their property, citing a similar action taken by the prophet Mohammad against the three Jewish tribes in Medina, [during] which they were annihilated. This attack, placed in the context in which the Jews of Iran were still feeling shock of the Shiraz show trials reveals the true feelings of the Islamic Regime toward the Jews of Iran.

A large part of the Antisemitic campaign waged by the government takes place in Farsi [so as] to not raise [the] attention of the non-Farsi speaking world. For example, when some specifically Antisemitic articles appear in Farsi newspapers with wide distribution, the articles are omitted from their international edition and from the website of those newspapers. It is clear that the Iranian authorities do not wish to highlight their Antisemitic activities and want to present Iran as a shining example of religious tolerance. When Maurice Motamed, the sole Jewish MP in Iran's Parliament, was interviewed by the *Forward* in his trip to the United States [during early 2003] for example, there were Iranian diplomats present and the interview took place at the residence of Iran's Ambassador to the UN to make sure that he does not say anything that the regime finds unproductive to its PR efforts.

The threat of retaliation against the entire community is an ever present factor in the minds of Iranian Jews and all community leaders. The Islamic Republic reminds Iranian Jews of their uncertain fate and future from time to time in speeches that are delivered by the leaders of the regime. . . . There is good reason to believe, therefore, that there is an effective mechanism of intimidation operating against the Iranian Jewish Community, and their refusal to report incidents of severe discrimination and persecution is in itself evidence of the dangerous situation that Jews in Iran live under.[776]

Additional forms of legal and extralegal discrimination adversely affect criminal proceedings for Jews and limit their employment and educational opportunities.[777] Even private religious education and observance are hindered or abused by Iranian authorities to spy upon and threaten Jewish communities, despite continued Western media claims that "Jews face no restrictions on their religious practice."[778] Dayanim elaborates on what amounts to a nearly full recrudescence of the system of *dhimmitude*.[779]

(*Legal disabilities*) The Jews suffer from official inferior status under Iranian Law and are not protected by police or the courts. The amount of financial compensation a Jew can receive from a Muslim in case of murder or accidental death of a relative is equal to one-eighth of that which would be paid if the victim was a Muslim. In practice this means that a life of a Jew in Iran has very little value. In addition, since Iranian courts routinely refuse to accept the testimony of a Jew against a Muslim, most cases of this sort are not even prosecuted and the police do not even investigate such claims. As a result of their legally inferior status, Jews find themselves outside the protection of the courts and police. This is not simply a perception on their part, but rather, sadly, a harsh reality. In none of the cases of the murder of Jews in Iran has a perpetrator ever been found, much less prosecuted.

(*Limitations on employment/business opportunities*) Ayatollah Khomeini's edicts concerning the Jews, published in his book *Tozieh Almasael* (Explanation of Problems), state clearly that while there is no Islamic law prohibiting a situation in which a Muslim may work under a Jew, this is a shameful situation for a Muslim to be in. These edicts still carry the force of law in Iran, and as a result, Jews have been barred from any position in which they would be superior to Muslims. Jews are excluded from most government positions. Virtually all government entities (most sectors in Iran are government-owned) have a "Muslim only" policy and they print this requirement in their job notices in newspapers. This formal exclusion of Jews from large areas of employment is badly damaging to the Jews. Most private companies, thanks to the anti-Semitic media campaign in Iran, do not hire Jews either. Most Jews are forced into self-employment, but due to general public prejudice, few buy anything from them. The US State Department Religious Freedom Report of 2001 confirms that Jewish businesses have been targets of vandalism and boycotts.

(*Limitations on educational opportunities*) All Jewish university students must pass a course on Islamic ideology. In general, the professors in these courses are, by definition, very dedicated to their ideology and many Jewish Students that I have interviewed have reported that attending such a course has been a humiliating experience, in which their religion has been ridiculed and trivialized. Jewish students who protest are expelled and blocked from entering the University. Jewish students have also reported that instructors have arbitrarily failed them to block their educational goals. Parents of Jewish elementary and secondary school students, I interviewed in Vienna (processing center for Iranian Jewish refugees) in July of 2002, report frequent verbal and even physical abuse of their children by allegedly anti-Semitic teachers. Iranian "Jewish" schools are forced to stay open on the Jewish Sabbath. Principals of "Jewish" schools in Iran by law must be Muslim and are generally selected based on their Islamic credential.

(*Restrictions on private religious practice*) Judaism is one of the recognized minority religions in Iran. Jews, therefore, are allowed to conduct religious services and give religious education to their children. The privileges of religious education, can, however, be suspended if it is thought by the authorities that such an education may prevent Jewish children from converting to Islam. Many informed observers believe that one reason that Jewish rabbis and teachers were arrested in Shiraz was the fact that they were instructing in the spirit of Orthodox Judaism. The US State Department Religious Freedom Report of 2001 notes that the Jewish community, and its religious, cultural and social organizations, are closely monitored by the Ministry of Islamic Culture and Guidance and the Ministry of Intelligence and Security. The form that this monitoring has taken is either sending agents to synagogues posing as Jews, or forcing Jewish communal leaders to inform on the activities of the Jewish community. This situation has created an atmosphere of terror and mistrust in the Jewish community. Many Jews who flee Iran relate that they told no one of their plans to emigrate, not even friends or relatives in fear of an unknown collaborator informing authorities of their plans.[779]

During mid-May 2006 public allegations were made that Iran's government was going to mandate that non-Muslims wear identifying clothing.[779a] The Canadian newspaper *National Post* subsequently retracted its May 19, 2006, report about a putative Iranian law requiring non-Muslim minorities—Jews, Christians, and Zoroastrians—to wear color-coded strips of cloth attached to their garments to distinguish them from Muslims.[779b] However, journalist and author Amir Taheri, who wrote the original article describing the alleged law, stood by his report, issuing the following clarification:

Regarding the dress code story it seems that my column was used as the basis for a number of reports that somehow jumped the gun. As far as my article is concerned I stand by it. The law has been passed by the Islamic Majlis and will now be submitted to the Council of Guardians. A committee has been appointed to work out the modalities of implementation. Many ideas are being discussed with regard to implementation, including special markers, known as zonnars, for followers of Judaism, Christianity and Zoroastrianism, the only faiths other than Islam that are recognized as such. The zonnar was in use throughout the Muslim world until the early 20th century and marked out the dhimmis, or protected religious minorities. I have been informed of the ideas under discussion thanks to my sources in Tehran, including three members of the Majlis who had tried to block the bill since it was first drafted in 2004. I do not know which of these ideas or any will be eventually adopted. We will know once the committee appointed to discuss them presents its report, perhaps in September (2006).[780] Interestingly, the Islamic Republic authorities refuse to issue an official statement categorically rejecting the concept of dhimmitude and the need for marking out religious minorities. I raised the issue not as a news story, because news of the new law was already several days old, but as an opinion column to alert the outside world to this most disturbing development.[781]

Possible overzealous reporting by the *National Post* aside, the plausibility of such a law being implemented should not have been dismissed based on the living legacy of Shi'ite religious persecution of non-Muslims in Iran since the founding of the Shi'ite theocracy in (then) Persia under Shah Ismail, at the very outset of the sixteenth century. The stipulations of Al-Majlisi (d. 1699)—perhaps the most influential Shi'ite cleric of the Safavid theocracy in Persia—from his late seventeenth-century treatise on non-Muslims are consistent with the requirements purportedly under discussion by the contemporary Iranian Parliament (although, the "color-coding" differs):

[I]t is appropriate that the ruler of the Muslims imposed upon them clothing that would distinguish them from Muslims so that they would not resemble Muslims. It is customary for Jews to wear yellow clothes while Christians wear black and dark blue ones. Christians [also] wear a girdle on their waists, and Jews sew a piece of silk of a different color on the front part of their clothes.[782]

Loeb's analysis of Jewish *dhimmitude* in Shi'ite Iran documents the social impact of *najis* regulations, beginning with the implementation of a

badge of shame [as] an identifying symbol which marked someone as a *najis* Jew and thus to be

avoided. *From the reign of Abbas I [1587–1629] until the 1920s, all Jews were required to display the badge* [emphasis added].[783]

Following a relatively brief hiatus under Pahlavi reign (1925–1979), the Khomeini-inspired Shi'ite theocracy in Iran has been accompanied, as discussed earlier, by a revival of *najis* regulations. Thus, if formal badging requirements for non-Muslims were now to be implemented, these measures would simply mark the further retrogression of Iran's non-Muslim religious minorities, completing in full their descent to a pre-1925 status. The non sequitur reaction of Jewish advocacy groups[784] and world leaders[784a] invoked comparisons to Nazi requirements that Jews wear a yellow Star of David on their clothing. Rabbi Marvin Hier, the dean of the Simon Wiesenthal Center, proclaimed, "This is reminiscent of the Holocaust. . . . Iran is moving closer and closer to the ideology of the Nazis,"[784b] while the American Jewish Committee maintained that "the story, with its chilling echoes of the Shoah, is another heinous example of the Iranian regime's contempt for human rights."[784c] Australian prime minister John Howard, speaking in Ottawa after a meeting with Canadian prime minister Stephen Harper, stated,

It obviously echoes the most horrible period of genocide in the world's history and the markings of Jewish people with a mark on their clothing by the Nazis.[784d]

Prime minister Harper remarked, "I think it boggles the mind that any regime on the face of the earth would want to do anything that could remind people of Nazi Germany."[784e] And US State Department spokesman Sean McCormack stated from Washington, DC, "I think it has clear echoes of Germany under Hitler."[784f]

These uninformed comments confirm the profound historical ignorance of sanctioned Islamic practices and doctrines such as *najis*, the *dhimmi* condition, discriminatory badging, and so on, and their implementation for centuries in Iran.

Since 1979 the restored Iranian theocracy—in parallel with returning the small remnant Jewish community to a state of obsequious *dhimmitude*—has always focused its obsessive anti-Jewish animus on the autonomous Jewish state of Israel. The pillars of this continuous campaign of annihilationist antisemitism are Holocaust denial[785] and the development of a nuclear weapons program intended expressly for Israel's eradication.[786]

Iran's steadfast pursuit of nuclear weapons may have even accelerated under the "progressive" regime of Muhammed Khatami,[787] who denounced US and European Union demands that Iran sign an agreement to terminate such efforts, transparently and verifiably.[788] An early 2002 report by Michael Rubin warned,

Nearly five years after his first election, Khatami has enacted few if any tangible reforms. Indeed, while many younger Iranians do enjoy some additional flexibility in dress, freedoms have actually declined under the Khatami administration. Khatami has accomplished one important task, though. With a gentle face, soft rhetoric, and numerous trips abroad, Khatami has succeeded in softening the image of the Islamic Republic. No longer is Iran associated with waves of 14-year-olds running across minefields, nor do many Western academics and commentators dwell on Iran's export of terror, so long as Tehran keeps its assassination squads away from Europe. However, the fundamentals of the regime's behavior have not changed. Indeed, under Khatami, Iran has accelerated not only its drive for a nuclear capability, but also actively increased its pursuit of chemical and biological weapons, as well as long-range ballistic missiles.[789]

Previously, the "Al-Quds Day," December 14, 2001, sermon of former Iranian president Ali Akhbar Hashemi Rafsanjani made clear the purpose of such weapons. During this "pious" address, Rafsanjani—who was also deemed a "moderate" while president—argued that nuclear weapons could solve the "Israel problem," because, as he observed, "the use of a nuclear bomb in Israel will leave nothing on the ground, whereas it will only damage the world of Islam."[790] Indeed, Rafsanjani was merely reiterating motifs of Jew hatred and jihad martyrdom expressed continuously by his spiritual inspiration, Ayatollah Khomeini. Between 1963 and 1980, for example, Khomeini made these statements:

(1963) Israel does not want the Koran to survive in this country. . . . It is destroying us. It is destroying you and the nation. It wants to take possession of the economy. It wants to demolish our trade and agriculture. It wants to grab the wealth of the country [Iran].

(1977) The Jews have grasped the world with both hands and are devouring it with an insatiable appetite, they are devouring America and have now turned their attention to Iran and still they are not satisfied.

(1980) We do not worship Iran, we worship Allah. For patriotism is another name for paganism. I say let this land [Iran] burn. I say let this land go up in smoke, provided Islam emerges triumphant in the rest of the world.[791]

For current Iranian president Mahmoud Ahmadinejad, the destruction of Israel is an openly avowed policy. Despite an international outcry of condemnation following Ahmadinejad's statements in late October 2005 that Israel "should be wiped off the map"[792] and "very

soon this stain of disgrace will be purged from the center of the Islamic world,"[793] he continued to express such annihilationist sentiments throughout 2006, while simultaneously referring to the "myth of the Holocaust,"[794] and even sponsoring a December 2006 Holocaust deniers' "conference" in Tehran.[795] Ahmadinejad also recently maintained he has "a connection with God,"[796] and his genocidal pronouncements have been endorsed by the upper echelons of Iran's national security establishment.[797] The conclusion that Israel's eradication has become "Iran's principal foreign policy objective"[798] does not seem unwarranted.

Matthias Kuntzel made these cogent observations regarding the unique dangers posed by Iran's fusion of a martyrdom mentality, with nuclear weapons capability, and Holocaust denial.

It is precisely this suicidal outlook that distinguishes the Iranian nuclear weapons program from those of all other countries and makes it uniquely dangerous.

Just as Hitler sought to "liberate" humanity by murdering the Jews, so Ahmadinejad believes he can "liberate" humanity by eradicating Israel. The deniers' conference as an instrument for propagating this project is intimately linked to the nuclear program as an instrument for realizing it.

Anyone inclined to dismiss the significance of such statements might want to consider the proclamation made by Mohammad Hassan Rahimian, representative of the Iranian Supreme Leader Ali Khamenei, who stands even higher in the Iranian hierarchy than Ahmadinejad. A few months ago, on November 16, 2006, Rahimian explained: "The Jew"—not the Zionist, note, but the Jew—"is the most obstinate enemy of the devout. And the main war will determine the destiny of mankind. . . . The reappearance of the Twelfth Imam will lead to a war between Israel and the Shia." The country that has been the first to make Holocaust denial a principle of its foreign policy is likewise the first openly to threaten another U.N. member state with, not invasion or annexation, but annihilation.[799]

Holocaust scholar Daniel Goldhagen has put forth the controversial argument[800] that the Nazis melded centuries of annihilationist German Jew hatred to a state machinery capable of implementing the systematic mass murder of Jews.[801] Citing the independent statements of Rafsanjani (from December 2001) and Ahmadinejad (from October 2005), Goldhagen, in a November 3, 2005, opinion editorial, cautioned,

Two Iranian presidents have now openly spoken about destroying Israel, with Ahmadinejad defiantly repeating his genocidal hopes again . . . despite the world's condemnation of him.[802]

Goldhagen's visceral concern that "it would be folly for the world to treat the Iranian leaders' words as anything but an articulation of their intent"[803] remained oddly decontextualized for a historian of antisemitism with his particular mind-set. Yet four centuries of *najis*-inspired Jew hatred in Shi'ite Iran, accompanied by pogroms, forced conversions, and other less violent but continuous forms of social and religious persecution—none of which are ever[804] mentioned by Goldhagen—surely meets his own prior standard—regardless of its validity—of an established "annihilationist" mentality in Germany. Irrespective of the controversy surrounding his earlier work on Nazi Germany,[805] Goldhagen's utter ignorance of Iran's centuries-old history of Jew hatred is pathognomonic of the current state of scholarship on Islamic antisemitism.

Nazism, the World War II Era, the Creation of Israel, and the Modern Exodus of Jews from Muslim Lands

During an interview conducted in the late 1930s (published in 1939),[806] Karl Jung, the Swiss psychiatrist and founder of analytical psychiatry, was asked "had he any views on what was likely to be the next step in religious development?" Jung replied, in reference to the Nazi fervor that had gripped Germany,

> We do not know whether Hitler is going to found a new Islam. He is already on the way; he is like Muhammad. The emotion in Germany is Islamic; warlike and Islamic. They are all drunk with wild god. That can be the historic future.[807]

Albert Speer, who was Hitler's minister of armaments and war production, wrote a contrite memoir[808] of his World War II experiences while serving a twenty-year prison sentence imposed by the Nuremberg tribunal.[808a] Speer's narrative includes this discussion that captures Hitler's racist views of Arabs on the one hand, and his effusive praise for Islam on the other:

> Hitler had been much impressed by a scrap of history he had learned from a delegation of distinguished Arabs. When the Mohammedans attempted to penetrate beyond France into Central Europe during the eighth century, his visitors had told him, they had been driven back at the Battle of Tours. Had the Arabs won this battle, the world would be Mohammedan today.[809] *For theirs was a religion that believed in spreading the faith by the sword and subjugating all nations to that faith. Such a creed was perfectly suited to the Germanic temperament* [emphasis added]. Hitler said that the conquering Arabs, because of their racial inferiority, would in the long run have been unable to contend with the harsher climate and conditions of the country. They could not have kept down the

more vigorous natives, so that *ultimately not Arabs but Islamized Germans could have stood at the head of this Mohammedan Empire* [emphasis added]. Hitler usually concluded this historical speculation by remarking, "You see, it's been our misfortune to have the wrong religion. Why didn't we have the religion of the Japanese, who regard sacrifice for the Fatherland as the highest good? The Mohammedan religion too would have been much more compatible to us than Christianity. Why did it have to be Christianity with its meekness and flabbiness?"[810]

A similar ambivalence characterized Nazi Germany's support for Arab Muslim causes in the World War II era.[811] Hitler, for example, in December 1937 even proposed omitting his "racial ladder" theory—which denigrated the Arabs—from a forthcoming Arabic translation of *Mein Kampf*.[811a] Moreover, it is a tragic irony that despite the "very low rung" occupied by Arabs in Hitler's racial ladder design,[812] the convergence between Nazi racist antisemitism and theological Muslim Jew hatred[813] still resonates across the Arab Muslim and larger non-Arab Muslim world to this day.

As Lukasz Hirszowicz has pointed out, the contentious question of historical Palestine "was as if made to order for the needs and aims of Nazi propaganda."[814] Accordingly, German policy already opposed the creation of a Jewish state based on a partition of Palestine even before the release of the Peel Commission recommendations on July 7, 1937. German diplomatic correspondence from June 1937 makes clear the Nazis' negative reaction to the Peel Commision's plan to partition Palestine into distinct Arab and Jewish states.

> Heretofore it was the primary goal of Germany's Jewish policy to promote the emigration of Jews from Germany as much as possible. In order to achieve this goal, sacrifices are even being made in foreign exchange policy. . . . The formation of a Jewish state or a Jewish-led political structure under British mandate is not in Germany's interest, since a Palestinian state would not absorb Jewry, but would create an additional position of power under international law for international Jewry, somewhat like the Vatican state for political Catholicism or Moscow for the Comintern.
>
> In reality . . . it is of greater interest to Germany to keep Jewry dispersed. For when no member of the Jewish race is settled on German soil any longer, the Jewish question will still not be solved for Germany. Rather, the developments of recent years have shown that international Jewry will of necessity always be the ideological and therefore political enemy of National Socialist Germany. The Jewish question is therefore at the same time one of the most important problems of German foreign policy.

Germany therefore has an interest in strengthening the Arab world as a counterweight against such a possible increase in power for world Jewry.[815]

A related area of convergence between the Arabs and Nazis was anti-British sentiment. Hirszowicz notes that a March 11, 1941, letter from German secretary of state Weizsäcker to the exiled mufti of Jerusalem, Hajj Amin el-Husseini, asserted

> that the Arabs and the Germans faced the same enemies—the English and the Jews.... Weizsäcker declared, in his letter to the ex-Mufti of Jerusalem, that the German Government was ready to cooperate with and extend to the Arabs military and financial aid when they were compelled to fight the British in order to achieve their national aims.[816]

Three months earlier the US envoy to Baghdad wrote of the mufti's importance to both emerging events in Iraq and the Arab world generally, in a November 11, 1940, report:

> With regard to the Mufti, my investigations convince me that he is the most highly respected and influential leader in Iraq today, both in religious and political circles.... He has gained a large following in Palestine and Syria and he is now developing a similar influence in Iraq. He is thus becoming a power to be reckoned with in the Arab world.[817]

By May 23, 1941, Hitler issued a directive extending military aid to Iraq for an Arab anti-British campaign. The introduction to this order stated, "The Arab liberation movement is our natural ally."[818] During the ensuing pro-Nazi uprising in Iraq of May and June 1941, it was the mufti who inspired local Muslim clergy to incite the Muslim populace with declarations of jihad against the British,[819] broadcasting over Iraqi and Axis radios his own "fatwa announcing jihad against Britain . . . the greatest foe of Islam" on May 9, 1941. Even after this failed effort to install and maintain a pro-Nazi regime in Baghdad, the mufti was welcomed in Berlin by Hitler (and his foreign minister, Ribbentrop) on November 28, 1941. Hitler pledged to fight the creation of a Jewish homeland in Palestine, and liquidate the Jewish communities in the Arab Muslim Near East. Hirszowicz provides this account of their exchanges:

> During his conversation with Ribbentrop and Hitler, the Mufti stressed that the Germans and Arabs were natural friends, since both were fighting three common enemies: Britain, the Jews, and Bolshevism. He offered to raise an Arab Legion and then directed the conversation to the question of the declaration [of Axis support].

After the usual tirade against the Jews, whom he considered to be the leaders of the states opposing him, Hitler declared to the Mufti: ". . . just a promise will be of no value. Only an assurance which rests on victorious armed forces is of real value." And he added: "Only if we win the war will the hour of liberation be also the hour of fulfillment of Arab aspirations."

> *Hitler assured the Mufti that Germany's uncompromising war against the Jews included active opposition to the Jewish national home in Palestine and that her objective was the destruction of the Jewish element residing in the Arab countries* [emphasis added]. . . . Hitler further declared to the Mufti at that time that the time would come when he (Hajj Amin) would not only present the Arabs with an Axis declaration. He [the Mufti] would also have the decisive voice in Arab affairs as the most authoritative spokesman for, and as *the* leader of the Arabs.[820]

On May 28, 1942, a subsequent written correspondence between Ribbentrop and the mufti (and Rashid Ali al-Kilani, the pro-Nazi Iraqi premier ousted in May and June 1941) reaffirmed their mutual commitment to liquidating the Jewish national home in Palestine, the only promise, Hirszowicz remarks, that "was unambiguous."[821] The mufti's pro-Nazi activities extended beyond the Arab countries and continued after the last Axis forces surrendered in Tunisia on May 13, 1943. Hirszowicz provides this concise overview of the mufti's "usefulness to the Germans," outside the Arab domain, through 1944:

> He was active in many other spheres even at the time of the Axis victories in the Soviet Union and North Africa. Documents show that he worked closely with the organizations of Muslim traitors from the Crimea, the Northern Caucasus, Azerbaijan, and Central Asia. He also did his share in pro-German propaganda in India. The Mufti most probably helped to form military units of Soviet Muslims and did much work among Balkan Muslims. Nazi propaganda boasted of his contribution in forming Waffen S.S. units of Bosnian Muslims. The list of questions the Mufti desired to raise with Auswärtiges Amt [the German Foreign Office] in May 1943 gives some idea of the range of his interests and activity. Besides the question of an Arab declaration the Mufti wanted to discuss problems of Croatia and the question of the S.S. Muslim division, problems of the Bulgarian Mohammedan population and intervention in that country for the purpose of preventing the emigration of 4,500 Jews (4,000 of them children) to Palestine; the question of turning over the former Jewish residences in Berlin to the Muslim Institute; the proposition for

setting up a special Arab-Muslim department in Auswärtiges Amt. *The Mufti's efforts to prevent Jewish emigration from Europe were an inseparable part of his activity during World War II. Among documents published after the war are some of his letters to the Governments of Bulgaria (May 6th, 1943), Italy (June 10th, 1943), Romania (June 28th, 1943), and Hungary (of the same date) [as Romania] demanding that they rescind permission for Jewish emigration. He urged that the Jews should be sent to Poland instead, "where they are under active supervision." The confession of one of Eichmann's collaborators, Dieter Wisliceny (hanged in Bratislava) and the evidence of R. Kasztner, a leader of Hungarian Jews, confirm the Mufti's role in preventing Jewish emigration from the European countries occupied by the Nazis. The testimony shows that the Mufti worked closely with the Nazi machinery responsible for exterminating the Jews* [emphasis added]. In 1944 he participated in organizing the anti-Jewish Congress at Krakow.[822]

Robert Satloff recently chronicled his remarkable personal odyssey[823] to find a phantom World War II/Holocaust-era hero among the Arabs, an "Arab (Raoul) Wallenberg."[824] Satloff's narrative discusses the infamous Wannsee Conference (held in Berlin during January 1942) "inventory" of Jewish populations (totaling 11 million persons) from thirty-one Nazi-controlled or targeted countries, all of which were earmarked for liquidation.[825] The Wannsee list also included the roughly five hundred thousand Jews living under French dominion in North Africa—the protectoraes of Morocco and Tunisia and the colony of Algeria. Libyan Jews under Italian colonial rule were not included in the Wannsee census.[825a] For three years, from the fall of France in June 1940 until the surrender of German troops in Tunisia on May 13, 1943, the European Axis powers—German Nazis, French Vichyites, and Italian Fascists—applied to these North African Arab countries under their control

> many of the same methods that would be used to devastating effect against the much larger Jewish populations in Europe, often at the same time and pace they were being used in Europe. These included not only statutes depriving Jews of citizenship, property, education, livelihood, and residence, but also forced labor, confiscations, deportations, and executions. The goal was to isolate Jews, to persecute them, and—in Tunisia at least—to lay the foundation for their eventual extermination. Virtually no Jew in North Africa was left untouched. Thousands suffered in more than 100 forced labor camps set up throughout the region. Many thousands more lost homes, farms, jobs, professions,

savings, and years of education. Still more lived in a state of perpetual fear and daily privation, victims of a ration system that gave them the least and gave it to them last. By a stroke of fortune, relatively few perished directly as a result of Fascist rule, with estimates ranging between 4,000 and 5,000 people. Some . . . were deported by Germans and Italians to their deaths in Europe. About 1,200 North African Jews, trapped in metropolitan France, were sent by the Vichy regime to Nazi death camps in Poland and elsewhere. The youngest was a three month old infant, Abrahim Taieb of Bône; the oldest, 85-year old Isaac Adda of Algiers. Some were killed in cold blood, others died of hunger or torture or disease in desert "punishment camps" in the Sahara. Many were killed in the almost-daily American and British bombings of Tunisia's air and seaports in the early months of 1943, when the Germans compelled Jewish laborers to work through the attacks at their hazardous jobs clearing rubble.[826]

Satloff attributes the dramatically lower death count for these Jews to the course of the war in North Africa, as well as logistical problems, but not lack of murderous intent on the part of the Nazis and their Axis allies:

> The low death count—just about 1 percent of the Jewish population in French North Africa, compared to more than half of all the Jews numbered on the Wannsee list—is as much testament to the fortunes of war as to the lesser threat faced by these Jews. The Mediterranean complicated the logistics of transport; Germany and its partners could not just stuff North African Jews into trains and send them to death camps in Central and Eastern Europe. But . . . the Tunisian experience suggests that the Nazis would have found alternatives, if they had had the time. That factor—time—was responsible for saving North African Jewry, most of all.[827]

The North African Muslim populace reacted primarily with "glacial indifference" to the Jews' plight.[828] However, as Satloff observes,

> many Arabs were not indifferent to the coming of the Jews' tormentors. "Go, go, I would wish to be with you, Hitler," were the lyrics of one popular Berber song of this period.[829]

He cites the following examples of such approving "Greek chorus" reactions:

> Gad Shahat, a veteran of Tunisia's Safsaf and Sedjanane work camps, recalled that local Arabs hailed German soldiers as they paraded Jews through the country's capital. "Muslims applauded the Nazi forces that arrested the Jews and made them march

through Tunis," he told an interviewer. "Muslims smashed bottles at us, at the Mateur station, jugs from which [we planned] to quench the thirst of old and tired Jews."

Yehoshua Duweib, another survivor of a Tunisian labor camp, testified that the "Arabs were gloating" when the Germans marched him and fellow Jews through town on the way to a work site. "They would say to us: 'Push the shovel, ya Shalom [a common Jewish name]. They meant: 'Until now you were a merchant or a clerk, but now you'll work hard.'" Even Arab women, breaking local custom that kept them in their homes virtually all the time, came out to watch and laugh at the humbled Jewish workers, he said.

Victor Cohen, also from Tunis, reported that when the Germans herded Jewish laborers through the streets, the "true nature" of the city's Arabs was finally revealed. "They were happy," he said. "They would mock and laugh: 'Take the shovel, pick up the shovel.'"

Yehuda Chachmon, who lived under Italian rule in Benghazi, Libya, said Arab street gangs grew so brazen and powerful during the war years that Jews were too afraid to leave their homes after dark. "Arabs would throw oranges, tomatoes, stones at us," he said. "Every Jew would hide in his house after five in the evening. The houses were closed [i.e., locked up] with bars and you could not leave until the morning."

Ernest-Yehoshua Orzan, a sales representative for his family's business, was ordered by the Germans to do his forced labor on a farm in Tunisia. He recalled the special pleasure some Arabs derived from the misfortune of Jews. "Near the farm where we worked were several Arab families [who would] always try to tell us things like: 'Your Tunis has been completely destroyed by bombings. . . . No one was left alive in the city of Tunis.' They knew we were from Tunis. They always 'made sure' to tell us things like that," he said.[830]

Other more aggressively hateful Muslims committed acts of violence against Jews, which ranged from brutalizing internment camp prisoners to participating in murderous anti-Jewish riots.[831]

Arab guards played the role of torturers, for example, in Saharan internment camps. Jews imprisoned in the southern Morocco camps of 'Ain al-Ourak and Foum Deflah

were subjected to the *tombeau*, French for "tomb," a method of punishment in which camp overseers ordered prisoners to dig holes in the ground two meters long, fifty centimeters wide and thirty-five centimeters deep and to lie in these faux graves for weeks on end. They stayed there day and night,

exposed to blistering summer heat that could rise more than 120 degrees F and frigid winter nights that could dip to below freezing. They lay in their own waste, surviving only on bread and water. The slightest movement by prisoners would trigger, in the words of one witness, "a rain of stones or blows from rifles" from camp guards.[832]

A Jewish survivor of another camp, Djelfa, in the Algerian desert, gave the following account of his torture by Arab guards, which he further claimed was gratuitous and not ordered by their superiors:

For the slightest infraction of the rules, they would bury you in the sand up to your neck. And the Arabs would urinate on your head. And if you moved your head, they would take a big stone and smash your head. You weren't supposed to move. If a scorpion or a viper or ants or whatever there was would bite you, you could not move.

The only way we could fight back, the only way we could protest this cruel treatment, was by not giving in to their punishment. They could beat us all they want . . . and we would sit quietly and silently absorb it, without a peep. We would not even make a sound, a noise. It would hurt. It would bleed. You would be in excruciating pain. And the more we defied them in our own way, the more they would beat us . . . and figure out more punishments, bigger punishments, longer punishments, more beatings, no water for the day, no food for two days, standing naked being tied to a post in the sun all day, in the hot African sun, putting a bucket of ants over your head, burying you in the sand to your neck and urinating on your head, and beating your head open—and nothing they did could make us make a sound.

The cruelty and the barbaric manners of the guards, that came out by themselves. Nobody told them to beat us all the time. Nobody told them to chain us together. Nobody told them to beat us up with chains and whips. . . . Nobody told them to tie us naked to a post and beat us and to hang us by our arms and hose us down, to bury us in the sand so our heads should look up and bash our brains in and urinate on our heads. Nobody told them to do that. They told us we're supposed to be confined to work on the Transsahrien [railroad]. But nobody told them how much or how hard or how. . . . No, they took this into their own hands and they enjoyed what they did. You could see it on their faces; they enjoyed it.[833]

And Tunisia was the sight of anti-Jewish riots by local Arab mobs, swelled with conscripts returning from the defeated French army after its surrender to Nazi Germany.

In August 1940, the towns of Kef, Ebba, Ksour, Moktar, and Siliana were the scene of riots and pillaging against Jews. . . . In November 1940, there was an anti-Jewish riot in Degache. In early 1941, the same fate befell the Jewish community in Gafsa.

[I]n May 1941, the coastal city of Gabès was the scene . . . of a three-day paroxysm of violence, pillage, and murder. What started with an attack by a gang of thirty Arabs on a synagogue, perhaps prompted by news of the demise of the short-lived pro-Nazi regime in Iraq, deteriorated into a mass frenzy of violence that left eight Jews killed and twenty injured. Again, local Arab policemen were, at best ineffective, and at worst, complicit. The rampage in Gabès was blood-curdling. Yosef Huri, a survivor, recalled what happened to his neighbor, Afila Rakach. Rakach was in her small kitchen, cooking dinner for her family, when a gang of local Arabs barged into her home. According to Huri, they grabbed a pot of boiling soup, poured it over her, tortured her in her house, stoned her, and then killed her. Another survivor, Youssef Mimoun, recalled that in one quarter of Gabès, Arab and Jewish neighbors had joined together for an evening of celebration—eating and drinking—the night before the rioting. The same people who had broken bread with the Jews one night, attacked them the next. "Although we had good relations, there were those among them who hated Jews just because we were Jews," he said. Tzvi Haddad, who lived at the end of a largely Arab street near a coffee house, remained haunted by the image of his mother, who left their home at the first sign of trouble to look for his sister. As soon as his mother got out the door, he recalled, an Arab knocked her down and then another grabbed her and tried to cut her throat. Tzvi heard his mother's screams, ran out to the street, saw blood flowing on her face and legs. Eventually, Tzvi's father arrived to rescue his wife, who, miraculously, survived. She carried a scar on her throat for the rest of her life.[834]

Satloff reached these somber conclusions after searching "fruitlessly" for his "Arab Wallenberg":

[M]any Arabs did more than just cheer on the sidelines as Jews were marched off to forced labor. They provided the manpower—guards, foremen, train conductors, and so forth—that made the persecution possible. And, if numerous eyewitness accounts are to be believed, a sizable number often performed their tasks willfully, even eagerly. Sometimes their zealousness was characterized by gratuitous violence that bordered on the sadistic. It was against the background of the raucous cheering of thousands that these essential Arab cogs in the Nazi, Vichy, and Fascist war machinery did their jobs [emphasis added].

Where Arabs lived, . . . persecution certainly existed. It did not descend to the level of extermination . . . but—as in Tunisia—that was more for lack of time than lack of will. Even in that small country, hardly central to German imperial designs, where the Nazis never controlled more than one-third of the country, and where Allied bombs fell day and night, the invaders still found the wherewithal to dispatch the SS to set up the scaffolding of the "final solution." This included officially sanctioned torture, confiscation, deportation, and murder. If the tides of war had turned in different directions, this almost surely would have evolved into full-fledged genocide. Not only did such persecution exist where Arabs lived, but Arabs played a role at every level [emphasis added]. Some went door-to-door with the Germans, pointing out Jews for arrest. Others led Jewish workers on forced marches or served as overseers at labor camps. They manned the railroads that took bewildered European Jews deep into the Sahara, prepared the gruel that passed for food at torture sites, patrolled the streets of Bizerte [Tunisian seaport], Tunis, and Sousse [NE Tunisia coastal town], armed with guns and clubs, looking for Jewish escapees. Some took these jobs because they needed money to feed their families; others volunteered because they were zealous about their work. Every person's story was different, but the common thread that connected them was their undeniability.[835]

However, a slightly more hopeful postscript to this bleak narrative has emerged: at the end of January 2007, several months after the publication of Satloff's book, Khaled Abdelwahhab, a Tunisian Arab, became the first Arab nominated for recognition as "Righteous among the Nations" by Yad Vashem, Israel's official Holocaust memorial.[836] While researching his book, Satloff had discovered that Abdelwahhab apparently sheltered some twenty-three Jews in an olive oil factory during the last months of the German occupation of Tunisia in 1943.

Sadly, the more prevalent and enduring legacy of the Nazi era in the Arab world—which plagues the region to this day—is epitomized by the asylum provided to Nazis and Nazi collaborators in the aftermath of World War II, particularly by Syria and Egypt. Bat Ye'or describes this phenomenon:

[T]hey lived under false names and worked in anti-Zionist propaganda centers, such as the Institute for the Study of Zionism, which was founded in Cairo, in 1955. Its director, Alfred Zingler (alias Mahmoud Saleh), worked together with Dr. Johannes von Leers (d. 1965, alias Omar Amin), who had been a specialist on the "Jewish Question" in Josef Goebbels' propaganda department. Zingler's main assistants were Dr. Werner Witschale and Hans Appler (Saleh Shafar), who had also served on the staff of Goebbels' ministry, as well as Louis Heiden. Heiden was the editor of one of the many Arabic versions of *The Protocols of the Elders of Zion* and of a translation of Hitler's *Mein Kampf* into Arabic. In 1955, the Cairo Egyptian special services for anti-Jewish and anti-Zionist propaganda hired Appler.

Other Nazis settled in Egypt as well. Most of them worked with the Egyptian government as advisers on anti-Zionist propaganda or assisted with the organization of police forces or as military trainers in Palestinian terrorist camps. In 1957, according to *Frankfurter Illustrierte* [August 25, 1957], *the number of Nazis in Egypt was two thousand* [emphasis added].[837] Erich Altern (Ali Bella), the chief of the Jewish section of the Gestapo in occupied Galicia [Eastern Central Europe, between Poland and Ukraine] during the war, escaped to Egypt in the early 1950s, where he served as a military instructor in the Palestinian camps. [Standartenfuhrer (an SS regiment leader)] Baumann (Ali Ben Khader), who had collaborated in the extermination of Jews in the Warsaw ghetto and went into hiding, became a military specialist in Egypt for the army of the Palestine Liberation Organization (PLO).[838]

The pervasive impact of this ugly mentality is perhaps best illustrated by then Col. Anwar El-Sadat's 1953 "Letter to Hitler." When, in September 1953, several news agency reports were circulated claiming that Hitler was still alive, the Cairo weekly *Al Musawwar* posed this question to a number of Egyptian personalities, including Sadat: "If you wished to send Hitler a personal letter, what would you write to him?"[838a] In response, Sadat wrote the following, published September 18, 1953:

My dear Hitler,

I congratulate you from the bottom of my heart. Even if you appear to have been defeated, in reality you are the victor. *You succeeded in creating dissensions between Churchill, the old man, and his allies, the Sons of Satan* [emphasis added]. Germany will win because her existence is necessary to preserve the world balance. Germany will be reborn in spite of the Western and Eastern powers. There will be no peace unless Germany once again becomes what she was. The West, as well as the East, will pay for her rehabilitation—whether they like it or not. Both sides will invest a great deal of

money and effort in Germany in order to have her on their side, which is of great benefit to Germany. So much for the present and the future. As for the past, I think you made mistakes, like too many battlefronts and the shortsightedness of Ribbentrop vis-à-vis the experienced British diplomacy. But your trust in your country and people will atone for those blunders. *We will not be surprised if you appear again in Germany or if a new Hitler rises up in your wake* [emphasis added].[839]

The two decades following World War II witnessed a rapid dissolution of the major Jewish communities in the Arab Muslim world (and the significant attrition of the Jewish population in Turkey, discussed earlier).[840] As Norman Stillman has observed, even the first decade after World War II saw

the overall Jewish population in the Arab countries . . . reduced by half through emigration. In several countries the decline was far greater. By the end of 1953, Iraq, Yemen, and Libya had lost over 90 percent of their Jews, and Syria 75 percent. Most of the Jews who remained in the Arab world were in the French-ruled Maghreb. It was not long, however, before the three countries of that region achieved their independence. Within little more than two decades after the end of World War II, most of the North African Jews were gone as well.[841]

Although the Arab-Israeli conflict combined with the end of French colonial rule in North Africa may have served as catalysts for this mass exodus, these phenomena were antedated by a more powerful underlying dynamic set in motion during the nineteenth-century era of Western colonization.[842] Bat Ye'or[843] and Stillman[844] highlight the profound political and psychosocial impact of the West's penetration into the Islamic world through the nineteenth and twentieth centuries, which undermined (at least temporarily, and in part) the prevailing system of *dhimmitude*:

(*Bat Ye'or*) They were no longer forbidden to have a position that might give them equality or superiority over a Muslim. They could revive their prohibited language, as well as their history and their culture. They were no longer dehumanized *dhimmis*, deprived of the right to speak, to defend themselves and to preserve their own history. . . . The national liberation of a *dhimmi* people [i.e., the Jews of Israel] meant the abolishment of the laws of dhimmitude . . . [in] their historical homeland.

(*Norman Stillman*) . . . the Jews and most native Christians . . . viewed it [European colonial governance] as a liberation from their traditional subordinate *dhimmi* status, which since the later Middle

Ages [at least] had been rigorously imposed upon them. The Jews and Christians of the Muslim world were quick to see that increased European interference and penetration into the affairs of their region meant a weakening of the traditional Islamic norms of society and could only better their own position, which was one religiously and legally defined inferiority.

Christian and Jewish *dhimmi* populations availed themselves eagerly of the modern educational programs provided by an array of Western religious and cultural representatives inundating the Middle East and North Africa. The Alliance Israélite Universelle, for Jews, specifically

became the chief provider of modern education in the major towns and cities of most Arab countries from the 1860s onward. French, rather than Arabic or Turkish, became the primary language of high culture for thousands upon thousands of Jews. The Alliance gave its pupils far more than education. It gave them new self-image, created new expectations within them, and helped to arouse a sense of international Jewish solidarity.[845]

Jews and Christians took advantage of these educational opportunities, which aroused the ire of the Muslim masses:

[Western education] . . . produced cadres of westernized native Jews who now had a distinct advantage over the largely uneducated Muslim masses as the Islamic world was drawn ineluctably into the modern world economic system. Together with the rapidly evolving native Christians who benefited from missionary schools, Jews came to have a place in the economic life of the Middle East and North Africa that was far out of proportion to their numbers or their social status in the general population. Their foreign ties, Western acculturation and economic success were deeply resented by the Muslim Arab majority. This conspicuous overachievement by some Jews and Christians would contribute to their undoing as a group in the twentieth century with the rise of nationalism in the Arab world.[846]

Decolonization led to the recrudescence of *dhimmitude* as an inevitable consequence when the aroused jihadist forces (whether traditional or thinly veiled under the guise of "secular Arab nationalism")[847] helped end Western colonial rule. For Jews, traditional Islamic antisemitism accompanied this *dhimmitude*, intensified by a furious anti-Zionism seamlessly interwoven with both Islamic and modern European antisemitism, especially Nazism.[848] This predictable course of events was foreshadowed during the waning years of European colo-

nialism when the policy of protecting non-Muslim minority rights was sacrificed in order to appease the restive majority Muslim populations:

The Jews of Arab lands had no vested interest in the old social and political order of their traditional Muslim overlords. Therefore, they welcomed European political domination that began with the French conquest of Algeria in the 1830s and culminated in the carving up of the Ottoman Empire at the end of World War I. It was their misfortune to discover that the hopes they placed in their British, French, and Italian masters would be disappointed again and again. In the nineteenth century, the European powers sought to extend their protection to the non-Muslim minorities, in part, to gain greater influence in the region. Once much of the Middle East and North Africa were under European control in the twentieth century, the colonial and mandatory authorities were frequently more concerned with appeasing, or at least not offending, the Muslim majority than in protecting the Jewish and Christian minorities, especially as the tide of Arab nationalism began to rise and swell. It was this powerful tide that would eventually engulf and destroy the Jewish and some of the Christian communities in the Arab world.[849]

Addressing the Political Committee of the UN General Assembly with regard to the proposed Partition Plan for Palestine (Resolution 181), on November 24, 1947, Egyptian delegate Heykal Pasha, a "well-known liberal,"[850] threatened,

The United Nations . . . should not lose sight of the fact that the proposed solution might endanger a million Jews living in the Muslim countries. Partition of Palestine might create Antisemitism in those countries even more difficult to root out than the Antisemitism which the Allies tried to eradicate in Germany. . . . If the United Nations decides to partition Palestine, it might be responsible for very grave disorders and for the massacre of the large number of Jews. . . . A million Jews live in peace in Egypt [and the other Muslim states] and enjoy all rights of citizenship. They have no desire to emigrate to Palestine. However, if a Jewish state were established, nobody could prevent disorders. Riots would break out in Palestine, would spread through all the Arab states and might lead to a war between two races.[851]

Five days later, on November 29, 1947, the UN General Assembly adopted Resolution 181, known as the "Partition Plan." Littman summarizes Resolution 181, its relationship to the 1922 League of Nations Mandate, and its reception by the Arab League:

Called the "Partition Plan," it [divided] the land west of the Jordan River into two parts: an Arab state and a Jewish state, with an international *corpus separatum* for Jerusalem. It comprised about 22 percent of the roughly 120,000 km² of the original 1922 League of Nations area of Palestine. All the land east of the Jordan River—78 percent, about 94,000 km² of the entire mandatory area— had been transferred to the Emir Abdullah of Arabia by Britain, thus creating the *de facto* Emirate of Trans-Jordan, later to be re-named in 1949 the Hashemite Kingdom of Jordan. This 1947 Partition Plan was categorically refused by all the Arab League States and also by the Arab-Palestinian leadership, still nominally headed by the Mufti of Jerusalem, Hajj Amin el-Husseini, who found refuge in Egypt in 1946 (he moved to Beirut in 1962).[852]

Heykal Pasha's speech provides a useful benchmark for delineating three phases of pogroms and persecutions that caused the exodus of Jews from Arab Muslim nations: in the decade prior to his speech, in the immediate aftermath of the speech and the UN Partition vote in November 1947, and the Arab-Israeli War of May and June 1948 and ensuing two decades.

The Baghdad pogrom (the "Farhud") of June 1941— fomented by Hajj Amin el-Husseini, during his World War II sojourn in Iraq[853]—was followed by three outbursts of anti-Jewish violence in November 1945—in Egypt, Libya, and Syria.[854] Baghdad (1941) and Libya (Tripolitania, 1945) experienced major pogroms: Hundreds of Jews were killed and thousands wounded, accompanied by widespread devastation to Jewish homes, synagogues, and businesses.[855] During the Farhud, Stillman maintains, 179 Jews (including women and children) were murdered, 242 children orphaned, 586 businesses looted, and 911 buildings housing 12,000 individuals were pillaged.[856] Estimates for property damage ranged from 680,000 to 2.7 million pounds.[857] Naim Kattan, an Iraqi Jew, described the Farhud in this eyewitness account from his autobiographical *Farewell Babylon*:

The Jews would bear the cost of this repressed hunger, this devouring thirst. Two days and a night. We could hear shots in the distance. They came closer and gradually grew clearer. The conflagration invaded new grounds. Soon it would swallow up everything. They advanced. Armed with picks, daggers, sometimes with rifles, they unfurled in waves, surrounded the city, beleaguered it. As they passed through, they brought along Muslims, spared the Christians. Only the Jews were being pursued. As they advanced, their ranks swelled, teeming with women, children, and adolescents

who ululated as they did on great occasions such as weddings and feasts. They reached the target. It was the poorest part of town, Abou Sifain. They pushed down the gates and moved in. What could not be carried away was demolished. Then a second wave entered the devastated site. The men were sent away. Those who put up the slightest resistance had their throats cut on the spot. And the women were made to submit to the will of the men. . . . The Chief Rabbi published a notice of mourning: the community had lost three hundred members. *People laughed in his face. Only three hundred!* Was he in league with the government? Or perhaps he only wanted to lessen the horror. . . . The dead were entitled to a prayer and the repose of their souls. And what of the hundreds of girls who had been savagely raped? At best they hoped to keep their misfortune secret.[858]

Elie Kedourie has written that six hundred Jews were murdered during the Farhud (in support of Kattan's implication that many more than three hundred had been killed), noting, that the figure of six hundred "is the official figure which was kept confidential at the time."[858a]

Recurrent anti-Zionist/antisemitic incitement from 1943 to 1945 culminated in a series of anti-Jewish riots during November of 1945.[859] Egypt was the site of the first of these riots. Stillman provides this account.[860]

Anti-Zionist demonstrations had been called for by such groups as Misr al-Fatat, the Muslim Brotherhood, and the Young Men's Muslim Association. A few days before the demonstrations were to take place, the British assistant commandant of the Cairo city police noted an atmosphere of "considerable ill-feeling in Cairo against Jews." However, he believed that with proper security precautions, there was no need for undue concern. Events proved otherwise, however. *Mass demonstrations took place on November 2 (Balfour Declaration Day) in Cairo and Alexandria, with smaller ones in Port Said, Mansura, and Tanta.* In Cairo, mobs pillaged Jewish businesses in the main part of town, in the Muski [a main, narrow street], and in the Jewish Quarter. The Ashkenazi synagogue was ransacked and burned. As often has been the case in the history of the Islamic world, violence initially directed against one non-Muslim minority easily spilled over into a generalized anti-*dhimmi* violence. Coptic, Greek Orthodox, and Catholic institutions were also attacked, as well as shops owned by foreigners. Some 500 businesses were looted, 109 of these belonging to Jews. Damage was estimated to be in excess of 1 million Egyptian pounds. Injuries numbered in the hundreds, but amazingly only one person, a policeman, was killed. In Alexandria, the rioting claimed six lives, five of them Jewish, and another 150 persons were injured. Some disturbances continued on the following day. The king and some prominent public figures expressed their regrets at what happened, and the government offered to bear the expenses for rebuilding the ruined synagogue. At the same time, however, there were calls from the Islamic religious establishment for Chief Rabbi Hayyim Nahum to issue a public statement repudiating Zionism. The chief rabbi responded with a letter to Prime Minister al-Nuqrashi Pasha, in which he included an earlier note that he had sent to the World Jewish Congress declaring the loyalty of the Jewish community to Egypt, declaring the need for finding some less confined refuge than Palestine for the survivors of the Holocaust, and expressing the hope that Jews and Arabs would cooperate in solving the problem "in an atmosphere of complete accord."

Neither the protestations of loyalty by the chief rabbi nor the expressions of regret and sympathy by government officials could restore Egyptian Jewry's sense of security, since the general atmosphere of hostility remained unchanged. As Thomas Mayer[861] has rightly pointed out, "the critics of the riots did nothing to prevent the distribution of anti-Jewish propaganda in Egypt," and "the Egyptian Jews continued to be harassed by Pan-Arab and Islamic societies, as well as by Government officials, and pressed to make anti-Zionist declarations."

One day after the rioting in Egypt subsided, much more extensive and devastating anti-Jewish violence erupted in Libya. A minor altercation between Arabs and Jews near the electric power station outside the Jewish quarter of Tripoli was followed the next day (November 5) by an anti-Jewish pogrom:

[M]obs numbering in the thousands poured into the Jewish quarter and the Suq al-Turk (the bazaar where many Jewish shops were located) and went on a rampage of looting, beating, and killing. According to one confidential report, weapons were distributed to the rioters at certain command centers, one of which was the shop of Ahmad Krawi, a leading Arab merchant . . . only Jews and Jewish property were attacked. The rioters had no difficulty in distinguishing Jewish homes and businesses because prior to the attack, doors had been marked with chalk in Arabic indicating "Jew," "Italian," or "Arab." Mob passions reached a fever pitch when a rumor spread that the Chief Qadi of Tripoli had been murdered by Jews and the Shari'a Court burned. The terror then spread to the nearby towns of Amrus, Tagiura, Zawia, Zanzur, and Qusabat.[862]

Zachino Habib, Tripoli's Jewish community president, provided this eyewitness account of what transpired in Tripoli, Zanzur, Zawia, Qusabat, and Zitlin on November 4–5, 1945:

[T]he Arabs attacked the Jews in obedience to mysterious orders. Their outbursts of violence had no plausible motive. For fifty hours they hunted men down, attacked houses and shops, killed men, women, old and young, horribly tortured and dismembered Jews isolated in the interior. . . . In order to carry out the slaughter, the attackers used various weapons: knives, daggers, sticks, clubs, iron bars, revolvers, and even hand grenades.[863]

Stillman assessed the toll of the pogrom in lives and property, as well as its psychosocial impact:

When the pogroms—for that is what the riots essentially were—were over, 130 Jews were dead, including thirty-six children. Some entire families were wiped out. Hundreds were injured, and approximately 4,000 people were left homeless. An additional 4,200 were reduced to poverty. There were many instances of rape, especially in the provincial town of Qusabat, where many individuals embraced Islam to save themselves. Nine synagogues—five in Tripoli, four in the provincial towns—had been desecrated and destroyed. More than 1,000 residential buildings and businesses had been plundered in Tripoli alone. Damage claims totaled more than one quarter of a billion lire (over half a million pounds sterling). The Tripolitanian pogroms dealt, in the words of one observer [Haim Abravanel, director of Alliance schools in Tripoli], "an unprecedented blow . . . to the Jews' sense of security." Many leading Arab notables condemned the atrocities, but as the British Military Administration's *Annual Report* for 1945 noted, "no general, deep-felt sense of guilt seems to animate the Arab community at large; nor has it been too active in offering help to the victims."[864]

Minor anti-Jewish violence also occurred on November 18, 1945, in Syria (coinciding with the Muslim holiday al-Id al-Kabir, the culmination of the hajj [pilgrimage] rites at Mina, Saudi Arabia), when "a mob broke into the Great Synagogue of Aleppo, smashed votive objects, burned prayer books, and beat up two elderly men who were studying there."[865]

Shortly after Heykal Pasha's November 24, 1947, speech and the November 29, 1947, UN vote that adopted the "Partition Plan" for Palestine, demonstrations were held (December 2 to 5) throughout the Arab Muslim world to protest the UN decision.[866] These demonstrations sparked anti-Jewish violence in Bahrain, Aleppo, and the British protectorate of Aden. The riots in

Aleppo and Aden were severe—many Jews were killed, significant physical devastation occurred, and roughly half of Aleppo's Jewish population fled.

In Bahrain, the first two days of demonstrations were marked only by some minor stone throwing at individual members of the small Jewish community. Beginning on December 5, however, crowds in al-Manama, the capital, began looting Jewish homes and shops, destroyed the synagogue, and beat up any Jews they could lay their hands upon. Miraculously, only one elderly woman was killed.

The rioting in Aleppo, Syria, took a far greater toll. The venerable Jewish community was physically devastated. At least 150 homes, 50 shops, all of the community's 18 synagogues, 5 schools, its orphanage, and a youth club were destroyed. Property was estimated at $2.5 million. Many people were reported killed, but no figures have ever been advanced. More than half of the city's 10,000 Jews fled across the borders into Turkey, Lebanon, and Palestine.

Similar devastation engulfed the Jewish community in the British-controlled protectorate of Aden. As in the Tripolitanian pogroms of 1945, the police, composed mainly of natives, proved unable to contain the rioting and in some places took part in it themselves. Troops had to be called in to quell the violence. By the time order was finally restored on December 4th, 82 Jews had been killed and a similar number injured. Of the 170 Jewish-owned shops in the Crater (the main town of Aden), 106 were totally destroyed and 8 more partially sacked. Hundreds of houses and all of the Jewish communal institutions, including the synagogue and the two schools, were burned to the ground. Many people had lost everything. Four thousand Jews had to be fed by the authorities. Rioters also wrought havoc upon the small Jewish communities in the surrounding towns and in the Hashed camp housing Yemenite Jewish refugees. The Adeni Jewish community claimed that the damage it had suffered exceeded over 1 million pounds.[867]

Such violent anti-Jewish outbursts following the November 1947 UN vote to partition Palestine further demoralized Jews living in eastern Arab countries, whose confidence had already been shaken by the 1941 Baghdad Farhud and the 1945 riots in Libya, Egypt, and Syria. The steady reemergence of Islamic (or its corollary "Arab") national identity in these countries also subjected the Jews to chronic discrimination in employment. Stillman elucidates these trends:

Expressions of sympathy from political leaders and reassurances that they had nothing to fear as long as they were not associated with Zionism offered little solace. The press, students, members of the political opposition, and religious leaders rarely maintained the fine distinction between Jews and Zionists. Calls for jihad . . . heightened interreligious tensions. Prominent Jews were increasingly called upon to make declarations of solidarity with the Palestinian Arab cause, not to mention generous contributions.

The waves of anti-Jewish violence that had struck almost every major Jewish community from Libya to Iraq, beginning with Baghdadi Farhud of 1941 and culminating in the widespread rioting of 1945 and 1947, had eroded the Jews' confidence in these countries. The Palestine issue was, of course, a major contributing factor in all of this, but it was by no means the only one. Indeed, it was more of a catalyst precipitating and sharpening other problematic issues.

More and more, Jews were finding themselves in the position of "odd man out" as the societies around them cultivated nationalisms with a strong ethnic and religious component (namely, Arabic and Islamic). . . . This was true in Iraq, where most of the Jews had roots going back two and a half millennia, as it was in Egypt, where most of them were of relatively recent foreign origin. Already in the late 1930s, Jewish civil servants were being weeded out of the Iraqi bureaucracy, utilities, and public corporations to make room for "real Iraqis." Throughout the late 1930s and 1940s, Egypt enacted a series of legislative measures aimed at Egyptianizing the economy. The Company Law of 1947, for example, specified that at least 75 percent of the employees, 90 percent of the laborers, and 51 percent of the capital in companies incorporated in the country had to be Egyptian. Since the majority of Jews in Egypt either held foreign nationalities or were technically stateless persons, they could not help but be adversely affected by the Company Law. The President of Cairo's Jewish community estimated privately that the Company Law jeopardized the jobs of perhaps as many as 50,000 Jews. Already in 1945, Minister of Commerce and Industry Hafni Mahmud was differentiating between "nominal Egyptians," and "real Egyptians" with regard to employment.[868]

The ongoing isolation and alienation of Jews from the larger Arab Muslim societies in which they lived accelerated considerably after the establishment of Israel on May 15, 1948, and the immediate war on the nascent Jewish state declared and waged by members of the Arab League. A rapid annihilation of Israel and its Jewish population was predicted and savored by Arab leaders such as Azzam Pasha, the secretary of the Arab League, who declared:

[T]his will be a war of extermination and a momentous massacre which will be spoken of like the Mongolian massacres and the crusades.[869]

Such widely held expectations may have subdued violent mob reactions of the Arab masses against Middle Eastern and North African Jews at the outset of the war. However, once the Arab offensive in Palestine experienced setbacks, several weeks after the war began, anti-Jewish violence erupted in Morocco and Libya:

The first such incidents took place on June 7 and 8 *in the northeastern Moroccan towns of Oujda and Jerada. Forty-two Jews were killed and approximately 150 injured, many of them seriously. Scores of homes and shops were sacked* [emphasis added].
    On June 12, the day after the first truce was declared between the Israeli and Arab forces in Palestine, mobs attacked the Jewish Quarter in Tripoli, Libya. (Thousands of Moroccan and Tunisian volunteers had been streaming through the city on their way east to join the Arab armies fighting in Palestine.) However, Jewish self-defense units, which had been organized here as in other cities that had suffered pogroms in recent years, repelled the attackers with stones, handguns, grenades, and Molotov cocktails, inflicting heavy casualties. The rioters then turned upon undefended neighborhoods outside Hara. Only thirteen or fourteen Jews were killed and twenty-two seriously injured, but property damage was very high. Approximately 300 families were left destitute. There were also attacks against the Jews in the surrounding countryside and in Benghazi.[870]

These events were followed by a series of violent disturbances in Egypt. Despite a second truce in Palestine declared on July 18, 1948,

anti-Jewish and anti-foreign agitation in the mosques and in the press reached a fever pitch. The atmosphere was even more highly charged by the coincidence of Ramadan, the holy month of fasting. There were sporadic assaults against Jews and foreigners in the streets in the days immediately following the [Israeli air force] air raids.[871]

During the next three months Egyptian Jewry was under siege:

[B]ombs destroyed Jewish-owned movie theaters and large retail businesses, including the Adès, Gategno, and Benzion establishments. In all, attacks on Jews claimed approximately fifty lives in the summer of 1948, with tremendous property losses. The injured, homeless, and unemployed numbered in the hundreds. Public protestations of loyalty and condemnations by Jewish notables and large contributions totaling nearly a quarter of a million dollars to the Welfare Fund for Egyptian troops fighting in Palestine did not bring security. A series of bombs in the Jewish Quarter killed 29 people on September 22, and fifty Jews were arrested on trumped-up charges. Morale in the community reached a particularly low ebb during this period, and according to a confidential American Jewish Committee report, there was a marked increase in conversions to Islam and Christianity.[872]

The signing of Arab-Israeli armistice agreements in the spring and summer of 1949 rekindled a cautious optimism among many upper, and some middle-class Egyptian, Iraqi, and Syrian Jews

that they could make the best of the new situation and return to some semblance of life as usual. In Egypt, Iraq, and even Syria for a brief time during the short-lived regime of Husni al-Za'im, these hopes were fostered by the easing of some restrictions imposed during the war and the release of many individuals who had been imprisoned on flimsy charges. In Egypt, hope was reinforced by the restoration of much of the property that had been placed under government stewardship. Furthermore, it was clear that much of the violence against Jews had not been government sponsored, although the authorities were certainly responsible for allowing the development of (and in part fostering) an atmosphere conducive to such violence and for taking inadequate steps to protect their Jewish minorities. For their part, government officials saw that, once unleashed, popular violence could get dangerously out of hand for all concerned, as the assassination of Egypt's Prime Minister al-Nuqrashi Pasha by the Muslim Brotherhood in December 1948.[873]

This optimism quickly faded for the Jews of Syria and Iraq, lasted perhaps until the 1956 Suez War among Egyptian Jews, and never existed for Libyan or Yemenite Jewry.[874] French disengagement from colonial rule in North Africa between 1954 and 1962 created anxiety in the Jewish populations of Morocco, Tunisia, and Algeria.[875] These tensions and fears are mirrored in the waves of mass exodus of Jews: almost immediately and completely for the Jews of Libya and Yemen (between 1949 and 1951); a slightly delayed mass exodus of Iraqi Jews by the end of 1951 (after which only 6,000 remained out of approximately 140,000, circa 1945); the rapid attrition of Syria's population, "of mass proportions in relation to the smallness of the community," by 1953; the flight of 60 percent of Egyptian Jewry within twelve months after the 1956 war, despite being required to abandon almost all their assets except for some items of clothing; a dramatic rise in Jewish emigration from Morocco and Tunisia in anticipation of their independence from France, which continued steadily once independence was achieved; and a precipitous and nearly complete exodus of Algerian Jewry in anticipation of Algerian independence in July 1962.[876]

The "best case" scenarios of Morocco and Tunisia may be most instructive. Muhammad V of Morocco and Habib Bourguiba of Tunisia—relatively progressive leaders—each initially appointed a Jew to their respective cabinets, and allotted Jews positions within their government bureaucracies.[877] A Muslim-Jewish group promoting interfaith understanding, named al-Wifaq (Entente), was even created in Morocco within the nationalist Istiqlal party. Despite these "goodwill gestures," no sustained policies were implemented to combat anti-Jewish discrimination, and the exodus of Jews continued apace.

> Neither Jewish minister survived the first reshuffling of their respective cabinets. More significantly, no Jew was appointed again to a ministerial post in either Morocco or Tunisia. The proponents of intercommunal entente made little impression on the Jewish and Muslim masses from whom they were totally removed. The cordiality shown to Jews in some of the highest echelons of government did not percolate down to the lower ranks of officialdom, which exhibited attitudes that ranged from traditional contempt to outright hostility. The natural progression in both countries toward increased identification with the rest of the Arab world (first Morocco, then Tunisia entered the Arab League in 1958) only widened the gulf between Muslims and Jews. Furthermore, government steps to reduce Jewish communal autonomy, such as Tunisian Law No. 58-78 of July 11, 1958, which dissolved the Jewish Communal Council of Tunis and replaced it with the Provisional Commission for the Oversight of Jewish Religious Matters, having far more circumscribed authority, had negative psychological consequences for Jews, who saw their traditional structures under siege. The official pressure on Jewish educational institutions for arabization and cultural conformity only succeeded in feeding the Jews' worst fears, rather than fostering integration.[878]

The continuing steady departure of Jews from Tunisia picked up momentum following violent clashes between the French and Tunisian governments in 1961 over the naval base at Bizerte. Widespread anti-Jewish riots in Tunis beginning on June 5, 1967, during the Six-Day War reduced Tunisian Jewry to a small remnant population within a year.

> At the height of the [Bizerte] crisis, Jews were accused in the nationalist press of being sympathetic to France and a potentially disloyal element. By the time the Six-Day War broke out between Israel and the Middle Eastern Arab states in June

1967, Tunisian Jewry had dwindled to about 23,000 persons.

The third Arab-Israeli war proved to be the final blow to the still not insubstantial remnant of Tunisian Jewry. On June 5, 1967 widespread anti-Jewish rioting in Tunis, the capital, where the vast majority of Jews lived, resulted in the looting of most Jewish shops and businesses and the desecration and burning of the Great Synagogue. A sense of almost total despair took hold of the community—despite President Bourguiba's strong condemnation of the riots and government promises to punish the perpetrators and make restitution. In the words of one eyewitness, "It is the unanimous opinion of Jews one talks to that if there was any doubt previously, it is quite clear now there is no future for them in Tunisia." Most fled to France. Within a year, only about 7,000 to 8,000 Jews remained in the country.[879]

Despite the prohibition of mass legal emigration from Morocco in 1956,

> clandestine departures organized by agents of the Israeli Mossad continued throughout the remainder of the decade and into the early 1960s. In the four years following the dissolution of Cadima [the local Moroccan Zionist organization ordered to "dissolve itself" in 1956] and the imposition of the ban on aliya activities, nearly 18,000 Moroccan Jews were spirited out of the country. Moroccan officials frequently looked aside as this underground exodus was taking place. Only during the premiership of Abd Allah Ibrahim (December 1958 to May 1960), who represented the radical wing of the Istiqlal party, was there a serious attempt to clamp down on illegal movement, and a special emigration section was established in the police department that carried out numerous arrests of Jews attempting or even suspected of planning to emigrate illegally.[880]

Muhammad V reversed the ban on Jewish emigration just prior to his sudden death in February 1961. Stillman argues that this policy reversal had both pragmatic and benevolent motivations:

> [T]o settle the Jewish problem once and for all, to reverse the growing influence of Nasserism in the country, which had become painfully evident during the Casablanca Conference of African States in January of that year, and to counter the negative international publicity that had been generated by the drowning of forty-four Jews, whose small boat, the Pisces, foundered off the northern Moroccan coast on the night of January 10, 1961, as they were attempting to flee the country.[881]

Within three years after mass emigration was allowed to resume, seventy thousand Jews left Morocco.[882] In 1965 Moroccan writer Said Ghallab described the attitude of his fellow Muslims toward their Jewish neighbors:

> The worst insult that one Moroccan can make to another is to call him a Jew. . . . My childhood friends have remained anti-Jewish. They mask their virulent antisemitism by maintaining that the State of Israel was the creation of Western imperialism. My Communist comrades have fallen into this trap. Not a single issue of the Communist press denounces *either the Antisemitism of the Moroccans or that of their government* [emphasis added]. . . . And the integral Hitlerite myth is cultivated among the popular classes. Hitler's massacre of the Jews was acclaimed with delight. It is even believed that Hitler is not dead, but very much alive. *And his arrival is awaited—like that of the Imam el Mahdi* [emphasis added]—to deliver the Arabs from Israel.[883]

Moroccan Muslim attitudes such as these, likely exacerbated by the Arab-Israeli wars of 1967 and 1973, may have contributed to the steady decline of Morocco's Jewish population throughout the 1960s and 1970s. Nearly a quarter million Jews lived in Morocco (almost three hundred thousand including Tangier) after World War II.[884] By the early 1970s that number had dropped dramatically to twenty-five thousand. With continued attrition, fewer than four thousand Jews remain in Morocco at present.[885]

Littman recently summarized the remarkable demographic decline of *all* the populations of Jews living in Muslim countries, especially the Arab nations, since 1945:

> In 1945 about 140,000 Jews lived in Iraq; 60,000 in Yemen and Aden; 35,000 in Syria; 5,000 in Lebanon; 90,000 in Egypt; 40,000 in Libya; 150,000 in Algeria; 120,000 in Tunisia; 300,000 in Morocco, including Tangier—a total of roughly 940,000 (and approximately 200,000 more in Iran and Turkey). Of these indigenous communities, less than 50,000 Jews remain today—*and in the Arab world, their number is barely 5,000—0.5% of the overall total at the end of the Second World War* [emphasis added].[886]

The Jews of Arab Muslim lands have been reduced to (an exceedingly) "small, vestigial and moribund remnant."[887] Devoid of political and economic power (or even aspirations)—unseen, unheard, and certainly unarmed—they are the ideal *dhimmis*, worthy of the benevolent and tolerant treatment ostensibly afforded them in the idyllic era before European colonization, as described in this October 1991 address to the UN General Assembly by then Syrian foreign minister, Farouk Shara:

> For hundreds of years Jews have lived amidst Muslim Arabs without suffering. On the contrary they have been greatly respected.[888]

Saul S. Friedman examined contemporary "respectful" Muslim treatment of Jews in Shara's own Syria in a 1989 study.[889] His sobering analysis reveals the living legacy of antisemitic, anti-*dhimmi* Islamic attitudes exploited by a pseudosecular totalitarian government, further enamored of European antisemitic motifs—from "historical proofs" of the Jews responsibility for ritual murder in the 1840 Damascus blood libel, published (and republished) by Syrian defense minister Mustafa Tlass, to Nazi antisemitism expressed by unrepentant Nazis such as Alois Brunner, who stated, "All of them [Jews] deserved to die because they were the devil's agents and human garbage. . . . I have no regret and would do it again," while being granted safe haven in Syria.[890]

At the outset of Hafez al-Assad's accession to power in the early 1970s, these were the conditions under which Syrian Jews lived:

> Jews were required to live in ghettos and not permitted to travel more than 3 or 4 kilometers from their homes. (By contrast 500,000 Muslims visited Lebanon in 1971 alone.) Anyone attempting to flee the country could be jailed and tortured for three months or more. Jews were required to carry identity cards with the word *Mussawi* (follower of Moses) broadly scrawled in red ink. In Al-Qamishli, Jewish homes and stores were required to bear a red sign (the color connoting uncleanliness). Under a law drafted February 8, 1967, all government employees and members of the Syrian armed forces were barred from trading with any Jewish establishment in Syria. A list of boycotted businesses was supplied by the government. In some instances, Jews were barred from making food purchases themselves and had to rely on Syrian friends to keep them from starving. Jews could not own or drive automobiles or have telephones.
>
> Jews could not serve in the Syrian armed forces, but had to pay $600 to secure exemption certificates. Jews could not sell property. In the event of death or illegal emigration, property was transferred to the state, which disposed of it either through sale or grant to Palestinians. Members of saiqa, a Palestine Liberation Organization (PLO) faction favored by the Syrians, openly strutted through the streets of a Damascus ghetto, intimidating people with arms and beatings. Al Fatah also maintained an office in this ghetto where in one week in 1971 seven Jewish homes were torched.

The overall situation was so critical that the Jewish Telegraphic Agency of November 19, 1971, reported:

For the first time since the Russian Revolution of 1917, Soviet Jews have petitioned their government to aid Jews of another country. Russian Jewish sources reported that a group of Muscovite Jews wrote to the Kremlin's Big Three—Communist Party Chief Leonid I. Brezhnev, Premier Aleksei N. Kosygin, and President Nikolai V. Podgorny—to intervene with the Damascus government for a cessation of restrictions on Syrian Jews. The names of the petitioners were not disclosed, but the sources said they were all activist Jews, many of whom have applied for migration to Israel. The petitioners based their appeal on humanitarian grounds and on the fact of good Russian-Syrian relations.[891]

Friedman also describes how gullible high-profile US journalists—Seymour Topping of the *New York Times* and Mike Wallace of *60 Minutes*, as well as the *National Geographic*—were manipulated by Assad's government during a mid-1970s Syrian campaign to whitewash the brutally oppressive conditions under which Syrian Jews lived:

On January 5, 1975, the *New York Times* correspondent Seymour Topping offered the American public a rare view of the lives of Syrian Jews. After rhapsodizing characteristically about "synagogues still being open" and giving the anodyne explanation of official hostility to Jews being due to the technical state of war that made it impossible for Jews to leave the city or country, Topping ended with a conventional stereotype. "The most popular men's clothing store in Damascus is owned by a Jew. 'He is a friend of mine,' said Dr. Saber Falhout, editor of the leading newspaper, *Al Baath*. 'This suit I am wearing was made by him.' It was a well-tailored plaid." Shortly after this misleading piece appeared, Topping spent some time with George Gruen of the American Jewish Committee. *Topping was informed that the people he interviewed were among the few Jewish families permitted to function outside ghetto walls, where foreign visitors were taken to display the government's benevolence* [emphasis added].

[A] Wallace segment on *60 Minutes* in 1975 would paint an equally misleading picture of conditions in Syria. Once more carefully selected spokesmen expressed gratitude to the Ba'athist regime for bringing stability to their lives. One, Maurice Nuseyri . . . offered his own identity card as evidence of a thaw in Arab-Jewish relations.

Although there was a line where Nuseyri's religion was typed, the hateful *Mussawi* was lacking. Wallace did inquire how long Nuseyri had had the card but did not follow-up when the latter responded, "Oh, about one week." *Nor did the normally relentless journalist inquire after two of Nuseyri's children who had fled the country, abandoning all property in their quest for freedom* [emphasis added].

One other prestigious institution would fall victim to Syrian propaganda. The *National Geographic* devoted part of its April 1974 issue to Syria. An article written by freelance journalist Robert Azzi told of the "freedom of worship and freedom of opportunity" enjoyed by Syrian Jews, especially in Damascus, "the city still tolerantly (embracing) [*sic*] significant numbers of Jews." Seven months later, the editors of the *National Geographic*, noting the difficulty of obtaining "reliable nonpartisan information," tried to swallow Azzi's words.

Many of our Jewish members sharply criticized us for not delineating in greater detail the harsh conditions under which that small community has been forced to exist since 1948. We began to wonder if we had unwittingly failed to reflect the true situation. *Now after months of carefully reviewing the evidence, we have concluded that our critics were right. We erred* [emphasis added].

For the first time in its eighty-six years of publication, the *National Geographic* retracted a major article. The evidence that Jews in Syria were not being treated fairly was compelling. Although the Assad government attempted to befog the issue, persecution of Jews continued through the remainder of the decade.[892]

Friedman concluded his 1989 assessment with these observations, despite the putative 1980s "thaw" in overt Syrian government persecution of Jews:

[T]here is no mistaking the dhimmi status of Syria's Jews even today [emphasis added]. Few Jews advertise their existence by displaying mezzuot on the street entrances of their houses. In a land where annual per capita income is less than $1,000, the *Muhabarat* [Syrian Secret Police] still require a deposit of $5,000 or $6,000 for any Jew temporarily leaving the country.

Recently, the officer in charge of the Jewish Section in the *Muhabarat* lost his wife in an auto accident and has clamped down on innocents. Six Jews remain imprisoned in the filthy Adra prison, bent over in tiny cells seventy feet below ground level.

All have been tortured and one (an eighteen-year-old Laham boy) was beaten so badly that he suffered from phlebitis. His father, visiting the jail, pleaded with the *Muhabarat*, "Take me! Kill me instead!"[893]

The plight of Syrian Jewry notwithstanding, vestigial Jewish populations in Muslim countries far removed from the battlegrounds of the Arab-Israeli conflict continue to be targeted with attacks—recent examples being the jihadist bombings of the ancient al-Ghariba synagogue in Djerba, Tunisia, on April 11, 2002 (which killed twenty-one and seriously wounded many others, most being elderly German tourists),[894] and the simultaneous jihadist bombings of two Istanbul synagogues in November 2003, discussed earlier.[895] And during January 2007 even the infinitesimal remnant population of Yemenite Jews (some two hundred or fewer) living in the province of Sa'ada was under duress. Reports indicated that these Jews were being forced to make apparent *jizya* payments, had been falsely accused of selling wine to Muslims, and were threatened with killings, abductions, and lootings.[896] A letter delivered to the Jewish communal leader, believed to have been composed by disciples of the Yemenite Shi'ite cleric Hossein Bader a-Din al Khouty, stated:

Islam calls upon us to fight against the disseminators of decay. . . . After accurate surveillance over the Jews [in Sa'ada province] . . . it has become clear to us that they were doing things which serve mainly global Zionism, which seeks to corrupt the people and distance them from their principles, their values, their morals, and their religion.[897]

Georges Vajda's 1937 analysis of the portrayal of the Jews in the hadith remains the definitive treatment of this subject matter.[898] Vajda (d. 1981) made these sadly prescient observations in 1968 regarding Islamic doctrines that continue to shape the behaviors of Muslim governments and societies toward any Jewish communities remaining in their midst, no matter how small or unobtrusive:

[I]t seems clear that, unless it changes its principles, goes against the deepest feelings of its coreligionists and calls in question its own raison d'être, no Muslim power, however "liberal" it may like to think itself . . . could depart from the line of conduct followed in the past *and continued de facto in the present* [emphasis added], in conferring on Jews anything but the historic status of "protection," patched up with ill-digested and unassimilated Western phraseology.[899]

SUMMARY AND CONCLUSIONS

A widely prevalent conception of Islam's doctrinal and historical treatment of Jews rests on two false pillars, epitomized by categorical affirmations such as these:

(I) In Islamic society hostility to the Jew is non-theological. It is not related to any specific Islamic doctrine, nor to any specific circumstance in Islamic history. For Muslims, it is not part of the birth pangs of their religion, as it is for Christians.[900]

(II) . . . "dhimmi"-tude [derisively hyphenated] . . . subservience and persecution and ill treatment . . . of Jews . . . is a myth.[901]

False Pillar I

False pillar I remains standing despite voluminous contrary evidence from Islam's foundational texts, discussed at length earlier: virulently Antisemitic Qur'anic verses *whose virulence is only amplified by the greatest classical and modern Muslim Qur'anic commentaries* (by Tabari, Zamkshari, Baydawi, Ibn Kathir, and Suyuti, to Qutb and Mawdudi), *the six canonical hadith collections, and the most respected sira* (by Ibn Ishaq/Ibn Hisham, Ibn Sa'd, Waqidi, and Tabari).[902] The antisemitic motifs in these texts have been carefully elucidated by scholarship that dates back to Hartwig Hirschfeld's mid-1880s analysis of the sira[903] and Georges Vajda's 1937 study of the hadith,[904] complemented in the past two decades by Haggai Ben-Shammai's 1988 examination of the major antisemitic verses and themes in the Qur'an and Qur'anic exegesis[905] and Saul S. Friedman's broad, straightforward enumeration of Qur'anic antisemitism in 1989.[906] The following is a recapitulation of the main findings from these modern analyses, with an emphasis on the Qur'an.

As a central anti-Jewish motif, the Qur'an decrees an eternal curse upon the Jews (Qur'an 2:61, 3:112) for slaying the prophets and transgressing against the will of Allah. This motif is coupled to Qur'anic verses 5:60 and 5:78, which describe the Jews' transformation into apes and swine (5:60), having been "cursed by the tongue of David, and Jesus, Mary's son" (5:78).[907] The related verse, 5:64, accuses the Jews (as Palestinian Authority president Mahmoud Abbas did in a January 2007 speech, citing Qur'an 5:64)[908] of being "spreaders of war and corruption"—a sort of ancient Qur'anic antecedent of *The Protocols of the Elders of Zion*.

The centrality of the Jews' permanent "abasement and humiliation," and being "laden with God's anger" in the corpus of Muslim exegetic literature on Qur'an 2:61 (including the hadith and Qur'anic commentaries) is clear. By nature deceitful and treacherous, the Jews rejected Allah's signs and prophets, including Isa, the

Muslim Jesus. Classical Qur'anic commentators such as Tabari, Zamakashari, Baydawi, and Ibn Kathir, when discussing Qur'an 5:82—"Thou wilt surely find the most hostile of men to the believers are the Jews and the idolaters; and thou wilt surely find the nearest of them in love to the believers are those who say 'We are Christians'; that, because some of them are priests and monks, and they wax not proud"—concur on the unique animus of the Jews toward the Muslims, which is repeatedly linked to the curse of Qur'an 2:61.[909] For example, in his commentary on 5:82, Tabari writes,

> In my opinion, [the Christians] are not like the Jews who always scheme in order to murder the emissaries and the prophets, and who oppose God in his positive and negative commandments, and who corrupt His scripture which He revealed in His books.[910]

Tabari's classical interpretations of Qur'an 5:82 and 2:61, as well as his discussion of the related verse 9:29 mandating the Jews payment of the *jizya*, represent both antisemitic and more general anti-*dhimmi* views that became—and remain—intrinsic to Islam to this day. Here is Tabari's discussion of 2:61 and its relationship to verse 9:29, which emphasizes the purposely debasing nature of the Qur'anic poll tax:

> "[A]basement and poverty were imposed and laid down upon them," as when someone says "the imam imposed the poll tax (*jizya*) on free non-Muslim subjects," or "The man imposed land tax on his slave," meaning thereby that he obliged him [to pay] it, or, "The commander imposed a sortie on his troops," meaning he made it their duty. . . . God commanded His believing servants *not* to give them [i.e., the non-Muslim people of the scripture] security—as long as they continued to disbelieve in Him and his Messenger—unless they paid the poll tax to them; God said: "Fight those who believe not in God and the Last Day and do not forbid what God and His Messenger have forbidden—such men as practice not the religion of truth [Islam], being of those who have been given the Book [Bible]—until they pay the poll tax, being humble" (Qur'an 9:29). The dhimmis [non-Muslim tributary's] posture during the collection of the *jizya*—"[lowering themselves] by walking on their hand, . . . reluctantly."
> . . . Ibn Zaid said about His words "and abasement and poverty were imposed upon them," "These are the Jews of the Children of Israel." I said: "Are they the Copts of Egypt?" He said: "What have the Copts of Egypt to do with this? No, by God, they are not; but they are the Jews, the Children of Israel.". . . By "and slain the prophets unrightfully" He means that they used to kill the Messengers of God without God's leave, denying their messages and rejecting their prophethood.[911]

Indeed the Qur'an's overall discussion of the Jews is marked by a litany of their sins and punishments,[912] as if part of a divine indictment and conviction process. The Jews wronged themselves (16:118) by losing faith (7:168) and breaking their covenant (5:13). The Jews (echoing an ante-Nicaean polemic) are a nation that has passed away (2:134; repeated in 2:141). Twice Allah sent his instruments (the Assyrians or Babylonians, and Romans) to punish this perverse people (17:4–5)—their dispersal over the earth is proof of Allah's rejection (7:168). The Jews are further warned about both their arrogant claim that they remain Allah's chosen people (62:6), and continued disobedience and "corruption" (5:32–33). Other sins, some repeated, are enumerated: abuse, even killing of prophets (4:155; 2:91), including Isa (Jesus; 3:55; 4:157), is a consistent theme. The Jews ridiculed Muhammad as Ra'ina (the evil one, in 2:104; 4:46), and they are also accused of lack of faith, taking words out of context, disobedience, and distortion (4:46). Precious few of them are believers (also 4:46). These "perverse" creatures also claim that Ezra is the messiah and they worship rabbis who defraud men of their possessions (9:30). Additional sins are described: The Jews are typified as an "envious" people (2:109) whose hearts are as hardened as rocks (2:74). They are further accused of confounding the truth (2:42), deliberately perverting scripture (2:75), and being liars (2:78). Ill-informed people of little faith (2:89), they pursue vague and wishful fancies (2:111). Other sins have contributed to their being stamped (see 2:61/3:112 above) with "wretchedness/abasement and humiliation," including— usury (2:275), sorcery (2:102), hedonism (2:96), and idol worship (2:53). More (and repeat) sins, are described still: the Jews' idol worship is again mentioned (4:51), then linked and followed by charges of other (often repeat) iniquities—the "tremendous calumny" against Mary (4:156), as well as usury and cheating (4:161). Most Jews are accused of being "evil-livers"/"transgressors"/"ungodly" (3:110), who, deceived by their own lies (3:24), try to turn Muslims from Islam (3:99). Jews are blind and deaf to the truth (5:71), and what they have not forgotten they have perverted—they mislead (3:69), confound the truth (3:71), twist tongues (3:79), and cheat Gentiles without remorse (3:75). Muslims are advised not to take the Jews as friends (5:51), and to beware of the inveterate hatred that Jews bear toward them (5:82). The Jews' ultimate sin and punishment are made clear: They are the devil's minions (4:60) cursed by Allah, their faces will be obliterated (4:47), and if they do not accept the true faith of Islam— the Jews who understand their faith become Muslims (3:113)—they will be made into apes (2:65, 7:166), or apes and swine (5:60), and burn in the Hellfires (4:55, 5:29, 98:6, and 58:14–19).

A general guiding principle of the hadith for Muslims is *khalifuhum*, which means, "do not do like them."[913] As Vajda demonstrates, however, this seemingly banal principle, which covers matters ranging from daily customs and practices (such as basic grooming and dress practices to avoid), is laden with anti-Jewish animus that only intensifies when the hadith deal with more profound subjects such as eschatology.[914]

Even sanctioned Muslim practices of onanism/masturbation and bestiality, in particular with slaves whom the Muslims wished to avoid impregnating, became a source of friction vis-à-vis the Jews, who were revolted by these practices. The customs to be observed at funerals, the matters of burial plots and tombs, and, more decidedly, Muhammad's view of the fate of buried Jews, also illustrate anti-Jewish animus. For example, public lamentation over the dead became forbidden to the Jews (and Christians). The hadith further condemn certain physical gestures for being specific to Jews.[915]

The hadith also portray the Jews' hatred and jealousy of Muhammad: Despite being convinced of the authenticity of Muhammad's divine mission, the Jews did not become votaries of Islam due to pride in their birth and appetite for domination. (These charges became a recurrent theme in later Muslim polemics.) A related commonplace charge in the hadith is that Jews altered their sacred texts, deleting Muhammad's name and precise description. Another series of hadith elaborate on Qur'an 3:93 and associated Qur'anic exegeses, which accuse the Jews of misrepresenting their alimentary prohibitions, most notably camel's flesh, as in fact described in the Torah. Vajda observes that "distrust must reign" in Muslims relations with Jews—Muslims must especially beware of asking them for information of a religious kind, because "the Jews . . . are rebels to the solicitations of Islam and keep their religious traditions in a way liable to lead Muslims into error."[916]

Striking evidence of Jewish perfidy in the hadith is illustrated by their continual, surreptitious cursing of the Muslims while ostensibly offering proper greetings. Other traditions attribute evil spells to the Jews.[917]

Following the Muslims' initial conquest of the Jewish farming oasis of Khaybar, one of the vanquished Jewesses reportedly served Muhammad poisoned mutton (or goat), *which resulted, ultimately, in his protracted, agonizing death.* (Sa'd's biography, however, maintains that the offending Jewess gave Muhammad poisoned goat, and insists that she was not spared.) *Thus the Qur'anic curse (verse 2:61, repeated in 3:112) upon the Jews for (primarily) rejecting, even slaying, Allah's prophets, is updated with perfect archetypal logic in this canonical hadith.*[918]

Muslim eschatology, as depicted in the hadith, highlights the Jews' supreme hostility to Islam. Jews are described as adherents of the Dajjâl—the Muslim equivalent of the Antichrist—or according to another tradition, the Dajjâl is himself Jewish. At his appearance, other traditions maintain that the Dajjâl will be accompanied by seventy thousand Jews from Isfahan wrapped in their robes, and armed with polished sabers, their heads covered with a sort of veil. When the Dajjâl is defeated, his Jewish companions will be slaughtered—everything will deliver them up except for the so-called gharkad tree. According to a canonical hadith—repeated in the 1988 Hamas Charter (in chapter 7)—if a Jew seeks refuge under a tree or a stone, these objects will be able to speak to tell a Muslim: "There is a Jew behind me; come and kill him!" Another hadith variant, which takes place in Jerusalem, has Isa leading the Arabs in a rout of the Dajjâl and his company of seventy thousand armed Jews. And the notion of jihad "ransom" extends even into Islamic eschatology—on the day of resurrection the vanquished Jews will be consigned to hellfire, and this will expiate Muslims who have sinned, sparing them from this fate.[919]

Stubborn malevolence, however, is the Jews' defining worldly characteristic: rejecting Muhammad and refusing to convert to Islam out of jealousy, envy, and even selfish personal interest leads them to acts of treachery, in keeping with their inveterate nature: "sorcery, poisoning, assassination held no scruples for them." These archetypes sanction Muslim hatred toward the Jews, and the admonition to, at best, "subject [the Jews] to Muslim domination," as *dhimmis*, treated "with contempt," under certain "humiliating arrangements."[920]

Hartwig Hirschfeld's study of the sira and their depiction of Muhammad's interactions with the Jews of Medina concludes that "mutual disappointment" characterized their relationship, with predictably disastrous consequences for the Jews. During his attempts at proselytization, Muhammad's misunderstanding (or sheer ignorance) of Jewish doctrine was ridiculed by rabbis and Jewish poets.[921] Ibn Ishaq, author of the earliest Muslim biography of Muhammad, accuses them of "hostility . . . , envy, hatred, and malice because God ha[d] chosen his apostle from the Arabs."[922] Regardless, the Jews' stubborn refusal to convert to Islam decisively altered the trajectory of Muhammad's religious thinking. Following the Battle of Badr—which established the power of nascent Islam—Muhammad initiated a campaign of political assassinations of Jewish (or presumptively Jewish) poets and leaders.[923] Ibn Ishaq recorded these telling words of one of Muhammad's Muslim assassins: "Our attack upon God's enemy cast terror among the Jews, and there was no Jew in Medina who did not fear for his life."[924] Such fear proved to be well founded, as, on the very morning after one political assassination (of Ka'b b. al 'Ashraf), Muhammad encouraged the Muslims to slay Jews indiscriminately, according to Ibn Ishaq:

> The apostle said, "Kill any Jew that falls into your power." Thereupon Muhayyisa b. Mas'ud leapt upon Ibn Sunayna, a Jewish merchant with whom they had social and business relations, and killed him.[925]

These murders of individual Jews were followed by the siege, expropriation, and expulsion of the Medinan Jewish tribes B. Qaynuqa and B. Nadir, and the subsequent massacre of the Jewish men of the B. Qurayza, whose wives, children, and possessions were then seized as booty by the Muslims.[926] Muhammad subsequently prepared for his campaign against Khaybar—a farming oasis and the last Jewish stronghold in Northern Arabia, where survivors (most notably, the B. Nadir) of the Muslims' earlier attacks on Medinan Jewry had also sought refuge—with two further political assassinations. Bloody assaults by the Muslims that ensued shortly afterward resulted in the complete subjugation of the Jews of Khaybar, the survivors becoming *dhimmis*.[927] The theological animus that motivated Muhammad's political subjugation of the Jews, specifically, became an indelible part of Muslim attitudes toward Jews across space and time. It also defined eternal parameters in which Jews would be permitted to live as humiliated Muslim *dhimmis*, the Jews of Khaybar—who, according to the hadith and sira, were eventually expelled from Arabia by Caliph Umar—being the prototype.[928]

A profoundly anti-Jewish motif occurring after the events recorded in the hadith and sira, put forth in early Muslim historiography (for example, by Tabari), is most assuredly a part of "the birth pangs of their religion": the story of Abd Allah b. Saba, an alleged renegade Yemenite Jew and founder of the heterodox Shi'ite sect. He is held responsible—identified as a Jew—for promoting the Shi'ite heresy and fomenting the rebellion and internal strife associated with this primary breach in Islam's "political innocence," culminating in the assassination of the third Rightly Guided Caliph Uthman, and the bitter, lasting legacy of Sunni-Shi'ite sectarian strife.[929]

Consistent with Islam's theological Jew hatred, S. D. Goitein's seminal analyses of the Cairo Geniza materials from the High Middle Ages (c. 950–1250) reveal that Jews living a millennium ago were already experiencing an indigenous Muslim antisemitism in the Middle East and North Africa. The intensity of this Muslim Jew hatred motivated Jews of the era to coin two unique Hebrew words: *sinūth* for Muslim antisemitism and *sōnē* for the Muslim haters who promulgated it.[930] Moreover, two independent Muslim observers writing in the mid-ninth century (the polymath al-Jahiz and the Sufi theologian al-Muhasibi) suggest the most plausible sources of such anti-Jewish animus among the Muslim masses were Qur'an 5:82 and the sira accounts of Muhammad's interactions with the Jews of Medina.[931] Nearly a thousand years later, in mid-nineteenth-century Egypt, E. W. Lane also attributed the Jew hatred he commonly witnessed among ordinary Muslims to their understanding of Qur'an 5:82.[932]

Although antisemitic Islamic motifs from the Qur'an, hadith, and sira were much more commonly employed in daily life as a form of chronic discrimination against Jews, they have also been used to incite more extensive persecutions, including mass violence against Jewish communities.[933]

Rigid conformity to a motif in the hadith (and sira) based on the putative deathbed wish of Muhammad himself, as recorded by Umar (the second Rightly Guided Caliph), "Two religions shall not remain together in the peninsula of the Arabs," had tragic consequences for the Jews of Yemen. (The hadith and sira further maintain that Umar did eventually expel the Jews of Khaybar.) Thus a pious seventeenth-century Yemenite ruler, Al-Mahdi, wishing to fulfill the mandate of this hadith in Yemen in 1679–1680, expelled the entire Jewish population of Yemen—men, women, and children—deporting them to the inhospitable wastelands of the plain of Tihama. This expulsion was accompanied by the destruction of synagogues, desecration of Torah scrolls, and inducements for conversion to Islam. Three-quarters of the thousands of Jews expelled perished from exposure to the intense heat (and cold), absence of potable water, and the subsequent spread of epidemic disease. The major Yemenite Jewish community in San'a experienced a 90 percent mortality rate from this catastrophic exile—of about ten thousand persons exiled, only about one-tenth survived.[934]

References to the Jews' transformation into apes (Qur'an 2:65 and 7:166), or apes and swine (Qur'an 5:60)—perhaps the most striking Qur'anic motifs for the Jews' debasement—have been exploited in polemical incitement against Jews or odes celebrating their having been disgraced and slaughtered.[935] Here again, the sacralized prototype is clear: right before subduing the Banu Qurayza and orchestrating the mass execution of the adult males from this besieged Medinan Jewish tribe, Muhammad addressed these Jews with hateful disparagement, as "You brothers of monkeys." Some three thousand to four thousand Jews were massacred in the 1066 Granada pogrom, inspired in part by an anti-Jewish ode containing the line "Many a pious Muslim is in awe of the vilest infidel ape," referring to the Jewish vizier Joseph b. Samuel Naghrela. Anti-Jewish riots and massacres by Muslims accompanied the 1291 death of Jewish physician-vizier Sa'd ad-Daula in Baghdad—the plundering and killing of Jews, which extended throughout Iraq (and likely into Persia)—were celebrated in a verse by the Muslim preacher Zaynu'd-Din 'Ali b. Said, which begins with this debasing reference to the Jews as apes: "His name we praise who rules the firmament./These apish Jews are done away and shent [ruined]." Referring to the Jews as "brothers of apes," who repeatedly blasphemed the Prophet Muhammad and whose overall conduct reflected their hatred of Muslims, the Moroccan cleric Al-Maghili (d. 1505) fomented and then personally led a Muslim pogrom (in c. 1490) against the Jews of the southern Moroccan oasis of Touat, plundering and killing Jews en masse and destroying their synagogue in neighboring Tamantit. Al-

Maghili's virulent Islamic antisemitism was perhaps captured best in a line from a verse diatribe he composed: "Love of the Prophet requires hatred of the Jews."[936]

Currently the invocation of Qur'anic references to the Jews as apes and pigs pervades Muslim (especially Arab Muslim) religious and political discourse in print, audio, video, and Internet venues. Young children are targeted with these messages, and even encouraged to repeat them by approving adults during additional media coverage.[937] Menachem Milson recently warned that repeated invocation of these motifs cannot be "dismissed as mere vulgar invective" or "primitive magical thinking." Rather, these recurring expressions need to be understood as a form of dehumanization serving as a pretext for the destruction of Jews.[938] Given the murderous historical legacy of Muslim societies that invoked these Qur'anic motifs (i.e., in Granada, Baghdad, and Touat, Morocco) his concern is not alarmist.

Thirty-four years ago Bat Ye'or published a remarkably foresighted analysis of the Islamic antisemitism resurgent in her native Egypt and its packaging for dissemination throughout the Muslim world. The core antisemitic motifs were Islamic, derived from Islam's foundational texts, onto which European—especially Nazi—elements were grafted:

> The pejorative characteristics of Jews as they are described in Muslim religious texts are applied to modern Jews. Anti-Judaism and anti-Zionism are equivalent—due to the inferior status of Jews in Islam, and because divine will dooms Jews to wandering and misery, the Jewish state appears to Muslims as an unbearable affront and a sin against Allah. Therefore it must be destroyed by Jihad. Here the Pan-Arab and anti-Western theses that consider Israel as an advanced instrument of the West in the Islamic world, come to reinforce religious anti-Judaism. The religious and political fuse in a purely Islamic context onto which are grafted foreign elements. If, on the doctrinal level, Nazi influence is secondary to the Islamic base, the technique with which the Antisemitic material has been reworked, and the political purposes being pursued, present striking similarites with Hitler's Germany.
>
> That anti-Jewish opinions have been widely spread in Arab nationalist circles since the 1930s is not in doubt. But their confirmation at [Al-]Azhar [University] by the most important authorities of Islam enabled them to be definitively imposed, with the cachet of infallible authenticity, upon illiterate masses that were strongly attached to religious traditions.[939]

Nazi academic and propagandist Johann von Leers's writings and personal career trajectory[939a]—as a favored contributor in Goebbels' propaganda ministry to his eventual adoption of Islam (as Omar Amin von Leers)

while working as an anti-Western and antisemitic/anti-Zionist propagandist under Nasser's regime from the mid-1950s until his death in 1965—epitomizes this convergence of Islamic antisemitism and racist, Nazi antisemitism, as described by Bat Ye'or. Already in an essay published on December 15, 1942,[939b] more than a decade before his formal conversion to Islam while in Egypt, von Leers produced an analysis focused primarily on Muhammad's interactions with the Jews of Medina, which revealed a pious reverence for Islam and its Prophet, and a thorough understanding of the sacralized Islamic sources for this narrative (i.e., the Qur'an, hadith, and sira). Von Leers, for example, offers this reverent summary characterization of Muhammad's activities in Mecca, and later Medina, which is entirely consistent with standard Muslim apologetics:

> [Mecca] For years Muhammad sought in Mecca to succeed with his preaching that there was only one God, the sole, all-merciful king of Judgment Day. He opposed to the Christian Trinity the unity of God, rejected the Christian doctrine of original sin and salvation, and instead gave every believer as a guiding principle the complete fulfillment of the commands of the righteous, given by a compassionate and just God, before whom every individual person had to account for his acts.

> [Medina] September 622 he left Mecca for Medina, where he took up residence. Here he encountered the Jewish problem for the first time. He believed in the victorious power of good in the world, he was firmly convinced that the religion of the one and only God, with its easy, practical, reasonable, basic laws for human life was nothing other than the original religion. He wanted to take mankind out of the current turmoil and lead it toward the original, clear vision of God. But since he had to deal with people who had been influenced by both Christianity and Judaism, he said that it was the religion in which Abraham (Ibrahim) had already believed, and which Christ and Moses had proclaimed, only each time it had been distorted by human beings. He said that this had been revealed anew to him by God. He wanted to make the path easy to follow for both Christians and Jews; thus at first he allowed his followers to pray facing toward Jerusalem. He repeatedly emphasized that he only wanted to purify the existing religions, to establish the restored, newly revealed faith. At the same time he was a skilled statesman. When the Arab tribes were unified, the Jews became a minority in Medina. Muhammad provided them with a kind of protectorate agreement: they were to retain their administration and their forms of worship, help the faithful defend the city, not ally themselves with Muhammad's opponents, and contribute to the faithful's wars. The

Jews could have been satisfied with this. But they began a general hate campaign against Islam, which proclaimed a pure conception of God.[939c]

Citing (or referring to) the relevant foundational text sources (i.e., Qur'an 13:36; 8:55–58; 59:1–15; the sira and canonical hadith descriptions of the fate of individual Jews such as Abu Afak and Ka'b ibn Ashraf and the Jewish tribes Banu Qaynuqa, Banu Nadir, Banu Qurayzah, as well as the Jews of the Khaybar oasis), von Leers chronicles Muhammad's successful campaigns that vanquished these Jews, killing and dispersing them, "or at most allow[ing] them to remain in certain places if they paid a poll tax."[939d] Von Leers further describes the accounts (from the hadith, and, more elaborately, the sira)[939e] of Muhammad's poisoning by a Khaybar Jewess, and also notes the canonical hadith that records Caliph Umar's rationale for his putative expulsion from northern Arabia of those remaining Jews who survived Muhammad's earlier campaigns:

> On his deathbed Mohammed is supposed to have said: "There must not be two religions in Arabia." One of his successors, the caliph Omar, resolutely drove the Jews out of Arabia.[939f]

And von Leers even invokes the apocalyptic canonical hadith that forty-six years later became the keystone of Hamas's 1988 charter sanctioning a jihad genocide against the Jewish State of Israel:

> Ibn Huraira even communicates to us the following assertion of the great man of God: "Judgment Day will come only when the Moslems have inflicted an annihilating defeat on the Jews, when every stone and every tree behind which a Jew has hidden says to believers: 'Behind me stands a Jew, smite him.'"[939g]

Von Leers's 1942 essay concludes by simultaneously extolling the "model" of oppression the Jews experienced under Islamic suzerainty and the nobility of Muhammad, Islam, and the contemporary Muslims of the World War II era, foreshadowing his own conversion to Islam just over a decade later:

> They [the Jews] were subjected to a very restrictive and oppressive special regulation that completely crippled Jewish activities. All reporters of the time when the Islamic lands still completely obeyed their own laws agree that the Jews were particularly despised. . . .
>
> Mohammed's opposition to the Jews undoubtedly had an effect—oriental Jewry was completely paralyzed by Islam. Its back was broken. Oriental Jewry has played almost no role in Judaism's massive rise to power over the last two centuries.

Scorned, the Jews vegetated in the dirty alleys of the mellah, and were subject to a special regulation that did not allow them to profiteer, as they did in Europe, or even to receive stolen goods, but instead kept them fearful and under pressure. Had the rest of the world adopted a similar method, today we would have no Jewish question—and here we must absolutely note that there were also Islamic rulers, among them especially the Spanish caliphs of the House of Muawiyah, who did not adhere to Islam's traditional hostility to Jews—to their own disadvantage. However, as a religion Islam has performed the immortal service of preventing the Jews from carrying out their threatened conquest of Arabia and of defeating the dreadful doctrine of Jehovah through a pure faith that opened the way to higher culture for many peoples and gave them an education and humane training, so that still today a Moslem who takes his religion seriously is one of the most worthy phenomena in this world in turmoil.[939h]

False Pillar II

An earlier, more complete statement of the second false pillar, "'*dhimmi*'-tude [derisively hyphenated] . . . is a myth," was published in 1974:

> *The dhimma on the whole worked well* [emphasis added]. The non-Muslims managed to thrive under Muslim rule, and even to make significant contributions to Islamic civilization. The restrictions were not onerous, and were usually less severe in practice than in theory. As long as the non-Muslim communities accepted and conformed to the status of tolerated subordination assigned to them, they were not troubled. The rare outbreaks of repression or violence directed against them are almost always the consequence of a feeling that they have failed to keep their place and honor their part of the covenant. The usual cause was the undue success of Christians or Jews in penetrating to positions of power and influence which Muslims regarded as rightly theirs. The position of the non-Muslims deteriorated during and after the Crusades and the Mongol invasions, partly because of the general heightening of religious loyalties and rivalries, partly because of the well-grounded suspicion that they were collaborating with the enemies of Islam.[940]

The contentions in this statement by Bernard Lewis are ahistorical and do not withstand scrutiny. Elsewhere Lewis elaborates on his point regarding the Mongols and his charge of *dhimmi* "collaboration" with them:

> The Mongol rulers found Christians and Jews— local people knowing the languages, and the coun-

tries but not themselves Muslims—very useful instruments, and appointed some of them to high office. Afterwards, when the Mongols were converted to Islam, became part of the Islamic world, and adopted Islamic attitudes, the Christians and Jews had to pay for past collaboration with the pagan conquerors.[941]

In 1937 Walter Fischel wrote a serious analysis of the Mongol period and its impact on Jews and Christians in the conquered Abbasid Caliphate. The Mongol conquest of Baghdad (seat of the Abbasid Caliphate) in 1258 ended the domination of Islam as a state religion, and with it the system of *dhimmitude*—a point Fischel makes explicitly:

> [T]he principle of tolerance for all faiths, maintained by the Il Khans [Mongol rulers], (depriving) the [Islamic] concept of the "Protected People," the ahl adh-Dhimma [*dhimmi* system] . . . *of its former importance; with it fell the extremely varied professional restrictions into which it had expanded,* [emphasis added], . . . primarily those regarding the admission of Jews and Christians to government posts.[942]

The thirteenth-century Christian chronicler Bar Hebraeus and the Iraqi Muslim Ghazi b. al-Wasiti (fl. 1292), author of a Muslim treatise on the *dhimmis*, made these concordant observations from diametrically opposed perspectives—Bar Hebraeus as a *dhimmi* celebrating the changes wrought by Mongol conquest and al-Wasiti as a Muslim lamenting them:

> With the Mongols there is neither slave nor free man, neither believer nor pagan, neither Christian nor Jew; but they regard all men as belonging to one and the same stock.

> A firman of the Il Khan [Hulagu] had appeared to the effect that everyone should have the right to profane his faith openly and his religious connection; and that the members of one religious body should not oppose those of another.[943]

Fischel concludes that because the Mongols abolished a system Lewis contends never really existed (or a system Lewis ignores), the plight of the *dhimmi* Jews and Christians improved substantially:

> For Christians and Jews, the two groups chiefly affected by the ahl adh-Dhimma policy, current until then, this change in constitutional and religious principles implied a considerable amelioration of their position; whereas for the Muslims it meant they had sunk to a depth hitherto unknown in their history.[944]

S. D. Goitein, in a 1963 essay, highlighted the limitation of studying the potential economic and other adverse social consequences of the *jizya* without any reference to non-Muslim sources:

> There is no subject of Islamic social history on which the present writer had to modify his views so radically while passing from literary to documentary sources, i.e., from the study of Muslim books to that of the records of the Cairo Geniza as the jizya . . . or the poll tax to be paid by non-Muslims. It was of course, evident that the tax represented a discrimination and was intended, according to the Koran's own words, to emphasize the inferior status of the non-believers. It seemed, however, that from the economic point of view, it did not constitute a heavy imposition, since it was on a sliding scale, approximately one, two, and four dinars, and thus adjusted to the financial capacity of the taxpayer. *This impression proved to be entirely fallacious, for it did not take into consideration the immense extent of poverty and privation experienced by the masses, and in particular, their persistent lack of cash, which turned the 'season of the tax' into one of horror, dread, and misery* [emphasis added].[945]

And Goitein wrote the following on the subject of non-Muslim *dhimmis* under Muslim rule (i.e., *dhimmitude*), in 1970:

> [A] great humanist and contemporary of the French Revolution, Wilhelm von Humboldt, defined as the best state one which is least felt and restricts itself to one task only: protection, protection against attack from outside and oppression from within . . . in general, taxation [by the Muslim government] was merciless, and a very large section of the population must have lived permanently at the starvation level. From many Geniza letters one gets the impression that the poor were concerned more with getting money for the payment of their taxes than for food and clothing, for failure of payment usually induced cruel punishment . . . *the Muslim state was quite the opposite of the ideals propagated by Wilhelm von Humboldt or the principles embedded in the constitution of the United States. An Islamic state was part of or coincided with dar al-Islam, the House of Islam. Its treasury was mal al-muslumin, the money of the Muslims. Christians and Jews were not citizens of the state, not even second class citizens. They were outsiders under the protection of the Muslim state, a status characterized by the term dhimma, for which protection they had to pay a poll tax specific to them. They were also exposed to a great number of discriminatory and humiliating laws. . . . As it lies in the very nature of such restrictions, soon additional humiliations were*

added, and before the second century of Islam was out, a complete body of legislation in this matter was in existence. . . . In times and places in which they became too oppressive they led to the dwindling or even complete extinction of the minorities [emphasis added].[946]

With regard to North African Jewry specifically under Islam, Goitein, in a 1974 paper, described the Jews' cultural narrowing to an "exclusively Talmudic sphere" as a result of *"the almost permanent state of oppression and vexations, if not outright persecutions"* [emphasis added].[947]

Bat Ye'or's extensive analyses of the *dhimmi* condition for both Jews and Christians published (in English) in 1985 and 1996, concluded:

These examples are intended to indicate the general character of a system of oppression, sanctioned by contempt and justified by the principle of inequality between Muslims and dhimmis. . . . Singled out as objects of hatred and contempt by visible signs of discrimination, they were progressively decimated during periods of massacres, forced conversions, and banishments. Sometimes it was the prosperity they had achieved through their labor or ability that aroused jealousy; oppressed and stripped of all their goods, the dhimmi often emigrated.

[I]n many places and at many periods [through] the nineteenth century, observers have described the wearing of discriminatory clothing, the rejection of dhimmi testimony, the prohibitions concerning places of worship and the riding of animals, as well as fiscal charges—particularly the protection charges levied by nomad chiefs—and the payment of the jizya. . . . *Not only was the dhimma imposed almost continuously, for one finds it being applied in the nineteenth-century Ottoman Empire . . . and in Persia, the Maghreb, and Yemen in the early twentieth century, but other additional abuses, not written into the laws, became absorbed into custom, such as the devshirme, the degrading corvées (as hangmen or gravediggers), the abduction of Jewish orphans (Yemen), the compulsory removal of footware (Morocco, Yemen), and other humiliations.* . . . The recording in multiple sources of eye-witness accounts, concerning unvarying regulations affecting the Peoples of the Book, perpetuated over the centuries from one end of the dar al-Islam to the other . . . proves sufficiently their entrenchment in customs.[948]

The second pillar remains standing despite Goitein's pioneering analysis of the *jizya*,[949] and related studies of the Jewish *dhimmi* condition, using the Geniza material,[950] expanded and elaborated upon by the research of his student Norman Stillman,[951] and the unique, copiously documented insights of Bat Ye'or.[952] Their work is supported, in turn, by others who chose to study specific regional examples of Jewish *dhimmitude*,[953] or explode mythical constructs such as the Andalusian golden age or unremitting Ottoman "benevolence," which included the jihad conquests and *sürgün* deportations of those Jews being incorporated into the Ottoman Empire.[954]

On Thursday, September 7, 2006, an All-Party Parliamentary Enquiry into Antisemitism issued its finding that anti-Jewish violence had become endemic in Britain, on both the streets and university campuses.[955] A major surge of attacks had accompanied—and followed—the summer 2006 conflict between Hezbollah and Israel, and the report held a "minority of Islamic extremists" responsible for "inciting hatred toward Jews."[956] As a press report noted,[957] the parliamentary enquiry's results are consistent with data recently published in the *Journal of Conflict Resolution* by Yale University biostatistician Dr. Edward H. Kaplan, and Dr. Charles A. Small of the Yale Institute for the Study of Global Antisemitism.[958]

Drs. Kaplan and Small examined the views of 5,004 Europeans, roughly 500 individuals sampled from each of ten European Union countries (Austria, Belgium, Denmark, France, Germany, Italy, the Netherlands, Spain, Switzerland, and the United Kingdom). The authors' main publicized results confirmed their (rather commonsensical) a priori hypothesis: Anti-Israel sentiments *strongly and independently* predicted the likelihood that an individual was antisemitic in a graded manner; that is the *more* anti-Israel (on a scale of 0 to 4), the *more* a person was likely to be antisemitic. But perhaps an even more striking finding in light of the burgeoning Jew hatred now evident in Europe's Muslim communities received much less attention: *In a controlled comparison to European Christians (as the "referent" group), European Muslims were nearly eightfold (i.e., 800 percent) more likely to be overtly Antisemitic.*[959] Furthermore, in light of the Pew Global Attitudes Project data on Muslim attitudes toward Jews in Islamic countries, the Yale study likely underestimated the extent of antisemitism among Europe's Muslim communities, had more poorly educated, less acclimated European Muslims been sampled. Pew's earlier international survey indicated:

In the Muslim world, attitudes toward Jews remain starkly negative, including virtually unanimous unfavorable ratings of 98% in Jordan and 97% in Egypt. *Muslims living in Western countries have a more moderate view of Jews—still more negative than positive, but not nearly by the lopsided margins that prevail in Muslim countries.*[960]

The clear excessive virulence of the antisemitism in Europe's Muslim versus Christian populations, combined with the evidence that globally, Muslims in Islamic countries exhibit even more fanatical Jew hatred than their European co-religionists, defies the "conventional wisdom" regarding the ultimate origins of Muslim Jew hatred in western Europe and beyond. This very flawed construct—that Muslim Jew hatred is merely a loose amalgam of recycled medieval Christian Judeophobic motifs, calumnies from the czarist Russian *Protocols of the Elders of Zion*, and standard Nazi propaganda[961]— continually ignores both empirical contemporary observations and primary, uniquely Islamic components of Jew hatred, both past and present. When the twenty-three-year-old Parisian Jew Ilan Halimi was being tortured to death in February 2006, his Muslim torturers, as Nidra Poller wrote in the *Wall Street Journal*, "phoned the family on several occasions and made them listen to the recitation of verses from the Qur'an, while Ilan's tortured screams could be heard in the background."[962] In the heart of western Europe, Ilan Halimi's murderers did *not* invoke any non-Islamic sources of anti-Jewish hate, only the Qur'an.

The two false pillars upon which the prevailing construct of Islamic antisemitism stands—this sham castle of glib affirmations—must be swept away if the enduring phenomenon of Islamic antisemitism is to be properly understood.

NOTES

1. Robert Wistrich, *Antisemitism—The Longest Hatred* (New York, 1991), p. xv.

2. Ibid., p. xvi. Regarding the spelling, "antisemitism," Dr. Shmuel Almog provided this cogent assessment in "What's in a Hyphen?" *SICSA Report: Newsletter of the Vidal Sassoon International Center for the Study of Antisemitism*, Summer 1989, http://sicsa .huji.ac.il/hyphen.htm, whose conclusions are now widely accepted:

A seemingly minor point crops up from time to time but grows in importance the more you reflect upon it. Should one write "anti-Semitism" with a hypen or "antisemitism" as one word?

What is the importance of such a technical question and why should anyone, apart from type-setters and proof-readers, worry about it? . . .

Let me start at the beginning: When did the word "antisemitism"make its first appearance? It is generally attributed to Wilhelm Marr, who was called by the Israeli historian Moshe Zimmerman "The Patriarch of Antisemitism." Marr coined the term in the 1870s to distinguish between old-time Jew-hatred and modern, political, ethnic, or racial opposition to the Jews. This term made great advances and soon became common usage in many languages. So much so, that it applied not just to the modern brand of Jew-hatred but—against all

logic—was attached to all kinds of enmity toward Jews, past and present. Thus we now say "antisemitism," even when we talk about remote periods in the past, when one had no inkling of this modern usage. Purists no longer cry out in dismay against such anachronistic practice; it is currently established procedure to use "antisemitism" for all types of Jew-hatred.

Let's go back to the hyphen then. What's the difference? If you use the hyphenated form, you consider the words "Semitism," "Semite," "Semitic" as meaningful. They supposedly convey an image of a real substance, of a real group of people—the Semites, who are said to be a race. This is a misnomer: firstly, because "semitic" or "aryan" were originally *language groups*, not *people*; but mainly because in antisemitic parlance, "Semites" really stands for Jews, just that.

And mind you, Jews are not a race at all. They do not all have inherent characteristics in common that may distinguish them from other people. What unites them is a tradition, culture, history, destiny maybe, but not genetics. If you do assume for a moment that Semites are a special race, consider also the implication that this so-called race comprises both Jews and Arabs. One often talks of the kinship between these two, who are now at loggerheads with each other. Be that as it may, antisemites talking against "Semites" do not generally refer to Arabs; they mean Jews. So did the Nazis who killed the Jews and invited cooperation from the Arabs.

It is obvious then that "anti-Semitism" is a nonterm, because it is not directed against so-called "Semitism." If there is any substance to the term, it is only to denote a specifically anti-Jewish movement. Antisemitism is a generic term which signifies a singular attitude to a particular group of people. As the late philosopher Zvi Diesendruck pointed out, "There has never been coined a standing term for the merely negative attitude" to any other people in history. Only antisemitism; only against Jews.

So the hyphen, or rather its omission, conveys a message; if you hyphenate your "anti-Semitism," you attach some credence to the very foundation on which the whole thing rests. Strike out the hyphen and you will treat antisemitism for what it really is—a generic name for modern Jew-hatred which now embraces this phenomenon as a whole, past, present and—I am afraid—future as well.

3. Bernard Lewis, *Semites and Antisemites: An Inquiry into Conflict and Prejudice* (New York/London: W. W. Norton, 1986), p. 117.

4. Raul Hilberg, *The Destruction of the European Jews*, 3rd ed. (New Haven, CT: Yale University Press, 2003).

5. "Nazis Reassure Arabs—Antisemitism Confined to Jews, Spokesman Explains," *New York Times*, November 5, 1942; Bernard Lewis recently expanded on this same incident in his essay "The New Antisemitism," *American Scholar* 75, no. 1 (2006): 25–36.

While in Berlin, Rashid Ali [the Pro-Nazi Iraqi Premier deposed in May/June 1941] was apparently disquieted by the language and, more especially, the terminology of antisemitism. His concerns were authoritatively removed in an exchange of letters with an official spokesman of the German Nazi Party. In answer to a question from Rashid Ali as to whether antisemitism was also directed against Arabs, because they were part of the Semitic family, Professor Walter Gross, director of the Race Policy Office of the Nazi Party, explained with great emphasis, in a letter dated October 17, 1942, that this was not the case and that antisemitism was concerned wholly and exclusively with Jews. On the contrary, he observed, the Nazis had always shown sympathy and support for the Arab cause against the Jews. In the course of his letter, he even remarked that the expression "antisemitism, which has been used for decades in Europe by the anti-Jewish movement, was incorrect since this movement was directed exclusively against Jewry, and not against other peoples who speak a Semitic language." (p. 33)

6. S. D. Goitein, *A Mediterranean Society: The Jewish Communities of the Arab World as Portrayed in the Documents of the Cairo Geniza*, vol. 2: *The Community*. (Berkeley and Los Angeles: University of California Press, 1971), p. 283.

A genizah or geniza (Hebrew: הזבג "storage"; plural: genizot) is the storeroom or depository in a synagogue, usually for worn-out Hebrew-language books and papers on religious topics that were stored there before they could receive a proper cemetery burial, it being forbidden to throw away writings containing the name of God (even personal letters and legal contracts could open with an invocation of God). But in practice, genizot also contained writings of a secular nature, with or without the customary opening invocation, and also contained writings in other languages that use the Hebrew alphabet (Judeo-Arabic, Judeo-Persian, Ladino, Yiddish).

The Cairo Geniza is an accumulation of almost two hundred thousand Jewish manuscripts that were found in the geniza of the Ben Ezra synagogue (built 882) of Fostat, Egypt (now Old Cairo); the Basatin cemetery east of Old Cairo; and a number of old documents that were bought in Cairo in the later nineteenth century. These documents were written from about 870 to as late as 1880 CE. The normal practice for genizas was to periodically remove the contents and bury them in a cemetery. Many of these documents were written in the

Arabic using the Hebrew alphabet. The Jews who wrote the materials in the geniza were familiar with the culture and language of their contemporary society. The documents are invaluable as evidence for how colloquial Arabic of this period was spoken and understood. Goitein demonstrates that the Jewish creators of the documents were part of their contemporary society. The importance of these materials for reconstructing the social and economic history for the period between 950 and 1250 cannot be overemphasized; the index Goitein created covers about thirty-five thousand individuals, which included about 350 "prominent people" (including Maimonides and his son Abraham), 200 "better-known families," and mentions of 450 professions and 450 goods. He identified material from Egypt, Palestine, Lebanon, Syria (but not Damascus or Aleppo), Tunisia, Sicily, and even covering trade with India. Cities mentioned range from Samarkand in Central Asia to Seville and Sijilmasa, Morocco to the west; from Aden north to Constantinople; Europe not only is represented by the Mediterranean port cities of Narbonne, Marseilles, Genoa, and Venice, but even Kiev and Rouen are occasionally mentioned.

The materials include a vast number of books, most of them fragments, which Goitein estimated number 250,000 leaves, including parts of Jewish religious writings and fragments from the Qur'an. The nonliterary materials, which include court documents, legal writings, and the correspondence of the local Jewish community, are somewhat smaller, but still impressive: Goitein estimated their size at "about 10,000 items of some length, of which 7,000 are self-contained units large enough to be regarded as documents of historical value. Only half of these are preserved more or less completely."

7. See, for example, Claude Cahen, "Dhimma," in *Encyclopedia of Islam*, eds. P. Bearman, Thomas Bianquis, C. E. Bosworth, E. van Donzel, and W. P. Heinrichs (Leiden: Brill, 2006). Cahen maintained: "There is nothing in medieval Islam which could specifically be called antisemitism."

8. Goitein, *A Mediterranean Society*, vol. 2, p. 278.

9. Ibid., pp. 278–79, 586–87, nn. 14–25.

10. Ibid., p. 587, n. 16.

11. Ibid., p. 278.

12. Ibid., pp. 279–80.

13. Ibid., pp. 278–83, 586–87, nn. 14–25.

14. Hartwig Hirschfeld, "Essai sur l'histoire des Juifs de Medine," *Revue Des Etude Juives* 7 (1883): 167–93; 10 (1885): 10–31.

15. Georges Vajda, "Juifs et musulmans selon le Hadit," *Journal Asiatique* 229 (January–March 1937): 57–127.

16. Haggai Ben-Shammai, "Jew-Hatred in the Islamic Tradition and Qur'anic Exegesis," in *Antisemitism through the Ages*, ed. Shmuel Almog (Oxford: Pergamon, 1988), pp. 161–69.

17. Lawrence Wright, *The Looming Tower: Al-*

Qaeda and the Road to 9/11 (New York: Knopf, 2006), pp. 38–39.

18. Esther Webman, *Anti-Semitic Motifs in the Ideology of Hizballah and Hamas* (Tel Aviv: Tel Aviv University, 1994), pp. vii–viii, citing these works: H. Lazarus-Yafeh, *Religious Thought and Practice in Islam* (Tel Aviv: Ministry of Defense, 1985), pp. 52–72; Lewis, *Semites and Antisemites*, pp. 11–23, 117–40, 192–261; Yehoshafat Harkabi, *The Arabs' Position in Their Conflict with Israel* ([Hebrew] Tel Aviv: 1968); Rivka Yadlin, *An Arrogant Oppressive Spirit: Anti-Zionism as Anti-Judaism in Egypt* (Oxford: Pergamon, 1989); Bernard Lewis, "The Arab World Discovers Antisemitism," *Commentary* (May 1986): 30–35.

19. Muhammad Sayyid Tantawi, *Banu Isra'il fi al-Qur'an wa al-Sunna* [The Children of Israel in the Qur'an and the Traditions] (Cairo: 1986). Qur'an 3:113: "They are not all alike. Of the People of the Scripture there is a staunch community who recite the revelations of Allah in the night season, falling prostrate (before Him)." The classical Qur'anic commentator Ibn Kathir (d. 1373) provides support for Tantawi's contemporary interpretation of 3:113. Ibn Kathir (*Tafsir Ibn Kathir*, vol. 2, [Riyadh: 2000, p. 246) wrote:

Muhammad bin Ishaq and others, including al-'Awfi who reported from Ibn 'Abbas, said, "These Ayat [verses] were revealed about the clergy of the People of the Scriptures who embraced the faith. For instance, there is Abdallah bin Salam, Asad bin 'Ubayd, Tha'labah bin Sa'yah, Usayd bin Sa'yah, and so forth. This Ayah [3:113] means that those among the People of the Book [Book = Bible] whom Allah rebuked earlier are not all the same as those among them who embraced Islam.

20. Aluma Solnick, "Based on Qur'anic Verses, Interpretations, and Traditions, Muslim Clerics State: The Jews Are the Descendants of Apes, Pigs, and Other Animals," Middle East Media Research Institute, special report no. 11, November 1, 2002, http://memri.org/bin/articles.cgi?Page=archives&Area=sr&ID=SR01102.

21. "Leading Egyptian Government Cleric Calls For: 'Martyrdom Attacks that Strike Horror into the Hearts of the Enemies of Allah,'" Middle East Media Research Institute, no. 363, April 7, 2002, http://memri.org/bin/articles.cgi?Page=archives&Area=sd&ID=SP36302.

22. "The Meeting between the Sheik of Al-Azhar and the Chief Rabbi of Israel," Middle East Media Research Institute, special report no. 2, February 8, 1998, http://memri.org/bin/articles.cgi?Page=archives&Area=sr&ID=SR00398.

23. Ibn Warraq, *Why I Am Not a Muslim* (Amherst, NY: Prometheus Books, 1995), p. 105.

24. Theodore Nöldeke, "The Koran," originally published in the *Encyclopedia Britannica*, 9th ed., vol. 16 (1891), pp. 597ff. Reproduced in Ibn Warraq, ed., *The*

Origins of the Koran (Amherst, NY: Prometheus Books, 1998), pp. 37–38.

25. Warraq, *Why I Am Not a Muslim*, pp. 105, 216.

26. Ben-Shammai, "Jew-Hatred in the Islamic Tradition and Qur'anic Exegesis," pp. 164–68.

27. Saul S. Friedman, "The Myth of Islamic Toleration," in *Without Future: The Plight of Syrian Jewry* (New York: Praeger, 1989), pp. 2–3.

28. Ben-Shammai, "Jew-Hatred in the Islamic Tradition and Qur'anic Exegesis," pp. 164–68.

29. Friedman, "The Myth of Islamic Toleration," pp. 2–3.

30. Ben-Shammai, "Jew-Hatred in the Islamic Tradition and Qur'anic Exegesis," p. 164.

31. Ibid. In the accompanying notes p. 169, nn. 9 and 10, Ben-Shammai elaborates on the notion of the permanence of the Jews abasement in the hadith, and a related Qur'anic verse:

There are interpretations ascribed to Muhammad's companions such as his cousin, Abdallah Ibn Abbas. These attributions are most doubtful, but by the mid-eighth century the earliest interpretations were already in writing. . . . The identical expression, in the sense of an everlasting decree, also occurs in Sura 3 of the Koran, verse 112. ["Ignominy shall be their portion wheresoever they are found save (where they grasp) a rope from Allah and a rope from men. They have incurred anger from their Lord, and wretchedness is laid upon them. That is because they used to disbelieve the revelations of Allah, and slew the prophets wrongfully. That is because they were rebellious and used to transgress."]

32. The Qur'anic poll tax or *jizya*, based upon Qur'an 9:29.

33. Ben-Shammai, "Jew-Hatred in the Islamic Tradition and Qur'anic Exegesis," p. 169, n. 11, observes:

As was apparently done with most the traditions during the second century of the Hegira [i.e., the second century after 622 CE]. Most of the traditions cited here are from the comprehensive commentary of Muhammad b. Jarir al-Tabari (d. 923) and are found in parallel versions in most of the collections of the traditions assembled in the ninth and early tenth centuries CE.

34. Ibid., p. 165.

35. Ibid.

36. Ibid.

37. Ibid.

38. Ibid., p. 167.

39. Qur'an 3:54–56—

And they (the disbelievers) schemed, and Allah schemed (against them): and Allah is the best of schemers. . . . (And remember) when Allah said: O Jesus! Lo! I am gathering thee and causing thee to ascend unto Me, and am cleansing thee of those who disbelieve and am setting those who follow thee above those who disbelieve until the Day of Resurrection. Then unto Me ye will (all) return, and I shall judge between you as to that wherein ye used to differ. . . . As for those who disbelieve I shall chastise them with a heavy chastisement in the world and the Hereafter; and they will have no helpers.

40. Ben-Shammai, "Jew-Hatred in the Islamic Tradition and Qur'anic Exegesis," p. 167.

41. Tabari, *The Commentary on the Qur'an*, with an introduction and notes by J. Cooper, ed. W. F. Medlung and A. Jones (Oxford: Oxford University Press, 1987), pp. 353–55.

42. Tabari, *Jāmiʿ al-Bayān fii Tafsiir al-Qur'aan*, ed. M. Shākir (Beirut: 1421/2001), vol. 10, pp. 125, 126; English translation by Michael Schub.

43. Baydawi, *Commentaius in Coranum: Anwaar al-Tanziil Wa-Asraar al-Ta'wiil,* ed. H. O. Fleischer (1846–48; reprint, Osnabrück: 1968), p. 63; English translation by Michael Schub.

44. Ibn Kathir, *Tafsir Ibn Kathir* (Riyadh: 2000), vol. 1, pp. 245–46.

45. Sayyid Qutb, *In the Shade of the Qur'an* (Leicester, UK: 1999), vol. 1, surah 1–2, p. 91.

46. Ibid., pp. 91–92.

47. Sayyid Abul A'la Mawdudi, *Towards Understanding the Qur'an* (Leicester, UK: 1988), vol. 1, p. xiii.

48. Ibid., pp. 78–80.

49. Ben-Shammai, "Jew-Hatred in the Islamic Tradition and Qur'anic Exegesis," p. 167. Qur'an 5:82 as cited by the author is the Pickthall translation.

50. Tabari, *Jāmiʿ al-Bayān fii Tafsiir al-Qur'aan*, vol. 7, pp. 5ff.

51. Zamakshari, *Tafsir al-kashshaf an haqa'iq ghawamid at-tanzil wa-uyun al-aqawil fi wujuh at-ta'wil* (Cairo, 1953–1955). English translation in Helmut Gatje, *The Qur'an and its Exegesis* (Berkeley, CA: 1976), p. 134. The last line included ("the Jews focused their hostility to the Muslims in the most overt and intense manner") was omitted by Gatje, and was translated by Dr. Michael Schub from the Beirut 2001 edition of *Tafsir al-kashshaf*, pp. 701ff.

52. Baydawi, *Anwaar al-Tanziil Wa-Asraar al-Ta'wiil,* vol. 1, p. 270.

53. Ibn Kathir, *Tafsir Ibn Kathir*, p. 246.

54. Sayyid Qutb, *In the Shade of the Qur'an*, pp. 217–18, 220.

55. Ibid., pp. 220–21.

56. Ben-Shammai, "Jew-Hatred in the Islamic Tradition and Qur'anic Exegesis," p. 167.

57. Edward William Lane, *An Account of the Customs of the Modern Egyptians* (New York: Dover, 1973), pp. 553–56.

58. "A Risala of Al-Jahiz," trans. Joshua Finkel, *Journal of the American Oriental Society* 47 (1927): 311–34.

59. Ibid., p. 319.

60. Indeed, Finkel (ibid., p. 316) underscores the devastating nature of the trenchant anti-Christian arguments mustered by Al-Jahiz:

While there are other anti-Christian writings extant in Mohammedan literature, no work goes so directly to the vital features of the problem, no work is of so potential of deadly effect.

61. Ibid., pp. 322–23.

62. "A Risala of Al-Jahiz," p. 323.

63. See Qur'an 2:105,

Neither those who disbelieve among the people of the Scripture nor the idolaters love that there should be sent down unto you any good thing from your Lord. But Allah chooseth for His mercy whom He will, and Allah is of Infinite Bounty.

64. Ibid.," p. 324.

64a. Ibid., pp. 316, 317.

64b. Ibid, p. 328.

64c. Roger Arnaldez, "al Muhasibi," *Encyclopedia of Islam*, eds. P. Bearman, Thomas Bianquis, C. E. Bosworth, E. van Donzel, and W. P. Heinrichs (Leiden: Brill, 2007).

64d. Al-Muhasibi, *The Book of the Patronage of the Law of Allah* [Arabic], ed. Margaret Smith (London: 1940–41), p. 256. English translation cited in Avraham Grossman, "The Economic and Social Background of Hostile Attitudes toward the Jews in the Ninth and Tenth Century Muslim Caliphate," in *Antisemitism through the Ages*, ed. Shmuel Almog (Oxford: 1988), p. 186 n. 39.

65. Lane, *An Account of the Customs of the Modern Egyptians*, p. 554

66. Ibid., pp. 554–55.

67. A. B. Clot-Bey, *Aperçu general sur l'Egypte* (1840), vol. 2, pp. 139–42. Excerpts translated by Martine Chauvet from Jacob M. Landau, *Jews in Nineteenth Century Egypt* (New York: 1969), doc. 12, pp. 152–54.

68. Moritz Lüttke, *Aegyptiens neue Zeit. Ein Beitrag zur Culturgeschichte des gegenwartigen Jahrhunderts sowie zur Charakteristik des Orients unde des Islam* (Leipzig, 1873), vol. 1, pp. 97–99. English translation in Landau, *Jews in Nineteenth Century Egypt*, pp. 18–19.

69. Landau, *Jews in Nineteenth Century Egypt*, p. 19.

70. Friedman, "The Myth of Islamic Toleration," pp. 2–3.

71. Ibn Kathir (*Tafsir Ibn Kathir*, pp. 579–80) mentions Nebuchadnezzar's depredations, but warns,

The earlier and later commentators differed over the identity of these invaders. Many *Isrā'īliyyāt* (reports from Jewish sources) were narrated about this, but I did not want to make this book too long by mentioning them, because some of them are fabricated, concocted by their heretics, and others may be true, but we have no need of them, praise be to Allah.

He continues,

What Allah has told us in his book is sufficient and we have no need of what is in the other books that came before. Neither Allah nor His Messenger required us to refer to them. Allah told His Messenger that when [the Jews] committed transgression and aggression, Allah gave their enemies power over them to destroy their country and enter the innermost parts of their homes. Their humiliation and subjugation was a befitting punishment, and your Lord is never unfair or unjust to his servants. They had rebelled and killed many of the Prophets and scholars.

Yusuf Ali's discussion of Qur'an 17:4 (in Abdallah Yusuf Ali, *The Holy Qur'an: Text, Translation, and Commentary* [1934; reprint, Elmhurst, NY: 2001], p. 694 n. 2174) suggests,

. . . it may be that the two occasions refer to (1) the destruction of the Temple by the Babylonian Nebuchadnezzar in 586 BC, when the Jews were carried of into captivity, and (2) the destruction of Jerusalem by Titus in AD 70, after which the Temple was never rebuilt. . . . On both occasions it was a judgment of God for the sins of the Jews, their backslidings, and their arrogance.

72. Friedman, "The Myth of Islamic Toleration," p. 2. Friedman derives all his Qur'anic citations (numberings and excerpts) from N. J. Dawood, *The Koran* (Harmondsworth, UK: Penguin, 1956).

73. Ibid., p. 2.

74. Ibid., pp. 2–3.

75. This verse is 2:61 in most Qur'anic numbering systems.

75a. This verse is 2:96 in most Qur'anic numbering systems.

75b. This verse is 2:54 in most Qur'anic numbering systems. Friedman, "The Myth of Islamic Toleration," p. 3.

76. Ibid.

77. This verse is 4:46 in most Qur'anic numbering systems.

78. This verse is 4:161 in most Qur'anic numbering systems.

78a. This verse is 3:110 in most Qur'anic numbering systems.

78b. This verse is 3:78 in most Qur'anic numbering systems.

79. Ibid., p. 3, citing N. J. Dawood's translation. Ibn Kathir's commentary refers to Qur'an 58:8–10 as indicating that the Jews are consigned to hell for their plotting to kill (Muslim) believers (Ibn Kathir, *Tafsir Ibn Kathir*, vol. 9, p. 520, section entitled, "The Evil of the Jews").

80. Friedman, "The Myth of Islamic Toleration," p. 3.

81. This verse is 98:6 in most Qur'anic numbering systems. Friedman, "The Myth of Islamic Toleration," p. 3.

82. Friedman, "The Myth of Islamic Toleration," pp. 2–3.

83. Ben-Shammai, "Jew-Hatred in the Islamic Tradition and Qur'anic Exegesis," pp. 164–68.

84. Ronald M. Nettler, "Islamic Archetypes of the Jews: Then and Now," in *Anti-Zionism and Antisemitism in the Contemporary World*, ed. Robert Wistrich (New York: 1990), pp. 64–65.

85. Sahih Bukhari, vol. 3, bk. 47, no. 786; Sahih Muslim, bk. 26, no. 5430; Sunan Abu Dawud, bk. 39, no. 4498; Ibn Sa'd, *Kitab Al-Tabaqat Al-Kabir* (New Delhi: 1993), vol. 2, pp. 249–52. English translation by S. Moinul Haq and H. K. Ghazanfar.

86. Hartwig Hirschfeld, "Abdallah Ibn Saba," Jewish Encyclopedia.com, http://www.jewishencyclopedia.com/view.jsp?artid=189&letter=A; Tabari, *Ta'rikh al-Rusul wa al-Muluk*, ed. M. J. de Goeje (Leiden: 1898), vol. 1, no. 6, pp. 3941–42, English translation in Nettler, "Islamic Archetypes of the Jews," p. 66.

87. Ibid. Nettler, "Islamic Archetypes of the Jews," pp. 65–66; Tabari as above in n. 92.

87a. "Speech of President Bashar Al-Assad Welcoming His Holiness Pope John Paul II on His Arrival in Damascus," May 5, 2001, *Syrian Arab News Agency*, emphasis added.

88. Ibn Kathir, *Tafsir Ibn Kathir*, pp. 405–406.

89. Mawdudi, *Towards Understanding the Qur'an*, vol. 3, pp. 201–202.

90. See notes 56–71, above.

91. Moshe Gil, *A History of Palestine, 634–1099* (Cambridge, 1992), p. 159 n. 32.

92. Tabari, *Ta'rikh al-Rusul wa al-Muluk*, vol. 3, pp. 1389–90; English translation in Norman Stillman, *The Jews of Arab Lands: A History and Source Book* (Philadelphia: 1979), p. 167.

93. Georges Vajda, "À propos de la situation des Juifs et des Chrétiens à Séville au début du XIIe siècle," *Revue des Études Juives* 99 (1935): 127–29; English translation by Michael J. Miller.

94. "Friday Sermons in Saudi Mosques: Review and Analysis," Middle East Media Research Institute, special report no. 10, September 26, 2002.

95. Kaufmann Kohler, Isaac Broydé, "Solomon ben Jeroham," JewishEncyclopedia.com, http://www.jewishencyclopedia.com/view_friendly.jsp?artid=916&letter=S.

96. Vajda, "À propos de la situation des Juifs et des Chrétiens à Séville au début du XIIe siècle."

97. Salomon Feuerstein, *Der Commentar des Karäers Salmon ben Jerucham zu den Klageliedern: Zum ersten*

Male nach der Pariser Handschrift edirt (Krakau, 1898), p. xiii. English translation by Haggai Ben-Shammai in "The Attitude of Some Early Karaites towards Islam," from *Studies in Medieval Jewish History and Literature*, ed. Isadore Twersky (Cambridge, MA: 1984) vol. 2, p. 10.

Additional examples of this Muslim doctrine on salutation were provided in the opinions of the tenth-century Kairouan (northeast Tunisia) jurist al-Qayrawani and the eighteenth-century Egyptian sheikh Damanhuri. From Qayrawani, *La Risala*, trans. Leon Bercher, 5th ed., (Algiers: 1960). English translation in Bat Ye'or, *Islam and Dhimmitude: Where Civilizations Collide* (Cranbury, NJ: 2001), p. 9:

> One should not be the first to say *salam* [blessing be upon you] to Jews or Christians; but when one has (inadvertently) said *salam* to a tributary, he should be asked to consider it null and void. If a Jew or Christian greets you, you must reply "alayka" ["the same to you"] (nothing more). But you can also reply: *"alayka' s-silâm,"* with kasra of the *sîn* [vocalized with an "i" and not an "a" to make it an insult], for it would then mean: "the stone," because, according to one opinion, this is permitted.

Sheikh Damanhuri issued a similar ruling on this subject some eight centuries later (from *Shaykh Damanhuri on the Churches of Cairo, 1739*, ed. and trans. Moshe Perlmann [Berkeley and Los Angeles: University of California Press, 1975], p. 57):

> If you greeted one whom you considered a Muslim, only to learn he was a *dhimmi*, withdraw your word, pretending "he considered my salutation." If one of them salutes he is answered with "same to you" only. If you correspond with one, you say: "Salutation to him who follows right guidance." But avoid congratulating, consoling, or visiting them, unless you expect the person visited to convert to Islam.

98. Sir John Drummond-Hay, *Western Barbary: Its Wild Tribes and Savage Animals* (London: 1844), p. 3.

99. Sahih Bukhari, vol. 2, bk. 23, no. 376, http://www.usc.edu/dept/MSA/fundamentals/hadithsunnah/bukhari/023.sbt.html; Sahih Muslim, bk. 004, no. 2029, http://www.usc.edu/dept/MSA/fundamentals/hadith-sunnah/muslim/004.smt.html#004.2029.

100. Sahih Bukhari, vol. 2, bk. 23, no. 457; Sahih Muslim bk. 040, no. 6861.

101. Tudor Parfitt, *The Road to Redemption: The Jews of the Yemen 1900–1950* (Leiden: 1996), p. 89.

102. Suyuti wrote a famous and ubiquitous commentary, "Tafsiir al-Jalalayn," he composed with his teacher, Jalaal al-Diin al-MaHallii; the latter composed the second part, then Suyuti wrote the first part to complete it, including this translation/quote for Qur'an 9:29. *Tafsīr al-Jalālayn* (Beirut: 1404/1984), p. 244, from Suyuti's *Durr al-Manthūr* . . . (Beirut: n.d.), vol. 3, p. 228, where Suyuti quotes various traditions. These quotes, in English translation, are reproduced from Andrew Bostom, ed., *The Legacy of Jihad* (Amherst, NY: Prometheus Books, 2005), p. 127.

103. Georges Vajda, "Un Traite Maghrebin 'Adversos Judaeos: Ahkam Ahl Al-Dimma Du Sayh Muhammad B. 'Abd Al-Karim Al-Magili,'" in *Études d'Orientalisme Dediees a La Memoire de Lévi-Provençal* (Paris: vol. 2, 1962), p. 811; English translation by Michael J. Miller.

104. Bat Ye'or, *Islam and Dhimmitude*, pp. 70–71.

105. David Littman, "Jews under Muslim Rule in the Late Nineteenth Century," *Wiener Library Bulletin* 28 (1975): 75.

106. Norman Stillman, *The Jews of Arab Lands in Modern Times* (Philadelphia: 1991), p. 51.

107. Jacques Chalom, *Les Israelites de la Tunisie: Leur condition civile et politique* (Paris, 1908), p. 193.

108. For Yemen: Parfitt, *The Road to Redemption*, p. 163, and Aviva Klein-Franke, "Collecting the Djizya (Poll-Tax) in the Yemen," in *Israel and Ishmael: Studies in Muslim-Jewish Relations*, ed. Tudor Parfitt (New York, 2000), pp. 175–206; for Afghanistan: S. Landshut, *Jewish Communities in the Muslim Countries of the Middle East* (Westport, CT: 1950), pp. 67–70.

109. Klein-Franke, "Collecting the Djizya (Poll-Tax) in the Yemen," pp. 182–83, 186.

110. Landshut, *Jewish Communities in the Muslim Countries of the Middle East*, p. 67.

111. Al-Mawardi, *The Laws of Islamic Governance [al-Ahkam as-Sultaniyyah]* (London: 1996), p. 211; Bat Ye'or, *The Dhimmi: Jews and Christians under Islam* (Cranbury, NJ: 1985) p. 169; K. S. Lal, *The Legacy of Muslim Rule in India* (New Delhi: 1992), p. 237.

112. For example, see Marghinani Ali ibn Abi Bakr, *al-Hidayah, The Hedaya, or Guide—A Commentary on the Mussulman Laws*, trans. Charles Hamilton (1791: reprint, New Delhi: 1982), vol. 2, pp. 362–63.

> Malik and Shafi'i have said that their (i.e., the non-Muslim dhimmis) is absolutely inadmissible, because as infidels are unjust, it is requisite to be slow in believing anything they may advance, God having said (in the Koran) "When an unjust person tells you anything be slow in believing him"; whence it is that the evidence of an infidel is not admitted concerning a Mussulman; and consequently that an infidel stands (in this particular) in the same predicament with an apostate. . . . Besides, a dhimmi may be suspected of inventing falsehoods against a Mussulman from the hatred he bears to him on account of the superiority of the Mussulmans over him.

And, from Joseph Schacht, *An Introduction to Islamic Law* (Oxford: 1982), p. 132:

. . . the dhimmi cannot be a witness, except in matters concerning other dhimmis . . .

113. W. M. Watt, trans., *The Faith and Practice of Al-Ghazali* (Oxford: 1953), p. 13.

114. Al-Ghazali, *Kitab al-Wagiz fi fiqh madhab al-imam al-Safi'i* (Beirut: 1979), pp. 186, 190–91, 199–200, 202–203. English translation by Dr. Michael Schub. Reproduced from Bostom, *The Legacy of Jihad*, p. 199.

114a. Parfitt, *The Road to Redemption*, p. 187.

114b. Ibid., p. 87; Yehuda Nini, *The Jews of the Yemen, 1800–1914*, trans. H. Galai (Chur, Switzerland: 1990), pp. 24–25.

114c. Nini, *The Jews of the Yemen*, p. 24.

114d. M. Gaudefroy-Demombynes, "Marocain Mellah," *Journal Asiatique* 3 (1914): 651; Meakin, "The Jews of Morocco," p. 372.

114e. Eliezer Bashan, "New Documents regarding Attacks upon Jewish Religious Observance in Morocco during the Late Nineteenth Century," *Pe'amim* (1995): 71; English translation by Rivkah Fishman.

115. Al-Mawardi, *The Laws of Islamic Governance*, pp. 60, 77–78, 200–201.

116. Moshe Perlmann, "Eleventh-Century Andalusian Authors on the Jews of Granada," *Proceedings of the American Academy for Jewish Research* 18 (1948–49): 286–87.

117. Sultan 'Abd Allah of Granada, *Kitab al-Tibyan*, trans. by Bernard Lewis. Extracts reproduced from Stillman, *The Jews of Arab Lands*, pp. 224–25. The account was part of a memoir composed during 'Abd Allah's imprisonment beginning in 1090 when Granada was conquered by the Berber Muslim Almoravids from North Africa.

118. Perlmann, "Eleventh-Century Andalusian Authors on the Jews of Granada," p. 284; Reinhart Dozy, *Spanish Islam: A History of the Muslims in Spain*, trans. Francis Griffin Stokes (London, 1915; Kessinger Publishing), p. 653.

119. Richard Gottheil and Joseph Jacobs, "The Crusades," JewishEncyclopedia.com, http://www.jewish encyclopedia.com/view_friendly.jsp?artid=908&letter=C.

120. Walter Fischel, *Jews in the Economic and Political Life of Medieval Islam* (London: 1937), p. 91.

121. Ibid., p. 91.

122. Bar Hebraeus, *The Chronography of Bar Hebraeus*, trans. E. A. W. Budge (London: 1932), p. 490.

123. Ghazi b. al-Wasiti, "An Answer to the Dhimmis," trans. Richard Gottheil, *Journal of the American Oriental Society* 41 (1921): 449.

124. Fischel, *Jews in the Economic and Political Life of Medieval Islam*, pp. 91–92.

125. Bar Hebraeus, *The Chronography*, p. 484.

126. Fischel, *Jews in the Economic and Political Life of Medieval Islam*, p. 108.

127. Ibid., p. 110.

128. Cited in ibid.

129. P. Jackson, "Wassaf—The Court Panegyrist," *Encyclopedia of Islam*, ed. P. Bearman, Thomas Bianquis, C. E. Bosworth, E. van Donzel, and W. P. Heinrichs (Leiden: Brill, 2006).

130. Fischel, *Jews in the Economic and Political Life of Medieval Islam*, p. 111.

131. Ibid.

132. Cited in ibid.

133. Ibid., pp. 112, 114.

134. Bar Hebraeus, *The Chronography*, p. 491.

135. Cited in Fischel, *Jews in the Economic and Political Life of Medieval Islam*, p. 116.

136. Cited in ibid., p. 117.

137. Bar Hebraeus, *The Chronography*, p. 491.

138. Fischel, *Jews in the Economic and Political Life of Medieval Islam*, p. 117 and n. 5.

139. E. G. Browne, *A Literary History of Persia* [electronic resource], with a new introduction by J. T. P. de Bruijn (Bethesda: 1997), vol. 3, pp. 35–36.

140. Qur'an 44:25—"They left how many gardens and fountains."

141. H. Z. Hirschberg, *A History of the Jews of North Africa* (Leiden: 1974), vol. 1, pp. 392–99; Jane S. Gerber, *Jewish Society in Fez 1450–1700* (Leiden: 1980), pp. 20–21.

142. Hirschberg, *A History of the Jews of North Africa*, p. 395.

143. Ibid., p. 395.

144. Sunni Muslims in the Arab world tended to reserve the terms "sharif" for descendants of Hassan (son of Caliph Ali ibn Ali Talibi) and "sayyid" for descendants of Husayn (also a son of Caliph Ali ibn Ali Talibi, and revered as the third imam by most Shi'a Muslims).

145. Hirschberg, *A History of the Jews of North Africa*, pp. 395–96.

146. Ibid., pp. 396–97.

147. Unfortunately, 'Abd el-Basit was wrong. Some six thousand Jews were slaughtered in the Jewish quarter of Fez in 1032–1033 during the ravages led by a Berber sheikh. See Edmond Fagnan, "Le Signe Distinctif des Juifs au Maghreb," *Revue Études Juifs* 48 (1994): p. 297; Salo W. Baron, *A Social and Religious History of the Jews* (New York: 1957), vol. 3, p. 108; and Hirschberg, *A History of the Jews of North Africa*, p. 108.

148. Hirschberg, *A History of the Jews of North Africa*, p. 398.

149. Gerber, *Jewish Society in Fez*, p. 21.

150. Y. D. Sémach, "Une chronique juive de Fès: Le 'Yahas Fès' de Ribbi Abner Hassarfaty," *Hespéris* 19, nos. 1–2 (1934): 91–93; English translation by Susan Emanuel.

151. Gerber, *Jewish Society in Fez*, p. 21.

152. Hirschberg, *A History of the Jews of North Africa*, p. 402; Gerber, *Jewish Society in Fez*, p. 18; John O. Hunwick, "Al-Maghili and the Jews of Tuwat: The

Demise of a Community," *Studia Islamica* 61 (1985): 155–83.

153. G. Deverdun, "Ibn 'Askar," in *Encyclopedia of Islam*, ed. P. Bearman, Thomas Bianquis, C. E. Bosworth, E. van Donzel, and W. P. Heinrichs (Leiden: Brill, 2006).

154. Ibn 'Askar, *Dawhat al-nashir li-mahasin man kana bi 'l-maghrib min mashayikh al-qarn al-'ashir* (Fez: 1891–92), p. 95; English translation in Hunwick, "Al-Maghili and the Jews of Tuwat," p. 161.

155. Vajda, "Un Traite Maghrebin 'Adversos Judaeos," p. 811; English translation by Michael J. Miller.

156. Hunwick, "Al-Maghili and the Jews of Tuwat," pp. 173–74, 162. On pp. 173–74, Hunwick summarizes the opinion of one of at least two major contemporary Moroccan jurists who supported al-Maghili's views, al-Tanasi (d. 1494):

> As part of his case al-Tanasi quoted a ruling in Tunis by the jurist 'Abd al-'Aziz al-'Abdusi (d. 1434) that there could be neither building nor repair of religious edifices in the land of the Muslims (*bilad al-muslimin*). Should dhimmis subsequently build a place of worship after being forbidden to do so, this would constitute an abrogation of the pact [dhimma], making it lawful to enslave their women and children and seize their property.

157. Ibid., pp. 176–77; 165–66.

158. H. I. Gwarzo, "The Life and Teachings of al-Maghili with Particular Reference to the Saharan Jewish Community," (PhD diss., University of London, 1972), p. 136.

158a. Ibid., p. 134.

158b. Ibid., p. 137.

159. Ibid., pp. 49–50. Gwarzo further notes (p. 261) that the Muslim rank-and-file afforded al-Maghili "respect, reverence, and blind loyalty."

159a. Hunwick, "Al-Maghili and the Jews of Tuwat," p. 183.

160. Raphael Israeli, "Anti-Jewish Attitudes in the Arabic Media, 1975–1981," in *Anti-Zionism and Antisemitism in the Contemporary World*, ed. Robert Wistrich (New York: 1990), pp. 103, 112.

161. Emmanuel Sivan, "Islamic Fundamentalism, Antisemitism, and Anti-Zionism," in *Anti-Zionism and Antisemitism in the Contemporary World*, ed. Robert Wistrich (New York: 1990), p. 82.

162. See discussion in text associated with notes 131 and 132, above, from Walter Fischel, *Jews in the Economic and Political Life of Medieval Islam* (London: 1937), p. 91.

163. Sivan, "Islamic Fundamentalism, Antisemitism, and Anti-Zionism," pp. 77–78.

164. Ahmad Yusuf Ahmad, *Al-Sh'b al-Dalil Isra'il* [Israel—The Misled People] (Cairo: 1962), p. 78; Cited in Y. Harkabi, *Arab Attitudes to Israel,* trans. Misha Louvish (Jerusalem: 1972), p. 92.

165. 'Abdallah al-Tall, *Khatr al-Yahudiyya al-'Alamiyya 'Ala al-Islam wa-al-Mashiyya* [The Danger of World Jewry to Islam and Christianity] (Cairo: 1964), p. 65; Cited in Harkabi, *Arab Attitudes to Israel*, p. 92.

166. D. F. Green ["D. F. Green" is a compound pseudonym for David Littman and Y. Harkabi, *Arab Theologians on Jews and Israel: Extracts from the Proceedings of the Fourth Conference of the Academy of Islamic Research* (Geneva: 1976), p. 15.

167. The Fourth Conference of the Academy of Islamic Research, Rajab 1388, September 1968 (Cairo: General Organization for Government Printing Offices, 1970).

168. Green, *Arab Theologians on Jews and Israel*, p. 70.

169. Ibid., p. 91.

170. Sylvia Haim, "Islam and the Theory of Arab Nationalism," *Die Welt Des Islams* 2 (1955): 124–49. See especially her conclusion on p. 149:

> Another feature of the modern doctrine which fits in with the Muslim past is the emphasis which both of them lay on communal solidarity, discipline and cooperation. ***The umma in Islam is a solidary entity, and its foremost duty is to answer the call of the jihad*** [emphasis added]. This brings us to the third feature which both modern and ancient systems have in common, to wit the glorification of one's own group. The traditional attitude of the Muslims to the outside world is one of superiority, and the distinction between the *Dar al-harb, Dar al-Islam*, and *Dar as-sulh*, is an ever present one in the mind of the Muslim jurist. ***It may therefore be said in conclusion of this modern doctrine of nationalism, that although it introduces into Islam features which may not accord with strict orthodoxy, it is the least incompatible perhaps of modern European doctrines with the political thought and political experience of Sunni Islam*** [emphasis added].

Also from Sylvia Haim, *Arab Nationalism—An Anthology* (Berkeley and Los Angeles: University of California Press, 1962), pp. 63–64, Haim quotes the founder of the Arab Nationalist Ba'ath Party, Michel Aflaq:

> Muhammad was the epitome of all the Arabs, so let all the Arabs today be Muhammad. . . . Islam was an Arab movement and its meaning was the renewal of Arabism and its maturity . . . [even] Arab Christians will recognize that Islam constitutes for them a national culture in which they must immerse themselves so that they may understand and love it, and so that they may preserve Islam as

they would preserve the most precious element in their Arabism.

Haim concludes (p. 164), " For Aflaq, Islam *is* [emphasis in original] Arab nationalism."

171. Official English translation in Zuhair Diab, ed. *International Documents on Palestine, 1968* (Beirut: 1971); cited in Bat Ye'or, *The Dhimmi*, p. 390.

172. Bat Ye'or, *The Dhimmi*, p. 390.

173. Musa Kazem el-Husseini (president, Palestinian Arab Congress) to High Commissioner for Palestine, December 10, 1920 (Translated January 2, 1921), Israel State Archives, R.G. 2, Box 10, File 244.

174. "A Friday Sermon on PA TV: . . . We Must Educate our Children on the Love of Jihad . . . ," July 11, 2001, Middle East Media Research Institute, special dispatch #240, http://memri.org/bin/articles.cgi?Page=archives&Area=sd&ID=SP24001.

175. Bostom, *The Legacy of Jihad*, pp. 43–51.

176. The expression "fay" is found in Qur'an 59: 6–10, which describes Muhammad's attack upon the Jewish tribe Banu Nadir. In the traditional Muslim interpretation of these verses the theocratic conception of property rights is confirmed, as voiced by the Prophet— Allah returns to the Believers the possessions of His foes, what is properly His. See Leone Caetani, *Annali dell' Islam* (Milan: 1905–1926), vol. 5, p. 332.

177. Joseph B. Schechtman, *The Mufti and the Fuehrer* (New York: 1965), pp. 114–15, 151; Jennie Lebel, *Hajj Amin ve Berlin* [Hajj Amin and Berlin] (Tel Aviv: 1996), pp. 140–42; Yossef Bodansky, *Islamic Antisemitism as a Political Instrument* (Houston: 1999), p. 29.

178. Shai Lachman, "Arab Rebellion and Terrorism in Palestine 1929–39: The Case of Sheikh Izz al-Din al-Qassam and His Movement," in *Zionism and Arabism in Palestine and Israel*, ed. Elie Kedourie and Sylvia G. Haim (London: Frank Cass, 1982), pp. 52–99.

179. Bat Ye'or, "Aspects of the Arab-Israeli Conflict," *Wiener Library Bulletin* 32 (1979): 68; Efraim Karsh, *Arafat's War* (New York: 2003), p. 117.

180. David Littman, "The Genocidal Hamas Charter," *National Review Online*, September, 26, 2002.

181. "The Covenant of the Islamic Resistance Movement—Hamas," Middle East Media Research Institute, special dispatch series no. 1092, February 14, 2006.

182. Sahih Muslim, bk. 041, no. 6985; Sahih Bukhari, vol. 4, bk. 52, no. 176/177.

183. Excerpts from Bat Ye'or, *The Dhimmi*, pp. 391–94.

184. Excerpts from Bat Ye'or, *Eurabia—The Euro-Arab Axis* (Cranbury, NJ: 2005), pp. 284–95.

185. Excerpts from ibid., pp. 312–19.

186. "Sheik Yousef Al-Qaradhawi: Our War with the Jews is in the Name of Islam," Middle East Media Research Institute, TV Monitor Project, clip no. 1052, February 25, 2006.

187. Tabari, *Jāmi` al-Bayān fii Tafsirr al-Quraan*, vol. 9, p. 122. Regarding Qur'an 7:166—". . . God made them into apes and pigs, howling, with wagging tails, whereas previously they had been men and women . . . the youths became apes; the mature people became pigs." In contrast, regarding Qur'an 5:60, from *Al-Muntakhab fii Tafsiir al-Qur'aan al-Kariim*. Al-Azhar paraphrase of, and commentary on the Qur'an, in Modern Standard Arabic, 11th ed. (Cairo: 1406/1985), p. 158: "He is angry with you for your unbelieving disobedience, He has obliterated your minds, so become like apes and pigs."

188. Suyuti, Jalal al-Din, *Tafsiir al-Jalaalayn* (Beirut: 1404/1984), p. 149, regarding 5:60: "[The Jews] '[are] the one[s] whom God has cursed' exiled him from His mercy 'and on whom God's wrath has fallen' . . . '[they] who worship the Taaghuut' obey Satan. He made them into apes and monkeys 'by transformation'"; Mawdudi, *Towards Understanding the Qur'an*, vol. 2, p. 175, regarding 5:60: "This alludes to the Jews, whose history shows that they were subjected, over and over again, to the wrath and scourge of God. When they desecrated the law of the Sabbath, the faces of many of them were distorted, and subsequently their generation reached such a low point, they took to worshipping Satan quite openly"; the Al-Azhar paraphrase of and commentary on Qur'an in Modern Standard Arabic (1985) [see n. 202, above], p. 158, also states that the Jews were punished because they "worship Satan, and follow error."

189. Ibn Kathir, *Tafsir Ibn Kathir* (Riyadh: 2000), vol. 4, p. 193. Elaborating on the Jews' punishment, i.e., the apes transformation of 7:166, and the related statement of 7:167 ["And when Thy Lord proclaimed He would send forth against them, unto the Day of Resurrection, those who should visit them with evil chastisement"], Ibn Kathir comments that afflictions will continue to be sent against the Jews, "on account of their disobedience, defying Allah's orders and Law and using tricks to transgress the prohibitions. . . . When Islam came and Muhammad was sent, they came under his power and had to pay the Jizyah as well. Therefore, the humiliating torment [chastisement] mentioned here includes disgrace and paying the Jizyah. . . . In the future, the Jews will support the Dajjal [False Messiah]; and the Muslims, along with Isa [the Muslim Jesus], will kill the Jews."

190. Jalal al-Din Suyuti, *Tafsiir al-Jalaalayn*, p. 149, "their fate is the Fire"

190a. M. J. Kister, "The Massacre of the Banū Qurayza: A Re-Examination of a Tradition," *Jerusalem Studies in Arabic and Islam* 8 (1986): 61–96; W. H. T. Gairdner, "Muhammad without Camouflage," *Moslem World* 9 (1919): 36.

190b. *The Life of Muhammad*, A Translation of Ibn Ishaq's *Sirat Rasul Allah*, trans. by A. Guillaume (Oxford: 2001), p. 461.

190c. Ibn Sa'd, *Kitab Al-Tabaqat Al-Kabir*, trans. S. Moinul Haq and H. K. Ghazanfar (New Delhi: 1993), p.

95. (The translators wrote: "Brothren [*sic*] of monkeys and boars fear me, fear me!")

191. H. R. Idris, "Contributions a histoire de l'Ifriqiya" (*Riyad an Nufus d'Al-Maliki*), *Revue des Études Islamiques* (1935); English translation in Bat Ye'or, *The Dhimmi*, p. 186.

192. H. R. Idris, "Tributaries in the Medieval Muslim West, according to the *Mi'yar* of al-Wansharisi"; English translation by Michael J. Miller of "Les tributaries en Occident Musulman medieval d'apres 'miyar d'al Wansarisi,'" in *Melanges d'islamologie: Volume dediae a la memoire de Armand Abel par ses colleagues, ses aeleves, et ses amis* (1974), pp. 172–96, selected extracts.

193. Dozy, *Spanish Islam*, p. 653; Perlmann, "Eleventh Century Andalusian Authors on the Jews of Granada," p. 284.

194. Perlmann, "Eleventh Century Andalusian Authors on the Jews of Granada," p. 286.

195. Ibid., pp. 287–88.

196. Ibid., p. 288 n. 56a.

197. Bar Hebraeus, *The Chronography*, p. 491; Fischel, *Jews in the Economic and Political Life of Medieval Islam*, pp. 116, 117 n. 5.

198. Bar Hebraeus, *The Chronography*, p. 490; Ghazi b. al-Wasiti, "An Answer to the Dhimmis," p. 449; Fischel, *Jews in the Economic and Political Life of Medieval Islam*, p. 91.

199. Browne, *A Literary History of Persia*, vol. 3, pp. 35–36.

200. Ibid., p. 35.

201. See Vajda, "Un Traite Maghrebin 'Adversos Judaeos"; Hunwick, "Al-Maghili and the Jews of Tuwat: the Demise of a Community."

202. Zamakhshary, *Al-Kashshaaf `an Haqaa'iq GhawaamiD al-Tanziil wa-`Uyuun al-Aqaawiil fii Wujuuh alTa'wiil*, ed. M. H. Ahmad (Cairo: 1365/1946), p. 684, referring to Qur'an 5:60/61:

Some say that when this occurred, the Muslims taunted them, saying, "O brothers of apes and pigs," and the Jews would bow their heads. "These" the cursed transformed ones "are the lowest in stature" they were put in the evil place they deserved. The emphasis here is intended as "lowest and most erring" for it became a byname for them beyond mere metaphor. The reason for this revelation is that a group of Jews approached Muhammad with the worst intentions, being hypocritical in feigning belief, and God revealed to Muhammad that they would leave in the same state in which they entered, and would heed nothing he would say in unbelief and pretending.

See also notes 190b and 190c, above, and Muhammad's references to the Banu Qurayza Jews as "monkeys," or "monkeys and pigs."

203. Ibid., p. 809; Vajda, "Un Traite Maghrebin 'Adversos Judaeos," p. 809.

204. See Hirschberg, *A History of the Jews of North Africa*, p. 402; Gerber, *Jewish Society in Fez*, p. 18; and Hunwick, "Al-Maghili and the Jews of Tuwat: the Demise of a Community."

205. Sahih Bukhari, vol. 3, bk. 47, no. 786; Sahih Muslim, bk. 026, no. 5430.

206. Gregory Wortabet, *Syria and the Syrians* (London: 1856), vol. 2. pp. 263–64.

207. Parfitt, *The Road to Redemption*, p. 89.

208. Aluma Solnick, "Based on Koranic Verses, Interpretations, and Traditions, Muslim Clerics State: The Jews Are the Descendants of Apes, Pigs, and Other Animals," Middle East Media Research Institute, special report #11, November 1, 2002.

209. "Islamic Antisemitism: The Jews Depicted as Apes and Pigs," Intelligence and Terrorism Information Center at the Center for Special Studies, bulletin # 5, chap. 3, October 2002, www.intelligence.org.il/eng/default.htm.

210. Ibid.

211. Ibid.

212. Solnick, "Muslim Clerics State: The Jews Are the Descendants of Apes, Pigs, and Other Animals."

213. Menachem Milson, "What Is Arab Antisemitism?" Middle East Media Research Institute, special report #26, February 27, 2004.

214. Ibid.

215. "Islamic Antisemitism: The Jews Depicted as Apes and Pigs."

216. Ibn Warraq, *Leaving Islam: Apostates Speak Out* (Amherst, NY: Prometheus Books, 2003), p. 401.

217. The classical Qur'anic commentary of Ibn Kathir, and the twentieth-century commentary of Mawdudi confirm and validate the anti-Jewish attitudes expressed in Qur'an 5:32–33. From Ibn Kathir (*Tafsir Ibn Kathir*, vol. 3, 2000, p. 160), entitled, "Warning Those Who Commit Mischief":

This Ayah chastises and criticizes those who commit the prohibitions, after knowing that they are prohibited from indulging in them. [Like] [t]he Jews of Al-Madinah, such as Banu Qurayza, An-Nadir, and Qaynuqa [Jewish tribes ultimately attacked, expropriated, expelled, and even massacred by Muhammad].

From Mawdudi (*Towards Understanding the Qur'an*, vol. 2, pp. 155–56), who includes a contextual reference to Qur'an 5:30–31 as well:

God honored some of the illiterate people of Arabia and disregarded the ancient People of the Book because the former were pious while the latter were not. But rather than reflect upon the causes of their rejection by God, and do something to overcome the failings which led to that rejection, the Israelites were seized by the same fit of arrogance and folly which had once seized the criminal son of Adam [verses 5:30–31], and resolved to kill those whose good deeds had been accepted by God. It was obvious that such acts would contribute nothing towards their acceptance by God. They would rather earn them an even greater degree of God's disapproval. Since the same qualities which had been displayed by the wrongdoing son of Adam were manifest in the Children of Israel, God strongly urged them not to kill human beings and couched his command in forceful terms.

The "land" (in verse 5:33) signifies either the country or territory wherein the responsibility of establishing law and order has been undertaken by an Islamic state. The expression "to wage war [fight] against Allah and His Messenger" denotes war against the righteous order established by the Islamic state.

218. For example, Ibn Kammuna (d. 1284), the thirteenth-century Jewish physician-philosopher of Iraqi origin, wrote (1280) simply (see Moshe Perlmann, trans. *Ibn Kammuna's Examination of the Three Faiths* [Berkeley and Los Angeles: University of California Press, 1971, pp. 131–33):

There is no tradition by the authority of any Jew that 'Uzayr (Ezra) was the son of God. . . . If any of them said that, he would be considered among them an unbeliever and outside of their community.

219. Ibn Warraq, *Why I Am Not a Muslim*, pp. 215–16.
220. J. Robson, "Hadith," in *Encyclopedia of Islam,* eds. P. Bearman, Thomas Bianquis, C. E. Bosworth, E. van Donzel, and W. P. Heinrichs (Leiden: Brill, 2006); J. Robson, "Tradition, the Second Foundation of Islam," *Muslim World* 41 (1951): 22, 24.
221. Robson, "Hadith"; "Tradition," pp. 22, 23
222. Robson, "Hadith"; "Tradition," p. 24.
223. H. Lammens, *Islam: Beliefs and Institutions* (New Delhi: 2002), p. 69.
224. Ibid., p. 65.
225. Robson, "Tradition," p. 31.
226. Ibid.
227. Ibid., p. 32.
228. Robson, "Hadith"; "Traditions," pp. 25–30.
229. Ignaz Goldziher, *Muslim Studies*, trans. C. R. Barber and S. M. Stern (London: 1967–1971), vol. 2, p. 19.
230. Joseph Schacht, "A Revaluation of Islamic Traditions," *Journal of the Royal Asiatic Society* (1949), pp. 143–54; republished in Ibn Warraq, ed., *The Quest for the Historical Muhammad* (Amherst, NY: Prometheus Books, 2000), pp. 358–67.
231. Ibid., pp. 366, 361.

232. Ibid., p. 360.
233. Goldziher, *Muslim Studies*, vol. 2, pp. 18–19.
234. Georges Vajda, "Juifs et musulmans selon le hadit," *Journal Asiatique* 229 (1937): 57–127. A first-time English translation of this essay, in full, is provided in this compendium, pp. 235.
235. Ibid., p. 61.
236. Ibid., p. 63.
237. Ibid., pp. 63–65.
238. Ibid., p. 72.
239. Ibid., pp. 72–73.
240. Ibid., pp. 75–81; Sahih Bukhari, vol. 2, bk. 23, no 376; Sahih Muslim, bk. 4, no. 2029.
241. Vajda, "Juifs et musulmans selon le hadit," p. 78.
242. Ibid., pp. 83–84.
243. Ibid., p. 85.
244. Ibid., pp. 86–87.
245. Ibid., p. 87.
246. Ibid., pp. 87–89.
247. Ibid., pp. 88, 90.
248. Ibid., pp. 91–92.
249. Ibid., pp. 93–96.
250. Ibid., pp. 97–98.
251. Ibid., p. 104.
252. Ibid., pp. 104–105.
253. Ibid., p. 105.
254. Ibid., pp. 106, 105.
255. Ibid., pp. 108–109.
256. Ibn Sa'd, *Kitab Al-Tabaqat Al-Kabir*, vol. 2 (New Delhi: 1993), pp. 249–52; English translation by S. Moinul Haq and H. K. Ghazanfar.
257. Vajda, "Juifs et musulmans selon le hadit," pp. 112–13.
258. Mark Durie, "Isa, the Muslim Jesus," in *The Myth of Islamic Tolerance*, ed. Robert Spencer, (Amherst, NY: Prometheus Books, 2005), pp. 541–55.
259. Robson, "Tradition," p. 259.
260. Vajda, "Juifs et musulmans selon le hadit," pp. 112–13; Regarding the ransoming of prisoners of Muslim enemies vanquished by jihad (see Bostom, *The Legacy of Jihad*, p. 149), the great Maliki jurist and polymath Averröes (d. 1198), wrote:

Most scholars are agreed that, in his dealings with captives, various policies are open to the Imam [head of the Islamic state, caliph]. He may pardon them, kill them, or release them . . . on ransom . . .

260a. Vajda, "Juifs et musulmans selon le hadit," p. 110.
261. Ibid., pp. 124–25.
262. Ibid., pp. 110, 125.
262a. Sahih Bukhari, vol. 3, no. 2730, in the Book of the Conditions; Sahih Muslim vol. 3, no. 4366; Ibn Ishaq (Guillaume translation), p. 525 (sections 779–80).
262b. Yehuda Ratzaby, "The Expulsion of Yemenite Jewry to Mawza' in 1679–80 in Light of Recently Dis-

covered Sources," *Zion* 37 (1972): 197–215 (Hebrew; English translation by Rivkah Fishman); Yehuda Ratzaby, "The Expulsion to the Desert," *Et-Mol* 9, 3 [53] (January 1984): 16–18. (Hebrew; English translation by Rivkah Fishman).

262c. H. Helfritz, *Land ohne Schatten* (Leipzig, 1934), pp. 212–13, cited in Ratzaby, "The Expulsion of Yemenite Jewry to Mawza' in 1679–80."

262d. Ratzaby, "The Expulsion of Yemenite Jewry to Mawza' in 1679–80," and "The Expulsion to the Desert."

263. Eliz Sanasarian, *Religious Minorities in Iran* (Cambridge: 2000), p. 111.

264. "The Covenant of the Islamic Resistance Movement—Hamas," Middle East Media Research Institute.

265. David Byers, "Report: London Mosque's DVDs Predict Mass Extermination of Jews," *European Jewish Press*, January 11, 2007.

265a. David Cook, "Muslim Fears of the Year 2000," *Middle East Quarterly* 5, no. 2 (June 1998): 51–62.

265b. Mohamad Yasin Owadally, *Emergence of Dajjal: The Jewish King* (Delhi: 2001).

265c. Ibid., p. 12.

265d. Ibid., pp. 35–36.

266. W. Raven, "Sira" in *Encyclopedia of Islam*, ed. P. Bearman, Thomas Bianquis, C. E. Bosworth, E. van Donzel, and W. P. Heinrichs (Leiden: Brill, 2006).

267. J. M. B. Jones, "Ibn Ishak Muhammad b. Ishak b. Yasar b. Khiyar (according to some sources, b. Khabbar, or Kuman, or Kutan)," in *Encyclopedia of Islam*, ed. P. Bearman, Thomas Bianquis, C. E. Bosworth, E. van Donzel, and W. P. Heinrichs (Leiden: Brill, 2006).

268. Guillaume, *The Life of Muhammad*.

269. Raven, "Sira."

270. Guillaume, *The Life of Muhammad*.

271. Raven, "Sira."

272. S. Leder. "al-Wakidī, Muhammad b . 'Umar b. Wakid," in *Encyclopedia of Islam*, eds. P. Bearman, Thomas Bianquis, C. E. Bosworth, E. van Donzel and W. P. Heinrichs (Leiden: Brill, 2006).

273. J. W. Fück, "Ibn Sa'd, Abū 'Abd Allāh Muhammad b. Sa'd b. Manī c al-Basrī al-Hās hmī Kātib al-Wākidī," in *Encyclopedia of Islam*, eds. P. Bearman, Thomas Bianquis, C. E. Bosworth, E. van Donzel and W. P. Heinrichs (Leiden: Brill, 2006).

274. Raven, "Sira."

275. Hirschfeld, "Essai sur l'histoire des Juifs de Medine."

276. Michael Cook, *Muhammad* (Oxford: 1996), pp. 64–65.

277. Guillaume, *The Life of Muhammad*, p. xiv.

278. See nn. 229–33 and the associated text, which refers to the analyses of the hadith by Ignaz Goldziher and Joseph Schacht.

279. Cook, *Muhammad*, pp. 64–65.

280. Ibid. p. 65.

281. Robert Spencer, *The Truth about Muhammad* (Washington, DC: 2006), p. 31.

282. Guillaume, *The Life of Muhammad*, p. 212.

283. Ibid., pp. 212–13.

284. Spencer, *The Truth about Muhammad*, p. 78.

285. Guillaume, *The Life of Muhammad*, p. 213; see also for a discussion of jihad, Bostom, *The Legacy of Jihad*.

286. Guillaume, *The Life of Muhammad*, p. 213.

287. W. Montgomery Watt, "Al Ansar," in *Encyclopedia of Islam*, eds. P. Bearman, Thomas Bianquis, C. E. Bosworth, E. van Donzel and W. P. Heinrichs (Leiden: Brill, 2006). Watt writes:

"[T]he helpers," the usual designation of those men of Medina who supported Muhammad, in distinction from the muhājirūn or "emigrants," i.e., his Meccan followers. After the general conversion of the Arabs to Islam the old name of al-Aws and al-Khazraj jointly, Banu Kayla, fell out of use and was replaced by Ansar, the individual being known as Ansari. In this way the early services of the men of Medina to the cause of Islam were honorably commemorated.

288. Hirschfeld, "Essai sur l'histoire des Juifs de Medine," pp. 10–31.

289. Moshe Gil, *A History of Palestine, 634–1099*, trans. Ethel Broido (Cambridge and New York: 1992), p. 11.

290. Watt, "Al Ansar."

291. Guillaume, *The Life of Muhammad*, p. 231.

292. The exegeses of Ibn Kathir (fourteenth century) and Mawdudi (twentieth century) make clear that these verses refer to the "B. Qurayza" (Ibn Kathir, *Tafsir Ibn Kathir*, vol. 4, p. 347), specifically, or the Jews of Medina (Mawdudi, *Towards Understanding the Qur'an*, vol. 3, pp. 160–61).

293. Julius Wellhausen, "Muhammad's Constitution of Medina" (first published as "Muhammads Gemeindeordnung von Medina," in *Skizzen und Vorarbeiten* [Berlin, 1889] vol. 4, pp. 67–83), published as an excursus in Arent Jan Wensinck, *Muhammad and the Jews of Medina*, trans. Wolfgang H. Behn (Berlin: 1982), pp. 137, 136.

294. Arent Jan Wensinck, *Muhammad and the Jews of Medina* (first published as *Mohammed en de Joden te Medina* [Leiden, 1908]), with an excursus [appendix] from Julius Wellhausen's "Muhammad's Constitution of Medina" (first published as "Muhammads Gemeindeordnung von Medina" from *Skizzen und Vorarbeiten* [Berlin, 1889], vol. 4, pp. 67–83). English translation by Wolfgang H. Behn (Berlin: 1982), pp. 70–71.

295. Guillaume, *The Life of Muhammad*, p. 363.

296. Moshe Gil, "The Constitution of Medina: A Reconsideration," *Israel Oriental Studies* 4 (1974): 64–65.

297. Hirschfeld, "Essai sur l'histoire des Juifs de Medine," p. 11.

298. Ibid., pp. 11–12.

299. Guillaume, *The Life of Muhammad*, p. 239.

300. Ibid., p. 239.

301. Ibid., p. 240.

302. Ibid.

303. Hirschfeld, "Essai sur l'histoire des Juifs de Medine," p. 13.

304. Ibid.

305. Guillaume, *The Life of Muhammad*, pp. 263–64.

306. Hirschfeld, "Essai sur l'histoire des Juifs de Medine," p. 14.

307. Ibid., p. 15.

308. Hirschfeld, "Essai sur l'histoire des Juifs de Medine," pp. 15–16.

309. Qur'an 2:217—"They question thee (O Muhammad) with regard to warfare in the sacred month. Say: Warfare therein is a great (transgression), but to turn (men) from the way of Allah, and to disbelieve in Him and in the Inviolable Place of Worship, and to expel His people thence, is a greater with Allah; for persecution is worse than killing. And they will not cease from fighting against you till they have made you renegades from your religion, if they can. And whoso becometh a renegade and dieth in his disbelief: such are they whose works have fallen both in the world and the Hereafter. Such are rightful owners of the Fire: they will abide therein." Ibn Kathir's commentary (*Tafsir Ibn Kathir*, vol. 1, p. 602) explains the killings thus:

This Ayah means if you had killed during the Sacred Month, they (the disbelievers of Quraysh) have hindered you from the path of Allah and disbelieved in it. They also prevented you from entering the Sacred Mosque, and expelled you from it, while you are its people, "a greater transgression with Allah" than killing whom you killed among them. Also, ". . . and Al-Fitnah (persecution) is worse than killing" means, trying to force the Muslims to revert from their religion, and re-embrace Kufr (disbelief) after they had believed, is worse with Allah than killing.

310. Ibid., p. 16; Warraq, *Why I Am Not a Muslim*, p. 93.

311. Hirschfeld, "Essai sur l'histoire des Juifs de Medine," pp. 16–21, 27–28; Warraq, *Why I Am Not a Muslim*, pp. 93–95.

312. Hirschfeld, "Essai sur l'histoire des Juifs de Medine," pp. 16–27.

313. Sir William Muir, *The Life of Mahomet* (London, 1878: Kessinger Reprints, 2003), pp. 248–49; Hirschfeld, "Essai sur l'histoire des Juifs de Medine," p. 16; Warraq, *Why I Am Not a Muslim*, pp. 93–94.

314. Hirschfeld, "Essai sur l'histoire des Juifs de Medine," p. 16.

315. Aloys Sprenger (1813–1893), an Austrian Orientalist and professor of Oriental languages at Bern

(1858–1881), was a prolific writer, editor, and collector of Islamic literature, especially hadith literature. See Wolfgang Behn, *Concise Biographical Companion to Index Islamicus* (Leiden: 2004), vol. 3, p. 435.

316. Muir, *The Life of Mahomet*, pp. 248–49.

317. Muir, *The Life of Mahomet*, p. 249.

318. Ibid.

319. Guillaume, *The Life of Muhammad*, p. 363.

320. Muir, *The Life of Mahomet*, pp. 250–51.

321. Ibid., pp. 251–52.

322. Hirschfeld, "Essai sur l'histoire des Juifs de Medine," pp. 17–18; Warraq, *Why I Am Not a Muslim*, p. 94.

323. Warraq, *Why I Am Not a Muslim*, pp. 94–95.

324. Guillaume, *The Life of Muhammad*, p. 368.

325. Ibid., p. 369.

326. Muir, *The Life of Mahomet*, pp. 258–59.

327. Hirschfeld, "Essai sur l'histoire des Juifs de Medine," p. 20; Warraq, *Why I Am Not a Muslim*, p. 95.

328. Hirschfeld, "Essai sur l'histoire des Juifs de Medine," p. 20.

329. Ibid., pp. 20–21.

330. Ibid., p. 21.

331. See n. 176 above, on "*fay* territory."

332. Guillaume, *The Life of Muhammad*, pp. 438–39.

333. Warraq, *Why I Am Not a Muslim*, p. 95.

334. Muir, *The Life of Mahomet*, p. 325; Warraq, *Why I Am Not a Muslim*, p. 95.

335. Guillaume, *The Life of Muhammad*, p. 461, actually uses the word "monkeys." "Apes" and "monkeys" are used interchangeably in translation. See, for example, Norman Stillman's translation of this same excerpt in *The Jews of Arab Lands in Modern Times*, p. 137, which refers to the Jews as "apes."

336. Kister, "The Massacre of the Banū Qurayẓa," pp. 61–96.

337. Abu Yusuf Ya'qub, *Le Livre de l'impot foncier*, trans. and annotated by Edmond Fagnan (Paris: 1921); English translation in Bat Ye'or, *The Dhimmi*, pp. 172–73.

338. Kister, "The Massacre of the Banū Qurayẓa," p. 69.

339. Ibid., p. 70.

340. W. H. T. Gairdner, "Muhammad without Camouflage," *Moslem World* 9 (1919): 36.

341. Hirschfeld, "Essai sur l'histoire des Juifs de Medine," pp. 27–28.

341a. Guillaume, *The Life of Muhammad*, pp. 482–83.

341b. Hirschfeld, "Essai sur l'histoire des Juifs de Medine," pp. 28–30.

342. Guillaume, *The Life of Muhammad*, p. 515.

343. Sahih Bukhari, vol. 3, bk. 47, no. 786; Sahih Muslim, bk. 26, number 5430; Sunan Abu Dawud, bk. 39, no. 4498; Guillaume, *The Life of Muhammad*, p. 516; Ibn Sa'd, *Kitab Al-Tabaqat Al-Kabir*, pp. 249–52.

344. Ibn Sa'd, *Kitab Al-Tabaqat Al-Kabir*, pp. 249–52.

345. Hartwig Hirschfeld, "The Annals of Islam,"

review of *Annali dell'Islam compilati de Leone Caetani, Principe de Teano*, vol. 2 (Milan: 1907), in *Jewish Quarterly Review* 20 (1908): 876.

346. Ibid. Regarding the breached treaty, Hirschfeld refers to its existence in his own essay "The Arabic Portion of the Cairo Genizah at Cambridge," *Jewish Quarterly Review* 15 (1905): 170–74.

347. See n. 341 above, and the related text, in which Hirschfeld discusses two assassinations of Khaybar Jews, prior to the Muslims assault, which is confirmed by Ibn Ishaq (Guillaume, *The Life of Muhammad*, pp. 665–66, and 482–83).

348. D. S. Margoliouth, *Mohammed and the Rise of Islam* (London: 1905; reprint, New Delhi: 1985), pp. 362–63.

349. Vajda, "Juifs et musulmans selon le hadit," p. 85.

350. Bostom, *The Legacy of Jihad*, pp. 37–56.

351. W. R. W. Gardner, "Jihad," *Moslem World* 2 (1912): 347–57; reproduced in Bostom, *The Legacy of Jihad*, pp. 293–300.

352. Paul Stenhouse, "Muḥammad, Qur'ānic Texts, the Shari'a and Incitement to Violence," October 25, 2005, http://www.jihadwatch.org/archives/008695.php.

353. Bostom, *The Legacy of Jihad*, pp. 141–250.

354. Edward William Lane, *An Arabic English Lexicon*, 6 vols. (London: 1865), p. 472. Lane's *Lexicon* is still used to this day by Muslim and non-Muslim scholars for definitive Arabic to English translation.

355. Ibid.

356. Al-Tabari, *The History of al-Tabari*, vol. 12: *The Battle of Qadissiyah and the Conquest of Syria and Palestine*, trans. Yohanan Friedman (Albany, NY: 1992), p. 167.

356a. The Noble Qur'an, http://www.usc.edu/dept/MSA/quran.

357. Translation of Sahih al-Bukhari, http://www.usc.edu/dept/MSA/fundamentals/hadithsunnah/bukhari/; reproduced in Bostom, *The Legacy of Jihad*, pp. 136–38.

358. Translation of Sahih Muslim, http://www.usc.edu/dept/MSA/fundamentals/hadithsunnah/muslim/; reproduced in Bostom, *The Legacy of Jihad*, pp. 138–40.

359. Bostom, *The Legacy of Jihad*, pp. 141–250.

360. Ibid., p. 161.

361. Ibid., p. 199.

362. Ibid., p. 213.

363. Ibid., pp. 96–97.

364. Ibid., pp. 98–99.

365. Ibid., pp. 43–93; 368–663; 675–81.

366. Ibid., pp. 43–93; 368–663.

367. Moshe Gil, *A History of Palestine, 634–1099* (Cambridge: 1992), p. 2.

368. Ibid., pp. 14–15.

369. Ibid., p. 20.

370. Bat Ye'or, *The Decline of Eastern Christianity under Islam* (Cranbury, NJ: 1996), pp. 44, 47; "Islam and the Dhimmis," *Jerusalem Quarterly* 42 (1987): 85.

371. S. D. Goitein and N. Ginsbury, "Jerusalem in the Arab Period (638–1099)," *Jerusalem Cathdera* 2 (1982): 170.

371a. Goitein and Ginsbury, "Jerusalem in the Arab Period," pp. 170–71.

372. Al-Baladhuri, *The Origins of the Islamic State*, trans. Philip K. Hitti (New York: 1916), p. 217.

373. [Michael the Syrian], *Chronique de Michel le Syrien*, ed. and trans. Jean-Baptiste Chabot (Paris: 1899–1905), vol. 2, p. 418; English translation in Bat Ye'or, *The Decline of Eastern Christianity under Islam*, p. 47.

374. Michael the Syrian, *Chronique*, vol. 2, p. 421; English translation in Bat Ye'or, *The Decline of Eastern Christianity under Islam*, p. 47.

375. Gil, *A History of Palestine*, pp. 61, 169.

376. Naphtali Lewis, "New Light on the Negev in Ancient Times," *Palestine Exploration Quarterly* 80 (1948): 116–17.

377. Gil, *A History of Palestine*, p. 170.

378. Ibid., pp. 420–21.

379. Ibid., p. 473.

380. Ibid.

381. Bat Ye'or, *The Decline of Eastern Christianity under Islam*, p. 74.

382. *Chronique de Denys de Tell-Mahre*, trans. Jean-Baptiste Chabot (Paris: 1895), part 4, p. 112; English translation in Bat Ye'or, *The Decline of Eastern Christianity under Islam*, p. 74.

383. Gil, *A History of Palestine*, pp. 474–75.

384. Ibid., p. 159.

385. Ibid.; Qur'an 16:63—"By God, We (also) sent (Our apostles) to peoples before thee; but Satan made, (to the wicked) their own acts seem alluring: he is also their patron today, but they shall have a most grievous penalty." Qur'an 5:72—"They do blaspheme who say: 'Allah is Christ the son of Mary.' But said Christ: 'O Children of Israel! worship Allah, my Lord and your Lord.' Whoever joins other gods with Allah, Allah will forbid him the garden, and the Fire will be his abode. There will for the wrong-doers be no one to help." Qur'an 58:19—"The devil hath engrossed them and so hath caused them to forget remembrance of Allah. They are the devil's party. Lo! is it not the devil's party who will be the losers?" In both 850 and 907–908, the Abbasid caliphs al-Mutawwakil and al-Muqtadir, respectively, decreed that Jews and Christians either attach wooden images (al-Mutawwakil) or drawings (al-Muqtadir) of devils to the doors of their homes to distinguish them from the homes of Muslims. Tabari (d. 923), cited in Bat Ye'or, *The Dhimmi*, p. 186; Ibn al-Jawzi, cited in Gil, *A History of Palestine*, p. 159 n. 32.

386. Bat Ye'or, *The Decline of Eastern Christianity under Islam*, p. 84.

387. Goitein and Ginsbury, "Jerusalem in the Arab Period," p. 169.

388. Kaufmann Kohler and Isaac Broydé, "Solomon ben Jeroham," JewishEncyclopedia.com, http://www.

jewishencyclopedia.com/view_friendly.jsp?artid=916 &letter=S.

389. Salomon Feuerstein, *Der Commentar des Karäers Salmon ben Jerucham zu den Klageliedern: Zum ersten Male nach der Pariser Handschrift edirt* (Krakau, 1898), p. xiii; English translation by Haggai Ben-Shammai in "The Attitude of Some Early Karaites towards Islam," in *Studies in Medieval Jewish History and Literature*, ed. Isadore Twersky (Cambridge, MA: 1984), vol. 2, p. 10.

390. Meshech is named as a son of Japheth in Genesis 10:2 and 1 Chronicles 1:5, and as a son of Shem in 1 Chronicles 1:17. Meshech is named with Tubal as a principality of the prince of Gog and Magog in Ezekiel 38:2 and 39:1, considered a Japhetite tribe, identified by Flavius Josephus with the Cappadocian Moschoi. Meshech is seen as ancestor of the Russian people by some Bible scholars who consider it possible that geographic names in Russia such as Moscow, the Meschera tribe, and the Meschera Lowland, could be related to Meschech. In addition, the people of Georgia have traditions of descent from Meshech, among others.

391. Kedar is a son of Ishmael mentioned in the Bible. Kedar also referred to the settlement in the Syrian Desert named after him.

392. Gil, *A History of Palestine*, p. 375.

393. Ibid., p. 373.

394. Ibid., p. 376.

394a. Salo W. Baron, *A Social and Religious History of the Jews*, vol. 3: *Heirs of Rome and Persia* (New York: 1957), p. 184.

395. Moshe Gil, "Dhimmi Donations and Foundations for Jerusalem (638–1099)," *Journal of the Economic and Social History of the Orient* 37 (1984): 166–67.

396. Gil, *A History of Palestine*, p. 415.

397. Ibid., p. 412.

398. Ibid., p. 415.

399. Ibid., p. 416.

400. Ibid.

401. Julius Greenstone, in his essay "The Turcoman Defeat at Cairo," *American Journal of Semitic Languages and Literatures* 22 (1906): 144–75, provides a translation of this poem [excerpted, pp. 164–65] by Solomon ha-Kohen b. Joseph [believed to be a descendant of the Geonim, an illustrious family of Palestinian Jews of priestly descent], which includes the poet's recollection of the previous Turcoman conquest of Jerusalem during the eighth decade of the eleventh century. Greenstone comments [p. 152], "As appears from the poem, the conquest of Jerusalem by Atsiz was very sorely felt by the Jews. The author dwells at great length on the cruelties perpetrated against the inhabitants of the city."

402. Gil, *A History of Palestine*, p. 420.

403. Ibid., pp. 420–21.

404. For example, Steven Runciman, *A History of the Crusades*, vol. 1: *The First Crusade and the Foundation of the Kingdom of Jerusalem* (Cambridge: 1951), pp. 286–87; Gil, *A History of Palestine*, p. 827, notes, "The Christians violated their promise to the inhabitants that they would be left alive, and slaughtered some 20,000 to 30,000 people, a number which may be an exaggeration."

405. Emmanuel Sivan, "Palestine during the Crusades," in *A History of the Holy Land*, ed. Michael Avi-Yonah (New York: 2001), p. 244.

406. Steven Runciman, *A History of the Crusades*, vol. 3: *The Kingdom of Acre* (Cambridge: 1955), pp. 419–21.

407. Kaufman Kohler and M. Seligsohn, "Isaac Ben Samuel of Acre," JewishEncyclopedia.com.

408. Isaac b. Samuel of Acre, *Osar Hayyim* (*Treasure Store of Life*) [Hebrew], MS. Gunzburg 775 fol. 27b, Lenin State Library, Moscow; English translation in Bat Ye'or, *The Dhimmi*, pp. 352–54.

409. C. E. Bosworth, "Christian and Jewish Dignitaries in Mamluk Egypt and Syria: Qalqashandi's Information on Their Hierarchy, Titulature, and Appointment (I)," *International Journal of Middle East Studies* 3 (1972): 65–66.

409a. Donald P. Little, "Communal Strife in Late Mamluk Jerusalem," *Islamic Law and Society* 6 (1999): 69–96.

409b. For the Islamic legal basis and tragic impact of such orphans decrees on Yemenite Jews under Muslim rule, over a continuum from the twelfth through the twentieth centuries, see Yosef Tobi, "Conversion to Islam among Yemenite Jews under Zaidi Rule: The Position of Zaidi Law, the Imam, and Muslim Society" [Hebrew], *Pe'amim* 42 (1990): 105–26; English translation by Rivkah Fishman, full text herein, pp. 577.

409c. Little, "Communal Strife in Late Mamluk Jerusalem," p. 95.

409d. S. D. Goitein. "Ibn 'Ubayya's Book on the Destruction of the Synagogue of the Jews in Jerusalem in 1474" [Hebrew], *Zion* 13–14 (1948–1949): 18–32.

410. Emil G. Hirsch, M. Selighson, and Solomon Schechter, "Machpelah," JewishEncyclopedia.com; A. A. Bonar and R. M. McCheyne, *A Narrative of a Mission of Inquiry to the Jews from the Church of Scotland in 1839* (Edinburgh: 1842), pp. 180–81, 273.

411. Hirsch, Selighson, and Schechter, "Machpelah."

412. Richard Gottheil and Wilhelm Belcher, "Benjamin of Tudela," JewishEncyclopedia.com.

413. Hirsch, Selighson, and Schechter, "Machpelah."

414. Eliezer Bashan, "The Prohibition on Non-Muslims Entering Mosques in the Ottoman Empire as Reflected in European Sources," *Shofar* (Winter 1997): 63.

415. Ibid., pp. 63–66.

416. The Muslim official of a mosque who summons the faithful to prayer from a minaret five times a day.

417. Samuel b. Ishaq Uceda, *Lehem dim'ah* [*The Bread of Tears*] (Venice: 1606); English translation in Bat Ye'or, *The Dhimmi*, p. 354.

418. Bat Ye'or, *Islam and Dhimmitude*, p. 318.

419. Gedaliah of Siemiatyce, *Sha'alu Shelom Yerushalayim* [*Pray for the Peace of Jerusalem*] (Berlin: 1716); English translation in Bat Ye'or, *The Decline of Eastern Christianity under Islam*, pp. 377–80.

420. Moshe Maoz, "Changes in the Position of the Jewish Communities of Palestine and Syria in the Mid-Nineteenth Century," in *Studies on Palestine during the Ottoman Period*, ed. Moshe Maoz (Jerusalem: 1975), p. 142.

421. Ibid., p. 144.

422. Ibid., pp. 144–145.

423. Ibid., pp. 145–146.

424. Maoz, "Changes in the Position of the Jewish Communities," pp. 147–48.

425. According to the Monk Neophytos's contemporary account, the Jewish victims included "five [Jewish] girls, who were still minors, [and] died under the bestial licentiousness of the Egyptian solders." From S. N. Spyridon, "Annals of Palestine, 1821–1841," *Journal of the Palestine Oriental Society* 18 (1938): 114.

426. A. [*sic*] E. R. Malachi, *Studies in the History of the Old Yishuv* (Tel Aviv: 1971), pp. 67ff.

426a. Edouard Engelhardt made these observations from his detailed analysis of the Tanzimat period, noting that a quarter century after the Crimean War (1853–1856), and the second iteration of Tanzimat reforms, the same problems persisted:

Muslim society has not yet broken with the prejudices which make the conquered peoples ubordinate . . . the raya [*dhimmis*] remain inferior to the Osmanlis; in fact he is not rehabilitated; the fanaticism of the early days has not relented . . . [even liberal Muslims rejected] . . . civil and political equality, that is to say, the assimilation of the conquered with the conquerors. [Edouard Engelhardt, *La Turquie et La Tanzimat* (Paris: 1882), vol. 1, p. 111; vol. 2, p. 171; English translation in Bat Ye'or, *Islam and Dhimmitude*, pp. 431–42.]

A systematic examination of the condition of the Christian rayas was conducted in the 1860s by British consuls stationed throughout the Ottoman Empire, yielding extensive primary source documentary evidence. [*Reports from Her Majesty's Consuls relating to the Condition of the Christians in Turkey* (1867), pp. 5, 29. See also related other reports by various consuls and vice consuls, in the 1860 volume, p. 58; the 1867 volume, pp. 4, 5, 6, 14, 15; and the 1867 volume, part 2, p. 3; all cited in Vahakn Dadrian, "The Clash between Democratic Norms and Theocratic Dogmas," in *Warrant for Genocide* (New Brunswick, NJ) pp. 26–27, n. 4. See also extensive excerpts from these reports in Bat Ye'or, *The Decline of Eastern Christianity*, pp. 409–33.] Britain was then Turkey's most powerful ally, and it was in her strategic interest to see that oppression of the Christians was eliminated, to prevent direct, aggressive Russian or

Austrian intervention. On July 22, 1860, Consul James Zohrab sent a lengthy report from Sarajevo to his ambassador in Constantinople, Sir Henry Bulwer, analyzing the administration of the provinces of Bosnia and Herzegovina, again, following the 1856 Tanzimat reforms. Referring to the reform efforts, Zohrab stated:

The Hatti-humayoun, I can safely say, practically remains a dead letter . . . while [this] does not extend to permitting the Christians to be treated as they formerly were treated, is so far unbearable and unjust in that it permits the Mussulmans to despoil them with heavy exactions. False imprisonments (imprisonment under false accusation) are of daily occurence. A Christian has but a small chance of exculpating himself when his opponent is a Mussulman (. . .) Christian evidence, as a rule, is still refused (. . .) Christians are now permitted to possess real property, but the obstacles which they meet with when they attempt to acquire it are so many and vexatious that very few have as yet dared to brave them. . . . Such being, generally speaking, the course pursued by the Government towards the Christians in the capital (Sarajevo) of the province where the Consular Agents of the different Powers reside and can exercise some degree of control, it may easily be guessed to what extent the Christians, in the remoter districts, suffer who are governed by Mudirs (governors) generally fanatical and unacquainted with the (new reforms of the) law. [Excerpts from Bulwer's report reproduced in Bat Ye'or, *The Decline of Eastern Christianity*, pp. 423–26.]

Finally, the modern Ottomanist Roderick Davison (in "Turkish Attitudes concerning Christian-Muslim Equality in the Nineteenth Century," *American Historical Review* 59 [1954]: 848, 855, 859, 864) also concludes that the reforms failed, and he offers an explanation based on Islamic beliefs intrinsic to the system of *dhimmitude*:

No genuine equality was ever attained . . . there remained among the Turks an intense Muslim feeling which could sometimes burst into an open fanaticism. . . . More important than the possibility of fanatic outbursts, however, was the innate attitude of superiority which the Muslim Turk possessed. Islam was for him the true religion. Christianity was only a partial revelation of the truth, which Muhammad finally revealed in full; therefore Christians were not equal to Muslims in possession of truth. Islam was not only a way of worship, it was a way of life as well. It prescribed man's relations to man, as well as to God, and was the basis for society, for law, and for government. Christians were therefore inevitably considered second-class citizens in the light of religious revelation—as well as by reason of the plain fact that they had been conquered by the Ottomans. This whole Muslim outlook was often summed up in the common term gavur (or kafir), which means "unbeliever" or "infidel," with emotional and quite uncomplimentary overtones. To associate closely or on terms of equality with the gavur was dubious at best. "Familiar association with heathens and infidels is forbidden to the people of Islam," said Asim, an early nineteenth-century historian, "and friendly and intimate intercourse between two parties that are one to another as darkness and light is far from desirable.". . . The mere idea of equality, especially the antidefamation clause of 1856, offended the Turks' inherent sense of the rightness of things. "Now we can't call a gavur a gavur," it was said, sometimes bitterly, sometimes in matter-of-fact explanation that under the new dispensation the plain truth could no longer be spoken openly. Could reforms be acceptable which forbade calling a spade a spade? . . . The Turkish mind, conditioned by centuries of Muslim and Ottoman dominance, was not yet ready to accept any absolute equality. . . . Ottoman equality was not attained in the Tanzimat period [i.e., mid- to late nineteenth century, 1839–1876], nor yet after the Young Turk revolution of 1908.

427. Maoz, "Changes in the Position of the Jewish Communities of Palestine and Syria in the Mid-Nineteenth Century," p. 156.

428. Bonar and McCheyne, *A Narrative of a Mission of Inquiry to the Jews from the Church of Scotland in 1839*, pp. 180–81, 273.

429. J. J. Binjamin II, *Eight Years in Asia and Africa: From 1846 to 1855* (Hanover: 1863), pp. 54–57.

430. *The British Consulate in Jerusalem (in relation to the Jews of Palestine, 1838–1914)*, part 1: 1838–1861, ed. Albert M. Hyamson (London: 1939), pp. 260–61.

431. Tudor Parfitt, *The Jews of Palestine* (Suffolk: 1987), pp. 168, 172–73.

432. "Jews in Flight from Palestine," *New York Times*, January 19, 1915; "Turks and Germans Expelling Zionists," *New York Times*, January 2, 1915; "Zionists in Peril of Turkish Attack," *New York Times*, February 2, 1915; "Threatens Massacre of Jews in Palestine," *New York Times*, May 4, 1917; "Cruel to Palestine Jews," *New York Times*, May 8, 1917; "Turks Killing Jews Who Resist Pillage," *New York Times*, May 19, 1917; "Twice Avert Eviction of Jerusalem Jews," *New York Times*, May 30, 1917; "Cruelties to Jews Deported in Jaffa," *New York Times*, June 3, 1917.

433. Ahmed Djemal Pasha (May 6, 1872–July 21, 1922). Between 1908 and 1918, Djemal was one of the most important administrators of the Ottoman government. When Europe was divided in two camps before World War I, he supported an alliance with France. Djemal traveled to France to negotiate an alliance with the French but failed and sided with Enver and Talat Pashas, favoring the German side. Djemal, along with Enver and Talat, took control of the Ottoman government in 1913. The Three Pashas effectively ruled the Ottoman Empire for the duration of World War I. Djemal was one of the designers of the government's disastrous internal and foreign policies, including the genocidal policy against the Armenians (Vahakn Dadrian, *The History of the Armenian Genocide* [Providence, RI: 1995], p. 208). After the Ottoman Empire declared war on the Allies in World War I, Enver Pasha nominated Djemal Pasha to lead the Ottoman army against English forces in Egypt, and Djemal accepted the position. Like Enver, he proved unsuccessful as a military leader.

433a. "Jews in Flight from Palestine"; "Turks and Germans Expelling Zionists"; "Zionists in Peril of Turkish Attack."

434. For the Armenian deportations, see Dadrian, *The History of the Armenian Genocide*, pp. 199–200, 220–22, 235–43, 255–64, 383–84; For the April 1917 deportations of Jews from Jaffa and Tel Aviv, Palestine, see "Cruelties to Jews Deported in Jaffa."

435. Yair Auron, *The Banality of Indifference* (New Brunswick, NJ: 2000), p. 75.

436. "Twice Avert Eviction of Jerusalem Jews."

437. Auron, *The Banality of Indifference*, p. 83.

438. "Cruelties to Jews Deported in Jaffa."

438a. Auron, *The Banality of Indifference*, pp. 82–83.

439. Musa Kazem el-Husseini (president, Palestinian Arab Congress) to High Commissioner for Palestine, December 10, 1920 (translated January 2, 1921), Israel State Archives, R.G. 2, Box 10, File 244.

440. Shai Lachman, "Arab Rebellion and Terrorism in Palestine 1929–39: The Case of Sheikh Izz al-Din al-Qassam and His Movement," in *Zionism and Arabism in Palestine and Israel*, ed. Elie Kedourie and Sylvia G. Haim (London: 1982), p. 55.

441. Ibid., pp. 59–61.

442. Ibid., pp. 61–63.

443. Ibid., pp. 64, 71.

444. Ibid., p. 76.

445. Ibid., p. 71.

446. Ibid., p. 72.

447. Ibid.

448. Ibid., pp. 78–86.

449. Ibid., pp. 96–97.

450. Ibid., pp. 87–88.

451. Ibid., p. 88.

452. Schechtman, *The Mufti and the Fuehrer*; Zvi Elpeleg, *The Grand Mufti Haj Amin Al-Hussaini*, trans. David Harvey (Frank Cass: 1993).

453. Yossef Bodansky, *Islamic Antisemitism as a Political Instrument* (Houston: 1999), p. 29.

454. Schechtman, *The Mufti and the Fuehrer*, pp. 114–15.

455. Lebel, *Hajj Amin ve Berlin*.

456. Schechtman, *The Mufti and the Fuehrer*, p. 151.

457. Lebel, *Hajj Amin ve Berlin*, pp. 140–42.

457a. Jan Wanner, "Amin al-Husayni and Germany's Arab Policy in the Period 1939–1945," *Archiv Orientalni* 54 (1986): 244.

458. Ibid., p. 243.

459. Schechtman, *The Mufti and the Fuehrer*, pp. 152–63.

460. Historian Howard Sachar, quoted in Stan Goodenough, "Nazis, Arabs Planned Final Solution for Pre-state Israel," Jerusalem Newswire, April 10, 2006.

461. Thomas Krumenacker, "Nazis Planned Holocaust for Palestine: Historians," *Boston Globe*, April 7, 2006; Klaus-Michael Mallman and Martin Cueppers, "Elimination of the Jewish National Home in Palestine: The Eihsatzlcommendo of the Panzar Army Africa, 1942," *Yad Vashem Studies* (2007): 111–41.

462. David Pryce-Jones, *The Closed Circle* (New York: 1989), p. 191.

463. Efraim Karsh, *Arafat's War* (New York: 2003).

464. Walid Phares, *Lebanese Christian Nationalism* (Boulder, CO: 1995); Farid El-Khazen, *The Breakdown of the State in Lebanon—1967–1976* (Cambridge: 2000).

465. Michael Oren, *Six Days of War—June 1967 and the Making of the Modern Middle East* (Oxford: 2002), p. 1

466. Charles Emmanuel Dufourcq, *La Vie Quotidienne dans l'Europe Medievale sous Domination Arabe* (Paris: 1978), p. 20; English translation in Bostom, *The Legacy of Jihad*, p. 40.

467. Bat Ye'or, "Aspects of the Arab-Israeli Conflict," *Wiener Library Bulletin* 32 (1979): 68.

468. Karsh, *Arafat's War*, p. 117.

469. Raphael Israeli, *Islamikaze—Manifestations of Islamic Martyrology* (London: 2003).

470. Karsh, *Arafat's War*, p. 233.

471. See nn. 183–86, above, and related text.

472. David Bedein, "A Not So Merry Christmas in the Holy Land," FrontPageMagazine.com, December 26, 2003, http://www.frontpagemag.com/Articles/ReadArticle.asp?ID=11477.

473. "Muslim-Christian Tensions in the Israeli-Arab Community," Middle East Media Research Institute, August 2, 1999, http://memri.org/bin/articles.cgi?Page=archives&Area=sd&ID=SP4199; Middle East Media Research Institute, "A Friday Sermon on PA TV: . . . 'We Must Educate Our Children on the Love of Jihad . . . ,'" July 11, 2001, http://memri.org/bin/articles.cgi?Page=archives&Area=sd&ID=SP24001.

474. "Muslim-Christian Tensions in the Israeli-Arab Community."

475. "Moslem Terror Chasing Out 1,000 Christian Arabs a Year," IsraelNationalNews.com, April 12, 2006, http://www.israelnationalnews.com/news.php3?id=101940.

476. Aaron Klein, "YMCA Warned to Vacate Hamas Town," *WorldNet Daily*, April 21, 2006.

477. Hamas Election Video: "Armed Struggle until Destruction of Israel," Palestinian Media Watch, December 12, 2005, http://www.pmw.org.il/Latest%20bulletins%20new.htm#b220106.

478. "Hamas Discusses Forming Government," *Jerusalem Post*, January 7, 2006.

479. "Hamas Head: We Will Never Recognize Israel," *Jerusalem Post*, February 3, 2006.

480. Cited in Bostom, *The Legacy of Jihad*, p. 96.

481. "Hamas Head: We Will Never Recognize Israel."

482. "The Covenant of the Islamic Resistance Movement—Hamas," Middle East Media Research Institute.

483. Carolyn Glick, "Let's Ignore Hamas," *Jerusalem Post*, April 3, 2006, http://www.jpost.com/servlet/Satellite ?cid=1143498792670&pagename=JPost%2FJPArticle %2FPrinter; H. T. Norris, P. Chalmeta, "al-Murābiṭūn," *Encyclopedia of Islam*, ed. P. Bearman, Thomas Bianquis, C. E. Bosworth, E. van Donzel, and W. P. Heinrichs. Leiden: Brill, 2007); Bostom, *The Legacy of Jihad*, p. 59.

484. "Hamas Leader Urges International Community to Respect Palestinian People's Choice," *Xinhua*, April 2, 2006, http://news.xinhuanet.com/english/2006-04/02/content_4373348.htm.

485. Avi Issacharoff, "Haniyeh in Tehran: Iran Gives Us 'Strategic Depth,'" *Haaretz*, December 10, 2006.

486. Avi Issacharoff, "Hamas Minister Target of Attempted Assassination in Gaza," *Haaretz*, December 12, 2006.

487. Bat Ye'or, *The Dhimmi*, p. 116.

488. Ibid., pp. 122–23.

489. Jane Gerber, "Towards an Understanding of the Term: 'The Golden Age' as an Historical Reality," in *The Heritage of the Jews in Spain*, ed. Aviva Doron (Tel Aviv), p. 15

490. Ibid., pp. 20–21.

491. Heinrich Graetz (1817–1891), is best kown for his multivolume *Geschichte der Juden*, which "superseded all former works of its kind . . . remarkable production in its day," and was subsequently translated into English, Russian, and Hebrew. A complete English translation by Bella Lowy was published in 1891–92 in London and republished by the Jewish Publication Society of America (Philadelphia: 1891–98), with copious indexing, and a biography of the author added. (Isidore Singer and Gotthard Deutsch, "Graetz, Heinrich," JewishEncyclopedia.com.)

492. Gerber, "Towards an Understanding of the Term," p. 20.

493. Graetz, *Geschichte der Juden*, p. 20.

494. *Fourth Conference of the Academy of Islamic Research, 1968*. See also *Arab Theologians on Jews and Israel: Extracts from the Proceedings of the Fourth Conference of the Academy of Islamic Research* (Geneva: 1976).

495. Said Abdel Fattah Ashour, "Jews in the Middle Ages Comparative Study of East and West," *Fourth*

Conference of the Academy of Islamic Research (1968) (Cairo: 1970), p. 505.

496. Gerber, "Towards an Understanding of the Term," p. 21.

497. Evariste Lévi-Provençal, *Histoire de l'Espagne Musulmane* (Paris: 1950), vol. 1; and Dufourcq, *Europe Medievale sous Domination Arabe*, esp. chap. 1, "Les Jours de Razzia et d'Invasion." For a full English translation of Dufourcq's chapter, see Bostom, *The Legacy of Jihad*, pp. 419–32.

498. Lévi-Provençal, *Histoire de l'Espagne Musulmane*, p. 150; English translation in Bostom, *The Legacy of Jihad*, p. 56.

498a. J. M. Safran, "Identity and Differentiation in 9th Century al-Andalus," *Speculum* 76 (2001): 583 n. 38. Safran states,

al-Kinani grew up in Cordoba and was a student of Ibn Habib's before traveling east to pursue his studies in Egypt, Baghdad, and Hejaz. He settled in Qayrawan, where he wrote numerous work.

498b. A. Huici-Miranda, "Ibn Habib, Abu Marwan 'Abd al-Malik b. Habib al-Sulami," in *Encyclopedia of Islam*, ed. P. Bearman, Thomas Bianquis, C. E. Bosworth, E. van Donzel, and W. P. Heinrichs (Leiden: Brill, 2006/2007).

498c. Safran, "Identity and Differentiation in 9th Century al-Andalus," pp. 582–83.

499. Dufourcq, *Europe Medievale sous Domination Arabe*, pp. 50, 194, 196; English translation in Bostom, *The Legacy of Jihad*, pp. 56–57.

500. Bat Ye'or, *The Decline of Eastern Christianity*, pp. 49–50.

501. Georges Vajda, "À propos de la situation des Juifs et des Chrétiens à Séville au début du XIIe siècle," *Revue des Études Juives* 99 (1935): 127–29. See full English translation herein, pp. 489.

502. Roger Arnaldez, "La guerre sainte selon Ibn Hazm de Courdoue," in *Études d'Orientalism Dediees a la Memoire de Lévi-Provençal* (Paris: 1962), vol. 2, pp. 445–59. For a full English translation of Arnaldez's chapter, see Bostom, *The Legacy of Jihad*, pp. 267–81.

503. See, for example, Dozy, *Spanish Islam*, pp. 547–73.

503a. Joseph Jacobs and Isaac Broyde, "Samuel Ha-Nagid (Samuel Halevi Ben Joseph Ibn Nagdela [Naghrela])," JewishEncyclopedia.com.

503b. Richard Gottheil and Meyer Kayserling, "Cordova," JewishEncyclopedia.com.

503c. Avraham Grossman, "The Economic and Social Background of Hostile Attitudes toward the Jews in the Ninth and Tenth Century Muslim Caliphate," in *Antisemitism through the Ages*, ed. Shmuel Almog (Oxford: Pergamon, 1988), pp. 178, 183 n. 2.

504. Ibid., 183 n. 2.

505. Perlmann, "Eleventh-Century Andalusian Authors on the Jews of Granada," p. 271.

506. Ibid., p. 272.

507. Ibid., p. 278.

508. Ibid., pp. 279–80.

509. Ibid., p. 282.

510. Ibid., p. 283.

511. See notes 116–20, above.

512. Perlmann, "Eleventh-Century Andalusian Authors on the Jews of Granada," pp. 285ff.

513. Grossman, "The Economic and Social Background of Hostile Attitudes toward the Jews in the Ninth and Tenth Century Muslim Caliphate," pp. 183–84, n. 2.

514. Charles Emmanuel Dufourcq, "Les Mozarabes du XIIe siecle et le pretendu 'Eveque' de Lisbonne," *Revue d'Histoire et de Civilisation du Maghreb* 5 (1968): 125–26. Dozy (*Spanish Islam: A History of the Muslims in Spain*, pp. 721–22) summarizes the events leading up to and surrounding the mass deportations as follows:

[T]he Fakihs and the [Muslim] populace fostered against them [the Mozarabs] [an] envenomed hatred. In most towns they formed but a small community, but in the province of Granada they were still numerous, and near the capital they possessed a beautiful church, which had been built about 600 C.E. by Gudila, a [Visi]Gothic noble. This church was an offense to the Fakihs . . . they issued a fatwa decreeing its demolition. Yusuf [b. Tashifin, the Almoravid ruler] having given his approval, the sacred edifice was leveled with the ground (1099 C.E.). Other churches seem to have met with a similar fate, and the Fakihs treated the Mozarabs so oppressively that the latter at length appealed to Alfonso the Battler, King of Aragon, to deliver them from their intolerable burdens. Alfonso acceded to their request. In September, 1125, he set out with four thousand knights and their men-at-arms. . . . Alfonso, did not however, achieve the results he aimed at . . . the ultimate object of the expedition had been the capture of Granada, and this was not effected. Upon the withdrawal of the Aragonese army, the Moslems cruelly avenged themselves on the Mozarabs. Ten thousand of the Christians were already out of their reach, for knowing the fate in store for them they had obtained permission from Alfonso to settle in his territories, but many who remained were deprived of their property, maltreated in endless ways, thrown into prision, or put to death. The majority, however, were transported to Africa, and endured terrible sufferings, ultimately settling in the vicinity of Saleh and Mequinez (1126 C.E.). This deportation was carried out by virtue of a decree which the Kady Ibn Rushd—grandfather of the famous Averröes—had procured. . . . Eleven years later a second expulsion took place, and very few were left in Andalusia.

515. Hirschberg, *The Jews of North Africa*, p. 117.

516. See note 514 above, especially Dozy.

517. Dozy, *Spanish Islam: A History of the Muslims in Spain*, p. 721.

518. Hirschberg, *The Jews of North Africa*, p. 118.

519. Spiritual leader of the Muslim Almohads, d. 1130. As a very pious Muslim, Ibn Tumart naturally did not draw a sharp distinction between the religious and the secular. He was a fundamentalist who wished to re-establish his conception of the original purity of Islam by reference to the Qur'an and the Sunna (J. F. P. Hopkins, "Ibn Tūmart," *Encyclopedia of Islam*, ed. P. Bearman, T. Bianquis, C. E. Bosworth, E. van Donzel, and W. P. Heinrichs (Brill: 2006/2007).

520. Hirschberg, *The Jews of North Africa*, pp. 127–28.

521. Ibid., pp. 123–29.

522. Bat Ye'or, *The Dhimmi*, p. 351 n. 4; Hirschberg, *The Jews of North Africa*, pp. 123ff.

523. Bat Ye'or, *The Dhimmi*, * at bottom of p. 351.

524. Ibid., pp. 345–51, English translation of Ibn Aqnin, *Tibb al-nufus* (*Therapy of the Soul*), [Judeo-Arabic], Bodl Ms. Neubauer 1273 (Oxford).

525. Ibid., p. 189; English translation of al-Marrakushi, *Al-mu'jib fi talkhis akhbar al-mahgrib* (*Histoires des Almohades*), from the French translation by Edmond Fagnan (Algiers: 1893).

526. Ibid.

527. Maimonides, "Epistle to the Jews of Yemen," in *Iggeret Teman*, ed. A. Halkin (New York: 1952), pp. 1–106; excerpts translated into English by Norman Stillman, in *The Jews of Arab Lands*, pp. 241–42.

527a. Rambam (Maimonides)'s *Teshuvot, Responsa*, ed. A. Freimann, no. 364. Cited in Georges Vajda, "Juifs et musulmans selon le hadit," *Journal Asiatique* 229 (1937): 120 n. 2; translated from the French by Susan Emanuel. Professor Hans Jansen translates the phrase *Ve-yirmezuu bah ha-remaziim hay-yedu `iim al-hem* as "They read into it [the Torah] the allusions [to Jesus, or to the Trinity, in particular] that are known to them." He argues that this may be a reference to the Christian habit of reading Jesus and the Trinity into the text of the Torah—such an allusion being necessary for the tradi-tional forms of Christianity to make sense to believers. (Dr. Hans Jansen, Houtsma Chair for Contemporary Islamic Thought, Department of Arabic, Persian, and Turkish, University of Utrecht, the Netherlands, personal communication.)

528. See nn. 489–92, and 496, above.

529. Richard Fletcher, *Moorish Spain* (Berkeley and Los Angeles: University of California Press, 1993), pp. 171–73.

530. Mercedes Garcia-Arenal, "Jewish Converts to Islam in the Muslim West," *Israel Oriental Studies* 17 (1997): 239.

531. Ibid.

532. Benzion Netanyahu, *The Origins of the Inquisi-tion* (New York: 1995), p. 3; for discussions of the per-secutions of this fifty-year period, i.e., 1367–1417, see pp. 116, 142–64, and 191–96.

533. For the numbers of *Marranos of Spain*, see Ben-zion Netanyahu, *The Marranos of Spain* (Ithaca, NY: 1999), pp. 238–48, 255–70. See also Netanyahu, *The Origins of the Inquisition*, pp. 1095ff. Netanyahu con-cludes (p. 248, Marranos of Spain) that the 1480 census of Marranos was 600,000–650,000.

534. Netanyahu, *The Origins of the Inquisition*, pp. 3, 1048–92.

535. Henry Kamen, "The Mediterranean and the Expulsion of Spanish Jews in 1492," *Past and Present* (May 1988): 30–55.

536. Ibid., p. 44.

537. Ibid., pp. 39, 44.

538. For Ottoman attitudes toward the Jews of the conquered Byzantine Empire, including Salonika, see Joseph R. Hacker, "Ottoman Policy toward the Jews and Jewish Attitudes toward the Ottomans during the Fif-teenth Century," in *Christians and Jews in the Ottoman Empire: The Functioning of a Plural Society*, ed. Ben-jamin Braude and Bernard Lewis (New York: 1982), vol. I, pp. 117–26. For the devastating nature of the Ottoman jihad campaigns of the fifteenth century, see Dimitar Angelov, "Certain aspects de la conquete des peuples balkanique par les Turcs," in *Les Balkans au moyen age: La Bulgarie des Bogomils aux Turcs* (London: Variorum Reprints, 1978), pp. 220–75; full English translation as "Certain Phases of the Conquest of the Balkan Peoples by the Turks," in Bostom, *The Legacy of Jihad*, pp. 462–517.

539. Paul Wittek, *The Rise of the Ottoman Empire* (London: 1966), p. 14. Wittek (also p. 14) includes this discussion, with a block quote from Ahmedi's text:

The chapter Ahmedi devotes in his *Iskender-name* to the history of the Ottoman sultans, the ancestors of his protector Sulayman Tshelebi, son of Bayazid I, begins with an introduction in which the poet solemnly declares his intention of writing a Ghaz-awat-name, a book about the holy war of the Ghazis. He poses the question "Why have the Ghazis appeared at last?" And he answers: "Because the best always comes at the end. Just as the definitive prophet Mohammed came after the others, just as the Koran came down from heaven after the Torah, the Psalms and the Gospels, so also the Ghazis appeared in the world at the last, "those Ghazis the reign of whom is that of the Ottomans. The poet continues with this question: "Who is a Ghazi?" And he explains: "A Ghazi is the instru-ment of the religion of Allah, a servant of God who purifies the earth from the filth of polytheism (remember that Islam regards the Trinity of the Christians as a polytheism); the Ghazi is the sword of God, he is the protector and refuge of the believers. If he becomes a martyr in the ways of God, do not believe that he has died—he lives in beatitude with Allah, he has eternal life."

540. Sonia Anderson, *An English Consul in Turkey: Paul Rycaut at Smyrna, 1667–1678* (Oxford: 1989).

540a. Sir Paul Rycaut, *The Present State of the Ottoman Empire* (London: 1686) [electronic version], pp. 200, 201.

540b. The Ottoman Office of the Mufti and Shaykh al-Islam were synonymous. J. H. Karmers and R. C. Repp, "Shaykh al-Islam," in *Encyclopedia of Islam* , ed. P. Bearman, Thomas Bianquis, C. E. Bosworth, E. van Donzel, and W. P. Heinrichs (Leiden: Brill, 2006/2007).

540c. Fr. Babinger, "Khosrew, Molla," in *Encyclopedia of Islam*, ed. P. Bearman, Thomas Bianquis, C. E. Bosworth, E. van Donzel, and W. P. Heinrichs (Leiden: Brill, 2006/2007).

540d. Molla Khosrew, *Il Kitab Al-Gihad*, trans. Nicola Melis (Cagliari, Italy: 2002), pp. 95–96. English translation by "UL."

541. Halil Inalcik, *The Ottoman Empire—The Classical Age, 1300–1600* (London: 1973), p. 6.

542. A. E. Vacalopoulos, *Origins of the Greek Nation—The Byzantine Period* (New Brunswick, NJ: 1970), p. 66.

543. Speros Vryonis, "The Experience of Christians under Seljuk and Ottoman Domination, Eleventh to Sixteenth Century," in *Conversion and Continuity: Indigenous Christian Communities in Islamic Lands, Eighth to Eighteenth Centuries*, ed. Michael Gervers and Ramzi Jibran Bikhazi (Toronto: 1990), p. 201.

544. Angelov, "Certains Aspects de la Conquete Des Peuples Balkaniques par les Turcs," pp. 220–75; Vacalopoulos, *Origins of the Greek Nation*, pp. 69–85.

545. Angelov, "Certains Aspects de la Conquete Des Peuples Balkaniques par les Turcs," pp. 236, 238–39.

546. Hacker, "Ottoman Policy toward the Jews and Jewish Attitudes toward the Ottomans during the Fifteenth Century," pp. 117–26; Hacker, "The Sürgün System and Jewish Society in the Ottoman Empire during the 15th–17th Centuries" [Hebrew], *Zion* 55 (1990): 27–82; published in English translation in *Ottoman and Turkish Jewry—Community and Leadership*, ed. Aron Rodrigue (Bloomington, IN: 1992), pp. 1–65.

547. See notes 489–92, above.

548. Hacker, "The Sürgün System and Jewish Society in the Ottoman Empire," pp. 7–8. Hacker elaborates (p. 44 n. 21) on this point, maintaining that "the approach adopted by nineteenth- and twentieth-century historians to the question of the Jewish-Ottoman encounter in the fifteenth century," including "H. Graetz, S. Dubnow, S. Rozanes, M. Franco, A. Galante , S. Baron, and H. Z. Hirschberg" was unduly influenced by "the romantic picture sketched by the sixteenth- and seventeenth-century writers."

549. Ibid., pp. 23, 22; see also Louis Ginsberg, "Cap-

sali," JewishEncyclopedia.com, and Joseph Jacobs and M. Franco, "Joseph Ben Isaac Sambari," JewishEncyclopedia.com.

550. For the overall impact of the jihad conquests see nn. 542–45, above, and 556 below. For a discussion of jihad enslavement by the Ottomans in the Balkans, especially Romania, see M. M. Alexandrescu-Dersca Bulgaru, "The Roles of Slaves in Fifteenth Century Turkish Romania," *Byzantinische Forschungen* 11 (1987): 15–22; English translation in Bostom, *The Legacy of Jihad*, pp. 566–72.

550a. For the impact of Ottoman policies of *sürgün* on Christian populations, see Doukas, *Decline and Fall of Byzantium to the Ottoman Turks*, annotated translation of *Historia Turco-Byzantia*, by Harry J. Magoulias (Detroit: 1975), pp. 241, 243, 257–58. Doukas mentions deportations of Christian populations from Anatolia and Rumelia, the Balkans, and the Peloponnesus.

After 5,000 families were registered from both the eastern and western provinces [Anatolia and Rumelia], Mehmed [II] instructed them and their households to take up residence in the City [Constantinople] by September on penalty of death.

Mehmed [II] returned to Adrianople with the booty [from Serbia, outside Smederovo] by way of Sofia. There he awarded one half to his officials and the troops who labored with him. After claiming half of the captives for himself, he sent them to populate the villages outside Constantinople. His allotted portion was four thousand men and women.

After taking all of the Peloponnesus, the tyrant [Mehmed II] installed his own administrators and governors. Returning to Adrianople, he took with him Demetrios [Paleologus?] and his entire household, the palace officials and wealthy notables from Achaia [northern Peloponnesus] and Lakedaimonia [southern Peloponnesus] and the remaining provinces. He slaughtered all the nobles of Albania and then allowed no fortress to remain standing with the exception of Monemvasia [southeast Peloponnesus], and this grudgingly and against his will. . . . He transferred about two thousand families from the Peloponnesus and resettled them in the City [Constantinople]. He also registered the same number of youths among the Janissaries.

550b. Hacker, "Ottoman Policy toward the Jews and Jewish Attitudes toward the Ottomans," p. 123.

551. Hacker, "The Sürgün System and Jewish Society in the Ottoman Empire," pp. 27–30.

552. Ibid., p. 2.

553. Ibid., p. 5.

554. Ibid., p. 8.

555. Ibid., pp. 8–9, 36–37.

556. See these accounts in English translation from S.

Vryonis Jr., "A Critical Analysis of Stanford J. Shaw's *History of the Ottoman Empire and Modern Turkey*, Volume 1: *Empire of the Gazis: The Rise and Decline of the Ottoman Empire, 1280–1808*," *Balkan Studies* 24 (1983), pp. 57–62, 68; reproduced in Bostom, *The Legacy of Jihad*, pp. 616–18.

[*Both Turkish and Christian chroniclers provide graphic evidence of the wanton pillage and slaughter of non-combatants following the Ottoman jihad conquest of Constantinople in 1453. First from the Turkish sources*]: Sultan Mehmed (in order to) arouse greater zeal for the way of God issued an order (that the city was to be) plundered. And from all directions they (gazis) came forcefully and violently (to join) the army. They entered the city, they passed the infidels over the sword (i.e. slew them) and . . . they pillaged and looted, they took captive the youths and maidens, and they took their goods and valuables whatever there was of them. . . . " [Urudj] The gazis entered the city, cut off the head of the emperor, captured Kyr Loukas and his family . . . and they slew the miserable common people. They placed people and families in chains and placed metal rings on their necks." [Neshri]

[*Speros Vryonis Jr. has summarized the key contents of letters sent by Sultan Mehmed himself to various Muslim potentates of the Near East*]: In his letter to the sultan of Egypt, Mehmed writes that his army killed many of the inhabitants, enslaved many others (those that remained), plundered the treasures of the city, 'cleaned out' the priests and took over the churches. . . . To the Sherif of Mecca he writes that they killed the ruler of Constantinople, they killed the "pagan" inhabitants and destroyed their houses. The soldiers smashed the crosses, looted the wealth and properties and enslaved their children and youths. "They cleared these places of their monkish filth and Christian impurity.". . . In yet another letter he informs Cihan Shah Mirza of Iran that the inhabitants of the city have become food for the swords and arrows of the gazis; that they plundered their children, possessions and houses; that those men and women who survived the massacre were thrown into chains.

[*The Christian sources include this narrative by Ducas, who gathered eyewitness accounts and visited Constantinople shortly after its conquest*]: (Then) the Turks arrived at the church [the great church of St. Sophia], pillaging, slaughtering, and enslaving. They enslaved all those that survived. They smashed the icons in the church, took their adornments as well as all that was moveable in the church. . . . Those of (the Greeks) who went off to their houses were captured before arriving there. Others upon reaching their houses found them empty of children, wives, and possessions and before (they began) wailing and weeping were themselves bound with their hands behind them. Others coming to their houses and having found their wife and children being led off, were tied and bound with their most beloved. . . . They (the Turks) slew mercilessly all the elderly, both men and women, in (their) homes, who were not able to leave their homes because of illness or old age. The newborn infants were thrown into the streets. . . . And as many of the (Greek) aristocrats and nobles of the officials of the palace that he (Mehmed) ransomed, sending them all to the "speculatora" he executed them. He selected their wives and children, the beautiful daughters and shapely youths and turned them over to the head eunuch to guard them, and the remaining captives he turned over to others to guard over them. . . . And the entire city was to be seen in the tents of the army, and the city lay deserted, naked, mute, having neither form nor beauty.

[*From the contemporary fifteenth-century historian Critobulus of Imbros:*] Then a great slaughter occurred of those who happened to be there: some of them were on the streets, for they had already left the houses and were running toward the tumult when they fell unexpectedly on the swords of the soldiers; others were in their own homes and fell victims to the violence of the Janissaries and other soldiers, without any rhyme or reason; others were resisting relying on their own courage; still others were fleeing to the churches and making supplication—men, women, and children, everyone, for there was no quarter given. . . . The soldiers fell on them with anger and great wrath. . . . Now in general they killed so as to frighten all the city, and terrorize and enslave all by the slaughter.

557. Hacker, "Ottoman Policy toward the Jews and Jewish Attitudes toward the Ottomans," p. 120; Hacker, "The Sürgün System and Jewish Society in the Ottoman Empire," p. 12.

557a. Hacker, "Ottoman Policy toward the Jews and Jewish Attitudes toward the Ottomans," p. 121; see also the reference to a letter of the Karaite polymath Caleb Afendopolo (d. 1499) by Jacob Mann in *Texts and Studies in Jewish History and Literature* (Philadelphia: Karaitica, 1935), vol. 2, p. 292, n. 15. Mann writes,

Caleb speaks of an "expulsion" which would indicate an act of persecution on the part of the government, as if wanting to keep the Jews under stringent supervision by congregating them in the capital.

558. Hacker, "The Sürgün System and Jewish Society in the Ottoman Empire," pp. 12–18; see also Richard Gottheil, "Ephraim B. Gershon," Jewish Encyclopedia.com, and Joseph Jacobs and M. Selig-

sohn, "Michael Ben Shabbethai Cohen Balbo," Jewish Encyclopedia.

559. Hacker, "The Sürgün System and Jewish Society in the Ottoman Empire," pp. 12–15.

560. Ibid., p. 15.

561. Ibid., pp. 15, 18.

562. Ibid., p. 15.

563. Ibid.

564. Ibid., p. 16.

565. See nn. 542–45, 550a, and 556, above.

566. Speros Vryonis Jr., in "Seljuk Gulams and Ottoman Devshirmes," *Der Islam* 41 (1965): 245–47, for example, makes these deliberately understated, but cogent observations:

[I]n discussing the *devshirme* we are dealing with the large numbers of Christians who, in spite of the material advantages offered by conversion to Islam, chose to remain members of a religious society which was denied first class citizenship. Therefore the proposition advanced by some historians, that the Christians welcomed the *devshirme* as it opened up wonderful opportunities for their children, is inconsistent with the fact that these Christians had not chosen to become Muslims in the first instance but had remained Christians . . . there is abundant testimony to the very active dislike with which they viewed the taking of their children. One would expect such sentiments given the strong nature of the family bond and given also the strong attachment to Christianity of those who had not apostacized to Islam. . . . First of all the Ottomans capitalized on the general Christian fear of losing their children and used offers of devshirme exemption in negotiations for surrender of Christian lands. Such exemptions were included in the surrender terms granted to Jannina, Galata, the Morea, Chios, etc. . . . Christians who engaged in specialized activities which were important to the Ottoman state were likewise exempt from the tax on their children by way of recognition of the importance of their labors for the empire. . . . Exemption from this tribute was considered a privilege and not a penalty . . .

. . . [T]here are other documents wherein their [i.e., the Christians] dislike is much more explicitly apparent. These include a series of Ottoman documents dealing with the specific situations wherein the devshirmes themselves have escaped from the officials responsible for collecting them. . . . A firman . . . in 1601 [regarding the devshirme] provided the [Ottoman] officials with stern measures of enforcement, a fact which would seem to suggest that parents were not always disposed to part with their sons.

"to enforce the command of the known and holy

fetva [fatwa] of Seyhul [Shaikh]- Islam. In accordance with this whenever some one of the infidel parents or some other should oppose the giving up of his son for the Janissaries, he is immediately hanged from his door-sill, his blood being deemed unworthy."

Vasiliki Papoulia in "The Impact of Devshirme on Greek Society," in *War and Society in East Central Europe*, ed. Bela K. Kiraly (Boulder, CO: 1982), vol. 2, pp. 554–55, highlights the continuous desperate, often violent struggle of the Christian populations against this forcefully imposed Ottoman levy:

It is obvious that the population strongly resented . . . this measure [and the levy] could be carried out only by force. Those who refused to surrender their sons—the healthiest, the handsomest and the most intelligent—were on the spot put to death by hanging. Nevertheless we have examples of armed resistance. In 1565 a revolt took place in Epirus and Albania. The inhabitants killed the recruiting officers and the revolt was put down only after the sultan sent five hundred janissaries in support of the local sanjak-bey. We are better informed, thanks to the historic archives of Yerroia, about the uprising in Naousa in 1705 where the inhabitants killed the Silahdar Ahmed Celebi and his assistants and fled to the mountains as rebels. Some of them were later arrested and put to death . . .

Since there was no possibility of escaping [the levy] the population resorted to several subterfuges. Some left their villages and fled to certain cities which enjoyed exemption from the child levy or migrated to Venetian-held territories. The result was a depopulation of the countryside. Others had their children marry at an early age. . . . Nicephorus Angelus . . . states that at times the children ran away on their own initiative, but when they heard that the authorities had arrested their parents and were torturing them to death, returned and gave themselves up. La Giulletiere cites the case of a young Athenian who returned from hiding in order to save his father's life and then chose to die himself rather than abjure his faith. According to the evidence in Turkish sources, some parents even succeeded in abducting their children after they had been recruited. The most successful way of escaping recruitment was through bribery. That the latter was very widespread is evident from the large amounts of money confiscated by the sultan from corrupt . . . officials. Finally, in their desperation the parents even appealed to the Pope and the Western powers for help.

Papoulia concludes:

there is no doubt that this heavy burden was one of the hardest tribulations of the Christian population. (p. 557)

567. Hacker, "The Sürgün System and Jewish Society in the Ottoman Empire," pp. 16, 17, 19, 20.

568. Ibid., pp. 24–33.

569. Ibid., p. 27.

570. Ibid.

571. Ibid., p. 28.

572. Ibid., p. 31.

573. Ibid., pp. 31, 32.

574. Ibid., pp. 32–33.

575. Ibid., pp. 1–65; Hacker, "Ottoman Policy toward the Jews and Jewish Attitudes toward the Ottomans during the Fifteenth Century," pp. 117–26.

576. Hacker, "The Sürgün System and Jewish Society in the Ottoman Empire," p. 23.

577. Molla Khosrew, *Il Kitab Al-Gihad*, pp. 177–89.

578. See nn. 102–114e, above.

579. Molla Khosrew, *Il Kitab Al-Gihad*, pp. 177ff.

580. The Hanafi school of jurisprudence, which predominated in the Ottoman heartland, did *not* sanction the administration of blows during *jizya* collection. See, for example, the writings of the seminal Hanafi jurist (d. 798) Abu Yusuf (in Bostom, *The Legacy of Jihad*, pp. 174–76, 179).

581. Ibid.

582. On the prohibition against bearing arms, in addition to Molla Khosrew's (confirmatory) opinion, see, for example, Schacht, *An Introduction to Islamic Law*, p. 131. See n. 112, above, regarding inadmissibility of *dhimmi* testimony when a Muslim is a party. These legal disenfranchisements are also discussed extensively in the pioneering works of Antoine Fattal, *Le Statut legal de non-musulmans en pays d' Islam* (Beirut: 1958); and Bat Ye'or, *The Dhimmi*.

583. On the general failure of the Tanzimat reforms see n. 426a, above. For the continued inadequacy of the reforms through 1912–1914, see, for example, Roderick Davison, "The Armenian Crisis, 1912–1914," *American Historical Review* 53 (1948): 482–83:

Wild rejoicing among Armenians, and great hopes for the future, arose with the Young Turk revolution of 1908. Armenians co-operated with the Turkish Committee of Union and Progress [the political party of the Young Turks]. A few steps were, in fact, made toward realizing the Armenian hopes. . . . But these embryonic measures of improvement from 1908–1912 were far outweighed by old and new grievances. When measured against the hopes of 1908, furthermore, the situation seemed to the Armenians as black as ever. . . . Armenian disillusionment sprang from the [Adana] massacres of 1909. The Young Turks, furthermore, soon turned from equality and Ottomanization to Turkification, stifling previous Armenian hopes. This policy

extended even to limiting privileges of the Armenian Patriarch Arsharouni, installed at Constantinople in 1912. In short, the constitutional regime had done little for the Armenians.

For Jews in Ottoman Palestine through 1917, see nn. 427–431, and the earlier accompanying discussion.

584. Dadrian, "The Clash between Democratic Norms and Theocratic Dogmas," p. 15.

585. *Reports from Her Majesty's Consuls relating to the Condition of the Christians in Turkey* (1867), pp. 5, 29, cited in Dadrian, "The Clash between Democratic Norms and Theocratic Dogmas," p. 17.

586. Davison, "Turkish Attitudes concerning Christian-Muslim Equality in the Nineteenth Century," p. 864.

587. Moritz Levy, *The Sephardim in Bosnia: A Contribution to the History of the Jews in the Balkans* [German] (Sarajevo: 1911), pp. 52–61; English translation by Colin Meade.

588. Ivo Andric, *The Development of Spiritual Life in Bosnia under the Influence of Turkish Rule* (1924), trans. Zelimir B. Juricic and John F. Loud (Durham: University of North Carolina Press, 1990), pp. 23–38, 78–87.

589. See n. 419, above.

590. Levy, *The Sephardim in Bosnia*, pp. 52ff.

591. Ibid.

592. Ibid.

593. Ibid.

594. Ibid.

595. Andric, *The Development of Spiritual Life in Bosnia under the Influence of Turkish Rule*, pp. 37, 86 nn. 72, 29.

596. Levy, *The Sephardim in Bosnia*, pp. 28, 35; English translation in Andric, *The Development of Spiritual Life in Bosnia under the Influence of Turkish Rule*, p. 86 n. 71.

597. Correspondence from James Porter, British ambassador to Constantinople, William Pitt the Elder, London, dated February 3, 1758 (SP 97-40); and June 3, 1758 (SP 97-40), reproduced in Bat Ye'or, *The Decline of Eastern Christianity under Islam*, pp. 384–86.

598. S. Zeitlin, "Review: The Sabbatians and the Plague of Mysticism," *Jewish Quarterly Review* 49 (1958): 145–55.

599. Paul Rycaut, *The History of the Turkish Empire from the Year 1623 to the Year 1677* (London: 1680), [electronic version], pp. 200–19; William G. Schauffler, "Shabbaetai Zevi and His Followers," *Journal of the American Oriental Society* 2 (1851): 1–26; Gershom G. Scholem, *Sabbatai Zevi: The Mystical Messiah* (Princeton, NJ: 1973), pp. 140–267, 327–460, 603–86; Geoffrey L. Lewis and Cecil Roth, "New Light on the Apostasy of Sabbatai Zevi," *Jewish Quarterly Review* 53 (1963): 219–25; Jane Hathaway, "The Grand Vizier and the False Messiah: The Sabbatai Sevi Controversy and the Ottoman Reform in Egypt," *Journal of the American Oriental Society* 117 (1997): 665–71.

600. Lewis and Roth, "New Light on the Apostasy of Sabbatai Zevi," pp. 220–21.

601. Rycaut, *The History of the Turkish Empire from the Year 1623 to the Year 1677*, p. 214.

602. Lewis and Roth, "New Light on the Apostasy of Sabbatai Zevi," p. 223; Hathaway, "The Grand Vizier and the False Messiah," p. 665.

603. Moshe Perlmann, "Dönme," in *Encyclopedia of Islam*, ed. P. Bearman, Thomas Bianquis, C. E. Bosworth, E. van Donzel, and W. P. Heinrichs (Leiden: Brill, 2006/2007).

604. S. Zeitlin, "Review: The Sabbatians and the Plague of Mysticism," p. 154.

605. Perlmann, "Dönme."

606. Hacker, "Ottoman Policy toward the Jews and Jewish Attitudes toward the Ottomans during the Fifteenth Century," p. 123. Describing the financial status of the *sürgün* Jews who repopulated Constantinople after its jihad conquest (during the relatively halcyon days) under Mehmed II in the latter half of the fifteenth century, Hacker writes,

We must note that the *majority of the Jews of Constantinople were not wealthy* and that *the gap between the few who were, and the many who were not, was large.*

607. M. A. Ubicini, *Letters on Turkey*, part 2. *The Raiahs*, trans. Lady Easthope (London, 1856), pp. 365–66.

608. Carsten Niebuhr, *Travels through Arabia and Other Countries in the East*, trans. Robert Hebron (Edinburgh, 1792), p. 245.

609. Charles McFarlane, *Constantinople in 1828* (London, 1829), pp. 115–16; cited in Bernard Lewis. *The Jews of Islam* (Princeton, NJ: 1984), p. 164.

610. Ibid.

611. Julia Pardoe, *The City of the Sultan and Domestic Manners of the Turks in 1836* (London: 1837), pp. 361–63; cited in Lewis, *The Jews of Islam*, p. 167–68.

612. See n. 608 above.

613. Ubicini, *Letters on Turkey*, part 2. *The Raiahs*, p. 371; *tchîffut*: "the quality of a Jew." Like Tschefied, above, in n. 608, i.e., commonly, "dirty Jew."

614. Ibid. pp. 346–47, 365–66.

615. Ibid., p. 365 n. 1, Ubicini names one prominent Jewish physician in Turkey, a "Doctor Castro, chief surgeon of the military hospital."

616. Paul Dumont, "Jewish Communities in Turkey during the Last Decades of the Nineteenth Century in Light of the Archives of the Alliance Israelite Universelle," in *Christians and Jews in the Ottoman Empire: The Functioning of a Plural Society*, ed. Benjamin Braude and Bernard Lewis (New York: 1982), vol. 1, pp. 209–42.

617. Ibid., p. 210.

618. Ibid., pp. 210, 211.

619. Ibid., pp. 213–14.

620. Ibid., p. 214.

621. Rev. de Sola Pool, "The Levantine Jews in the United States," *American Jewish Yearbook* 15 (1913/1914): 208.

622. Dumont, "Jewish Communities in Turkey during the Last Decades of the Nineteenth Century," pp. 224–25.

623. Speros Vryonis, *The Mechanism of Catastrophe: The Turkish Pogrom of September 6–7, 1955, and the Destruction of the Greek Community of Istanbul* (New York: 2005), p. 30.

624. Bernard Lewis, *The Emergence of Modern Turkey* (London: 1968), pp. 254–55.

625. Vryonis, *The Mechanism of Catastrophe*, p. 32 n. 15.

626. Ziya Gokälp, *The Principles of Turkism*, trans. and ed. R. Devereux (Leiden: 1968), p. 102; cited in Vryonis, *The Mechanism of Catastrophe*, p. 30 n. 8.

627. Speros Vryonis, *The Turkish State and History: Clio Meets the Grey Wolf* (New Rochelle, NY: 1991), pp. 65–73.

628. Frank Weber, *The Evasive Neutral* (Columbia, MO: 1979), pp. 113, 115–16. Weber makes clear that based on the reports of both British and German diplomats during the World War II era, Pan-Turanism remained a potent ideology (and perhaps even an official policy) in ruling Turkish political elites, and even more so within the Turkish army, and among the masses.

Thus British as well as German sources strongly suggest that Pan Turanianism [Turanism] was not simply a mass enthusiasm popularly engendered, but an official program of the Turkish government, continuously though surreptitiously cultivated. Ankara preferred to use subordinate diplomats or non-official spokesmen in order to obscure the origins of the Pan-Turanian movement, but there was little room for doubt that those origins were in the highest echelons of the Turkish leadership.

Nuri Paşa, brother of the celebrated Enver Paşa, Ottoman minister of war who was most responsible for allying the sultan's empire with the Wilhelmian Reich in 1914 . . . had survived the First World War to become a moderately prosperous factory owner in Republican Turkey . . . [on a] mission to propound his theories of the Pan-Turanian reorganization of the Middle East before the highest dignitaries of the German government . . . he delimited for the German minister [Woermann] what areas of Asia he considered "Pan Turanian." These were the Crimea, Transcaucasia, Azerbaijan, the land between the Ural Mountains and the Volga River, and Daghestan and Tatar Autonomous Soviet republics. In addition to these provinces, Nuri also claimed Turanian enclaves in Syria, Iraq, and northern Iran. Finally, he would have had the Turanian state embrace "East Turkestan," that is, the Chinese province of

Sinkiang. Quite obviously, his schemes were a blend of old and new, with some points drawn from Ottoman times and others conceived under the republic. . . . [Woermann] pointedly commented that all these Pan-Turanian proposals ran counter to Atatürk's precept that Turkey was a purely national state. Nuri asserted that Atatürk's foreign policy had been only temporary, necessitated by the weakness of the infant Turkish Republic and fear of Soviet Russia. But the Wehrmacht [German army] now stood on Soviet soil and was gaining more ground every day. According to Nuri, Turanian expansion was very popular with the Turkish people and with the Turkish army, and if the government in Ankara did not advance the cause or proved negativistic and timid, the Turkish army could be expected to sweep it away.

629. Bernard Lewis, "History-Writing and National Revival in Turkey," *Middle Eastern Affairs* 4 (1953): 225.
630. Faik Ökte, *The Tragedy of the Turkish Capital Tax* (London: 1987); English translation by Geoffrey Cox, with an introduction by David Brown, p. ix.
630a. Alexis Alexandris, *Greek Minority of Istanbul and Greek-Turkish Relations, 1918–1974* (Athens: 1983/1992), p. 111.
631. Ibid.
632. Vryonis, *The Mechanism of Catastrophe,* pp. 32–33.
633. Hatice Bayraktar, "The Anti-Jewish Pogrom in Eastern Thrace in 1934: New Evidence for the Responsibility of the Turkish Government," *Patterns of Prejudice* 40 (2006): 95–96.
634. Membership in the authoritarian nationalist party Ittihat ve Terakki (Union and Progress).
635. Vahakn Dadrian, "The Role of Turkish Physicians in the World War I Genocide of Ottoman Armenians," *Holocaust and Genocide Studies* 1 (1986): 169–92 n. 44. According to Bayraktar, "The Anti-Jewish Pogrom in Eastern Thrace in 1934," p. 102 n. 39,

In the 1920s, Tali temporarily held the post of leader of the CHF [*Cumhuriyet Halk Firkasi*, People's Republican Party] in Istanbul and was also a member of the Turkish National Assembly.

636. Bayraktar, "The Anti-Jewish Pogrom in Eastern Thrace in 1934," p. 103.
637. Ibid., p. 104.
638. Ibid., pp. 105ff.
639. Rifat Bali, "Stere otpe du Juif dans le Folklore Turc," in *Relations Entre Turcs et Juifs* (Istanbul: 2001), pp. 25–28.
639a. Bayraktar, "The Anti-Jewish Pogrom in Eastern Thrace in 1934," pp. 105ff.
640. Weber, *The Evasive Neutral* (Columbia, MO: 1979), pp. 22–23.

641. Ibid., p. 101.
642. Alexandris, *Greek Minority of Istanbul and Greek-Turkish Relations*, pp. 213–14.
643. Bernard Wasserstein, review of *Turkey and the Holocaust* (by Stanford Shaw), *Times Literary Supplement*, January 7, 1994, p. 4.
644. Ibid.
645. Ökte, *The Tragedy of the Turkish Capital Tax,* p. 23.
646. Ibid., p. 24.
647. Ibid.
648. Ibid., p. 26.
649. Lewis, *The Emergence of Modern Turkey*, p. 300.
650. Ökte, *The Tragedy of the Turkish Capital Tax*, pp. 26, 32, 34–35, 38–39.
651. Vryonis, *The Mechanism of Catastrophe*, p. 38.
652. Alexandris, *Greek Minority of Istanbul and Greek-Turkish Relations*, pp. 220–21, 22–226.
653. Lewis, *The Emergence of Modern Turkey*, p. 300 n. 10.
654. Alexandris, *Greek Minority of Istanbul and Greek-Turkish Relations*, p. 220.
655. Edward Clark, "The Turkish Varlik Vergisi Reconsidered," *Middle East Studies* 8 (1972): 208–209.
656. Alexandris, *Greek Minority of Istanbul and Greek-Turkish Relations*, pp. 216–24.
657. Ibid., pp. 216–17.
658. "The Turkish Minorities," *New York Times*, September 17, 1943, p. 20.
659. Alexandris, *Greek Minority of Istanbul and Greek-Turkish Relations*, pp. 223–24.
660. Vryonis, *The Mechanism of Catastrophe*, pp. 34, 35, 39.
661. D. E. Webster, *The Turkey of Atatürk* (Philadelphia: 1939), pp. 280–81.
662. *The Position of the Jewish Communities in Oriental Countries*, submitted March 1946 to the Anglo-American Committee of Inquiry by the Jewish Agency for Palestine, and published in Jerusalem, 1947, pp. 16–17.
663. Data compiled from the 1927 Turkish census, reproduced in Webster, *The Turkey of Atatürk*, table 3, p. 50; an assessment by the Simon Wiesenthal Center, "Turkey-Demography," using statistics from *Encyclopedia Judaica* (1972), http://motlc.learningcenter .wiesenthal.org/text/x33/xm3316.html; and, for 1964, a report dated April 5, 1964, published in *Tages Nachtrichten*, a large German-language daily from Tel Aviv, Israel.
664. "Antisemitism in the Turkish Media (Part II): Turkish Intellectuals against Antisemitism," Middle East Media Research Institute, Special Dispatch series no. 904, May 5, 2005.
665. Bernard Lewis, "Islamic Revival in Turkey," *International Affairs* 28 (1952): 48.
666. M. Hakun Yavuz, *Islamic Political Identity in*

Turkey (Oxford: 2003).Yavuz, who felt the 2002 election of the Islamist Recep Tayyip Erdogan (of the *Adalet ve Kalkınma Partisi*, AKP, or "Justice and Development Party"), vindicated his viewpoint regarding the emergence of a modern, progressive Turkish Islam, singles out Bernard Lewis in a pejorative manner, invoking the hackneyed language of Edward Said's silly polemic *Orientalism*—an intractably flawed work from 1978, which has been discredited permanently by Ibn Warraq's *Defending the West: A Critique of Edward Said's* Orientalism (Amherst, NY: Prometheus Books, 2007). Here is Yavuz's comment, from p. 261:

> The AKP's experiment with democracy reveals the failure of an authoritarian secularism that is informed by *crude orientalist conceptions, like those of Bernard Lewis* [emphasis added], that posit Islam as inherently opposed to democracy, pluralism, and modernity. Ironically, for many decades the main obstacle to full democratization in Turkey has not been Islam but rather the authoritarian secular ideology of an oppressive state elite, which found many apologists in Western circles.

667. Yavuz, *Islamic Political Identity in Turkey*, pp. 47–48, 56, 55, 56–57.

668. Vryonis, *The Mechanism of Catastrophe*, p. 555.

669. Ibid., pp. 189–289.

670. Ibid., p. 562.

671. Ibid., p. 563.

672. Cited in ibid., p. 563.

673. Yavuz, *Islamic Political Identity in Turkey*, pp. 239–64, 258.

674. Jacob Landau, "Muslim Turkish Attitudes towards Jews, Zionism, and Israel," *Die Welt des Islams* 28 (1988): 294, 292.

675. Ibid., pp. 297–98.

676. Ibid., pp. 298–99.

677. Ibid., p. 300.

678. Landau, "Muslim Turkish Attitudes towards Jews, Zionism, and Israel."

679. Yavuz, *Islamic Political Identity in Turkey*, p. 241.

679a. "Antisemitism in the Turkish Media (Part III): Targeting Turkey's Jewish Citizens," Middle East Media Research Institute, Special Disptatch series no. 916, June 6, 2005, n. 4.

680. Ibid.

681. Landau, "Muslim Turkish Attitudes towards Jews, Zionism, and Israel"; "Antisemitism in the Turkish Media (Part I)," Middle East Media Research Institute, Special Disptatch series no. 900, April 28, 2005; "Antisemitism in the Turkish Media (Part II)"; "Antisemitism in the Turkish Media (Part III)."

682. Judith Miller, "The Istanbul Synagogue Massacre: An Investigation," *New York Times*, January 4, 1987.

683. Ilene Prusher, "Turkish Jews Search for Answers," *Christian Science Monitor*, November 19, 2003.

684. Ely Karmon, "The Synagogue Bombings in Istanbul: Al-Qaeda's New Front?" Policywatch #806: *Analysis of Near East Policy*, from the Washington Institute, November 18, 2003.

685. Miller, "The Istanbul Synagogue Massacre"; Karmon, "The Synagogue Bombings in Istanbul."

686. "Antisemitism in the Turkish Media (Parts I–III)."

687. "Antisemitism in the Turkish Media (Part III)."

688. See nn. 608 and 613, above.

689. "Antisemitism in the Turkish Media (Part III)."

690. Yigal Schleifer, "One of the Kurds' Leaders Is Jewish? So They Claim in Turkish Newspapers," Jewish Telegraphic Agency, April 7, 2003.

691. "Antisemitism in the Turkish Media (Part II)."

692. *The Position of the Jewish Communities in Oriental Countries* (Jerusalem: 1946) pp. 16–17.

693. Prusher, "Turkish Jews Search for Answers."

694. Vryonis, *The Mechanism of Catastrophe*, pp. 31–32.

695. Lewis, *The Jews of Islam*, p. 166.

696. V. Minorsky, *Tadhkirat al-Muluk. A Manual of Safavid Administration* (1725; reprint, London: 1943); Walter Fischel, "The Jews in Medieval Iran from the 16th to the 18th Centuries: Political, Economic, and Communal Aspects," *Irano-Judaica* (1982): 266; Al-Amili, *Jami i Abbasi*, discussed in E. G. Browne, *A Literary History of Persia* (Cambridge: 1930), vol. 4, p. 407; Al-Majlisi, *The Treatise Lightning Bolts against the Jews*, trans. V. B. Moreen, in *Die Welt des Islams* 32 (1992), pp. 187–93. Also see Bostom, *The Legacy of Jihad*, pp. 213–20, for an original English translation of Al-Amili and a reproduction of Moreen's translation of Al-Majlisi.

697. I.e., the combined Safavid (1502–1722) and Qajar (1795–1925) periods comprised 350 years of Shi'ite theocracy, interrupted by Sunni Afghan rule from 1722 to 1795, most notably under Nadir Shah from 1734 to 1747.

698. Browne, *A Literary History of Persia*, p. 371.

699. Fischel, "The Jews in Medieval Iran," p. 266.

700. Tome Pires, *Suma Oriental (1512–1515)* (London: 1944), vol. I, p. 27.

701. Raphael du Mans, *Estat de la Perse*, ed. Schefer (1660; reprint, Paris, 1890), pp. 193–94; cited in, Fischel, "The Jews in Medieval Iran," p. 266.

702. Samuel C. Chew, *The Crescent and the Rose* (Oxford: Oxford University Press, 1937), p. 211.

703. Laurence Loeb, *Outcaste—Jewish Life In Southern Iran* (New York: 1977), p. 292.

703a. Benjamin, *Eight Years in Asia and Africa—From 1846–1855*, pp. 211–13.

703b. D. G. Littman, "Jews under Muslim Rule: The Case of Persia," *Wiener Library Bulletin* 32 (1979): 7–8.

703c. Ibid., p. 7.

704. Fischel, "The Jews in Medieval Iran," p. 275.

705. Thevenot, cited in ibid., p. 275.

706. Fryer, cited in ibid., p. 275.

707. Fischel, "The Jews in Medieval Iran," p. 275.

708. Ibid., pp. 275–76.

709. W. F. Fischel, "Isfahan—The Story of a Jewish Community in Persia," *Joshua Starr Memorial Volume, Jewish Social Studies Publication No. 5* (195): 122–23.

710. Ibid., pp. 123, 124; and Fischel, "The Jews in Medieval Iran," pp. 279–80.

711. Fischel ignores this earlier, more apposite Muslim equivalent (and possible learned prototype) of the persecutions in late fifteenth-century Spain, i.e., the Muslim Almohad persecutions in both Spain and North Africa of the mid- to late twelfth century. See nn. 520–27, above, and the accompanying discussion.

712. Fischel, "Isfahan," p. 124.

713. This threat is confirmed in an independent account from the *Kitab-i-Anusi*, excerpts translated by V. B. Moreen, *Iranian Jewry's Hour of Peril and Heroism—A Study of Babai Ibn Luft's Chronicle (1617–1662)* (New York/Jerusalem: 1987), p. 188.

714. English translation from Bat Ye'or, *The Decline of Eastern Christianity under Islam*, pp. 372–73.

715. *A Chronicle of the Carmelites in Persia and the Papal Mission of the 17th and 18th Centuries* (London: 1939), pp. 364–66.

716. Arnold T. Wilson, "History of the Mission of the Fathers of the Society of Jesus, Established in Persia by the Reverend Father Alexander of Rhodes," *Bulletin of the School of Oriental Studies* 3 (1925): 695.

717. The full text is reproduced herein. See pp. 331.

718. Loeb, *Outcaste*, p. 21.

718a. Al-Majlisi, "Lightning Bolts against the Jews."

719. Ignaz Goldziher, *Introduction to Islamic Theology and Law* (Princeton, NJ: 1981), p. 213.

720. Napier Malcolm, *Five Years in a Persian Town* (New York: 1905), p. 107.

721. Sorour Soroudi, "The Concept of Jewish Impurity and Its Reflection in Persian and Judeo-Persian Traditions," *Irano-Judaica* 3 (1994): 156 n. 36.

722. Loeb, *Outcaste*, p. 21.

723. Fischel, "The Jews in Medieval Iran," p. 281.

724. Ibid.

725. *A Chronicle of the Carmelites in Persia,* July 29, 1678, p. 408. Ibid., June 13, 1702, p. 474.

726. Fischel, "The Jews in Medieval Iran," p. 282.

727. Ibid., p. 283.

728. Fischel, "Isfahan," p. 126.

729. Ibid., p. 127; and W. F. Fischel, "The Jews of Persia, 1795–1940," *Jewish Social Studies* 12 (1950): 121.

730. David d'Beth Hillel, *The Travels of Rabbi David d'Beth Hillel: From Jerusalem, through Arabia, Koordistan, Part of Persia, and India to Madras*, p. 115; cited in W. J. Fischel, *The Jews of Kurdistan a Hundred*

Years Ago (New York: 1944); reprinted in *Jewish Social Studies* 6, no. 3: 223.

731. James B. Fraser, *Narrative of a Journey into Khorasan in the Years 1821 and 1822* (London: 1825), p. 182.

732. Henry A. Stern, *Dawnings of Light in the East* (London: 1854), pp. 184–85.

733. Malcolm, *Five Years in a Persian Town*, p. 108.

734. Reverend Isaac Adams, *Persia by a Persian* (Washington, DC: 1900), p. 120.

735. Soroudi, "The Concept of Jewish Impurity," p. 157.

736. D'Beth Hillel, *The Travels of Rabbi David d'Beth Hillel*, pp. 74–75, cited in Fischel, *The Jews of Kurdistan*, pp. 223–24.

737. A. Grant, *The Nestorians* (New York: 1841), pp. 382–83.

738. Fischel, *The Jews of Kurdistan*, pp. 224–25; and Fischel, *The Jews of Persia*, p. 124. After exhaustive research on the late eighteenth-century fate of the Jews of Tabriz, Amnon Netzer concluded, in "The Fate of the Jewish Community of Tabriz," in *Studies in Islamic History and Civilization in Honor of Professor David Ayalon* (Jerusalem: 1986), p. 419:

that there was, indeed, a terrible massacre of the Jews in Tabriz at some time between the years 1790–1797, and that Tabriz ceased to become a dwelling place where Jews could have a communal life for many generations to come.

739. Cited in G. N. Curzon, *Persia and the Persian Question* (1892), vol. 1, p. 166.

740. W. J. Fischel, "Secret Jews of Persia," *Commentary* (January 1949): 29.

741. Fischel, *The Jews of Persia*, pp. 124–25.

742. Loeb, *Outcaste*, p. 57.

743. C. J. Wills, *Persia as It Is* (London: 1887), pp. 229–30.

744. Ibid., pp. 23, 24.

745. Fischel, *The Jews of Persia*, pp. 134, 137.

746. Ibid., p. 142.

746a. Littman, "Jews under Muslim Rule," pp. 12–14.

747. Ibid., pp. 143–44, and Loeb, *Outcaste*, pp. 289–90.

748. Loeb, *Outcaste*, p. 291.

749. Littman, "Jews under Muslim Rule: The Case of Persia," p. 5. Littman provides a remarkably concise overview of the history of the Jewish community of Persia under Muslim rule, complemented by an impressive array of primary source documents from the archives of the Alliance Israélite Universelle (pp. 5–15), translated by the author into English, with but one exception, for the first time. The full text of Littman's landmark article, from which Bernard Lewis borrowed liberally for his discussion of Persian Jewry in *The Jews of Islam* (see especially pp. 181–83) is now available online at http://www.dhimmitude.org/archive/littman_jews_under_muslims_case_of_persia.pdf.

749a. Littman, "Jews under Muslim Rule," p. 5.

749b. David Littman, "The Ancient Jewish Community of Iran and the Shiraz 'Show Trial,'" United Nations Commission on Human Rights, January 8, 2001.

750. Sultanhussein Tabandeh, *A Muslim Commentary on the Universal Declaration of Human Rights*, trans. F. J. Goulding (London: 1970).

751. Eliz Sanasarian, *Religious Minorities in Iran* (Cambridge: 2000), p. 173, n. 92.

752. Tabandeh, *A Muslim Commentary on the Universal Declaration of Human Rights*, p. 4.

753. Netzer, "The Fate of the Jewish Community of Tabriz," p. 413. See also nn. 699–701, above.

754. Sanasarian, *Religious Minorities in Iran*, p. 25.

755. Tabandeh, *A Muslim Commentary on the Universal Declaration of Human Rights*, pp. 17, 18, 37.

756. Sanasarian, *Religious Minorities in Iran*, p. 28.

757. Ibid., p. 85.

758. S. R. (Ayatollah) Khomeini, *Principles, Politiques, Philosophiques, Sociaux et Religieux*, trans. and ed. J.-M. Xaviere (Paris: 1979); English translation of these excerpts in Bat Ye'or, *The Dhimmi*, pp. 396–97.

759. Sanasarian, *Religious Minorities in Iran*, p. 85.

760. Ibid., pp. 84–85.

761. Ibid., p. 29.

762. Sanasarian, *Religious Minorities in Iran*, p. 111.

763. Reza Afshari, *Human Rights in Iran—The Abuse of Cultural Relativism* (Philadelphia: 2001), p. 136.

764. Sanasarian, *Religious Minorities in Iran*, p. 113.

765. Afshari, *Human Rights in Iran*, p. 165.

766. Jovan Cvijic, *La Peninsule Balkanique* (Paris: 1918), pp. 387–88ff; English translation by Michael J. Miller.

767. Pooya Dayanim, "Imagine Being a Jew in Iran," *Iranian*, March 12, 2003.

768. Brian Murphy, "Iran's Jews Caught Again in No Man's Land," Associated Press, July 30, 2006. Shortly afterward (August 3, 2006), three representatives of the small remnant Moroccan Jewish community—mimicking the *dhimmi* behaviors of the Jews of Shiraz, Iran—emerged from their own usual state of self-imposed political silence to file a petition in Rabat's high court against Moroccan-born Israeli defense minister Amir Peretz, accusing him of "war crimes" committed during the same July 2006 confrontation with Hezbollah on the Lebanon-Israel northern border ("Moroccan Jews Ask Court to Try Amir Peretz for War Crimes," *Haaretz,* August 3, 2006).

769. Webman, *Anti-Semitic Motifs in the Ideology of Hizballah and Hamas*, pp. 1–15; "Nass al-Risala al-Maftuha wajahaha Hizballah ila-l-Mustad'afin fi Lubnan wa-l-Alam," *al-Safir*, February 16, 1985; English translation reproduced at: http://www.acsa2000.net/hizballah.htm.

770. Webman, *Anti-Semitic Motifs in the Ideology of Hizballah and Hamas*, p. 10.

771. "The Islamic Genocide Plan," *FrontPage Magazine.com*, December 1, 2006.

772. Ann E. Mayer, *Islam and Human Rights* (Boulder, CO: 1999), p. 141.

773. Ibid., p. 142.

774. Ibid., p. 143.

775. Ibid.

776. Dayanim, "Imagine Being a Jew in Iran."

777. Ibid.

778. Murphy, "Iran's Jews Caught Again in No Man's Land."

779. Dayanim, "Imagine Being a Jew in Iran."

779a. Chris Wattie, "Iran Eyes Badges for Jews—Law Would Require Non-Muslim Insignia," *National Post*, May 19, 2006.

779b. Chris Wattie, "Experts Say Report of Badges for Jews in Iran Is Untrue," *National Post*, May 19, 2006.

780. As of March 2007, no further information on this matter has emerged from the Iranian committee Mr. Taheri cites.

781. Amir Taheri, "Amir Taheri Addresses Queries About Dress Code Story," press release, May 22, 2006, Benador Associates, http://www.benadorassociates.com/article/19508.

782. Al-Majlisi, "Lightning Bolts against the Jews," cited in Bostom, *The Legacy of Jihad*, p. 218.

783. Loeb, *Outcaste*, p. 21.

784. Wattie, "Iran Eyes Badges for Jews"; Andrew Bostom, "The Yellow Badge of Denial," *American Thinker*, May 23, 2006.

784a. "Howard Compares Iran to Nazi Germany," *Age*, May 20, 2006.

784b. Wattie, "Iran Eyes Badges for Jews."

784c. Bostom, "The Yellow Badge of Denial."

784d. "Howard Compares Iran to Nazi Germany."

784e. Ibid.

784f. Ibid.

785. "Iranian President Ahmadinejad on the 'Myth of the Holocaust,'" Middle East Media Research Institute, Special Dispatch series no. 1091, February 14, 2006; Justus Reid Wiener et al., "Referral of Iranian President Ahmadinejad on the Charge of Incitement to Commit Genocide," Jerusalem Center for Public Affairs, 2006; Matthias Kuntzel, "Iran's Obsession with the Jews," *Weekly Standard,* February 19, 2007.

786. "Former Iranian President Rafsanjani on Using a Nuclear Bomb against Israel," Middle East Media Research Bulletin, January 3, 2002; Nazila Fathi, "Iran's President Says Israel Must Be Wiped off the Map," *New York Times*, October 26, 2005; "Iranian President at Tehran Conference," Middle East Media Research Institute, Special Dispatch series no. 1013, October 28, 2005; Wiener et al., "Referral of Iranian President Ahmadinejad on the Charge of Incitement to Commit Genocide"; Kuntzel, "Iran's Obsession with the Jews."

787. Gary Sick, "US Can Exploit Peaceful Iran Revolution," *Newsday*, June 11, 1997.

788. "Iran's Mushrooming Threat," *Washington Times*, June 15, 2004.

789. Michael Rubin, "Iran's Burgeoning WMD Programs," *Middle East Intelligence Bulletin* 4, no. 3 (March/April 2002), http://www.meib.org/articles/0203 _irn1.htm

790. "Former Iranian President Rafsanjani on Using a Nuclear Bomb against Israel."

791. Kuntzel, "Iran's Obsession with the Jews."

792. "Iran's President Says Israel Must Be Wiped off the Map."

793. "Iranian President at Tehran Conference."

794. "Iranian President Ahmadinejad on the 'Myth of the Holocaust.'"

795. Kuntzel, "Iran's Obsession with the Jews."

796. "President Ahmadinejad: 'I Have a Connection with God, since God Said that the Infidels Will Have No Way to Harm the Believers . . .'" Middle East Media Research Institute, Special Dispatch series no. 1328, October 19, 2006.

797. Wiener et al., "Referral of Iranian President Ahmadinejad on the Charge of Incitement to Commit Genocide."

798. Ibid.

799. Kuntzel, "Iran's Obsession with the Jews."

800. Raul Hilberg, "The Goldhagen Phenomenon," *Critical Inquiry* 23 (1997): 721–28.

801. Daniel Goldhagen, *Hitler's Willing Executioners—Ordinary Germans and the Holocaust* (New York: 1996).

802. Daniel Goldhagen, "Iran Bares 'Genocidal Intent,'" *New York Sun*, November 3, 2005.

803. Ibid.

804. Using four powerful academic search engines—Google Scholar, JSTOR, ATLA Religion Database, and Academic Search Premier—and examining his own Web site (http://www.goldhagen.com), I discovered only two additional examples (i.e., beyond the brief opinion editorial "Iran Bares 'Genocidal Intent,'" cited above) of Goldhagen's writings on Islam: an essay published in the *New Republic* online from March 13, 2006, entitled "The New Threat—The Radical Politics of Islamic Fundamentalism," and a brief note replying to a reader's criticism of that essay, published April 17, 2006. Neither of these works reveals the slightest familiarity with Islamic doctrines or history, let alone any specific understanding of the historical plight of Iranian Jewry under Shi'ite rule.

805. Hilberg, "The Goldhagen Phenomenon."

806. Karl Jung, "The Symbolic Life," *The Collected Works* (Princeton, NJ: 1939), vol. 18, p. 281.

807. Ibid.

808. A recently discovered letter, however (Kate Connolly, "Letter Proves Speer Knew of Holocaust Plan," *Guardian*, March 13, 2007), indicates that despite repeated claims he was unaware of Nazi plans to exterminate the Jews, Speer attended a conference in 1943 where Heinrich Himmler, the head of the SS and Gestapo, made clear the Nazi regime's genocidal program during what has become known as the Posen speech. Writing in 1971 to Helen Jeanty, widow of a Belgian resistance leader, Speer admitted,

There is no doubt—I was present as Himmler announced on October 6, 1943, that all Jews would be killed. . . . Who would believe me that I suppressed this, that it would have been easier to have written all of this in my memoirs?

808a. Albert Speer, *Inside the Third Reich* (New York: 1970), p. 96.

809. Charles Emmanuel Dufourcq, however, recounts how the Arab jihad ravages of western Europe continued apace after their defeat at Tours. The Arab invaders found the Mediterranean regions of France, Italy, and Sicily, "more attractive" prey, in particular the churches and monasteries. Dufourcq wrote (from Bostom, *The Legacy of Jihad*, pp. 421–22):

Around 734–735 they stormed and took Arles and Avignon. From the coast of Provence and in Italy, their sailors preceded the cavalry or substituted for them. In 846 they disembarked at the mouth of the Tiber, seized Ostia, went up the river, refrained from attacking the wall of Rome, but pillaged the Basilicas of Saint Peter and Saint Paul, which at that time were both outside the walls. This alarm prompted, as a counter-measure, the construction of a new Roman enclosure encompassing Saint Peter's and rejoining the old one at the Castello Santangelo, the old mausoleum of the Emperor Hadrian. In 849 the Moslems attempted a new landing at Ostia; then, every year from around 857 on, they threatened the Roman seaboard.

In order to get rid of them, Pope John VIII decided in 878 to promise them an annual payment of several thousand gold pieces; but this tribute of the Holy See to Islam seems to have been paid for only two years; and from time to time until the beginning of the tenth century, the Moslems reappeared at the mouth of the Tiber or along the coast nearby.

Marseilles, for its part, was also hit: in 838 the Arabs landed there and devastated it; St. Victor's Abbey, outside the walls, was destroyed, and many inhabitants of the city were carried off in captivity; ten years later a new raid occurred, the Old Port was again sacked. And this perhaps was repeated once more around the year 920.

The whole Italian peninsula was similarly exposed: around 840, Moslem ships followed the Adriatic coasts as far as the Dalmatian archipelago and the mouth of the Pô River. Then, returning South, they dared to attack a city, Ancona, some two hundred kilometers northwest of Rome; a sort of commando dashed ashore: the city was devastated and set on fire.

During their conquest of Sicily, when they took Syracuse in 878, after a deadly attack, they were exasperated by the resistance that they met with. When they rushed into the city, they found along their way the Church of the Holy Savior, filled with women and children, the elderly and the sick, clerics and slaves, and they massacred them all. Then, spreading out through the city, they continued the slaughter and the pillage, had the treasure of the cathedral handed over to them; they also took many prisoners and gathered separately those who were armed. One week later all of the captives who had dared to fight against them were butchered (four thousand in number, according to the chronicle *al-Bayyan*). In 934 or 935, they landed at the other end of Italy, at Genoa, killed "all the men" they found there, and then left again, loading onto their ships "the treasures of the city and of its churches." A few years later they settled for a time, it seems, in Nice, Fréjus, Toulon. . . .

One could list many other similar facts. Generally speaking, in these Arab raids carried out by a cavalcade or after a landing, the churches were especially targeted, because the assailants knew that they would find there articles used in worship that were made of gold or silver, sometimes studded with precious stones, as well as costly fabrics. And because the churches were considered to be an offense against God, the One God, given that they were consecrated to the "polytheistic" belief in the Trinity, they were then burned down. The bells were the object of particular animosity, because they dared to amplify the call to infidel prayer by resounding through the skies, towards heaven; therefore they were always broken.

810. Albert Speer, *Inside the Third Reich* (New York: 1970), p. 96.

811. Lukasz Hirszowicz, *The Third Reich and the Arab East* (London: 1966), pp. 315–16.

811a. Ibid., p. 46.

812. Ibid., p. 315.

813. *The Fourth Conference of the Academy of Islamic Research*; D. F. Green, *Arab Theologians on Jews and Israel*; Bat Ye'or, "The New Egyptian Jew Hatred—Local Elements and External Influences," in *Jews in Egypt* [Hebrew] (Jerusalem: 1974); full English translation of the original French by Susan Emanuel is presented herein pp. 613; Tantawi, *Banu Isra'il fi al-Qur'an wa al-Sunna*.

814. Hirszowicz, *The Third Reich and the Arab East*, p. 27.

815. Ibid., p. 30.

816. Ibid., p. 129.

817. Ibid., p. 77.

818. Ibid., p. 165.

819. Schechtman, *The Mufti and the Fuehrer*, p. 110.

820. Hirszowicz, *The Third Reich and the Arab East*, pp. 218–19. See also earlier reference (n. 461) to the Einsatzgruppe Egypt.

821. Hirszowicz, *The Third Reich and the Arab East*, p. 227.

822. Ibid., pp. 312–13.

823. Robert Satloff, *Among the Righteous—Lost Stories from the Holocaust's Long Reach into Arab Lands* (New York: 2006).

824. Ibid., p. 171; Raoul Gustav Wallenberg (August 4, 1912–?) was a Swedish humanitarian sent to Hungary under diplomatic cover to save Hungarian Jews from the Holocaust (see http://www1.yadvashem.org/search/index_search.html). According to Per Anger (d. 2002), a Swedish diplomat awarded as a "Righteous among the Nations" by the State of Israel and Yad Vashem in 1982, and also Wallenberg's friend and colleague during World War II (see Elizabeth R. Skoglund, *A Quiet Courage: Per Anger, Wallenberg's Co-Liberator of Hungarian Jews* [Grand Rapids, MI: 1997]), Wallenberg must be credited with saving at least one hundred thousand Jews.

825. Ibid., pp. 18–19.

825a. Ibid., p. 19.

826. Ibid., pp. 19–20.

827. Ibid., pp. 20–21.

828. Jacques Sabille, *Les Juifs de Tunisie sous Vichy et L'occupation* (Paris: 1954), p. 137; cited in Satloff, *Among the Righteous*, p. 73.

829. Satloff, *Among the Righteous*, p. 74.

830. Ibid., p. 75.

831. Ibid., pp. 68–71; 80–85.

832. Ibid., pp. 69–70.

833. Ibid., pp. 82–83.

834. Ibid., pp. 84–85.

835. Ibid., pp. 79, 160.

836. Matti Friedman, "Khaled Abdelwahhab of Tunisia First Arab Nominated for the 'Righteous among Nations' Holocaust Honor," Associated Press, January 30, 2007.

837. *Frankfurter Illustrierte*, August 25, 1957. This citation, and the following references, which provide a more comprehensive listing of Nazis and their World War II and post–World War II activities in the Arab Middle East, especially Egypt and Syria, come from Bat Ye'or. *Eurabia*, p. 328, n. 9: Institute of Jewish Affairs, *Pattern of Prejudice* (May/June 1967); Michel Tatu in *Le Monde*, June 9, 1967; M. S. Arnoni, *Le Nationalisme Arabe et les Nazis* (Tel Aviv: 1970); Yahudiya Masriya [aka Bat Ye'or], *Les Juifs en Egypte* (Geneva: 1971), pp. 66–69.

838. Bat Ye'or, *Eurabia—The Euro-Arab Axis* (Cranbury, NJ: 2005), p. 42.

838a. D. F. Green, *Arab Theologians on Jews and Israel*, p. 87.

839. Ibid.

840. See n. 663, above.

841. Stillman, *The Jews of Arab Lands in Modern Times*, p. 141.

842. Bat Ye'or, "The *Dhimmi* Factor in the Exodus of Jews from Arab Countries," in *The Forgotten Millions— The Modern Jewish Exodus from Arab Lands*, ed. Malka Shulewitz (London: 1999), p. 44; Stillman, *The Jews of Arab Lands in Modern Times*, pp. 178, 179.

843. Bat Ye'or, "The *Dhimmi* Factor in the Exodus of Jews from Arab Countries," p. 44.

844. Stillman, *The Jews of Arab Lands in Modern Times*, p. 178.

845. Ibid.

846. Ibid., pp. 178–79.

847. See n. 170, above.

848. *The Fourth Conference of the Academy of Islamic Research*; Green, *Arab Theologians on Jews and Israel*; Bat Ye'or, "The New Egyptian Jew Hatred."

849. Stillman, *The Jews of Arab Lands in Modern Times*, p. 179.

850. Ya'acov Meron, "The Expulsion of the Jews from the Arab Countries: The Palestinians' Attitude towards It and Their Claims," in *The Forgotten Millions—The Modern Jewish Exodus from Arab Lands*, ed. Malka Shulewitz (London: 1999), p. 84.

851. Ibid.

852. David Littman, "Historical Facts and Figures: The Forgotten Jewish Refugees from Arab Countries," UN Commission on Human Rights, written statement, July 17, 2003, E/CN.4/Sub.2/2003/NGO/35.

853. "The Report of the Iraqi Commission of Inquiry on the Farhud (1941)," in Stillman, *The Jews of Arab Lands in Modern Times*, p. 414; Schechtman, *The Mufti and the Fuehrer*, p. 115.

854. Stillman, *The Jews of Arab Lands in Modern Times*, pp. 142–46.

855. Renzo de Felice, *Jews in an Arab Land: Libya, 1835–1970*, trans. Judith Roumani (Austin, TX: 1985), pp. 193–94, 365 n. 19; Stillman, *The Jews of Arab Lands in Modern Times*, pp. 143–46; Naim Kattan, *Farewell Babylon*, trans. Sheila Fischman (New York: 1976), pp. 16–25; Elie Kedourie, *The Chatham House Version and Other Middle Eastern Studies* (Hanover, NH: 1984), pp. 307–309, 447 n. 55.

856. Stillman, *The Jews of Arab Lands in Modern Times*, p. 119.

857. Ibid.

858. Kattan, *Farewell Babylon*, pp. 16, 23.

858a. Kedourie, *The Chatham House Version*, pp. 307–309, 447 n. 55.

859. Stillman, *The Jews of Arab Lands in Modern Times*, pp. 142–46.

860. Ibid., pp. 142–43.

861. Thomas Mayer, *Egypt and the Palestine Question—1936–1945* (Berlin: 1983), p. 300.

862. Stillman, *The Jews of Arab Lands in Modern Times*, p. 144.

863. De Felice, *Jews in an Arab Land*, pp. 193–94, p. 365 n. 19.

864. Stillman, *The Jews of Arab Lands in Modern Times*, p. 145.

865. Ibid., p. 146.

866. Ibid., p. 147.

867. Ibid., pp. 147–48.

868. Ibid., pp. 148, 149, 150.

869. Barry Rubin, *The Arab States and the Palestine Conflict* (Syracuse, NY: 1981), pp. 200–202.

870. Stillman, *The Jews of Arab Lands in Modern Times*, p. 152.

871. Ibid., p. 153.

872. Ibid., pp. 153–54.

873. Ibid., pp. 154–55.

874. Ibid., pp. 155–69.

875. Ibid., pp. 170–76.

876. Ibid., pp. 155–76.

877. Ibid., p. 172.

878. Ibid., p. 173.

879. Ibid., pp. 173–74.

880. Ibid., p. 174.

881. Ibid.

882. Ibid.

883. Said Ghallab, "Les juifs sont en efer," *Les Temps Modernes* 277 (1965): 2247, 2249, 2251; English translation in David Littman and Bat Ye'or, "Protected Peoples in Islam," in *The Myth of Islamic Tolerance*, ed. Robert Spencer (Amherst, NY: Prometheus Books, 2005), p. 95.

884. Littman, "Historical Facts and Figures: The Forgotten Jewish Refugees from Arab Countries"; Stillman, *The Jews of Arab Lands in Modern Times*, p. 175.

885. Littman, "Historical Facts and Figures: The Forgotten Jewish Refugees from Arab Countries."

886. Ibid.

887. Stillman, *The Jews of Arab Lands in Modern Times*, p. 177.

888. Meron, "The Expulsion of the Jews from the Arab Countries," p. 83.

889. Friedman, *Without Future*.

890. Ibid., esp. p. 36 and p. 115 for Brunner quote; see also "The Damascus Blood Libel (1840) as Told by Syria's Minister of Defense, Mustafa Tlass," Middle East Media Research Institute Inquiry and Analysis Series, no. 99, June 27, 2002; and n. 87a, above, "Speech of President Bashar Al-Assad Welcoming His Holiness Pope John Paul II on His Arrival in Damascus." During his speech, Bashar puts the "torture" of Jesus (Isa) in an Islamic context consistent with Qur'an 2:61/3:112, which accuses the Jews of murdering the prophets, a motif "updated" with "flawless" logic in the hadith, when Muhammad is poisoned by a Khaybar Jewess, and ultimately suffers a protracted, painful death traced to this incident.

891. Friedman, *Without Future*, pp. 29–30.

892. Ibid., pp. 31, 32.

893. Ibid., pp. 109, 119–20.

894. "Two Men Convicted in Tunisia Bombing," CNN.com, May 10, 2006, http://www.cnn.com/2006/WORLD/europe/05/10/spain.tunisia.bombing/; Littman, "Historical Facts and Figures."

895. See nn. 683 and 684, above.

896. Aaron Klein, "Jews Flee Homes after Muslim Death Threats," *WorldNet Daily*, January 22, 2007; "Islamists Threaten Yemeni Jews for Selling Wine," Reuters, January 29, 2007. A March 18, 2007, report ("Muslims Forcing Christian Assyrians in Baghdad Neighborhoods to Pay 'Protection Tax,'" Assyrian International News Agency) demonstrates the living legacy of such practices in the contemporary Muslim world. This account from Iraq states:

> Muslims in the Dora neighborhood [of Baghdad] are forcing Assyrians to pay the *jizya*. . . . At least two cases have been reported to a government employee—who wishes to remain anonymous—in which the Christian Assyrian wives were instructed to go to a certain mosque and pay, which they did out of fear. The stated reason for the payment was "we do the fighting and you pay to support."

An independent report ("Islamic Groups Impose Tax on Christian 'Subjects'") published in the March 19, 2007, *Asia News* (http://www.asianews.it/index.php?l=en&art =8773&size=A#) indicated enforcing *jizya* payments was a more widespread phenomenon in Iraq, and part of a larger Islamization effort:

> "Non-Muslim subjects must pay a contribution to the *jihad* if they wish to be allowed to live and practice their faith in Iraq." These orders are being imposed on the Christians of Mosul and Baghdad by Islamic militias. Besides these threats of extortion, thousands of non-Muslims are also being forced to leave their homes by letters assigning their houses to Muslim citizens. The initiative is part of the general campaign to Islamafy the entire country, which began with the imposition of the veil on all women. . . . *According to local Christians it really is a contribution to the holy war, which—the jihad maintains—will also protect their community from external aggression.* The monies collected are then given over to Mosques, but "without the knowledge of authorities." Other accounts tell of letters being left in gardens or the entrance to Christian homes, notifying the families that they must leave their dwellings because they have been assigned to others, whose names and surnames are listed in black and white in the letters.

897. Klein, "Jews Flee Homes after Muslim Death Threats."

898. Vajda, "Juifs et musulmans selon le hadit."

899. Georges Vajda, "L'image du Juif dans le Tradition Islamique," *Les Nouveaux Cahiers* 13–14 (1968): 7; English translation in David Littman and Bat Ye'or, "Protected Peoples in Islam," p. 106.

900. Lewis, *The Jews of Islam*, p. 85.

901. Lewis, "The New Antisemitism," p. 29.

902. See earlier sections of this introductory survey entitled "Antisemitism in the Qur'an" and "Antisemitism in the Hadith and Early Muslim Biographies of Muhammad."

903. Hirschfeld, "Essai sur l'histoire des Juifs de Medine."

904. Vajda, "Juifs et musulmans selon le hadit."

905. Ben-Shammai, "Jew-Hatred in the Islamic Tradition and Qur'anic Exegesis."

906. Friedman, "The Myth of Islamic Toleration."

907. See nn. 35–37.

908. Aaron Klein, "Abbas Urges: 'Raise Rifles against Israel,'" *WorldNet Daily*, January 11, 2007.

909. See nn. 30–38.

910. See n. 50.

911. See nn. 41–42.

912. See nn. 72–80.

913. See n. 236.

914. See nn. 237, 257–60.

915. See nn. 238–42.

916. See nn. 243–54, 248, 260a.

917. See nn. 246, 247, 255.

918. See nn. 255, 256, and earlier related discussion associated with nn. 85–87.

919. See nn. 257–60.

920. See nn. 261–62.

921. See nn. 297–98.

922. See nn. 299–300.

923. See nn. 310–23.

924. See n. 324.

925. See n. 325.

926. See nn. 320–21, 331–39.

927. See nn. 340–44.

928. See nn. 345–49.

929. See nn. 85–87.

930. See nn. 6–12.

931. See nn. 58–64d.

932. See nn. 65, 66, and further related elaboration in nn. 67–69.

933. For multiple examples of both chronic discrimination and incitement based upon these motifs, see nn. 87a, 91–93, 95–98, 101–10, 114a–e, 189–215.

934. See nn. 262a–d.

935. See nn. 189–204.

936. For al-Maghili's verse, see n. 158a; for more on al-Mahgili, see nn. 153–159a.

937. See nn. 208–213.

938. See n. 213.

939. Bat Ye'or, "The New Egyptian Jew Hatred—Local Elements and External Influences."

939a. Bat Ye'or, *Les Juifs en Egypte* (Geneva: 1971),

pp. 66–69, annexe I, "Nazis Au Caire," and p. 69, annexe II, "Liste D'Ouvrages Antisemites Publies Au Caire"; Irving Sedar and Harold Greenberg, *Behind the Egyptian Sphinx* (Philadelphia: 1960), pp. 76–78; O. John Rogge, *The Official German Report* (New York: 1961), p. 380; Gregory Paul Wegner, "A Propagandist of Extermination: Johann von Leers and the Antisemitic Formation of Children in Nazi Germany," *Paedagogica Historica* 43 (2007): 299–325.

939b. Johann von Leers, "Judentum und Islam als Gegensatze," *Die Judenfrage in Politik, Recht, and Wirtschaft* 6, no. 24 (December 24, 1942): 275–78. A full translation of this essay by Steven Rendall ("Judaism and Islam as Opposites") is provided in part 8. I first learned of this essay by von Leers while reading Joel Fishman, "The Big Lie and the Media War against Israel: From Inversion of the Truth to Inversion of Reality," *Jerusalem Center for Public Affairs*, July 29, 2007, http://www.jcpa.org/JCPA/Templates/ShowPage.asp?D BID=1&TMID=111&LNGID=1&FID=388&PID=0&II D=1704. Fishman, in turn cited Jeffrey Herf, *The Jewish Enemy—Nazi Propaganda during World War II and the Holocaust* (Cambridge, MA: 2006), pp. 180–81, as his source. Herf included a very limited English translation extract of von Leers's conclusions. Oddly, Herf made no mention of von Leers's subsequent conversion to Islam, and was also oblivious to the Nazi author's thorough grounding in, and accurate representation of, the pious Muslim sources (i.e., Qur'an, hadith, and sira). Fishman, in contrast, did make note of von Leers's conversion to Islam.

939c. Von Leers, "Judentum und Islam als Gegensatze."

939d. Ibid.; see earlier extensive discussions, especially "Antisemitism in the Hadith and Early Muslim Biographies of Muhammad," p. 56.

939e. See earlier discussion of Muhammad's poisoning by a Khaybar Jewess in relation to nn. 256, 263, and 343–44.

939f. See earlier discussion of this hadith in relation to nn. 262a–d.

939g. See earlier discussion of this hadith in relation to nn. 257–59, and 264–65.

939h. Von Leers may be referring to any number of regulations discussed in particular in relation to the Jews of North Africa (see nn. 38–40 from "A Note on the Cover Art"; see also nn. 114d–e for additional discussion of the Moroccan mellah), Yemen (see n. 114c), and historical Palestine (see n. 419), but other examples could be adduced from virtually every domain in which Jews lived under Islamic law (see nn. 587–96, and 606–19, for Turkey and Bosnia during Ottoman rule, for example).

940. Bernard Lewis, *Islam, from the Prophet Muhammad to the Capture of Constantinople* (New York: 1947), p. 217.

941. Lewis, *The Jews of Islam*, pp. 54–55.

942. See n. 121.

943. See nn. 122–23.

944. See n. 124.

945. S. D. Goitein, "Evidence on the Muslim Poll Tax from Non-Muslim Sources," *Journal of the Economic and Social History of the Orient* 6 (1963): 278–79.

946. S. D. Goitein, "Minority Self-Rule and Government Control in Islam," *Studia Islamica* 31 (1970): 101, 104–106.

947. S. D. Goitein, "Origin and Significance of North African Jewry," in *Proceedings of the Seminar on Muslim-Jewish Relations in North Africa* (Princeton, NJ: 1974), p. 12.

948. Bat Ye'or, *The Dhimmi*, p. 67; Bat Ye'or, *The Decline of Eastern Christianity under Islam*, pp. 252, 254.

949. Goitein, "Evidence on the Muslim Poll Tax from Non-Muslim Sources."

950. Ibid., and Goitein, *A Mediterranean Society*, vol. 2, pp. 278–83, and also pp. 586–87 nn. 14–25.

951. Stillman, *The Jews of Arab Lands*; Stillman, *The Jews of Arab Lands in Modern Times*.

952. Bat Ye'or, *The Dhimmi*; Bat Ye'or, *The Decline of Eastern Christianity under Islam*.

953. For example: Fagnan, "Le Signe Distinctif des Juifs au Maghreb"; Gil, *A History of Palestine*; Hirschberg, *A History of the Jews of North Africa*; Gerber, *Jewish Society in Fez*; and Jane Gerber, "The Pact of Umar in North Africa: A Reappraisal of Muslim-Jewish Relations," in *Proceedings of the Seminar on Muslim-Jewish Relations in North Africa* (Princeton, NJ: 1974), pp. 40–50; Bashan, "New Documents on Attacks on Jewish Religious Life in Morocco in the Last Third of the 19th Century"; Littman, "Jews under Muslim Rule, II"; Levy, "Die Sephardim in Bosnien"; Loeb, *Outcaste*; Ratzaby, "Expulsion to the Desert—The Most Decisive Event in the History of the Jews of Yemen"; and Yosef Tobi, "Conversion to Islam among Yemenite Jews under Zaidi Rule," *Pe'amim* 42 (1990): 105–26.

954. Gerber, "Towards an Understanding of the Term"; Hacker, "Ottoman Policy toward the Jews and Jewish Attitudes toward the Ottomans"; and Hacker, "The Sürgün System and Jewish Society in the Ottoman Empire."

955. George Conger, "UK MPs Find Leap in Antisemitism," *Jerusalem Post*, September 5, 2006.

956. Ibid.

957. Ibid.

958. Edward H. Kaplan and Charles H. Small, "Anti-Israel Sentiment Predicts Antisemitism in Europe," *Journal of Conflict Resolution* 50 (2006): 548–61.

959. Ibid., p. 557 and p. 558, table 3.

960. "The Great Divide: How Westerners and Muslims View Each Other," *Pew Global Attitudes Project*, June 22, 2006.

961. Lewis, "The New Antisemitism," and previously, all the references cited in n. 18.

962. Nidra Poller, "The Murder of Ilan Halimi," *Wall Street Journal*, February 26, 2006.

PART 2

❖❖❖

Anti-Jewish Motifs in the Qur'an and Its Exegesis

CHAPTER 2

Qur'anic Verses

THE QUR'ANIC CURSE UPON THE JEWS (QUR'AN 2:61, 3:112) AND RELATED VERSES

2:61

(Pickthall) And when ye said: O Moses! We are weary of one kind of food; so call upon thy Lord for us that He bring forth for us of that which the earth groweth—of its herbs and its cucumbers and its corn and its lentils and its onions. He said: Would ye exchange that which is higher for that which is lower? Go down to settled country, thus ye shall get that which ye demand. And humiliation and wretchedness were stamped upon them and they were visited with wrath from Allah. That was because they disbelieved in Allah's revelations and slew the prophets wrongfully. That was for their disobedience and transgression.

(Shakir) And when you said: O Musa! we cannot bear with one food, therefore pray Lord on our behalf to bring forth for us out of what the earth grows, of its herbs and its cucumbers and its garlic and its lentils and its onions. He said: Will you exchange that which is better for that which is worse? Enter a city, so you will have what you ask for. And abasement and humiliation were brought down upon them, and they became deserving of Allah's wrath; this was so because they disbelieved in the communications of Allah and killed the prophets unjustly; this was so because they disobeyed and exceeded the limits.

(Arberry) And when you said, "Moses, we will not endure one sort of food; pray to thy Lord for us, that He may bring forth for us of that the earth produces—green herbs, cucumbers, corn, lentils, onions." He said, "Would you have in exchange what is meaner for what is better? Get you down to Egypt; you shall have there that you demanded." And abasement and poverty were pitched upon them, and they were laden with the burden of God's anger; that, because they had disbelieved the signs of God and slain the Prophets unrightfully; that, because they disobeyed, and were transgressors.

3:112

(Pickthall) Ignominy shall be their portion wheresoever they are found save (where they grasp) a rope from Allah and a rope from men. They have incurred anger from their Lord, and wretchedness is laid upon them. That is because they used to disbelieve the revelations of Allah, and slew the prophets wrongfully. That is because they were rebellious and used to transgress.

(Shakir) Abasement is made to cleave to them wherever they are found, except under a covenant with Allah and a covenant with men, and they have become deserving of wrath from Allah, and humiliation is made to cleave to them; this is because they disbelieved in the communications of Allah and slew the prophets unjustly; this is because they disobeyed and exceeded the limits.

(Arberry) Abasement shall be pitched on them, wherever they are come upon, except they be in a bond of God, and a bond of the people; they will be laden with the burden of God's anger, and poverty shall be pitched on them; that, because they disbelieved in God's signs, and slew the Prophets without right; that, for that they acted rebelliously and were transgressors.

❖❖❖

5:78

(Pickthall) Those of the Children of Israel who went astray were cursed by the tongue of David, and of Jesus, son of Mary. That was because they rebelled and used to transgress.

(Shakir) Those who disbelieved from among the children of Israel were cursed by the tongue of Dawood and Isa, son of Marium; this was because they disobeyed and used to exceed the limit.

The three translations are as follows: Marmaduke William Pickthall, *The Glorious Qur'an* (Elmhurst, NY: 2001); M. H. Shakir, *The Qur'an Translation* (Elmhurst, NY: 1999); A. J. Arberry, *The Koran Interpreted: A Translation* (New York: 1996).

(Arberry) Cursed were the unbelievers of the Children of Israel by the tongue of David, and Jesus, Mary's son; that, for their rebelling and their transgression.

5:64

(Pickthall) The Jews say: Allah's hand is fettered. Their hands are fettered and they are accursed for saying so. Nay, but both His hands are spread out wide in bounty. He bestoweth as He will. That which hath been revealed unto thee from thy Lord is certain to increase the contumacy and disbelief of many of them, and We have cast among them enmity and hatred till the Day of Resurrection. As often as they light a fire for war, Allah extinguisheth it. Their effort is for corruption in the land, and Allah loveth not corrupters.

(Shakir) And the Jews say: The hand of Allah is tied up! Their hands shall be shackled and they shall be cursed for what they say. Nay, both His hands are spread out, He expends as He pleases; and what has been revealed to you from your Lord will certainly make many of them increase in inordinacy and unbelief; and We have put enmity and hatred among them till the day of resurrection; whenever they kindle a fire for war Allah puts it out, and they strive to make mischief in the land; and Allah does not love the mischief-makers.

(Arberry) The Jews have said, "God's hand is fettered." Fettered are their hands, and they are cursed for what they have said. Nay, but His hands are outspread; He expends how He will. And what has been sent down to thee from thy Lord will surely increase many of them in insolence and unbelief. And We have cast between them enmity and hatred, till the Day of Resurrection. As often as they light a fire for war, God will extinguish it. They hasten about the earth, to do corruption there; and God loves not the workers of corruption.

9:29

(Pickthall) Fight against such of those who have been given the Scripture as believe not in Allah nor the Last Day, and forbid not that which Allah hath forbidden by His messenger, and follow not the Religion of Truth, until they pay the tribute readily, being brought low.

(Shakir) Fight those who do not believe in Allah, nor in the latter day, nor do they prohibit what Allah and His Apostle have prohibited, nor follow the religion of truth, out of those who have been given the Book, until they pay the tax in acknowledgment of superiority and they are in a state of subjection.

(Arberry) Fight those who believe not in God and the Last Day and do not forbid what God and His Messenger have

forbidden—such men as practise not the religion of truth, being of those who have been given the Book—until they pay the tribute out of hand and have been humbled.

Sins and punishments: the Jews wronged themselves (16:118) by losing faith (7:168) and breaking their covenant (5:13). The Jews (echoing an ante-Nicaean polemic) are a nation that has passed away (2:134; repeated in 2:141). Twice Allah sent his instruments (the Assyrians/or Babylonians, and Romans) to punish this perverse people (17:4–5)—their dispersal over the earth is proof of Allah's rejection (7:168). The Jews are further warned about both their arrogant claim that they remain Allah's chosen people (62:6), and continued disobedience and "corruption" (5:32–33).

16:118

(Pickthall) And unto those who are Jews We have forbidden that which We have already related unto thee. And We wronged them not, but they were wont to wrong themselves.

(Shakir) And for those who were Jews We prohibited what We have related to you already, and We did them no injustice, but they were unjust to themselves.

(Arberry) And those of Jewry—We have forbidden them what We related to thee before, and We wronged them not, but they wronged themselves.

7:168

(Pickthall) And We have sundered them in the earth as (separate) nations. Some of them are righteous, and some far from that. And We have tried them with good things and evil things that haply they might return.

(Shakir) And We cut them up on the earth into parties, (some) of them being righteous and (others) of them falling short of that, and We tried them with blessings and misfortunes that they might turn.

(Arberry) And We cut them up into nations in the earth, some of them righteous, and some of them otherwise; and We tried them with good things and evil, that haply they should return.

5:13

(Pickthall) And because of their breaking their covenant, We have cursed them and made hard their hearts. They change words from their context and forget a part of that whereof they were admonished. Thou wilt not cease to discover treachery from all save a few of them. But bear with them and pardon them. Lo! Allah loveth the kindly.

(Shakir) But on account of their breaking their covenant We cursed them and made their hearts hard; they altered the words from their places and they neglected a portion of what they were reminded of; and you shall always discover treachery in them excepting a few of them; so pardon them and turn away; surely Allah loves those who do good (to others).

(Arberry) So for their breaking their compact We cursed them and made their hearts hard, they perverting words from their meanings; and they have forgotten a portion of that they were reminded of; and thou wilt never cease to light upon some act of treachery on their part, except a few of them. Yet pardon them, and forgive; surely God loves the good-doers.

2:134

(Pickthall) Those are a people who have passed away. Theirs is that which they earned, and yours is that which ye earn. And ye will not be asked of what they used to do.

(Shakir) This is a people that have passed away; they shall have what they earned and you shall have what you earn, and you shall not be called upon to answer for what they did.

(Arberry) That is a nation that has passed away; there awaits them that they have earned, and there awaits you that you have earned; you shall not be questioned concerning the things they did.

2:141

(Pickthall) Those are a people who have passed away; theirs is that which they earned and yours that which ye earn. And ye will not be asked of what they used to do.

(Shakir) This is a people that have passed away; they shall have what they earned and you shall have what you earn, and you shall not be called upon to answer for what they did.

(Arberry) That is a nation that has passed away; there awaits them that they have earned, and there awaits you that you have earned; you shall not be questioned concerning the things they did.

17:4–5

(Pickthall) And We decreed for the Children of Israel in the Scripture: Ye verily will work corruption in the earth twice, and ye will become great tyrants. So when the time for the first of the two came, We roused against you slaves of Ours of great might who ravaged (your) country, and it was a threat performed.

(Shakir) And We had made known to the children of Israel in the Book: Most certainly you will make mischief in the land twice, and most certainly you will behave insolently with great insolence. So when the promise for the first of the two came, We sent over you Our servants, of mighty prowess, so they went to and fro among the houses, and it was a promise to be accomplished.

(Arberry) And We decreed for the Children of Israel in the Book: You shall do corruption in the earth twice, and you shall ascend exceeding high. So, when the promise of the first of these came to pass, We sent against you servants of Ours, men of great might, and they went through the habitations, and it was a promise performed.

7:168

(Pickthall) And We have sundered them in the earth as (separate) nations. Some of them are righteous, and some far from that. And We have tried them with good things and evil things that haply they might return.

(Shakir) And We cut them up on the earth into parties, (some) of them being righteous and (others) of them falling short of that, and We tried them with blessings and misfortunes that they might turn.

(Arberry) And We cut them up into nations in the earth, some of them righteous, and some of them otherwise; and We tried them with good things and evil, that haply they should return.

62:6

(Pickthall) Say (O Muhammad): O ye who are Jews! If ye claim that ye are favoured of Allah apart from (all) mankind, then long for death if ye are truthful.

(Shakir) Say: O you who are Jews, if you think that you are the favorites of Allah to the exclusion of other people, then invoke death If you are truthful.

(Arberry) Say: You of Jewry, if you assert that you are the friends of God, apart from other men, then do you long for death, if you speak truly.

5:32–33

(Pickthall) For that cause We decreed for the Children of Israel that whosoever killeth a human being for other than manslaughter or corruption in the earth, it shall be as if he had killed all mankind, and whoso saveth the life of one, it shall be as if he had saved the life of all mankind. Our messengers came unto them of old with clear proofs (of Allah's Sovereignty), but afterwards lo! many of them became prodigals in the earth. The only reward of those who make war upon Allah and His messenger and strive after corruption in the land will be that they will be killed or crucified, or have their hands and feet on alternate sides cut off, or will be expelled out of the land. Such will be their degradation in the world, and in the Hereafter theirs will be an awful doom.

(Shakir) For this reason did We prescribe to the children of Israel that whoever slays a soul, unless it be for manslaughter or for mischief in the land, it is as though he slew all men; and whoever keeps it alive, it is as though he kept alive all men; and certainly Our apostles came to them with clear arguments, but even after that many of them certainly act extravagantly in the land. The punishment of those who wage war against Allah and His apostle and strive to make mischief in the land is only this, that they should be murdered or crucified or their hands and their feet should be cut off on opposite sides or they should be imprisoned; this shall be as a disgrace for them in this world, and in the hereafter they shall have a grievous chastisement.

(Arberry) Therefore We prescribed for the Children of Israel that whoso slays a soul not to retaliate for a soul slain, nor for corruption done in the land, shall be as if he had slain mankind altogether; and whoso gives life to a soul, shall be as if he has given life to mankind altogether. Our Messengers have already come to them with the clear signs; then many of them thereafter commit excesses in the earth. This is the recompense of those who fight against God and His Messenger, and hasten about the earth, to do corruption there: they shall be slaughtered, or crucified, or their hands and feet shall alternately be struck off; or they shall be banished from the land. That is a degradation for them in this world; and in the world to come awaits them a mighty chastisement.

Other sins: abuse, even killing of prophets (4:155; 2:91), including Jesus (3:55; 4:157), is a consistent theme. The Jews ridiculed Muhammad as Ra'ina (the evil one, in 2:104; 4:46), and they are also accused of lack of faith, taking words out of context, disobedience, and distortion (4:46). Precious few of them are believers (also 4:46). These "perverse" creatures also claim that Ezra is the messiah and they worship rabbis who defraud men of their possessions (9:30).

4:155

(Pickthall) Then because of their breaking of their covenant, and their disbelieving in the revelations of Allah, and their slaying of the prophets wrongfully, and their saying: Our hearts are hardened—Nay, but Allah set a seal upon them for their disbelief, so that they believe not save a few.

(Shakir) Therefore, for their breaking their covenant and their disbelief in the communications of Allah and their killing the prophets wrongfully and their saying: Our hearts are covered; nay! Allah set a seal upon them owing to their unbelief, so they shall not believe except a few.

(Arberry) So, for their breaking the compact, and disbelieving in the signs of God, and slaying the Prophets without right, and for their saying, "Our hearts are uncircumcised"—nay, but God sealed them for their unbelief, so they believe not, except a few.

2:91

(Pickthall) And when it is said unto them: Believe in that which Allah hath revealed, they say: We believe in that which was revealed unto us. And they disbelieve in that which cometh after it, though it is the truth confirming that which they possess. Say (unto them, O Muhammad): Why then slew ye the prophets of Allah aforetime, if ye are (indeed) believers?

(Shakir) And when it is said to them, Believe in what Allah has revealed, they say: We believe in that which was revealed to us; and they deny what is besides that, while it is the truth verifying that which they have. Say: Why then did you kill Allah's Prophets before if you were indeed believers?

(Arberry) And when they were told, "Believe in that God has sent down," they said, "We believe in what was sent down on us;" and they disbelieve in what is beyond that, yet it is the truth confirming what is with them. Say: "Why then were you slaying the Prophets of God in former time, if you were believers?"

❖❖❖

3:55

(Pickthall) (And remember) when Allah said: O Jesus! Lo! I am gathering thee and causing thee to ascend unto Me, and am cleansing thee of those who disbelieve and am setting those who follow thee above those who disbelieve until the Day of Resurrection. Then unto Me ye will (all) return, and I shall judge between you as to that wherein ye used to differ.

(Shakir) And when Allah said: O Isa, I am going to terminate the period of your stay (on earth) and cause you to ascend unto Me and purify you of those who disbelieve and make those who follow you above those who disbelieve to the day of resurrection; then to Me shall be your return, so I will decide between you concerning that in which you differed.

(Arberry) When God said, "Jesus, I will take thee to Me and will raise thee to Me and I will purify thee of those who believe not. I will set thy followers above the unbelievers till the Resurrection Day. Then unto Me shall you return, and I will decide between you, as to what you were at variance on."

4:157
(Pickthall) And because of their saying: We slew the Messiah, Jesus son of Mary, Allah's messenger—they slew him not nor crucified him, but it appeared so unto them; and lo! those who disagree concerning it are in doubt thereof; they have no knowledge thereof save pursuit of a conjecture; they slew him not for certain.

(Shakir) And their saying: Surely we have killed the Messiah, Isa son of Marium, the apostle of Allah; and they did not kill him nor did they crucify him, but it appeared to them so (like Isa) and most surely those who differ therein are only in a doubt about it; they have no knowledge respecting it, but only follow a conjecture, and they killed him not for sure.

(Arberry) And for their saying, "We slew the Messiah, Jesus son of Mary, the Messenger of God"— yet they did not slay him, neither crucified him, only a likeness of that was shown to them. Those who are at variance concerning him surely are in doubt regarding him; they have no knowledge of him, except the following of surmise; and they slew him not of a certainty—no indeed.

2:104
(Pickthall) O ye who believe, say not (unto the Prophet): "Listen to us" but say "Look upon us," and be ye listeners. For disbelievers is a painful doom.

(Shakir) O you who believe! do not say *Raina* [emphasis added] and say Unzurna and listen, and for the unbelievers there is a painful chastisement.

(Arberry) O believers, do not say, "Observe us," but say, "Regard us"; and give ear; for unbelievers awaits a painful chastisement.

4:46
(Pickthall) Some of those who are Jews change words from their context and say: "We hear and disobey; hear thou as one who heareth not" and "Listen to us!" distorting with their tongues and slandering religion. If they had said: "We hear and we obey: hear thou, and look at us" it had been better for them, and more upright. But Allah hath cursed them for their disbelief, so they believe not, save a few.

(Shakir) Of those who are Jews (there are those who) alter words from their places and say: We have heard and we disobey and: Hear, may you not be made to hear! and: *Raina*, [emphasis added] distorting (the word) with their tongues and taunting about religion; and if they had said (instead): We have heard and we obey, and hearken, and Unzurna it would have been better for them and more upright; but Allah has cursed them on account of their unbelief, so they do not believe but a little.

(Arberry) Some of the Jews pervert words from their meanings saying, "We have heard and we disobey" and "Hear, and be thou not given to hear" and "Observe us," twisting with their tongues and traducing religion. If they had said, "We have heard and obey" and "Hear" and "Regard us," it would have been better for them, and more upright; but God has cursed them for their unbelief so they believe not except a few.

9:30
(Pickthall) And the Jews say: Ezra is the son of Allah, and the Christians say: The Messiah is the son of Allah. That is their saying with their mouths. They imitate the saying of those who disbelieved of old. Allah (Himself) fighteth against them. How perverse are they!

(Shakir) And the Jews say: Uzair is the son of Allah; and the Christians say: The Messiah is the son of Allah; these are the words of their mouths; they imitate the saying of those who disbelieved before; may Allah destroy them; how they are turned away!

(Arberry) The Jews say, "Ezra is the Son of God"; the Christians say, "The Messiah is the Son of God." That is the utterance of their mouths, conforming with the unbelievers before them. God assail them! How they are perverted!

Additional sins: the Jews are typified as an "envious" people (2:109), whose hearts are as hardened as rocks (2:74). They are further accused of confounding the truth (2:42), deliberately perverting scripture (2:75), and being liars (2:78). Ill-informed people of little faith (2:89), they pursue vague and wishful fancies (2:111). Other sins have contributed to their being stamped (see 2:61/3:112 above) with "wretchedness/abasement and humiliation," including—usury (2:275), sorcery (2:102), hedonism (2:96), and idol worship (2:53).

2:109

(Pickthall) Many of the people of the Scripture long to make you disbelievers after your belief, through envy on their own account, after the truth hath become manifest unto them. Forgive and be indulgent (toward them) until Allah give command. Lo! Allah is Able to do all things.

(Shakir) Many of the followers of the Book wish that they could turn you back into unbelievers after your faith, out of envy from themselves, (even) after the truth has become manifest to them; but pardon and forgive, so that Allah should bring about His command; surely Allah has power over all things.

(Arberry) Many of the People of the Book wish they might restore you as unbelievers, after you have believed, in the jealousy of their souls, after the truth has become clear to them; yet do you pardon and be forgiving, till God brings His command; truly God is powerful over everything.

2:74

(Pickthall) Then, even after that, your hearts were hardened and became as rocks, or worse than rocks, for hardness. For indeed there are rocks from out which rivers gush, and indeed there are rocks which split asunder so that water floweth from them. And indeed there are rocks which fall down for the fear of Allah. Allah is not unaware of what ye do.

(Shakir) Then your hearts hardened after that, so that they were like rocks, rather worse in hardness; and surely there are some rocks from which streams burst forth, and surely there are some of them which split asunder so water issues out of them, and surely there are some of them which fall down for fear of Allah, and Allah is not at all heedless of what you do.

(Arberry) Then your hearts became hardened thereafter and are like stones, or even yet harder; for there are stones from which rivers come gushing, and others split, so that water issues from them, and others crash down in the fear of God. And God is not heedless of the things you do.

2:42

(Pickthall) Confound not truth with falsehood, nor knowingly conceal the truth.

(Shakir) And do not mix up the truth with the falsehood, nor hide the truth while you know (it).

(Arberry) And do not confound the truth with vanity, and do not conceal the truth wittingly.

2:75

(Pickthall) Have ye any hope that they will be true to you when a party of them used to listen to the word of Allah, then used to change it, after they had understood it, knowingly?

(Shakir) Do you then hope that they would believe in you, and a party from among them indeed used to hear the Word of Allah, then altered it after they had understood it, and they know (this).

(Arberry) Are you then so eager that they should believe you, seeing there is a party of them that heard God's word, and then tampered with it, and that after they had comprehended it, wittingly?

2:78

(Pickthall) Among them are unlettered folk who know the Scripture not except from hearsay. They but guess.

(Shakir) And there are among them illiterates who know not the Book but only *lies* [emphasis added], and they do but conjecture.

(Arberry) And some there are of them that are common folk not knowing the Book, but only fancies and mere conjectures.

2:89

(Pickthall) And when there cometh unto them a scripture from Allah, confirming that in their possession—though before that they were asking for a signal triumph over those who disbelieved—and when there cometh unto them that which they know (to be the truth) they disbelieve therein. The curse of Allah is on disbelievers.

(Shakir) And when there came to them a Book from Allah verifying that which they have, and aforetime they used to pray for victory against those who disbelieve, but when there came to them (Prophet) that which they did not recognize, they disbelieved in him; so Allah's curse is on the unbelievers.

(Arberry) When there came to them a Book from God, confirming what was with them—and they aforetimes prayed for victory over the unbelievers—when there came to them that they recognized, they disbelieved in it; and the curse of God is on the unbelievers.

2:111

(Pickthall) And they say: None entereth paradise unless he be a Jew or a Christian. These are their own desires. Say: Bring your proof (of what ye state) if ye are truthful.

(Shakir) And they say: None shall enter the garden (or paradise) except he who is a Jew or a Christian. These are their vain desires. Say: Bring your proof if you are truthful.

(Arberry) And they say, "None shall enter Paradise except that they be Jews or Christians." Such are their fancies. Say: "Produce your proof, if you speak truly."

2:275

(Pickthall) Those who swallow usury cannot rise up save as he ariseth whom the devil hath prostrated by (his) touch. That is because they say: Trade is just like usury; whereas Allah permitteth trading and forbiddeth usury. He unto whom an admonition from his Lord cometh, and (he) refraineth (in obedience thereto), he shall keep (the profits of) that which is past, and his affair (henceforth) is with Allah. As for him who returneth (to usury)—Such are rightful owners of the Fire. They will abide therein.

(Shakir) Those who swallow down usury cannot arise except as one whom Shaitan has prostrated by (his) touch does rise. That is because they say, trading is only like usury; and Allah has allowed trading and forbidden usury. To whomsoever then the admonition has come from his Lord, then he desists, he shall have what has already passed, and his affair is in the hands of Allah; and whoever returns (to it)—these are the inmates of the fire; they shall abide in it.

(Arberry) Those who devour usury shall not rise again except as he rises, whom Satan of the touch prostrates; that is because they say, "Trafficking (trade) is like usury." God has permitted trafficking, and forbidden usury. Whosoever receives an admonition from his Lord and gives over, he shall have his past gains, and his affair is committed to God; but whosoever reverts—those are the inhabitants of the Fire, therein dwelling forever.

2:102

(Pickthall) And follow that which the devils falsely related against the kingdom of Solomon. Solomon disbe-

lieved not; but the devils disbelieved, teaching mankind magic and that which was revealed to the two angels in Babel, Harut and Marut. Nor did they (the two angels) teach it to anyone till they had said: We are only a temptation, therefore disbelieve not (in the guidance of Allah). And from these two (angels) people learn that by which they cause division between man and wife; but they injure thereby no-one save by Allah's leave. And they learn that which harmeth them and profiteth them not. And surely they do know that he who trafficketh therein will have no (happy) portion in the Hereafter; and surely evil is the price for which they sell their souls, if they but knew.

(Shakir) And they followed what the Shaitans chanted of sorcery in the reign of Sulaiman, and Sulaiman was not an unbeliever, but the Shaitans disbelieved, they taught men sorcery and that was sent down to the two angels at Babel, Harut and Marut, yet these two taught no man until they had said, "Surely we are only a trial, therefore do not be a disbeliever." Even then men learned from these two, magic by which they might cause a separation between a man and his wife; and they cannot hurt with it any one except with Allah's permission, and they learned what harmed them and did not profit them, and certainly they know that he who bought it should have no share of good in the hereafter and evil was the price for which they sold their souls, had they but known this.

(Arberry) And they follow what the Satans recited over Solomon's kingdom. Solomon disbelieved not, but the Satans disbelieved, teaching the people sorcery, and that which was sent down upon Babylon's two angels, Harut and Marut; they taught not any man, without they said, "We are but a temptation; do not disbelieve." From them they learned how they might divide a man and his wife, yet they did not hurt any man thereby, save by the leave of God, and they learned what hurt them, and did not profit them, knowing well that whoso buys it shall have no share in the world to come; evil then was that they sold themselves for, if they had but known.

2:96

(Pickthall) And thou wilt find them greediest of mankind for life and (greedier) than the idolaters. (Each) one of them would like to be allowed to live a thousand years. And to live (a thousand years) would by no means remove him from the doom. Allah is Seer of what they do.

(Shakir) And you will most certainly find them the greediest of men for life (greedier) than even those who are polytheists; every one of them loves that he should be granted a life of a thousand years, and his being granted a long life will in no way remove him further off from the chastisement, and Allah sees what they do.

(Arberry) And thou shalt find them the eagerest of men for life. And of the idolaters; there is one of them wishes if he might be spared a thousand years, yet his being spared alive shall not remove him from the chastisement. God sees the things they do.

2:54

(Pickthall) And when Moses said unto his people: O my people! Ye have wronged yourselves by your choosing of the calf (for worship) so turn in penitence to your Creator, and kill (the guilty) yourselves. That will be best for you with your Creator and He will relent toward you. Lo! He is the Relenting, the Merciful.

(Shakir) And when Musa said to his people: O my people! you have surely been unjust to yourselves by taking the calf (for a god), therefore turn to your Creator (penitently), so kill your people, that is best for you with your Creator: so He turned to you (mercifully), for surely He is the Oft-returning (to mercy), the Merciful.

(Arberry) And when Moses said to his people, My people, you have done wrong against yourselves by your taking the Calf; now turn to your Creator and slay one another. That will be better for you in your Creator's sight, and He will turn to you; truly He turns, and is All-compassionate.

More (and repeat) sins, still: the Jews' idol worship is again mentioned (4:51), then linked and followed by charges of other (often repeat) iniquities—the "tremendous calumny" against Mary (4:156), as well as usury and cheating (4:161). Most Jews are accused of being "evil-livers"/"transgressors"/"ungodly" (3:110), who, deceived by their own lies (3:24), try to turn Muslims from Islam (3:99). Jews are blind and deaf to the truth (5:71), and what they have not forgotten they have perverted—they mislead (3:69), confound the truth (3:71), twist tongues (3:79), and cheat Gentiles without remorse (3:75). Muslims are advised not to take the clannish Jews as friends (5:51), and to beware of the inveterate hatred that Jews bear towards them (5:82).

4:51

(Pickthall) Hast thou not seen those unto whom a portion of the Scripture hath been given, how they believe in idols and false deities, and how they say of those (idolaters) who disbelieve: "These are more rightly guided than those who believe"?

(Shakir) Have you not seen those to whom a portion of the Book has been given? They believe in idols and false deities and say of those who disbelieve: These are better guided in the path than those who believe.

(Arberry) Hast thou not regarded those who were given a share of the Book believing in demons and idols, and saying to the unbelievers, These are more rightly guided on the way than the believers?

4:156

(Pickthall) And because of their disbelief and of their speaking against Mary a tremendous calumny.

(Shakir) And for their unbelief and for their having uttered against Marium a grievous calumny.

(Arberry) and for their unbelief, and their uttering against Mary a mighty calumny.

4:161

(Pickthall) And of their taking usury when they were forbidden it, and of their devouring people's wealth by false pretences, We have prepared for those of them who disbelieve a painful doom.

(Shakir) And their taking usury though indeed they were forbidden it and their devouring the property of people falsely, and We have prepared for the unbelievers from among them a painful chastisement.

(Arberry) And for their taking usury, that they were prohibited, and consuming the wealth of the people in vanity; and We have prepared for the unbelievers among them a painful chastisement.

3:110

(Pickthall) Ye are the best community that hath been raised up for mankind. Ye enjoin right conduct and forbid indecency; and ye believe in Allah. And if the People of the Scripture had believed it had been better for them. Some of them are believers; but most of them are evil-livers.

(Shakir) You are the best of the nations raised up for (the benefit of) men; you enjoin what is right and forbid the wrong and believe in Allah; and if the followers of the Book had believed it would have been better for them; of them (some) are believers and most of them are transgressors.

(Arberry) You are the best nation ever brought forth to men, bidding to honour, and forbidding dishonour, and believing in God. Had the People of the Book believed, it were better for them; some of them are believers, but the most of them are ungodly.

3:24

(Pickthall) That is because they say: The Fire will not touch us save for a certain number of days. That which they used to invent hath deceived them regarding their religion.

(Shakir) This is because they say: The fire shall not touch us but for a few days; and what they have forged deceives them in the matter of their religion.

(Arberry) That, because they said, "The Fire shall not touch us, except for a number of days"; and the lies they forged have deluded them in their religion.

3:99

(Pickthall) Say: O People of the Scripture! Why drive ye back believers from the way of Allah, seeking to make it crooked, when ye are witnesses (to Allah's guidance)? Allah is not unaware of what ye do.

(Shakir) Say: O followers of the Book! why do you hinder him who believes from the way of Allah? You seek (to make) it crooked, while you are witness, and Allah is not heedless of what you do.

(Arberry) Say: People of the Book, why do you bar from God's way the believer, desiring to make it crooked, yourselves being witnesses? God is not heedless of the things you do.

5:71

(Pickthall) They thought no harm would come of it, so they were wilfully blind and deaf. And afterward Allah turned (in mercy) toward them. Now (even after that) are many of them wilfully blind and deaf. Allah is Seer of what they do.

(Shakir) And they thought that there would be no affliction, so they became blind and deaf; then Allah turned to them mercifully, but many of them became blind and deaf; and Allah is well seeing what they do.

(Arberry) And they supposed there should be no trial; but blind they were, and deaf. Then God turned towards them; then again blind they were, many of them, and deaf; and God sees the things they do.

3:69

(Pickthall) A party of the People of the Scripture long to make you go astray; and they make none to go astray except themselves, but they perceive not.

(Shakir) A party of the followers of the Book desire that they should lead you astray, and they lead not astray but themselves, and they do not perceive.

(Arberry) There is a party of the People of the Book who yearn to make you go astray; yet none they make to stray, except themselves, but they are not aware.

3:71

(Pickthall) O People of the Scripture! Why confound ye truth with falsehood and knowingly conceal the truth?

(Shakir) O followers of the Book! Why do you confound the truth with the falsehood and hide the truth while you know?

(Arberry) People of the Book! Why do you confound the truth with vanity, and conceal the truth and that wittingly?

3:78

(Pickthall) And lo! there is a party of them who distort the Scripture with their tongues, that ye may think that what they say is from the Scripture, when it is not from the Scripture. And they say: It is from Allah, when it is not from Allah; and they speak a lie concerning Allah knowingly.

(Shakir) Most surely there is a party amongst those who distort the Book with their tongue that you may consider it to be (a part) of the Book, and they say, It is from Allah, while it is not from Allah, and they tell a lie against Allah whilst they know.

(Arberry) And there is a sect of them who twist their tongues with the Book, that you may suppose it part of the Book, yet it is not part of the Book; and they say, It is from God, yet it is not from God, and they speak falsehood against God, and that wittingly.

3:75

(Pickthall) Among the People of the Scripture there is he who, if thou trust him with a weight of treasure, will return it to thee. And among them there is he who, if thou trust him with a piece of gold, will not return it to thee unless thou keep standing over him. That is because they say: We have no duty to the Gentiles. They speak a lie concerning Allah knowingly.

(Shakir) And among the followers of the Book there are some such that if you entrust one (of them) with a heap of wealth, he shall pay it back to you; and among them there are some such that if you entrust one (of them) with a dinar he shall not pay it back to you except so long as you remain firm in demanding it; this is because they say: There is not upon us in the matter of the unlearned people any way (to reproach); and they tell a lie against Allah while they know.

(Arberry) And of the People of the Book is he who, if thou trust him with a hundredweight, will restore it thee; and of them is he who, if thou trust him with one pound, will not restore it thee, unless ever thou standest over him. That, because they say, There is no way over us as to the common people. They speak falsehood against God and that wittingly.

5:51

(Pickthall) O ye who believe! Take not the Jews and the Christians for friends. They are friends one to another. He among you who taketh them for friends is (one) of them. Lo! Allah guideth not wrongdoing folk.

(Shakir) O you who believe! do not take the Jews and the Christians for friends; they are friends of each other; and whoever amongst you takes them for a friend, then surely he is one of them; surely Allah does not guide the unjust people.

(Arberry) O believers, take not Jews and Christians as friends; they are friends of each other. Whoso of you makes them his friends is one of them. God guides not the people of the evildoers.

5:82

(Pickthall) Thou wilt find the most vehement of mankind in hostility to those who believe (to be) the Jews and the idolaters. And thou wilt find the nearest of them in affection to those who believe (to be) those who say: Lo! We are Christians. That is because there are among them priests and monks, and because they are not proud.

(Shakir) Certainly you will find the most violent of people in enmity for those who believe (to be) the Jews and those who are polytheists, and you will certainly find the nearest in friendship to those who believe (to be) those who say: We are Christians; this is because there are priests and monks among them and because they do not behave proudly.

(Arberry) Thou wilt surely find the most hostile of men to the believers are the Jews and the idolaters; and thou wilt surely find the nearest of them in love to the believers are those who say "We are Christians"; that, because some of them are priests and monks, and they wax not proud.

The Jews' ultimate sin and punishment: they are the devil's minions (4:60) cursed by Allah, their faces will be obliterated (4:47), and if they do not accept the true faith of Islam—the Jews who understand their faith become Muslims (3:113)—they will be made into apes (2:65/7:166), or apes and swine (5:60), and burn in the Hellfires (4:55, 5:29, 98:6, and 58:14–19).

4:60

(Pickthall) Hast thou not seen those who pretend that they believe in that which is revealed unto thee and that which was revealed before thee, how they would go for judgment (in their disputes) to false deities when they have been ordered to abjure them? Satan would mislead them far astray.

(Shakir) Have you not seen those who assert that they believe in what has been revealed to you and what was revealed before you? They desire to summon one another to the judgment of the Shaitan, though they were commanded to deny him, and the Shaitan desires to lead them astray into a remote error.

(Arberry) Hast thou not regarded those who assert that they believe in what has been sent down to thee, and what was sent down before thee, desiring to take their disputes to idols, yet they have been commanded to disbelieve in them? But Satan desires to lead them astray into far error.

4:47

(Pickthall) O ye unto whom the Scripture hath been given! Believe in what We have revealed confirming that which ye possess, before We destroy countenances so as to confound them, or curse them as We cursed the Sabbath-breakers (of old time). The commandment of Allah is always executed.

(Shakir) O you who have been given the Book! believe that which We have revealed, verifying what you have, before We alter faces then turn them on their backs, or curse them as We cursed the violators of the Sabbath, and the command of Allah shall be executed.

(Arberry) You who have been given the Book, believe in what We have sent down, confirming what is with you, before We obliterate faces, and turn them upon their backs, or curse them as We cursed the Sabbath-men, and God's command is done.

3:113

(Pickthall) They are not all alike. Of the People of the Scripture there is a staunch community who recite the revelations of Allah in the night season, falling prostrate (before Him).

(Shakir) They are not all alike; of the followers of the Book there is an upright party; they recite Allah's communications in the nighttime and they adore (Him).

(Arberry) Yet they are not all alike; some of the People of the Book are a nation upstanding, that recite God's signs in the watches of the night, bowing themselves.

2:65

(Pickthall) And ye know of those of you who broke the Sabbath, how We said unto them: Be ye apes, despised and hated!

(Shakir) And certainly you have known those among you who exceeded the limits of the Sabbath, so We said to them: Be (as) apes, despised and hated.

(Arberry) And well you know there were those among you that transgressed the Sabbath, and We said to them, Be you apes, miserably slinking!

7:166

(Pickthall) So when they took pride in that which they had been forbidden, We said unto them: Be ye apes despised and loathed!

(Shakir) Therefore when they revoltingly persisted in what they had been forbidden, We said to them: Be (as) apes, despised and hated.

(Arberry) And when they turned in disdain from that forbidding We said to them, Be you apes, miserably slinking!

5:60

(Pickthall) Shall I tell thee of a worse (case) than theirs for retribution with Allah? (Worse is the case of him) whom Allah hath cursed, him on whom His wrath hath fallen and of whose sort Allah hath turned some to apes and swine, and who serveth idols. Such are in worse plight and further astray from the plain road.

(Shakir) Say: Shall I inform you of (him who is) worse than this in retribution from Allah? (Worse is he) whom Allah has cursed and brought His wrath upon, and of

whom He made apes and swine, and he who served the Shaitan; these are worse in place and more erring from the straight path.

(Arberry) Say: Shall I tell you of a recompense with God, worse than that? Whomsoever God has cursed, and with whom He is wroth, and made some of them apes and swine, and worshippers of idols—they are worse situated, and have gone further astray from the right way.

4:55

(Pickthall) And of them were (some) who believed therein and of them were (some) who turned away from it. Hell is sufficient for (their) burning.

(Shakir) So of them is he who believes in him, and of them is he who turns away from him, and hell is sufficient to burn.

(Arberry) And some of them there are that believe, and some of them that bar from it; Gehenna suffices for a Blaze!

5:29

(Pickthall) Lo! I would rather thou shouldst bear the punishment of the sin against me and thine own sin and become one of the owners of the fire. That is the reward of evil-doers.

(Shakir) Surely I wish that you should bear the sin committed against me and your own sin, and so you would be of the inmates of the fire, and this is the recompense of the unjust.

(Arberry) I desire that thou shouldest be laden with my sin and thy sin, and so become an inhabitant of the Fire; that is the recompense of the evildoers.

98:6

(Pickthall) Lo! those who disbelieve, among the People of the Scripture and the idolaters, will abide in fire of hell. They are the worst of created beings.

(Shakir) Surely those who disbelieve from among the followers of the Book and the polytheists shall be in the fire of hell, abiding therein; they are the worst of men.

(Arberry) The unbelievers of the People of the Book and the idolaters shall be in the Fire of Gehenna, therein dwelling forever; those are the worst of creatures.

58:14–19

(Pickthall) Hast thou not seen those who take for friends a folk with whom Allah is wroth? They are neither of you nor of them, and they swear a false oath knowingly. Allah hath prepared for them a dreadful doom. Evil indeed is that which they are wont to do. They make a shelter of their oaths and turn (men) from the way of Allah; so theirs will be a shameful doom. Their wealth and their children will avail them naught against Allah. Such are rightful owners of the Fire; they will abide therein. On the day when Allah will raise them all together, then will they swear unto Him as they (now) swear unto you, and they will fancy that they have some standing. Lo! is it not they who are the liars? The devil hath engrossed them and so hath caused them to forget remembrance of Allah. They are the devil's party. Lo! is it not the devil's party who will be the losers?

(Shakir) Have you not seen those who befriend a people with whom Allah is wroth? They are neither of you nor of them, and they swear falsely while they know. Allah has prepared for them a severe punishment; surely what they do is evil. They make their oaths to serve as a cover so they turn away from Allah's way; therefore they shall have an abasing chastisement. Neither their wealth nor their children shall avail them aught against Allah; they

are the inmates of the fire, therein they shall abide. On the day that Allah will raise them up all, then they will swear to Him as they swear to you, and they think that they have something; now surely they are the liars. The Shaitan has gained the mastery over them, so he has made them forget the remembrance of Allah; they are the Shaitan's party; now surely the Shaitan's party are the losers.

(Arberry) Hast thou not regarded those who have taken for friends a people against whom God is wrathful? They belong neither to you nor to them; and they swear upon falsehood, and that wittingly. God has made ready for them a chastisement terrible; surely they—evil are the things they have been doing. They have taken their oaths as a covering, and barred from God's way; so there awaits them a humbling chastisement. Neither their riches nor their children shall avail them anything against God; those—they are the inhabitants of the Fire, therein dwelling forever. Upon the day when God shall raise them up all together, and they will swear to Him, as they swear to you, and think they are on something. Surely, they are the liars! Satan has gained the mastery over them, and caused them to forget God's Remembrance. Those are Satan's party; why, Satan's party, surely, they are the losers!

CHAPTER 3
Jew Hatred in the Islamic Tradition and the Koranic Exegesis

Haggai Ben-Shammai

In the middle of the eighth century, most of the world's Jews, including the autonomous Jewish center in Babylonia, were in lands under the rule of Islam. In the central countries under Muslim rule, the Jews were fewer in number than the Christians. This was the case in Egypt, the Land of Israel, Syria, and also Iraq. The Christian majority underwent a gradual process of Islamization, which in a few countries was very slow. In a few of the Islamic countries there are Christian minorities to this very day who have to a great extent preserved their status as the backbone of the veteran urban bureaucracy. Across the borders, there were Christian powers such as Byzantium, Ethiopia, and the Frankish kingdom. The fact that they constituted a threat to Islam provided added strength for the Christians living in Muslim lands.

1. THE TRADITION OF ANTI-JEWISH LITERATURE

From the ninth century onward, out of the ancient tradition, there began to develop a literature of polemics against the Jews, "the people of the Book" (or "the protected people"—both terms referring primarily to the Jews and the Christians) or against the non-Muslims. Not inconceivably, this literature followed old Christian examples, extant before Islam, with parallels in ancient Persian literature as well. Several years ago, Professor Moshe Perlmann wrote an article with an interesting and instructive summary of the anti-Jewish polemic literature.[1] This literature in itself, however, is not our concern here but serves merely as one indication of hatred and scorn for Judaism (and Christianity). No less important an indication, and much more useful, are the decrees generally, though erroneously, called the "Covenant of Umar." They were not promulgated all at once but gradually took shape over a few centuries, apparently reaching their more or less final form in the ninth century. There is no doubt that the crystallization of these regulations against the non-Muslims, especially against

"the people of the Book," was connected with the name of the caliph Al-Mutawakkil, who reigned in the mid-ninth century CE.

These regulations were intended to degrade and humiliate both the individual non-Muslim (by the different garb they were made to wear) and the religious group as a whole. One of the most important of the regulations, intended to degrade the entire group, forbade the appointment of Jews and Christians to public positions or positions of authority. We know that this regulation (and not only this one) was not always strictly adhered to in practice. In some countries and some periods there were so many exceptions that it seemed they had become the rule.

We do in fact again and again find Jews and Christians in positions of authority in various Islamic countries at different times; Jews or Christians were even appointed to the office of vizier, the equivalent of a head of state today. Generally, whenever such a thing happened, there was always some religious figure of authority who, at the proper moment, would privately or publicly explain to the rulers how they should conduct themselves, and the affair sometimes ended unpleasantly. Let us illustrate with one story.[2] The 'Abbasid Caliph al-Ma'mun (who ruled from 813–833) honored a certain Jew greatly. To be sure, nowhere is it said that he appointed the Jew to an official position but "he seated him higher than those most dignified—al-Ashraf" (perhaps the occurrence of this term indicated that he seated him even over the descendants of Muhammad who are normally designated as a group by this term).

One of them became angry and sent a note to al-Ma'mun on which the following verses were written:
O Son of him, obedience to whom was incumbent upon all people, and whose truth was decree and law binding (Upon us), He whom thou honorest claims that the father of your fathers[3] (= Muhammad) is nothing but a Liar.

Haggai Ben-Shammai, "Jew-Hatred in the Islamic Tradition and Koranic Exegesis," in *Antisemitism through the Ages*, ed. Shmuel Almog (Oxford: Pergamon, 1988), pp. 161–69.

Al-Ma'mun answered him: "You are right!"—ordering at once that the Jew be drowned. Then al-Ma'mun told those who were present the story of al-Miqdad ibn al-Aswad, a friend of the Prophet—how, (when he was on one of his journeys), he was accompanied for a whole day by a Jew. When evening came, al-Miqdad remembered the saying handed down from the Prophet: "No Jew meets with a Muslim in privacy unless he has some scheme to trap him." (Incidentally, this is one version of this tradition. There are tens of parallel versions with variations.) After al-Miqdad promised the Jew that he would not hurt him, the Jew confessed to him: "I did in fact have a trap in mind. All day I have been planning to tread upon the shadow of your head." (Stepping on the shadow here apparently has some magical significance: the shadow is the soul and stepping on it is a symbolic act of trampling on the soul, i.e., a kind of killing.) "How right was the Prophet of Allah," rejoined al-Miqdad.

As already mentioned, there are many variations of the old sayings. For example, "No Jew remains alone with a Muslim unless he plans to kill him," or "No two Jews meet except to plot the death of Muslims," and many more such. The story quoted was intended against the "protected people" in general and is one of a series of similar accounts. Did the Jew have a separate status? As mentioned, legally the status of the Jew was not different in principle. All the "protected people" were equal, especially the Jews and the Christians. There is even an opinion that the fact that the Jewish communities thrived under Muslim rule for over thirteen hundred years while there was a consistent, evident shrinkage of the Christian population is proof enough of Islam's attitude toward Judaism as against its attitude toward Christians. It seems to me that this fact indicates, no less, and perhaps even primarily, the nature of the Jewish communities everywhere, not only in the Muslim lands, in contrast to that of the Christian communities.[4] However, it is not my intention to discuss the laws and regulations but rather the Islamic tradition, which, while it provides an underlying ideological base for the law, also has a developmental dynamic of its own beyond the letter of the law. The polemic literature, especially that which deals with the Jews, is anchored in this Islamic tradition.

The literature of the Islamic tradition in essence constitutes the continuity of the development of Islam as reflected in the Koran. One of the important findings of the famous Orientalist Goldziher was that the oral Islamic tradition, hadith in Arabic, reflects the development of early Islam and its relationship to historical developments during its first two centuries. A large part of the entire spiritual creativity of Islam in that period developed as oral tradition. It is a vast, complex mosaic composed of an infinite number of tiny pieces (including

Islamic historiography). Naturally, Koranic exegesis is the first area in which this creativity took on an oral tradition form. An examination of this literature, especially the exegesis of the Koran, indicates that the main fore of the attitude toward Jews and Christians had already been almost fully shaped before 750 CE. If we accept the proposition that the main decrees against the Jews were first institutionalized in the days of the Umayyad Caliph 'Umar b.'Abd no doubt that there is a close connection between this fact and the crystallization of the attitude toward the Jews in the mid-eighth century which we shall describe below. Our examination indicates that the attitude toward the Jews as reflected in this tradition during that period had already been crystallized in the main centers of Islam: in Medina, in Syria, and in Iraq.

This tradition, shaped over a thousand years ago, has continued with a vital dynamism of its own to this very day. There are many instances of it in twentieth-century literature. For example, the publication containing the discussions at the Fourth Conference of the Academy of Islamic Research held in Cairo in 1968[5] has very instructive articles about attitudes toward the Jews. Every year sees the publication of scores of books written by Muslims containing anti-Jewish traditions. Their authors are from various circles: In some of the books the religious outlook is the decisive factor; in some, the secular outlook is couched in European anti-semitic terms. In this connection, one should mention an example which is a curiosity. About forty years ago, a work of intrinsic interest was printed in Egypt. It is called *Ifham al-Yahud* ("Silencing the Jews"), composed by Samau'al al-Magribi, an apostate Jew, in the middle of the twelfth century CE.[6] Samau'al explains how he came to the truth of Islam—after a dream one night—and why the religion of the Jews is so contemptible that it deserves to be degraded and suppressed. This treatise was published in one volume, along with a similar one, also by an apostate Jew who converted to Islam apparently at the end of the nineteenth century. The volume has an introduction by a Muslim scholar named Muhammad Mahmud al-Faqi, who, at that time, was the head of some Muslim society. The introduction very precisely repeats all the traditions found in the literature for a thousand years, plus an interesting insertion of a number of motifs from *The Protocols of the Elders of Zion*. This is of interest because at that time the *Protocols* had not yet penetrated the Muslim religious circles but were more widespread among people who had access to modern secular literature.[7]

2. THE CURSE AGAINST THE JEWS

A central place in the traditions concerning the Jews is held by the words of the Qur'an in sura 2:61/58: "And abasement and poverty were pitched upon them, and they were laden with God's anger; that because they had disbelieved the signs of God and slain the Prophets unrightfully; that because they disobeyed and were transgressors."[8] The reference is actually to the Israelites in the wilderness, but to all of the Muslim exegeses, without exception,[9] it was absolutely clear that the reference was to the Jews of their day. The Arabic word translated as "pitched upon them" also means, literally, that the "abasement and poverty" were decreed for them forever.[10] The "abasement" is the payment of the poll tax and the humiliating ceremony involved. As for the "poverty," this ensured their remaining impoverished forever. There are traditions which attribute this interpretation to Muhammad himself.[11] The text continues: "and they were laden with God's anger." Here the text is speaking of a fearful rage decreed upon them forever, and many traditions, in parallel versions repeated again and again in different sources, connect this "anger" with the anger in the Qur'an 1:7 where are mentioned "those against whom Thou art wrathful." In this verse, Muslims ask that God lead them in the right path, not in the way of those who must bear His wrath. This last is connected to Qur'an 5:60/65 in which it is said of the Israelites: "Say, Shall I tell you of a recompense with God, worse than that? Whomsoever God has cursed, and with whom He is wroth, and made some of them apes and swine, and worshippers of idols[12]—they are worse situated, and have gone further astray from the right way." Who are the people who have incurred perpetual degradation, who suffer God's wrath forever and who have become the apes and swine referred to in this verse? Many Muslim exegetes interpreted this as referring to the Jews, and some cite various stories of Jews who actually became apes or swine.[13] They associate this with another verse, Koran 5:78/82: "Cursed were the unbelievers of the Children of Israel by the tongue of David and Jesus, Mary's son, "and explain it to mean the Jews who were cursed by David when he passed the house of a certain Jew, who because of these curses were transformed into swine or apes. What is the explanation of this fearful decree? Why were the Jews so terribly cursed? The main reason was that from time immemorial the Jews rejected God's signs, the wonders performed by the prophets. They did not accept the prophecy of Jesus whom the Koran counts among the prophets. But this is all part of the Jews' nature: they are by their very nature deceitful and treacherous. In sura 2:89/93 it says: "When there came to them a Book from God, confirming what was with them—and they aforetimes prayed for victory over the unbelievers—when there came to them what they recognized, they disbelieved in it: and the curse of God is on the unbelievers." In this connection the tradition recounts that at first the Jews truly hoped for Muhammad's victory over the Arab nonbelievers and said: "Would that Allah send his prophet of whom our Book says that his coming is assured." But when the prophet finally came and they saw he was not one of them, they then denied him out of jealousy of the Arabs,

though they knew that in truth he is the prophet. Furthermore, this Jewish trait brought them to grave heresy. They thought that they would succeed only in leading humankind astray but also in fooling God. Sura 5:64/69 reads: "The Jews have said, 'God's hand is tied.'" And in the continuation of the verse: "As often as they light a fire for war, God will extinguish it." Exegetes cite traditions which prove that the Jews always hated the true prophets and put them to death. Therefore they always failed in their wars and their Temple was destroyed time and again. According to one tradition: "These enemies of God (mentioned in the verse) are the Jews. Whenever they kindle the flame of war, God extinguishes it. Never are the Jews found in any land but that they are the lowest of inhabitants. (You know) that Islam came upon the scene when the Jews were under (the rule of) the Majus (i.e., the Zoroastrians), who are, of all creatures, the most detested by God."

The vile characteristics inherent in Jews are also stressed by the commentaries and traditions dealing with sura 5:41/45, which reads:

O Messenger, let them not grieve thee, that vie with one another in unbelief, such men as say with their mouths "We believe" but their hearts believe not; and the Jews, who listen to falsehood, listen to other folk, who have not come to thee, perverting words from their meanings, saying "If you are given this then take it; if you are not given it, beware!" Whomsoever God desires to try, thou canst not avail him anything with God. Those are they whose hearts God desired not to purify; for them is degradation in this world; and in the world to come awaits mighty chastisement.

In his commentary, Tabari[14] cites many traditions on this verse, of which these are the main ones:

1. 'Abd Allah b. Suraya was the most expert and wisest of the Jews in Medina. When Muhammad reached Medina, he passed the House of Study (Bayt al-Midras). The Jewish sages were dealing with the case of an adulterer and adulteress and could not come to a decision. At their request, Muhammad made the decision for death by stoning in accordance with the Torah. The end of the matter was that Ben Suraya admitted that Muhammad was the most expert in the Torah but that the Jewish sages would not admit it out of jealousy.

2. A Jew tried to lie to Muhammad and claim that the penalty for adultery in the Torah is lashes. Only after Muhammad had him swear by the Torah, did the Jew admit that the punishment is stoning; and added that since adultery is widespread among the Jewish dignitaries who were afraid that they might be exposed if they differentiated in the penalty between dignitaries and the simple folk, they

replaced stoning with lashes. At that Muhammad said: "My God, I am the first who has revived Your commandment[15] after these have killed it."

3. A combined version of these two traditions—perhaps a later one—opens with the story as in the first version. The Jewish sage finally admitted that the Jews ignored the Torah's proper punishment for adulterers, that is, stoning, and had substituted lashes. Then, after the Jew had confessed, the verses under discussion were revealed to Muhammad (i.e., 41–44/45–49 of sura 5).

4. An exegetical tradition ties this verse to those called *munafiqun* [hypocrites]: according to the accepted interpretation, a Qur'anic term for those whose mouths and hearts are not one, that is, who stated that they accepted Islam but secretly remained hostile to it and even actively assisted the tribes fighting Muhammad. Tabari opted for this interpretation and even connected it to the first tradition: The verse refers to 'Abd Allah b. Suraya who told Muhammad that he believed in his prophecy (for he had presented the case for his decision), but in his heart he did not believe.

Tabari explains: "Those they are whose hearts God desired not to purify,"[16] meaning that God wanted to lead the Jews astray and hence created their hearts this way. They will never walk in the straight path. Further on in the Qur'an, in 42/46, the Jews are described as (the ones) "who listen to falsehood and consume the unlawful." Most of the commentaries explain "the unlawful" as bribery, and there are those (in a tradition ascribed to 'Ali b. Abi Talib, Muhammad's cousin, son-in-law, and the fourth caliph) who interpret this also to mean the pay for blood-letting, the dowry for an adulteress, the price of a dog, the price of wine, the price of a dead animal (i.e., one not properly slaughtered), and more.

3. DIFFERENCES IN ATTITUDES TO JEWS AND CHRISTIANS

The examples cited here are but a tiny fraction of the material which could be quoted on this subject. An interesting question is: Do the Qur'an and the tradition differentiate between Jews and Christians? In fact, the attitude would appear to be the same. In sura 5:51/56 we have: "O believers, take not Jews and Christians as friends; they are friends of each other. Whoso of you makes them his friends, is one of them." Interestingly, the traditions cited in connection with this verse[17] deal with the question: What is the law on consuming animals slaughtered by Christian Arabs and marrying their daughters? This is proof that these traditions are early, since they are from a period when the problem was still acute and the process of Islamization was just beginning. One tradition tended to forbid it, specifically mentioning the Arab-

Christian tribe of Taghlib, which it compared to the "Christians-of-the-children-of-Israel." (Is this merely confusion or is it directed at the Judeo-Christians?) Another tradition set a special law for the Arab Christians and permitted consumption of animals slaughtered by them and the marriage of their women.

However, there is another verse which differentiates between Jews and Christians. In the same sura, 82/85: "Thou wilt surely find the most hostile of men to the believers are the Jews, and the idolaters; and thou wilt surely find the nearest of them in love to believers are those who say 'We are Christians'; that, because some of them are priests and monks, and they wax not proud." The tradition connects this verse with another, sura 3:55/48: "When God said, 'Jesus, I will take thee to Me and will raise thee to Me, and I will purify thee of those who believe not, I will set thy followers above the unbelievers, till the Resurrection day,'" about which there is a tradition: "The Christians are to be above the Jews until the day of Judgment, for there is no land where the Christians are not above the Jews, neither in the east nor the west. The Jews are degraded in all the lands."

In these traditions the Christians have a clear priority over the Jews. If we posit that the early tradition reflects the historical development of early Islam and that the political, economic, and social reality was apt to produce this preference, there is no doubt that these traditions reflect this reality.

As has been stated, this tradition has remained alive to this very day. It is interesting to see this tradition of preference for Christians over Jews in nineteenth-century Egypt. The accounts of the Orientalist Edward William Lane's travels in Egypt,[18] written in 1835, contain interesting confirmation of this. To be sure, Lane was a Christian observer and clearly a concerned party, but his testimony is generally accepted as reliable. Besides which, the Jewish minority in Egypt at that time was too small to create the impression of being an economic or any other sort of power which might arouse antisemitic associations.

On the difference in the Muslims' attitudes toward the Jews and the Christians, Lane first of all mentions the verse mentioned above, sura 5:82/85, according to which the Jews are the greatest foes of the believers. Apparently, that is what Lane heard in Egypt, and he says that that is the reason why the Jews are most hated. Later on he recounts the tale of the Jew who greeted another Jew and (in error) said to him, "Good morning, sheikh Muhammad," for he thought he was a Muslim acquaintance. The Jews seized the Jew and beat him severely because he thought to wish a Muslim well. Lane heard this account from a Muslim who sought to prove to Lane that Jews would beat anyone who means to wish a Muslim well. Lane also cites a standard phrase, which he says he heard in Egypt: "Such a one hates me with the hate of the Jews."

Describing the living conditions of the Jews, Lane

reports: "Though their houses have a mean and dirty look from without, many of them contain fine and well furnished rooms. The more wealthy among them dress handsomely at home, but put on plain or even shabby dress before going out." In his opinion, the reason for this is that the Jews thought they must appear condemned to perpetual misery and degradation in keeping with the interpretation of sura 2:61/58, as mentioned above.

We have cited only a few examples. Tracing the chain of the tradition is a very arduous task in which scholars more able and gifted than I am have already labored, researched, and brought to light much that is new on the subject. The important thing, however, is that if the oral tradition reflects the developments in early Muslim society, then the traditions about the Jews, without doubt, not only formed the ideological infrastructure of the anti-Jewish legislation but were also a reflection of the actual attitude toward the Jews in the first two centuries of Islam's existence. It is not inconceivable that in these traditions something of the Byzantine or the early Iranian legacy was absorbed. It is also not beyond possibility that apostates had a hand in the matter. It may even be that the influence of these traditions on the Arabic-speaking Muslims over the generations was greater than their influence upon other Muslims. For all practical purposes, however, it makes no substantial difference.

*For further clarification of any references, see original essay.

NOTES

1. M. Perlmann, "The Medieval Polemics between Islam and Judaism," in *Religion in a Religious Age*, ed. S. D. Goitein (Cambridge, MA: 1974), pp. 103–38; and especially the article (mentioned in the bibliography ibid.) of G. Vajda, "Juifs et musulmans selon le hadit," *Journal Asiatique* 229 (1937): 57–129, which also extensively treats early Islam's attitude to the Jewish Halakha and the laws of Islam suspected to be of Jewish origin.

2. From the treatise by Ghazi Ibn al-Wasiti (end of the thirteenth century), published with English translation by R. Gottheil, "An Answer to the Dhimmis," *Journal of the American Oriental Society* 41 (1921): 396, 429.

3. The Abbasid caliphs claimed descent from Abbas, Muhammad's uncle.

4. See S. D. Goitein, *Jews and Arabs* (New York: 1967), especially p. 65.

5. The complete text of the conference was published in Arabic and English in Cairo in 1970. (Its English title is the Fourth Conference of the Academy of Islamic Research.) Selections from the English edition were published by D. F. Green, *Arab Theologians on Jews and Israel* (Geneva: 1971).

6. The edition under discussion was published in Egypt in 1939 (and apparently was reprinted there in 1961; see Y. Harkabi, *Arab Attitudes to Israel* [Jerusalem: 1972], p. 492 n. 7). M. Perlmann published a critical edition of the treatise by Samau'al al-Magribi, with English translation, in the *Proceedings of the American Academy for Jewish Research* 32 (1964).

7. On the development in Islam from a traditional hatred of the Jews to antisemitism of the European type, see Harkabi, *Arab Attitudes*, pp. 218ff. On *The Protocols of the Elders of Zion* and its connection with the Arab-Jewish conflict, see E. Rubinstein's survey "'The Protocols of the Elders of Zion' in the Arab-Jewish Conflict in Erez Israel in the Twenties" [Heb.], *Ha-Mizrah he-Hadash* 26 (1978): 37–42.

8. The verse numbers cited are from the European edition by G. Flügel. Where these differ from those of the Royal Egyptian edition, the Egyptian numbers are given first and then the numbers according to the Flügel text. The English rendering is mostly that by A. J. Arberry, *The Koran Interpreted* (Oxford: Oxford University Press, 1964).

9. There are interpretations ascribed to Muhammad's companions, such as his cousin 'Abdallah Ibn 'Abbas. These attributions are most doubtful, but by the mid-eighth century the earliest interpretations were already in writing.

10. The identical expression, in the sense of an everlasting decree, also occurs in sura 3 of the Qur'an, 108/112.

11. As was apparently done with most of the traditions during the second century of the Hegira. Most of the traditions cited here are from the comprehensive commentary of Muhammad b. Jarir at-Tabari (died in the year 923 CE) and are found in parallel versions in most of the collections of the tradition assembled in the ninth and early tenth centuries CE.

12. The source of the Arabic word (untranslated in the Hebrew by Rivlin) is apparently Aramaic (there are those who think it reached the Arabic language from the Ethiopic) and means worship of the idols.

13. See, for example, Tabari, part 4, p. 293.

14. Ibid., part 1, pp. 232ff. With parallels in all the collections of the tradition. These collections are discussed at length by Vajda, "Juifs et musulmans selon le hadit," pp. 93–99.

15. That is, he restored it. In this connection the phrase "revitalizing the commandment" or "revitalizing the custom" was widely used.

16. Tabari, p. 238.

17. Ibid., pp. 277ff. On the Christians of the Taghlib tribe see Vajda, "Juifs et musulmans selon le hadit," p. 114 n. 4.

18. E. W. Lane, *An Account of the Manners and Customs of the Modern Egyptians* (London: 1860). For this material see pp. 554–56.

PART 3

Anti-Jewish Motifs
in the Hadith

CHAPTER 4

Excerpts from the Canonical Hadith Collections

SAHIH BUKHARI*

Vol. 1, bk. 10, no. 53: Narrated Abu Musa: The Prophet said, "The example of Muslims, Jews and Christians is like the example of a man who employed laborers to work for him from morning till night. They worked till mid-day and they said, 'We are not in need of your reward.' So the man employed another batch and said to them, 'Complete the rest of the day and yours will be the wages I had fixed (for the first batch). They worked up till the time of the 'Asr prayer and said, 'Whatever we have done is for you.' He employed another batch. They worked for the rest of the day till sunset, and they received the wages of the two former batches."

Vol. 1, bk. 12, no. 749: Narrated Abu Huraira: Allah's Apostle said, "Say 'Amen' when the Imam says" *Ghair-il-maghdubi 'alaihim wala-ddal-lin*; not the path of those who earn Your Anger (such as Jews) nor of those who go astray (such as Christians); all the past sins of the person whose saying (of Amen) coincides with that of the angels, will be forgiven.

Vol. 2, bk. 23, no. 376: Narrated 'Aisha (the wife of the Prophet): Once Allah's Apostle passed by (the grave of) a Jewess whose relatives were weeping over her. He said, "They are weeping over her and she is being tortured in her grave."

Vol. 2, bk. 23, no. 414: Narrated 'Urwa: Aisha said, "The Prophet in his fatal illness said, 'Allah cursed the Jews and the Christians because they took the graves of their Prophets as places for praying.'"Aisha added, "Had it not been for that the grave of the Prophet (p.b.u.h) would have been made prominent but I am afraid it might be taken (as a) place for praying."

Vol. 3, bk. 31, no. 222: Narrated Ibn 'Abbas: The Prophet came to Medina and saw the Jews fasting on the day of Ashura. He asked them about that. They replied, "This is a good day, the day on which Allah rescued Bani Israel from their enemy. So, Moses fasted this day." The Prophet said, "We have more claim over Moses than you." So, the Prophet fasted on that day and ordered (the Muslims) to fast (on that day).

Vol. 3, bk. 34, no. 426: Narrated Ibn 'Abbas: Once 'Umar was informed that a certain man sold alcohol. 'Umar said, "May Allah curse him! Doesn't he know that Allah's Apostle said, 'May Allah curse the Jews, for Allah had forbidden them to eat the fat of animals but they melted it and sold it.'"

Vol. 3, bk. 34, no. 427: Narrated Abu Huraira: Allah's Apostle said, "May Allah curse the Jews, because Allah made fat illegal for them but they sold it and ate its price."

Vol. 3, bk. 39, no. 531: Narrated Ibn 'Umar: Umar expelled the Jews and the Christians from Hijaz. When Allah's Apostle had conquered Khaybar, he wanted to expel the Jews from it as its land became the property of Allah, His Apostle, and the Muslims. Allah's Apostle intended to expel the Jews but they requested him to let them stay there on the condition that they would do the labor and get half of the fruits. Allah's Apostle told them, "We will let you stay on this condition, as long as we wish." So, they (i.e., Jews) kept on living there until 'Umar forced them to go towards Taima' and Ariha'.

Vol. 3, bk. 47, no. 786: Narrated Anas bin Malik: A Jewess brought a poisoned (cooked) sheep for the Prophet who ate from it. She was brought to the Prophet and he was asked, "Shall we kill her?" He said, "No." I continued to see the effect of the poison on the palate of the mouth of Allah's Apostle.

Vol. 4, bk. 52, no. 176: Narrated 'Abdullah bin 'Umar: Allah's Apostle said, "You (i.e., Muslims) will fight with the Jews till some of them will hide behind stones. The

*Excerpted from M. Muhsin Khair, "Translation of Sahih Bukhari," Muslim Students Association, University of Southern California, http://www.usc.edu/dept/MSA/fundamentals/hadithsunnah/bukhari.

stones will (betray them) saying, 'O 'Abdullah (i.e., slave of Allah)! There is a Jew hiding behind me; so kill him.'"

Vol. 4, bk. 52, no. 177: Narrated Abu Huraira: Allah's Apostle said, "The Hour will not be established until you fight with the Jews, and the stone behind which a Jew will be hiding will say, 'O Muslim! There is a Jew hiding behind me, so kill him.'"

Vol. 4, bk. 52, no. 195: Narrated Anas: The Prophet set out for Khaybar and reached it at night. He used not to attack if he reached the people at night, till the day broke. So, when the day dawned, the Jews came out with their bags and spades. When they saw the Prophet; they said, "Muhammad and his army!" The Prophet said, "Allahu—Akbar! (Allah is Greater) and Khaybar is ruined, for whenever we approach a nation (i.e., enemy to fight) then it will be a miserable morning for those who have been warned."

Vol. 4, bk. 52, no. 196: Narrated Abu Huraira: Allah's Apostle said, "I have been ordered to fight with the people till they say, 'None has the right to be worshipped but Allah,' and whoever says, 'None has the right to be worshipped but Allah,' his life and property will be saved by me except for Islamic law, and his accounts will be with Allah (either to punish him or to forgive him)."

Vol. 4, bk. 55, no. 546: Narrated Anas: When 'Abdullah bin Salam heard the arrival of the Prophet at Medina, he came to him and said, "I am going to ask you about three things which nobody knows except a prophet: What is the first portent of the Hour? What will be the first meal taken by the people of Paradise? Why does a child resemble its father, and why does it resemble its maternal uncle," Allah's Apostle said, "Gabriel has just now told me of their answers." 'Abdullah said, "He (i.e., Gabriel), from amongst all the angels, is the enemy of the Jews." Allah's Apostle said, "The first portent of the Hour will be a fire that will bring together the people from the east to the west; the first meal of the people of Paradise will be Extra-lobe (caudate lobe) of fish-liver. As for the resemblance of the child to its parents: If a man has sexual intercourse with his wife and gets discharge first, the child will resemble the father, and if the woman gets discharge first, the child will resemble her." On that 'Abdullah bin Salam said, "I testify that you are the Apostle of Allah." 'Abdullah bin Salam further said, "O Allah's Apostle! The Jews are liars, and if they should come to know about my conversion to Islam before you ask them (about me), they would tell a lie about me." The Jews came to Allah's Apostle and 'Abdullah went inside the house. Allah's Apostle asked (the Jews), "What kind of man is 'Abdullah bin Salam amongst you?" They replied, "He is the most learned

person amongst us, and the best amongst us, and the son of the best amongst us." Allah's Apostle said, "What do you think if he embraces Islam (will you do as he does)?" The Jews said, "May Allah save him from it." Then 'Abdullah bin Salam came out in front of them saying, "I testify that None has the right to be worshipped but Allah and that Muhammad is the Apostle of Allah." Thereupon they said, "He is the evilest among us, and the son of the evilest amongst us," and continued talking badly of him.

Vol. 4, bk. 56, no. 660: Narrated 'Aisha and Ibn 'Abbas: On his death-bed Allah's Apostle put a sheet over his face and when he felt hot, he would remove it from his face. When in that state (of putting and removing the sheet) he said, "May Allah's Curse be on the Jews and the Christians for they build places of worship at the graves of their prophets." (By that) he intended to warn (the Muslim) from what they (i.e., Jews and Christians) had done.

Vol. 4, bk. 56, no. 662: Narrated Abu Said: The Prophet said, "You will follow the wrong ways, of your predecessors so completely and literally that if they should go into the hole of a mastigure, you too will go there." We said, "O Allah's Apostle! Do you mean the Jews and the Christians?" He replied, "Whom else?" (Meaning, of course, the Jews and the Christians.)

Vol. 5, bk. 59, no. 365: Narrated Ibn Umar: Allah's Apostle had the date-palm trees of Bani Al-Nadir burnt and cut down at a place called Al-Buwaira. Allah then revealed: "What you cut down of the date-palm trees (of the enemy) Or you left them standing on their stems. It was by Allah's Permission."

Vol. 8, bk. 73, no. 53: Narrated 'Aisha (the wife of the Prophet): A group of Jews entered upon the Prophet and said, "As-Samu-Alaikum" (i.e., death be upon you). I understood it and said, "Wa-Alaikum As-Samu wal-la'n" (death and the curse of Allah be upon you). Allah's Apostle said "Be calm, O 'Aisha! Allah loves that one should be kind and lenient in all matters." I said, "O Allah's Apostle! Haven't you heard what they (the Jews) have said?" Allah's Apostle said, "I have (already) said (to them) 'And upon you!'"

Vol. 9, bk. 85, no. 77: Narrated Abu Huraira: While we were in the mosque, Allah's Apostle came out to us and said, "Let us proceed to the Jews." So we went along with him till we reached Bait-al-Midras (a place where the Torah used to be recited and all the Jews of the town used to gather). The Prophet stood up and addressed them, "O Assembly of Jews! Embrace Islam and you will be safe!" The Jews replied, "O Aba-l-Qasim! You have conveyed Allah's message to us." The Prophet said, "That is what I want (from you)." He repeated his first statement for the second time, and they said, "You have conveyed Allah's message, O Aba-l-Qasim." Then he said it for the third time and added, "You should Know that the earth belongs to Allah and His Apostle, and I want to exile you from this land, so whoever among you owns some property, can sell it, otherwise you should know that the Earth belongs to Allah and His Apostle."

Vol. 9, bk. 93, no. 532: Narrated Abu Sa'id Al-Khudri: We said, "O Allah's Apostle! Shall we see our Lord on the Day of Resurrection?" He said, "Do you have any difficulty in seeing the sun and the moon when the sky is clear?" We said, "No." He said, "So you will have no difficulty in seeing your Lord on that Day as you have no difficulty in seeing the sun and the moon (in a clear sky)." The Prophet then said, "Somebody will then announce, 'Let every nation follow what they used to worship.' So the companions of the cross will go with their cross, and the idolaters (will go) with their idols, and the companions of every god (false deities) (will go) with their god, till there remain those who used to worship Allah, both the obedient ones and the mischievous ones, and some of the people of the Scripture. Then Hell will be presented to them as if it were a mirage. Then it will be said to the Jews, "'What did you use to worship?' They will reply, 'We used to worship Ezra, the son of Allah.' It will be said to them, 'You arc liars, for Allah has neither a wife nor a son. What do you want (now)?' They will reply, 'We want You to provide us with water.' Then it will be said to them 'Drink,' and they will fall down in Hell (instead)."

SAHIH MUSLIM*

Bk. 001, no. 0284: It is narrated on the authority of Abu Huraira that the Messenger of Allah (may peace be upon him) observed: By Him in Whose hand is the life of Muhammad, he who amongst the community of Jews or Christians hears about me, but does not affirm his belief in that with which I have been sent and dies in this state (of disbelief), he shall be but one of the denizens of Hell-Fire.

Bk. 001, no. 0352: Abu Sa'id al-Khudri reported: Some people during the lifetime of the Messenger of Allah (may peace be upon him) said: Messenger of Allah! shall we see our Lord on the Day of Resurrection? The Messenger of Allah (may peace be upon him) said: Yes, and added: Do you feel any trouble in seeing the sun at noon with no cloud over it, and do you feel trouble in seeing the moon (open) in the full moonlit night with no cloud over it? They said: No, Messenger of Allah! He (the Holy Prophet) said: You will not feel any trouble in seeing Allah on the Day of Resurrection any more than you do in seeing any one of them. When the Day of Resurrection comes a Mu'adhdhin (a proclaimer) would proclaim: Let every people follow what they used to worship. Then all who worshipped idols and stones besides Allah would fall into the Fire, till only the righteous and the vicious and some of the people of the Book who worshipped Allah are left. Then the Jews would be summoned, and it would be said to them: What did you worship? They will say: We worshipped 'Uzair, son of Allah. It would be said to them: You tell a lie; Allah had never had a spouse or a son. What do you want now? They would say: We feel thirsty, O our Lord! Quench our thirst. They would be directed (to a certain direction) and asked: Why don't you go there to drink water? Then they would be pushed towards the Fire (and they would find to their great dismay that) it was but a mirage (and the raging flames of fire) would be consuming one another, and they would fall into the Fire.

Bk. 004, no. 2020: Abu Musa reported that when 'Umar was wounded, there came Suhaib from his house and went to 'Umar and stood by his side, and began to wail. Upon this 'Umar said: What are you weeping for? Are you weeping for me? He said: By Allah, it is for you that I weep, O Commander of the believers. He said: By Allah, you already know that the Messenger of Allah (may peace be upon him) had said: He who is lamented upon is punished. I made a mention of it to Musa b. Talha, and he said that 'A'isha told that it concerned the Jews (only).

Bk. 004, no. 2029: 'Amra daughter of 'Abd al Rahman narrated that she heard (from) 'A'isha and made a mention to her about 'Abdullah b. 'Umar as saying: The dead is punished because of the lamentation of the living. Upon this 'A'isha said: May Allah have mercy upon the father of 'Abd al-Rahman (Ibn 'Umar). He did not tell a lie, but he forgot or made a mistake. The Messenger of Allah (may peace be upon him) happened to pass by a (dead) Jewess who was being lamented. Upon this he said: They weep over her and she is being punished in the grave.

Bk. 010, no. 3763: Ibn Umar reported that 'Umar b. al-Khattab (Allah be pleased with him) expelled the Jews and Christians from the land of Hijaz, and that when Allah's Messenger (may peace be upon him) conquered Khaybar he made up his mind to expel the Jews from it (the territory of Khaybar) because, when that land was conquered, it came under the sway of Allah, that of His Messenger (may peace be upon him) and that of the Muslims. The Jews asked Allah's Messenger (may peace be upon him) to let them continue there on the condition

*Excerpted from Abdul Hamid Siddiqi, "Translation of Sahih Muslim," Muslim Students Association, University of Southern California, http://www.usc.edu/dept/MSA/fundamentals/hadithsunnah/muslim.

that they would work on it, and would get in turn half of the fruit (of the trees), whereupon Allah's Messenger (may peace be upon him) said: We would let you continue there so long as we will desire. So they continued (to cultivate the lands) till 'Umar externed them to Taima' and Ariha (two villages in Arabia, but out of Hijaz).

Bk. 019, no. 4363: It has been narrated on the authority of Abu Huraira who said: We were (sitting) in the mosque when the Messenger of Allah (may peace be upon him) came to us and said: (Let us) go to the Jews. We went out with him until we came to them. The Messenger of Allah (may peace be upon him) stood up and called out to them (saying): O ye assembly of Jews, accept Islam (and) you will be safe. They said: Abu'l-Qasim, you have communicated (God's Message to us). The Messenger of Allah (may peace be upon him) said: I want this (i. e., you should admit that God's Message has been communicated to you), accept Islam and you would be safe. They said: Abu'l-Qasim, you have communicated (Allah's Message). The Messenger of Allah (may peace be upon him) said: I want this . . .—He said to them (the same words) the third time (and on getting the same reply) he added: You should know that the earth belongs to Allah and His Apostle, and I wish that I should expel you from this land. Those of you who have any property with them should sell it, otherwise they should know that the earth belongs to Allah and His Apostle (and they may have to go away leaving everything behind).

Bk. 019, no. 4364: It has been narrated on the authority of Ibn Umar that the Jews of Banu Nadir and Banu Quraizi fought against the Messenger of Allah (may peace be upon him) who expelled Banu Nadir, and allowed Quraiza to stay on, and granted favour to them until they too fought against him. Then he killed their men, and distributed their women, children and properties among the Muslims, except that some of them had joined the Messenger of Allah (may peace be upon him) who granted them security. They embraced Islam. The Messenger of Allah (may peace be upon him) turned out all the Jews of Medina. Banu Qainuqa' (the tribe of 'Abdullah b. Salim) and the Jews of Banu Haritha and every other Jew who was in Medina.

Bk. 024, no. 5245: Abu Horaira reported Allah's Messenger (may peace be upon him) as saying: The Jews and the Christians do not dye (their hair), so oppose them.

Bk. 026, no. 5382: Ibn 'Umar reported Allah's Messenger (may peace be upon him) as saying: When the Jews offer you salutations, some of them say as-Sam-u-'Alaikum (death be upon you). You should say (in response to it): Let it be upon you.

Bk. 026, no. 5430: Anas reported that a Jewess came to Allah's Messenger (may peace be upon him) with poisoned mutton and he took of that what had been brought to him (Allah's Messenger). (When the effect of this poison was felt by him) he called for her and asked her about that, whereupon she said: I had determined to kill you. Thereupon he said: Allah will never give you the power to do it. He (the narrator) said that they (the Companion's of the Holy Prophet) said: Should we not kill her? Thereupon he said: No. He (Anas) said: I felt (the effects of this poison) on the uvula of Allah's Messenger.

Bk. 037, no. 6668: Abu Burda reported Allah's Messenger (may peace be upon him) as saying: There would come people amongst the Muslims on the Day of Resurrection with as heavy sins as a mountain, and Allah would forgive them and He would place in their stead the Jews and the Christians. (As far as I think), Abu Raub said: I do not know as to who is in doubt. Abu Burda said: I narrated it to 'Umar b. 'Abd al-'Aziz, whereupon he said: Was it your father who narrated it to you from Allah's Apostle (may peace be upon him)? I said: Yes.

Bk. 040, no. 6861: This hadith has been narrated on the authority of Abu Ayyub through some other chains of transmitters (and the words are): "Allah's Messenger (may peace be upon him) went out after the sun had set and he heard some sound and said: It is the Jews who are being tormented in their graves."

Bk. 041, no. 6984: Abdullah b. 'Umar reported that Allah's Messenger (may peace be upon him) said: The Jews will fight against you and you will gain victory over them until the stone would say: Muslim, here is a Jew behind me; kill him.

Bk. 041, no. 6985: Abu Huraira reported Allah's Messenger (may peace be upon him) as saying: The last hour would not come unless the Muslims will fight against the Jews and the Muslims would kill them until the Jews would hide themselves behind a stone or a tree and a stone or a tree would say: Muslim, or the servant of Allah, there is a Jew behind me; come and kill him; but the tree Gharqad would not say, for it is the tree of the Jews.

Bk. 041, no. 7034: Anas b. Malik reported that Allah's Messenger (may peace be upon him) said: The Dajjal [Muslim Anti-Christ] would be followed by seventy thousand Jews of Isfahan wearing Persian shawls.

SUNAN ABU DAWUD*

Bk. 2, no. 0652: Narrated Aws ibn Thabit al-Ansari: The Apostle of Allah (peace be upon him) said: Act differ-

*Excerpted from Ahwad Hasan, "*Partial* Translation of Sunan Abu Dawud," Muslim Students Association, University of Southern California, http://www.usc.edu./dept/MSA/fundamentals/hadithsunnah/abudawud.

ently from the Jews, for they do not pray in their sandals or their shoes.

Bk. 19, no. 2996: Narrated Muhayyisah: The Apostle of Allah (peace be upon him) said: If you gain a victory over the men of Jews, kill them. So Muhayyisah jumped over Shubaybah, a man of the Jewish merchants. He had close relations with them. He then killed him. At that time Huwayyisah (brother of Muhayyisah) had not embraced Islam. He was older than Muhayyisah. When he killed him, Huwayyisah beat him and said: O enemy of Allah, I swear by Allah, you have a good deal of fat in your belly from his property.

Bk. 19, no. 3000: Narrated Abdullah Ibn Umar: The Prophet fought with the people of Khaybar, and captured their palm-trees and land, and forced them to remain confined to their fortresses. So they concluded a treaty of peace providing that gold, silver and weapons would go to the Apostle of Allah (peace be upon him), and whatever they took away on their camels would belong to them, on condition that they would not hide and carry away anything. If they did (so), there would be no protection for them and no treaty (with Muslims).

They carried away a purse of Huyayy ibn Akhtab who was killed before (the battle of) Khaybar. He took away the ornaments of Banu an-Nadir when they were expelled.

The Prophet (peace be upon him) asked Sa'yah: Where is the purse of Huyayy ibn Akhtab?

He replied: The contents of this purse were spent on battles and other expenses. (Later on) they found the purse. So he killed Ibn Abul Huqayq, captured their women and children, and intended to deport them.

They said: Muhammad, leave us to work on this land; we shall have half (of the produce) as you wish, and you will have half. The Apostle of Allah (peace be upon him) used to make a contribution of eighty wasqs of dates and twenty wasqs of wheat to each of his wives.

Bk. 19, no. 3001: Narrated Abdullah ibn Umar: Umar said: The Apostle of Allah (peace be upon him) had transaction with the Jews of Khaybar on condition that we should expel them when we wish. If anyone has property (with them), he should take it back, for I am going to expel the Jews. So he expelled them.

Bk 25, no. 3638: Narrated Zayd ibn Thabit: The Apostle of Allah (peace be upon him) ordered me (to learn the writing of the Jews), so I learnt for him the writing of the Jews. He said: I swear by Allah, I do not trust Jews in respect of writing for me. So I learnt it, and only a fortnight passed that I mastered it. I would write for him when he wrote (to them), and read to him when something was written to him.

Bk. 27, no. 3772: Narrated Abdullah ibn Mas'ud: The Prophet (peace be upon him) liked the foreleg (of a

sheep). Once the foreleg was poisoned, and he thought that the Jews had poisoned it.

Bk. 33, no. 4185: Narrated Anas ibn Malik: Al-Hajjaj ibn Hassan said: We entered upon Anas ibn Malik. My sister al-Mughirah said: You were a boy in those days and you had two locks of hair. He (Anas) rubbed your head and invoked blessing on you. He said: Shave them (i.e. the locks) or clip them, for this is the fashion of the Jews.

Bk. 38, no. 4349: Narrated Ali ibn Abu Talib: A Jewess used to abuse [i.e., write satirical verses about] the Prophet (peace be upon him) and disparage him. A man strangled her till she died. The Apostle of Allah (peace be upon him) declared that no recompense was payable for her blood.

Bk. 39, no. 4495: Narrated Jabir ibn Abdullah: Ibn Shihab said: Jabir ibn Abdullah used to say that a Jewess from the inhabitants of Khaybar poisoned a roasted sheep and presented it to the Apostle of Allah (peace be upon him) who took its foreleg and ate from it. A group of his companions also ate with him.

The Apostle of Allah (peace be upon him) then said: Take your hands away (from the food). The Apostle of Allah (peace be upon him) then sent someone to the Jewess and he called her.

He said to her: Have you poisoned this sheep? The Jewess replied: Who has informed you? He said: This foreleg which I have in my hand has informed me. She said: Yes. He said: What did you intend by it? She said: I thought if you were a prophet, it would not harm you; if you were not a prophet, we should rid ourselves of him (i.e., the [false] Prophet). The Apostle of Allah (peace be upon him) then forgave her, and did not punish her. But some of his companions who ate it, died. The Apostle of Allah (peace be upon him) had himself cupped on his shoulder on account of that which he had eaten from the sheep. Abu Hind cupped him with the horn and knife. He was a client of Banu Bayadah from the Ansar.

Bk. 39, no. 4498: Narrated AbuSalamah: Muhammad ibn Amr said on the authority of AbuSalamah, and he did not mention the name of AbuHurayrah: The Apostle of Allah (peace be upon him) used to accept presents but not alms (sadaqah).

This version adds: So a Jewess presented him at Khaybar with a roasted sheep which she had poisoned. The Apostle of Allah (peace be upon him) ate of it and the people also ate.

He then said: Take away your hands (from the food), for it has informed me that it is poisoned. Bishr ibn al-Bara' ibn Ma'rur al-Ansari died.

So he (the Prophet) sent for the Jewess (and said to her): What motivated you to do the work you have done?

She said: If you were a prophet, it would not harm

you; but if you were a king, I should rid the people of you. The Apostle of Allah (peace be upon him) then ordered regarding her and she was killed. He then said about the pain of which he died: I continued to feel pain from the morsel which I had eaten at Khaybar. This is the time when it has cut off my aorta.

Bk. 41, no. 5186: Narrated Abu Hurayrah: Suhayl ibn Abu Salih said: I went out with my father to Syria. The people passed by the cloisters in which there were Christians and began to salute them. My father said: Do not give them salutation first, for Abu Hurayrah reported the Apostle of Allah (peace be upon him) as saying: Do not salute them (Jews and Christians) first, and when you meet them on the road, force them to go to the narrowest part of it.

HADITH BY TIRMIDHI AND MUSLIM FROM THE AL-BAGHAWI COMPILATION
*MISHKAT AL-MASABIH**

Abu Bakra reported God's messenger as saying, "The parents of the dajjal will wait thirty years without having any children born to them, then a boy who will be one-eyed and have a long molar tooth and be most useless will be born to them. His eyes will sleep but his heart will not." God's messenger then described his parents to them saying, "His father will be very tall and spare and will have a long nose like a beak, and his mother will be a huge woman with long arms." Abu Bakra said they heard of a child being born among the Jews in Medina, so az-Zubair b. al'Awwam and he went to visit the parents and saw that they were as God's messenger had described. They asked them if they had a child and they replied that they had waited thirty years without having a child born to them but now a boy had been born to them who was one-eyed, had a long molar tooth and was most useless, whose eyes slept but whose heart did not. When they went out they found him lying in the sun in a wrapper mumbling. He uncovered his head and asked what they had said, and when they asked if he had heard what they said he replied that he had, for his eyes slept but his heart did not. Tirmidhi transmitted it [pp. 1157–58].

Abu Musa reported God's messenger as saying that when the Day of Resurrection comes God will hand a Jew (or a Christian) to every Muslim and say, "This is your means of release from hell." Muslims transmitted it [pp. 1171–72].

CHAPTER 5
Jews and Muslims according to the Hadith

Georges Vajda

INTRODUCTION[1]

After the many studies of relations between Islam and Judaism over the past century (inaugurated by the famous treatise by the German scholar A. Geiger, *Was hat Mohammad aus dem Judenthume aufgenommen* [*What Muhammad Adapted from Judaism*, now in English translation by Moshe Perlmann, New York: Ktav, 1950, titled *Judaism and Islam*] in 1833), it is necessary to justify the publication of a new work that does not even have the merit of making known materials that were previously unknown, or of treating in all their breadth the problems that arise from this subject. In effect, the research I am proposing to undertake has a rather limited objective: examination of materials from the hadiths [sayings of the Prophet] that relate to the Jews, to the exclusion from political history of Arab Judaism, contemporaneous with Muhammad, and of the problem, often but never exhaustively treated, of the Haggadic influences on Qur'anic and post-Qur'anic legends.

In short, it is a matter of gathering the characteristics of the image that Muslim tradition formed of Jews. The interest of this research has resided primarily in the fact that it allows us to go back to the most important source after the Qur'an, which completes or modifies it on numerous points, about the attitude that official Islam adopted toward the Jews. And so I have concentrated less on this aspect of the subject, for it is one of the best known thanks to the work of the Orientalists.

It is from another viewpoint that I believe I have profited from attentive reading of the sources and the comparison of variants of those hadiths that interest us. As we know, the hadiths are not a sure guide for knowledge of the authentic biography of the prophet, but in its diversity, it is a faithful mirror of the fluctuations in Islam in evolution. The hadith is always suspect, if not for being completely inauthentic or the product of fantasy without any relation to reality, then at least for concealing a bias, an argument for or against a particular doctrine, custom, institution, or political and religious party. Considered from this angle, many hadiths that seem without value in themselves acquire worth by the allusions they contain. This is as true of the hadiths regarding Jews as of all the others, and so there is utility in analyzing them not only to find information on the Jews, but also for allusions to facts about Muslims. I think that this method, which is used by Ignatius Goldziher and P. Lammens, has still not been systematically applied to the group of hadiths that I intend to study.

My debt is great to all those who have preceded me in this research. It goes without saying that I have always gone back to first-hand sources, yet (without pretending to any kind of priority) I refer rarely to the work of Orientalists, except when I have not had access to the sources that they did.

As for the texts that I have plumbed, naturally I have not tried to reproduce them extensively, in the text or in translation. While giving as many references as possible (which will permit the reader to realize quickly any deficiencies in my documentation), I have closely studied only typical texts and variants that have seemed for one reason or another to be worthy of interest.[2]

A reclassification of materials that are already known, even if insufficiently exploited and brought to light, the present essay cannot avoid repeating certain information given previously. Thus that most of the points that I will treat have been touched upon in the information that Goldziher (especially during the first half of his scientific activity) scattered in various anthologies. But as this master unfortunately never wrote on the subject, this overall work is still wanting, and since after him and J. Horovitz, very few Orientalists would be capable of furnishing it, I have been forced to take up his research, with the aid of sources of which he still was not aware in his youthful works, and so to complete them along lines he did not envisage. On the other hand, I am content to refer readers back to his various articles for details of things that he has, believe me, entirely elucidated.

If the principal interest of the hadiths that occupy us here is of an Islamological order, the information that can be drawn from them about the religious and moral

Georges Vajda, "Juifs et Musulmans selon le Hadith" (Jews and Muslims according to the Hadith), *Journal Asiatique* 229 (1937): 57–129. Translated by Susan Emanuel.

situation of the Jews, dramatized (*mise-en-scène*) by Tradition, is by no means negligible. Naturally, the difficulty in situating them with exactness in time and space invites us to the greatest prudence in their use.

As soon as one renounces using the hadiths as absolutely sure and trustworthy documentation, it is evidently vain to try to take account of the value judgments that Muslim criticism emits regarding any isolated tradition, any collection, or the individual credibility of any traditionalist. Therefore I have been very wide-ranging in making use of documents and the "six books," as well as of the *Musnad* by Ahmed ibn Hanbal and the *Muwatta* by Mālik, not forgetting the commentaries to which I was able to have access, Kastalāni on Bukhārī, Nawawi on Muslim, and Zurkāni on the *Muwatta*. Ibn Sa'd's *Tabakāt* and Tabarī's *Tafsīr* have also been consulted.[3] It would no doubt have been possible and even desirable to prolong this promenade through the vast fields of the *hadith*. But reading the commentaries and rather exhaustive surveys in late collections like the *Muhtasar Kanz al-'Ummāl* convinced me that the benefit, although certain, that one might hope to draw from more extensive investigations would have been counterbalanced by a considerable loss of time and indefinite postponement of this present work. This pretext is weak, I agree, but it remains true that despite the admirable *Handbook of Early Muhammedan Tradition* by M. Wensinck and the *Concordance* edited by the same scholar, the studies of the hadiths, as with other Islamic studies, are still (with the exception of a few of value) at the same stage as classical philology in the seventeenth century. Thus it is not absolutely reprehensible to publish essays that might have gained from maturing a few more years. The ultra-cautiousness of doing so is redeemed by the admission of not having reached the goal and the sincere desire to outdo oneself in future and of being outdone still more rapidly by other scholars.[4]

The materials of the hadiths relating to Jews (excluding traditions that are purely historical or haggadic) may be divided into three groups:

1. Jewish customs and the attitude of Muslims toward them.
2. Behavior of Jews toward Muhammad and Muslims.
3. Behavior of Muslims toward Jews.

Needless to say, this division cannot be imposed in a rigorous way on documents of the particular nature with which we are dealing. It will be for us a guiding thread, without constituting an absolute norm.

I.

Goldziher has very clearly discovered[5] the principle that animates the prescriptions and recommendations of the hadiths regarding the customs of non-Muslims. This principle boils down to a single word: *khālifūhum,* meaning "do not do like them."[6]

The following texts (which are only a selection) will illustrate this attitude:

1. A.B.H., 5:264 ff: "Leaving his apartments, the prophet found old men *Ansar* whose beards were white. He told them: 'Assembly of Ansār, dye yourselves red or yellow and do the contrary of the people of the Book.' We told him: 'Apostle of Allah, the people of the Book wear the *sirwāl* (pantaloons) and do not wear the *izār*' [loincloth]. The prophet says 'Wear the sirwāl and wear the *izār*, and do the contrary of the people of the Book.' We told him 'The people of the Book wear ankle-boots (*huff*) and do not wear sandals (*na'l*).' He says: 'Wear ankle-boots and wear sandals, and do the contrary of the people of the Book.' We told him: 'The people of the Book trim their beards and grow their mustaches.' He says: 'Trim the mustache and grow the beard, and do the contrary of the people of the Book.'[7]

Ibid., 2:356 (Abū Huayra): "grow your beard, remove your mustaches, alter your white hair and do not resemble Jews or Christians."[8]

The prophet also forbids as a Jewish custom the *qaza* (partial removal of the hair).[9]

Also branded was the use of false hair/hairpieces/wigs. According to a tradition reported in several compilations (Sa'id b. al-Musayyab and Humayd b. 'Abdalrahmān), during the last *khutba* [Friday sermon in the mosque] that he pronounced in Medina, the caliph Mu'awiya I showed the faithful a toupée of false hair, saying, "I never saw that done except among the Jews, the prophet had called it 'falseness' (*zūr*)"; or in another version: "people of Medina, where are your wise men? I heard the prophet, who prohibited doing the like and said: 'the children of Israel perished when their women took [false hair].'"[10]

Rabbinic literature did know about wigs. They were an integral part of the feminine toilette since the Mishnah allows women to go out on Saturday with their false chignons.[11]

The solemnity of the dramatization proves that pious circles tried to combat energetically this mode of coiffure.

The real motive for this condemnation arises from a hadith that was much circulated[12] that bans the wearing of false hair, tattooing, and hair removal, for all these practices "alter the creation of God."

Alongside these hadiths one finds, though, traditions of a different tendency. Pagans, says Ibn 'Abbās,[13] had the custom of making a parting in their hair *Yafuquuna r'uusa-hum* but the People of the Book left their hair loose. The Prophet loves to conform to the habits of the People of the Book [some versions add "when he had not received the order to do the contrary"]; so he let flow his locks of hair, but he did not yet make a parting.[14]

We have seen above two hadiths recommending the

dyeing of the beard as opposed to the custom of the People of the Book. These traditions often go back to various *isnād* [chain of transmission], and versions that scarcely differ in the fundamentals.

Almost always it is recommended to dye the hair in contrast to the Jews,[15] or to Jews and Christians.[16]

The Prophet himself, if we may believe the authors of the sira [Prophet's biography], did not have to apply this recommendation since (according to his servant, Anas b. Mālik) he never had enough white hair to justify dyeing.[17] On the other hand, many of his companions used cosmetics (Ibn Sa'd raises scrupulously all traditions relating to this subject), among them Abū Bakr.[18]

It is difficult to say if the condemnation, presupposed by the hadith, of dyeing hair on the part of the People of the Book, corresponds or not to reality. Rabbinic law does not prohibit it, as far as I can see. Krauss[19] cites only two Talmudic passages, of which one, *Nāzīr*, 39a, speaks of old people's hair-dyeing, without a disapproving tone, and the other, *Bābā M'sī'ā*, 60b, relates the incident of a non-Jew who dyes his hair to sell himself better as a slave.

2. The scruples of Jews on matters regarding ablutions are favorably reflected by a hadith. Mohammed, son of the famous Jewish convert 'Abdallāh b. Salām, recounts[20] that the Prophet asked one day the Jews of Kubā to inform him about purification, for "it is you God has praised because of purification" (allusion to Qur'an 9:108): "There you shall find men who keep themselves pure. Allah loves those that purify themselves."[21] They told him that the Torah prescribed purifying with water after the satisfaction of natural needs. There is perhaps a vague allusion to Deuteronomy 23:10 ff that contains prescriptions regarding hygiene for the Israelite army on campaign,[22] but in any case, the hadith has no historical value since the Qur'anic verse onto which it is affixed does not concern Jews at all, but the incident of the "mosque of rivalry."[23]

3. On another point of ritual legislation, the conflict is very pronounced[24] between Muslim conceptions and Jewish conceptions. It is a matter of the regime of women in menstruation. Very severe among the Jews,[25] it is much less strict among the Muslims.

The compilations of Bukhāri and Muslim[26] transmit hadiths that say the Prophet had himself washed or combed by Aysha when she was in menses, taking objects from her hand even if his wife had warned him of her state, leaning on her while reciting the Qur'an, and so on.

Muslim[27] reports the following tradition in the name of Anas: "Jews do not eat in the company of women in menses and do not stay in the same place as they. The companions of the prophet consulted him on this subject. Then was revealed the Qur'anic verse 2:222: "They ask you about menstruation. Say: 'It is an indisposition.

Keep aloof from women during their menstrual periods and do not approach them until they are clean again . . .' And the prophet added: 'Do whatever you want except in carnal relations.'[28] Having learned that, the Jews said: 'This man does not want to leave any of our doctrines without opposition.'"[29] Usayd b. al-Hudayr[30] and 'Abbād b. Bisr[31] reported these statements to the Prophet, adding that from now on they would abstain from any kind of relation with their wives while they were in menses. The Prophet showed himself very disappointed in this attitude.

The Judaic scruples concerning the ritual purity of women remains a lively issue in Islam, though, as attested by the protestations one finds in the hadiths.

Bakhāri reports that the daughter of Zayd B. Tābit, having learned that some women called for light in the middle of the night to check their state of purity, declared: "[Once upon a time] women did not act like that," and she reproved them.[32]

Despite the interpretation that Kastalāni gives this hadith (see the preceding note), it seems to me that we are dealing with a protest against the scruples inspired by the rabbinic recommendation, such as one finds in the Nidda. 2:1: "it is meritorious to examine the purity of women as minutely as possible."[33] In the same chapter of the Mishnah we find the opinion that when a husband returns from a voyage, conjugal relations should take place in artificial light, a practice otherwise prohibited.[34]

In another passage from Bukhāri,[35] Umm 'Atiyya declares: "we used to attribute no importance to grey or yellow flows" [outside menstruation], an affirmation in which resonates a note of polemic against the meticulousness specific to Jews in this matter.[36]

4. Qur'anic verse 2:222, on which legislation concerning menstruation is founded, is followed by a revelation on the modes of conjugal relations: "Your wives are your fields; go, then, into your fields when/as you please" (2:223).[37]

If one consults Tabarī's commentary, which devotes no less than eleven pages[38] to the interpretation of verses 222–23, one realizes with surprise that with regard to the first verse, he does not cite the traditions of the anti-Jewish tendency that we have just studied. He does not mention the Jews at all, but gives as reason for the revelation (with hadith as evidence) that pagan Arabs avoided any contact with women in menses;[39] the verse must thus be combating this custom, and the authorities of Tabarī are not wrong to communicate very scabrous traditions about Muhammad's conduct toward his wives in an impure state.

The following verse is interpreted, with various nuances, by a majority of exegetes in this sense, that is, that the modes of the sexual act are left to the pleasure of each individual, although bestiality is forbidden. ['Abdallāh] ibn 'Omar allows the act against nature, though,[40] and the prevailing opinion regarded as licit the interruption of coitus for the purpose of preventing conception (*'azl*).

Jews were represented as rigorous on this matter. A tradition[41] gives as motive for the revelation of verse 223 that a Jew who encountered a Muslim asked him: "Is there among you someone who has congress with his wife on his knees?" The revelation specifies that any kind of congress is licit provided that it is not against nature.

According to another tradition,[42] several Muslims conversed one day in the presence of a Jew about their intimate relations with their wives.[43] The Jew cried: "You resemble the beasts! As for us, we have congress with them only in one way."

It is also recounted that the Jews said: "Arabs have congress with their wives *ex parte posteriore*; a child born of such relations has squinty eyes." And so the verse was revealed to stigmatize their lie.

If one may lend credence to a tradition of Ibn 'Abbās,[44] the Quraysh *muhājirun* [immigrants] took liberties that shocked their wives from Medina. But it would be impossible for Jewish influence to have been involved.[45]

Onanism/masturbation and sometimes bestiality, on which the hadiths cited by Tabarī give such exact if repellent details, were practiced, it seems, especially with slaves with whom they wanted to avoid conception.

The Jews protested against this procedure. Here is what a tradition of Abū Sa'īd al-Hudrī relates: someone comes to find the Prophet and tells him: "I have a slave with whom I interrupt coitus, for I do not want her to conceive, but I want what men want. But the Jews claim that *coitus interruptus* is an attenuated case of the exposure of newborn girls."[46] The Prophet replied: "The Jews have lied. If Allah wants to create it, you are not capable of preventing [the child from being conceived]."[47]

The same Companion found himself implicated in an analogous incident after the expedition of al'Muraysi in year 5. The partial restraint of the Muslims, permitting them the satisfaction of their concupiscence without compromising the hope for ransoming the captives, was approved by the Prophet, with the same motive as in the preceding hadith. But when Abū Sa'īd wanted to sell a young girl from the booty, a Jew observed at the market that she was certainly pregnant by him; the Muslim assured him that he had practiced *'azl*, to which the Jew replied that it was an attenuated form of coitus. Informed of this discussion, the Prophet could only denounce the lies of the Jews.[48]

The frankly reproving attitude of the Jews toward the sexual dissipation of the Arabs may be illustrated by many Talmudic texts. They found conjugal relations during the day repugnant, at least unless they were invisible.[49] The indecencies committed in the course of the act implied physical infirmities for any child: muteness, deafness, blindness, paralysis.[50] Onanism was severely reproved.[51]

But the contrary opinion was also seen. A man might do anything with his wife in the same way as each person had the right to consume meat and fish according to his taste.[52] Rabbis declared themselves powerless to answer the complaints of women who reproached their husbands for having taking unpleasant liberties with them.[53]

The silence of Tabarī on Jewish objections to the governing of women in menses cannot be fortuitous. There must have been a certain embarrassment about the laxity of the Qur'an as opposed to Jewish rigor, which had not ceased to find partisans among the Muslims. Moreover the Qur'anic text, whose tenor is very general, would be susceptible of being interpreted otherwise if it were not unanimously read like this by Muslim exegesis. But this unanimity, combined with other facts that we shall encounter in the remainder of this essay, makes us believe that the tradition did indeed grasp Muhammad's thinking on this.

As for the severity with which Arab paganism excluded the impure woman from the community, I do not know if one should take it literally. The references gathered by Wellhausen[54] show only that the woman in menses was excluded from sacrifices and feasts, a rule that Islam maintains in spirit when it forbids the *Salāt* [requisite five Muslim daily prayers] for the impure woman. This is not the only example of the transposition in paganism of a custom for which the Muslims insisted on not recognizing the Jewish provenance.[55]

5. The chapter on ritual purity, which for the ancients is at the same time cleanliness in itself, includes proprieties to be observed in the satisfaction of natural needs. Arab paganism already knew rules of this kind.[56] Wensinck has shown[57] that the prescriptions of the *sunna* [literally "trodden path," meaning religious acts instituted by Muhammad, or "the way of the Prophet"] relating to behavior in water closets were inspired by the corresponding rabbinical rules.[58]

6. The customs observed at funerals are also of interest for our subject on several points that I will treat briefly since Goldziher has already dealt with this question.[59]

The Prophet stood up at the passage of a funeral procession. He was told that the dead person was a Jew. He replied: "[W]hen you see a funeral procession, stand up." Later, in Kādisiyya, Sahl b. Hunayf and Kays b. Sa'd rose at the passage of a procession. They noticed that the dead person was a *dhimmi*. They relate the same incident, except for making the Prophet say "*alaysat nafsan* [is this not a soul]?"[60]

According to a hadith of Abū Mūsa al-As'arī, one should stand at the passing of a funeral procession whether for a Jew, a Christian, or a Muslim, for it is not to the dead person that one expresses respect, but to the angels who accompany him.[61]

A hadith from Jābir relates the same incidents as those reported by Bukhārī but with the motive: "the dead person is a terror (*faza'*); when you see a funeral, stand up."[62]

Another tradition ('Bāda b. al'Sāmit) recounts that in following funerals, the Prophet had the habit of standing until the dead person was put in his tomb. One day a *haber* [rabbi] passed and told him that the Jews did likewise, at which Muhammad invited those attending to sit down so as not to do as the Jews.[63]

The respectful attitude that was attributed to the Prophet with respect even to a dead Jew displeased certain fanatics, among which one is disagreeably surprised to find Hasan al-Basrī. In his commentary on the Muwatta, Zurqāni summarizes[64] the hadiths that we have just seen (adding the motive that one should stand out of respect toward the one who takes souls), but rejects the reasons given by 'Abdallāh b. Ayyās and Hasan who had conjectured that the Prophet stood up because he was bothered to see the cadaver of a Jew pass before him and because the smell of a Jew disturbed him.

The procession should move quickly for, according to Abū Hurayra, "if death is good, it is toward a good thing that you are leading him, if not it is an evil that you should get rid of as soon as possible"[65] or, as Sa'īd b. al Musayyab (died 94) told his people: "[I]f some good awaits me with my Lord, that is worth more than what is at your home."[66] Still, in another opinion, "one should not go with slow steps with the coffin like the Jews do."[67] 'Imrān b. al Husayn (d. 52) ordered when dying: "[W]hen after my death you take me outside, go quickly and do not walk slowly like the Jews and the Christians."[68]

Islam reproves, at least in theory, lamentation of the dead. Public lamentation was also forbidden to Jews and Christians.[69]

There are also some texts of hadiths that mention the lamentations of Jews but with a tendency that examination of variants quickly reveals. One finds in effect rather frequent allusions to a (popular?) belief that the lamentations of survivors augment the pain of the defunct. This belief however well rooted in the consciousness of the faithful, was set aside by orthodoxy as being in contradiction with the idea of individual responsibility, often and clearly expressed by the Qur'an (e.g., 6:164, etc. "no soul shall bear another's burden").

The Prophet heard one day that a Jewess was mourned by her parents. He observed: "[T]hey cry for her and she is punished in her tomb"[70] according to Kastalāni because of her infidelity, not at all on account of her parents' lamentations. But this exegesis is incompatible with the texts that immediately precede it, from which it arises that independently of the behavior, real or fictive, of Jews in mourning, the belief in question had to be energetically combated.[71] 'Omar professed it, it seems,[72] and against him Tradition has mobilized a personage no less than the Prophet's wife Aysha.[73]

The tomb of the Prophet was dug in *lahd*, that is to say, a hole was made in the lateral partition wall of the grave and not in *sakk* or *darīh*, a vertical grave. The majority of traditions in Ibn Sa'd attribute the adoption of this mode of interment to the fact, due to chance, that the gravedigger who made the *lahd* turned up before the one who practiced the other technique. There is only one variant[74] that justifies this choice by the Prophet's entourage with this consideration: "[T]he *sakk* is proper to [P]eople of the Book." The documentary value of this clue is nil, for the two systems of inhumation were used concurrently in Arabia[75] and also in Palestine.[76]

7. The question of burial leads us to examine another group of hadiths in which the severe censure inflicted on Jews and on Christians does not succeed in hiding the true tendency, which is to stigmatize a Muslim abuse.

A hadith that was widespread relates that during his agony the Prophet cursed the Jews and Christians who had taken the tombs of their prophets as sites of worship.[77]

Here are the principal versions of this hadith.

A.B.H. 1:218 (Ibn 'Abbās and Aysha): When the Prophet was taken by an attack, he threw a *hamīsa* (a sort of robe) over his face; when he came around, we lifted him while he said: "May God curse the Jews and the Christians, they have taken the tombs of their prophets for sites of worship." (Aysha adds: "he put them on guard [Muslims] against similar practices.")[78]

Elsewhere, one finds this curse without the tale that frames it;[79] Abū 'Bayda relates it as the Prophet's last recommendation, at the same time as the order to expel the Jews from the Arabian Peninsula.[80]

Ibn Sa'd devotes an entire chapter (2:2, 34–36) to this reproach made to Jews and Christians.

Aysha said that during the Prophet's illness his wives conversed by his bedside on an Abyssinian church called Mariya. In effect, Umm Salama and Umm Habiba had stayed in Abyssinia. The Prophet says: "[T]hose are people who, when a pious man finds himself among them, construct a place of prayer on his tomb and fashion images [they] put there. These are the most perverse men before God."[81]

Historicity of this tradition is very debatable. It ill fits with the fact that most of the sources that tell us of the Prophet's illness. According to the current version of the sira, Muhammad continued to take turns with his wives until the aggravation of his state of health forced him to ask them for permission to be cared for by Aysha. His malady was, moreover, painful and companied by frequent fainting. So one imagines with difficulty a conversation at his bedside about religious architecture in Abyssinia.

34:23–25 = A.B.H. 1:218, and so forth.

35:1–4. Jundub heard the Prophet say five days before his death: "Those who preceded you took for mosques the tombs of their prophets and their righteous. As for you, do not take tombs for mosques, for I forbid you to do so."[82]

35:5–7. When he met the Prophet for the last time,

'Utba heard him say: "May God combat the Jews and the Christians, they have taken . . . "

35:9–11. The Caliph 'Omar II also cited these prophetic words with the addition: "That there not remain two religions in the countries of the Arabs" (cf. *Sahih*, 44–45).

35:12–14 ('Atā b. Yasār). The Prophet says: "Ah, my God, do not make my tomb an idol one adores. The anger of God is violent against those who have taken . . ." (An abbreviated version of the same hadith goes back to Abū Hurayra, *Muslim*, p. 366, 4–5).

35:16–18 ('Urwa, Aysha). "The Prophet said during the illness from which he did not recover 'may God curse [etc.]'; if he had not [said that] people would not visit his tomb, but he feared that it would be taken for a mosque."[83]

35:24–26. Kastalāni'b b. Mālik reports that five days before his death, the Prophet very solemnly protested against the procedure of ancient generations that took their dwellings for tombs.

The tendency of this hadith is contrary to that of the previous ones: whereas they constitute so many protests against the incorporation of Aysha's home and the tomb of the Prophet, which were separated only by a thin partition, in the mosque of Medina,[84] Ka'b's hadith aims to justify this measure by making the Prophet condemn burial at home.[85]

The lesson that we may draw from this group of traditions is that the Jews and Christians play only the role of extras. They are used for the dramatization of a hadith that is forged to combat the cult of the Prophet's tomb in Medina.[86]

8. Muslim tradition condemns certain gestures as specific to Jews (or Christians). Since the Orientalists have noted most of these texts, I can confine myself to a summary reminder.

A hadith disapproves of Muslims who salute each other by making a sign with their fingers like the Jews, or with the hand like the Christians.[87]

Aysha did not like her protégé Masrūq to put his hands on his hips, for, she said, only the Jews do that.[88]

Raising the hands in prayer is a Jewish gesture.[89]

One should not sway (*nawadān*) while praying, as the Jews do.[90]

9. To end this first group of hadiths, I will cite an eschatological tradition, which has the Prophet say that before the final judgment the Muslims will follow step by step[91] the manner of acting of their predecessors. They ask him: "Are you speaking of Jews and Christians?" "Whom else would I be speaking of?"Another version, still more bizarre, from Abū Hurayra, replaces Jews and Christians with Persians and Romans.[92]

This is a hadith of a very banal type. The depravity of manners and the disappearance of good Muslim customs, being replaced by foreign customs: this is a commonplace in eschatological tradition; our text does not borrow from any historical interpretation.

II.

The more Muhammad advanced his career in Medina, the more his resentment against Jews grew. This evolution was rather natural since the Jews, not content with disappointing his expectations of seeing them rally unreservedly to his cause, riddled him with sarcasm, cast doubt on the authenticity of his prophetic mission, and lastly had the fault of possessing vast resources in chattels and land, which the Prophet could not do without in order to secure his domination in Medina and the execution of vast projects of religious and political conquest.

It is not up to me here to present, after so many others, a historical study of Muhammad's fight with the Jews, nor to study all the exegetical lucubrations which some commentators have used to illustrate the passages of the revelation that refer to this—or are thought to be related to it. I shall confine myself to analyzing a certain number of traditions whose very diversity is an excellent proof of their inauthenticity, but which will show us how the image of Jews became more precise and nuanced in the pious circles where these traditions were forged, or at least enlarged and developed.

1. The first tradition has it that Jews hated and were jealous of Muhammad; they did not wait to do so until he was established in Yatrib, for already the legendary Bahīrā invites Abū Tālib, uncle and tutor of the infant Muhammad, to beware of Jews.[93] Nevertheless, the Jews knew very well that it was Muhammad who should accomplish the prediction of their books.[94] If, then, they did not follow him, this was not out of ignorance but out of jealousy and national particularism.

Here are two texts illustrating this recrimination:

The apostle of Allah entered the *Bayt al-Midrās* [house of study] and said: "Send me the wisest person among you." They said: "It is Abdallāh b. Sūriyā."[95] The apostle of Allah remained alone with him and adjured him by his religion, by the blessings that God had showered [on the Jews] by nourishing them with manna and *salwaa* quail and protecting them by clouds [to answer him]: "Do you know that I am the apostle of Allah?" He answered: "By God, yes, and of course these people [the Jews] know what I know and that your description is clearly found in the Torah, but they are envious of you." [The Prophet:] "What prevents you yourself?" He answered: "I feel repugnant at doing otherwise than my people, but perhaps they will follow you and convert to Islam, and then I will convert [also]."[96]

A Jew said to his comrade: "Let us go find the prophet to ask him about this verse (Qur'an 17:101): 'We brought Moses nine signs.'" His comrade says: "Do not say *prophet* in speaking of him, for if he heard this, he would have four eyes."[97] They ask him and he tells them: "You would not associate anything with God, you would not commit larceny, you would not fornicate, you would not kill the soul that God has forbidden, except through justice, you would not practice magic, you would not lend at usury, you would not deliver the innocent to the men invested with authority to be put to death, you would not slander honest women (*variation:* you would not desert the army on campaign) and on you, Jews, it is especially imposed to not violate the Sabbath."[98] He embraced his hands and his feet, saying: "We confess that you are a prophet." He said: "And what prevents you from following me?" They replied: "David prayed that [prophecy?] never quit his descendants and so we fear that the Jews would kill us if we converted to Islam."[99]

The accusation that the Jews, although convinced of the authenticity of Muhammad's mission, did not want to adhere to Islam out of pride in their birth and appetite for domination is also found later in Muslim polemics.[100]

2. An evident proof of the perfidy of the Jews is the surreptitious way in which they continually curse the Muslims while maintaining the air of greeting them correctly. We possess abundant material on this subject and, here again, the variety of stories excludes authenticity.

The salutation *al-salāmu 'alayka* [singular] (or *'alaykum*) [plural] (of respect) [Peace be upon you] should only be used among Muslims. If a Jew uses it, he should not be answered *wa'alayka* (or *wa'alaykum*) *al-salām* [and upon you be peace], but only *wa'alayka* or *wa'alaykum* [the same to you], for the Jews are in reality saying *al-sām 'alaykum* [may poison be upon you], a word that is glossed by "death" or "disgust, annoyance."[101]

Tradition is pleased to raise this manifestation of Judaic perfidy in numerous hadiths, of which several are notable for a veritable concern for dramatization. It is impossible for a real incident to be the basis of this group of anecdotes, which are mutually irreconcilable. But it is also probable that they were born of the desire to legitimate a governing arrangement whose practical application must have suffered some difficulties in conquered countries, where even the most elementary relations were daily making the new masters confront a significant non-Muslim population.[102]

It would not be without interest to review the principal versions of this hadith. They show us how the skill of certain traditionalists (it would be difficult to say which link of the *ismād* [chain] is the veritable author in each

case) knew how to dramatize a rather banal incident so that it becomes historic.

"A Jew greeted the apostle of Allah by saying *al-sām 'alayka* ['May poison be on you,' for 'may peace be upon you']. [The Prophet said:] 'Bring him to me.' He told him: 'Did you say *al-sām 'alayka*?' 'Yes.' The apostle of Allah said: 'When the People of the Book greet [you], say *wa'alayka* [(and the same) to you].'"[103]

A slightly more developed version: "When the prophet was sitting amid his companions, here comes a Jew who greets them. The prophet had him come back and asked him: 'What did you say?' 'I said *al-sām 'alayka*.' The prophet concluded: 'When an individual of people of the Book greets you, say *and to you*, meaning *what you have said*.'"[104]

A slightly dramatized tale: "A Jew passed by the prophet and his companions, greeted them, and the prophet's companions returned the greeting. The prophet declared: 'He said *al-sām 'alaykum*.' They apprehended the Jew, brought him back, and he admitted it. The prophet said: 'Render back to them what they said.'"[105]

Another version features 'Omar with his habitual violence: "An individual of the people of the Book arrived and greeted the prophet by saying *al-sām 'alaykumi*. Then 'Omar said: 'Apostle of Allah, should I cut off his head?' He answered: 'No. When they greet you, say *wa'alaykum*.'"[106]

Elsewhere, the scene is embellished by Aysha's intervention: "The Jews came to find the prophet and told him *al-sām 'alayka*. The prophet replied [to them]: '*Al-sām 'alaykum*.' Then Aysha cried: '*Al-sām 'alaykum*, brothers of monkeys and pigs[107] and the curse of Allah and his anger!' The prophet said: 'Gently.' She replied: 'Apostle of Allah, did you not hear what they said?' The prophet: 'Did you not hear what I replied to them? [Know] Aysha [that] gentleness ornaments everything, but everything is spoiled if one suppresses it.'"[108]

I confine myself to translating these texts and I will only mention two traits arising from the other versions. In a certain number of texts the Prophet assures his indignant wife that he has sufficiently replied to the Jews by telling them *and on you, too*, for the imprecations of infidels are not granted, whereas those of believers never fail to be.[109]

However, I do see, one Qur'anic revelation serving as the reference point for all these hadiths: Qur'an 58:8: "When they come to you, they salute you in a way that Allah does not greet you with."[110]

This important series of hadiths illustrates so vividly the insolence and crudeness of Jews that later, when the *fukahā* [jurisconsults] (especially Western ones) decreed pitiless sanctions against whoever insulted or mocked the Prophet, it was wondered why Muhammad had not dealt severely with the Jews who saluted him with *al-sām 'alaykum*. The cadi/judge 'Iyād replied: especially [he used] diplomacy so as not to scare minds away at the start of Islam by rigorous measures; in addition, the incriminating words of the Jews had not been pronounced distinctly enough to constitute a public outrage.[111]

3. Not content with accosting the Prophet in a surreptitious and unpleasant manner, the Jews tried to trick him. But in fact, as soon as one tries to obtain details on the nature of these tricks, one must eliminate almost all the material as historically useless. What springs from the traditions relating to this subject is only the worn trope of presenting the Jews in the most unfavorable light as possible.

The People of the Book, recounts Ibn 'Abbās, were asked by the Prophet about something. They held as secret the information being requested and gave him information about something else. They then left him, having pretended to have informed him and joyously boasted about having kept from him what he had asked them for.[112]

Evidently, this tradition is completely deprived of sense. It is only an exegetical play upon Qur'an 3:187–88, especially the second verse: "Never think that those who rejoice in their misdeeds and wish to be praised for what they have not done—never think they will escape punishment; a woeful punishment awaits them." The ancient interpretations gathered by Tabarī[113] do not bring any concrete data to explain this verse, which is moreover related by others with regard to "hypocrites."[114]

4. That the Jews and Christians had altered their sacred books to efface from them the name and exact description of Muhammad is a commonplace that is so banal in Muslim polemics that I content myself with mentioning here one or two texts, not because of their documentary value but for their picturesque interest.

This was transmitted in the name of 'Abdallāh b. Mas'ūd: "Allah sent his prophet to have someone entered into paradise. He entered into the synagogue [al-kanīsa] [where] a Jew was just in the course of reading [them] the Torah. When they [the Jews] arrived at the description of the prophet, they stopped. But in a corner of the synagogue was a sick person. The prophet said: 'Why did you stop?' The sick person replied: 'They arrived at the description of the prophet, which is why they stopped.' Then the sick person dragged himself up to the book of the Torah, grabbed it and read until he came to the description of the prophet and of his community and he said: 'Here is your description and the description of your community. I confess that there is no other God but Allah and that you are the apostle of Allah.' Then he rendered up his soul."[115]

Another version of the same story is found in Ibn Sa'd.[116] The Prophet accompanied by Abū Bakr and 'Omar passed beside a Jew who was reading in a book of the Torah for one of his sick parents. The Prophet adjured the Jew to tell him if his description was found in the Torah. When he shook his head no, the sick person

contradicted him, pronounced profession of Muslim faith, and expired. The Prophet himself recited the prayer at his burial and wrapped him in his winding sheet.[117]

5. The most typical case of the illegitimate modification of the Torah and on which Muslim tradition insists with the most self-satisfaction, is that of the punishment for adultery.[118] It is quite probable, despite the lack of authenticity of some details, that a historical incident forms the basis for the traditions we are now going to study.

The Qur'an punishes with flagellation any adultery attested by four eyewitnesses.[119]

Tradition has it, however, that there was a verse called "on lapidation"[120] that prescribed the stoning of adulterers. This verse, which tradition transmits in different versions, did not enter the Qur'an—but several hadiths relate that it was still applied both by Muhammad as by 'Omar.[121] Here we do not want to deal with the question from the point of view of the composition of the Qur'an, nor evaluate the solutions that commentators have offered to fix the contradiction between the canonical text of the Holy Book and the disowned (but applied) verse regarding lapidation. But according to tradition, the legislation concerning adultery raised a controversy between the Jews and Muslims that we must examine.

The Jews brought to the Prophet an adulterous couple and claimed that their book prescribed punishing them by blackening their faces so as to cover them with shame. Muhammad told them: "You are lying, [the punishment ordered] for this crime is lapidation; so bring the Torah and recite it if you are telling the truth" (cf. Qur'an 3:93, which in context relates to the alimentary prohibitions of the Jews). The one-eyed reader of the Jews named Ibn Sūriyā started to read; arriving at a certain passage, he covered it with his hand. Muhammad invited him to lift it; when he lifted it, it shone. So, the Jews admitted that lapidation was indeed prescribed in the Torah, but then kept this law hidden. The Prophet had the guilty ones stoned.[122]

Muslim gives this story with several isnād [chains of transmission].[123] In the first hadith, the punishment indicated by the Jews is a little more exactly described: "We blacken their faces, we place them on a mounting, their faces turned toward each other, and we make them take a tour of the town.[124] The reader is anonymous (fatā) [some fellow]; it is 'Abdallāh b. Salām who engages the Prophet in ordering the reader to raise his mind, under which is found the verse about lapidation. One of the versions gathered by Abū Dāwūd[125] situates the scene in the Bayt al-Midrās [house of study]; another specifies that the guilty ones received a hundred lashes with a tarred cord.[126]

The intervention from 'Abdallāh b. Salām in several variants of this hadith ought to arouse our distrust regarding its authenticity. This personage only converted in year 8, hence at a time when large Jewish groupings had already disappeared from Medina. Moreover, if one admits that the issue of how to punish adultery had been ruled in a sense unfavorable to lapidation by sura 24, one cannot push back the date of the discussions that occupy us beyond the year 6, the latest date that tradition assigns to the Aysha incident [an incident during which Aysha stayed behind and later rejoined the Prophet; afterward, his enemies charged her with adultery. As a result, Allah revealed that there had to be four witnesses to adultery], which motivated the revelation of this sura (at least its parts relating to the point concerning us here). It is even possible that it fails to go back to the year 4.[127]

Another variant in Muslim and in Ibn Māja[128] highlights the perfidy of the Jews even more, as well as the little respect they have for their revealed book.

They passed by the prophet with a flagellated Jew with a blackened face. He called them and asked them: "Is that the punishment for adultery that you find in your book?" "Yes." He fetches one of their wise men and adjures him by the God who revealed the Torah to Moses to tell him if this is really the punishment for adultery [ordered] in their book. The latter answered; "No, if you had not adjured me in this fashion I would not have told you. We found [that the punishment for adultery is] lapidation, but this sin was widespread among our great and when we seized great personages, we let them off, but to the weak we applied the punishment. [Finally] we said to ourselves: 'Let us agree on a punishment that we will apply to the great as to the weak.'[129] We then instituted the blackening of the face[130] and flagellation instead of lapidation." The apostle of Allah cried: "God, I am the first who has revived your order after they killed it off." On which came the revelation of Qur'an 5:41.

This verse furnished the occasion for Tabarī to recount his story of adulterers. It is the Jews who come to consult Muhammad. If he decrees, they told themselves, flagellation and ignominious treatment, he is a king; if he pronounces the judgment of the Torah, he is a prophet. Muhammad comes before *Bayt al'Midrās* [house of study], discusses things with Abdallāh b. Sūriyā, who admits to him that the Jews refuse only out of jealousy to recognize his prophetic claims. Finally, he orders the lapidation of the guilty parties.[131]

What is the significance of this controversy between Muhammad and the Jews?

The Prophet reproaches the Jews for having substituted a rule they had themselves invented for God's own law concerning adultery. He applies this law to a Jew, and if one believes the traditions (which are no more or less worthy of credit than any others), he applied it, as did 'Omar, to the Muslims too. Nevertheless, the "lapidation verse" has not been accepted in the Qur'an's canonic text, which replaces it, in the most recent pas-

sages relating to adultery, precisely with the flagellation whose practice by the Jews is regarded as an arbitrary alteration of the primitive revelation. Unless one rejects en bloc the traditions relating to the *rajm* [lapidation; stoning] as forged for the sole purpose of shaming the Jews as falsifiers of their revelation and to glorify Muhammad, who saw clearly through their criminal actions, it is necessary to regard the procedure censured by the Prophet as having been really used in the ghettos (*juiveries*) of *Hijāz*. But in that case, the effective legislation of the Qur'an concerning the punishment of adultery, definitively consecrated by sura 24, derives in a direct line from Jewish practice, consecrated by Muhammad.

Here is the only solution that I dare propose, as a hypothesis, to this difficulty. Informed in Medina of the Mosaic law of punishment for adultery, although it had fallen into disuse among the Jews themselves,[132] Muhammad (who claimed to be reestablishing the original revelation in its purity) tried to put it back in vigor. The troublesome experiences that he had in his own entourage soon convinced him of the inopportuneness of these draconian measures, and so he came back to the procedure of his Jewish compatriots, removing what might appear showy and surrounding it with precautions—such that its application became practically impossible. Thus the verse on lapidation disappeared from the Qur'an, which did not prevent 'Omar, whose severity would not allow itself to be inflected by the higher interests of the state, from applying it later.[133] Tradition took on the task of blurring this evolution in Muhammad's thinking and it must be admitted that it succeeded rather well. If the Jews recognized that he had ignored the Torah law in order to find a median solution, between the excessive indulgence that wiped out the sins of the great, on one hand, and the rigor that only struck the small, on the other, still one must agree, without any bias against Qur'anic revelation, that Muhammad did exactly the same thing in promulgating in the name of Allah his bizarre ruling on the verification of adultery.

6. We have seen that certain versions of the hadith on lapidation took their point of departure from a *question* that the Jews are said to have posed to Muhammad. This dramatic situation is frequently encountered in tradition: as we shall see, it is an artificial use of a banal narrative cliché that frames those stories with a polemical tendency as well as the riddles that arise purely and simply from folklore via the so-called eschatological mysteries of a less original type. Of rather mediocre importance in the older hadiths, the genre knew great popularity in the polemical and educational literature of more recent eras, not only in Arabic, but also in other Muslim languages.[134]

The Qur'an gives a rather vague definition of the term *rūh* ("spirit").[135] Tradition has perhaps conserved a memory of the difficulty Muhammad felt in specifying the meaning of this word. It represents the question as posed by some Meccans who are said to have consulted the Jews of Yatrib on the way in which they might put Muhammad to the test. The Jews had advised them to interrogate him about *rūh*, the Seven Sleepers, and Dū-I-Karnayn [Alexander the Great]—and sura 18 was revealed.[136]

However, the majority of traditions hold that the question was posed by Jews in Medina, which is incompatible with the date of sura 18 and verse 17:65, commonly assigned to the Meccan period.[137]

Since the greatest number of such questions are grouped in a passage of the *Musnad Ahmed*,[138] we can conveniently take this as our point of departure:

The Jews declare themselves disposed to rally to Muhammad if he answers five questions.

Q1. What is the distinctive sign of the Prophet? A: His eyes sleep but his heart never sleeps.

Q2. In what conditions does the woman deliver a boy or a girl? A: If, when the two seeds meet, that of the man wins over that of the woman, she gives birth to a boy, while in the contrary case, a girl is born.

Q3. What did Israel (Jacob) forbid himself? A: He suffered from a sciatic nerve and found nothing that suited him [more than] some milk (according to some traditionalists, it was camel's milk) and so he forbid himself their flesh (text altered, see p. 103 of original French).

Q4. What is thunder? A: It is one of Allah's angels in charge of the clouds. He carries in his hand a riding whip of fire with which he pushes the clouds, directing them where Allah wants. And what is the voice one hears? It is his voice.

Q5. [The Jews]: "Only one question remains: this one will commit us to recognize your dominion if you answer it. There is no prophet without an angel bringing him the message [or news in general?]. Tell us who is your companion." A: It is Jibrīl (Gabriel). The Jews said: Jibrīl who descends to earth [to bring] war, combat and punishment is our enemy. If you had named Mikā'īl who brings mercy, vegetation and rain, it would have been [good]." Upon this came the revelation of Qur'an 2:97.[139]

Questions 2 and 4 refer, it is unnecessary to stress, to popular beliefs that are without interest for us here.[140]

On the first question, Hartwig Hirschfeld[141] has already observed that the Prophet's response[142] was a translation of Song of Songs 5:2, *'anī y'iēna w'libbī 'ēr*, [I sleep while my heart is awake] with the word *'anī* ("I") being replaced by *'enī* ("my eye"). It is unknown how and why this verse penetrated into Muslim tradition in order to be applied to prophets.

The fifth question is clarified by traditional exegesis of Qur'an 2:97. This verse was revealed against 'Abdallāh b. Sūriyā, who had asked the Prophet which angel transmitted revelations to him. The Prophet told him it was Jibrīl, at which the Jew declared: He is our enemy, he has shown himself hostile toward us on several occasions and especially when he revealed to our

prophet that Buht-Nasr would destroy the *Bayt al-maqdis* [Holy Temple in Jerusalem]. To prevent this catastrophe, the Jews decided to assassinate Buht-Nasr, but Jibrīl prevented them.[143]

The third question is very badly conserved in the collection we began with, but numerous parallels allow us to complete it.

Questioning Muhammad on subjects that only a prophet could know, the Jews asked him what was the nourishment that Isrā'il (Jacob) forbade himself before the Torah revelation. Jacob, replied the Prophet, fell gravely ill and made a vow that if God returned him to health, he would renounce that food and drink that was most dear to him. Thus he gave up the meat and milk of the camel.[144]

A tradition from Ikrima relates that Isrā'il forbade himself the *lobus caudalus* [tail, or end lobe][145] on liver, the two kidneys and fat,[146] except for that found on the back, for all that is offered in sacrifice and consumed by fire.

The tendency of this hadith becomes clearer if one knows that it represents an attempt to interpret a Qur'anic verse that deals with the alimentary prohibitions of the Jews. One reads in effect in Qur'an 3:93: "All food was lawful to the children of Israel except for what Israel forbade himself before the Torah was revealed; bring the Torah and recite it, if you are telling the truth."

Tabarī has gathered a great number of interpretations of this verse. According to Suddī, Jacob suffered in the night from sciatica; he made the vow never to eat any nerve if God would deliver him from this malady. The Jews claim to follow their ancestor but they are lying, for it is God who imposed on them alimentary restrictions, on account of their sins.

According to Dahhāk the verse means to say that neither before nor after the revelation did God forbid anything to the Jews, except that for the reason that we know, Jacob made the vow to abstain from consuming nerves.

Ibn 'Abbās explains: Any food was permitted to the children of Israel before the revelation of the Torah, but Jacob forswore nerves, and his children imitated him, without the interdiction being in the Torah.[147]

Tabarī lingers over this exegesis, not without modifying it. Before the revelation of the Torah, nothing was forbidden to the children of Israel, but Jacob, suffering from sciatica, forswore nerves, and so on. Then, in revealing the Torah, God prohibited certain foods to the Jews.

Another series of hadiths represents things a little differently: Jacob forbids himself camel's flesh and milk.

'Abdallāh b. Katīr (and others): Jacob, suffering from sciatica, renounces by a vow, so as to get better, his preferred food: flesh and milk of the camel.

According to Hasan, the Jews falsely pretended that the interdiction by Jacob of camel flesh is found in the Torah, whereas in fact it is prior to the revelation and is not in the Torah at all;[148] this is also the opinion of Ibn 'Abbās.

The latter doctor reconciles the two series of traditions by teaching that Jacob forbid himself both the nerves and flesh of camels. He had consumed meat not cleaned of the sciatic nerve and fell ill and swore never to eat it again.

Tabarī accepts this interpretation since the Jews still prohibit nerves [in general] and the flesh of the camel [in particular]. He then cites, under the name of Ibn 'Abbās, the question the Jews put to Muhammad that we have seen. Muhammad invites the Jews to bring the Torah and read it so as to make manifest their falsehood; God has never forbid these things. It is a proof of the authenticity of Muhammad's mission that he, an *'ummī*, [the Prophet][149] has unmasked the lie of Jewish doctors that most of their co-religionists had not perceived.

It seems evident to me that the controversy bears on the origin of the food prohibitions in general and particularly on the interdictions by the Jews of camel meat, the national dish of the Arabs.[150]

The Muslim polemic does not want to admit that this interdiction is written in the Torah, for that would put the national dish of the Arabs on the same footing as pork, for example. But it must make a concession to the affirmation of the Jews: if there is a prohibition, it results only from a private initiative by Jacob. It would be interesting to know how Muslim tradition managed to find this combination between the interdiction of the sciatic nerve, still relying on a biblical fact, and the claimed prohibition of camel flesh by Jacob. The texts I possess do not allow me to answer this question.

Let us try to retrace the evolution of this polemic theme, whose elements we have just analyzed. The familiar narration of Genesis (Jacob's struggle with the angel in Gen. 32:25–33) closes with the remark: "This is why the children of Israel do not eat the sciatic nerve." So this is a custom that was never raised, within the Pentateuch, to the rank of a positive interdiction. The biblical motif is unknown or ignored by Muslim tradition. The Qur'an speaks, without being precise, of a prohibition voluntarily assumed by Israel. Tradition designates as the object of the interdiction either the sciatic nerve (with a motive alien to Jewish sources) or else the meat and milk of the camel. These two indications are reconciled, but the tendency (supported indeed by the remainder of the Qur'anic verse) that is everywhere subsidiary, is to demonstrate that the interdiction is not revealed and hence is expressly willed by God (or else, according to some who are still in conformity with the thinking of the Qur'an on this point, imposed after the fact on Jews on account of their sins). It is due to Jacob's private initiative, something followed by his descendants, but it does not oblige the Muslims by any means to do so.[151]

Another order of issues of an especially eschatological kind is transmitted by Muslim.[152] Tawbān, the Prophet's *mawlā* [spiritual teacher], recounts:

I found myself close to Allah's apostle when a Jewish *haber* [rabbi] arrived and said: "Peace be with you, Mohammed." I pushed him [so violently] that he almost collapsed. He said to me: "Why did you shove me?" "Didn't you say 'apostle of Allah'?" The Jew replied: "We call him by the name his family gave him." The apostle of Allah says: "My name is Mohammed, and so my family called me." The Jew replied: "I came to pose questions to you." Allah's apostle: "Will you benefit from what I will teach you?" The Jew: "I will listen with my ears." Allah's apostle hit the ground with his baton/stick *hiraawa* and said: "Ask!" The Jew: "Where will men be on the day when the earth will be changed into something other than heaven and earth?" (cf. Koran 14:48). A: "In the shadow, beyond the bridge." The Jew: "Who will go first?" A: "The poor with the refugees." The Jew: "What gift will be offered them when they enter into paradise?" A: "The appendix of the fish liver."[153] The Jew: "What will they drink after this food?" A: "They will drink from a spring called Salsabil." The Jew: "You spoke true" and he added "I came to ask about something that no inhabitant of the earth knows, except for the prophets and one or two people." The [P]rophet: "So benefit from it." The Jew: "I will listen, etc." and he added: "I came to ask you about the child" (answer as above). The Jew said: "You have spoken truly and you are a prophet." Then he withdrew. Allah's apostle concluded: "I did not know [the answer to] all the questions that he set me until God instructed me."

It is useless here to comment upon questions without historical and doctrinal interest. This text brings us toward the apocryphal literature that was formed around the theme of questions by Jews to Muhammad, a literature that concerns the folklorist more than the historian.[154]

I mention only a claimed question from the Jews about the six days of creation, forged or used with a view to fighting the Jewish Sabbath.[155]

7. To finish with this second group of hadiths, we should say a word about the evil spells attributed to the Jews. The biography of the Prophet recounts that he had been bewitched with the Jew Labīd b.al-al'A'sam. The charm was broken when, thanks to the intervention of Jibrīl (or Jibrīl and Mikā'il, or two anonymous personages), who indicated the place where Labīd had hidden the hair of the Prophet, which he had taken and braided into magic knots and introduced into the male flower of the palm tree.[156]

Another case is much less clear. Ibn 'Omar recounts that when he went to Khaybar to attend the division of the crop between Jews and the treasurer of Egypt, in conformity with the pact in force, the Jews bewitched him so well that his right hand froze at the fist. It was after this event that 'Omar expelled them from Khaybar.[157]

Bukhārī's version leaves out the bewitching;

'Abdallāh b.'Omar was the victim of a nocturnal assault when he went to Khaybar to inspect a property he owned.

According to a tradition from Wākidī,[158] the Jews were expelled for having incited slaves to assassinate their masters. Finally, a tradition recorded by Ibn Sa'd[159] reports that 'Omar expelled the Jews of Khaybar because at that time the Muslims already had enough manpower to cultivate their palm groves without turning to tenant farmers.

Consequently it is difficult to admit the historicity or at the very least the magic origin of the accident of Ibn 'Omar. This story had to have been invented so as to lay the responsibility for the expulsion of the Jews of Khaybar on themselves.[160]

III.

The hadiths relating to the behavior of Muslims toward Jews are animated by two different tendencies. Alongside tolerance, which is recommended toward monotheists who are voluntarily subject to Muslim domination, one finds a few humiliating arrangements. In relations between Muslims and Jews, distrust must reign, for the Jews—and Christians are not judged differently—are rebels to the solicitations of Islam and keep their religious traditions in a way liable to lead Muslims into error. Even when Islam knowingly borrows from Judaism, these borrowings are presented as amendments of the corresponding Jewish customs, unless they expressly forge traditions that aim to efface the true origin of the rite in question, by transposing it either into Arab paganism or into "Israelite" or pre-Israelite antiquity.

Let us verify each of these points using some typical traditional texts.

1. One should not mistreat the *dhimmis*,[161] but it is also forbidden to pay any attention to them.[162] One should not greet them first;[163] we have already seen how one must return their greeting; when one meets them on the road, they have to be pushed toward the edge as a way of containing them.[164]

When one hears a Jew sneeze, one does not say to him: "Allah have mercy on you," but "Allah guide and amend your spirit."[165]

2. Very aware of its superiority over the two monotheist religions, Islam does not hesitate to illustrate it with the help of texts "borrowed" from their literature. Thus they apply to the Jews, Christians, and Muslims the Gospel parable of workers hired at different hours of the day (Matt. ch. 20).[166]

Ibn Sa'd[167] cites a rather deformed version of the wedding parable (Matt. 22:2ff; Luke 19:15ff) as relating to God, Islam, Muhammad, and his believers. According to the hadith, the parable was offered by Jibrīl or Mikā'il

[the angels Gabriel or Michael], who appeared to the Prophet in a dream.

Despite this feeling of superiority, tradition attributes a very great value to the conversion of Jews and Christians. It has the Prophet say on the day that Mecca was taken: "Whoever among the people of the two Books converts to Islam will receive a double recompense; his rights and his duties are identical to ours. Whoever converts among the pagans will receive his [simple] recompense; his rights and his duties are identical to ours."[168]

Nevertheless the elite of the Jews is not pressed to adopt the new religion. The Prophet's biography shows that the number of converted *ahbār* [rabbis] remains tiny, although tradition tries hard to represent the converts that it has made figure in the sira as so many notable personages and scholars of the first order. The hadith also takes on a melancholy tone by putting into the Prophet's mouth the following phrase: "If a dozen *ahbār* believed in me, all the Jews on earth would do the same."[169] Another version, still more pessimistic, substitutes "Jews" for "*ahbār*."[170]

3. The hostility of the Jews with respect to Islam will arise again during the troubles that will precede the Resurrection and Last Judgment. The *Dajjâl*, the Antichrist of the Muslims, will count the Jews among his adherents. When he is vanquished, his companions will be massacred; when a Jew seeks refuge under a tree or a stone, these objects will be able to speak to tell a Muslim: "There is a Jew hidden under me, kill him!"[171]

According to another tradition, the *Dajjâl* [Antichrist] is in fact Jewish. At his appearance, he will be accompanied by seventy thousand Jews of Isfahan[172] wrapped in their *taylasān* shawl [like a Heb. Tallit].[173] Ibn Māja[174] speaks of seventy thousand Jews, armed with polished sabers, their heads covered with *saj* (a sort of veil). They will be defeated; everything will deliver them up except for the *garkad* [tree].[175]

In Tirmidī's hadith,[176] the Prophet described the *Dajjâl* as Jewish; he remarks that his eyes sleep but his heart does not sleep, a trait that we have encountered in the description of the true prophet. Tradition has it, moreover, that Abū Bakr and Zuhayr b. al-'Awāmm had found the *Dajjâl* in Medina.[177]

4. Not only are the Jews vanquished in the eschatological war, but they will serve as ransom for the Muslims in the fires of hell. "The Apostle of Allah said: 'In the place of each Muslim who dies [and who should go to hell], God introduces a Jew or a Christian.'"[178] On the Day of Judgment, for each Muslim a Jew or a Christian will be delivered to serve as his ransom.[179]

The sins of certain Muslims will weigh on them like mountains, but on the day of resurrection, these sins will be lifted and laid upon the Jews.[180]

There exist many hadiths, naturally inauthentic, figuring especially in the works of an ascetic and mystical kind that judge with more or less arithmetical precision the number of merits that believers may acquire, taking into account the recitation of certain supplementary prayers, divided among each day and each night of the week. If the *du'ā* [prayer] assigned to Saturday and Sunday are accompanied by solemn repudiation [*tabarru'*] of some Jews and Christians, then the reciter sees the number of his merits grow by the number of these unbelievers.[181] However, one must not exaggerate the importance of these speculations of *zāhid* [ascetic], which seem, after all, rather late, but perhaps it would be worth the trouble to research whether they effectively influenced popular piety.[182]

5. We may pass rapidly over the question of food prepared by Jews and Christians:[183] a hadith forbids the consumption of food prepared by a Christian.[184] According to another one, the Prophet did not permit use of utensils of the people of the Book unless they were rinsed and then only if one did not have any others.[185] This tradition is clarified by a variant[186] that contains the same instruction, but adding that the prohibition refers to a utensil in which the people of the Book had cooked pork, and therefore it undoubtedly concerns Christians.[187]

The question of alimentary laws was been touched on above; I add only that according to Ibn 'Abbās, the Jews had once declared to the Prophet: "[W]e eat what we kill, but we do not need eat what God has killed," at which point Qur'an 6:121 was revealed: "Do not eat of that which has not been consecrated in the name of God." If these statements attributed to the Jews are indeed authentic (whether or not made to Muhammad), they must have been badly understood or badly applied in the verse. The slaughter of a beast among Jews is always a religious act and could never fall under a Qur'anic interdiction. The Jews must have wanted to say that they consumed animals that they had (ritually) butchered, but regarded as forbidden the dead beast, hence "killed by Allah."

6. The revelation proclaimed by Muhammad, claiming not only to complete but to replace previous (and falsified) revelations, should in principle have done away with them. Such is the rule that rigorous Muslims meant to follow in the first two centuries of Islam, a regulation that it is still difficult not to lift, due to the flow of proselytes of both Jewish and Christian origin who brought with them traditions that were more or less deformed from their native religion, and also due to the natural curiosity of Muslims that pushed them to secure information from the People of the Book on points that seemed unclear to them, or which were treated too concisely in the Qur'an.

Thus it is necessary to examine the attitude of the hadiths regarding stories imported from Judaism and Christianity. This question was often treated by Goldziher and there is nothing much to add to his references. Therefore I will confine myself to a few precise points and give some details in places where he was content to refer simply to the texts.

In the information borrowed (or attributed) to People of the Book, one may distinguish two groups, between which the boundary is not always very firm. First there are edifying and miraculous stories (stuffed with scriptural citations, most often false or borrowed not from the canonic books, but from the apocrypha or from rabbinic wisdom) which relate, in the majority of cases, to the ancient Banū Isrā'īl, and which generally have lost all connection not only with history, but also with legend, whether Jewish or Christian. These are *isrā'iliyyāt* [Judeo-Christian material]; for centuries they were fabricated en masse; the books of *nawādir* [rarities] are full of them. On the other hand, there are more serious indications, of a historical as well as doctrinal order, of interest for the interpretation of the Qur'an and for the relation of Islam and Muhammad to ancient revealed religions. Tradition tolerates the former, but it energetically combats anything derived from direct consultation of the People of the Book.

"[You may] transmit from me, be it only a verse, and talk about the children of Israel, without committing a sin, but whoever has voluntarily put a lie to my account, may he occupy [henceforth] a place in the fire [of hell]."[188] And one finds a tradition that represents the Prophet recounting one whole night the hadith of B. Isrā'il, until a great part of the time for the dawn prayer had passed.[189]

The tone changes totally as soon as it is no longer a matter of Banū Isrā'īl of fabulous antiquity but rather of flesh-and-blood Jews. Then the correct attitude recommended by the Prophet is summarized in these words, transmitted by Abū Hurayata: "Do not give faith to [assertions of] People of the Book and do not tax them as lies; say 'we believe in God and revelation.'"[190] One should never ask anything of them. Even converts are suspected of lying, like the famous Ka'b al-ahbār, about whom Mu'āwiya said that he was one of the most truthful among those who transmitted the traditions of People of the Book.[191] "A Jew came to the prophet and asked him: 'What does the dead body here say?' The prophet: 'Allah knows best.' The Jew: 'I attest that he is speaking.' The apostle of Allah concluded: 'When the People of the Book tell you of [their] traditions, do not believe them and do not tax them with lying; say: we believe in God, his books and his messengers.' [In that way] if what they say is true, you will not have contradicted them and if it is not, you will not have believed them."[192]

An admonition from Ibn 'Abbās, which Bukhārī cites several times, is characteristic. "Assembly of Muslims, how can you ask things of the People of the Book, when yours, revealed to the prophet of God, is the most recent of God's messages?[193] It is pure, whereas God has told you that the [P]eople of the Book have changed what God wrote and altered the book by their own hand, saying 'it comes from God' so as to draw profit from it.[194] The science that you have obtained, does it not prevent you from asking them?[195] By God, we have never seen any among them who has asked *you* about what was revealed to you." The Muslim's slightly naive indignation clings to Qur'anic revelation but still senses its lacks, and recognizes with regret the superiority of the *ahl al-kitāb* [P]eople of the Book, i.e., Jews and Christians], which he can scarcely avoid asking about (and this was indeed the case of the presumed author of the diatribe we have just read).[196]

If tradition prohibits the demand for oral information, it is still more rigorous when it comes to the sacred texts in the possession of Jews and Christians. Written in a foreign language, they must be translated by non-Muslims who claim to make use of them in conversation. If they are in Arabic (it is admitted that there *were* some before Islam),[197] they are certainly falsified. In any case, it is forbidden to use them, and still more to confront them with the Qur'an.

"Al-Sa'bī relates in the name of Jābir b. 'Abdallāh: 'Omar b. al-Hattāb came one day to the [P]rophet with a book that he had received from one of the [P]eople of the Book.[198] Having examined it, the Prophet says in irritation: "Do you want to dash to your perdition, son of al-Hattāb?[199] By God, I brought you [revelation] white and pure. Do not ask them about anything, from fear of taxing with lying when they speak true and adding faith to their sayings when they lie. By God, if Moses were alive, he could not do otherwise then to follow me.'"[200]

It is transmitted in the name of Abū Hurayra that the People of the Book read the Torah in Hebrew and translated it to the Muslims. The Prophet advised his people to distrust the Jews, neither believe them nor contradict them. May the Muslims merely say: "We believe in God, which was revealed to us and which was revealed to you."

In the same spirit is the instruction that (according to Ibn Sa'd)[201] Muhammad gave to 'Ayyās b. Abī Rabī'a, sent as ambassador to the Yemenite chiefs, who were apparently Christian. He should require the translation of all that they recited in a foreign language, and still refuse all discussion of it.[202]

IV.

The typical texts whose analysis permits us describe the position of ancient Muslim tradition with respect to Jews and Judaism, do not allow us to be enclosed (as goes without saying) in the frameworks of the hadiths that, in the preceding argument, we have classified, somewhat arbitrarily, into three groups: Jewish customs that are disavowed, Jews and Muslims, Muslims and Jews. There was exchange and struggle between the two religions, even when the texts do not say so openly. And this

was indeed the case for Islam and Judaism concerning a question that we have yet to treat: Muslim fasting and its relations with Jewish fasting. In order not to prolong this essay, I will deal with this elsewhere and confine myself here only to mentioning the results of my research.

The expiatory virtue of fasting is accepted by Islam as by Judaism, but this does not mean they are parallel, which would be quite comprehensible, in that the hadiths borrow literally from the Haggadah a very well-known sentence relating to the quality of fasting.

Despite this agreement on the religious value of the observance, differences are numerous in the details: several of them are given by the hadiths as intentional modifications of Jewish or Christian customs.

For example, while rabbinic Judaism had replaced since the fourth century the empirical recording of the new moon with astronomical calculation, the hadiths energetically reject this latter method.

Then, according to the Qur'an, the nocturnal suspension of fasting takes place, when it is possible to distinguish a black thread from a white thread; the hadiths are almost unanimous in relating these indices of the blackness of the night and the whiteness of the day, contrary to the way in which the Talmud decides the analogous case.

It is recommended to hasten the breaking of the fast, whereas the Jews (and Christians) delay it until the rise of the stars.

Some divergences of slight importance arise regarding abstinences imposed on the faithful while fasting. A much greater difference: whereas the Jews and the Christians prohibit sexual relations during even the night after the fast and did not permit the breaking of it on the part of those who slept before doing so, the Qur'an abrogated these severe rules (which according to the hadiths the Muslims had at first followed and then entirely suspended) for the night, with obligatory abstinences during the day only.

It is known that the *Asūrā* [Day of Ashurah, tenth day of the Islamic month, Muharram] is a copy of the Jewish Yom Kippur and that it was, before being replaced by Ramadan, the principal fast for Islam.

The interdiction of fasting did not prevail in an absolute way except for two great feasts, *fitr* and *'adhā*; for Friday, it was much less rigorous than the analogous prohibition for Saturday within Judaism.

The incontestably Jewish origin of this feast still embarrasses the hadiths, hence various attempts at legerdemain: some affect to ignore the Jewish provenance of *Asūrā* and make it into a continuation of a pre-Islamic Koreshi [of the Quraysh, Muhammad's tribe] fast; others bow to the evidence, using a thousand artifices to relate it to events of the period of Banū Isrā'īl, to Noah or even Adam, so as to efface its true nature, and in addition, some credit the Prophet with the aim to displace it, or they try to establish by lexicographic subtleties that it does not coincide with the Jewish fast; finally, it is combined, in such a way as to diminish it, with a certain fast of 'Arafa, whose existence does not appear to me at all certain.

Muslim tradition recommends, finally, that one fast on Mondays and Thursdays, and that the sequence of fasts (Monday, Thursday, Monday) be observed at least once a month. Without any support from the Qur'an or Muslim history, these fasts are of manifestly Jewish origin; the reasons for which they are recommended are of haggadic nature, and I think it certain that they were taken as such in the teaching of the rabbis, although until now, I have not been able to discover analogues, except in texts much later than the birth of Islam but certainly exempt from any Muslim influence.

CONCLUSION

The first principle that governs the correct attitude of the Muslim toward the People of the Book is a reaction against all those practices that are specific to them, even if they do not touch upon either faith or customs. We have remarked upon the parallelism that exists on this point between Judaism and Islam (*hukkot hadith-gōy—hālifūhum*).

However, it often happens that a use is prohibited as particular to the Jews and Christians, whereas in reality the target is an abuse that is widespread among Muslims: hairpieces, tombs of prophets.

While one seems to have regarded rather sympathetically the care the Jews took about bodily purity (unfortunately, the hadiths in question are very obscure), Islam and Judaism followed rather different paths with respect to the purity of women and to sexual morality: Both Jewish law and custom were much more exigent about these than Islam; the hadiths even conserve the memory of conversations that arose on this subject; one also finds traces of a reaction against Jewish rigor that appears to have influenced the Muslims.

On the other hand, the hadiths reproach the Jews for not applying Torah law concerning adulterers and it is Muhammad who reestablishes the ancient order of things. We have noticed that this way of seeing things was irreconcilable with the Qur'an, which has the air of being inspired by the Jewish procedure, which the hadiths make so severely condemned by Muhammad.

The transformation of borrowed elements is again exercised in the regulation of fasting, where the Qur'an and tradition softened/relaxed on several points the more severe regimen that obtained in Judaism and Christianity, while continuing to follow their models, principally the Jewish ones: they tried to remove the *Asūrā* from its original significance, and changed the fasts on Mondays and Thursdays into the Monday/Thursday/Monday sequence.

Another method deliberately applied by the hadiths, either to justify the acceptance of a practice of foreign provenance or else for polemical purposes, is the transposition of the institutions in question into those of Arab pagans (e.g., the treatment of menstruation, *Asūrā*) or else as belonging to the fabulous epoch of "the children of Israel" or of the prophets who preceded them (e.g., the exclusion of women from the mosque, precautions taken in urinating, the sciatic nerve, camel flesh, *Asūrā*). We have often noted that tradition makes use of methods of the Haggadah to combat the Jews.

In traditions of an eschatological kind, Jews and Christians occupy a place of choice, but historical study can scarcely draw useful information from them.

In the hadiths, Jews are represented in the darkest colors. Convinced by the clear testimony of their books that Muhammad was the true prophet, they refused to convert, out of envy, jealousy, and national particularism, even out of private interest. They have falsified their sacred books and do not apply the laws of God; nevertheless, they pursued Muhammad with their raillery and their oaths, and harassed him with questions, an enterprise that turned to their own confusion and merely corroborated the authenticity of the supernatural science of the Prophet. From words they moved to action: sorcery, poisoning, assassination held no scruples for them. They should be granted life, the enjoyment of their goods and the practice of their religion, but treat them with contempt and especially beware of asking them for information of a religious kind.

However, all the severity of tradition would not prevent Muslims from *diraasat* taking lessons/learning from Jews and Christians so as to enrich their religious knowledge, or from attaching a high value to conversion of Jews—the rarity of which was deplored.

Given the eminently polemic character of the texts of the hadiths that mention Jews, the data that they furnish on their religion situation must be carefully checked, which is rarely possible in a direct way.

The Jews' religious organization does not present an aspect much different from what the Qur'an allows one to perceive. Their spiritual directors were the *ahbār*, those who read the Torah best. Reading and recitation are much spoken of, which would imply at first glance that religious studies in the *Bayt al-Midrās* [house of study] consisted principally of commentated readings of scripture. This conclusion would be premature; the hadiths, in sum, give only a very schematic sketch of *Bayt al-Midrās* activity that might just as well apply to the synagogue-schools in Hijāz, as in Babylonia or anywhere else. The Muslims were not very well placed to observe the details of what was done in a Jewish school; as for the converts of Jewish origin, they had no interest whatever in informing the Muslims about their previous studies. By contrast, with respect to external aspects, tradition notes with exactitude the striking details of the attitudes of Jews: particular intonations in reading, gestures, and swaying during prayer.

There is also an intrinsic reason why the hadiths

insisted with particular complaisance on the scriptural study of the Jews; they were *ahl-kitāb* [People of the Book], they possessed one (or several) book(s) that were completely revealed, with a well-fixed text—although they did not hesitate to alter it and to add their own inventions, whereas in the Prophet's time, where the hadiths claim to take us, the Qur'an was in the course of being revealed. Nothing is more natural, then, than to represent the People of the Book as assiduously studying their own, and the care to dramatize this that we have discerned so many times in the hadiths, in this case, does not falsify historical truth.

The other important facts about Jews that come from the polemical hadiths: their scruples about ritual purity, their rigor in sexual ethics and in the observance of fasting, the replacement of capital punishment, no longer applied after the destruction of the Temple, by flagellation and exposure to public contempt.

It is not impossible that most of these traits were specific to Hijazian Judaism [of the Hijaz, in northwest Saudi Arabia], contemporary with Muhammad and the first caliphs. But this impression might also be fallacious since, as we have said, the hadiths tend to schematize, and consequently they may well simplify the most complex facts by applying the Qur'anic standard to them. The judgment on this question will always be colored by the evaluation one makes about the authenticity of hadiths in general—and I admit to being rather skeptical on this point.

What one may assert, though, about the religious situation of the ghettos of the Hijāz is that they were not deprived of knowledge other than scriptural, that the assiduous reading of the Bible took place in the spirit of rabbinic tradition, of which one has found many traces in the course of the preceding essay, and finally that this Hijazian Judaism, as badly understood as it may be, scarcely represents an aberrant type of Judaism.

The few positive results that we think to have obtained in this study would appear in a false light if we did not immediately note what we consider to be the deficiencies of our inquiry.

In effect it has been constrained to noting and explaining hadiths where the Jews are mentioned, and it is only occasionally that we have examined texts in which Jewish dealings were not explicit. This method is not very wide ranging and one can only expect partial results from it. If one wanted to draw up a more complete inventory of what Islam in its beginnings owed to Judaism, whether it fought against it or whether it was inspired by it, *all the hadiths* ought to be scrutinized in the light of rabbinic literature. In order to offer the desired guarantees of precision and critical independence, this enterprise would require equal proficiency in Islamology and in Jewish studies, which amounts to saying that it could only be achieved by collaboration among several scholars.

May such collaborations be numerous, so as to tighten the relations between two sister disciplines, Islamology and the science of Judaism.

"Juifs et musulmans selon le hadit," *Journal Asiatique* 229 (1937): 57–127; translated from the French by Susan Emanuel.

*For further clarification of any of the references, see original essay.

NOTES

1. The present essay came from a series of classes given at the École de Hautes Études in January and February of 1936, in the framework of lectures by Maurice Liber. The pages that follow reproduce the essential content of these classes, except for developments of a general order that were necessary with an audience composed largely of Hebraists, but which are superfluous here.

2. In labeling these hadiths, I use the following abbreviations for the collections in which they are found:

A.B.H. = Ahmed b. Hanbal, *Musnad Ahmed* (Cairo, 1313).

A.D. = Abu Dāwūd, *Sunan* (Cairo, 1280).

Buh = Al-Bakhārī, *Sahīh*, ed. Krehl-Juynboll (Leyden, 1862–68, 1907–1908).

Buh Kast = Ibid., with commentary by al-Kastalānī (Bulak, 1304).

Ibn Maja = Ibn Maja, *Sunan* (Cairo, 1313).

Ibn Sa'd = Ibn Sa'd, *Biographien Muhammeds*, ed. E. Sachau et al. (Leyden, 1904–15).

Kast. = Kastalāni, *Irsad* etc.

Muht. Kans = Muhtasar Kanz al-Ummal.

Muslim = Muslim, *Sahih* (Cairo, 1329–33).

Muslim, Naw = Ibid., with commentary of al-Nawawi.

Muwatta = Malik b. Anas, *al Muwatta*, with commentary by al'Zurkānī (Cairo, 1279).

Nasa'i = *al-Nasa'i*, *Sunan* (Cairo, 1312).

3. Unfortunately it was impossible for me to procure the collections by Dahimī and Tayālisī.

4. Before tackling the subject, I must mention two recent studies with which my own offers points of contact. One, *Materialien zum islamischen und jüdischen Eherecht* [*Materials for the Study of Islamic and Jewish Marriage Laws*] (1928) by M. S. Bialoblocki, is almost exclusively founded on the *Sahih* by Bukhārī, plumbed without the aid of Oriental commentaries and subjected to an exegesis that often calls for reservations. Methodologically, it still represents a serious attempt to confront an important chapter in Jewish and Muslim laws. Reprised with a broader and better assimilated Arabic documentation, works of this kind would incontestably spread much clarity on the genesis of Muslim juridical thought and would aid in making a distinction between the properly indigenous heritage and various foreign contributions.

On the other hand, S. D. Goitein has initiated in Tarbiz VI (pp. 89–101, 510–22), [entitled] "Isrā'iliyyat," a series of [Hebrew] articles devoted principally to the search for Jewish elements in the anecdotes and sentences of the ascetics, grouped in the *Hilyat al-awliya* by Abu Nu'aym al-Isbahani (d. 430 H), of which three volumes have been published. This research is very interesting, for it allows us to be specific, chronologically and geographically, about Jewish elements that entered into the thinking of pious circles in the first four or five Muslim generations. Nevertheless in these works ([hopefully] only preliminary) M.G. has an overly narrow framework. The *Hilya* is from the fifth century and given the special character of this compilation, one cannot use the data that it furnishes without risk, unless one presupposes already elucidated the very obscure problem of the origin of those hadith with ascetic and mystical tendencies. [But, c]onfronted with older compilations, the texts of the *Hilya* will perhaps receive previous confirmation. It is to be hoped then that M.G. enlarges the bases of his promising work. [Let me also mention another important article by M.G., "Eléments juifs dans le K. Ansab al-Asraf de Balāduri," *Siyôn* 1 (75–81): [in Hebrew, which reached me when I was correcting the proofs].

5. See *R.E.J.*, 28 (1894): 77–78.

6. It is important to note . . . , too, there is a parallel between Judaism and Islam. The interdictions known by the designation *Huqqot Hag-goyim* [The Gentiles' Laws, *sic*] that seem to have originally applied only to practices contrary to morality were extended very early on to many usages, entirely inoffensive, which the progress of Hellenization had spread among the Jews; they came to regulate from this viewpoint details of daily life like the wearing of hair and dress. See the interesting [Hungarian] article . . . by M. P. Takacs, *A Blau Lajos Talmudtudomanyi Tarsulat: Evkonyve* (Budapest: 1935), pp. 55–64. He refers to J. L. Palache, *Huqqqot Hag-goy Bijdragen en Mededeslingen can het Genotschap von de Joodsche Wetenechap in Nederland* [Hebrew/Dutch, i.e. Gentile's Laws (*sic*)] (Amsterdam: 1925).

7. According to information given by S. Krauss, *Talmudische Archaeologie*, vol. 1, all the effects named in our hadith were current among Jews in the Talmudic era and nothing justifies accepting the distinctions mentioned by the Ansar. What Kr. concludes (p. 620) about *Baba Batra* 58 is no less sure.

8. Buh. Kast 8:423: "do the opposite of the infidels" (*al-majus*, according to Kastalani).

9. See Goldziher, *M.G.W.J.* (1880), p. 355–56, which cites Muslim (Nawawi 4:453), which I have not been able to verify; in Muslim (Naw. 8: 419) the *qaza'* is forbidden without saying it is a Jewish custom, as in Buh. Kast 8:471. Kastalānī mentions hadith on this subject and gives as motive for the interdiction either that the procedure deforms the skin [of the cranium] or that it is "*ziyy al-shaytan*" or "*ziyy al-yahud*," an accoutrement of Satan or of the Jews. Cf. Wellhausen, *Reste*, 196–99.

10. Buh. *Anbiya,* 60–64 (2:376–80); Buh. Kast. VIII, 475; A.D. II, 124; Nasa'i, II, 281–93.

11. M. *Sabbat*, VI, 5, cf. Krauss, Talm. Arch., 1:195, 65; A. Büchler, *W.Z.K.M.*, xix, 109.

12. For example, Buh. (*Libas*, 87); Muslim, Naw. 8:421; A.B.H.1: 416, and many other passages, indicated by Wensinck, *Handbook*, see under "Hair."

13. Buh. *Libas*, 70 (4: 98); Buh. Kast. 6:238; 8:464; A.B.H. 1:246; Ibn Sa'd 1:2, 134.

14. According to a[n Ibn Sa'd] tradition (1:2, 129), the Prophet's hair was not at all straight, nor very frizzy; when its braid could easily be separated, he made a parting; if not, even when [loose, his hair] did not go below his earlobes. Cf. ibid., 5:282, 16–18, where Omar II seems to punish the Muslims who do not make a parting.

15. See, e.g., A.B.H. 1:165; 2:261, 356; Ibn Sa'd 3:1, 135, 27.

16. A.B.H. 2:240, 260, 309, 401; 5:264; Buh, *Anbiya*, 50 (2:273); *Libaz,* 67 (4: 96); Muslim 6:55; Muslim, Naw. 8: 396; Tirmidī 1:325; A.D. 2:127; Ibn Maja, 2:199.

17. A.B.H. 3:262; cf. Ibn Sa'd 4:2, 49, 9. Moreover, according to Ibn 'Omar, the Prophet dyed his beard yellow, Ibn Sa'd 4:1, 131.

18. Ibn Sa'd, 1:2, 126, I, 2, 135; 3:1, 133. This author has gathered another series of hadiths with a different tendency (1:2, 139–40): the Prophet had the habit of dyeing his hair and beard; "he ordered," we read in this text, "altering [the whiteness of] hair so as not to do as the non-Arabs *al-'Ajam*." I do not remember [reading elsewhere the motive thus stated].—In passing, I recall the ban on dyeing black (cf. Ibn Sa'd, 1:2, 140–2; 5:334, 344; Nasa'i 2:278) which does not seem to have had a polemic intention. Curiously, one variant of the hadith in Ibn Sa'd (5:237, 11–12), has it said to imam Abu Ja'far Mohammed [al-Bakir] that black is the shade of '*ahl al-bayt*, but following *Kut al-dulub*, IV, 11, it is that of the *ahl al-nār*.

19. *Op laud*, 1:191, 194, 643, 649.

20. A.B.H. 6:6

21. According to Ibn Sa'd, the *Ansari* 'Uwaym b. Sa'ida was counted among those about whom the verse was revealed. [He] was the first [to purify] himself with water after having satisfied his natural needs.

22. Can one relate to this biblical test the information transmitted by Wāqidi, p. 198 (abridged in German by Wellhausen): the Jews always have an axe on them, or else is it simply a matter of a piece of equipment of palm cultivators?

23. Cf. Wāq. (Well), p. 410 ff and El S. *Masdjid*, p. 365, where the other sources are cited. Goldziher has discussed the text we have just studied (*R.E.J.*, pp. 86–87), but using the abbreviated version of the *Usd al-gāba* [*Lions of the Thicket*] and hence he did not see the exegetical difficulty. Ibid., p. 87 one finds texts on ablutions with or after meals, recommended by the Torah.

24. Goldziher treated this briefly in *R.E.J.*, pp. 85–86.

25. Cf. the anecdote recounted in *b. Sabbat 13 a–b:* a very pious scholar died before his time; his wife almost accused Heaven of injustice, but [it was later established] that he had not in his lifetime suspended all contact with his wife, not during menstruation but during the period when, to monitor their evacuations, women dress in white. . . . Muslim tradition is at the antipodes of these scruples. Cf. *Tanhuma, Mesora.*

26. Buh. *Hayd* (I1:83); Buh. Kast 1:340–65 (cf. 8:472–78).

27. *Hayd* (1:167); Muslim, Naw. 2:33; cf. A.B.H. 6:106; Ibn Sa'd, 1:2, 160; Tab, *Tafs,* 2:102.

28. Naturally the *fiqh* adopted the same lax position, cf. Muwatta, 1:103–104.

29. *maa yuriidu al-rajul `an yaDa`a min amrinaa shay'an illaa khalafanaa* [The only reason this person wants to enter into our affairs is to oppose/change them]. The repugnance of the Jews toward practices that he condemns here is well illustrated by *Tanhuma* (ed. Buber), *Mesora.*

30. Died in 20 H, one of the first Medinan Muslims (see Ibn Sa'd 3:135–37).

31. Died in 12 H, an even older Muslim than the preceding one (see Ibn Sa'd 3:16–17).

32. *Hayd* 19 (1:89), Kast. (1:358) [opined] that this way of acting was criticized by Umm Kultūm because the artificial light was not sufficient to note ritual purity with certainty, so that these women were risking performing the prayer impurely.—Later, the *Quut al-Quluub [The Hearts' Nourishment]* (2:46) will denounce as a condemnable innovation the excessive scruples regarding ritual purity.

33. *kol hay-yad ham-marbeh libdoq be-nashiim meshubbechet* [The more someone's hand delves into women's matters, the more praiseworthy it is].

34. *le-or han-ner* [by candle light].

35. *Hayd* 25 (1:91); id. Ibn Māja 1:115 (also in A. D. de Nasa'i according to Kastalāni 1:362).

36. It is up to specialists in rabbinic legislation to decide if this hadith might legitimately be compared with *Nidda* 2:6–7 on the colors of blood.

37. One of many euphemisms about women and relations with them. Cf. J. Nacht, *Euphémismes sur la femme dans la littérature rabbinique (R.E.J.* 59, 36–41)—a useful collection of material but with interpretations subject to caution.

38. *Tafs.* 2:214–25.

39. Cf. the *hanif* Abū Kays Sarma b. Mālik (Sprenger 3:34, n. 2), who would not enter a house where there was a person in an impure state or a woman in menses.

40. This personage himself contrasts his virile ardor *buD`* with the temperance of his father, Caliph Omar I (Ibn Sa'd 3:1, 235). As often in Muslim tradition, one discovers diametrically opposed references: one insists on his modesty (ibid., 4:1, 112), it is even reported that he did not want to take a wife (ibid., 4:1, 125, 19). See

also Bukhāri *Tafsir,* esp. 2:223 where the author attenuates the brutal opinion of Ibn 'Mar by suppressing the word *dubihā,* which furnishes the occasion for commentators (summarized by Kastalāni VII, 34) to dissertate on the rhetorical figure occasioning this suppression. One is again obliged to justify Ibn 'Mar by attributing to him a tradition that very severely reproved pederasty, self-abuse, or any sort of bestiality (Kast. 7:35). This commentator reports that Imam Malik professed the same opinion as Ibn 'Omar, hence a new scandal and attempts at justification. Most doctors condemn the procedure. Al'Sāf'ī appears to have accepted it, but only in theory (by applying his method of analogy).

41. Tab. *loc. cit.*, 221, 14.

42. Ibid.

43. These sorts of statements ended up shocking the opinion of some. One also finds hadiths that criticize the divulging of secrets of the alcove/bedroom: Muslim, Naw. 6:190 ('Abri Hurayra); Abū Nu'aym, *Hilyat al-Awliyā* (Cairo, 1351/1932), 1:186. The custom is still maintained down to our day; see H. Grandquist, *Marriage Conditions in a Palestinian Village* (Helsingfors: 1935), vol. 2, p. 155.

44. Tab. p. 223.

45. This is even expressly affirmed by a tradition from Ibn 'Omar (Kast 7:35); cf. on the uninhibited treatment of women, Lammens, *Fātima,* p. 59.

46. *al-ma'uuda al-Sughraa* [exposing newborn girls abandoned to die]. In the *Kut al kulub* 4:172 it is Ibn 'Abbās who appropriates this judgment.

47. A.D. 1:215. Cf. Muslim, Naw. 6:191, 201. The traditions contradict each other. Generally, they have the Prophet say that no precaution prevents conception if God wants it. In other hadiths his judgment is disapproving, and (like the Jews in A.D.) he compares coitus interruptus with the inhumation of girls. Elsewhere he seems less severe and several companions of the Prophet assert having practiced the *'azl* during the time when the Qur'an was revealed, without this having been prohibited. Some [even] declare that if the *'azl* and relations with a woman nursing a child never hurt the "Romans" and the Persians, then . . . the Arabs have nothing to fear either. Other indications on the *'azl* from Muht. Kans 6:417: disapproved of by Abu Bakr and 'Omar; if the woman is free, practice it only with her consent; Ibn 'Omar prohibited it, Sa'd f. Abi Wakkās and Zayd b. Tābit practiced it.—This question would merit detailed study; the [author of] *Kut al-kulub* (4:172–73) . . . condemns the *'azl,* [with] curious indications that I . . . note in passing.

48. Wakidi, (Wellh.) p. 179.

49. See, e.g., *Nidda* 16, 17, *Sabbat* 86; *Ketubōt* 65.

50. *Nadārim* 20.

51. Cf. *Nidda* 13 and the texts cited by Saul Lieberman, *R.E.J.* 97 (1934): 52.

52. *Ned. 20* (all these texts are gathered in the post-Talmudic treatise *Kalla*). On this ungallant saying,

Goitein refers to this sentence by Omar: *innamaa al-nisaa' laHm `alaa waDam illaa maa dhubba `anhu* [Women are only meat on the butcher's block, except for any parts that have dried up] (cf. *Nihāya*, W.D.M. Freytag ed. Prov. 1:21). Goitein is probably right to maintain that the two sayings are both of popular origin. But it is important to note that according to the interpretations given of them, 'Omar's sentence does not have the same meaning as the saying reported in the Talmud: according to Zamahsarī, it relates to the weakness of women, while according to al-Azhari, to their facility to give themselves to men; the analogy, he postulates, does not arise from Maydāni either.

53. *Nedārim* 20. I cannot adhere to the conclusion [of] M. Bialoblocki (op. cit., p. 45) . . . from this text (that the Talmud authorizes abnormal commerce, so the Jews of Arabia could not forbid the Muslims except as a Noahide [laws] precept [Jewish belief/law, welcoming all non-Jews into Heaven who follow seven of the ten commandments], whereas Muhammad claimed precisely for his own people the so-called Jewish privilege). Despite his subtlety, it is as false from the Talmudic standpoint . . . with regard to the Arab sources, . . . which M.B. [mostly] ignores. It is evident that the letter of the law scarcely permitted limiting the powers of the husband, hence the doctor of the Law, as a legal authority, could not have received recriminations from discontented wives. However, . . . the same page of the Talmud . . . even [notes that] in rabbinic circles there were attempts to reform this state of affairs. As for [Jewish] public opinion . . . (freely expressed . . . in both the Talmud and the hadith), . . . it energetically condemned loose living in conjugal life.

54. *Reste*, pp. 170–71.

55. Note that this interdiction is also projected back into "Israelite" antiquity. Kast. 1:341 (cf. 2:153) cites a hadith that the wives of B. Isrā'il formerly participated in offices at the mosque. But when out of pride (or coquetry) they wore "feet in wood" (Hebrew *Ar. Arjulun min khashab* identified by Goldziher, *R.E.J.* 28, 85 with the *qabqaab* [wooden clog]), Allah inflicts menses on them, which render them excluded from sites of worship (see also Muslim, Naw. 3:81–85). I do not know if this *israa`iiliyyaat* [report based on Jewish sources] refers to a Jewish Haggadic fact. Still, the procedure of motivating an infirmity by a sin is not foreign to the *Haggadah*. It is even very old: according to the *Sifre Numbers*, it is as a result of the sin of the Golden Calf that gonorrhea and leprosy appeared in the Israelite camp.

56. *Reste*, p. 173.

57. *Der Islam*, vol. 1, pp. 101–102.

58. Let me mention in this regard a bizarre hadith present in several collections. Abū Mūsa al-As'ari warned about [not being soiled by] urine: "it was a custom of the children of Israel when urine wet the clothing of one of them to cut it off [with scissors]" (Buh. Kast 1:294; cf. A.B.H. 4:399; Ibn Maja 1:67, 70).

From Kastalāni's commentary, it appears that these precautions from Abū Mūsa were a little exaggerated. On the modesty of this personage, see Ibn Sa'd 4:82. The Talmud (*b. Nidda* 13) regulates the act of urinating but in a totally different spirit.

59. *R.E.J. loc. cit.*; *R.H.R.*, vol. 16 (1887): 160ff; cf. *MSt* 2:224.

60. Buh. *Jana'iz*, 50 (1:330) Jābir, cf. Muslim, Naw. 4:288 ff. The opinions of the *fukahā* on the attitude to take to the passage of a procession are summarized by Kast. 2:417.

61. A.B.H. 4:391.

62. A.D. 2:42, cf. Muslim, Naw. 4:290 (where it concerns a Jewess).

63. A.D. 2:42–43, cf. p. 46 where it is reported that at a burial the Prophet sat down, before the digging of the *lahd*, facing the *kibla*. Goldziher (*R.H.R.* 16, 161) mentions another motive that might have provoked the fabrication of hadiths forbidding standing a dead person: it is the tendency not to use with respect to a creature the gestures of veneration due, according to strict monotheism, to God alone. For the Jewish custom to stand at the passing of a funeral procession, see Krauss, *Talm. Arch.* vol. 2: 64–481.

64. 2:19.

65. Buh. *Janā'iz* 52 (1:331); translation after commentators, quoted by Kast. 2:420, which mentions the same hadith in Muslim (Naw. 4:270–2), Tirmidī, Nasa'I, Ibn Māja; the same motive is put in the mouth of 'Omar (Ibn Sa'd, 3:1, 261); the tradition that follows in the text ("if the dead person is just, he says to his family 'go before me' and if he is not he cries 'alas, where are you taking me?'" Kast 2:468. Cf. Ibn Sa'd 4:2, 62.

66. Ibn Sa'd 5:105 *fa-in yakun lii `inda rabbi khayr fa-huwa khayr mimmaa `indakum* [If I have any good from my Lord, it is also your good.]; see also Ibn Sa'd 5:163, 24 ('Ali b. al-Husayn) 4:62, 73, 99, 211; 7:1.68; and A.D. 2:41.

67. Goldziher, *R.E.J.*, p. 88, that notes other uses of mourning that I will not discuss. Cf. J. Bergmann, *M.G.W.J.* (1935): 325.

68. Ibn Sa'd 7:1, 6. *idhaa mittu fa-kharajtum bii fa-asra`uu al-mashy wa-laa tuhawwiduu ka-maa tahawwada al-yahuud wal-naSaaraa* [When I die, take me out walking quickly; do not amble [*tuhawwiduu*] the way the Jews and Christians do [*tahawwada*]. The play on words *hawwada—yahūd* allows us to reflect on the documentary value of this text. I do not know if the pace of the procession was governed by custom or Talmudic legislation; cf. Krauss, *Talm. Arch.*, 2:481.

69. In the *'ahd 'Omar*, Goldziher, *MSt* 1:259. 'Omar II forbids it by describing it as *fi'l al-jahiliyya* [in the pre-Islamic period of ignorance/brutality], Ibn Sa'd 5:290.

70. Buh. Kast, 2:404.

71. Ibid., p. 402. Cf. Nawawi on Muslim, 4:247 ff.

72. The Prophet authorized women to weep, but 'Omar hit them (Ibn Sa'd 3:1, 290).

73. See Muslim, Naw. 4:250–52; Ibn Sa'd 3:263, cf. ibid., pp. 148 and 251.

74. Ibn Sa'd 2:2, 72, 18; other references in Goldziher, *R.E.J.,* 1:88.

75. *Reste*, pp. 178–89.

76. See, e.g., A. G. Barrois, *Précis d'archéologie biblique* (Paris: 1935), p. 66. Note though that the *tabi* al-Dahhak b. al-Muzahim (d. 105) required that he be buried in *lahd* and not in *darih*, Ibn Sa'd 6:211.

77. *ittakhadhuu qubuur anbiyaa'ahum masaajida* [They take the tombs of their prophets as places of prayer]. See on this question Lammens, *Fatima*, p. 118 ff.

78. Cf. Ibn Hisām (Wüstenfeld), 1021; Buh. 2:371; I, 21 (A'isa, Ibn 'Abbās, Abū Hurayra); Muwatta 4:71. Buh. 1:118 [inquires] whether one may construct a mosque on the placement of a tomb of the *jahiliyya*. Kastalāni (1:429) tries to link these two motifs (see 'Omar disapproving of Anas b. Malik praying near a tomb and the developments of Kast. on this, pp. 429–30). Further on in Kast. (1:433), a hadith recommends making certain prayers at home and not taking houses as tombs, which Kast. understands figuratively: do not make your houses into tombs, dwellings of the dead who do not pray. Yet it must be noted that in putting this hadith here, Bukhārī related it to the interdiction against praying on tombs.

Buh. *Magazi* 64 (3:187) has Aysha add: "if not for this recommendation, his tomb would have been marked by a distinctive sign [but] they feared that it would be made into a mosque" [Were it not for this, his tomb would be opened and be used as a place of prayer, etc.; Were it not for this, he would not be remembered] (This latter text seems indeed a deliberate alteration of the other versions that express that the Prophet's tomb has been arranged so as to avoid popular devotion taking it over).

The term [Arab] is susceptible to two interpretations: a) allusion to the *tasnim*, . . . curving the tomb; this explanation, suggested by M. W. Marçais, is confirmed by a passage from Ibn Sa'd in which it is reported that the tomb of Abu Bakr, like that of the Prophet was made *musattah*, flat (3:1, 149); ibid., one describes the Prophet's and Abu Bakr's and 'Omar's tombs as "neither raised nor flush with the ground, garnished with pebbles of the area" *mabTuuHa bi-baTHaa' al-`arSa* [flattened like a courtyard]. According to Muslim (Naw. 4:299) the tomb of a Muslim dead in Rhodes was flat (*taswiya*); Fudala b. 'Ubayd cites in the Prophet's name the prescription to do so. In the hadith that follows 'Ali affirms having received the mission from the Prophet "to efface the figurative representations and to flatten the tombs." Nawawi (p. 301) notes that al-Safi'i reproved the *tasnim*, whereas Mālik and many others . . . preferred it.

b) The other interpretation is equally possible: "his tomb was placed in a place accessible to the public." This is how Kastalāni explains it (2:430). See also Nawawi 3:177–78, which recalls the circumstances that forced the Muslims to incorporate the Prophet's tomb in the mosque and the precautionary measures taken to prevent the tomb from becoming an object of adoration. The lexicons that I managed to consult do not furnish any explanation.

79. A.B.H. 2:366 (Abū Hurayra); cf. ibid., pp. 453, 518; A.D. 2:47.

80. A.B.H. 2:195 (repeated on the same page with variants; p. 196 without mention of tombs).

81. Cf. Buh. *Janā'iz* (in Kast 2:437). *Salāt* 8 (1:119) it is not indicated that the two women had described the Abyssinian church at the bedside of the Prophet, Kast. 1:430 mentions the hadith in Bukhārī, Muslim (Naw. 3:175): one version with, and the other without relation to the Prophet's illness. Attempts to distinguish between the veneration of tombs of saints among the People of the Book and among Muslims seem an attempt to attenuate the severity of the prophetic condemnation.

82. Cf. Muslim, Naw 3:177.

83. On this text, probably altered on purpose, 'Abbās and Alī did not ask the Prophet to name his successor (see Ibn Sa'd 4:1, 18–19, where these two people enter the dying Prophet's room, but when they hear him repeat "may God curse [etc.]," they leave without saying anything.

84. See, for example, El. *Al-Madina*, p. 93; the polemic might be directed against the work executed by 'Omar v. 'Abdal-'Aziz on the orders of Walīd 1st; see also Samhudī, *Hulāsa,* p. 145. On the precautions taken during this work, see Kast. 2:430; Nawawī on Muslim 3:177–78.—Speaking of the visit to the Prophet's tomb in Medina, Gazāli (in Goldziher, *M.G.W.J.* [1880]: 355) recommended venerating it, but forbid anyone to go too close and embrace it, "for touching and embracing tombs of the Saints [*al-masāhid*] is a custom of Jews and Christians."

85. Cf. pp. 70–72, where Ibn Sa'd combines a series of hadiths tending to show that it was after deliberation that the place of the tomb was chosen.

86. This conclusion is not undermined by the Haggadic texts that say Jacob did not want to be buried in Egypt from fear that he would become an object of idolatrous worship (Genesis-*Rabba* 96:6) and that the place of Moses' sepulcher is unknown so that the Israelites did not raise it into a sanctuary or the pagans soil it with their idolatry (*Pesikia Zutreta, We-zot haberakha* [Venice: 1546]); cf. a hadith of Ibn 'Abbās quoted by Kast. 2:436; the tombs of Moses and Aaron are unknown, which is why the Jews do not make these prophets into Gods. The hadith [used] (and more than once) a Haggadic theme and even the customs existing at the time (the veneration of tombs of saints among Jews and Christians is a fact) for a properly Muslim purpose.

87. Tirmidī, 2:116.

88. Buh. 2:272. It appears to be an attitude during prayer, cf. Muht. Kans 3:217, below, and Leszynsky, *Die Juden in Arabien z. Zeit Mohammeds,* p. 26.

89. Goldziher, *M.G.W.J.* (1880): 311; *R.H.R.* 16 (1887): 163; *Or. Stud.* (Nöldeke gewidmet 1:621); cf.

Muslim, Naw. 3:72 where raising the hands is disapproved without it being stigmatized as a Jewish custom (for a contrary opinion, see Buh Kast 9:197). See also J. Bergmann, *M.G.W.J.* (1935): 329.

90. Cf. Goldziher, *M.G.W.J.* (1871): 179. The *Lisān* cites the hadith in this form: *la takuunuu mithla al-yahuud idhaa nasharuu al-Torah naadaw* [don't be like the Jews—when they open their Torah they call out]. See again *R.E.J.,* 28, 84–85.

91. The Arabic text says picturesquely: "step by step, so closely that if they fall in a lizard hole, you will follow them."

92. A.B.H. 2:327; Buh. *Anbiya* 50 (2:371–72); *I'tisam* 14 (4:432); Muslim 7:57. According to Muht. Kans 1:100, this conformity would be a sign of depravity: *Hattaa an kaana minhum man ataa ummahu `alaaniyy-atan laa kaana fii ummati man yaSna`a dhaalika* [to the point that one would openly have intercourse with his mother; I don't want that to happen in my community] and the Muslim community would split into seventy-three sects, a commonplace, cf. Goldziher's classic study, *R.H.R.* 26, 129 and *Vorlesungen,* start of chap. 5.

93. Ibn Hisān (Wüst). 116; Ibn Sa'd 1:1, 76.

94. Cf., e.g., Ibn His. 102, 129–30, 134–36, 178, 286, 370, 378–79; Ibn Sa'd 1:1, 73, 107, 109; Wāqidī (Wellh.) pp. 162–63.

95. Reader of the Jews who had only one eye, A.B.H. 2:5 (a trait which he shares with *Dajjāl*—Anti-Christ); although very young, he was the wisest of the Jews; Tab. *Tafa*. 6:135 (in 6:145 it is a matter of two Jews, sons of Sūriyā, one was a "rabbi" and the other "habēr"; see below the analysis of texts relating to *rajm*).

96. Cf. for this kind of idea, the case of Kināna b. Sūriyā, who convinced himself of the authenticity of Muhammad's mission, when he augured, thanks to divine inspiration, that the Banū Nadīr wanted to kill him. If he did not then convert, it was in order not to expose his daughter al-Sa'tā to outrages (Wāqidī, p. 161, cf. ibid., pp. 213, 217, 271). The Banū Korayza recognized in front of Ka' b. Asad that Muhammad was a prophet and the realization of the predictions of the revealed books, but they still refused to submit to him, declaring: "We will not separate from the rule (*hukm*) of the Torah" (Ibn Sa'd 1:1, 107 ff). [Very early on, the ascetic literature uses the theme of jealousy (*hasad*) of the Jews. Cf. Muhasibi, *Ri'āya* ms. Bodl. Hunter 611, 139 ff.]

97. Sign of joy, explains the gloss by al-Nasā'ī.

98. Confusion between the plagues of Egypt and the Ten Commandments; on the latter, cf. Hirschfeld, *New Researches*, p. 82.

99. A.B.H. 4:239, cf. Nasā'ī 2:172.

100. See Goldziher in *Jeschurun of Kobak* 8 (1871): 78.

101. Cf. A.B.H. 2:9 ('Abdallāh ibn 'Omar), 19, 58. 113 ff; Buh. *Isti'dan* 22 (4:174). For the attitude of the *fiqh*, see, e.g., Muwatta 4:184–85. Mālik teaches that whoever has greeted a Jew or a Christian [the commen-

tator observes that Jews and Christians have assimilated with each other on this point, although the traditions that inspire the rule speak only of the Jews] should formally repent of it. One will find in Zurkānī subtle appreciations of the two lessons *'alaykum and 'wa'alaykum* (cf. Kast. 9:150) as well as the opinion that one may respond to the greeting of a Jew *al-silām 'alaykum* = "the stone on you" or *al-salām*, in the sense of farewell and separation.

102. Someone seeing Muslims in Syria greeting Christians *fi sawāmi'ihim* (= "in their churches" or "convents") cites a tradition from Abū Hurayra that begins with these words: "Don't be the first to greet Jews and Christians" (see below); A.B.H. 2:222.

103. A.B.H. 3:140 (Katāda 'Anas b. Mālik).

104. Ibid., 3:144 (same end of *isnād*), cf. pp. 99 and 212, 113, 115, 202, 214, 222, 234, 262, 273, 277, 290 ff.

105. Ibid., pp. 192, 289.

106. Ibid., pp. 210 (Hisām b. Zayd b. Anas), 218. It is the Muslims attending the scene who pose the question.

107. Allusion to the Qur'an 5:60.

108. A.B.H. 3:241 (Tābit Anas), cf. 6:37, 199; Muslim 7:4 ('*Urwa Aysha & Zuhrī*).

109. A.B.H. 3:383; 6:116; cf. Buh Kast 9:28, 30, 149, 223; 10:83 (with reference to *Nasā'ī*).

110. A.B.H. 6:229; Tab. *Tafs* 28:9–11. See also Buh. *Jihād*, 56 (2:232 ff); *Isti'dān*, 22 (4:174); *Da'wāt*, 58 (4:207); Muslim 7:3–5; *Tirmidī* 2:117; Ibn Maja 2:207–208; Ibn Sa'd 6:131, 26. Cf. Ibn Sa'd 4: 2, 71, 6; 5:393, 26: one should answer the greeting of a Jew or a Christian *alāka 'l-salami* (wood from which one makes lances)? By contrast, the Kufi 'Abdalarahmān b. al-Aswad salutes Jews and Christians, for "greeting is the distinctive sign of the Muslim and I love people to know that I am one," Ibn Sa'd 6:203; cf. Buh Kast 1:95, 113 where the fact of greeting acquaintances just like those who are unknown to you is noted as one of the "best parts of Islam." Kastalāni, who refers to several parallels, naturally adds that the recommendation concerns only Muslims.

111. *Sifā* (Constant. 1290) 2:216 ff; cf. Kast. 10:83.

112. A.B.H. 1:298.

113. *Tafsir* 4:126 ff.

114. Buh. *Tafsir* on 3:16 (3:221); Muslim 8:122. Tabarī (ibid., p. 129) also mentions the hadith of Ibn 'Abbās in the same vague form, but here the dramatization is curious. Marwān b. al-Hakam sends a message to Ibn 'Abbās: "If it is true that whoever is pleased with what he does and likes to be praised for what he has not done, is therefore likely to be punished, then God will punish us all." Ibn 'Abbās declares that the verse does not concern Muslims but Jews. This anecdote has perhaps a hidden aspect I do not discern.

115. A.B.H. 1:416.

116. 1:1, 123 ('Abū Sahr al-'Ukalī)

117. Christians are no better treated by traditions in this genre. A certain Sahī, a freedman of Utayba, recounts that being Christian in his youth, he discovered

the exact description of the Prophet on a page of the Gospel that was deliberately stuck to the next page. When his kin perceived that he had unstuck this page, they inflicted punishment on him (Ibn Sa'd 1:2, 89).

118. See Goldziher, *Z.D.M.G.* 32, 345; *R.E.J.* 28, 79.

119. Qur'an 24:2; cf. for the chronology of verses relating to the question and other details *E.I. Zinā* (J. Schacht). Among the commentators Nawawi (7:208–10) has given an instructive exposition of the question.

120. *Ayat al-rajm*, cf. Nöldeke-Schwally, *Gesch. Des Qur'an*, part 1, p. 248ff; Hirschfeld, *New Researches*, p. 137.

121. Observance of which is supposed to be recommended in one of his last *hutba* (Ibn Sa'd 3:1, 242). It seems that he had approved (at least tacitly) of a more summary solution to affairs of this kind: according to Ibn Sa'd (6:107) he prescribed that the competent authority publicly exercise retaliation against an individual who has killed his wife and the man found with her, but he confidentially enjoins the authority to take no more than the blood price. If it is permitted to draw a conclusion from the data furnished by the texts to which Wellhausen refers (*Die Ehe bei dem Arabern*, *N.G.G.* [1893]: 447), 'Omar would remain in fact in the lineage of the *jāhiliyyai*. According to one of Muslim's hadiths (Naw. 7:221), the spontaneous confessions of the adulteress and her lapidation expiate the crime (as in general, legal punishment expiates the offense, Buh Kast 9:455), an idea that, precisely in relation to lapidation, is found in the *Mishna* (*Sanhedrin* 6:2). Ibid., p. 207 speaking of a lapidated adulterous woman, the Prophet declared that she had made a penitence that would suffice to expiate the sins of a tax gatherer (*Sahib maks*); see also p. 228. See also the sealed book containing the description of the Prophet that Ka'b al-abār claimed to have received from his father—and which . . . seems . . . a poor pretext [for] his late conversion (Wākidi [Wellh.] p. 419; Ibn Sa'd 8:2, 156). 119. A.B.H. 2:5, cf. Buh. *Tawhīd* (4:495) where the reader remains anonymous.

122. Cf. p. 122ff.

123. Ibid.

124. Cf. Tab. *Tafs.* 6:144, below. On the modes of shameful parades there is some fluctuation, cf. the following text of Tabarī (ibid., p. 135ff). *Wa-`alaa al-jild bi-Habl min liif muTallaa bi-qaaar thumma yusawwid wujuuha-humaa thumma yaHmilaani `alaa Himaarayni wa-yuHawwilu wujuuha-humaa min qabl dubur al-Himaar* [they tie a bast rope dyed in pitch on its hide, then they blacken their faces, then they load up two donkeys and turn their heads to face the donkeys' rear end (the ass's ass, as it were)], hence one donkey per delinquent, each mounted facing the beast's tail; cf. ibid., p. 141, 9.

125. 2:152 ff.

126. See also. Buh. *Hudūd*, 24 (4:391–92), also with an intervention from Abdallāh b. Salām; cf. ibid., 4:309;

Kast. 7:60–61 and 10:11–12; Ibn Hisam, 393.

127. The *mufassirūn*, of which Zurkāni (4:2 ff.) has assembled interpretations that are too precise for our taste, all place the scene in year 4 but do not bother to make Abdallāh b. Salām intervene. The Jews in question come from Khaybar and their names are enumerated.

128. 2:62—Isnād: A'mas, 'Abdallāh b. Muiteb, Basā b.'Azib.

129. The different treatment of notables and the common people from the standpoint of the *hudūd* is a commonplace in the hadiths, cf., e.g., Ibn Sa'd 4:1, 48–49. And see Lammens, *Fātima*, 104–105, with whom we essentially agree. Projection of this crime into the past (a recurrent procedure in hadiths): e.g., Buh Kast 4:456, "those who preceded you have perished, for they applied the legal sanctions to the humble and left unpunished the great."

130. Blackening the face was not unknown in rabbinical texts, but is not, as far as I know, mentioned as a punishment for adultery; cf. A. Büchler, *W.Z.K.M.* 19 (1905): 136.

131. *Tafsīr* 6:185 (Abū Hurayra). Further on, Tabarī also gives the tradition of Barā b.'Azib and a combination of the two in the name of Abū Hurayra, converted only in year 7, but who claims to be an eyewitness to the affair. Another variant on p. 137 that speaks of "forty strokes of the whip"—information that corresponds better with the Jewish rule flagellation rule—p. 138: It is the Jews who are curious to know the Prophet's opinion, but he does not let himself be duped.—p. 142: A new development on the inequality of treatment of adulterers: if the two guilty ones are not of the same rank, then the one who is of high birth only suffers flagellation, the other is stoned. See also pp. 140ff.

It is to this incident, too, that another verse of the same sura is related (verse 15): "People of the Book! Our Apostle has come to reveal to you much of what you have hidden of the Scriptures." In the hadith of Ikrima that Tabarī cites about this verse (6:92), the Prophet adjures Ibn Sūriyā, the wisest of the Jews, to tell him the truth of the matter. Terrified *Hattaa akhadha-uh ifkl* [*sic*]; [last word is corrupted][so that terror seized him], the Jew admits that to avoid condemnations to death, which were increasing due to the misconduct of Jewish women who were for the most part very beautiful, his co-religionists had attenuated the rigorous law of the Torah, by replacing lapidation with the ignominious but not fatal punishment that we already know (including shaving of the hair that rabbinical legislation also knew, see the cited article by Büchler). Let us note, finally, a hadith (Ikrima Ibn'Abbās) badly noted by Abū Nu'aym (Hilya 3:344), which Goitein first mentioned (*Tarbiz* 6:503): Jews did not blacken the face of their wives convicted of adultery because they were beautiful. One might compare this text with the opinion of Rabbi Yehūda, that the priest did not submit to any ignominious treatment (brutal tearing of clothing, destruction of the coiffure) as prescribed in the *Mishnah* any woman accused of adultery if she was beautiful. (M. *Sofa* 1:5; *Sifrē, Numbers, Nāsō,* ed. Horovitz, p. 17 and n. 1). It is quite unlikely that the Muslim polemicist who invented this hadith knew and used the *mishna* in question, but he must have been embroidering a tradition of the type reported by Tab. *Tufs.* 6:92. In any case, R. Yehūda's opinion, which has not prevailed, is interpreted by the *Gemara* in the sense that he wanted to avoid the beauty of the guilty woman troubling the spectators and augmenting the scandal (*b. Sofa* 8).

132. By virtue of that principle of rabbinic penal law that capital punishments no longer applied after the destruction of the Temple (see Goitein, *op. cit.*).

133. They even have 'Otmān say that lapidation was the punishment for adultery (Ibn Sa'd 3:148).

134. Hirschfeld has dealt with this subject (*Historical and Legendary Controversies between Muhammad and the Rabbis,* J.Q.R. [1898]: 100ff) without having exhausted it, either as found in ancient texts or the more recent fabrications. Steinschneider has drawn up a bibliography of the questions from Jews to Muhammad (*Die arabische Literatur der Juden* 11, pp. 8–9); he does not mention the Turkish text printed in the East by J.-Th. Zenker, *Quarante questions addressées par les docteurs Juifs au prophète Mahomet* (Vienna: 1851) (Qyrq Su'al). Note that 'Alī was also questioned by the Jews; the answers that are attributed to him are no less apocryphal that those of the Prophet; as far as I can see, the theological element predominates, cf., e.g., *Hilya* 1:72–73 (*balkafiyya!*); see also Kāmil, ed. Wright, p. 553. It goes without saying that Shi'ite literature abounds with this, cf. Tabarsī, K. al-Ihtjāj, pp. 137–39.

135. 17:85.

136. A.B.H. 1:255; Ibn Hisām, 192 ff, cf. 351, 397–99.

137. See A.B.H. 1:389, 410, 444; Buh. *'Ilm* 47 (1:45); *I'tisām* 3 (4:425); *Tawhīd* 27, (4:470, 471), Muslim 8:128 ff.

138. A.B.H. 1:274 (Ibn 'Abbās).

139. Cf. A.B.H. 1:278, questions 1, 2, 3, and 5 with a more solemn drama (frequent adjurations). For #2, one more detail: the male seed is white and rude, that of the woman yellow and fine (cf. *Nidda,* 31, yellow in the man, red in the woman); cf. also ibid., iI, 465, Buh. Antiya I (2:331 ff); Muslim 1:172 ff; Ibn Sa'd 1: 115–16.—The response contradicts the rabbinical text to which it is usually compared: following *Nidda* (25b, 31a, *Berakhōt* 60a, *Tanhuma* (Büber) *Tazri,* 4 if the ejaculation is produced first in the woman, the child will be a boy, in the contrary case, a girl, and a scriptural proof is even alleged (Lev. 12:2). Useless to say that we are in the realm of popular medicine that is preoccupied in every age and everywhere with determining the sex of the embryo.

140. About this question I recall only a hadith and its Talmudic parallel, [both] well known, but which differ on one essential point. *Nidda* 16b: "The angel appointed at conception is called 'night' (*layla* cf. Job 3:3). He takes a drop [of sperm] and presents it to the Most Holy, saying: 'Master of the world, what will be the destiny of this drop? Will it [the being that comes forth] be strong or weak, wise or foolish, rich or poor? *But it does not ask if it will be righteous or wicked,* due to what is taught by R. Hanīna: 'Everything is between the hands of Heaven, except for fear of Heaven.'" Babylonian Talmud, Tractate *Berachot* 33b.

Buh. *Hayd* 17 (1:88) cf. Muslim, Naw. 10:69 ff ('Annas b. Mālik): "God appointed to the matrix an angel who said: 'Lord, here is a drop of sperm, a speck of blood a morsel of flesh.' When God wants to achieve the formation [of the fetus, the angel] says: 'Will it be boy or girl, unhappy to happy, what is the substance [assigned to it], what is the term [of its life]?' [All that] is inscribed [when it is] in the womb of its mother.'" Nothing can adequately translate the opposition, irreducible on this point, between Jewish faith and Muslim faith. It is astonishing that this escaped Goldziher, who wrote . . . [in German: The concept of the gestation of the child much interested Jewish literature, from the Talmudic period to the Middle Ages. See M. Higger, "The Formation of the Child," *Gaster Anniversary Volume* (1936), pp. 250–59.]

141. *R.E.J.* 7:190; *J.Q.R.,*10 (1898): 104–105; *New Researches,* 92. Note that certain hadiths totally and materially contain this prophetic property. Cf. Buh. Kast. 6:34 ff.

142. Ibn Sa'd 1:1,113, this characteristic of the Prophet is indicated by 'Atā and Hasan, without saying that Muhammad had affirmed it before the Jews. Cf. Ibn Sa'd 1:1, 131, 10–12: "He [the Prophet] told me 'Mohammed, may your eye sleep, your ear hear, may your heart remember.' My eye sleeps, my heart remembers, my ear hears."

143. Here I am summarizing Baydāwi, for it was impossible . . . to procure the volume of the *Tafsīr* of Tabarī where the verse in question is commented upon. The rest of Baydāwi's commentary that derives from the same tradition as that cited in *Musnad Ahmet* has already been studied by Geiger (*Was hat Mohammed* . . . pp. 12–15). The characteristic regarding two angels rests on Jewish beliefs that are deliberately distorted. Information in ancient rabbinical literature on Michael and Gabriel has been gathered in G. Brecher, *Das Transcendentale Magie und magische Heilarten* (Vienna: 1850), pp. 21–28. Notably it is Gabriel who figures as the agent of destruction of the Temple. About the angel, transmitter of revelations, note the tradition in Ibn Sa'd (1:1, 127), that relates that for three years it was the angel Sarafil who was attached to Muhammad and afterward replaced by Jibrīl. This hadith, of unknown tendency, is contested.

144. A.B.H. 1:273.

145. See G. F. Moore, *Or. Stud. Nöldeke gewidnet,* 2:760–69.

146. Ibn Hisām, 376.

147. They even observed details of how Jews treat

meat: they sever the nerves from the flesh, we read in two traditions (ibid., pp. 3–4).

148. The text of this hadith seems altered.

149. Here no doubt in the sense of "illiterate." For the origin and use of the term, see J. Horovitz, *Koranische Untersuchungen*, pp. 51–53.

150. Eating camel is for a Jew a sign of apostasy: Wākidī (Wellh.) p. 217; Ibn Hisan, p. 692.

151. We have previously seen a hadith relating the interdiction of fat to the Jews (see also Qur'an 6:146). According to several hadiths, the Jews abstained from [eating] fat but did not . . . from selling it, a practice [that Muhammad] severely reproved . . . : Buh. *Anbiyā*, 60 (2:372); cf. 2:40–43; Muslim, Naw. 6:468ff; Ibn Sa'd 2: 2, 35ff. [C]astigating this Jewish practice[,] the Prophet forbids, [while] taking . . . Mecca, serving grease of the dead beast [to feed] others. But elsewhere (Buh. Kast 8:29, contra Ibn Sa'd 6:77, 9ff), [he] permits using the skin of the lamb or a dead goat. Kast. summarizes the [casuists'] opinions. . . . (For other references, see Wensinck, *Concordance*). It would be . . . interesting to examine [how] these fluctuations correspond to rabbinical divergences [on] the use, for other purposes, of things [normally] prohibited. [Recall], Muslim tradition [repeats] and amplifies the biblical passage—Deut. 23:19—[forbidding], in [fulfilling] a vow, [using] the salary of a prostitute [or] the price of a dog ([which] are thus compared in the hadith): Muwatta 3:130: *Inna rasuul Allaah nahaa `an thaman al-kalb wa-mahr al-baghy wa-Halawaan al-kaahin (rishwa)* [Verily, Allah's Prophet refused the price of a dog, the dowry of a prostitute, and the bribery of a soothsayer/priest] *(kaahin)* cf. Tab. *Tafsir,* 6:140 and the collection of this kind of hadith in Muht. Kans 2:232–33.

152. 1:173.

153. Cf. Buh. 2:232; 4:235, 240–41.

154. Like the questions of Abdallah b. Salām, recorded by Bukhārī, (*Anbiyāi,* 2:331–32), cf. on his conversion, ibid., 3:42–50, 196–67; Hirschfeld, *J.Q.R.* [1898]: 11).

155. On these hadiths see Goldziher, *Die Sabbathinstitution im Islam (Gedenkbuch . . . Kaufmann* [Breslau, 1900], pp. 86–105). My colleague Etienne Hahn of Budapest, who devoted a successful [Hungarian] dissertation . . . to the "Creation of the world in Muslim legend," [discusses] these texts in an article soon appearing in the *Revue des Études Juives.*

156. A.B.H. 6:57; Nasā'ī 2:172; Ibn Sa'd 2:2, 4–6.

157. A.B.H. 2:30.

158. pp. 294 ff.

159. 2:1. 82–3. The last requests of the Prophet (see above) also constitute a motive for the expulsion of non-Muslims from the Arabian Peninsula, a measure that was imperfectly executed, cf. Lemmens, *L'Arabie occidentale à la veille de l'hégire,* p. 306, pp. 323 n. 4.

160. One also finds the Jews performing the role of charlatans or bone-setters: the sick eye of the wife of Abdallāh b. Mas'ūd was cured by the incantation of a Jew, A.B.H. 1:381. (Other indications on the sorcery of the Jews, Goitein, *Siyōn,* 1:78–79.)

161. A.D. 2:30–31.

162. General opinion, represented by the [sira's] editors, has never pardoned Abdallāh ibn 'Ubayy, leader of the "hypocrites," for his loyalty, moreover inoperative, toward his Jewish compatriots. Dying, he has to hear from the Prophet's mouth: "Did I not forbid you to love the Jews?" Abdallāh replies, impenitent: "As'ad b. Zurera hated them and he is no less dead for it" (A.B.H. 5:201; A.D. 2:36; Wak [Wellh.] p. 414).

163. A.B.H. 2:266; A.D. 2:36; Tirmidī 2:117; cf. Buh Kast 9:147 (mixed assembly of Jews and Muslims).

164. A.B.H. 2:266 (p. 263, instead of "Jews and Christians," there is "pagan"), 346–444 (with the "pagan" variant), 459; Muslim 7:5.

165. Tirmidī 2:123, but Zurkani 4:190 gives the use of the second formula toward Muslims. Remember the hadith, already rejected by ancient authority, cited by Goldziher (*R.E.J.* 28:76) the Prophet had to wash himself after having shaken the hand of a Jew; this trait of hatred (founded on the "Zoroastrian"?) is, as far as my reading enables me to judge, isolated in Muslim tradition, at least in the Sunnite hadiths.

166. A.B.H. 2: 6, 111, 121 (the Prophet himself (Fr. *en chair*) said it himself [i.e., material in para. 2 of p. 111, concerning commendable actions at different times of day].

167. 1:1, 113. (Jabir b. Abdallāh). See on these hadiths of Gospel origin, Goldziher, *Hadith un neues Testament* (2:38) along with *Oriens Christianus* (1902), p. 198.

168. A.B.H. 2:259, cf. Buh. *Jihād,* 146 (2:56); *Nikaly* 52 (3: [illegible]).

169. A.B.H. 2:346 (Abū Hurayra).

170. Buh. *Manākib* 5a (3:51) cf. explanations of commentators, Kast. 6:237.

171. A.B.H. 2:67 (Abdallāh b. 'Omar), 131, 135, 149, 398 (Abū Hurayra), 418 (where one finds this curious addition that only the *garkad* tree, "tree of the Jews," will not deliver them up; the refuge tree is a motif from folklore, see B. Heller, *M.G.W.J.* (1936): 45, 530 (same motif as 418); Buh. *Jihādi* 94 (2:229–30); *Manākib* 25 (2:402); Muslim 7:188ff. There are many variants of this tradition. In A.B.H. 3:368 (Jāhir b. 'Abdallāh) the stone and tree speak to 'Isā, victor of *Dajjāl* and [the Jews'] persecutor. Ibid., 4:216–17 ('Utmān b. abī-l-As) [I]nstead of *yahūdī* there is *kāfir,* but [earlier] the text remarks that most . . . [*Dajjâl*] adherents are Jews. See 5:16 (. . . eschatological tradition, of Basran, . . . transmitted via Samura b. Jundah).

172. I cannot explain this feature.

173. On the *taylasān,* see Goldziher, *M.G.W.J.* (1880): 356–57.

174. 2:267.

175. Mueller 8:191. The eschatological struggle with the Jews is part of a vaster ensemble in which also figures fights against the Turks and other barbarians, cf., for example, Buh.

176. 2:40.

177. To this kind of idea belongs the case of Ibn Sayyād, a Jewish adolescent, manifestly weak in spirit, that Muhammad seems to have taken for the *Dajjâl*. I am less convinced than Sprenger (3:31) of the historicity of the tale's tradition hawks on this subject (Muslim's *Sahih*, for example, contains in this respect rich material) and the question merits deeper examination.

178. A.B.H. 4:391 (Abu Musa al-Asari).

179. Ibid., p. 402; cf., 407–408 (in some versions, they do not speak expressly of Jews and Christians but of "adherents of religions" in general), Muslim; 8:104–105.

180. Muslim, art cit. The commentary of Nawawī (10:197) tries to attenuate the brutality of this conception. Cf. in the same order of ideas Muht. Kans 6:232, someone who is unable to pay the *sadaka* will curse the Jews; this will take the place of alms for him.

181. See *Kut al-kulūb* 1:41–45; cf., *Ihyā* 1:207–209 and Muht. Kans, art cit.

182. Here one must touch upon the claimed schism of the Jews into 70 sects or more. The study done by Goldziher (*R.H.R.* 26 [1892]: 129–37) dispenses me of going back to it.

183. Which the Qur'an (5:5) permits to be consumed by Muslims; see the discussion of this verse in Tab. *Tafs*, 6:56–58; cf. p. 160: the beast slaughtered by the Jews and Christians, regardless of whether these people of the Book were originally so, or were in fact proselytes. Yet the Caliph 'Alī did not permit, contrary to the majority opinion, meat coming from B. Taglib, Christians, for he said that the latter did not manifest their Christianity other than in drinking wine. Moreover, even the flesh of a beast offered to a church was allowed. 'Omar II allowed the *dabīha* of Samaritans (Ibn Sa'd 5:260, 15).

184. A.B.H. 5:226–27.

185. Tirmidī, 2:295.

186. A.D. 2:97.

187. Cf. Buh Kast 8:272, where the Prophet forbids using utensils of People of the Book, except in case of necessity. The text of the hadith does not say which kind of *ahl-kitāb* is involved. The heading of the paragraph speaks of "utensils of the *Majūs*," see. Kast. art cit. Purification by ritual immersion of impure utensils is a Jewish procedure (*tabīla*).

188. *fal-yatabawwa' maq`aduhu min al-naar* [May his seat be removed to Hell-fire]. That is to say, "that he consider himself as damned." Cf. Sa'fe . . . ; A.B.H. 2:159, 202; cf. 474; 3:13, 46 (where it is said: "transmit nothing from them of which one cannot find something more marvelous among them"); Ibn Sa'd 2:2, 100; 3:1, 75; Muht. Kans 4: 62–65 offers a rich collection of variants.

189. A.B.H. (Imren b. al-Husaya 4:487–55).

190. See, e.g., Buh. *Sahadat* 29 (Im . . . .).

191. Buh. *l'tisam* 96 (4:441).

192. A.B.H. 4:136; cf. Muht. Kans 1:100.

193. *aHdath al-akhbaar bi-Allaah* [the most recent news concerning God].

194. Cf. Qur'an 2:41, 79, 174, 3:77, 187, 199; 5:44; 9:9; 16:95.

195. Buh. 2:162–63; cf. *l'tisām* 25 (4:441); *Tawhād* 42 (4:489–90).

196. Cf. Goldziher, *Z.D.M.G.* 23 (1878): 344.

197. See A. Baumstark, "*Das Problem eines vorislamischen christlich-kirschkichen; Schrifttums in arabischer Sprache* [A Problem of the Pre-Islamic Christian Church: Texts in the Arabic Language], *Islamica* 4 (1931): 562–75.

198. Tradition is silent about the language of this book. Moreover, I do not know of any text that would permit attributing to the first Muslims or Arabic origin a sufficient knowledge of Hebrew, Aramaic, or even Ethiopian to understand religious books. The tradition that has the Gospel written in or translated into Arabic or into Hebrew by Waraka b. Nawfal is contradictorily transmitted precisely on this point that interests us (cf. Sprenger, 1:124–28). Zayd B. Tābit, entrusted with the Prophet's correspondence, learns to write in Hebrew or Syriac (but not the language), cf. e.g. Ibn Sa'd 2:2, 115.

199. A.B.H. 3:387; cf. Muht. Kans 1:100: "If Moses came back and you followed him you would be in error; I am your prerogative among the prophets, and you are mine among the nations." In addition, this hadith expresses more the idea that Muhammad is the Prophet specially sent to the Arabs.

200. Buh. 4:441–95. The end of the text is a Qur'anic reminiscence, see Qur'an 2:137, 3:198; 5:59; see also Buh. *Tafsir* on 2:126 (Kast. 7:15).

201. 1:2, 32.

202. The same suspicion toward the Jews does not diminish later, cf. Goldziher, *Z.D.M.G.* 32 (1878): 345, which cites the texts of Ibn Hazm and Ibn Khaldun, see also *Richtungen*, pp. 54–63. The doctrine is also summarized by Tabari, *Tafsir* 5:70 on the Qur'an 4:45: the Book of God warns the Muslims against the Jewish imposture. He recommends not consulting them on any affair concerning religion and not listening to their calumnies against the truth. Cf. *Kūt al-k.* 2:15.

In the disagreement that arises among scholars about the fixing of the sunna in writing, someone points out that the *ahbār* have added a book to revelation, with an interested purpose. This book is the *matnat (mishna)*. I refer to an article in which Goldziher studied the question ("*Kämpfe um die Stelhung des Hadit im Islam*," *Z.D.M.G.* 61 [1907]: 860–72).

As a counterpart to this attitude toward Jewish doctrine, let us recall here a Jewish text, much more recent than the Muslim sources [cited here], but which is still significant. It is a consultation of Maimonides (d. 1204) on the question of whether a non-Jew has the right to study their Law or if a Jew may teach it to a non-Jew *goy* [Rambam (Maimonides)'s *Teshuvot* Responsa.] (A. Freimann, ed. no. 364). In principle, the response is negative: one must as far as possible prevent non-Jews from studying the Law. However, "it is permitted to teach the commandments and the explanations according to [rabbinic] law to the Christians, but it is prohibited to do likewise for the Muslims. You know, in effect, that according to their belief this Torah is not from heaven and if you teach them something, they will find it contrary to their tradition, because their practices are confused and their opinions bizarre *mippnei she-ba'uu la-hem debariim be-ma`asiim* [because a mish-mash of various practices and strange, inapplicable statements were received by them]. What [one teaches them] will not convince them of the falseness of their opinions, but they will interpret it according to their erroneous principles and they will oppress us. [F]or this reason . . . they hate all [non-Muslims] who live among them. It would then just be a stumbling block for the Israelites who, because of their sins, are in captivity among them. On the contrary, the uncircumcised [Christians] admit that the text of the Torah, such as we have it, is intact. They interpret it only in an erroneous way and use it for purposes of the allegorical exegesis that is proper to them *Ve-yirmezuu bah ha-remaziim hay-yedu`iim la-hem* [They would exchange secret signs known only to them]. If one informs them about the correct interpretation, there is hope that they will return from their error, and even if they do not, there is no stumbling block for Israel, for they do not find in their religious law any contradiction with ours."

PART 4

Anti-Jewish Motifs in the Sira (Early Muslim Biographies of Muhammad)

CHAPTER 6

Muhammad's Jewish Adversaries in Medina

Ibn Ishāq/Ibn Hishām

Ibn Ishāq states that at that time the Rabbis of the Jews began to manifest their hostility toward the Apostle of Allah—may Allah bless him and grant him peace. They did it out of jealousy, envy, and malice because Allah Exalted had conferred distinction upon the Arabs by choosing him as His messenger from amongst them. They were joined by some men from the Aws and Khazraj who had remained in their paganism. These were the hypocrites who clung to the faith of their fathers which was marked by polytheism and denial of the resurrection. However, when Islam appeared and their people united under it, they were forced to pretend to have accepted Islam. But they accepted only to protect themselves from being killed, while remaining hypocrites in secret. Thus they felt inclined toward the Jews because they belied the Prophet—may Allah bless him and grant him peace—and because they strove against Islam.

It was the rabbis of the Jews who would question the Apostle of Allah and harass him. They brought to him abstruse questions in order to confuse the truth with falsehood. Portions of the Qur'an were revealed concerning them and their questions. Although a few queries concerning what is permitted and forbidden were asked by the Muslims themselves.

(These are the names of those Jews:)

From the Banu 'l-Nadīr there were: Huyayy b. Akhtab[1] and his brothers Abū Yāsir and Judayy; Sallām b. Mishkam; Kināna b. al-Rabīʿ b. Abi 'l-Huqayq; Sallām b. Abi 'l-Huqayq; Abū Rāfiʿ al-Aʿwar, who was killed by the companions of the Apostle of Allah at Khaybar; al-Rabīʿ b. al-Rabīʿ b. Abi 'l-Huqayq; ʿAmr b. Jahhāsh; Kaʿb b. al-Ashraf, who was from the Tayyi' of the Banū Nabhān clan, and whose mother was from the Banu 'l-Nādīr;[2] al-Hajjāj b. ʿAmr, an ally of Kaʿb b. al-Ashraf; and Kardam b. Qays, also an ally of Kaʿb.

From the Banū Thaʿlaba b. al-Fityawn there were: ʿAbd Allāh b. Sūriyā al-Aʿwar—there was no one in the Hijāz in his time more learned in the Torah; Ibn Salūbā; and Mukhayrīq, who had been their rabbi, but later converted to Islam.[3]

From the Banū Qaynuqāʿ there were: Zayd b. al-Lasīt—according to some his name was Ibn al-Lusīt; Saʿd b. Hunayf; Mahmūd b. Sayhān; ʿUzayr b. Abī ʿUzayr;[4] ʿAbd Allāh b. Sayf—according to some his name was Ibn Dayf; Suwayd b. al-Hārith; Rifāʿa b. Qays; Pinhās; Ashyāʿ; Nuʿmān b. Ada; Bahrīb. ʿAmr; Sha's b. ʿAdī; Shā's b. Qays Zayd b. al-Hārith; Nuʿmān b. Abī Awfā; Abū Anas; Mahmūd b. Dahya; Mālik b. Sayf, whose name according to some was Ibn Dayf; Kaʿb b. Rāshid; ʿAzar; Rāfiʿ b. Abī Rāfiʿ; Khālid; Azār b. Abī Azār, whose name was Āzir b. Āzir according to some sources; Rāfiʿ b. Hāritha; Rāfiʿ b. Huraymila; Rāfiʿ b. Khārija; Mālik b. ʿAwf; Rifāʿa b. Zayd b. al-Tābūt;[5] and ʿAbd Allah b. Salām b. al-Hārith, who was their rabbi and chief scholar.[6] His name was originally al-Husayn, but when he became a Muslim, the Apostle of Allah—may Allah bless him and grant him peace—gave him the name ʿAbd Allāh.

From the Banū Qurayza there were: al-Zubayr b. Bāta b. Wahb; ʿAzzāl b. Shamwīl; Kaʿb b. Asad, who had negotiated a treaty on behalf of the Banū Qurayza which was broken in the Year of the Parties (627);[7] Shamwīl b. Zayd; Jabal b. ʿAmr b. Sukayna; al-Nahhām b. Zayd; Qardam b. Kaʿb; Wahb b. Zayd; Nāfiʿ b. Abī Nāfiʿ; ʿAdī b. Zayd; al-Hārith b. ʿAwf; Kardam b. Zayd; Usāma b. Habib; Rāfiʿ b. Rumayla; Jabal b. Abī Qushayr; and Wahb b. Yahūdhā.

From the Jews of Banū Zurayq, there was Labīd b. Aʿsam. It was he who cast a spell upon the Apostle of Allah—may Allah bless him and grant him peace—so that he was unable to have sexual relations with his wives.[8]

From the Jews of Banū Hāritha, there was Kināna b. Sūriyā.

From the Jews of Banū ʿAmr b. ʿAwf, there was Qardam b. ʿAmr.

And from the Jews of Banu 'l-Najjār, there was Silsila b. Barhām.

These then were the rabbis of the Jews, men whose malice and enmity was aimed at the Apostle of Allah and

Ibn Hishām, *al-Sīra al-Nabawiyya*, vol. 1 (Cairo: 1955), pp. 513–16. English translation and annotation in Norman Stillman, *The Jews of Arab Lands: A History and Source Book* (Philadelphia: 1979), pp. 119–20.

his companions. They raised questions and stirred up mischief against Islam in order to extinguish it—the two exceptions to this being ʿAbd Allāh b. Salām and Mukhayrīq.

*For further clarification of any references, see Stillman's original essay.

NOTES

1. He is the father of Muhammad's "Jewish wife" Safiyya. Concerning Huyayy and his daughter, see chapter 10, "The Raid against the Banu Nadir."

2. According to Muslim tradition, he was one of the Prophet's greatest enemies in Medina. For his assassination, see chapter 8, "The Assassination of Kaʿb b. Al-Ashraf."

3. See his story in Ibn Ishaq (Guillame, *The Life of Muhammad*, p. 241).

4. Not ʿUzayz b. ʿUzayz as in the Arabic text, p. 514.

5. This is a rather odd name. *Tābūt* in Arabic means "ark" (from Heb., *tēvā*).

6. Renegades are invariably presented by their new co-religionists as great scholars of their former faith.

7. This treaty was supposedly concluded with Muhammad and kept with Kaʿb. It was torn up during the Meccans' siege of Medina. Several names appearing here seem to be variants of the Qurazīs mentioned in the account of the extermination of their tribe.

8. The spell that rendered Muhammad impotent supposedly lasted for one year. The commentator al-Suhaylī argues that this is a genuine tradition.

CHAPTER 7

The Affair of the Banū Qaynuqāʿ

Ibn Ishāq/Ibn Hishām

Meanwhile, the affair of the Banū Qaynuqāʿ took place. It is considered one of the military exploits of the Apostle of Allah—may Allah bless him and grant him peace. This is the story.

The Apostle of Allah—may Allah bless him and grant him peace—assembled them in the market of Qaynuqāʿ. Then he said to them, "O Jews, beware lest Allah bring down upon you vengeance like that which has descended upon the Quraysh. Accept Islam, for you know that I am a prophet who has been sent. You will find that in your scriptures and Allah's covenant with you."

"O Muhammad," they replied, "you seem to think that we are your people. Do not delude yourself because you have till now encountered people with no knowledge of war and thus have gained advantage over them. By Allah, if we should go to war with you, you will surely learn that we are men!"

Ibn Ishāq related that he was informed by a freedman of Zayd b. Thābit's family on the authority of either Saʿīd b. Jubayr or ʿIkrima, on the authority of Ibn ʿAbbās, that the following verses were revealed concerning the Banū Qaynuqāʿ:

Say to those who disbelieve—You will be defeated and gathered into Hell, and what an evil resting place that is! You already had a sign in the two parties that met in battle. One party fought on the path of Allah, while the other disbelieving seemed to see them as though double with their eyes. Allah strengthens with His aid whom He wills. Lo, there is a lesson in that for men of insight. (sura 3:12–13/10–11)

The "two parties" refer to the participants at the Battle of Badr (624), namely, the companions of the Apostle of Allah—may Allah bless him and grant him peace—and the Quraysh.

Ibn Ishāq continued: ʿĀsim b. ʿUmar b. Qatāda informed me that the Banū Qaynuqāʿ were the first Jews who violated the agreement between them and the Apostle of Allah—may Allah bless him and grant him peace, and they went to war with him between Badr and Uhud.

Ibn Hishām adds: ʿAbd Allāh b. Jaʿfar b. al-Miswar b. Makhrima mentioned on the authority of Abū ʿAwn that the cause of the Qaynuqāʿ affair was that an Arab woman had come with some merchandise to the market of the Banū Qaynuqāʿ. She sat down next to a goldsmith there. Then they began urging her to unveil her face, which she refused. The goldsmith moved close to the hem of her garment and tied it behind her back. When she got up her privates were exposed. They laughed at her, and she screamed. Then a Muslim jumped upon the goldsmith, who was Jewish, and killed him. Then the Jews overwhelmed the Muslim and killed him. The family of the slain Muslim called upon their co-religionists for help against the Jews. The Muslims were furious, and thus there was bad blood created between them and the Banū Qaynuqāʿ.

(Ibn Ishāq's narrative now continues:) So the Apostle of Allah—may Allah bless him and grant him peace—besieged them until they surrendered unconditionally.

ʿAbd Allāh b. Ubayy b. Salūl[1] stood up for them with him after Allah had delivered them into his power, and said, "O Muhammad, deal kindly with my clients." (For they were allies of the Khazraj.)

But the Apostle of Allah—may Allah bless him and grant him peace—was slow to respond, so he said again, "Muhammad, deal kindly with my clients." At this, he turned away from him, so ʿAbd Allāh stuck his hand into the collar of the Apostle's coat of mail.[2]

"Unhand me!" the Apostle said to him. His face became dark with rage. "Woe unto you, unhand me!"

"No, by Allah," came the answer, "I will not let you go until you deal kindly with my clients. Four hundred men without coats of mail, and three hundred with, protected me from all manner of men.[3] Are you going to cut them down in a single morning? By Allah, I am a man who fears the changes of circumstances."

"They are yours," replied the Apostle of Allah—may Allah bless him and grant him peace.

During the time that the Apostle had besieged them, he placed Bashīr b. ʿAbd al-Mundhir in charge of Medina. The entire siege lasted fifteen days.

Ibn Hishām, *al-Sīra al-Nabawiyya*, vol. 2 (Cairo: 1955), pp. 47–49. English translation and annotation in Norman Stillman, *The Jews of Arab Lands: A History and Source Book* (Philadelphia: 1979), pp. 122–23.

NOTES

1. He was one of the leading men of Medina. He goes down in Muslim history with the unsavory distinction of being the chief of the Hypocrites (Ar., *munāfiqūn*), those Medinese who did not accept Islam and the Prophet wholeheartedly.

2. Ibn Hishām adds here that the name of this coat of mail was *dhāt al-fudūl*. As is the case with many other heroic figures, tradition has given appropriate names to his weapons and garments.

3. Ar., *min al-ahmar wa 'l-aswad* (literally, "from the red and the black").

CHAPTER 8

The Assassination of Ka'b b. al-Ashraf

Ibn Ishāq/Ibn Hishām

Ibn Ishāq stated: this is the story of Ka'b b. al-Ashraf.

After the defeat of the enemy at Badr (624), Zayd b. Hāritha came to the people of the Lower Quarter (of Medina) and 'Abd Allāh b. Ruwāha to the people of the Upper Quarter bearing the good news. The Apostle of Allah—may Allah bless him and grant him peace—had sent them to the Muslims of Medina to proclaim the victory of Allah Almighty and Exalted and the slaying of the polytheists.

According to 'Abd Allāh b. al-Mughīth, 'Abd Allāh b. Abī Bakr, 'Āsim b. 'Umar, and Sālih b. Abī Umāma, each of whom told me part of this story, Ka'b b. al-Ashraf, a member of the Banū Nabhān branch of the Tayyi', whose mother was of the Banu 'l-Nadīr, exclaimed: "Is it true? Did Muhammad really kill those whom these two men have named? Those were the nobles of the Arabs and the kings of men. By Allah, if Muhammad has indeed struck down these people, then it were better to be buried in the earth than to walk upon it!"

When the enemy of Allah was sure of the news, he departed and went to Mecca. He stayed with al-Mutallib b. Abī Wadā'a b. Dubayra al-Sahmī, whose wife 'Ātika b. al-'Īs b. Umayya took him in and entertained him. He in turn began to agitate against the Apostle of Allah—may Allah bless him and grant him peace—and he composed verses in which he wept for those of Quraysh whose bodies were cast into the pit after Badr.[1]

Then Ka'b returned to Medina where he wrote erotic poetry about the Muslim women in order to offend them. At this, the Apostle of Allah—may Allah bless him and grant him peace—said, "Who will take care of Ibn al-Ashraf for me?"[2]

"I shall," answered Muhammad b. Maslama, the brother of the Banū 'Abd al-Ashhal. "I will kill him."

"Do it then, if you can," he said.

So Muhammad b. Maslama returned home and remained three days, neither eating nor drinking except what was absolutely necessary to maintain life. When this was reported to the Apostle of Allah—may Allah bless him and grant him peace—he summoned him and asked, "Why have you given up food and drink?"

"O Apostle of Allah," he replied, "I gave my word to you and do not know whether or not I can fulfill it."

He answered, "It is only incumbent upon you to try."

"O Apostle of Allah," he said, "we shall have to tell lies."

"Say what seems best to you, for in this you are at liberty to do that."

So Muhammad b. Maslama plotted his murder together with Silkān b. Salāma b. Waqsh, who was called Abū Nā'ila, who was a member of the Banū 'Abd al-Ashhal and the milk-brother[3] of Ka'b b. al-Ashraf, with al-Hārith b. Aws b. Mu'ādh, also of Banū 'Abd al-Ashhal, and with Abū 'Abs b. Jabr of the Banū Hāritha. They sent Silkān (Abū Nā'ila) to the enemy of Allah Ka'b b. al-Ashraf before they themselves came to him. He went and talked with him for some time, and they recited verses to one another. (Abū Nā'ila would often recite poetry.)

Then he said, "Woe is me,[4] O Ibn al-Ashraf. I have come with a matter I want to tell you, but wish you to keep secret for me."

"I shall do that," Ka'b replied.

The other went on, "This man's coming has brought upon us a terrible trial. The Arabs have become our enemy. They shoot at us with a single bow.[5] They have cut the roads for us so that our families perish, our lives have become strained, and we find ourselves and our households in distress."

"By Allah," Ka'b replied, "did I not keep telling you, Ibn Salāma, that this affair would turn out as I have said?"

Silkān then said to him, "I would like you to sell us food. We shall put up security and be faithful to you. You in turn will deal generously in this."

"Will you give me your women as security?"[6]

"How can we give our womenfolk as security, when you are the most vigorous man in Yathrib and one of the best scented?"[7]

"Will you give me your sons as security, then?"

"Surely you wish to shame us! I have some friends who are of the same mind as I am, and I would like to bring you to them so that you can sell to them on good

Ibn Hishām, *al-Sīra al-Nabawiyya*, vol. 2 (Cairo: 1955), pp. 51–57. English translation and annotation in Norman Stillman, *The Jews of Arab Lands: A History and Source Book* (Philadelphia: 1979), pp. 124–27.

terms. We shall offer you enough arms to make a good pledge." (Silkān's purpose here was that he should not object when they came with weapons.)

"Weapons are a good security," Ka'b said.

So Silkān returned to his companions and told them his news. He ordered them to take their arms. Then they hurried off, joining him later at the house of the Apostle of Allah—may Allah bless him and grant him peace.

The Apostle walked with them as far as Baqī' al-Gharqad.[8] Then he sent them on their mission, saying, "Go in Allah's name. O Allah, help them." Then the Apostle of Allah—may Allah bless him and grant him peace—returned to his house.

It was a moonlit night. They proceeded until they reached his castle where Abū Nā'ila called out to him. Now it so happened that Ka'b was only recently married. He jumped up in his bed sheet, but his wife held on to the end of it and said, "You are a man at war. Those in a state of war do not go out at this hour."

He replied, "It is Abū Nā'ila. Had he found me sleeping, he would not have awakened me."

But she said, "By Allah, I can detect evil in his voice!"

"If a warrior is called, he must answer even if it is for a stabbing," said Ka'b.

With that, he went down and chatted with them for a while. Then Abū Nā'ila said, "Would you like to walk with us, Ibn al-Ashraf, to Shi'b al-'Ajūz[9] so we can talk there for the rest of the night?"

"If you wish," he replied.

So they went out walking. They had been going some time when Abū Nā'ila ran his hand through the hair of his temples. Then he sniffed his hands and said, "I never smelled a better scent than I have tonight."

They walked on a while, and he did the same thing again so that he would be put at ease. On they walked, and again he did it, but this time he grabbed his sidelock and cried, "Strike the enemy of Allah!" With this, they struck at him, but their swords clashed over him with no effect.

Muhammad b. Maslama recalled later, "When I saw our swords were of no avail, I remembered a dagger attached to my sword[10] and I drew it. The enemy of Allah had already cried out with such a scream that there was not a castle around in which a fire was not lit. So I thrust it into his groin and bore down upon it until I reached his genitals, whereupon the enemy of Allah fell."

"Al-Hārith b. Aws b. Mu'ādh had been hit and was wounded either in the head or the foot by one of our own swords. We made away until we had passed the Banū Umayya b. Zayd, the Banū Qurayza, and Bu'āth, and had reached the Harrat al-'-Urayd.[11]

Our companion al-Hārith b. Aws lagged behind us, having lost much blood. We waited for him for some time. Finally, he reached us, following our tracks. We carried him and brought him to the Apostle of Allah—may Allah bless him and grant him peace—as the last part of the night was waning. He was standing in prayer. We greeted him, and he came out to us. Then we told him how we had killed Allah's enemy. He spat upon our companion's wound. Then he went in again, and we returned to our families.

"The Jews were terrified by our attack upon Allah's enemy. And there was not a Jew there who did not fear for his life."

NOTES

1. At this point, there follow two and one-half pages of verses in the Arabic text, which we have omitted here.

2. Ar., *man lī bi-'bn al-Ashraf.*

3. Milk-brotherhood (Ar., *ridā'* or *ridā'a*), a kind of foster brotherhood resulting from being suckled together, was considered to be a close bond of relationship among the pre-Islamic Arabs.

4. The Arabic text has *wayhaka* (literally, "woe unto you"). The sense, however, seems to be as we have translated.

5. That is, they are united against us.

6. This line and the following retort are not in Ibn Ishāq's narrative. Ibn Hishām adds it at the end of the paragraph.

7. Reading *wa-a'taruhum* instead of *wa-a'tawhum,* which is clearly a misprint in the Arabic text.

8. This bramble-covered field became the first Islamic cemetery in Medina two years after this incident. See A. J. Wensinck and A. S. Bazmee Ansari, "Bakī' al-Gharkad," El[2] 1: 957–58.

9. This was a ravine behind Medina. See Yāqūt, *Mu'jam al-Buldān*, vol. 3, ed. F. Wüstenfeld (Leipzig: 1868), pp. 295–96.

10. Ar., *fa-dhakartu mighwalan fī-sayfī.*

11. A *harra* is an area covered with black volcanic stone, of which there are many in the vicinity of Medina. Al-'-Urayd is another name for the wadi of Medina. Thus, the Harrat al-'-Urayd was apparently some spot in the wadi. See L. Veccia Vaglieri, "Harra," El[2] 3: 226–27; and Yāqūt, *Mu'jam al-Buldān,* vol. 3, pp. 661–62.

CHAPTER 9

The Brothers Muhayyisa and Huwayyisa

Ibn Ishāq/Ibn Hishām

Ibn Ishāq relates:

The Apostle of Allah—may Allah bless him and grant him peace—declared, "Kill any Jew who falls into your power. So Muhayyisa b. Mas'ūd[1] fell upon Ibn Sunayna,[2] one of the Jewish merchants with whom his family had social and commercial relations and killed him. Huwayyisa b. Mas'ūd was not a Muslim at this time. He was older than Muhayyisa. When the latter had committed the murder, Huwayyisa began beating him, saying, "What an enemy of Allah you are! Did you kill him when, by Allah, most of the fat on your belly came from his wealth?"

Muhayyisa said that he answered, "By Allah, had he who commanded me to kill him commanded me to kill you, I would have cut off your head." This was the beginning of Huwayyisa's becoming a Muslim.

"By Allah," he asked, "had Muhammad commanded you to kill me, would you have done so?"

"Yes, by Allah, had he commanded me to strike off your head, I would have surely done it."

"By Allah," he exclaimed, "any religion that can bring you to this is indeed wonderful!" Thereupon Huwayyisa converted to Islam.

NOTES

1. In the Arabic text Ibn Hishām interjects here that "according to some his full name was Muhayyisa b. Mas'ūd b. Ka'b b. 'Āmir b. 'Adī b. Majda'a b. Hāritha b. al-Hārith b. al-Khazraj b. 'Amr b. Mālik b. al-Aws."
2. Ibn Hishām injects here: "[S]ome say his name was Ibn Subayna."

Ibn Hishām, *al-Sīra al-Nabawiyya*, vol. 2 (Cairo: 1955), pp. 51–57. English translation and annotation in Norman Stillman, *The Jews of Arab Lands: A History and Source Book* (Philadelphia: 1979), p. 128.

CHAPTER 10

The Raid against the Banu Nadir (AH 3/625)

Al-Wakidi

This took place in Rabi' I, thirty-seven months after the Hijra of the Prophet—may Allah bless him and grant him peace.

I was told the following account by Muhammad b. 'Abd Allāh, 'Abd Allāh b. Ja'far, Muhammad b. Yahyā b. Sahl, Ibn Abī Habība, Ma'mar b. Rāshid, and others whom I shall not name. Each told me part of the story:

'Amr b. Umayya went from Bi'r Ma'ūna to Qanāt. There he met two men from the Banū 'Āmir. He asked them their pedigree and they gave it to him. He sat conversing with them till they fell asleep. Then he fell upon them and killed them. He then went to the Apostle.... He told him about the incident involving the two men. The Apostle of Allah—may Allah bless him and grant him peace—said, "You have done badly. Those men had a guarantee of protection from us."

"I did not know," replied the other. "I only saw them in their polytheism. Their people have done us harm through treachery." Now he had brought their spoils, and the Apostle of Allah—may Allah bless him and grant him peace—ordered him to set aside the spoils from the two men until he could send it back along with the bloodwit [fine paid to settle bloodshed].

The Apostle of Allah—may Allah bless him and grant him peace—went to the Banu 'l-Nadīr to ask their help in paying the bloodwit. It so happens that the Banu 'l-Nadīr were the allies of the Banū 'Āmir. The Apostle went out on Saturday with a group of Emigrants and Helpers. He performed his prayers in the mosque of Qubā[1] on the way. After that, he came to the Banu 'l-Nadīr, finding them in their meeting.[2] He and his companions sat down. He addressed them, asking their help with the bloodwit for the two Kilābīs killed by 'Amr b. Umayya. They replied, "We shall do as you wish, o Abu 'l-Qāsim.[3] It is about time that you came to visit us. Do seat yourself and let us feed you." The Apostle of Allah—may Allah bless him and grant him peace—was reclining against the wall of one of their houses. Meanwhile, some of them withdrew to confer among themselves.

Huyayy b. Akhtab spoke, "O Jews, Muhammad has come to you with only a tiny group of companions. There are not even ten." (With him were Abū Bakr, 'Umar, 'Alī, al-Zubayr, Talha, Sa'd b. Mu'ādh, Usayd b. Hudayr, and Sa'd b. 'Ubāda.)[4] "Let us throw a stone at him from the roof of this house under which he is sitting and kill him. You will never find him more vulnerable than at this moment! If he is killed his companions will scatter. Those of the Quraysh who are with him will betake themselves to their sacred precinct (that is, Mecca). Those of the Aws and Khazraj here will remain your allies. Do not put off for a future day what you have been wanting to do. Now is the time!"

'Amr b. Jihāsh spoke up. "I shall climb to the roof and drop a stone on him." But Sallām b. Mishkam warned, "O my people, heed me now, disobey me in the future. By God, if you do this, it will be reported that we dealt treacherously with him. Indeed, this would be a violation of the treaty between us and him. Do not do this! By God, if you will not listen and carry out what you are seeking, then there will continue to be a remnant of this religion until the Day of Resurrection. The Jews will be exterminated, and his religion will triumph."

However, the stone was all ready to be thrown onto the Apostle of Allah—may Allah bless him and grant him peace. Just as it was about to be dropped, the Apostle received a revelation from heaven telling him what they were planning to do. He quickly got up as if he had some pressing need and set off toward Medina. His companions, who were sitting and chatting, thought that he had got up in order to take care of some need. But when they had waited for him in vain, Abū Bakr—may Allah be pleased with him—said, "We have no reason to stay here. The Apostle of Allah—may Allah bless him and grant him peace—has been sent off on some affair." So they got up to leave.

Huyyay said to them, "Abu 'l-Qāsim has rushed away, and here we had wanted to entertain him and offer him food!" The Jews now regretted what they had done.

Kināna b. Suwayrā' said to them, "Do you know why Muhammad got up?"

Al-Waqidi, *Kitāb al-Maghāzī*, vol. 1, ed. Marsden Jones (London: 1966), pp. 363–75. English translation and annotation in Norman Stillman, *The Jews of Arab Lands: A History and Source Book* (Philadelphia: 1979), pp. 129–36.

"No, by God, we do not know, and neither do you," they retorted.

"On the contrary. By the Torah! I do indeed know. Muhammad was informed of the treachery you were plotting. Do not deceive yourselves. By God, he is surely the Apostle of God. He would not have got up unless he had been informed of your plans. He is none other than the last of the prophets. You were hoping that he would spring from the Sons of Aaron, but God has done as He wishes. From our books and from what we have learned from the Torah, which has not been changed or substituted, we know that his birthplace was to be Mecca and that he would emigrate to Yathrib [Medina]. The description of him does not differ one iota from that in our scripture. What he has brought you [Islam] is better than having him wage war against you. I can see you going into exile, your little ones screaming, your houses and property left behind. These are the basis of your distinction. Therefore, heed me in two courses of action. There is a third, but there is no good in it."

"What are the first two?" they asked.

"Accept Islam and join Muhammad. You will be assured of your property and your children. You will become the elite among his companions. Your property will remain in your possession and you will not have to leave your homes."

"We will not abandon the Torah and the Covenant of Moses," came the reply.

"Then he will send you a message ordering you to leave his city. However, he will not consider your blood or your wealth licit. Your property will remain yours. You will be able to sell it if you wish or to retain it."

"So be it," they said.

When the Apostle of Allah—may Allah bless him and grant him peace—returned to Medina, his companions followed him. . . . When they caught up with him they learned that he had just summoned Muhammad b. Maslama. Abū Bakr asked him, "Why did you get up without telling us, o Apostle of Allah?"

"The Jews were plotting treachery. Allah informed me of it, and so I got up and left."

Muhammad b. Maslama arrived, and the Apostle told him to go to the Jews of Banu 'l-Nadīr and deliver this message: "The Apostle of Allah has sent me to tell you to leave your city."

When he came to them, he said, "The Apostle of Allah has sent me with a message for you, but I will not deliver it until I have reminded you of something which you know. I adjure you by the Torah which Allah revealed to Moses, do you recall that I once came to you before Muhammad—may Allah bless him and grant him peace—had been sent on his prophetic mission. You had the Torah before you and you said to me, 'O Ibn Maslama, if you wish to dine, we shall entertain you, and if you wish to become a Jew, we shall convert you.' I answered you, 'Feed me, but do not make a Jew of me. By Allah, I shall never become a Jew.' You fed me from one of your bowls. By Allah, it looked as if it were of pearl. Then you said to me, 'Nothing keeps you from our religion other than the fact that it is the religion of the Jews. You seem to be seeking the religion of the Hanīfs[5] about which you have heard. . . . The true Master of the Hanīf religion will come to you soon. He is very cheerful and very deadly. In his eye is a red tinge. He shall come from the direction of Yemen [i.e., from the South], riding an ass, wearing a *shamla*,[6] and content with a crust of bread. His sword will be hanging from his shoulder. He will not perform miracles. He will pronounce wise judgments as if he were from your own noble roots.[7] By God, there will be pillage, bloodshed, and mutilation in your town.'"

"Yes by God, we did say that to you," the Jews replied, "but it did not apply to him."

"I shall say no more about it," he said. "The Apostle of Allah has directed me to say to you: 'You have violated the treaty I concluded with you by plotting treacherously against me.' He bade me recount to you what you had been contemplating, how 'Amr b. Jihāsh climbed to the roof of the house in order to throw a stone."

They were dumbstruck, unable to utter a sound.

He concluded, "Leave my city. I shall grant you ten days. Whoever is seen after that will have his head struck off."

"O Muhammad (Ibn Maslama), we never would have thought that a member of the Aws (their allies) would bring a message like this!"

"Hearts change," Muhammad answered.

They took several days to make preparations. They sent for pack camels they had kept in reserve in Dhu 'l-Jadar,[8] and rented others from some people of the Ashjaʿ tribe. While they were busy making preparations, a message was brought to them from Ibn Ubayy[9] by Suwayd and Dāʿis: "Do not leave your homes and property. Stay in your fortresses. I have two thousand men with me from my people and the Arabs. They will join you in your fortifications and are prepared to die to the last man before he could reach you. The Qurayza will support you. Surely, they would never abandon you. Your allies from Ghatafān will also reinforce you."

Ibn Ubayy sent word to Kaʿb b. Asad[10] that he should support his co-religionists. But Kaʿb replied that no one from the Banū Qurayza would violate the treaty. As a result Ibn Ubayy despaired of any help from the Qurayza. He wanted the dispute between the Banu 'l-Nadīr and the Apostle to be decided by war. He continued sending messages to Huyayy until finally Huyayy decided to send a message to Muhammad informing him that they would not leave their homes nor their property, and let him do what he must. Huyayy was depending upon the help promised by Ibn Ubayy.

Huyayy said to his people, "Let us repair to our fortresses, bringing in our cattle, and patrol our lanes. We shall transport rocks into our fortifications. We have enough food to last us a year and an unlimited water supply which cannot be cut off. Does anyone think that Muhammad would besiege us an entire year? I hardly think so!"

Sallām b. Mishkam answered him, "By God, you are indulging in false hopes, Huyayy. Heaven knows, I would certainly disassociate myself from you along with those Jews who heed me were it not for the fact that your authority would be weakened and you would be scorned. However, do not do this, Huyayy, for by God, you know and we know with you that he is indeed the Apostle of God and that he is described in our literature. If we have not followed him because we begrudge the fact that prophecy has departed from the Sons of Aaron, then let us go and accept the guarantee of safe conduct he has offered us and leave his city."

In the end, Huyayy dispatched his brother Judayy to the Apostle of Allah—may Allah bless him and grant him peace—with this message: "We shall not leave our homes and property. Do what you will." He also ordered his brother to go to Ibn Ubayy and inform him of his message to Muhammad and to BID him quickly fulfill his promise of aid. When Judayy came before the Apostle of Allah—may Allah bless him and grant him peace—he found him seated amongst his companions. He delivered his message, and the Apostle exclaimed, "Allah is most great!" The Muslims repeated the cry. Then he said, "The Jews have declared war!"

Judayy left and came to Ibn Ubayy who was seated in his house with a small group of his allies. Meanwhile, the Apostle's herald had already proclaimed his order to march on the Banu l'-Nadīr. Even as Judayy was sitting with 'Abd Allāh b. Ubayy and his allies, in came 'Abd Allāh b. 'Abd Allāh b. Ubayy. He put on his shirt of mail, picked up his sword, and went out to join the war party. Judayy b. Akhtab realized when he saw Ibn Ubayy just sitting there in his house while his son was taking up arms that he could not hope for any assistance from him, so he hurried off to Huyayy.

The Apostle of Allah—may Allah bless him and grant him peace—set out with his companions and performed the afternoon prayer in the territory of the Banu 'l-Nadīr. When they saw the Apostle and his companions, they mounted the ramparts of the forts with arrows and stones. The Qurayza disassociated themselves from them and did not come to their aid with either arms or men. They kept far away.

When neither 'Abd Allāh, who just sat in his house, nor any of his allies showed up the next day, the Banu 'l-Nadīr despaired of his aid. Sallām b. Mishkam and Kināna b. Suwayrā' began speaking to Huyayy, "Where is the help from Ibn Ubayy that you were claiming?"

"What am I to do?" asked Huyayy. "A massacre has been decreed for us!"

Sa'd b. 'Ubāda supplied the Muslims with dates while the Jews remained in their stronghold. The Apostle then ordered that their palm trees be cut down and burned. He appointed two of his companions, Abū Laylā al-Māzinī and 'Abd Allāh b. Salām,[11] to do the job. Abū Laylā cut down the variety known as *'ajwa*, while 'Abd Allāh b. Salām cut down the variety called *lawn*. . . . When the *'ajwa* palms were cut down the Jewish women began to tear their clothes, beat their cheeks, and wail. . . . Abū Rāfi' Sallām screamed at them, "Even if our *'ajwas* are cut down here, we still have more in Khaybar."[12] But one old woman answered him, "He will do the same thing there." "God smite your mouth!" Abū Rāfi' told her. "I have ten thousand warriors as my allies in Khaybar." When these words of Abū Rāfi''s were reported to the Apostle, he smiled.

The Jews became anxious at the destruction of their *'ajwa* palms. Sallām b. Mishkam said to Huyayy, "Our *'ajwa* palms are even more precious than the *'ajwa*. Once planted, they will not bear fruit for thirty years more if cut down."

So Huyayy sent the following message to the Apostle of Allah—may Allah bless him and grant him peace: "O Muhammad, you have forbidden corruption. Why then do you cut down palm trees? We shall give you whatever you ask, and we shall depart from your city."

The Apostle replied, "I shall not consent to it today. However, depart with whatever your camels can carry except weapons."

Sallām said, "Accept the offer, damn you, before you are forced to accept worse terms!"

"What could be worse than this?" complained Huyayy.

"That he take your offspring captive, kill your warriors, in addition to taking your property. Our property is the least consideration for us today if we compare it to slaughter and captivity."

Nevertheless, Huyayy refused to accept the terms for one or two days. Seeing him hesitating like this, Yāmīn b. 'Umayr and Abū Sa'd b. Wahb said to each other, "You know very well that he is the Apostle of Allah. Let us wait no longer and convert to Islam. We will then be guaranteed our lives and our property." So they went down by night, became Muslims, and thereby preserved their lives and their property.

Finally, the Jews surrendered on condition that they could take whatever their camels could carry excluding their weapons. Now that the Apostle of Allah had dislodged them, he said to Yāmīn,[13] "What do you think of your cousin 'Amr b. Jihāsh and the way he plotted to kill me?" ('Amr was married to Yāmīn's sister al-Ruwā' b. 'Umayr.)

Yāmīn answered, "I can take care of him for you, o Apostle of Allah." He then paid a man from Qays ten dinars to assassinate 'Amr b. Jihāsh. (Some say he paid him five loads of dates.) The man lay in wait for him and killed him. Yāmīn came back to the Prophet—may Allah bless him and grant him peace—and informed him of the assassination which delighted him.

The Apostle of Allah had besieged the Banu 'l-Nadīr

fifteen days before ousting them from Medina. He appointed Muhammad b. Maslama to supervise their departure. They complained that they had outstanding debts against people. The Apostle told them to hurry up and collect them. . . . Abū Rāfiʿ Sallām b. Abi ʾl-Huqayq had lent Usayd b. Hudayr one hundred dinars for one year. He settled with him for eighty dinars on his capital and absolved him from the rest.

During the siege the Jews had destroyed their houses which they were leaving behind. The Muslims had further ruined what was left behind and burned until the truce was called. The Jews loaded up their timbers and the lintels of their doors.

The Apostle of Allah—may Allah bless him and grant him peace—said to Safiyya b. Huyayy,[14] "If only you had seen me fastening the saddle for your maternal uncle Bahrī b. ʿAmr, and how I sent him on his way!"

They loaded up their women and children and departed via the territory of the Balhārith b. al-Khazraj, and after that through the territory of the Jabaliyya, and then over the bridge. From there they went past the Musallā[15] and crossed the marketplace of Medina. Their women were decked out in liters wearing silk, brocade, velvet, and fine red and green silk. People lined up to gape at them. They passed by in a train one after the other, borne by six hundred camels. . . . They went off beating tambourines and playing on pipes.

NOTES

1. Qubā was a suburb of Medina. Muhammad spent several days there after making his *Hijra.* It was there also that he laid the foundations for his first mosque. See Ibn Hishām, *al-Sīra al-Nabawiyya,* vol. 1 (Cairo: 1955), p. 494; English trans. Alfred Guillaume, *The Life of Muhammad* (Lahore: 1968), p. 227.

2. Perhaps al-Waqidi is referring to their Sabbath service.

3. This was Muhammad's by-name (*kunyā*).

4. These were leading companions. They include no less than three of the first four caliphs (namely, Abū Bakr, ʿUmar, and ʿAlī).

5. The Hanīfs in pre-Islamic Arabia were freelance seekers of God. Al-Waqidi seems to have the Jews using it in the koranic sense of pure monotheism. See W. M. Watt, "Hanīf," EI² 3:165f.

6. A simple wrap worn in Arabia at this time similar to an *izār.* See Yedida K. Stillman, "Libās," EI² 5.

7. I am following Wellhausen's rendering here. The Arabic reads: *kaannahu washījatukum hādhihi,* and as M. Jones points out in his footnote, is rather obscure. See Julius Wellhausen, *Muhammed in Medina: Das ist Vakidi's Kitab al-Maghazi in verkürzter deutscher Wiedergabe* (Berlin: 1882), p. 162: *als sei emergency room von eurer eigenen edelsten Wurzel.* See also M. Jones, ed., *Maghāzī,* vol. 1, p. 367 n. 2.

8. A pasture six miles from Medina near Qubā. See Jones, *Maghāzī,* vol. 1, p. 367 n. 3.

9. The leader of the so-called Hypocrites.

10. The chief of the B. Qurayza.

11. He was Muhammad's first Jewish convert.

12. This was the important Jewish agricultural settlement approximately ninety miles north of Medina. It too fell to Muhammad.

13. From this point on he is called Ibn Yāmīn in the text.

14. She was to become the Prophet's "Jewish wife" after the fall of Khaybar.

15. A large outdoor prayer area.

CHAPTER 11

The Extermination of the Banū Qurayza (AH 5/627)

Ibn Ishāq/Ibn Hishām

The angel Gabriel appeared to the Apostle of Allah—may Allah bless him and grant him peace—at the time of the noonday prayer. As al-Zuhrī related to me, he wore a turban of silk embroidered with gold which covered his face. He rode a mule with a velvet brocade saddle. He asked, "Have you already put aside your arms, O Apostle of Allah?" He answered that he had, to which Gabriel replied, "The angels have not yet put aside their weapons, and I have just now returned from seeking out the enemy. Allah Almighty and Exalted commands you, O Muhammad, to march against the Banū Qurayza. Indeed, I am on my way to them to shake their strongholds."

The Apostle of Allah—may Allah bless him and grant him peace—ordered a muezzin to call out to the people who hear and obey that they should not perform the afternoon prayer except on the territory of the Banū Qurayza. He then left Ibn Umm Maktūm in charge of Medina, according to Ibn Hishām.

The Apostle of Allah—may Allah bless him and grant him peace—sent 'Alī b. Abī Tālib ahead of him with his banner to the Banū Qurayza, and the people flocked to it. 'Alī marched forward until, as he drew near the fortifications, he heard them speaking about the Apostle in a despicable way. He turned back until he met the Apostle of Allah—may Allah bless him and grant him peace—on the road. He told him, "O Apostle of Allah, you must not come near these scoundrels!"

"Why?" he asked. "I think you must have heard them insulting me."

"Yes, I did."

"Had they seen me, they would not have said such things!" Then, when he drew near their fortifications, he called out, "O you brothers of apes, has Allah shamed you and brought down His vengeance upon you?"

"O Abu 'l-Qāsim," they called back, "you have never been a barbarian."

The Apostle of Allah—may Allah bless him and grant him peace—besieged them twenty-five days[1] until his siege exhausted them and Allah cast terror into their hearts.

It so happened that Huyayy b. Akhtab[2] joined the Banū Qurayza in their fortress when the Quraysh and Ghatafān had turned back.[3] He did this in fulfillment of the agreement he had made with Ka'b b. Asad.

When they became certain that the Apostle was not going to turn away from them without a fight, Ka'b b. Asad spoke to them. "O Jews, you see the circumstances that have descended upon us. I shall propose three courses of action. Choose whichever you please. They are: (1) that we follow this man and testify to his truth, for by God, it is surely already clear to you that he is a prophet sent by God and that he is indeed the one whom you find mentioned in your scripture. This way you will insure your lives, your property, your children, and your wives."

But they replied, "We will never separate ourselves from the rule of the Torah, neither will we exchange it for another."

"If you refuse this course of action, (2) then let us slay our women and children. After that, we shall go out against Muhammad and his companions as men with our swords drawn, having left no impediments behind us, and let God decide between us and Muhammad. If we perish, we perish. At least we shall not have left behind us any offspring to worry about. If we should triumph, then by my life, we can certainly find other wives and children."

But they responded, "Should we kill these poor things! What good would life be after that?"

"If you refuse to accept this proposal of mine," he [Ka'b b. Asad] said, (3) "tonight is the sabbath eve, perhaps Muhammad and his companions will feel secure from us at that time. Let us go down and it may be that we can take Muhammad and his companions by surprise."

They countered, "We would be profaning our sabbath, and we would be doing none other than that which was done by those before us who were transformed into apes,[4] as you well know."

He exclaimed, "Not a man among you has spent a single night since the time his mother gave birth to him resolute against fate!"

Ibn Hishām, *al-Sīra al-Nabawiyya*, vol. 2 (Cairo: 1955), pp. 233–45. English translation and annotation in Norman Stillman, *The Jews of Arab Lands: A History and Source Book* (Philadelphia: 1979), pp. 137–44.

Then they sent to the Apostle of Allah—may Allah bless him and grant him peace—requesting that he send Abū Lubāba b. 'Abd al-Mundhir to them that they might take counsel with him. He was a brother of the Banū 'Amr b. 'Awf, and they were allies of the Aws.[5] So the Apostle of Allah—may Allah bless him and grant him peace—sent him to them. When they saw him, the men rose up to greet him, while the women and children broke out crying in his face, and his heart softened toward them.

"Do you think we should surrender to Muhammad's judgment, Abū Lubāba?" they asked.

"Yes," he replied, but made a sign with his hand toward his throat indicating that it would be slaughter. Abū Lubāba recalled later, "By Allah, my feet had not moved an inch from the spot when I realized I had betrayed Allah and His Apostle." With that, Abū Lubāba immediately left them. Instead of going to the Apostle of Allah—may Allah bless him and grant him peace—he went and tied himself to one of the pillars in the mosque, saying, "I shall not leave this place until Allah pardons me for what I have done." Then he promised Allah, "I shall not come to the Banū Qurayza ever again, nor shall I ever again be seen in a city in which I betrayed Allah and His Apostle."

When the news about him reached the Apostle of Allah—may Allah bless him and grant him peace—who had been waiting for him, he said, "If he had only come to me, I would have prayed that he be forgiven. However, since he acted as he did, I shall not free him from his place until Allah pardons him."

Yazīd b. 'Abd Allāh b. Qusayt told me that Abū Lubāba's pardon was revealed to the Apostle of Allah—may Allah bless him and grant him peace—at dawn while he was in the house of Umm Salama.[6] She later recalled, "I heard the Apostle laughing at dawn and asked him, 'Why are you laughing, O Apostle of Allah?' 'May Allah cause you to laugh,' he replied, 'Abū Lubāba has been pardoned.'. . . When the Apostle passed him on his way to morning prayer, he set him free."

Tha'laba b. Sa'ya, Usayd b. Sa'ya, and Asad b. 'Ubayd converted to Islam on the night that the Banū Qurayza surrendered to the Apostle's judgment. They were members of the Banū Hadl, not Qurayza or al-Nadīr—indeed, their pedigree was higher than that for they were part of the Banū Umm al-Qawm.

On that same night 'Amr b. Su'dā al-Qurazī went out past the Apostle's guard which was under Muhammad b. Maslama that evening. When Ibn Maslama spotted him, he called out, "Who is that?" And 'Amr b. Su'dā identified himself. It so happened that 'Amr had refused to join the Banū Qurayza in their treachery toward the Apostle of Allah—may Allah bless him and grant him peace—saying that he would never act treacherously toward Muhammad. When Ibn Maslama recognized him, he exclaimed, "Please Allah, do not deprive me from removing the stumbling blocks of the noble." Then he let

him go his way. He immediately set out and went until he came to the door of the Apostle's Mosque in Medina that night. After that he vanished, and no one knows to this very day where in the world he went. When his story was told to the Apostle of Allah—may Allah bless him and grant him peace—he replied, "That man was saved by Allah on account of his faithfulness." Some people claim that he was tied with a rotten rope along with the others from the Banū Qurayza when they surrendered themselves to the Apostle's judgment, and that the rope was found thrown aside, no one knowing where he had gone. Concerning this, the Apostle said, "Allah knows best what really happened."

When it became morning, they surrendered to the judgment of the Apostle of Allah—may Allah bless him and grant him peace. Then the Aws jumped up and pleaded, "O Apostle of Allah, these are our clients, not those of the Khazraj, and you know well how you recently treated our brethren's clients." Now the Apostle of Allah—may Allah bless him and grant him peace—prior to the campaign against the Banū Qurayza had besieged the Banū Qaynuqā', who were allies of the Khazraj.[7] When they had surrendered to his judgment, 'Abd Allāh b. Ubayy b. Salul asked him for them, and he gave them over to him. Therefore, when the Aws pleaded with him, he said, "Would you be satisfied, O People of Aws, if one of your own men were to pass judgment on them?"

"Certainly," they replied.

The Apostle of Allah—may Allah bless him and grant him peace—said, "Then it shall be left to Sa'd b. Mu'ādh." Now the Apostle had put Sa'd b. Mu'ādh in the tent of a woman of Aslam, named Rufayda, which was pitched inside his mosque.[8] She used to care for the wounded and personally see to those Muslims in need of attention. The Apostle had instructed his people, when the latter was struck by an arrow at the Battle of the Trench, to put him in Rufayda's tent until he could visit him soon after.

When the Apostle of Allah—may Allah bless him and grant him peace—appointed him as arbiter over the fate of the Banū Qurayza, his people came to him and lifted him onto a donkey on which they had placed a leather cushion for he was a handsomely corpulent man. Then they went with him to the Apostle. On the way they kept imploring him, "O Abū 'Amr,[9] deal graciously with your clients, for the Apostle has appointed you arbiter so that you might be gracious to them." As they continued to press him, he replied, "It is time for Sa'd to ignore the censure of men for the sake of Allah."

Some of his tribesmen who were with him then returned to the quarter of the Banū 'Abd al-Ashhal and announced to them the impending death of the Banū Qurayza before Sa'd had even arrived because of what he had been heard to say.

When Sa'd reached the Apostle of Allah—may Allah bless him and grant him peace—the Apostle said, "Rise to greet your leader." The Emigrants of Quraysh said to themselves that the Apostle must be referring to the Helpers. The Helpers, on the other hand, thought the Apostle was including everyone, and so they got up and said, "O Abū ʿAmr, the Apostle has appointed you arbiter over the fate of your clients so that you may pass judgment upon them."

"Will you accept as binding, by Allah's covenant and His Pact, the judgment upon them once I have given it?" They replied that they would. "And will it be binding upon one who is here," he said turning toward the Apostle, not mentioning him by name out of respect. The Apostle of Allah—may Allah bless him and grant him peace—answered yes. Saʿd said, "My judgment is that the men be executed, their property divided, and the women and children made captives."

ʿĀsim b. ʿUmar b. Qatāda told me on the authority of ʿAbd al-Rahmān b. ʿAmr b. Saʿd b. Muʿādh on the authority of Alqama b. Waqqās al-Laythī that the Apostle said to Saʿd, "You have judged them according to the verdict of Allah above the seventh heaven."

When they surrendered, the Apostle of Allah—may Allah bless him and grant him peace—had them imprisoned in Medina, in the quarter of Bint al-Hārith, a woman of the Banu 'l-Najjār. Then the Apostle went to the market of Medina, which is its market to this day, and had trenches dug. After that, he sent for them and had them decapitated into those trenches as they were brought out in groups. The enemy of Allah, Huyayy b. Akhtab was among them, as was Kaʿb b Asad, the chief of the tribe. In all, they were about six hundred or seven hundred, although some say there were as many as eight or nine hundred. As they were being brought out in groups to the Apostle, they asked Kaʿb, "O Kaʿb, what do you think he will do with us?"

"Will you never understand? Can't you see that the summoner does not cease, and those who are led away from you do not return? By God, it is death!"

[T]hese proceedings continued until the Apostle of Allah—may Allah bless him and grant him peace—had finished them off.

Huyayy b. Akhtab, the enemy of Allah, was brought out with his hands bound behind his neck. He was wearing an embroidered robe, the Color is good. Neck is normal of rosebuds,[10] which he had torn from all sides with rents the size of fingertips so that it would not be taken as spoil. He looked at the Apostle of Allah—may Allah bless him and grant him peace—and said, "By God, I do not blame myself for opposing you. However, he who forsakes God will be forsaken." Then he drew near the people there and said, "There is no evil in God's command. God has ordained a book, a decree, and a slaughter for the Children of Israel." Then he sat down and was beheaded.

Muhammad b. Jaʿfar b. al-Zubayr informed me on the authority of ʿUrwa b. al-Zubayr that ʿĀ'isha, the Mother of the Faithful, said, "Only one of their women was killed. By Allah, she was with me, talking with me and shaking with laughter, while the Apostle was killing her menfolk in the marketplace. Suddenly an unseen voice called her by name—'Where is so-and-so?' 'By God, I am here,' she cried. 'Woe unto you,' I said, 'what is wrong with you?' 'I am to be killed,' she said. 'What for?'—'For something I have done.' She was led away and beheaded."

ʿĀ'isha used to say, "I shall never forget my amazement at her good spirits and copious laughter, when all the time she knew that she would be killed." (Ibn Hishām adds: It was she who had thrown a millstone on Khallād b. Suwayd, killing him.)

I was told by Ibn Shihāb al-Zuhrī that Thābit b. Qays b. al-Shammās came to al-Zabīr b. Bāta al-Qirazī, who was called Abū ʿAbd al-Rahmān. Now al-Zabīr had spared Thābit's life before the advent of Islam. (One of al-Zabīr's sons told me that he had spared him at the Battle of Buʿāth[11] when he had taken him prisoner, cut off his forelock, but then let him go.) Thābit came to him—he was already an old man—and asked him, "Do you recognize me, Abū ʿAbd al-Rahmān?"

"Would a man like me, not recognize a man like you?"

"I want to repay you for the kindness you showed me."

"The noble repays the noble."

Then Thābit b. Qays came to the Apostle of Allah—may Allah bless him and grant him peace—and said, "O Apostle of Allah, al-Zabīr once spared my life, I dearly want to repay him for it. Therefore, grant me his life."

"He is yours," the Apostle replied.

Then he went back to him and informed him that the Apostle had granted him his life.

"An old man with no family and no children—what use does he have for life?" retorted al-Zabīr.

Thābit returned to the Apostle and said, "By my father and my mother, o Apostle, grant me the lives of his wife and children."

"They are yours," he said.

He came and told him. But al-Zabīr said, "A household in the Hijaz without property! How can they survive like that?"

So Thābit went again to the Apostle and said, "What about his property?"

"It is yours," he replied.

Thābit returned and told him that the Apostle had granted him his property. Now he asked, "Tell me, Thābit, what has happened to him whose face was like a Chinese mirror in which the virgins of the tribe would look at themselves, Kaʿb b. Asad?"

"He was killed."

"What about the lord of the desert and the sown, Huyayy b. Akhtab?"

"Killed."

"And what has become of the two assemblies, the clan of Banū Kaʿb b. Qurayza and Banū ʿAmr b. Qurayza?"

"They were taken out and killed."

"Then I ask, O Thābit, by the claim I have upon you, will you not let me join my people, for by God, there is no good in life after they are gone. I do not have the patience to wait even the time it takes to pour a bucket of water to join my loved ones." So Thābit came up to him and beheaded him.

When Abū Bakr the Righteous learned that he had said "to join my loved ones," he remarked, "By Allah, he will join them in the fire of Hell for all eternity!"

The Apostle of Allah—may Allah bless him and grant him peace—had commanded that every male who had attained puberty should be slain.

I was informed by Shu'ba b. al-Hajjāj on the authority of 'Abd al-Malik b. 'Umayr that 'Atiyya al-Qurazī said, "The Apostle of Allah—may Allah bless him and grant him peace—had given orders that every male of the Banū Qurayza who had reached puberty should be slain. I was still a youth, and they discovered that I was not yet adolescent, so they let me go."

I was told by Ayyūb b. 'Abd al-Rahmān b. 'Abd Allāh b. Abī Sa'sa'a, brother of the Banū 'Adī b. al-Najjār, that Salmā b. Qays Umm al-Mundhir, the sister of Salīt b. Qays, who was one of the Apostle's maternal aunts, and who had prayed with him toward both qiblas,[12] and had acknowledged him with the allegiance of women, asked him to grant her the life of Rifā'a b. Samaw'al al-Qurazī. He was already an adult and had taken refuge with her. He had been acquainted with her family previously. "O Prophet of Allah," she said, "by my father and mother, I appeal to you, grant me Rifā'a's life. He has already declared that he will pray as a Muslim and eat camel meat." So he turned him over to her, and she spared his life.

The Apostle of Allah—may Allah bless him and grant him peace—divided the property of the Banū Qurayza along with their wives and their children among the Muslims. On that day he announced the shares for both horses and men, and he took out the fifth for himself.[13] Each cavalryman got three shares—two for the horse and one for its rider. Each infantryman, having no horse, got a single share. There were thirty-six horses taken on the Day of the Banū Qurayza. They constituted the first spoils for which lots were cast and from which the fifth was taken. The allotments were made in accordance with established practice and what the Apostle had done, and this became the customary practice for raids.

After that, the Apostle of Allah—may Allah bless him and grant him peace—sent Sa'd b. Zayd al-Ansārī, brother of the Banū 'Abd al-Ashhal, with some of the female captives from the Banū Qurayza to Nejd, where he sold them for horses and arms.

The Apostle of Allah—may Allah bless him and grant him peace—chose for himself from their women Rayhāna b. 'Amr b. Khunāfa, a woman of the clan of Banū 'Amr b. Qurayza. She remained with the Apostle until she died as his chattel. The Apostle offered to marry her and impose the veil on her, but she said, "No. Keep me as your chattel for that will be easier on both me and you." So he kept her that way. Now at the time of her capture, she resisted being converted to Islam, accepting nothing but Judaism. So the Apostle put her aside, and he was upset on account of that. But while he was in the company of his companions, he heard footsteps behind him and said, "This is surely Tha'laba b. Sa'ya bringing me the good tidings that Rayhāna has accepted Islam!" He approached him and said, "O Apostle of Allah, Rayhāna has become a Muslim." This made him glad.

NOTES

1. According to al-Wāqidī, it was a fortnight. See al-Wāqidī, *Kitāb al-Maghāzī*, vol., 2, ed. M. Jones (London: 1966), p. 496.

2. The leader of the Banu 'l-Nadīr.

3. After failing to take Medina at the Battle of the Trench (March–April 627). This was the last great effort of the Quraysh of Mecca to quash Muhammad and his new religion. The Ghatafān joined the attackers upon the urging of the Banu 'l-Nadīr, in Khaybar, who promised them half the date harvest. See al-Wāqidī, *Kitāb al-Maghāzī*, vol. 2, p. 443.

4. See sura 2:65/61 (as well as 7:166 and 5:60).

5. The Banū 'Amr b. 'Awf were a clan of the Aws.

6. Each of the Prophet's wives had a separate hut along the east wall of the enclosure which was his residence. See K. A. C. Creswell, "Architecture," EI² 1: 609.

7. See chapter 7, "The Affair of the Banū Qaynuqā'."

8. That is, in the large open court of the Prophet's residence that also served as the mosque of the early Muslim community in Medina. See J. Pedersen, "Masdjid," Shorter EI, p. 331.

9. Sa'd's *kunyā* or byname.

10. Ar., *faqqāhiyya*: *"a reddish Color is good. Neck is normal like that of roses when they blossom,"* Lisān al-'Arab, cited in the notes to Ibn Hishām, *al-Sīra al-Nabawiyya*, vol. 2, p. 241 n. 2.

11. In this battle that took place ca. 617, on the territory of the Banū Qurayza, the Aws and their Jewish allies, the Banū Qurayza and Banu 'l-Nadīr, defeated the other great Medinese confederation, the Khazraj. See C. E. Bosworth, "Bu'āth," EI² 1: 1283; and Yisrā'ēl Ben-Ze'ev, *Ha-Yehūdīm ba-'Arāv* (Jerusalem: 1957), pp. 87–94.

12. That is, the two directions of prayer, Mecca and—for a short while—Jerusalem.

13. The Qur'an (sura 8:41) specifically states: "Know that whatever you take as spoils, one fifth is for Allah, for the Apostle and his kinsmen, for the orphan, the poor, and the wayfarer."

CHAPTER 12

Muhammad and the Jews of Khaybar (AH 7/628)

Ibn Ishāq/Ibn Hishām

Muhammad b. Ishāq stated: The Apostle of Allah—may Allah bless him and grant him peace—stayed in Medina upon returning from al-Hudaybiyya[1] during the month of Dhu 'l-Hijja and part of Muharram since the polytheists were overseeing the pilgrimage. Then he set out against Khaybar during the latter part of Muharram. (Ibn Hishām adds:) Numayla b. 'Abd Allāh was left in charge of Medina, and the standard was entrusted to 'Alī b. Abī Ṭālib[2]—may Allah be pleased with him. The banner was white.

(Ibn Ishāq continued:) I was told by someone whom I do not suspect on the authority of Anas b. Mālik that whenever the Apostle of Allah—may Allah bless him and grant him peace—raided a people, he would not attack until it was morning. If he heard the call to prayer, he held back. If he did not hear it, he attacked.[3] We arrived in Khaybar at night, and so the Apostle spent the night there. When it became light, and he did not hear the call to prayer, he mounted up—and we with him. I rode behind Abū Talha, and my foot touched against the Apostle's foot. We encountered some workmen from Khaybar coming out with their spades and baskets. When they saw the Apostle of Allah—may Allah bless him and grant him peace—and the troops, they exclaimed, "It is Muhammad and the army with him!" Then they turned in flight. The Apostle of Allah shouted, "Allah is most great! Khaybar is destroyed! When we come down into a people's square, it is an ill-fated morning for those who have been warned!"

The Apostle of Allah—may Allah bless him and grant him peace—seized the various properties one by one, and he conquered the fortresses in the same manner. The first to be captured was the fortress of Nā'im. Mahmūd b. Maslama was killed there by a millstone which was thrown upon him from above. Next was al-Qamūs, the fortress of the Banū Abi 'l-Huqayq. The Apostle of Allah—may Allah bless him and grant him peace—took some of them captive. Among those taken were Safiyya b. Huyyay b. Akhtab and two cousins of hers. She had been the wife of Kināna b. al-Rabī' b. Abi 'l-Huqayq.

The Apostle chose Safiyya for himself. Now Dihya b. Khalīfa al-Kalbī had asked the Apostle for Safiyya, and so when he chose her for himself, he gave Dihya her two cousins. The female captives from Khaybar were distributed among the Muslims.

Until this time, the Muslims ate the meat of domestic donkeys, but then the Apostle of Allah—may Allah bless him and grant him peace—arose and forbade the people to do several things which he enumerated.

'Abd Allāh b. Abī Najīh informed me on the authority of Makhūl that the Apostle of Allah—may Allah bless him and grant him peace—forbade four things that day: approaching pregnant captives sexually, eating the meat of domestic donkeys, eating the flesh of any beast of prey, and selling booty before it was properly distributed.

When the Apostle of Allah—may Allah bless him and grant him peace—had taken nearly all their fortresses and had got possession of most of their property, he came to al-Watīh and al-Sulālim, which were the last fortresses of the people of Khaybar to be captured. The Apostle besieged them for approximately ten days. (Ibn Hishām adds:) The war-cry of the Apostle's companions at the battle of Khaybar was "O you have been given victory, kill! kill!"

'Abd Allāh b. Sahl b. 'Abd al-Rahmān b. Sahl, brother of the Banū Hāritha, told me on the authority of Jābir b. 'Abd Allāh that the Jew Marhab came out of their fortress fully armed and said:

Khaybar knows that I am Marhab
A seasoned warrior fully armed
Sometimes piercing, sometimes striking
As when lions advance in rage.
My inviolable sanctuary may not be approached.

He was saying, "Who will meet me in combat?"
The Apostle of Allah—may Allah bless him and grant him peace—then asked, "Who will take care of this man?"

Ibn Hishām, *al-Sīra al-Nabawiyya*, vol. 2 (Cairo: 1955), pp. 328–38. English translation and annotation in Norman Stillman, *The Jews of Arab Lands: A History and Source Book* (Philadelphia: 1979), pp. 145–49.

"I shall take care of him for you," answered Muhammad b. Maslama.

"By Allah, I have the duty of an avenger who has not yet had satisfaction because my brother was killed yesterday."

"Go to him then," he said. "O Allah, help him against the other."

When the two approached each other, there was an old tree whose wood had become soft standing between them. Each of them began to take shelter from the other behind it. When one of them dodged behind it, the other would hack at it with his sword, until finally each one was exposed to the other. The tree had become like a man standing up erect. No branches were left on it. Then Marhab attacked Muhammad b. Maslama and struck at him. The latter protected himself with his shield. The sword cut into it and became stuck. Muhammad b. Maslama struck him back and killed him.

Kināna b. al-Rabī', who had custody of the treasure of the Banu 'l-Nadīr, was brought before the Apostle of Allah—may Allah bless him and grant him peace. He questioned him concerning its whereabouts. He, however, denied knowing its location. Then one of the Jews came to the Apostle and told him, "I saw Kināna walking around in a certain ruin early each morning."

At this, the Apostle said to Kināna, "Do you know that if we find that you have it, I shall have you killed?"

"Yes," he replied.

The Apostle of Allah—may Allah bless him and grant him peace—ordered the ruin to be excavated, and part of the Banu 'l-Nadīr's treasure was dug up. So the Apostle questioned him about the rest, but he refused to hand it over. Then the Apostle ordered al-Zubayr b. al-'Awwām, saying, "Torture him until you extract it from him." Al-Zubayr struck a fire with flint on his chest until he nearly expired. Then the Apostle gave him over to Muhammad b. Maslama who cut off his head as part of his revenge for his brother Mahmūd b. Maslama.

The Apostle of Allah—may Allah bless him and grant him peace—had besieged the people of Khaybar in their fortresses al-Watīh and al-Sulālim until they came to realize all was lost, and they entreated him to be lenient with them and to refrain from shedding their blood. This he agreed to do. The Apostle had already taken possession of all their property—al-Shaqq, Natāh, al-Katība, and all their fortresses—with the sole exception of what belonged to these two fortresses.

When the people of Fadak[4] heard about what happened to them, they sent to the Apostle of Allah—may Allah bless him and grant him peace—entreating him to be lenient with them too, and refrain from shedding their blood. They in turn would surrender all of their property to him. He agreed to this. Muhayyisa b. Mas'ūd,[5] brother of the Banū Hāritha, was one of the intermediaries between them and the Apostle.

When the people of Khaybar had surrendered on these terms, they asked the Apostle of Allah—may Allah bless him and grant him peace—to employ them on their former property for half the produce. "We are more knowledgeable about that than you and are better cultivators. So the Apostle of Allah—may Allah bless him and grant him peace—made peace with them in return for fifty percent of their produce, adding, "On condition that we may expel you if and when we wish to expel you."[6] He made peace with the inhabitants of Fadak on the same terms. Thus, Khaybar became part of the communal spoils of the Muslims, whereas Fadak was exclusively for the Apostle of Allah—may Allah bless him and grant him peace—because they had not driven horses or camels against it.[7]

When the Apostle of Allah—may Allah bless him and grant him peace—had rested, Zaynab b. al-Hārith, Sallām b. Mishkam's wife, presented him with a roasted lamb. She had previously inquired as to which joint of lamb was the Apostle's favorite. When told it was the shoulder, she put a great deal of poison in it, poisoning the rest of the lamb as well. Then she brought it. When she had placed it before the Apostle of Allah—may Allah bless him and grant him peace—he took the shoulder and chewed a piece of it, but he did not swallow it. Bishr b. al-Barā' b. Ma'rūr was with him, and also took a piece from it as did the Apostle. Now Bishr swallowed it, whereas the Apostle of Allah—may Allah bless him and grant him peace—spit it out and said, "This bone tells me that it is poisoned." Then he summoned her, and she confessed. "What brought you to do this?" he asked.

"You know very well what you have brought upon my people," she replied. "I thought to myself, if this man is only a king I shall be rid of him, and if he is a prophet, he will be informed [that the lamb was poisoned]."

At these words, the Apostle of Allah—may Allah bless him and grant him peace—let her off. Bishr died from what he had eaten.

Marwān b. 'Uthmān b. Abī Sa'īd b. al-Mu'allā told me that the Apostle of Allah—may Allah bless him and grant him peace—said to Umm Bishr b. al-Barā' when she came to visit him during the illness from which he was to die, "O Umm Bishr, this is the time in which I feel a deadly attack from what I ate with your brother at Khaybar."

Indeed, the Muslims consider the Apostle to have died a martyr in addition to the prophethood with which Allah had honored him.

NOTES

1. About six weeks before the expedition against Khaybar, Muhammad signed an agreement with the Quraysh at this spot on the edge of the sacred territory of Mecca. Among other things, Muhammad agreed not to make the pilgrimage that year. Many of his followers were dismayed and disappointed. The raid against Khaybar was in part a consolation. See W. Montgomery Watt, "al-Hudaybiyya," EI[2] 3: 539.

2. He was Muhammad's cousin, son-in-law, and the fourth caliph.

3. This is not as generous as it may seem at first, for only Muslims would make the call to prayer.

4. This agricultural settlement was located not far from Khaybar, and like it was inhabited by Jews. After the death of Muhammad, Fadak became a point of contention between Fāṭima, the Prophet's daughter, and Abū Bakr, the first caliph. She claimed that it had been left to her by her father, but Abū Bakr argued that its pious foundation was established by Muhammad for charitable purposes. The dispute over who was entitled to the revenues of Fadak was to continue for nearly two centuries. See L. Veccia Vaglieri, "Fadak," EI² 2: 725–27.

5. Concerning him, see chapter 9, "The Brothers Muhayyisa and Huwayyisa."

6. This clause is most probably a later interpolation that was put in to justify the expulsion of the Jews from northern Arabia by Caliph ʿUmar in 642.

7. In sura 17:64–66, the Muslims are enjoined to urge horse and foot against the unbelievers so as to "share in their wealth and children." Since Fadak surrendered without being attacked, there was no need to share the booty.

CHAPTER 13

Excerpts from the Sira of Ibn Sa'd

Ibn Sa'd

THE ASSASSINATION OF ABU AFAK, THE JEW

Then (occurred) the *sariyyah* of Sālim Ibn 'Umayr al-'Amri against Abū 'Afak, the Jew, in Shawwāl in the beginning of the twentieth month from the *hijrah* of the Apostle of Allāh, may Allāh bless him. Abū 'Afak, was from Banū Amr Ibn 'Awf, and was an old man who had attained the age of 120 years. He was a Jew, and used to instigate the people against the Apostle of Allāh, may Allāh bless him, and composed (satirical) verses. Sālim Ibn 'Umayr who was one of the great weepers and who had participated in Badr, said: I take a vow that I shall either kill Abū 'Afak or die before him. He waited for an opportunity until a hot night came, and Abū 'Afak slept in an open place. Sālim Ibn 'Umayr knew it, so he placed the sword on his liver and pressed, till it reached his bed. The enemy of Allāh screamed and the people, who were his followers rushed to him, took him to his house and interred him.

THE SUBJUGATION OF THE BANŪ QAYNUQĀ'

Then (occurred) the *ghazwah* of the Apostle of Allāh, may Allāh bless him, against Banū Qaynuqā' on Saturday, in the middle of Shawwāl, after the commencement of the twentieth month from the *Hegira*. These people were Jews and allies of 'Abd Allāh Ibn Ubayyi Ibn Salūl. They were the bravest Jews, and were goldsmiths. They had entered into a pact with the Prophet, may Allāh bless him. When the Battle of Badr took place, they transgressed and showed jealously, and violated the pact and the covenant. Thereupon Allāh the Blessed and the High revealed to His Prophet: "And if thou fearest treachery from any folk, then throw back to them (their treaty) fairly. Lo! Allāh loveth not the treacherous." The Apostle of Allāh, may Allah bless him, had said: I fear the Banū Qaynuqā' but after this verse he marched against them. His standard that day was borne by Hamzah Ibn 'Abd al-Muttalib. The standard of the Apostle of Allāh, may Allāh bless him, was white, and there were no flags that day. He left Abū Lubābah Ibn 'Abd al-Mundhir al-'Amri as his vicegerent at al-Madinah. Then he marched against them and besieged them for fifteen days till the appearance of crescent of the month of Dhu al-Qa'dah. They were the first among the Jews to violate the pact and fight. They shut themselves up in their fortress, so he (Prophet) strongly besieged them, till Allāh cast fear in their hearts. They submitted to the orders of the Apostle of Allāh, may Allāh bless him, that their property would be for the Prophet while they would take their women and children with them. Then under his orders their hands were tied behind their backs. The Apostle of Allāh, may Allāh bless him, appointed al-Mudhir Ibn Qudāmah al-Silmi, of the Banū al-Silm, the tribe of Sa'd Ibn Khaythamah to tie their hands behind their backs. 'Abd Allāh Ibn Ubayyi had a talk with the Apostle of Allāh, may Allāh bless him, about them and entreated him (to release them). Thereupon he (Prophet) said: Leave them, may Allāh curse them and curse him who is with them! He abandoned (the idea of) their killing and ordered them [p. 20] to be banished from al-Madinah. 'Ubādah Ibn al-Sāmit was entrusted (with the duty of) banishing them. They went to Adhri'āt where they lived for a short while. The Apostle of Allāh, may Allāh bless him, took (for himself) from their arms three bows: a bow called *al-Katūm* which (later) broke in Uhud, a bow called *al-Rawhā* and a bow called *al-Bayda*; he took two coats of mail from their arms—a coat of mail called *al-Sughdiyah* and the other called *Fiddah*. (He took) three swords—one *Qala'i* sword, another known as *Battār* and a third one. (He also took) three spears. They found in their fortress arms in plenty and instruments of goldsmiths. The Apostle of Allāh, may Allāh bless him, took his personal share and one-fifth and distributed four-fifths among his Companions. It was the first one-fifth share separated, after that of Badr. He who seized their property was Muhammad Ibn Maslamah.

Ibn Sa'd, *Kitab Al-Tabaqat Al-Kabir*, vol. 2 (New Delhi: 1993), pp. 31–33, 35–39, 68–71, 91–96, 131–46, 244–52. English translation by S. Moinul Haq and H. K. Ghazanfar.

THE ASSASSINATION OF KA'B IBN AL-ASHRAF, THE JEW

Then (occurred) the *sariyyah* for slaying Ka'b Ibn al-Ashraf, the Jew. It took place on 14 Rabi' al-Awwal (4 September A.C. 624) after the commencement of the twenty-fifth month from the *Hegira* of the Apostle of Allāh, may Allāh bless him. The cause of slaying him was that he was a poet and used to satirize the Prophet, may Allāh bless him, and his Companions, and used to instigate (polytheists) against them, and offended them. When the expedition of Badr took place, he was humbled and humiliated and so he said: Today it is better to be beneath the earth than above it (i.e., death is preferable to life). Then he went to Makkah and made the Quraysh lament for the dead at Badr and exhorted them in verses (to take revenge). Then he came to al-Madinah. The Apostle of Allāh, may Allāh bless him, said: O Allāh! guard me as Thou willest against Ka'b Ibn al-Ashraf, his declaration of evil and versified sayings; he also said: Who is for me against Ka'b Ibn al-Ashraf, as he has offended me? Muhammad Ibn Maslamah said: I am; O Apostle of Allāh, I shall kill him. He (Prophet) said: Do it and consult Sa'd Ibn Mu'ādh about this affair. Muhammad Ibn Maslamah and a few persons of the Aws assembled together; they were 'Abbād Ibn Bishr, 'Abu Nā'ilah Silkān Ibn Salāmah, al-Hārith Ibn Aws Ibn Aws Ibn Mu'ādh [p. 22] and Abū 'Abs Ibn Jabr. They said: O Apostle of Allāh, we shall kill him but permit us to speak to him. He said: Do speak. Abū Nā'ilah was the foster-brother of Ka'b Ibn al-Ashraf. He went to him (Ka'b). He (Ka'b) disliked him (Abū Nā'ilah) and was afraid of him. He said: I am Abū Nā'ilah, and I have come to you to inform you that the advent of this man (Prophet) is a calamity for us. The Arabs are fighting with us and they are shooting from one bow (i.e., they are united against us). We want to keep away from him (Prophet). There are certain persons of my tribe who agree with my opinion. I want to come to you to purchase food and dates. We will pawn with you something which will be a security. He was satisfied with his words and said: Bring them to me whenever you like. He went out from him having fixed a time. He went to his companions and informed them. They agreed to come to him when it was evening. Then they went to the Apostle of Allāh, may Allāh bless him, and informed him. He went with them till he reached al-Baqi', then he sent them and said: Go with the blessing of Allāh and His support. He (Ibn Sa'd) said: It was a moonlit night. They moved on till they reached his fort. Abū Nā'ilah called him and he (Ka'b) stood up. His wife, who had been newly wedded, held his blanket and said: Where do you go? You are a warrior. He said: I am pledged and he is my (foster-brother) Abū Nā'ilah. He covered himself with a blanket with his hand and said: Even if a person is called to be stabbed he should respond. Then he came down and talked for some time till he was pleased with them and became intimate with

them. Now Abū Nā'ilah put his hand into his hair and caught hold of him by the locks and said to his companions: Kill the enemy of Allāh. They struck him with their swords, which fell together and were therefore ineffective as some of them were obstructing others. He embraced Abū Nā'ilah. Muhammad Ibn Maslamah said: I thought of the rapier in my sword. I drew it and thrust it into his navel and pressed it and it cut him up to the pubes. The enemy of Allāh shrieked so loudly that none of the fortresses of the Jews remained without fire being lighted. Then they cut his head and took it with them. When they reached Baqi' al-Gharqad, they said *takbīr* (Allāh is Great); he also recited *takbīr* (Allāh is Great). He knew that they had killed him. When they reached the Apostle of Allāh, may Allāh bless him; he said: (Your) faces be lucky. They said: Yours too! O Apostle of Allāh. They cast his head before him. He (Prophet) praised Allāh on his being slain. When it was morning, he said: Kill every Jew whom you come across. The Jews were frightened, so none of them came out. Nor did they speak. They were afraid that they would be suddenly attacked as Ibn al-Ashraf was attacked in the night.

Muhammad Ibn Humayd al-'Abdī informed us on the authority of Ma'mar Ibn Rāshid, he on the authority of al-Zuhrī, relating to the words of Allāh the High, "and ye will bear much wrong from those who were given the Scripture before you, and from the idolators." He said: This refers to Ka'b Ibn al-Ashraf who used to excite the polytheists against the Apostle of Allāh, may Allāh bless him, and his Companions. It means that he wrote in verse satires on the Prophet, may Allāh bless him, and his Companions: A party of five *Ansārs* went to him [p. 23]. In it there were Muhammad Ibn Maslamah and another person called Abū 'Abs. When they reached [there] he was in a meeting of his people at al-'Awāli. He was frightened on seeing them and disliked their condition. They said: We have come to you for a purpose. He said: So one of you should come close to me and inform me of that purpose. One of them went to him. They said: We have come to you to sell our coats of mail to you, so that we may have money to spend. He said: By Allāh! if you do this, (it will be good for you). Since this man (referring to Prophet) has come to you, you have had too much trouble. Then they promised to come to him in the early hours of the night. When the people had parted with him, they (Muslims) called him. His wife said to him: What brought them to you at this odd hour and what is that you like? He said: They had informed me of their affair and condition.

Muhammad Ibn Humayd informed us on the authority of Ma'mar, he on the authority of Ayyūb, he on the authority of 'Ikrimah: He (Ka'b) came to them and they talked with him. He asked them: What will you mortgage with me? Will you mortgage your children? He wanted to give them dates in loan. They said: We feel ashamed that our children will be disgraced by the people saying: That this was pawned for a *wasq* and that for two *wasqs*. Then he said: Will you mortgage our women? They said: You are the most handsome of men, so we cannot trust you, which of the women will decline (to submit to you), because of your charm. We will mortgage our weapons and you are fully acquainted how much we require them. He said: Yes. Bring your arms and carry (dates) as much as you like. They said: Come down, we will take from you, and will take from us. He began to descend but his wife embraced him and said: Call your people, equal to them in number, to be with you. He said: If they had found me sleeping they would not have awakened me. She said: Talk to them from the roof of the house. He refused and came down and his odor was diffusing. They asked: What is this odor? He said: It is the perfume of so and so's mother, (meaning) his wife. Someone of them went close to him to smell his head, and seized him by the neck and said: Kill the enemy of Allāh. Thereupon Abū 'Abs stabbed him in his hip and Muhammad Ibn Maslamah struck him with the sword. Then they killed him and retired. The odor became panicky and they came to the Prophet, may Allāh bless him, reminded them of his misdeeds and how he had been instigating them and exciting them to fight with them (Muslims) and how he had been harming them. Then he asked them to reduce to writing (terms) which might be binding between him and them.

He (Ibn Sa'd) said: After that this document remained with 'Ali, may Allāh be pleased with him.

THE ATTACK UPON THE BANU AL-NADIR

Then (occurred) the *ghazwah* of the Apostle of Allāh, may Allāh bless him, against Banu al-Nadir, Rabi' al-Awwal of the fourth year, after the commencement of the thirty-seventh month from his *Hegira*. The dwellings of Banu al-Nadir were in the territory of al-Ghars and its adjoining places where there lay the graveyard of Banū Khatmah. They were in alliance with Banū 'Āmir.

They (narrators) said: The Apostle of Allāh, may Allāh bless him, set out on Saturday and offered prayers in the mosque of Qubā, and with him there were his Companions, the *Muhājirs* and *Ansārs*. Then he went to Ranu al-Nadir and had a talk with them about their assisting him in the realization of the ransom of the two persons of Kilāb whom 'Amr Ibn Umayyah al-Damri had slain. They said: O Abu al-Qāsim, we will do as you like. Then some of them went into secret consultation and decided to act treacherously against him (Prophet). 'Amr Ibn Jihāsh Ibn Ka'b Ibn Basil al-Nadari said: I shall ascend on the roof of a house from where I shall throw a stone down (on him). Thereupon [p. 41] Sallām Ibn Mishkam, said: Do not do it. By Allāh! he will come to know what you intend to do with him. It would be a violation of our agreement with him. The Apostle of Allāh, may Allāh bless him, received information of what they intended to do. He rose in a hurry as if he was

in need. Then he returned to al-Madinah, and his Companions joined him. They said: You left and we did not know if it. He said: The Jews had intended to act treacherously; Allāh informed me and I left. The Apostle of Allāh, may Allāh bless him, sent Muhammad Ibn Maslamah (with a message); Go out from my land and you shall not live here because of the treachery you had intended to commit. You are given ten days' time (to leave). He who is seen after this time would be beheaded. They passed several days in making preparations, and sent messengers to their supporters of Dhu al-Jadr. They hired sturdy camels. (In the meantime) Ibn Ubayyi also sent (a message) to them: Do not leave your houses and stay in your fort. Verily, there are two thousand people of my tribe and other Arab tribes are also with me. They will enter your fort to join you, and will die to the last man. The Qurayzah and your allies from the Ghatagān will come to your assistance. Huyayyi was tempted by what Ibn Ubayyi had said. He sent (a message) to the Apostle of Allāh, may Allāh bless him: We shall not leave our houses; you may do what you like. The Apostle of Allāh, may Allāh bless him, said the *takbir* loudly, and the Muslims said the *takbir* in response. He (Ibn Sa'd) said: The Jews had waged war so the Prophet, may Allāh bless him, marched against them with his Companions. He offered *'Asr* prayers in the plain of Banu al-Nadir. 'Ali was the standard bearer. He (Prophet) had appointed Ibn Umm Maktūm as his vicegerent.

When they (Banu al-Nadir) saw the Apostle of Allāh, may Allāh bless him, they climbed over their forts with arrows and stones. The Qurayzah kept aloof and did not help them. Ibn Ubayyi and their allies of the Ghatafān deserted them, so they lost all hope of their help. The Apostle of Allāh, may Allāh bless him, besieged them and cut their trees of date palms. Then they said: We go out of your land. He said: Today I shall not accept (this offer). But you can leave it and save your lives; carry what your camels can, except arms. The Jews accepted this condition. He (Prophet) had besieged them for fifteen days, during which time they were demolishing their houses (with their own hands). He (Prophet) banished them from al-Madinah and appointed Muhammad Ibn Maslamah (to execute) their banishment. They made their women folk and children ride and loaded their luggage on six hundred camels. Thereupon the Apostle of Allāh, may Allāh bless him, said: Among their people they (Jews) are like the Banu al-Mughirah among the Quraysh. They went to Khaybar, and the hypocrites felt much grieved for them. The Apostle of Allāh, may Allāh bless him, confiscated their property and arms which consisted of fifty coats of mail, fifty hoods, and 340 swords. The property of Banu al-Nadir was personally for the Apostle of Allāh, may Allāh bless him, to meet his needs. He did not have its fifth part separated nor he allotted a share for any one. However he gave some of it to some of his Companions. The names of the *Muhājirs* on whom he bestowed and whose names have been handed down to us are: Abū Bakr al-Siddiq, (received) Bir Hajr, 'Umar Ibn al-Khattāb, Bir Jarm, 'Abd al-Rahmān Ibn 'Awf, Sawālah, Suhayb Ibn Sinān, al-Daratah, al-Zubayr Ibn al-'Awwām and Abū [p. 42] Salamah Ibn 'Abd al-Asad, al-Buwaylah, and Sahl Ibn Hunayf and Abū Dujānah, property which was known as that of Ibn Kharashah.

Muhammad Ibn Harb al-Makki and Hāshim Ibn al-Qāsim al-Kināni informed us; they said: Al-Layth Ibn Sa'd informed us on the authority of Nāfi', he on the authority of 'Abu Allāh Ibn 'Umar: Verily, the Apostle of Allāh, may Allāh bless him, burned the date-palm garden of al-Nadir which was known as al-Buwayrah. Thereupon Allāh the most High revealed: "Whatsoever palm trees ye cut down or left standing on their roots, it was by Allāh's leave."

Hawdhah Ibn Khalifah informed us: 'Awf informed us on the authority of al-Hasan: Verily, the Prophet, may Allāh bless him, banished Banu al-Nadir; he said: Go. Verily, it is the first of exile; and I am on its traces.

THE MASSACRE OF THE BANŪ QURAYZAH

Then occurred the *ghazwah* of the Apostle of Allāh, may Allāh bless him, against the Banū Qurayzah in Dhual-Qa'dah in the fifth year from his *Hegira*. They said: When the polytheists went back from the Ditch and the Apostle of Allāh, may Allāh bless him, returned (to al-Madinah), he entered the apartment of 'Āyishah and Gabriel came to him close to Janā'iz and said: (Meet your) helper against your combatant. Thereupon the Apostle of Allāh, may Allāh bless him, went to him fearing. He said: Verily Allāh commands you to march to Banū Qurayzah. I also intend to go there and I shall shake their forts. Thereupon the Apostle of Allāh, may Allāh bless him, called 'Ali, may Allāh be pleased with him, and gave his banner to him. He sent Bilāl to proclaim among the people that the Apostle of Allāh, may Allāh bless him, commands you not to offer al-'*Asr* prayers but in (the locality of) Banū Qurayzah. The Apostle of Allāh, may Allāh bless him, appointed 'Abd Allāh Ibn Umm Maktūm as his lieutenant over al-Madinah then marched against them with three thousand Muslims and thirty-six horses on Wednesday, 23 Dhu al-Qa'dah. He besieged them very closely for fifteen days. They (Muslims) shot arrows which went inside and none knew what became of them. When the siege became very severe they sent (a message) to the Apostle of Allāh, may Allāh bless him: [p. 54] Send Abū Lubābah Ibn 'Abd al-Mundhir to us. He sent him to them. They consulted him in their affair. He pointed them with his hand signaling their slaughter. Then he repented saying: We are for Allāh and to Him we will return. He said (to himself) I have betrayed Allāh and His Apostle. Then he retired and sticked to a mosque and did not come to the

Apostle of Allāh, may Allāh bless him, until Allāh revealed (acceptance of) his repentance. Then they surrendered to the Apostle of Allāh, may Allāh bless him. The Apostle of Allāh, may Allāh bless him, gave directions to Muhammad Ibn Maslamah about them. They were chained and kept aside. Then their womenfolk and children were brought and placed on one side. He gave them in the custody 'Abd Allāh Ibn Salām and collected their goods and what armours, household effects and clothes which were in the forts, were collected. There were found fifteen hundred swords, three hundred coats of mail, two thousand spears, fifteen hundred shields and leather shields, there was wine and wine-jars, (wine) was poured and its one-fifth was not allotted. There they discovered many water-carrier camels and cattle. Al-Aws said to the Apostle of Allāh, may Allāh bless him, to give them (captives) to them, because they were their allies. The Apostle of Allāh, may Allāh bless him, authorized Sa'd Ibn Mu'ādh to give a decision about them. He passed an order: He who is subjected to razors (i.e., the male) should be killed, women and children should be enslaved, and property should be distributed. Thereupon the Apostle of Allāh, may Allāh bless him, said: You have decided in confirmation to the judgment of Allāh, above the seven heavens. The Apostles of Allāh, may Allāh bless him, returned on Thursday 7 Dhu al-Hijjah. Then he commanded them to be brought into al-Madinah, where ditches were dug in the market. The Apostle of Allāh, may Allāh bless him, sat with his Companions and they were brought in small groups. Their heads were struck off. They were between six hundred and seven hundred in number. The Apostle of Allāh, may Allāh bless him, chose Rayhānah Bint 'Amr for himself and ordered the booty to be collected. One-fifth portion of goods and captives was separated and the remainder was sold to the highest bidder. He divided it (price) to the Muslims. There were 3,072 shares—two shares for the horse and one share for its owner. The Khums was entrusted to Mahmiyah Ibn Jaz' al-Zubaydi. The Apostle of Allāh, may Allāh bless him, set free or gave (to someone) or made him servant as he liked. Likewise he did with the luggage he had received.

Kathīr Ibn Hishām informed us: Ja'far Ibn Burqān informed us: Yazid (i.e., Ibn al-Asamm) informed us; he said: When Allāh cleared away the enemy forces and the Prophet, may Allāh bless him, returned to his house he began to wash his head. (In the meantime) Gabriel, may peace be on him, came to him and said: May Allāh excuse you! You have put them away. Come with us to the fort of Banū Qurayzah. Then the Apostle of Allāh, may Allāh bless him, took a bath and marched with them to the fort.

Abū Ghassān Mālik Ibn Ismā'il al-Nahdi informed us: Juwayriyah Ibn Asmā informed us on the authority of Nāfi', he on the authority of Ibn 'Umar: Verily when the enemy forces (al-Ahzāb) retreated, he (the Prophet), may Allāh bless him, proclaimed among them that none should offer *al-Zuhr* prayers but in (the locality of) Banū [p. 55] Qurayzah. People feared the elapsing of the time of prayers and so they offered it, while the others said: We will not offer prayers but where the Apostle of Allāh, may Allāh bless him, has fixed, although the time may elapse. He (Ibn ʻUmar) said: The Apostle of Allāh, may Allāh bless him, did not disapprove (the action of) either party.

Shihāb Ibn ʻAbbād al-ʻAhdi informed us: Ibrāhīm Ibn Humayd al-Ruwāsī informed us on the authority of Ismāʻīl Ibn Abi Khālid, he on the authority of al-Bahiyyi and others: The Prophet, may Allāh bless him, came to Qurayzah riding on a naked (or unsaddled) donkey while the people walked.

Mūsā Ibn Ismāʻil informed us: Jarīr Hāzim informed us on the authority of Humayd, he on the authority of Anas Ibn Mālik; he said: I am visualizing the dust of the army of Gabriel, may peace be on him, rising in the lane of the Banū Ghanam, when the Apostle of Allāh, may Allāh bless him, marched to Banū Qurayzah.

Al-Fadl Ibn Dukayn informed us: ʻAbd al-ʻAziz Ibn Abi Salamah informed us: My uncle al-Mājishūn informed me; he said: Gabriel, may peace be on him, came to the Apostle of Allāh, may Allāh bless him, on the day of al-Ahzāb on a horse and wearing black turban, ends of which were falling between his shoulders. There was dust on his front teeth and red villous garment under him. Then he said (to the Prophet): Have you put away your arms before we put them away? Verily Allāh commands you to march on Banū Qurayzah.

ʻĀrim Ibn al-Fadl informed us: Hammād Ibn Zayd informed us on the authority of Yahyā Ibn Saʻīd, he on the authority of Saʻīd Ibn al-Musayyib, he said: The Prophet of Allāh, may Allāh bless him, besieged Banū Qurayzah for fourteen nights.

Al-Fadl Ibn Dukayn informed us: Sufyān informed us; (Second chain) ʻAmr Ibn Haytham informed us on the authority of Shuʻbah, both of them on the authority of ʻAbd al-Malik Ibn ʻUmayr: ʻAtiyyah al-Qurazi informed us; he said: I was among those who were taken captive on the day of Qurayzah. They (Muslims) killed those who were of the age and spared those who were not of the age and I was among those who were not of the age.

ʻAmr Ibn ʻĀsim informed us: Sulaymān Ibn al-Mughīrah informed us on the authority of Humayd Ibn Hilāl; he said: There was a weak and not binding pact between the Prophet, may Allāh bless him, and the Qurayzah. When al-Ahzāb marched in great force, they (Qurayzah) violated the pact and helped the polytheists against the Apostle of Allāh, may Allāh bless him. Allāh sent invisible armies and wind, so they fled away and the latter (Qurayzah) remained in their fort. He (Humayd) said: The Apostle of Allāh, may Allāh bless him, and his Companions put down their arms. Then Gabriel, may Allāh bless him, came to the Prophet, may Allāh bless him, and then reached him. Then the Apostle of Allāh,

may Allāh bless him, came down and he (Gabriel) was reclining by the chest of the horse. He (Humayd) said: Gabriel said while dust was on his eyebrow: We have not yet removed the arms, so march on the Banū Qurayzah. He (Humayd) said: The Apostle of Allāh, may Allāh bless him, said: My Companions are exhausted, will you allow them a few days' respite? He (Humayd) said: Gabriel, may peace be on him, said: March on them, I shall enter on this horse of mine into their forts which I shall demolish. He (Humayd) said: Then Gabriel, may peace be on him, and those of the angels, who were with him, turned their backs and dust was seen rising in the lane of Banū Ghanam, a branch of al-Ansār. The Apostle of Allāh, may Allāh bless him, emerged and one of his Companions came forward [p. 56] and said: O Apostle of Allāh! sit, we will represent you. He said: What is that? He (Companion) said: I have heard they will encounter you. He (Prophet) said: Moses was put to great suffering. He (Humayd) said: He approached them and said: O brethren of monkeys and boars! Fear me, fear me. He (Humayd) said: Someone of them said to the other: This is Abū al-Qāsim, we had not promised to do him evil. He (Humayd) said: An arrow pierced into the median vein of the arm of Saʻd Ibn Muʻādh. Then the blood stopped and wound was cured and he invoked Allāh not to let him die before his breast was cooled in respect of Banū Qurayzah. He (Humayd) said: Then grief overpowered them (Banū Qurayzah) in their fort and they surrendered to be adjudged by Saʻd Ibn Muʻādh. He (Humayd) said: He decided that their warriors should be killed and their children would be enslaved. Humayd said: Some of them said: The dwellings will be for the Muhājirs not for al-Ansār. He (Humayd) said: Al-Ansār said: They are our brethren and we were with them. Thereupon he (the first proposer) said: I liked they should be independent of you. He (Humayd) said: When he (Saʻd) was free from his engagement after he had decided about them, a goat walked over him while he was reclining on his side. He received a wound from its hoof; it did not heal and he died. The chief of Dūmat al-Jundal sent a mule and a garment of silk to the Apostle of Allāh, may Allāh bless him. The Companions of the Apostle of Allāh, may Allāh bless him, wondered at the garment. Thereupon the Apostle of Allāh, may Allāh bless him said: Verily turban cloth of Saʻd Ibn Muʻādh in heaven is better than this.

THE JIHAD AGAINST THE JEWS OF KHAYBAR

Then (occurred) the *ghazwah* of the Apostle of Allāh, may Allāh bless him, against Khaybar in Jumāda al-'Ūlā in the seventh year from his *Hegira*. It lies at eight *bairds* (ninety-six miles) from al-Madinah. They (narrators) said: The Apostle of Allāh, may Allāh bless him, ordered his Companions to make preparations for a *ghaqwah* against Khaybar. He began to mobilize those who were around him and used to fight along with him. Then he said: None but the desirous of jihad should come out with us. The Jews who had remained in al-Madinah felt greatly distressed. He set out appointing Sibā' Ibn 'Urfutah al-Ghifāri to be in charge of al-Madinah. His wife Umm Salamah accompanied him. When he halted at an open space belonging to them, they (Jews) did not move about in the night and no cock crowed till the sun rose. When it was morning, their hearts were trembling. They opened their forts and went for their routine duties with shovels, flasks, and date-baskets. When they saw the Apostle of Allāh, may Allāh bless him, they said: Muhammad and al-Khamīs, they meant the army. Then they turned their backs and fled toward their forts. The Apostle of Allāh, may Allāh bless him, delivered a sermon to the people and divided banners among them. Before Khaybar there were no banners but flags. The banner of the Prophet, may Allāh bless him, was black and made of the covering garment of Āyishah and it was called al-'Uqāb (Eagle). His flag was white which he gave to 'Ali. He gave a banner to al-Hubāb Ibn al-Mundhir and another banner to Sa'd Ibn 'Ubādah. Their password was: Ya Mansur amit. Then the Apostle of Allāh, may Allāh bless him, fought against the polytheists who offered the fiercest possible battle. They killed a large number of his Companions and he also put to death a very large number of them. He captured the forts one after the other. There were several well-defended forts. One of them was al-Natāh, and the others were the fort of al-Sa'b Ibn Mu'ādh, the fort of Nā'im and the fort of Qal'at al-Zubayr. In its other part there were other forts. Among these were the fort of al-Ubayyi, the fort of al-Nizār and there were the forts of the armies as al-Qumūs, al-Watih and Sulālim, which was the fort of Banū Abi al-Huqayq. He (Prophet) seized the treasure of the family of Abū al-Huqayq, which they had put in a camel skin, and concealed it in a desolate place. Allāh led His Apostle to it and he took it out. He killed ninety-three men of the Jews, among whom were Abū Zaynab al-Hārith, Marhab, Usayr, 'Yāsir, 'Āmir, Kinānah Ibn Abi al-Huqayq and his brother. We have mentioned them only because of their high position. Among the Companions of the Prophet, may Allāh bless him, who were slain at Khaybar, were Rabi'ah Ibn Aktham, Thaqf Ibn 'Amr Ibn Sumayt, Rifā'ah Ibn Masrūh 'Abd Allāh Ibn Umayyah Wahb (an ally of Banū Asad Ibn 'Abd al-'Uzzā), Mahmūd Ibn Maslamah, Abū Dayyāh Ibn al-Nu'mān (a participant of Badr), al-Hārith Ibn Hātib (a participant [p. 78] of Badr), 'Adi Ibn Murrah Ibn Surāqah, Aws Ibn Habib, Unayf Ibn Wā'il, Mas'ūd Ibn Sa'd Ibn Qays, Bishr Ibn al-Barā Ibn Ma'rūr (who died from [eating] a poisoned goat), Fudayl Ibn al-Nu'mān, 'Āmir Ibn al-Akwa' (who committed suicide and was interred with Mahmūd Ibn Maslamah in the same pit at al-Raji' in Khaybar), 'Umārah Ibn 'Abbād Ibn Mulayl, Yasār (a Negro slave), and a person of the Ashja' (tribe). They were fifteen persons in all (Qur'an 37:177). In this

Ghazwah, Zaynab Bint al-Hārith, the wife of Sallām Ibn Mishkam, gave poison to the Apostle of Allāh, may Allāh bless him. She presented him a poisoned goat, from which the Apostle of Allāh, may Allāh bless him, and several of his Companions, among whom was Bishr Ibn al-Barā Ibn Ma'rūr, ate. (Bishr) died of it. It is said that the Apostle of Allāh, may Allāh bless him, as it had not been set apart from them. Then he directed the four-fifths of the booty to be auctioned and the highest bidder was to get it. Farwah auctioned it and divided (the price) among his Companions. The person who was made in charge of counting the men was Zayd Ibn Thābit. He counted them to be fourteen hundred and two hundred horses. Four hundred shares (were allotted) for horses. The one-fifth (al-Khams) that was given to the Apostles of Allāh, may Allāh bless him, he gifted it as he liked. He gave weapons and garments to the members of his family of Banū 'Abd al-Muttalib, to men, women, orphans, and mendicants. He gave provision from al-Katibah (the name of a place) to his wives and Banū 'Abd al-Muttalib and others. Then there arrived the men of al-Daws including Abū Hurayrah, then al-Tufayl Ibn 'amr and the men of al-Ash'ar tribe the Apostle of Allāh, may Allāh bless him, had taken as slaves. Subsequently he set her free and married her. Al-Hajjāj Ibn 'Ilāt al-Sulami arrived at Makkah and told the Quraysh that the Jews had taken Muhammad prisoner, his Companions had dispersed, and some had been killed. They (Jews) were bringing them (Muslims) to the Quraysh. Thus al-Hajjāj recovered his debt, (by pleasing them) and departed quickly. Al-'Abbās Ibn 'Abd al-Muttalib met him and he (Hajjāj) gave him the correct information about the Apostle of Allāh, may Allāh bless him, but requested him to keep it a secret till he had departed. Al-'Abbās complied with it. When al-Hajjāj had set out, al-'Abbās made it known and expressed joy and freed a slave who was called Abū Zabībah.

Wahb Ibn Jarīr Ibn Hāzim informed us [p. 79], Hishām al-Dastawā'ī informed us on the authority of Qatādah, he on the authority of Abū Nadrah, he on the authority of Abū al-Khudri; he said: We set out for Khaybar when eighteen days of Ramadān had passed. Some people fasted and the others did not fast. Those who fasted were not blamed for fasting nor persons not fasting were blamed of their action.

Muhammad Ibn 'Abd Allāh al-Ansārī informed us: Humayd al-Tawil informed us on the authority of Anas; he said: We resolved Khaybar by night. When it was *fair* the Apostle of Allāh, may Allāh bless him, offered morning prayers. He rode and the Muslims rode with him. When the people of Khaybar rose in the morning, they came out with their shovels and date-baskets as they used to work in their field. When they saw the Apostle of Allāh, may Allāh bless him, they said: Muhammad and al-Khamis, they meant the army. Then they returned fleeing to their city. Thereupon the Prophet, may Allāh bless him, said: Allāh is Great. Khaybar is ruined. When we halt in the plain of a nation, then the morning of those [who were] warned is hapless. Anas said: I was co-rider with Talhah and my foot was touching the foot of the Apostle of Allāh, may Allāh bless him.

Rawh Ibn 'Ubādah informed us: Sa'īd Ibn Abi 'Arūbah informed us on the authority of Qatādah, he on the authority of Anas Ibn Mālik, he on the authority of Abū Talhah: he said; The Apostle of Allāh, may Allāh bless him, was at Khaybar in the morning, when they (Jews) took their shovels and went to their farms and fields. When they saw the Apostle of Allāh, may Allāh bless him, with an army they turned their backs and fled away. Thereupon the Apostle of Allāh, may Allāh bless him, said: Allāh is Great, Allāh is Great, verily when we halt at a plain belonging to a people, the morning of those [who were] warned is hapless.

Hawdhah Ibn Khalīfah informed us: 'Awf informed us on the authority of al-Hasan; he said: When the Apostle of Allāh, may Allāh bless him, stopped in the vicinity of Khaybar, its inhabitants became terrified. They said: Muhammad and the Yathribites have come. He (al-Hasan) said: When the Apostle of Allāh, may Allāh bless him, saw them frightened; he said: When we stop at a plain belonging to a people, the morning of those warned is hapless.

'Affān Ibn Muslim informed us: Hammād Ibn Salamah informed us: Thābit informed us on the authority of Anas; he said: I was a co-rider with Abū Talhah on the day of Khaybar, and my foot was touching the foot of the Apostle of Allāh, may Allāh bless him. He (Anas) said: We arrived there when the sun had risen, and they had come out with their cattle shovels, date-baskets, and asses. He (Anas) said: The Apostle of Allāh, may Allāh bless him, said: Allāh is Great, Allāh is Great, when we stop at a plain belonging to a people, the morning of those [who were] warned is hapless. He (Anas) said: Then Allāh brought about their (Jews') defeat.

Sulaymān Ibn Harb informed us: Hammād Ibn Zayd informed us on the authority of Thābit, he on the authority of Anas: Verily the Prophet, may Allāh bless him, offered his morning prayers at Ghalas in the vicinity of Khaybar, then he raided them. Then he said: Allāh is Great, Khaybar is ruined. Verily when we halt at a plain belonging to a people, the morning of the warned is hapless. When he entered (the place) they came out, running in streets and saying: (Here is) Muhammad and the army. (Here is) Muhammad and the army. He (Anas) said: Then he killed the combatants and took the children.

'Affān Ibn Muslim informed us: Hammād Ibn Salmah informed us: 'Ubayd Allāh Ibn 'Umar informed us; he said: I think he (informed us) on the authority of Nāfi', he on the authority of Ibn 'Umar; he said: [p. 80] The Apostle of Allāh, may peace be on him, confronted the inhabitants of Khaybar in the morning. He (Prophet) fought with them till they were forced to take shelter in their mansions and he took possession of their land and palm groves. Then he made peace with them on the con-dition that their blood would not be split and they would be entitled to take with them as much of their property as their beasts could carry, and the Prophet, may Allāh bless him, would have the yellow and the white (gold and silver) and arms, and that he would banish them. They promised to the Prophet, may Allāh bless him, not to conceal, and anything if they did there would be no responsibility (on the Muslims) and no covenant. When the wealth was found which they had concealed in a camel's skin, he (Prophet) enslaved their women, took possession of their land and palm groves. He returned them for one-half (of the yield). Ibn Rawāhah used to make an estimate (of the yield) and realize one-half.

'Abd Allāh Ibn Numayr informed us: Yahya Ibn informed us on the authority of Sālih Ibn Kaysān, he said: On the day of Khaybar there were two hundred horses with the Apostle of Allāh, may Allāh bless him.

'Affān Ibn Muslim informed us: Suhayl informed us on the authority of his father, he on the authority of Abū Hurayrah; he said: The Apostle of Allāh, may Allāh bless him, said on the day of Khaybar: Surely I shall hand over the banner to a person who loves Allāh and His Apostle and Allāh and His Apostle love him, and through him there will come the victory. He (Abū Hurayrah) said: 'Umar said: Before that day I never aspired for command. I stood and waited, hoping that he would hand it over to me. But on the following day, he called 'Ali and handed it over to him and said to him: Fight and do not turn back till Allāh makes you victorious. He went close (to the ranks of enemy) and cried: O Apostle of Allāh! for what should I fight? He replied: (Fight) until they bear witness (to the truth) that there is no God save Allāh and that Muhammad is the Apostle of Allāh. When they confess this, their persons and properties will be saved from me except in the discharge of their obligations and their reckoning will be with Allāh.

Hāshim Ibn al-Qāsim informed us: 'Ikrimah Ibn 'Ammār informed us: Iyās Ibn Salamah Ibn al-Akwa' informed us; he said: My father informed me; he said: My uncle challenged Marhab the Jew to fight with him on the day of Khaybar. Thereupon Marhab said:

Khaybar knows that I am Marhab,
Noted for my using the arms and a seasoned warrior,
When the battles face him he becomes a flame of fire.
Thereupon my uncle 'Āmir recited:
Khaybar knows that I am 'Āmir.
Noted for the use of arms and a dauntless fighter not
  fearing death.

They exchanged two blows. The sword of Marhab penetrated the shield of 'Āmir's shield and he fell down. Then the sword fell on his calf and cut his median vein, which cost him his life. Salamah Ibn al-Akwa said: I came across the Companions of the Apostle of Allāh, may Allāh bless him, who declared: All the good deeds of 'Āmir were lost as he had committed suicide.

Salamah said: Then I approached the Apostle of Allāh, may Allāh bless him, weeping, and asked: Were the deeds of 'Āmir vain? He said: And who said this? I said some of your Companions (said this). The Apostle of Allāh, may Allāh bless him, said: He who said this uttered a lie. His reward has been doubled. When he set out to Khaybar he was reciting the war song before the Companions of the Apostle of Allāh, may Allāh bless him. With them the Prophet was driving his beasts, and he ('Āmir) reciting (the verses):

[p. 81] By Allah, if there had not been Allāh, we
  would not have received guidance,
We would not have given charity nor offered prayers.
Verily those who opposed us
And they created trouble for us, we refused to yield
And we cannot do without Thy grace,
If we have to encounter (the enemy), keep our feet
  firm.
So bestow calm on us.

Thereupon the Apostle of Allāh, may Allāh bless him asked: Who is he? They said: O Apostle of Allāh! he is 'Āmir. He (turning to the dead body) said: May your Lord pardon you. He (narrator) said: He (Prophet) did not ask for a man specifically but he was martyred. When 'Umbar Ibn al Khattāb heard this; he said: O Apostle of Allāh! Why did you not give us an opportunity to be benefited by 'Āmir and he forestalled us in getting martyrdom. Salamah said: Then the Apostle of Allāh, may Allāh bless him, sent me to 'Alī and said: Today I shall hand over the banner to a man who loves Allāh and His Apostle, and Allāh and His Apostle love him. He (Salamah) said: I brought him guiding him because he was suffering from ophthalmia. The Apostle of Allāh, may Allāh bless him, applied his saliva to his eyes, then he handed over the banner to him. Then Marhab came out, brandishing his sword, and said:

Khaybar knows that I am Marhab,
Noted for the use of arms and seasoned warrior,
When he is face to face with a battle he becomes a
  flame of fire.
Thereupon 'Ali, may Allāh's blessings and benedic-
  tions be on him, said:
I am he whose mother named him Haydarah (lion)
Like the tiger of a forest, having an awful countenance,
I weigh them (enemies) by the measure of al-sandarah
  (birch tree).

Then he struck the head of Marhab with the sword, and the victory was in his hands.

Bakr Ibn 'Abd al-Rahmān the qādi of al-Kūfah informed us: Isa Ibn al-MuKhtār Ibn 'Abd Allāh Ibn Abī Laylā al-Ansārī related to me on the authority of Muhammad Ibn 'Abd al-Rahmān Ibn Abī Laylā al-Ansari, he on the authority of al-Hakam, he on the authority of Miqsam, he on the authority of Ibn 'Abbās; he said: When the Prophet, may Allāh bless him, gained victory over Khaybar, he made peace with them on (the condition) that they could (leave the place alive) with their families, but they could not take with them yellow or white (metals, i.e., gold or silver). Then Kinānah and al-Rabī' were brought to him. Kinānah was the husband of Safiyyah, and al-Rabī' his cousin and his uncle's son. The Apostle of Allāh, may Allāh bless him, said to them: Where are your utensils, which you used to lend to the people of Makkah? They said: We had to flee in such a way from place to place that we had to settle at a place and then we had to leave it so we have spent everything. He said to them: If you conceal anything from me and I come to know of it, it will be lawful for me (to shed) your blood and (to enslave) your children. They said: Yes. Then he called a person of al-Ansar and said: Go to such and such a cultivable land. Then proceed to the palm grove and look for a date tree to your right or to your left and then try to find a high date tree, and bring whatever is in it. He (Ibn 'Abbās) said: He went and brought utensils and wealth to him. Thereupon he ordered their heads to be struck off and enslaved their children. He sent a man who brought Safiyyah and passed with her by the place of their assassination. The Prophet of Allāh, may Allāh bless him, asked him: Why did you do so? He said O Apostle of Allāh! I wanted to infuriate her. He (Ibn 'Abbās) said: Then he handed her over to (the custody of) Bilāl and a man of al-Ansār. She remained with him.

Hāshim Ibn al-Qāsim informed us: 'Ikraimah Ibn 'Ammār informed us on the authority of Yahyā Ibn Abī Kathir, he on the authority of Abū Salamah Ibn 'Abd al-Rahmān. He on the authority of Jābir Ibn 'Abd Allāh; he said: At the time of the day (campaign) of Khaybar the people suffered from hunger, so they seized domestic donkeys and slaughtered them. They filled their kettles. It (report) reached the Prophet of Allāh, may Allāh's blessings be on him. Jābir said: The Apostle of Allāh, may Allāh bless him, declared unlawful flesh of donkeys, mules, beasts with canine teeth and birds with talons. He also declared unlawful dead birds, and things snatched plundered.

'Affān Ibn Muslim informed us: Hammād Ibn Zayd informed us: 'Amr Ibn Dīnār informed us on the authority of Muhammad Ibn 'Ali, he on the authority of Jābir Ibn 'Abd Allāh: Verily the Apostle of Allāh, may Allāh bless him, prohibited (the eating of the) flesh of donkeys and permitted flesh of horses on the day of Khaybar.

Muhammad Ibn 'Abd Allāh al-Ansāri informed us: Hishām Ibn Hassān informed us: Muhammad informed us: Anas Ibn Mālik informed us: he said; A person came to the Apostle of Allāh, may Allāh bless him, on the day of Khaybar and apprised him, that (the flesh of) donkeys was eaten. Then another person came to him and apprised him that the donkeys had been exhausted. Thereupon he ordered Abū Talhah and he cried: Verily Allāh and his Apostle prohibit you from eating the flesh of donkeys because it is filthy. So the kettles were overturned.

'Affān Ibn Muslim and Hāshim Ibn al-Qāsim informed us; they said: Shu'bah informed us on the authority of Abū Ishāq, he on the authority of al-Barā Ibn 'Āzib he said: We found donkeys on the day of Khaybar. The crier of the Apostle of Allāh, may Allāh bless him, announced that the kettles should be overturned.

'Abd Allāh Ibn Muhammad Ibn Abī Shaybah informed us: 'Abd Allāh Ibn Numayr informed us on the authority of Muhammad Ibn Ishāq. He on the authority of 'Abd Allāh Ibn 'Amr Ibn Damrah al-Fazāri, he on the authority of 'Abd Allāh Ibn Abī Salit, he on the authority of his father Abū Salīt, who was a participant in Badr; he said: The order of the Apostle of Allāh, may Allāh bless him, prohibiting the flesh of donkeys reached us on the day of Khaybar and we were hungry, but we overturned them (kettles).

Yazīd Ibn Hārūn informed us: Yahyā Ibn informed us on the authority of Bushayr Ibn Yasār: When Allāh conferred upon the Apostle of Allāh, may Allāh bless him, booty of Khaybar, he divided it into thirty-six parts, each consisting of one hundred shares. He set apart half of them for contingencies and divided the other half among the Muslims. The share of the Prophet, may Allāh bless him, was included in those of the Muslims. His share included Natāh and what it contained and what he made into a *waqf*, included al-Watihah, al-Katībah and Sulālim and what they contained. When the property passed into the possession of the Prophet, may Allāh bless him, and his Companions, they had no laborers to till the land on their behalf.

Thereupon the Prophet, may Allāh bless him, made it over to the Jews on basis of sharing one half of its produce. They continued to do it until it was the time of 'Umar Ibn al-Khattāb [p. 83]. When the number of the Muslim laborers grew large and they learned the tilling of the land, 'Umar banished the Jews towards Syria and divided the property among the Muslims which they hold till today (time of the author).

Sulaymān Ibn Harb informed us: Hammād Ibn Zayd informed us on the authority of Yahyā Ibn Sa'id, he on the authority of Bushayr Ibn Yasār; he said: When the Prophet, may Allāh bless him, conquered Khaybar, and seized it, he divided booty into thirty-six shares. He took for himself eighteen shares and divided eighteen shares among people. There were one hundred horses and he allotted two shares for every horse.

Mūsā Ibn Dāwūd informed us: Muhammad Ibn Rāshid informed us on the authority of Makhūl: Verily the Apostle of Allāh, may Allāh bless him, allotted to a horseman on the day of Khaybar three shares, two for his horse and one for him.

'Attāb Ibn Ziyād informed us: 'Abd Allāh Ibn al-Mubārak informed us: Ibn Lahī'ah informed us on the authority of Muhammad Ibn Zayd: 'Umar the *mawla*

(enfranchised slave) of Abi al-Lahm informed me; he said: I fought with my master on the day of Khaybar and I witnessed its victory with the Apostle of Allāh, may Allāh bless him. I asked him to allot me (a share). He gave me some unserviceable furniture but did not allot (a share) to me.

'Attāb Ibn Ziyād informed us: 'Abd Allāh Ibn al-Mubārak informed us: Ibn Lahī'ah informed us; Al-HāriĀh Ibn Yazīd al-Hadramī related to me on the authority of Thābit Ibn al-Harith al-Ansārī; he said: The Apostle of Allāh, may Allāh bless him, allotted a share to Sahlah Bint 'Āsim Ibn 'Adī and her newly born daughter on the day of Khaybar.

'Attāb Ibn Ziyād informed us: 'Abd Allāh Ibn al-Mubārak informed us: Muhammad Ibn Ishāq informed us on the authority of Yazid Ibn Abī Habīb, he on the authority of a man of al-Jayshān or he said on the authority of Abū Marzūq, the *mawla* (enfranchised slave) of Tujib, he on the authority of Hanash, he said: I was present at the victory to Jarbah with Ruwayfi 'Ibn Thābit al-Balawī. He (Hanash) said: He delivered a sermon to us. Then he (Hanash) said: I was present at the victory at Khaybar with the Apostle of Allāh, may Allāh bless him. I heard him saying: He, who believes in Allāh and the last day, should not irrigate the crop of the other (i.e., should not cohabit with a pregnant hand-maid before delivery). He, who believes in Allāh and the last day, should not cohabit with an enslaved woman till she is cleared (i.e., two periods have passed). He who believes in Allāh and the last day should not sell the booty till it is divided. He, who believes in Allāh and the last day, should not ride the beast of the booty of the Muslims in a way that it becomes lean and then return it to the booty of the Muslims, or wear a cloth and he return it to the booty of the Muslims when it is worn out.

'Affān Ibn Muslim and Hāshim Ibn al-Qāsim informed us; they said: Shu'bah informed us; he said: Al-Hakam said: 'Abd al-Rahmān Ibn Ab Laylā said (explaining) His words: "And hath rewarded them with a near victory" (Qur'an 48:18). He said: It refers to Khaybar. And (explaining God's words). And other (gain), which you have not been able to achieve, Allāh will compass it" (Qur'an 48:21), he said: It referred to Persia and Rome.

Mūsā Ibn Dāwūd informed us: Layth Ibn Sa'd informed us, if Allāh wills, on the authority of Sa'd Ibn Abī Sa'id al-Maqburi, he on the authority of Abū Hurayrah; verily he said: When Khaybar was conquered, a goat which was poisoned, was presented to the Apostle of Allāh, may Allāh bless him. Thereupon, the Prophet may Allāh bless him said: Collect all the Jews who are here [p. 84]. Thereupon they collected them for him. The Apostle of Allāh, may Allāh bless him, said to them: I ask you about something, will you speak the truth to me? They answered: Yes, O Abu al-Qāsim. Thereupon the Apostle of Allāh, may Allāh bless him, said: Who is your father? They answered: Our father is so and so. Thereupon the Apostle of Allāh, may Allāh bless him, said; You have told a lie, your father is so and so. They said: You have spoken the truth and you are virtuous. Then he asked: Will you speak the truth, if I ask you about something? They answered: Yes, O Abu al-Qāsim, if we will speak a false you will know our falsehood, as you did in our answer about our father. Then the Apostle of Allāh, may Allāh bless him, asked about the people of hellfire. They said: We will there be for a short period, then you will replace us. Thereupon the Apostle of Allāh, may Allāh bless him, said: You will live in it and we shall never replace you. Then he asked: Will you speak the truth if I ask you about something? They answered: Yes, O Abu al-Qāsim. He asked them: Did you put poison in this goat? They said: Yes. He asked: What made you do this? They answered: We wanted to get rid of you if you are a pretender, and it would not harm you if you are a prophet.

Bakr Ibn 'Abd Al-Rahmān, the *qāḍī* of the inhabitants of al-Kūfah informed us: 'Isā Ibn al-Mukhtār informed us on the authority of Muhammad Ibn 'Abd al-Rahmān Ibn Abi Laylā, he on the authority of al-Hakam, he on the authority of Miqsam, he on the authority of Ibn 'Abbās; he said: When the Apostle of Allāh, may Allāh bless him, wanted to leave Khaybar, the people said: Now we shall know if Safiyyah is a slavegirl or a wife. If she is a wife, he would conceal her from public gaze, otherwise she would be a handmaid. When he set out he ordered a veil for her. So she put on a veil and people knew that she was his wife. When she wanted to ride, he brought his thigh close to her to ride on it. She declined but placed her knee on his thigh, then he made her ride. When it was night, he entered a tent and she entered with him. Abū Ayyūb came there and passed the night by the tent with a sword keeping his head at the tent. When it was morning and the Apostle of Allāh, may Allāh bless him, perceived (somebody) moving, he asked: Who is there? He replied: I am Abū Ayyūb. He asked: Why are you here? He replied: O Apostle of Allāh! there is a young lass newly wedded (to you) with whose late husband you have done what you have done. I was not sure of safety, so I wanted to be close to you. Thereupon the Apostle of Allāh, may Allāh bless him, said twice: O Abū Ayyūb! May Allāh show you mercy.

'Affān Ibn Muslim informed us: Hammād Ibn Salamah informed us: Thābit informed us on the authority of Anas; he said: Safiyyah had fallen in the share of Dihyah. She was a handsome girl. The Apostle of Allāh, may Allāh bless him, purchased her for seven heads (camels) and entrusted her to Umm Sulaym for make up and preparing her to become a bride. The Apostle of Allāh, may Allāh bless him, gave the *walīmah* dinner of dates and butter. The ground was cleansed well, and pieces of leather were spread, then butter, cheese, and dates were brought. The people ate to their satisfaction. He (Anas) said: The people said: We do not know if he has married her or taken her as a slavegirl. He

(Anas) said: If she put veil on her, she is his wife and if she has not put she is his slavegirl. He (Anas) said: When he wanted to make her ride, he covered her till she sat on the hinder part of the camel, and they knew that he had wedded her.

Sulaymān Ibn Harb informed us: Hammād Ibn Zayd informed us on the authority of Thābit, he on the authority of Anas; he said: Safiyyah Bint Huyayyi was among the slaves. She fell in the share of Dihyah al-Kalbī. Then she passed on to the Prophet, may Allāh bless him. He set her free and then married her and gave her liberty as her dower. Hammād said: 'Abd al-Azīz said to Thābit: O Abū Muhammad! Did you ask Anas, what he paid her as dower? He said: He gave her soul (freedom) as her dower. He (Hammād) said: Thābit moved his head as if he approved it.

MUHAMMAD'S BEWITCHING BY THE JEWS

'Affān informed us; (he said): Wuhayb informed us; (he said): Hishām Ibn 'Urwah informed us on the authority of his father, he on the authority of 'Āyishah: The Apostle of Allāh, may Allāh bless him, was bewitched and he imagined that he had done a work which he had not. This (state) persisted till I saw him praying one day, and then he said: Do you know Allāh has informed me about what I was asking? Two men came to me, one of them stood by my head, the other by my feet. One of them asked: What is the ailment of this man? The other replied: He is bewitched. He asked: Who has bewitched him? The other replied: Labid Ibn al-A'sam. He asked: In what (manner)? The other replied: In the comb, the hair falling from the comb and the well of plump date palm. He asked: Where is it? The other replied: In Dhu Dharwān. He (Ibn Sa'd) said: Then the Apostle of Allāh, may Allāh bless him, went there; and on his return he informed 'Āyishah saying: Its trees are like the heads of Satans, and its water is like a dilution of *henna*. I said: O Apostle of Allāh! Disclose it to the people. He replied: Allāh has cured me and I fear lest it (disclosure) may cause disorder among the people.

Mūsa Ibn Dāwūd informed us; Ibn Lahi'ah informed us on the authority of 'Umar, the Mawla (enfranchised slave) of Ghufrah: Verily, Labid Ibn al-A'sam, the Jew, bewitched the Prophet, may Allāh bless him, by which his sight became weak and his Companions paid him visits as if he was a sick man. Then Gabriel and Michael, peace be on them, informed him (about the person). The Prophet, may Allāh bless him, caught him and he confessed. Then he (Prophet) got (the material of) sorcery from a pit inside a well, he had it pulled out then he spat over it. The effect of magic disappeared and the Apostle of Allāh recovered and he pardoned the sorcerer.

Muhammad Ibn 'Umar informed us; he said: Abu Marwān related to me on the authority of Ishāq Ibn 'Abd

Allāh, he on the authority of 'Umar Ibn al-Hikam; he said: When the Apostle of Allāh, may Allāh bless him, returned from al-Hudayabiyah in Dhu al-Hijjah and the month of Muharram commenced, the chiefs of the Jews, who had remained in al-Madinah, and who had declared their acceptance of Islam, but were (in reality) hypocrites, went to Labid Ibn al-A'sam, the Jew, who was an ally of Banu Zurayq. He was a sorcerer and the Jews knew it that he was the most proficient among them in sorcery and knowledge of poisons. They said to him: O Abu al-A'sam! You are a greater sorcerer than any one of us. We bewitched Muhammad, our men and women bewitched him but it was of no avail. You must have been observing his influence over us, his antagonism to our faith, and the number of people he has killed and sent into exile. We will recompensate you if you bewitch him in a way that he is perished. They promised to give him three dinārs if he bewitched the Apostle of Allāh, may Allāh bless him. He wanted the comb and [p. 5] the hair of head sticking to it. He put knots into them, spat over them, buried them in a pit beneath a fat palm tree, and later he took them and buried in the bottom of a well. The Apostle of Allāh, may Allāh bless him, felt something which he did not like and thought that he had done something which he had not. His eyesight also suffered. Then Allāh guided him. He called Jubayr Ibn Iyās al-Zurqi, who had participated in the battle of Badr and directed him to go to the well at Dharwān. Jubayr went there and took them out. Then he (Prophet) sent for Labid Ibn al-A'sam and said to him: What induced you to do what you have done? Allāh has informed me about your magic and what you have done. He replied: O Abu al-Qāsim! The love of dinārs. Ishāq Ibn 'Abd Allāh said: Then I informed 'Abd al-Rahmān Ibn Ka'b Ibn Mālik about it. He said: The daughters of A'sam and sisters of Labid, who were greater sorcerers and more wicked than Labid had bewitched him. Labid was the person who carried the material and placed it in the bottom of the well. No sooner had they tied the knots than the Apostle of Allāh, may Allāh bless him, began to suffer from the weakening of eyesight. One of the daughters of A'sam came to 'Āyishah, for spying, she told her about it or she heard 'Āyishah talking about the failing eyesight of the Apostle of Allāh, may Allāh bless him. Then she went back to her sisters and Labid and informed them. Thereupon one of them said: If he is a prophet, he will be guided (by Allāh) about this magic: and if he is otherwise, he will lose his senses and that will be a punishment for what our people and co-religionists have suffered at his hands. Allāh guided him in regard to it. Al-Hārith Ibn Qays said: O Apostle of Allāh! Should that well not be demolished? The Apostle of Allāh, may Allāh bless him, turned away his face from him. Subsequently al-Hārith Ibn Qays and his Companions demolished it although it yielded sweet water. He (Ibn Sa'd) said: They dug another well, in the digging of which the Apostle of Allāh, may Allāh bless him, helped them. They dug it to

its water-level and subsequently it was ruined. It is said: He who brought the magical material by the order of the Apostle of Allāh, may Allāh bless him, was Qays Ibn Mihsan.

Muhammad Ibn 'Umar informed us; (he said): Muhammad Ibn 'Abd Allāh related to me on the authority of al-Zuhri, he on the authority of Ibn al-Musayyib and 'Urwah Ibn al-Zubayr; they said: The Apostle of Allāh, may Allāh bless him, used to say: The Jews of Banu Zurayq bewitched me.

'Umar Ibn Hafs informed us on the authority of Juwaybir, he on the authority of al-Dahhāk, he on the authority of Ibn 'Abbās; he said: The Apostle of Allāh, may Allāh bless him, fell ill. He was bewitched about women and food. Then two angels descended while he was in a state between sleep and waking. One of them sat by the side of his head and the other by his feet. One of them said to his companion: What is his ailment? He replied: It is the effect of witchcraft that is magic. The first asked: Who did it? The other replied: Labid Ibn al-A'sam, the Jew. The first asked: By what thing did he do it? The other replied: In the spathe of a palm tree. The first asked: Where did he place it? The other replied: In the well of Dharwān under a rock. The first asked: What is its remedy? The other replied: Water of the well should be drawn, the rock should be removed and the spathe of the palm tree should be taken out. The angels then rose. The Prophet of Allāh, may Allāh bless him, sent for 'Ali, may Allāh be pleased [p. 6] with him, and 'Ammār; and ordered them to go to the pit, and do what he had heard the angels say. They approached the pit. The water of which appeared as if it was colored with *hinna*. They drew it, then removed the stone and took out the spathe of the palm tree. There were eleven knots. The two surahs nos. 113 and 114 were revealed to him. No sooner did the Apostle of Allāh, may Allāh bless him, recite a verse than a knot loosened. When all of them were loosened, he regained his urge for food and women.

Mūsa Ibn Mas'ūd informed us; (he said): Sufyān al-Thawri informed us on the authority of al-A'mash, he on the authority of Thumāma al-Muhallimi, he on the authority of Zayd Ibn Arqam, he said: A man from among the Ansārs whom the Prophet may Allāh bless him, trusted made knots (of sorcery) and threw them into a well. Then two angels descended to pay him sick visit. One of them said to his companion: Do you know that such-and-such a person of the Ansārs made knots of witchery and threw them into such-and-such a well. If the same be taken out, he will be cured. Some persons were then sent to the well and they noticed the water of the well had become green. They took them out and threw them away. The Apostle of Allāh, may Allāh bless him, was cured. He (Prophet) did not say anything about it to him (to Ansāri,) nor any sign (of displeasure) was visible in his countenance.

'Attāb Ibn Ziyād informed us; (he said): 'Abd Allāh

Ibn al-Mubārak informed us; (he said): Yūnus Ibn Yazīd informed us on the authority of al-Zuhri about a sorcerer in his time. He said: He will not be put to death, because one of the men of Scriptures bewitched the Apostle of Allāh, may Allāh bless him, but he did not put him to death.

Muhammad Ibn 'Umar informed us; (he said): Ibn Jurayj related to me on the authority of 'Ata; (second chain) he (Ibn Sa'd) said: Ibn Abi Habībah related to me on the authority of Dāwūd Ibn al-Husayn, he on the authority of 'lkrimah: Verily the Apostle of Allāh, may Allāh bless him, pardoned him (sorcerer) 'lkrimah said: After pardoning him whenever he happened to see him, he turned his face.

Muhammad Ibn 'Umar said: This version is more sound in our view than the narration that the Apostle of Allāh, may Allāh bless him, put him to death.

MUHAMMAD'S POISONING BY A JEWESS FROM KHAYBAR

Abu Mu'āwiyah al-Darīr (blind) informed us; (he said): al-A'mash informed us on the authority of Ibrāhim; he said: They (people) say, Verily, the Jews poisoned the Apostle of Allāh, may Allāh bless him, and Abu Bakr.

'Umar Ibn Hafs informed us on the authority of Mālik Ibn Dīnār, he on the authority of al-Hasan: Verily, a Jewish woman presented poisoned (meat of) a she-goat to the Apostle of Allāh, may Allāh bless him. He took a piece from it, put it into his mouth, chewed it, and threw it away. Then he said to the companions: Halt! verily, its leg tells me that it is poisoned. Then he sent for the Jewish woman and asked her: What induced you to do what you have done? She replied: I wanted to know if you are true; in that case Allāh will surely inform you, and if you are a liar I shall relieve the people of you.

Sa'īd Ibn Muhammad al-d Ibn Muhammad al-Thaqafi informed us on the authority of Muhammad Ibn 'Umar, he on the authority of Abu Salamah Ibn 'Abd al-Rabmān; he said: The Apostle of Allāh, may Allāh bless him, did not eat things given in charity but ate from things given as present. A Jewish woman presented him [p. 7] a roasted she-goat. The Apostle of Allāh, may Allāh bless him, and his Companions ate from it. It (goat) said: I am poisoned. He said to his Companions: Hold your hands! Because it has informed me that it is poisoned. They withdrew their hands, but Bishr Ibn al-Bara expired. The Apostle of Allāh, may Allāh bless him, sent for her (Jewess) and asked her: What induced you to do what you have done? She replied: I wanted to know if you are a prophet, in that case it will not harm you and if you are a king, I shall relieve that people of you. He gave orders and she was put to death.

Sa'īd Ibn Sulaymān informed us; (he said): 'Abbād Ibn al-'Awwām informed us on the authority of Hilāl Ibn Khabbāb, he on the authority of 'lkrimah, he on the authority of Ibn 'Abbās: Verily, a woman of the Jews of Khaybar presented poisoned (meat of) a goat to the Apostle of Allāh, may Allāh bless him. Then he recognized that it was poisoned, so he sent for her and asked her: What induced you to do what you have done? She replied: I thought if you are a prophet, Allāh will inform you, and if you are a pretender, I shall relieve people of you. When the Apostle of Allāh, may Allāh bless him, felt (sick) he got himself cupped. He (Ibn 'Abbās) continued: Once (Prophet) set out for Makkah and when he put ihrām he felt (sick) he got himself cupped.

Sa'īd Ibn Sulaymān informed us; (he said): 'Abbād Ibn al-'Awwām informed us on the authority of Sufyān Ibn Husayn, he on the authority of al-Zuhri, he on the authority of Sa'īd Ibn al-Musayyib and Abu Salamah Ibn 'Abd al-Rabmān, they on the authority of Abu Hurayrah; (he related a narration) similar to it or nearly similar to it and (added) that the Apostle of Allāh, may Allāh bless him, did not take action against her.

Abu al-Walid Hishām al-Tayālisi informed us; (he said): Abu 'Awānah informed us on the authority of Husayn, he on the authority of 'Abd al-Rabmān Ibn Abi Layla; he said: The Apostle of Allāh, may Allāh bless him, was bewitched and then a man came to him and cupped him at his temples with a horn.

Mūsa Ibn Dāwūd informed us; (he said): Ibn Lahi'ah informed us on the authority of 'Umar the *mawla* (enfranchised slave) of Ghufrah; he said: The Apostle of Allāh, may Allāh bless him, ordered the woman, who had served (poisoned meat of) goat to him to be put to death.

Muhammad Ibn 'Umar informed us; (he said): Ibrāhim Ibn Ismā'il Ibn Abi Habibah related to me on the authority of Dāwūd Ibn al-Husayn, he on the authority of Abu Sufyān, he on the authority of Abu Hurayrah; (second chain) Muhammad Ibn 'Abd Allāh related to me on the authority of al-Zuhri, he on the authority of 'Abd al-Rahmān Ibn 'Abd Allāh Ibn Ka'b Ibn Mālik, he on the authority of Jābir Ibn 'Abd Allāh; (third chain) Abu Bakr Ibn 'Abd Allāh Ibn Abi Sabrah related to me on the authority of Yūnus Ibn Yūsuf, he on the authority of Sa'īd Ibn al-Musayyib; (fourth chain) 'Umar Ibn 'Uqbah related to me on the authority of Shu'bah, he on the authority of Ibn 'Abbās; some of them furnished additional information; they said: When the Apostle of Allāh, may Allāh bless him, conquered Khaybar and he had peace of mind, Zaynab Bint al-Hārith, the brother of Marhab, who was the spouse of Sallām Ibn Mishkam, inquired: Which part of the goat is liked by Muhammad? They said: The foreleg. Then she slaughtered one from her goats and roasted it (the meat). Then she wanted [p. 8] a poison which could not fail. The Jews discussed about poisons and became united on one poison. She poisoned the she-goat, putting more poison on the forelegs and shoulder. When the sun had set and the Apostle of Allāh, may Allāh bless him, returned after leading the people in *Maghrib* (sunset) prayers, she sat by his feet. He asked her about her. She said: O Abu al-Qāsim! here as a present which I wish to offer to you. The Prophet, may Allāh bless him, ordered it to be taken. It was served to him and to his Companions who were present and among those who were present was Bishr Ibn al-Bara Ibn Ma'rūr. Then the Apostle of Allāh, may Allāh bless him, said: Come closer and have night meal. The Apostle of Allāh, may Allāh bless him, took the foreleg, a piece of which he put into his mouth. Bishr Ibn al-Bara took another bone and put it into his mouth. When the Apostle of Allāh, may Allāh bless him, ate one morsel of it Bishr ate his and other people also ate from it. Then the Apostle of Allāh, may Allāh bless him, said: Hold back your hands! because this foreleg; and according to another version, the shoulder of the goat, has informed me that it is poisoned. Thereupon Bishr said: By Him Who hath made you great! I discovered it out, but the idea that I did not like to make your food unrelishing. When you had eaten what was in your mouth, I did not like to save my life after yours, and I also thought you would not have eaten it if there was something wrong. Bishr did not rise from his seat, but his color changed to that of *taylsān* (a green cloth). For a year the pain did not permit him to change his sides but with the help of others and then he expired. According to another version, he died before leaving his seat. He (Ibn Sa'd) said: A piece of it was dropped before a dog who ate it and died

(instantaneously) without being able to move its foreleg. The Apostle of Allāh sent for Zaynab Bint al-Hārith and said to her: What induced you to do what you have done? She replied: You have done to my people what you have done. You have killed my father, my uncle, and my husband, so I said to myself: If you are a prophet, the foreleg will inform you; and others have said: If you are a king we will get rid of you. The Jewess returned as she had come. He (Ibn Sa'd) said: The Apostle of Allāh, may Allāh bless him, handed her over to the heirs of Bishr Ibn al-Bara, who put her to death. This is the approved version with us. The Apostle of Allāh, may Allāh bless him, got himself cupped in the back of the neck because of what he had eaten. Abu Hind cupped him with a horn and a knife. The Apostle of Allāh, may Allāh bless him, ordered his Companions and they got themselves cupped in the middle of their heads. The Apostle of Allāh, may Allāh bless him, lived after this three years, till in consequence of his pain he passed away. During his illness he used to say: I did not cease to find the effect of the (poisoned) morsel. I took at Khaybar and I suffered several times (from its effect) but now I feel the hour has come of the cutting of my jugular vein, which is a vein in the back. The Apostle of Allāh, may Allāh bless him, dies a martyr. May Allāh's blessings, His mercy, and His pleasure be on him.

CHAPTER 14

Muhammad at Khaybar

Al-Tabari

According to Ibn Isḥāq: Kinānah b. al-Rabīʿ b. Abī al-Huqayq, who had the treasure of the Banū al-Nadīr, was brought to the Messenger of God, who questioned him; but he denied knowing where it was. Then the Messenger of God was brought a Jew who said to him, "I have seen Kinānah: 'What do you say? If we find it in your possession, I will kill you.'" "All right," he answered. The Messenger of God commanded that the ruin should be dug up, and some of the treasure was extracted from it. Then he asked him for the rest of it. Kinānah refused to surrender it; so the Messenger of God gave orders concerning him to al-Zubayr b. al-ʿAwwām, saying, "Torture him until you root out what he has." Al-Zubayr kept twirling his firestick in his breast until Kinānah almost expired; then the Messenger of God gave him to Muhammad b. Maslamah, who beheaded him to avenge his brother Mahmūd b. Maslamah.

The Messenger of God besieged the people of Khaybar in their fortresses of al-Watīḥ and al-Sulālim. Finally, when they were certain that they would perish, they asked him to banish them and spare their lives, which he did. The Messenger of God had already taken all the property—al-Shiqq, Natāh, al-Katībah, and all their fortresses—except what belonged to those two fortresses. When the people of Fadak heard of what they had done, they sent word to the Messenger of God, asking him to banish them and spare their lives, and they would leave him their property; and he did so. Among the men who mediated between them and the Messenger of God in the matter was Muhayyisah b. Masʿūd, a member of the Banū Hārithah. When the people of Khaybar surrendered on these terms, they asked the Messenger of God to employ them on the properties for a half share. They said, "We know more about them than you are better cultivators of them." So the Messenger of God made peace with them for a half share, provided that "if we want to make you leave, we may." The people

of Fadak made peace with him on similar terms. Khaybar became the booty (*fay*) of the Muslims; Fadak belonged exclusively to the Messenger of God, because the Muslims had not attacked its people with horses or camels.

When the Messenger of God rested from his labor, Zaynab bt. Al-Hārith, the wife of Sallām b. Mishkam, served him a roast sheep. She had asked what part of the sheep the Messenger of God liked best and was told that it was the foreleg. So she loaded that part with poison, and she poisoned the rest of the sheep, too. Then she brought it. When she set it before the Messenger of God, he took the foreleg and chewed a bit of it, but he did not swallow it. With him was Bishr b. al-Barāʾ b. Maʿrūr, who, like the Messenger of God, took some of it; Bishr, however, swallowed it, while the Messenger of God spat it out, saying, "This bone informs me that it has been poisoned." Then he summoned the woman, and she confessed. He asked, "What led you to do this?" She said: "How you have afflicted my people is not hidden from you. So I said, 'If he is a prophet, he will be informed; but if he is a king, I shall be rid of him.'" The Prophet forgave her. Bishr b. al-Barāʾ died of the food he had eaten.

According to Ibn Humayd–Salamah–Muhammad b. Isḥāq–Marwān b. ʿUthmān b. Abī Saʿīd b. al-Muʿallā, who said: The Messenger of God said during the illness from which he dies—the mother of Bishr b. al-Barāʾ had come in to visit him—"Umm Bishr, at this very moment I feel my aorta being severed because of the food I ate with your son at Khaybar." The Muslims believed that in addition to the honor of prophethood that God had granted him the Messenger of God died a martyr.

According to Ibn Isḥāq: After the Messenger of God had finished with Khaybar, he returned to Wādī al-Qurā and besieged its people for some nights; then he returned to Medina.

Al-Tabari, "The Victory of Islam," trans. Michael Fishbein, in *The History of al-Tabari*, vol. 8 (Albany, NY: 1997), pp. 122–24.

CHAPTER 15

The History of the Jews of Medina

Hartwig Hirschfeld

He [Muhammad] won them [the pagan Arabs] over to Islam by commanding them "not to associate any other being with God, not to steal, not to commit adultery, not to kill their children and to obey what is good."[1] It is obvious that, as a basis for conversion to Islam, Muhammad had made a digest of the Decalogue, insofar as it suited Arab customs. A third encounter took place one year later between Muhammad and other residents of Medina, who had come to him to convert. They invited him to emigrate to Medina, and one of them added: "Between us and them—by which he meant the Jews—there are ties that we want to break. If God grants victory to you, will you return then to your native town?"[2] Muhammad promised to stay for the rest of his life in Medina; for he was very pleased with an offer that afforded personal security [i.e., he feared for his life] and a vast field in which to work. Around the middle of June in the year 622 he departed from Mecca, which his disciples had already left earlier. As soon as people in Medina learned that Muhammad had forsaken his native town, the inhabitants went out every day to await him. It was a Jew who from the height of his castle noticed his arrival one day, and he exclaimed: "O sons of Keila, here comes your *ancient one* whom you are awaiting!"[3] Muhammad, however, went down to Kobâ, where he stayed for a few days. He then mounted his camel Al-Kaçwa and made that memorable entrance that created for a heretofore unknown people a great history and an inexhaustible literature. The Jews had no reason to rejoice about that arrival.

THE HISTORY OF THE JEWS UNTIL THEIR EXPULSION FROM MEDINA UNDER CALIPH OMAR

By settling in Medina, where he had met with such a cordial reception, Muhammad had founded Islam, but he had not yet removed the many obstacles in the way of the development of his project. His life was no longer threatened; his enemies were far away; but he did not know how to handle these men who were pursuing interests that were often contrary to his own. Those who called themselves followers of the Prophet were not, for the most part, thoroughly convinced Muslims; on the contrary, almost all of them had maintained close relations with their relatives who still adhered to pagan beliefs. Add to these the hypocrites, those who pretended to believe in Muhammad's teaching, and finally the declared opponents of Islam, among which the Jews were numbered. The last mentioned had disappointed Muhammad the most.

Therefore the Prophet was busy at first managing his relations with the inhabitants of Medina. He set forth his views in a treaty that he made with the natives of the city and those who had come from Mecca, devoting a few paragraphs to those who had been born Jewish and to the Arab converts to Judaism. His words have been preserved, but since they have been translated so often, it appears that there is no need to quote them again.[4]

The Jews, for their part, were singularly disappointed in their expectations. The way in which Muhammad understood revelation, his ignorance and his clumsiness in religious questions in no way encouraged them to greet him as their Messiah. He tried at first to win them over to his teachings by sweetness and persuasion; they replied by posing once again the questions that they had already asked him; his answers, filled with gross errors, provoked their laughter and mockery. From this, of course, resulted a deep hostility between Muhammad and the Jews, whose only crime was to pass a severe judgment on the enterprise of this Arab who styled himself "God's prophet" and to find his conduct ridiculous, his knowledge false, and his regulations thoughtless. This judgment, which was well founded, was nevertheless politically incorrect [*une faute politique*], and the consequences thereof inevitably would prove to be disastrous for a minority that lacked direction or cohesion.

Among those who had especially scoffed at Muhammad's ignorance were: from the tribe of the An-Nadhîr, rabbi Hoyyeyy b. Akhtab and his brothers Abou-Yâsir and Djodey, Sallâm b. Mischkam, Kinâna, Ar-Rabî

"Essai Sur l'Histoire des Juifs de Medina," *Revue des Études Juives* 7 (1883): 192–93; 10 (1885): 10–31; English translation by Michael J. Miller.

and Sallâm, son of the poet Ar-Rabī b. Abī-l-Houkeik, the brother of that poet, Sallâm, Amr b. Djahhâsch, the poet Cab b. Al-Aschraf[5] and his two clients Haddjâdj b. Amr and Cardam b. Keis; from the tribe of the Banou Thalaba, Al-Fityaoun, the blind rabbi Abd-Allâh b. Çourâ, who was reputed to know the Torah better than any learned man of Hedjâz, Ibn Çalouba and Mokheirik; from the tribe of the Banou Keinokâ, Zeid b. Al-Loceit, Sad b. Honeif, Mahmoud b. Seihân, Ozeir b. Abi-Ozeir, Abd-Allah b. Dheif, Soweid b. Al-Hârith, Rifâa b. Keis, Finhaç, Aschya, Nomân b. Adhâ, Bahriy b. Amr, Schâs b. Keis, Zeid b. Al-Hârith, Noman b. Amr, Sokein b. Abi Sokein; Adyy b. Zeid, Nomân b. Abi Aoufa, Abou Anas, Mahmoud b. Dahya,[6] Mâlik b. Dheif,[7] Cab b. Râschid, Azar, Râfi b. Abi Râfi, Khâlid, Izâr b. Abi Izâr, Râfi b. Hâritha, Râfi b. Horeimala, Râfi b. Hâridja, Mâlik b. Aouf, Rifâa b. Zeid b. Al-Tabout and the rabbi Abd-Allah b. Salâm; from the tribe of the Banou Koreiza, Az-Zabīr b. Bâtâ, Azzâl b. Schamwīl, Cab b. Asad, Schamwīl b. Zeid, Djabal b. Amr, An-Nahhâm b. Zeid, Fardam b. Cab, Wahb b. Zeid, Nâfi b. Abi-Nâfi, Abou-Nâfi, Adyy b. Zeid, Al-Hârith b. Aouf, Cardam b. Zeid, Osâma b. Habīb, Râfi b. Romeila, Djabal b. Koscheir, Wahb b. Yahoudâ; from the other Jewish families, probably of Arab origin, Labīd b. Açças, Kinâna b. Çouriyâ, Fardam b. Amr, Silsila b. Barhâm.[8]

All these men held important positions in their tribes, and union among them could certainly have triumphed over the attacks of their enemies and thus have assured their existence. But defections occurred, even among the most distinguished of them.

Motives that might have urged ignorant Israelites, who were incapable of evaluating Muhammad's teachings, to embrace Islam must not have had any influence on an educated man like Abd-Allâh, son of Salâm, and we doubt the sincerity of his new religious convictions, especially since his conversion is related for posterity only by himself.[9] Be that as it may, the conversion of Abd-Allâh, glorified and exalted by the Arab traditionalists, had extremely fortunate consequences for Muhammad. The latter, to reward him for his adherence to Islam, dubbed him "Servant of God." Several members of the tribe of the Banou Keinokâ followed the apostate's example: Sad b. Honeif, Zeid b. Al-Loçeit, Nôman b. Aoufa, Othmân b. Aoufa, Râfi b. Horeimala, Rifa'a b. Zeid, who all became Muslims—not, it seems, out of conviction, but so as to imitate Abd-Allâh. Since the sincerity of the religious beliefs was called into question, they were nicknamed "hypocrites." Other conversions took place, those of Silsila b. Barham and Kinâna b. Çouriyâ. But these last-mentioned men were of Arab descent, and their conduct is easily explained by the ties that they probably had with Muslim relatives and friends.

These conversions, however, were still exceptional cases, and Islam had few initiates among the Jews. The followers of Muhammad were almost all uneducated,

rough-hewn Arabs, ignorant even of the very principles of the religion that they had embraced. As for the Israelites, they responded to the Prophet's advances with jesting. That is when Muhammad began to replace persuasion with violence; those who were not sincere in the Muslim beliefs, whether Jews or Arabs, were beaten and driven from the mosques.[10] Abou Bekr himself, who was usually so prudent and moderate, made his way into the Jewish school and rained blows upon the rabbi Finhâç.[11] To reward him for this exploit, Muhammad favored him with a revelation.[12]

It was at this time, according to the traditionalists, that Muhammad is thought to have written a letter to the Jews of Khaybar, most of them members of the An-Nadhīr tribe. Nothing proves the authenticity of this document; it is possible, however, that the Prophet addressed himself by letter to those Jews living far away whom he tried to convert to Islam. Here, moreover, are the contents of that letter: "In the name of Allah, the good and the merciful. From Muhammad, one sent by God, colleague and brother of Moses, all of whose commandments he confirms. Has not God spoken to you thus: 'You, who possess the Torah, you read in it: Muhammad is the one sent by God, and his followers must prove pitiless against the unbelievers, merciful to their friends; they [i.e., the latter] bow and kneel, their faces bear the signs of their submission?' So it is that the Torah speaks of them. The Gospel compares them to the seed that springs from the earth, rises up as an ear of wheat and flourishes to the great joy and wonder of the one who sowed and the one who labored. To those who believe in him and do good, God has granted the remission of their sins and has rewarded them. By God, through revelation, through the manna and the quails that served as food for the tribes, for your ancestors, by the one who dried up the sea to allow your forebears to pass over and to save them from the wrath of Pharaoh, I adjure you to listen to me. You yourselves have told me that your revealed books command you to believe in *a* Muhammad. If it should be the case that these books do not speak to you about that, believe all the same in Muhammad; bind yourselves to Allah and to his prophet."[13]

This letter had no effect; the attacks continued and Muhammad responded with verses from the Qur'an. That, at least, is how many verses are connected by the traditionalists to particular incidents, but it is not always possible to know whether the verse is older than the event to which it is related or if it was composed on the occasion of the event itself. The Jews had asked Muhammad to work miracles, for example, to make food descend from heaven. Muhammad responded to this proposal with rather embarrassed explanations; he went into the Jewish schools and carried on controversies to prove the divine character of his mission, but no one listened to him.[14] Hoyyeyy and his brother Yâsir took more and more steps to prevent the Jews from converting to Islam.

The Jews, in response to Muhammad's proselytizing zeal, tried to reawaken the old rivalry between the Aousites and the Khazradjites and recalled their ancient combats and especially the battle of Boâth.[15] They also incited the Koreischites and other Arab tribes against the Muslims.

The resistance that the Jews put up to all attempts at converting them changed in a singular manner the direction of Muhammad's religious thinking. Until then he had adopted Jewish ceremonies for his new religion; he had been turning toward Jerusalem to pray and had used the same method as the Jews of calling the faithful together to prayer.[16] Later on, however, he borrowed from the Christians their custom of gathering their brethren to church with the help of two logs [struck together]; finally, he had the faithful summoned from the top of a tower by a man's voice. Then he commanded the Muslims to turn toward Mecca while they prayed.[17] This sudden change, to his way of thinking, had a twofold purpose: to show the Jews that he was making himself independent of their laws, and to flatter the national self-esteem of the Arabs. Although he responded weakly to the Jews who were astonished at this change,[18] there is nevertheless no doubt about his real sentiment.[19]

It was around that time that Muhammad inaugurated a new system of propaganda to recruit followers and to put an end to opposition against his teachings: he used force. Upon learning that a caravan of Koreischites was about to get under way, he instructed a certain number of his friends to position themselves in ambush so as to attack the travelers. One of the Koreischites was killed, two others were taken captive, while the fourth fled. This incident took place during the holy month of the Arabs, in which it was forbidden to engage in battle. Muhammad, who had even shared with the murderers in the spoils from his enemies, justified his conduct and that of his friends by means of a new revelation.[20] The Jews vehemently scoffed at this modus operandi of the Prophet, who of course resolved that he would take revenge on his adversaries as soon as circumstances would allow.

After the battle of Badr, which had established the power of nascent Islam, Muhammad decided to chastise the scoffers and the adversaries of his new religion. Because an Arab woman named Açmâ had written satirical verses against Muhammad, he had her assassinated. The traditionalists try to justify this murder by saying that this woman was Jewish and had defiled the mosques.[21] Soon a second victim fell beneath the Prophet's blows: an old man, Abou Afak, from the Arab tribe of Amr b. Aouf, who had converted to Judaism, had been inciting the members of his tribe against the Muslims by his verses.[22] Muhammad expressed the desire to see this adversary punished, and Abou Afak was assassinated by a member of his own family.

After this twofold exploit, Muhammad made one last attempt among the Jews to convert them to Islam. He gathered them on the marketplace of the Banou Keinokâ, exhorted them to accept his teachings and reminded them of the defeat of the inhabitants of Mecca. The Banou Keinokâ rejected Muhammad's proposal, and the struggle began. According to certain accounts, here is the incident that precipitated hostilities between Jews and Muslims. An Arab woman was sitting at the market in front of a goldsmith's shop to sell some milk, or else to wait for the goldsmith to repair her jewelry. The Jews tried to force her to uncover her face; she refused. Then one of them positioned himself behind that woman and, without her noticing it, lifted up the hem of her robe and attached it to the back. When she stood up, all the bystanders burst into laughter. Some Muslims who were on the scene fell upon the instigator of this scandal and killed him. The Jews, in turn, in order to avenge their companion, put the murderers to death.[23]

Whatever the truth about this story may be, Muhammad resolved to turn against the Jews the power that his various successes had given him. He started with the Banou Keinokâ. They had withdrawn into their citadels. After a fifteen-day siege, they surrendered, and the Prophet had them thrown into irons and intended to have them executed. We should recall here that the Banou Keinokâ had signed a treaty that guaranteed them personal safety and ownership of their goods. Abdallâh b. Obeyy, who even before the battle of Boâth had demonstrated that he was favorably disposed toward the Jews and who was particularly jealous of the Prophet's victory, tried to rescue the captives. He went therefore to see Muhammad and asked him to have the prisoners set free. Muhammad refused. Abdallâh then grabbed him by the breastplate. "What the hell, will you let me go?" the Prophet exclaimed, red with anger. "I will let you go," his interlocutor replied, "when you have granted me the freedom of the seven hundred warriors who have been my allies and have defended me against the red [troops] and the black. I fear that fortune may betray us." These last words made a strong impression on the Prophet, and he promised to spare the lives of the Banou Keinokâ on the condition that they leave their country. The Jews emigrated therefore toward the north and settled at Adzraât; their fortune, which consisted in gold ware and jewelry, had remained in the hands of the conqueror.[24]

The emigration of the Banou Keinokâ considerably diminished the strength of the Jews. Their brethren from the An-Nadhîr and Koreiza tribes had made no effort to come to the aid of the defeated warriors, not seeing, in their blindness, that their own interests were closely connected with those of the unfortunate emigrants. Yet the circumstances would have been favorable to engage in resistance against Muhammad. In Medina there was a powerful party that greatly desired to expel those who had come from Mecca to meet up again with Muhammad. Furthermore the Koreischites were eager to avenge their defeat and to battle with the Prophet. Abou Sofyân, the chieftain of the tribe, had sworn not to allow a single drop of water to fall on his head before he had punished Muhammad. He went to Medina with two hundred horsemen. There, he slipped by night into the dwelling of Hoyyeyy, rabbi of the An-Nadhīr tribe, and into the cell of Sallâm b. Mischkam, chieftain of that tribe, to find out what the townspeople were thinking. In the morning he departed again to rejoin his men, and he sent a party of them to Al-Oreidh, where they set fire to several date plantations and killed two Muslims. News of this attack spread rapidly; Muhammad marched against his adversaries with a large troop. The Koreischites beat such a hasty retreat that they had to leave behind many sacks of flour so as not to be encumbered by them in their flight. This expedition bears the name of *Sawîk*, from the Arabic word *sawîk*, which is the name of a dish made out of flour.

After this new success, Muhammad began a new series of his murders. There was a Jewish poet in Medina from the An-Nadhīr clan, by the name of Cab b. Al-Aschraf, who was a declared enemy of the Prophet. Very little is known about his background; his father, according to most chroniclers, was from the family of Nabhân, from the tribe of Tayy, and his mother belonged to the An-Nadhīr. Cab, who as a child had lost his father, was raised by his mother's family.[25] According to the traditionalists, he had been a Muslim for some time and prayed facing Mecca; but nothing confirms this claim. At the news of Muhammad's victory in Badr, the poet exclaimed: "Is it possible that Muhammad has killed these warriors, the most noble among the Arabs, the bravest of men? By heaven, if Muhammad has put these men to death, I love the depths of the earth better than the surface of it." He then went to Mecca and recited the following verses to incite the Koreischites to revenge:

The mill of Badr has ground up the warriors—such a misfortune elicits sobs and makes tears flow. The princes of humanity have been killed beside their cisterns. You cannot allow yourselves to be exterminated! Kings have been laid out in the dust. More than one pure, renowned and esteemed man has been struck down in that battle, [more than one] who showed hospitality to strangers, distributed [food] with open hands when the glistening stars of the rain were lacking, and was a lord to whom belonged one quarter of the booty.

Some men, whose indignation pleases me, say: Ibn Aschraf is a trembling man; they are right. When my friends were killed, why didn't the earth then split open to swallow all its inhabitants? May the man who has brought about this unfortunate incident be wounded with a lance, may he become blind and deaf and live eternally in agony!

People have told me that the death of Aboul-Hakīm saddened and deeply afflicted all the sons of Al-Moughīra. Close by Aboul-Hakīm are the two

sons of Rabiâ; neither Moun-nabbīh nor Tobba and the others who were killed could escape their fate.

People told me that Al-Hârith b. Hâschim is acting like a respectable man and gathering warriors.

To visit Yathrib with an armed troop, for this brave and esteemed man defends his dignity.[26]

Concerning that same event, Cab also composed the following verses.[27]

Drive the fool far away from you, so as not to have to listen to his nonsense. Do you blame me for shedding tears over those who were sincere and faithful friends to me? Yes, I will weep as long as I live and remember the exploits of the courageous men whose glory lives in Al-Djoubadjib. Upon my life, the sons of Morīd were not wicked, but they are now as cunning as foxes. They would deserve to have their noses cut off, because they showed disdain for the tribes of Loayy b. Ghâlib. By the house of God set among the mountains, I give my share of the Mourīd in payment to Djadar.[28]

Cab returned to Medina, where he seriously offended the Muslims, according to the chroniclers, by having relations with their wives. But this accusation is entirely unfounded and seems to have been brought against Cab only to justify his death. Even his journey to Mecca is not certain, any more than all the incidents previous to his death.[29] The poet was a dangerous adversary for the Prophet; the Prophet decided to have him killed. One day he cried, "Who will deliver me from the son of Al-Aschraf?" A man from Medina, Mohammed b. Maslama volunteered to carry out this exploit, but asked Muhammad to allow him to use deceit and lies. The Prophet gave him permission to do so. This detail demonstrates once more that, in order to do away with the opponents of his despotism, whom he called the enemies of his faith, Muhammad did not hesitate to use any means. The murder of Cab is related in several works, and so we do not have to tell the story again here.[30]

The murder of the chieftain of the An-Nadhīr was, in Muhammad's mind, certainly only the prelude to a general attack on the whole tribe. But for the moment this project could not be carried out; the Muslims had just been beaten at Ouhoud by the Meccans in the year 3 of the Hegira, and this defeat momentarily diminished the prestige and the power of the Prophet. In that battle a Jewish proselyte named Mokheirīk was killed, who had once been a tenacious adversary of Muhammad; later, we do not know when, he had converted to Islam and gave up his life in defending his new religion.[31]

In order to restore his military glory and avenge their insults—the mere memory of which roused his indignation—the Prophet resolved to have done with the Jews. Furthermore, he felt encouraged by the calm and indifference with which they had witnessed the expulsion of the Banou Keinokâ and the murder of Cab. Here is the alleged pretext for that war. A Muslim had killed two Amyrites. Muhammad, accompanied by Abou Bekr, Omar and Ali, went to the An-Nadhīr and asked them to join with him in apologizing for that double murder. His friends waited for him at the entrance to his dwelling; they saw him return in great haste. Muhammad told them that a divine revelation warned him that the Jew Amr b. Djihâsch, refusing to obey the orders of Sallâm b. Mischkam, was planning to throw a rock down on him from the height of his citadel so as to kill him. This accusation was certainly false and only served as a pretext to attack the An-Nadhīr, whose destruction had been decided long ago. Muhammad laid siege to the citadels of his enemies and, contrary to all customs, gave orders to burn and cut down the palm trees at Boeira.[32] Abd-Allah b. Obeyy urged those who were under siege not to persist, and he promised to intercede in their favor with the Prophet. The latter agreed to allow the An-Nadhīr to come out of their fortresses, unarmed, and he permitted each group of three persons to take with them a camel's load of their belongings. The An-Nadhīr accepted these conditions, loaded their beasts, carrying off the wooden materials of which their houses were built, and withdrew, to the sound of music, to the north, where they settled, partly in Khaybar, partly in Adzraât in Syria. Among those who decided to stay in Khaybar were the brother and the sons of Rabī b. Abī-l-Houkeik and the rabbi Hoyyeyy. Two Nadhirites, Yamīn b. Omeir and Abou Sad b. Wahb, embraced Islam in order to save their fortune and remain in Medina. The lands and houses of the emigrants were divided up among the Muslims.[33]

The Jews certainly could have defended themselves successfully against an enemy that had no experience in the military arts and was insufficiently prepared to sustain a long struggle, but they lacked energy, resolve, and unity. Their emigration can be explained, however, to a certain extent by their fear that they would not be able to continue living in a land where betrayal and murder prevailed, and where their adversaries would surely increase in numbers and strength over time.

Some friends of the exiles, who remained in Medina, had the courage to deplore bitterly in public the expulsion of the Nadhīrites, and they expressed in eloquent verses their deep regrets about the defeat of that tribe. One Muslim had praised Muhammad for the murder of Cab and the expulsion of the An-Nadhīr. Sammâk, a Jew, responded as follows:

You are proud of having assassinated Cab b. Al-Aschraf! Boast, then of this exploit,
    when you went out that morning to put him to death, although he was never untrue to his word and never betrayed anyone.
    The time will come, perhaps, when luck will change and turn against you, when the just judge will demand from you an accounting

of the murder that you committed against the An-Nadhīr and their allies and of the destruction of their palm trees, which you cut down before the dates had been gathered.
    If heaven grants me to live [to see it], we will invade your lands, armed with lances and well-honed swords. Valiant warriors will wield those arms and will use them to defend themselves and will strike down their enemies with their blows.
    With them is Çakhr and his retinue, who are all fearless in attacking
    like a mighty lion of Tardj who is defending his lair, a brother of the forest.

The Muslim poet Cab b. Mâlik composed another poem on this same incident which ends with these verses:

Now they are suffering the consequences of their defeat, and it is a grave matter, for there is only one camel for every three of them. They have been expelled after the Keinôka, and for them the palm trees and the dwellings have been reserved. [Meant ironically?]

Sammâk responded:

I awoke and a racking grief overcame me during a night that seemed to me longer than all other nights
    I see that all the rabbis reject him, although they are all learned and erudite,
    Although they are those diligent, perspicacious wise men about whom the Torah and the Psalms speak.
    You have assassinated Cab, the prince of the rabbis. Yes, in times past the protector was reliable!
    Cab approached his brother Mahmoud, but Mahmoud's heart concealed evil intentions.
    He left him behind, and it was as though black blood flowed in streams on his garment.
    By my father and yours, the blow inflicted on Cab struck the Nadhīr.
    When we make you pay for your crime, in honor of Cab, we will leave lying [in the dust] men around whom the birds will fly,
    As though they were butchered sheep on a feast day, but no one drives them [i.e., the birds] away.
    (We will come) with swords! So it was near Ouhoud, when you felt the weight of Çakkr's valor, when no one came to your aid.

The Arab poet Abbâs b. Mirdâs[34] also deplored in a poem the humiliation inflicted on the Jews; we reprint the following excerpt:

By my life, must I show you the emigrant women who wander at the foot of the mountains Al-Schatâ and Teiab?

Among them are women with big eyes like the gazelles of Tabâla, who inspire love in thoughtful and prudent men.

If a man who asks for something good comes to pay them a visit, they say to him, with faces shining like gold coins, "Welcome! Greetings! Nothing that you ask will be refused; you will not have to undergo the shame of a refusal."

Do not take me, however, for a flatterer allied with Sallâm b. Mischkam or Hoyyeyy b. Akhtab.

The Israelites expelled by Muhammad tried again to resist the Prophet. Sallâm and Kinâna, sons of Aboul-Houkeik, Hoyyeyy, Haoudzâ b. Keis and Abou Ammâr, both of them from the tribe of Wâil, went to the Koreischites to unite in a league with them against their common enemy; they initiated talks with the Banou Ghatafân for the same purpose. They all combined forces and marched on Medina, which the inhabitants, surprised by the unexpected attack, were able to defend only by means of a hastily dug moat around the city. The An-Nadhîr tried again to win the Koreiza tribe over to their cause, and to this end Hoyyeyy went to consult the chieftain of the tribe, Cab b. Asad. The latter had the door to his castle shut as soon as he saw the Nadhîrite arrive.

"Open the door," cried Hoyyeyy.

"Bad luck to you," Cab replied; "You bring misfortune with you. I have entered into an alliance with Muhammad and I will remain faithful to it."

"You are afraid, then, that I will eat some of your polenta."

These words had their effect on Cab, and he told the servants to open the door.

"Cab, I come with fifteen thousand Arabs, a mighty throng that is like the waves of the sea; I come with the chieftains and lords of the Koreischites, and with the Banou Ghatafân; they will not leave the country until they have killed Muhammad." Cab refused at first to join up with the Prophet's enemies; finally, he yielded, especially since Hoyyeyy swore that if they should be defeated he could withdraw with him into his citadel and share his fate.[35]

Muslim historians accuse the Koreiza of treachery, but that accusation is unfounded. Cab had foreseen that the enterprise would be unsuccessful, he had recognized long before that the rivalry among the various Arab tribes and the dissension that prevailed among them would necessarily result in the defeat of the coalition forces. He had wisdom from years of experience, and he was convinced that Islam, which fought for an idea, would triumph over the pagan Arabs who fought without any conviction. Despite his pessimistic expectations, however, he agreed to ally himself with the An-Nadhîr.

While they were preparing their attack, Muhammad, intending to have done with his Jewish adversaries, devised a plan which, if successfully executed, would assure him of victory. He sent messengers to the Ghatafân and offered them one-third of the date harvest, which they accepted. Having achieved that, he easily managed to sow discord between the Banou Ghatafân and the Koreischites, on the one hand, and on the other hand between the Jews and their Arab allies. He enlisted a man named Noeim b. Masoud, who had secretly converted to Islam, to urge the Jews to demand hostages from the Koreischites until after the war was over so as to prevent them from going over to the Prophet's side. These insinuations had the desired effect. When the allies sent word to the Jews, one Friday, that they should prepare for battle the next day, the latter responded that they did not want to fight on the sabbath and that, furthermore, they would not march against Muhammad before obtaining hostages from their allies. This demand was rejected, relations between the Jews and the Arabs cooled and the forces took advantage of a storm that broke one night to lay a siege.[36]

The Koreiza, therefore, were without any allies. It is likely that they had wanted to join up with Muhammad's enemies so as to fight him; this is corroborated also by the following anecdote: One day Çafiyya, Muhammad's aunt, was at the top of a citadel in Fâri, owned by the poet Hassân b. Thâbit, when she saw a Jew arrive, who was carefully examining the fortress. Çafiyya saw this man as a spy and urged Hassân to kill him; when he refused, she went down herself, stole over to the Jew, and killed him.

Toward noon on the day when the Koreischites and the Ghatafân had laid the siege, the Muslims (so the historians relate) saw the archangel Gabriel arrive on a white mule, his head wrapped in a silk turban; he ordered Muhammad to attack the Koreiza. Hoyyeyy, true to his promise, had gone to Cab's citadel to share his fate. The Muslims came to lay siege to that fortress. The siege had already lasted a month when Cab summoned his comrades in arms and said to them, "We cannot continue to defend ourselves; we must therefore resign ourselves to accepting Islam . . . "—"Never!" they all cried—" . . . or else have the courage to kill your wives and children and attempt one last sortie against Muhammad." They rejected the latter course of action as well. Cab added, "This evening the sabbath begins. The Muslims know that we do not fight on that day, and they are not on their guard; let us take advantage of that to surprise them." "We do not want to transgress a prohibition that our ancestors have not transgressed." "Then let us die here," Cab replied, "since none of you want to make a manly decision."[37]

The Koreiza knew very well what Muhammad would do to them when he took the fortress: he would put them all to death. They preferred, however, to surrender to their enemy than to try one last time the fortunes of war. Several of them, Thalaba b. Saya, Oseid b. Saya, Asad b. Obeid, became Muslims, and one woman from the tribe followed their example. Her husband, the poet Aous, whom she tried to convert likewise,[38] addressed to her the following verses:

She invited me to embrace Islam on the day when I met her; I refused and said to her: Return to Judaism.

As for us, we live according to the Torah and its laws; upon my life, the beliefs of Muhammad are false.[39]

Each one of us believes that his faith is the best, but only the man who follows the straight path possesses the true faith.

The Koreizite Amr b. Sodâ set out at night and passed by a Muslim guard, who allowed him to continue his journey, and went into a mosque, from which he did not return. Muhammad probably spirited him away; indeed, he said with regard to him, "God saved him because of his faithfulness," and the chroniclers add, "God knows best what happened."[40]

The next day the Jews surrendered. The Aousites interceded on their behalf with the Prophet; Muhammad declared that he would leave the matter up to a judge that he would appoint and who would decide their fate. Sâd b. Moâdz, appointed the arbiter, decided that the men would be killed, the women and children held captive, and the goods taken as booty. Muhammad said that this judgment was in keeping with the one that God had pronounced above the seven heavens. Almost 750 Jews, among them Cab and Hoyyeyy, were slaughtered in a marketplace in Medina. Hoyyeyy was the last to be killed. When he was being led to his death, Muhammad said to him, "God has brought you to your ruin." "I do not fear death," the valiant rabbi replied, "I do not repent at all of having declared war on you, and today again, at the moment in which I leave this world, I declare that you are an imposter." Then he knelt down and was decapitated.[41]

The Jewish poet Djabal ben Djawwâl composed the following verses on the death of Hoyyeyy:

Upon your life, the son of Akhtab blamed himself for nothing, but God abandons the one who betrays him.

He fought in such a way that he placed himself above all reproach and, in order to win, he used all possible means.[42]

He also deplored the defeat of the An-Nadhīr and the Banou Koreiza in the following verses:

O Sad of the sons of Moâdz, why did the Khoreiza and the An-Nadhīr yield?

Upon your life, Sad ben Moâdz calmly witnessed that catastrophe, which they themselves brought on that morning.

But Abou-Houbâb the Khazradjite had said

before to the Banou Keinôka: Don't go there. The allies had Oseid instead of Hodheir, while fortune turns its wheel (i.e., changes).

Al-Boéira has not been abandoned by Sallâm, Saya and the son of Akhtab, he is completely forsaken.

In their land they were as mighty as the crags of the Meitân mountains.

And although Abou Hacam Salâm yielded, they will not put down their arms and they will not let them rust.

In the two priestly tribes, there were men as agile as eagles; they were kind, but conducted themselves heroically.

They won for themselves a lasting glory that shines with a brilliance as pure as the moon.

Remain in the land, Aousite lords, without vigor or strength.

You have left your cauldrons empty while those of the others burned with a devouring fire.

The women and children of the Koreiza were divided among the Muslims, and the children were converted to Islam. Muhammad wanted to marry one of the captive Jewish women named Reihâna; she begged the Prophet to allow her to remain Jewish and a slave. Later, however, she agreed to embrace Islam. Another Jewish woman, during the siege, had dropped a stone onto a Muslim and had killed him. She was sentenced to death. As she went to her execution she conversed with Aïscha, and she marched to her death laughing.

The booty was considerable. It was further increased by the arrival of many Jews who quickly came from various parts to ransom the captive women. The Muslims turned this traffic into the object of financial speculation.

Muhammad wreaked terrible revenge on those who had incited the Koreischites against his authority. But of the instigators of that struggle, only Hoyyeyy had perished; his companion, Abou-Râfi Sallâm b. Abi-l-Houkeik was in Khaybar. Muhammad, who feared that he might cause him difficulties, sent murderers after him. Five men from the tribe of the Khazradjites traveled to Khaybar, slipped into Sallâm's dwelling at night, and closed the doors. Sallâm was on the upper floor; his wife went down and asked the men what they wanted. They replied that they had come to buy some wheat, entered the chamber where Sallâm was in bed, and stabbed him. At the cries of the victim's wife, some Jews came running with torches, but the murderers had managed to escape.[43]

After the death of Sallâm, the chieftain of the Jews of Khaybar was Al-Yoseir b. Rizâm. Since the latter was one of those who had incited the Ghatafân to attack the Prophet, Muhammad sent against him a band of assassins headed by the poet Abdallâh b. Rawâha, which included the murderers of Abou Râfi. Their plan failed, but they managed to persuade Al-Yoseir that Muhammad was summoning him to appoint him to an important position. Seduced by that promise, he left for Medina, accompanied by several friends. Along the way, the men who had been sent by Muhammad attacked those who had trusted their words and killed them.[44]

These murders were the prelude to a general attack against the Israelites of Khaybar.[45] Muhammad, at the head of fourteen hundred foot soldiers and three hundred horsemen, marched against that city and arrived during the night. In the morning the Israelites, going out to the fields as usual, noticed armed Muslims everywhere. They fled, shouting, "Muhammad and the Khamīs."[46] They shut themselves up in their citadels and prepared to withstand a siege. Khaybar was defended by numerous citadels, those of Nâim, Al-Kamouc, which belonged to the family of Abi-l-Houkeik, Al-Schikk, Natât, As-Solâlim, Al-Wâtih, and Al-Catîba. The Jews had correctly concluded from the murders ordered by Muhammad that they would be attacked next. They did not foresee, however, that the attack would occur so suddenly. They had also entered into an alliance with the Ghatafân against the Muslims, but, as was their wont, the Ghatafân pretended to try to help their allies and retreated without even having fought. Mahmoud b. Moslama was killed outside of Nâim by a piece of a millstone that one of the besieged inhabitants dropped on him.

Among the Israelite warriors there was a soldier with invincible courage named Marhab. This hero was of Yemanite origin and had converted to Judaism. He hurled the following challenge at the Muslims:

Khaybar knows that I am Marhab, the skilled warrior, the experienced soldier.
Sometimes I fight with the lance, sometimes I strike with the sword, when the angry lions come.
My person is consecrated, and no adversary dares approach; the bravest avoids any encounter with me.

The poet Kab b. Malik parried these challenging words with similar bravado. "Who wants to measure swords with him?" the Prophet asked one day. Muhammad b. Maslama, the brother of Mahmoud who had been killed outside Nâim, volunteered to battle with the Yemanite. Marhab struck with such force that his blade became embedded in his opponent's shield and, while he was trying to draw it out, Muhammad ran him through with his sword.[47] Yâsir tried to avenge the death of his brother Marhab, but was likewise killed.

Little by little all the forts fell into the hands of the Muslims, with the exception of Wâtih and Solâlim. A great number of Jews were taken prisoner, among them Kinâna b. Ar-Rabi, b. Abi-l-Houkeik and his fiancée, Çafiyya [Shafiyya?], daughter of Hoyyeyy. Çafiyya was very beautiful, and Muhammad wanted to take her as his wife; he summoned her fiancé, Kinâna, and under the pretext of making him tell where he had hidden the treas-

ures of the Nadhirites that had been entrusted to his protection, he subjected him to atrocious torture, put him to death, and then married Çaffiya. All the combatants who were captured with weapons in hand were killed; almost nine hundred died in this way.

The two other forts that were still putting up resistance[48] surrendered shortly after to the Muslims. The soldiers' lives were spared, but they had to hand over all their treasures to Muhammad[49] and abandon their lands to the victors. However, since they were better farmers than the Muslims, they could continue to cultivate these lands, on the condition that they would deliver half of the harvest to their masters and leave the countryside as soon as Muhammad demanded it. The Jews of Fadak, whose chieftain was named Youschah b. Noun, and those of Teimâ and Wâdi-l-Kôrâ, terrified by the defeat of the inhabitants of Khaybar, likewise submitted to Muhammad; the Prophet was then the absolute master of all the Hedjaz, except for Mecca.

Shortly after the conquest of Khaybar, Muhammad was almost poisoned. Zeinab, the wife of Sallâm b. Mischkam, had served him roast mutton in which she had put some poison. Muhammad sensed from the first mouthful that the meat had a bitter, unpleasant taste, and he ate no more of it; one of his companions who had eaten of it died. The Prophet called Zeinab to ask her the reason for this criminal attempt. "You are not unaware of the evil that you have done to my people," she replied. "If Muhammad is only a prince, I said to myself, then the Jews will be delivered from his tyranny; if he is a prophet, he will be warned about my plan." Muhammad was satisfied with this courageous response and pardoned Zeinab.[49a]

The Jewish property of Hedjaz was all in the hands of the enemy.[50] The Israelites of Arabia, therefore, no longer had any fatherland in that country; their situation was the same as the day on which they had first arrived in that land, and their sojourn there depended on the will of the man who had conquered that entire region and who could, as it pleased him, grant or refuse them permission to settle there. Muhammad did not completely expel the Jews from Arabia. It was enough for him to have humiliated them and to have subjected them to his rule. Abou Bekr, the Prophet's successor, did not change that situation, and the Israelites continued to reside among the Arabs. But Omar, a prudent and diplomatic man, realized that the sojourn of the Israelites in the midst of the Muslims was dangerous for Islam. He pretended that Muhammad had said in his presence one day that they should not allow two religions to exist in Arabia and ordered all the Jews to leave the land. In order to justify that expulsion, writers relate that some Israelites had attacked by night a Muslim who had come to Khaybar to inspect his property, that they had broken his arms and killed one of his companions. The Jews went to Syria.

Thus the history of the Jews in Northern Arabia

encompasses a period of only 150 years, but it is of capital interest for the history of the progress of the idea of [the one] God throughout the world. These are the Jews who taught and propagated in the Arabian Peninsula the fundamental concepts of civilization. As soon as their task was completed, they returned to the land from which they had come; the seed that they had sowed in the Arabian soil would produce its fruits in all the regions subjected to Muslim rule.

*For further clarification of any references, see original text.

NOTES

1. Ibn-Hischâm, *Vie de Mohammed*, ed. Wüstenfeld, p. 289.
2. Ibid., p. 296.
3. In Arabic: *Djaddoukoum*, which also means "good fortune"; but on the lips of the Jew this meaning is not very likely. See Hischâm, p. 334; Samhoudi, p. 56.
4. Sprenger, *Das Leben und die Lehre des Mohammed*, vol. 3, pp. 20 f; Caussin de Perceval, Essai, vol. 3, p. 22; and as cited by Ibn-Hischâm, p. 341.
5. See below [text above note 25].
6. Or Dahjâ; see above, footnote [inserted here]:

One would think that nothing is more clear or certain than the name of that man which is on the lips of millions every day. But we have only to glance at the Qur'an and the related traditions to see that the Prophet's name is surrounded by obscurity and that nothing at all is known about his name when he was young. Indeed, in one tradition found in the works of Beidhâwi we read: "On the occasion of the hair-cutting ceremony, his grandfather (his father was already dead) called him *Kotham* (Ibn al-Athīr, vol. 2, p. 2), but his mother named him *Mouhammad*." However it is immediately evident that this tradition is not authentic. Generally, even when it speaks about the years of his youth, tradition calls him "the one sent by God." In a poem— of very dubious authenticity—attributed to Abou Tâlib, the Prophet's uncle and tutor, we find the words: "*Ahmad* is for us a splendid monument, against which the power of arrogant men can do nothing" (Hischâm, p. 176; cf. p. 52). Some, in fact, take Ahmad for the Prophet's name when he was a youth; there is no justification, however, for this opinion. It should be noted, moreover, that this name occurs *once* in that part of the Qur'an concerned with Medina (sura 61:6): "And Jesus, the son of Miriam, says: O children of Israel, I am the one sent by God to confirm for you what you already possess of the Torah and to announce a messenger who will come after me; his name is *Ahmad*." If Ahmad had really been the Prophet's name during his youth, it certainly would already have been mentioned previously. Other traditions— which are a far cry from manifesting all the indications of authenticity—relate that Muhammad, during his youth, bore the name of *Al-Amin* (Hischâm, p. 125) because of his sincerity. Of course this is nothing but a nickname. The only thing that can be stated with certainty is that after Khadidja had given him a son, he bore the name of Abou-l-Kâsim, in keeping with the Arabian custom, and that he was still called by that name later in Medina (Hischâm, p. 410). One tradition recorded in Bokhâri (ed. Krehl, vol. 2, p. 278) relates: "A man wanted to give his son the name Al-Kâsim, and the Ansâr ('assistants,' a name for the Muslims in Medina) told him: 'We will not call you Abou-l-Kâsim (because that is the Prophet's name).' Muhammad, upon hearing about this discussion, approved of the Ansâr, saying: 'Name yourselves with my name, but not with my *Kounya* (i.e., Abou + the son's name).'"

Bokhâri, vol. 3, p. 352, relates that Abou-l-Yaman said: "One day I heard the following being said to the one sent: I am Muhammad, I am Ahmad, I am the Mâhi (purifier) through whom God will obliterate unbelief, I am the Hâschir (reconciler), because all men will be united by following in my footsteps; I am the Akib (last prophet, cf. Qur'an, sura 33:40, *Seal of the prophets*)." See in Maçoudi, vol. 4, p. 119, the same tradition, with these verses:

"Glory to Allah who created pure beings; the most pure generation is that of the Hâschim (the ancestors of Muhammad). And the spotless offspring of this pure family is Muhammad, Abou-l-Kâsim, the light."

Without any doubt, the Prophet's name during his youth has fallen into oblivion, which could have happened the more easily given that the childhood name of every Arab in general is relegated to the background as soon as a son is born to him: even more so in Muhammad's case because early on the tradition already gave him the latter name, or that of "God's Messenger." The name *Mouhammad* is found only four times in the Qur'an and only in the suras revealed in Medina (3:138; 33:40; 47:2; 48:29) and it is likely that before that it was completely unknown or very rare in Mecca. It is remarkable, however, that Muhammad and Ahmad are derived from the same root (HH in Hebrew) and both mean "glorified, honored." Furthermore there is a third form of this name with the same root: *Mahmoud*, "praised"; this descriptive name resulted, no doubt, from the transformation of one of the two other names for the sake of poetic meter (Hischâm, p. 659, twice). This way of playing upon the root *hamada* clearly demonstrates that the name

Muhammad was less a proper name than an epithet; it recalls the passage from the Book of Daniel where the Prophet bears the nickname HH (10:11, 19, 23), or HH for short (cf. Gen. 36:26 HH). One is seriously tempted to establish a connection between the knowledge of this name among the Jews and the origin of the appellations Muhammad, Ahmad, and Mahmoud. Nevertheless, the Jews of Medina were already acquainted with the name of Mahmoud before the arrival of the Prophet in that city. For example, Mahmoud b. Seihân and Mahmoud b. Dahjâ were both from the Keinokâ tribe (Hischâm, p. 351). If we carefully examine the passage in which the name Muhammad appears for the first time in the Qur'an, we will discover a sort of generalization in the idea that is expressed by it. Here is the passage (47:2): "Those who believe perform good works; and those who add faith to everything that has been revealed to a *Mouhammad* possess the truth of their master" (Cf. Hischâm, p. 379). One cannot help thinking that the Prophet here is alluding to the Jews, by speaking in general terms about distinguished persons who have been deemed worthy of a heavenly revelation. If he had meant to speak only about himself personally, he might well have said: *Al-Mouhammad*, "the highly-exalted." We see in the following verses of his favorite poet, Hassân b. Thâbit, how far this title was from having taken on the narrow meaning of a proper name:

"Have you not seen that He sent His servant with this witness? God is the Greatest and the Most-High. He assigned His name to him so as to honor him: He who sits upon the throne is glorified (Mahmoud), while he is *exalted* (Mouhammad)." (Following Al-Baghâwi's commentary on Qur'an 3:138; the second stanza is found also in the *Divân*, p. 23).

See also, concerning the name Muhammad, Sprenger, *Das Leben und die Lehre des Mohammeds*, vol. 1, p. 155, and vol. 3, p. 31 (footnote), where all the traditions related to this question are collected in one place, as well as the commentaries on the passages cited from the Qur'an. He mentions finally the name Al-Moustafâ, "the elect," but this epithet only appears at a later date.

7. See [*previous, excised text*]: According to the tradition, the rabbi Mâlik b. Al-Dheif traveled to Mecca in order to debate with the Prophet. Mâlik was very portly, and Muhammad, upon observing this, addressed him, "I adjure you by Him who gave the Torah to Moses: do you not find it written that some rabbis are very fat?" Mâlik, visibly offended, replied, "God has revealed nothing to man" [*or: "*... to that man"]. When he returned to Medina he was vehemently criticized by the Jews because of his clumsy response, and they said to him, "Well, now! Didn't God reveal the Torah to Moses? How

could you give such an answer?" "He angered me," Mâlik retorted, "and in my indignation I spoke thus." "If in anger you utter such statements, you are not worthy to be our rabbi." Mâlik was dismissed and the poet Cab b. Al-Aschraf was appointed in his place. [Footnote: Al-Baghâwi on the Qur'an 6:31; Sprenger, *Das Leben*, vol. 2, p. 294.]

8. Ibn-Hischâm, pp. 351 ff. I listed all these names only to show that the Jews have been to some extent *arabicized*. Among them, indeed we find only a very small number of biblical or distinctively Israelitic names, and this fact is in keeping with the fundamental idea of the work by Zunz, *Namen der Juden*. We recognize a biblical origin in the names *Ozeir* = HH, *Finhâç, Aazar*; the last mentioned is a corruption of HH, which seems to have given rise also to the name of *Izâr. Schamwîl* is indisputably the name HH, which we find again in the Arabic form *As-Samaoual*. These observations prove that the Jewish traditions were preserved in a purer form in Medina than in the works of the poet of Teimâ, where the Arab influence is clearly evident. It even seems that the Jews of Medina had a sort of jargon as their language (cf. Sprenger, 3:235).

Nahhâm is the name HH; *Yahouda* = HH is found once in the works of Ibn-Hischâm spelled as *Bahoudza* (cf. Ibn-Hischâm, p. 393). It is worth noting that Muhammad uses the word *yahoud* to refer to a *Jew*. When they are grouped with the Christians, Muhammad calls them *Ahl-al-Kitâb*. In order to justify his biblical stories, which he took from the tradition of the "children of Israel," he concludes a series of such narratives with these words: "Don't they have this sign [in the first place] so that the learned men of the children of Israel might recognize it?" The Jews of northern Arabia took the name of *Al-Yaoud* quite early on. Muhammad was completely unaware of the origin of that designation; he did not know, either, that the Jews in Arabia were not Arabs by birth. The word *Yahoud* resembles a verbal form, the kind from which proper names are very often derived. Muhammad certainly thought that the name of the Jews came from such a form, and he traces *Yahoud* back to the root *hâda* (*alladzîn ahâdou* "those who are Jewish," 6:147, 16:119 . . .). The name *Yahoud* does not appear in any sura written in Mecca, and it is only after having lived in Medina that Muhammad knew that it was a foreign proper name. Nevertheless he treats this name as though it came from the root *hâda* and says *hâdou*, *houd*, and *yahoud* interchangeably. Later, in order to distinguish Jews from Christians, he uses the term *yahoudyy* (HH), saying, for example, "Abraham was neither a Jew (*yahouddyyan*) nor a Christian (*naçrânyyan*). The origin of *yahoud* was so little understood by the Moslem traditionalists that Bokhâri (3:51) says that *hâdou* means: "they remain Jews," a word that is derived from *hâda*, "to return to the truth," like *tâba*.

9. His real name was Al-Hocein. Here is what Ibn-Hischâm relates on the subject of his conversion:

When I heard what people were saying about the one sent by God, who is called Abd Allâh, I recognized from his qualities and from the time when he was supposed to appear that this was a true prophet. I confided my thoughts to no one before the arrival of Muhammad in Medina. When I learned that Muhammad had come, I found myself upon a palm tree, at the foot of which my aunt Khâlida b. Al-Hârith was seated. I exclaimed: "God is great!" My aunt rebuked me, saying, "Shame on you! You could not have said more about him if Moses himself had arrived." "By God," I replied, "he is Moses' brother and brings us his faith." "Is he, then, the prophet whose coming is foretold for these times?" 'Yes." "Ah! So it is!" I went over to the messenger, made by profession of faith and converted my family. We kept our conversion secret from the Israelites. I informed the Prophet that my former co-religionists were slanderers and, in order to convince him of it, I invited him to seek information from them concerning me, without letting them know about my conversion. That is what he did. To his questions they answered: "Al-Hocein is our master and the son of our master; he is our rabbi!" When I had heard these words, I went out from the placed where I had hidden and told them that Muhammad was the prophet announced by God. "You liar!" they shouted, overwhelming me with insults "Wasn't I right?" I said to Muhammad, "in describing them to you as liars, slanderers and faithless people?" See Bokhâri 3: 42–50.

10. Ibn-Hischâm, p. 362.

11. Ibid., p. 389.

12. Qur'an 3:177.

13. Ibn-Hischâm, p. 376; *Ouyoun al-Athâr* (MS Sprenger, 122, 123, p. 273), according to Ibn-Ishâk, who relates it to the name of Ibn 'Abbâs, which does not make this document any more trustworthy. A passage from this letter is found at the end of the forty-eighth sura, one of the most recent, but it could be that this final verse, which has no connection with the one preceding, was a later addition and not Muhammad's. If this letter or another [like it] really has Muhammad as its source, it was probably written before the march of the Muslims upon Khaybar, and the words, "Has not God told you?" persuaded the compilers of the Qur'an to insert into that book the introduction to this letter that was written in the style of the Qur'an. In my monograph *Jüdische Elemente im Korân* [*Jewish Elements in the Qur'an*], p. 57, I said that Muhammad, in speaking about "the signs on their faces," has in mind the phylacteries that the Jews of Medina no doubt were already wearing; perhaps he spoke about them again in this letter. But the allusion that he makes to the *books* certainly indicates another object. The expression from the Qur'an, *roukkaan souddjadan*, recalls the Hebrew expression, HH; in fact it is a faithful translation thereof. I believe therefore that Muhammad understands "your books" to be the Mishna of Yôma, 6:2, which perhaps was part of the liturgy of Kippur. We know that in Muhammad's writings the word *Torah* has a very broad meaning; the Prophet therefore could be alluding here to Yom Kippur, which he saw being celebrated in Medina and which he speaks about in other passages as well. See Bokhâri, 3:51. Cf. Geiger, *Was hat Mohammed dem Judenthum entlehnt* [*What Did M. borrow from Judaism?*], p. 37; and *Jüdische Elemente*, pp. 54 ff.; Sprenger, 3:53, footnote; Caussin de Perceval, 2:18, footnote. . . . For the other comparisons, see the Gospel of Mark 4:8.

14. Ibn-Hischâm, p. 383; *Ouyoun*, p. 276.

15. Ibn-Hischâm, p. 386; *Ouyoun*, p. 277.

16. *Ouyoun*, p. 261. The Jews used a horn for this purpose.

17. Ibn-Hischâm, pp. 381, 427; *Ouyoun*, p. 299; Ibn-Sad (MS Sprenger, 103), f. 47 b. The Kibla (direction faced during prayer) was changed in the seventeenth or eighteenth month after the Hegira. Cf. Sprenger, 3:47.

18. Qur'an 2:136.

19. Ibn Sad, *ibid.*

20. Qur'an 2:214.

21. Wâkidi, translated by Wellhausen; Sprenger, 3:146.

22. Ibn-Hischâm, p. 995; Wâkidi, p. 174. Here are the verses:

I have lived for many long years and nowhere have I found an association
    that was more nobly attached to its allies and more faithful to its word toward those in need of its help
    than the sons of Keila, taken as a group. Mountains have crumbled, but they have not flinched.

They were divided by a horseman who came to visit them and confused them as to what was permitted and what was forbidden.

You ought to have shown more resolve and remained faithful to your first master.

23. Ibn-Hischâm, pp. 383, 545; Ibn-al-Athîr, 2:106. Sprenger, 3:250, correctly doubts the authenticity of this incident, because at that time Muslim women did not yet wear the veil.

24. Ibn-Hischâm, p. 546; Ibn-al-Athîr, 2:547; Wâkidi, (ed. Kremer), p. 177.

25. Aghâni, 19:106; Ibn-Hischâm, p. 548; Ibn-al-Athîr, 2:110; Wâkidi, p. 185; Bokhâri, 3:74.

26. Ibn-Hischâm, pp. 548 ff. For verse 2, see Hamasa, p. 89. Verse 5, "heel," in Arabic, *cab*, is an allusion to the poet's name. Verse 9, see Ibn-Hischâm, p. 510.

27. Ibn-Hischâm, p. 550, doubts the authenticity of these verses. Verse 4, Ibn-Hischâm, has *fakhtâlat*, which probably should read *fahtâlat*. Al-Akhâschib is the mountain Al-Cammân in the land of the Banou Tamîm.

28. Aghâni, p. 103, also cites the following verses by Cab (see Yâcout, *Geographisches Wörterbuch*, trans. Wüstenfeld, 2:63, and cf. Noeldeke, *Beiträge*, p. 80):

We have a well that provides abundant water; all who have a container can draw from it.

The black camels bring buckets and ropes to it.

I have been able to make all my wishes come true except the one that I made concerning Batn-al-Djourouf (the dwelling of his beloved?).

29. See the traditions cited in Sprenger, 3:156.

30. Ibid.; Caussin de Perceval, 3:85 ff. Cf. Ibn-Hischâm, Ibn-al-Athîr, Bokhâri, Ouyoun, etc.

31. Ibn-Hischâm, pp. 354 and 378. It goes without saying that the chroniclers praise him highly for his knowledge and his riches. "He recognized, according to the biblical prophecies and his own investigations, that Muhammad was the true Messiah, and he embraced Islam. On the day of Ouhoud, which was Saturday, he urged the Jews to come to the help of Muhammad. When they refused, he took up arms, bequeathed his fortune to the prophet and threw himself into the fray; he met his death there, and Muhammad distributed his fortune as alms."

32. Cf. Bokhâri, 3:72; Yâcout, 1:765; Sprenger, 3:162. Cf. Deuteronomy 21:19.

33. Wâkidi, p. 353; Ibn-Hischâm, pp. 652 ff.; Ibn-al-Athîr, 2:133; Beladzori, p. 17.

34. See [*previous, footnote from excised text*], with the verses composed on that occasion [as follows]:

[*Kitab al-Aghâni*, 19: 94]; Noeldeke, *Beiträge*, p. 54; Yâcou, 4:462. Ibn-Hischâm, *Vie de Mohammed*, ed. Wüstenfeld, p. 660, records an elegy of the Arabian poet Abbas b. Mirdâs (son-in-law of the famous poet Al-Khansâ), in which he weeps over the expulsion of the two tribes mentioned above:

You breathe invectives against those who are of noble stock, related to the priests, disregarding the benefits that they have showered upon you at all times. Have they not more than abundantly deserved that you should lament their lot and that your people should weep for them, if it wants to repay its debt of gratitude? Thanksgiving is the most beautiful action to which men of honor aspire. You resemble the man who, for the sake of becoming famous, has someone cut off the head to which he was heretofore united. Weep over the sons of Aaron, remember their deeds; when you were wallowing in misery, they satisfied your hunger.

The Jewish poet Cab b. Asad of the tribe of Koreiza sang: "While you were swimming in abundance, you were living in security in your houses thanks to the two priests. What is it now that drives you far away into the greatest fatigue?"

The word *Kâhin* in this verse must indisputably be translated as "priest;" this remark is of some importance, because we find it several times in the Koran, and there the word means "sorcerer" (sura 69:42; 52:29). From this we see clearly that the Jews had entirely preserved all their traditional privileges and that it was only long after their settlement in Arabia that they took Arabic names.

On *Kâhin*, see also Kamous, Yâcout, 4:44, 384; Maçoudi, *Les prairies d'or*, trans. Barbier de Meynard, 3: 396; Aboulféda, *Histoire anteislamique*, p. 136.

35. Ibn-Hischâm, p. 675; Wâkidi, pp. 364 ff.

36. Ibn-Hischâm, pp. 682–84; Wâkidi, p. 378.

37. All of these accounts, stripped of their embellishments, can be considered as the expression of the historical truth. Cab, because of his attitude before the battles of Boâth, appeared to the chroniclers as the man to whom traditions of this sort could be traced back with the most verisimilitude.

38. Aghâni, 19:97. Cf. Noeldeke, *Beiträge*, p. 76.

39. The text says "true." Originally the word was probably "false," as Noeldeke explains (*Beiträge*, p. 76).

40. Ibn-Hischâm, p. 687.

41. Wâkidi, p. 373; Ibn-Hischâm, pp. 690ff. There is a fantastic account of the execution of Az-Zabîr b. Bâtâ which I do not want to reprint here because it has already been translated several times. See Sprenger, 3:221; Welthausen, *Muhammed in Medina*, "Introduction"; Caussin de Perceval, 3:146; Graetz, 5:110. In the battle of Boâth, Az-Zabîr spared the life of Thâbit b. Kheis, who had been taken prisoner. See the complete account of that battle in Aghâni, 15:161–65.

42. Ibn-Hischâm, pp. 690 and 713, mentions this poet several times without stating that he was Jewish. Ibn Hadjar (ed. Sprenger, 1:453) includes him, on the authority of Hassân b. Thabit, *Diwân*, p. 45, among the Thalabite poets and declares that he had been Jewish but then converted to Islam. Yâcout, 1:765, probably misled by a copyist's error, calls him Djamal; see volume 5:94. Hassân b. Thabit, *Diwân*, p. 45 (cf. Yâcout; Ibn Hadjar, Beladzori, 1:19; Bokhâri, 3:72), addresses the following reply to Sad:

That tribe entered into an alliance with Koreisch, but it has no defender in his country.

These are the possessors of Scripture, but they have tried to corrupt it, they are blind and they do not know the Torah.

You deny the Qur'an, and yet you have declared the Mohammed has brought the truth.

Certainly, the lords of the Banou Loayy are not concerned at all about a fire that is spreading in Boéira. Abou-Sofyân ben Al-Hârith answered him (cited in Ibn-Hischâm, p. 713): May God make this situation last and light a fire in their land.

And you will see which of us two is further from

the fire and you will learn which of our two lands will suffer most from it.

If the palm trees of that country were mounts [e.g. horses and camels], they would say: you must not remain here; depart. (See Sprenger, 3:162; Beladzori, p. 17.)

43. The account of this death given by Ibn-al-Athir, 2:112, is slightly different from ours; according to him, this murder was committed in the month of Djoumâda of the year 3 [of the Hegira]. We have followed Ibn Ishâk, who explicitly states that this murder took place after the massacre of the Banou Koreiza; he bases his assertion on the fact that Sallâm was among those in the coalition against Muhammad. Some—for example, Bokhari, 3:76, have dated the murder of Sallâm immediately after that of Cab, because these two crimes took place in the midst of almost identical circumstances and also following what is implied in the verses by Hassân b. Thâbit, *Diwân*, p. 63; Ibn-Hischâm, p. 716:

May God bless the soldiers that you have fought, O son of Al-Hokeik, and you, son of Al-Aschraf.

They marched against you at night, armed with well-sharpened swords; they pounced on you like lions in a thicket surrounded by water (or, according to one *scholie*, in the midst of reeds growing in the water).

They invaded your land, entered your dwellings, struck you with awe and offered you the deadly brew.

They hoped thus to protect the religion of the prophet, having little concern for anything else.

Ibn-al-Athir, 2:114, corrects the date to the month of Dzoul-Iliddja in the year 4 of the Hegira; see Sprenger, 3:236.

44. Ibn-Hischâm, p. 981; see Sprenger, 3:236.

45. According to Yâcout, the expression *Khaybar* means, among the Jews, a *citadel*; the place designated by this word is found north of Medina. The name *Khaybar* is perhaps derived from HH, or it may be analogous to the form HH. It was a fertile land with many palm trees, which is evident from these words by Hassân b. Thâbit, *Diwân*, p. 127: "Like someone who would want to bring dates to the market of Khaybar." The origin of the word Khaybar was already obscure for the Arabs; therefore nothing can be concluded about the following explanation given by Yâcout, p. 503: "Khaybar, so called after the name of the son of Kâniya b. Mihlâlii b. Iram b. Abil (the latter is the brother of Ad b. Awdh b. Iram b. Sâm b. Nouh), and brother of Yathrib who gave his name to the city of Medina." A similar explanation is given by Insân al-Ouyoun, p. 229 (MS Sprenger, p. 148).

46. Ibn-Hischâm, p. 760. According to another account (Ibn-al-Athir, p. 168), the hero of this story is

Ali. Indeed, if we are to believe Boreida al-Aslami, the Prophet put a halt to the battle for several days because he was suffering from migraine headaches. Abou Bekr, impatient with this lull, marched nevertheless against the enemy, but without success. The next day Omar, in turn, fought, but accomplished no more than Abou Bekr. Upon hearing news of this, the Prophet exclaimed, "Tomorrow I will give the command to a man who loves God and his messenger and who is loved by them; that man will attack the enemy valiantly." Meanwhile Ali arrived, who had been kept back by an eye ailment. The Prophet told him to approach and spat in his eyes. Ali was cured and, at Muhammad's orders, marched against the enemies. A Jew who saw him from the height of his citadel shouted to him, "Who are you?" "I am Ali (the disciple), the son of Abou Tâlib." The man then exclaimed, "O Jews, you will be beaten." Marhab recited some verses that he had composed against Ali. The latter replied: "I am the one whose mother nicknamed the *lion,*/my sword will take the measure of my enemies./ I am physically strong as the lion in the forest." After this verbal duel began the duel with swords, and with one mighty blow Ali split the helmet and the head of Marhab.

Abou-Râfi gives the following version. In a sortie that the Jews made against the Muslims, an enemy soldier struck the shield from Ali's hands. The latter seized a door and used it as a shield.

In my opinion, these various stories were invented by Ali's adherents to exalt Ali at the expense of Abou Bekr and Omar. There is no doubt that Ali was very brave and can be considered the hero of Islam, but the story about the door is too reminiscent of what is recounted about Sampson in the book of Judges (15:13 [*sic*]). To add further to the marvelous character of this story, the chroniclers have Muhammad heal Ali's eye ailment. Cf. Ibn-Hischâm; Ibn-al-Athir, 2:169; Wâkidi, p. 389. Cf. Yakoubi, 2:56; Baladzkori, p. 23.

47. Ibn-Hischâm, p. 763; Wâkidi, pp. 390ff. Cf. Ibn-Hadjar; see p. 28 n. 3.

48. The capture of the fortress of Natât (Yâcout, 4:792) was celebrated in triumphant song that Ibn-Hadjar attributes to Djabal b. Djawwâl, whereas Ibn-Hischâm ascribes it to Lokeim. Ibn-Hischâm seems to be correct; he quotes this song to demonstrate that Lokeim had become a Muslim. Here, in any case, is the passage:

Nâtat was put to rout by the messenger; he had a strapping, broad-shouldered army.

The Absite should have expected to be humiliated, since that fighting force included Aslam and Ghifâr.

At dawn they went to confront the sons of Amr b. Zoura, and the inhabitants of Al-Schikk were wrapped in darkness in broad daylight.

They carried off the roosters and left only the hens in the land, which no longer utter a sound.

Each of the citadels is besieged by the horsemen of Abd-Aschbal and of Banou-l-Naddjâr, or by the emigrants (from Mecca) who never turn their backs on their enemy.

I knew very well that Muhammad would carry off the victory and that he would never leave the region before having completely vanquished his enemies.

On that day the Jews fled the battlefield in the midst of the clouds of dust that the allies raised.

49.   According to Wâkidi, p. 392, two sons from the family of Abou-l-Hokeik are said to have delivered all these treasures to Muhammad, except for a silver vase that was marvelously engraved, which they had concealed while declaring under oath that they did not have it. Muhammad supposedly threatened to exclude them from the alliance if they kept the slightest object, and he did this in the presence of Jews and Muslims alike. Then the angel Gabriel appeared, who pointed out the place where the vase was hidden. The Prophet had the guilty parties executed.

49a. Ibn Sa'd (*Kitab Al-Tabaqat Al-Kabir,* pp. 249–52) maintains that Muhammad's poisoning was a well-orchestrated Jewish conspiracy, and insists that Zeinab was handed over

to the heirs of Bishr Ibn al-Barra [whom the Jewess had also poisoned, leading to his rapid death] who put her to death. *This is the approved version*

[emphasis added]. . . . The Apostle of Allah lived after this three years, till in consequence of his pain he passed away. During his illness he used to say: I did not cease to find the effect of the poisoned morsel I took at Khaybar.

The canonical hadith collections, and major sira all agree that Muhammad's painful and protracted death was due, ultimately, to this poisoning. (Sahih Bukhari, vol. 3, bk. 47, no. 786; Sahih Muslim, bk. 26, no. 5430; Sunan Abu Dawud, bk. 39, no. 4498; Guillaume, *The Life of Muhammad,* p. 516; Ibn Sa'd, *Kitab Al-Tabaqat Al-Kabir,* pp. 249–52.)

50. Muhammad reserved for himself the beautiful Çafiyya; he was so smitten by her that he celebrated his marriage with her during his return to Mecca. The Arab chroniclers relate many stories about Çafiyya and the jealousy that Muhammad's other wives experienced in her regard. One day Zeinab, one of the Prophet's wives, called her "that Jewess"; her husband was so annoyed at her that he kept her secluded from his presence for several months. Another taunted Çafiyya about her heritage; the latter complained about it to Muhammad, who said to her, "Why don't you reply to them all that you are at least their equal, that your husband is Muhammad, your father Aaron, your uncle Moses?" She died in the year 52 of the Hegira, leaving behind great wealth. See Ibn-Hadjar, pp. 666–69; cf. Sprenger, 2:7ff.

PART 5

Muslim Jurists, Theologians, and Scholars on the Jews: Classical and Premodern Era

CHAPTER 16

The First Jews' Oath in Islam

(Second Half of the Eighth Century)

According to Muhammad b. ʿUmar al-Madā in his book *The Pen and the Inkwell*,[1] the first time that these oaths were created for people of the Jewish faith was during the time of al-Fadl b. al-Rabīʿ,[2] the vizier of Hārūn al-Rashīd. They were created by a secretary of his who had asked him, "How do you put a Jew under oath?"

Al-Fadl replied,

I say to him: If not (i.e., if you are not speaking the truth), then may you be separated from your God whom alone you worship and whom alone you profess. May you detest your religion which previously you had approved. May you repudiate the Torah. May you be cursed by 800 rabbis through the words of David and Jesus son of Mary. May you be transformed as the Sabbath-breakers were transformed into apes and pigs.[3] May you transgress what was ordained by Daniel, Ashloma,[4] and John. May you meet God with the blood of John the son of Zacharias on your hands. May you shatter Mt. Sinai into stones. May you beat the clapper[5] in the Temple. May the twelve tribes and the patriarchs, Israel, Isaac, and Abraham, wash their hands of you. May you immerse the Catholicos' beard in the baptismal font of the Christians. May you change your sabbath from Saturday to Sunday.

And if not (i.e., you are not speaking the truth), then may Allah ordain that you meet that which comes out of the water on Friday night.[6] May Allah make your food pig's flesh, camel's tripe, and swine's entrails. May Allah cause Nebuchadnezzar to rule over you and your people a second time, killing the men of fighting age, enslaving the youth, and destroying the cities. May Allah reveal to you the hands that will seize the knees (of the patriarchs) of the tribes. May Allah punish you with every tongue you denied and every verse you distorted. May you say that Moses was false and that he is in the Place of Ruin and the House of Deception. May you disavow "I am that I am, the Lord of Hosts, God Almighty."

This oath is binding upon you and your descendants until the Day of Resurrection.

NOTES

1. Neither this writer nor his book are cited in Carl Brockelmann, *Geschichte der arabischen Literatur*, 2nd ed. and supplement (Leiden: 1937–49).

2. He became the vizier of Hārūn al-Rashīd after the fall of the Barmacids in 803, and continued in that office under Hārūn's son al-Amīn (809–13).

3. According to Qur'an 2:65 and 7:166, the Jews, consistent with the Qur'anic curse of 2:61, were transformed into apes, ostensibly for "Sabbath breaking." Qur'an 5:60 mentions ape and pig/swine transformations, as per this curse, in the context of accusations of Satan worship.

4. Stillman could not identify this prophet.

5. The clapper (Ar., *nāqūs*) is commonly used by Christians in the Middle East during services.

6. Some demon apparently.

---

al-Qalqashandi, *Subh al-Aʿshā* (Cairo: 1918), vol. 13, pp. 266–67. English translation in Norman Stillman, *The Jews of Arab Lands: A History and Source Book* (Philadelphia: 1979), pp. 165–66.

CHAPTER 17

Why the Muslims Prefer the Christians to the Jews

*Al-Jahiz**

I shall begin to enumerate the causes which made the Christians more liked by the masses than the Magian [Zoroastrians], and made men consider them more sincere than the Jews, more endeared, less treacherous, less unbelieving, and less deserving of punishment. For all this there are manifold and evident causes. They are patent to one who searches for them, concealed to one who shuns investigation.

The first cause is as follows: The Jews were the neighbors of the Muslims in Medina and other places, and (as is well known) the enmity of neighbors is as violent and abiding as the hostility that arises among relatives. Man indeed hates the one whom he knows, turns against the one he sees, opposes the one whom he resembles, and becomes observant of the faults of those with whom he mingles; the greater the love and intimacy, the greater the hatred and estrangement. Therefore feuds among relatives and neighbors, in the case of the Arabs as well as of other people, lasted longer and proved more rancorous. When the [Muslim] Emigrants [from Mecca] became the neighbors of the Jews [in Medina] . . . the Jews began to envy the Muslims the blessings of their new faith,[1] and the union which resulted after dissension. They proceeded to undermine the belief of our [i.e., the Muslim] masses, and to lead them astray. They aided our enemies and those envious of us. From mere misleading speech and stinging words they plunged into an open declaration of enmity, so that the Muslims mobilized their forces, exerting themselves morally and materially to banish the Jews and destroy them. Their strife became long-drawn and widespread, so that it worked itself up into a rage, and created yet greater animosity and more intensified rancor. The Christians, however, because of their remoteness from Mecca and Medina, did not have to put up with religious controversies, and did not have occasion to stir up trouble, and be involved in war. That was the first cause of our dislike of the Jews, and our partiality toward the Christians.

Another circumstance, which is the most potent cause, is the wrong[2] interpretation given by the masses to the Qur'anic verses (Qur'an 5:82–85): "Thou wilt surely find the most hostile of men to the believers are the Jews and the idolaters; and thou wilt surely find the nearest of them in love to the believers are those who say We are Christians; that, because some of them are priests and monks, and they wax not proud; and when they hear what has been sent down to the Messenger, thou seest their eyes overflow with tears because of the truth they recognize. They say, Our Lord, we believe; so do Thou write us down among the witnesses. Why should we not believe in God and the truth that has come to us, and be eager that our Lord should admit us with the righteous people? And God rewards them for what they say with gardens underneath which rivers flow, therein dwelling forever; that is the recompense of the good-doers."

The wrong interpretation of the above verses supplanted that of the learned, and the Christians craftily used it to seduce the common and vulgar. In the very verse lies the proof that here God is not referring to the Christians we are acquainted with nor to their associates the Melkites and Jacobites. . . .

As for Judaism, at the birth of Islam, it prevailed in no tribe. It only had converts in Yemen, and a small minority of the tribes of 'Iyad and Rabī'a. The bulk of the Jews, and these were Jews by extraction and were descended from Aaron, lived in Yathrib, Himyar, Taymā'a, and Wādī l-Kurā. Thus what filled the hearts of the Arabs with affection for the Christians were the ties of blood and our regard for loyalty.

Moreover, our masses began to realize that the Christian dynasties were enduring in power, and that a great number of Arabs was adhering to their faith; that the daughters of Byzantium bore children to the Muslim rulers, and that among the Christians were men versed in speculative theology, medicine, and astronomy. Consequently they became in their estimation philosophers and men of learning, whereas they observed none of these sciences among the Jews.

The cause for the lack of science among the Jews lies in the fact that the Jews consider philosophic speculation

From his "A Reply to the Christians," trans. Joshua Finkel in "A Risala of Al-Jahiz," *Journal of the American Oriental Society* 47 (1927): 311–34. Extracts from pp. 322–24, 326, 327–28.

to be unbelief, and Kalām theology [Muslim dogmatic theology] an innovation leading to doubt. They assert that there is no lore other than that revealed in the Torah and the books of the prophets; and that faith in medicine and astrology leads to opposition against the standard views of the authorities of old, and is conducive to Manicheanism and atheism. So much are they averse to these sciences that they would allow the blood of their practitioner to be shed with impunity, and would prohibit discourse with them.

Another cause for the admiration accorded by the masses to the Christians is the fact that they are secretaries and servants to kings, physicians to nobles, perfumers, and money changers, whereas the Jews are found to be but dyers, tanners, cuppers [bloodletters], butchers, and cobblers. Our people [the Muslims] observing thus the occupations of the Jews and the Christians concluded that the religion of the Jews must compare unfavorably as do their professions, and that their unbelief must be the foulest of all, since they are the filthiest of all nations. Why the Christians, ugly as they are, are physically less repulsive than the Jews may be explained by the fact that the Jews, by not intermarrying, have intensified the offensiveness of their features. Exotic elements have not mingled with them; neither have males of alien races had intercourse with their women, nor have their men cohabited with females of a foreign stock. The Jewish race therefore has been denied high mental qualities, sound physique, and superior lactation. The same results obtain when horses, camels, donkeys, and pigeons are inbred.

*Finkel's discussion of al-Jahiz (p. 314) includes these comments:

. . . al-Jahiz (d. 869) is one of the greatest Arabic authors of all times. His encyclopedic knowledge is amazing. While there are other authors no less versatile than he in the numerous branches of learning, none could make full use of them as he did, and none could focus on a single subject so many rays of erudition. The present essay "A Reply to the Christians" illustrates this point fully. Jahiz managed to crowd into this short treatise theology, philosophy, psychology, sociology, history, folklore, and what not. Behind this multifarious material Jahiz stands supreme.

NOTES

1. See Qur'an 2:105:

Neither those who disbelieve among the people of the Scripture nor the idolaters love that there should be sent down unto you any good thing from your Lord. But Allah chooseth for His mercy whom He will, and Allah is of Infinite Bounty.

2. Clearly al-Jahiz's views are not in accord with the classical Qur'anic tafsir (commentary) on verse 5:82 These commentaries were reviewed at some length in the introductory survey, especially nn. 49–66, and the related text. Tabari's opinion (from Tabari, *Jāmi` al-Bayān fii Tafsiir al-Qur'aan*, vol. 7, pp. 5ff; English translation by Michael Schub) is typical:

In my [Tabari's] opinion, [the Christians] are not like the Jews who always scheme in order to murder the emissaries and the prophets, and who oppose God in his positive and negative commandments, and who corrupt His scripture which He revealed in His books.

CHAPTER 18

A Renegade Jew as the Source of the Shi'ite "Heresy" and the "Conspiracy" to Destroy the Early Islamic Caliphate

Al-Tabari

'Abd Allah b. Saba'[1] was a Yemenite Jew. . . . He later converted to Islam in the time of [Caliph] Uthman.[2] Then he traveled through the lands of the Muslims trying to lead them into error. . . . [For example] in Egypt he promulgated to the people the [heterodox] doctrine of the Return [of Muhammad as Messiah]. So the Egyptians discussed this idea. Then, after that, he said that there were one thousand prophets, each of whom had an agent; and that Ali was Muhammad's agent. Then he said, Muhammad was the Seal of the Prophets and Ali was the Seal of the Agents. Also, he asked: "Who is more evil than those who denied Muhammad's designation of Ali as his agent-successor, pounced upon this successor-designate of Ali's messenger and seized (illegitimately) the rulership of the Muslim community?" [In answer to this question as it were,] he told the Egyptians that Uthman had seized power illegitimately while Ali was, in fact, the agent-successor of Allah's messenger. "Rebel against this illegitimate rule, provoke it, and challenge your rulers . . ." [said 'Abd Allah b. Saba'].

was reading when attacked. Moreover, during the attack his wife was injured, and their home ransacked. Uthman's body was secretly buried during the night by his wife and a small cadre of close friends. The election of the new caliph Ali took place within this atmosphere of tumult and terror. Thus ended the era of political unity in Islam, and shortly afterwards religious unity as well, marking the transition to a period of civil wars and schisms. (See G. Levi Della-Vida and R. G. Khoury, "Uthman b. 'Affan," *Encyclopedia of Islam*, ed. P. Bearman, Thomas Bianquis, C. E. Bosworth, E. van Donzel, and W. P. Heinrichs [Leiden: Brill, 2006/2007].)

NOTES

1. Hartwig Hirschfeld, "Abdallah Ibn Saba," Jewish Encyclopedia.com, http://www.jewishencyclopedia .com/view.jsp?artid= 189&letter=A.

2. Uthman b. 'Affan was the third of the Rightly Guided Caliphs who reigned from 644–655. The bloody events which ended his reign ushered in a period of civil warfare which has embarrassed Arab historiographers. Uthman is believed to have been assassinated by a party led by Muhammad b. Ali Bakr, the son of the first caliph and the brother of Aisha. Tradition maintains that Uthman's blood flowed on to a copy of the Qur'an he

Al-Tabari, "Ta'rikh al-Rusul wa al-Muluk," M. J. de Goeje, ed. 1, no. 6 (1898): 3941–42; English translation in Ronald M. Nettler, "Islamic Archetypes of the Jews: Then and Now," in *Anti-Zionism and Antisemitism in the Contemporary World*, ed. Robert Wistrich (New York: 1990), p. 66.

CHAPTER 19

"To Disclose the Fraudulence of the Jewish Men of Learning"

Al-Jaubari

Know that these people are the most cunning creatures, the vilest, most unbelieving and hypocritical. While ostensibly the most humble and miserable, they are in fact the most vicious of men. This is the very essence of rascality and accursedness. If they remain alone with a man, they destroy him. They offer him sleep-inducing food, they slay him. They compound black henbane seed, ear wax, and wild onion, one particle of each, then insert it in some food. He who partakes of it, immediately falls asleep. Then they seize him and kill him. Understand this. They are the most unbelieving and most perfidious of men. So beware of their company. They have no belief or religion. This is the description of the learned of the Jewish liars. Their common people are connected with the apothecary business. They have their characteristics as follows. They adulterate all the drugs and while nobody pays attention, sell them to people. They mix myrobalan with pepper, saffron, musk, wood, ambergris, tutty, chalk, dragon blood juice, sugar, camphor, and mastic. . . . Among them are the naturalist physicians, most infidel and hypocritical. They have secrets unknown to anybody else, how to make the distant near, and how to make the strong weak. If one of them wishes to heal a man . . . he will effect [it] in a couple of days; but if he wants to play a trick on him, he will first neglect to maintain the strength of the patient until it diminishes; then he will prescribe an effective medicine for him for three days, after which he will cause the patient to suffer from some other malady; and so on, thus reaping a rich harvest from the patient. If the patient has an heir, the latter will give the doctor a hint to kill the patient; for a certain remuneration the doctor will turn against the patient, weaken him little by little until he finally dies. Again, if the patient has a wife who wishes for his death, she will say to the physician: "Oh, doctor, by God, if my husband is dead, then give him something to take which would weaken him until he perishes." Then the woman, poor in reasoning power and in faith, and then bent on her husband's death, will say to the doctor: "You do what you like, and you shall have from me whatever you desire." Then he says: "This is something I dare not do." But she keeps promising him whatever he wishes. Then he says: "Such matters are not accomplished by promises (*wuʿūd*) but by cash (*nuqūd*)." Then he receives from her whatever they have agreed upon. Look at this cunning and craft and vileness; how they take other people's moneys, ruin their lives. . . . [At the behest of the woman the physician can compound a drug that will make the husband feeble-minded.]

Excerpts from chap. 5 of *al-Mukhtar fi kashf al-asrar* [The Chosen One's Unmasking/Clarification of Divine Mysteries]; "To Disclose the Fraudulence of the Jewish Men of Learning," English translation by Moshe Perlmann in "Notes on the Position of Jewish Physicians in Medieval Muslim Countries," *Israel Oriental Studies* 2 (1972): 316–17. It took several centuries for the Jews to attain the status of medical physicians, the ninth-century Muslim scholar al-Jahiz referring to their ignorant obscurantism (see chap. 17)—"dyers, tanners, cuppers, cobblers"—in contrast to the numerous Christian professionals. But the subsequent proliferation of Jewish physicians—despite their achievement of distinction and community leadership as providers of an important service, Perlmann notes, "brought upon them the misgiving and hostility of the *fakih* and [their] disciples. There is much evidence of this antagonism." From the twelfth century, Perlmann cites (p. 316) a fatwa which prohibited a Jewish physician in Fas from appearing in the same elegant attire as a Muslim scholar. This opinion emphasized how the Jewish physician must be humiliated, just like his more humble co-religionists—no horse to ride upon, no donning a turban, and no wearing the colors of the pious of ancient Islam.

CHAPTER 20

A Collection of Legal Opinions Demonstrating the Attitudes of Muslim Jurists and Citizens toward the Jews of Muslim Spain and North Africa, Ninth—Fifteenth Centuries

Al-Wansharisi

NINTH CENTURY—IFRIQIYA [MODERN TUNISIA]

A Jew who dresses like the Muslims and fails to wear the clothing that distinguishes him from them will be incarcerated, beaten, and paraded ignominiously through the places inhabited by the Jews and the Christians as an example. The cadi of Kairouan, Ibn Abi Talib (d. 275 = 888–889 CE) commanded one of the cadis under his authority to oblige Jews and Christians to wear their belts (*zananir*) amply displayed upon their robes so that they might be easily distinguished, and if one of them rides a horse, to stop him from doing so, to give him twenty lashes while he is stripped, and then to throw him in prison, and in case of a repeat offense, to beat him severely and to incarcerate him for a long time (vol. 6, pp. 51, pp. 286–303).

NINTH–TENTH CENTURIES—AL-ANDALUS

The council of jurists (*sura*) in Cordova, having been consulted, approved the demolition of a synagogue (*sanuga*) built in Cordova, because the tributaries, Jews and Christians, cannot construct temples in Muslim cities in the midst of Muslims (vol. 2, p. 197).

An eight-year-old Jewish boy who has converted will not be taken from the custody of his parents. Once he is an adult, he will be invited to confirm his faith and, if he refuses, he will be forced to do so by a beating (vol. 2, p. 274).

TENTH–ELEVENTH CENTURIES—IFRIQIYA

A Muslim has a Jewish neighbor who was raised in the midst of Muslims. They provide services for each other and, when they meet, exchange words and smile to one another. This man declares, "Allah knows my hatred of the Jews, but I have a kindly nature."

It is better not to associate with people of another religion. One may perform a service for a neighbor who is a tributary and speak politely to him, but without deference. If he greets you saying, "May salvation be upon you," you must reply, "Upon you," and nothing more. There is no need to ask him news of himself or of his household. One can be a good neighbor to a tributary, but one must maintain a certain reserve (vol. 11, pp. 227–28).

From H. R. Idris, "Tributaries in the Medieval Muslim West, according to the *Mi'yar* of al-Wansharisi." English translation by Michael J. Miller of "Les tributaries en Occident Musulman medieval d'apres 'miyar d'al Wansarisi'," in *Melanges d'islamologie: Volume dediae a la memoire de Armand Abel par ses colleagues, ses aeleves, et ses amis* (1974), pp. 172–96, selected extracts.

Note by Idris: The publication by Professor S. D. Goitein of *A Mediterranean Society: The Jewish Communities of the Arab World as Portrayed in the Documents of the Cairo Geniza* (vol. 1, 1967; vol. 2, 1971; vol. 3, in preparation [as of 1974]) has prompted me to excerpt from my work on the fatwas of the Mi'yar of al-Wansharisi (d. 914 = 1508 CE), lithograph edition Fès 1314–1315 (= 1896–1898 CE), twelve volumes, the principal references concerning the tributaries. For brevity's sake, each document has been condensed and reduced to what is essential and the names of the muftis have been omitted. Along the same lines, in order to avoid repetitions, and also in order to characterize each testimony, a classification by century and by region has been adopted.

TWELFTH CENTURY—IFRIQIYA

The cadi should order the tributaries to have distinctive signs, such as dying the end of their turban, since Jews living among Muslims necessarily have dealings with them (vol. 2, pp. 206–207).

FOURTEENTH CENTURY—IFRIQIYA

The decapitation (probably in Tunis) of a Jew who had insulted the Prophet upon hearing the call to prayer (vol. 2, p. 281).

A Muslim declares to a Jew that Islamic law and Islam are "above the nations" and the Jew replies that they are "beneath the whole world." The *cadi* imprisons him for a time and then has him scourged (vol. 2, pp. 281–82).

FOURTEENTH CENTURY—AL-ANDALUS

A Jew alleges against a Muslim that he, the Jew, holds three titles (*rusum*), one of them fifteen years old, the other two going back eleven years, demanding the balance of an account of which he claims to be the creditor for each of these three mortgages. The other man maintains that he paid them in full. The *mufti* replies that the Jews customarily consider it licit to gouge the Muslims. Usually one does not leave one's property for such a long time in the hands of someone else, all the more reason when it is a question of an Infidel doing business with a Muslim. The jurists hold that the rules of the law are directed against anyone who is a prevaricator or notoriously unjust, and so the one who is claiming a right against a man of this sort has only to take an oath in order to obtain satisfaction. In the present case, one should follow the opposite rule, and that is the way that affairs in which Jews are involved should be settled. The Muslim, then, should swear that he paid off his debts to the Jew and, as soon as he has taken the oath, the right of the Jew will cease (vol. 5, p. 214).

FIFTEENTH CENTURY—CENTRAL MAGHRIB

A controversy between the *cadi* of Touat [an oasis in southern Morocco] and some jurists about the upkeep of the synagogues of Touat and other places of the Sahara, which has almost stirred up a civil war. Almost all of the Jews of Touat live in a quarter (*darb*) set aside for them, and their synagogue (*kanisa*), located in the midst of their dwellings, does not touch any Muslim house. They pay the head-tax and are very humble and submissive. Some Jews who arrived from Tamantit, a city of Touat, built a synagogue (*kanisa*) there on a plot that had previously been sold to Muslims or others. The building must be destroyed. The Jews of Touat must be made subject to the head-tax, the obligation to provide lodging (*diyafa*) and provisions (*al-arzaq*). (See al-Maghili.)

FIFTEENTH CENTURY—UPPER MAGHRIB

Under the Marinid caliph Abu Ya'qub Yusuf ben Ya'qub (1286–1307), the jurists of Maghrib handed down a *fatwa* against the Jews who were selling wine to the Muslims; they were killed, and their families were reduced to slavery in all of the Marinid states (vol. 2, pp. 199–200). If just one tributary harms the Muslims, all the others lose every protection; their belongings are taken and treated as booty, subject to the fifth; the goods of uncertain provenance go into the public treasury (*bayt al-mal*), to be dealt with by the inspector (*nazir*) (vol. 2, p. 203).

For a long time, the stipend for the imams who preach at the Grand Mosque (no doubt in Fes) has been taken from the proceeds of the head-tax (*jizya*) of the Jews.

FIFTEENTH CENTURY—AL-ANDALUS

The Jews who do business (*mu'amala*) in the localities cite claims drawn up in legal forms (*rusum sar'iyya*) stating amounts owed to them by Muslims, going back ten, fifteen, twenty, or thirty years. The debtors claim to be clear, but without testimony from witnesses, and the Jews deny having been paid back. The question of the Jews is left to the evaluation (*igtihad*) of the *cadi*. The claim of one of these vile, wicked creatures is weakened if it originates with an outright swindler and if it goes back to a date in the distant past; in that case one should rely on the statement of a Muslim under oath. If the affair is doubtful it is better to refrain from judging. If it is determined that the Jew is a patient and understanding creditor, which is rare, the rule is that things should be left as they are. If his character is unknown, it is better to suppose that he belongs to the first category. The length of the period for liquidating debts, for those who allow it, has no fixed limit. Al-Haffar (Andalusian, fourteenth century) sets it at sixteen years, with the understanding that the *cadi* makes the decision and that the expiration of the period does not invalidate the claim (vol. 5, pp. 214–15).

A Jew alleges that he has a twenty-eight-year-old claim (*rasm*), according to which a Muslim who died during the last plague, more than eight years ago, owed him fifty-eight dinars in the coinage that was current at that time. Should one accept (*retenir*) the allegation of the tributary who claims the remainder of this debt, make him take an oath so as to reimburse him from the inheritance of the deceased party? He deserves to be punished, to incur the wrath of Allah, and that his claim should be torn up, and that he be declared in debt for the amount that the deceased party paid him against his will (vol. 5, p. 215).

On the occasion of the Passover (*'id al-fitr/al-fatira*) the Jews offer flat cakes (*raga'if*) to some of their Muslim neighbors. One should not accept presents from Christians and Jews on the occasion of their feast days (vol. 11, p. 88).

FIFTEENTH CENTURY—
CENTRAL MAGHRIB OR IFRIQIYA

In a recently founded locality in Muslim territory, the Jews built a synagogue (*kanisa*) which was destroyed at the instigation of a devout [Muslim]. The Jews would like to rebuild it. They should not be allowed to do so (vol. 2, pp. 199–200).

CHAPTER 21

Anti-Jewish Anecdotes from an Anti-*Dhimmi* Treatise

Ghazi al-Wasiti

In the days of the Abbasid al-Ma'mūn,[1] some Jew advanced to such a position that he would sit in a higher place than the nobles. So a distinguished Muslim devised a strategem and wrote a note to al-Ma'mūn with the following verse:

> O son of him[2] to whom all men were obedient,
> Whose law was a binding duty,
> Lo, the man whom you honor
> Is—this writer claims—a liar!

Al-Ma'mūn replied: "You have spoken truly and have proven your devotion!" The Jew was immediately drowned.

Al-Ma'mūn then related to those present a story about al-Miqdād b. al-Aswad al-Kindī,[3] a companion of the Apostle of Allah—may Allah bless him and grant him peace. While on one of his journeys, he was accompanied by some Jew for the entire day. On the dawn of the next day, al-Miqdād—may Allah be pleased with him—suddenly remembered the words of the Apostle—may Allah bless him and grant him peace: "No Jew can be alone with a Muslim without plotting to harm him." So al-Miqdād said to the Jew: "I swear by Allah, you shall not part company with me without telling what kind of harm you were planning to do me. If you do not, I shall kill you!" The Jew replied: "Do I have your assurance that no harm will come to me if I tell?" "Yes," he said, and bound himself with a solemn oath.

Then the Jew admitted: "Ever since I have been traveling with you, I have been planning for you to lose your head so I might trample it beneath my shoe." At this al-Miqdād—may Allah be pleased with him—exclaimed: "The Apostle of Allah was right—may Allah bless him and grant him peace!"

It is told that in the time of some king there lived a Jew named al-Hārūni, who held a high position in his household. Once he played a game of chess with him in his drinking-hall on the promise that he might request whatever he desired for himself should he win. When he did in fact win, he asked the king to fulfill his promise. "Ask what you wish," the king told him. So he replied: "Let the king command that there be stricken from the Koran the verse that reads: 'Verily, the true religion in the sight of Allah is Islam.'"[4]

The king immediately had his head cut off.

I have been informed by the most unimpeachable sources that the physician Moses (Maimonides) was ill, and the Qādī al-Fādil paid him a visit. The Jew was a scholar and a gentleman. So he said to al-Fādil: "Your sense of decency has made you come and visit me. Let me advise you not to receive any medical treatment from a Jew, because with us, whoever desecrates the Sabbath—his blood is licit for us." The Qādī thereupon banned Jews from practicing medicine or being employed in that capacity.

NOTES

1. He was caliph from 813–833.
2. The reference is to al-Ma'mūn's father, Hārūn al-Rashīd.
3. He appears several times in the *sīra,* where he is usually referred to as al-Miqdād b. ʿAmr.
4. Sura 3:19/18.

Al-Wāsitī, *Kitāb Radd ʿalā Ahl al-Dhimma,* ed. R. Gottheil, *Journal of the American Oriental Society* 41, no. 5 (1921): 396–97. Excerpted and annotated originally in Norman Stillman, *The Jews of Arab Lands: A History and Source Book* (Philadelphia: 1979), pp. 275–76.

CHAPTER 22
On Killing a Jew

Sirhindi

Whenever a Jew is killed, it is for the benefit of Islam.

From Yohanan Friedmann, *Shaykh Ahmad Sirhindi: An Outline of His Thought and a Study of His Image in the Eyes of Posterity* (Montreal: McGill University, Institute of Islamic Studies, 1971), pp. 73–74.

CHAPTER 23

Lightning Bolts against the Jews

Muhammad al-Majlisi

In the name of Allah, the Beneficent, the Merciful, praise be to God who strengthens Islam and the Muslims, who degrades Unbelief. [It is He Who] brings to the clear religion and bestows prayer upon him whom He sent as a mercy to all created beings, [upon] Muhammad and the most pure people of his household.

Know that God, the Exalted, established the *jizya* upon the People of the Book, since they are closer to [true] guidance than the rest of the infidels, because they have heard about the manners and practices of the prophets, peace be upon them, and because they have seen the descriptions of His Excellency [Muhammad] in their books. Wherever they remain for some time among Muslims and hear Qur'anic verses and the *ahadith* of the Prophet and of those of his House [the Imams], peace be upon them, and witness the true laws and perfect worship of the people of Islam, if they do not act fanatically, they will quickly arrive at the knowledge of the true claims of Islam. So if they observe the conditions of the *jizya* and live in baseness and abjectness among Muslims, bias and obstinacy will not prevent them from accepting the true religion, and they will soon accept Qur'an [9:29]: "Fight against such as those who have been given the Scripture as believe not in Allah nor the Last Day, and forbid not that which Allah hath forbidden by His messenger, and follow not the religion of truth, until they pay the tribute readily, being brought low." That is, fight against those who do not believe in God and in the Day of Resurrection, who do not prohibit the things that have been prohibited by God and His Prophet, such as wine and pork, and do not believe in the religion of truth, from among those who had been given the Book,—until they pay the *jizya*, with their own hands, while they are in a low and abased state.

THE LAWS OF *JIZYA*

It should be known that the laws of *jizya*, according to the unanimous opinion of the Shi'i *ulama,* may God be pleased with them, apply only to the People of the Book, that is, to the Jews who have the Torah, the Christians who have the Gospels, and the Zoroastrians who have the like of a Book. They [the Zoroastrians] had been sent a prophet who brought a book written on twelve thousand parchments [lit., "cow skins"]. They killed their prophet and burned his book. Then Zoroaster wrote for them the *Zand* and *Pazand*, in place of the Book; it is like a Scripture, for they believe it to be God's book. Their original book, together with the rest of the books of the prophets, are with His Excellency, the Twelfth Imam, may God's prayers be upon him. As for other than these three denominations, idolaters and other infidels, it is not allowed to accept the *jizya* from them. If the ruler of the Muslims [*hakim-I Musalmanan*] deems it advisable he may grant an exemption to some of them [idolaters and non *dhimmis*] while they are within Muslim lands, whether or not by settling with them for a substitute. It is a well-supported opinion that this is lawful.

The *jizya* is obligatory for mature and sane people; it is not to be taken from preadolescent children, from the mentally disturbed, or from women. But it is the opinion of most jurists that the *jizya* can be taken from old men, from the blind, and [from] the disabled who are unable to move. As for slaves, there is a difference of opinion [regarding the *jizya*], but the majority of the jurists maintain that the *jizya* is taken from the master on the slave's behalf. They also maintain that it should be extracted from the poor as well as from the distressed; and if they do not have it they are to be given a reprieve until they obtain it, even if it is done by begging.

It is maintained by most jurists that the *jizya* is not a fixed amount but the Imam, peace be upon him, or his deputy impose whatever they deem best. It is permissible for the jizya to be levied on their person or on their land—to determine, for example, how much they should pay for any *jarib* [acre] of land. There is a difference of opinion regarding whether or not the *jizya* can be levied on both. A tradition has come down that this is not permissible, and this [view] is more prudent. It is lawful to subject them [the *dhimmis*] to different rates of taxation

---

Risala-yi Sawa'iq al-Yahud [The Treatise Lightning Bolts against the Jews]; English translation by V. B. Moreen in *Die Welt des Islams* 32 (1992): 187–93.

as His Excellency Ali, The Commander of the Faithful, settled [a *jizya*] of twelve *dirhams* on the rich (which, in the reckoning of those days, was almost equal to five *ashrafis*).

In the realization of the state of *dhimma* [protection] it is necessary that they [the *dhimmis*] should accept the *jizya* and not perpetrate deeds that are opposed to [the state of] security, such as waging war against Muslims, or aiding infidels in their war against Muslims. And some [of the jurists] said that they should commit themselves to the laws of the Muslims, and that they should not reject anything decreed upon them by a Muslim ruler in accordance with the shari'a. And they [also] said that it is appropriate for the Muslim ruler to impose upon them seven conditions: First, that they should not fornicate with Muslim women, nor assault their [Muslims'] children; second, that they should not marry Muslim women; third, that they should not tempt Muslims to turn away from their religion; fourth, that they should not rob Muslims; fifth, that they should not harbor the spies of infidels; sixth, that they should not help infidels attain victory over Muslims nor inform them about the state/conditions of the Muslims; seventh, that they should not kill Muslim men, women, and children. If these seven conditions have been stipulated, and they violate them, then they forfeit protection. But if the conditions have not been stipulated [and they commit any of the above acts], they will be punished in accordance with the *shari'a* of Islam, but they do not forfeit protection. Most of the *ulama* maintain that they should not perpetrate anything that would be to the detriment of the religion of Islam, such as maligning the Supreme God or His Excellency, the Prophet, or one of the innocent imams, may God's prayers be upon them, and that this should [also] be a condition imposed upon them. And if they violate it they forfeit protection. And if, God forbid, they insult God, the Prophet or the imams, peace be upon them, whoever [from among the Muslims] hears [such an insult] from the *dhimmis* must kill [them] if no harm results from it.

The following are [also] among the things that they [the *dhimmis*] must be prevented from, and provided that they are stipulated, if they violate them they forfeit protection, but if they are not stipulated they do not forfeit protection. First, that they should not openly publicize those things which are prohibited by the *shari'a* but are permitted to them and there is not harm from them to the Muslims such as wine, eating pork, contracting marriages with close family members, etc.; second, that they should not erect churches, temples or places of fire worship in the lands of Islam, but if they [already] have some, and these are in need of repair, they may repair them. If they are ruined entirely there is a difference of opinion regarding whether or not they may rebuild them in the same place; third, that they should not read out very loudly from their [holy] books, nor ring any bells (and some say that they may ring them softly so that Muslims would not hear them); fourth, that they may not build their own homes higher than the houses of their Muslim neighbors (or their part of the house), nor higher than those of the Muslims dwelling in other parts of the same house (and some say that they may not build them of the same height with them either but that they must be lower); fifth, most of the *ulama* believe that it is appropriate that the ruler of the Muslims imposed upon them clothing that would distinguish them from Muslims so that they would not resemble Muslims (It is customary for Jews to wear yellow clothes while Christians wear black and dark blue ones. Christians [also] wear a girdle on their waists, and Jews sew a piece of silk of a different color on the front part of their clothes. And some [jurists] say that they should be recognizable by their wearing different shoes than Muslims, for instance, one of their shoes be of one color and the other of another color, such as one yellow and one red. [And they also say that] they should wear a ring of iron, lead or copper, and that they should tie a bell on their feet at the [public] baths so as to be distinguishable from Muslims. Similarly, their women should be distinguished through their clothing from Muslim women in the manner stated above or by other means.); sixth, that they should not ride upon Arabian steeds, or that they should not ride any horses at all, only mules or asses, and that they should not ride upon saddles, only on pack saddles, with [both] legs on one side, and have no sword, dagger or any [other] weapon with them, nor should they keep any of these within their homes. But foremost of these matters I found no legal basis. However, if the ruler of the Muslims deems it advisable to impose these conditions upon them, thus shall it be.

Some say that they [the *dhimmis*] should not be informed of the amount of the *jizya* so that they should live continuously, in the course of the year, in a state of anxiety and agitation. [They say that] at the time of paying the *jizya* they should stand on the ground in front of him who takes the *jizya*. [The official] should say to him: "Count it!" And he [the payer] should count the money until the Muslims speak up and say that it is enough. And some [also] say that he should lower his head while handing it over, and that he who takes the *jizya* should pull his beard and slap his face at the time of praying. But I have not seen any legal basis for these.

And it is [also] said to be recommended that if Muslims walk with them on the [same] road that they [the *dhimmis*] should not walk in the middle but rather on the side of the road. And, that they should not enter the pool while a Muslim is bathing at the public baths. At meetings, they should not be seated high[er than Muslims], nor should Muslims greet them first. And, if they greet them, Muslims should answer [only] with "Alayka." ['Upon you!'] Muslims should not associate with them, neither should they enter into sleeping partnership with them. It is also incumbent upon Muslims that they should not accept from them victuals with which they had come into contact, such as distillates [and oils], which cannot be purified. If something can be purified, such as clothes, if they are dry, they can be accepted, they are clean. But if they [the *dhimmis*] had come into contact with those cloths in moisture they should be rinsed with water after being obtained. As for hide, or that which has been made of hide such as shoes and boots, and meat, whose religious cleanliness and lawfulness are conditional on the animal's being slaughtered [according to the *shari'a*], these may not be taken from them. Similarly, liquids that have been preserved in skins, such as oils, grape syrup, [fruit] juices, myrobalan, and the like, if they have been put in skin containers or water skins, these should [also] not be accepted from them. Other infidels, such as the Hindus and others, have such laws in common with them [the *dhimmis*], but these [infidels] are even worse.

It would also be better if the ruler of the Muslims would establish that all infidels could not move out of their homes on days when it rains or snows because they would make Muslims impure. And if Muslims should hear that they insult or hold a Muslim in contempt, they should prevent and hinder them as well as chastise them. They should never be in position of authority over Muslims. But Muslims should also be urged to show disrespect toward them [the *dhimmis*].

If a litigation breaks out between them and the Muslims, the Muslim judge should judge between them according to the *shari'a*. And, if they have a litigation among themselves, it is held by most jurists that the judge of the Muslims has the choice to settle [the case] himself according to Islamic law or entrust it to their own judges. But it is better if he judges [the case] himself.

And God favors the good and the just.
Praise be to God, First and Last.
May God's prayer be upon Muhammad and upon his Pure Family.

Eleventh-Century Andalusian Authors on the Jews of Granada

Moshe Perlmann

It is the purpose of the present study to survey the literary expressions of attitudes toward Jews and Judaism that came down from eleventh-century Islamic Spain.

For the first time the Muslim West stepped into the domain of polemics which by then was well developed in the East. Moreover the polemics here are not merely theological, literary, bookish, but are related to public affairs, political conditions, social attitudes and resentments, and are centered on the personages of the two Nagids, Samuel and Joseph.[1] Pertinent material has been preserved in both prose and verse.

The extraordinary careers of Samuel Nagdela and his son Joseph, who for decades virtually conducted the affairs of the Kingdom of Granada and employed many Jews in government posts, enabled their adversaries to fan the hatred against Jews in general.[2] The high standard of life of the bulk of the urban Jews, and their conspicuous role in public life, made them convenient targets for attacks in a society which clung strongly to the view that the infidel should not meddle in affairs of the true believers, and should be kept in his proper place—outside the pale, in humbleness and humiliation (sighâr, ḏull).[3]

But apart from the aggravating role of the Nagids, the intermingling of Christians, Muslims, Jews, Berbers, Arabs, and Spaniards, led to various discussions on religions, and even on religion in general: natural law vs. revelation, etc.[4] Taking an active part in the intellectual life of Spanish Muslim society, Jewish intellectuals participated in such inquiries.

Ibn Hazm (384–456/994–1064),[5] the great savant, theologian, and man of letters, dealt with the subject of Jews and Judaism in three works. He produced an exposure of Jewish and Christian falsifications in the Torah and the Gospels, *Izhâr tabdîl alyahûd wa-n-nasārā li-t-taurāt wa-l-injîl.* This book, not known as a separate work at present, was incorporated into the magnum opus of the author, *K. al-Fisal* [or: *al-fasl*] *fî-l-milal wa-l-ahwā' wa-n-nihal.*[6] Planned as a system of dogmatic theology, the Book of Studies [or: Decision] about Religions, Opinions and Sects, proceeds as an analysis of various groups: skeptics, atheists, deists, polytheists, unitarians without a belief in revelation, non-Muslim unitarian believers in revelation, Muslim sectarians. Thereupon Ibn Hazm is able to offer his own construction as the one apt to save the believers. As he incorporated some earlier polemic treatises, the book grew in size, lost in symmetry, and became to a great extent a history of religions and sects.

The refutation of Jewish and Christian scriptures, originally a few pages in length (vol. 1, pp. 98–116), grew with the incorporation of the earlier *Izhâr* into a sizable volume (vol. 1, pp. 116–224, vol. 2, pp. 2–91). As *Fisal* was written in 418–422/1027–1030, the treatise *Izhâr* must have been written still earlier, before Ibn Hazm reached the age of thirty. In *Fisal*, Ibn Hazm refers to his disputes with Samuel b. Nagdela (pp. 135, 152ff), whom he calls Ismael (p. 135), by which name he was known among Muslims. Samuel was to him "the most learned and most skilled in disputations" (*a'lamuhum wa-ajdaluhum*) among Jews.[7] One discussion with him took place in 404/1013, that is, when both Samuel and Ibn Hazm were quite young. Samuel is mentioned as *Kātib* but *Izhâr* (if it contained the passage) and *Fisal* could refer only to the earlier stage in Samuel's career.

Even later, Ibn Hazm felt compelled to resume his polemics against Judaism, and this time directly against Samuel, for he heard that the latter had written a pamphlet against the claim of the Qur'an to divine origin.[8]

Thus, at present, of three works by Ibn Hazm which discussed Judaism, we still have two: *Fisal* and the pamphlet *Radd*, Refutation (or *Risāla,* Epistle).

In *Fisal* we have a unique document: its section on Judaism is the only extensive work written by a Muslim author on the subject; it is the only work of anti-Jewish polemics written by one of the great minds of Islam. A piece of theological writing, it narrows down to textual criticism of Jewish scriptures. But the ingenious notes soon raise historical problems of higher criticism and matters of principle regarding the Muslim attitude toward Judaeo-Christian scriptures. The book is written for Muslims, to refute the Jews and the Muslim's reverence for Jewish scriptures, not to persuade the Jews.[9]

From *Proceedings of the American Academy of Jewish Research* 18 (1948–49): 843–61.

The author quotes threescore passages which are analyzed in detail. In case of doubt in translation or interpretation he withholds judgment.[10]

He dwells mostly on the Pentateuch (pp. 117–204), especially on Genesis (pp. 117–53), picks a few passages from other biblical books (pp. 204–16) and from post-biblical literature (pp. 216–24). He shows a good knowledge of the Pentateuch in Arabic, but less satisfactory knowledge of the other writings criticized.[11]

He states he knew Christianity before studying the Jewish scriptures (p. 116). He had many contacts with Jews, and the book still echoes the disputes he had with Jewish scholars. We mentioned two references to Samuel b. Nagdela. Possibly some of the other disputes also involved the Nagid. However, in all the other cases no name is recorded.[12] His impression of the Jewish disputants is unfavorable: he thought they were trying to explain away difficulties with tricks and lies.[13] "It has happened to us so often in our disputes with their savants. . . . They are prone to lie . . . whenever they want to wiggle out of difficulty in a dispute"; a contemptible trait.[14] The author enjoys thoroughly the confusion, helplessness, defeat of his adversaries when pressed by his unrelenting critique.[15]

Another echo of the disputes is that he anticipates possible objections based on Qur'an passages not unlike the biblical passages under fire. Sometimes he merely admires the superiority of the Qur'an version of the biblical stories.[16]

The analysis of the biblical passages quoted persuades him that the biblical writings cannot be considered divinely inspired, nor can the claim of their ancient origin be maintained.

They abound in inconsistencies and contradictions inconceivable in God's words.[17] Ibn Hazm is on the alert for inaccuracy in numbers, figures: divine data would be free from such mistakes. "I have never seen anybody more ignorant of arithmetic than the person who compiled the Torah for the Jews."[18] The scriptures are found wanting also in matters of geography[19] and history.[20]

The contents of many biblical stories are so shocking, immoral, and coarse that the revolted reader will reject the scriptures. The scriptures want us to believe that Abraham doubted God's word, Sarah lied to God, the daughters of the prophet Lot conceived by their father, Isaac and Esau were cheated by Jacob who in turn was cheated by Laban; Israel fought divine force; the chastity of the family life of the prophet Jacob was violated by outsiders as well as by his own children; the lineage of kings and prophets begins with incest and fornication; Moses doubted God's might.[21]

These stories are marked by crass anthropomorphism,[22] plurality in the concept of deity (*shirk*), and characterizations of God and his prophets as weak, helpless.[23]

The scriptures of the Jews, then, are mere forgeries, distortions.[24] The Muslim attitude toward the scriptures

should be one of absolute rejection. The Muslim accepts only the Qur'an, and only from the Qur'an he knows of previous revelations, among them one called Torah and one called Gospel, but he finds that the Torah of the Jews at best presents a text that has been tampered with extensively and has no validity.

Some Muslims ignorantly reject this concept of forgery (*tahrîf*) and believe in the transmission of the scriptures (*tawātur*). Yet even the Qur'an teaches that *tahrîf* has taken place. This weakness of accepting the opinions of the Jews (about their scriptures) may lead to further acceptance of their claims and traditions. Can a Muslim use scriptural arguments? Only a few passages have been left, since they escaped the attention of the Jews, no doubt by Allah's grace, so as to serve as evidence against the Jews (*hujja*).[25] Such are the few *a'lâm*, predictions of Muhammad's advent.[26] Thus, beginning with total rejection of scriptural texts, our author ends with accepting some evidence of the texts,—an old contradiction of Muslim authors.[27]

Ibn Hazm is quick to point out cases supporting the theory of abrogation (*naskh*) by divine will of one revealed precept by another. He is quite a dialectician in this matter: God gives life, and takes it (and grants revival); a dynasty's power is transferred into the hands of humble subjects; converted enemies become part and parcel of the religious community. Transgression against the Sabbath would make forbidden violence against sinners obligatory. "Precepts are commands to perform certain acts for a definite period, and when the period is over the command may turn into its opposite."[28]

The text of the LXX differs considerably from the masoretic text. It appears from a detailed analysis of biblical history that ancient Israel did not know the Torah, did not observe and preserve it, but rather did everything to make it extinct. Only the high priest in Jerusalem was in possession of a copy which he used three times a year. The Northern Kingdom was cut off from Jerusalem altogether but even in the Kingdom of Judah matters were hardly any better than in the north; nor were the priests faithful. This clearly demonstrates (p. 199: *adwa'u mina-sh-shams*) that there was no reliable transmission, and that consequently falsification was possible. Only Deuteronomy 32:1–43 was a passage the Hebrews were enjoined to memorize. But it is an objectionable passage as it stands in the present text.[29] The oldest Jewish tradition goes back no further than the days of Hillel and Shammai, Simeon (the Just?) and Mar Akiba (vol. 2 p. 83). Not so the Muslim tradition: close to us, it can be traced back in detail and verified by trustworthy witnesses [vol. 1, p. 115; vol. 2, p. 82]. In Islam tradition goes back to divinely inspired evidence; whilst the Jews cannot bring evidence from anybody in direct and immediate contact with a prophet (vol. 2, pp. 7ff.; vol. 2, p. 84).

Who then produced the present text? Who was the forger? He must have been a liar, a contemptible character, either an ignorant ass or a conscious, purposeful, malicious, archmisleader; nay, he must have been a coarse atheist, scoffing and mocking at any belief or religious feeling, who viciously mixed truth and falsehood to the detriment of future generations.[30]

The forger arose at a late date, in the days of the second commonwealth, in an age when there were no more prophets, and the sages were succeeding in implanting prayers and bookish study in the people.[31]

Ibn Hazm writes about this author-forger mostly *without* naming him. But in a few passages he names him definitely: Ezra, the Aaronid scribe who flourished sometime before the second destruction.[32] From his memory he put together the pieces of old tradition, filling up the lacunae. This took place about forty years after the seventy-year captivity. Actually only under the Hasmoneans did the Torah spread and thus, four hundred years after the destruction of the ancient kingdom, a new religion (*sharī'a jabdīda*) arose, the work of the sages (*ahbār*).

The survey of the biblical writings outside the Pentateuch is brief, sketchy, and abounds in mistakes. Here one does not have the impression of study and real knowledge of the text. Perhaps Ibn Hazm used a set of excerpts supplied to him?[33]

The still-shorter section on Talmudic material was of course based on such a set of excerpts.[34] It assaults aggadic material, exposing its anthropomorphism. Biblical passages appear here, evidently as a result of confusion of biblical and postbiblical material.[35] The stories remind the author of old wives' tales.[36] On such absurdities, and on their authors, the Jews base their religion. These authors were as bad at computations as the Bible forger. The Talmud was also compiled by atheists (*mulhidūn lā dīna lahum*). They bribed Paul and sent him to mislead the early Christians by teaching them to believe in Jesus's divinity.[37] Now the Christians must have been, in the opinion of the rabbis, either right or wrong; if they were right—why did the rabbis want to mislead them? If they were wrong why did the rabbis want to deepen this error instead of putting matters straight? The Jews possibly wanted to corrupt Islam in the same way by fomenting schism by the propaganda of 'Abdallah b. Sabā'.[38]

Ibn Hazm works himself up to fever heat over the legends about R. Ismael meeting the Shekhina mourning the destruction of the Temple. The Jews, "that is the Rabbanites amongst them," glorify Metatron, the Little Lord (*ar-rabb as-saghīr*), on the Day of Atonement.[39]

This last passage might make us think of a Karaite source. Ibn Hazm mentions Ananites in Toledo and Talavera (p. 99): they accept only what the prophets enjoined, repudiating the rabbis and their inventions. But it might well have been a Christian source that made use of some anti-Rabbanite material.[40] Indeed, he may have used some such excerpts even in the section on the Pentateuch, though there is no question as to his sound reading of that book, exceptional for a Muslim author.

Ibn Hazm, known for his vehemence, is blunt in these pages. Dirty, vile, filthy, stinking are epithets he frequently hurls against the Jews.[41] Everyone who knows them, he contends, recognizes that they are the filthiest people, a villainous breed, false, mean and cowardly (p. 202). Psalm 103:15–16 ("his days are as grass, as a flower of the field") shows an atheist materialist concept, he says, "and indeed the religion of the Jews tends strongly towards that, for there is not in their Torah any mention of the next world, or of reward after death. . . . They combine materialism, plurality in deity, anthropomorphism, and every stupidity in the world."

He judges not by chapter and verse only but by the qualities he ascribes to the Jewish people.

Jacob filched the blessing assigned to Esau: "By God, it is the way of the Jews. You will not find among them, with rare exceptions, but a treacherous villain" (*al-khabīti al-mukhādi'*, p. 138).

"They, both the ancient and the modern, are altogether the worst liars. Though I have encountered many of them, I have never seen among them a truth seeker, except two men only" (p. 156).[42]

"They are the filthiest and vilest of peoples, their unbelief horrid, their ignorance abominable" (p. 154). Among minds, theirs are like the odor of garlic among odors (p. 180).

What a people, what a lineage! Abraham marries his own sister. Isaac is a thief. Jacob married Leah in error. Reuben fornicates with his father's wife, Judah with his son's. (A slip: Joshua and Rahab.) Amram married his aunt, which is against the law, and Moses was born from this union. David commits the crime against Uriah. Absalom defiles his father's wives.[43]

Let them persist in their vain hopes for a glorious future; hopes that are the stock-in-trade of fools (p. 138). Sometimes their leaders perceive the truth but will be stubborn against reason in blind fidelity to their ancestors (*taqlīd al-aslāf*), and group feeling (*'asabīya*), and the desire to perpetuate their worldly position (p. 116: *istidāmatan li-ri'āsa dunyawīya*).[44]

Ibn Hazm returned to this subject in the refutation of a pamphlet by Samuel ibn Nagdela that contained notes critical of the Qur'an. He had heard of the pamphlet but was unable to obtain a copy. Instead he found a refutation of it written by a Muslim, and having learned from it the arguments of Samuel, he set out to refute them with all the knowledge and skill he could muster.[45]

The refutation consists of an introduction, eight chapters, epilogue and conclusion. Each of the eight chapters refutes an argument of Samuel's: the latter is reproduced, followed by deprecatory remarks and a logical rejoinder. In a counterblast, the reader is also introduced to a weak spot in the Bible, to show that it contains passages far more damning than the Qur'an passages to which Samuel has raised objections. The epilogue lists Jewish errors and sacrileges.

Thus the pattern used in *Fisal* appears here in reverse:

first comes the defense of the Qur'an, then follows the critique of a Bible passage. Again we find theological material, or rather critique and countercritique of passages of sacred texts of Jew and Muslim.

The real difference between the two works (apart from size) is the specific tone of the introduction and the conclusion of the pamphlet. Here Ibn Hazm attacks the Jews, especially Samuel, for their domination of the country, the state, and its resources. But even more bitter, perhaps, is his feeling against the ruler or rulers who allowed matters to reach such a stage. Muslim kings, absorbed in worldly matters, neglect their faith; building castles, enjoying pleasures; greed makes them neglect even the defense of the believers against infidels. The Jews, devoid of power, use fraud, hypocrisy, false submissiveness to work their way into high society, and know how to conceal their hatred for the Prophet and his community. In his impudence Samuel even dared to write against the Qur'an. Of him one might say with Mutanabbi:

> If nobly you act towards a noble man, you gain
>   his fealty;
> But if nobly you act toward a villain, he will
>   rebel.
> To greatness, generosity in place of the sword
>   is as harmful
> As the use of the sword in the place of generosity.

Oh, God, we complain to Thee for the rulers of our faith absorbed in worldly affairs neglect the observance of their religion; absorbed in erecting castles—may they soon abandon these—they do not cultivate their sacred faith which accompanies them in the life to come, in their abode eternal; absorbed in piling up riches—sometimes with results fatal to their own lives, and helpful to their enemies—they are deflected from their faith and people which gave them strength in their earthly life, and can secure to them life eternal. Non-Muslims become arrogant, and infidels wag their tongues. If the powers temporal looked into this matter they would be even more perturbed by it than we are. For they will share with us whatever may befall the community as a result of angry zeal for the glorious religion in defense of the exalted faith. Moreover, they will be particularly affected by what this state of their corrupt policy and troublesome leadership may result in. . . .

. . . A man who was filled with hatred towards the Apostle—a man who is, in secret, a materialist, a free-thinker, a Jew—of that most contemptible of religions, the most vile of faiths . . . loosened his tongue . . . and became conceited in his vile soul, as a result of his wealth. His riches, his gold and his silver robbed him of his wretched senses; so he compiled a book in which he set out to demonstrate

the alleged contradictions in the Word of God, the Koran. . . . When I came to know of the affair, of the work of that accursed creature, I did not cease searching for that filthy book, so that, with the gift bestowed upon me by Allah, I might be of service by helping His faith with words and insight, and in defending His community with eloquence and knowledge. I was fortunate, and obtained a manuscript containing a refutation written by a Muslim. So I copied out the passages the polemist had reproduced from the work of that ignominious ignoramus. I proceeded at once, with God's help, to refute his evil thoughts. By God, his argumentation proves how poor is his knowledge, how narrow his mind, about which I already knew something. For I used to know him when he was naked, except for charlatanry, serene, except for anxiety, void except of lies.[45a]

Toward the end there is another stab at the ruler.

It is my firm hope that God will treat those who befriend the Jews and take them into their confidence as He treated the Jews themselves . . . (Koran injunctions against Jews and Christians). For whosoever amongst Muslim princes has listened to all this and still continues to befriend the Jews, holding intercourse with them, well deserves to be overtaken by the same humiliation and to suffer in this world the same griefs which God has meted out to the Jews, apart from their chastisement in the next world. Whosoever acts in this manner will be recompensed by suffering along with the Jews themselves, according to God's warning in their Torah, in the Fifth Book (Deut. 28:15–58, quoted in full). . . . On their own evidence, this is God's message, and the chastisement He has apportioned them. . . . Then let any prince upon whom God has bestowed some of His bounty take heed. . . . Let him get away from this filthy, stinking, dirty crew beset with God's anger and malediction, with humiliation and wretchedness, misfortune, filth and dirt, as no other people has ever been. Let him know that the garments in which God has enwrapped them are more obnoxious than war, and more contagious than elephantiasis. May God keep us from rebelling against Him and His decision, from honouring those whom He has humiliated, by raising up those whom He has cast down.

The arguments of the Jew are futile, his reasoning poor. And his is the leader ('amīd) of the Jews, their great man, their scholar. If he at least knew Arabic! He asks why the Qur'an ascribes healing power to honey (16:71) since those who are fevered, or whose bile is inflamed are made worse by honey. Does God say that *all* diseases are cured by honey? Not at all. The text says very clearly: some people. Such a statement is true. He might have remembered that a biblical prophet (vol. 2 Kings 20:7) performed cures with honey; and in that hodge-podge (*ikhtilāt*) which the Jews call the Torah, the highest praise given to Palestine is that it flows with milk and honey.

The epilogue lists biblical (and a few Talmudic) passages, illustrative of anthropomorphism, contradictions, the coarseness and stupidity of the Jewish scriptures. The Jews were promised a land of their own but find themselves under Muslim yoke. Their exilarchs are bastards, and so were their kings and Moses, all begotten in unions unlawful under their own law. A short review explains how the Torah was compiled by Ezra.

The theological scriptural section is thus sandwiched between attacks on Granada's ruler and his Jewish minister. The ruler is threatened with the people's discontent and Allah's wrath, while Samuel is denounced as a man blinded by wealth, arrogant, devoid of "the slightest knowledge of human nature, with no understanding of the resources of the Arabic language."[45b]

The poetical counterpart of the publicist's motifs in Ibn Hazm's Refutation can be found in the poem by Abu Ishāq al-Elbīrī directed against Joseph b. Samuel.[46] It also threatens the ruler with popular discontent for employing a Jew in high office, and decries Jewish domination of the country. Several sources ascribe to the poem a role almost decisive in bringing about the outbreak of 1066 which put an end to the forty years of administration of Samuel and Joseph, and in which Joseph was killed among three thousand other Jewish victims. Yet recently discovered memoirs of the king of Granada who ruled in 1077–1090 after Bādīs, the master of the Nagids, give an authoritative picture of political relations and intrigue in Granada, without mentioning Elbīrī or his poem.[47] The poem was probably used in instigation, but was only a contributory factor in undermining Joseph's position and in whipping emotions against the Jews into a frenzy.[48]

The poem contains forty-seven lines (meter: *mutaqārib*), is marked by concreteness of images, virulence, and forceful simplicity of expression, well fit to impress the Berber soldiery which could not be expected to appreciate the usual elaborate poetic idiom.

A sincere friend of the Sinhāja Berbers, the poet offers them advice. Here, too, from the very outset, responsibility for the evil of Jewish domination is placed squarely on the ruler.

> Your lord has sadly erred
> And his foes are rejoicing
> He selected an infidel to be his Kātib
> Who, if your lord wished, could have been a
>   believer . . . .
> It was not even of their own (the Jews') making
> For from our midst arises the accomplice.[49]

The king is also addressed directly; how could he, shrewd man that he is, overlook the evil while all over the land people deplore the rise to power of the bastard upstarts. This makes the prince unpopular. Appointing the Jew is also against the word of Allah. There is an undertone of intimidation and threat:

> The earth trembles from their (the Jews')
>   immorality
> And is almost heaving under us all.
> Noble and glorious ruler, he is urged to act,
>   and is reminded: You are responsible for
>   what they are doing.[50]

A plan of action is drafted, again both for the people and the prince. The Jews must be swept back into their proper place.

> Bring them down to their place
> Return them to the most abject station.
> They used to roam around us in their tatters
> Covered with contempt, humiliation, and scorn.[51]
> They used to rummage amongst the dungheaps
>   for a bit of filthy rag
> To serve as a shroud for a man to be buried in.[52]

In those good old days, the low-race (*hijna*) infidels were not accepted in society. An end must be put to the present situation when

> Many a pious Muslim is in awe of the vilest
>   infidel ape.
> The poet who knew that the Jews ("dogs")
>   were held in contempt everywhere was
>   overwhelmed by the situation he found in
>   Granada. He turns away from the prince. He
>   addresses the mob comparing their lot with
>   that of the Jews.

> They divided up Granada, capital and provinces
> And everywhere there is one of those accursed
> They seize Granada's revenues
> Biting into and crunching them.
> They dress in exquisite garments
> Whilst you the basest wear.

Let the people hear what the prince, specifically, is urged to do. He should remember that the Jewish minister has become as rich as the prince himself, and

> Therefore, haste to slaughter him as sacrifice
> And offer him, fat ram that he is.
> The family should not be spared either: They
>   all have treasures concealed.

These should be confiscated, the prince being more entitled than the Jews to all this wealth.

Do not consider that killing them is treachery
Nay, it would be treachery to leave them
scoffing.

The Jews have broken the covenant (i.e., overstepped their station) and compunction would be out of place.[53]

They are in charge of your secrets
But how can the faithless be trusted.

Muslims are poorly fed while the infidels gather at sumptuous feasts. They slaughter animals in the town's market places and the Muslims eat what remains.[54] Above all rises the evil image of the Jewish courtier.

That ape of theirs had his home paved with
marble
And made the purest of springs flow thither.
Our affairs are his charge
And we have to wait at his gate[55]
While he ridicules us and our religion.

Proudly the Jews ride about the city; their prayers rise louder than those of the Muslims.

One of the texts preserving the poem mentions that in his insolence the courtier was emboldened to mock at certain Koran passages and to express openly what is called his atheism *ilhâd* (probably some ironic remarks about matters Islamic).[56]

Elbīrī lived to see the end of "Jewish domination." Ibn Hazm died two years earlier.

Elbīrī used the epithet "ape" (*qird*) profusely when referring to Jews. Such indeed was the parlance. "Swine" described Christians, but sometimes Jews too.[56a]

To the contemporary royal memorialist, Joseph b. Samuel is invariably "the pig" (*khinzīr*). The prince believed that his father had been poisoned by Joseph who through his agents knew of every move in the royal household.[57] Joseph was master over all.[58] "My grandfather aged then considerably . . . and left the affairs of state to the Jew, as his deputy, and the Jew was able to command and forbid at will." There were intrigues against Joseph, and the king was told: "He devours your wealth, has become master over most of your possessions, and erected a palace better than yours. By God, remove him and gain the sympathies of the Muslims by getting rid of him."[59] Apparently, there was an attempt to rise against Joseph when rumor spread that he had had the crown prince poisoned. Feelings ran high and his life was in danger "This was the foreboding of his destruction."[60] Aware of the intrigue against him, Joseph allegedly said:

Our scoffing at the people has been for the sake of
the sultan's glory. We have believed ourselves safe

from them under his protection. Yet now there is no more hope: no sultan to grant us safety, while a vile rival is plotting against us at the court and the populace seeks our destruction. And we are few and weak upon the earth.[61]

Rumor had it that Joseph was plotting with a neighboring ruler in the hope of establishing a Jewish principality. "He betrayed us." A drunkard's shouting in this strain mobilized the mob, resentful of the unprecedented elevation of Jews in office.[62]

There were also laudatory poems honoring the Nagids. In rhymed prose a Muslim says "I profess the religion of the Sabbath openly when I am with you, and in secret when I am with my own people." This seems to be an exceptional case.[63] For that matter the Muslim sources recognize the high attainments of the Nagids, mention Joseph's wide intellectual interests, his excellent Islamic library, etc. Still the main point remains: the Nagids, infidels, ruled over Muslims. Joseph "did not know the humbleness of the *dimmī* or the filth of Jewishness."[64]

It seems that the feeling pervading all the utterances of the Muslim authors was one of resentment at the sight of temporary suspension of *dull*, humiliation, through the rise of the Jewish courtiers.[64a] It is also instructive that Jewish authors felt most bitter on this point. In the twelfth century Yehuda HaLevi wrote in defense of the *dīn dalīl*, the humbled faith; Abraham b. Daud writes on the exalted faith (opposite of humbled).[65] Maimonides writes: "And you, my brethren, now that on account of our many sins, God hurled us amidst this nation of hostile Ishmael. . . . Never has a nation arisen more injurious to us than this people; no nation has ever been so intent on humiliating and degrading us, and on hating us. That is why when David, King of Israel, was shown in an inspired vision all the tribulations which were to overwhelm Israel, he did not cry out, or ask for help for our people, until he saw what we were to suffer in the Kingdom of Ishmael; and then he exclaimed (Psalm CXX 5). 'Woe is me that I sojourn in Mesech, that I dwell in the tents of Kedar!'. . . Daniel also described our humiliation solely under Ishmael—may God crush him soon! (Daniel VIII). . . . We have to bear the humiliations they impose upon us, and their calumnies which are beyond human endurance. As the prophet says (Psalm XXXVIII 14): 'But I am as a deaf man, I hear not; and I am as a dumb man, that openeth not his mouth.'"[66]

NOTES

1. In this respect the Spanish discussions of the eleventh century are reminiscent of anti-Christian writings in Mamluk Egypt with their protest against the

employment of unbelievers as scribes in governmental offices. Cf. BSOS 1942, p. 843 sq. *History of the Jews in Egypt and Syria under Mamluk Rule* (Jerusalem: 1944), pp. 336–39.

2. Cf. the articles of Ch. Schirmann in *Kirjath Sepher* 13 (1936); *Zion* 1, no. 2 (1937); *Moznaim* (1939), pp. 48–58, and I. F. Baer, *A History of the Jews in Christian Spain* (Tel Aviv: 1945), pp. 26–29. These use the source mentioned in n. 47.

3. A. S. Tritton, *The Caliphs and Their Non-Muslim Subjects* L. 1930; G. von Grunebaum, *Medieval Islam* (Chicago: 1946), p. 177ff.

4. M. Asín Palacios in *Cultura Española*. 1907; id., *Abenházam de Córdoba*, v. II (Madrid: 1928).

5. C. van Arendonk in the *Enc. Of Islam*; Brockelmann *G A L*, Suppl I, 692 ff. A. R. Nykl, *Hispano-Arabic Poetry* (Baltimore: 1946), pp. 73–103.

6. Ed. Cairo 1317–1321, H., 5 volumes.—Unless otherwise stated quotations are from vol. I. Tr. In vv. II–V *of Abenházam* by M. Asín Palacios, 1928–32.— Goldziher surveyed *Milal* literature in ZDMG 65, pp. 349 ff. The relation between *Fisal* in its present form and earlier works of its author has been discussed by Steinschneider, Goldziher, and foremostly I. Friedlaender, *Zur Komposition von Ibn Hazm's Milal wa'n-Nihal in Orientalische Studien Th. Nöldeke . . . gewidmet* (Giezen: 1906) vol. 1, pp. 267–81. In 1359 H. (1940) Sā'īd al-Afghānī published in Damascus a volume, *Ibn Hazm al-andalusī wa-risāla fi-l-mufādala bayna-s-sahāba.* Here pp. 169–280 contain the text of a treatise which appears as part of *Fisal* (vol. 4, pp. 111–53). H. Hirschfeld wrote on Ibn Hazm's Bible criticism in J.Q.R. v. 13, pp. 222 ff; M. Schreiner in *Semitic Studies in Memory of A. Kohut* (Berlin: 1897), pp. 495–513; and ZDMG 42, p. 612 ff. Cf. nn. 11, 17, 34, and E. Strauss, *Memorial Volume* (Jerusalem: 1946), pp. 182–97. The reading *Fisal* in the title is supported by L. Gardet and M. M. Anawati, *Introduction à la théologie musulmane* (Paris: 1948), p. 147 n. 2.

7. The contemporary Ibn Sā'id al-Andalusī wrote in *K. Tabaqāt al-umam*, ed. Cheikho (Beirut: 1912), p. 90. (Tr. R. Blachère, P. 1935, p. 160; cf. J. Finkel in J.Q.R. NS 18, pp. 45 ff): "More than any Spanish Jew before him, he was learned in the law of the Jews and understood how to prevail in disputes on its behalf and to rebut its opponents (*'ilm bi-sharī'a . . . wa-l-ma'rifa bi-l-intisār lahā wa-ḏ-ḏabb 'anhā . . .*).

8. See note 45.

9. 155, 209, 224 end.

10. 117, 121, 144 end; 151; 165.

11. E. Algermissen, *Die Pentateuchzitate Ibn Hazms* (Münster thesis), 1933.

12. 141, 142 [Arabic, *Usar Allah*; Hebrew, *Yisrael*] 156, 174 top; 207f. 205: Jos. 5: 2–3 versus Gen. 17:14, circumcision neglected in the desert; Jew: on account of desert conditions; Ibn Hazm: (a) The Israelites stayed over lengthy periods at certain stations in their wander-

ings, and (b) it was not any easier to perform circumcision on the eve of the battles for the conquest of Palestine.—The Jewish argument goes back to Yeb. 71b: Aramaic: "*meshum hulsha de-orha*" (because of weakness due to travel).

13. 174; 208: a shameless person will not find it difficult to turn around any word to his own contentment, without any proof. But reinterpreting the text (*wasf al-kalām 'an maudi'ihi wa = ma'nāhu ilā ma'nan ākhar*) is permissible only if a true proof has been presented of admitted linguistic usage.

14. 213. *Fa-l-qaum lā mu'nata 'alayhim mina-l-ki ḏb . . . iḏā tama'ū bi-t-takhallus min majlisihim lā yakūn ḏālika illā bi-l-kiḏb.*

15. 174, 205, 223: When a Jew suggested that Metatron is the name of an angel, the author retorted: (a) Why then does Metatron mourn and moan over the destruction of the Temple in the first person; (b) Why does he regret the Lord's deed?

16. The four rivers of Eden in Genesis are an absurd concoction. The Qur'an also refers to rivers, but those are *celestial* streams. (119) 129, 131, 138, 155, 160, 161 ff, 182 f.

17. 121(Gen. 4:2 and 4:20: 6:3 and the figures of longevity of numerous personages of the biblical story). 143, 144, 156 (If Moses had turned the waters of Egypt into blood, where did the Egyptians get water to show that they too could turn it into blood), 158, 160 (Exod. 16:31 and Num. 11:7–8) 161 end (Deut. 4:12 and ex. ch. 24) 168 f. (Ex. 16:31 and Num. 11:7–8) 161 end (Deut. 4:12 and Ex. ch. 24) 168 f (Ex. 6, Num. 1:3) 178 (the writer of such absurdities—on the numbers of Aaronids, Jos. 21—deserves scourging, chains, branding), 182. I. Di Matteo, *Le pretese contraddizioni della S. Scrittura secondo Ibn Hazm,* in *Bessarione* 27 (1923): 77–127.

18. 150. Similarly 151, 179, 184. Demonstrations: 121, 122 f. Methuselah, 124 Noah, 124 end 158 (Israel in Egypt), 144 (Joseph's place among his brethren) 149 f., (Jacob's house entering Egypt), 151 (data from Judges and I Kings):165 (number of Israelites). 166–75: A dissertation on geographical impossibility of the large number of Israelites in antiquity and of the number of cities Jos. 15–19. This is followed by the argument of economic impossibility 176–77. The pages 166–77 foreshadow Ibn-Khaldūn's exposition in the opening of the *Muqaddima.* 178, 179 (from desert to Kingdom), 184 (length of Moses' life).

19. 118 Rivers in Eden.

20. 128 Israel never reached the Euphrates—(on Gen. 15:18); 136 Jacob has served Esau, despite Gen. 25, 23; 152 f. on Gen. 49:10: The scepter did depart from Jacob and, except for Zerubabel's days, was never regained. In 404 H. Samuel Nagrela pointed during a discussion to the exilarchs in the East as Jewish rulers (*wa-hiya qiyāda wa-mulk wa-riyāsa*). "But I said that was wrong inasmuch as the exilarch's command would not be carried out with regard to anybody, Jew or non-Jew. It is merely

a title without substance." The Jews were ruled after their return from exile not by the House of David but by Aaronids. Ibn Hazm knows of the Agrippas of the House of Herod (Asín, *Abenhazam* vol. 2, p. 292 misunderstood this reference) and refers to ancient authors describing them as non-Jews (*min ar-rūm*).—143 Cf. Goldziher, REJ, v. 8, 121 ff.

21. 129 on Gen. 15:7–8, 130 f. on Gen. 18 (Abraham addresses the three guests in singular; prostrated before men? . . . or else, if he knew these were angels, why the food; meat and dairy dishes offered simultaneously). 132 (Sarah). 133 on Gen. 18–19 (Lot and his daughters). 137 on Gen. 27 (Esau). 140 on Gen. 29 (Laban; 141 the marriages of Jacob violate the law against marrying two sisters). 142 on Gen. 32 (Jacob Israel. But if your angels eat and drink, they may fight too). 143 on Gen. 34–35 (Jacob's family). 145 ff. on Gen. 38 (Tamar—Judah; Solomon should spring from such lineage) 181 ff. on Ex. 32 (Aaron's role in the story of the golden calf); 185 on Num. 11 (Why should Moses have doubted that the Lord would provide meat?); Such stories make him shudder: 133 *taqsha'irregular min samā'ihā julūd al-mu'minīn.* Cf. 141, 155.

22. 117 Gen. 1:26; 120 Gen. 3:22; 121 Gen. 6:1–4; 153 Ex. 4:22 (The Christians ascribe one son to God; the Jews claim that they are all God's sons); 159 f. Ex. 15:1–3; 160 end, Ex. 20:22–23; 161 Ex. 24:9–11; 164 f. Ex. 33; 205 Ps. 27, Ps. 82:6, 199–201; 208 Prov. 8:22–31; 209 Is. 66:8–9 (Worse than the Christian tenets concerning the Madonna and her child).

23. 154, 155 end.

24. 144 *mufta'ila, mubaddala*; 158 *muharraf, muftara*; 180 *musta'mala, makdūba.*

25. 203 f., 211, 212. Muslims against tahrīf—215. Remaining sound passages for Muslim use 212, 213, 215. 104: We do not believe in any Torah or Gospel that does not contain a warning of Muhammad's message.

26. 104, 111, 112 In Ps. 72:16 Hebrew: *va-yatzitzu me'ir* = they of the city—min al-Madīna—is an evidence for Islam (207).—Such *a'lām* occur in the ninth-century works of Alī Tabari and Ibn Qutayba: Cf. Brockelmann in *Beitr. Z. Assyr.* III 1898.

27. A century before Ibn Hazm this problem was discussed by Saadia [in *Amānāt,* treatise 3] and Qirqisani (*K. al-Anwār,* ed. Nemoy II, [New York: 1940], p. 292 sq.; I. Friedländer in *Zeitschr. F. Assyr.,* v. 26, 93–110). In comparison with earlier authors Ibn Hazm is neither consistent nor original in his exposition. Goldziher's different impression ZDMG 32, pp. 363 ff. is based on comparison with *later* authors, and is due to the fact that at the time when he wrote (1878) earlier polemics were unknown.

28. 100 . . . *Ash-sharāi' innamā hiya awāmir fī waqt mahdūd bi-'amal mahdūd. Fa-idā kharaja dālika-l-waqt 'āda dālika-l-amr manhiyan 'anhu.* 101 Case of *badā* sudden change in divine will, "which is the strongest abrogation"; Moses' intercession for Israel changes a

divine decision. On badā cf. s. v. in *Enc. of Isl.* (Goldziher). 102, 141, 163f.

29. 110, 185, 198, 199. The Deuteronomy passage 199–202.

30. 120 *kaddāb muftarin*; 179 "We have never heard of a more reprehensible character and more corrupt disposition—except those who follow him and believe him." Stupid or misleading—159, cf. 156/7, 182; 162: *dalāl, talbīs, ishkāl, tadlīs*; The scoffer—123 *min 'amal zindīq jāhil au mustakhiff mutalā'ib bihim.* Similarly 128, 129, 134, 155, 162, 168, 171 end, 177, 184, 185, 140 end: *min taulīd zindīq mutalā'ib bi-d-diyānāt.* 135: *sifāt al-kilāb.* Mixing truth and falsehood: 184 f.

31. 113, 192, 193, 196, 199. Late origin of the Torah 209. When a verse states that "to this day" nobody has found the tomb of Moses, it testifies to the late date of composition.

32. 117, 198, 210. (Daniel was the last prophet.) Chronology: 197. For classical antecedents of this view of Ezra's role, cf. E. Stein, *Alttestam. Bibelkritik i. D. späthellenist. Litt.,* Lwow 1935.

33. Mistakes: 204 Jos. 205 ff. Ps., 208 Eccl., 217 Is. 207 on The Song of Songs: *Kalām ahmaq lā ya'qil walā yadrī ahad minhum murādahu* (The talk of a fool, and not one of them understands or knows its meaning).

34. This was first edited and translated by Goldziher in Kobak's *Jeschurun* v. VIII, 1873.

35. Biblical passages: 218 ff.

36. Old wives' tales: 218 *al khurāfāt allatī yatahaddat bihā an-nisā' bi-l-layl idā ghazalna.*

37. 221 Shi'ur Qoma, Seder Nashim, Talmud. Paul the seducer—cf. Krauss, *Leben Jesu* 47, 85, 121, 157; E. Fritsch, *Isl. U. Christ. im Mittelalter,* 49–52; G. Levi della Vida in RSO 13, pp. 327–31.

38. Corrupting Islam 222, cf. I. Friedländer, Ibn Saba, in *Zeitschr. F. Assyr. V. 23* (1909). Ibn Hazm does not mention the stories of Muhammad's Jewish companions (such as those treated by J. Mann in HUCA XII–XIII, M. Schwabe in *Tarbis* II, Baneth ib. III, J. Leveen in JQR NS, 16).

39. R. Ismael 222. Metatron 223. In Mas'ūdī, *Murūj* II, 388 ff. this material is cited (a century earlier).

40. 223 and 224, the months of the High Holidays are called September and October, which names would rather point to a Christian source. Christian writings against Jews produced in Spain are discussed by A. Lukyn Williams, *Adversus Judaeos* (Cambridge: 1935), pp. 206 sq. Peter Alphonsi in the eleventh century utilizes material similar to that of Agobard of Lyons (ib. 348 ff.), two centuries earlier.

41. 127, 154, 156, 148, 222, 223. Like the Shiites, Ibn Hazm maintains that the infidel is ritually impure: v. Goldziher, *Zahiriten,* 61 ff.

42. Cf. 131, 213.

43. Cf. 135, 147 f.

44. 99 f. Some share the view of the 'Isawīya that Jesus and Muhammad also were prophets. "I often came

across prominent Jews that were close to this view."
From an ancient Aaronid's history Ibn Hazm concludes
that prominent Jews of the first century had recognized
the truth in the teachings of the Baptist and of Jesus. Asīn
Palacios (*Abenhazam* II, 45, 212 f., n. 87) concluded that
Ibn Hazm had read Josephus. This is improbable. Ibn
Hazm used a Yosippon text. Cf. ed. Gunzbourg-Kahana
col. 361. S. Krauss, *Leben Jesu* p. 238 f., 300 n. 6. The
Christ passage occurs, e.g., in *Ta'rīkh Yūsīfūs al-Yahūdī*
(Beirut: 1872), p. 211 f.

In the passage on the Ananites (p. 99) Asīn Palacios
(vol. 2, p. 211, and n. 85) evidently misinterpreted the
Arabic words "*al-quras wal-mass*" of the text. The Jews
could not call them the followers of Anan "the exilarch."
Possibly, the Arabic conceals a distortion of the Hebrew
words "*karaim ve-minim*" (i.e., "the Ananites whom the
Jews call Karaites and heretics"). Ibid., n. 86: Ibn Hazm
does not identify the Rabbanites with the Essenes but
refers to them as "*al-asb'athiyya*" in Arabic, followers of
"ishm'atha" (in Aramaic)—oral tradition. Cf. Mas'ūdi,
Tanbīh, 112 f.

45. E. Garcia Gómez, *Polemica religiosa entre Ibn
Hazm e Ibn al-Nagrila, in al-Andalus,* vol. 4 (1936):
1–28.

45a. *Fa-innanā nadrīhi 'āriyan illā mina-l-makhraqa,
salīman illā mina-l-karb, sifran illā mina-l-buht.* The
editor translates: desnudo, excepto de delirios despro-
visto de todo, salvo de tristeza, vacīo, a no ser de men-
tiras. For *makhraqa* cf. Dozy I, 366.

Samuel, of course, was well aware of enmity and
intrigues against him, of the tendency to make all the
Jews of the kingdom responsible for his deeds, and of
the issue made of his career even in the foreign policy
of the state he served. Cf. the well-known lines: *"And
they said: How will you be above a foreign people
which sought to destroy not only me with his slander
which he concocted and invented . . . and he sent [word
to] him: Do you know that Samuel's living according to
his religion is a transgression [sin]? There is neither
peace nor quiet. And this Jewish soul is safe in its body.
Send it away and remove it from quarrels and contentions. And make a compromise concerning it. And if
not—know that all kings over your war have plotted a
conspiracy."* Diwan, ed. D. Sassoon, pp. 7–8; Brody,
125 ff.

45b. The Hebrew anti-Islamic treatise ascribed to Ibn
Adret seems to draw on Ibn Hazm when quoting the
Muslim view. (Cf. M. Schreiner, in ZDMG 48 (1894):
39–42; M, Zikier (Zucker), "Beirurim be-Toldot ha-
Vikuhim ha-Datiyyim she-bein ha-Yahadut ve-ha-
Islam," *Festschrift Armand Kaminka zum Siebzigsten
Geburtstage* (Vienna: 1937), pp. 31–48.

46. The poem was first published by R. Dozy, in
*Recherches sur l'histoire et la littérature de l'Espagne
pendant le moyen age*, vol. I in the 3rd ed. (1881), pp.
282–94, and pp. 61–68). The translation appears also in
Dozy's *Histoire des Musulmans d'Espagne*, 2nd ed., par

E. Lévi-Provençal III 71 f. (Leyde: 1932). The text is
available also in Lisān ad-Dīn Ibn al-Khatīb's K. *A'māl
al-A'lām,* ed. E. Lévi-Provençal (Rabat: 1934), pp.
265–67. Em. Garcia Gómez published the diwan of
Elbiri: *Un alfaqui español Abu Ishaq de Elvira* (Madrid-
Granada: 1944). Here the poem will be found under no.
25, pp. 151–53 (with notes on pp. 149 f. and on pp.
38–40 in the introduction, where the background of the
poem is discussed). It is now reprinted in *Selections from
Hispano-Arabic Poetry*, ed. A. R. Nykl (Beirut: 1949),
pp. 141–43. (Cf. H. Pérès, *La poesie andalouse en arabe
classique au XI siecle* [1937], pp. 270 ff.) Nykl, *Hisp.-
Arabic Poetry*, pp. 197–200.

47. E. Lévi-Provençal, "Les 'mémoires' de 'Abd
Allāh, dernier roi Ziride de Grenade," *al-Andalus* 3
(1935): 232–344; 4 (1936–39): 29–145; and 6 (1941):
1–63.

48. Garcia Gómez, *Un alfaqui*, p. 30: "Pero es más
probable que la invectiva antijudaica del poeta de Elvira
no fuese más que uno de tantos motivos concurrentes en
la producción de la catástrofe; el más *brillante*, si se
quiere, desde el punto de vista de la instigación y la
propaganda."

49. *Walākinna minnā yaqūmu-l-mu'īn.*

50. *Fa-anta rahīnun bimā yaf'alūn.*

51. *Waradduhum asfala-s-sāfilīn Fa-tāfu ladaynā,
'Alayhim sighārun wa-ḏullun wa-haun.*

52. This line occurs only in the diwan: *wa-qammū l
mazābila 'a khirqatin mulawwanatin li-ditāri-d-dafīni.*
Why "a coloured rag"? For a badge-*ditār?* The above
translation is based on reading *mulawwaṭatin*—soiled,
filthy.

53. Reference to "Umar's covenant."

54. atrāf. Dozy: itrīf = terefa, i.e., what the Jews throw
away "to the dog." Cf. Steinschneider, *Pol. Lit.*, 152 f.,
332 f.

55. *Wa-sārat hawā'ijunā' indahu wa-nahnu 'alā
bābihi qā'imūn.*

56. Dozy, *Rech.* vol. 68, p. 289.

56a. Cf. Pérès, *la poesie andalouse*, p. 240. This
nomenclature is based on Qur'an passages 2:61, 5:65,
7:166.

57. Memoires (cf. n. 47) 265/283. Cf. Ibn Khatīb,
Ihāta I/273 (Cairo: 1901): "One almost could not breathe
without Joseph knowing thereof." Ibn Iḏāri, *al-Bayān al-
Mugrib,* vol. 3 (Paris: 1930), p. 265.

58. 266/285 (also *Andalus*, vol. 6, p. 15) *tabarmaka-l-
yahūdī.* Ibn-Daud mentions that Joseph, born into power,
was unable to remain modest. See n. 64a.

It is remarkable that in the memoirs Samuel figures as
the venerable Abū Ibrāhim ash-Shaykh (*Andalus*, vol. 6),
and only Joseph comes in for rough treatment. In an illuminating passage Samuel's appointment is explained
(ibid., 11 f. tr. P. 30):

There was in the Jew so much shrewdness and skill
in handling people that was well suited to the time

of Samuel and Badis and to the people who were intriguing against them. Badis therefore used Samuel out of distrust for (istīhāshan) others, and because he saw the ill will of his own kith and kin; further because Samuel was a Jew, a dhimmi, not aspiring to any power. Nor was Samuel a Spaniard who might have become dangerous in a crisis by joining hands with a prince of another race (or: line). Badis needed monies with which to woo his kith and kin and to secure power (the editor translates wayuhāwilu bihā amra-l-mulki: et de régler certaines affaires). Badis could not do without one like Samuel who would collect for him sums with which to carry out his plans (yajma'u lahu mina-l-amwāl), without imposition, right or wrong, on any Muslim; and because the people of the city (Granada) and the treasury officials were mostly Jews, and Samuel would collect the monies from them and give them to Badis.

59. 269/292.

60. 266/285.

61. 269/292.

62. Ihāta, p. 266; and al-Bayān: wa-dālika anna hādā-l-la'īn talaba an yuqīma li-l-yahūd daula. (This accursed one sought to establish a government for the Jews.) The undesirable recent elevation of the Jews—Memoirs 273/300 Betrayal 267/287.

63. Ibid., 269 f. Strangely Pérès speaks of a real conversion to Judaism.

64. Ibn Itransdri, al-Bayān al-Mughrib III, p. 264.

64a. Maqqarī, Analectes, vol. 2, p. 351. The tender quality (riqqa) of a poet's (Ibn Sahl) verse is explained thus: there were combined in him the humility of the lover and the humiliation of the Jew (ijtama'a fīhi dullāni, dullu-l'ishqi wa-dullu-l-yahūdīyati). For the poet, Ibn Sahl (thirteeenth century), cf. Nykl Poetry, p. 344, where dull is translated submissiveness.

65. Cf. Bacher, Der arab. Titel d. religionsphil. Werkes Abr. B. Dauds, in ZDMG 42.

66. Epistle to Yemen, ms. B. M., f. 124a; Hebrew ed. Holub, p. 49.

CHAPTER 25

"Adversos Judaeos": A Treatise from Maghrib—"Ahkam ahl al-Dhimma" by Sayh Muhammad b. 'Abd al-Karim al-Magili

Georges Vajda

The quarrels of Muhammad al-Magili with the Jews of Touat, a conflict that ultimately took a tragic turn for both parties, have been related in documents that are accessible enough that we need not tell the story again here.[1] One detail that is less well known, on the other hand, is the doctrinal stance that determined in practice (or else justified after the fact) the steps taken by the inflexible *faqiih* [jurisprudent]. One document that has been preserved but is not often noted allows us to study that stance, and to do so will suffice to convince the reader that, granting the part played by *tantum religio potuit suadere malorum* ["only religion could convince people of such evils"; "only religion could persuade the wicked" (suadere + genitive)], the doctor of law from Tlemcen was neither a man obsessed nor a bloody brute. He did nothing more than draw conclusions, with uncompromising sternness, excluding all opportunism, from the principles acknowledged by all his co-religionists, even those principles that were most often adapted or even ignored in everyday life. The impartial observer is forced to agree, moreover, that the precarious modus vivendi that was put into effect was derived less from some rather ideal (not to say imaginary) Abrahamic hospitality than from reasons of state and also, of course, from particular interests.

The essential components of this stance are very well summarized in the notes concerning Magili in the *Da'wat al-nasir* by Ibn 'Askar [ibn Asaakir].[2] We reprint this passage [most likely *Da`wat al-naaSir* (the call of the victorious one)] here, retouching in a few places, as necessary, the [French] version by A. Graulle.[3]

[Al-Magili . . .] displayed a rigid obstinacy in prescribing good and forbidding evil. He thought that the Jews (may God curse them) no longer enjoyed the status of a protected minority (*dhimma*); this status had been dissolved by the fact that they were associated with the Moslems who held authority. Such a share in the government is contrary to the abasement and the disdain that accompany the payment of the *jizya*. The fact that one individual (*or* one group) among them has broken the statute is enough to invalidate it for all of them. [The Doctor of the law] declared that it was licit to shed the blood or take the property of the Jews, and he described the duty of repressing this minority group as more imperative than in the case of the other infidels. He wrote on this subject a work composed of several chapters(?)[4] which brought him into conflict with most jurists of his day, among whom were the *shaykh* Ibn Zakri[5] and other (important personages). A great discussion ensued. The work reached Fes, the capital where the jurists examined it in depth. Some of them made a show of disdain, while others showed themselves equitable (*fa-min-hum man anifa wa-min-hum man anSafa*). Among the latter was noted the shaykh of the (*jamaa`a*) group [people, multitude, sect, cult], the imam Abu 'Abd Allah ben Gazi.[6] He wrote on the back of his copy: "Here is a work of superior value, which deals, however, with a ticklish subject.[7] This is the work of a man who cuts an unusual figure in our generation."[8] We must note, however,[9] that he [unduly] imputed the character of disbelief to something that only deserves to be called error (*aTlaqa l-kufr 'alaa l-ta`dliil*). [He labels mere error as unbelief.] With the words just quoted[10] [Ibn Ghaazii] meant that al-Magili interpreted the word of God (Koran,

A chapter by G. Vajda from the anthology *Études d'Orientalisme dédiées à la mémoire de Lévi-Provençal* (Paris: G.-P. Maisonneuve et Larose, 1962), vol. 2, pp. 805–13. Translated by Michael J. Miller.

5:56): *"O you who believe! do not take Jews and Christians as associates; they are affiliated with each other. Whoever among you takes them as affiliates will be one of them,"*[11] as though it charged [those concerned] with disbelief, whereas in his opinion the verse only reckons those whom it describes among the number of the misled. Disbelief, indeed, is the contrary of faith, in other words, the accusation that it [Allah's message delivered by the Prophet] is a lie."[12]

The little work by al-Magili that gave rise to this controversy has been preserved in at least three manuscripts; we have been able to make use of only one of them;[13] it puts us, however, in a position to proceed to the rapid overview to which we must limit ourselves in the present article.

The purpose of our text can be summarized in three points: to explain the obligation imposed on Muslims to avoid contact with Infidels; to recall the statue of subjection and humiliation which, according to the shari`a [Islamic law], must be applied to the *dhimmis*; and to highlight the intolerable infractions whereby the contemporary Jews, who were often protected and wrongly employed by the powerful men of the day, make themselves culpable with regard to the regulations that concern them.[14]

The first point, treated in the first chapter (149 verso, line 18 to 151 verso, line 24), on the whole develops the adage, "Birds of a feather flock together." Anyone who admits an infidel into his intimate circle, appoints him to some office or entrusts to him a part of his property, is thoroughly lacking in (A) religion (*din*), (B) common sense (*'aql*), and (C) honor (*muruwwa*).

Each of these statements is then demonstrated (1) by rational proofs, (2) by passages from the Qur'an and from the tradition (in fact, the two methods are not always strictly separated).

A

None of us would allow a man who calls himself our friend to embrace our enemies and drive away our friends; all the more reason not to when it is a question of God's interests.

Besides the arguments from authority drawn from verses of the Qur'an and from the ancient stock of traditions, the author avails himself of more recent illustrations as well.

"Ibrahim al-Masmudi, the great saint (*qutb*) [literally, 'pole'] of Tlemcen in his day,[15] had the habit of keeping company with an apothecary in the latter's shop. While going one day to see him, as was his custom, he saw a Jew in conversation with him. The sheikh immediately doubled back and went home. When the man [the apothecary] learned of this, he went to the master's house and asked permission to enter. But the saint closed the door in his face and refused to open it, saying to him words to the following effect: You will not present to a friend of Allah and of his apostle the face with which you accost an enemy of Allah." Another anecdote of the same type. When the pious doctor Hiba[16a] happened to be staying in the *oued [Wadi]* Dra', he never came near the castle of the Banu S(a)bih[16b] who were protecting the Jews. When he had to pass by this place, "he would hike up his garment around his legs and say to his companions: 'Run, for fear that, if the wrath [of God] should fall upon the Jews, it could smite you with them.' And he never stopped running with his companions until he was far from their castle, fortress."[16c]

B

Rational man and even the brute animal instinctively draw near to what is beneficial to them and go away from what is harmful to them. The man who is in his right mind will therefore draw near to his friends and go away from his enemies. Now, we have no worse enemies than the Infidels, adversaries of our prophet and intercessor, and among these the "brothers of the apes" are the most relentless. This truth is illustrated both by means of verses from the Koran and by trustworthy reports that al-Maghili received from certain friends.[17]

C

Every honorable man[18] feels a natural repugnance toward those who do not share his beliefs, even if they be his close relatives. What, then, should be done about the "brothers of the apes" who unceasingly blaspheme our religion and our Prophet, and whose entire conduct expresses the profound hatred that they have for us: they disdain our food, they make fun of our prayer, they speak ill of our Prophet. A true believer must consider that every Jew is Iblis in person[19] and seeks only to harm his religion, to make him eat meat that his own beliefs render illicit for him and also carrion,[20] as well as fermented food,[21] and to involve him in some usurious transaction. And so it is fitting, in keeping with the measures taken by 'Umar ibn al-Khattaab, to forbid them to practice the professions of moneychanger and butcher and to exclude them from the *suuq*s [marketplaces] of the Muslims.

The second chapter (folio 151 verso, line 25 to folio 152, 15) deals with financial obligations and methods of social discrimination concerning the *dhimmis*.

After recalling the Qur'anic command to grant peace to the Infidels only if they are humiliated and pay the tolerance tax,[22] al-Magili sums up the precepts of the law concerning this chapter,[23] insisting above all and vehemently on the affronts that should be inflicted upon members of minorities (in this case, upon the Jews) when the tax is collected.

> On the day for tax collecting, they should be assembled in a public place, like the *souk*. They should present themselves there, standing up at the lowest, vilest place. The auxiliaries of the Law should stand above them, striking a menacing pose, so that appears to their eyes and to the eyes of the others that our purpose is to debase them by pretending to take their belongings.[24] They will realize that we do them a favor [again] by accepting the *jizya* from them and letting them go [their way]. Then they shall be brought one by one [before the official responsible] for collecting the tax. While paying, the *dhimmi* will receive a slap and will be pushed back in such fashion that he will think that he has escaped the sword thanks to this [insult]. This is how the friends of the Lord in the first and last generations act toward their miscreant enemies, for power belongs to God, to His Apostle and to the Believers.[25]

In order to be valid, the *jizya* must be collected by the public authority; the sums that certain protectors of the Jews allow their protégés to pay them are bribes, pure and simple.[26]

After some instructions as to the use of the funds collected in this way,[27] the author turns to the state of humiliation (*Saghar*) in which the *dhimmis* must be kept. The main thing here is to see to it that the protected people present the most miserable outward appearance and that they in no way publicize their religious practices. Likewise they should be forbidden to praise one of their doctors in the presence of Muslims, and care should be taken that the prohibition against constructing new buildings for worship be applied strictly.

The theme of the third and last chapter (folio 152 verso, line 15 to folio 153 verso, line 31, and then the concluding formulas, 153 verso, line 31 to 154, line 3) is the boldness and the wickedness of the Jews of this era in most regions; the state of open rebellion against the legal statutes in which they find themselves by the fact that they occupy positions of responsibility under those in authority and accept employment in the service of the sovereign.[28]

The missive written by the caliph 'Umar upon making peace with the Christians of Syria[29] regulates the status of the protected minorities. A breach on the part of the *dhimmi* causes him to lose his rights to protection and makes his blood and his property "licit" [fair game]. It is true that the jurists debate the question of determining whether any infraction against one of the stipulations results in all of these serious consequences. What is certain is that doubt is permitted only if the infraction is not of an ongoing character and does not manifest obstinate persistence in illicit behavior. Now this is precisely the

concrete case of the minorities which al-Magili has in mind (152 verso, lines 18–19): the Jews of Touat, Tigurarin, [also Tegorarin] Dra', Tafilalet, of various places in Ifriqiya as well as those of Tlemcen.[29a]

The author insists especially (153, lines 26–28) on two grievances:

4. that they settled in regions not subject to the legitimate government (*sukna l-bilaad al-Sa'iba*) [inhabitants of outlying regions]
5. that they affiliated themselves with those in authority and show hostility, in the way that they manage their masters' fortune, toward the learned men who earn their living by teaching the children of those masters.[30]

The Jews who occupy a position serving a sovereign, a vizier, a *qadi*, or some other important personage thus find themselves in a state of permanent rebellion against their status, which from then on no longer protects them.[31]

In a word, all means of coercion must be used with regard to the Jews to make them observe strictly their status as *dhimmis*. To kill a Jew (who by his own fault has lost his status as a member of a protected people) is more meritorious than an expedition into infidel territory; one must persecute people of this sort, wherever they may be found, slay them, take their wives, children, and goods. Those who assist them and become accomplices in their transgressions will experience the same eternal damnation as their favorites.[32]

And the author ends his little work with sonorous verses against the abettors of the Jews, in an appeal for repentance addressed to all Muslims.[33]

*For further clarification of any references, see original text.

NOTES

1. It can be found in Ahmad Baba, *Nayl al-ibithag*, pp. 331–33 in the Cairo edition, 1351/1932 [CE], copied by Ibn Maryam, *Bustan*, ed. M. Ben Cheneb, pp. 253–57, trans. F. Provenzali, pp. 288–93 (*cf.* p. 553 n. 1033). Derived likewise from the *Nayl*, it seems, directly or indirectly, are the pages devoted to our subject by various nineteenth- and twentieth-century writers on Arab themes, for instance, J. J. L. Barges, *Complément de l'Histoire des Beni Zeiyan* (Paris: 1887), pp. 389–92; A. Cour, *L'établissement des dynasties des Chérifs au Maroc* (Paris: 1904), pp. 47f.; dependent on these writers, in turn, is N. Slousch, *Études sur l'Histoire des Juifs au Maroc, Archives Marocaines* (1905–1906) vol. 6, pp. 149ff. The figure of Magili has been evoked more recently in the article by M. Mariano Aribas Palau, *"Los Israelitas bajo los primeros Sa'dies"* (in *Homenaje a Millás Vallicrosa*, vol. 1, 1954), especially on p. 48 [4]. I would not dare to dispute peremptorily, before any

formal proof has been provided, the possibility of a relation between the anti-Jewish movement in Tlemcen and in Touat in the late fifteenth century and the immigration that followed the expulsion from Spain in 1492. The text that we will deal with here hardly lends support to such a view of the matter (see further on, p. 29 B). There are some other references in the article by Madame Dj. Jacques-Meunié, *Hespéris* (1958), p. 263 (on the fifteenth century).—The date of al-Magili's death varies slightly from one source to another: 909/1503–1504 [CE] or 910/1504–1505. The article on him in Brockelmann (*Suppl.*, vol. 2, p. 363) needs to be supplemented. Besides the text that we will deal with here, Brockelmann could have taken only one other short work into account. Sifting through the Arab manuscripts of the *Bibliothèque nationale* in Paris, which were put aside by Blochet has brought to light, together with a second copy of the said text, three other compositions by Muhammad (or rather Mahammad) ben 'Abd al-Karim al-Magili. They are:

First, *'Amal al-yawm wal-layla*, [Working Day and Night] MS arab. 5673, fol. 257–59 (see my *Index Général . . .*, p. 257), a short work which testifies, by its quotations from al-Sadili and Ibn 'Ata' Allah, to the author's adherence to the *fariqa* that was so widespread in Maghrib;

Second, his *Fatawi*, legal opinions addressed to the Sudanese sovereign 'Abd Allah ben Muhammad 'Askiya, MS 5259, fol. 48–65 (incomplete copy, ibid., pp. 39–44; *Index Général*, p. 331, in which we should read "39" instead of "33"): these texts are of some interest for the history of the Islamization of Sudan;

Third, *Minah al-wahhab fi radd al-fikr ila l-sawab*, [Gifts from the Giver (Allah) in refutation of the wrong to correct thinking]. MS 5602, fol. 36–47, a very poorly preserved copy (*Index Général*, p. 478, where *Tawhid* [Unicity (Unity of God)] should be replaced with *Falsafa* [philosophy], since it is a question of an *urgaza* with commentary on the basics of formal logic).

2. Pages 95–97 of the lithograph of Fes.

3. *Archives Marocaines* 19 (1913): 224–25.

4. The text is uncertain; *wa'allafa fi dalika ta'lifan wjh* (vowels) *fihi rasa'il*. [He composed a work in sections dealing with this matter.]

5. Ahmad, mention of whom is found, for example, in the same collection of biographies, p. 88 (French translation p. 203); he died in 960 = 1500 CE, a date which from then on provides a *terminus ante quem* for the composition of the text by al-Magili.

6. Muhammad ben Ahmad, died in 919 = 1513 CE.

7. I reproduce, for lack of a better one, the translation of Graulle, but I find it utterly unsatisfactory. The original has: *sadara 'an nassin 'alil*; neither the verb nor the complement, nor even the epithet can have anything like the meaning imputed to them in the translation; according to what follows, it should be understood instead to mean: "the author's thesis is developed setting

out from (*sadara 'an*) a Koranic text (*nass*) that has been misinterpreted (*'alil*; obviously this is not the revealed text, which is "sick," but rather the interpretation of it that the author [Vajda] claims to give).

8. An ambiguous and rather subtle compliment in which admiration is mixed with irony: al-Magili is certainly not "in line with" the flexible *fuqaha* of the court, but had not Islam itself begun by being *garib* [literally, "strange," unacceptable], and won't it become that way again before the end of the ages?

9. *bayda anna* [even though] here begins the in-depth criticism; Graulle was to a great extent mistaken as to its meaning.

10. What follows is the explanation by Ibn 'Askar of the critique written by Ibn Gazi.

11. I reprint the version of M. R. Blachère, *Le Coran* (Paris: 1957), p. 141.

12. The meaning of the critique is as follows: it is clear that developing relations or ties of *wala'* (they can be of various sorts) with the infidels is at most a serious error, but by no means a negation of the revealed message; consequently, the entire argument of Magili is unsound and is binding on no one but himself. On the question of "theological notes [*or* characteristics]," the reader may consult the summary by Gardet-Anawati, *Introduction à la théologie musulmane* (Paris: 1948), pp. 435–42; *cf.* also H. Laoust, *Essai . . . sur . . . Ibn Taymiya* (Cairo: 1939), pp. 260–64; and F. Jabré, *La notion de certitude selon Ghazali* (Paris: 1958), passages noted in the index, p. 468 under the heading *takfir*.

13. P.-B. N.-Ar. [*Paris, Bibliothèque nationale, Archive?*] 5452, not described by Blochet (I used it in my *Notes de bibliographie maghrébine*, VII, *Hespéris*, 1950, pp. 216[8] ff.). The treatise by Magili appears there as fol. 149 verso to 154 (I emphasize only in passing, since it is not possible to develop the point here, that a note in the margin of fol. 152 verso reports a fatwa concerning the construction of a synagogue in Ilig (Ilegh) following the reestablishment of that locality by Abu l'Hasan 'Ali ben Muhammad, the leader of the *zawiya* [Sufi sect] of Dila [which] was conquered by Mawlay Ralid; *cf. Nuzha*, éd. Houdas, pp. 286/475 and 303/502).—In this manuscript, the short work has no title of its own; the one that I have kept, for the sake of convenience, was given by Brockelmann, whose source is the *defter* [record book] of the Zaytuniyya [name of Sufi sect, literally the Olivers], which I have not been able to verify. The third copy, incomplete, it seems, is found in the *Bibliothèque nationale* of Rabat (D 1602, described briefly, under the number 1386, by Allouche-Regragui, *Catalogue des Manuscrits Arabes de Rabat* [1954], p. 260); the title that is indicated there (*ta'lif fi ma yagib 'ala l-muslimin min igtinab al-kuffar*) [What the Muslims lack concerning the knowledge of how to ostracize the unbelievers] is artificial; it is taken from the beginning of the text (after the initial formalities, fol. 149 verso, line 15 of the Paris MS). Haggi [Hajji] Halifa also lists it (ed. Flügel, vol. 3, p. 365,

no. 5693 = Yaltkaya-Bilge, vol. 1, col. 845, with the no less artificial title *risala fi sti'mal al-yahud wal-nasara*) [Treatise on how to use (*sic*) the Jews and Christians (*sic*)]; M. Steinschneider, *Polemische und apologetische Literatur* . . . "(Leipzig, 1871), pp. 55 ff. knows it only by this reference.

14. P.-B. N.-Ar. 5452 (quoted by folio and line),149 verso lines 14–17: *faqad sa'alani ba'd al-ahyat 'amma yagib 'ala l-muslimin min igtinab al-kuffar wa'amma yalzam ahl al-dhimma min ada' al-jizya wal-sagar wa'amma 'alayhi 'aktar yahud hada l-zaman min al-ta'addi wal-tugyan wal-tamarrud 'ala l-ahkam al-sar'iyya bitawliyat arbab al'sawka wahidmat al-sultan.* [A brother asked me about what the Muslims lack concerning ostracizing the unbelievers, and what the People of the Dhimma must do in addition to paying the jizya while in a state of humiliation: for most of the Jews of our time act out of rebellious and hostile resistance to the laws of the Shari`a; they sit at the notables' tables, and serve the Sultan.]

15. Died in 804 = 1401 CE or 805/1402: *Nayl*, 51–52; *Bustan*, 64–66, translated by Provenzali, 69–72 (and n. 269, p. 389).

16a. I have found no information about this individual.

16b. On this locale, see Jean-Léon l'Africain, *Description de l'Afrique*, trans. A. Epaulard (Paris: 1956), p. 423 (*cf.* L. Massignon, *Le Maroc* . . . , p. 258); Charles de Foucauld, *Reconnaissance au Maroc*, pp. 294 ff. (on p. 403 he notes another *mellah* consisting of about fifty families); more recently, Dj. Jacques-Meunié, *Les Oasis des Lektaoua et des Mahamid, Hespéris* 34 (1947): 397–429.

16c. The personal bitterness of a man who has paid dearly for his intransigence emerges in a passage like fol. 150 verso, lines 9–13: "They are liars: the people who claim to place their trust and their affection in the Prophet never cease inviting their [worst] enemies to be with them and their families. They take under their protections their most relentless adversaries and, because of them, break with their friends, to the point where they harbor Jews in their homes while at the same time they fight against the Doctors [of the law] to protect them. *Those are the ones who have denied their Lord* . . . " (Qur'an 13:6[5]).

fama akdaba qawman yaz 'umuna annahum yu'minuna bil-nabi sl'm wayuhibbunah wahum ma'a dalika yuqarribuna min anfusihim wa'ahlihim a'da'ah wayatawalluna asarr al-nas 'adawatan lahu wayuqafi 'una li' aglihim ahbabah hatta innahum ya' wuna l-yahud ilayhim wayuharibuna l-'ulama' 'alayhim ula'ika lladina kafaru birabbihim . . . [What liars are those people who claim to believe in and love the Prophet, but among themselves they are the most secretive of people in their hostility; they even gather together to oppose the (Islamic) doctors of the Law. These are the ones who disbelieve in their Lord.]

17. Folio 151, lines 2–10. I am content with tran-scribing these two reports which both have reference to the hateful behavior of the Jews who are reduced to servile work with respect to their masters: *waqad ahbarani ha'd ihwani wakana qadiyan fi hadihi l-awtan innahu lamma qadima ilayhi wawaliya l-qada' biha sta'mala yahudiyyan fi asgalih. qala wakanat minni zalla fi sti 'malih hina zanantu anna tahdimahu min idlalih. qala fakana yatasarraf fi asguli wayuzhir al-nasiha li fa a'taytuhu yawman tiyabi liyagsilaha walam amanhu 'ala dalika fakana bayna yaddaya yagsil wa ana anzuru fih hatta 'aradat li haga fadahaltu ilayha waraga'tu bisur'a fawagadtuhu fawqa tiyabi wahuwa yabul 'alayha farabattuh wadarabtuh ma sa'a llahu watubtu 'an qurb a'da'i llah.* [A brother, who was a *qadi* (judge), informed me that in these countries whenever one came before the court he would "use" a Jew for the trial. This went on for a long while so that I supposed that [the Jew's] service was really to mislead [his client]. The way the Jew would behave in my service would generally be to give me good advice. I gave [a Jew] my clothes one day to wash, but I didn't trust him in this. He washed them in front of me while I looked on. Soon I had to answer the call of nature, so I left but returned quickly enough to find him pissing on my clothes. I tied him up and beat him good and proper. I now repent from ever desiring the propinquity of God's enemies.]

Another informant about al-Magili: *ra'a yahudiyya ta'gin hubz muslim wata'hud al-qaml min ra'siha wataq-tulha bayna azfariha wata'gin min gayr an tagsila yadayha.* [He once saw a Jewess kneading a Muslim's bread. She took some lice from her head, killed them between her fingernails, and continued to knead the bread without washing her hands.]

18. Folio 151, line 13: *du himma 'aqliyya wa anfas mardiyya* [possessing intelligence of note and pleasant (-smelling) breath].

19. Folio 151 verso, line 8: *kull yahudi innama huwa Iblis bi 'aynih* [every Jew is the devil incarnate].

20. The sale to non-Jews of meat that is ritually unclean for consumption, according to Jewish law, is a grievance that recurs more than once in the anti-Jewish polemic of Islam: *cf.* M. Steinschneider, *Polemische und apologetische Literatur*, pp. 332–33.The rabbinical legislation, furthermore, forbids this sort of sale, unless the buyer has been accurately informed by the vendor as to the quality of the merchandise: see the Talmud of Babylon, *Hullin*, 94g–95a and the "Code of Laws" of Moses Maimonides, *Hilkot De'ot*, vol. 2, p. 6. The current commercial practice was no doubt less scrupulous, both in the Talmudic period (cf. the cited text, 95a) and later on. The text by al-Magili speaks of *tarifa* (mistake for the next Arabic word; means 'a curiosity') (the MS erroneously has *zarifa* [a subtlety], but there is no doubt whatsoever as to the correct reading; *cf.* Dozy, vol. 2 p. 38 and Fagnan, p. 103) and jifa. These two words correspond to the technical terms which, in rabbinical ritual, designate the animals that are unsuitable for eating:

teréfah [unkosher], an animal slaughtered according to regulations, but found during the examination after the slaughter to have a wound that would quickly have brought about a natural death, and *nebélah* [an animal corpse], that has been slaughtered irregularly.

21. The manuscript has, unless it is an error, *hamr* [wine, alcoholic beverage], but the turn of phrase (the word in question is governed by *yut'imuh* [feed him/it]) and the context demands the reading *hamir* [leaven]. It no doubt refers to fermented foods or those containing leaven (in Hebrew *hames*), which the Jew gives or sells to a non-Jew on the occasion of Passover, during which a Jewish house must be cleansed of every fermented substance. Without putting too fine a point on it, the Muslim doctor reproaches the Jews for offering to Muslims foods that they themselves do not want.

22. Qur'an 9:29 (in the French translation of R. Blachère): "Fight those who . . . do not practice the religion of Truth among those who have received the Scripture. [*Fight them*] until they pay the *jizya* directly and they are humiliated."

23. See the *Muhtasar* of Halil (Paris: 1900), pp. 80–81; text translated [into Italian] and extensively annotated by I. Guidi, *Il Muhtasar o Sommario del Diritto Malechita* . . . (Milan: 1919), vol. 1 pp. 412–19; a recent French translation by G. H. Bousquet, *Khalil ben Ish'aq, Abrégé de la Loi Musulmane selon le rite de l'Imam Malek* (Algiers: 1956), vol. 1, pp. 215–16. According to the terms of the pact of Omar, says our author, the Jew pays annually "around eight *mitqals*" [a measure]; half of this because of the tax, strictly speaking (*asl al-jizya*) [literally, the "root" of the *jizya*, or head tax] the rest in the form of various payments (*fima yatba'ha min al-arzaq wanahwaha*) [and other various material goods]; the *dhimmi* whose conduct is above reproach can be dispensed from the latter payments. According to Halil, the *'anawi* (member of a minority living in a land conquered militarily) pays four dinars or forty dirhems each lunar year.

24. The syntax is not clear here; according to the context, it should no doubt be understood that after being placed in the situation of people who are about to be deprived of everything, the *dhimmis* will consider themselves fortunate that the Muslims are content to collect the *jizya* from them.

25. Folio 152, lines 4–9: *wasifat ahdiha an yugma'u yawma i'ta' iha bimakan mustahir kal-suq wanahwahu wayuhdaru bi ahassih wa asfalih qa'imin 'ala aqdamihim wa a'wan al-sari'a fawqa ru'usihim bima yuhawwifhum 'ala anfusihim hatta yazhar lahum wali-gayrihim anna maqsadana idlaluhum izhar (?) li 'ahd amwalihim wayaruna anna l-fadl lana fi qabul al-jizya minhum wa irsaluhum. tumma yugbad minhum fard ba'da fard liqabdiha wayus'af 'ala 'unugihim ba'da ahdiha wayudfa' daf'a yara annahu huraga min taht al-sayf. hakada yaf'al ahbab sayyid al-awwalin wal-aharin bi a'da' ih al-kafirin fa'inna l-'izza lillah walirasulih*

walil-mu'minin. [They would gather together in a lowly place like a market or some similar scabrous place, in order to present themselves, honored and humble, standing on their feet while the executors of the Shari`a stood over them to scare them almost to death. Thus it became to them and to others apparent that superiority is ours in receiving the jizya from them. Then, one by one, a sword was placed on their necks, and they were struck as if by a sword. Thus did the lovers of the Sayyid (Lord: Muhammad) of the first and the last against the unbelievers, his enemies. Power is Allah's and His Emissary's and the Believers'.]

26. Folio 152, line 10: *karakuls ma ya'huduh al-gala'if min yahudihim bi aydihim laysa bigizya innama huwa ruswa* [everything taken from the caliphs' Jews, besides the *jizya*, (is considered) bribery].

27. He establishes priorities (providing for defense, allocations to the Prophet's descendants, to the learned and to persons responsible for the common interests of the Muslims, the support of the poor, an equal division of what remains), but he admits that contemporary reality is a far cry from such a precise regimen; the indispensable thing, he says, is that the *jizya* be collected under the conditions indicated.

28. *fima 'alayhi yahud hada l-zaman fi'aktar al-awtan min al-gur'a wal-tugyan wal-tamarrud 'ala l-ahkam al-sar'iyya bitawliyat arbab al-sawka wa-hidmat al-sultan* [The Jews of our time in most countries have the gall to act out of rebellious hostility against the Shari`a laws. (They sit at) the notables' tables, and serve the sultan].

29. This well-known document is reproduced at folio 152 verso, line 21 to 153, line 25.

29a. Cf. *Jean-Léon l'Africain* . . . in the translation cited above, pp. 436–37: "There were in Tegorarin several very wealthy Jews. The interference of a preacher from Tlemcen provoked the pillage of their properties, and most of them were massacred by the populace. This incident took place in the year when the Jews were driven out of Spain and Sicily by the Catholic King." Although we can consider the pamphlet that we are dealing with as a manifesto written before going into action, its composition should be dated at the very latest in the first months of 1492; in that case, the argument that the anti-Jewish movement was motivated by the influx of Jews banished from Spain would lose much of its force. It remains possible, however, that our pamphlet is trying to justify a past action after the fact, although that does not seem very likely, especially in light of the passage from the *Dawha* [proselytizing] translated above.

30. I cannot derive any other meaning from this phrase, but I would gladly abandon my interpretation as soon as someone proposed a better one. Here is the text: [they stuck to the powerful, and held tenaciously to their wealth, against relying on the doctors (of law) [in matters of their children].

Grammatically, *ta'assub* [group solidarity] is coordinated with *sawka* [raw power]. In keeping with this construction, one would have to understand that the crime of the Jews was to enlist in the service of leading citizens, who showed signs of partiality, in managing their properties, to the detriment of the learned. It is difficult to see what the responsibility of the Jews would be in such a situation, even according to a zealot like al-Magili, unless we are to understand that the employment of Jews is precisely what deprives the Moslem doctors of advantageous positions, reducing them to obscure teaching jobs. Such a predicament is quite conceivable, but it would be expressed very unclearly. The interpretation that I propose tentatively has against it the fact that it does not respect the syntax, but it has the advantage of implying a direct culpability of the Jews.

31. The author reports here (folio 153, line 33 to 153 verso, line 11) in the name of al-Qaysi (identity?) an incident that occurred during the reign of Abu 'Inan (749/1348–759/1358): a Jew who had been employed by the sovereign was put to death for having altered on a pupil's slate a verse from the Qur'an, 3:79[85]: "Whoever seeks a religion other than Islam, it will not be accepted by him." By erasing the negative word *gayr* [not], he changed its meaning to read: "Whoever seeks Islam as a religion."

32. Folio 153 verso, lines 13–15. *fawalladi nafsi biyadih laqatl yahudi wahid a'zam agran min gazwa fi ard al-musrikin fahuduhum waqtuluhum hayt wagadtumuhum wanhabu amwalahum wasbu awladahum wunisa'ahum fi kull makan hatta yud'inu lil'ahkam al-sar'iyya atamm id'an* [I swear by the One who holds my soul in His hands: killing a Jew gains a better wage than a razzia into the unbelievers' country, so take them and kill them wherever you find them; plunder their wealth and take their women and children into captivity from everywhere till they submit totally to the Shari`a laws] and further on, lines 17–18: *faman hawala fakk say' min tilka l-salasil wal-aglal min raqabat ahad min al-kuffar faqad hadda llah warasulah wasatanqalib fi 'unuqih wayukabb ma'ahum fi l-nar* [whoever leaves out one of these directives against the unbelievers, God and His emissary have decreed that he will be turned upside down and sent into hellfire to join them].

33. Folio 153 verso, lines 21–29: [rhyming couplets] *baritu lil-rabbi l-wadud min qurbi ansari l-yahud qawman ahanu dinahum wa akramu dina l-yahud* [I am at one with my Lord: I have distanced myself from my Jewish helpers. They shame their religion]. *yakfi l-fata min saynihim wahubti asli tinihim an qala'u min dinihim warafa'u dina l-yahud* [a young man may despise (the Jews) and the ingrained filth of their character and their religion].

ya laytahum law dabbaru wastarga'u wastagfaru wasattaru ma azharu min nasri rahati l-yahud [would that (the Jews) only reconsider and repent, and hide anything positive they may have].

alam yaraw kayfa qada rabbu l-wara fima mada anna yafuzu bil-rida man radiyat 'anhu l-yahud [do you not know that in the past God of all mankind was satisfied with everyone not satisfied (by the Jews)?]

la sakka anna l-haqqa nur fi kulli suqin la yabur yansuruhu l-rabbu l-sabur 'ala l-nasara wal-yahud [doubtlessly the light of the Truth will never shine on the Christians or the Jews].

faya ilahi bil-nabiyyi l-mustafa l-hadi l-taqi wakulli qutbin wawali sammit bi ansari l-yahud [By God! By the Prophet, the Chosen One! Rejoice at the Jews' misfortune].

subba l-bala' min fawqihim wamhaq baqaya rizqihim waftah lahum min mahqihim baban ila nari l-waqud [may the plague descend upon them and destroy the remainder of their possessions].

illa lladina stagfaru wagabbaru ma kassaru wabayyanu ma sarraru hatta staqamati l-hudud [only those who ask forgiveness and expose what they had hidden will be led straight].

fagfir lahum ma qad mada waktub lahum minka l-rida wa-aggilan biman qada minhum bigannati l-hulud [forgive (the Muslims) for what is past; inscribe for them an eternity in Paradise].

PART 6

❖❖❖

Muslim Jurists, Theologians, and Scholars on the Jews: Modern Era

CHAPTER 26

Our Struggle with the Jews

Sayyid Qutb

The Muslim community continues to suffer from the same Jewish machinations and double-dealing which discomfited the Early Muslims. But the Muslim community (today) does not—one must say with great regret—utilize those Qur'anic directives and this Divine Guidance (of the following sort, regarding these problems):

Do you really want them to believe you, when a group of them have already heard Allah's Word and falsified it knowingly, after having understood it?

When they meet Believers they say, "We too believe"; but when they are alone with one another they say "Do you tell them about what Allah has revealed to you, that they may argue with you about it before your Lord? Do you understand?" Do they not know that Allah knows what they keep secret and what they proclaim?[1]

The Muslim community does not take advantage of the Islamic sources which its ancestors used. Only in this way were the ancestors able to overcome the Jewish conspiracy and double-dealing in Medina. And thus did the religion (Islam) arise; and thus was the Muslim community born.

The Jews continue—through their wickedness and double-dealing—to lead this (Muslim) community away from its religion and to alienate it from its Qur'an. (They do this) in order to prevent the community from utilizing its traditional Qur'anic weapons and its perfect Qur'anic readiness for struggle. (The Jews) are secure so long as this (Muslim) community is estranged from the sources of its real power and the roots of its pure knowledge.

Anyone who leads this community away from its religion and its Qur'an can only be a Jewish agent—whether he does this wittingly or unwittingly, willingly or unwillingly.[2] The Jews will, then, be safe from this community, so long as the community is alienated from the one unique truth from which it derives its existence, its power and its victory—the truth of religious creed, the practice of belief and the Shari'a. . . .This is The Way and these are the landmarks.

The Jews in Medina had had a certain standing there, as well as economic and treaty ties with the town's population. The Jews' enmity had not yet become glaringly apparent. Nor had the Muslims (themselves) yet deeply understood that only their creed is treaty, homeland and the basis of commercial relations and communal cooperation; and that there is no permanency to any relations or close ties when these clash with the creed!! Thus did the Jews have the opportunity for directing (affairs), filling minds with doubt and sowing confusion.

(In Medina) there were those among the Muslims who listened to what the Jews said and were influenced by it, and there were those who repelled the Jews, while the Prophet, Peace be Upon Him, desired that measures be taken to eliminate their conspiracy from the Muslim ranks: As happened in the case of 'Abd Allah b. Ubayy's advocacy of the Banū Qaynūqā' and his rudeness in this toward the Prophet, Peace be Upon Him.[3]

The enemies of the Muslim community would not always fight it only in the field, with sword and lance. They would not always join forces against (this community) just in order to fight it with sword and lance. For the enemies of Islam fought it first in the realm of creed!![4] And they fought it there through conspiring, sowing doubt and confusion, and hatching plots.

As was their wont, (the Jews) would head for the community's creed, from which its very being originated and from which its existence was established. They would then seek to instill in the community destructive elements and (false) counsel; because they always understood—as they so well understand today[1*]—that this (Islamic) community would achieve its destiny only from this source (of its teachings); that it would grow feeble only when its creed had grown feeble; that it could be victorious only when its spirit would be victorious; and that its enemies would not win anything from

---

English translation in Ronald L. Nettler, *A Muslim Fundamentalist's View of the Jews* (Oxford: 1987), pp. 72–89.

it so long as it adhered to the bond of faith and relied on the support of that bond, following the way of faith, carrying the banner of belief, and belonging to the party of faith and waxing proud in this connection.

It is clear, then, that the worst enemies of this community (Islam) are those who lead it away from its creed to belief, dissuading it from taking Allah's way and path and deceiving it about the reality of its enemies and their ultimate goals.

The struggle between the Muslim community and its enemies is, before anything else, the struggle for this creed. For even when its enemies want to overcome the community in its land, its products, its economy and its raw materials, they try first to affect it in its Creed; because they know from long experience that they will never gain anything they want so long as the Muslim community adheres to its creed. For this creed is that means through which the community remains cognizant of its enemies' plot. These enemies and their agents, then, strive assiduously, with the effort of giants, to deceive this community about the true nature of the struggle. (The enemies) do this in order to win from the community everything they want in the way of colonization and profit, while they are able to feel safe from the power of the Islamic creed in its full dissemination.

Whenever the means of conspiring, sowing doubt against (our) Creed and weakening its internal bonds are on the rise, (Islam's) enemies will exploit these more abundant possibilities—but always for the very same old goal: "One segment of the People of the Book would love to lead you astray!!"[5] This is (their) established hidden goal.

Thus the Qur'an would first always repel this poisoned weapon. The Qur'an would always admonish the Muslim Community to reaffirm the Qur'anic Truth. The Qur'an would always repudiate the suspicions and doubts which the People of the Book cast upon it, and likewise reveal the great truth which this religion (Islam) contains. The Qur'an convinced the Muslim Community of its own truth, and of its value on this earth and its role and the role of the Creed which it transmits, in the history of humanity.[6]

Thus the Qur'an always would warn the community against the conspiracy of the conspirators and unmask for the Muslim community the hidden designs of its enemies, their dirty ways, their dangerous intentions, and their hatred of Islam and the Muslims because of Islam's uniquely great superiority.

The Qur'an would always encourage the community to affirm the reality of power and its great role in this worldly existence. Thus the Qur'an made clear to the community the weakness of its enemies, their insignificance in Allah's estimation, their blindness to truth, their rejection of what Allah previously revealed to them and their killing of the prophets. The Qur'an likewise showed the community that Allah is with (the Muslims), that he alone is the Omnipotent King of Kings who has no partner, and that he will lead the ungrateful Jews to exemplary punishment, as he did the polytheists before them.

Our community is concerned about Jewish deception and plotting: "Oh People of the Book, Why do you wittingly cover the truth with falsehood and thereby hide the truth?"[7]

This is a characteristic of the People of the Book which Muslims must understand and take warning from: deception and plotting.

And this feature which Allah—Glory Be To Him—criticized in the behavior of the People of the Book in days gone by is exactly what they have been doing until this very moment. This is their way in the cycle of history.

The Jews began in this was from the first moment . . . ; then the Christians followed them. Through the lengthy centuries—regretfully—(the Jews) poisoned the Islamic heritage in a way that may itself be revealed only with the effort of centuries!! (The Jews) replaced truth with falsehood in the whole (Islamic) heritage—except for this Preserved Book (the Qur'an) whose preservation Allah has guaranteed forever. Glory to Allah for His great superiority.

(The Jews) plotted against Islamic history, its events and its great men, and sought to bring confusion to them. They conspired to distort the Islamic oral revelation (the hadith of Muhammad), until Allah sent his men who retrieved the precise formulation of the oral revelation and codified it, except for what remained irresistibly beyond the bounds of their inevitably limited human effort.

The Jews also conspired against and falsified the exegesis of the Qur'an. This is a very dangerous conspiracy.

The Jews have instilled men and regimes (in the Islamic world), in order to conspire against this (Muslim) community. Hundreds, then, even thousands, were plotting within the Islamic world, continuing (to appear) in the form of Orientalists and the students of Orientalists. Today they play an important role in the intellectual life of those countries whose people say "they are Muslims!"

The tens of personalities who have been foisted upon the Muslim community (as conspirators against it) in the guise of "heroes" were manufactured by Zionism, in order that these "heroes" should do for the enemies of Islam what these enemies are themselves not able to do openly.[2*;8]

This conspiracy continues uninterruptedly. The source of security and salvation from it remains in rigorous adherence to and reliance on this Preserved Book (the Qur'an), for the guidance it provides in this fierce battle of so many centuries.

The Jews' way of attacking (Islam) through sowing doubt and suspicion (about it) in the Muslim community continues:

One group of the People of the Book say: "Believe at the beginning of the day what was reveled to those who believe, and then apostatize from it at day's end." Haply such people will return. Believe only those who follow your religion![9]

This is a deceitful and depraved way. First these people paraded their Islam; then they reneged on it, taking some poor souls, (weak) minds, and the unstable away from the truth and uniqueness of their religion and throwing them into confusion and derangement. For when these weak people saw the Jews (seemingly) believing, then suddenly apostatizing, they concluded that the Jews had apostatized only because they knew of some hidden defect and shortcoming in this religion of Islam. (These weak-minded Muslims) then teetered between belief and apostasy. For as a result of all this, they were unable to maintain their stability.

This deception has continued in the same way until today, in all forms which are appropriate to the particular evolution of conditions and peoples in every era.

The enemies of Islam lost hope that today this (older type) of deception would still work. So the anti-Islam forces in the world turned toward a variety of (new) ways, all of which would be based on that same ancient deception.

Indeed, this antagonistic force threatening the Islamic world today has a massive army of agents in the form of professors, philosophers, doctors, and researchers—sometimes also writers, poets, scientists, and journalists—carrying Muslim names because they are of Muslim descent!! And some of them are from the ranks of the "Muslim religious authorities"!!

This army of "learned authorities" intends to break the creed of the Muslims,[3*] in all ways—through research, learning, literature, science, and journalism; and by prying the principles of the creed from their very foundation and derogating from the importance of the creed and the Shari'a, in equal measure.[10] They present the creed as though it could do what it really cannot do, and then when it is found "wanting" they say it is "reactionary"! They call for liberation from the creed and for excluding it from the realm of (real) life, (presumably) out of concern that it would be harmed with its entrance into worldly troubles or, on the other hand, that the integrity of practical life would be harmed should the creed invade that realm!!

They invent conceptions, teachings and principles for understanding and behaving which contradict and shatter the conceptions and teachings of the creed. . . . Then they decorate these contrived conceptions in a manner befitting the mutilation of the Islamic ideas and teachings. . . . They free the sensual desires from their restraints and they destroy the moral foundation on which the pure creed rests, in order that the creed should fall into the filth which they spread so widely on this earth. They mutilate the whole of history and falsify it, just as they falsify words!!

And so they are Muslims!! Do they not carry Muslim names? Bearing these Muslim names, they proclaim (their Islam at the beginning of the day). And with these tricks they apostatize at day's end!! With this and that, they fulfill the ancient role of the Jews. Nothing has changed except the form and the framework of that ancient (Jewish) role.

They display their Islam—you have proof of this in the (Muslim) names (they carry)—at the beginning of the day, and apostatize at the end of it, so that perhaps Muslims will (under the influence) leave their religion. . . . But let this be a secret among ourselves which nobody will understand except those who think as we do concerning the (danger of the) destruction of this (Islamic) religion. "Do not have trust in anyone except those who follow your relgion."[11]

The agents of Zionism today are like that. . . . They agree with each other on one issue . . . , which is the destruction of this (Islamic) creed at the first auspicious and unrepeatable opportunity. . . . This Jewish consensus (on destroying Islam) would never be found in a pact or open conference. Rather it is the (secret) agreement of one (Zionist) agent with another on the important goal, as something fundamental (and unquestioned).[4*]

One (Jew) trusts only another, One Jew confides only in another. . . . Then they make a great display—some of them at least—of the very opposite of what they really want and what they are plotting. . . . The environment surrounding them is prepared, and all the apparatus is readied. And those who understand the truth of this religion (Islam) on this earth have either gone into hiding or fled!![12]

The Qur'an spoke much about its Jews and elucidated their evil psychology. It is not mere chance that the Qur'an elaborates on this. For there is no other group whose history reveals the sort of mercilessness, (moral) shirking and ungratefulness for divine guidance as does this one. Thus had they killed, butchered, and expelled many of their prophets. This is the most disgusting act that has come out of any community which had sincere preachers of the truth. The Jews perpetrated the worst sort of disobedience (against Allah), behaving in the most disgustingly aggressive manner and sinning in the ugliest way. Everywhere the Jews have been they have committed unprecedented abominations.

From such creatures who kill, massacre, and defame prophets one can only expect the spilling of human blood and any dirty means which would further their machinations and evilness.

The noble Qur'an relates to us astonishment at the strange way of the Jews:

Say: Whoever is an enemy to Gabriel—Gabriel it was who brought it down upon your heart, with Allah's permission, confirming what was before it, and serving as guidance and good tidings to the believers. . . . Whoever is an enemy to Allah and His angels and His messengers, and Gabriel and Michael—indeed Allah is an enemy to the unbelievers.[13]

In the story of this challenge, we may understand another Jewish characteristic. . . . These people (the Jews) went to an extreme in anger and rage—an extreme which exceeded all proper bounds—over "his sending down his bounty to those of his servants whom he chooses." This led the Jews to an internal contradiction which cannot stand against reason. . . . The Jews heard that Gabriel was sent down as Allah's representative to Muhammad (Peace Be Upon Him). And when the Jews' opposition to Muhammad had gone to the end point of enmity and wrath, they were consumed by the desire to fabricate a fantastic story and a vacuous "proof" (against Gabriel). They claimed then that Gabriel was their enemy because he came with destruction and punishment and that this is what prevented them from believing in Muhammad—that is, because Muhammad's companion was Gabriel. And (they claimed, further) that if the one who brought the revelation had been Michael, they would then have believed; for (in their opinion) Michael brings abundance, plenty and rain.

This (would have been) a ludicrous rage (against the Jews on Gabriel's part), but (still they claimed) that (Gabriel's) hatred and rancor toward them drove him to every kind of impetuosity. But was Gabriel really a person working with them or against them, or according to some program of his own? No. Gabriel was only a servant of Allah, obeying his will and not opposing what He commanded!

But the black fury of the Jews toward Gabriel (Peace Be Upon Him) extended to (Muhammad) the Messenger of Allah (May Allah Bless Him and Bring Peace Upon Him).[14]

What brought the Jews to all this was their jealousy of the Messenger of Allah (May Allah Bless Him and Bring Peace Upon Him). They were jealous of Muhammad because Allah chose him for this mission, which the Jews expected would be theirs, and they were angry because Allah generously bestowed his revelation on that one among his servants whom he chose (that is, Muhammad).

It is ingratitude which appears here in the Jews as a natural disposition. (This is) the characteristic of narrow selfishness which lives strongly in (their) fanaticism, causing them to feel that any good which comes to others is tantamount to having been taken from the Jews themselves. This disposition of theirs does not allow them to feel the larger human connection which binds humanity together. Thus did the Jews (always) live in isolation.

The Jews feel that they are a group cut off from the tree of life, and they just wait for humanity to meet with disaster. They harbor hatred for others. They consequently suffer the punishment due to those who hate and bear rancor. This in turn leads the Jews to make others suffer these same punishments repeatedly, in the form of dissensions among peoples and wars which the Jews themselves foment in order to make profits from them.

Through these wars and disturbances the Jews cultivate their continuing hatred (for others) and the destructiveness which they impose on people and which others (then needs be) impose on them. . . . All of the evil arises only from their destructive egoism: "grudging that Allah should send his bounty down to those of his servants whom He so chooses."[15]

The Jews' black hatred of Allah's messenger, the Qur'an, and Islam caused them to prefer polytheism to Islam—and they are a People of the Book.

Today, the Jews prefer communism—another evil connection—to this religion (Islam). Indeed, they institute these heretical doctrines in order to fight against Islam![5]*

There is a hadith about the Battle of the Ditch, transmitted by Muhammad Ibn Ishaq from a number of transmitters. Here a group of Jews were mentioned; among them were Sallām b. Abī al-Huqayq al-Nadrī, Huyayy b. Akhtab al-Nadrī, Kinānah b. Abī al-Huqayq al-Nadrī, Hawdha b. Qays al-Wa'ilī, and Abū Ammār al-Wa'ilī. These people were from Banū Nadīr and Banū Wa'īl. They are the people who joined together for a massive attack on the Messenger of Allah, Peace Be Upon Him. They rode out until they came to the Quraysh in Mecca. They then called the Quraysh to war against the Messenger of Allah—Peace Be Upon Him—saying: "We shall be with you against Muhammad until we have annihilated him." The Quraysh said to them: "O you Jews. . . . You are the first People of the Book and you know about the (religious) dispute in which we are bitterly engaged with Muhammad. Is our religion the best or is his?" The Jews answered: "Indeed, your religion is better than his, and your claim is more in the right than his"!!![16]

The Jews are the people about whom Allah revealed:

Did you not see those who were given a portion of the Book believing in demons and false gods and saying about those who rejected Islam: "These people are more rightly guided than those believers who are in the path of Islam"?[17]

Then there is Allah's statement "Or are they jealous of the people for what Allah, Most High, gave them of His abundance?"[18]

Thus when the Jews said to the Quraysh (that the religion . . . of the Quraysh was better than Muhammad's), it made the Quraysh happy. And so the Quraysh waxed enthusiastic for war against the Messenger of Allah, the war to which the Jews had invited them. And they prepared for it.

Allah, the most mighty, was right: "You will surely find the worst enemies of the Muslim to be the Jews and the polytheists . . ."[19]

The literary form of this (Qur'anic) passage could

mean that it was a general pronouncement to the Messenger, issuing forth in the most general sort of articulation; and that, therefore, it was a broad public pronouncement, because it contained a clear and bare fact which one may discover (for oneself).

Once this has been established, the matter which directs (our) attention in the formulation of this passage is the precedence (here) of "the Jews" over "the polytheists," in the sense that the Jews (are designated) as "the worst enemies of the Muslims"; and that the strength of the Jewish enmity is clear and explicit—an established matter which anyone who looks can see and which anyone who so desires can find!!

Certainly it is true that the simple conjunction "and" in (ordinary) Arabic (literary) expression designates the joining of two things (which are assumed to be of equal weight and standing), and not one thing following (or inferior to) the other. . . . But the Jews' being in first position here, when it has usually been assumed in our tradition that they are less antagonistic toward the Muslims than are the polytheists—because the Jews are essentially a People of the Book—carries a special significance other than that usually obtains with the ordinary usage of the conjunction "and" in Arabic (literary) expression!! Here—*at the very least*—is the acknowledgment that the Jews' status as People of the Book does not change the existing reality, that is, that the Jews, like the polytheists, are the worst enemies of the Muslims!![20]

(And we might even argue that our saying) "at the very least" here does not negate the possibility that the meaning (of this passage) might even be that the Jews' enmity (toward the Muslims) *is* in fact stronger than that of the polytheists.[21]

For if people would become aware of this sacred principle of historical reality which has been evident from Islam's inception and until the present moment, then they would not hesitate to confirm that the enmity of the Jews toward the Muslims was always stronger, crueler, and deeper in its persistence, as well as being of longer duration, than was the enmity of the polytheists.

The Jews have confronted Islam with enmity from the moment that the Islamic state was established in Medina. They plotted against the Muslim community from the first day it became a community. The Qur'an (in fact) contained directives and suggestions concerning this (Jewish) enmity and plot. These directives were themselves sufficient to portray this bitter war which the Jews launched against Islam, the Messenger of Allah and the Muslim community during its long history. This is a war which has not been extinguished, even for one moment, for close on fourteen centuries, and which continues until this moment, its blaze ranging in all corners of the earth.[6*]

The Messenger had made a treaty of coexistence with the Jews when he first arrived in Medina. He called them to Islam which would have confirmed the Torah which they possessed. But the Jews did not honor this pact,

being in this instance as they were with every covenant they made with their Lord or their prophets long ago. Thus did Allah say about them:

We have revealed to you clear signs. Only the unbelievers have rejected them. Why, whenever they make a treaty does one group of them violate it? In fact, most of them are unbelievers. And when a Messenger of Allah would come to them to confirm what they already had (i.e., their revelation) a group of those who had been given the Book would reject the Book of Allah behind the backs of (the others), as if they did not know.[22]

The Jews have preserved in their heart of hearts an enmity toward Islam and the Muslims from the day that Allah brought the Aws and Khazraj together in Islam.[23] Thus the Jews had no choice (but to oppose Islam) from the day that the leadership of the Muslim community was established with the Messenger of Allah at its head. For then the Jews already had no opportunity to take control.

The Jews used every weapon and all means which the scheming Jewish genius could devise, and such devices had helped them since the years of (their) captivity "in Babylon" (their) slavery in Egypt . . . and (their) ignominious conditions under the Romans. . . . Although Islam certainly made their situation more comfortable after various people had got fed up with them through the course of history, the Jews met Islam's offer of kindness with the ugliest plot and the most painful treachery, from the first day.

The Jews had gathered all the polytheistic forces of the Arabian Peninsula against Islam and the Muslims. They began collecting together the dispersed tribes for war against the Muslim community: "They say to those who reject Islam, 'These people are more rightly guided than the Believers who are in the path of Islam.'"[24]

When Islam overcame the Jews with the force of right (in the days when the people were real Muslims), the Jews turned around and conspired against Islam in a conspiracy of calumnies against Islam's books. The only thing which was spared from this conspiracy was Allah's Book (the Qur'an), which was guaranteed by his protection, glory be to him. And they conspired against Islam with a conspiracy in the ranks of the Muslims . . . , and an incitement to civil disturbances, by way of using the new converts to Islam and others who did not have any understanding of the necessity of Islamization of all areas. . . . The Jews also conspired against Islam by inciting its enemies against it throughout the world. . . . This has brought the Jews in the latest era to the point of being the chiefs of the struggle with Islam, on every foot of the face of the earth. . . . The Jews are (also) the ones who utilize Christianity and idolatry in this comprehensive war. . . . And they are the ones who create the circumstances and make the "heroes" who carry Muslim names. . . . And they attack every foundation of this religion (Islam), in a Crusader-Zionist war!! How right was Allah, the most mighty, in saying: "You will surely find the worst enemies of the Muslims to be the Jews and the polytheists."[25]

The one who incited the various parties against the emerging Muslim State in Medina, and brought together the Jews of Banū Qurayzah and others with the Quraysh of Mecca and the other (Arab) tribes in the peninsula . . . was a Jew.

The one who incited the peoples, brought together the small groups, and set loose the sectarian movements in the assassination of Uthman—may Allah be pleased with him—and all the catastrophes which followed this assassination . . . was a Jew.[26]

Those who conducted a campaign of disparagement and lies against the sacred narratives of the Messenger of Allah (Peace be upon him), and other sacred transmissions (about the Messenger), and against the biographical traditions concerning him, . . . [were Jews].[27]

And a Jew was behind the incitement of various kinds of tribal arrogance in the last caliphate; the (fomenting) of revolutions which began with the removal of the Shari'a from the legislation and substituting for it "The Constitution" during the period of the sultan, 'Abd al-Hamid; and the "hero" Ataturk's ending of the caliphate. Then behind the subsequent war declared against the first signs of Islamic revival, from every place on the face of the earth, . . . stood the Jews.[28]

Behind the doctrine of atheistic materialism was a "Jew"; behind the doctrine of animalistic sexuality was a Jew; and behind the destruction of the family and the shattering of sacred relationships in society, . . . was a Jew.[7]

The war which the Jews launched against Islam was longer, more extensive, and of greater ferocity than the war which the polytheists and idol worshipers perpetrated—then and now. . . . Indeed, (Islam's) struggle with the Arab polytheists did not last more than twenty years altogether. And likewise the battle with Faris[29] in the first period. . . . As for the modern period, the intensity of the struggle between the Hindu idol worshipers and Islam is vividly apparent, but it does not equal the viciousness of world Zionism which considers Marxism as a virtual Branch of its (own activities).[30]

❖❖❖

The story of the Banū Isrā'īl on which the Qur'an so elaborates, possesses the most extensively detailed and variegated wisdom. Among the many facets of this wisdom is the realization that the Banū Isrā'īl were the first ones who confronted the Islamic preaching with enmity, treachery, and war in Medina and in the whole of the Arabian Peninsula. . . . The Jews were enemies of the Muslim community from the first day. The Jews were the same ones who instigated the polytheists, made promises to them, and conspired with them against the Muslim community. The Jews were those who undertook the war of rumors, hidden conspiracy, and treachery within the Muslim ranks; just as they instigated the dissemination of doubts, suspicions about Islam, and falsifications of the Muslim creed and leadership. . . . All of that was before the Jews revealed their true face in (their) declared and open war (against Islam).

Is there any alternative, then, but to expose them to the Muslim community, so that the community may know who its enemies are, what the enemies' nature is, what their history is, what means they use, and what is the reality of the battle with them in which the Muslim community is immersed?

Allah indeed knew that the Jews would become the enemies of this (Muslim) community throughout its history; just as they had been the enemies of Allah's guidance throughout their entire past (before Muhammad's arrival). Thus the whole Jewish affair came into this (Muslim) community already exposed, as were the (Jewish) methods.

Another facet of this wisdom relates that the children of Israel possessed the last prophetic religion before Allah's final revealed religion (Islam), and that their history had extended for a long period before Islam . . . (we know also that in spite of their possessing true religion), there had occurred deviations from the truth in their belief, and that they had evinced a recurrent rejection of Allah's covenant with them. There were in their lives, consequently, certain influences of this rejection and deviation . . . , as become apparent in their ethics and traditions.

All this dictates that the Muslim community—which is the repository of all revelations and the nursemaid of the divine creed in its entirety—must be aware of the history of the Jews and the turnabouts (from Truth to falsehood) in this history. The Muslim community must then know the perils on the way (to success in upholding Allah's truth) and their dire consequences, as these are exemplified in the life and personality of the Banū Isrā'īl. This is so that the Muslim community may incorporate (the) Jews' experience—in creed and in life—into its total experience, and that it should benefit from this capital and take advantage of it over the course of the centuries. This Muslims must do in order to be protected—by a special characteristic—from the dangers of the journey, the entrance of Satan, and the stirrings of (religious) deviation (as happened to the Jews).

This wisdom also says that the experience of the Banū Isrā'īl was a story of numerous pages, covering a long period of time. Allah, indeed, knows that when peoples exist for a long time, their hearts will harden and deviant groups will emerge from their midst. Allah also knows that the Muslim community, whose history will stretch out until the End of Days, will inevitably meet hard times reminiscent of those in the life of the Banū Isrā'īl. This did Allah put before the leaders of the Muslim community and the renewers of Islam's message living examples of the tribulations which befall peoples (as we have seen in the history of Jewish transgressions). From these gruesome lesions, the Muslim leaders will know how to treat the disease after knowing its nature. (The Muslims will thereby avoid the worst possibilities of decadence inherent in their times of trouble. They will learn from the Divine lessons of the absolute evil which enveloped the nature of the Jews how to avoid such a fate, and with their pure nature they will indeed survive intact until the End of Days, as Allah's Chosen People. The Jews may try, but they will never destroy this People).

Therefore: The struggle between Islam and the Jews continues in force and will thus continue, because the Jews will be satisfied only with the destruction of this religion (Islam). Even after Islam had subjugated them, they continued to fight against this religion through conspiracies, treacheries and activating their agents in evildoing.

As for today, the struggle has indeed become more deeply entrenched, more intense, and more explicit, ever since the Jews came from every place and announced that they were establishing the state of Israel. Their greed now extends from afar to Jerusalem, and today they are merely steps away from it. . . . Nothing will curb their greed short of Islam's defeating them.

Battles for Jerusalem had made the rounds before. . . . The Jews had indeed done evil in the Holy Land. Thus did Allah send against them his servants, men of great strength, who roamed around the dwellings. And this was a promise fulfilled. But the Muslims—while preparing for the battle—must understand this Qur'an.

Certainly the Messenger's journey from the Masjid al-Haram to al-Masjid al-Aqsa was a journey for the best of reasons, for it connected (all) the great beliefs of (divine) guidance, from Ibrāhīm and Ismāʻīl (Peace Be Upon Them) down to Muhammad, Seal of the Prophets (Peace Be Upon Him). It also brought together, totally, as it were, the holy places of all the monotheistic religions. This was as though the meaning of this wondrous journey were to announce the legacy of the Final Prophet (Peace Be Upon Him) to the sacred teachings of the prophets before him and the inclusion in Muhammad's mission of all these previous sacred traditions, comprising (spiritual) horizons which transcend time and place and including ideas greater than the easily grasped ideas which seem revealed in it at first glance.[31]

The children of Israel will contest with Muslims over the legacy of the al-Aqsa Mosque. And the struggle will again be current.

"Then when the promise of the first of these came to pass, we sent against you Our servants, men of great strength who roamed round the dwellings. And this was a promise fulfilled."[32]

(Allah said about the Jews: "You shall do evil in the earth twice and you shall thereby ride very high.")[33] The first time (may be explained as follows): They rode high in the Holy Land. They had power and sovereignty there. Then they did evil in the land. Consequently, Allah sent against them him servants who possessed great strength, courage and power. His servants took possession of dwellings, . . . amused themselves in them, and next morning left in disdain. . . . They trampled underfoot everything and everyone, without fear. . . . "And this was a promise fulfilled," not a broken one and not a deception.

The story of (Jewish) evildoing was repeated; as were (Jewish) humiliation and expulsion (as punishment or this evildoing).

Whenever the Children of Israel reverted to evildoing in the land, punishment awaited them. The Sunna is resolute here: "If you return, then We return."[34]

And the Jews did indeed return to evildoing, so Allah gave to the Muslims power over them. The Muslims then expelled them from the whole of the Arabian Peninsula. . . . Then the Jews again returned to evildoing and consequently Allah sent against them others of his servants, until the modern period. Then Allah brought Hitler to rule over them. And once again today the Jews have returned to evildoing, in the form of "Israel" which made the Arabs, the owners of the land, taste of sorrows and woe. So let Allah bring down upon the Jews people who will mete out to them the worst kind of punishment, as a confirmation of His unequivocal promise: "If you return, then We return"; and in keeping with his Sunna, which does not vary. So for one who expects tomorrow, it is close!!

The Muslim is certainly never frightened by what he sees of (Jewish) power and threat, because "they fight united only (in the safety of) protected towns or from behind walls. Their courage is great, among themselves. You think they are united, but their hearts are scattered."[35]

Appearances indeed deceive. We see the solidarity of the unbelievers who are People of the Book, in their own affairs. We see their communal cohesiveness, as we sometimes see the unity of the Hypocrites in one camp. . . . But the most veracious report from on high tells us that they were in essence not like that, and that this was only an external and deceptive appearance. Once in a while this veil of deception is lifted. And then from behind it, the veracity of (Allah's) truth (in this matter) appears in this earthly, visible realm.

The believers (Muslims) were in touch with reality and their hearts were really united in Allah only when the other (Jewish) camp was starkly revealed to them—without these disparities, this inconsistency and hypocrisy which do not represent the reality of the situation.

The believers cannot be steadfast and secure unless they witness the "solidarity" of the People of Falsehood dissolving and collapsing.

The days continue clearly to reveal the truth of the Qur'an in its portrayal of the nature of the nonbelievers, wherever Muslims meet them, in any time and in any place.

And the recent complications in the Holy Land,[8*] between the believers sacrificing themselves and the Jews, is a confirmation of this (Qur'anic) teaching, in an astonishing form. For the Jews would fight the Muslims only from (the security of) fortified settlements in the Land of Palestine.... This when the Jews lost their cover for one instant they turned their tails and ran away like rats. It was almost as though this verse had been revealed about them at that moment.

Glory be to the Omniscient, the Knowing!!

*For further clarification of any references, please see original essay.

NOTES

1*. Consider the campaign of casting doubt on the Muslim creed and mobilizing (anti-Islamic) heresy in an Arab army, against belief in Allah, just some weeks before the defeat of 1967!!! Afterward, then, there was, for example, the dogged determination to remove Islam from the question of Palestine.

2*. "In the near future we shall make the president someone who is accountable (to us). At that time we will never again be hesitant in boldly effecting our plans, which this person, as our 'effigy' will be responsible for.

"In order that we achieve these results, we shall choose the candidates for these presidents from among those whose previous reputations were blackened by some scandal or some other shady and suspicious affair. . . .

"Thus a president of this kind will be a loyal promoter of our goals, he will fear notoriety. He will remain loyal to the authority of fear which always controls the man who has achieved power and who yearns to maintain his distinctions and his honors which are tied to his high position . . . " (*The Tenth Protocol of the Elders of Zion*).

3*. "We shall never permit the existence of any religion other than our own. For this reason, it is necessary for us to destroy all (other) systems of belief. The decisive result of this will be the deserved fruits of the heretics" (*The Fourth Protocol of the Protocols of the Elders of Zion*).

4*. "None of the members will disclose his knowledge of (our) secret to another. Because nobody permits an individual to enter into our world unless he was a perpetrator of infamous acts in his past life" (*The Protocols*, part 13).

5*. "Do not think that our statements are empty. Bear in mind that we arranged the success of Marx, in advance! . . . We always build and nurture Communism, pretending to help the workers in building brotherhood and working for the general good of humanity. This is what the socialistic Masons preach!!" (*The Protocols*, parts 2 and 3).

6*. While entering (Old) Jerusalem in June 1967, the Jewish armies shouted, "Muhammad died and had fathered only daughters." (N.B. *Translator's note*: It is historically true that Muhammad had only daughters and no sons. It is culturally true in Islamic terms that if a man has not fathered sons, this is a great humiliation and a disgrace to his manhood.)

7*. These three are, in order: Marx, Freud, and Durkheim. And additionally, behind the literature of decadence and ruin, was a Jew—Jean-Paul Sartre!!

8*. 1948. See *The Muslim Brothers in the Palestine War* by Professor Kamil al-Sharif (Cairo: 1949).

1. Qur'an: sura 2, al-Baqarah, vv. 74–76.

2. This is the common notion of many Muslim fundamentalist thinkers that the Jews and Zionists lie somewhere behind the secular nationalist politicians who currently conduct Muslim affairs of state. This idea takes pride of place in Qutb's essay.

3. 'Abd Allah b. Ubayy was the Khazraji tribal chieftain in Medina who, because of contractual alliances with the Jewish tribe of Qaynuga', prevented Muhammad from destroying these Jew. In later Muslim historical writings, Ubayy was invariably cast in the role of archvillain and friend of Islam's Jewish enemies.

4. The term "creed" here (al-'Aqidah), a key word in Qutb's vocabulary, has resonances of formal theological meaning. For the medieval theologians of Islam, 'aqidah was Islam's systematic and organized set of beliefs, its "catechism" which set out in orderly form the doctrinal tenets of the Qur'an. For Qutb it was this and more; for in his mind, 'aqidah was also Islam's main defense against the alien cultural onslaughts which modern times, in particular, had brought against Islam. The Jews and Islam's other enemies have always known that 'aqidah is what enables Muslims to live as Muslims, and that if 'aqidah falls, then Islam's historical importance will vanish.

5. Qur'an: sura 3, The House of 'Imran, v. 69.

6. The term "community" (al-Ummah) is a central idea and practice in Islam. *Ummah* is the total group of Muslims in the world, who by virtue of their acceptance of Islam's revelation and aspirations, are united in this national body. The *ummah*, as this collectivity, has its own Islamic destiny to be fulfilled, beyond the salvational goals of its individual members: world historical and political leadership.

7. Qur'an: sura 3, The House of 'Imran, v. 71.

8. In many contemporary Muslim writings, particularly those of the fundamentalists, the term "heroes" (*abtāl*) is used ironically to refer to the secularized and Westernized leaders and intelligentsia who, in fundamentalist opinion, are often agents of the Jewish-Zionist cabal against Islam.

9. Qur'an: sura 3, The House of 'Imrān, v. 72.

10. "Creed" (*al-'aqīdah*) and "Shari'a" refer here to the doctrinal foundation of Islam and the behavioral framework of life for Muslims. These are Islam's two sides which together constitute the total tradition.

11. Qur'an: sura 3, The House of 'Imrān, v. 73.

12. This is another typically fundamentalist allusion to the "Muslims" who, in their ignorance of what is required, capitulate so easily to the alien influences.

13. Qur'an: sura 2, The Cow, vv. 97–98.

14. Qutb here raises the ancient Islamic idea of the Jews' alleged hatred of Islam being base on their hatred of Gabriel, the channel of Muhammad's revelatory inspiration. There is no evidence in Jewish sources, however, of this sort of attitude toward Gabriel. The origins of the Islamic doctrine, therefore, remain obscure.

15. Qur'an: sura 2, The Cow, v. 90.

16. For this tradition see Ibn Hisham's edition of Ibn Ishaq's *Sirah Rasul Allah* [*The Life of Muhammad*], trans. A. Guillaume (Lahore, Karachi, Dacca: Oxford University Press, 1967), pp. 450–60.

17. Qur'an: sura 4, The Women, v. 51.

18. Qur'an: sura 4, The Women, v. 54.

19. Qur'an: sura 5, The Table, v. 82.

20. That is, in spite of the (erroneous) belief of many Muslims that the People of the Book were better than the polytheists, the conjunction "and" used in this verse syntactically determines that there must *at least* be an equivalence between the two terms joined by "and." This would, by Divine Declaration, make the Jews *at least* as strong in their enmity toward the Muslims as were the polytheists.

21. That is, because the verse mentions the Jews *before* the polytheists.

22. Qur'an: sura 2, al-Baqarah, v. 99.

23. The Aws and Khazraj were the two leading Arabian tribes in Medina and its environs.

24. Qur'an: sura 4, The Women, v. 51.

25. Qur'an: sura 5, The Table, v. 82.

26. This was a standard Islamic historiographical thesis and interpretation of Uthman's assassination. See chapter 3 of the commentary from Nettler's book.

27. This is Qutb's standard contention that the Jews always tried to destroy Islam's tradition.

28. Many fundamentalist Muslim writers in our century saw the catastrophe of the Ottoman caliphal collapse and the ensuing secularization of Turkey as a Jewish conspiracy.

29. Faris was a Muslim with an allegedly Jewish background.

30. The Jewish-Zionist-communist equation was a standard formulation of modern Muslim writers, whether fundamentalist or other.

31. The Qur'anic story of Muhammad's night journey, explained in later tradition as having been to Jerusalem, was pregnant with a symbolism which supported the Islamic claim of the Qur'an's being the universal truth, incorporating and completing all previous revelations.

32. Qur'an: sura 17, The Table, v. 5. The background story to this verse appears in the following Qur'anic quotation.

33. Ibid., v. 4.

34. Ibid., v. 8.

35. Qur'an: sura 59, The Mustering, v. 14.

CHAPTER 27

The Jews in the Qur'an

Abdul Sattar El Sayed

The blind sedition stirred by the Jews in the Arab nation set off the flames of war in this area, which remained since the dawn of history, as the land of peace and security, guidance, mercy, and human welfare. Such sedition however, was not the first deed by the Jews throughout their history whether old or new. Jewish history has almost been an interconnected series of acts of sedition and intrigue in any land or community where they happened to live.

Jews in any community have always been a factor of sedition. They have moreover been a curse that spread among the people bringing about corruption, sowing the seeds of enmity and hatred, and breaking the bonds of brotherhood between peoples, who henceforth engage in ceaseless conflict. Hence, the unabating flames of war destroy the good elements among the people, and extinguish all manifestations of civilization.

We acknowledge this fact ourselves and so do any people who may have been plagued by the Jews as individuals or in groups. For the Jews are like evil which has the same effect whether it were big or small, or like germs of a malignant disease where only one germ is sufficient to eliminate an entire nation. This, after all, is bound to happen if such germ was left to control the body and infuse its poison into it, or once it was left to burn and destroy like a fire in a pack of wood that is left free with no one to extinguish it in the bud.

Prior to this hardship which God imposed on the people of Palestine and later the whole of the Arab nation, the Jews' evil was spread all over the world. Each people in the community of nations had its due share of their evil and plague and to tolerate it. Therefore, we as Arabs did not regard the Jews in a different light from that of other peoples, that is, a pest which humanity had to tolerate and live with like other calamities of life and other diseases. The Jews in this way constituted a general hardship, and calamities are usually light and easy to take when they are general.

However, the arrival of the Jews from East and West and the subsequent effort of recruiting them from all parts of the world to come and live in this region represented a great evil which the Arabs have to bear all alone. It follows consequently that this area exists on the edge of an ever-restless volcano that erupts every now and then to cause disaster and destruction.

This argument is based neither on predictions about matters which are likely to happen nor prophesies which we derive from the past experiences of Jewish life in all communities where they lived. The basis of our argument, however, is the present reality and the current telling circumstances; the land of Palestine that witnessed destruction and disaster, and the 2 million homeless Palestinians who live out in the open, or in tents and caves, are the harvest of such plague and remnants of such volcano.

On the other hand, we do not state these facts for the sake of history, nor do we reveal them to urge for help and assistance against such plague. The matter is much more important and more serious; it is our life that is threatened with dangers and our existence which is being overwhelmed by the portents of extinction.

It is therefore natural that to defend our life and existence is a matter that concerns us in the first place. In this domain we must offer the best we can and mobilize all material and moral capabilities to fight the danger; exactly in the same way as the body when it is invaded with disease. No matter how great the inherent energies which the body may lose in the act of resisting disease, it has to fight even if it must sacrifice a part or two of its organism.

It was once said, "If you fall, use your cunning." Cunning here means that we should know our enemy in a revealing manner in order to find out the truth about it, and recognize its predominant nature that governs its conduct and determines its approach in the community where it exists. By so doing we would have gone halfway or even more than halfway toward overcoming our enemy and eliminating it, exactly as a physician who has to diagnose the disease before setting out to carry out the operation.

We are fortunate enough to have an available docu-

From the *Fourth Conference of the Academy of Islamic Research* (Cairo: 1970), pp. 527–34.

ment that tells the truth about the Jews, and reveals their nature, life, and the inherent poison they carry as well as the remedy for such poison. This document is represented in the Holy Qur'an which provides the real description of the Jews, and constitutes the microscope through which we can see the pests and poisons that reside in their minds and hearts.

The Holy Qur'an spoke about the Jews in many verses, and on several situations and occasions scanning their moves, and depicting their line of thinking. It would thus be appropriate at this juncture to examine this plague closely, and by identifying it we can guard against, and avert, its danger. This has been provided by God to us as a sign of mercy and a blessing so that we may save our religion and life.

WHAT IS IN THE QUR'AN ABOUT THE JEWS?

Verses that were [the] subject of controversy:

Before expounding the verses of the Qur'an that exposed the Jews and revealed their shameful deeds and brought upon them humiliation and condemnation, I would like to speak about the controversial verses. Taken literally out of their context with other verses that were expressive of God's wrath against the Jews, such controversial verses might provide an argument for some people who say that if God had cursed the Jews in some verses, he however glorified them in other verses, and conferred his blessings on them.

Those people argued that if the latter verses did not confer on the Jews a higher status among the other nations on earth, they were bound at least to maintain for them a middle position between outright commendation and utter condemnation.

We shall not hasten to answer this argument. We shall first quote the holy verses that spoke about the blessings of God on the Jews and look into the implications of such verses. One of those verses says:

O Children of Israel! Remember My favour wherewith I favoured you and how I preferred you to (all) creatures. And guard yourselves against a day when no soul will in aught avail another, nor will intercession be accepted from it nor will compensation be received from it, nor will they be helped. And (remember) when We did deliver you from Pharaoh's folk who were afflicting you with dreadful torment slaying your sons and sparing your women: That was a tremendous trial from your Lord. And when We brought you through the sea and rescued you, and drowned the folk of Pharaoh in your sight. (The Cow, 47–50)

Another verse says:

O Children of Israel! We delivered you from your enemy and We made a covenant with you on the holy mountain's side, and sent down on you the manna and the quails. (Saying) East of the good things wherewith We have provided you and transgress not in respect thereof lest My wrath come upon you, and he on whom My wrath cometh, he is lost indeed. (Taha, 80–81)

These verses show the Children of Israel as having obtained the blessings of God who conferred on them his mercy. We should not interpret those verses and the like outside their context. We only say that, by virtue of their words, those verses speak about God's favors on the Children of Israel and reveal his great mercy and blessings upon them. God's great favors on the Children of Israel, however, were only intended as a trial to those people following which they were to receive a knockout blow from him if they ever showed ingratitude to such blessings and failed to offer due thanks and gratitude to God. There is, for instance, Korah whom God presented as a lesson for his people. God gave him so much treasure that the stores thereof would verily have been a burden for a troop of mighty men. He however did not pay back to God his due right in return for those favors. The more God gave him his blessings and favors the farther he got from him. So in grateful and unjust was Korah that God destroyed him and he went down in hell as an example for others. God says about him:

Now Korah was of Moses' folk, but he oppressed them, and we gave him so much treasure that the stores thereof would verily have been a burden for a troop of mighty men. When his own folk said unto him: Exult not. Lo! Allah loveth not the exultant. But seek the abode of the Hereafter in that which Allah hath given thee and neglect not thy portion of the world, and be thou kind as Allah has been kind to thee, and seek not corruption in the earth. Lo! Allah loveth not corrupters. He said: I have been given it only on account of knowledge I possess. Knew he not that Allah had destroyed already of the generations before him men who were mightier than him in strength and greater in respect of following? The guilty are not questioned of their sins.

Then went he forth before his people in his pomp. Those who were desirous of the life of the world said: Ah, would that unto us had been given the like of what hath been given unto Korah! Lo! He is Lord of rare good fortune. But those who had been given knowledge said: Woe unto you! The reward of Allah for him who believeth and doeth right is better, and only the steadfast will obtain it. So we caused the earth to swallow him and his dwelling-place. Then he had no host to help him against Allah, nor was he of those who can save themselves. And morning found those who had coveted his place but yesterday crying: Ah welladay. Allah enlargeth the provision for whom he will of his slaves and straighteneth it (For whom he will). If Allah had not been gracious unto us he would have caused it to swallow us (also). Ah, well-aday! The disbelievers never prosper. (The Story, 76–82)

The Children of Israel are nothing else but Korah himself. God brought him the riches and favors in plenty, but he did not receive them well. And later God sent a deluge on him to destroy him and his riches, for God's wrath befalls the unjust villages and his punishment is always painful and severe.

The favors of God on the Children of Israel and the revelations which he made to them were therefore a mere introduction to this hardship that God incurred on them. These favors only called for the punishment of God on them and constituted reasons leading to their expulsion by God from the community of human beings, and rendering them strangers in the society of men. The many messengers which God sent the Jews stand as a testimony that they were of a different nature than human nature, and that they were carriers of diseases and pests. Therefore, God sent them numerous messengers to try and treat such diseases and to alleviate the effect of such pests which could spread to corrupt the entire world.

THE QUR'AN AND THE TRUE DESCRIPTION OF THE CHILDREN OF ISRAEL

The Qur'an has drawn a gloomy picture of the Children of Israel, showing them only as a dispersed horde possessed with an evil soul that shuns all that is good and brings disaster to any straight way.

The description of the Qur'an of the Children of Israel is not a description of a phenomenon that appeared during the era of prophethood, but rather of an old disease which lived through the generations of the Jews' age after another.

The Torah, although the Jews have meddled and changed it, still contains much of their shameful deeds, and provides several examples of their deviations and the impudence of their souls. Our only explanation for the fact they did not omit or change those shameful deeds ascribed to them in the Torah earlier is because these qualities and deeds were sanctioned by them in the past; they found nothing wrong in pursuing such deeds or acquiring such qualities. Furthermore, the Jews acquired cunning and slyness and sanctioned every forbidden act and then pretended that these were God's orders to them, and provisions of their law. By so doing they wished to confer on those sins and vices the character of sanctity.

That is particular to divine acts and heavenly laws. They also persuaded themselves to follow such deeds and considered their inaction as inducing to bring them nearer to God.

But let us leave aside the heavenly legislation, and the questions of its perfection and grandeur, and let us resort to the rule of reason, and its provisions as well as the norms of right and wrong which have been accepted by the people. This will help us to realize the falsehood and injustice of the legislation of the Jews which is unjustly ascribed to God.

The Jews allege in the Torah that God commanded Moses, saying:

Thou shalt not lend upon usury to thy brother; usury of money, usury of victuals, usury of anything that is lent upon usury. Unto a stranger thou mayest lend upon usury, but unto thy brother thou shalt not lend upon usury; that the Lord thy God may bless thee in all that thou settest thine hand to in the land whither thou goest to possess it. (Deut. 2:30)

Usury is the most obnoxious of injustices, and the most disrespectful of the meanings of humanity. In its application of usury modern civilization heeded the principles of justice and equity more than the Jews had set out in the Torah as legislation. The principle of usury in modern civilization is a general one that applies to all people, and not confined to "strangers" as the Jews had decreed.

People throughout the ages have endeavored to the best of their ability to alleviate the hardships and evils brought about by war. Therefore people agreed on a certain set of rules connected with the conduct of war which should be binding to belligerent parties. These rules have been made possible by the feelings of brotherhood and affection that still exist among people.

The Jews however established for themselves a law of war whose source they ascribed to God; in a bid to develop in them the hatred and animosity to all humanity, they alleged that such laws were among the commands of God to them so that their provisions may become part and parcel of their feelings and thinking. Thus they would find no deterrent if they attempted to kill and destroy since by so doing they would be executing the orders of God.

According to the allegations of the Jews, in respect of their relations with people who are alien to them, they come to the lands of other people in lightning raids like that of a swarm of locust on a rich green land with the only object of destroying all that is available. But the divine command, according to the allegations of the Jews, has not yet finished. If the previous command drew for them the law of war between them and the outlaying lands, it remains to be seen what type of legislation now applied in their relations with the neighboring countries.

The question which may arise in this connection is how can a humanistic legislation issue such orders in respect of conflict, dispute, or war between neighbors?

Skirmishes might take place between neighbors, and such skirmishes may develop into conflict and fighting.

For this very reason, all laws whether heavenly or earthly called for good neighborhood, and respect of rights and obligations of neighbors to avert any abuse of affection or contacts between people which might disturb their mode of living and cause insecurity and instability.

Such commands turned the life of the Jews into a devastating danger and an obnoxious evil both on them and on those people who have been unfortunate enough to be their neighbors. According to those heavenly commands, the Jews are required to stir war with their neighbors once they have the opportunity to do so. Again they are required to eliminate and uproot the neighboring peoples so that no man or animal would exist therein. Such action would, in the opinion of the Jews, bring them security. It is amid the totally wasted lands and wilderness that they can live in peace.

Such has been the tradition of the Jews with their neighbors throughout history. Time could not change those rules since the Jews themselves have not changed and so long as their false Torah from which they derived their teachings also existed.

Hence we can discover the watchword which helps reveal the secrets of Jewish history and the calamities that befell the Jews in ancient and modern times dispersing them all over the world and depriving them of a homeland. For the Jews wherever they existed act like poisonous thorns, and chronic diseases that spread germs into the body of their neighbors and continues to do so unless the thorns are uprooted and the diseases are eliminated.

By setting out this horrible picture of man and the most obnoxious aspect of humanity represented by the Children of Israel, the Qur'an has stated an established fact which had earlier been related by the Torah and established by the events of history.

WHAT DOES THE HOLY QUR'AN SAY?

The Qur'an has provided several verses that exposed the true character of the Jews and revealed their defects. In the Qur'an the Jews have been evidently portrayed as deserving humiliation, shame, and condemnation. We shall however confine ourselves here to those verses that depict the broadliness [*sic*] of the unstable character of this lost herd or the snakes as they have been called by Jesus Christ.

Among the distinctive qualities of the Jews as set forth in the Qur'an is their breach of covenants. "And because of their breaking their covenant, We have cursed them and made hard their hearts" (The Table, 14). Some of those who are Jews change words from their context and say: "We hear and disobey" (Women, 45). The Jews are thus the most daring of liars, hypocrites, and dishonorable creatures. Hypocrisy has been one of their distinct characteristics, for this quality coexists only with absence of manhood and unscrupulousness.

Among the other qualities of the Jews which were mentioned in the Qur'an was their keenness to preserve their life. So keen were they on life that they considered as legitimate and regarded as precept of religion every means towards this end. For them the end justifies the means. In this respect God says:

And thou shalt find them greediest of mankind for life and greedier than the idolaters. (Each) one of them would like to be allowed to live a thousand years. And to live (a thousand years) would by no means remove him from the doom. Allah is seer of what they do. (The Cow, 96)

Love of life for the Jews undermines all morals, virtues and meanings of dignified life. Their homes have been something like caves of wild beasts of fortified bastions in which they spent the biggest amounts of money and effort. God says in this connection: "And when thou shalt seest them their figures shall please thee, and if they speak thou giveth ear unto their speech. (They are) as though they were blocks of woods in striped cloaks. They deem every shout to be against them. They are the enemy; so beware of them. Allah confound them. How they are perverted" (The Heights, 4).

It was this love for life that brought upon them humiliation inflicted upon them by God. For they loved life. Therefore, God punished them after they had hurt his prophets with word and deed. Here God says: "Ignominy shall be their portion where so ever they are found save (whether they grasp) a rope from Allah and a rope from men. They have incurred anger from their Lord and wretchedness is laid upon them. That is because they used to disbelieve the revelations of Allah and slew the Prophets wrongfully. That is because they are rebellious and used to transgress" (The Family of Imran, 112).

For that reason God sent upon them those who may torture them. He said: "And (remember) when they proclaimed that He will raise against them till the day of Resurrection those who would lay on them a cruel torment. Lo! Verily thy Lord is swift in prosecution and lo! Verily He is Forgiving, Merciful!" (The Heights 1, 167).

For this reason God decreed that they should be scattered all over the globe so that no nation would be made out of them. They would rather live as an evil on earth, or like diseases and pests. Their evil is thus not confined to one people or one nation. "And We have sundered them in the earth as separate nations" (The Heights, 168).

This is our enemy, and the disease that plagued our lands. According to the descriptions provided of the Jews in the Qur'an, they stand as an enemy which is devoid of any human feelings. They are rather a pest or a plague that is cursed like Satan who was expelled by God from the realm of his mercy. This enemy is also sent out to launch war on people exactly like Satan. We have been warned by God against Satan when he said: "Satan is your enemy so regard him as such." God also warned us against the Jews when he said: "The most violent enemies for the believers are the Jews and those who disbelieved." Again he said: "And when thy seest them their figures please thee and if they speak thou givest ear unto their speech. They are as though they were blocks of wood in striped cloaks. They deem every shout to be against them. They are the enemy; so beware of them. Allah confounded them. How they are perverted" (The Heights, 4).

The presence of the Jews in this part of the world was motivated by the fact that it was the only area in the world that remained steadfast before atheism and heathenism which was spread by the Jews all over the world. The faith that still exists in the Arab nation, brought the Jews to this area in a bid to extinguish the light of God but, God will keep his light on in spite of the heathen people.

In the same way that the devil, rallied by his supporters, is weak and fragile before the force of faith (the cunning of the devil is weak) so are the Jews who may now appear strong by virtue of the support of imperialism. In fact they are weaker than the devil and inferior to him in cunning in the face of the faithful people who adhere to religion. God has shown us the result of their conflict with us when he said: "They will not harm you save a trifling hurt, and if they fight against you they will turn and flee. And afterwards they will not be helped" (The Family of Imran, 111).

God also says: "You are more awful as they fear in their bosoms than Allah. That is because they are a folk who do not understand. They will not fight against you in a body safe in fortified villages or from behind walls. Their adversity among themselves is very great. Ye think of them as a whole whereas their hearts are divers. That is because they are a folk who have no sense" (Exile, 13–14).

If faith was to be the equipment of each battle in the war of right, it represents the only effective weapon in the face of the wrongdoers. Once this weapon weakens, the wrongdoers will increase in strength and the evil will spread and flourish everywhere at its will.

Faith, therefore, is our faith in this battle. It is the force with which we may face the evil and defeat our sly enemy with the will of God. Our share of faith is in fact plentiful. Islam has called upon us to offer ourselves as martyrs in the sake of right, and we have responded to this call. God has not let us down in any situation with an enemy no matter how strong it might be.

This has been a description of our past with an enemy whom we confronted with faith and patience. And thus will be our present with the enemy which has been struck with humiliation forever by God. It will be one of the virtues of God which he conferred upon us to delegate us to bring destruction upon this people in accordance with His instructions that say:

"And (remember) why they proclaimed that He will raise against them till the Day of Resurrection those who would lay on them a cruel torment."

CHAPTER 28

The Jewish Attitude toward Islam and Muslims in Early Islam

Abdul-Hamid 'Attiyah al-Dibani

Praise be to God who confers success upon the truly pious, and shows the right way to wholehearted believers. Peace and prayer be to our Prophet Muhammad, his household and Companions, and all who had raised the standard of Islam with firm resolve and penetrating insight, until they had triumphed through Islam, and Islam had triumphed through them; those who have been, since, the finest examples of excellence and great merit, and leaders to light and truth.

May God be pleased with them, and with those who had been, and are, still, following their guidance up to the Day of Judgment.

It is a great pleasure to me to express, on behalf of the Libyan Islamic University, our regards and acknowledgment to his Eminence, Sheikh Hassan Ma'moun, Rector of Al-Azhar, and chairman of the conference. Equally do we thank the members of the Islamic Research Academy.

These are the greetings occasioned by the hopes aimed at through their researches. They are also those of the Muslim masses, seeking a ray of light that comes forth from this conference to illuminate darkness, dispel the perplexity, and who show them the way, through which they would go forward to recover their hope for power, and to stamp out the transient setback.

This would draw ample dimensions for a future based on firm foundations, in which the ultimate aims of Islam could be realized in Muslim society. A glorious and happy life would, thus, be effected, so as to lead mankind to peace and prosperity, through constructive cooperation and human brotherliness, fostered by closely blended relationships.

Verily, Muslim scholars are the sole pioneers, leaders, and true promoters of the genuine reform movement in the Muslim community, whose eminent rank and close adherence to her principles and beliefs can only be judged through their efforts and moral courage in uttering truth, fearing not, in the cause of God, any blame the blamers may cast upon them. Everything depends on their leading role, and the right fulfillment of their duty in guiding and directing the Muslim community.

Whenever they say the truth, yet nobody hearkens to them, utter only what is demanded from them, setting aside the rules and injunctions of their faith, or issue resolutions and recommendations meant to be idle plans, committed only to paper, and nothing of which is put into effect, save what is conformable to caprice and self-seeking interests, then, it is quite reasonable to declare that the Muslim community is just going to her inevitable doom.

We are suffering today a momentary setback to which we have stooped our heads. Hence, there would be no place to deny the facts, nor to keep them out of sight; since the defeat should provide us with an opportunity to rectify mistakes and abuses, so that it might not prove to be a total annihilation.

The Muslim community, in seeking, nowadays, the right counsel that emanates from true piety to God, hopes that the Azhar, by virtue of its glorious past, and the unique eminence accorded to it by believers, be the source of this shining light and right guidance.

The vehement atheistic trends that overwhelm our present-day world with their pernicious evils, the widespread doctrines based on the materialistic approach, and the iniquitous triad, identified with atheism, Zionism, and colonialism are all pushing the Muslim community to bypaths that mislead her from the way of God. Each item in that triad adopts a particular method of its own in seizing the available opportunities, most appropriate to realize its evil designs.

Some maintain that the major factor in the setback is our adherence to our old-established traditions, and our incompetence to develop up-to-date institutions based on the confirmed facts of science and technology. They add to their allegations our (so-called) antiquated usages, and everything that is closely related to our faith and beliefs.

Others account for the setback as due to a mere accident in which the enemy had been favoured by good luck. They go on to assert that we had been following the right way which we have only to pursue until we gain our victory.

From the *Fourth Conference of the Academy of Islamic Research* (Cairo: 1970), pp. 507–26.

It is as if they wanted the deep wounds, well known to everyone as impairing the Muslim community to remain unhealed; so that they might be of great help to the enemy who is lying in wait for her total destruction, availing himself of both the internal and external factors.

Yet, the candid truth we have to declare is that "the latter generations of this community can only be reformed in the same way as the former ones had been reformed."

Our Muslim community is closely attached to a creed and a system that had never been contrived by man; and, thereby, they are beyond any mistaking or misapprehension. She is attracted to her glorious past, and linked up with her great Apostle. Her present-day enemy is (the selfsame enemy of old), identical with the one who had confronted her Prophet in the early days of Islam. Thus she is bound to oppose him, until the Almighty inherits the earth and all who are thereon.

God, Glory be to Him, had pointed out that the Jews are more hostile to Muslims than the idolaters (since He mentioned them prior to the latter).

He said, "Thou wilt find the most vehement of mankind in hostility to those who believe to be the Jews and the idolaters" (5:82). He had, thus, relieved us from the trouble of identifying that relentless enemy whose intents, plans, and character He had equally made plain.

Through his great Apostle, God has shown us how to repel his aggression, and warned us against the adoption of any other way, save his straight path. "And (He commandeth you, saying): This is My straight path, so follow it. Follow not other ways, lest ye be parted from His way. This hath He ordained for you, haply, ye may fear" (6:153).

Shortly after his emigration to Medina, the Apostle of God (P.B.U.H.) was unexpectedly faced with the wiliest intrigues concocted by these Jews. He had not anticipated such hostility; since they were Scriptureries [*sic*] and adherents of a revealed religion, the teachings of which often state that there would appear, at the end of time, a Prophet whose attributes and signs are given in full detail.

Therefore, the Medinan Jews had been, out of all kinds of people, most entitled to hasten to the aid of Muhammad (P.B.U.H.); especially because they used at the beginning of his residence in Medina, to seek his assistance against the idolaters, whenever there arose any quarrel or dispute between them and the latter.

When the Jews perceived that the expected Prophet had been an Arab, and not one of themselves; and that he had made them equal to the Gentiles; since he had renounced their claim to be the chosen People of God; when their influence came to be on the wane, after the Prophet's emigration to Medina; when they became unable to pursue exploitation and the devouring of peoples wealth through usury; when their material interests proved to be conflicting with the teachings of the new religion, they could not help expressing their refutation

and hatred, and showing open enmity obstinacy; thus, overlooking what is explicitly mentioned in the Torah.

For this reason, the Medinan Jews had become a thorn in the side of this budding Call. Such a malicious tendency is fully explained by the narrative of Ibn Salam which had been reported by Ibn Ishaq (in the biography of the Prophet [P.B.U.H.]).

Ibn Salam said that he had been informed of the Apostle of God, recognized his name and characteristics, and identified the time of his long-awaited appearance.

When he reached Medina, he alighted at Quba, in the dwellings of Bani 'Amr Ibn 'Awf. A man came, announcing the Prophet's arrival, while I was climbing up a palm tree of my own; and my (paternal) aunt was sitting underneath.

When I heard the news of the Prophet's advent, I said, "God is Most Great." My aunt, on hearing my Takbir, said that if I had known of the coming of Moses, son of 'Imran, I would not have uttered more. "O aunt!" said I. "By God! He is the brother of Moses, who had been sent with an identical mission."

She asked me whether he was the Prophet whose call was about to be announced. I answered her in the affirmative.

Thereupon, I went to the Apostle of God! The Jews are a folk, known to be given to slander and calumny. I would like that you hide me in your house, call them unto you and question them about me (before announcing to them that I have been converted to Islam).

He did as I had told him. The Prophet, then, asked the Jews, "What kind of man is Al-Husein Ibn Salam in your group?" to which they answered that he was their master, the son of their master, and that he was their most learned scholar.

Thereupon, I came out and said, "O Jewish Folk! Fear God, and acquiesce in what had been revealed to you. By God! you do know that he is the Apostle of God whose name and signs are explicitly stated in the Torah. (You should bear evidence that his person and character agree in every particular with the prophetic description in your Scripture).

I solemnly testify that he is the Apostle of God; and wholeheartedly believe in his Mission. Thereafter, they accused me of telling lies and kept on reviling me. Then, I said to the Prophet, "O Apostle of God! Have I not told you that the Jews are a slandering people, addicted to fraud, treachery, and impiety?" Then, I announced that my household and I had adopted Islam.

Ibn Ishaq reported, as well, what had been related by Safiyyah, daughter of Huyaiyy Ibn Akhtab, and wife of the Apostle of God (P.B.U.H.). She said,

I had been most beloved of my father and (paternal) uncle Abu Yàsir. Never did I meet them with their children, without favouring me with greater affection and fondling.

When the Apostle of God reached Medina, and alighted at Qubà' in the dwellings of bani 'Amr Ibn 'Awf, my father and uncle went to him during the night, and did not come back safe at sunset.

They were tired out and quite unable to walk. I cheered up at once, as was my wont; but they did not show any regard to me; because of their grief and perplexity.

I heard my uncle Abu Yàsir, asking my father Huyaiyy Ibn Akhtab, whether he did identify the Prophet and recognize him. To both these questions, he answered in the affirmative. When he was, later, asked about his impression of him, he said, "By God! I would be his relentless enemy, so long as I live."

Such was the attitude of the Medinan Jews toward the Prophet. Out of arrogance and obstinacy, they had categorically denied his Mission. But when they perceived the warm reception accorded to him by the Arabs who had adopted Islam, and realized that these converts would be a dominating power in Medina, to be reckoned with, they were so perplexed that they tended to follow policy of reconciliation and appeasement. Hence, they welcomed the idea of concluding an agreement of good neighborliness between them and the Muslims.

In this historical pact that came to be arranged, is clearly shown, more than the most optimistic could have anticipated or realized, the tolerance and fair dealing of Islam toward the dissidents; since it comprised the following terms:

1. The abolition of racial 'asabiyyah, or group feeling between the Jews and Arabs. Admission to the new Faith was allowed to everybody. In case a Jew was converted to Islam, be would he, ipso facto, accorded the same rights and standing of his Muslim brothers, without any discrimination whatsoever, as stated in article (16) of the pact, which goes to say:

Whoever of the Jews follows us has the same help and support (as the believers), so long as they are not wronged (by him); and he does not help (others) against them.

2. Cooperation in expenditure on the vital interests of the Medinan society, so long as Muslims were exposed to danger through enemy attacks. (In other words, the Jews should contribute with the Muslims while at war with a common enemy.) In article (24) of the pact, this was expressly stated as follows:

The Jews bear expenses along with the Believers, so long as they continue at war.

3. Every group could dispose of his wealth, so long as it paid what was due for the defense of the town as previously stated. This is implied in the article (37):

"It is for the Jews to bear their expenses and for the Muslims to bear their expenses."

4. Wholehearted union against imminent danger that might befall Medina, through enemy attack, as stated in the pact (art. 37):
   (a) *Between them, (that is, to one another), there is nasr, help against whoever wars against the people of this sahifah, document.*
   (b) *The valley of Yathrib (the old name of Medina), is sacred for the people of this document (art. 39).*
   (c) *Anything which is (particularly) inviolable (to a certain people), should never be given neighborly protection, without the consent of its people (art. 41).*
   (d) *No neighborly protection is given to Quraysh and those who help them (art. 43).*
   (e) *Between them (the People of this document) is help against whoever suddenly attacks Yathrib (art. 44).*

5. Equality had been accorded to all the Jews, inhabiting Medina and its suburbs. Formerly there had been some sort of discrimination amongst them. Banu Al-Nadir, for instance, considered the Banu Qurayzah as of a lower status; they did not pay for a murdered Qurayzite, save a half of the diya, blood money.

But it was expressly stated in the pact that

the Jews of Banu 'Awf are an ummah, a community along With the Believers. For the Jews of Banu'l n'Najjar, for those of Banu Sa'idah, for those of Banu Jusham, for those of Banu Al-Aws, for those of Banu Tha' labah, the like of what is for the Jews of Banu Awf (art. 25:31).

6. Religious freedom had been guaranteed, and made secure for everybody.

To the Jews their religion, and to the Muslims their religion (art. 25).

7. The Apostle is the head of the Medinan People to whom the major cases and feuds have to be submitted for settlement.

Whenever among the People of this document, there occurs any incident (disturbance) or quarrel, from which disaster for it (the People) is to be feared, it is to be referred to God and to Muhammad, the Messenger of God (God bless and preserve him). (God is the Most Scrupulous and Truest Fulfiller of what is in this document) (art. 42).

8. Each of the two parties (Muslims and Jews) should heed the interests of the other. Equally to be pursued are mutual advice and fulfillment of promises.

Between them is sincere friendship and honorable dealing not treachery (art. 37).

9. Liable to punishment is he who betrays the terms of this document which excludes from the guarantees it had offered to the Jews all sorts of infringement that might be committed by anyone of them. (That is to say):

with the exception of anyone who has done wrong, or acted treacherously; he (thus) brings evil only on himself and his household (art. 31).

These are the most important terms of the pact, the Prophet (P.B.U.H.) had concluded with the Medinan Jews.

But, did the Jews undertake to fulfill the clauses of this covenant? Did they engage themselves in the pursuit of their daily affairs: in industry, trade, and husbandry? Did they mind their own business, exercising freely their religious observances, within the secure and extended scope of the rights the Prophet had accorded to them?

Or did they relapse into their wonted malicious dispositions that had previously incited them to defy their own prophets, thereby, adopting in their lives such an uninterrupted series of disavowal, treachery, and refractoriness?

To answer these questions, we have to deal, in the following, with certain historical facts that reveal their attitude toward the call to Islam, during its initial stages. It would, therefore, be made clear to what extent did the Apostle show forbearance, clemency, and tenderness towards them. Yet there had been no bounds to their envy, malice, transgression, treachery, and (especially) their violation of all the terms of the pact they had pledged the Muslims to comply with.

1. Certain Medinan Arabs had equally had the same reasons as those that had incited the Jews to disavow the new Faith. Some of them, such as Abdullah Ibn Ubayy had been eagerly aspiring to sovereign power. The latter's clan was on the point of (stringing pearls) to crown him.

But after the emigration, the majority of the Medinese

people disregarded him and professed their allegiance to the Prophet to whom they submitted the management of all their affairs. The disaffected were thereby estranged; their hearts were filled with envy and malice.

Thus, they had to profess their conversion, while disguising their unbelief,—as had been done by certain Jews—, so that they might have free scope to concoct plots against Islam.

These Hypocrites became a ready instrument in the hands of the Jews and their rabbis, in designing intrigues, and disseminating doubts and suspicions in the way of the Islamic Call. So obstinate had they been as to use every possible exertion to ply questions of which the point (—as seemed to them—) was often difficult to turn aside; questions intended to dissipate the Prophet's efforts in returning answers and refuting their viewpoints.

Such confusion was meant to impede any constructive work for the establishment of Islam. This had taken so distinct a feature and so common a usage that their chiefs became well known for their doggedness and opposition to what was being revealed to the Prophet.

We cite as instances: Huyayy Ibn Akhtab of the Banul-Nadir, Abdullah Ibn Sariyy of the Banu Tha'labah, Zeid Ibn Al-lassit of the Banu Qainuqa; Al-Zubeir Ibn Bata of the Banu Qurayzah, and Labid Ibn A'sam of the Banu Ruzayq.

Some of them said, "How surprising is Muhammad's assertion that Solomon son of David had been a Prophet. By God, he had been nothing more than a wizard." Hence God's saying was revealed, "Solomon disbelieved not; but devils disbelieved, teaching mankind magic."

2. The Medinan Jews used to stir up strife and sedition, by recalling the old feuds between the Aws and the Khazraj, the flames of which had only been allayed by the good offices of the great Prophet (P.B.U.H.) and the tenets of the new faith.

Once, Shass Ibn Qais, the Jew, happened to pass by a group of the Aws and the Khazraj who had been conversing with each other in a common meeting. He came to be exasperated, because of their close fellowship and reconciliation through Islam, after they had been implacable enemies in pre-Islamic times.

He said, "The Aws and the Khazraj have become united in this town. By God, there would not be room for us after they had come to be closely attached together." Then, he told a young Jew who was in his company to attend their meeting, recall the Battle of Bu'ath, and recite the poems that had been composed by the two clans, on that occasion.

The young Jew was thus able to incite sedition by arousing the old quarrels that had already been quelled by Islam. Disputes arose between the two clans; and mutual boasting became so intense that two men of the respective groups rushed upon each other. One of them said to the other, "If you like, we would renew the battle."

The two clans were exasperated and gave assurance to fight each other in Tabirah, to which they repaired, calling for arms. When the Prophet (P.B.U.H.) was informed of the intended combat, he went out to them accompanied by his companions from among the emigrants.

He said, "O Muslims! Will you be moved by the call of the Jahiliyyah (to be swayed by the passions of pre-Islamic times), whilst I am in your midst, after God had guided you to Islam, accorded you His favor, saved you from unbelief and the heathen usages of the Jahiliyyah, and reconciled your hearts?"

The people perceived that they had been tempted by the devil; so they obeyed the Prophet, and went away with him thereupon, respecting Ibn Qais and what he had done, a revelation was sent down, in which God, the Almighty said, "Say: O People of the Scripture! Why disbelieve ye the revelations of God, when God (Himself) is Witness of what ye do? Say: O People of the Scripture! Why drive ye back believers from the way of God, seeking to make it crooked, when ye are witnesses (to God's guidance)? God is not unaware of what ye do" (3:98, 99).

As regards the Muslims who had been incited by the intrigue plotted by this Jew, to combat each other, God, the Almighty said, "O ye who believe! If ye obey a party of those who have received the Scripture, they will make you disbelievers after your belief. How can ye disbelieve, when God's revelations are recited unto you, and His messenger is in your midst? He who holds fast to God, he indeed is guided unto a right path" (3:100, 101).

❖❖❖

3. The Jews used to refute openly the injunctions sent down in the revelations, as when the Apostle told the believers to change their "*qiblah*," direction of prayers (from Jerusalem) to the Ka'ba, the Sacred House (of Mecca).

Rifa'a Ibn Qais, together with other rabbis, went to the Prophet to express their disapproval of this change, saying: "O Muhammad! What made you alter your former *qiblah*, whilst you are claiming to be adopting the religion of Abraham?" To these, Good, Glory be to Him, had referred when he said, "The fools among the people will say: 'what had induced them to abandon their former *qiblah*?' Say: To God belong both east and west. He guideth whomsoever He pleaseth unto the right path" (2:142).

Yet they went on disseminating rumors among Muslims in which they asserted that if the former *qiblah* were the right one, then the latter would be wrong. If the latter were true, then Muslims' prayers that had been directed to the former *qiblah*, would, thereby, be rendered unfounded. For this reason, God, the Almighty, reassured Muslims by saying: "And never would God make your faith of no effect, for God is to all people, most surely full of kindness, Most Merciful" (2:143).

Again did they go to the Prophet, intending to incite sedition, and arouse doubts and perplexity amongst Muslims; since they offered to follow him and to believe in his Faith, were he to return to his former *qiblah*.

A revelation was sent down on this occasion in which God, Glory be to Him, said, "And even if thou broughtest unto these who have received the Scripture all kinds of portents, they would not follow the *qiblah*, nor canst thou be a follower of their *qiblah*; nor are some of them followers of the *qiblah* of others. And if thou shouldst follow their (vain) desires after the knowledge which hath come unto thee, then surely wert thou of the evildoers" (2:145).

❖❖❖

4. When all their designs came to naught, they adopted other means to realize their aims; that is to say to cause perplexity and confusion among Muslims.

The Jews, led by Al-Harith Ibn, Abdullah Ibn Saif, and Adi Ibn Zeid, held a meeting, and planned that they would, in the morning simulate faith in what had been revealed to Muhammad; then they would recant in the evening; presuming that after having collated certain tenets in the new religion with those of the Torah, together with their religious lore, they had found out that the former was nothing but mere falsehood and fabrication.

They had based their assumption on the fact that they were Scriptureries [*sic*], while other people were illiterate and Gentiles. Hence, they were entitled to advise Muslims to disown their faith.

God, the Almighty had disclosed their evil designs, and admonished Muslims to be on their guard. Thus, He said, "O People of the Scripture! Why confound ye truth with falsehood, and knowingly conceal the truth? And a party of the People of the Scripture say: Believe in that which hath been revealed unto those who believe at the opening of the day, and disbelieve at the end thereof, in order that they may turn back" (3:71, 72).

Facing these frauds and intrigues, the Prophet did not lose his forbearance, relying on divine revelations to expose the designs of the Jews and to refute their lies. When they realized that all their secret plots had come to be disclosed through this means, they were compelled to have recourse to avowed opposition and manifest challenge.

❖❖❖

5. When Muslims won victory over the unbelievers in the Battle of Badr, and the Apostle sent two of his men to convey the glad tidings to the people of Madina together with the names of those who had been killed or

captured from amongst the Qurayshites, Ka'b Ibn Al-Ashraf declared at the top of his voice: "Is this true? Do you believe that Muhammad had killed those most eminent people amongst the Arabs, as named by these two men? By God! Were this to be true, then death would be better than life."

But once the news proved to be true, he proceeded to Mecca where he stirred up the tribe of Quraysh to avenge their heroes, killed at Badr, by elegies lamenting their death.

On his return to Medina, he disquieted Muslims by the publication of amatory sonnets addressed to certain of their women. Being a foul-tongued poet, he started to compose satirical poems against the Prophet.

Since these jeering remarks were wanton violation of the terms of the treaty, concluded between the Muslims and the Jews, in which it was explicitly stated that "anyone who has done wrong or acted treacherously, would bring evil only on himself and his household," the Apostle did not want to hold Ka'b's clan responsible for his crime, despite the fact that he had been one of its notable figures. (He only intended that the punishment should be confined to the culprit.) So he sent some Muslims to kill him.

This was the least the Apostle could do to keep the peace and to avoid the outbreak of war between the Muslims and the Jews. Only was the culprit held accountable for his crime, though he had been one of the chiefs of his clan.

After having dwelt at length with these convincing evidences, respecting the crass offenses of Ka'b against Islam and its Apostle, I think that it is not possible for anyone to criticize what the Muslims had done to Ka'b unless he be prejudiced, or given to slander and calumny as had been the wont of certain Orientalists, most of whom are of Jewish persuasion.

6. As regards the sympathetic relations between the Jews and the Hypocrites, their audacious contempt of Islam, and the hurting of Muslims' feelings, the issue had not been confined to Ka'b.

A Muslim woman, once visited the marketplace of the Banu Qainuqa. She sat down at the shop of a Jewish goldsmith waiting for some ornaments. The goldsmith wanted her to uncover her face, but she declined to do so.

Thereupon, he unperceived, pinned her skirt behind to the upper dress. When she arose, the awkward exposure excited laughter, and she screamed with shame. A Muslim apprised of the affront, slew the offending Jew; the brethren of the Jew in their turn fell upon the Muslim and killed him.

Consequently, the Apostle wanted to put an end to these betrayals and crimes against the public order. He met the Banu Qainuqa in their marketplace and said to them, "O Jews! By the Lord, beware of the punishment of God, to Whom belong Glory and Power; a punishment that would happen to you in a way similar to that of Quraysh. Believe therefore, since ye know full well that I am the Apostle of God, as stated to you in your Scripture, and the Covenant of God to you."

With this prophetic admonition and wise words, the Apostle (P.B.U.H.) called these Jews to comply with the pact and to maintain their belief in God. They should have responded to his appeal, or at least to fulfill their pledge by keeping friendly relations with Muslims and promoting good neighborliness.

But, since the Banu Qainuqa were the most valiant among the Medinan Jews, possessing much more riches and weapons, they made so insolent a retort as to lead to their annihilation.

They said, "O Muhammad! You know that we are your people, so do not deceive yourself, because you have fought a people who have no experience in war; hence you could overcome them. By the lord, were we to combat you, you would soon realize that we are the people (most qualified as warriors)."

Facing this menacing presumption announced solemnly by the Banu Qainuqa in their marketplace, the Prophet had to accept the challenge; otherwise, it would mean loss of Muslims' prestige. (If no response were made to this defiance), Muslims would expect to suffer much more effrontery and audacity.

On this occasion was revealed God's saying: "If thou fearest treachery from any group, throw back (their Covenant) to them, (so as to be) on equal terms; for God loveth not the treacherous" (8:58).

The Prophet said that he had misgivings, as regards the Banu Qainuqa, so he marched forth to attack the offending tribe which was besieged for fifteen days until they surrendered at discretion. They asked to be released, together with their women and offspring and to withdraw from Medina. Muslims would take, as spoils of war, their property, armor, and goldsmiths' tools.

This victory availed the Prophet of the opportunity of shedding their blood, were he keen to make a clean sweep of his enemies; as he was, then, the conqueror wielding full authority; and the Jews were lowly and submissive. But his noble character made him accede to this peaceful victory. So he released them; and they proceeded to Adhri'at (on the confines of Syria).

7. The Prophet intended that the other Jewish clans would consider the measures he had taken (against the Banu Qainuqa) as a lesson for them, respecting their destiny. He wanted them to comply with their pledges in the pact, so that he might occupy himself exclusively in repelling the external enemy who had been lying in wait to attack Medina from all directions. But the Banu Al-Nadir were not exhorted by what had happened to the Banu Qainuqa; they went on violating the terms of the covenant.

When the Qurayshites came with their hordes to attack Medina, shortly before the Battle of Ohod, the Prophet asked the Banu Al-Nadir to lend unto God and his Apostle loans, so as to repel the enemies' aggression, in accordance with the clauses of the pact, in which it was stated that the Jews should contribute with the Muslims, while at war with a common enemy.

But the Banu Al-Nadir replied scoffingly, "You claim our Lord to be asking for loans from us. Only is the penniless who borrows from the well-to-do. Were what you assume to be true, then God would be poor and we would be rich."

Hence, was revealed God's saying: "God hath heard the taunt of those who say: 'Truly, God is indigent and we are rich!' We shall certainly record their word with their slaying of the Prophets in defiance of right, and We shall say: 'Taste ye the penalty of the scorching Fire'" (3:181).

When the Qurayshites came to attack Medina, Mukhayriq, the Jew, one of the Banu Tha'labah clan called the Jews to jihad, saying, "O Jews! You know that you should abide by the help and support of Muhammad."

They remonstrated that the day was a Sabbath (which should be kept); but he told them to break it. Then he took his sword and other equipments and said: "Were I to be killed, my property would be handed over to Muhammad to be at his disposal." Then, he fought until he was killed. The Prophet (P.B.U.H.), on hearing of his death, said: "Mukhayriq had outdone all the Jews in worth and merit."

8. After the Battle of Ohod, the Banu Al-Nadir rejoiced at the setback that had befallen Muslims. They said: "Muhammad cannot pretend now to be anything more than an aspirant to the kingly office. No true claimant of the prophetic dignity hath ever been beaten in the field, or suffered loss in his own person and that of his followers as Muhammad hath."

9. Nevertheless, the Apostle did not hold the Banu Al-Nadir accountable for what they had said or done. But it occurred later after the tragedy of Bi'r Ma'unah, that a Muslim killed two men of the Banu' Amir, and the Muslims had to pay their blood money which they could not afford to do. Thereupon, the Apostle went to the Jews, seeking their aid in its defrayment, in accordance with the pact concluded between them and the Muslims.

The Jews answered courteously, promised assistance, and invited him to sit down, while they made ready the money. The Apostle sat beside a wall and the Banu Al-Nadir started to plot against him.

One Nadirite said: "We may not find the man sitting

in the same place." Another said: "Who would ascend the roof and roll down a stone upon him; thus, it would be our great relief?" 'Amr Ibn Jihash expressed his willingness to do so, and ascended the roof. Owing to a divine monition, the Apostle arose abruptly, and walked out of the assembly, together with his companions.

Thus, there was no reason for treating the Banu Al-Nadir kindly. The Prophet (P.B.U.H.) thereupon commissioned Muhammad Ibn Maslamah, one of the Ansars' Helpers, to deliver this command: "Thus sayth the Prophet of the Lord: 'ye shall go forth out of my land within the space of ten days: whosoever after that remaineth behind shall be put to death.'"

They began their preparations to depart had it not been for Abdullah Ibn Ubayy, the head of the Hypocrites, who reassured them that he had two thousand men of his clan ready for their defense. "Were you attacked" he said, "we will join hands with you; and if you were evicted, we will go out with you."

The Banu Al-Nadir were deceived with these promises (and resolved to hold fast in their fortress). So they sent to Muhammad saying: "We will not depart from our possessions; do what thou wilt against us."

Thereupon, the Prophet invested their stronghold, and the siege lasted for twenty-five days. The Jews, seeing no prospect of relief from the Hypocrites, were now ready to lay down their arms and abandon their lands, taking with them all their movable possessions that could be carried by camels. But they submitted to the stipulation laid down by Muslims that they should relinquish their weapons.

Not withstanding, the evil actions the Banu Al-Nadir had committed against Islam and its Apostle, there was no place to malice in the hearts of the prophets. The Apostle acceded to their surrender; some of them went to Khaybar, and others to Adhri'at.

On this occasion, the Qur'anic chapter entitled Sūratū'l- Hashr (the exile) was revealed, dealing at length with the shameful treason (and the projected murder of the Prophet) by Banu Al-Nadir, together with the attitude of the Hypocrites.

10. Thus, Medina came to be relieved from one of the Jewish clans, known to have been most hostile and dangerous to Islam. There remained only the Banu Qurayzah who had been most reconciled to Muslims. Islam had accorded them rights identical with those of the Muslims, as we have already explained.

But the untoward events and crucial circumstances then besetting the Muslims had revealed that their apparent friendship was due to their weakness, and incapacity to do battle; and that their hearts were full of malice and ungratefulness. As a matter of fact, they wished to destroy Muslims root and branch.

It is to be noted that Huyayy Ibn Akhtab, who had

gone out with the Nadirites, wandered with a group of Jews throughout the Arabian Peninsula, inciting the Arabs, especially the tribes of Quraysh and Ghatafan, against the Apostle. He could muster confederate hosts and march with them to attack Medina. All of them had been bent on eradicating the new faith.

Huyayy Ibn Akhtab started to put into effect the plot he had promised the confederates to perform; that is to persuade the Jews who had remained in Medina to act treacherously against the Muslims (by launching an attack in the rear, while the Muslims were being engaged in battle against the confederates).

Huyayy said to Ka'b Ibn Asad, the head of the Qurayzite clan: "I have brought to you all that makes you mighty and proud. With me are the overwhelming numbers of the confederated army, as 'a surging sea.' I have conducted to thee the tribe of Quraysh with its leaders and notables. They have halted near the mountain of Ohod, and have made a compact with me that they would never depart, until they had annihilated Muhammad and his adherents."

Ka'b Ibn Asad head of the Qurayzites said to him: "By God, you have brought to me but shame and disgrace, it is like a waterless cloud with thunder and lightning but yielding no rain. . . . Woe to you O Huyayy! Leave me, for Muhammad had always been quite truthful and sincere."

At last Huyayy could persuade Ka'b, chief of the Banu Qurayzah to relent; thereby, responding to violate the pact in the most crucial and hazardous moment. The Muslims were then undergoing a severe strain, being unequipped and outnumbered. The confederates, behind the trench that had been dug by the Muslims there, were about ten thousand men.

This is the occasion referred to in the Holy Qur'an. "When they came upon you from above you and from below you, and when eyes grew wild and hearts reached to the throats, and you were imagining vain thoughts concerning God there were the believers sorely tried, and shaken with a mighty shock" (33:10, 11).

Once the Banu Qurayzah had acceded to break faith with Muslims, and to act treacherously against them, Islam was about to be eradicated within the twinkling of an eye, had it not been for Nu'aim Ibn Mas'ud al-ashja'i, one of the leading notables of Ghatafan, who had been destined by God to sustain the cause of Islam at this critical moment.

Possessing the ear of both sides, the Jews and the unbelievers, feigning to be one of the disaffected among Muslims, he worked out a deceitful plan intended to cause discord and discouragement between the two parties in this confederacy.

Nu'aim went first to the Banu Qurayzah, and representing himself as their friend, he said: "Beware of trusting the tribes of Quraysh and Ghatafan; since they are free to do what they like. If the issue proved to be worsening, respecting their interests, they would go back to their country, without being affected with any harm.

But you are fellow citizens with the man (Muhammad). So before compromising yourselves irretrievably by joining in the renewed attack on Medina, you ought to demand from Quraysh seventy men of their notable as hostages, who would be a guarantee against being in the last resort deserted (and left in the grip of Muhammad's power)." Suspecting no harm, they agreed to act on his advice.

Next, Nu'aim went to the allied chiefs of Quraysh and Ghatafan who did not mistrust him. He cautioned them against the Jews. "I have heard," said he, "that the Banu Qurayzah intend asking you for hostages; beware how ye give them, for they have already repented of their compact with you and promised Muhammad to give him up the hostages to be slain; thereby gaining the Prophet's forgiveness."

This insidious plot immediately took effect; and the confederacy was broken. When the Jews demanded hostages, the unbelievers regarded this as a confirmation of Nu'aim's intelligence, and became fully persuaded of the treachery of the Banu Qurayzah. The confederate chiefs became disheartened and discord was rife.

The Lord had sent against the enemy the tempestuous wind, and the unseen armies of heaven who had been fighting for Muslims. Terror had been struck into the heart of the enemy. Thus, the Lord is he who had defeated the confederates. . . .

Then God, the Almighty, commanded His Apostle to proceed to the Banu Qurayzah to reckon with them as active collaborators with the enemy. He invested their fortress for twenty-five days and when they were reduced to great distress, they offered to capitulate. They assented that their fate be decided by Sa'd Ibn Mu'adh. Sa'd's judgment was that the men should be put to death, the women and children sold into slavery (and the spoils of war divided among the army).

On this occasion was revealed God's saying: "And He brought those of the People of the Scripture who supported them down from their strongholds, and cast panic into their hearts. Some ye slew, and ye made captive some. And He caused you to inherit their land and their houses and their wealth, and land ye have not trodden. God is Able to do all things" (33:26–27).

This is the retribution for high treason, as decreed in all the codes, both ancient and modern.

11. Thus, Medina came to be purified of the Jewish malice, unbelief and perversion of truth. But a party of the Banu Al-Nadir, after their exile, settled down among their Jewish brethren at Khaybar, where they formed a gang that started to conspire against the Apostle of God.

This chief was Abu Rafi' Salam Ibn Abul-Huqayq, who had taken part in the confederate force which besieged Medina. He was now encouraging certain bedouin tribes in their depredations against Muslims.

Most prominent among these was the clan of Sa'd Ibn Bakr, inhabiting Fadak who had joined hands with the Jews. A portion of the dates of Khaybar was to be given to them, as a remuneration for their participation in launching raids against Muslims.

Thereupon, an expedition was sent against the Jews of Khaybar which captured some of their camels and flocks (but it produced no other results). But owing to the fact that Abu Rafi', chief of the Jews of Khaybar had been the chief instigator of these plots, the Apostle sent five of his men who dispatched him.

Usair Ibn Rizam was elected in his place, as chief of the Jews. He declared that "he would deal a hard blow at Muhammad that had never been dealt before; and that he would maintain the same relations with the tribe of Ghatafan to start fresh attacks against Medina."

The Prophet (P.B.U.H.) sent Abdullah Ibn Rawaha with thirty men to persuade Usair to be on good terms with Muslims (and to visit Medina). They assured him that Muhammad would make him ruler over Khaybar, and that he would treat him with distinction.

Usair consented to set out with them, with thirty of his Jewish followers to conclude a peace treaty with the Apostle. Yet when they traveled some distance, Usair repented of having assented to a proposal of peace that would make him a client of Muslims.

In betrayal to 'Abdullah Ibn Rawaha and his men, Usair stretched out his hand toward his sword. 'Abdullah, on perceiving this, cried out: "Is treachery O enemy of the Lord?" As he spoke, he leaped from his camel, and aimed a deadly blow with his sword at Usair. Upon this the Muslims turned upon the Jews, and murdered all of them.

The Prophet (P.B.U.H.) marched against the Jews of Khaybar, and conquered their strongholds, one after the other. The Jews surrendered on condition that their lives be spared, and that they be allowed to be banished from their lands, without taking any of their movable possessions.

Here the Prophet had shown magnanimity toward them, the like of which has never been recorded in history before or since. He dealt with them tenderly; because they were not accountable for the offenses of their chiefs.

Though their request was the most they asked for, it was the Apostle who offered to make peace with them. They were left in possession of their lands, on condition that they surrendered part of the yield to Muslims. The Apostle said to them: "You are to hold your fields, pending our pleasure." The same terms were accorded to the Jews of Fadak, Taima' and Wadi Al-Qura.

Thus ended the question of the Jews who had been living in the Hijaz. The Prophet (P.B.U.H.) wanted to make that region (in the Arabian Peninsula) a country for both the Jews and Muslims, where the former would have the rights and duties entitled to them. But they persisted in intriguing against the Muslims, violating the pact and the pledges they had undertaken to fulfill; despite the fact that they were in need of being protected by Muslims.

With the expansion of Islam beyond the land of Khaybar, when Persia and the Byzantine Provinces were conquered by the Arabs, during the reign of the rightly guided caliphs, the Jews of Khaybar became a thorn in the side of Muslims.

'Umar Ibn Al-Khattab feared they might attack Muslims in the rear. So the caliph put into effect what the Apostle had stipulated; that is, they were to be left on sufferance with their fields at a rent of part of the produce.

Despite what they had done to some Muslims, among whom was his own son, 'Umar treated them fairly; he paid them the value of their lands and date palms, as compensation. Then they were sent away to Syria.

Throughout the long ages of Muslim history, the Jews had been quite powerless under the rule of Islam. But in modern times the colonialist powers could put into effect their designs. Once Muslim jurisprudence had been discarded as a rule of life, the Jews could establish a state of their own in the heart of the Muslim world, to defy Muslims, and to gain victory over the Arabs in three consecutive battles.

Would it be possible for us, now, after having dealt at length with this topic, to realize the actual cause of our setback? It is the severance that took place between religion and life. Thus our relationship with God that distinguishes us from our enemies came to be last.

'Umar Ibn Al-Khattab had candidly declared, that "a body of troops would be much more at stake, through committing transgression, then when facing the enemy. God might give power to a more wicked people over them, as when he empowered the unbelieving Hagians against the Israelites, once the latter had acted in a way that incurred the wrath of God."

Now then, what conclusions that can be drawn from this brief survey, and found to be most relevant to our present-day circumstance?

These might be summed up in the following.

1. If the Jews, during the prophetic age, started by intrigues, plots, and the dissemination of doubts, as to the appropriateness of this faith to be a rule of life, something identical had been done by Jewish Orientalists, and the adherents of subversive doctrines, most of whom are known to be Jews.

A prominent part in the propagation of such ideologies is played everywhere by Zionists who wield (some sort of) control over all the information media in our present-day world conditions.

2. If the Jews, during the early days of Islam, had completely failed in their secret plots to weaken the hold Islam, and the solidarity of the Muslim. Community owing to the fact that the latter had tenaciously adhered to the Book of their Lord and the Sunna of their Prophet—, they have nowadays achieved remarkable success in disuniting Muslims and dissipating their efforts, through the latter's departure from the main sources of their spiritual values which are the fundamental shield against materialism.

When these major fountainheads of strength were lost, the Jews, by virtue of their wealth, influence, and equipment, could launch their attacks against Muslims, occupy their territory, profane that which is held as sacred, and afflict them with dispersal and dreadful torment.

3. Early Muslims had been wide awake to the fact that their deadliest enemies were the Jews. God, Glory be to Him, had not commanded Muslims to make their requisite military preparations, save after he had made mention of the Jews. He said, "Make ready for them all thou canst of (armed) force and of horses tethered, that thereby ye may dismay the enemy of God and your enemy . . ." (3:60).

But (unfortunately) we have at present, closed our eyes to this holy guidance and the tenets of our Islamic heritage which provided us with the means of distinguishing between friends and foe; and revealed to us the character of this deceitful and wicked enemy.

God, the Almighty, stated that the Jews would never be satisfied unless Muslims were to abjure their religion. "It is never the wish of those without faith among people of the Scripture, nor of the Pagans that anything good should come down to you from your Lord. But God will choose for His special Mercy whom He will, for God is Lord of grace abounding" (2:105).

"Never will the Jews or the Christians be satisfied with thee unless thou follow their form of religion" (2:120).

"Quite a number of the People of the Scriptures wish they could turn you back into misbelievers after ye have once believed, through envy from themselves, after the truth has been made manifest to them" (II, 109).

God, the Almighty, had notified us of the extent of their military preparations which were the outcome of their dismay, cowardice, and feebleness, when they encountered true believers, face to face. So much had they dreaded Muslims that they renounced their close alliance with Hypocrites.

God, Glory be to Him, said, "Ye indeed are a keener source of fear in their hearts than God. That is because they are a people devoid of understanding. They will not fight against you, in a body, save in fortified villages or from behind walls; their valour is great amongst themselves. Thou dost reckon them as one body; but their hearts are separated. That is because they are a people who have no sense" (LI–X, 13, 14).

"They will not harm you save a trifling hurt; and if they fight against you, they will show you their backs. And afterward they will not be helped" (3:111).

Equally did God make plain that humiliation, wretchedness, and submission had been stamped upon them, and that they would suffer dispersion and torment till the Day of Judgment.

God, the Almighty, said, "And then thy Lord proclaimed that He would surely raise against them, till the Day of Resurrection those who should break them evil torment; verily thy Lord is quick in retribution; but verily He is Oft-Forgiving Most Merciful" (7:167).

Were we to go back to the Book of God, and the biography of his Apostle deducing from them the true character and manners of the Jews, we would come to a well-worked-out plan, based on the most veritable postulates, and minutest data since these had been elucidated by the Knower the Aware.

4. The Apostle (P.B.U.H.) had tried all sorts of pacts with them, as had been done by former prophets and Apostles; but they had been unworthy of any of them. No limits are known to their selfishness, cupidity, and (pseudoethnocentrism), which are so intense that they are incessantly bent on the violation of any pledge, out of their (superstitious and conceited) belief that they are the allegedly only people whom God had chosen, and that other peoples are Gentiles toward whom they are not bound by any obligation whatsoever.

Hence, present-day Muslims should never treat with them for peace; since it had been proved, beyond doubt that they are a mere gang of robbers and criminals, to whom trust, faith, and conscience mean nothing.

Our return to (the true teachings of) Islam would restore to the Muslim community its vital principles the force of which would realize endurance and steadfastness, confidence and will, courage and faith. Thus could be established the equitable power that would be a factor in promoting peace and prosperity for the world at large.

There would be built up inside the world of Islam armaments plants, so that Muslims might be in no need of importing them from enemy countries which would certainly make a ban on such exports for fear of their possible use against them.

Our return to Islam would realize the economic integration between the various Islamic countries. The Muslim community, far-flung between both East and West, and disunited on account of foreign conflicting ideologies would become "analogous to the human body, any organ of which, suffering from ailment, would be immensely painful to the rest; thereby originating in its entire organism symptoms of fever and insomnia."

We would be a nation most ardent to establish itself, to

render services to others, to live for its cherished and ultimate aims, and to die in the Way of God. Thus, we would be favored by divine help. "God will certainly aid those who aid His (Cause); for verily, God is Full of Strength, Exalted in Might (Able to enforce His Will)" (22:40).

In short, we express our thanks and acknowledgments to the leading men in the U.A.R., and to the organizers of this conference who have made available every opportunity to ensure its success. We pray God, the Almighty, to inspire those in authority, in the Muslim world with vigor and confidence, so that they may hasten their steps in putting into effect the tenets of God, and in following the radiant light of his guidance. This is because we are at present in dire need of prompt action, speedy help, deep insight, and the return to God. "He who holdeth fast to God, he indeed is guided unto a right path" (3:101).

CHAPTER 29

Extracts from "Arab Theologians on the Jews and Israel"

D. F. Green (David Littman and Yehoshafat Harkabi)

THE ATTITUDE OF THE JEWS TOWARD ISLAM IN THE EARLY DAYS OF ISLAM

Moh. Taha Yahia

Before commencing to write this treatise I endeavored to consult the reference books within my reach lest I should be remiss in making a scientific study of the subject, or accused of being swayed by political tenderness or by religious and cultural prejudices.

Reading through the story of the Jews in history books, and comparing it with the statements of the Qur'an, from the old and new testaments I gained an insight into their conditions throughout the ages from the time when an apostle was first sent to them, to the time of Jesus and Muhammad and from then up to the present time.

From those studies and comparisons I have come to this decisive conclusion that worldly avarice, obstinate contention, and cruelty are deeply ingrained in the innermost being of the Jews who try to achieve their individual and social ambitions by fair means or foul. They are so obstinate as to reject even the teachings of Allah's prophets and apostles, so cruel as to exact severe retribution for an injury, so aggressive as to flout all positive and religious laws and human feelings. With them, the end justifies the means, for arrogance and evildoing are inherent qualities of their nature.

Jewish Doctrine:

Before discussing the attitude of the Jews toward Islam and Muslims in the early days of Islam, it behooves us to refer to the distortion of the Jewish creed that filled the life of Jews with perfidy and evil.

Jews' Hostility to Islam and Muslims:

From the very beginning Jews declared their hostility to Islam and even to all the other religions, and have not ceased to do so ever since.

I should like to say before I conclude that I have thoroughly scrutinized the nature of the Jews. They are avaricious, ruthless, cruel, hypocrite [*sic*], and revengeful. These traits govern their lives. They never change nor are they inclined to change. They always try to seize any opportunity to take revenge on Islam and Muslims.

JEWISH ROLE IN AGGRESSION ON THE ISLAMIC BASE IN MEDINA

Dr. Abdel Aziz Kamil

The struggle between the Arabs and the Jews in Medina goes back to pre-Islamic days and Islam has nothing to do with their conflicts. The Arabs of Medina could not, in themselves, be able to ward off this great evil until they were helped by other Arabs to take back their usurped original Arab right.

The Jewish problem was part of their heritage. They carried its seeds wherever they went. The Arabs of Medina have fought the Jews before Islam and after the advent of Islam. The base of Islam in Medina inherited this struggle for no other reason but to regain its legal valid rights and to annihilate the forces of conspiracy and civil discord from the Arabian Peninsula. This has nothing to do with the religion of Islam.

One by one the forts were conquered and eventually the fort of Wateeh and Sulalim fell. The Jews then agreed to surrender and submit. The Prophet (P.B.U.H.) offered them the opportunity to continue tilling their lands and taking half of its harvest.

The news of the fall of Khaybar quickly spread throughout the country and influenced the Jews of Fadak so much that they also accepted the same conditions. Their example was followed by Wadi Al-Qura and Taimaa.

In this way the Prophet (P.B.U.H.) was able to crush the strongholds of the Jews and their military power from the Arabian Peninsula after the decisive battles of Khaybar.

This continued till the era of the second caliph Omar who was then forced to complete their evacuation from the Arabian Peninsula to the borders of Syria.

But did their evacuation bring the episode to an end?

Never! It continued appearing in one form or another.

D. F. Green, eds., "Arab Theologians on Jews and Israel," extracts from the *Proceedings of the Fourth Conference of the Academy of Islamic Research*. This chapter includes extracts from D. F. Green's rendition, pp. 25–38, 68–70.

Today, Zionism has adopted and followed the same evil. Imperialism creates in Palestine a state of conspiracies to disunite and crush the unity of the Arab and Islamic world and divide it into two parts: African and Asian.

We should work at a nonstop pace until such a time that we can clear our land and its sacred places from Zionists and return them to their lawful owners as it was done by the Prophet (P.B.U.H.) in Medina, the base of Islam. He crushed the foreign evil.

The crux of the argument is that the Arabs and the Muslims throughout their long history were not the aggressor. But we have observed in this study that they always initiate good deeds and spread peace. The only answer they got for this from their enemies was further hostilities, conspiracies and treacheries. They have before them no other alternative but to force the evil away from themselves and regain their right.

JEWS' ATTITUDES TOWARD ISLAM AND MUSLIMS IN THE FIRST ISLAMIC ERA

Sheikh Abd Allah Al Meshad

The Jews harmed the Muslims economically, because they had possessed most of the wealth in Medina and thus controlled the economic position. They used to adopt the same policy at all times. They dealt with loans, usury, and monopolized foods. They are characterized by avarice and many other vices. (According to the translator, the Prophet [P.B.U.H.] died and his armor was pawned to a Jew for thirty bushels of barley [Al-Bukhari, vol. 5] which arose from selfishness, loving of world-life, and envying people.)

This is a clear description of hypocrisy and the Hypocrites of the Jews and others and this image clarifies their foul means in resisting the call and corrupting the society (of Islam). Many statements about them are mentioned in the holy chapters of Baqara, Tauba, Al Ahzab, Al Hashr, Al Monafekoun, Al Maida, Nissa, and others.

The Jews colluded with every hostile movement against the Islamic call and the Muslims.

Those are some aspects of the enmity displayed by the Jews toward the Muslims. It is due to dangerous psychological factors symbolized in the scorn of Arabs and the rejection of the idea of the last Apostle to be from them. How could the Arabs obtain this favor, while they were illiterate, and the Jews could not accede to that honor which was the privilege of the Children of Israel? That scorn was an aspect of envy rooted in them. Envy was the cause of the first crime committed by Lucifer in heaven and the cause of the first crime upon earth committed by Cain in killing his brother. Therefore the Jews could neither keep the covenant taken upon them by Allah, nor carry out the treaty they had made with the Prophet. They had resorted to their former policy and thus they deserved to be called, "the worst of beasts" in the Qur'an. Allah saith: "For the worst of beasts in the sight of God are those who reject Him: They will not believe. They are those with whom thou didst make a covenant, but they break their covenant every time, and they have not the fear (of God)" (Anfal, 55–56).

Jews at the Time of Orthodox Caliphs

The Prophet (P.B.U.H.) passed away and the Jews remained the same people of mean disposition and buried rancor so they never forgot how the Muslims had treated them. They were in wait for their calamities despite their (Jews') dispersion. They tried to seize the chance to revenge on them. They were usually cowards and could not face openly their enemy especially when he was strong. Therefore their methods in attacking the faith were conspiracies, plots, intrigues, seditions, separation for the believers, distortion of the call, and trials to drive the Muslims out of their purified creed which was the cause of their strength.

The Jews and the enemies of the faith in general fancied that the chance of vengeance came upon them when Muhammad died. The Jews took certain hostile attitudes and though they were few in number, they were of great peril and they showed that they were people who never lost hope in spreading corruption. They were of no significance at the time of Abu Bakr, the righteous.

Then Omar came to complete the message of Abu Bakr in conquering other countries, in strengthening the social bonds among the Muslims and in setting up the bases of ruling on equality, justice, and freedom, and on the true, strong Islamic principles.

He viewed that Arabia—being the outset of the call and the center of radiation—should be void of all factors of sedition. He got experience that the Jews were the callers and instigators of the sedition at any time and everywhere. He purified Arabia from them. Most of them dwelled at Khaybar and its neighborhood. That was because he was informed that the Prophet said while he was dying: "Never do two religions exist in Arabia."

Omar also relied on a condition in the covenant between them and the Prophet. That condition gave the Prophet the right to drive them out whenever he pleased.

Therefore, Arabia was purged from their pollution. They did not find any residence but outside its boundaries.

Omar implored Allah (and he was worthy to be answered) to be a martyr. But how could he achieve his aim in that respect while he was staying at Medina far from battlefields where martyrdom was preferable?

He felt that a hand of a pagan would kill him and thus Allah bestowed upon him the honor of martyrdom one day.

When we look at the recent pictures of the Jews' conspiracies and how they design precisely and accurately for the long run or forever in such a subtle technique that we never suspect of its safety, we think it is not impossible that the Jews were those who drew the plans and plotted for killing Omar, or at least they had known that conspiracy but they did not ferret it out.

Omar passed away as a martyr in 24 AH. Othman—of the two lights—succeeded him. He was a reserved decent and abstemious believer who spent all wealth for God's Word.

Yet the Jews remained the same people weaving conspiracies against Islam and the Muslims wherever they observed the large expansion of the Islamic Empire.

It is a fact that the doctrine of the Shi'a was a shelter to be refuged to by all people who intended to destroy Islam due to enmity or grudge, by whosoever wanted to intermingle the cults of his fathers with Judaism, Christianity, and Zoroastrianism or Hinduism and also by those who wanted the independence of their countries and the separation from the caliphate.

Such events had occurred in the western part of the Islamic Empire before the immigration of the Fatimites to Egypt. All the above-mentioned people used their excessive love for the Prophet's descendants as a slogan to mask all their tendencies behind it. Judaism was symbolized in the Shi'a's belief which states that the spirit of the imams would reappear.

The Shi'ites alleged that hellfire was prohibited for anyone of them to touch but for a few days just as what the Jews had said (The fire shall not touch us but for a few numbered days . . . etc.).

It is but a few of the many acts committed by the Jews to oppose the Islamic call and to conspire against the Muslims during the first era of Islamic history. This unveils the vicious qualities which they were accustomed to inherent in them. It is preferable to compile some of them in a list (quoted or extracted from the Holy Qur'an) to define lucidly their personality as follows:

1. Telling Lies about God
   —"But they tell a lie against God, and (well) they know it" (Al-I-Mran, 74).
   —"The Jews say: 'God's hand is tied up.'"
   —"They said 'God is indigent and we are rich.'"
   —"We are sons of God, and His beloved."
   —"The fire shall not touch us but for a few numbered days."

2. Their Fondness for Listening to Falsehood (Lies)
   —"It be among the Jews, men who will listen to any lie, will listen even to others who have never so much as come" (Maida, 41).
   —"They are fond of listening to falsehood, of devouring anything forbidden" (Maida, 42).

3. Mutiny (Disobedience) against Allah
   —"But because of their breach of their covenant We cursed them" (Maida, 13).

4. Mutiny (Disbelief) against His Messengers (Apostles)
   —"We shall never believe in thee until we see God manifestly" (Baqara, 55).
   —"Go thou and thy Lord and fight ye too, while we sit here (and watch)" (Maida, 24).

—"To them an Apostle with what they themselves desired not—some (of these) they called imposters and some they (go so far as to) slay" (Maida, 70).

5. Facility of Assassination
   —"And slaying His messengers without just cause" (Baqara, 61).

6. Confuting the Covenants (Breaking Promises)
   —"It is not (the case) that every time they make a covenant, some party among them throw it aside."
   —"They are those with whom thou didst make a covenant, but they break their covenant every time" (Anfal, 56).

7. Hardheartedness
   —"Thenceforth were your hearts hardened: They became like a rock and even worse in hardness."

8. Argumentativeness and Double-Facedness
   —"How can he exercise authority over us when we are better fitted than he to exercise authority?" (Baqara, 247).
   —"They said, 'Beseech on our behalf thy Lord to make plain to us what she is: To us are all heifers alike" (Baqara, 70).

9. Suppression of the Truth and Misguidance
   —"And cover not truth with falsehood, nor conceal the truth, when ye know (what it is)."

10. Hypocrisy
    —"When they meet those who believe, they say: 'we believe.'"
    —"Do ye enjoin right conduct on the people, and forget (to practice it) yourselves?"
    —"Saying with their lips what was not in their hearts" (Al-I-Mran, 167).

11. Egoism
    —"It is that whenever there comes to you an Apostle with what ye yourselves desire not, ye are puffed up with pride?" (Baqara, 87).
    —"Nor sell My signs for a small price."

12. Desire for Corrupting People
    —"Every time they kindle the fire of war, God doth extinguish it."
    —"But they (ever) strive to do mischief on earth."

13. Their Lack of Good Conscience
    —"Nor did they (usually) forbid one another iniquities which they committed."

14. Loving Malignancy for Others
    —"It is the wish of a section of the People of the Book to lead you astray."

—"And wish that ye should lose the right path."

—"Why obstruct you those who believe from the Path of God."

15. Their Resentment for Benefaction Done for People

—"If aught that is good befalls you it grieves them."

—"Or do they every mankind for what God hath given them of His bounty."

—"It is never the wish of those without Faith among the People of Book, nor of the Pagans, that anything good should come down to you from your Lord."

16. Hastening to Commit Sins and Disobedience to Allah's Injunctions

—"Many of them dost thou see, racing each other in sin and rancor, and their eating of things forbidden."

17. Self-Conceit and Haughtiness

—"We are sons of Allah, and His beloved."

—"There is no call on us (to keep faith) with these ignorant (Pagans)."

—"Has thou not turned thy vision to those who claim sanctity for themselves? Nay but God doth sanctify whom He pleaseth."

18. Exploitation and Opportunism

—"That they usury thou they were forbidden."

—"Of devouring anything forbidden."

19. Trickery for Transgression

—"And well ye knew those amongst you who transgressed in the matter of the Sabbath: We said to them: Be ye apes despised and rejected."

20. Cowardice

—"Go thou and thy Lord and fight ye two, while we sit here (and watch)."

—"Of a truth ye are stronger (than they) because of the terror in their hearts, (sent) by God."

—"They will not fight you (even) together, except in fortified tourships, or from behind walls."

—"They said, 'This day we cannot cope with Joliath and his Forces.'"

21. Indecency in Talking

—"We hear, and we disobey."

—"Hear what is not heard."

—"Raina"—with a twist of their tongues.

22. Miserliness

—"Have they a share in dominion or power? Behold, they give not a farthing to their follow men."

—"But when He did bestow of His bounty, they were covetous."

—"And let not those who covetously withhold of the gifts which God hath given them of His Grace, think that it is good for them."

—"There are indeed many among the priests and anchorites who in falsehood devour the substance of men, and hinder (them) from the way of God: (And there are those who bury gold and silver and spend it not in the way of God): Announce unto them a most grievous penalty."

23. The Most Excessive Selfishness

—"Who love them, but they love you not."

—"There is no call on us (to keep faith) with these ignorant (pagans)."

24. Fear of Death

—"Thou wilt indeed find them of all people, most greedy of life."

25. Garbling of the Holy Books

—"Who displace words from their (right) places."

—"Then woe to those who write the Book with their own hands, and then say: 'This from God.'"

THE ATTITUDE OF THE JEWS TOWARD ISLAM, MUSLIMS, AND THE PROPHET OF ISLAM AT THE TIME OF HIS HONORABLE PROPHETHOOD

Muhammad Azzah Darwaza

It is deduced and inspired from the verses revealed in Medina that the Jews did not say the truth and they coated what was right with what was wrong. The Jews were also stubborn in telling lies and contradicting the truth. They preferred the pleasures of the world. They enjoined the good although they were not good people. They deceived the people. They did not cooperate with others. They put their heads together and secretly agreed among themselves to deceive the people and to be hypocrites. The Jews did not help others or teach them. They told lies about Allah and let people suspect their religion. They broke their promises and practiced malice and harmful activities against the people. They misled them. They resorted to foul means to usurp people and embezzle their money. The Jews stirred up sedition and scattered the seeds of corruption among the people. They were not good neighbors to the Arabs and they did not coexist with the Arabs. They rejoiced when others were molested or suffered from catastrophes. The Jews were notorious for covetousness, avarice, and bad manners. They were not ashamed of embracing polytheism or performing the rites of paganism. They sometimes praised the idols and were in collusion with idolaters against monotheists. They displaced the words of Allah and disfigured the laws of heaven and God's advice. They were hard-hearted and sinful, they committed unlawful and forbidden crimes. The Jews indulged deeply in the pleasures and lusts of the world neglecting the laws of Allah. They sowed the seeds of suspicion and doubt among the people.

Thus the Jews rightfully deserved the wrath and the curse of Allah, recorded throughout many verses. God branded them with the stigma of humility and meanness. Allah has sent among them those who torture them severely and will keep on persecuting them up to the Last Day. It has been prescribed for them to be thus dispersed upon the earth.

"Humility" Apparently Should Have Been Translated as "Humiliation" (D. F. G.)

It is extremely astonishing to see that the Jews of today are exactly a typical picture of those mentioned in the Holy Qur'an and they have the same bad manners and qualities of their forefathers although their environment, surroundings, and positions are different from those of their ancestors. These bad manners and qualities of the Jews ascertain the Qur'anic statement about their deeply rooted instinct which they inherited from their fathers.

All people feel this innate nature of the Jews everywhere and at anytime.

These who are not of Jewish origin, have acquired this trait as they lived with them and coexisted among them for a time, namely, they acquired it through their contact with those who are of Jewish origin.

Consequently, the Jews are avoided by all people who scorn and hate them.

People are always cautious when they get in touch with them so as to avoid their wickedness and deceit.

All people want to get rid of the Jews by hook or by crook. All races of mankind, throughout the world, always reject the Jewish actions and behavior unanimously and thus it is an evidence and a strong proof that their wickedness and bad manners are a result of the evil nature which is inherent in them.

People are not prejudiced against them but the Jewish evil and the various wicked aspects of their bad manners are quite clear in different circumstances.

Some Orientalists of the Jews and of non-Jews who had wicked and evil intention to Islam, alleged that the Prophet—P.B.U.H.—had had the intention of torturing the Jews and eradicating their entity as an outcome to a racial and religious bias from the very beginning.

These slanderous Orientalists alleged that the Apostle did not realize his intention in punishing them altogether once and for all as he had not enough power. Therefore, he punished them step by step as they alleged falsely.

These Orientalists insinuated that the Apostle had broken his covenant with the Jews to secure their economic, social, and religious freedom and that the Prophet was inclined to slaying and fighting and that he was greedy enough to lay hands on the Jews' money to be lavished upon the Muslims.

These slanders of some Orientalists emanated from their own wicked intentions toward Islam and their blind fanaticism.

Their allegations were due to the fact that they could not understand the Qur'an and the meanings of its Holy Verses. These Verses give a clear evidence and a confirmed proof that their allegations are false and their charges against the Apostle are silly and foolish.

The series of the verses of Baqara, Al-Imran, Nissa, Ma'ida, and Ahzab stated the above-mentioned situations, the verses (1–7) of Hashr Chap. revealed also the facts of the aforesaid circumstances. I shall try to explain that matter later, when giving full details of punishment. Out of reasoning, I state that there was nothing of the false allegations aroused by the slanderous Orientalists at the time of the Qur'anic Revelation and of jotting down the versions. Therefore we cannot say that the evidences and reasons of punishment were invented to defend the attitudes of the Prophet and the Muslims toward the Jews. Every false pretender should be hushed due to the authenticity and truth of the Qur'anic verses. Besides, the manners and instinct of the Jews while dealing with other remarkable nations, from the time of their Exodus to the present time, suffice us to prove the justification for the torture which befalls them everywhere under any circumstances.

The Murder of the Jewish Poet Named Kaab Ibn Al Ashraf

It was the third time when the Jews were severely punished. Kaab Ibn Al Ashraf used to disparage the Prophet— P.B.U.H.—and his companions. He instigated people to molest the Muslims. Kaab grew jealous and wept when the Prophet and the Muslims conquered Quraysh. Therefore he went to Mecca where he recited dirges for the murdered idolaters and composed poems to disparage the Prophet and the Muslims. Kaab enticed Quraysh to fight the Muslims again.

The Prophet adjured Allah to save him from the evil of Ibn Al Ashraf who had declared his wickedness and composed hostile poems. The Prophet then said: "Who can revenge on Ibn Al Ashraf who molested me?" Muhammad Ibn Moslema cried out saying that he could do that. The Prophet gave him sanction to murder Ibn Al Ashraf. The Prophet consulted the leader of Aws, Saad Ibn Mapaz, as the Prophet wanted that matter to be known to Saad. Saad agreed on the plan of killing Ibn Al Ashraf who was one of the allies of Aws.

Muhammad Ibn Moslema was allowed to play a trick or resort to a stratagem in killing Ibn Al Ashraf, who lived in a fortified inaccessible castle. Muhammad Ibn Moslema and some men of Aws played tricks and managed to enter the castle where they slew the tyrant. They cut off his head and carried it to Bakei, where they cheered up aloud. When the Prophet heard their cries, he knew at once that they had killed Ibn Al Ashraf and thus he praised them. They threw the head of Al Ashraf before the Prophet. The murder of Ibn Al Ashraf horrified the Jews' poets and their adventurers.

The Prophet advised Bani Qurayza to embrace Islam and some of them followed his advice, but the other men were slain and the other women and children were taken as slaves. Afterward those slaves were sent to Iraq, where they were sold and weapons for the Muslims were purchased instead. The property, arms, possessions, orchards, and plantations of Bani Qurayza were laid hands on.

When Bani Qurayza were punished, an end was put to the Jews of Medina. Those Jews had been the strongest, the richest, and the most pernicious and harmful ones. They had been deeply rooted in the society and they had had a high rank and an important status.

No Jews remained in Medina except a few persons who were peace loving and thus they enjoyed their freedom in residing wherever they liked and in adopting their own religion. This is a clear definite evidence of the Islamic principle of clemency. Punishment should be tackled against the fighting enemies to ward off danger and harm from Islam and the Muslims. Clemency was the doctrine which the Apostle—P.B.U.H.—his companions, and his successors adhered to since it was the basis of rule.

The Prophet—P.B.U.H.—allowed the Jews who were not troublesome to remain to look after the plantations and orchards. Those Jews were permitted to remain on condition that they should be unarmed and they should pay half of the product yield to the Prophet. The dangerous and troublesome Jews were driven out.

The Prophet marched toward Wadi Al Kora after the conquest of Khaybar.

There were also some strong fortresses, and the Jews resisted the Muslims but the Muslims gained victory like that of Khaybar.

Therefore, the Jews of Fadk, Taimaa, and Garba'a were much terrorized and they sent immediately their representatives to make a conciliation with the Prophet. They promised the Prophet to give half their property to the Muslims and to be peaceful with them.

Some Orientalists ignore the various reasons why the Jews of Khaybar and others were punished. They jotted down the verses of the Qur'an through which Allah promised the Muslims who participated in Hudaibeya to be given the booty of Khaybar as a heavenly reward. These Orientalists alleged that the invasion of Khaybar was launched because the Prophet wished to reward the Muslims of Hudaibeya and comfort them. These Orientalists always allege what they like to announce according to their wishes, but we have mentioned the most evident reasons of the punishment befalling the Jews. The question of the booty is casual and always subsidiary for waging the wars of the Prophet. It is mentioned in the verses of the Qur'an about jihad as a secondary reason for striving against the Unbelievers.

Abi Obaidah Ibn Al Garrah related as well that the Prophet said while he was on the verge of death: "Drive out the Jews from Hijaz and the People of Najran from Arabia." Omar carried out the blessed last will of the Prophet and thus Arabia was purged from the Jews during the era of the Prophet—P.B.U.H.

The "People of Najran" Were Christians (D. F. G.)

The Arabs and the Muslims have recently been inflicted in their countries by the Jews.

They formerly treated the Jews kindly and graciously. The Arabs and the Muslims housed and protected the Jews. They gave them their religious freedom inside their temples to perform their rites. They let the Jews trade and even live freely. Moreover, the Arab Muslims made friends with them and kept their covenants. In Hijaz, Muslims treated the Jews exactly the same as their forefathers did during the time of the Prophet—P.B.U.H. They also dealt with them according to the injunctions of the Book of Allah and the traditions of his Prophet. In other countries, the Jews were cruelly molested and they suffered from privation and atrocious oppression. However, the Jews treated the Arabs and the Muslims evilly, unjustly, treacherously, and mercilessly. The Jews followed the attitudes of their ancestors toward the Prophet and the Muslims. The Jews kept on sticking to their corrupt demoralized instinct and their vicious wicked prejudice. They committed their treacherous oppressive atrocities in Palestine and they paid no heed to honor, manliness, or truth.

The atrocities of the Jews are so terrific that they curdle one's blood. Their wicked intentions toward all the Arabs and their countries are quite evident. They attacked their countries several times and occupied some areas of the Arab world in addition to all parts of Palestine.

The Jews slaughtered, tortured, and expatriated the inhabitants from those occupied Arab areas. They ruined and damaged the land, possessions, and property of the Arabs. The Jews were backed by their friends all over the world. They instigated some states, especially the imperialist ones, to stand against the Arabs. The imperialist states supported the Jews and secured their mastery and superiority.

It is firmly undoubted that the Jews and their imperialist supporters exert all efforts—all over the fields of activity.

They try hard to be superior to the Arabs and to exploit their countries. They do their utmost to make the Arabs weak, invalid, and at variance. Therefore, the Arabs will lack peace, security, unity, prosperity, and self-sufficiency. The Jews' success is mainly and foremost due to some defects in the Arabs. They lack cooperation, the necessary forces, and the spirit of backing each other in striving against the Jews. If the Arabs remain thus divided, they will face overwhelming dangers which now threaten all Muslims, Arabs as well as their countries.

It is essentially necessary to resort to seriousness in this respect from the religious and national viewpoints. The Arabs should take all measures and do their best to eradicate the state of the Jews in order to get rid of them as the Prophet did before.

The support of those unjust and ambitious imperialists

to the Jews is ephemeral and will not certainly live long. Allah promised his faithful servants who believe in him to be triumphant. God prescribed humility and his wrath to befall the Jews, the enemies of the believers. Allah saith about these enemies: "Every time they kindle the fire of war, God doeth extinguish it."

About Making Reconciliation with the Jews:

In Anfal Chap. verses 55–64, Allah saith:

"But if the enemy incline towards peace, do thou also incline towards peace, and trust in God."

Chroniclers and interpreters state that these verses concern some party of the Children of Israel who broke their covenants and made treacherous plots against the Muslims.

The aforesaid Qur'anic sentence is an important point in this topic, as the Jews announce from time to time that they long for reconciliation with the Arab Muslims. They naturally declare that this pacification with the Arab Muslims is to be termed with their recognition of their state in Palestine.

This is mere sophism. The Qur'anic sentence is applied to make peace with an enemy who has his own country and state, but the Jews in Palestine are our enemies who have made their aggression upon a country of the Arab Muslims. The Jews usurped the Arab country with the help of the imperialist tyrants.

These imperialists are the enemies of the Arab Muslims as they waged the fiercest war against the Muslims, tortured them, and drove them out of their homes. The Jews, under the aegis of imperialists, laid their hands upon the houses, orchards, plantations, vineyards, movable and immovable property, shops and factories. The Jews violated the Islamic holy shrines and profaned their sanctities. They pulled down the mosques and erased the Arab and Islamic features of Palestine. The aggressions of the Jews were launched repeatedly every now and then. They long for usurping more land and plundering more money of the Arab Muslims. The Jews are thirsty for drinking more blood of the Muslims. They are eager to destroy their homes, persecute severely their men, women, and children; and expatriate them.

Before invading Palestine and setting up their state upon the debris of the Islamic Arab state, the Jews had not been the enemies of the Arab Muslims. At that time the Islamic authorities granted them freedom, safety and security whereas they were exposed to oppression and chase wherever they lived. Therefore we cannot resort to the peaceful means in dealing with them as long as they keep what they have abducted and usurped of the Arab countries and as long as they form their state upon the ruins of an Islamic state.

The Muslims and the Arabs cannot agree to that even if the Jews leave some parts of what they have usurped and remain in the sections which the UN has allotted to the Jews. It is the homeland of the Muslims and the Arabs and thus the UN has no right at all to permit the Jews to possess any small part of it. None of the Muslims or Arabs have the right to accept that matter. Any pliancy or submission in this matter is a treachery to Allah, his apostle, and to the Muslims.

Thus Even If Israel Was Reduced to the Boundaries of the UN 1947 Partition Resolution, It Would Not Be Acceptable. Its Existence Is Rejected as a Question of Principle Regardless of Its Size (D. F. G.)

It is incumbent on the Muslims to strain every nerve and make all efforts in order to be well equipped by all means to fight the Jews. The Muslims should corner the Jews without feeling exhausted or tired as Allah enjoins upon them. The Muslims should spare no effort to exterminate their state and deliver every place of the Muslims' homeland from the Jews' desecration and keep it under the control of the Islamic authorities as it was. Any slight indifference to this matter is indeed a shameful sin against religion.

ISRAELITIC NARRATIVES IN EXEGESIS AND TRADITION

Muhammud El-Sayyed Husein Al-Dahabi

Yet the Qur'an—despite its purity—and the Sunna—despite its integrity and authenticity—had not been safe from the blemishes and corruption wrought by counterfeiters. Hence, the Qur'an was pervaded by inaccurate interpretations; its texts had been commented upon in a way inconsistent with the aims it had been revealed to realize. The Sunna had equally been permeated with heterogeneous so much so that it became difficult to distinguish the genuine from the spurious. Needless to say that behind these misrepresentations and misinterpretations were evil aims and malicious tendencies, fostered in the hearts of those who had been sworn enemies of Islam and Muslims.

Among the leading figures of heresy and sectarianism was Abdullah ibn Saba the Jew, who feigned to be a Muslim, disguising his unbelief, making a show of supporting the Prophet's offspring (Alu-l-Bait), so as to deceive Muslims and to copagate [*sic*, means propagate] among them his heretical and noxious views.

On Explaining the Relation of the Holy Qur'an to Other Heavenly Books and Its Specific Rank Thereof

Scholars of exegesis and tradition designated as Israelitic the whole body of these narratives, because most of what had been transmitted concerning these superstitions and forgeries, had been drawn from Jewish sources (notably what is known as Haggada). It is also to be noted that the Jews are known to be mostly a people of liars and slanderers. The malice they bear to Islam and Muslims exceeds all bounds, as stated by God, be he exalted, in his saying: "Thou wilt surely find that the most vehement of mankind, in enmity against those who believe are the Jews and the idolaters . . . " (5:82).

(Since ages past), the Jews, from among the people of the Scripture, had been in close relations with Muslims. Then (religious) culture—more than any other—had acquired the widest range of diffusion (in the Arabian Peninsula). Because of these connections, the Jews found it easy to practice a great deal of cunning in inserting narratives that blemish the Islamic texts. (There sprang from the ranks) the earliest heresiarch, Abdullah ibn Saba, who was the foremost leader of sedition and heterodoxy.

He, with his adherents, the "Sabàis," feigned to be devout Muslim, and went to all lengths in their deceitfulness, by simulating to be the most fervent supporters of the Al'ul-Bait, the offspring of the Prophet, so as to corrupt the beliefs of Muslims. Thus they were destined to have the greatest share in composing these heaps of Israelitic narratives they had intruded upon the Book of God and the Sunna of his Apostle (P.B.U.H). For this reason, the Jewish color that came to be the prominent feature of these narratives led to designate the whole body of this heterogeneous material—even if it be non-Jewish—as Israelitic.

Consequently, the enemies of Islam, especially from amongst the Jews and others, started to seek for other ways, contributory to the undermining of Muslims' power. Their evil cunning and appalling deceit led them to concoct wily intrigues and foul machinations. Some of them feigned the adoption of Islam and supported the Shi'ites (who support the claims of the Prophet's offspring to the caliphate), while their hearts were boiling over with resentment and malice to Muslims. They exploited the latter's love to the Prophet's offspring and shed crocodile tears, bewailing what were supposed to be the wrongs committed against the Prophet's family.

They exceeded all bounds in venerating and sanctifying the "Al-ul-Bait," until they accorded them the rank of prophethood, and even to what is more eminent. They depicted Abu Bakr, 'Umar, and 'Uthman as usurpers who arrogated to themselves the caliphate which is the legitimate right of 'Ali ibn Abi Talib, and his offspring after him. To vindicate their doctrines, they forged curious traditions and concocted strange tales, most of which had been drawn from Jewish sources.

Needless to say, the Jews are a sort of people who utter honeyed words, while they are as crafty as foxes.

So, they could cleverly and deceitfully draw perfect plots to the stories they had composed: then they transmitted these narratives to the simple and ignorant folk. When these stories gained wide prevalence and became popular, they came to be ascribed to the Prophet (P.B.U.H.), while the Prophet was immune from their transmitters and propagators.

Such are the hazardous results caused by the transmission of the Israelitic narratives which had threatened to spoil the purity of Muslims' beliefs and the sanctity of Islam. The Jews spare no pains to corrupt the faith of the Muslims and to weaken their trust in the Qur'an and the Sunna, together with what is related to them. They tend to shake their confidence in their pious predecessors who had been in charge of conveying the message of Islam and propagating it in East and West. Foremost among these are Jewish Orientalists, advocates of Judaism who are still disseminated throughout Africa, the alleged dark continent endeavoring to eradicate Islam. "But God doth encompass them from behind" (85:20).

As to what had been stated by Goldziher . . . this presumption, as stated by that Jewish Orientalist, is only put forward to relieve and deliver his Jewish folk from their sordidness and lowliness.

Ignaz Goldziher—A Most Prominent Hungarian Jewish Orientalist (1850–1921). Orientalists Have Been Accused in This Volume and Elsewhere as Having the Intention of Distorting and Perverting Arab Culture (D. F. G.)

In interpreting the above Qur'anic verse, Tabari had gone to say: "The last of a series of the Israelitic Prophets was one sent to the Israelites who said, 'O Children of Israel! God tells you that He had deprived you of your voices and loathed you because of the considerable number of your sins.' Thereupon, the Israelites plotted against him, and were on the point of assassinating him.

"Then, he added, 'They killed their Prophet. Thereupon, God smote them with humiliation took away kingship from them.' Thus, they became the most lowly and degraded amongst nations, having to pay tribute and yielding to the authority of foreign kings. In such a plight will they ever remain."[1]

NOTE

1. Tabari's *Tafsir*, vol. 15 (Government Press), pp. 33–34.

CHAPTER 30

Extracts from *The Children of Israel in the Qur'an and the Sunna*

Muhammad Sayyid Tantawi

THE NOBLE QUR'AN METHOD OF CALLING ON THE JEWS TO ACCEPT ISLAM, AND PROOFS OF ITS FAIRNESS TOWARDS THEM

. . . Then God warned the Jews of severe punishment in this world and the next if they did not believe in Muhammad: Qur'an 4:47: "Before we destroy [their] faces, we overturn them over onto their backs, or we curse them as we cursed the Men of the Sabbath. God's word comes true."

This means: "O you who were given the Godly Book, namely, the Torah, believe in the Qur'an which we have brought down as a confirmation of the principles and pillars of religion that you have of aforetime—before We scourge you with one of the following punishments:

(1) One mentioned in Qur'an, above: "We will destroy [their] faces and [over]turn them over onto their backs" [i.e., curse them].

Mujaahid said it means that "we turned (their) faces away from the True Path, and so we will turn them onto their backs for their error."

Al-Suddi said that it means that "we will blind them to the truth, and bring them back to (their former state of) unbelief."

Al-DaHHaak said that it means that "we will return them to clear guidance," for he had already turned them over on their backs so that they disbelieved in Muhammad and the messages he brought.

(2) God said, Qur'an 4:47: ". . . or we will curse them the way We cursed the men of the Sabbath." The meaning of "curse" here is exile *al-Tard* and *al-idhlaal al-ma`nawiyy* moral humiliation.

The general import is that the verse is a call for belief by the Jews before God stamps their hearts and takes their light away, Qur'an 2:17, so they cannot face the truth, or even lean toward it; or, they were cursed from aforetime and were exiled from his mercy, and miserable

wretchedness *al-dhullah wal-maskana* was decreed as their lot, for horrible punishment became their dominant trait.

God is capable of punishing a group of them with one of these two punishments, and the other group punished with the other, for they persisted in their rebellious error.

Qur'an 4:47: "God's command comes true" means that everything that God orders is put into effect without exception, for nothing on earth or in heaven can hinder him.

The pronoun in "we will curse **them**" refers to the owners of the faces, or, by way of object switching, it refers to those who were given the Book.

Then he reiterated that he would not forgive anyone who joined partners with him, but except for these, he may forgive whomever he wills, Qur'an 4:48 [also 4:116]: "God will never pardon one who [ascribes] partners to him; he pardons whom he [wishes] among the others. [But] for whoever ascribed partners to him has committed a grievous crime/sin."

This means that God will not forgive those Jews who did not believe in Muhammad any of their sins, big or small. Qur'an 4:48 [4:116]: ". . . and whoever ascribes partners to God . . ." because he condemns (those partners) who are not of his creation to lowliness and slavery. Qur'an 4:48 [4:119]: ". . . for he has committed a grievous sin"; i.e., he is to be faulted with a grievous sin.

These two verses command belief in Muhammad and made clear to (the Jews) that their disbelief could only lead them to *khizy* degradation in this world and to `adhaab` punishment in the next, for he does not forgive those who ascribe partners to him, but other than these (sinners), he punishes whoever he pleases.

Jews Led into Disputing Religion [Islam] Due to Their AL-BAGHY WAL-HASAD Wanton Envy

In their essence, heavenly laws are the same. All descend from God's presence for mankind's guidance in order to help them in this world and the next; they differ only in

Muhammad Sayyid Tantawi, *Banu Isra'il fi al-Qur'an wa al-Sunna* [The Children of Israel in the Qur'an and the Sunna] (Cairo: Zahraa' lil-I`laam al-`Arabi, 1986–87), pp. 107–26, 129–46.

details, not in the essentials. This minute difference is a sign of God's mercy for his worshipers, for he ordained for each community of believers that which is appropriate for them in their particular circumstances.

Muhammad brought the final revelation of religious law, its guardian and the criterion of all fundamental aspects of God's unicity, belief in his emissaries, revelation of noble qualities, and principles of noble behavior.

The Jews should have rushed to believe in this emissary, the unlettered Prophet who brought irrefragable proofs to believe in him and in what he received from his Lord. But most of them were blind and deaf to the truth, and refused to believe in Muhammad, whom they knew like they knew their own sons, Qur'an 2:146: Then they fiercely disputed him.

In many of its verses the noble Qur'an describes the refusal of the People of the Book to enter Islam and from joining Muhammad. The reason is their wanton envy, not logical evidence. Here is one of those verses:
Qur'an 3:19–20:

God's religion is Islam. The people who were given the Book knowingly dispute that which came to them out of *baghy* stiffneckedness/stubbornness. He who disbelieves in God's verses/signs—God is quick to bring him to account. So if they dispute you (Muhammad), I and my followers have directed *alsam-tu* our faces to God, so say to those who were given the Book and to the unlettered, "Have you become Muslims *a-aslam-tum*?" If they did, it was because they were rightly guided; if they turned away—you have to set them right. God sees all concerning his worshipers.

He said, Qur'an 3:19: "God's religion is Islam."

Qataada said that "Islam" means the Shahaada: "There is no God but Allah," and the repetition of this from God's presence. This is God's religion which he legislated for himself, with which he sent his emissaries. God's *awliyaa´* "friends" demonstrate this: He accepts only these, and reward comes only from him.

Then God points out that the Jews did not leave Islam following any evidence; it was only out of their wanton envy, Qur'an 3:19: "Those who were given the Book did not dispute what they knowingly had, out of stiff-neckedness/stubbornness *baghy* among them," i.e., those who were given the Book did not differ concerning the Islamic religion per se, they left it and refused to enter it, Qur'an 3:20: "except after there came to them what they knowingly had," i.e., even after they knew it was the undeniable Truth, nor did their disputing result from ignorance or doubt on their part, but rather from "stiff-neckedness/stubbornness"; i.e., their disputing and denial of the truth was caused solely out of their **wanton envy** of Muhammad and of the nobility God endowed him with, and because of their *Talab lil-riyaasa* lust for power and their *HuZuuZ al-dunyaa* striving for the lux-

uries of this life, and out of *radhiilat al-baghy wal-Hasad* their degenerate wanton envy and *Hubb al-dunyaa* love for this world which had penetrated into their hearts—the light of knowledge was removed from them, and this made them deny the truth all the more and distance themselves from the Way of Belief: (the Jews) sank into a *al-kufr wal-fusuuq wal-`iSyaan* prurient and disbelieving disobedience.

He then concluded the noble verse with a strong threat to anyone who would disbelieve in his verses/signs, Qur'an 3:21: "Whoever disbelieves in God's verses/signs—God is quick to bring him to account," i.e., whoever denies his signs and proofs which he establishes as a remembrance for those with intellect, and evidence for those who can consider—God becomes his punisher and his caller to a hard account, for he is quick to bring to account.

. . . [T]hese are some of the verses which point to the fact that (the Jews rejected Islam) out of wanton envy. Another is Qur'an Surat al-Jaathiya, 45:16–17:

And certainly We gave the Book and the wisdom and the prophecy to the children of Israel, and We gave them of the goodly things, and We made them excel the nations. And We gave them clear arguments in the affair, but they did not differ until after knowledge had come to them out of envy among themselves; surely your Lord will judge between them on the day of resurrection concerning that wherein they differed.

Another is Surat al-Naml, 27:76–79:

Verily, this Qur'an narrates to the Children of Israel most of that about which they differed truly, it (this Qur'an) is a guide and a mercy to the believers. Verily, your Lord will decide between them (various sects) by His Judgment. And He is the All-Mighty, the All-Knowing. So put your trust in Allah; surely, you (O Muhammad SAW) are on manifest truth.

These noble verses, and many similar ones, point out that the reason for the Jews rejecting Islam was wanton envy and their *istibdaal* clannishness, which is grossly exaggerated. The noble Qur'an called them many times to return to the ways of righteousness, and to extirpate their shared identity `*aSabiyya*, and walk the straight path, and to rush to believe in Muhammad, who brought clear evidence and demonstrable proofs of his truth, and they knew this clearly and without any doubt. Qur'an also called them to Islam, right guidance, and their own happiness, yet in their *i`raaD* rejection of it is their *shaqaa´ wa-Dalaala* erroneous misery.

Qur'an Tells the Jews the Truth about That with Which They Disagree

. . . [T]he noble Qur'an does not restrict itself to clarifying that the Jews' religious objections come out of only wanton envy, and that they have to reject these *radhaa´il* unseemly behaviors, and follow the truth Muhammad brought them; no, Qur'an does more than that: it informs them that they already know the *al-Haqq wal-Sawaab* correct truth about their religious quibbles, that they should open their hearts to and not stand in the way preventing others from following it.

So see Surat al-Shuura, 42:14,

And they did not become divided but, after knowledge had come to them, through jealousy among themselves. And had it not been for a word that had already gone forth from thy Lord for an appointed term, the matter would, surely, have been decided between them. Surely, those who were made to inherit the Book after them are in a disquieting doubt concerning it. And, verily, those who were made to inherit the Scripture (Torah and Evangel) after them (i.e., the Jews and Christians) are in grave doubt concerning it (i.e., Allah's true religion—Islam or the Qur'an).

This means that the noble verses in this Qur'an which God revealed to his Prophet Muhammad tell the real story of the Banu Israel . . . [that which] agrees with it is true, what disagrees with it is false.

The Banu Israel disputed many matters, among them the *nusakh* versions. Some claim (that some verses of the Torah) were impossible logically, and inapplicable legally; others held the opposite view. They also differed in the matter of Jesus, they related him to Joseph the carpenter, and accused his mother of what she was innocent of. They disputed also in the matter of Abraham, and said he was a Jew. They also fell out over the Prophet in many matters, which I have described in detail in *Masaalik al-Yahuud li-Kayd al-Islam wal-Muslimiin* (The Methods Jews Use to Entrap Islam and Muslims).

. . . [T]hen God says that He alone will judge what the Jews differ about. Qur'an . . . then God says that He alone will judge what the Jews differ about. Qur'an 27:78: "Your Lord will judge between them with His Judgment, for He is the Omnipotent, the Omniscient."[1]

Then he ordered his Prophet to depend on him, and to strive to spread his religion and his word without paying attention to the *´a`daa al-diin* enemies of the religion, those who block and pervert his way . . . they should *yuHakkimuu `uquula-ahum* restrain their intellects and forsake *al-`inaad wal-Hasad* rebellious envy . . .

The Proofs against the Jews

See Surat Yuunus, 10:94:

This means, O emissary, that if you have any doubt about what We have revealed to you, including narratives, morals, or laws then ask the people of the Book who recite the Torah and the Evangel, for they know without a shadow of a doubt, that you have come with this Qur'an from God's presence, for their adherence to these books gives them this certain knowledge . . . .

[The Qur'anic commentator Abu al-Qasim Mahmud ibn Umar al-]Zamakhshari notes that they know their own scriptures like they know their own sons. Qur'an 2:146:

Those to whom We gave the Scripture (Jews and Christians) recognize him (Muhammad SAW or the Ka'bah at Makkah) as they recognize their sons. But verily, a party of them conceal the truth while they know it—[i.e., the qualities of Muhammad SAW which are written in the Taurat (Torah) and the Injeel (Gospel)].

From their own books, they should know that Qur'an is true, yet they *yaktamuuna* conceal the truth knowingly. Qur'an calls the People of the Book in general to Islam, but [also] the Jews, specifically. They cannot open their hearts, and cling to their *hawaa* illusion, and reject the Prophet out of *HirS `alaa ziinat al-Hayaat* lust for the luxuries of this world, *bay` lil-diin bil-dunyaa* their selling out of religion for this world, and their *`aSabiyya* tribal solidarity which they fabricated, and their envy of the Prophet . . . which brings down God's *ghaDab* wrath, and condemns them to *khizy* degradation in this world and punishment in the next.

. . . ([A]t the time of Muhammad's coming) there were waves of false beliefs and inherited fables, and a low moral level and ugly practices.

Muhammad brought his message to two types of people: (1) the idol worshipers who believed God had partners they must humbly obey; (2) the People of the Book who *Harrafuu al-kalim `an mawaaDi`I-hi* corrupted their texts by moving around the words (to inappropriate places), and forgot their previous good fortune, persisted in being hard-hearted, and many were *faasiquuna* fornicators. Thus the different approaches: idolatry cannot be tolerated—[therefore we must,] in short, [declare] total war.

Al-Bukhari relates on the authority of Ibn `Abbas that the Prophet would let his hair down following the practice of the Jews, and not part his hair as the idolaters were wont to do, which was a sign of his solidarity with the People of the Book, but later he began to part his hair.[2]

Qur'an describes the People of the Book correctly as such. The Book is the Torah . . . and the Evangel . . .

given to guide them. Sometimes Qur'an mentions this in their praise, and sometimes to chide them for rejecting (the final heavenly revelation) and to condemn them for their low morals and evil ways. They are also called to account for their knowingly **kitmaan al-Haqq** concealing the truth and for giving the lie **takdhiib** to Muhammad, while knowing his truth like they know their own sons, and their being steadfast in their **`inaad wa-juHuud wa-tanaaquD** hard-core denial and obstinacy—this is their true nature. Qur'an 3:98–99:

> Say: O followers of the Book! why do you disbelieve in the communications of Allah? And Allah is a witness of what you do. Say: O followers of the Book! why do you hinder him who believes from the way of Allah? You seek (to make) it crooked, while you are witness, and Allah is not heedless of what you do.

Qur'an describes People of the Book in general terms, with negative attributes like their fanaticism in religion, following a false path. It describes the Jews with their own particular degenerate characteristics, i.e., killing the prophets of God, corrupting his words by putting them in the wrong places, consuming the people's wealth frivolously, refusal to distance themselves from the evil they do, and other ugly characteristics caused by their **qaswa wa-fujuur** deep-rooted lasciviousness. See Qur'an 2:83: "And when We made a covenant with the children of Israel: You shall not serve any but Allah and (you shall do) good to (your) parents, and to the near of kin and to the orphans and the needy, and you shall speak to men good words and keep up prayer and pay the poor-rate. Then you turned back except a few of you and (now too) you turn aside." [Only a minority of the Jews keep their word.]

Qur'an 3:113–15:

> They are not all alike. Among the People of the Book, there is a party who stand by their covenant; they recite the word of Allah in the hours of the night and prostrate themselves before Him. They believe in Allah and the Last Day, and enjoin good and forbid evil, and hasten to vie with one another in good works. And these are among the righteous. And whatever good they do, they shall not be denied its due reward, and Allah well knows those who guard against evil.

This means that all Jews are not the same. The good ones become Muslims; the bad ones do not.

... [The good Jews] follow Islam, the bad ones distance themselves from it, for they turn away from the Truth, disbelieve in God and the Last Day.

Jews Argue with What Is Good

... [T]he Jews always remain **muta`annitiina Zaalimiina** maleficent deniers. ... [T]hey should desist from their **al-ìnaad wal-juHuud** negative denial ... some Jews went **bil-ifraaT fil-i`tidaa´ wal-ìnaad** way overboard in their denying hostility, so gentle persuasion can do no good with them, so use force with them and treat them in the way you see as effective in ridding them of their evil. One may go so far as to ban their religion, their persons, their wealth, and their villages.

Al-Bukhari related on the authority of Abu Hurayra [sic] that the Jews used to recite the Torah in Hebrew and explicate it in Arabic for the Prophet of Islam. The emissary of God said, "neither believe nor disbelieve the Jews, but say, 'We believe in what was revealed to us and what was revealed to you. Our God is One God, and we submit ourselves/are Muslims to Him.'"

... [B]e rough only with those Jews who are **al-Zaalimuun al-mu`aaniduun** evildoers in denial ... Surat al-Nahl, Qur'an 16:125:

> Call to the way of your Lord with wisdom and goodly exhortation, and have disputations with them in the best manner; surely your Lord best knows those who go astray from His path, and He knows best those who follow the right way.

Allowing Their Food, Dealing with Them, Intermarriage

... [A]ll signs of God's liberality toward the Jews ... Bukhari:

> `A´isha said that Muhammad once bought food from a Jew and later bought a pawned iron suit of armor from him [thus testifying to the Prophet's good intentions towards Jews]; ... when Muhammad died, the pawned suit of armor was worth/valued at thirty Saa`s of barley. Qur'an allows Muslims to marry Jews, but not polytheists.
>
> `Uthman married a Christian; `Umar married a Jewess, and so did Hudhayfa ... despite all this goodwill of the Prophet of Islam towards the Jews, they refused to take advantage of it by persisting in harming the Muslims.

Receiving the Jizya from the Jews, Not from the Polytheists

Some people understood Qur'an 9:29: "Fight against those who (1) believe not in Allah, (2) nor in the Last Day, (3) nor forbid that which has been forbidden by Allah and His Messenger (4) and those who acknowledge not the religion of truth (i.e., Islam) among the people of the Scripture (Jews and Christians), until they pay the the Jizya **`an yadin wa-hum Saaghiruuna´** as **qaswa wa-idhlaal wa-imtihaan al-karaama**," with willing submission, and feel themselves subdued . . . [and suffer] humiliating harshness and repudiating dignity, but this interpretation is wrong: the People of the Book are to hand over a certain amount of their wealth in order to participate in the construction of the Islamic dynasty/state which will take care of their needs; they must be **khaaDi`uuna** obedient to it, not permitting rebellion against it, or allowing the harming of its interests, nor disturbing its security.

This is their **al-khuDuu` al-taamm** total submission to the laws of the Islamic state in which they live in a protected state, a condition which every state demands of its citizens and from those under its protection to enable it to fulfill its social obligations in calm security, and that it not expose itself to destruction nor to vitiating its power/control, nor its reputation to be sullied, nor subject to deterioration nor disturbance.

This is one facet of Islam's munificence toward the People of the Book, i.e., that it requires paying the *jizya* only by the men and not by women or children; nor does it require *jizya* payment by those who can demonstrate they are too poor to pay.

. . . [I]n Abu Yuusuf's **WaSaya** last will and testament:

O Commander of the Faithful, your Prophet and the son of your uncle Muhammad treated the people of the Dhimma with clemency—he did not harm them or hurt them or force them beyond their capacity, nor did he take any of their property, except when it became necessary. Muhammad said, "Whoever harms a contractee/confederate or forces him beyond his capacity, has me as his opponent.

At the time of Muhammad's death, he said to `Umar, "I will to the people of the *Dhimma* after my death that you fulfill your contractual duties to them, that you fight beside them, and not force them above their capacity."

Treating Them Legally

When the People of the Book wanted to live under an Islamic state and its protection, and bound itself to live peaceably therein, and not declare war on it, nor display any hostility to it that would harm it, nor relate slanders against it, then Islam orders its followers to treat them according to this extremely fair and merciful **al-qaa`ida** basis (what's good for them is good for us and what's bad for them is bad for us).

(. . . as long as they remain peaceful, they may participate in various ways in the Islamic state. . . . [S]ometimes some Jewish government ministers would take advantage of their Islamic ruler's leniency for their own profit. . . .)

Abu Yuusuf says `Umar once pushed a blind man's arm, then asked him which part of the People of the Book he belonged to. He replied that he was a Jew. `Umar asked, "What brought you to this condition?" "I

blame the *jizya*, poverty, and old age." So `Umar took him by his hand, brought him to his house, and gave him whatever he found. Then he sent him to the treasury, and told him, "Look at all this wealth from taxes! By God! We did not do justly. We consumed his youth and we despise him in his old age. Qur'an 9:60: "The *Sadaqaat* are only for the *Fuqara'* poor and the *Al-Masakin* wretched." The poor are the Muslim poor, this man is one of the wretched People of the Book. Then he relieved him of the *jizya* and of his other taxes. Abu Bakr said, "I witnessed this of `Umar, and I saw that old man."

[S]o this is Islam's fair approach to the People of the Book . . . and the Jews were of an evil inclination and stood apart from Islam's call, doubting the certainly true; they remained hostile to its emissary spreading [*fitan*] revolution among its followers. They tried every way they could to nip it in the bud.

Next chapter, inshalla, we'll talk about their **masaalik al-khabiitha** evil ways.

THE METHODS JEWS USE TO ENTRAP ISLAM AND THE MUSLIMS

. . . In the previous section we clarified some of the ways in which the noble Qur'an calls for the Jews to embrace Islam, and we explicated some of the methods which show them the justice inherent in Islam, and its respect and friendship toward them.

We noted that the Jews did not accept this noble treatment for what it was; they employed every means to oppose the call to Islam.

In this chapter we will mention some of the evil methods the Jews have employed to entrap Islam and the Muslims after the Prophet's (PBUH) emigration to Medina.

First we will discuss their evil ways—we will try to answer the following questions:

A. Were the Jews of Medina aware of the appearance of the Prophet and of his messages before he emigrated there?
B. How did the Jews receive the Prophet on his arrival in Medina as an emigrant?
C. Why did the Jews greet—all of them—the call to Islam at first and then oppose it later?

In response to the first question:

Some Jews came to Mecca for business, and various occupations. The inhabitants of Mecca themselves would set out for Khaybar to buy the jewelry of the Abu al-Haqiiq clan, with which their wives and daughters would adorn themselves for their weddings. The Meccans of the Aws and Khazraj tribes would also come to Mecca for business purposes, to circumambulate the Ka`ba, and so on. Doubtlessly these interconnections would result in the dissemination of the news concerning a new religion which Muhammad ibn `Abd Allah had brought.

During the Prophet's presence among them the Quraish had already sent al-NaDr ibn al-Haarith and `Uqba ibn Abi Mu`iiT to the Jewish rabbis in Medina, who asked them about Muhammad, and to describe him. The two of them informed (the rabbis) of Muhammad's statement that the Jews were the first People of the Book, and they had exclusive knowledge about the prophets. The two of them then left and entered [another part of . . .] Medina, and they asked the Jewish rabbis about the Prophet and the two of them informed (the rabbis) of some of Muhammad's statements, saying to them that they were the people of the Torah, so the two came to them so that (the rabbis) would inform them of this their companion.

The Jewish rabbis replied to them that they should ask Muhammad three questions; if he answered correctly, he was a Prophet and an emissary. If he answered incorrectly, he should be killed.

(I) Ask him about young men who perished long ago, and what was their amazing story.
(II) Ask him about the wanderer who reached the very ends of the earth, and what was his message.
(III) Ask him about the [nature of the] *ruuH* (Spirit).

If he answers these three questions correctly, then follow him, for he is a true prophet. If not, then he is a dead man [*sic*], do with him what you will.

Al-NaDr and `Uqba left and went to Mecca and informed the Quraish of what they heard from the Jewish rabbis, and the Quraish went to Muhammad, and said to him that Muhammad should inform them of the amazing story of the young men of long ago, and of the wanderer who had reached the ends of the earth, and of the nature of the *ruuH* (Spirit).

The emissary of God told them he would answer them on the following day. (Muhammad did not include the words "*in sha'a Allah*"—God willing—here.) They departed from Muhammad, and the latter stayed for fifteen nights during which God brought him no revelation, nor did Gabriel come to him, until the Meccans became agitated and said, "Muhammad promised 'tomorrow' but it's now been fifteen nights and we haven't received anything concerning what we asked him about. Muhammad became saddened that no revelation had come to him, and he was distressed as to what he would say to the Meccans. Then Gabriel brought him Sura [17] of the people of the Children of Israel, which brought an end to his sadness in that it informed him of the answers to the questions about the young men and the wanderer, when [Gabriel] brought down, Qur'an 17:85: "They ask you about the *ruuH*. Say, 'the *ruuH* is by God's command [there must be infinite different translations of this phrase]—you have only been given a little bit of knowledge.'"

D.

When a quarrel would break out between the Jews of Medina and the Aws and Khazraj tribes, (the Jews) would threaten them saying, "Our [*sic*] Prophet was but his time has gone, so we will pursue him and kill you together with him, with the same type of killing as that of `Aad and Iram [Qur'anic peoples]."

The noble Qur'an indicated this, Qur'an 2:89:

Whenever a Book from God comes to them, God confirms what had already been with them, and they were from aforetime (literally, attempting victory) victorious over those who disbelieved. And when what they knew came, they disbelieved. So may God's curse be upon the unbelievers!

(The term *istiftaaH* [in the above verse] means "the attempt for victory"; that is, "If they attempt victory, they will have victory.")

The meaning here is that they will try to gain victory over the unbelievers when they fight them, they say, "O God! Grant us victory over the Prophet sent for all time until eternity, and whose description and features we find in the Torah." When this prophet came whom they tried to defeat—they didn't follow him nor did they believe in him—and may God's curse be upon the disbelievers.

Another opinion holds that the term **yastaftiHuuna** means [not merely "to try to gain victory" but rather] "to gain victory," that is, it informs them that the time of the Arab Prophet is approaching—this is the thrust of this view.

Before the coming of the Prophet, the Jews used to inform the unbelievers of his appearance, and when this prophet, whom they spoke about, appeared, they disbelieved him—may God's curse be upon the unbelievers.

E.

In the few years which preceded the Hegira, the Prophet used to meet—during the pilgrimage season when he would present his call to the tribes, and would teach them Islam—with individuals from the Aws and Khazraj. They would look at one another and exclaim, "By God! This is the Prophet the Jews promised would come, yet they don't accept him."

After the first generation had sworn allegiance to Muhammad, he sent to the inhabitants of Medina MuS`ab ibn `Umayr to recite the Qur'an to them, to teach them Islam, and to train them in religious practice, so that Islam spread throughout many homes in Medina.

There followed the swearing of allegiance of the very large group/generation in which many of the nobles of the Aws and Khazraj took part, at which the Khazrajite leader Abu al-Haytham ibn al-Tayhaan told the Prophet,

"O Emissary! Between us and those people, i.e. the Jews, are ties/relations; but we will cut these off. But how is it possible for us to do so, and then God brought you to return to your people and leave us?"

The emissary laughed and said, "Blood is blood, and blood-letting from a corpse is blood-letting from a corpse,[3] you are of me and I am of you, I battle those you battle, and I make peace with those with whom you make peace."

What we must emphasize here is that the Jews were not unaware of those swearings of allegiance between Muhammad and the Medinans before the Hegira, nor were they unaware of the Islamic calls toward Yathrib [Medina] and its propagation among its population.

How could (the Jews) have been unaware that Islam was spreading openly in Medina, when MuS`ab ibn `Umayr was calling the people to God and his emissary in public. This message spread from clan to clan, from sub-tribe to sub-tribe so that joy overflowed in (MuS`ab's) heart: he realized that Islam had found fertile ground among the Medinans, and that its followers were daily increasing in number and power in Yathrib.

But what is the main reason that the Aws and Khazraj took to Islam so readily, and rushed to embrace it with open arms?

In answer to this question: the mixing of the Aws and Khazraj with the Jews of Yathrib had a deep psychological *ruuHiyy* impact, since the Jews were the People of the Book, and of preachers, and of the call to monotheism, taking idols for gods was prohibited to them. They were promised a new prophet who would follow them and kill them by his own hands, and would make the king of the world under their power. These religious disputes—in addition to the rebellions and the wars which decimated the Aws and Khazraj by the Jews' incursions on them—made the inhabitants of Yathrib readily accept the call of Islam, and they saw its caller, Muhammad, as their savior from all their trials and tribulations.

Thus we may conclude our answer to the first question: the Jews were not only cognizant of the appearance of the Prophet and his messages—nay, their presence in Medina and its environs was in itself one of the main reasons for the spread of Islam there, even if indirectly and inadvertently, as Dr. Israel Wolfensohn says.

Now we will answer the second question, that is, how did the Jews receive the Prophet upon his emigration?

On a certain day in recorded history, when the Muslims of Medina were waiting, as usual, for the Prophet, after the news of his emigration piled up around their ears a Jew shouted out to them that the Prophet's entourage had come into view, by exclaiming, "O sons of Qayla [matriarch of Aws and Khazraj], your grandfather has arrived!"

Al-Bukhari notes a hadith in his section on the Hegira:

When the Muslims of Madina heard of the Emissary of God's exit from Mecca, they would go out every morning to al-Hurra in order to see him before the noon-day heat would drive them back. One day they returned toward home after awaiting him for a long time, while a certain Jew watched them. Later, when the Prophet and his Companions seemed to (appear and then) disappear in a desert mirage, so the Jew could not restrain himself from calling out in his loudest voice, "O you group of Arabs! Here's your grandfather you've been waiting for." Thereupon the Muslims went for their weapons, and they met the Emissary of God on the plain of al-Hurra.[4]

All the Jews participated with the Muhaajiruun and the AnSaar in the welcoming reception of the Bringer of God's call. Concerning them all we say that, because of the genuine hadiths that have come down to us about some of the Jews rejected the Islamic call and subversively undermined its caller from the first day of the emigration.

On the authority of Safya bint Hayy ibn AkhTab:[5] This contract is even better than the League of Nations Charter! . . . and after all we did to deal fairly with the Jews, and they had been aware of news of the Islamic call even in Mecca, especially in the few years immediately following the Hegira, all of them welcomed the Prophet warmly at his arrival in Medina. And there were good relations for (a while) after the Hegira. Qur'an 16:120: "Surely Ibrahim was an exemplar, obedient to Allah, upright, and he was not of the polytheists." Qur'an 16:123: "Then We revealed to you: Follow the faith of Ibrahim, the upright one, and he was not of the polytheists."

We now answer the third question, that is, why did the Jews make peace with the emissary in the months following the Hegira? And why did they turn against him with hostile trickery in all its shapes and forms?

In answer to the first part of this question: The Jews did not participate in welcoming the emissary on his arrival in Medina out of love, but rather they hoped for his goodwill and his willingness to become allied with them, so they would be helped by him and his Muslim followers to form a united power in the Arabian Peninsula to resist the Christians, who had displaced them from Palestine and had soundly defeated them. They believed that the Islam which Muhammad brought could never compensate for the tritheism of the Christians, so there was no recourse except to get help from the Muslims in stopping Christianity which expelled them from the Promised Land.

Second part: the Jews made peace with Muhammad on his arrival in Medina in the few months after the Hegira only because they believed he would leave them out of the scope of his call, considering themselves better guided than to join his *risaala* religion. They were prevented from accepting his call, and *akbar min* too great to be included under his stewardship. They believed that he would never allow the new teachings to replace those of the Torah, and that he would not hold them to account for their *taHriif aw taghyiir* corruption or changing of the (holy) text [*sic*]; perhaps they expected that he would join them, especially after they saw him pray toward their *qibla*, and fast on the day of `Aashuuraa´ (tenth day of [J]ewish year is Yom Kippur) with them. He said, "We are more deserving of Moses than you." He announced his belief in God, his angels, his emissaries, and the Last Day.

Third: When the emissary of God entered Medina the Jews were in a difficult situation because of divisive dissention within the ranks, and this tight spot they were in made them incapable of showing open hostility to the emissary, so they found it advisable to delay making their opposition to the Islamic call public until the appropriate time they chose.

Fourth: after the emigration of the emissary to Medina the Aws and the Khazraj allied themselves together, and the Islamic state brought them under one flag after they had differed with one another. They now held the real power in Medina and they renewed their agreement with the Prophet that they would defend him with their wealth and persons. This position of total power for the Aws and Khazraj occurred after their entrance into Islam prevented the Jews from opposing the Prophet with their hostility at the time of his emigration, so they preferred to wage war against him [Muhammad] using underhanded means, the most important of which was *al-irjaaf wal-tashkiil* to undermine him with tricky theological questions [*sic*], stirring up religious dissension, and semantic argumentation, which we will detain [*sic*] shortly.

This is one of the most important reasons that made the Jews accommodate themselves to the Islamic call in the first months following the Hegira. They took a wait-and-see attitude toward it, but they saw it spread, and its power continue, so you might assume that they would be content to enjoy security under its umbrella and see their commerce prosper, and their wealth increase. But no! As this situation continued, and the Islamic call gained more adherents and began to take its natural place under the sun, the Jews began to become worried, and anxiety disturbed their sleep, and worries gnawed at them. So they began thinking deeply about *al-kayd* entrapping Islam and the Muslims, and this plotting took control of their emotions and their intellects. They knew the course of events was going in the opposite direction of their aspirations and *ahwaa´* vain hopes, for the following reasons:

(1) They were disheartened that Islamic teachings were becoming accepted by so many, and that the number of Muslims was increasing, not decreasing. Every day their power grew, and they were achieving independence in thought and deed.

(2) The Jews' political and economic power, which had been based on dissention among the Arabs, and keeping this state of dissension in place began to dwindle away to nothing—this alarmed them. The Aws and Khazraj entered Islam, and had become by the grace of God the Muslims' brothers and military confederates—as contrasted to the past when they had been sworn enemies of the Muslims.

(3) The Jews realized that their fervor to have the Muslims join them in order to make them more formidable in their war on the Christians in the Arabian Peninsula had become a will'o the wisp because the teachings of Islam do not deny the laws of Moses—indeed, it confirms the truth in it—but now Islam was taking on the appearance of independent renewal, and because after the Hegira the Muslims in Medina had become a state with its own independent moral personality. In everything, in their wars and their peace, and so on, the Muslims behaved solely in accordance with the religious practices of their Prophet, and they were hardly inclined to follow the leadership of the Jews, or of anyone else.

(4) In their very nature the Jews are the people the most eager for life, and the greediest of them in accumulating wealth, and they were aware that the commerce they were doing in Medina for hundreds of years and which they had exploited to acquire *Haraam* things forbidden, began to slip through their fingers to the Muhaajiruun and the Muslims, who did not lack knowledge of financial and economic matters, began to compete with them. This competition encouraged the Muslims to expend their greatest efforts to work for their own benefit and to free themselves of having to borrow from the Jews.

(5) The Jews were terrified when they saw that the Prophet did not exclude them from his call to Islam, just as he called to others, because his *risaala* message is universal, directed to all mankind. The Jews were frightened by this confrontation with the Islamic call, and wrongly supposed that the Israelite people *fadhdha* were above all other peoples, and that it was God's chosen people over all the rest of the nations, and that it would be impossible to appoint an emissary from among any of them, and that He would inspire him with a new law, whose teachings would be no less that those in the Torah.

(6) The Jews were angered because they recognized in the character of the Prophet a dangerous competitor would vitiate their religious superiority, and special status, and their cultural dominance. People already had begun to desert them and accept the Prophet as their primary authority, and most trustworthy guide and

leader to be obeyed, for he was an emissary from God's very presence, of true Arab blood, and he brought with him religious and secular happiness.

(7) The Jews were depressed to witness the teachings of Islam call for the revival of the spirit of brotherhood and equality among all mankind, so that the Arab had no advantage over the non-Arab, nor the Israelite over the non-Israelite, except in respect to *al-taqwaa* piety (see Qur'an), and that Islam had drawn some of the Jews' leading scholars to it, for example, their rabbi and their son of a rabbi, `Abdallaah ibn Salaam, who became a Muslim shortly after meeting the Prophet, and he ordered all the members of his household to become Muslim with him. He did not restrain himself to announcing his acceptance of Islam, but he went on to describe the Jews as a *buhut* mendacious people, and he warned the Prophet of their *makr wal-khiyaan* scheming. Bukhari reported on the authority of Anas ibn Maalik, who said, "In the first few months after the Hegira that `Abdallaah ibn Salaam heard the emissary of God, while he was in a verdant meadow, and asked him three questions which could be answered only by a Prophet:

> (I) What are the first signs of the end of the world? (II) What was the first food for the people in the Garden of Eden? And (III) What does a child get from its mother and its father? [T]he Prophet said that Gabriel had given him the answers already. `Abdallaah ibn Salaam replied, "Gabriel?" the Prophet: "Yes." `Abdallaah ibn Salaam: "But he is the angel who is the Jews' enemy!" Then the Prophet recited the verse, Qur'an 2:97: "Whoever is an enemy to Gabriel—for he has [brought the Qur'an down to your] heart," and then the Prophet answered: (I) The first sign of the Hour is the Fire which will gather all the people of the east and the west, and (II) the first food the people of the Garden of Eden ate was *ziyaadat kabid al-Huut* an abundance of whale liver, and (III) if the father's liquid squirts out before the mother's liquid is released the child will resemble his father; and vice versa. `Abdallaah ibn Salaam exclaimed that there is no god but God, and that Muhammad is his Prophet; the Jews are a *buhut* mendacious people, and when they find out about my becoming a Muslim they will reject me.

> . . . then the Jews came to the emissary of God and he said to them, "Which of you is `Abdallaah ibn Salaam?" and they answered, "The best of us, and the son of the best of us, our leader and the son of our leader." So he asked them, "Do you know whether he accepted Islam or not?" and they answered, "God forbid!" [T]hen `Abdallaah ibn Salaam appeared and said, "I bear witness that there is no god but God, and I bear witness that Muhammad is the emissary of God." So the Jews said, "He is the worst of us, and the son of the worst of us, and they belittled him," so `Abdallaah ibn Salaam told Muhammad, "This is exactly what I feared."

These are the most important reasons the Jews initiated hostilities against the Islamic call in Medina. They took every measure they could to extinguish its fire and vitiate its power. They did not accept the fact that this *al-Haniif* monotheistic religion should gain support, and it troubled them that they would have to live in its shadow and under its rule. If they accepted its safety and security, they could have lived prosperously in this environment. Yet they preferred to unite in *an yakiiduu* entrapping the Prophet of God and the believers, and despite the fact that they lived within the Islamic call, they tried to obstruct it and to distort it. They pooled all their resources of power and wealth to kill it in the cradle, and what wouldn't they do to achieve their ends?

We say in response that we are not exaggerating when we say that the Jews left no stone unturned in the attempt to snuff out the Islamic call, nor was any means considered out of bounds in order to denigrate Islam and its Prophet—they tried everything they could.

Here are some of their ways of entrapping Islam and the Muslims (which we will detail below):

A. religious argumentation and semantic bickering;
B. use of various schemes to discredit the Prophet;
C. their attempt to stamp out trust between the Muslims;
D. the attempt to convert the Muslims from their religion;
E. finagling with God's laws, and attempting to arouse rebellion against the emissary;
F. allying themselves with the hypocrites against the Muslims;
G. allying themselves with the polytheists against the Muslims;
H. falsely slandering the emissary;
I. making fun of/mocking the religion and its principles;
J. attempting to assassinate them.

It appears to us that the first way the Jews tried to harm the emissary was by inciting rebellion among the various groups of Muslims. This is effected through multiplying religious contention and semantic nit-picking. From his very nature the Israelite is contentious and rebellious in the face of the Truth, and the story of their sacrificing the cow, Qur'an 2:67–71 [2:246]: "The story of a group of the Banu Israel which said to one of their prophets, send us a king we will kill for God," and other stories in Qur'an about their *lujaaj* stubbornness—that is proof enough for us to say that—and here we are not saying that we are analyzing their psychology—we are merely providing some examples and instances of their disputations and demonstrating that evil intentions were the source of their resistance to facing the truth. At the time of the appearance of the Prophet, he was unable to disprove their arguments, nor to confront their religious evidence, to the extent that the Muslims would begin to doubt the truth of their Prophet, and convert out of their religion of Islam to which God had guided them. But the Jews failed in this method just as they failed in others, because God taught his Prophet the response that would silence their tongues, debunk their arguments. Qur'an 10:33: "God's word stands, even if they disapprove."

Here are some of the ways in which the Jews tried to make their case against the Prophet. We will list them all first, and give details below:

   I. they argued against the Prophet's prophethood, to undermine it;
   II. they argued about Abraham and his *milla* people;
   III. they argued against the prophecy of Jesus;
   IV. they disputed the matter of the *nusakh* various versions;
   V. their disputing the matter of the change in the qibla;
   VI. their disputing allowed and prohibited foods.

In more detail: (I) The Jews' dispute with the Prophet concerning the legitimacy of his prophethood in order to undermine him: the Jews tried to undermine the legitimacy of the Prophet's prophethood, and cast doubts on his truth, so that people would turn away from his call. They attempted this in various ways, the most important of which are the following:

(a) They claimed that Muhammad was not the Prophet they had been expecting, and who had been foretold in the heavenly books, even after they knew his truth as well as they knew their own sons. The noble Qur'an spoke of their lies, Qur'an 2:89: "And when there came to them a Book from Allah verifying that which they have, and aforetime they used to pray for victory against those who disbelieve, but when there came to them (Prophet) that which they did not recognize, they disbelieved in him; so Allah's curse is on the unbelievers."

On the authority of Ibn `Abbaas: "The Jews tried dominate the Aws and the Khazraj before the Prophet's mission, and when God sent him from among the Arabs, the Jews denied him, and denied what they had been saying about him, so Mu`aadh ibn Jabal and Bishr ibn al-Barraa´ said to them, 'O you Jews! Obey God and become Muslims! You used to dominate us before

Muhammad, when we were a polytheistic people, and you would announce to us his coming, and would provide us with his description.' Then a member of the (Jewish) Banu NaDiir, Salaam ibn Mushkam, said to them, 'No-one we recognize has come to us: Muhammad is not the Prophet we described.' At this point the noble verse, Qur'an 2:89 was revealed."[6]

(b) The perception among the people that the Jews were the guardians of God's contracts, and that they disbelieved in Muhammad out of envy of him. They really did believe in Muhammad because he did not perform any miracles as previous prophets had done, so they warned the people not to believe in Muhammad, because this meant for them that he was not a genuine prophet.

[The] noble Qur'an spoke of their doubt, and rejected it at Qur'an 3:183: "(Those are they) who said: Surely Allah has enjoined us that we should not believe in any apostle until he brings us an offering which the fire consumes. Say: Indeed, there came to you apostles before me with clear arguments and with that which you demand; why then did you kill them if you are truthful?" The core of this doubt is expressed in their saying that God made contracts with them in their books which told them not to believe in any Prophet who does not perform miracles. If anyone of the nation accepts such a false prophet, fire will come down from the sky and consume him.

God ordered his Prophet to respond to the Jews by telling them of their evil history, for this would silence them, by his telling Muhammad, "Say to them (O Muhammad) prophets before me came with signs (i.e., evidence and proofs) and with what you say (i.e., the fire that would consume the victims who accepted the false prophets), but you did not kill them if you were truthful," Qur'an 3:183 (in your opposing that you follow the truth and are led by genuine emissaries).

In his commentary the Imam al-Razi notes on this verse that God made clear the proofs they would demand of such a miracle, not by way of honest inquiry, but rather by way of deception. This is because their forefathers demanded of former prophets, for instance Zechariah, John the Baptist, and Jesus, and after they had demonstrated these miracles, the Jews made haste to kill them, after having welcomed them with deceit, dissension, and obstinacy [*sic*]. This shows that their demands were by way of deception, for if this were not so, they would not have rushed into murder. The contemporary Jews were satisfied with these deeds of the former generation in their demands, too. So God does not have to answer them in this.

Thus the noble verse nullifies the Jews' demand, and demonstrates their lie to them, and emphasizes the Prophet's truth in what his Lord communicated to him.

(II) The Jews' making deceitful demands of Muhammad, in order to challenge him with impotence (to produce miracles), and Muhammad's appearance to (be able to produce miracles) at their demand, was to make people abandon Muhammad and to believe in his untruthfulness.

Al-Tabari and Ibn Abi Haatim related, on the authority of `Ikrama, on the authority of Ibn `Abbaas, who said, "The Jew Raafi`ibn Huraymala told Muhammad, 'O Muhammad! Were you an emissary from God as you say, tell God to speak so that we may hear Him,'" to which God replied with, Qur'an 2:118: "Those who do not know ask that God speak to them or give a sign, as those who came before them—their minds are alike— We have given signs to people who are true believers."

The meaning of this noble verse is that "Those who do not know" any useful knowledge, like those Jews who make deceitful demands of you, O Muhammad "if only God would speak to us," that is, either directly, or through inspiration to us or to you, or would show us a proof the establish the Truth of your prophethood, and they say this in stubborn denial because the signs that God established prove the Truth of your prophethood for they are true signs.

Then God replied to them by saying, "[T]heir speech is just like that of those who came before them," that is, like this deceitful speech, the speech of their forefathers to whom God sent emissaries to take them out of their darkness into the light . . . "their minds are alike," that is, the minds of these and those in their erroneous stubbornness.

"We made clear signs for the true believers"—that is, we made them completely transparent in their natures, for those whose real intention is to seek out the truth sincerely wherever it may be found, so they aspire for it by examining genuine evidence with hearts purified from prejudicial fantasies, in respect for the truth and the necessity to follow it.

(III) One of the methods the Jews used to undermine Muhammad was to dispute his prophethood, trying to negate the fact that Qur'an was brought down from God's presence to Muhammad. Ibn `Abbaas related that Ibn Surayyaa al-FiTyuuni[7] said that the Hebrew word *al-fiTyuun* referred to whatever the Jews owned or controlled [*sic*] ["pitayon" in Hebrew means "bait; temptation"] said to the emissary, "O Muhammad! You have not brought anything we recognize, God has not revealed to you any clear sign for which we would follow you." Muhammad replied that the noble Qur'an was a miracle for the emissary, so God thereupon revealed Qur'an 2:99: "We have revealed to you clear signs, which only the *faasiq* will deny."[8]

A *faasiq* is one who goes from one thing to another, and it refers to disobedient unbelief, because this is going out from God's *fiTra* (nature), which is the good and true, into wanton destruction. The meaning of this noble verse is that "we have already revealed to you—O Muhammad —signs so of themselves clear in their import, because their *I`jaaz* (inimitability/miraculousness) for mankind, and in their irrefragable proofs of theological matters, one needs no further evidence of its veracity.

NOTES

1. M. T. Al-Hilaalii and M. M. Khan, trans., *The Noble Qur'an* (Riyadh: Darussalam Publishers, 1996). "Judgment" is translated elsewhere "In His Wisdom."

2. Abu `Abdallah Muhammad ibn Isma`il al-Bukhari, *Al-Sahih*, 10 vols. (Cairo: 1303/1885–86), 5:900.

3. I.e., the Jews tried to kill me, so kill them.

4. Al-Bukhari, *Al-Sahih*.

5. *Siira of Ibn Hishaam* (N.p.: Halabi publishers, 375/1955), vol. 2., p. 140, concerning the Banu `Amr ibn `Awf.

6. According to Ibn Kathiir's commentary.

7. Al-Suhayli.

8. From al-Niisaabuuri, *The Occasions of the Revelation*.

CHAPTER 31

Extracts from *The Jews in the Qur'an*

'Afiif 'Abd al-Fattah Tabbara

THE EFFECT OF HIDDEN HATREDS AND REBELLION

. . . One of the Jews' plots against Islam is the exploitation and propagation of hidden hatreds which were interstitiated within the hearts of Yathrib's (Medina) inhabitants, the Aws and the Khazraj. Ibn IsHaaq explains this, and here is the summary: Shaas ibn Qays, a Jew with a strong grudge against the Muslims, passed by a mixed group of the Aws and Khazraj after the appearance of Islam, and noticed that their past enmity was gone. This upset him very much, for he saw a new goodwill among them. So he sat down with them, and gradually related to them the hostile argumentations of their recent past, and he began to recite some of their battle poetry[1] which affected their consciousness, and aroused their `aSabiyya tribal solidarity, until he came to the part, ". . . weapons, weapons," and there was nearly a clash. News of this event reached the emissary of God, and he went out to the Aws and Khazraj telling them, "Are you still in the Jaahilayya? After God guided you to Islam, with me being the most clearly honorable among you . . . and he saved you from unbelief, and softened your hearts." So then everyone knew that the dispute had come from Satan, and scheming on the part of their enemy, so the men of the Aws and the Khazraj cried and embraced one another. They departed from the emissary of God *saami` iina muTii`iina* piously obedient. God had extinguished the scheming of the enemy of God, Shaas ibn Qays.[2] This recounting is reflected in the heavenly revelation, Qur'an 3:99–101:

Say, "O people of the Book! why do ye turn from the way of God him who believes, craving to make it crooked, while ye are witnesses? But God is not careless of what ye do." O ye who believe! if ye obey the sect of those to whom the Book was brought, they will turn you, after your faith, to unbelievers again. How can ye misbelieve while unto you are recited the signs of God, and among

you is His Apostle? But whoso takes tight hold on God, he is guided into the right way.

What Shaas ibn Qays did is the same thing the Muslims' enemies always do, and what the Zionists do now. It would be wise for the Muslims and Arabs to avoid their scheming and take a lesson from this story so that they do not allow their enemies to shatter their unity and brotherhood in the religion.

Strewing Doubts within Islam

The Jews intend to weaken faith within the Muslims' souls, and to totter their solidarity in Islam, by strewing doubts in their hearts by claiming that Islam is merely *taHriif* corruption of some of the texts found in the Torah, that there are contradictions in Qur'an, and other kinds of obfuscations.

The truth is that Islam is purely the true call to return to the true religion, which all of the emissaries brought, and a purifying of religion by removing the superstitions and disputes that spread *al-baghDaa´* hatred among mankind.

Qur'an 3:69–70 tells about the Jews' attempts to alienate the Muslims from Islam:

Some followers of the scripture wish to lead you astray, but they only lead themselves astray, without perceiving. O followers of the scripture, why do you reject these revelations of God though you bear witness (that this is the truth)?

In other words, a group of Jews wanted you to fix you firmly in error by casting doubt to weaken your belief, but when they wanted to lead you astray with doubt, they only departed from seeing the way of right guidance which Muhammad had brought. This shows that their error was out of ignorance of the error they clung to. Then God said to them, "Why do you Jews disbelieve in the clear proofs you see which prove the prophethood of

'Afiif 'Abd al-Fattah Tabbara, *Al-Yahud fi al-Qur'an: tahlil 'ilmi li-nusus al-Qur'an fi al-yahud 'ala dau' al-ahdath al-hadira, ma'a qisas Ibrahim wa Yusuf wa Musa `alayhim al-salaam* [The Jews in the Qur'an: Scientific Analysis of Qur'anic Texts concerning the Jews in the Light of Modern Events Combined with the Stories of the Prophets Abraham, Joseph and Moses, May Peace Be Upon Them], 8th ed. (Beirut: Publishing House of Knowledge for the Millions, 1980), pp. 30–35, 37–99, and 261–65.

403

Muhammad, while you witness its truth in his description and the good news of his arrival which is in your own books?"

One of the methods used by the Jews to spread doubts among the Muslims is mentioned at Qur'an 3:72:

> And a party of the people of the Scripture say: "Believe in the morning in that which is revealed to the believers (Muslims), and reject it at the end of the day, so that they may turn back."

Among the various "occasions for the revelation" of this verse is the story that some Jews spoke among themselves, saying, "Let them have satisfaction in their religion at the beginning of the day, and cause disbelief at the end of the day, because it is more effective if you confirm them so that they know that you understand what they hate, and that is more effective in turning them away from their religion.["]

This method of the Jews' blocking of the Muslims from Islam, which the verse describes, is built on the natural *qaa'ida* law of people's behavior, that is, an indication of the truth in disbelief, will cause disbelief in one [already/previously] convinced of [the truth]. Heracles ruled Rome with this principle, and one of the things he asked of Abu Sufyaan (one of Muhammad's disputants), who, when asked, "Will one who has accepted Islam later reject it?" answered, "No."

The Jews wanted to deceive people in this way, by saying, "If the worthlessness of Islam will not become clear to these people, they will not abandon it after accepting it."

But what is the purpose of this continual attempt to make the Muslims erroneously reject Islam? In the past, the Muslims had worshiped idols, and idol worship is one of the most despicable things in the eyes of the Jews. But Islam is the religion of *al-tawHiid* unicity, and it approaches Judaism in this manner, so it would have been beneficial for the Jews to have aided Islam rather than to have schemed such *al-faaDiH* despicable plots.

Qur'an clarifies the purpose of the Jews' plotting at Qur'an 2:109:

> Many of the followers of the Book wish that they could turn you back into unbelievers after your faith, out of envy from themselves, (even) after the truth has become manifest to them; but pardon and forgive, so that Allah should bring about His command; surely Allah has power over all things [Omnipotent].

This verse explains that the reason for the Jews' zeal in turning the Muslims away from Islam and towards error, and relates that it is—*al-Hasad* envy! Envy of the Islamic call which they recognized as true, and was beginning to bear fruit in its adherents because it softened their hearts and began to improve their lot in life.

The envier hopes to rob the envied of his happiness, even if it means that the envier too will be harmed. How could he know that that happiness, when it had been firmly taken possession of, would lead to power over the envied, and would induct him under his control? This is what the Jews expected, and this is what God clarified at Qur'an 2:105:

> Neither those who disbelieve among the people of the Scripture (Jews and Christians) nor Al-Mushrikun (the disbelievers in the Oneness of Allah, idolaters, polytheists, pagans, etc.) like that there should be sent down unto you any good from your Lord. But Allah chooses for His Mercy whom He wills. And Allah is the Owner of Great Bounty.

But preceding these *al-danii'a* lowly attempts, Qur'an exhibits its elevatedness for it is the book of peaceful tolerance, commanding the Muslims to kindhearted forgiveness. This is mentioned in the same verse as the Jews' envy, " . . . kindheartedly tolerate until God brings His *amr* command." This verse also mentions the promise of aid and help, and good reward, and this promise was to be fulfilled in the near future—and this again proves that Qur'an is heavenly revelation and that it confirms Muhammad's message.

The Jews' Spying on the Muslims

The hadith traditionalists/transmitters relate the names of a group of Jews who converted to Islam, but secretly disbelieved. Their conversion to Islam was only a means to spy on the Muslims, and to tell tales about the emissary about what he intended to do with the Jews, their allies, and the polytheists. They would sit among some of the Muslims in order to listen in on them, and to spread doubts among the Muslims of little faith, and to connive with those hypocrites of the Aws and the Khazraj who were of like mind to work together to gnaw away at Islam and to spread rebellion among the Muslims. In order to quash this rebellion, God revealed the heavenly revelation to forbid communicating with, or putting trust in, the Jews, at Qur'an 3:118:

> O believers, take not for your intimates outside yourselves such men spare nothing to ruin you; they yearn for you to suffer. Hatred has already shown itself of their mouths, and what their breasts conceal is yet greater. Now We have made clear to you the signs, if you understand.

In other words, "O believers! Do not take as friends those who are not of your religion, who seek to get to know your secrets, because they want to corrupt you, and intend to harm you. Signs of hatred slip from their tongues, and what their hearts hide is more than they show. God showed you the signs which distinguish the friend from the enemy. So warn them, if you are intelligent and have true perception."

The meaning of the verse is not that a Muslim cannot be a friend of someone who differs totally with his religion, but rather it prohibits making friends with one who is attributed with evil and hopes that harm [will] come upon the Muslims. What is intended by "these attributes" refers to those Jews who were the most violent in making war on Islam at its initial appearance. Those who displayed their sincerity to the believers—Qur'an commands befriending them and dealing with them in good faith and justly. This is what Qur'an, sura *al-mumtaHina* (The Tested One) [60:8] expresses:

> Allah does not forbid you respecting those who have not made war against you on account of (your) religion, and have not driven you forth from your homes, that you show them kindness and deal with them justly; surely Allah loves the doers of justice.

This is how the Muslims behaved in the past during the days of their most intense *Hamaas* zeal. They respected the Christian sects which lived among them most highly, and would approach their scholars, and the Christians served the Islamic dynasty well, as history demonstrates.

Let us now list some of the Qur'anic verses that forbid befriending the Jews: (1) Qur'an 3:119–120:

> Lo! You are the ones who love them but they love you not, and you believe in all the Scriptures [i.e., you believe in the Taurat (Torah) and the Injeel (Gospel), while they disbelieve in your book, the Qur'an]. And when they meet you, they say, "We believe." But when they are alone, they bite the tips of their fingers at you in rage. Say: "Perish in your rage. Certainly, Allah knows what is in the breasts (all the secrets)." If a good befalls you, it grieves them, but if some evil overtakes you, they rejoice at it. But if you remain patient and become *Al-Muttaqun* [*The Pious*—see v. 2:2], not the least harm will their cunning do to you. Surely, Allah surrounds all that they do.

In other words, "O you whom they love, but you don't love them . . ." Qur'an expresses with the *mot juste* here, the attribute of the Muslims, the attribute which is one of the shibboleths/marks of Islam, that is, that the Muslims love even those who are most hostile to them. Here Islam and Christianity jibe in that the desire for the good of mankind. As in the saying of *as-sayyid al-masiiH* the Lord Messiah, "Love your enemies, bless those who curse you."

His saying, (2) ". . . and you believe in the entire book . . ." is, "O you Muslims, you believe in all the holy books God revealed, e.g., the Torah, the Evangel, and the Qur'an, and you have in your souls no disbelief in any part of the godly books or in those prophets who brought them, and your love of them is the proof of this faith of yours. It would be better if they loved you because you believe in God's books, and after God clearly displayed their hypocrisy toward the believers he ordered his emissary Muhammad to curse them, to abandon them and their treachery and their hypocrisy with this eloquent sentence which implies the most intense kind of *al-izdiraa´* disparagement/belittling of them, that is, ". . . Say: 'Die, together with your anger/fury.'"

Lastly, (3) Qur'an clarifies the evil intentions of the Jews toward the believers, and that these intentions would never harm the believers if they bore their suffering with patience, and were pious toward their Lord, because God would protect the Muslims from the Jews' scheming, ". . . their scheming will not harm them at all. . . ." This godly promise was realized in his victory for the believers and *al-khudhlaan wal-haziima* the humiliating defeat for the Jews in all their hostile attempts.

The Jews' Attempt to Influence the Prophet

One of their plots against Islam was their attempt to arouse rebellion in the Prophet himself, and to attempt to influence him in spreading God's teachings and the lack of justice in them when they are examined in the right way. The tradents [traditionalists/conveyors of the traditions] of the hadith and sira [Prophet's biography] relate that the leaders of the Jews said to one another, "Let's go to Muhammad—perhaps we will be able to make him rebel against his religion, for he is only a man," so they approached him, saying, "O Muhammad, you know that we are rabbis, nobles, and leaders of the Jews: if we follow you, (other) Jews will follow you, in order not to go against us; and if between us and some of our people a quarrel were to break out, we would defer to you for judgment so that you judge in our favor against our opponents, we will believe in you and your truth." But the emissary of God turned them away in this, so God reveals at Qur'an 5:49:

> And that you should judge between them by what Allah has revealed, and do not follow their low desires, and be cautious of them, lest they seduce you from part of what Allah has revealed to you; but if they turn back, then know that Allah desires to afflict them on account of some of their faults; and most surely many of the *faasiqy* people are transgressors.

This verse demonstrated the loftiness of the teachings of Islam, for God commands his emissary, Muhammad, to judge between the Jews in matters relating to what God revealed, and if they refrain from following their wish-fulfilling whims in the judgment, and He warns him that they had better not turn away from him on account of part of what God revealed to him, and if they turn aside from God's judgment in the desire (for a different outcome), then know, O, Muhammad, that God only wants to delay their punishment in this world for a part of the sins they committed. He will recompense them in the next world for their *al-`iSyaan wal-tamarrud* rebellious disobedience, for most of the people are in rebellion against the laws of the Shari`a.

This Qur'anic text is lofty with just laws and it makes their execution a foregone conclusion, regardless of the type of man or any other influence, for it makes *al-qaanuun* law one for all people and all classes, just as this Qur'anic text is the guide for judges so they are not misled by the influence of the prideful whims of their leaders who would try to further their personal interests at the cost of justice and truth.

THE JEWS' WORSHIP OF MONEY

(1) Calls for the Love of Money among the Jews.

In all of history there has never been a people so notorious for their love of money and piling it up as the Jews. They have always done this by both legal and illegal means, to the point that it came close to *muruu´a* virtue/manliness and the Jews increased their greed to pile up money to the point of worship. So the Lord MasiiH (Messiah, Jesus), who was sent to the Children of Israel to bring them right guidance, spoke to them in the following terms, "Do not worship two Lords, God and money."

But what is reason for this greed to acquire wealth?

Perhaps it goes back to their belief that they are God's chosen people, and so they want power over the entire world, and wealth is one of the most important means to enable them to reach their objective. You can see them now controlling the treasuries of all the large nations with the money they made and with which they pull the strings of the world's economies and politics.

And perhaps this also goes back to their material belief because they do not believe except in the material life and in their (set of beliefs) there is no afterlife. Qur'an has referred to this in Sura al-MutaHana, 60:13: "O you who believe, do not follow a people God is angry with. They despair of the next life as the unbelievers despair of the Companions [in] the Grave. [The infidels despair of (the resurrection of) those who dwell in the graves.]" In other words, do not befriend nor fight with these Jews who are deserving of God's wrath: they have lost all hope of reward in the world to come because of their *nakraan* evil, just as the unbelievers and idol worshipers have lost all hope of meeting the dead who inhabit the graves on the Day of Resurrection.

Qur'an speaks of this rule which has produced many theological lessons and confirms that Qur'an is right and that it is Inspiration from God, for in the Jews' Torah one cannot find mention of *al-ruuH* spirit or of the Afterlife.[3]

Will Durant says, "The Jews seldom mention the Afterlife because they did not want anything in their religion that smacked of permanence/eternity, so their concept of reward and punishment is limited to this world."[4]

This doctrine of denying the Afterlife vitiates the idea that the good people will be rewarded for their goodness, and that the bad people will be punished for their evil, and it places the individual on the slippery slope which leads into the abyss of evil deeds and committing sins, and it transforms the material and corporeal pleasures into the very goal of life. This is what transmogrified the Jews into a materialist people, avaricious in the pursuit of treasure by any means. Adolf Hitler described them thus: ". . . the Jews cannot form a religious organization because they have no *mithaaliyya* idealism and because they do not know what comes after this world. This is according to the Talmud, [which] contains not one word of the Other World."

But despite this belief, there were Jews who, at the time of the Muhammadan mission, abrogated for themselves and the other Jews exclusively the reward of the Final Abode. Qur'an demanded proof of this claim by asking them to hope for death so that they would collect this reward that was exclusively theirs, and that if they did not wish for death then they were not veracious in their claim. Qur'an 2:94–95:

Say: "If the Last Abode with God is yours exclusively, and not for other people, then long for death—if you speak truly." But they will never long for it because of what their hands have sent before them (i.e. what they have done). And Allah is All-Aware of the *Zalimun* (polytheists and wrongdoers).

Qur'an demolished their refusal to wish for death, because they knew for themselves that they were sinners and evildoers who deserved punishment. Wishing for death is the balance by which he gave them a true judgment on a person's faith. The virtuous believer does not fear death because he knows that after this world comes one better than this life, while the inveterate sinner sees only the terrifying specter of death.

Qur'an explains the truth of their situation in their love for permanence in this life at the end of the previous verse 96, sura 2: "You will find them to be the greediest of people for life.[5] Of those who disbelieve, each one wants to live one thousand years, but he cannot slip away from [ultimate/final] punishment [even if he lives that long]. God sees what they do."

The Jews are the most greedy of people for absolute life, and they are the greediest of those who disbelieve because they hope for an absolute life. They do not believe in another life, so each one of them hopes to lengthen his own life to a thousand years in this world, but even if this hope comes true they cannot avoid God's punishment as recompense for their actions.

(2) Prohibiting Work on the Sabbath Day

God's will urges right guidance for erring peoples deals with this hegemonic materialism by legislating exclusively for them the prohibition of working on the Sabbath.

The Sabbath is one of the holy days which the Jews were commanded to observe by prohibiting work on it, so a Jew may not work on this day, nor may he carry out any act which would have material benefit. Whoever breaks this prohibition and dishonors it by working on it may have committed a grave sin. The Jews do not have a graver sin than transgressing the prohibition of working on the Sabbath, except for idol worship. The *sabt* is (English) "Sabbath"[;] in Hebrew in the sense of *raaHa* rest, because on it God *istaraaHad* rested.[6]

(3) The Sabbath Day in Qur'an

The Sabbath is mentioned in several places in Qur'an where the Children of Israel are discussed. Sometimes it relates that Moses took the Covenant away from them on account of the obligation of observing the prohibition on this day, and because of their transgressing it and their lack of observance—all of them—of this Covenant, and their transgressing of it. Thus Qur'an Sura al-A`raaf, 7:163: "And ask them (O Muhammad SAW) about the town that was by the sea, when they transgressed in the matter of the Sabbath (i.e., Saturday): when their fish came to them openly on the Sabbath day, and did not come to them on the day they had no Sabbath. Thus We made a trial of them for they used to *fisq* rebel [see also Qur'an 4:154]." In other words, "Ask, O Muhammad, the Children of Israel about the news of the people of the village which was close to the sea, and whose inhabitants would transgress God's laws by fishing on the Sabbath and the fish came up to them in plain sight on the surface of the sea, when they would hide at other times. This was their test from God to distinguish the obedient from the disobedient.

The religious scholars note the amount of hostility which the inhabitants of this city displayed in that they took a fishnet used to catch the fish on the Sabbath, in order to take it another day, and with this lowly trick they tried to deceive God and received for themselves God's wisdom intended to save them from their perdition in this life and their total involvement in it, thus receiving God's wrath.

Following the previous verse comes surat al-A`raaf, verses 164–65:

And when a community among them said: "Why do you preach to a people whom Allah is about to destroy or to punish with a severe torment?" (The preachers) said: "In order to be free from guilt before your Lord (Allah), and perhaps they may fear Allah." So when they forgot the reminders that had been given to them, We rescued those who for-

bade evil, but We seized those who did wrong with a severe torment because they used to rebel (disobey Allah) [*fisq*].

In other words, but a group of them said to those who warned them about the **maghabbat** deceit of their actions, "Why do you advise people whom God will destroy because of their sins, and which He will grievously punish in the next world?" The advisers replied, "We warned them as an excuse to their Lord not to cover up **al-munkar** evil in silence, in the hope that they would obey their Lord, but when the transgressors refused our good advice totally, God saved those who withheld themselves from **al-suu´** evil, and severely punished those who sinned, in recompense for their transgressing obedience to God."

The Taaghiya Mistaken Material of the Jews

Because of their aversion to hard work in acquiring wealth, God forbade to the Jews good things which are allowed to others, and which had previously allowed to them, Qur'an 4:160–61:

And for the injustice of those who are Jews have we forbidden them good things which we had made lawful for them, and for their obstructing so much the way of God, And because of their taking interest [*al-ribaa* usury/interest] although they had been forbidden it, and because of their devouring people's wealth wrongfully. And We have prepared for those of them, who disbelieve, a painful punishment.

In other words, these Jews who commit al-Zulm evil, God forbids them good things which previously were allowed to them, and this punishment is punishment for them and a lesson to them. Through this evil they prevented many people from entering God's religion, then they disobeyed and hindered their prophets. Likewise they accepted usury/interest despite the fact that it was prohibited to them. Then Qur'an mentions another type of their evil, that is "consuming in vain people's wealth," for example, in bribery, corruption, improper use of the balance (weights and measures), and in monopolizing taxes. This succinct quick text announces the evil materialist spirit which fills their souls. By material means, they allowed usury/interest, and it suffices to say the Jews, *they* are the ones who set up the modern economic system which depends on usury/interest. The Jewish family Rothschild appeared during the past century and spread out all over Europe and America—they are the ones who imposed this system which is based on the usury/interest of the international economy, and most of the prominent Jews in the economic sector deal in [undermining Islam] which they lend to governments in order to control their politics according to the Jews' **mukhaTTaT rasuum** established plan. [*sic*]

Adolf Hitler described the Jews' infiltration into Germany's economy, threatening to take it over,

[T]he Jews began by lending money at an evil profit, which the Aryans could not compete with. This kind of loan came into being only after the passing of some time, and after the Jews had monopolized business and crafts which they worked at in their own sections of cities, which they added country by country. But evil usury which they would charge would alienate the local inhabitants . . . desire for revenge against them increased as the Jews would rent out wide tracts of land and would burden the owners and workers with harsh rule which made them into victims of the Jews. In the end they would turn against the Jews, when they would discover that these strange people were dangerously annoying parasites.[7]

THE TABAA T (INHERENT) CHARACTERISTICS OF THE JEWS

Al-ghuruur, *the Avidity of the Jews in Their Superiority over Mankind*

In the teachings of the Jews we find: the Children of Israel are the "chosen people." This thought is an insult to the honor of other peoples, because it encourages those who believe in it to hatefully exploit the other, and this superiority alleviates the severity of any sins or crimes the Jews commit. [*sic*]

One who examines Qur'an will see that it points out this superiority, but in the opposite way than the way in which the Children of Israel regard it. Qur'an indicates this to clarify its concept of them (Qur'an 2:47–48):

O ye children of Israel! remember my favors which I have favored you with, and that I have preferred you above the worlds. Fear the day wherein no soul shall pay any recompense for another soul, nor shall intercession be accepted for it, nor shall compensation be taken from it, nor shall they be helped [victorious].

The "superiority" of the Children of Israel the Qur'an intends is not their superiority over the believers and the "worlds" [misprint here] who have God's Shari`a, but rather their superiority over **sharr al-wujuud** the evil of the contemporary situation, that is, the pharaoh and his hosts. The Lord of the Worlds made them superior over Pharaoh only because the Jews were the oppressed and Pharaoh was the oppressor. Just as Qur'an mentions concerning the Children of Israel: "We want to give to those who are weak in the land" and "The word of your Lord concludes in goodness with the Children of Israel. Because of their patience/what they endured."

Qur'an uses the term **tafDiil** "superiority" not in the sense of personal superiority referring to their **dhawaat** essences or their **jins** race/type; God prefers one people over another only on account of their deeds. After using this term in the first half of the verse, in the second half of the verse it warns them of their avidity in using this term, because every soul will be recompensed by its deeds, Qur'an 2:48: "so fear the [judgment] day on which soul will not vie with soul, [nor will] intercession [be accepted], nor will they be victorious"—that is, "Beware, O Children of Israel, of the Day of Resurrection on which there will be recompense. A day in which no soul will have any effect on any other, like suffering for another's sin. No intercession will be accepted for it, and nothing shall lessen its responsibility for its evil deeds, no ransom or exchange. No one will be able to remove punishment from him who deserves it."

Were the Children of Israel superior over the other peoples as they believe, why did God direct this clear speech to them in which he tells them he will pay them back for their deeds, and that no intercessor will be of benefit to them, nor will ransom be accepted to alleviate God's punishment if they had sinned?

Some of their scholars justified this superiority by the plethora of their prophets, but plenty of prophets [are] evidence of suspicion on their **suu´ al-`unSur** [ingrained/inherent] evil nature [character], for whenever their situation changed for the better by a certain prophet, and then he died, the Jews would backslide into their **baghy wa-iSyaan** licentious disobedience, whereupon God would send another prophet to reform them.

This superiority which the Jews arrogate to themselves they base on the belief that they are God's beloved sons. God negates this at Qur'an 5:18: "The Jews and Christians say . . . he punishes whom he wills."

Observe this clear disproof of their superiority, for Qur'an says to them clearly, "O you Jews! If you were superior to other peoples as you claim, then why do you suffer these punishments God had afflicted you with over the centuries because of your disobedience, and why did he disperse you so that you become an evil example for humankind because of your evil deeds, as Qur'an 5:18: 'But you are humans We created,' which is a clear disproof of the thought of the Jews' **tamyiiz `unSuriyy** racial chosenness and the thought of 'God's chosen people.'"

In Qur'an's view people are equal before God; there is no advantage of any person over another, not white over black, except in his deeds and piety. The best people is the one which believes in God, commands the good and forbids evil, and fulfills the obligations of fairness. Qur'an calls Muhammad's people "the best of people": Qur'an 3:110:

You are the best of the nations raised up for (the benefit of) men; you enjoin what is right and forbid the wrong and believe in Allah; and if the followers of the Book had believed it would have been better for them; of them (some) are believers and most of them are transgressors.

"Good" and "chosen" here refer to the attributes mentioned in the verse, that is, they are inherent in "commanding the good and forbidding evil."

The Jews' Hopes for God's Forgiveness

Deeply ingrained in the Jews' imagination is that salvation is collective, not individual, and that only a genetic relationship with the seed of Abraham could guarantee its bearer with eternal salvation. [*sic*]

This belief *Zallat talaazuma-hum* became more ingrained and organized their way of life through various historical stages and it made them into the most ingrained of people with moral perversity and the most deeply involved in *al-munkaraat* evil deeds. This became an incentive for neighboring peoples to oppress them.

Qur'an explains this concept and rejects it: Qur'an surat al-A`raaf, 7:168–69:

And we cut them up into nations in the earth, some of them righteous, and some of them otherwise; and we tried them with good things and evil, that haply they should return. And there succeeded after them a succession who inherited the book, taking the chance goods of this lower world, and saying, "It will be forgiven us"; and if chance goods the like of them come to them, they will take them. Has not the compact of the book been taken touching them, that they should say concerning God nothing but the truth? And they have studied what is in it; and the Last Abode is better for those who are god-fearing. Do you not understand?

In other words, "We divided the Jews into groups, some good some not good, and we chose them for bounties and revenge in the hope that the sinners among them would repent from their sin. We then brought forth another folk after these, and they inherited the Torah but did not adhere to it, but rather pursued the pleasures of this world by unlawful means, saying, "God will forgive us for what we have done, despite the fact that God's forgiveness was premised on their doing repentance— which they did not do, but persisted in acquiring wealth in unlawful ways. Then God reproached them for requesting forgiveness despite their persisting in what they were doing, and He said, 'We have taken the Torah as a Covenant with you (they had learned what was in it), that they tell the truth, and that the Final Abode is for those who renounce sin, do you not understand that the bounty of the afterlife is better than the pleasures of this world?'"

Qur'an emphasizes this also. The people of the hadith narrated that the Muslims and the people of the Book would vie with each other in boasting, and each side claimed the Afterlife exclusively for themselves, so God revealed the following two verses, Qur'an 4:122–23:

But those who believe (in the Oneness of Allah— Islamic Monotheism) and do deeds of righteousness, We shall admit them to the Gardens under which rivers flow (i.e., in Paradise) to dwell therein forever. Allah's Promise is the Truth, and whose words can be truer than those of Allah? (Of course, none). It will not be in accordance with your desires (Muslims), nor those of the people of the Scripture (Jews and Christians), whosoever works evil, will have the recompense thereof, and he will not find any protector or helper besides Allah.

In other words, "Recompense and salvation does not come through hopes, O Muslims, and O Jews and Christians of the Children of Israel, but whoever does a bad deed will be recompensed accordingly, and he will find only God to harm him or to save him, and he who does good works, and believes in God, they [*sic*] are saved and they are the ones who will enter the Garden of Paradise. There makes no difference whether male or female, they won't be harmed in the slightest way ['worth a date-pit'] for their actions."

The meaning of religions is not to vie with one another in boasting, and there is no advantage to be gained by belonging or strongly believing in one religion, but the goal and spirit of religions is belief in God and doing good works.

The Jews' Cowardice

Qur'an describes the Jews as cowards. Cowardice is characterized by *ghadr* deceit and *al-khiyaana* treachery; it is the opposite of courage.

A folk cannot lack courage without having cowardice rule over it. This is the reason for the Jews' inordinate love of this world and the enjoyment of its lustful pleasures, for courage goes hand in hand with danger, and it accompanies the firmly held belief that one must accept death gracefully if that is necessary to realize this faith.

The Jews' cowardice is the reason for their tenacity in clinging to this life, no matter how *Haqiira dhaliila* wretchedly humiliating it be. In his book *The War against the Muslims* Bernard Lazar says, "[T]he only reward the pious of the Family of Israel hope for is that God will grant them a long life of goodness, joyful and wealthy . . . and the Jew sees the end of existence in the end of this life . . . and he sees goodness in mankind only in relation to the good things of this life."[8]

The Jews are notorious for their cowardice and for deserting ongoing battle, yet they are swift in arranging plots and hostile actions camouflaged with deceit and *al-khadii`a* deception.

This trait is dominant among them since early history,

and neighboring peoples would despise them because of their treacherous cowardice, so they attacked the Jews many times, sometimes from Egypt, at other times from Syria and east of the Jordan, sometimes from Iraq, up to the time they began to be attacked from Europe.

Qur'an describes the Jews' hostile treachery against their prophets, Qur'an 3:112:

> *al-dhulla* Humiliation is stamped upon them wherever they may be, except when under a covenant (of protection) from Allah, and from men; they have drawn on themselves the Wrath of Allah, and destruction is put over them. This is because they disbelieved in the Ayat (proofs, evidences, verses, lessons, signs, revelations, etc.) of Allah and killed the Prophets without right. This is because they disobeyed (Allah) and used to transgress beyond bounds (in Allah's disobedience, crimes and sins). [9]

In other words, God imposed *al-hawaan* humiliation upon them wherever they were, except for the times they clung to God's rope and peoples' rope and thus avoided God's wrath, as he imposed *al-istikaana wal-khuDuu`* humiliating wretchedness on others because of their disbelief in God's verses/signs and their murdering prophets who might have brought the truth except for their hostile transgression. But a thought may occur to the reader's brain [*sic*]: "How could Qur'an attribute to the Jews *al-dhulla wal-maskana* humiliation and wretchedness, when today they rule Palestine and their word is heard/obeyed in every major power?"

The solution is simple: Qur'an describes them with the term *al-dhulla* humiliation, but it indicated that once the Jews had had sovereignty: "except with a rope of God and a rope of mankind."

The Jews never achieved power in the land except with a rope from mankind, that is aid from the Western powers, in the present, and a rope from God which intended his judgment that they win in Palestine in order to show the Arab peoples that during this defeat the evildoers have forced upon them that corruption, bribery, and treachery had become widespread among them.

How true the following words are! "The Jewish rape of our *arD* land can be explained only as a long process and continuous preparation on the part of international Jewry which achieved its goals together with the benefits of imperialism in our *waTan* homeland on the one hand, and which went, on the other hand, with the total social and economic corruption in which we live." [10]

The Palestine tragedy has become the reason for the Arab impetus to purify their society from corruption, and Arab peoples still have the time and the opportunity to call up their strength to reform their society and to join their word together [*sic* = "speak with one voice"] which is the entranceway to liberate Palestine.

The Jews' ghadr wa-ajraam *Treacherous Crimes*

The Arabs will never forget the humiliating shame they suffered in the Palestine War. A *baaghiya mujrima* wantonly criminal gang of Zionist Jews used all kinds of hostile treachery and *al-qatl al-jamaa`iyy* mass murder, in order to conquer (the Arabs') homelands and properties, and still the blood of the victims of the massacres of Deir Yasin [*sic*][11] and Beit Drass [*sic*]. These provide the best witness of all that occurred in the land which was stolen from our homeland of the *FadaaHa baghiyy* chthonian depravity and crimes of the Zionists: there they killed Arab men, women, and children, the like whose *al-hawl* horror at which the skin crawls.

For the Jews, this criminal character is not something new, but it is *mutawaarith* inherited from the ancestors and grandfathers. The French philosopher and historian Gustave LeBon says:

> The painful history of the Jews is a story only of *Duruub al-munkaraat* one catastrophe after another. From the stories of prisoners who had been sawed apart while alive or of those who were burned in the ovens, to the stories of the queens who had been thrown to the dogs to be eaten, and to the stories of the inhabitants of the cities in which the Jews had been slaughtered, with no difference to sex or age. [12]

Anyone who reads their holy books will be affected by paying attention to the *al-faZaa'i`* disasters that befell them, in the cities they *aghaaruu `alaa* swarmed into, and the majority of them supporting themselves by deceit, let him remember what they did in Jericho: "They destroyed everything in the city, men, women, children, old men, even the cattle, sheep, and camels with the edge of the sword." [13]

Qur'an accuses them of crimes as serious as that of murdering God's emissaries: Qur'an 5:70:

> Verily, We took the covenant of the Children of Israel and sent them Messengers. Whenever there came to them a Messenger with what they themselves desired not—a group of them they called liars, and others among them they killed.

They also executed those people who believed in justice, Qur'an 3:21:

> Verily! Those who disbelieve in the Ayat (proofs, evidences, verses, lessons, signs, revelations, etc.) of Allah and kill the Prophets without right, and kill those men who order just dealings, . . . announce to them a painful torment.

Qur'an also accuses them of deceit, Qur'an 2:100:

Is it not (the case) that every time they make a covenant, some party among them throw it aside? Nay! the truth is most of them believe not.

This testimony of both Qur'an and history agree that the Jews commit deceitful crimes.

The Jews Create Corruption in the Earth

It is doubtless that two of the firmest binds among any people that work as a prophylactic to protect them from degenerative decay are: (1) character/ethics is one of the marks of godly guidance, and which allowed the propagation of religions, for as long as a people remained within the bounds of this guidance they would live in goodness and security, and thus the degradation of ethics in any people is a signal of collapse.

Among the stated goals of some Jewish Zionists is the gnawing away at the others' ethics in addition to having control of him, and this is their stated policy in the book *The Protocols of the Elders of Zion.* [*sic*][14]

This is what Adolf Hitler meant when he wrote,

Ever since the Jews invented Bolshevism [*sic*] they intended to gnaw away at the integrity of the German nation. We see *al-radhiila* degeneracy beginning to participate in the (thoughts of) German youth wherever you turn, and we see the throne of *al-ibaaHiyya wal-khalaa`a* ethical anarchy arising in the role of showing cinematic films, *wal-maraabi`* poor/red-light districts, and bars—and even in the public squares. How can one have hope in the youth in such a condition that prefers pleasures [debauchery] to the fatherland; how can one expect them to sacrifice their lives for defending its institutions and traditions?[15]

It is noteworthy that Qur'an repeats this same truth fourteen centuries ago, at Qur'an 5:64: "They run through the earth doing corruption, but God does not like the corrupters."

And Qur'an 5:62–63:

And you see many of them (Jews) hurrying for sin and transgression [as bribes and Riba (usury), etc.], and eating illegal things. Evil indeed is that which they have been doing. Why do not the rabbis and the religious learned men forbid them from uttering sinful words and from eating illegal things. Evil indeed is that which they have been performing.

In other words: "You see, O Muhammad! Many of these Jews rush into *al-ma`aaSii wal-i`tidaa'* hostile transgression against others, and into consuming forbidden wealth, like bribery and usury, and how bad it is they do such *al-qabaa'iH* ugly deeds. If it were necessary for their scholars and *imaams* leaders to prevent

them from acting thus, by calling a sin like lying and every *munkar qabiiH* ugly evil like *ghayba* secrecy/concealing wealth, gossip and slander against others; and consuming forbidden wealth, bribery, and usury. How evil it is that their scholars are content with these transgressions, and ignoring (their duty to give) good advice, and their not commanding the good and forbidding evil."

What Qur'an says applies to the Zionists perfectly: they do not restrain themselves from corrupting others into sin by any means in order to control them, as they are used to using all of the *wasaa'il al-munkar wal-khidaa`* stealthy and underhanded means of deception in order to expel the Arab Palestinians from their homes; they achieve their goals through bribery as they buy off the great powers, and the governors, and the press agencies, all in order to help them in the realization of their cherished aims.

THE MOCKING UNBELIEVERS OF THE PEOPLE OF THE BOOK

The Lesson to Be Learned in the Jews' Mockery in Qur'an

Qur'an contains many verses describing the mockery by the unbelievers among the Children of Israel, and the condemnation of their *al-qabiiIIa* ugly deeds whether in disobeying the emissary of God, or those who came before Muhammad in the Old Testament; and here Qur'an jibes with the Old Testament[16] in stating the Jews' mockery and condemning their *al-sa'iyya* evil deeds, and God's anger which this brought down on them, his punishment and banishment of them in every period of their long history in which they never get even a taste of settling down.

Speech in the Qur'anic verses which we mention are of general applicability to the Jews; their (sad) state was a lesson for other peoples because it makes known the natural state of nations in a position like that of the Jews'. Thus Qur'an is a guide for *lil-`aalamiina* the worlds (levels of existence/see first suura, *al-FaatiHa*: "Lord of the worlds") until the Day of Judgement, not a historical narrative devoted to the mockery of the Israelites, for it is considered an *umma* in itself in its individuality and totality, so that its status not become like the one the verse refers to, but that its judgement become like their judgement in the presence of God, because the recompense for the actions of hearts and corporeal members, is the same, regardless of individuals, tribes, or their hatreds.[17]

Mockery in Qur'an is especially virulent because of the extent to which it will go in its *al-faHsh wal-danas* despicable pollution, so the reader must be especially careful in understanding [these] parts of [Qur'an].

The Evil of the Jews' Deeds

Much of what Qur'an speaks about in connection with the unbelievers among the Children of Israel, is their being deserving of God's curse. "Curse" in Arabic means "expulsion from God's mercy, so everything God curses He has expelled from His mercy, deserves punishment, and perishes."[18] Concerning his cursing of the unbelievers among the Children of Israel, God says, Qur'an 5:78–80:

> Curses were pronounced on those among the Children of Israel who rejected Faith, by the tongue of David and of Jesus the son of Mary: because they disobeyed and persisted in excesses. Nor did they (usually) forbid one another the iniquities which they committed: evil indeed were the deeds which they did. Thou seest many of them turning in friendship to the Unbelievers. Evil indeed are (the works) which their souls have sent forward before them (with the result), that God's wrath is on them [forever], and in torment will they abide.

In other words, God expelled the unbelievers of the Children of Israel from his mercy. He made note of this in the **al-zabuur** the Psalms which he revealed to his prophet David, and in the Evangel he revealed it to his prophet Jesus. This is on account of the Jews' hostile disobedience against God's prohibitions and against his prophets, and their not taking (these prophets') good advice. One of them does not prevent another from his ugly actions and **al-munkar** evil deeds, neither do they restrain him. How ugly are the things they perpetrate!

This is in addition to the fact that forbidding evil is a touchstone for manners and virtues because it creates in an *umma* a general outlook and it establishes responsibility for a society. It guards the individual and the group, and if the prohibition of evil be abandoned, then the evildoers will flaunt their *fisq* evil, and will infect the general population with it. Then evil will spread, and this **al-munkar** evil will be the reason for the downfall of the *umma* and the justification for its suffering God's anger.

After Qur'an had reiterated the Jews' refusal to hinder evildoing, it mentioned one of their attributes, that is, allying themselves with the idol-worshiping polytheists against the monotheist Muslims, and their accepting them as helpers to cooperate with them in their war against Islam. This alliance is **sharr ma`Siyya** the most grievous sin the Jews ever committed, and they will find their comeuppance in God's wrath and in an eternity of torture in hell.

The Jews' Breaking of God's Covenant

Qur'an makes clear how God made a covenant with the Children of Israel that they would follow, and how they broke the covenant to deserve God's wrath, Qur'an 5:12–13:

> Indeed Allah took the covenant from the Children of Israel (Jews), and We appointed twelve leaders among them. And Allah said: 'I am with you if you perform As-Salat (Iqamat-as-Salat) and give Zakat and believe in My Messengers; honor and assist them, and lend to Allah a good loan. Verily, I will remit your sins and admit you to Gardens under which rivers flow (in Paradise). But if any of you after this, disbelieved, he has indeed gone astray from the Straight Path.' So because of their breach of their covenant, We cursed them, and made their hearts grow hard. They change the words from their (right) places and have abandoned a good part of the Message that was sent to them. And you will not cease to discover deceit in them, except a few of them. [*sic*] But forgive them, and overlook (their misdeeds). Verily, Allah loves Al-Muhsinun (good-doers) [see also 2:112].

In these two verses, God clarifies how he made a covenant with the Children of Israel for their obedience, and set over them twelve chieftains, and promised them to help them with his aid and victory, if they would establish prayer and pay alms and believe in all his emissaries and help them, and if they would give charity. If they did this, God would forgive their evil deeds, and induct them into the Gardens of Paradise. But for the Jews who subsequently disbelieved, they strayed from the Straight Path. But the Children of Israel broke the covenant, and so became deserving of God's expelling them from his mercy, and their hearts became hardened so as not to turn toward the truth. Then they murdered the prophets. This is what Qur'an repeats at Qur'an 4:154:

> And for their covenant, we raised over them the Mount and (on the other occasion) we said: "Enter the gate prostrating (or bowing) with humility"; and We commanded them: "Transgress not (by doing worldly works on) the Sabbath (Saturday)." And we took from them a firm covenant.

The Jews' Turning Away from God's Shari`a

Because of the Jews' hostility to the believers, and their rejecting obedience to God, and their hypocrisy, they became deserving of God's anger and of His expelling them from His mercy, as Qur'an 5:59–60:

> Say: "O People of the Book! Do ye disapprove of us for no other reason than that we believe in God, and the revelation that hath come to us and that which came before (us), and (perhaps) that most of you are rebellious and disobedient?" Say: "Shall I

point out to you something much worse than this, (as judged) by the treatment it received from God? those who incurred the curse of God and His wrath, those of whom some He transformed into apes and swine, those who worshiped evil;—these are (many times) worse in rank, and far more astray from the even path!"

In other words, "Say, O emissary, to these Jews, 'Is the reason for your *al-baghD* hatred of us our belief in God and in what was revealed to us, and in what the prophets of old brought us; and our belief that most of you have rejected God's Shari`a?' And say to them, O emissary, 'Did He not inform you that the evil of your ways is the cause of your comeuppance by God?' Qur'an answers this question by naming the Jews by their ancestors and their taking part in their *al-fisq* evil, so that a similar comeuppance, represented by their being set wide apart from God's mercy and becoming afflicted with God's wrath, will not afflict them. So God made some of them into apes in respect to their base desires, and pigs in their unrestrained lust for pleasure; he made them into Satan's slaves, and these are evil to the most extreme degree, and they are the most erring of people from the true way.

The Jews' Concealment of God's Teachings

The hadith tradents [compilers] relate that some Muslims asked a group of Jewish rabbis about part of the Torah, and the Jews concealed it from them, refusing to give them information about it. Concerning them,[19] God revealed Qur'an 2:159:

Verily, those who conceal the clear proofs, evidences and the guidance, which we have sent down, after we have made it clear for the People in the Book, they are the ones cursed by Allah and cursed by the cursers.

Al-kitmaan concealment is sometimes covering up and hiding something, and other times it is removing it and substituting something else in its place. Despite their contract with the emissary Muhammad, the Jews committed both types of concealment of parts of the Torah, for example, they [hid] the law of lapidation of/stoning the adulterer, they denied the Torah's announcement of the good news of Muhammad's coming, and they insisted on applying nonrelevant interpretations on those Torah verses mentioning Muhammad. They also fabricated evidence denying the prophecy of Jesus, claiming that it belonged to/was intended for someone else. This is what *al-kitmaan* concealment means when used in Qur'an.

The verse states that the Jews concealed right guidance that had appeared in the revealed books, and refused to share it with anyone: "The lesson to be learned/the moral of this verse is that even if the event is

specific, the judgment is general, for whoever conceals God's signs and guidance from people is deserving of God's curse."[20]

Qur'an records the People of the Book's minimizing the propagation of God's right guidance at Qur'an 3:187:

(And remember) when Allah took a covenant from those who were given the Scripture (Jews and Christians) to make it (the news of the coming of Prophet Muhammad saw and the religious knowledge) known and clear to mankind, and not to hide it, but they threw it away behind their backs, and purchased with it some miserable gain! And indeed worst is that which they bought.

In other words, God made a firm contract with the People of the Book that they would clarify (the Book's) meanings, and not hide anything of God's signs or right guidance from people. But the Jews ignored this in rejection, and sought instead the goods and pleasures of this world.

This, in short, is what Qur'an records about the Jews' *al-taqaa`us* refusal to propagate God's *al-waSaayaa* instructions—primarily, worshiping God alone, especially among the idol-worshiping Arabs/Bedouins. This is a well-known fact which Dr. Israel Wolfensohn admits,

Doubtlessly, there was in the Jewish *maqduur* subconscious the desire to spread Judaism among the Arabs until it achieved supremacy, even if there was the widespread conviction among the Jews the intention to propagate the religious call directly, and even if the religious call was partially restricted to fellow Jews.[21]

The Jews Do Not Benefit from God's Right Guidance

Concerning a group of Jews who are not influenced by the teachings of the Torah and do not follow them, God says, Qur'an 62:5: "The likeness of these who carry the Torah without following it is like an ass/a donkey carrying books." God likens their not following the right guidance they have in their hands to a noncomprehending donkey. Then the likeness is clarified and deepened when God compares these Jews "who carried the Torah," that is, they took upon themselves to learn Torah and carry out its commandments, but they found no benefit in it. Their likeness is like that of a donkey who carries huge volumes, not knowing a thing about what they contain, and it does not distinguish between it and other loads, for it has only toil to bear.

This metaphor is directed at a certain group of Jews, but it applies as well to bearers of Qur'an who have abandoned acting on it, and thus cannot benefit from its truth because they have not abided by its *Huduud* laws.

God says about a certain group of Jews, Qur'an 57:14:

"Some of them are **ummiyyuun** illiterates who only know vain hopes of the Book, and they only just suppose." In other words, among the Jews is a group of ignorant illiterates, who cannot read or write and have no knowledge of anything in the Book, that is, the Torah. They have no knowledge of its laws, and they have no part in religion, but only wishful thinking with their fabricated suppositions. "Such wishful thinking is found in every *umma* in a state of weakness and decay, in order for the inhabitants to boast of the laws they have, and of their ancestors who were rightly guided, as they are, by the records they kept as fruit of that right guidance. They hope out of wishful thinking that this be sufficient to help them and save them, and give them respect in the eyes of other peoples."[22]

The Hardness of the Jews' Hearts

Qur'an 2:74:

Then, after that, your hearts were hardened and became as stones or even worse in hardness. And indeed, there are stones out of which rivers gush forth, and indeed, there are of them (stones) which split asunder so that water flows from them, and indeed, there are of them (stones) which fall down for fear of Allah. And Allah is not unaware of what you do.

God compares their hard hearts to solid stone, but adds, "but even harder" because stone can be worked and shaped. There are stones that break under a lot of water, and stones that shatter and fountains of water flow out of them, and stones that fall from high mountains, obeying God's will in affecting them by lightning, hurricanes, or earthquakes.

The meaning of "hearts" is the metaphorical one of intelligent consciousness. The hearts of the Children of Israel were hardened, and they lost the ability to be shaped or molded. Thus the laws and admonitions and lessons to be learned can never penetrate into their hearts, so that they may learn from them. From the heights of humanity the Children of Israel descended into a deep, stagnant pit, nay! Even lower than that!

SOME OF THE INSTRUCTIONS FOR THE CHILDREN OF ISRAEL IN QUR'AN

Qur'anic Directions for the Children of Israel Are Also Instructions for the Believers

What distinguishes the Islamic call is its total exclusivity for the whole of mankind; it is not restricted to one people or another, and the Lord of the Worlds commanded this truth to his emissary, Muhammad, to communicate to all men, Qur'an 21:107: "We have sent you out of mercy from us towards the whole world."

God—in Islam—is the creator of the universe, Lord of the Worlds, and God of all men whatever their differences; as for Yahweh of the Hebrews, he is the God of the Children of Israel.

Just as Muhammad's message is universal, it is at one and the same time perfectly complete, in that it contains the messages God gave to Moses, Jesus, Abraham, and so on. Thus in Qur'an we encounter many of the legal instructions for Muhammad's followers to adhere to because the essence of the godly message among God's emissaries is one in its beliefs and characteristics, but legislations may vary according to the level of a certain *umma*'s development.

Worshiping God and Goodness toward Mankind

Among the Qur'anic instructions addressed to the Children of Israel is Qur'an 2:83:

And when We made a covenant with the children of Israel: You shall not serve any but Allah and (you shall do) good to (your) parents, and to the near of kin and to the orphans and the needy, and you shall speak to men good words and keep up prayer and pay the poor-rate. Then you turned back except a few of you and (now too) you turn aside.

God explains in this verse that the contract he made with the Children of Israel not to worship anyone else, and not to have any partners in his worship, neither king, rabbi, nor money, or anything else of God's creation. He made with them a covenant to honor parents, relatives, orphans, and the needy who are unable to acquire what they need; he contracted them also to speak kindly to people, and to command the good and forbid evil, and not to sink into stealthy slander, for this is what human groups do and then sink into hostile disputations; God also contracted them to establish prayer and to give charity **al-zakaat**. "Charity" means spending part of rich people's money for the benefit of the poor, but the Children of Israel shirked carrying out these lofty teachings, with the exception of a few of them.

One of the instructions the Qur'an brings to the Children of Israel is Qur'an 2:43–46:

And be steadfast in prayer (**Iqamat-as-Salat**); practice regular charity (**Zakat**); and bow down your heads with those who bow down (**Irkaa'**) (in worship) [submit yourselves with obedience to Allah]. Enjoin you Al-Birr (piety and righteousness and each and every act of obedience to Allah) on the people and you forget (to practice it) yourselves, while you recite the Scripture [the Taurat (Torah)]! Have you then no sense?

Qur'an calls the Children of Israel to establish prayer, yet they were in error because they clung only to prayer's outward appearances, so they prayed without having "established prayer": "Establishing" means giving something its full essence, so that good effects are produced by it, and "establishing prayer" means directing oneself to God alone with total sincerity in submitting oneself to him and thus realizing self-betterment. Then Qur'an calls on them to spend on charity for the needy in order to improve society and fortify it against revolutions and rebellion from the ***al-maHruuma*** criminal classes. After Qur'an commands them to prostrate themselves, this being an important part of prayer, for it symbolizes submission to God's command, and it demonstrates his power, and shows obedience to his omnipotence. "Prostrating oneself with the prostrators" means that they should be among a group of Muslims and pray their prayers, because one of the signs of "prayer" in Islam is prostration to God.

Later Qur'an blames those of the Children of Israel who command the instructions of God then forget to do them, despite the fact that they recite the book when it would be better for them were they to be warned and corrected by God's words which they read, and then do them.

Last, God commands them to ask for aid in patience and with prayer against the disasters that befall them in this life, but true patience is by remembering God's promise to recompense the patient with goodness for the acts of goodness which tear at the soul; and by restraining oneself from prohibited lusts which the soul yearns for in spite of remembering the sudden catastrophes caused by God's actions and his behavior toward his creation, so it is incumbent to submit oneself to his command.

Asking for aid through prayer is helpful in alleviating suffering, and in strengthening the soul for the confrontation with the pains and terrors it encounters, for prayer is the firmest bond between a man and his Lord through which he extends certainty, right guidance, and light. Then Qur'an explicates that prayer shatters the souls of those who engage in following lusts, but prayer is gentle with submissive souls which fear God, and which are of a certainty that they will meet their Lord on the Day of Account.

The Value of the Human Soul and the Ugliness of Crime

From ancient times, the Children of Israel became well known for criminality among their various groups, and thus the commands in Qur'an address them in order to highlight the ***al-shanaa`a*** despicableness of this aspect of criminality, and the value and status of the human soul.

For no matter how ***istaHdathat*** developed/transpired, and [how] ideally honorable a soul became, and no matter how clement or humane it may become, any legislation, law, or set of instructions it invents could not possibly compare with the level of loftiness of Qur'an.

O Reader! Stand in glorious submission before this Qur'anic text which totally ennobles the human soul, regardless of its color, nationality/tribal identity, or beliefs [*sic*] as it absolutely condemns criminality, and outlines its maleficent ugliness against the human species! Qur'an 5:32:

> Because of that We ordained for the Children of Israel that if anyone killed a person not in retaliation of murder, or (and) to spread mischief in the land—it would be as if he killed all mankind, and if anyone saved a life, it would be as if he saved the life of all mankind. And indeed, there came to them Our Messengers with clear proofs, evidences, and signs, even then after that many of them continued to exceed the limits (e.g., by doing oppression unjustly and exceeding beyond the limits set by Allah by committing the major sins) in the land! [verse plagiarized from *Mishna Sanhedrin*]

This instruction came to the Children of Israel after the story of Cain, who killed his brother Abel out of envious evil; Cain and Abel were the sons of Adam. This crime demonstrates that mankind is inclined toward extreme violence which culminated in unlawful murder. God wrote about the Children of Israel, among whom hostilely evil murder spread, that murder of an innocent soul, without recompense (blood money) or with unintended corruption, must be punished with death, for it as if the murdered soul were the soul of all humanity, because the individual represents the human species in general. Thus whoever allows the spilling of a man's blood unjustly, allows the spilling of the blood of every member of human society, and he influences others to commit the same crime. Thus Qur'an clarifies that the murder of one soul unjustly qualifies as murdering all of society as far as God is concerned, and it merits his punishing wrath; then Qur'an clarifies that whoever is the cause of saving another soul from death, either out of honor for in or defending it from danger that threatens it—it is as if he saved all mankind, for the impulse to save a person's life is empathetic mercy and respect for the soul, and for saving it he deserves the most splendid reward from his Lord.

These are the great teachings of Qur'an concerning the human soul, which we need most of all during periods of tumultuous rebellion against the systems of government which allow the spilling of blood arbitrarily, and people deal with their adversaries in opinion and in belief with the harshest brutality. But what is obtained by force will be returned by the truth, to the individual, no matter how weak his standing in society. There is no excuse for anyone to permit the spilling of his brother's blood in hostile evil, by murdering him by himself, or having the deed done indirectly. Murder calls out for revenge, if not in the same time frame, then in subsequent time frame, sooner or later.

The Qur'anic verses that condemn criminality comprise a reaction to the Zionist cliques, which had Arab blood flow in order to expel them from their homeland. Does their religion command them to commit such crimes? No way! They are not a religious group, but merely a political group which has hijacked the religion for itself to achieve its goals.

The Call to the Children of Israel to Follow the Light of Islam

Qur'an, surat al-`Aaraaf, 7:156–57:

> And ordain for us good in this world, as well as in the next; we have turned to Thee with repentance." ALLAH replied, "I will inflict MY punishment on whom I will; but MY mercy encompasses all things; so I will ordain it for those who act right-eously and pay the Zakaat and those who believe in Our Signs—Those who follow the Messenger, the Prophet, the Ummi whom they find mentioned in the Torah and the Gospel which are with them. He enjoins on them good and forbids them evil and makes lawful for them the good things and forbids them the bad things and removes from them their burdens and shackles that were upon them. So those who shall believe in him and honor and support him and help him and follow the light that has been sent down with him—these shall prosper."

These two Qur'anic verses clarify those to whom God calls [misprint here] in his mercy: the People of the Book, those who embrace Islam and follow the emissary, Muhammad, and how not? For Muhammad's description is clearly written in the Torah and the Evangel, and he commands them to do good, and "the good" means that which people generally recognize as beneficial and praise-worthy actions; and Muhammad forbids them from doing evil, and "evil" means that which people's minds reject as harmful maleficence. Muhammad also allows them good things of this life, that is, every delectable flavor, and healthful nourishment; and Muhammad forbids them harmful things which are unnatural and pollute the body. Just as he lifts their chains from them, that is, he removes the bindings that do not permit movement. The imposition of strict Shari`a rules that God imposes on the Children of Israel resulting from their evil behavior is likened to fet-ters which hinder their freedom. Thus Islam brought its Shari`a which comprises the right and the good for the masses; those who believe in Muhammad and his Shari`a and protect him from every enemy, they are victorious as they follow the light which was revealed to him and these are the willers of the major mercy and satisfaction of God.

Some Jews Who Accepted Islam

The tradents [compilers] of the hadith relate some of the names of the Jewish rabbis who became Muslims, for example, `Abdallah ibn Salaam, a learned rabbi, who, after accepting Islam, abandoned his people, telling them, "O group of Jews! Be pious to God and accept what Muhammad brought you, for by God! You know he is God's emissary. You find him written in your Torah by his name and by his attributes, and I testify that Muhammad is the emissary of God, and that I believe in, confirm, and know."[23]

Another was Mukhayriq, who was a learned rabbi, and was very rich from his palm fields, and knew of the emissary of God by his attributes when he recognized them. In the battle of Uhud, in which Muslims and polytheists were killed, Mukh said to his people, "O you group of Jews! By God! You know that Muhammad's victory over you is right!" The Jews responded, "Today is the Sabbath." Mukh replied, "This is no reason!" Then he took up his arms, and went out, and came to the emissary of God after he had instructed his people, "If I be killed today, my wealth goes to Muhammad to do with as God wishes." When the battle raged, and people were killed, Mukh killed until he himself was killed . . . and the emissary of God said, "Mukh is the best Jew."[24]

There were many more Jews besides these two who accepted Islam, and they are lauded in Qur'an and excepted from the humiliating curse for disbelief in Muhammad, Qur'an 3:113–14:

> Not all of them are alike: Of the People of the Book are a portion that stand (for the right): They rehearse the Signs of God all night long, and they prostrate themselves in adoration. They believe in God and the Last Day; they enjoin what is right, and forbid what is wrong; and they hasten (in emu-lation) in (all) good works: They are in the ranks of the righteous.

In other words, not all of the Children of Israel are equal. Some comprise a righteous group which holds fast to the true religion, while reciting God's book through the hours of the night, and worship prostrating themselves to God, believing in God and in the existence of the Last Day on which man will be recompensed for his deeds, and they command obedience, forbid disobedience, and rush into doing works of charity. These are among the good in God's reckoning.

Testimony of the Prophet Muhammad in the Torah

Qur'an 7:157: "Those who follow the apostle, the unlet-tered Prophet, whom they find mentioned in their own (scriptures) [Torah],—in the law and the Gospel . . ."[25] Qur'an clarifies here that the attributes of Muhammad and the good news of his prophethood are mentioned in the Torah and in the Evangel.[26] The important question we must answer is whether or not good news or indica-tions that the described emissary would come from God after Moses and Jesus which are found in the Torah or Evangel actually refer to Muhammad. We answer this question with a "yes," but we will summarize our inquiry by mentioning only one example from the Torah: Deuteronomy 18:17:

> The Lord said to me, "They have spoken well (vs. 18:) I will establish from among their brothers a prophet like you, and I will send my words into his mouth, and he will speak to them everything I tell him. (vs. 19:) But anyone who does not obey my words which he will speak in my name, I will bring him to account. (vs 20:) Any prophet who dares to speak any word not from me in my name, or speaks the words of other gods, that prophet will be slain. (vs 21:) [misprint: 31] If you ask yourself, How shall I know that the Lord has not spoken this word? (vs. 22:) If a prophet speaks in the name of the Lord, and his word is not fulfilled, or does not come to be, then that word was not spoken by the Lord, but that prophet dared to speak it out of presumptuousness. Do not fear him.

This good news from the Torah applies to Muhammad from several angles:

- The expression "like you" occurs in this piece of good news, and the Lord's speech here is directed to Moses, that is, the Lord will establish a prophet for them like Moses, for Moses brought a book with a Shari'a (legislation). Muhammad, like Moses, brought the book and the legislation to complete (the former ones).
- The expression "from among your brothers" also occurs in this piece of good news. This is proof that he will come not from the Children of Israel, and the expression "brothers" refers to the Children of Ishmael, because this term occurs in its true sense in God's promise to Haagar about the true (future) of her son, Ishmael, "For he will dwell among his brothers."[27] Muhammad also was a brother to the Children of Israel because he is descended from Ishmael, Abraham's son.
- The expression "I will put My words in his mouth" also occurs in this piece of good news. It is an indication that to the Prophet will be revealed the Book as revelation, and that he will be unlettered, unable to write, yet able to memorize speech. This applies to Muhammad: he was an illiterate bumpkin, who did not know how to read or write, nor to distinguish his ass from his elbow. Thus Qur'an described Muhammad: "You did not recite from a Book from aforetime, nor did your right hand inscribe it, but the doubters questioned it."
- The item of good news explains that the promised prophet who would say something that God did not order him to say would be killed. Had Muhammad

not been a true and believable prophet, he would have been killed. In the matter of Muhammad, Qur'an, surat al-Haaqqa, 69:44–46: "If he says bad things about you, We will take him by his right hand, then We will cut out his **al-watiin** aorta/jugular vein/mandibular artery." This means that even if Muhammad had lied against God and Qur'an [misprint here], and said something that was not from heavenly revelation, then God would have punished him horribly, taking Muhammad's right hand, the way he does with criminals, and God would then execute Muhammad by decapitation.

But Qur'an emphasizes the truth of Muhammad's prophethood and announces as the principal piece of evidence that God will protect and preserve him, Qur'an 5:67: "God will **ya`Simu-ka** inure you from the people." This promise came true, for God protected Muhammad and did not allow anyone to do him harm, despite the numerous attempts his adversaries dealt treacherously with him. This is one of the strongest proofs of the truth of Muhammad's prophesy.

The Qur'anic text makes clear that the sign of a false prophet is his foretelling the unseen future, and then it not coming to pass. Muhammad foretold of many unseen things in the future, and all of them came true, for example, promising his companions victory, and bequeathing them with God's caliphate in the earth, Qur'an, surat Ghaafir 40:51: "Indeed We grant victory to our emissaries and those who believe in the life of this world [*sic*]." And Qur'an 3:12: "Say to those who disbelieve, 'you will be defeated.'" And Qur'an 24:55:

> Allah has promised to those of you who believe and do good that he will most certainly make them rulers in the earth as he made rulers those before them, and that he will most certainly establish for them their religion which He has chosen for them, and that he will most certainly, after their fear, give them security in exchange; they shall serve me, not associating aught with me; and whoever is ungrateful after this, these it is who are the transgressors.

These verses were revealed when the Muslims encountered weak periods in which they did not believe in their lives because of the arguments of their disputants, but it was only a few years until the results of these verses came true, and the Muslims were victorious over their enemies. And the caliphate of God in the earth passed over to the Islamic *umma*.

Armed Warfare between the Muslims and the Jews

The Muslims were in need of deliverance from their enemies within Yathrib (Medina), that is the Jews and the Arab/Bedouin hypocrites who aided them, as a step preceding their ability to confront their enemies outside Yathrib, like the Quraysh and other tribes.

The Jews began making known to the emissary their hostility to him, since the time he called them to accept Islam. The emissary would dispute with them fairly, but this was in vain, because they continued to oppose him, and then the Jews began scheming their treacherous plots against Muhammad personally, and helping his enemies against him. At that point self-defense became all but unavoidable by ridding Yathrib of all his internal enemies, or to enter armed combat against them when they frustrated his plans. The timing of the beginning of the action was on the day of Muhammad's victory over the Quraysh at a place called Badr, when conditions were ripe for Muhammad to carry out his plan. The very next thing he did was to confront the Banu Qaynuqaa`.

Al-ijlaa' Ethnic Cleansing *of the Banu Qaynuqaa`*

The reasons for the Prophet's beginning to *al-ijlaa'* exterminate the Banu Qaynuqaa`, as opposed to the other groups of Jews, goes to the fact that they were living within the confines of the illuminated Medina, in one of their clans, and the emissary wanted to *yaTharu* cleanse Medina from the internal enemy, who was weighing who was stabbing him in the back. The tradents of the hadith related that the Banu Qaynuqaa` had a peace agreement with the Prophet, but at the Battle of Badr, they showed their *al-baghy wal-Hasad* envious hatred and broke the contract.[28] Thereupon, God revealed to Muhammad Qur'an, surat al-anfaal 8:58: "And if you fear treachery on the part of a people, then throw back to them on terms of equality; surely Allah does not love the treacherous."[29]

The Banu Qaynuqaa` were not numerous, and hostility reigned between them and the other Jews because they were allied with the Arab Khazraj, and the Banu NaDiir and the QurayZa were allies of the Arab Aws. When war would break out between the Aws and the Khazraj, the Banu Qaynuqaa` would fight along with the Khazraj, and the NaDiir and the QurayZa would fight alongside the Aws, so that each would fight with an Arab tribe and against their own brethren, to the point that they would spill each other's blood. They knew the Torah, and what it commanded and forbid them, and the Aws and the Khazraj were idol-worshiping polytheists, so when hostilities ended, they would ransom the Jewish prisoners, as Qur'an 2:73–74 indicates:

> And if you fear treachery on the part of a people, then throw back to them on terms of equality; surely Allah does not love the treacherous. Then your hearts hardened after that, so that they were like rocks, rather worse in hardness; and surely there are some rocks from which streams burst forth, and surely there are some of them which split asunder so water issues out of them, and surely there are some of them which fall down for fear of Allah, and Allah is not at all heedless of what you do.

In other words, "O Children of Israel! We accepted a contract with you that we would not spill each other's blood, nor expel one another from his home. You insist this contract jibes with your Book, and you witness its truth, then you kill one another, and expel a group from their homes as assistance to your Arab allies who must kill, pillage, and fight. But when some Jews are imprisoned with your Arab ally, then you work to free them with pecuniary ransom, excusing yourselves in this by claiming that your Book commands you to ransom prisoners from among the chosen people. If you truly believed what you say, then why did you fight against them and expel them from their homes? All religions forbid that a man fight his brother in religion, and condemns it."

To return to the main theme: how did the emissary confront the Banu Qaynuqaa`? The historians note that the emissary approached the Banu Qaynuqaa` a few days after the Battle of Badr, gathered them together in their market, and spoke to them. One of the things he told them was, "O you group of Jews! Beware that God does not take vengeance out on you as He did to Quraysh! Accept Islam! You well know that I am a prophet sent—you find this in your Book, and in God's covenant with you."[30]

At this their attitude toward the emissary was one of daring presumptuousness. They answered him, "O Muhammad! We do not deny that you have met an ignorant people in martial matters, and that you have taken advantage of them. But by God! If we were to fight you, then you would find out that we are the victorious people!"

It is clear from this response that the Banu Qaynuqaa` were depending on their opposition to their allies, the Khazraj, in their struggle against the emissary, for he would not be able to imagine that such a small tribe as the Banu Qaynuqaa` would dare to declare war on the most victorious tribe in Yathrib, but the Khazraj betrayed them by not lifting a finger to save them. The emissary besieged them on all sides in their fortress for fifteen nights, until they surrendered to the decision of the emissary, and `Abdallah ibn Ubayy arbitrated for them, and insisted to the prophet that he arbitrate, until the latter complied. Then [*sic*] the emissary ordered their *al-ijlaa'* expulsion from Medina, and deputized this to the command of `Abaada ibn al-Saamit, who exiled them to Adhra`aat in Syria.

The exile of the Banu Qayunqaa` had a profound effect on the Jews' souls, and thus from then on they refrained from theological disputes, and contented themselves with casting aspersions on the Muslims. The Islamic structure entered the hearts of the Arab tribes who had not yet accepted Islam, and it widened the area in which the emissary could spread his call.

The Ethnic Cleansing of the Tribe of the Banu al-NaDiir

After the Banu Qaynuqaa` it was the turn of the Banu al-NaDiir. The emissary suspected that they were secretly plotting against him and were looking for a pretext to betray him.[31] Thus he decided to expel them from their homes before they had the chance to rebel, especially because they refused to come to his aid at the Battle of UHud, despite the fact that they had a mutual defense treaty between them, on the pretext that they did not have to participate, according to said contract, in a battle that occurs at a large distance from Medina.

The battle of UHud took place on a Saturday, so the Jews refused to bear arms on that day or to join the emissary in battle.

But the Jew Mukhayriq said, "That is no excuse! He took up his sword and `udda battle gear, saying, 'If I am killed, then I bequeath my wealth to Muhammad to do with whatever he wants.'" Then he joined the emissary of God and fought with him until he was killed in battle. The emissary said, "Mukhayriq is the best Jew."[32]

For this reason the emissary warned the Banu al-NaDiir that they had better leave their fortresses and distance themselves from Yathrib (Medina) within ten days, but they immediately refused to heed this warning. Then it appeared that they were beginning to heed this warning, and accepted the decision to leave Yathrib, but a group of the hypocrites of the Banu `Awf informed them, "If you remain here and disobey the order to leave, we will never betray you; and if you are attacked, we will fight alongside of you, and if you are expelled, we will leave with you." But the Banu al-NaDiir refused to accept this.[33]

Qur'an indicates this act of treachery by the hypocrites of the Banu al-NaDiir at Qur'an, surat al-Hashr, 59:11–12:

> Have you not seen those who have become hypocrites? They say to those of their brethren who disbelieve from among the followers of the Book: If you are driven forth, we shall certainly go forth with you, and we will never obey any one concerning you, and if you are fought against, we will certainly help you, and Allah bears witness that they are most surely liars. Certainly if these are driven forth, they will not go forth with them, and if they are fought against, they will not help them, and even if they help them, they will certainly turn (their) backs, then they shall not be helped [gain victory].

The Banu al-NaDiir's fortresses were well bulwarked so that it would have been impossible to mount a successful siege within a short time; moreover, they were fortified from behind, as per Qur'an, surat al-Hashr, 59:14, "You will not fight them all, except in fortified villages, or from behind walls."

This verse points to the Jews' cowardice, and their deficit in courage in comparison to the Muslims, when confronting each other face to face. Therefore the Prophet ordered the chopping down and incineration of their palm trees. The Jews called out to him, "O Muhammad! You have prohibited **al-fasaad** corruption/wanton destruction, and you condemn anyone who commits it, so how can you chop down and incinerate our palm trees?" And so the heavenly inspiration was revealed: Qur'an, surat al-Hashr, 59:5: "Whether you chop down noble palms, or leave them standing on their roots, it is with the permission of God, so let the **faasiq**s evildoers be humiliated."

Leveling and incinerating the palms is only placing **al-ru`b** terror in the Jews' hearts, to coerce them to accept Islam: it is not **al-fasaad fil-arD** doing corruption in the earth, Qur'an 2:204–205: especially since the Jews were so stubborn in their rejection, and they had enough food to last them for a year, as recorded in the hadith.

It appears that the leveling and incineration of the palms was the reason for the spreading of **al-ya´s** despair in the Jews' hearts, when they found themselves between two stools: (1) obeying the decision of the emissary, or (2) to leave Medina to attack the Muslims, to prevent them from burning down the palms, whose fruit was a primary recourse of life for them. They chose the first option:

> They requested that the prophet let them leave without harming them, and allowing them to take all the wealth their beasts of burden could bear, except for their weapons, and he agreed. So they loaded their beasts with all they could carry, and each one of them destroyed his own house, down to the **nijaaf** protective cover for the mezuzza, which he loaded on his camel, and took all of this to Khaybar; but some of them went to Syria.[34]

The mezuzza derives from a Talmudic belief that every Jew must put one on his door which contains writings from the instructions of Moses to the Children of Israel, to maintain their belief in one God, and no one else, at the cost of punishment or death. So when the Jews left their homes they took their mezuzzas with them, and this is a customs kept by Jews until today. It appears that the Jews of the Arab countries would put their mezuzzas inside a **nijaaf** protective covering, for fear of harm by weather or by human hands, and when they traveled from their homes, they would destroy the protective covering, and take out the mezzuza.[35]

Qur'an indicated the stubborn tenacity of the Banu al-NaDiir in maintaining possession of their fortresses, and their refusal to abandon them, supposing that they would protect them from God's command; it also points to their defeat and their destruction of their own houses at Qur'an, surat al-Hashr, 59:2:

He it is who drove out the disbelievers among the people of the Scripture (i.e., the Jews of the tribe of Bani An-Nadir) from their homes at the first gathering. You did not think that they would get out. And they thought that their fortresses would defend them from Allah! But Allah's (Torment) reached them from a place whereof they expected it not, and He cast terror into their hearts, so that they destroyed their own dwellings with their own hands and the hands of the believers. Then take admonition, O you with eyes (to see).

Ibn Hisham describes their leaving their fortresses: "They *istaqalluu bi*—took leave of their women, children, and wealth, taking with them only their books and a *al-mazaamiir* psalms/musical instruments, and at their back was a mournful lament."[36]

The Emissary's Razzia against the Banu QurayZa

When the nobles of the Banu al-NaDiir entered Khaybar they began to think of how they might take revenge on the emissary and his followers, and they discussed with one another the means they would employ to enable them to return to their fortresses and fields in Yathrib. A group of Jews, among them Salaam ibn Ubayy ak-Haqiiq, Kinaana ibn al-Rabii`, and Khuyayy ibn AkhTab, plotted to incite the *al-aHzaab* the parties opposed to the emissary (title of sura 33) to make war on the Muslims.

> So they went out until they met the tribe of Quraysh in Mecca, and they called on them to make war on the emissary of God, saying, "We will fight together with you against him, until we uproot him," and the Quraysh answered them, "O you group of Jews! You are the people of the first Book and of the knowledge we have now begun to differ with, we together with Muhammad, so are you asking us to sacrifice our good fortune or his religion?" The Jews answered, "Only your religion is better than his religion, and you are the more deserving of it . . ." And when they had said this to Quraysh, they were gladdened and enthused to make the war they called for on the emissary of God, so they gathered together and prepared for it. Then this group of Jews went out until they came upon GhaTafaan ibn Qays ibn `Aylaan, and they called upon them to make war on the emissary of God, and swore that they would fight alongside of them, even if the Quraysh had swore fealty to them in this matter, so they were all mustered for battle.[37]

From this narrative we can see that the Jews are not blamed for their attempt to return to their land and their plantations, nor are they blamed for trying to find allies to help them to realize their goal and take revenge on their disputants, because this is merely part of inherent human nature.

But what they are blamed for, and deserve blame for from every monotheist, Jew and Muslim alike, is that that conversation between the group of Jews and the polytheist Quraysh, wherein this group of Jews voiced preference for the various religions of the Quraysh over the religion of the Possessor of the Islamic Message . . . thus it became impossible to forgive the Jews for such a *al-khaTa´ al-faaHish* heinous sin; and to declare to the leaders of the Quraysh that the worship of idols is preferable to Islamic Unicity (was an additional unforgivable sin). Had the matter been left at refusing to grant them their desires—the Children of Israel had been the standard-bearers of monotheism for many centuries throughout the world, among peoples worshiping idols just as their ancestors had done, and they had suffered countless catastrophes: massacre, oppression because of their belief in one God, throughout many and various historical periods— and this is in addition to their relying on idol-worshipers as if they were fighting each other and breaking the Torah's teachings which instructed them to stay far apart from the idol-worshipers and to dispute them. [*sic*][38]

This criticism of the Jews' behavior is not our own words, but the words of one of the Jewish professors, that is, Israel Wolfensohn.

Qur'an indicates that the deed of this group of Jews, and their joining up with the Meccan unbelievers: Qur'an 4:51: "Do you not see that those who were given a portion of the Book believe in the Jibt[39] and the Taaghuut,[40] and say to those who disbelieve, 'these are more rightly guided than those who believe,'" that is, "O emissary do you not see how those Jews who were given a part of the knowledge of the Torah pass judgment on those who follow idols, assuming them to be right guidance; and moreover, that they are more rightly guided in faith!"

The Banu QurayZa Break the Contract

The Jewish leaders of the Banu al-NaDiir succeeded in bringing the strongest disputation against the emissary in the attempt to participate in the opposition to him. All of the Quraysh, GhaTafaan, and other tribes comprised ten thousand mounted fighters to take on the emissary in Yathrib.

Muhammad and the Muslims got wind of this development, and were fearful. What could the Muslims possibly do against the many thousands of these combatants when their number did not reach three thousand? One of the emissary's companions, Salmaan the Persian, had strategic knowledge of warfare that was unknown to the Arabs, and he showed them how to dig a **khandaq** ditch around Medina, and how to fortify it internally. The Muslims hurriedly carried out his advice and dug a ditch; the emissary joined in the digging with his own hands.

The opposing armies came up against Yathrib, and the sight of the ditch surprised them: they had not been able to imagine that kind of new defense. They saw no way to avoid crossing the ditch, and the mutual exchange of arrows lasted several consecutive days.

After a few days of the mutual exchange of **al-munaawashaat wal-mubaararaat** missiles and/types of arrows had past, it became clear to the leaders of the opposing parties that the war would never come to an end unless the Banu QurayZa joined up with them.

On the one hand, they remained partners in a contract with the Muslims, and on the other hand, it was the inability of the armies of the opposing parties [to reach an agreement]. In addition, the Muslims had taken with them provisions, weapons, and the digging implements, and the fortresses of the Banu QurayZa were between the Muslims' armies and those of the opposing parties, serving as an impenetrable barrier. So Huyayy ibn al-AkhTab, one of the Banu al-NaDiir's nobles, tried to convince his Banu al-NaDiir brethren to break their contract. At first he did not succeed because the Banu al-NaDiir leader refused to break his word with the **AnSaar** (Medinan Muslim converts) who told him, "Leave me, for in Muhammad I see only truth and faithfulness." Huyayy continued in his efforts by attempting to convince Ka`b ibn Asad, until he succeeded, and he received a contract from him: "If the Quraysh and GhaTafaan turn back without harming Muhammad, I will enter your fortress with you, so your fate will be mine." But Ka`b ibn Asad broke his contract, so his agreement with the emissary remained in effect.[41]

This deed terrified the Muslims because they knew that with the joining of the Banu QurayZa would add significant strength to their enemies, and here they saw their fears being realized, with the Banu QurayZa already making overtures to their enemies, and breaking apart **al-madad wal-miira** their pact/agreement (with the Muslims). They also saw Quraysh and GhaTafaan—ever since Huyayy ibn al-AkhTab informed them of the Banu QurayZa's joining up with their enemies, changing their **al-nafiisa** best friends, and they began applying themselves, a contingent of three **katiibas** battle groups, to the battle against the emissary. Then misfortune became disaster for the Muslims, and they began to become so anxious they started having doubts about God.

The Muslims were stymied by fear, but the emissary found a way to weaken his enemies, so he sent some men to two leaders of the GhaTafaan and offered them one-third of Medina's produce on the condition that they turn away from he and his companions. Thus a **al-SulH** tem-porary truce was achieved between them—orally, and later it was put in writing.[42]

Then the emissary sent one of his messengers, that is, Nu`aym ibn Mas`uud, to QurayZa, of whom they were unaware that he had already converted to Islam, and he had been a drinking companion of theirs in the Jaahiliyya. He reminded them of the friendship that they had between them. Then he reminded them that they had helped Quraysh and GhaTafaan against Muhammad. . . .

. . . Quraysh and GaaTafaan might not have been able to hold out much longer, so they went their separate ways, and Muhammad **nakala bi-him** chided/warned them not to fight on the side of his enemies in order to take hostages. Then Muhammad approached the Quraysh and informed them that the QurayZa regretted what they had done when they broke their covenant with his, and that they were trying to mollify him, and had gained his friendship, because they agreed to hand over to him the nobles of Quraysh for decapitation. Then their leader held a consultation, and they sent a Qurayshite leader, Abu Sufyaan to Ka`b, a leader of the Banu QurayZa, as a messenger to tell him, "O Ka`b! Our remaining and besieging this man, that is the emissary, has already taken a long time. We realize that he has pre-pared for himself many provisions, and we have less." So the brought back to the emissary the answer that the following day would be Saturday, and he does not do any work on the Sabbath, saying, "We are not of those who fight Muhammad with you, for we fear that the battle will turn against you until it spreads to your country and you have to abandon it. No man in our village has the ability to do this, so send us the hostages so as to put our minds at ease." When Abu Sufyaan, the leader of the Quraysh, heard this, **lam yabqa laday-hi kalaam na`iim rayba** he could not answer diplomatically/calmly/politely, so he went and spoke to the GhaTafaan, and, lo and behold, they reneged on going out to war against Muhammad, influenced by the promised one-third of Medina's produce Muhammad had already begun to provide them with. At that point, doubts began to come to the fore among the leaders of the opposition.

Then God sent a frigid wind against them filled with hail. It overturned their vessels and blew away their implements, so it seemed to them that the Muslims had taken advantage of this opportunity to cross over to attack them. Abu Sufyaan led the way, and they fled the field, and when morning came, Muhammad found that none of them were there.

As a result of the Banu QurayZa's joining up with the armies of the opposing parties, and their breaking their agreement which they had with the emissary that he would not **yumahhil** hurry/rush them, but he began rather to besiege them on the same day that the opposition parties retreated, so the emissary ordered that everyone not to pray the **al-`ASr** the afternoon prayer until they reached the **mawTin** territory of the Banu QurayZa.

There was never a battle per se in the razzia against the Banu QurayZa; the Muslims merely surrounded the Jews and began launching rocks and arrows at them, but the Banu QurayZa did not dare to come out of their fortresses during the siege because the Muslims numbered in the thousands while the number of Jews did not exceed seven hundred.

After some fifteen nights of the siege had passed, the Banu QurayZa surrendered, agreeing to submit to the emissary's judgments because they truly believed that the Muslims would treat them the way they dealt with the Banu Qaynuqaa` and the NaDiir [*sic*].

In the morning the Jews agreed to accept the emissary's judgement, and the Aws *fa-tawaathbat* yawned, saying, "O emissary of God! They are our clients, not those of the Khazraj, and you have already done what you did [*sic*] to our brethren's clients yesterday." Muhammad answered them, "O you group of Aws! Are you not satisfied that one of your own judges them." They answered, "Yes." Muhammad: "This is a matter for Sa`d ibn Mu´aadh." Then Sa`d said, "My judgement is that the men be killed, their wealth distributed, and the women and children taken prisoner."[43]

Ka`b ibn Asad, the leader of the Banu QurayZa, suggested to his brethren before they left their fortresses that they embrace Islam, saying, "So that your lives, women, and children be spared . . . " They replied, "We will never abandon the Law of the Torah, and not exchange it for anything."[44]

Four of the Jews were spared that day because they embraced Islam, and were allowed to keep their women, children, and possessions.

Then a pit was dug, and the Muslims decapitated all of the Jews of the Banu QurayZa, about seven hundred in all. When Huyayy ibn al-AkhTab was about to be beheaded—and he had fulfilled his contract and joined his brethren in their fortifications—he was wearing an amulet (a type of medal) [*sic*] which he had shattered into pieces the size of a fingernail so it would not be looted—when he looked toward the emissary of God, he said, "By God! I have not cursed myself with hostility to you, for whoever denigrates God will himself be denigrated"; then, addressing himself to the people at large, he said, "O you people! There is nothing untoward in God's command: his Book, his Omnipotence, and the war he declared on the Children of Israel!" Then he sat down, and they chopped off his head. . . .[45]

All in all, this razzia put paid to the Jewish tribes in Yathrib. Qur'an points to the armies' retreat, Qur'an 33:25–27:

And Allah turned back the unbelievers in their rage; they did not obtain any advantage, and Allah sufficed the believers in fighting; and Allah is Strong, Mighty. And He drove down those of the followers of the Book who backed them from their fortresses and He cast awe into their hearts; some you killed and you took captive another part. And He made you heirs to their land and their dwellings and their property, and (to) a land which you have not yet trodden, and Allah has power over all things.

[See also A. Guillaume, *Ibn Ishaq's Sirat Rasul Allah, The Life of Muhammad* (Karachi: Oxford University Press, 2003), p. 468.]

Excursus: A Note on Sa`d ibn Mu`aadh's Judgment

His decision to execute the Jewish fighters is the same as what the opposing parties would do to the Muslims had they been defeated by the Banu QurayZa's treachery: so Sa`d's judgment is balanced by what they would have done to the Muslims.

Had the Banu QurayZa been faithful in their contract, nothing bad would have happened to them. And after breaking their contract, and opposing Muhammad in war, and rejecting Muhammad's judgment at the outset, had they only admitted their mistake in breaking the contract, their blood would not have had to be spilled. But hostility had penetrated into their hearts to the extent that Sa`d ibn Mu`aadh, their ally who believed he would be able to preserve their lives was not able to do so because they assembled to make war on the Muslims once more. This is what occurred to many of the Jews who were expelled from Yathrib. The judgment Sa`d decreed was only for self-defense, and the emissary of God repeated it, "By the One who holds my soul in His hand! God and the Muslims are pleased with this judgement; and he commanded it be carried out."

We have already mentioned that Muhammad never killed anyone who had embraced Islam.

The Razzia on Khaybar

Khaybar lies to the north of Yathrib. Many Jews sought refuge there for they were afraid of Islam, and they wanted to join its enemies in the campaign to do battle against Yathrib, the home base of Islam, to uproot it, and to retrieve the flocks, lands, and money they had lost there.

On the other hand, the Jews were worried about what happened to their brethren in Yathrib who felt that their homes were about to be taken in a Muslim razzia. One of the Jewish leaders of the Banu NaDiir, Sallaam ibn Mishkam, announced that the Jews' lives were in danger in the Hijaz. He pointed out to them that it was incumbent upon them to form a battle group together with the Jews of the Wadi Quraa and the Taymaa´, to overrun Yathrib, without relying on the Arab subtribes for support in this razzia. But some of the other leaders opposed him in this opinion.[46]

In this period, the Jews were sending delegations to Medina with money to ransom a huge number of women and children.[47]

The Muslims were aware of the Khaybar Jews' plotting so they began making preparations for battle with them. They sent a group to kill their leaders, no matter whether they were inciters or reasonable men; this was at the razzia's beginning. Among the victims were two very influential leaders of Khaybar, Salaam ibn Ubayy al-Haqiiq and Yasiir ibn Razaam. Before the emissary had turned his attention to Khaybar, he swore a pact with the Quraysh which insured them of a truce of ten years. With this *al-hudna* truce, the emissary was protected from attack by the Quraysh.

The reasons the prophet launched the razzia against Khaybar, are (in short): the rebellion by the Jews of Khaybar in urging the Quraysh and the GhaTafaan to fight the Muslims;

There were certain groups among the Khaybar Jews who were exceedingly violent. They had a great deal of money and weapons. There was absolutely no hope that they would embrace the Islamic religion, especially after what had happened to the Jews of Yathrib. The Jews would never enter Islam, so the only purpose in the emissary's turning to them was to include all the Arabs into one religion, and to form one unity out of them. He was determined thus to exterminate the Jews of Khaybar so that they would not be a stumbling block [this term is from the Old Testament] in the way of his realizing this goal.

In the process of spreading his religion, the prophet had only two forces opposing him:

The force of the Quraysh, and

The force of the Jews. He thus focused on removing these two forces to allow him the space in which to spread his call, either the remainder of the Hijaazi tribes, even if they did not possess as powerful a force as the Quraysh and the Jews.[48]

The emissary called the people to travel to the Jews of Khaybar, and they struck quickly.

The Jews, who had in their possession their picks and their agricultural implements, were surprised by the sudden arrival of Muhammad and his army. When they saw him, they fled to their fortresses, shouting, "Muhammad and his army!" As for the emissary, he said, "Allah Akbar! Khaybar is destroyed. We have attacked in a people's field. The morning of those who had been warned has turned evil indeed."[49]

The Jews had fortified the area of Khaybar by dividing it into three separate fortified regions, each one with a number of bulwarks. The regions were called: al-NaTaat, al-Shiqq, and al-Katiiba. In the first region, al-NaTaat, was the fortress of al-Sa`b ibn Mu`aadh, the fortress of Naa`im, and the fortress of Qal`at al-Zubayr. In the second region, al-Shiqq, were the fortresses of Ubayy and al-Nizaar. In the third region, al-Katiiba, were the fortresses of al-QummuuS, al-WaTiiH, and Salaalim.[50]

The fortresses of Khaybar were protected on the tops of mountains, and its men were experienced in war and had drilled for all kinds of battle. They had in their possession a plethora of weapons and implements of destruction to use against anyone who would attempt to attack their compounds.[51]

The Muslims stood before the fortresses of Khaybar observing all of the defense positions. The Jews discussed their situation among themselves, and

decided to bring their wealth and their families into the fortress of al-Katiiba, and they brought their supplies and stores into the fortress of al-Naa`im, and they assembled their warriors in the fortress of al-NaTaat. Since Sallaam ibn Mishkam was sick, he too entered al-NaTaat, and he urged his men to fight.[52]

The two armies met in fierce battle in front of the fortress of al-NaTaat. One opinion is that the number of wounded Muslims reached fifty that day.

Al-Sallaam ibn Mishkam died, so the leadership passed to al-Haarith Abii Zaynab, who thereupon went out of the fortress of al-Naa`im to fight the Islamic army, but he was defeated by the Banu Khazraj, who had appeared in order to fight him and to force him to return to the fortress. Then some daring Jews gathered together and attacked the AnSaar[53] until they reached the standard-bearer in the proximity of the emissary.

The emissary sent Abu Bakr al-Sidddiiq to carry the banner to the fortress, and he did battle, but returned without finding an opening. The emissary said, "Tomorrow I will give the banner to a man who loves God and His emissary. By His hand, God will find an opening for him, and he will not fall." The emissary called aloud for `Ali, for he was *armad* eager/anxious, and to whom it seemed an easy task/project. The emissary told him, "Take this banner with you until you find an opening by God's hand." So `Ali approached the fortress, the people came out and did battle, and one of the Jews struck `Ali, and `Ali ripped the Jew's shield out of his hand, and then found a door to the fortress, and, shielding himself, fought on until God granted him victory.[54]

Then violent battles took place around the al-Naa`im fortress, without having the Muslims victorious over the Jews, so the emissary ordered his AnSaar to chop down four hundred of the Jews' palm trees in order to put terror in their hearts.[55]

The al-Naa`im fortress fell after its leader, al-Haarith Abii Zaynab, was killed.

After the fall of the al-Naa`im fortress, the Muslims directed themselves toward the fortress of al-Sa`b ibn Mu`aadh, crept up to it, but the Jewish forces had spread themselves out. The emissary had to urge on his men, and they advanced until they took an (outer) wall. But they saw numerous interior walls, which they brought down after exerting strenuous efforts, and the Jews retreated to another fortress, that of al-Zubayr.

The Muslim fighters were in a grave position until they overran the fortress of al-Sa`b ibn Mu`aadh. For within it they found a large amount of food.

Then the Muslims turned their attention to the fortress of al-Zubayr. It was well bulwarked so that the Muslims were unable to penetrate it no matter how hard they fought. Only after a treacherous Jew came to them and advised the Muslims to cut off the water to the fortresses. This water flowed into the castles from underground, so the Jews had to come out to fetch it, and after a violent battle, they were defeated [sic] and fled to their brethren in the strongholds of al-Shiqq.[56]

Later the Muslims took Ubayy's castle in the region of al-Shiqq, and then left the rest alone because of their lack of importance from the military point of view. They turned their attention to the area of al-Katiiba where the Jews had assembled in the fortress of al-QummuuS, into which all of those who were defeated from the other Khaybariyy fortresses had fled. Here the siege lasted twenty days, until the Muslims were able to conquer it.

Then the Muslims laid siege to the fortress of al-WaTiiH and Salaalim in the region of al-Katiiba, and the Jews requested **al-SulH** a truce, so they asked the emissary to spare them, and he agreed.[57]

The Surrender of the Other Regions

While the Muslims were besieging al-WaTiiH, one of the strongholds of Khaybar, the emissary, Muhammad, sent some soldiers to Fadak, situated to the north of Khaybar. The leader of this mission was MuHaySa ibn Mas`uud, who

called the people to Islam, and when he saw that they had no inclination toward **al-SulH** a truce, and only wanted to fight him, they received the news of the events that occurred at Khaybar. Their hearts filled with great fear, and they sent a group of Jews to the prophet to grant them a truce, for which they would give him half the territory of Fadak, and they would keep the other half. Muhammad was satisfied with this and granted them a truce.

When the Jews of al-Taymaa´ heard the news of Khaybar, Fadak, and Wadi al-Quraa, they were afraid, and accepted the **al-jizya** head-tax.[58]

One of the results of the Khaybar razzia was to put paid to Jewish activities in the areas of the Hijaz.

A Foiled Plot

Because of this defeat, the souls of the Jews were filled with **al-Haqd** hatred against the emissary. A Jewish woman attempted to assassinate the emissary out of vengeance for her people.

Zaynab, the daughter of al-Haarigh and the mother of al-Sallaam ibn Mishkam, [prepared] a roasted lamb [not "goat" here] which she had poisoned, and presented it to the emissary. He took a piece of the foreleg and licked a mouthful of it, but he did not swallow it. At that time the emissary was in the company of Bishr ibn al-Baraa´, one of the companions, who partook of it as the emissary did. Bishr chewed it, but the emissary of God spit it out, saying, "This bone informs me that it has been poisoned." Then he summoned her, and she confessed. The emissary told her, "What made you do this?" She answered, "You came to my people and they were not fearful, so I thought, 'If he were an angel, I would be content, and if he were a prophet, then it would become known (i.e., the poison would have had not effect).'" So the emissary of God left her alone, but Bishr died from the morsel he had eaten.[59] [This is one version of the story.]

Islam's Tolerance

After the Muslims had sovereignty over the Jews, the emissary treated them in the spirit of tolerance. He ordered his assistant, Mu`aadh ibn Jabal, "not to tempt the Jews away from their Judaism."[60] In like manner, the Jews of Bahrain were not forced to convert—only to pay the *jizya*, and they maintained the religion of their ancestors.[61]

The tradents of the hadith describe the Muslims' tolerance, for example, among the spoils of the Khaybar razzia were scraps of Torah passages, and when the Jews requested their return, the emissary permitted it.[62]

Dr. Israel Wolfensohn:

This proves that the lofty level of these Torah passages in the opinion of the emissary made the Jews point to the prophet with their fingertips, and express their gratitude to him for preserving these fragments, as compared to the evil treatment such passages were given by the Romans when they conquered Jerusalem in the year 70 after the birth (of Jesus). The Romans incinerated the holy books and stomped on them with their feet.

If we compare Muhammad's behavior to that of the Christians who oppressed the Jews in the wars of al-Andalus, to the point that they, too, burned the

Torah scrolls. This is the expansive divide between the Roman and Christian conquers and the emissary of Islam.[63]

The Expulsion of the Jews from the Arabian Peninsula

After the emissary conquered Khaybar, he divided it up among his AnSaar and his wives by casting lots. The Jews were allowed to remain on their land on the condition they give the Muslims one-half of their produce. Thus did the Jews remain until the caliphate of `Umar ibn al-KhaTTaab, who sent the Jews a messenger to tell them "God orders you to leave. I have out from the emissary of God, who said, 'The Arabian Peninsula will never permit two religions. A Jew who has a contract with the emissary of God shall give it to me, and I will carry it out for him. Whoever does not, prepare to leave.' Then `Umar expelled them."[64]

The State of Israel Will Never Endure

It is the harsh judgment of history against the Children of Israel that despite all the dispersions and oppressions they have suffered through the centuries, and all of the hundreds of razzias against them, they will never find peace of mind by establishing, through *al-baghy wal-`udwaan* hostile maleficence, a national homeland in Palestine. The present situation is merely temporary, for they will soon be expelled by the Arabs after they unite their troops. Then the Arabs, following God's right guidance, will quash the *al-fasaad al-ijtimaa`iyy* social corruption which threatened their existence.

Let me strengthen this assertion by quoting Qur'an, surat al-Aa`raaf 7:167: "And when your Lord announced that He would certainly send against them to the day of resurrection those who would subject them to severe torment; most surely your Lord is quick to requite (evil) and most surely He is Forgiving, Merciful." In other words: "Remember, O emissary, that God is certain that He will rule over the Children of Israel until the day of Resurrection, when He will make them taste the harshest punishment. This will be their comeuppance. God makes haste to punish the sinner, just as he hurries to forgive and show His mercy to the repentant."

In this verse, one notices punishment and oppression will remain the fate of the Children of Israel until the Day of Resurrection. They had been oppressed in the pre-Islamic era, and they should have taken this as a warning to repent. But it is the judgment of history that they will continue to be oppressed until the Day of Resurrection. This is one of the "hidden secrets" that no human would ever be able to foretell, but the Qur'an's foretelling it is an indication that it is indeed a heavenly inspiration.

This verse also has the effect of spurring on the Arabs to prepare for the return of their stolen land. God will never allow the Children of Israel to rule over Palestine

forever, but only if the Arabs reform themselves and change their impotent aspects, and eliminate the causes of their disunity. . . .

Some Reasons for the Persecution of the Jews

The Jews' *`adam al-indimaaj* refusal to integrate themselves into society anywhere and their *àdam al-ikhlaaS wal-wafaa'* insincerity and disloyalty to their hosts, and their *al-suluuk al-shaa`in* unseemly misbehavior toward them, caused them to become an exclusive people who lived only among themselves. The Jews believe they have the right to forcibly steal other people's property. Perhaps the teachings of the Talmud, one of their holy books, made a significant impression on the quality of their behavior.

One of the teachings of the Talmud says, "Other people's property is to be considered abandoned goods which a Jew may take possession of." Another teaching is: "God allows the Jews to control the property and life of all peoples."[65] A third is: "Just as a man assigns names to beasts, the Jew may assign names to all the other peoples of the earth because of their bestial nature."[66]

Another Talmudic teaching: "God commands us to employ usury against the 'goyiim' (non-Jews), and has forbidden to loan money except to gain profit. It is thus impossible for Jews to loan money except in usury, and, moreover, we must also *al-`irhaaq* bankrupt the gentiles."[67]

The primary reason for the Zionists' rape of Palestine today is to prevent the assimilation of the Jewish people. For a time, the Zionists colonized Palestine by deceiving and dividing the Arabs, but how long will the Zionists be able to hold out among 100 million Arabs who have awakened from their deep slumber, and have begun to organize themselves to prepare to expel these parasites from their lands?

The battle is near. Israel will lose her dream of establishing a homeland in the heart of the Arab lands. Then the Zionists will return to the life of the wilderness, wandering, and searching for a new homeland in which to gather together its scattered remnants (history repeats itself).

THE STORIES IN QUR'AN ARE NOT PLAGIARIZED FROM THE TORAH

Many tomes have been composed by Orientalist researchers on the origins of Islam, and whether or not it was plagiarized, for instance, from Judaism. The intent of this is clear, to show Muhammad as a fraud, as a prophet and as an emissary from God.

What is undeniable is that a researcher of the Torah and the Qur'an will find many similar teachings which have the same, and sometimes different, purposes. The heart of the matter is whether or not the Islamic teachings which resemble the Jewish ones are plagiarized from it. For the answer to this question, we place the following facts before the reader:

- Islam is not a new religion. The researcher of Islam who is competent in his field will see that Islam is not a new religion, but rather the extension and perfection of Judaism and Christianity, and their reformation by removing the false material, including *al-bida`* reprehensible innovations and theological disputes. In his speech to the believers at Qur'an, surat al-Shuura (consultation), 42:13: "He legislated the religion for you—the same one in which he instructed Noah, and which we instructed you [O Muhammad]. It is also what we instructed Abraham, Moses, and Jesus: to establish the religion, but do not be divided in it." Despite this, some of the fundamentals of Judaism and Islam resemble each other, but this is merely on account of their common source, that is God.
- Then the Qur'an certifies that the Jews corrupted their Scripture. Qur'an 4:46: "Of those Jews are some who move the words to the wrong places."
- Then at Qur'an 5:43, he makes clear that, from another viewpoint, there are laws in the Torah that are not subject to change: "How can they judge you while they have the Torah, which expresses God's judgment, then later they turn away? They are not believers." The "reason for the revelation" of this verse is that "the Jews brought, from among their own, an adulteress and an adulterer before the prophet [for judgment]. Muhammad asked them, "What do you find in your Book?" The Jews answered, "[Their proper punishment prescribed in the Torah is that] we blacken their faces to humiliate them." The Prophet replied, "You lie! It says in the Torah that they should be lapidated (stoned to death)." [According to Shahih Bukhari, vol. 8, hadith 6818, Muhammad said]: "So bring out the Torah and recite it, if you claim you are telling the truth." So they brought him a Torah and a Torah reciter from among them, who recited until he came to a place in the text over which he put his hand, and he was told, "Raise your hand!" So he did, and thus it became clear, that is, the "Stoning Verse" [no longer valid in Judaism, this Torah verse prescribing stoning to death as the penalty for adultery, is the basis of the Shari`a law, which itself is in contradiction to the Qur'an's prescribing whipping].[68] Then the Jews exclaimed, "O Muhammad! The Torah prescribes stoning, but we wanted *al-kitmaan* to conceal it for ourselves." Thus Muhammad ordered that the pair be stoned to death.[69]

The Distinguishing of the Qur'an from All the Other Religious Books

Any researcher of the noble Qur'an finds that absolute truth emanates from it, and that it is a heavenly inspiration. Read for instance the narrative of Moses and the Children of Israel in the Qur'an, and then compare it to the story in the book of Exodus in the Old Testament. You will conclude that the Qur'anic version is more impressive on the human soul, and more subtly felt, and of greater advantage from the aspects of moral lesson and reproach, despite its containing variegated factual contradictions.

In addition the Qur'an is perfectly complete in relating the truth about the secrets of the universe. All of its statements have been proven true by modern scientific discoveries. The Qur'an's legislation concerning family and social law, jurisprudence and economics, and its method of worship that elevates the soul and body of a human being—all these are supreme. The Qur'an is also perfectly complete in that it conveys ethical practices not found in Judaism, or in any other contemporary religion. Were the Qur'an plagiarized from Judaism, then its practices and shibboleths/identifying characteristics would have been similar.

The Emissaries in the Qur'an and in the Torah

The Qur'an and the Torah have different points of view with respect to God's emissaries. This shows that the Qur'an is not plagiarized from Judaism. It is rather a reformation of the reprehensible *al-bida`* innovations that entered Judaism, innovations which the prophets and emissaries labeled as the most heinous of actions.

God sent emissaries and prophets to elevate the human species, and to liberate it from wallowing in sinful evil like frivolous lusts and *kabH al-jaHaam* deleterious practices/sins.

Indubitably, the emissaries and the prophets whom God sent to reform their societies, were endowed by God with *al-`iSma* immunity from sin. He also made them of the loftiest character in their righteous lifestyles and in their elevated level of ethics to serve as a role model for their followers.

The heavenly message is for all mankind because God is Lord of the Worlds, not the Lord of one particular people. Qur'an, surat al-NaHl, (The Bee), 16:36: "We sent to every people an emissary, to tell them to worship God and to abjure error. Some God guided, others remained in error." The Children of Israel, on the other hand, believe that God gives his bounty and his mercy exclusively to them, thus making prophecy limited to the Children of Israel, as if the rest of humankind was not of his creation.

When one examines the Jews' books, it is noteworthy that they ascribe to their prophets *al-kidhb wal-khidaa`* duplicitous deception and *irtikaab kabaa'ir al-ma`aaSii* the gravest sins. The Jews ascribe deception to Jacob. They suppose that Lot committed adultery with his two daughters, and they claim that Aaron called on the Israelites to worship the [golden] calf. They lie about David committing adultery with Uriah's wife, and that Solomon became an idol worshiper in order to please his wife. The Qur'an tells the stories of these prophets without including any one of these accusations. This is a characteristic of Qur'an that differentiates it from the Old Testament. If the Qur'an described any of these prophets with any of these deficiencies, or with others, then it would have set up an evil model which would be deleterious to the psyche of the righteously pious believer, who might think, "If this is the way that God's emissaries and prophets behaved, then there is no harm in doing the same myself." This is an excuse that sick souls would be able to exploit in justifying their sins and transgressions.

But Qur'an provides the biographies of these prophets, with their pure behavior, replete with patience, self-sacrifice, and sincerity. They were above the usual human frailties, and this makes them a fine model for the human race. Qur'an elevates their stature and commands the believers to emulate them. Even if we were to mention all of the Qur'anic verses that mention the glorious excellence of the prophets, we would simply not have enough space. Thus we will limit ourselves to a few examples: Qur'an, surat al-An`aam, 6:83–90:

That is our argument. We gave it unto Abraham against his folk. We raise unto degrees of wisdom whom We will. Lo! thy Lord is Wise, Aware. And we bestowed upon him Isaac and Jacob; each of them we guided; and Noah did we guide aforetime; and of his seed (we guided) David and Solomon and Job and Joseph and Moses and Aaron. Thus do We reward the good. And Zachariah and John and Jesus and Elias. Each one (of them) was of the righteous. And Ishmael and Elisha and Jonah and Lot. Each one (of them) did we prefer above (our) creatures, With some of their forefathers and their offspring and their brethren; and we chose them and guided them unto a straight path. Such is the guidance of Allah wherewith he guideth whom he will of his bondmen. But if they had set up (for worship) aught beside him, (all) that they did would have been vain. Those are they unto whom we gave the Scripture and command and prophethood. But if these disbelieve therein, then indeed we shall entrust it to a people who will not be disbelievers therein. Those are they whom Allah guideth, so follow their guidance. Say (O Muhammad, unto mankind): I ask of you no fee for it. Lo! it is naught but a Reminder to (his) creatures.

Qur'an begins with these verses which prove beyond any shadow of a doubt God's existence and his unicity.

He gives this proof to Abraham to make it firm with his people, and he held it up before them. God's **sunna** Way is inherent in his creatures; he elevates whom he wills in knowledge and wisdom. Then God mentions that he gave this also to Abraham, Isaac, and Jacob, the son of Isaac and granted them success in achieving the true and the good, just as he had done with Noah aforetime.

*English translation by Dr. Michael Schub. For further clarification of any references, see original text.

NOTES

1. Specifically, a poem about a battle between the two in which the Aws was victorious.

2. Ibn Hishaam, II, pp. 204, 205.

3. Footnote on Pharisees and Saducees: editor's note: Torah (i.e., Five Books of Moses) repeatedly mentions "Ruah," or spirit, for example, in Gen. 1:2; Exod. 31:1–5 and Num. 11:29 and 16:22; as do nineteen additional Old Testament books, e.g., Isa., 11:2–3 and Ezek. 36–37, often meaning the Spirit of God. The Afterlife is also implicit in Torah, as in Gen. 12:10 (Jordan's plain as well-watered as "Gan Eden," or "The Garden of God"); 49:33 (Jacob "expired and was gathered to his people"); Num. 23:10 (King Balak declares, "May my soul die the death of the righteous," i.e., let my soul be rewarded in Heaven); as it is elsewhere in the Old Testament, e.g., Isa. 26:9 ("as long as my Spirit is within me, I seek you out, for when Your judgments are against the land, the inhabitants of the world learn righteousness") and Dan. 12:2 ("these for everlasting life"). See also: Gen. 25:8, 25:17, 35:29, 49:33; Deut. 42:50; 2 Kings 22:20.

4. Will Durant, *The Story of Civilization*, vol. 2, p. 345.

5. "Life" here is indefinite (i.e., not *al-Hayaat*—the life) in order to emphasize subtly their greed for the absolute life they live no matter how **Haqiirat al-qadr** wretchedly powerless and **Da´iilat al-qiima** lowly. From *Al-Balaagha al-Qur´aaniyya*.

6. [Long note, indicating] "God doesn't need rest."

7. *KifaaHii* = Adolf Hitler, *Mein Kampf*, p. 177 of Ar. Trans.

8. Taken from Msgnr. Boulous `Abboud, *The Jews in History*.

9. Tabr; "rope" refers here to **al-`ahd** contract and **al-dhimma** protection.

10. From Prof. MuHsin Ibraahiim and Prof. Haanii al-Hindii, *Israel*.

11. In the village of Deir Yasin the Zionists gathered together twenty-five pregnant women, put them in a long line, and then opened fire on them. Then they split open their bellies with **al-madaa wal-Haraab** knives and bayonets, and extracted from them the embryos halfway, so they could chop up the babies, member by member, in

front of their fathers who were still living. This is in addition to their murder of men too old to fight, etc. In the village of Zaytoun the Zionists gathered all the inhabitants together in the mosque, and then lit dynamite over their heads. (From *The Book of Palestine and the New Raids*, ed. Ministry of Education, Culture, and Guidance, Baghdad.)

12. *The Jews in the Earliest Civilizations*, trans. Prof. `Aadil Zu`aytar.

13. Josh. 6:21.

14. [F]rom their secret manuscripts . . . the (others') youth have already descended deep into *al-`atah* lasciviousness and *al-fisq al-munkar* evil licentiousness, to which they have been driven by our lackeys, the teachers, the servants, and the nannies who teach them in the homes of the rich, and the clerks, and the women who teach them about the places of *al-lahw* (sensual) enjoyment, and the so-called women of society who induce them into the tradition [*sic*] of *al-fisq wal-taraf* excessive luxuriousness.

15. Hitler, *Mein Kampf*, pp. 146, 147.

16. The books of the N.T. condemn the actions of the Children of Israel: see chap. 2 and chap. 11 of Jeremiah, chap. 2 and chap. 6 of Ezekiel, chap. 1 of Isaiah, and chap. 17 of 4 Kings.

17. *Tafsiir al-Manaar*. Sheich Rashiid RiDaa. I, col. 1, p. 297.

18. *Lisaan al-`Arab* (Dictionary).

19. Ibn Hishaam, II, p. 200.

20. *Tafsiir al-Manaar*, II, 51.

21. *History of the Jews in Arab Countries*, p. 72.

22. *Tafsiir al-Manaar*, I, 359.

23. Ibn Hishaam, II, 164.

24. Ibid., p. 165.

25. Intended here is Muhammad.

26. *IZhaar al-Haqq* [The Demonstration of the truth] by al-Hindiyy contains many examples of the good news of Muhammad's attributes which are mentioned in the Torah and the Evangel, and, were it not for the fear of going on/bloviating for too long, we would have noted many of them.

27. Gen. 16:12.

28. Ibn Sa`d, *Al-Tabaqaat al-Qubraa*, 36, p. 68.

29. Ibn Hishaam, II, p. 188, in summary.

30. Ibid., III, p. 50.

31. The hadith tradents relate that one of the reasons for Banu al-NaDiir's expulsion was that once the emissary of God agreed to help them in the matter of blood money for the victims of two members of the tribe of Banu `Aamir, whom one of the Banu al-NaDiir members, `Amr ibn Umayya aD-Damariyy, had killed in order to force the tribe to make financial amends for a broken contract between them. When the emissary of God was sitting with them by the wall of one of their houses, the Jews began parting from one another, and intended to

deal treacherously with him by striking him with a huge boulder from atop one of their houses. Then the emissary got wind of this from heaven, immediately got up and returned to Medina, and stayed with his companions (from Ibn Sa`d, *Al-Tabaqaat* and from Tabari, *History*) [the latter is being published as a series in English].

32. Ibn Hishaam, III, p. 94.

33. Ibid., III, p. 200.

34. Ibid., III, p. 201.

35. Wolfensohn, *The Jews in the Arab Lands*, p. 138.

36. Ibn Hishaam, III, p. 201.

37. Ibid., pp. 225, 226.

38. Wolfensohn, *The Jews in the Arab Lands*, p. 142.

39. *Jibt* means idols and magic.

40. *Taaghuut* means everything worshiped outside of God, every erring mind [*sic*], and every Satan that leads astray from the true path.

41. Ibn Hishaam, III, p. 232.

42. Ibid., p. 234.

43. Ibid., pp. 249–51.

44. Ibid., p. 246.

45. Ibid., p. 93.

46. Al-Waaqidiyy, p. 224.

47. Ibid., p. 229.

48. Wolfensohn, *History of the Jews in the Arab Lands*, p. 162.

49. SaHiiH Muslim, 5:185.

50. `Ali, Jawaad, *Ta'riikh al-`Arab qabla al-Islaam* [*The History of the Arabs before Islam*], 6:155.

51. Ibid., 2:50.

52. Ibid.

53. These are the two tribes of Aws and Khazraj who embraced Islam and *naSaruu* helped the emissary, and thus they were called the "AnSaar."

54. Ibn Hishaam, III, p. 349.

55. *Ta'riikh al-Khamiis*, 2:51.

56. Al-Waaqidiyy, p. 276.

57. Ibn Hishaam, III, p. 352.

58. *Ta'riikh al-Khamiis*, 2:64.

59. Ibn Hishaam, III, p. 352.

60. Al-Balaadhuuriyy, p. 71.

61. Ibid., p. 78.

62. *Ta'riikh al-Khamiis*, 2:60.

63. Wolfensohn, *The Jews in the Arab Lands*, p. 170.

64. Ibn Hishaam, III, p. 371.

65. Tractate Baba Batra, section Hekerim [Abandoned Property], III, section 25; taken from *Majallat al-Mashriq* [*Orient Magazine*] 18 (770).

66. Tractate Sanhedrin.

67. Tractate Baba Metzia; from Michel Kufuuriyy, *The Book of Zionism.*

68. See Michael Cook article.

69. From al-Bukhaariyy and Muslim.

CHAPTER 32

Extracts from *Qur'anic Truths regarding the Palestinian Issue*

Salāh 'Abd al-Fattāh al-Khālidī

THE ASWAD BLACK HISTORY OF THE CHILDREN OF ISRAEL—AND WE ARE AGAINST IT [SIC]

The second type of history of the Children of Israel is a *aswad muZim qaatim*, jet-black evil, a history based on disbelief in God, fighting the truth, denying the emissaries, committing sins, practicing *al-Zulm* oppression, rushing into *al-fasaad* corruption, and spreading *radhaa'il al-munkaraat* the most despicable of heinous crimes.

This then is the *al-baghiiD* chthonicly unethical history of the Jews, long in its stages and years, extended over time, *Haalik* blacker than black are its pages.

This is the true history of the Jews, taking into account their *aSl* origin/inner nature, *qawm* tribe/people, *`unSur* race, *jins* kind/nationality, and these are *alSaq* absolutely attached to them, and most truthful in demonstrating their *nafsiyya* psyche and their *Tabii`a* true nature.

This is a history we are free of and we denounce it; we hate its actors, and condemn them with disbelief, oppression, *al-fusuuq* perversity, and *al-`iSyaan* disobedience.

We leave their history to them, let them take it and record it, and shake their heads *khajalan* in dejection whenever they remember it, or whenever it is mentioned to them. This despicable history of the Jews began when they asked Moses to see God openly, and he turned them down. He refused to give the covenant to them, withheld the manna and quails, and requested for them vegetables, squash, garlic, leeks, and onions. Qur'an 2:57–60:

And we made the clouds to give shade over you and We sent to you manna and quails: Eat of the good things that we have given you; and they did not do us any harm, but they made their own souls suffer the loss. Manna and quail were sent to the Jews for food. And remember the time when we said "Enter this town and eat therefrom—whatever you will—plentifully; and enter the gate submissively and say, 'God! forgive us our sins.' We shall forgive you your sins and we shall give increase to those who do good."

But those who were unjust changed it for a saying other than that which had been spoken to them, so we sent upon those who were unjust a pestilence from heaven, because they transgressed. Recall that Moses sought water for his people. We said, "Strike the rock with your staff." Whereupon, twelve springs gushed out therefrom. The members of each tribe knew their own water. Eat and drink from God's provisions, and do not roam the earth corruptingly.

The Jews' history is one of disbelief in God, worshiping the calf instead of God, and worshiping gold and wealth.

The Jews' history is also one of *dhull* humiliation/inferiority and *jubn* cowardice, of rejecting *al-jihaad* war and battle, and entering the Holy Land *faatiHiina* as conquerors.

Their history is one of *al-tiih* wandering, which God afflicted them with for forty years in Sinai, and *al-i`tidaa´* hostility to God's laws, and fishing on the Sabbath day in a certain village, and their being transformed into apes and pigs.

Their history is also one of disbelief and denial, breaking contracts, spreading *al-fujuur* licentiousness, rebellion against the prophets, and murdering those who do good works.

Their history is also one of God's curse and anger against them, a history of *al-maskh* transformation into apes and pigs, and *al-qadhf* slander, a history of *al-Diyaa´* being lost, *al-tiih* wandering, and *al-tashriid* dispersion, a history of *al-dhull* humiliation/inferiority and *al-maskana* wretchedness, with which God smote them, and *al-tasliiT* subjugation and *al-ta`dhiib* punishment, which God allotted them.

This is the true history of the Jews—let them glory in it and brag about it if they want!

The exceptional purely innocent ones among them, their prophets who did good works, separated themselves from the rest of the Jews and cursed them!!

Salāh 'Abd al-Fattāh al-Khālidī, *Haqā'iq Qur'āniyya Khawla al-Qadiyya al Filastiniyya* [Qur'anic Truths regarding the Palestinian Issue] (London: Muslim Palestine Publications, 1994), pp. 73–79, 193–279. Dedicated to Mujahadeen [on] the Blessed Palestinian Earth.

We and the Prophets of the Children of Israel

Qur'an describes the history of the Children of Israel into two groups, the first comprised the prophets who did good works, and whose history has nothing to do with oppression, unbelief, or hostility. This leads us to a word about our relationship with their prophets, and our aim in this is to refute those who hold to the false doctrine of "The Arab Nationalist View" in our *al-Siraa`* struggle (used in title of translations of *Mein Kampf*) against the Jews.

The Arab nationalists are unaware of these truths concerning the Children of Israel and their history. Thus they employ nationalist, tribal and racial, concepts and terminology; they examine the terms "Jewish tribe/nation" and "Jewish race" and thus they come to hate everything with a Jewish origin, even when it is goodly and pious, or a prophetic emissary—so they reject anything which had any previous contact with Jews, as if it were necessarily unbelieving and evil.

We read the words of the Arab nationalists who say they hate the prophets of the Children of Israel because they consider them Jews, so they hate Moses and Aaron, and despise the Israelite David because he killed Goliath the Palestinian, and they condemn Solomon because he was a tyrannical king of the Jews and built the Temple in Jerusalem, and colonized Arab land up to Yemen. But this is unbelief on the part of the Arab nationalists, and an abandonment of God's religion because anyone who denies a genuine prophet is considered an unbeliever, and whoever hates, condemns, or curses a true prophet he also is considered an unbeliever; Moses, Aaron, David, and Solomon are noble prophets.

Our Belief in Their Prophets

We believe in the prophets of the Children of Israel mentioned in Qur'an, we love them and pray to them, we *nabtanii* honor their history, and we emulate them in their behavior. We **consider their history Islamic history** [emphasis added], and their deeds faithful, as the Qur'an commands us, Qur'an 2:285:

> The apostle believes in what has been revealed to him from his Lord, and (so do) the believers; they all believe in Allah and his angels and his books and his apostles; We make no difference between any of his apostles; and they say: We hear and obey, our Lord! Thy forgiveness (do we crave), and to thee is the eventual course.

Also Qur'an 2:136:

> They said: Say: We believe in Allah and (in) that which had been revealed to us, and (in) that which was revealed to Ibrahim and Ismail and Ishaq and Yaqoub and the tribes, and (in) that which was

given to Musa and Isa, and (in) that which was given to the prophets from their Lord, we do not make any distinction between any of them, and to him do we submit.

Also Qur'an 4:150–52:

> Surely those who disbelieve in Allah and his apostles and (those who) desire to make a distinction between Allah and his apostles and say: We believe in some and disbelieve in others, and desire to take a course between (this and) that. These it is that are truly unbelievers, and we have prepared for the unbelievers a disgraceful chastisement. And those who believe in Allah and his apostles and do not make a distinction between any of them—Allah will grant them their rewards; and Allah is Forgiving, Merciful.

We Are More Deserving of Moses than They

The emissary of God teaches us the faithful view of the good people and the prophets of the Children of Israel, and he calls us to faith in their prophets, loving them, praising them, emulating them, for we consider them from us and belonging to us, and that we distance the Jews from relating to them, or assuming that they are following them in their behavior. We consider that we are the ones who are the first (in deserving) these noble prophets.

Bukhaarii and Muslim related on the authority of Ibn `Abbaas that when the emissary of God entered Medina the Jews saw him fasting the `Aashuuraa´, and he said, "What is this?" And they answered, "A good day (holiday)—one on which God saved Moses and the Children of Israel from their enemy, so Moses fasted (in its honor)."

The emissary of God said, "I am more deserving of Moses than you," so he fasted (in honor of that day), and commanded (the Muslims) to fast on it.

Muhammad is more deserving of Moses than the Jews, because Muhammad's **risaala** message comprised everything in Moses'. The Jews have no right to any religious or faith connection to Moses, because they disbelieved, **Taghuu** were disobedient, and **baghuu** spread licentiousness.

Muhammad's *umma* is more deserving of Moses than the Jews are because they comprise the **al-maZhar al-`amaliyy al-waaqi`iyy** actual, demonstrable reality of Moses' message, while the Jews disbelieve and **al-bughaat** spread licentiousness, and hardly reflect his message at all.

Let us now examine this slogan given to us by Muhammad, "We are more deserving of Moses than they."

Moses is ours, his history is our history, his life and biography are a power for us and a force for us, he is from us and we are from him, and so it is with all of the prophets of the Children of Israel.

We are more deserving of Aaron than the Jews, we are more deserving of David and Solomon than they, we are more deserving of Zachariah and John the Baptist than they, we are more deserving of Jesus than either the Jews or the Christians, we are the *umma* with the inheritance of faith from all of God's emissaries and prophets.

Their Prophets Are Free of Them

What is between the Jews and their prophets? Why do they suppose they are of them, or that they are on their path? The Jews are unbelievers, ***bughaat*** spreaders of licentiousness, and evildoers!

Qur'an informs us that their prophets made themselves free of the Jews, cursed them, and became angry with them.

Moses spoke to them: Surat al-Saff, 61:5: "O my people! Do not harm me, for you know that I am God's emissary to you. When they turned aside, God turned aside their hearts, and God does not lead a people of *faasiqs*."

When Moses himself asked the Children of Israel to enter the Holy Land *faatiHiina* as conquers, they refused him, and rebelled. Qur'an 5:24: "We will never enter it as long as they are there, so go, you and your Lord, and fight, for here are the sitters (abstainers from war)."

When Moses freed himself from them, and took refuge in God, and requested that he and the Jews be separated, Qur'an 5:24 [*sic*]: "He said, 'My Lord, I have no one but myself and my brother, so separate between us and the people of *faasiqs*.'"

David, their prophet, emissary, and king, separated himself from the Jews and cursed them. Qur'an 5:78: "He cursed the unbelievers from among the Children of Israel, with the tongues of David and Jesus son of Maryam, because of their disobedience and transgression."

All of the Jews Are Now Unbelievers

We conclude the subject of our view of the Jews' history and the prophets of the Children of Israel: Our division of the Children of Israel into two groups, and our division of their history into two groups, only applies to the former Children of Israel, who lived before Muhammad: those who believed with them are of us, those who disbelieved are our enemies.

When Muhammad's mission came, they were requested to confirm it and to believe in it and to follow it, to enter into its religion. Whoever did this is a believer and a Muslim, a brother of ours and one of our own.

Whoever rejects this, and is steadfast in remaining a Jew, is an unbeliever, destined for eternal hellfire. This applies to all the Jews after the Hegira, and our view of their history is one of innocence and repulsion.

Muslim related on the authority of Abu Hurayra that the emissary of God said, "I swear by the one who holds Muhammad's soul in his hand, not one person among this *umma* listens to me, neither Jew nor Christian." Then Muhammad died, and those who disbelieved in what he brought are all companions of the fire.

WE DO NOT SAY, "THE STATE OF ISRAEL": THE JEWS EXPLOIT THE NAME "ISRAEL"

The Jews exploit the name "Israel" in the contemporary state of their power at the present moment, and they mean by this that they are tied to God's prophet "Israel," and that they follow his religion, and that they are his heirs and sons, and hence God is pleased with them, and helps them.

When they established their state in Palestine, they named it "the State of Israel" and many of their foundations, ministries, and organizations took the name "Israel," like "Bank of Israel," "the flag of Israel," "the Land of Israel," and "the Voice of Israel" (radio station), the IDF [Israel Defense Forces], the Israel(i) Foreign Office, and the like.

Jewish Character Traits according to the Qur'an: History, Indications, and Fate

The Jews have astonishing attributes. In each Jew is a complex of ethical depravities and behavioral corruptions so astonishing that it is doubtful that this can be found in any other people. These traits have taken permanent root in their character, such as never occurred in any other people. These depravities, corruptions, maleficences, deficiencies, sicknesses, and handicaps have their own special taint, prominent indications, and deep imbeddedness [*sic*] in the Jews' astoundingly complex personality. These defects reached their furthest development, and then they infiltrated into the very heart and soul of every Jew, to the point that they influence every aspect of the Jew's soul.

Then these inherent attributes spread out their branches, and their shadows accompanying them, to the Jews' occupational work and their behavioral habits. Their external connection to the Jewish personality is evidenced by their outward effects on social communication. Thus this pervertedly twisted personality emanates despicable moral outrages, so they become an external reflection of themselves, and a concentrated image of their underlying meanings and dimensions, and a human model of heinous ethical depravity which may be expressed as a "collection of defects" or as a "combination of deficiencies," or even as an "assembly of noisome corruptions."

Another remarkable point on this topic is that these deficiencies and ethical illnesses do not represent only on generation of Jews, or in any particular group of Jews! But how depraved they are! These characteristics are found in the inveterately corrupt Jew, wherever he may be, because every Jew (except the believing and just prophets of the Children of Israel) is a combined human example of these depravities. One cannot exclude that lowly Jew in the time of the pharaoh, nor that liberated Jew who lived in the land of Palestine, nor that Jew who left Palestine for the valleys of the earth to intermix there, not the modern Jew of the twentieth century who thinks that he has exclusive superiority in the cultural world, and that he has prominence in the political world, and not that Jew who lives in Palestine and pretends to practice the Torah and cling to the Jewish religion.

The baneful Jewish moral system demonstrates itself in each and every Jew. This is the result of determined inherited "genes" carried by every Jew everywhere and throughout all of history.

The Jew is able to disguise everything except his iniquitous character. The Jew is able to live without everything except his reprobate nature, his execrable behavior, his plotting, his treachery, his prevaricating, his blameworthiness, and his hatred.

If you want to recognize the true Jew, imagine in your mind a gang of sullied personalities, and then you will have each and every Jew before you.

If you have any doubts in this matter, examine with a clear eye, with careful analysis, and with the correct Qur'anic viewpoint, and apply them to any random Jew, analyze his personality and observe his behavior and practices, and your insight will probe deeply into the depths of his soul and you will discover a cluster of symptoms composed of these execrable personality traits.

How many times have we observed these defilements in today's Jews! In various locations, on different social, educational, and occupational levels we hear of their habits, declarations, deeds, communications, and their sticking together. Reliable sources who have had dealings with them and have observed them inform us that every Jew behaves according to a chthonian level of ethical behavior. This reminds me of what the imaginative satirical poet Ibn al-Rumi said in his lampoon of a certain `Amr: "Your face, O `Amr, is long; dogs' faces are long. The ugliness of dogs is your nature; and so it will always remain." The noble Qur'an describes the complex Jewish personality, and it reveals to us the Jews' sullied morals, and it presents us with an archetype of Jewish practices which embody this egregiousness. Thus does the magnificently miraculous Qur'an diligently analyze the Jewish personality and warns humankind of the lethal Jewish danger from the demonic Jewish creature.

Jews Are Liars

Lying is a despicable trait, a destructive perversion, and a dangerous sickness. When prevarication penetrates into one's soul it becomes a permanent characteristic which vitiates the meaning of goodness in his soul. This illness is not amenable to treatment.

This disingenuous characterizes the Jew wherever he may be, and he practices deceitful duplicity in every area. The Jews lied about God, his prophets, his friends, and about other nations.

What is stupefying is that the Jews made lying into a religion! They made it into a faith, a form of worship, and into a form of sacrifice they offer to their Lord as an integral part of their religion. With this lying they attack truth, goodness, right, the emissaries, the preachers, and the reformers.

This prevarication permeates every aspect of the Jew's life, on every level and in all areas.

The Jews are liars in their religious lives, their worship, and in their views of God.

The Jews are liars in their political, economic, social, moral, educational, and psychological lives.

The Jews lie to their enemies as well as to their friends, to their allies, their opponents, and adversaries.

Qur'an indicates a collection of the Jews' lies, some of which we make note of here: (1) Qur'an 3:75, (2) Qur'an 3:78, (3) Qur'an 3:93–95, (4) Qur'an 3:183–84, (5) Qur'an 4:49–51, (6) Qur'an 5:42.

These verses repeatedly define the Jews as a lying people, and that they have internalized this falsity and are at ease with it as their character, religion, behavior, and life, and that they fill everything with deceit, and they apply themselves to everything falsely.

Thus Qur'an describes them as "those who habitually listen to lies." This indicates that lying won its victory over them and controls them. The Jews are not merely liars, and not merely habitual hearers of lies (this is an intensive grammatical term for "average listeners"), [but] take pleasure in lying and in being in the company of lies and liars. They search for lies and liars, they listen to them and practice them, and they participate in them with gleeful zealousness.

The Jews Are Corrupters

All of Jewish history is a demonstration of their corrupting the truth. We have many examples of this offensive corruption; we may even say that the Jews are the most corrupting and falsifying of the truth of all the peoples of the world; they are the shrewdest in making the counterfeit look true, and in the surreptitious *al-kitmaan*, concealing of the truth.

Qur'an reveals this characteristically reprobate Jewish taint at Qur'an 2:75–76,

[A] party of them used to listen to the Words (*kalam*) of Allah, then used to distort it knowingly after they understood it. Behold! when they meet the men of Faith, they say: "We believe": But when they meet each other in private, they say: "Shall you tell them what God hath revealed to you, that they may engage you in argument about it before your Lord?" Do ye not understand (their aim)?

The Jews corrupt God's word; no one with a heart

would corrupt God's word. And when do they corrupt it? They do so immediately after hearing and understanding it, Qur'an, "after comprehending it." Instead of being led to God's law, their sick minds change God's word upon hearing it, opposing it with counterfeit defiling, while being totally aware that they are corrupting God's word. Their knowledge pushes them in this direction; their ears which hear, their minds which understand, and their souls which know—all take part in this wicked perversion. Qur'an 4:46, i.e., the Jews corrupt the words by moving them from their rightful secure positions so that clear and repeated speech becomes sullied either phonetically or semantically. If the Muslims knew the truth and said, *sami`-naa wa-aTa`-naa*, "We hear and obey," the Jews deform this into *sami`-naa wa-`aSay-naa*, "We hear and disobey."

The companions said to the emissary of God, "O [ye] emissary of God, [the Jews say] *raa`i-naa* [which in Hebrew resembles the pronunciation of "our shepherd/our evil one/look at us"] which means that what you have heard guides and protects us(??), and what they intend by this is the reverent acknowledgment of you as the emissary of God." But the Jews intend a banefully corrupt signification for this word; they say, "O Muhammad *raa`i-naa*," which is related to *al-ra´uuna*, which refers to "vague fantasy," [linguists refer to this as a "folk/false etymology"] and they affix this attribute on Muhammad, "twisting their tongues" with execrable intention; and "criticizing religion." They themselves have no religion.

Qur'an eradicated this sick scheming and pusillanimous fabrication by prohibiting the companions from pronouncing this expression, and substituting for it another expression, that is, Qur'an 2:104: "O you who believe! Do not say *raa`i-naa*, but say rather *unZur-naa*, 'look at us,' and listen. The unbelievers have a painful punishment."

Recording the Jews' corruption is Qur'an 2:104: "They are cursed for breaking their contract. We have hardened their hearts. They move the word from their proper places."

And Qur'an 5:13:

". . . O you emissary! Do not be saddened. . . . He will purify their hearts." "The Jews practice corruption of the words, compare the new religion they hear about to the Torah they have corrupted in various ways; what agrees with what they have, they accept; whatever differs from it, they discard," (from same verse, above): ". . . when you are given this, then take it, but if you do not accept it, then beware!"

These verses inform us that the cause of the Jews' dastardly corruption is their hardness of heart, and their polluting debauchery.

In his *Al-Mufradaat* (dictionary), the Imam al-Raaghib says, "Anything's *taHriif* means it's moving aside, e.g., in a slip of the pen. '*taHriif* of words' means the manipulation of a certain word to make it mean more than one thing."[1]

It is a veritable miracle that the Qur'an assigns corruption to be the Jews' wares exclusively, and the Jews' defilement exclusively. The word *yuHarrifuuna*, "they corrupt," occurs only four times in Qur'an, and in all instances it refers to the Jews alone.

The Jews Are Enviers

Envy is a dangerous illness, a condemnable perversion, and a vile personality trait. It is a proof of defilement of the soul, a personality complex, and a conundrum for humankind.

A man cannot envy his equal, honorable in his form, belief, morals, behavior, and life. Only the avid inveterate egoist who is a sickly and debased coward is able to envy.

The Jews comprise a "collection of deformities" and a "gang of degenerates"; it is ineluctable that the disease of envy will infect them, take control of their souls, and direct their movements. It is an insidious Jewish disease in the villainous Jewish character which infects others similar to them in contemptibility.

Jewish envy determines their approach to those whom God has bestowed his favor because they do not want God to bestow his bounty on anyone but the Jews.

This nefarious envy is the motivation for the Jews' aggressive hostility toward the emissary of God, the rejection of his message, despite the fact that they well knew Muhammad was the emissary of God. They envy Muhammad on account of his message and his prophethood, and because he is not a Jew; thus they fight him.

The Jews envy the Muslims because God bestowed his bounty, that is, Islam, upon them; thus they fight him.

The Jews envy the Muslims because God made them his caliphs (deputies) on the earth, and the witnesses to peoples, and his trustees for his religious mission, and the professors for mankind; they are not Jews, so the Jews oppose them: Qur'an 4:50–54:

Behold! how they invent a lie against God! but that by itself is a manifest sin! Hast thou not turned thy vision to those who were given a portion of the Book? they believe in sorcery and evil, and say to the unbelievers that they are better guided in the (right) way than the believers! They are (men) whom God hath cursed: And those whom God hath cursed, thou wilt find, have no one to help. Have they a share in dominion or power? Behold, they give not a farthing to their fellow-men? Or do they envy mankind for what God hath given them of his bounty? but we had already given the people of Abraham the Book and Wisdom, and conferred upon them a great kingdom.

These verses present us with the reason that in all the political alliances the Jews made with the polytheists against the Muslims caused this verse to be revealed because it mentions the Jews' allying themselves to the Quraysh in the razzia of the *al-aHzaab*, opposing parties—the reason is the Jews' sick envy, blind hatred, and infernal contempt for the truth and its people.

This envy is still the main factor in the Jews' relations to the Muslims, even in contemporary times. The Jews envy them their Islam, which is God's bounty to them, and thus they ally themselves with the Christians, the communists, and the atheists; all their operative alliances follow this valid political motivation mentioned in the Qur'an.

We now note by way of example some Qur'anic subtleties and proofs: The word *am* "(exclusive) or" occurs twice in the two verses above with discrete significations:

VII. "*am*, do they have a part in the kingdom?" Here *am* has an interrogative import.
VIII. "*am*, they envy the people." Here *am* has an emphatic connotation: "Indeed."

In this latter instance, we discover the continual political and practical dimension in the emphasis carried by the particle *am*, so that interprets the section which follows it, that is the secret of the Jews' alliances until the final hour.

Another verse reveals to us the Jews' envy of the Muslims: Qur'an 2:109: "Many of the people of the Book want to return you to your unbelieving after you have believed, out of the envy in their souls, after the truth was revealed to them."

The Jews' envy of the believers culminated when they realized that the Muslims were right, and this envy transmogrified itself into permanent zealotry to convert the believers, after they had accepted their faith, to disbelief in God. They utilized various means to realize this demoniacally cursed goal. Qur'an [2:109] expressed this goal, the methods, and the Jewish weaponry as "desiring": "Many of the People of the Book want to return you to your unbelieving after you have believed, out of the envy in their souls, after the truth was revealed to them." Desire is a function of the heart and an inner longing. "Desiring" may occur only in the heart, and it may only be (fundamentally for any human being) for beneficial and useful goods and ends. But extending the concept of "desiring" to the propagation of unbelief, and rebellion against the Muslims, and converting them from their religion—all of this is impossible for anyone other than the envying Jews: Qur'an 2:105: "Those who disbelieve among the People of the Book or the polytheists—their Lord will not bring down anything good to them."

The Jews Are Tricksters

The Jews are tricksters. They employ deceit in all their interactions with others, and they go so far as to use it in their religious laws and in their rabbis' instructions which are commands that emanate from God. These perverted Jewish machinations allow them to forbid what is permitted and vice versa, and to limit what is obligatory and to accept what is reprehensible.

Qur'an points out this despicable Jewish trait; it records an example of their sleight of hand to undermine and corrupt God's laws.

Qur'an 2:58–59: "And when we said: Enter this city, then eat from it plenteous (food) wherever you wish, and enter the gate making obeisance, and say, '*HiTTa* forgiveness' [forgive! Hebrew *HeeT´* is 'sin'] we will forgive you your wrongs and give more to those who do good (to others). But those who were unjust corrupted it for a [different] saying." In other words, God commanded them to enter the holy land in a prostrating position, asking God for forgiveness, saying, "O our Lord! *HuTTa `an-naa* Remove[2] from us our sins." By the order of their rabbis, they falsely interpreted this and crawled (into the city) on their tushies, saying, "A *Habba* grain of barley [Hebrew *HiTTa* is Aramaic *HinTa*, meaning 'wheat']!" [As the emissary of God explained (in a hadith).]

God forbade the Jews some of the good things of this world as their punishment. An example is the fat of cattle, as he says, Qur'an, surat al-An`aam [6:]146:

And unto those who are Jews, we forbade every (animal) with undivided hoof, and we forbade them the fat of the ox and the sheep except what adheres to their backs or their entrails, or is mixed up with a bone. Thus we recompensed them for their rebellion [committing crimes like murdering the prophets, eating of *Ribâ* (usury), etc.]. And verily, we are truthful.

The Jews stealthily evaded this rabbinic command, ate the forbidden cattle fat, melted it down and then sold it and kept its price. May God curse them for this as the emissary of God declared, as reported by al-Bukhaariyy, Muslim, al-Nisaa´iyy, and Ibn Maaja, on the authority of `Umar ibn al-KhaTTaab, who said, "The emissary of God said, 'May God curse the Jews! Fats were proscribed for them, so they sold it and consumed its price!'"

The Qur'anic story of the companions of the village situated near the sea, and the Jews' manipulation there of God's laws, and their hostility to observing the Sabbath prohibitions—this is another vile example of the accursed Jewish trickery.

Qur'an surat al-Aa`raaf [7:]163–66:

Remind them of the community by the sea, who desecrated the Sabbath. When they observed the Sabbath, the fish came to them abundantly. And when they violated the Sabbath, the fish did not come. We thus afflicted them, as a consequence of their transgression. Recall that a group of them said, "Why should you preach to people whom God will surely annihilate or punish severely?" They answered, "Apologize to your Lord," that they might be saved. When they disregarded what they were reminded of, we saved those who prohibited evil, and afflicted the wrongdoers with a terrible retribution for their wickedness. When they continued to defy the commandments, we said to them, "Be you despicable apes."

In other words, God forbade the Jewish inhabitants of this village to work on the Sabbath, in particular, not to fish. In addition to their being tested, the fish would give them **shurra`** which would swim on the water's surface so as to almost cover its entire area. On other days, the fish would hide beneath the water's surface, and when the Jews tried to catch them, they would have limited success.

The Jews' diabolical thoughts are displayed here in their scheming trickery, in order to evade God's command. Their Satans advised them to dig trenches beside the water, then go to their houses. When the water rose above its usual level, it would reach these ditches, pools, and basins and fill them, and, naturally, the fish would fall into the nets which the Jews surreptitiously placed there. On the following days when fishing was permitted, they would gather up the fish trapped by premeditated trickery.

The good Jews among them forbade them from this unsavory scheme. The other Jews would not answer, or simply reject this recommendation. But God saved these good people, who preached and did good works among the other Jews, but he imposed his punishment on the plotting tricksters and transformed them into apes and pigs, as per Qur'an 2:65–66:

And ye know of those of you who broke the Sabbath, how We said unto them: Be ye apes, despised and hated! And We made it an example to their own and to succeeding generations, and an admonition to the God-fearing.

The Jews Are Diverters

The Jews are first and foremost tricksters against God's commands, and when they are unable to plot successfully, they must find other ways to reach their goals and to realize them. In such cases the Jews resort to a different style, one just as nefarious, and employ it in their relationships with others. This method uses diversion, evasion, passive resistance, and delay. The story of the Children of Israel's (golden) calf is the best example of this. Qur'an 2:67–73:

And when Moses said unto his people: Lo! Allah commandeth you that ye sacrifice a cow, they said:

Dost thou make game of us? He answered: Allah forbid that I should be among the foolish! They said: Pray for us unto thy Lord that He make clear to us what (cow) she is. (Moses) answered: Lo! He saith, Verily she is a cow neither with calf nor immature; (she is) between the two conditions; so do that which ye are commanded. They said: Pray for us unto thy Lord that he make clear to us of what color she is. (Moses) answered: Lo! He saith: Verily she is a yellow cow. Bright is her color, gladdening beholders. They said: Pray for us unto thy Lord that He make clear to us what (cow) she is. Lo! cows are much alike to us; and Lo! if Allah wills, we may be led aright. (Moses) answered: Lo! He saith: Verily she is a cow unyoked; she plougheth not the soil nor watereth the tilth; whole and without mark. They said: Now thou bringest the truth. So they sacrificed her, though almost they did not. And (remember) when ye slew a man and disagreed concerning it and Allah brought forth that which ye were hiding. And we said: Smite him with some of it. Thus Allah bringeth the dead to life and showeth you his portents so that ye may understand.

How many times did the Jews divert Moses, and how many times did he answer them, and then in the end, they carried out the order!

The first diversion is when they asked their prophet, Moses, "Are you making fun of us by making this request?" Moses is a prophet whose instructions came from God, and Moses would lead them to the rabbinic way of determining the unintentional murderer.

Their second diversion was asking him to clarify what exactly was meant by "the required calf." Moses intuited their evasive diversion and told them to do as they were ordered.

The third diversion is in their asking for clarification of the calf's color, and Moses clarified it for them.

The fourth diversion is that they asked Moses for further precision in the description of the required calf because cattle resemble each other closely, so Moses delimited it for them.

After these diversions, "they sacrificed it but almost did not." Notice the subtle precision of this Qur'anic expression, that is, they almost did not do it, and they almost did not sacrifice it, so they did not sacrifice it, except after these diversionary tactics. In his *Mufradaat* (Vocabulary Entries), the Imam al-Raaghib said, "'Almost' means to come close to doing something. One says, 'he almost did' means that 'he might not have done it,' and if it is accompanied by a negative particle, then it did actually occur, but it nearly did not happen.'"[3]

In spite of the fact that had they been serious about carrying out God's command issued to their prophet Moses, and had they intended to carry it out immediately, they would not have resorted to these diversionary tactics. Had they not engaged in these nit-picking arguments, then they would have been able to obtain an appropriate calf to sacrifice. They would then strike the dead on part of it, and God would revive it, and it would inform on its murderer. [*sic*]

The narrative of the Children of Israel's calf in the Sura of the Cow is a clear example of the Jews' diversions, and irrefragable proof on the ability of this infernal Jewish trait in their souls and in their lives. This is not the first diversion they carried out, nor will it be the last, for up to the present time, their life has been based on, and tainted with, this diversion.

The Jews Are Fickle

The Jews' approach to God's inspiration and law, their encounter with God's emissaries and prophets, and their stance toward God's troops and his men—all are based on fickle fantasy.

They do not take to the truth because it is truth, but rather because it satisfies their fantastical whims, and if one objects, they ostracize him. The Jews do not believe in the law because it comes from God, but only when it agrees with their whimsical fickleness, and if one opposes this, they deny him.

They do not believe any prophet, because he is from God, but they believe in him only when he is in agreement with their fickle whimsy. When not, they deny him or kill him. They never travel with good people because of their goodness, unless they agree to their whimsical fantasy. If they do not find the good people so, they deny them and harm them.

Some verses of Qur'an point out this despicable, fanciful, satanic Jewish fickleness, for example, Qur'an 2:41: "O Children of Israel! remember My favors which I bestowed upon you, and fulfill your covenant with Me, I will fulfill My covenant with you, and Me alone should you fear."

Also Qur'an 2:87:

And verily we gave unto Moses the Scripture and we caused a train of messengers to follow after him, and we gave unto Jesus, son of Mary, clear proofs (of Allah's sovereignty), and we supported him with the Holy spirit. Is it ever so, that, when there cometh unto you a messenger (from Allah) with that which ye yourselves desire not, ye grow arrogant, and some ye disbelieve and some ye slay?

And Qur'an 2:145:

And even if thou broughtest unto those who have received the Scripture all kinds of portents, they would not follow thy *qiblah*, nor canst thou be a follower of their *qiblah*; nor are some of them followers of the *qiblah* of others. And if thou shouldst follow their desires after the knowledge which hath come unto thee, then surely wert thou of the evildoers.

So Qur'an 5:49:

And that you should judge between them by what Allah has revealed, and do not follow their low desires, and be cautious of them, lest they seduce you from part of what Allah has revealed to you; but if they turn back, then know that Allah desires to afflict them on account of some of their faults; and most surely many of the people are transgressors.

Qur'an 5:70:

We made a covenant with the Israelites and sent Messengers to them. Whenever a Messenger came to them with a message which did not suit their desires, they would reject some of the Messengers and kill others.

Qur'an, surat al-An`aam [6:91]:

And they measure not the power of Allah its true measure when they say: Allah hath naught revealed unto a human being. Say (unto the Jews who speak thus): Who revealed the Book which Moses brought, a light and guidance for mankind, which ye have put on parchments which ye show, but ye hide much (thereof), and (by which) ye were taught that which ye knew not yourselves nor (did) your fathers (know it)? Say: Allah. Then leave them to their play of caviling.

The Jew Are Mockers

One of the most contemptible traits of the Jews is their sarcastic mockery, lampooning the emissary who did not fit their fancy, and disparaging non-Jews who behaved righteously. They laughed off the truth the prophets had brought them.

They made fun of Islam, its values, and its principles. They mocked the Muslims as they were performing these principles. God warns us from making friends with the sarcastically sardonic Jews who send us, our principles, and our worship, up, at Qur'an 5:57–58:

O Ye who believe! Choose not for guardians such of those who received the Scripture before you, and of the disbelievers, as make a jest and sport of your religion. But keep your duty to Allah if ye are true believers. And when ye call to prayer they take it for a jest and sport. That is because they are a folk who understand not.

The Jews took Islam as foolish child's play, and made it the subject of puns and jokes. Only a person with a soul bereft of all goodness could do such a thing. Were the rabbinic religion the truth—as the Jews' belief it is God's own truth—then how could they make it the subject of their mocking sarcasm and childish foolishness?

The Jews made the principles of prayer and the call to prayer into a target for their aping mockery, and when they hear the *muezzin* call to prayer, they twist their tongues in mocking puns, and they make degenerate movements in mocking mimicry.

How could there be any friendship, alliance, or cooperation in battle between a proud Muslim and this type of mocker? When a Muslim does so, he has lost all his life, vitality, and belief.

This trait is deeply rooted in the Jewish character, and they displayed it in their dealings with the polytheists— in every time period, all over the world—and they began mocking the Muslims from the very first call to Islam, at Qur'an 2:14–15:

And when they fall in with those who believe, they say: We believe; but when they go apart to their devils they declare: Lo! we are with you; verily we did but mock. Allah (himself) doth mock them, leaving them to wander blindly on in their contumacy.

The Jews Are Traitors

Treachery is connected with perverted unbelief, and Jews are perverted unbelievers with no morals. Treachery is inextricably connected to, and deeply rooted in, the Jews. It is an inveterate trait in the very heart of their being. The Jews are treachery's emissaries, protectors, and propagators among people.

Qur'an informs us of the repeated treacheries of the Jews at Qur'an 5:13: "And because of their breaking their covenant, we have cursed them and made hard their hearts. They change words from their context and forget a part of that whereof they were admonished. Thou wilt not cease to discover treachery from all save a few of them."

By examining this verse, we find that

(1) It explains the reason for the deep-rootedness of treachery in them by use of the "*baa´* of cause or reason": "*fa-bi-maa*," By breaking their covenant . . . , because the breach of their covenant with God is the reason for their rotten ethics, unspeakable crimes, and continual treacheries. This is true because faithfulness to a binding contract with God is a *sine que non* of security from unprincipled perversions, for if someone challenges God by breaking his contract with him, it is clear that there is nothing to stop him from breaking his contract with other men.

(2) This verse also allows us to see the long string of Jewish defilements, and it forms a closed circle: breaking covenants, corrupting the words by moving them to inappropriate places, and perpetrating betrayals. This proves that these chains of perverted villainies exist, and that one gives rise to another. . . .

(4) This verse also informs us of the justification for God's punishment of the Jews for reason of their infernal deformities, and this is God's Sunna for the life of mankind: whoever sells his soul to Satan and wallows in iniquitous corruption, God assigns him comeuppance commensurate with his level of depravity. When the Jews descended into disobedience, God recompensed them by cursing them and exiling them from his mercy, then this abusive curse caused their hearts to harden further.

(5) This verse also informs us that the Jews' treacheries are continually repeating forever: " . . . and you still *taTTali`* are informed [on betrayal]. . . . " This part of the verse is directed at the emissary of God, who was being *taTTali`* informed at all times of the Jews' treacheries: by the Banu NaDiir, the Banu Qaynuqaa`, the Banu QurayZa, and by the Jews of Khaybar and Fadak and Taymaa´. Speech is also directed at each Muslim wherever he may be to call on him to examine the Jews' life with open eyes in order to be informed by them of their ever and continual betrayals. Speech is also directed to the observer of history, and to the researcher of its events and truths, in order that he, too, become well aware of the reiterated Jewish treacheries.

(6) We conclude from this verse that the Jewish betrayal is complete, from every aspect and in every area of experience, just as it is continual in every time and place; we conclude this from the form *khaa´ina* "betraying" and we derive an important *qaa`ida* rule from it, that is the suppression of the direct object (of "betraying") has as its purpose the deliberate obfuscation of the direct object's identity, so that the mind may wander and the imagination have its maximal play.

The Jews are double-dealers with their prophets and they are double-crossers of the Muslims; they are disloyal to their allies; they sell their agents out; and they are duplicitous with their enemies.

You can always be sure of their perfidy: they are disloyal in word, deceptive in movement, unfaithful in deed, dishonest in their contracts and agreements, double-crossers in their alliances and confederacies, and duplicitous in their agreements and negotiations.

(7) God is correct in this verse. It applies perfectly to our contemporary reality, because the Jews are diabolical traitors who exploit every second in perpetrating multiple betrayals, and the observer will observe with wonder the perpetuity implied in the expression "and you are still informed," and by its focus, for everyone who is able to focus, wherever he may be.

In the end, some naive Arabs get taken in by the Jews in their contracts and agreements, for the simple-minded may believe that the Jews are righteous and have left off their duplicity, but this verse requires that he open his eyes; it tells him, "you still are informed of treachery from them."

The Jews Are in Error, and They Lead Astray

Qur'an informs us that the Jews strayed from the Straight Path, then they became zealous in leading others astray to join them in their blind error.

Qur'an 3:69: "A party of the followers of the Book desire that they should lead you astray, and they lead not astray but themselves, and they do not perceive." Qur'an 3:90 repeats that the Jews are in error: "Surely, those who disbelieve, after their believing, then increase in unbelief, their repentance shall not be accepted, and these are they that go astray."

At Qur'an 5:77 clarifies that in addition to being in error, the Jews lead others astray:

Say: O People of the Scripture! Stress not in your religion other than the truth, and follow not the vain desires of folk who erred of old and led many astray, and erred from a plain road.

The Jews are certainly in error and they stubbornly fixed in their error, and this has become transformed into a permanent trait and a continual misdeed: notice the emphatic, definite succinctness of the phrase "these are the ones in error."

As for the reason for their error: they disbelieved after they believed, and they persisted in error so that error multiplied.

The Jews in their illusions follow others who came before, following them in their fantasies, for fantasy is what binds them to the previous people in error. If one imitates a person in error, that person will be in error; and if one follows a person in error, that person will be in error like him, and error will become transformed into his permanent personal trait.

It was not enough for the Jews to be in error—and this is a heinous crime—but they wallowed in it until it became a vile character trait and the most unspeakable crime. They zealously endeavored to turn the believing right-guided people astray, and to separate them from the truth in which they believed, so that the Jews would be able to share their life and fate with them, and be equal to them in misconception.

At Qur'an 5:77: "Say: O People of the Scripture! Stress not in your religion other than the truth, and follow not the vain desires of folk who erred of old and led many astray, and erred from a plain road." He reveals to us the nature of the deluded and the fruits of their delusion, so that they want everyone to be like them, so they corrupt them as they lead them astray.

The Jews are indeed in error, and delusion is a perma-

nent Jewish character trait. Turning people away from the truth is the Jews' mission in the world, and it has reached its peak in this modern period.

The Jews Are tujjaar fujjaar, Corrupt Businessmen

The Jews do business in all types of vile criminal activities. They deal in beliefs and religions, in values and principles, in truth and goodness, in good qualities and virtues, in peoples and in countries, and in deeds and contracts.

In many of its verses, Qur'an tells us of this Jewish commercial trait, and it points out the most unsavory varieties and the most execrable variations of Jewish business.

They do business with God's verses. They barter for them and sell them out at a measly price. They corrupt the verses for whoever requests it, making the prohibited into the permitted and vice versa. God warned them of the Jews' con-man commerce at Qur'an 2:40: "Do not sell my verses for a measly price. Fear me!"

Who is it that deals in God's verses and dares to sell them to the Jews for a paltry price? Any price that a cursed merchant gets for God's verses must of necessity be a lowly price, even if it be thousands, or even millions, of dinars, nay, even if the price be the entire world!

Qur'an 2:79 denies the Jews this playing around with God's verses, corrupting them, and then doing business with them:

Then woe to those who write the Book with their own hands, and then say: "This is from God," to traffic with it for miserable price! Woe to them for what their hands do write, and for the gain they make thereby.

God made a firm contract with the Jews that they would remain with him forever: that they would pray to him and would remain faithful to his law and religion. He warned them about breaking contracts and **al-kitmaan**, concealing the truth, and he forbade them from selling his Book at a miserable price. But the Jews are businessmen in everything, even in God's covenant: Qur'an 3:187:

And remember God took a covenant from the People of the Book, to make it known and clear to mankind, and not to hide it; but they threw it away behind their backs, and purchased with it some miserable gain! And vile was the bargain they made!

And when did the Jews do this? And when did their rabbis approach this? After God had warned them about doing business with his covenant: Qur'an 5:44: "Do not fear people but fear me. Do not sell my verses at a stingy price."

The Jews believe they are in a good business by selling God's verses and laws, and that they are blessed with the *fiTna*, natural humanity, [note: not *fitna*, "rebellion"], wisdom, good form, and wide vision. But Qur'an repeats the opposite attributes of theirs; whenever they sell the truth and take its price they only sell themselves out in vain, for disbelief and for Satan: Qur'an 2:102: "[T]hey learned what hurt them, and did not profit them, knowing well that whoso buys it shall have no share in the world to come; evil then was that they sold themselves for, if they had but known." The meaning of **sharaw**, "they sold" (themselves for the price), is that they sold them whenever they sold the truth and right guidance, for a paltry price, and they have no portion in the Afterlife.

Who is the negligent businessman who forgets himself in the heat of the sale, panting after money and profit, and permits a sale at the fair selling price, and presents it to the seller with a guarantee of the transaction? Is this seller the treacherous, cursed Satan? No one would do this except a greedy Jewish merchant, or, better said, the despicable character of greedy Jewish businessmen.

Qur'an makes us despise this unsavory Jewish commercial deal, and it calls on us to wonder at their infernal deed: Qur'an 2:90:

> Miserable indeed is what they sold their souls for—rejecting these revelations of God out of sheer resentment that God should bestow His grace upon whomever He chooses from among His servants. Consequently, they incurred wrath upon wrath. The disbelievers have incurred a humiliating retribution.

What did they receive as the price of their souls which they bartered away, and what did they buy with it? Unbelief! Qur'an 3:19: " . . . that they disbelieve out of hatred, in what God revealed." And how could a person be so debilitatedly sick as to sell his soul for what amounts to only unbelief! And is unbelief a commercial commodity? And must one pay even one penny for it, and what sort of mind would sell it for this paltry penny? But the Jews do not sell it for a penny, a dinar, nor one thousand dinars: they sell it at the price of their souls which is their most valuable possession! Let people be amazed at this futile Jewish sale, and at this losing Jewish commerce!

The Jews do business in truth and goodness, and sell God's firm covenant and laws. What will be their lot on the Day of Resurrection? Qur'an 3:77 answers:

> Lo! those who purchase a small gain at the cost of Allah's covenant and their oaths, they have no portion in the Hereafter. Allah will neither speak to them nor look upon them on the Day of Resurrection, nor will He make them grow. Theirs will be a painful doom.

The Jews sold their souls to the devil. They have no portion of goodness and mercy on the Day of Resurrection, for as long as they purchase disbelief in this world, in the next they will feel God's anger, curse, and punishment. The comeuppance is commensurate with the types of misdeeds committed, and as you judge, you shall be judged!!

In this contemptible, unprofitable business, the Jews have become the slaves of this world. They purchase this world and its forbidden lusts and luxuries in exchange for the pleasure and peace of mind of the Garden in the next world. They have sold the everlasting world to come for one moment in this ephemeral lower world, and all of the life in this world cannot match that of the next. How much is an unprofitable Jewish life that lasts not more than a few decades worth? Qur'an 2:86: "These are the ones who sold this life for the life in the world to come. Punishment will not be alleviated for them, nor will they be victorious."

These are the Jews, this is Jewish business, and this is the Jewish character. They are businessmen who deal in right guidance, faith, truth, and law. They are the first to make these dear and precious truths and values—which cannot be measured in price, or be exchanged for anything in this world, or for all of this world—into a commercial commodity which they put in their shop window for sale. They praise, then sell them, and in exchange they collect unbelief, error, and disaster; and God's anger, punishment, and Fire.

Other merchants have tried to emulate the Jews, and they started to deal in right guidance and religion, they sold them and their souls along with them for a puny sum, and received catastrophic punishment in return.

The Qur'an warns us about the merchant character which belongs to the losing merchants: Qur'an 2:174–75: "Those who **yaktumuuna**, conceal Allah's revelations in the Book, And purchase for them a miserable profit—They swallow into themselves naught but Fire."

How stupid they are! And how great is their loss! And, O, how rotten their business is! And O, may their perpetual torture in hellfire outlast their patience!

The Jews Are Foolish

The Jews try to deceive mankind, and imagine that they are clever and wise; that they are professors of science, makers of civilization, guardians of knowledge, custodians of the truth and religion, emissaries of the good and the just, and so on. This stratagem works on some very naive people who are deceived by these coarse Jewish slogans, so these simpletons consider the Jews as they claim.

But the truth is the complete opposite of this: Jews are foolish, not wise; they are stupid, not clever. The wise person is one who knows how to protect himself and ward off punishment, and the intelligent person is one who is quick to reform this world and the next, but the Jews are not like this.

Qur'an considers the Jews to be foolish, so why

shouldn't we consider them to be so? This debased character trait has become embedded in them, in their lives and souls, and I firmly believe the Qur'an is correct in its analysis here.

The Imam al-Ghaarib says that the meaning of **safah** is "**khiffa**, lightness of the body; also uses as lightness of the soul because of a deficiency of intelligence, and in matters of this world and of the next."[4]

The Jews are foolish because they reject Abraham's **milla**, religion, yet they claim they are related to him in religion and in their religion's inheritance of his message. They lie in this claim because one of the conditions of Abraham's religion is that they enter it, that is, Islam, the seal of the religions and messages; and that they follow Muhammad, for Muhammad is the "call of Abraham," and whoever denies the emissary of God spurns and rejects Abraham's religion; that is, whoever does this is foolish. Qur'an 2:130: "He who rejects Abraham's religion is foolish in his soul."

The Jews are foolish because they reject Islam, and they spread doubts and suspicions against its teachings, principles, and laws. Qur'an 2:142:

The fools among people will say: "What has turned them from their **qibla** which they had?" Say: "The East and the West belong only to Allah; He guides whom He likes to the Straight Path."

The Jews began spreading their doubts and suspicions after the Muslims' **qibla**, direction of prayer, had been changed from Jerusalem to Medina, specifically, to the Ka`ba. They started to cast doubts on the Muslims' religion, so this verse was revealed to negate their actions, and to make note against them their **al-safah, wal-khiffa, wal-Taysh** their stupid and illusory foolhardiness. Only a fool speaks foolishness, and behaves only in a foolish way.

The Jews Are Humiliated

Humiliation is attached to the Jews for their entire lifetime: they were humiliated in Egypt, and when they arrived in Palestine, and when they were exiled from Palestine, and when they dispersed into the valleys of the earth.

What concerns us here—in our discussion of the Jewish character—is to indicate that this humiliation is to be considered as an inveterate Jewish character trait, and a destructive Jewish perversion. Humiliation is one of their historical attributes, a fixed fact of their existence, and a **qaa`ida**, basis of their life. We will return to this topic soon, **inshallah**.

The Jews acquired the characteristic of humiliation from their life circumstances, that is, punishment, oppression, and dispersion.

They lived as humiliated beings in Egypt under the rule of Pharaoh, and how correct is Qur'an in describing Pharaoh's humiliation of the Jews! Qur'an 2:49:

When We saved them from Pharaoh's people, who subjected you to severe torment, killing your sons and sparing your women, and in this there was a great trial from your Lord.

One of the reasons for their humiliation is their disobedience to their Lord's commands, their disbelief in Him, and their worship of the calf instead of God, as Qur'an, surat al-Aa`raaf, (7:152),

Those who took the calf (for a god), surely wrath from their Lord and disgrace in this world's life shall overtake them, and thus do We recompense the devisers of lies.

One sign of their humiliation is their rejection of power and honor, and their addiction to food, drink, and luxurious pleasures: Qur'an 2:61:

Recall that you said, "O **Moses**, we can no longer tolerate one kind of food. Call upon your Lord to produce for us such earthly crops as beans, cucumbers, garlic, lentils, and onions." He said, "Do you wish to substitute that which is inferior for that which is good? Go down to Egypt, where you can find what you asked for." They have incurred condemnation, humiliation, and disgrace, and brought upon themselves wrath from God. This is because they rejected God's revelations, and killed the prophets unjustly. This is because they disobeyed and transgressed.

The Jews are humiliated because they disbelieved in God, killed his prophets, disobeyed his emissaries, transgressed his prohibitions—all of this is humiliation. They are humiliated—and this is why they search out lustful indulgences, and have become their slaves. All of this is humiliation.

The Jews Are Cowards

Cowardice is connected to humiliation, for every humiliation produces cowardice, and anyone who is humiliated is necessarily a dastard; were he not humiliated, he would not be cowardly or fearful.

The Jews are people who live their lives as humiliated beings, whose humiliation has borne the bitter fruit of cowardice, fear, and terror. Cowardice is one of their most prominent characteristics; it is one of their contemptible, inveterate characteristics; it is a perpetual, permanent, and everlasting **qaa`ida**, basis of their lives throughout all of their history.

We will point out three historical examples which will clarify their cowardice in a practical, external form in order to support what we say with concrete instances that point to a fixed fact of history: the Jews' cowardice. . . .

The Jews' Cowardice on Entering the Holy Land

The Jews' cowardice toward Moses' directions to them when they entered the Holy Land, when he told them: Qur'an 5:21–24:

> O my people! Go into the holy land which Allah hath ordained for you. Turn not in flight, for surely ye turn back as losers: They said: "O Moses! Lo! a giant people (dwell) therein and lo! we go not in till they go forth from thence. When they go forth from thence, then we will enter (not till then). Then out spoke two of those who feared (their Lord, men) unto whom Allah had been gracious: Enter in upon them by the gate, for if ye enter by it, lo! ye will be victorious. So put your trust (in Allah) if ye are indeed believers. They said: O Moses! We will never enter (the land) while they are in it. So go thou and thy Lord and fight! We will sit here.

In other words, Moses told them that God had promised them—temporarily—the Holy Land, and he guaranteed them victory over the unbelievers who dwelled therein. He warned them against defeat, fear, and cowardice, and two courageous believing men sketched out for them the road guaranteeing victory: "enter the gate against them . . . and rely on God."

But the Jews are faint-hearted dastards who do not dare enter any battle nor to carry out God's command to jihad. At this point, their cowardice began to speak, and mumbled some sickly excuses. When push came to shove, there was no excuse left, so they began to angrily curse Moses and his instructions. How despicable the coward is! And how amenable to curses is his tongue. This points to a people of cowards. "We will never enter it until they leave it," but when they leave it, then we will enter. Their cowardice requires that their enemies leave the land and hand it over to the Jews. Notice especially the sapient subtlety of relating the deed to (the Palestinian dwellers), that is, by expressing "*yakhrujuu*," "they go out" in the active rather than in the passive voice [i.e., "*yukhrajuu*" = "they are forced out"]. Who wants to go out from his own land and country out of free choice without facing war, battle, and defeat before delivering them over to his enemies? What sensible person could think or imagine such a thing? Only one who is lily-livered, and whose faintness of heart demands such a naively stupid supposition. The dastardly Jews actually expected that! As for the present time, lo and behold the Arabs are the cowards—that is, those who take their cowardice from the Jews—they expect and assume the same thing, and they imagine that Palestine, or part of it—"the part called the West Bank"—when the Jews leave it, they will leave of their own accord and not by fighting and imposing defeat on them!!

Whenever things became burdensome for the Jews, they cursed most indecorously, saying, "O Moses, we will never enter it as long as they are in it." Notice the emphasis connoted by their using "*lan*," "will never" . . . and ever. "For if you (Moses) are telling the truth about (the land) God has promised us, and if you are serious about our entering it, then you and your Lord go and fight it out, for here we sit!"—that is "you two go and fight for us, and we will collect the reward and enter it."

The remarkable part of this sentence points out the Jews' cowardice in warfare: They do not want to fight, they do not fight well, yet despite this, they are eager to instigate wars and they are always at the ready to ignite the conflagration of armed conflict, but only among others. They scheme and plan out wars with their vile, satanic plotting, then they get other peoples to undertake them, and these other peoples pay the price. The Jews advance them sufficient funds for weapons, fighting men, blood, victims, and pain. And when the war ends, the reprobate Jews come forward to grab the fruits of usury and interest, and to take possession of its gains and booty: others fight and pay the price the Jews collect in profit and produce!

This is true for most wars. Behind them lies the premeditated plotting of the Jews, for they are the ones who profit most from wars, and the booty that comes with them. The two world wars are not too far past, and historians have explained explicitly the Jewish machinations which caused them, and the Jews' profit from them.

What is remarkable here too is that some modern Arabs have adapted this cowardice from the Jews, and have begun asking the Muslims to fight the Jews by themselves to expel them from Palestine, as if to say, "Go you together with your Lord, and fight. We sit here."

The Jews' Cowardice in the Battle against Taaluut (Saul)

. . . We will summarize in order to indicate some of the subtleties in these last two verses: They display the cowardice of the Jews and their hypocrite accomplices, they record the external appearances of this dastardliness, they explain its presence in them, and they explain the reasons for its being part of them.

They fear the believers more than they fear God, and their chests fill with fear, terror, and fright from the believers, but they do not fill with terror, fright, and fear from God!! Thus are all cowards: they do not fear God, they are not shamed by him, nor do they correctly gauge God's power.

The Jews and the hypocrites do not battle the Muslims together: "They do not fight you (O believers!) together" (Quran 59:14). *Jamii`an*, "together," is in the accusative case for "simultaneous situation," which may refer back to the subject, that is, "the Jews," or to the direct object, that is, "the Muslims." But the Jews do not fight the Muslims when the Muslims are united, because cowards fear others who are united. Just as the Jews do not unite in fighting the Muslims because they are dastards, and cowardice divides those who suffer from it, and it is the most important factor in dissension and fragmentation.

The verse demonstrates the means used by the Jews to do combat with the Muslims, and which their cowardice, fear, and fright inspired them to utilize, that is, to fight them only in bulwarked villages or from behind a wall. The Jews—and all cowards are like this—are not man enough [*sic*] to confront the Muslims face-to-face, so how could they possibly be described as having the courage, daring, trust, challenge, and pride that constitute *al-rujuula*, manliness (virtue, etc.). Their hearts are filled with cowardice, and there is no longer any room in them for any virtuous characteristics. But such nobly positive characteristics cannot accept cohabitation in the hearts, feelings, and souls with fear, fright, and terror. If the owners of these hearts accept only the spread of this vile sickness and fatal perversion, then these virtues will flee them, and never look back in sorrow.

It is the Jews' cowardice that led them into dissension and fragmentation: "Their evil among them is great. They think they are together, but their hearts are in different places."

Concerning the Jews' acceptance of cowardliness, their satisfaction with it, and their zealousness for it—the following two verses put the cap/seal on this: Qur'an 5:58: "That is because they are a people that, *laa yafqahuuna*, does not understand" and Qur'an 5:58: "That is because they are a people that *laa ya`qiluuna*, does not comprehend" Thus: it is a matter of lack of *fiqh* "understanding" and a lack of `*aql* "comprehension."

The Jews Are Misers

Miserliness has entered and now controls the Jewish soul. It is reflected in their bodily members, and it leaves its traces on their lives, history, and their relations with others.

Jews are slaves to money! Thus do they chase it, pile it up, and hoard it so as to worship it. They refuse that it be given to the needy, and they are misers in the face of others' tragedies, with the wealth God has blessed them with.

History has recorded for us the Jews' lusting after money and the Jewish greed in hoarding it, and the Jewish zeal in investing it for profit, and making it into a means to enslave and humiliate others, and to propagate ugly and pernicious corruption, and to fight noble truth and pure modesty.

Qur'an 4:53 points out an example of the Jews' lust for and worship of money: "Or do they have a share of the wealth, yet they do not give people a date notch."

This verse displays the Jews' niggardliness and attachment to wealth; they hoard it, and are zealous for it, and they pant after obtaining it. Qur'an points out that even if they had a share in the *al-mulk*, possession, that is, they would have control over it, its distribution, and giving parts of it for the livelihood of others. Yet they are pikers with it, and do not give the people any of it: "they do not give the people even a date-notch." *Al-naqiir*, "date-notch" refers metaphorically to "the smallest possible amount of anything," as it is the hole that appears on the surface of a date pit. It is a likeness for paucity and worthlessness. Despite this, Jews are tight with it and do not share it.

It is remarkable that the tightwad yearns for respect, and that he accuses the noble person of miserliness. He hides his sick deformity and deficiency in accusations. How can such a scrooge complain to his Lord about a noble person and accuse him of penurious niggardliness? This is exactly what the Jews do!! Qur'an 3:180–81:

And let not those who covetously withhold of the gifts which Allah Hath given them of his grace, think that it is good for them: Nay, it will be the worse for them: soon shall the things which they covetously withheld be tied to their necks like a twisted collar, on the Day of Judgment. To Allah belongs the heritage of the heavens and the earth; and Allah is well-acquainted with all that ye do. Allah hath heard the taunt of those who say: "Truly, Allah is indigent and we are rich!"—We shall certainly record their word and (their act) of slaying the prophets in defiance of right, and we shall say: "Taste ye the penalty of the Scorching Fire!"

Those referred to here are the Jews, for it is they who hoard what God has given them out of his grace, but they consider it a talent, an inborn quality, a virtue, and a propitious fate, but this miserliness is bad for them in this world and in the next.

The Jews Are Zealous for the Life (of This World)

This is another contemptible Jewish trait, and it is connected with a series of other execrable moral defilements. It is closely related also to dastardly humiliation and wretchedness. It is a zealous lust for this life. Qur'an 2:96: "You will find them the most zealous people for life—(the Jews) and the polytheists—each one of them wants to live a thousand years. Yet they will not evade the punishment with long life. God sees what they do."

Jews are eager for life. Were this a sign of life, the important thing would be that living their life would be enough, and they would not be concerned whether theirs was a good life or a humble one, a human life or a near-human life, a man's life or the life of an insect or an animal. But they prefer another kind of life, one maculated with humiliation and cowardice, over the first life which is good and noble. Because a life of goodness and nobility requires personal qualities that the Jews do not have, and excellent people who no Jews may be in company with. It also requires a significant expenditure the Jews are too dastardly to pay, and a high price Jews refuse to pay!!

Jews are satisfied with the superficial outer appearances of life: do they not eat and drink?—Like animals—do they not breathe and move?—Like reptiles—do they not sleep and wake up?—Like animals—do they not live a lustful animal life?—Like cattle—thus they live their desired lives, and they are the happiest people (on earth) living like this.

This is life lived by the criterion of the Jews—not by the criterion of noble men. It is the life that is fitting for Jews—but not for noble people. The only people who could be pleased, accept, or be zealous for such a life are those with a Jewish personality, soul, and character.

All of this is implied in the grammatical indefiniteness of "life" in "you will find them the most zealous of people for "*Hayaat*," "life" (not "*al-Hayat*," "[the] life"): this indefiniteness implies a plethora of debased degradation. [*sic*]

Throughout all of their history, the Jews have never succeeded in sloughing off this despicable and execrable wretchedness and blameworthiness.

The Jews Break Binding Contracts

You will never find any people more enthusiastic to break firm contracts than the Jews, either out of neglect or out of some perceived need. They do so out of gall: they break them, annul them, and cancel them.

Other people emulate the Jews in this perverted attribute, and they dare to break their solemn contracts, whether they are between them and God or between them and other people.

Qur'an 2:83–85 gives examples of the Jews' breaking their firm agreement:

F. Qur'an 2:83: And (remember) when we took a covenant from the Children of Israel, (saying): Worship none but Allah (Alone) and be dutiful and good to parents, and to kindred, and to orphans and Al-Masakin (the poor), and speak good to people [i.e., enjoin righteousness and forbid evil, and say the truth about Muhammad, Peace be upon him], and perform As-Salat (Iqamat-as-Salat), and give Zakat. Then you slid back, except a few of you, while you are backsliders.

G. Qur'an 2:63–64: When we took a covenant with them and raised over them the Mount, saying, "take what you have gotten with force, and remember what it contains. Perhaps you will be pious." After that they turned away, and were it not for God's grace and mercy for you, you would have been among the losers.

H. Qur'an 2:93: When we took their covenant and held the Mount over them, saying, "take what you have gotten by force and listen." They said, "We hear and disobey." So they [absorbed/drank] the calf in their hearts because of their unbelief.

I. Qur'an 3:187: When God took a covenant with those who were given the Book, you must explain it to the people and not hide (*kitmaan*) it. They put it behind their backs and sold it for a paltry price, and evil is what they exchange.

J. Qur'an 4:154–55: And we raised above them the Mount, taking compact with them; and we said to them, "Enter in at the gate, prostrating"; and we said to them, "Transgress not the Sabbath"; and we took from them a solemn compact. So, for their breaking the compact, and disbelieving in the signs of God, and slaying the prophets without right, and for their saying, "Our hearts are uncircumcised"— nay, but God sealed them for their unbelief, so they believe not, except a few.

K. Qur'an 5:12–13: Indeed Allah took the covenant from the Children of Israel (Jews), and we appointed twelve leaders among them. And Allah said: "I am with you if you perform As-Salat (Iqamat-as-Salat) and give Zakat and believe in my messengers; honor and assist them, and lend to Allah a good loan. Verily, I will remit your sins and admit you to Gardens under which rivers flow (in Paradise). But if any of you after this, disbelieved, he has indeed gone astray from the Straight Path." So because of their breach of their covenant, We cursed them, and made their hearts grow hard. They change the words from their (right) places and have abandoned a good part of the Message that was sent to them. And you will not cease to discover deceit in them, except a few of them. But forgive them, and overlook (their misdeeds). Verily, Allah loves *Al-Muhsinun* (good doers).

L. Qur'an 5:70: Verily, we took the covenant of the Children of Israel and sent them messengers. Whenever there came to them a messenger with what they themselves desired not—a group of them they called liars, and others among them they killed.

M. Qur'an, surat al-A`raaf, 7:169: Then after them succeeded an (evil) generation, which inherited the Book, but they chose (for themselves) the goods of this low life (evil pleasures of this world) saying (as an excuse): "(Everything) will be forgiven to us." And if (again) the offer of the like (evil pleasures of this world) came their way, they would (again) seize them (would commit those sins). Was not the covenant of the Book taken from them that they would not say about Allah anything but the truth? And they have studied what is in it (the Book). And the home of the Hereafter is better for those who are *Al-Muttaqun* (the pious). Do not you then understand?

These eight citations speak of God's accepting a covenant with the Jews, and the Jews' gall in breaking it. We display them just as they are before the reader; we have not discussed the proofs and subtle truth they contain in order to remain succinct, and not to overwhelm the reader's brain.

In its etymology, the word for contract, ***miithaaq***, has a root that is mentioned twenty-eight times in Qur'an in relation to God's contract with the Jews. And it records their breach of contract in each.

This is a remarkable sign, one that demonstrates that this character trait of treacherous cowardice is inveterate in the Jews.

This is enough for us to consider in dealing with God's contract with the Jews. God told them at Qur'an 2:40: "O Children of Israel! Remember the bounty I have bestowed upon you. If you are faithful in your Covenant, I will be faithful in My Covenant. So fear *me*!"

But they did not accept this condition, and broke God's covenant, just as they did with all their other firm commitments.

Qur'an 2:58–59:

And when We said: Go into this township and eat freely of that which is therein, and enter the gate prostrate, and say: "Repentance." We will forgive you your sins and will increase (reward) for the right-doers. But those who did wrong changed the word which had been told them for another saying, and We sent down upon the evil-doers wrath from heaven for their evil-doing.

In other words, this is a marvelous verse because it demonstrates that this vile trait is inveterate in the diseased Jewish spirit, and that it is hard-wired into the corrupted Jewish personality, and it continues all through the filthy and depraved, spitefully hateful, history of Jewish relations with their firm contracts.

Qur'an 2:99–101:

We have sent down to thee Manifest Signs (ayat); and none reject them but those who are perverse. Is it not (the case) that every time they make a covenant, some party among them throw it aside?—Nay, Most of them are faithless. And when there came to them an apostle from God, confirming what was with them, a party of the People of the Book threw away the Book of God behind their backs, as if (it had been something) they did not know!

What is remarkable about the expression "every time that" in this verse is that it indicates that breaking contracts is a recurring theme with the Jews, for every contract they make, they break, whoever their contracting partner may be. The expression "every time that" indicates continual repetition, as if to be formulaic. This is also implied in the paronomastic (pleonastic, repetitious) expression "they contract a contract."

This verse strikingly clarifies for us the scheming baseness of the Jews in breaking their agreements: When they make a contract, not all of them break it, only a group of them, the others having separated themselves from the former group. They had announced their resistance to this action, yet they themselves are of variegated kinds, and had recommended breaking the contract. This patent, hateful scheming of the Jews is evidenced through history.

The Jews Rush into Aggression and Sin

One of the invariable inherent characteristics of the Jews is that they rush into unbelief, and into sinful aggression. "Sin" implies lawlessly spending the peoples' wealth, and purposeless speech and corrupt acts, as per Qur'an 5:41:

And when there came to them an apostle from God, confirming what was with them, a party of the People of the Book threw away the Book of God behind their backs, as if (it had been something) they did not know!

"Those who rush into unbelief" are of two groups: the Jews, and their lackeys from among the polytheists who feign belief. The latter imitate the former in this vile characteristic, and thus became like them in rushing into unbelief, vanity and sinful aggression.

The verb "they rush" indicates the eagerness with which they embrace unbelief and sinful aggression: desiring them, concerning themselves with them, approaching them, hurrying to meet them, and their haste in realizing them and obtaining them. "They rush" ***yusaari`uuna*** (Form III verb) is more intensive than "they rush" ***yusri`uuna*** (Form IV verb), and it is clearer in the description of the Jews' activity of arriving at worthless unbelief, because the emphasis implied in the morphology of the verb form intensifies the meaning and the additional force given to this form by the *alif* it contains casts these shadows, and makes these revelations.

Concerning the Jews' scurrying: Qur'an 5:62–63:

And thou seest many of them vying one with another in sin and transgression and their devouring of illicit gain. Verily evil is what they do. Why do not the rabbis and the priests forbid their evil-speaking and their devouring of illicit gain? Verily evil is their handiwork.

The hurrying of the Jews here refers to their rushing into sinful hostility and misusing other people's money. This consists of three stages or steps: when they are in possession of the ***al-munkar*** forbidden and useless, they first fall into sin, then they transgress against others, and then they demonstrate their misuse of other people's money "and it is forbidden." Indeed the Jewish rush into this is further proof of the thoroughly ingrained nature of their perversity which resides in their hearts and controls their existence, and it controls their inclination for their choices, their deeds, steps, behavior, and movements.

The honest man does not like sin or vain aggression, and he does not meditate on them. If thoughts of sin or vain aggression occur to him, he shrugs them off and gets rid of them for good. The upright man does not willingly choose to accept uselessness, and if he meets up with it, it is only because of an unintentional stumble, as if he had two left feet, or a tired mind. It may happen due to conflicting circumstances in his life, but not out of his own accord, volition, so that he rushes very fast into it.

It is remarkable that the Jewish rabbis did not try to put a stop to this, and end the Jews' insane rushing in, but they rather encouraged them to do this, and they presented them with the excuses and legal trickery in order to double their zeal in desiring this, and to accelerate their steps toward this, coming on like gang-busters, because these pernicious rabbis were the most perverse of the Jews, and even more desirous of rushing into sin.

Perverse corruption and rushing into sin and aggressive sin is inherent in each and every Jew; it has reached every level of their society, and every rung of their company, even to the group which considers itself to be the prophylactic for the truth and the propagation of the message, confrontation with the useless, and reform of the perverted.

These are the Jews throughout their history: all their groups and individuals, rushing into negating unbelief and sinful hostility.

The Jews are an example for their lackeys to emulate in this insane desire to rush in, and so these flunky lackeys come to the Jews, hurrying to them and to their friends with aid and offers of alliance, as per Qur'an 2:52: "You see those in whose hearts is sickness hurrying to them, saying, 'We fear a disaster will strike us.'"

This verse indicates that the reason the lackeys rush to make friends with the Jews and make alliances with them is the sick perversion that entered their hearts and expelled faith, self-respect, virtue, and power from them. Rushing in to befriend the Jews settled in their hearts, and did their emulation of their useless rushing into unbelief and aggressive sin. We observe this in our own time in the Jews' obsequious lackeys, and we see it in their personalities and in their deeds.

The Jews Conceal True Evidence

The Jews are the people of a previous book in which God told them about Muhammad's message and informed them of his prophethood. He commanded them to believe in Muhammad, and made firm covenants with them, and God made them witnesses to the truth of Muhammad's prophethood and his message. He demanded that they bear witness to this among the unbelievers and the polytheists so that their testimony would

be convincing for them, and that they would thus accept Islam.

But what did the Jews do when Muhammad the son of `Abdallah appeared? Did they bear the witness that God had demanded of them? And how did they deal with this?

The cursed Jewish Satan had awakened in them, and spread within them the vilest satanic character traits, which colored their view of the new prophet, and their attitude toward the new religion.

They were the first to disbelieve in him. They declared war on him and confronted him with hostility from the first day of his mission. They denied their prophets' foretelling of Muhammad's coming and concealed the good news about him that is in the Torah. They concealed the evidence that he is the emissary of God despite their certain knowledge that he was in fact the emissary of God. When the polytheists demanded evidence from them concerning Muhammad's mission, they denied that he was the emissary of God; nay! they went even further in their perverted view in claiming that the polytheists were closer to God than the Muslims, more rightly guided than the Muslims, and that God loved them more than he loved the Muslims!!

. . . Some verses record the concealment the Jews attempted, for example:

Qur'an 2:140, Or do ye say that Abraham, Isma'il Isaac, Jacob and the Tribes were Jews or Christians? Say: Do ye know better than God? Ah! who is more unjust than those who conceal the testimony they have from God? but God is not unmindful of what ye do!

2:42, Confound not truth with falsehood, nor knowingly conceal the truth.

2:146, The People of the Book know this as they know their own sons; but some of them conceal the truth which they themselves know.

3:187, And (remember) when Allah laid a charge on those who had received the Scripture (He said): Ye are to expound it to mankind and not to hide it. But they flung it behind their backs and bought thereby a little gain. Verily evil is that which they have gained thereby.

The Jews Do Corruption in the Earth

The Jews do corruption in the earth, in all the earth. This is one of the most prominent marks of theirs throughout all of their history, early, middle, and contemporary. They are the people who are most avid for corruption, they overtake all other people in doing corruption, and they serve as the archetype for those who would imitate them in this.

Doing corruption in the earth is connected with the Jews since their first days with their prophet Moses. The Jew Korach was a member of the Jews in Moses' time, and he did corruption in the earth by using the wealth and knowledge God had bestowed upon him for corruption. The upright people advised him correctly not to create corruption, but he refused to take their advice: Qur'an, surat al-Qasas [narrative], 28:76–78:

> When [Korach] his own folk said unto him: Exult not; lo! Allah loveth not the exultant. But seek the abode of the Hereafter in that which Allah hath given thee and neglect not thy portion of the world, and be thou kind even as Allah hath been kind to thee, and seek not corruption in the earth; lo! Allah loveth not corrupters, He said: I have been given it only on account of knowledge I possess. Knew he not that Allah had destroyed already of the generations before him men who were mightier than him in strength and greater in respect of following? The guilty are not questioned of their sins.

Moses was aware from his experience with the Children of Israel and his expertise concerning them, that corruption and the longing for it were inveterate in the Jewish heart, so he continually warned them about it.

When he gave his people water by striking the rock with his stick and there flowed out twelve springs, each tribe knew that one of them was exclusively for them to drink from. Moses commanded them to eat and drink, but not to create corruption, telling them, Qur'an 2:60: "Eat and drink of God's sustenance, but do not go about the earth spreading corruption."

When Moses faced the Mount in expectation of God's salvation, he put his brother Aaron [aka Raul] in his place as the Children of Israel's leader. He warned Aaron of the Children of Israel's corruption and their inclination toward it, and invited him to observe it. Moses warned him not to follow the corrupters, saying to him, Qur'an, surat al-Aa´raaf, 7:142: "Follow in my place and do well, and do not follow the way of the corrupters."

Qur'an 17:4 mentions the trait of corruption in the Jews, and their zealousness for it: "We judged that the Children of Israel will create corruption in the earth twice, and will thus be exceedingly haughty."

These two instances serve as models, and are not meant to be limited in time. All of Jewish history is corruption and corrupting others: murder, destruction, and devastation. The first model is their corruption in Medina and its environs at the time of the Prophet, when he and his companions decided to let the Jews be, despite their corruption. The second example is the Jews' corruption in the Holy Land at this time, as everyone knows of their corruption [in Palestine]; anyone with two eyes can see it. This second model is mentioned at Qur'an [5:64]: "Each time they light the fire of war God extinguishes it. They go about the earth creating corruption. God does not like the corrupters."

This verse could serve as the title for their entire history, for it implies their corruption in all its aspects and facets.

The Jews have a profound love for corruption, as they lustfully pant after causing wars to realize this corruption. They also have a zealous desire to scheme for, and an evil passion after, planning and inflaming wars, and for the preparation of their non-Jewish fodder. All this we infer from the expression "each time that," which implies continual repetitiveness of desire, and the continual renewal of striving for pernicious plotting and igniting the spark of war. They are the ones who go about the earth, but they do not go about the earth to reform it, to build it, to purify it, or to cleanse it because they do not even know the meanings of these terms. Thus they go about the earth doing destructive corruption and demolition.

God (i.e., Qur'an) is correct: Most of the wars in the world, and especially this present world war, were planned out by the Jews, started by the Jews, and ignited by the Jews in order to spread their corruption in the earth. They realize their goals when they annihilate all of humanity.

Jews ignite the spark of war, and the igniter does not get burned—he only provides the fuel. God is correct: The Jews do not lose any victims in these wars. The only victims come from naive people, and the fuel consists of them, their resources, wealth, and existence.

The Jews Obstruct God's Path

The Jews have abandoned God's straight path and have preferred Satan's way; they want to be his [Satan's] soldiers, men, and friends. They then committed an even more heinous crime when they became warring enemies against God's way, destroying its sign-posts in fleeing from them, and calling on people to abandon it. They became obstructions on the path of God, and they use whatever they own to fortify this stumbling block.

Qur'an 3:98–99:

> Say: "O People of the Book! Why reject ye the Signs of God, when God is Himself witness to all ye do?" Say: "O ye People of the Book! Why obstruct ye those who believe, from the path of God, Seeking to make it crooked, while ye were yourselves witnesses (to God's Covenant)?" but God is not unmindful of all that ye do.

These two verses record the two steps that are inextricably linked, for first the Jews disbelieved in God's verses (signs); then, second, they went on to the next step in obstructing the path of God, and turning the Muslims away from it, this being one of the results of perverted unbelief.

Concerning the phrase "you turn them aside": this is a clear indication of the Jews' desire to twist God's path, and their disbelieving souls' passion for carrying this out. Their twisting them—and "twisted" is a recognizable trait—this is what they are about: perverted obstruction. For "you turn them aside" is in the accusative case for simultaneous action.

This obstruction of God's path is not limited to one tribe of Jews, but it applies to all of them, even to their rabbis and monks [*sic*—mistake *ruhbaan*, monks, for *rabbaaniyyuun*, Rabans(??)]. Qur'an 9:34: "O you who believe! Many of the rabbis [*sic*] and the monks consume the people's wealth unjustly and obstruct the way of God."

The main concern of the rabbis is to bolster the truth, not to vitiate it, and to call for straightness, not crookedness, and in leading others to the path of God, not to obstruct them from it, but they are Jewish rabbis. And this is a Jewish trait.

The Jews expended everything they had to combat Islam, in full knowledge that it is the only path to God. They still expend everything they own to obstruct it, and to make war on its men and its call—and they still go on fighting. They failed to realize their satanic goals in the past, and, with God's permission, they will fail in the future.

The Jews Are a "Combination of Defects"

We have displayed above a number of despicable Jewish traits, and we have demonstrated that they are inveterate and deeply rooted in the complex Jewish consciousness, and that they have instigated themselves deep in the debased Jewish personality. We have also shown that this has been the situation throughout all of Jewish history in general, and it is embodied in the Jews of today. The noble Qur'an is the sole source on which we have relied, and from which we have recorded these Jewish traits, and what we have written about them is sufficient.

We have extracted from Qur'an twenty Jewish traits. The Jews are: liars, perverters (of the text), envious, tricky, fickle, mercurial, sardonic, treacherous, in error, causing others to be in error, merchants, fools, humiliated, dastards, misers, avid for (this) life, disloyal to their firm contracts, rush into sinful aggression, concealers of true evidence, corrupters in the earth, and obstructors in God's path.

One might be surprised to see the Jewish personality described with all of these traits, and he might be even more surprised to note that the Jews have inherited all of these defects from their ancestors, and they are most pleased with this bequest. It is as if their genes never leave their lives.

Making note of these Jewish defilements is an indication of what we reported above, that is the Jewish personality is a "combination of defects," a "collection of perfidies," and a "catalogue of iniquitous perversities." One may ask himself what virtue or goodness could remain in the Jewish consciousness, or, rather, what human significance or noble sentiment could remain in the midst of this turgid heap of diseased debauchery. And perhaps one might come upon a wandering Jew: pure evil, absolute hatred, dangerous plague, cursed Satan, and an enemy to everything human in the life of humankind.

The only Jews to be excluded from this are the prophets of the Children of Israel whom God chose and nurtured. Like the others, these prophets, are part of a "combination of virtues," a "collection of goodnesses," and practical examples of good right guidance.

Thus also must be excluded the Children of Israel's virtuous people, who sincerely followed their prophets with seriousness, truth, and faithfulness, and who followed the truth which Muhammad brought, and who became his men and his soldiers.

The Jews Are Cursed

It is impossible that the Jews could not be cursed. How could they not be accursed when they are attributed with such degenerate inveterate character traits, twenty of which we have demonstrated above? They are worthy of eternal curse because of the villainous traits they display and the corrupt evils they have perpetrated.

"*Al-la`na*," "curse," according to the Imam *al.Raaghib*, means "long exile onto the path of anger, and in the Afterlife it refers to God's punishment, in this life, exclusion from receiving God's mercy and success; from other men, it refers to their claims." And *al-lu`na* refers to one who is to be greatly cursed. And *al-lu`ana* refers to one who curses a great deal.

The Jews are in a condition of *mal`ana*, that is, everyone pours out curses on them; God has cursed them, the angels have cursed them, their prophets have cursed them, the good people among them have cursed them, and everyone has cursed them.

They are deserving of this eternal and continual damnation until the Day of Resurrection when they will encounter God's wrath, fury, and punishment. They were accordingly exiled from God's mercy, and kept afar from his goodness.

Many Qur'an verses were revealed emphasizing this Rabbaani law [*sic*] on the Jews, and the judgment upon them of cursed damnation, and exile from his mercy, for example, Qur'an 5:13: For breaking their covenant, We curse them, and have made their hearts hard. And Qur'an 5:60:

Say: "Shall I point out to you something much worse than this, (as judged) by the treatment it received from God? those who incurred the curse of God and his wrath, those of whom some he transformed into apes and swine, those who worshiped evil;—these are (many times) worse in rank, and far more astray from the straight/even path!"

And Qur'an 5:64: The Jews say: "God's hand is tied up." Be their hands tied up and be they accursed for the (blasphemy) they utter. Nay, both His hands are widely outstretched.

And Qur'an 5:78: Those of the Children of Israel who are cursed by David and Jesus, the son of Maryam, because of what they disobeyed and what they transgressed. And Qur'an 2:78–79:

And there are among them illiterates, who know not the Book, but (see therein their own) desires, and they do nothing but conjecture. Then woe to those who write the Book with their own hands, and then say: "This is from God," to traffic with it for miserable price!—Woe to them for what their hands do write, and for the gain they make thereby.

And Qur'an 3:78: The recompense of these is that they have God's, the angels', and all of mankind's curse on them. And Qur'an 4:46–52:

Of the Jews there are those who displace words from their (right) places, and say: "We hear and we disobey"; and "Hear what is not heard"; and "*Ra'ina*"; with a twist of their tongues and a slander to faith. If only they had said: "What hear and we obey"; and "Do hear"; and "Do look at us"; it would have been better for them, and more proper; but God hath cursed them for their unbelief; and but few of them will believe. O ye People of the Book! believe in what we have (now) revealed, confirming what was (already) with you, before we change the face and fame of some (of you) beyond all recognition, and turn them hind wards, or curse them as we cursed the Sabbath-breakers, for the decision of God must be carried out. God forgiveth not that partners should be set up with him; but he forgiveth anything else, to whom he pleaseth; to set up partners with God is to devise a sin most heinous indeed. Hast thou not turned thy vision to those who claim sanctity for themselves? Nay—but God doth sanctify whom he pleaseth. But never will they fail to receive justice in the least little thing. Behold! how they invent a lie against God! but that by itself is a manifest sin! Hast thou not turned thy vision to those who were given a portion of the Book? they believe in sorcery and evil, and say to the unbelievers that they are better guided in the (right) way Than the believers! They are (men) whom God hath cursed: And those whom God hath cursed, thou wilt find, have no one to help.

God's curse upon the Jews is firm and eternal. It has accompanied them throughout their history. This curse is repeated in all its facets in the Qur'an verses we have quoted twelve times. This is one of the clearest proofs that curses are always related to the accursed Jews. They indeed have changed it in their history to a *mal`ana* (state of being continuously damned), for they have disbelieved in God, and battled his emissaries and religion.

The Jews' Mission in the World: Devastating Corruption

Contemporary Jews try to deceive, nay! the Jews of every time period camouflage themselves to mankind and present themselves as people having a mission of goodness, that they are bringing goodness to mankind, and that they propagate it among them.

The Jews assume that they are the guardians of science, ethics, values, and civilization, and that they are civilization's avant garde, bearers, and propagators. They maintain that they established their state in Palestine in order to realize this goal, and to spread this mission.

They tell the other peoples that a Jewish state was now established to protect these principles, ideals, ethics, and values, and to maintain civilization, culture, progress, democracy, science, and knowledge.

Some poor simpletons believe these Jewish claims, and consider them to be the Jews' mission to the world.

Muslims with insight, however, know the Jewish nature, and they know well the true nature of the Jews' mission. The Muslims define their roles in making others understand this, so they take in hand the noble Qur'an to clearly explain this situation, and they are grateful to God for this bounty and excellence in unveiling their enemy's consciousness.

Now . . . we believe that the reader of this piece of research . . . after he has assimilated what we wrote above, will be aware of the true nature of the Jews' mission.

We have discussed the Jews' position toward their prophets, and their harming them. We have remarked on their hateful ancestors' beginnings, for instance, Joseph's brothers, and we have recorded the most prominent of their character taints. Then we discussed the Jewish claims, lies, and perversities which demonstrate the true nature of their characters and souls . . . .

. . . [A]nd it indicates their true mission in the world. Then we analyzed the Jewish belief in its inner workings, and we demonstrated that they have no faith, as it is evidenced by their description at Qur'an 5:68: "(The Jews) do not have a leg to stand on." We then discussed at length the Jewish consciousness and had more Qur'anic support, with its own wonderfully applicable analysis which lays out the perversity which emanated from the Jewish consciousness, and clarifies for us the abject execrableness inherent in this, the Jewish consciousness. This makes it reasonable that we label it a "combination of depravities." Qur'an records for us the most important of the Jewish character taints which becomes apparent in every Jew in every time period.

Thus we can now recognize the truth of the Jews' mission for the world.

What can the Jews possibly contribute to the world when their ethical view of values and principles is as described above? What could they possibly give the world when they have neither religion nor faith? When they are without belief and without imagination [*sic*]? They have only unbelief, false claims, lies, evasions, and corruptions (of texts)? Without morals, nobility, goodness, or righteousness?

What could the Jew give the world when he feels only black hatred and lascivious envy? They invest this hatred and envy in combating morals, principles, and values, and they spread corrupt and debased evil.

The title/address of the Jews' message can be found at Qur'an 5:64: "Each time they light the fire of war, God extinguishes it. They go about in the world creating corruption."

Wars and corruption, destruction and dissolution—this is the true Jewish mission in today's world, and the amazing deception they ply upon others.

The Jews constitute a mortal danger that threatens the world; a virulent plague that demolishes it and puts paid to it; a despising Satan who plots against it. The Jews' mission is hatred and envy, prevarication and evasion, unbelief and error, destruction, lustful pleasures, and indecency. And what relationship does this satanic mission have to that of the believer, which is right guiding, pious, and virtuous, beneficial for him and for all mankind?!

God's Punishments against the Jews

It is only natural that the results of their actions, and the fruits of their investments, will be applied to the Jews. This is God's Sunna: there is no action without recompense.

The execrable moral deficiencies attributed to the Jews make them deserving of God's punishment, and the satanic deeds they have perpetrated make them into a people deserving of God's wrath and his vengeance. He will recompense them for their evil deeds.

Qur'an give[s] a number of examples of the Jews being punished by God. This is for their recalcitrance and transgression.

In the main, Qur'an mentions the reason behind the Jews' punishment by employing the "*baa´* of reason or cause" which explains the purpose of the punishment, and it clarifies the wisdom in its befalling them.

For example, Qur'an 4:155–61:

fa-bi-maa, In that they broke their covenant; that they rejected the signs of God; that they slew the Apostle in defiance of right; that they said, "Our hearts are the wrappings (which preserve God's Word; We need no more)";—Nay, God hath set the seal on their hearts for their blasphemy, and little is it they believe; that they rejected faith; that they uttered against Mary a grave false charge; that they said (in boast), "We killed Christ Jesus the son of Mary, the Apostle of God";—but they killed him not, nor crucified him, but so it was made to appear to them, and those who differ therein are full of doubts, with no (certain) knowledge, but only conjecture to follow, for of a surety they killed him not:—Nay, God raised him up unto himself; and God is Exalted in Power, Wise;—And there is none of the People of the Book but must believe in him before his death; and on the Day of Judgment he will be a witness against them;—For the iniquity of the Jews we made unlawful for them certain (foods) good and wholesome which had been lawful for them;—in that they hindered many from God's Way;—That they took usury, though they were forbidden; and that they devoured men's substance wrongfully;—we have prepared for those among them who reject faith a grievous punishment.

This section records a number of the Jews' crimes for which they deserve God's anger and punishment. Out of eleven crimes noted, the "*baa´* of cause or reason" occurs four times.

The Jews Murder One Another

Qur'an records for us that the Jews deserved the first of God's punishments at the time of Moses. This is because God commanded them to fight, and to kill one another. Qur'an 2:54:

And when Moses said unto his people: O my people! Ye have wronged yourselves by your choosing of the calf (for worship) so turn in penitence to your Creator, and kill (the guilty) yourselves. That will be best for you with your Creator and He will relent toward you. Lo! He is the Relenting, the Merciful.

The Children of Israel worshiped—or, to be more exact, a group of them worshiped—the calf that "the Samaritan" made for them when Moses went away to speak directly to his Lord. Moses returned to his people only to find them worshiping the calf, so he incinerated the calf and pulverized it. He expelled the Samaritan and made him crawl on his face through the desert, until he had lost all his strength. Then Moses excoriated his people because of their crime and their disbelief in God.

A group of the Children of Israel regretted their actions and wanted to do penitence to God. God showed them the proper path of repentance, and commanded them to kill themselves. He commanded that the virtuous ones from among them, that is, those who had not worshiped the calf, would separate themselves from the rest of the group who had. God ordered the good ones to fight and kill the others.

They carried out the order, and there was a slaughter

within the Children of Israel. A group of them killed another, thereby doing penitence to God, as per Qur'an [2:54]:

> Repent to your creator and kill one another. This is better for you by your creator. He received penitence from you.

Some people find it strange that God would demand communal punishment in this way, but is is really not strange at all. For in worshiping the calf they committed a heinous and vicious crime, and this is at the basis of this punishment. They disbelieved in God and rebelled against his religion when they worshiped the calf. It is common knowledge that the apostate in Islam must repent or be executed for his unbelieving rebellion. Those who worshiped the calf were merely unbelieving apostate[s] who deserved death, for it is the appropriate comeuppance for this crime, and perhaps it is even one of the first punishments imposed by God.

The Judgment to Make the Jews Wander in the Wilderness

This is another communal punishment against the Jews for one or more of their sins. Their prophet Moses commanded them to enter the holy land, and promised them victory over its inhabitants. Their faith melted in their hearts, and their courage and manliness were lost in their humiliating cowardliness. Dastardliness, humiliation, fear, and terror came to the fore and made them reject any attempt to encourage them or to boost their morale in their souls. They expressed this orally, and announced that they were unprepared to participate in battle. They told Moses to go to war together with his Lord, Qur'an 5:24:

> They said, "O Moses! We will never enter it as long as it lasts, so you, together with your Lord, go fight! We will remain sitting (it out) here."

Facing this panty-waisted attitude of theirs, Moses found himself alone—that is, with his brother Aaron—and turned to his Lord with this prayer, Qur'an 5:25: "O my Lord! I have only myself and my brother. So separate us from the froward folk!" He prayed that God would separate him from this cowardly generation of Jews who did not want to live. His Lord answered him positively: God must do so with the prophets [sic], and God gave him inspiration, Qur'an 5:46: "They will be *muHarram* in exile for forty years, wandering in the earth.". . .

The Children of Israel wandered in the Sinai for forty years, this being God's judgment on them. That cowardly generation of Jews, born into and living in humiliating faintheartedness died out wandering in the desert. A new generation was born of them, a generation which lived on despite disaster and the hardships of life, a generation hardened by the desert's hardships. This was a generation born into the coarseness of life, an adversity that awakened their manliness, gravitas, endurance, courage, and ingenuity. This generation took refuge in God and were sincere to him. It flourished from the signs of *al-mujaahid*, the warrior, and Moses led this new generation to the Holy Land, and they conquered that country after Moses' death under the leadership of Joshua bin Nun, to whom God gave victory over his polytheistic, idol-worshiping enemies.

The Intensification of Judgments against the Jews

The Jews have a history replete with rebellions against God's judgments. Their record is overflowing with cases and examples where they tried to overturn God's judgments. They acquired for themselves corruption (of texts), forgery, and mercurialness. With these they do harm to themselves by exposing themselves to God's anger and his cursing them. They have suffered for their corruption (of texts), evil deeds, and chicanery. Thus God intensifies his judgments against them, and prohibits them from enjoying the permitted good things of this earth which had been allowed aforetime.

Qur'an records examples of intensified judgments which God made obligatory for them only as a punishment for their crimes, for example, Qur'an 4:160: "For the evil of the Jews' we have forbade them what was once permitted."

Qur'an 6:146 demonstrates some of the good things God forbade them: "We have forbidden for the Jews the hoofed . . . and the *al-Hawaayaa* [entrails], and the sciatica [bones]. We are right/true."

God forbade the hoofed animal, that is, every animal with an unsplit hoof. This is related to the toes, for example, the camel, stork, goose, and duck.

God forbade them the animal fat of cattle and flocks, but he excepted from this the fat they carry on their backs: "except for what they carry on their backs." He also excepted the fat on the *al-Hawaayaa* (organs), and the sciatica, which is fat connected to the bones.

What concerns us here is the intensified prohibitions, and their cause: "This is the recompense of their hatred," that is, these intensified judgments are purely punishment on them, in recompense for their hatred, evil, degeneracy, and trickery.

And so did the Jews accommodate God? Did they take to the straight path? Did they accept God's judgments? No!! They were raised on evil hatred, on hostility against God's judgments, and trickery and corruption of them.

God forbade them the fat, so they did not eat it directly, they consumed it in the iniquitous and scheming Jewish way: Al-Bukhari, Muslim, al-Nisaa'iyy, and Ibn Maja relate that the emissary of God said, "May God curse the Jews. Animal fat was made forbidden for them, so they sold it and consumed its profit." What is significant is that they consumed it, and consuming it is equivalent to consuming its profit. Everything forbidden to eat is forbidden as a source of profit or enjoyment. Thus it is prohibited to sell wine and pig meat because the imbibing of wine and the eating of pig meat are forbidden. When consuming fat is forbidden to the Jews so is making a profit from selling it. But the Jews wallow in disobedience to God's judgments.

The Jews' Heavy Burden

Qur'an informs [us] that God has put a heavy burden on the Jews, and demanded that they follow it faithfully and in detail. This burden is represented by the intensified laws God imposed on them, and by the good things God disallowed them.

The expression *"al-iSr,"* "the burden," occurs in Qur'an only three times, twice in discussion of the Jews, and the third time in the discussion of the covenant God made with the prophets of the Children of Israel concerning the belief in Muhammad as a prophet and as an emissary.

Qur'an 3:81:

And when Allah made a covenant through the prophets: Certainly what I have given you of Book and wisdom—then an apostle comes to you verifying that which is with you, you must believe in him, and you must aid him. He said: Do you affirm and accept my compact in this (matter)? They said: We do affirm. He said: Then bear witness, and I (too) am of the bearers of witness with you.

"Burden" refers here to "a firm contract—whoever breaks it has no reward or benefit."

The people who are burdened in this context are the followers of the aforesaid prophets, because the prophets believe a priori in Muhammad, but their followers might not believe in the seal of the prophets. The context in which this occurs is the discussion of the People of the Book, that is the Christians and the Jews, therefore *they* are the ones who are intended in the firm contract.

The other two verses deal with the Jews and the stricter laws which were imposed on them.

Qur'an 2:286:

God will not burden any soul beyond its power. It shall enjoy the good which it hath acquired, and shall bear the evil for the acquirement of which it labored. O our Lord! punish us not if we forget, or fall into sin; O our Lord! and lay not on us a load like that which thou hast laid on those who have been before us; O our Lord! and lay not on us that for which we have not strength: but blot out our sins and forgive us, and have pity on us. Thou art our protector: give us victory therefore over the infidel nations.

Until we recognize God's preference for, and mercy on, the Islamic *umma*, and the ease of the laws and legislation, and adherence of the companions to the obligatory duties of the religion, and their dedication to what the Qur'an's verses indicated to them, and their satisfaction with that which God required of them—we will live in the ambience of that verse.

. . . In his *SaHiiH*, Muslim relates another hadith. Qur'an: "God does not require a soul that it do more than it is able, it gets what it earns and receives what it deserves. O our Lord, do not hold us responsible for what we do in error or out of forgetfulness." God agreed. Qur'an: "O our Lord, do not put a burden we cannot bear on us, as You did to those who came before us." God agreed. Qur'an: "O our Lord, do not make us bear what is unbearable, and forgive us, and excuse us, have mercy on us. You are our Friend/Lord." God agreed.

"God agreed" means that he answered you positively, O you believers, and did not load you with a heavy burden as he did with those who came before you. You differ from the Jews and Christians: The Jews were tricky corrupters (of the text) and transgressing evildoers and they deserved to be loaded with a heavy burden and enormous load, but you do your duty and are content, so we will not put this heavy burden on you [and the Christians?]

The third and the final verse refer to the burden God laid on the Jews, which he would not relieve them of unless they believed in Muhammad, and accepted his religion, and followed his Shari`a: Qur'an 7:156–57:

He said: "With My punishment I visit whom I will; but My mercy extendeth to all things. That (mercy) I shall ordain for those who do right, and practice regular charity, and those who believe in Our signs;—Those who follow the apostle, the unlettered Prophet, whom they find mentioned in their own (scriptures),—in the law and the Gospel;—for he commands them what is just and forbids them what is evil; he allows them as lawful what is good (and pure) and prohibits them from what is bad (and impure); he releases them from their heavy burdens and from the yokes that are upon them. So it is those who believe in him, honor him, help him, and follow the light which is sent down with him,— it is they who will prosper.

What concerns us in this group of verses is their discussion of the mission of the emissary of God, and our concern with the people of the Book, that is, that he take off their burden and fetters from them—he wants to make it easy for them—and that his message abrogates some of the intensified laws concerning the good things forbidden to them.

And this is what really happened. Anyone who does a cursory comparison of some of these laws in the Torah and in Qur'an will come to the same conclusion.

In his commentary on this verse in his *Kashshaaf*, al-

Zamakhshari indicated this group of verses of intensified laws on the Jews, and which point out their heavy burden, saying,

"Burden" is the weight loaded upon its bearer, i.e., it impinges on his freedom of movement. Here it is used metaphorically to indicate its compulsory hardship. This is comparable to insisting they kill one another to prove the sincerity of their repentance; "the fetters" symbolize the hardships included in their laws, e.g. the imposition of the al-qaSaaS, blood money for murder regardless whether it be intentional or unintentional, without regard to the law of al-diya, wehrgeld [payment]; and amputating limbs that sin, and excoriating the site of impurity from the skin or the garment; incineration of cattle, burning the animals' veins, and the Sabbath restrictions.[5]

The heavy burden is God's punishment on the Jews. It is evidenced by the stringent laws which God held them to as comeuppance for their evil aggression and perverted hatred.

Despicable Aggression among the Jews

God instituted another punishment on the Jews, a grievously painful punishment: He transformed the relations of brotherhood and fellowship among them to envious hatred, and He replaced their harmonious brotherhood with despicable aggression.

God spread out perfidious hatred among them, so they would look at one another with this poisoned outlook. Qur'an 5:64:

The Jews say: "God's hand is tied up." Be their hands tied up and be they accursed for the (blasphemy) they utter. Nay, both his hands are widely outstretched: He giveth and spendeth (of His bounty) as he pleaseth. But the revelation that cometh to thee from God increaseth in most of them their obstinate rebellion and blasphemy. Among them we have placed enmity and hatred till the Day of Judgment.

This hateful hostility is the **al-qaa`ida**, basis which determines the relations between members of their society, and the attitude one takes toward another. This is in place of relations based on humane values; this is indeed a painful punishment. This is the price the Jews must pay for their lying about God, and their combating the truth he offered them by corrupting his texts and murdering his people. Jewish society is fragmented from within and can never regain the noble, human bond between individuals that once existed. The Jews have been transformed into quarrelling disputants and battling fragmenters.

This hateful aggression that God spread among them is not only for a limited, temporary time period, it is forever, and it maculates the Jews' history throughout. It is a general sign of their entire life through the epochs and centuries. Witness Qur'an 2:85: "We sent hateful aggression down on them until the Day of Resurrection." " . . . until the Day of Resurrection" is God's explicit judgment, his fixed ordained fate, and his true punishment.

This is emphasized at Qur'an, surat al-Hashr [59:]14:

They fight you only in bulwarked fortresses or from behind a wall. Execrable evil lurks among them and hinders them all as their hearts are divided. This is because they are a people who do not understand.

The Jews' Transformation into Monkeys and Pigs

This punishment was imposed only on the Jews. It is a remarkable situation unknown with any other nation or people, because it is a real transmogrification of the Jewish personality, and an absolute change in it from the human to the animal. This is an actual transformation from a human status to that of actual monkeys and pigs.

This punishment was imposed by God on the Jews who were "the people of the village," and "the people of the Sabbath" who used chicanery to change God's orders to allow themselves to do what God had forbidden; they transgressed the Sabbath, so God changed them into monkeys and pigs.

Qur'an 2:65–66:

You know those among you who transgressed the Sabbath, so We said to them, "Become losing monkeys." We make an example of them for what is before them, not what is after them; and an admonition to the pious.

Qur'an 5:60:

Say: "Shall I point out to you something much worse than this, (as judged) by the treatment it received from God? those who incurred the curse of God and his wrath, those of whom some he transformed into apes and swine, those who worshiped evil;—these are (many times) worse in rank, and far more astray from the straight/even path!"

These verses point out the stories of "the Jews of the Sabbath" and "the Jews of the village." Some of the verses in surat al-Aa`raaf [7], refer to these succinctly: Qur'an 7:163–66:

Ask them concerning the town standing close by the sea. Behold! they transgressed in the matter of the Sabbath. For on the day of their Sabbath their fish did come to them, openly holding up their heads, but on the day they had no Sabbath, they came not: thus did we make a trial of them, for they were given to transgression. When some of them said: "Why do ye preach to a people whom God will destroy or visit with a terrible punishment?"—said the preachers: "To discharge our duty to your Lord, and perchance they may fear him. When they disregarded the warnings that had been given them, We rescued those who forbade evil; but we visited the wrongdoers with a grievous punishment because they were given to transgression. When in their insolence they transgressed (all) prohibitions, we said to them: 'Be ye apes, despised and rejected.'"

This was a Jewish village on the shore—we do not want to delimit its name or location because this is one of the (intentionally) ambiguous Qur'an texts, whose details we can search for only within the Qur'an or in the sound hadith, so we will leave it at that. God ordered them not to fish on the Sabbath, but we are dealing with Jews here! They revolted in quarrelsome dissent to evade God's command! And to add to their temptation, the fish came out of the water of their own accord, in hordes, on that Sabbath when fishing was forbidden, as if they were a ship or a sail, and as if they were inviting the people to gather them up. The Jews' lust for them increased. On the other days of the week, the Jews looked for them in the water, and hardly found any.

Can transgressing Jews show patience in adversity? Can they hold out through days of incitement? They simply do not possess the personal qualities to qualify for this.

They used satanic tricks to evade God's command because the perverse Jewish mind is inspired to scheme: "God forbade us to fish on the Sabbath, so we will obey his command, and not fish on that day. The order does not (explicitly) prohibit us from digging a trench at the shoreline, and when the waves of the sea come up they will force the fish into the trench; the ancient whales, too, will fall into this trench on the Sabbath, and will be unable to return to the open sea. The following day, we will come and gather up the trapped whales in the trench, and we will still be obeying (the letter of) God's commands."

A remnant of virtuous people of the Children of Israel remained in this village, who disapproved of this plotting Jewish chicanery, and they warned and forbade the others; they repeatedly requested that they desist. They did this because they knew it was their obligation to God.

But the scheming transgressors were not to be deterred, and persisted in their transgression. God imposed his punishment on them, saying, "Be losing monkeys," and He transformed them into losing monkeys. They began making movements like monkeys. God saved the believers who forbade them to perpetrate this transgression and this villainous corruption.

It appears that these Jewish monkeys did not have descendants after them, and only lived for a short period after their transformation.

*Translated by Dr. Michael Schub. For further clarification of any references, see original essay.

NOTES

1. *Al-Mufradaat*, p. 114.
2. [Another folk/false etymology—ms.]
3. *Al-Mufradaat*, p. 443.
4. *Al-Mufradaat*, p. 234.
5. *Kashshaaf*, II, 122.

CHAPTER 33

Our War with the Jews Is in the Name of Islam

Yusuf Al-Qaradawi

Our war with the Jews is over land, brothers. We must understand this. If they had not plundered our land, there wouldn't be a war between us. . . .

We are fighting them in the name of Islam, because Islam commands us to fight whoever plunders our land, and occupies our country. All the school of Islamic jurisprudence—the Sunni, the Shi'ite, the Ibadhiya—and all the ancient and modern schools of jurisprudence—agree that any invader who occupies even an inch of land of the Muslims, must face resistance. The Muslims of that country must carry out the resistance, and the rest of the Muslims must help them. If the people of that country are incapable or reluctant, we must fight to defend the land of Islam, even if the local [Muslims] give it up.

They must not allow anyone to take a single piece of land away from Islam. That is what we are fighting the Jews for. We are fighting them. . . . Our religion commands us. . . . We are fighting in the name of religion, in the name of Islam, which makes this jihad an individual duty, in which the entire nation takes part, and whoever is killed in this [jihad] is a martyr. This is why I ruled that martyrdom operations are permitted, because he commits martyrdom for the sake of Allah, and sacrifices his soul for the sake of Allah. We do not disassociate Islam from the war. On the contrary, disassociating Islam from the war is the reason for our defeat. We are fighting in the name of Islam. [. . .]

They fight us with Judaism, so we should fight them with Islam. They fight us with the Torah, so we should fight them with the Qur'an. If they say "the Temple," we should say "the Al-Aqsa Mosque." If they say: "We glorify the Sabbath," we should say: "We glorify the Friday." This is how it should be. Religion must lead the war. This is the only way we can win. [. . .]

Everything will be on our side and against Jews on [Judgment Day], at that time, even the stones and the trees will speak, with or without words, and say: "Oh servant of Allah, oh Muslim, there's a Jew behind me, come and kill him."[1] They will point to the Jews. It says "servant of Allah," not "servant of desires," "servant of women," "servant of the bottle," "servant of Marxism," or "servant of liberalism." . . . It said "servant of Allah." When the Muslims, the Arabs, and the Palestinians enter a war, they do it to worship Allah. They enter it as Muslims. The hadith says: "Oh Muslim." It says "Oh Muslim," not "Oh Palestinian, Jordanian, Syrian, or Arab nationalist." No, it says: "Oh Muslim." When we enter [a war] under the banner of Islam, and under the banner of serving Allah, we will be victorious.

NOTE

1. Excerpt from the canonical hadith, Sahih Bukhari, vol. 4, bk. 52, no. 176.

Middle East Media Research Institute, "Sheik Yousef Al-Qaradhawi: Our War with the Jews Is in the Name of Islam," February 25, 2006, Clip #1052, from Qatar Television.

CHAPTER 34

The Jews of Today Bear Responsibility for Their Forefathers' Crime against Jesus

Yusuf Al-Qaradawi

In this film [*The Passion of the Christ*], there is an important positive aspect. The positive aspect lies in its exposing the Jews' crime of bringing Jesus to the crucifixion. Even though we [Muslims] believe that Jesus was not crucified,[1] a crime was committed, and the people who paved the way for this crime, who helped to commit it, who brought Jesus to the crucifixion, and kept pursuing the issue, until the governor on behalf of the Romans in Jerusalem at that time sentenced him to death.[2] . . .

[. . .] More than thirty years ago, the Vatican issued a document exonerating the Jews of [spilling] the blood of Jesus. Not all Christians accepted this document. The pope in the Vatican and the Catholics are the ones who exonerated them. They exonerated them under political pressure. But the Protestants did not exonerate them, the Orthodox did not exonerate them, and Patriarch Shinoda in Egypt did not exonerate them, and kept saying that they bear the responsibility. [. . .]

Do the Jews of yesterday bear responsibility for the crimes committed by the Jews of the past? The principle is that they indeed bear responsibility for these crimes, as long as they do not renounce them. If they glorify and take pride in what their forefathers did, if they write about it, quote it, record it, and teach it to their children, and if they consider it to be part of their religion and heritage, they bear the responsibility. As we can see, the Qur'an held the Jews of the Prophet Muhammad's time responsible for what their forefathers did. It addressed them, saying: "We made Moses a promise extending over forty nights, then you took the calf for worship, wrongfully." It says, "You took," but it was their forefathers, not them. But they adopt the deeds of their forefathers, and so they bear responsibility for them—unless they renounce them. [. . .]

They adopt the deeds of their forefathers, and they take pride in them. Therefore, I say that the Jews of the twenty-first century adopt what the Jews of the first century did. They adopt what [their forefathers] did to Jesus, and so they bear responsibility for it, unless they renounce it, saying: This was a crime, and we ask Allah to absolve us of it. But they have not said this, and therefore, the Jews of today bear responsibility for the deeds of the Jews of yesterday.

NOTES

1. Qur'an 4:157–58:

That they [i.e., the Jews] said in boast, "We killed Christ Jesus the son of Mary, the Messenger of Allah"; but they killed him not, nor crucified him, but so it was made to appear to them, and those who differ therein are full of doubts, with no (certain) knowledge, but only conjecture to follow, for of a surety they killed him not. . . . Nay, Allah raised him up unto himself; and Allah is Exalted in Power, Wise. . . .

2. Ibn Kathir (d. 1373), an important Muslim historian, theologian, and Qur'anic commentator, provides an elaboration of Qur'an 4:157–58, which emphasizes the Jews' overall perfidy, especially their gloating (but unknowingly "false") claim to have killed Jesus, when in fact they facilitated the murder of his body double, substituted by Allah:

When Allah sent Isa (Jesus) with proofs and guidance, the Jews—may Allah's curses, anger, torment, and punishment be upon them—envied him because of his prophethood and obvious miracles . . . the Jews defied him . . . and tried their best to harm him. . . . Allah made [a] young man look exactly like Isa (Jesus), while a hole opened in the roof of the house, and Isa (Jesus) was made to sleep

Middle East Media Research Institute, "Sheik Yousef Al-Qaradhawi: The Jews of Today Bear Responsibility for Their Forefathers' Crime against Jesus," August 26, 2006, Clip #1249, from Qatar Television.

and ascended to heaven while asleep. . . . When Isa (Jesus) ascended, those who were in the house came out. When those surrounding the house saw the man who looked like Isa (Jesus), they thought that he was Isa (Jesus). So they took him at night, crucified him and placed a crown of thorns on his head. The Jews boasted that they killed Isa (Jesus) and some Christians accepted their false claim due to their ignorance and lack of reason.

CHAPTER 35

The Jews' Twenty Bad Traits as Described in the Qur'an

Sheikh 'Atiyyah Saqr

On March 22, 2004, Sheikh 'Atiyyah Saqr, former head of the Al-Azhar Fatwa Committee who previously issued a fatwa declaring Jews "apes and pigs,"[1] was asked the following question in an online chat room: "What, according to the Qur'an, are the Jews' main characteristics and qualities?" The following was his answer.[2]

THE BAD TRAITS OF THE JEWS OUTWEIGH THEIR ONE GOOD TRAIT

Sheikh Saqr lists one positive trait of the Jews,[3] and then twenty bad traits: fabricating, listening to lies, disputing and quarreling, hiding the truth and supporting deception, rebelling against the prophets and rejecting their guidance, hypocrisy, wishing evil on people, feeling pain at others' happiness and feeling happiness at others' afflictions, rudeness and vulgarity, murder of innocents, mercilessness and heartlessness, breaking promises, cowardice, and miserliness.

In discussing these bad traits, Sheikh Saqr wrote,

We would like to note that these are but some of the most famous traits of the Jews as described in the Qur'an. They have revolted against the divine ordinances, distorted what has been revealed to them and invented new teachings which, they claimed, were much more better [*sic*] than what has been recorded in the Torah.

It was [because of] these traits that they were not warmly received in all the countries where they tried to reside. Instead, they were either driven out, or lived in isolation.

It was the Almighty Allah who placed on them His Wrath and [humiliated] them due to their transgression. Almighty Allah told us that He had sent to them those who would pour upon them rain of

severe punishment that would last till the Day of Resurrection.

All this gives us glad tidings of the coming victory of Muslims over [the Jews], as soon as Muslims cling to strong faith and belief in Allah and adopt modern means of technology.

Explaining the discrepancy between the Jews' bad and good traits, Saqr added:

The Qur'an [devoted] a considerable [number] of its verses to talking about Jews [and] their personal qualities and characteristics. The Qur'anic description of Jews is quite impartial, praising them in some occasions where they deserve praise and condemning them in other occasions where they practice blameworthy acts. Yet the latter occasions outnumbered the former, due to their bad qualities and the heinous acts they committed.

Saqr then lists the following twenty "bad traits" of the Jews, as they appear in the Qur'an:

They used to fabricate things and falsely ascribe them to Allah. Allah Almighty says: "That is because they say: We have no duty to the Gentiles. They knowingly speak a lie concerning Allah." (Al-'Imran: 75) Also: "The Jews say: Allah's hand is fettered. [But it is] their hands that are fettered and they are accursed for saying [Allah's hands are fettered]. Nay, but both His hands are spread out wide in bounty. He bestoweth as He will." (Al-Ma'idah: 64) In another verse, Almighty Allah says: "Verily, Allah heard the words of those who said, (when asked for contributions to the war): 'Allah, forsooth, is poor, and we are rich! We shall record their

---

"Former Al-Azhar Fatwa Committee Head Sets Out the Jews' 20 Bad Traits as Described in the Qur'an," April 6, 2004, Middle East Media Research Institute, February 27, 2004, Special Dispatch Series #691.

words with their wrongful slaying of the Prophets and we shall say: Taste ye the punishment of burning!'" (Al-'Imran: 181)

They love to listen to lies. Concerning this Allah says: "And of the Jews: listeners for the sake of falsehood, listeners on behalf of other folk." (Al-Ma'idah: 41)

Disobeying Almighty Allah and never observing His commands. Allah says: "And because they broke their covenant, We have cursed them and hardened their hearts." (Al-Ma'idah: 13)

Disputing and quarreling. This is clear in the verse that reads: "Their Prophet said unto them: Lo! Allah hath raised up Saul to be a king for you. They said: How can he have kingdom over us when we are more deserving of the kingdom than he is, since he hath not been given wealth enough?" (Al-Baqarah: 247)

Hiding the truth and supporting deception. This can be understood from the verse that reads: " . . . [They] distort the Scripture with their tongues, that ye may think that what they say is from the Scripture, when it is not from the Scripture." (Al-'Imran: 78)

Rebelling against the Prophets and rejecting their guidance. This is clear in the verse: "And when ye said: O Moses! We will not believe in thee till we see Allah plainly." (Al-Baqarah: 55)

Hypocrisy. In a verse, we read: "And when they fall in with those who believe, they say: We believe; but when they go apart to their devils they declare: Lo! we are with you; verily we did but mock." (Al-Baqarah: 14) In another verse, we read: "Enjoin ye righteousness upon mankind while ye yourselves forget (to practice it)? And ye are readers of the Scripture! Have ye then no sense?" (Al-Baqarah: 44)

Giving preference to their own interests over the rulings of religion and the dictates of truth. Allah says [to the Jews]: " . . . When there cometh unto you a messenger (from Allah) with that which ye yourselves desire not, ye grow arrogant, and some ye disbelieve and some ye slay?" (Al-Baqarah: 87)

Wishing evil for people and trying to mislead them. This is clear in the verse that reads: "Many of the People of the Book long to make you disbelievers after your belief, through envy on their own account, after the truth hath become manifest unto them." (Al-Baqarah: 109)

They feel pain to see others in happiness and are gleeful when others are afflicted with a calamity. This is clear in the verse that reads: "If a lucky chance befall you, it is evil unto them, and if disaster strike you they rejoice there at." (Al-'Imran: 120)

They are known for their arrogance and haughtiness. They claim to be the sons and of Allah and His beloved ones. Allah tells us about this in the verse that reads: "The Jews and Christians say: We are sons of Allah and His loved ones." (Al-Ma'idah: 18)

Utilitarianism and opportunism are among their innate traits. This is clear in the verse that reads: "And of their taking usury when they were forbidden it, and of their devouring people's wealth by false pretences." (An-Nisa': 161)

Their rudeness and vulgarity is beyond description. Referring to this, the Qur'anic verse reads: "Some of those who are Jews change words from their context and say: We hear and disobey; hear thou as one who heareth not, and Listen to us!, distorting with their tongues and slandering religion. If they had said: We hear and we obey; hear thou, and look at us, it had been better for them, and more upright. But Allah hath cursed them for their disbelief, so they believe not, save for a few." (An-Nisa': 46)

It is easy for them to slay people and kill innocents. Nothing in the world is dearer to their hearts than shedding blood and murdering human beings. They never give up this trait even with the Messengers and the Prophets. Allah says: " . . . And [they] slew the prophets wrongfully." (Al-Baqarah [2]: 61)

They are merciless and heartless. In this meaning, the Qur'anic verse explains: "Then, even after that, your hearts were hardened and became as rocks, or worse than rocks, for hardness." (Al-Baqarah: 74)

They never keep their promises or fulfill their words. Almighty Allah says: "Is it ever so that when ye make a covenant, a party of you violates it? The truth is, most of them believe not." (Al-Baqarah: 100)

They rush hurriedly to sin and compete in transgression. Allah says: "They restrained not one another from the wickedness they did. Verily, evil was what they used to do!" (Al-Ma'idah: 79)

Cowardice and love for this worldly life are undisputable traits [of the Jews]. It is to this that the Qur'an refers when saying: "Ye [Muslims] are more awful as fear in their [the Jews'] bosoms than Allah. That is because they are people who understand not. They will not fight against you in a group save in fortified villages or from behind walls. Their adversity among themselves is very great. Ye think of them as a whole whereas their hearts are diverse." (Al-Hashr: 13–14) Allah Almighty also says: "And thou wilt find them greediest of mankind for life and (greedier) than the idolaters." (Al-Baqarah: 96)

Miserliness runs deep in their hearts. Describing this, the Qur'an states: "Or have they even a share in the Sovereignty? Then in that case, they would not give mankind even the speck on a date stone." (An-Nisa': 53)

Distorting Divine Revelation and Allah's Sacred Books. Allah says in this regard: "Therefore woe be unto those who write the Scripture with their hands and say, 'This is from Allah,' that they may purchase a small gain therewith. Woe unto them for what their hands have written, and woe unto them for what they earn thereby." (Al-Baqarah: 79)

POSTSCRIPT

This exchange was posted on March 23, 2004, 8:00 AM GMT, at the popular Web site for Islamic education "Islam Online," http://www.islamonline.com/cgibin/news _service/fatwah_story.asp?service_id=449, shortly after the appearance of Sheikh Saqr's remarks:

Dear Sheikh! As-Salam `Alaykum. What, according to the Qur'an, are the main characteristics and qualities of Jews?

Answer:

In the Name of Allah, Most Gracious, Most Merciful. All thanks and praise are due to Allah and peace and blessings be upon His Messenger.

Dear questioner, we are really pleased to have your question and we pray to Allah to make our humble efforts, exerted solely for His Sake, come up to your expectation.

As regards the question you posed, the following is the fatwa issued by Sheikh 'Atiyyah Saqr, former Head of Al-Azhar Fatwa Committee, in which he states the following: [i.e., a mere unedited repetition of the contents recorded above].

NOTES

1. April 15, 2002.
2. IslamOnline.com, March 22, 2004.
3. According to Sheikh 'Atiyyah Saqr: "The Qur'an has specified a considerable deal of its verses to talking about Jews, their personal qualities and characteristics. The Qur'anic description of Jews is quite impartial; praising them in some occasions where they deserve praise and condemning them in other occasions where they practice blameworthy acts. Yet, the latter occasions outnumbered the former, due to their bad qualities and the heinous acts they used to commit. The Qur'an praises them on the verse that reads: 'And verily We gave the Children of Israel the Scripture and the Command and the Prophethood, and provided them with good things and favored them above (all) peoples.' (Al-Jathiyah: 16), i.e., the peoples of their time."

PART 7

The Jews of Arab Muslim Lands: Historical Maps

CHAPTER 36

Twelve Maps of the History of the Jews of the Islamic Near East

❖❖❖

Martin Gilbert

From Martin Gilbert, *The Jews of Arab Lands: Their History in Maps* (World Organization of Jews from Arab Countries, London: Board of Deputies of British Jews, 1976), maps 1, 2, 3, 4, 5, 6, 7, 8, 9, 10, 11, 12. Reprinted with permission.

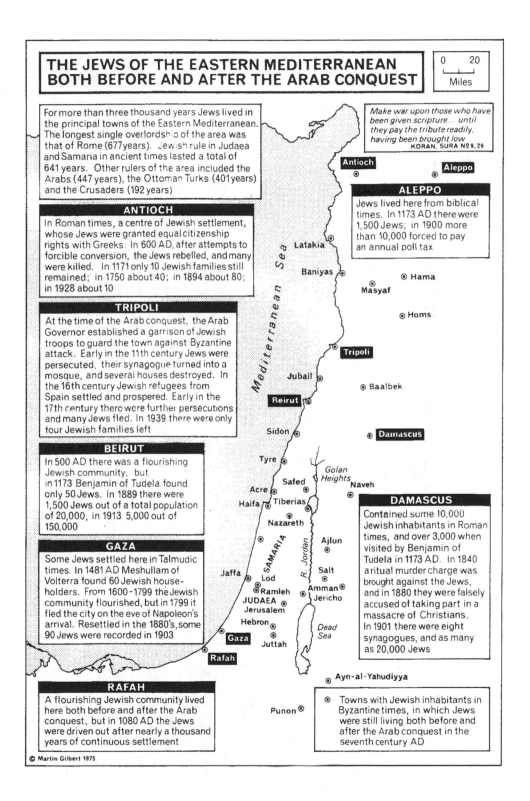

THE JEWS OF THE EASTERN MEDITERRANEAN BOTH BEFORE AND AFTER THE ARAB CONQUEST

0   20
Miles

For more than three thousand years Jews lived in the principal towns of the Eastern Mediterranean. The longest single overlordship of the area was that of Rome (677 years). Jewish rule in Judaea and Samaria in ancient times lasted a total of 641 years. Other rulers of the area included the Arabs (447 years), the Ottoman Turks (401 years) and the Crusaders (192 years)

Make war upon those who have been given scripture... until they pay the tribute readily, having been brought low
KORAN, SURA № 9, 29

ANTIOCH

In Roman times, a centre of Jewish settlement, whose Jews were granted equal citizenship rights with Greeks. In 600 AD, after attempts to forcible conversion, the Jews rebelled, and many were killed. In 1171 only 10 Jewish families still remained; in 1750 about 40; in 1894 about 80; in 1928 about 10

ALEPPO

Jews lived here from biblical times. In 1173 AD there were 1,500 Jews; in 1900 more than 10,000 forced to pay an annual poll tax

TRIPOLI

At the time of the Arab conquest, the Arab Governor established a garrison of Jewish troops to guard the town against Byzantine attack. Early in the 11th century Jews were persecuted, their synagogue turned into a mosque, and several houses destroyed. In the 16th century Jewish refugees from Spain settled and prospered. Early in the 17th century there were further persecutions and many Jews fled. In 1939 there were only four Jewish families left

BEIRUT

In 500 AD there was a flourishing Jewish community, but in 1173 Benjamin of Tudela found only 50 Jews. In 1889 there were 1,500 Jews out of a total population of 20,000, in 1913 5,000 out of 150,000

GAZA

Some Jews settled here in Talmudic times. In 1481 AD Meshullam of Volterra found 60 Jewish house-holders. From 1600-1799 the Jewish community flourished, but in 1799 it fled the city on the eve of Napoleon's arrival. Resettled in the 1880's, some 90 Jews were recorded in 1903

DAMASCUS

Contained some 10,000 Jewish inhabitants in Roman times, and over 3,000 when visited by Benjamin of Tudela in 1173 AD. In 1840 a ritual murder charge was brought against the Jews, and in 1880 they were falsely accused of taking part in a massacre of Christians. In 1901 there were eight synagogues, and as many as 20,000 Jews

RAFAH

A flourishing Jewish community lived here both before and after the Arab conquest, but in 1080 AD the Jews were driven out after nearly a thousand years of continuous settlement

⊚ Towns with Jewish inhabitants in Byzantine times, in which Jews were still living both before and after the Arab conquest in the seventh century AD

Mediterranean Sea

Antioch
Aleppo
Latakia
Baniyas
Masyaf
Hama
Homs
Tripoli
Jubail
Baalbek
Beirut
Sidon
Damascus
Tyre
Golan Heights
Safed
Naveh
Acre
Tiberias
Haifa
Nazareth
SAMARIA
Ajlun
R. Jordan
Salt
Jaffa
Lod
Ramleh
Amman
Jericho
JUDAEA
Jerusalem
Hebron
Dead Sea
Gaza
Juttah
Rafah
Ayn-al-Yahudiyya
Punon

© Martin Gilbert 1975

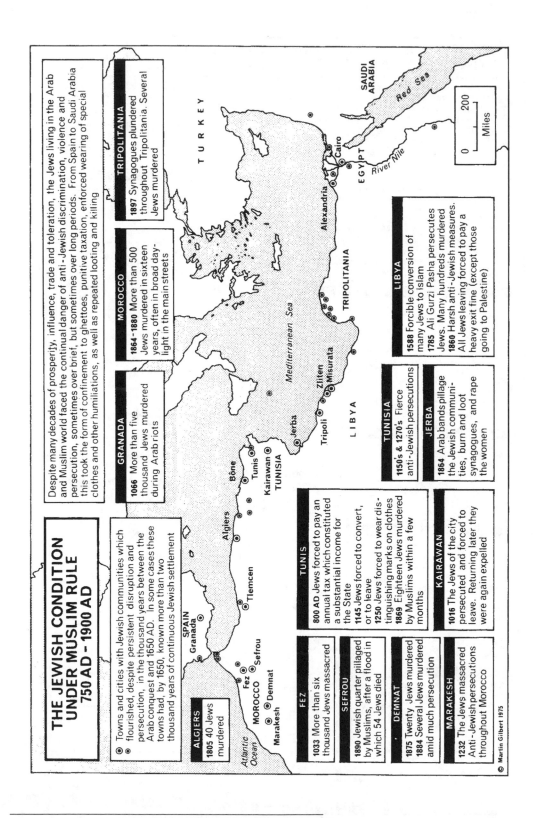

THE JEWISH CONDITION UNDER MUSLIM RULE 750 AD – 1900 AD

Despite many decades of prosperity, influence, trade and toleration, the Jews living in the Arab and Muslim world faced the continual danger of anti-Jewish discrimination, violence and persecution, sometimes over brief, but sometimes over long periods. From Spain to Saudi Arabia this took the form of confinement to ghettoes, punitive taxation, enforced wearing of special clothes and other humiliations, as well as repeated looting and killing

⊙   Towns and cities with Jewish communities which flourished, despite persistent disruption and persecution, in the thousand years between the Arab conquest and 1650 AD. In some cases these towns had, by 1650, known more than two thousand years of continuous Jewish settlement

ALGIERS
1805 40 Jews murdered

TRIPOLITANIA
1897 Synagogues plundered throughout Tripolitania. Several Jews murdered

MOROCCO
1864-1880 More than 500 Jews murdered in sixteen years, often in broad daylight in the main streets

GRANADA
1066 More than five thousand Jews murdered during Arab riots

LIBYA
1588 Forcible conversion of many Jews to Islam
1785 Ali Gurzi Pasha persecutes Jews. Many hundreds murdered
1860 Harsh anti-Jewish measures. All Jews leaving forced to pay a heavy exit fine (except those going to Palestine)

TUNISIA
1150's & 1270's Fierce anti-Jewish persecutions

JERBA
1864 Arab bands pillage the Jewish communities, burn and loot synagogues, and rape the women

TUNIS
800 AD Jews forced to pay an annual tax which constituted a substantial income for the State
1145 Jews forced to convert, or to leave
1250 Jews forced to wear distinguishing marks on clothes
1869 Eighteen Jews murdered by Muslims within a few months

KAIRAWAN
1016 The Jews of the city persecuted and forced to leave. Returning later they were again expelled

FEZ
1033 More than six thousand Jews massacred

SEFROU
1890 Jewish quarter pillaged by Muslims, after a flood in which 54 Jews died

DEMNAT
1875 Twenty Jews murdered
1884 Several Jews murdered amid much persecution

MARAKESH
1232 The Jews massacred throughout Morocco
Anti-Jewish persecutions throughout Morocco

TURKEY

SAUDI ARABIA

Red Sea

Cairo

EGYPT

River Nile

Alexandria

Mediterranean Sea

TRIPOLITANIA

Zliten
Misurata

Jerba

Tripoli

LIBYA

Bône

Tunis

Kairawan
TUNISIA

Algiers

Tlemcen

SPAIN
Granada

Sefrou
Fez
MOROCCO ⊙ Demnat

Marakesh

Atlantic
Ocean

0   200
Miles

© Martin Gilbert 1975

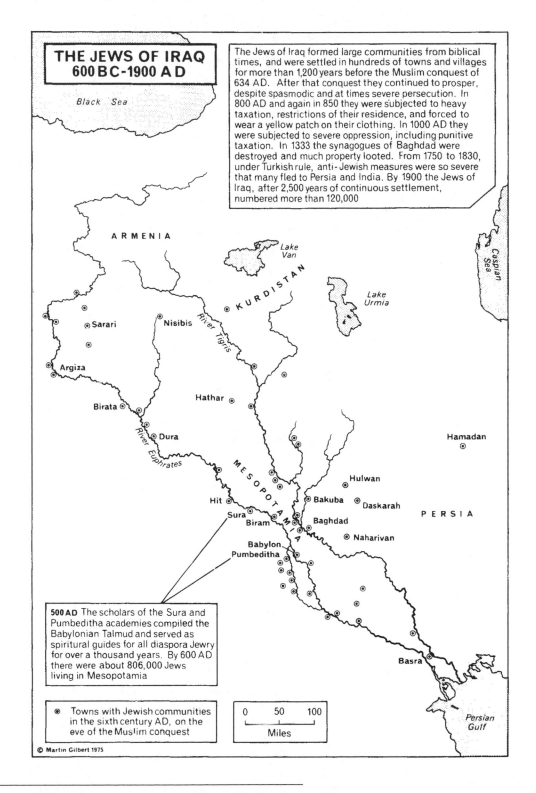

THE JEWS OF IRAQ
600 BC-1900 AD

Black Sea

The Jews of Iraq formed large communities from biblical times, and were settled in hundreds of towns and villages for more than 1,200 years before the Muslim conquest of 634 AD. After that conquest they continued to prosper, despite spasmodic and at times severe persecution. In 800 AD and again in 850 they were subjected to heavy taxation, restrictions of their residence, and forced to wear a yellow patch on their clothing. In 1000 AD they were subjected to severe oppression, including punitive taxation. In 1333 the synagogues of Baghdad were destroyed and much property looted. From 1750 to 1830, under Turkish rule, anti-Jewish measures were so severe that many fled to Persia and India. By 1900 the Jews of Iraq, after 2,500 years of continuous settlement, numbered more than 120,000

ARMENIA

Lake Van

K U R D I S T A N

Lake Urmia

Caspian Sea

Sarari

Nisibis

River Tigris

Argiza

Hathar

Birata

River Euphrates

Dura

M E S O P O T A M I A

Hamadan

Hulwan

Hit

Bakuba

Daskarah

Sura

Baghdad

P E R S I A

Biram

Babylon

Naharivan

Pumbeditha

500 AD The scholars of the Sura and Pumbeditha academies compiled the Babylonian Talmud and served as spiritual guides for all diaspora Jewry for over a thousand years. By 600 AD there were about 806,000 Jews living in Mesopotamia

Basra

⊚   Towns with Jewish communities in the sixth century AD, on the eve of the Muslim conquest

0   50   100

Miles

Persian Gulf

© Martin Gilbert 1975

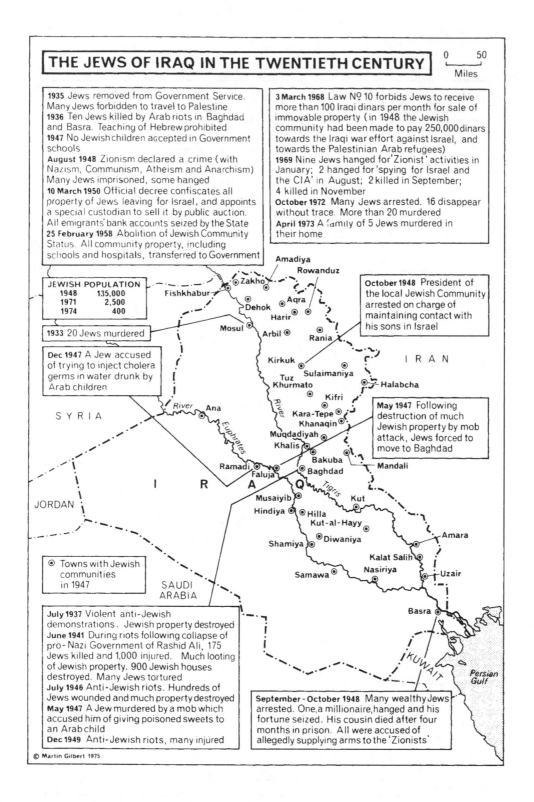

THE JEWS OF IRAQ IN THE TWENTIETH CENTURY

0   50
Miles

1935 Jews removed from Government Service.
Many Jews forbidden to travel to Palestine
1936 Ten Jews killed by Arab riots in Baghdad
and Basra. Teaching of Hebrew prohibited
1947 No Jewish children accepted in Government
schools
August 1948 Zionism declared a crime (with
Nazism, Communism, Atheism and Anarchism)
Many Jews imprisoned, some hanged
10 March 1950 Official decree confiscates all
property of Jews leaving for Israel, and appoints
a special custodian to sell it by public auction.
All emigrants' bank accounts seized by the State
25 February 1958 Abolition of Jewish Community
Status. All community property, including
schools and hospitals, transferred to Government

3 March 1968 Law N⁰ 10 forbids Jews to receive
more than 100 Iraqi dinars per month for sale of
immovable property (in 1948 the Jewish
community had been made to pay 250,000 dinars
towards the Iraqi war effort against Israel, and
towards the Palestinian Arab refugees)
1969 Nine Jews hanged for 'Zionist' activities in
January; 2 hanged for 'spying for Israel and
the CIA' in August; 2 killed in September;
4 killed in November
October 1972 Many Jews arrested. 16 disappear
without trace. More than 20 murdered
April 1973 A family of 5 Jews murdered in
their home

JEWISH POPULATION
1948	135,000
1971	2,500
1974	400

1933 20 Jews murdered

Dec 1947 A Jew accused
of trying to inject cholera
germs in water drunk by
Arab children

October 1948 President of
the local Jewish Community
arrested on charge of
maintaining contact with
his sons in Israel

May 1947 Following
destruction of much
Jewish property by mob
attack, Jews forced to
move to Baghdad

Amadiya
Rowanduz
Zakho
Fishkhabur
Aqra
Dehok
Harir
Mosul
Arbil
Rania
Kirkuk
Sulaimaniya
Tuz
Khurmato
Halabcha
Kifri
River   Ana
Kara-Tepe
Khanaqin
Muqdadiyah
Khalis
Bakuba
Ramadi
Faluja   Baghdad   Mandali
Musaiyib   Kut
Hindiya   Hilla
Kut-al-Hayy
Shamiya   Diwaniya   Amara
Samawa   Kalat Salih
Nasiriya   Uzair
Basra

SYRIA

Euphrates

IRAN

Tigris

JORDAN

I   R   A   Q

⊙ Towns with Jewish
communities
in 1947

SAUDI
ARABIA

KUWAIT

Persian
Gulf

July 1937 Violent anti-Jewish
demonstrations. Jewish property destroyed
June 1941 During riots following collapse of
pro-Nazi Government of Rashid Ali, 175
Jews killed and 1,000 injured. Much looting
of Jewish property. 900 Jewish houses
destroyed. Many Jews tortured
July 1946 Anti-Jewish riots. Hundreds of
Jews wounded and much property destroyed
May 1947 A Jew murdered by a mob which
accused him of giving poisoned sweets to
an Arab child
Dec 1949 Anti-Jewish riots, many injured

September - October 1948 Many wealthy Jews
arrested. One, a millionaire, hanged and his
fortune seized. His cousin died after four
months in prison. All were accused of
allegedly supplying arms to the 'Zionists'

© Martin Gilbert 1975

© Martin Gilbert, *The Routledge Atlas of Jewish History*/7th ed., ISBN 0415399653.

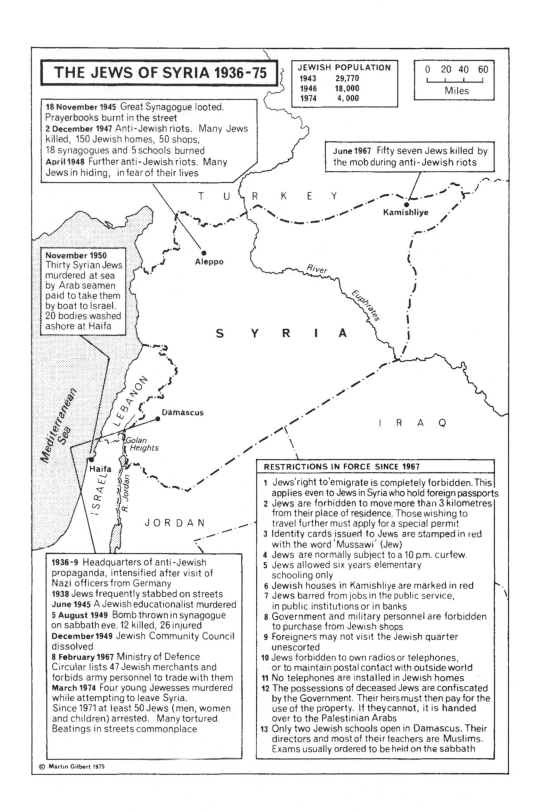

THE JEWS OF SYRIA 1936-75

JEWISH POPULATION	
1943	29,770
1946	18,000
1974	4,000

0 20 40 60
Miles

18 November 1945 Great Synagogue looted. Prayerbooks burnt in the street
2 December 1947 Anti-Jewish riots. Many Jews killed, 150 Jewish homes, 50 shops, 18 synagogues and 5 schools burned
April 1948 Further anti-Jewish riots. Many Jews in hiding, in fear of their lives

June 1967 Fifty seven Jews killed by the mob during anti-Jewish riots

T U R K E Y

Kamishliye

November 1950
Thirty Syrian Jews murdered at sea by Arab seamen paid to take them by boat to Israel. 20 bodies washed ashore at Haifa

Aleppo

River

Euphrates

S Y R I A

LEBANON

Damascus

Golan Heights

I R A Q

Mediterranean Sea

ISRAEL

R. Jordan

Haifa

JORDAN

RESTRICTIONS IN FORCE SINCE 1967

1 Jews'right to'emigrate is completely forbidden. This applies even to Jews in Syria who hold foreign passports
2 Jews are forbidden to move more than 3 kilometres from their place of residence. Those wishing to travel further must apply for a special permit
3 Identity cards issued to Jews are stamped in red with the word 'Mussawi' (Jew)
4 Jews are normally subject to a 10 p.m. curfew.
5 Jews allowed six years elementary schooling only
6 Jewish houses in Kamishliye are marked in red
7 Jews barred from jobs in the public service, in public institutions or in banks
8 Government and military personnel are forbidden to purchase from Jewish shops
9 Foreigners may not visit the Jewish quarter unescorted
10 Jews forbidden to own radios or telephones, or to maintain postal contact with outside world
11 No telephones are installed in Jewish homes
12 The possessions of deceased Jews are confiscated by the Government. Their heirs must then pay for the use of the property. If they cannot, it is handed over to the Palestinian Arabs
13 Only two Jewish schools open in Damascus. Their directors and most of their teachers are Muslims. Exams usually ordered to be held on the sabbath

1936-9 Headquarters of anti-Jewish propaganda, intensified after visit of Nazi officers from Germany
1938 Jews frequently stabbed on streets
June 1945 A Jewish educationalist murdered
5 August 1949 Bomb thrown in synagogue on sabbath eve. 12 killed, 26 injured
December 1949 Jewish Community Council dissolved
8 February 1967 Ministry of Defence Circular lists 47 Jewish merchants and forbids army personnel to trade with them
March 1974 Four young Jewesses murdered while attempting to leave Syria.
Since 1971 at least 50 Jews (men, women and children) arrested. Many tortured. Beatings in streets commonplace

© Martin Gilbert 1975

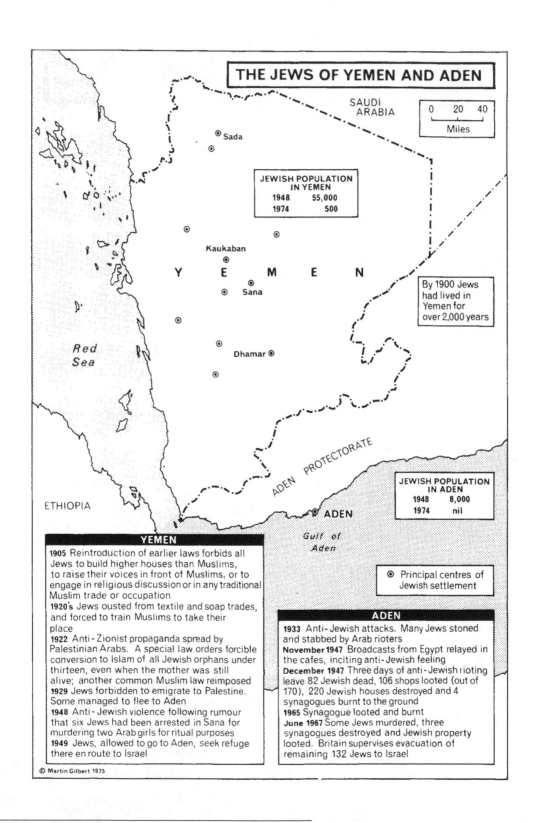

THE JEWS OF YEMEN AND ADEN

SAUDI ARABIA

0   20   40
Miles

⊚ Sada
⊚

JEWISH POPULATION IN YEMEN
1948   55,000
1974   500

Kaukaban
⊚

Y E M E N

⊚ Sana

By 1900 Jews had lived in Yemen for over 2,000 years

Red Sea

⊚ Dhamar ⊚

ADEN PROTECTORATE

ETHIOPIA

⊚ ADEN

JEWISH POPULATION IN ADEN
1948   8,000
1974   nil

Gulf of Aden

⊚ Principal centres of Jewish settlement

YEMEN
1905 Reintroduction of earlier laws forbids all Jews to build higher houses than Muslims, to raise their voices in front of Muslims, or to engage in religious discussion or in any traditional Muslim trade or occupation
1920's Jews ousted from textile and soap trades, and forced to train Muslims to take their place
1922 Anti-Zionist propaganda spread by Palestinian Arabs. A special law orders forcible conversion to Islam of all Jewish orphans under thirteen, even when the mother was still alive; another common Muslim law reimposed
1929 Jews forbidden to emigrate to Palestine. Some managed to flee to Aden
1948 Anti-Jewish violence following rumour that six Jews had been arrested in Sana for murdering two Arab girls for ritual purposes
1949 Jews, allowed to go to Aden, seek refuge there en route to Israel

ADEN
1933 Anti-Jewish attacks. Many Jews stoned and stabbed by Arab rioters
November 1947 Broadcasts from Egypt relayed in the cafes, inciting anti-Jewish feeling
December 1947 Three days of anti-Jewish rioting leave 82 Jewish dead, 106 shops looted (out of 170), 220 Jewish houses destroyed and 4 synagogues burnt to the ground
1965 Synagogue looted and burnt
June 1967 Some Jews murdered, three synagogues destroyed and Jewish property looted. Britain supervises evacuation of remaining 132 Jews to Israel

© Martin Gilbert 1975

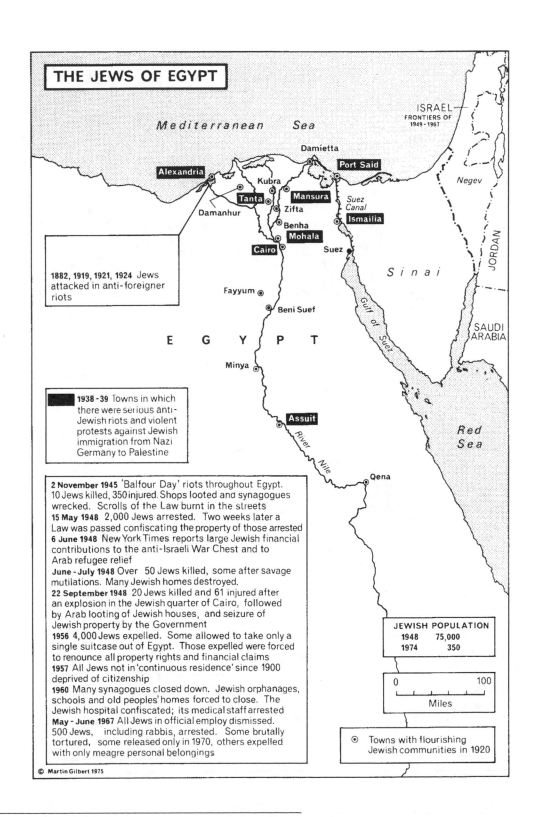

THE JEWS OF EGYPT

Mediterranean Sea

ISRAEL
FRONTIERS OF
1949-1967

Damietta

Alexandria

Port Said

Negev

Kubra

Tanta

Mansura

Suez Canal

Damanhur

Zifta

Ismailia

Benha

Mohala

Suez

Cairo

S i n a i

1882, 1919, 1921, 1924 Jews
attacked in anti-foreigner
riots

Fayyum

Gulf of Suez

JORDAN

Beni Suef

SAUDI
ARABIA

E   G   Y   P   T

Minya

1938-39 Towns in which
there were serious anti-
Jewish riots and violent
protests against Jewish
immigration from Nazi
Germany to Palestine

Assuit

*Red
Sea*

River Nile

Qena

2 November 1945 'Balfour Day' riots throughout Egypt.
10 Jews killed, 350 injured. Shops looted and synagogues
wrecked. Scrolls of the Law burnt in the streets
15 May 1948 2,000 Jews arrested. Two weeks later a
Law was passed confiscating the property of those arrested
6 June 1948 New York Times reports large Jewish financial
contributions to the anti-Israeli War Chest and to
Arab refugee relief
June - July 1948 Over 50 Jews killed, some after savage
mutilations. Many Jewish homes destroyed.
22 September 1948 20 Jews killed and 61 injured after
an explosion in the Jewish quarter of Cairo, followed
by Arab looting of Jewish houses, and seizure of
Jewish property by the Government
1956 4,000 Jews expelled. Some allowed to take only a
single suitcase out of Egypt. Those expelled were forced
to renounce all property rights and financial claims
1957 All Jews not in 'continuous residence' since 1900
deprived of citizenship
1960 Many synagogues closed down. Jewish orphanages,
schools and old peoples' homes forced to close. The
Jewish hospital confiscated; its medical staff arrested
May - June 1967 All Jews in official employ dismissed.
500 Jews, including rabbis, arrested. Some brutally
tortured, some released only in 1970, others expelled
with only meagre personal belongings

© Martin Gilbert 1975

JEWISH POPULATION	
1948	75,000
1974	350

0   100
Miles

⊙   Towns with flourishing
Jewish communities in 1920

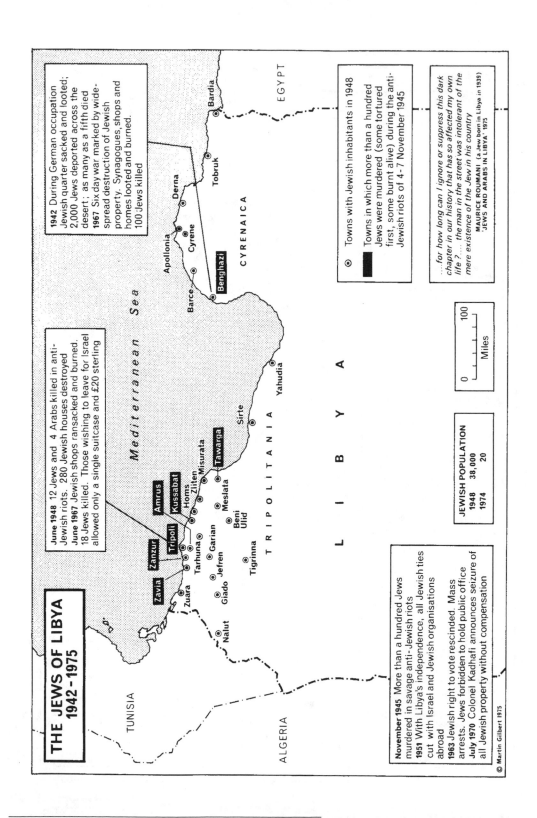

THE JEWS OF LIBYA
1942–1975

1942 During German occupation Jewish quarter sacked and looted; 2,000 Jews deported across the desert ; as many as a fifth died
1967 Six day war marked by widespread destruction of Jewish property. Synagogues, shops and homes looted and burned. 100 Jews killed

⊙ Towns with Jewish inhabitants in 1948

■ Towns in which more than a hundred Jews were murdered (some tortured first, some burnt alive) during the anti-Jewish riots of 4–7 November 1945

...for how long can I ignore or suppress this dark chapter in our history that has so affected my own life ?.... the man in the street was intolerant of the mere existence of the Jew in his country
MAURICE ROUMANI (a Jew born in Libya in 1939) 'JEWS AND ARABS IN LIBYA' 1975

June 1948 12 Jews and 4 Arabs killed in anti-Jewish riots. 280 Jewish houses destroyed
June 1967 Jewish shops ransacked and burned. 18 Jews killed. Those wishing to leave for Israel allowed only a single suitcase and £20 sterling

November 1945 More than a hundred Jews murdered in savage anti-Jewish riots
1951 With Libya's independence, all Jewish ties cut with Israel and Jewish organisations abroad
1963 Jewish right to vote rescinded. Mass arrests. Jews forbidden to hold public office
July 1970 Colonel Kadhafi announces seizure of all Jewish property without compensation

JEWISH POPULATION
1948 38,000
1974   20

© Martin Gilbert 1975

© Martin Gilbert, *The Routledge Atlas of Jewish History*/7th ed., ISBN 0415399653.

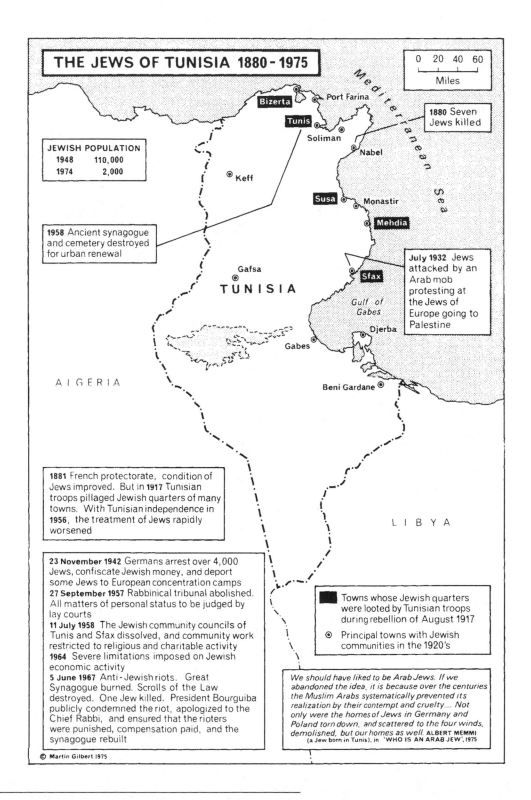

THE JEWS OF TUNISIA 1880-1975

0   20   40   60
Miles

1880 Seven Jews killed

Port Farina

Bizerta

Tunis

Soliman

Nabel

Mediterranean Sea

JEWISH POPULATION
1948   110,000
1974   2,000

Keff

Susa

Monastir

Mehdia

1958 Ancient synagogue and cemetery destroyed for urban renewal

Gafsa

TUNISIA

Sfax

Gulf of Gabes

July 1932 Jews attacked by an Arab mob protesting at the Jews of Europe going to Palestine

Djerba

Gabes

ALGERIA

Beni Gardane

LIBYA

1881 French protectorate, condition of Jews improved. But in **1917** Tunisian troops pillaged Jewish quarters of many towns. With Tunisian independence in **1956**, the treatment of Jews rapidly worsened

23 November 1942 Germans arrest over 4,000 Jews, confiscate Jewish money, and deport some Jews to European concentration camps
27 September 1957 Rabbinical tribunal abolished. All matters of personal status to be judged by lay courts
11 July 1958 The Jewish community councils of Tunis and Sfax dissolved, and community work restricted to religious and charitable activity
1964 Severe limitations imposed on Jewish economic activity
5 June 1967 Anti-Jewish riots. Great Synagogue burned. Scrolls of the Law destroyed. One Jew killed. President Bourguiba publicly condemned the riot, apologized to the Chief Rabbi, and ensured that the rioters were punished, compensation paid, and the synagogue rebuilt

■ Towns whose Jewish quarters were looted by Tunisian troops during rebellion of August 1917
◉ Principal towns with Jewish communities in the 1920's

We should have liked to be Arab Jews. If we abandoned the idea, it is because over the centuries the Muslim Arabs systematically prevented its realization by their contempt and cruelty.... Not only were the homes of Jews in Germany and Poland torn down, and scattered to the four winds, demolished, but our homes as well. ALBERT MEMMI (a Jew born in Tunis), in 'WHO IS AN ARAB JEW', 1975

© Martin Gilbert 1975

© Martin Gilbert, *The Routledge Atlas of Jewish History*/7th ed., ISBN 0415399653.

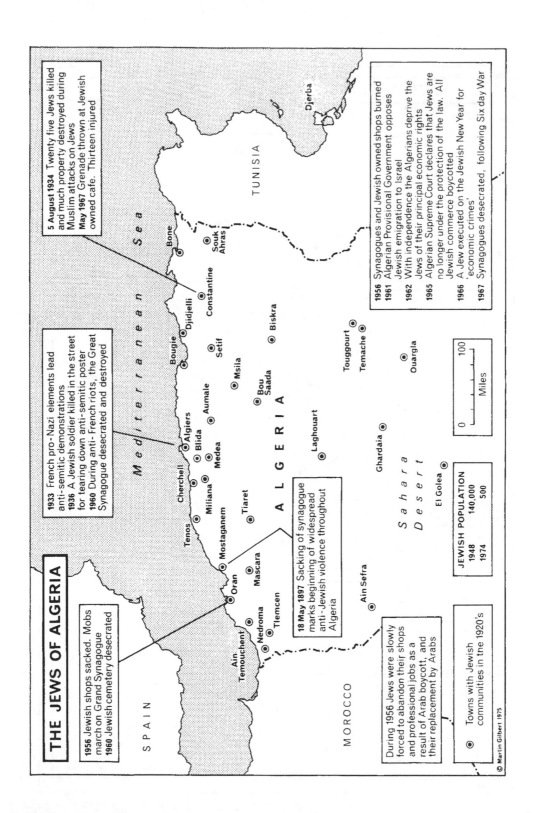

THE JEWS OF ALGERIA

1956 Jewish shops sacked. Mobs march on Grand Synagogue
1960 Jewish cemetery desecrated

1933 French pro-Nazi elements lead anti-semitic demonstrations
1936 A Jewish soldier killed in the street for tearing down anti-semitic poster
1960 During anti-French riots, the Great Synagogue desecrated and destroyed

5 August 1934 Twenty five Jews killed and much property destroyed during Muslim attacks on Jews
May 1967 Grenade thrown at Jewish owned cafe. Thirteen injured

1956 Synagogues and Jewish owned shops burned
1961 Algerian Provisional Government opposes Jewish emigration to Israel
1962 With independence the Algerians deprive the Jews of their principal economic rights
1965 Algerian Supreme Court declares that Jews are no longer under the protection of the law. All Jewish commerce boycotted
1966 A Jew executed on the Jewish New Year for 'economic crimes'
1967 Synagogues desecrated, following Six day War

18 May 1897 Sacking of synagogue marks beginning of widespread anti-Jewish violence throughout Algeria

During 1956 Jews were slowly forced to abandon their shops and professional jobs as a result of Arab boycott, and their replacement by Arabs

JEWISH POPULATION	
1948	140,000
1974	500

⊙ Towns with Jewish communities in the 1920's

0   100
Miles

TUNISIA

Djerba

Bone

Souk Ahras

Constantine

Djidjelli

Bougie

Setif

Biskra

Touggourt
Temache ⊙

Msila

Aumale

Bou Saada

Algiers
Blida
Medea

Ouargla

ALGERIA

Cherchell
Miliana
Tiaret

Laghouart

Ghardaia

Tenos
Mostaganem

Sahara Desert

El Golea

Mascara

Oran

Ain Sefra

Nedroma
Tlemcen

Ain Temouchent

MOROCCO

S P A I N

M e d i t e r r a n e a n   S e a

© Martin Gilbert 1975

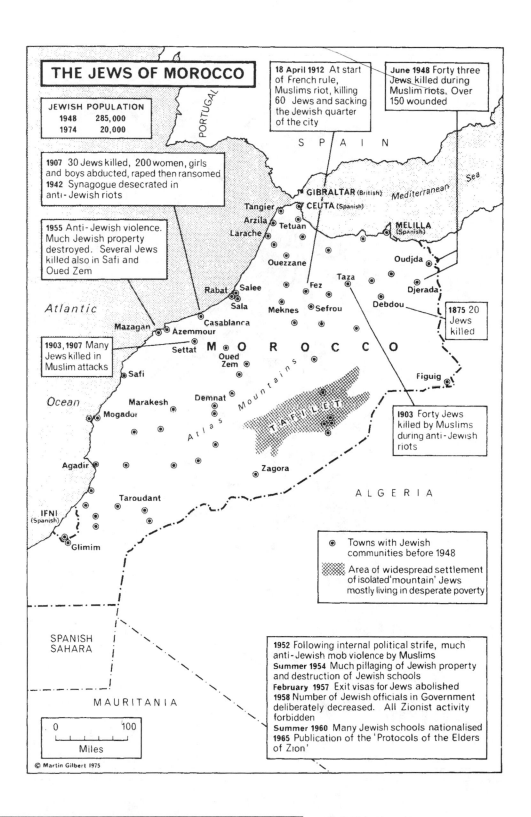

THE JEWS OF MOROCCO

JEWISH POPULATION
1948   285,000
1974   20,000

1907 30 Jews killed, 200 women, girls and boys abducted, raped then ransomed
1942 Synagogue desecrated in anti-Jewish riots

1955 Anti-Jewish violence. Much Jewish property destroyed. Several Jews killed also in Safi and Oued Zem

1903, 1907 Many Jews killed in Muslim attacks

18 April 1912 At start of French rule, Muslims riot, killing 60 Jews and sacking the Jewish quarter of the city

June 1948 Forty three Jews killed during Muslim riots. Over 150 wounded

1875 20 Jews killed

1903 Forty Jews killed by Muslims during anti-Jewish riots

PORTUGAL

S P A I N

Mediterranean Sea

GIBRALTAR (British)
CEUTA (Spanish)
Tangier
Arzila
Tetuan
Larache
MELILLA (Spanish)

Ouezzane
Oudjda
Taza
Djerada
Fez
Debdou

Atlantic

Rabat   Salee
Sala
Casablanca
Mazagan   Azemmour
Settat
Oued Zem
Meknes   Sefrou

M   O   R   O   C   C   O

Ocean

Safi

Marakesh   Demnat

Atlas   Mountains

TAFILELT

Figuig

Mogador

Agadir

Zagora

ALGERIA

Taroudant

IFNI
(Spanish)

Glimim

● Towns with Jewish communities before 1948

▨ Area of widespread settlement of isolated 'mountain' Jews mostly living in desperate poverty

SPANISH
SAHARA

1952 Following internal political strife, much anti-Jewish mob violence by Muslims
Summer 1954 Much pillaging of Jewish property and destruction of Jewish schools
February 1957 Exit visas for Jews abolished
1958 Number of Jewish officials in Government deliberately decreased. All Zionist activity forbidden
Summer 1960 Many Jewish schools nationalised
1965 Publication of the 'Protocols of the Elders of Zion'

MAURITANIA

0   100
Miles

© Martin Gilbert 1975

© Martin Gilbert, *The Routledge Atlas of Jewish History*/7th ed., ISBN 0415399653.

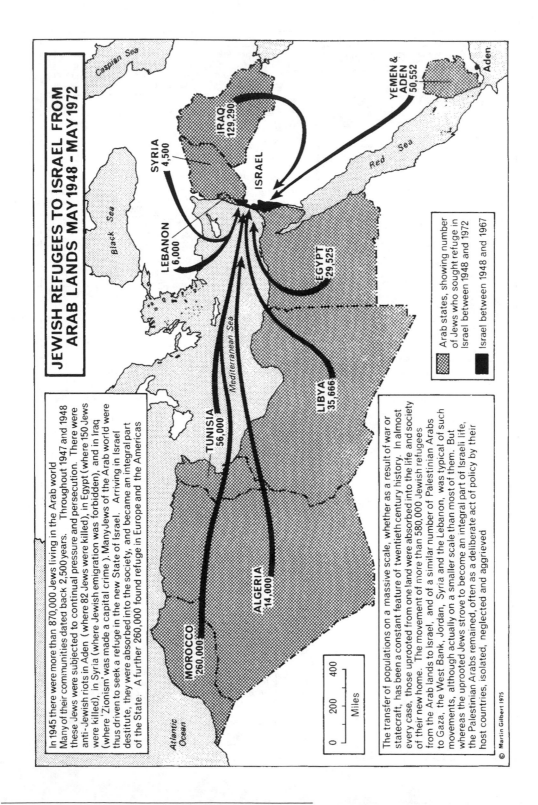

JEWISH REFUGEES TO ISRAEL FROM
ARAB LANDS MAY 1948 – MAY 1972

Caspian Sea

Black Sea

Mediterranean Sea

Atlantic Ocean

Red Sea

Aden

YEMEN & ADEN
50,552

IRAQ
129,290

SYRIA
4,500

ISRAEL

LEBANON
6,000

EGYPT
29,525

LIBYA
35,666

TUNISIA
56,000

ALGERIA
14,000

MOROCCO
260,000

Arab states, showing number
of Jews who sought refuge in
Israel between 1948 and 1972

Israel between 1948 and 1967

0   200   400
Miles

In 1945 there were more than 870,000 Jews living in the Arab world
Many of their communities dated back 2,500 years.   Throughout 1947 and 1948
these Jews were subjected to continual pressure and persecution.   There were
anti-Jewish riots in Aden (where 82 Jews were killed), in Egypt (where 150 Jews
were killed), in Syria (where Jewish emigration was forbidden), and in Iraq
(where 'Zionism' was made a capital crime). Many Jews of the Arab world were
thus driven to seek a refuge in the new State of Israel.   Arriving in Israel
destitute, they were absorbed into the society, and became an integral part
of the State.   A further 260,000 found refuge in Europe and the Americas

The transfer of populations on a massive scale, whether as a result of war or
statecraft, has been a constant feature of twentieth-century history.   In almost
every case, those uprooted from one land were absorbed into the life and society
of their new home.   The movement of more than 580,000 Jewish refugees
from the Arab lands to Israel, and of a similar number of Palestinian Arabs
to Gaza, the West Bank, Jordan, Syria and the Lebanon, was typical of such
movements, although actually on a smaller scale than most of them.   But
whereas the uprooted Jews strove to become an integral part of Israeli life,
the Palestinian Arabs remained, often as a deliberate act of policy by their
host countries, isolated, neglected and aggrieved

© Martin Gilbert 1975

PART 8

The Dhimmi Condition for Jews, and Muslim Jew Hatred: Early Islam through the Modern Era

CHAPTER 37

Evidence on the Muslim Poll Tax from Non-Muslim Sources: A Geniza Study

Shlomo Dov Goitein

There is no subject of Islamic social history on which the present writer had to modify his views so radically while passing from literary to documentary sources, i.e., from the study of Muslim books to that of the records of the Cairo Geniza as the jizya or *jāliya*, the poll tax to be paid by non-Muslims. It was, of course, evident that the tax represented a discrimination and was intended, according to the Qur'an's own words, to emphasize the inferior status of the nonbelievers. It seemed, however, that from the economic point of view, it did not constitute a heavy imposition, since it was on a sliding scale, approximately of one, two, and four dinars, and thus adjusted to the financial capacity of the taxpayer.[1]

This impression proved to be entirely fallacious, for it did not take into consideration the immense extent of poverty and privation experienced by the masses, and in particular their way of living from hand to mouth, their persistent lack of cash, which turned the "season of the tax" into one of horror, dread, and misery. The provisions of ancient Islamic law which exempted the indigent, the invalids, and the old, were no longer observed in the Geniza period and had been discarded by the Shāfi'ī School of Law, which prevailed in Egypt, also in theory. It is precisely persons of such descriptions about whose plight we read so much in our records. The payment of the poll tax constituted item number one in the budget of families with modest income, such as teachers or laborers. For a man could clothe inexpensively, he could eat at starvation level, as perhaps a very large section of the population did. But he could not escape the tax gatherer—at least not for long. If he was caught, he was beaten and suffered otherwise corporal punishment, *'nqūba*, and was thrown into prison, where, because of starvation and maltreatment, he faced death.

A few passages picked out at random from a mass of pertinent Geniza letters may serve as an initial illustration. A schoolmaster from Qalyūb, a small town north of Cairo, who also earned some money copying books, makes, around 1225, the following complaint to a relative in the capital: "This place does not provide me with the poll tax or clothing, and, as to food, the fees suffice only for me alone. For they amount only to five dirhams a week and I need three quarters of a dirham a day at least. Thus my income is not enough even for having a robe laundered. . . . The Nagid promised me a year ago that he would take care of the *jāliya*. But the year has passed and I have not received anything from him. I am now perplexed and pondering where to turn and where to flee." He sends four books copied by himself, hoping, somewhat faintly, that the proceeds would resolve his predicament.[2]

An old, half-blinded refugee from Ceuta, Morocco, asks, in a letter written with his own hand (as he emphasizes), a countryman for a few pounds of flour in order to keep body and soul together, but this only after other friends had helped him with the poll tax. Before becoming disabled by the failing of his eyesight, he had worked as a silversmith, but his beautiful handwriting, his good Arabic and Hebrew style, and his copious Bible quotations show him also as a man of learning.[3]

The writer of the following letter, too, must have seen better days, for he speaks to the addresses, a personality of high standing, almost as an equal. After only a few introductory phrases, he continues:

My present state is marked by illness, infirmity, want and excessive fear, since I am sought by the controller of revenue, who is hard upon me and writes out warrants of arrest, sending "runners" to track me down. I am afraid they will find out my hiding place. If I fall into their hands, I shall die under their chastisement or will have to go to prison and die there. Now I take my refuge with God and with you—may God save you from all misery—please ask Shams al-Dīn (the director of revenue in the capital, cf. p. 293) to write a letter to al-Mahalla that they should register us as *absent*, for every one says: your only salvation is to be registered as absent. Furthermore, if God ordains that some money will come together for my *jāliya*, it should

Shlomo Dov Goitein, "Evidence on the Muslim Poll Tax from Non-Muslim Sources: A Geniza Study," *Journal of the Economic and Social History of the Orient (JESHO)* 6 (1963): 278–95.

be said that it is for *the fugitives (al-hāribīn)*, for it is not myself alone, but my sons as well, for whom I am held responsible.[4]

The last sentence shows that, in a previous letter, the addressee had been asked to arrange a collection for securing the writer's *jāliya*. This was indeed an extremely common occurrence. As an example, we translate here the main part of an autograph letter by Moses Maimonides, written by the master with particular care: "Kindly assist the bearer of this letter, Isaac of Der'a (a town in Morocco), for he is an acquaintance of mine. Ask the *Hāvēr* (the local spiritual leader) to make the community care for him, so that he will get the money for his poll tax in your place. He has to pay two *jāliyas*, one for himself and one for his son. If possible, enable him to pay the tax in your town, Minyat Zifta. For he is a newcomer and thus far has not paid anywhere. He is now on his way to Damietta on an errand important for me. On his way back, action should be taken for him according to your means."[5] The letter implies that the foreigner was not yet registered anywhere and recommends that he should become listed as a permanent resident neither in the capital, nor in the city of Damietta, but in the provincial town Minyat Zifta, where the rates of the tax presumably were lower or where the collectors were less rigorous.

Trying now to define in detail who was bound to pay the poll tax, or for whom it had to be paid, the illustrative passages quoted above are sufficient to prove that poverty, old age, and illness did not provide any excuse for exemption. A person was regarded as taxable long before he was capable of making a livelihood. In a settlement between a husband and wife, dated 1244, the latter undertakes to provide full board for their elder son, to let him learn the craft of silversmithery and to pay his poll tax for two years.[6] From a query submitted to Abraham Maimonides we learn that the guardians of an orphaned minor had to pay the *jāliya* for full ten years, before the latter was declared by a Jewish court a major and competent to take care of his property. In a letter addressed to Moses Maimonides, a person is accused of having neglected his duties as pater familias, since he had never paid the poll tax and school fees (in this sequence!) for his two boys, one of whom was seventeen and the other thirteen at the time of the complaint.[7] From a document written around 1095 it appears that the *jāliya* was due from the age of nine.[8]

Whether death cancelled arrears in poll tax due was a moot point between the Muslim doctors of law. In the Geniza period it went without saying that it had to be borne by the legal heirs. Therefore we find provisions for the payment of such debts in deathbed declarations. Particularly moving is one made on a Sabbath (when no financial arrangements are allowed), which happened to be the day before the person concerned died and in which a provision is made for a payment of two dinars

due for the *jāliya* (dated 1142).[9] A responsum of Maimonides shows that even in the case of a very poor widow no exemption was made from this rule.[10]

The members of a family were held responsible for each other's poll tax. A silk weaver fled from Old Cairo and went as far south as Aswan (now famous for its dam), since bearing such a burden for his father and three brothers was too much for him. We learn this from a letter of one of the brothers assuring him that all members of the family had paid—not without the father having spent one night in prison—and that he could now safely return.[11] Cases of persons who had to account for a brother or for sons have been quoted before. The same applied to brothers-in-law.[12] The poll tax was due also on travelers to non-Muslim countries to be paid for them back home. We learn about a merchant who sojourned in India nine years and finally died there that his brothers had fulfilled this duty for the whole period—a fact mentioned in the document concerned as in no way anything extraordinary.[13] In a letter from Alexandria, a brother out in India is politely reminded to send something for his *jāliya*, since his father was spending money for this purpose all the time.[14] At his arrival in Alexandria after an absence of four years of which he had been kept back in Constantinople by illness for two and a half years and had suffered also shipwreck, a merchant asks his relatives in Old Cairo to tell the tax collector about his misfortunes with a request to register him as a newcomer (in order to save four years' tax): "Promise him half a dinar or a dinar and remind him that I am Joseph who had his store beneath the Mu'allaqa church."[15]

Persons traveling within the realm of Islam, and indeed anyone leaving his domicile even for a short period, had to carry with him a *barā'a*, or acquittance showing that he had absolved himself for the current year. When in a smaller locality the tax gatherer had not arrived in time, no one could set out on a journey, since it was dangerous to do so without a *barā'a*.[16] A scholar from Ascalon, Palestine, writing a letter of recommendation for a colleague from Damascus who traveled to Egypt emphasizes that the latter was in possession of a certificate issued by the poll tax office (and not merely by an individual tax gatherer). Even so he asks the addressee to see to it that the Egyptian authorities should not "interpret" the certificate in a way which would enable them to squeeze an additional amount from his friend.[17] It was common occurrence that Nile boats were not allowed to depart or even were turned back by the police because one of the passengers was unable to produce his *jāliya* receipt.[18]

Since everyone paid where he was registered as resident, one would expect that a traveler would not be held to contribute to the *jāliya* of the locality where he sojourned temporarily. However, the Geniza shows that the tax collectors found ways to have also foreigners pay under one pretext or another. The letter regarding the scholar from Damascus just mentioned, as well as the stories of the merchants from Sicily and Tunisia sketched in *Mediterranean Society*, ch. V B I (e), are cases in point. Even while setting out from one town of Egypt to another, a traveler would provide himself with a letter of recommendation to an influential personality asking him for protection against overreaching tax collectors.

However, it was not only the government officials and tax farmers whose rapacity was dreaded. The leaders of the local denominational communities, who had a say in the assessment, also contributed to the plight of the "newcomers." The following passage from a letter of a Tunisian merchant writing from Alexandria is very instructive in this respect:

I wish to tell you what happened to me with regard to the poll tax since your departure from here. There are many in this city who have arrived prior to myself, but were not treated the way I experienced. Every day they molest me and summon me to the court, asking me to pay the *jāliya* in full. They want to register me as a resident, whereas my father, as you know, was only a "newcomer." What they impose on me, is remitted to others, who do not allow themselves to be molested—you know whom I mean. The benefit which I derived from your intervention for me is that I have to pay this year almost two dinars. I would not have minded, if others had been treated in the same way. The tax gatherers (*busbsbār*, the "ralliers") and the director of the *jāliya* are not to be blamed; all this is entirely the work of the Jews.

The role of the local communities in the collection of the poll tax will be discussed presently.[19]

When did a person cease to be a newcomer, *tārī'*, and obtain the status of a permanent resident, *qātin*? Owing to the astonishing mobility of the Mediterranean middle class of those days, this question caused much headache both to the administration and to the persons affected. As we have already seen in the example of the Egyptian merchant who was immobilized by illness in Constantinople, much depended on the goodwill of the individual official (and the amount of the bribe offered to him). In general, however, it appears from the Geniza records, it was not easy to change one's status. An eleventh-century Tunisian merchant and scholar, who, after having lived for years in Egypt, later on spent some time in Byzantium and finally settled in the Holy Land, writes the following: "I intend to pass the winter in Jerusalem, for I have learned about the (bad) Nile (which meant famine for Egypt whereto the writer was expected to travel). Furthermore, I am registered in the revenue office, *kharāj*, of Old Cairo as resident. Originally they registered me as a newcomer, but when my stay in the country extended, I became a *qātin*. By now, I have been away from Egypt for ten years and this is my eleventh." Since the writer wished to pay the poll tax incumbent on

a resident where he actually lived, namely, in Palestine, he preferred not to return to Egypt, where he still was registered as such.[20]

Because of the great number of Syro-Palestinians living all over Egypt, a special office was created for them in the capital, where they had to appear every year in person for the payment of their *jāliya*. This was perhaps an Ayyubid innovation. No direct reference to the "Syro-Palestinian *jāliya*" has been found thus far in the Geniza with regard to the Fatimid period.[21]

Were there any exemptions from the duty to pay the poll tax? The ancient idea that those who dedicate themselves to the service of God should be free from the service of men, was realized in the Jewish community by the latter bearing the burden of the tax for its scholarly officials. This was an internal arrangement. The Muslim authorities had nothing to do with it. There are, however, two reports in the Geniza, from the eleventh and the twelfth centuries respectively, claiming that certain Jews in Bagdad were granted exemption from the poll tax. In one it is stated that they should not publicize this special favor; in the other, that the beneficiaries themselves declined to accept it, because the tax protected their life and property (as is indeed the official Muslim theory). Those reports are semilegendary and although they may contain a grain of truth, lack the details which would make them significant.[22]

A few cases of exemption from the poll tax occur in Geniza letters related to Egypt. A distinguished traveler from France acknowledges gratefully his having been freed from the *dhimmiyya*, a term he explained by the Hebrew word for capitation, as well as other impositions by a special rescript of the viceroy (al-Malik al-Afdal).[23] A man who had lost his riches and served as a minor community official earning one and a quarter dirhams a day ("which is really not a salary") informs the Nagid Samuel (1140–1159) of his intention to settle definitely in a village near Minyat Zifta belonging to one Nāsir ed-Dīn, whose inhabitants did not pay the *jāliya*.[24] Another destitute person writes that he had been offered a government post in Alexandria, "where he would not be held for the poll tax."[25] Whatever this expression may mean, the two last cases do not represent a real exemption, but rather payment rendered in the form of a service, which, to be sure, was salvation for persons without cash.

As to the amounts of the poll tax, the Geniza proves that the data given by the Muslim handbooks of administration, although hardly reflecting the realities in full, are basically correct. Ibn Mammātī (a Christian convert to Islam, d. 1209) notes as highest yearly rate four and one-sixth dinars. This is exactly the sum paid by a physician according to a document dated 1182.[26] As lowest grade he gives "one plus one-third and one-fourth dinars and two habbas," i.e., one and five-eighths dinars. We find this amount in the Geniza repeatedly for Saladin's time, but also 120 years earlier, when a Tunisian merchant in Old Cairo paid the poll tax for a Jewish packer who worked in the flax growing center of Busīr, but most probably, as a foreigner, had to deliver his *jāliya* in the capital.[27] According to the "Scroll" of the Norman proselyte Obadiah, in Bagdad, around 1110 the three classes of non-Muslims paid one and a half, two and a half, and one-half dinars, respectively.[28]

In practice, however, adjustments were made to these rates in conformity with local conditions. The following passage from a letter, written in Alexandria in May 1141, is instructive in this respect: "Rayhān (a freedman or slave of the caliph or the vizier) promised the Jews and the Christians to obtain for them a properly ratified rescript vouching that the rates of the jizya would remain as they are at present and that no one would have the right to ask them for more. The rates should be the same as those fixed by the cadi al-Makīn (the well-known judge of Alexandria who died in 1134).[29] Approximately at the same time there were complaints about gross misuse and embezzlement of the proceeds of the poll tax in that city. In a later letter the same writer alludes to both, namely, the attempt to raise the rates and the malpractices at its collection, when he says: "It was X (an influential personality in Old Cairo) who saved the Jews from the jizya and the ways of its collection."[30]

It seems to the present writer that such adjustments represented not only increases in the rates (as when the caliph al-Hākim doubled the poll tax for some time),[31] but occasionally also alleviations made with regard to the poverty of the affected population. A large section of the Jewish community of Alexandria consisted of people with low income; this is proved by the Geniza for three centuries. It may well be that the cadi al-Makīn reduced the rates to some extent. When we find that both foreigners and persons native in Egypt registered for the *jāliya* not in the cities where they lived, but in smaller towns, we may safely assume that this practice was advantageous, most probably because of lower rates. Unfortunately, it is not possible for the time being to answer this question with the aid of the many details about actual payments given in the Geniza records. For these amounts may either include fines for arrears, or, on the contrary, represent only installments.

A few examples may be sufficient to illustrate this complex situation. A local Egyptian Jew, registered in a small town, who was momentarily out of cash, asks for a load of two dinars for the payment of the current year's *jāliya*. As security he provides three books: a compendium of medicine, valued at fifty silver dirhams; the Maqāmāt of Harīrī (a famous work of Arabic belles-lettres), worth thirteen dirhams; and a book of rabbinical law, whose price is not indicated. He promises to return the loan in a month's time. The three books combined betray the writer as an educated medical practitioner, who would be expected to pay the rate for medium income at least, which is officially two and one-twelfth dinars. Thus we could assume that the amount of two dinars mentioned in the letter represents

a reduced rate. However, the writer remarks also that most of the year had already passed, which means that he had to pay arrears. Consequently, either the rate for medium income in that little town was considerably below two dinars, or the physician paid the *jāliya* for the poor, which is, however, unlikely. There exists a third possibility. Perhaps the original rate of two dinars per head, which, according to some ancient sources, was stipulated at the time of the conquest of Egypt by the Muslims, was still in force in that place. However the data from the relevant Arabic papyri are opposed to such an assumption.[32]

Similarly, when a religious slaughterer paid one and three-quarters dinars circa 1180, this may represent either a substantially reduced medium rate, or a slightly raised minimum. Arrears could not be assumed in this case, because the person concerned worked on the market and the accounts of his payments to the community for every week of the year have been preserved. Thus he could not escape the tax collectors.[33]

In a financial report of a *parnas*, or social officer, in Old Cairo for the last month of the Muslim year coinciding with April–May 1182 we find the following items: "*jāliya* for X: 13 dirhams, balance of the *jāliya* for Y: 11 ½ dirhams." Since we are here near the "closing of the accounts" (see below), it stands to reason that the first item, like the second, represents only a last installment.[34] There is, however, no complete certainty in the matter, particularly since similar sums are mentioned elsewhere as payments for the *jāliya*.[35]

The vital questions of whether special rates existed for individual meritorious cases cannot be decided as yet with the material at our disposal. On the one hand we find many requests addressed to notables to use their influence on the tax officials with regard to a certain person or local community.[36] On the other hand, one wonders whether so much hardship could have existed, if the granting of alleviations had been common practice. New finds might bring more clarity into this matter.

The fines for arrears are repeatedly referred to. These were actually payments to the "ralliers" sent to summon the non-Muslims to the tax office. A man who was in arrears with thirty dirhams had to pay one silverpiece, *fidda*, every week. Another one writes that he gave the *busbsbār* four dirhams at a time (perhaps they appeared in that number). Moreover, his house was offered for sale by auction.[37]

The opposite of this procedure, namely, the extortion of payments of the poll tax in advance, is known thus far from Geniza records only for Palestine and for the second quarter of the eleventh century, a period of anarchy and misrule. According to one report, payment was asked a full five months before the Muslim New Year, on which it was due.[38]

As to the collection of the *jāliya*, it has often been asserted that this was done by the non-Muslim communities and their official heads. This assumption is refuted by the evidence of the Geniza records which show that each individual was contracted by the state authorities directly and had to find the means for payment himself. A person lacking the required cash would sell or pawn his clothes or take from his wife's marriage portion, which he was not allowed to touch, or even lay his hands on material given to her for processing it, such as raw silk which she was supposed to unravel.[39] In case none of such supplementary sources were available he would ask for an advance or a loan, and if he could not expect anyone to provide him with either, he would approach a person known for his munificence with the request to contribute something himself and to introduce him to others.[40]

In addition to the references given above, two more examples may suffice to illustrate a subject so profusely represented in the Geniza records. The first is a letter by a Jewish judge from Old Cairo to a physician and scholar living in the provincial town of al-Mahalla with regard to a young cantor, whose father had pursued the same profession: "When the bearer of this letter learned that the time of collection of the poll tax was nearing, he sought rescue by traveling to the Rīf (the 'countryside') and appealing to the beneficence of God and of Israel. Before all others he is turning to the gate of God and your gate that you should do with him yourself all that is in your power and, moreover, help him by using your influential position. He is a fine young man, aspiring to noble goals, religious and devout and deserving all the good you will do for him." A religious functionary in Bilbīs, a town on the caravan route to Palestine, writes to his superior in Old Cairo: "What holds me back here is the hope to get the money for the poll tax for me and my son. Otherwise, I would have left the place, since one cannot really make a living here." Despite the reference to his son, the man must have been comparatively young, for he asks the addressee whether he could come to the capital and continue his studies with him.[41]

When all efforts to obtain the sums due for the *jāliya* failed, the insolvent taxpayer went into hiding, an expedience very often encountered in the Geniza. In one letter we even find the following remark: "This week the people experience hardships because of the *jāliya* and we all were hiding in the houses."[42] However, this means of escape had many hitches. First of all, as we have seen, the fugitive's male relatives were held responsible for him. Secondly, he was unable to earn a livelihood, especially if his income was derived from a workshop or store. When a person in such a predicament writes that his wife and children had died of hunger, because he was in hiding and unable to maintain them, he meant it literally, not figuratively. Finally, such a person often owed money also to private creditors who would track him down even without the aid of the state police.[43]

Imprisonment, the routine punishment for the failure to pay the poll tax, was not always confined to such short terms as those mentioned above. We read about a cantor who had been in jail for two months because he had found no one to pay for him and was not set free despite a serious illness.[44]

In view of the Geniza material provided, which could be easily expanded, it is impossible to maintain that the local or territorial non-Muslim communities were in charge of the collection of the poll tax of their members and automatically took care of them in this respect. Still, the denominational units played a very great role with regard to this branch of public revenue. First, direct and indirect references in the Geniza records prove that both the local *muqaddams* and the Nagid, or "Head of the Jews" were consulted by the state authorities when they assessed the financial capacity of the taxpayers, and it goes without saying that the same must have been the case with the Christian local and territorial leaders.[45] The total amount to be levied in one area, like other items of the budget, was fixed in advance (otherwise it could not be farmed out). This explains why the Jewish authorities were so eager to register foreigners, who sojourned in a city even for a short while, as residents. Moreover, although, in Egypt at least, the Jewish local leaders were not held responsible for the total of the poll tax to be raised—we do not read even about threats in this respect—, they themselves regarded the payment of the *jāliya* for the poor as a holy obligation and a pious deed comparable to the highly meritorious ransoming of the captives (For the organization of this charity cf. the present writer's article "The Social Services of the Jewish Community," *Jewish Social Studies* 26 [1964].)

It is, however, evident from many Geniza records that during long periods and in many places the assistance of the indigent taxpayer was not handled by the community, but left to the vagaries of private philanthropy. We had repeatedly opportunity to refer to such situations. Conversely, there were times when a local non-Muslim community was charged with a flat-rate poll tax or where its leaders saw themselves coerced to take a yearly collection, at least for a section of the community, into their own hands. When, owing to the dismal economic and security situation in eleventh-century Jerusalem, the population fluctuated in jerks, a fixed sum was made mandatory on the Jewish community, and its leaders were held responsible for its payment, as we may conclude from their desperate appeals for help to their brethren in the Egyptian capital: "A heavy poll tax is imposed on us in a lump; but we are few, and unable to pay even a fraction of it. Every year we take loans (from Muslims) for interest so that pilgrims to the Holy City should not be molested with warrants of arrest."[46] One letter from Jerusalem sent around 1040 is an appeal for a collection toward the repayment of such a loan incurred by the community together with the arrears due from previous years.[47]

A somewhat similar, but still different situation is reflected in the following orders given by the Nagid Abraham Maimonides to this treasurer (and, by the way, written in his own hand): "Please pay immediately eighty-one dirhams to the cadi Shams al-Din (the director of revenue in Old Cairo), in order to close the account for the balance of the *jāliya* for the year 614." The Muslim year in question ended on March 29, 1218, and the paper is dated April 22. "Send thirty-five dinars to the illustrious elder 'The Trusted' (a social service officer), to be taken from the revenue of the houses belonging to the community. This is the balance due for the Jewish poll tax of (New) Cairo to the government revenue office, for which The Trusted stood security with the consent of the community. Please rush. The claims of the revenue office suffer no delay." Even for a balance due, the sums mentioned are insignificant. Therefore we are certainly right in assuming that the Nagid took care solely of the *jāliya* incumbent on the poor. Since the community paid for them anyhow, they were not approached by the tax collectors individually. This assumption is corroborated by a third order of the Nagid, found in the same bunch of papers (but written in Arabic characters), which deals with the ground rent paid for the poor living inside the old Roman fortress of Fustāt.[48]

In the orders just mentioned the department in charge of the poll tax is referred to in a general way as "the government office." However it is evident from many records that this task was assigned to a group of special officials, one called *'āmil*, employee, taking care of the administrative side, while the technicalities accompanying all cash payments in those days were handled by a government cashier, who was styled *jahbadh al-jamālī* down to the twelfth century, while, later on, the general designation for banker or money changer, *sayrafī*, was used instead.[49] In case of irregularities, the chief of police and even the governor of a city were approached. This was done, e.g., in Alexandria around 1140, when they issued receipts to the taxpayers, but left their names "open," i.e., as still owing the tax in the government records, in order to extort from them two payments, one going to the state treasurer and one pocketed by himself and his complices. As the document shows, the local authorities approached, although having good intentions, were of no avail and an appeal was lodged with the central government.[50]

Occasionally, reference is made in the Geniza records to *tax farmers (dāmin)* being in charge of the collecting of the *jāliya*. Thus far, however, such references have been found only with regard to small places, where it can be safely assumed that the *dāmin* took care of all the taxes due. In his brilliant analysis of an Ayyubid source concerning the revenue from the Fayyūm district, Claude Cahen shows that the *jāliya* was included in the general estimate of the district.[51]

The express testimony of the Geniza letters to the great hardship caused by the *jāliya* is confirmed by the implicit evidence of the Arabic papyri. In his painstaking study quoted on p. 279, note 1, A. Grohmann comes to the conclusion that the data about arrears and install-ments in the payment of the *jāliya* indicate the straitened circumstances in which the great mass of the taxpayers usually found itself.

In general it should be emphasized that the subject of the poll tax occupies far more space in the Geniza records than we would anticipate. A very considerable section of the non-Muslim population must have been unable to pay it and often suffered humiliation and privation on its account. While, in the higher circles, the prospects of appointment to leading government posts acted as an inducement for embracing Islam, the mass conversions in the lower classes might well have been caused in part by the intolerable burden of the poll tax.[52]

BIBLIOGRAPHICAL NOTE

For information about the Cairo Geniza see *JESHO* 4 (1961): 168. The manuscripts are quoted according to the cities and collections, in which they are preserved, and the signs used by the latter. Note the following abbreviations:

TS: Taylor-Schechter Collection, preserved in the University Library, Cambridge, England.
UL Cambridge: Other collections of Geniza papers in the same library.
Oxford: Bodleian Library, Oxford, ms. Heb.
AtaS: S. Assaf, *Texts and Studies in Jewish History* (in Hebrew) (Jerusalem, 1946).
MJ: Jacob Mann, *The Jews in Egypt and in Palestine under the Fatimid Caliphs* (Oxford, 1920–22).
MT: Jacob Mann, *Texts and Studies*, vol. 1 (Philadelphia, 1931).
India Book: A collection of Geniza documents on the India trade, prepared by the present writer for publication.
Mediterranean Society or Medit. Soc.: A Mediterranean Society of the High Middle Ages, based on Records from the Cairo Geniza, a volume in preparation by the present writer.
N: Geniza records connected with Nahray ben Nissim, a Qayrawanese merchant, scholar, and public figure, who emigrated to Egypt and Palestine and lived in those countries between 1048 and 1095. Prepared for publication by Mr. M. Michael.
READINGS: *Readings in Mediterranean Social History*, selected documents from the Cairo Geniza translated into English by S. D. Goitein.

For clarification of any references, please see original essay.

NOTES

1. For the sources and previous treatments of the vast subject, cf. the article "Djizya" in the second edition of the *Enc. of Islam* (Claude Cahen). This paper was written before the present writer had opportunity to see

that article. For the history of the *jāliya* in Egypt cf. the detailed exposition of A. Grohmann, *Die Arabischen Papyri aus der Giessener Universitaetsbibliotbek* (Giessen, 1960), pp. 19–28 and 82–83. For the interpretation of the relevant passage from the Qur'an 9:29, cf. Cl. Cahen, *Arabica* 9 (1962): 76–79; and Fr. Rosenthal, *Joshua Starr Memorial Volume* (New York, 1953), pp. 68–72.

2. TS 13 J 22, f. 9.

3. TS 12.3, transl. in READINGS.

4. UL Cambridge 1081 J 13.

5. TS 12.192, 11.3–9, publ. ATaS 165.

6. TS 13 J 4, f. 7.

7. Abraham Maimuni, Responsa, pp. 161–62; Maimonides, Responsa, p. 50.

8. S. Kandel, *Genizai keziratok* (Budapest, 1909), p. 6: a father of a boy (fourteen) declares to have paid for him *jāliya* for five years. The scholar to whom the query is addressed is known from a letter dated 1094, cf. MJ II, p. 235.

9. TS 13 J 3, f. 2. The declaration contained other provisions as well.

10. Maimonides, Responsa, p. 103.

11. TS 8 J 26, f. 18, transl. in READINGS no. 19.

12. Brother-in-law: Philadelphia, Dropsie College 398.

13. Maimonides, Responsa, pp. 36–37.

14. TS 13 J 28, f. 15 (India book 291), verso, I. 14.

15. TS NS J 3, l. 16. The traveler had left Egypt in 1156.

16. Cf. *Studia Islamica* 3 (1955): 86.

17. Oxford c 28 (2876), f. 65, margin: *barā'a dimāniyya*.

18. E.g., TS 13 J 15, f. 2, l. II.

19. TS Box 25, f. 62 (N 118), ll. 3–11. Cf. below p. 292.

20. TS 13 J 14, f. 18 (N 54), verso, ii. 5–10.

21. Cf., however, below p. 286 and ibid., n. 5.

22. Oxford f. 56 (2821), f. 19, ll. 7–11, publ. JQR 43 (1952), p. 76, cf. ibid., pp. 59–60.—S. Schechter, A Geniza Ms., *A. Berliner Jubilee volume 1903,* Hebr. Section, pp. 108–12.

23. Philadelphia, Dropsie College 393, l. 13. The Arabic word is transliterated by the European traveler as *zymyyh*.

24. TS 18 J 3, f. 1: *man yaskun fībā mā yazin jāliya*.

25. TS 13 J 36, f. 2: *kitāb an yatlubūb fi'l-amal wamā mskh (miska) thamma 'alā jāliya*.

26. Ibn Mammātī, *Qawānīn al-dawāwin* (Cairo, 1943), p. 318. Oxford f. 56 (2821), f. 45, l. 7, called her *jizya*.

27. Budapest, David Kaufman Coll. XXI: "One and two thirds dinars" (I 16/24 for I 15/24; the man most probably had to pay the *qirāt* as fine; see below). TS 16.272, verso, l. 7: "five prisoners who have to pay eight dinars," which is 1 24/40 per person (1 5/8 equals 1 25/40). TS 8 J 19, f. I, ll. 5–6: 1 1/3 plus ¼ plus half a *qirāt,* which would be one and a half *habbas* instead of

two *habbas.* For payment to a special office for foreigners in the capital, cf. above p. 285.

28. Cf. A. Scheiber-J. L. Teicher, *Journal of Jewish Studies* 5 (1954): 37. See READINGS no. 4.

29. UL Cambridge or 1080 J 258, ll. 22–28: *tawqī 'mukammal* (cf. Dozy *Supplément* s.v.) . . . *yatadamman an yujraw fī 'l-jizya 'alā mā bum 'alayb . . . ma'an yujraw 'alā mā kān qarrarbu al-qādi l-makīn.*

30. TS 12.290, verso l.9.

31. Cf. Cl. Caben, Histories Coptes, *Ball. De l'inst. Franqais d'archéologie orientale* (1960): 140, l. 2.

32. Ms. Frankfurt, publ. Joseph Horovitz. *Zeitschrift f. Hebr. Bibliogr.* 4 (1900): 155–58. The writer bears the extremely rare name Mishael b. Uzziel, which was, however, common in the family of Maimonides' Egyptian wife. The very wording *al-mamlūk yazin an Damira 'l-qibliyya* shows that he did not live in that place. The addressee, R. Hananel, is well known. Documents signed by him as from 1223 have been preserved. For the rate of two dinars per head cf. Cl. Cahen, "*Le rigime des impóis dans le Fayyum ayyubide,*" *Arabica* 3 (1956): 22. For the Arabic papyri see the source quoted p. 279, n. 1.

33. TS 16. 39 (The account is most probably from 1183).

34. TS 8 J 11 f. 7 d, margin.

35. New York, ENAdler Coll. 4020, f. 30: "I sold the old kerchicf (*mandil*) which with omissions."—UL Cambridgc or 1080 J 80, I. 8: a father sends to his son eleven dirhams for the *jāliya.* TS 16.286: "They took twelve dirhams from me and left me alone for a while." (Alexandria 1219). Transl. in READINGS.

36. E.g., TS 8 J 21, f. 6, l. 15, MJ II, p. 110: "Talk for me to the *ba'alha-mas*" (Hebr. For Ar. *Sābib al-jāliya*).

37. Philadelphia, Dropsie College 358, ll. 4–5, and 398, 1.7. Fine: *magbram* TS 16.296, l. 7.

38. TS 13 J 26, f. 13, MJ II, pp. 174–75 (where f. 11 is printed for f. 13).

39. Cf. p. 289, n. 3, and Maimonides, Responsa, pp. 116 and 92.

40. Advance: Philadelphia, Dropsie College 410, Loan: above p. 288 and the source quoted p. 286, n. 4.

41. TS 10 J. 17, f. 19 verso and 10 J 18, f. 22 verso, ll. 5–6. Other examples: READINGS, TS 12. 289, and Cambridge, Westminster College 43.

42. Oxford d 66 (2878), f. 135: *basalat lil-nās shadā'id min ajli l-jāliya wakunna jami' mukhabbayīn fī 'l-buyūt.*

43. TS 13 J 36, f. 2, ll. 12–14. TS to J 17, f. 20. The writer complains that others owed him money as well.

44. UL Cambridge 1081 J 61.

45. Cf., e.g., *Mediterranean Society* VA 2.

46. TS 13 J 11, f. 5, ll. 18–20, MJ II 186: *pittāgē* (from Greek *pittakion*) *ha-mas* is the Hebrew equivalent for Ar. *riqa' al-jāliya*, warrants arrest for nonpayment of the poll tax.

47. Philadelphia, Dropsie College 392. Some of the 10 [signatories] are known from other sources.

48. TS K 25, f. 240, nos. 11, 12, and 1.

49. TS 13 J 33, f. 9, ll. 10 and 13. For a *sayrafi* as attending the collection of the *jāliya* the fourteenth century, cf. 16.296, l. 9. One talked also generally about *sāhib* and *asbāb al-jāliya,* TS NS J 290, l. 10, Philadelphia, Dropsie College 379, l. 9, cf. Hebr. *Ba'al ha-mas* p. 289, n. 4.

50. The first source mentioned in n. 2.

51. *Arabica* 3 (1956): 21.

52. The writer wishes to express his sincere thanks to the directors and staffs of the libraries whose manuscripts he was permitted to use.

CHAPTER 38

Concerning the Situation of Jews and Christians in Seville at the Beginning of the Twelfth Century

Georges Vajda

E. Lévi-Provençal has just published a text that is extremely valuable for the history of labor and our knowledge about social life in Spain under the Muslims.[1]

It consists of a manual to be used by the *mohtasib*, who are "civil servants responsible for ensuring that guilds in large Islamic cities maintain established business customs and for cracking down on fraudulent trades practices and commerce-related offenses."[2] Among the various sorts of information about urban life in Seville that are provided by this document, which dates from the Almoravid period and was written around 1200,[3] some concern Jews and Christians.

In making use of this information, we must not overlook the fact that what we have here is a wish list of a pious Muslim who has taken it upon himself to alert the government to things that were not in conformity with the strict Islamic law in that country.

Therefore quite often he is talking not about the current state of affairs, but about what ought to be, and when he censures what he regards as an abuse and a violation of the law, he may be exaggerating somewhat.

Since the Arabic text of the treatise is not accessible to all historians, I thought it might be useful to provide the readers of the *Revue des Études Juives* with a translation of the passages dealing with Jews and Christians.

I. *P. 238, l. 18– p. 239, l. 3*: "A Muslim must never give a massage to a Jew or Christian (at the baths). He must never pick up their garbage or clean their outhouses. These tasks, which are for people of lowly status, are more suitable for Jews and Christians." "A Muslim must not take care of a beast of burden belonging to a Jew or a Christian; he must not serve as their mule driver and must not help them into the saddle. If a Muslim is found to have done so, he shall be reprimanded for it."

II. P. 239, ll. 4–14: "Muslim women must be pre-vented from entering into those abominable churches, because the clerics are corrupt, fornicators, and sodomites." "Christian women (*ifranjiyyat*) must not enter them either except on days when people pray there together or on feast days, because they have the habit of dining sumptuously with the clerics and of giving themselves up to debauchery with them. There is not a single clergyman who does not have at least two [concubines] or more. It has become a custom with them, because they forbid what is permitted and permit what is forbidden. You must direct the clerics to marry as [is done] in the Orient. If they wanted to, they would do it. If a cleric refuses to marry, you must not let any woman, old or otherwise, into his house." "You must compel them to be circumcised, as did the Abbadid al-Mo'tadid [d. 1068]. Indeed, they pretend to follow the law of Jesus (peace be upon Him). Now Jesus was circumcised and they celebrate a feast to commemorate that event, whereas they neglect the practice."

III. P. 239, ll. 20–21: "A Jew must not slaughter animals for a Muslim. You must direct the Jews to have their own butcher's shops (literally, their 'vices' [clamps with closing jaws])."

IV. P. 240, ll. 17–18. "No item of clothing may be sold to a leper, a Jew or a Christian, unless it allows them to be recognized. The same rule applies for [incorrigible] drunkards."

V. P. 241, ll. 11–16: "You must not allow any tax-collector [French: *gabeleur*], policeman, Jew or Christian to wear the attire of great men, doctors of law, or the wealthy. On the contrary, they must be objects of contempt and disgust; they are not entitled to a greeting of peace[4] [Qur'anic verse cited to support precept]. They must wear a distinctive, ignominious sign."

VI. P. 248, ll. 3–8: "One must not sell to Jews or

Georges Vajda, "À propos de la situation des Juifs et des Chrétiens à Séville au début du XIIe siècle," *Revue des Études Juives* 99 (1935): 127–29; translation by Michael J. Miller.

Christians books about the sciences, except those that pertain to their religion.[5] Indeed, they translate scientific books, attribute them to others of their religion and to their bishops, when they are [in fact] composed by Muslims." "Hasan[6] did not allow a Jewish or Christian physician to treat a Muslim. Given that they harbor no benevolent feelings toward Muslims, how could anyone entrust to them the lives of Muslims? Let them treat those of their own religion."[7]

NOTES

1. "*Un document sur la vie urbaine et les corps de métiers à Séville au XIIe siècle; Le Traité d'Ibn 'Abdun, publié avec une introduction et un glossaire*" [A document about urban life and trade guilds in Seville in the twelfth century; The Treaty of Ibn Abdun, published with an introduction and a glossary], *Journal Asiatique* 224 (April–June 1934): 177–299.

2. I borrow this definition from a publication similar to the one in question here, by G. S. Colin and E. Lévi-Provençal: *Un manuel hispanique de hisba*, a publication of the Institut des Hautes Études Marocaines, vol. 21 (Paris, 1931), p. 1 of the introduction. The treatise that we are discussing deals with matters that extend

beyond the scope of the duties of a *mohtasib*, in the strict sense of the word, as the publisher has noted (p. 179).

3. "*Un document*," 180–81.

4. Non-Muslims are never greeted with the formula *al-salamu 'alaykum*.

5. The text in this passage is uncertain. According to Paul Kraus's suggestion, I read "*mâ*" instead of "*man*."

6. Here, too, the text seems altered to me. First, it is strange that the author cites an authority, which he does not do anywhere else, as far as I can see. Also, when Muslim literature mentions the name Hasan without specifying further, it generally refers to Hasan al-Basri, a famous Muslim ascetic, who died in 728 CE. But it is historically impossible, as L. Massignon and P. Kraus have also assured me, that the words in question could be his. We are therefore confronted with an apocryphal saying that I have been unable to find elsewhere, or, more plausibly, the text was altered [this would not be the only case of an anachronism in a sentence attributed to Hasan al-Basri. In the tenth century, al-Tawhidi (*Risalatani*, Éditions Constantinople [a publisher], p. 162), ascribes to him the saying that a true friend is as rare as the philosopher's stone].

7. The end of the text is not in order either. I have modified slightly the sequence of sentences.

CHAPTER 39

The Distinctive Sign of the Jews in Maghreb

Edmond Fagnan

Studies by Ulysse Robert[1] and I. Loeb[2] have shed light on the question of the distinctive mark that Jews were forced to wear during the Middle Ages. To their work, which concerned only the Christian West, one could add certain information with regard to what happened in the East, a part of which has already been compiled by S. de Sacy.[3]

We note in passing, at any rate, that the wearing of certain special signs goes back to before the thirteenth century of the Christian era, at least in the East, since the ordinances of the Fatamid caliph Al-Hakim on this subject date from the year 395 of the Hegira (1004–1005 CE), and they do not seem to be his invention.[4] Due to the nature of the subject treated by the illustrious scholar, he limited himself to speaking about Egypt, and to this [Salomon] Munk [1805–1867][5] was able to add a useful supplement by translating an Arabic passage relative to Maghreb and to Spain. It is comparable to what is reported by U. Robert, namely, that around the year 1320 "the king of Grenada, Ismaïl Abul-Walid ibn Abu Saïd ben Faraj, who reigned from 1315 to 1326, after the example of the Christian kings of neighboring lands, required the Jews in his domain to wear a sign to distinguish them from Muslims." Here is the language used by Abd el-Wâhid Merrâkechi:

Toward the end of his reign, Aboû Yoûsof [al-ManSuur] l'Almohade [1184–1199 CE] ordered the Jews living in Maghreb to differentiate themselves from the rest of the population by a distinctive outfit consisting of dark blue clothing fitted out with sleeves so wide that they almost reached the feet, and, instead of a turban, a skullcap of the ugliest possible form, which could have been mistaken for a packsaddle and which came down below the ears. This outfit became the garb of all the Jews of Maghreb and remained so until the end of that prince's reign and the beginning of the reign of his son, Aboû Abd Allâh. The latter modified it after all sorts of measures were taken by

the Jews, who had recourse to the intercession of everyone who, they believed, might be useful to them. Aboû Abd Allâh made them wear yellow clothing and turbans, and that is the outfit that they still wear in the present year of 621 [1224 CE].[6]

We see that these accounts, which are explicit enough, have reference to a particular garb, and that this tradition seems to have been maintained to a certain extent even in Algeria under the French. There is, moreover, another word used in our day [i.e., the late nineteenth century] exclusively to designate the black or dark blue turban that serves as the headdress of the indigenous Jews.[7]

The ordinance of the Almohade al-ManSuur was not strictly obeyed in its entirety for very long, as Merrâkechi himself tells us. It is likely that things soon reverted to what probably had been the previous state of affairs, I mean, to the wearing of a simple distinctive sign, which, in Egypt, was yellow or black and bore the name of *ghiyâr* [patch of discrimination].[8] No text, to my knowledge, allows us to determine what the color of it was in the Maghreb; but the name that was given to it, *chekla* [sign, clothing patch], was quite different and does not appear, moreover, in any dictionary,[9] at least not with the meaning in question. This word is used repeatedly by Maghrebian writers. Thus Zerkechi[10] relates as follows the decree of al-ManSuur that we have been speaking of: "In 595 (beginning on November 2, 1198), al-ManSuur ordered the Jews to use the *chekla* (*bi 'amali 'ch-cheklati*) [by employing the patch]; he decreed that their tunics (*k'amiç*) should be one cubit long and of equal width, and that they should wear blue *burnous* [hooded Arab cloaks] and blue caps." In addition,[11] he informs us that in 648 (April 4, 1250, by common reckoning), the *chekla* was imposed on the Jews of Tunis," a fact recorded also by Ibn Aboû Dinâr Kayrawâni: "In 648, the *chekla* was imposed on the Jews, who were subjected to ever greater humiliations."[12] Furthermore, I have discovered a rhymed and insulting bit of doggerel that is still repeated in Ténès, although no one knows any

Edmond Fagnan, "Le Sign Distinctif des Juifs au Maghred," *Revue des Études Juives* 28 (1894): 294–98. Translated by Michael J. Miller.

more the precise meaning that should be attached to the word *chekla*: "O Jew, man with the *chekla*, my father gave you a kick, because he found a pearl in your hand; may your father and the father of your grandfather be— accursed!" Note, finally, that this word, in its diminutive form, is found in the name Bou-chekila (the origin of which seems . . . beyond doubt)—a name belonging to this day to an Israelite family of Constantine.

I add here several passages taken from Arabic authors concerning the history of the Jews in Maghreb.

In 424 Aboû 'l-Kemâl l'Ifrenide, prince of Châla (formerly Salé in Maroc), seized Fez, where he despoiled the Jews of all their wealth, killed more than six thousand of them, and handed their wives over to his soldiers.[13]

According to Edrisi, "Aghmât Aylân (at the foot of the Grand Atlas [mountains in Northwest Africa] and not far from Merrâkech or Maroc) is a beautiful, rich city, inhabited exclusively by Jews. Ali b. Yoûsof l'Almoravide had forbidden them to settle in Maroc or even to spend the night there, under pain of the most severe punishments. They are allowed to enter the city by day, but only for the sorts of business and services in which their nation specializes; the lives and goods of those who are found there after sunset are at the mercy of everyone. Consequently, the Jews make very sure that they do not act contrary to this rule."[14]

On the 27th of Ramadan, 869 (September 2, 1464), an insurrection broke out in Fez against the Merinide Sultan Abd el-Hakk b. Aboû Sa'id, who was executed with his prime minister, the Jew Hâroûn, while the Jews of the city were massacred. "Abd el-Hakk, after being, as it were, under the thumb of the Benoû Watâs, a group which for many long years controlled all the affairs of state, wished to regain his independence and, consequently, arrested most of the Benoû Watâs and seized their property, while the others fled. Having become his own master, he took charge of things himself and went on military expeditions at the head of his army. As his replacement during his absences, he left the Jew Hâroûn in charge of Muslim affairs in Fez, adjudicating their disputes, and so he was a source of humiliation for them. The impression that this made on the people was considerable, so that one day, when the sultan had sallied forth with his army to reestablish peace in the provinces and to pursue the Benoû Watâs, who had seized Tanger and Tâzâ, among other places, an agreement was made with the *mizwâr* [official] of the shereefs [Arabian princes] and a riot broke out against the Jews of Fez, who were massacred. But the insurgents had reason to fear the sultan and his prime minister, Hâroûn, and they held the city until the day when the prince returned with a small number of [armed] men; they [insurgents] arrested them [the sultan and Hâroûn] and executed them."[15]

Kayrawâni, wishing to describe epigrammatically the ardor with which the Tunisians in 1091 (February 1, 1680) pursued the nomadic tribe of the Ouled Sâïd, whose plundering had been a trial to them from time

immemorial, tells us that the individuals descended from that tribe preferred to call themselves Jews than to admit their true origin.[16]

We find in the *Diwân el-inchâ* [inshaa' coming into being] (an Arabic manuscript in Paris, no. 1573 of the Académie Française, in folios 140 and 303), details related principally to the historical account of the Karaïte and Rabbanite sects. The almost complete absence of [Arabic] diacritical marks makes it a bit difficult to use this copy of a work that is interesting for more than one reason, since it sets forth the things that the *kâteb* or chancery employees had to know.

*For clarification of any references, please see original essay.

NOTES

1. *Revus des études juives* [Review of Jewish Studies] 4: 81: 94.

2. Ibid., 6: 268.

3. *Chrestomathie arabe*, 2nd ed., vol. 1, pp. 97, 144, 181; *Exposé de la religion des Druses*, [Exposition on the religion of the Druze], vol. 1, pp. cccix, cccxxx, ccclx, ccclxviii, cccxcviii.

4. We read, for example, in Ibn-el-Athîr (Arabic text, vol. 7, p. 34; this passage seems to appear also in Nowaïri, see Dozy, *Vêtements*, p. 436; Weil, *Geschichte der Khalifen* [The History of the Caliphs], 11, 353): "In 233 (July 25, 849), the Caliph El-Motowakkel enjoined his tributaries [the Jews and the Christians] to use yellow *taylesân* [like a scarf or a tallit], to wear special belts (*zonnâr*), to equip their saddles with wooden stirrups, behind which they had to place two balls, to mark the clothing of their slaves by means of two pieces of material, each having its own color different from that of the garment, and four fingers long; furthermore, their wives could not go out unless they were dressed in a yellow *izâr* [belt]. They were forbidden to wear purses at the belt (*mintak*); the destruction of their recently built temples was ordered; a tithe upon their settlements was exacted, and the doors of their houses were marked with figures of demons carved from wood. It was forbidden from then on to make use of their services in public administration; it was no longer allowed for any Muslim to give them instruction; the displaying of the cross on Palm Sunday was forbidden, as well as its use along a public road; finally, their tombs could be no higher than ground level. These instructions were sent to all parts of the empire." The word *taylesân* denotes the ends of the muslin [cloth] of the turban or headdress which fell to the shoulders. The *zonnâr* is a special belt which infidels have to wear in Muslim countries so that they can be recognized; it is made up of many small cords of various colors and is worn around the waist (cf. the gloss by Ca'idi [judge] on the commentary of Kharachi, vol. 2, p. 446). The *izâr* or *haïk* is the large veil made of wool or a

lighter material which covers a woman from head to foot. The *mintak* is the leather or cloth belt worn around the waist and designed to hold money (see the commentaries of Sidi Khalil at p. 59, l. 1; therefore it is not, as Dozy says in *Vêtements*, p. 420, "always a belt of gold or silver.") Here is what the law prescribes, as formulated by Khalil (text, p. 78; cf. the translation by Perron, 2: 296): "It is forbidden for a tributary [a Jew or Christian . . . subdued willingly or by force] to ride a horse or a mule, to use a saddle, to walk down the middle of the street; he must wear distinctive clothing; he is to be punished if he takes off his *zonnâr*."

5. *Journal asiatique* 2 (1842): 40.

6. *Histoire des Almohades*, French translation (Alger, Jourdan [Algeria, Jordan?], 1893), p. 264.

7. The word *zmâla* or *zemla* (see the *Dictionnaire Beaussier*; Dozy, *Supplément*). More detailed information can be found in the work by M. A. Cohen, *Les Juifs dans l'Afrique septentrionale* [Jews of Northern Africa], especially pp. 179 and 205 (the 1867 issue of the *Recueil des notices de la Société archéologique de Constantine*) [Anthology of the Accounts of the Archaeological Society of Constantine].

8. *Chrestomatie* by Sacy (vol. 1, p. 55 of the text, and pp. 146 and 181 of the notes).

9. An educated and conscientious native whom I questioned on this subject told me that this sign, which varies with each region, consists, among other things, of the fact that a Jew had to shave his head while sparing the hair that covered his temples.

10. *Ta'rikh ed-dasolateyn*, Tunis edition, p. 11, l. 20.

11. Ibid., p. 25, l. 17.

12. *Kitâb el-mou'nis fi akhbâr ifrik'iyya wa-tounis* [The Pleasant (Book) about the History of Africa and Tunis(ia)], Tunis ed., p. 128, l. 4. The Pellissier-Rémusat translation (in *Exploration scientifique de l'Algérie*), which includes countless errors, seems to refer this to the year 651 (see p. 224, where we find this version: "During this reign, the Jews had much to suffer. They subjected them to innumerable insults").

13. Ibn Khaldoun, *Histoire des Berbères* [History of the Berbers] French trans., vol. 3, p. 222; see also vol. 2, p. 354; Kartûs [Kartûz?], text, p. 69.

14. Dozy and de Goeje, *Description de l'Afrique et de l'Espagne par Edrisi* [Description of Africa and Spain by Edrisi], pp. 79–80. Edrisi ended his book at the year 548 (March 28, 1153), but subsequently revised it. Ali b. Yoûsof reigned from 500 to 537 (1106–1142 CE). In contrast, in the Spanish city of Lucena, the outskirts were occupied by the Muslims, who were forbidden to enter the fortified part of the city by the Jews, who had settled within walls (ibid., p. 252).

15. Zerkechi, p. 141 of the edition previously cited. In the MS of this chronicle, under no. 853 of the Arabic text (= no. 1874 of the printed Catalogue of the Bibliothèque nationale), on folio [p.] 103, v, this marginal note: "This Haroûn is the brother of Aboû Djenâh (may both of them be cursed!); he abolished the alms distributed to the ulemas [Muslim legal doctors] . . . to assign them to his poor coreligionists."

16. The edition cited above, p. 253, line 14.

CHAPTER 40

The Origins of 'Obadyah, the Norman Proselyte—'Obadyah's Experiences in Baghdad, Early Twelfth Century

Alexander Scheiber

The first fragment of the "Scroll" written by the Norman proselyte, 'Obadyah, was discovered by E. N. Adler among the Geniza documents in his possession,[1] but he was unable either to fix its age or to elucidate its historical background. Two further fragments were found subsequently by J. Mann in the Geniza Collection of the Cambridge University Library,[2] and recently S. D. Goitein discovered a fourth fragment in the same Library.[3] While the Adler fragment is unvocalized,[4] the Cambridge fragments are provided with vowels, and it would thus appear that the "Scroll" is extant in two different manuscripts, although both of them are written by the same hand.

The fragments discovered by Mann disclose that 'Obadyah, a Norman of noble extraction, embraced Judaism in 1102 and visited Jewish communities in Syria, Palestine, Egypt, and Mesopotamia. (Seven such communities are mentioned by name.)[5] He learned Hebrew and described his life and adventures in that tongue. The fragments of his "Scroll" so far discovered contain the most precise information, and the discovery of further fragments of such an important source for the history of this period has been awaited with great interest.

Goitein in fact expressed the hope that further fragments of the "Scroll" might come to light. He wrote: "In particular, there seem to exist good prospects that fragments may be found in such sections of the Cairo Geniza as have not yet been searched for this purpose."[6] This hope has soon been fulfilled, for I have recently found in the Kaufmann Geniza Collection in Budapest yet another fragment of 'Obadyah's "Scroll." The Budapest fragment consists of four pages and is provided with vowels like the Cambridge fragments. It seems to be an autograph, for several corrections were made in the text and on one occasion a long portion was supplemented in the margin. The manuscript was clearly written in the form of a codex, not a roll.

The measurements of the manuscript are 15 × 23.5 cm. The pages are lined and contain nineteen lines each. The folios 1b and 2a are very badly preserved; the ink has faded and words are rubbed out. I have succeeded, however, although with considerable difficulty, in deciphering the text almost completely. Examination of the manuscript by means of ultraviolet rays in the Institute of Forensic Medicine and the Museum of Stamps in Budapest unfortunately yielded no results.

The text of the Budapest fragment is not continuous. There is a gap of a few pages between folios 1b and 2a, but it is quite clear that it fits in, and supplements, the fragment discovered by Goitein. Folio 1a of Goitein's fragment continues, though not directly, folio 1b of the Budapest fragment, and folio 2a of the latter supplies the continuation of 2b of the former.

Folios 1a–1b of the Budapest fragment are of particular interest since the author there describes his descent. He was born in Oppido, in southern Italy. His father's name was Dro or Drochus and his mother's, Maria. His twin brother was named Rogerius or Roger, and he himself Johannes or Guan.[7] His brother was a soldier, while he himself became a scholar.

When Johannes was yet a child an unusual event occurred. The archbishop of Bari, Andreas, recognized the truth of the Torah, went to Constantinople, and there embraced Judaism.[8] At first he was persecuted by the Christians, who even had designs upon his life, but afterwards the persecutors themselves followed his example and were converted to the Jewish faith. Andreas finally went to Egypt, which was then ruled by the Fatimid al-Mustansirbillāh (1036–1094),[9] and remained there until his death. The news of his conversion spread through Longobardia (north eastern Italy), Byzantium, and Rome, and caused consternation among Christian scholars.

The manuscript proceeds to describe in great detail and exactitude the geographical boundaries of Oppido,

Alexander Scheiber, "The Origins of 'Obadyah, the Norman Proselyte—'Obadyah's Experiences in Baghdad, Early Twelfth Century," *Journal of Jewish Studies* 5 (1954): 32–37.

Johannes's birthplace. All the places mentioned are situated in Basilicata and can easily be identified with the help of a historical atlas.

Johannes seems to have been ordained a priest. In the first year of his priesthood he had a dream in which he saw himself officiating in the basilica of Oppido, when a figure appeared at his right hand near the altar and called him by his name. Here the manuscript breaks off. Goitein's fragment, folio la, continues the story, telling how Johannes awoke from his dream, but there are obviously some pages still missing, in which the appeal addressed by the figure to Johannes was described.

A Hebrew letter in the Cambridge Geniza has been ascribed by Assaf to 'Obadyah, whom he considers to have been a priest before his conversion.[10] Goitein, too, regards 'Obadyah as the author of the letter,[11] and I agree fully with both scholars. The Budapest fragment confirms Assaf's conclusion: Johannes was a Catholic priest before he became a Jew.

It appears from the Budapest fragment that Mann's theory that 'Obadyah came from Normandy and bore a French name at his birth is not correct. But his surmise that the first part of the "Scroll" must have contained a description of 'Obadyah's life before his conversion to Judaism has been confirmed. Mann concludes the exposition of his theory: "Let us hope that the beginning and end of 'Obadyah's Scroll will still turn up among the Mss. of the Geniza."[12] It is gratifying that now at least the beginning has been found.

The late Professor A. Marx wrote a few years ago concerning 'Obadyah: "We do not know and cannot even guess what influences caused him to change the whole course of his life."[13] It is evident now from the Budapest fragment that the conversion of the Archbishop Andreas was the first impulse that led Johannes toward Judaism. Jewish history knows nothing about Andreas's conversion. There are only two other instances of this kind reported: the conversion of Deacon Bodo in the ninth century in Spain and that of the priest Wecelinus about 1012 in Germany.[14] The mass conversion of Christians in Constantinople is also entirely unknown. But the reliability of the information contained in 'Obadyah's "Scroll" about historical events which can be checked from other sources has been proved to be very great, and justifies acceptance of his account of the conversions.

Folios 2a–2b of the Budapest fragment narrate 'Obadyah's experiences in Adina, that is, Baghdad.[15] The servant (*Hamasara*) brought him to the synagogue, where he was supplied with food by the Jews. The head of the academy, Isaac (that is, Isaac b. Moses),[16] instructed him together with the orphaned children in the Hebrew script and language and taught him the Pentateuch and the prophets.

The biographical details are followed in the manuscript by a survey of the history of the Jews in Baghdad. Before 'Obadyah's time, the caliph of Baghdad, al-Muqtadī (1075–1094), ordered, through his deputy, Abū

Shujā,[17] that Jewish males should wear distinctive yellow badges on their headgear as well as special belts round their waists. Other sources confirm that, during al-Muqtadī's reign, the Jews had to wear honey-colored belts[18] and yellow caps.[19] 'Obadyah adds further details. Every Jewish man had to wear a piece of lead on his neck, inscribed with the word *dhimmi*, an indication that the Jews were submitted to the poll tax.[20] Each Jewess had to wear two distinctive badges as well as shoes of different colors, one red and the other black. They also had to wear small brass bells wound their necks or on their shoes, in order to announce their identity. Arabic authors confirm that during Muqtadī's reign Jewesses had to wear shoes of different colors, black and white,[21] or black and red.[22] A special body of Muslim "inspectors," both male and female, were appointed to supervise the execution of the order. They behaved cruelly toward the Jews, who were also frequently beaten in the streets.

The collection of the poll tax is also described. The Jewish population was divided into three groups: the rich, who had to pay four and a half gold dinars; the middle class, who paid two and a half; and the poor, who paid one and a half. If a Jew died, his body was not allowed to be buried until his debts in taxes had been paid either from his property or (if there was nothing left) by other Jews. There was also the threat that the body of the deceased would be burned if the payment was not forthcoming. There are accounts of the poll tax collections in other sources,[23] but not so detailed as here. I shall deal with all these matters at greater length when I publish the text of the newly discovered fragment.

APPENDIX: ENGLISH TRANSLATION OF THE BUDAPEST FRAGMENT

Professor Scheiber has kindly sent me a photograph of the four pages of the Budapest fragment as well as his transcript of the text, provided with illuminating notes. This material enables me to offer an English translation of the text. I have departed in one or two places from Professor Scheiber's interpretation of the text, and I have duly indicated such departures in the notes. The assumption that the manuscript is an autograph does not seem to me to be necessary. The corrections and the marginal supplements may be due to the copyist.

[Folio la]: And its name is Oppido. He married a woman called Maria. She became pregnant and bore to her husband De Ro[24] two sons on the same day. The first was born in the normal way and was called Rogerius, that is, Roger. But the second . . . at first and his mother bore him with great pain, and called him Johannes, that is, Guan (Jean). The boys grew up, Rogerius plying the profession of arms and warfare, and Johannes devoting himself to the pursuit of knowledge and wisdom in books.

At that time, Andreas, the archbishop, that is, the

great priest, of the city of Bari, was stirred by God to the love of Moses' Torah. He left his country, his priestly office, and all his honors and went to the city of Constantinople, where he was circumcised. He went through "evils and troubles" and finally fled to save his life from the Christians, who tried to kill him. But the Lord God of Israel saved him from their hands, with his faith unimpaired.[25] Blessed by Thy Name forever, oh Lord, who protects the proselytes! The evildoers[26] followed after him, but they observed his deeds and did themselves what he had done and entered the covenant of the Living God. The man [Andreas] went to the city of Cairo and remained there until his death. The name of the King of Egypt at that time was al-Mustansir and that of his viceroy. . . .

The story of the Archbishop Andreas spread [fol. 1b] through the whole land of Longobardia, [and reached] all the sages of Greece [Byzantium] and Rome, which is the capital of Edom [Catholic Christianity]. The Greek and Roman sages [theologians] were covered with shame when they heard the tale. Johannes heard the story of Andreas, when he was still a boy in his father De Rochez's house.

These are the names of the cities round Oppido, the birthplace of Johannes: To the West, the city of Rome, the city of Salerno, the city of Potenza, the town of Pietragalla, and the town of Anzi. To the East, the city of Bari, the city of Montepeloso, the town of Genzano, and the town of Banzi. To the North, the city of Acerenza and the river called Bradano, between Oppido and Acerenza. To the South, the city of Tolve and the city of . . . , and Oppido lies between the two.

In the year in which Johannes received his first orders[27] . . . in the house of his father De Rochez, in the same year he had a dream: He was officiating in the basilica . . . his own people, when he saw a man standing at his right hand facing the altar, who called out to him: Johannes!

. . . [Fol. 2a] Academy. The servant installed 'Obadyah, the Proselyte, in a house used by the Jews for prayers, and food was brought to him. Afterward, Isaac, the head of the academy, arranged that Johannes should join the orphaned boys in order to be taught the law of Moses and the words of the prophets in the divine characters and the tongue of the Hebrews.

Before these events, the Caliph of Baghdad, of the name of al-Muqtadī, had given power to his vizier, Abū Shujā', to introduce a change of policy[28] in regard to the Jews of Baghdad and he had tried several times to destroy them. But the God of Israel had thwarted his intention (and) on this occasion also He hid them from his wrath. He (Abū Shujā') imposed that each male Jew should wear a yellow badge on his headgear. This was one distinctive sign on the head and the other was on the neck—a piece of lead of the weight (size?) of a silver dinar (?)[29] hanging round the neck of every Jew and inscribed with the word *dhimmi* to signify that the Jew had to pay poll tax. Jews also had to wear girdles round their waists. Abū Shujā' further imposed two signs upon Jewish women. They had to wear a black and a red shoe, and each woman had to have a small brass bell on her neck or shoe, which would tinkle [fol. 2b] and thus announce the separation of Jewish from Gentile women. He assigned cruel Muslim men to spy upon Jewish men and cruel Muslim women to spy upon Jewish women, in order to oppress them with all kinds of curses, humiliation, and spite. The Gentile population used to mock at the Jews, and the mob and their children used to beat up the Jews in all the streets of Baghdad.

The law of the poll tax, collected yearly by the caliph's official from the Jews, was as follows: Every Jew belonging to the wealthy class had to pay four and a half dinars in gold; a Jew of the middle class two and a half; and a Jew of the poorest a dinar and a half. When a Jew died, who had not paid up the poll tax to the full and was in debt for a small or large amount, the Gentiles did not permit burial until the debt of the poll tax was paid. If the deceased left nothing of value, the Gentiles demanded that other Jews should with their own money meet the debt owed by the deceased in poll tax; otherwise [they threatened], they would burn the body. Another law of the Gentiles of Baghdad was to make . . .

*For further clarification of any references, see original essay.

NOTES

1. *REJ* 69 (1919): 129–34.

2. Ibid., 89 (1930): 245–59.

3. *Journal of Jewish Studies* 4 (1953): 74–84.

4. See *Catalogue of Hebrew Manuscripts in the Collection of Elkan Nathan Adler* (Cambridge, 1921), fascimile no. 1.

5. Goitein, *op. cit.,* p. 84 n. 1.

6. Ibid., p. 74 n. 1.

7. Goitein has presumed correctly that, before his conversion to Judaism, 'Obadyah's name was Johannes (ibid., p. 81).

8. I have found the name of Andreas Archiepiscopus in the list of the bishops of Bari. He became archbishop in 1062 and died in 1078 (Bonifacus Gams, *Series Episcoporum Ecclesiæ Catholicæ,* [Ratisbonæ], 1873, p. 856).

9. J. Mann, *The Jews in Egypt* (Oxford, 1920), vol. 1, p. 76; E. Strauss, [*Toldot ha'Yehudim be'Mizrahim Yisurehah = The History of the Jews of Egypt (Suffering?)*] (Jerusalem, 1944), vol. 6, p. 30.

10. S. Assaf, *Texts and Studies in Jewish History* (Jerusalem, 1946), p. 143.

11. *Op. cit.,* p. 76.

12. *Hattequfa* 24 (1029): pp. 337, 339.

13. *Proceedings of the American Academy for Jewish Research* 16 (1947): 199. Mann expressed a similar opinion (*op. cit.*, p. 337).

14. See Cabaniss in *JQR* 48 (1953): 313 ff.; and ASSAF, *op. cit.*, p. 144.

15. Isaiah 47, 8. Cf. Mann, REJ (1919): p. 255.

16. D. S. Sassoon, *A History of the Jews in Baghdad* (Letchworth, 1949), pp. 60–61. The date of Isaac b. Moses is put by Sasson soon after 1100. According to our data, it must be later.

17. Goitein, *JQR*, N.S., 43 (1952–53): 63–64, 74.

18. Ibid., p. 64, n. 8.

19. E. Strauss, *Études Orientales à la Mémoire de Paul Hirschler* (Budapest, 1950), p. 79.

20. *Handwörterbuch des Islām* (Leiden, 1941), p. 18. The technical term *al-dhimma* (the protected people) was applied to non-Muslims whose faith was tolerated against the payment of the poll tax.

21. Goitein, *JQR* 43 (1952–53) 64 n. 8.

22. E. Strauss, *Études Orientales*, p. 81.

23. A. Harkavy, *Berliner-Festschrift* (Frankfurt a/M, 1903), Hebrew section, pp. 36, 39; Gotein, *op. cit.*, pp. 71, 76.

24. [*deRoh*] afterward the name is spelled [*deRocham*]. I submit that is a French name with the prefix *De*: De Rochez or De Rokez. The variation in the spelling of the name is an indication that the MS is not an autograph.

25. [*Beit aharah*].

26. [*hodim*]. Prof. Scheiber reads [*hovedim*]. If my reading is correct, no mass conversion to Judaism is referred to.

27. [*nitma ba Johannes tehilat t'meatoh*].

28. [*shinah*] Or is it the Arabic *shinā' (hatred)?*

29. [*bemischal kessef* (weight of silver) *min hal offeret*].

CHAPTER 41

Moses b. Samuel, a Jewish Katib in Damascus, and His Pilgrimage to Medina and Mecca

Jacob Mann

The vicissitudes of a Jewish secretary, whom his master, an emir in Damascus, compelled to adopt Islám and to accompany him on his pilgrimage to Medina and Mecca, are described in a number of skillfully wrought Hebrew poems printed here for the first time. They are extant in two manuscripts, Oxford MS. Heb. F. 3 and 4 (see Neubauer-Cowley's *Catalogue of Hebrew MSS. At the Bodleian,* vol. ii, nos. 2726 and 2766). They are designated as Karaite hymns (so on the backs of the binding), but have really no connection whatever with this sect. The handwriting seems to be of the fourteenth century, but furnishes no conclusive evidence.

The author, Moses b. Samuel, a native of Safed and the aforesaid Katib, depicts his experiences in five poems having in all 134 strophes. Each of the latter consists of three rhymed hemistichs, while the fourth is a biblical verse ending in *li*. In addition each strophe begins with a letter of either the alphabet or the author's acrostic. Poems i, iii, and v are alphabetical, while no. ii has the acrostic "I Moses b. Rabbi Samuel," and no. iv begins "I Moses b. Rabbi Samuel, who requests full forgiveness from God, who preferred the faith of Moses and Israel." Ultimately our poet returned to his former religion and, as an erstwhile convert, asked for divine pardon. The first poem was preceded by an introductory composition of three strophes with the acrostic "Moses." This as well as the first sixteen strophes of poem are missing. The conclusion of the work (*mahberet*) forms a piyyut of thanksgiving wherein the metre is employed (no. vi). The acrostic is "Moses b. Samuel of Safed."

As the poems are translated here, it is only necessary to give a summary of our author's story. A deputation waited upon the caliph (in Cairo), in the presence of the members of the Diwān, and read before him a petition advocating a number of restrictions against "the people of the tribute" (i.e., Jews and Christians). The kadis and the ulemas were summoned to give their opinions as to

what the Prophet's attitude was toward this part of the population. The viceroy (Wezīr) advocated that no Jew or Christian should be allowed to attain any dignity or authority in the State and none of them be employed as katibs. Moreover, the following restrictions should be imposed upon them: that they wear certain marks in the baths, put on no beautiful garments, raise not their voices in the houses of worship, while their women should not expose any jewelry. The caliph agreed, and the secretary of the Diwān was ordered to draw up the corresponding edicts. This took place in the month of Ab. The decrees were despatched to all provinces, and during the next month (Elul) reached Damascus, where our Moses acted as katib to an emir. He was commissioned to supervise the concerns of his master in the Damascus district, and thus moved in a purely Muslim environment. When the new treatment of "the people of the tribute" became known, the attitude of the other subordinates of his master towards him completely changed. A certain David Hakkohen in Fustāt, evidently also a government official, seems to have been compelled to adopt Islam. Moses returned to Damascus in the month of Tishri and spent the festival of Tabernacles in constant fear of the fate about to overtake him. On the eighth day of the festival he was arrested and brought before the emir and his brother. Two witnesses gave specious evidence that he spoke disrespectfully of the ruling religion. As a result, he seems to have been tortured and was dangerously ill for three months. Other Jews were similarly treated. After his recovery our poet was forced to renounce Judaism and continue to act as katib to his master. Thereupon the latter resolved to make a pilgrimage to Mecca, taking with him all the members of his household. In vain did Moses attempt to evade this enforced religious ceremony by pretending that his recent illness forbade him to undertake such an arduous journey. He was compelled to join the emir's company, and the interesting

Jacob Mann, "Moses b. Samuel, a Jewish Katib in Damascus, and His Pilgrimage to Medina and Mecca," *Journal of the Royal Asiatic Society* (1919): 155–84; reproduced in *The Collected Articles of Jacob Mann* (Gedera, Israel: 1971); pp. 83–87, 100–12 are included here.

account of his pilgrimage, written with a superb sarcasm, testifies to the author's state of mind while outwardly performing the rites of the hajj. During the journey Moses resolved to rid himself of his employment as secretary with a view of being able to return to his former faith. Circumstances helped him when his master incurred the caliph's wrath and was banished, together with his brother, to Aleppo. But subsequently the caliph visited Damascus, when the emir and his brother took the opportunity of waiting upon their sovereign and regaining his favor. They succeeded and our poet was again threatened with a hard taskmaster. He poured out his soul in prayer in the famous synagogue of Jaubar, near Damascus, in the cave said to have been used by Elijah the prophet. Also in the Ark, where the scrolls of the Law are kept, Moses deposited a petition to God. Now when the emir was restored to his former dignity, he asked Moses to resume his services as katib. But the latter refused by maintaining that he had taken an oath at the Prophet's tomb in Medina no more to serve in that capacity. Thereupon his master ordered him to be tortured. But while giving his command he had a stroke and expired after an illness lasting for seventeen days. Thus our poet was finally delivered from a cruel fate. He no doubt returned to his former religion. But whether he could do this in Damascus or had to flee the country is obscure. So far no more is known of his life story.

A general persecution against "the people of the tribute" in Egypt and in Syria during the reign of the Fatimid caliphs (CE 969–1171) only occurred under al-Hakim. But this ruler is nowhere reported to have visited the capital of his Syrian dominion. Moreover, the name of the chief katib, "the secretary of the secret" (sofer ha-sod), makes it evident that the poems date from the post-Fatimid period. It was during the reign of the Mamlūk caliphs in Egypt that the restrictions against Jews and Christians were from time to time renewed. A serious time for the tributary population was the year CE 1301, when several of the laws mentioned in our poems were enforced all over the empire. These were carried out in Rajab, 700 H. (April, 1301), in Cairo, and in the following month (Shabān) in Damascus.[1] These dates do not correspond with those given in the poems, which must therefore deal with events that took place at some other time. Already in Shabān, 689 H. (August–September 1290) an order was issued by the Caliph Kala'um forbidding any Jew or Christian to be employed in the administrative offices of the government, and the holders of such appointments to be dismissed.[2] A more critical emergency occurred a short time later during the reign of Kala'un's son al-Ashraf Khalil. Makrizi[3] reports how the haughty attitude of a Christian katib to an emir in Cairo towards a Muslim official resulted in a riot of the Muslim population. The Caliph proclaimed in the capital that no Jew or Christian should be allowed to remain in the employment of an emir. At the same time he commanded all emirs to propose to their Christian secretaries

to adopt Islam under the threat of death. Probably the same alternative was put before the Jewish katibs, and these events are reflected in the poems discussed here. One of these compelled converts was David Hakkohen in Cairo, while the same fate overtook Moses b. Samuel in Damascus. But, of course, no definite conclusion as to the date can be arrived at, since the beginning of poem i is missing, wherein very likely the time of these happenings was fully indicated. Let us hope that the lacuna may yet be discovered.

TRANSLATION

i

. . . They found the king in the company of his wise men, and they read the letter before him. The king heard and it pleased him. *All their thoughts are about me.*[4] The king approved of their petition and granted them authority over the people of the tribute. *Let them be desolate by reason of their shame that say unto me (Aha, Aha!).* The kādis and the wise men ('ulemas) were summoned, and they were ready to give answer to him (the king). And said he, "Hear ye, Muslims and ye learned, give ear unto me. Behold this letter, and tell me what the Prophet said about them (the people of tribute)." And each of them answered as a lion, *intending to do me (mischief).* "Hear, my lord the king, for thou art a man of wisdom" thus spoke the viceroy (Wezīr). *And he gave an opinion and said concerning me,* "By thy life that he (the Prophet) is certainly not in their favor." Pay attention to the words of the Wezīr [vizier], forcibly delivered: *I shall instruct thee, listen to me.* (Completed is the [first] alphabet.)

ii

Said he (the Wezīr): "The people of the tribute are vile; let none of them be great amongst us, nor have authority like Arabs. *Yea, the strength of their hands, whereto will it profit me?* Let us increase the laws upon them, so that they be not free from the yoke. And we shall establish our false religion, *bind it unto me as a crown.* Let them wear a sign in the baths, their clothes be not beautiful, and everybody cut off (a part) of his turban, *all that sinned against me.* Let all of them refrain from the work of Katib, their women to be deprived of their ornaments; and during prayers let them not raise their voices. *And wherin I have erred, give me to understand."* The king head the speech and became like a drunken man (i.e., strongly impressed). He decided and replied to the people: "He (Muhammad) *gave me all the kingdoms of the earth.* Now let us humiliate this people, for their laws are different from those of all other nations, and their seed is known among the peoples. *Thus it will be good unto me.* Let speedily the decrees be written and proclaimed in the provinces and the cities, and let nothing miss from all (my) words. *But as for you,* (a holy nation) *will ye be unto me."* The confidential Katib was summoned, he that was the chief support of this intrigue, and he (the king) said to him, "Write and exert thyself greatly *as thou hast planned*[5] *for me."* They hastily left the king with arrogance, for their plan has been accepted to humiliate and make despicable, and thereby the people's transgression be atoned. *Behold, O God, for I am in distress.* In the fifth month (Ab) the (event causing) sighing happened, for it is a month of weeping and crying[6] (and) the soul has no relief in it. *Because I am hated,* (God) *gave unto me* (this trouble). The confidential Katib, who had been summoned, took his seat and called all the secretaries, and said, "Write quickly in accordance with the king's command; *has he not told me?"* All of them heard the instructions and they quickly wrote the edicts. For God is a judge that brings low and raises up, *therefore did God do this unto me.* He (the chief Katib) hurried on (the drawing up of) the decrees, and went about signing (them) with the king's seal as he was bidden (literally: "as he listened"); for he is an important and respected man, (as) *I have been fully told.* In the sixth month (Elul) arrived at my city, Damascus, the decrees which formed my snare, and the fire burned in my heart, *on account of this net they hid for me.* It was fixed to assemble the people of the tribute, that they come, hear, and act (accordingly). And they came and surrendered, *for many fought against me.*

iii

I was at first a Katib, conscientious and well disposed, (in the employ) of a wicked emir, a slanderer. *Such* (a lot) *was I made to possess.* Before the edicts arrived he (my master) guided me (i.e., instructed me) to make a tour over his towns, and he commanded me, "Go, collect what is mine, *for God favored me and I have* (all). Yea, in thy thought curse not the king, when his command comes to disparage thy religion, and tell not others thy secret. *My son, give thy heart to me* (to my words)." I listened to his words and went with his servants to the villages, and spoke smooth words so that my ways were enticed, for I was foolish. *And nights of weariness were appointed unto me.* At first I was with them on equal terms, but on hearing of the intrigue they opened their mouths widely. May God not consent to forgive them, (viz.) *my enemies that speak evil against me.* The seventh months (Tishri) arrived and my goblet was filled from the cup of wrath. My friends and companions were removed from me *and my mouth spoke when I was in distress.* Fierce anger took hold of me when the wicked (fellows) told me that destruction was committed on the pleasant (person) in Egypt, David Hakkohen, the son of delight, *and* (that) *was my reproach.* Wounds were in my heart, and my bowels within me thrilled; plowers plowed upon my back *and I had the fear of Isaac.* I hid the pain, (however) I could not, on account of the foes with whom

I traveled. But my spirit was spent, and I submitted *when my enemies said evil about me.* I knew that they opened their eyes on me, on account of the report that reached them, and I sought to flee on account of their deeds, *I would hasten my escape.* I restrained my anger till (my arrival in) the city (Damascus), and my companions passed on one side and I on another, and I hid myself, going nowhere, *but it profited me not.* I entered (the synagogue) to beseech my God and set my heart to prayer, and I asked for them mercy of my God, saying, *"Be gracious unto me, O God, for I am in distress.* From thee do I ask cover for the storm, for a little while till the wrath passeth, and then shall I serve God in comfort. *Thou art a protection to me.* My heart is submissive before thee, look down upon me from thy habitations, and open thine eyes for my prayer. *Bend Thy ear unto me.* My flesh crept and terror took hold of me on account of the report that reached me, and the evil that overtook me. *O God, be a helper unto me."* Till the night of the eighth day of the festival I made supplication, and having finished the prayer I fell asleep. When morning arrived I was caught *and I was distracted.* With rivers of water did my eyes flow because God did not hear my prayer, and also my household (wept) *at the report they heard of me.* Distress and oppression overtook me, and to my master and his brother, the wicked person, did they bring me, *for the thing I feared came upon me, and that I was afraid of reached me.* My master's brother, the bad and wicked who so often sinned, called me, and he raised his voice, roared, made sport, *and said, "come near to me."* He increased his wickedness towards me, and spoke harshly, "Is it really so that thou didst despise the religion of Ishmael *when you told me 'I have no (pleasure in it)'?"* Two witnesses, sons of Beliya'al, he brought forward in rebellion and treachery; and they gave evidence before I entered (the room). *They became mine enemies.* My sin was complete and the end came; and I became among the Gentiles as a target for the arrow. The evil time oppressed me *by reason of what it did to me.*

iv

("I, Moses b. Rabbi Samuel, who asks complete forgiveness from God who hath chosen the faith of Moses and Israel.")

He (that person) robbed me and magnified my pain. Look and see, my brethren, the children of my mother and father, *whether there is pain like mine which is done unto me.* I have been ensnared on my holiday, on the twenty-second day of my month (Tishri), and he removed the crown of my head. *If I be wicked, woe unto me.* May God see from his habitation, and judge this man and all his crowd, who increased his wickedness and arrogance. *O God, I called thee, hasten to me.* On account of the punishment meted out to me, they carried me to my house with a bad disease, and my heart was torn under my clothes, *by reason of what they did to me.*

My illness lasted three months, on account of my pain my wound was grievous; and my request from my rock (God) is that he accept my repentance. *May God thus do unto me.* While the illness was within me, I heard a report, evil to my heart, that what afflicted me did (also) my brethren, *for it is bitter unto me.* And I prayed unto God, and I said: "*A pure heart create unto me.* See, my God, that my spirit is subdued and (see) the trouble that overtook me and my brethren. And how should this be, (seeing that) thou hast taken me out from my mother's womb? *What is this thou hast done unto me?* I have sought thee, O my God, with all my heart. Do not cause me, O my Rock, to go astray from thy commandments, for thy saying have I stored up in my heart. *Until thy wrath is passed, would that thou appointest me* (a set time and rememberest me). May, I pray, thy kindness comfort me with the repentance (by which) thou wilt make me return unto thee, and thou wilt appoint for me a set time and wilt remember me; *then I will be at rest.* Return unto me in thy mercy, make me return and I shall return unto thee. I will teach the transgressors thy ways, *which I behold unto me.* Deliver me from the yoke of the Gentiles, and draw me out from the depths of their darkness; and in thy great kindness console me. *May my enemies not rejoice about me.* And until old and hoary age remember, my God, (this) unto me for good, and may my salvation be near. *This also remember unto me.*"

After these words God visited (me) and was a redeemer unto me from my illness, and he gave me vigor and strength, *for he inclined his ear unto me.* Yet the affliction of my heart did not depart and pain was shut up within me. And I said, "How did I hate reproof *and all this availeth me not.*" The emir made me return to my secretaryship, perforce without my goodwill, and he raised (my rank) by making me forgo my religion. *And surpassing greatness was added unto me.* He spoke peace while being destruction unto me, and he enticed me with his words and he said unto me, "Thou art now *unto me as a friend, a brother.*" And it came upon his heart to go to Mecca, to perform the rites of a pilgrim and to weep there. And he spoke soft words unto me, "*Oh that thou wert as my brother!*" He commanded all his retinue to be ready, women, fathers, and sons, to perform the pilgrimage to Mecca in crowds. *And thus hath he done unto me.* He commanded his chosen subordinates, and the thought was in my heart that I shall (only) listen about the journey and shall securely dwell (at home), *saying, "God do so unto me* (if I make the pilgrimage)." He (the emir) prepared his matters and requisites so that there should be no mishap on his travels, and he sent to me through his messengers, *for he sought an occasion against me.* "Hear (the message) from me and go with me, thou and my men that visit my hall, for thou art like my people. *If thou dost not listen to me* (thou wilt be punished)." And his servants came to me and told his words about me. Then I cried. "My great and mighty ones, *hear unto me and entreat for me* the

emir my lord, request him and say unto him, 'This man is ill and cannot travel; leave him (therefore) in his house.' *And ye give unto me* (an answer)." They (the emir's servants) brought him back the reply, and his anger was kindled and he increased his wrath and indignation. And he said, "Bring ye him here; *I shall understand what he will say unto me.*" He sent unto me one of his officers, a man of deceit in his actions, and he said unto me, "Hasten, say unto him, '*Behold, I am here, for thou hast called me.*' Return to speak with him, then will his anger go back from thee, (for) thou art an elderly and respected person with him. *Hearken unto my voice and go (and) take me (with you).*" I hastened to go unwillingly, and when I reached him he sported with me, saying, "Behold, thou has dealt deceitfully with me *and thou didst not tell me* (the truth). This day will I renew they troubles and shall not let thee reach thy desire nor go (back) to thy house, *lest they make thee sin against me.*" He commanded (one) of his officers about me carefully to watch my doings, and he said to those near unto him to punish me (if I try to escape). *As for me, far be it from me* (to sin against the Lord).

At dawn he gathered his servants, and the men of his company and his friends, and they all traveled together. And he said, "*Far be it from thee* to travel unwillingly," for my pain was shut up within me, and owing to the greatness of my sin before my Rock and Stronghold, *all that saw me scoffed at me.* We went from province to province and from town to town, while the flame (of indignation) burned in my heart, till we passed Mount Sē'ir. *All that saw me scoffed at me.* I arrived in the town of their Prophet (Medina), where they prayed *for* him at arrival and departure, thinking that he heard and saw them. *Laughter hath he made unto me.* The pilgrims assembled at his tomb and beheld in the night a light shining over his minaret. Said one of his assembly, "*Art thou jealous of me?*" I hastened to call one of the townspeople and asked him wherefrom (came) the light. *Swear by the god here that thou tell me no falsehood.* He hastened to speak the true report without falsehood. "The light of our Prophet is indeed alike by night and by day, only in these days it is invisible, for I is rare. *And if they believe me not,* (behold) in the street yonder everyone waves a torch in his hand in order that the light illumine (the tomb of) the Prophet *whom they sanctify unto me.*" When his townspeople heard his words they arose to kill and accurse him. But he had the better of them and verified his statement. *Oh the sons of the stranger speak falsely to me.* My mouth speaketh the praise of the Lord that he brought unto me this man for the purity of my hands, and I bowed down upon my face, *because he inclined (his ear?) unto me.* His speech is sweet to my heart, though it be severe. And I said, "and there arose no prophet again in Israel like Moses, and his memory shall not be forgotten from the mouth of all the nations, *for he hath set it unto me for an everlasting covenant.*"

There (at Medina) they stayed three days and (then) went to Mecca barefoot and naked, and I went with them for twelve days appalled. *Were not God a help unto me,* (I should have died). They arrived at the house of their worship (the mosque), whither they turn their faces at prayer. And I examined the Black Stone that causes them to stumble; *it appeared unto me as a plague.* And they reeled and moved about like a drunkard, for said they, "Let us follow and commemorate the custom of our Prophet." O God, abandon them in their sin. *Let not the King* (God) *impute* (iniquity) *unto me.* I went out from there (the mosque) while they increased the festivity, and I said, "O Lord, be zealous for thy name and thy discouraged Torah, and remove from our heart this anxiety *which thou hast given unto me.* Set thy countenance upon thy desolate sanctuary, restore to it thy honor, and raise up its horns. As for thy despised people, set them on high, *and holy men will ye be unto me.* Behold this house and those that visit it, while thy house is desolate and we far from it. Make us return to dwell in its shade, *for thou art a protection unto me.* May I dwell in thy tent forever, I and thy desolate people, for thou hast chosen us from all the nations; *wonderful is thy love unto me.* To do thy will, O God, I desired, and behold I am now caught in my sin. But I have kept thy word before, *for it is to me forever.*"

Thereupon we journeyed from Mount as-Safa (?), we and the men of the town of Ashar Diran (?), and the men of the lands of Ishmael and Haran, *who rendered their guilt offering unto me.* At midday we halted till sunset, while our bodies, together with the head, were naked. For they said, "This is our holy mountain." *Holy shall this be unto me.* My God requited me good and revealed not my secret, since he knew that I went involuntarily and without my intent; (thus) he brought me back in peace and did not forsake me in the land of my wandering. *Behold, God is a helper unto me.* They returned by the same way of their country which they took (before), they that said that they made me do a meritorious act which they did (too). And I returned to my relatives who supported (my hands); *after my hardship I had* (a rest). To God I gave thanks and praise and asked for complete forgiveness from him. Then shall I pay what I vowed, *and he will be my* (God). I shall no longer do the work of a secretary, for its fear is engraved on my heart, till I go forth from slavery unto freedom; *he will render unto me in accordance of the purity of my hands.* This is my request from the everlasting Rock, that I and my seed walk in the perfect way; and that he deliver us from among the nations: *for God will heal me.* In his kindness he inclined his ear unto me, (so that) the king was wrath with my master and expelled him to Aleppo, to do as was my will. And I and my household dwelt (in) quiet upon my base, *and the Lord requited unto me.* God is good to those that hope for him, to the soul that seeks him, ever to be found by him that asks for him. I shall every day wait upon him and seek him, *and by night there will be no silence unto me.*

Thereupon the king left his country (Egypt) and came to our land to do his desire. (I thought that) the end has come upon the emir, the foe, *and my sleep was pleasant unto me.* When my master and his brother heard (the news), they returned from Aleppo and stood before him (the king), who did much good to them. And he said to them, "Walk in attachment before me, *keep ye my covenant and ye will be mine.*" On account of this my heart was sick and sad and I entered the synagogue of the prophet Elijah. I prayed before him (God) in the cave of hiding. "*O my God, what wilt thou give unto me.* My King, behold my master standing in his (former) basis, and I fear lest he asks me to be with him. My God, rescue my soul from his trap. *I will hasten an escape unto me.*" I placed the letter in the Ark and prayed before God as much as I could, saying, "I know that thou art able to do everything, *in distress thou makest broad for me.*"

Finally the king exalted the head of my master and gave him a portion among the lords. Then he (my master) asked me to divide the management of the townlets among his servants, but *I said, "Far be it from me."* I answered him while my heart showed submission, "My master knoweth of my oath at the Prophet's grave that I shall not bring myself (again to do) this work. But *if thou doest thus unto me* (thou mayest kill me)." Then he lifted up his face to his servants who surrounded me, and he said, "Bring him near unto me, in order to increase the severe (punishment) for my deed." *But God was a support unto me.* My Rock brought him low while the command came out from his mouth, and his body shivered and he became ill. He (God) cast him into the abyss and the deep, and *and God requited unto me.* God, tremendous and feared, accepted my prayer, and he killed him after seventeen days. My God granted me redemption from him. *He heard my voice and gave unto me* (as I wished). God, merciful and searching the hearts and kidneys, rescued the sheep from the lion's mouth. May he in his kindness rescue the remainder of the sheep. *I rejoiced when they told me* (the news). Song and praise will I render unto thee all my days, for thou didst deliver me from my enemies and foes. From thee I ask my bread and water. *Thine am I and what is mine.* My lips utter praise, for thou didst save me in pity and compassion, and hast given me thy superior Torah. *Thou hast turned my lamentation into a dance unto me.*

vi

(Completed by the strength of God, may he be exalted. The following piyyut said the author of the [above] work, "Moses b. Samuel of Safed"):—

My King, constantly are my trust and hope in thee till my return to the earth. May my song be favorable before thee as thou hast answered me in my cry. Behold, I stand as a poor man asking and requesting thy forgiveness for my sin. Wherewith am I to meet thy kindnesses that surround me always? In the presence of the assembly of thy people shall I praise thee, for thou art my help in my trouble. I am low, insignificant, and unworthy of all Thy kindnesses, so that I am ashamed. On this account I was confused and trembled; also I was yet more vile and said, "Who am I from my father's house, and wherewith have I come hither?" Said sons of understanding and also replied unto me to set right my path ". . . the ways of God." I heard and considered . . . which I pour out upon my head, cause my walks constantly to be in comfort (literally: "in butter"); lift up my face whenever I beseech thee; hear and accept my request; support my steps upon a path of uprightness; be my protection till I die. May all my prayers be for a favor; fulfill my request in Thy mercy.

*For further clarification of any references, see original essay.

NOTES

1. See *Journal Asiatique* 4, no. 18: 486–87; Weil, *Geschichte des Abbasidenchalifate in Egypten* 1: 269 ff. A Hebrew account is given by Sambari in Neubauer, *Mediaeval Jewish Chronicles* 1: 135–37.

2. See Quatremére, *Histoire des Sultane Mamlouka,* vol. 2, 1, 109.

3. Wüstenfeld, Makrizi's *Geschichte der Copten,* 71 ff.

4. The italics indicate the Bible verses at the end of the strophes.

5. [The Hebrew word] *'alal* is taken here in the meaning of "plan," "intrigue," cf., Rabbinic Hebrew *'alilah,* a pretext.

6. I.e., mourning for the destruction of the Temple.

CHAPTER 42

The Destruction of the Kairouan, and the Almoravid and Almohad Persecutions

H. Z. Hirschberg

THE DESTRUCTION OF KAIROUAN

This was the situation at the beginning of the reign of al-Mu'izz, which according to Arab historians was altogether a period of peace and prosperity in the emirate until the Fatimids began to incite the Bedouins against him. It seems that even in those good days the Jews repeatedly endured hardships of which the chronicles make no mention. A letter of the Palestinian Gaon Solomon ben Yehuda to Fustāt, discovered in the Geniza, mentions incidentally "what happened to the Kairouan community when the hand was extended against them and their enemies would have prevailed but for the mercy of the Merciful . . . the Nagid Rabbenu Jacob was of some help."[1] This letter dates from the thirties of the eleventh century, but no particulars of the danger then threatening Kairouan [northeast Tunisia] Jewry can be gathered from it, nor is that danger mentioned in the letters of R. Nissim ben Jacob or Rabbenu Hananel, distinguished Yeshiva Heads whose activities in Kairouan at that time will be discussed below.

A few years later, the general situation in the country deteriorated. In the forties, al-Mu'izz openly defected from his Egyptian overlord and swore allegiance to the Baghdad caliph, whose name again appeared in Friday prayers at mosques. The Fatimids sent the Upper Egyptian nomad Bedouin tribes of the Hilāl and Sulaym against the rebel. These launched recurrent marauding expeditions against Cyrenaican, Tripolitanian, and Tunisian cities. The authorities were compelled to withdraw from Kairouan to a suburb and defend Old Kairouan from there. Part of the population also left the city, and the emir sought refuge in the well-fortified and easily defensible citadel of al-Mahdiya. In 1057, the Bedouin broke into Kairouan and wrought havoc there. The palaces of the sheikhs of the Sanhāja tribe and the houses of the rich were looted; the inhabitants scattered in all directions.[2]

This happened shortly after the death of R. Hananel ben Hushiel (1056), as we gather from a fragmentary

Geniza letter which alludes to those events while noting that the Gaon and Yeshiva Head has appointed Nissim *Rashi V' Rabanim* "Head of the Rabbis House" (academy) and representative of the Yeshiva for the whole of the Maghreb in succession to R. Hananel. This information is followed by a brief description of Kairouan: "God wanted the ruin of this country and the destruction of those in it. We beg God to do good . . . and look upon us in his mercy, etc." And again: . . . "will write to the community and console them for what happened to them—their subsequent exile from their city and departure from their country. Their quarter and *Al Mikdash al-Galil* (sumptuous synagogue) were the admiration of every passerby."[3]

We do not know where this letter was written—whether in Kairouan or in Mahdiya—and are therefore unable to deduce from it whether the Kairouan Jews were vouchsafed to return to their city or were banished from it forever. The request that comfort be extended to the people of Kairouan permits of no definite conclusion, for the writer may have meant that the Gaon's message should be sent to the place where the community had found refuge.

At any rate, if they returned, part of them will surely not have remained there long. The city as a whole was becoming impoverished, for before there had been time to rebuild the ruins of 1057, it was sacked by a nomad Berber tribe in 1060. From then onward, the actual masters of the country were the Bedouin, who extorted and pillaged the population at will.

From a Geniza letter discussed by S. D. Goitein we learn that R. Nissim left his native Kairouan for Mahdiya and died there in June or July 1062. Another letter, of approximately 1061, mentions the (unnamed) Nagid of Kairouan, who was forced to leave the country and moved westward; he was so poor that (Jewish) merchants from Tunisia living in Egypt had to collect money for him.[4]

When al-Mu'izz died in 1063, the state began to disintegrate. Every important city and every region became

---

From H. Z. Hirschberg, *A History of the Jews of North Africa* (Leiden: 1974), vol. 1, pp. 114–39; 201–204.

an "independent" kingdom. Upon the destruction of Kairouan, nodal point of the threads connecting the individual Jewish settlements all over the country, continuous information about them ceases. This must not be taken to mean that these communities ceased to exist, but merely that they are no longer traceable. A handful of Jews seems to have lived in Kairouan for quite a considerable time. It is mentioned in a letter of the middle of the twelfth century as a place where Jews can live.[5] According to a late Arab writer, their complete expulsion from the city took place in the second half of the thirteenth century, when Kairouan was proclaimed one of the holy cities of Islam and Jews and Christians were forbidden to reside in it as well as in Hammāmet near Tunis.[6] Although a document of the year 1500 discovered in the Great Mosque of Kairouan mentions one Maimūn the Jew as the lessee of a shop in the Muslim endowment, he was probably a convert to Islam.[7] Joseph ha-Kohen (middle of the sixteenth century) reports that Jews were forbidden to reside in Kairouan because it was the seat of the "Ismaelite High Priest."[8]

After the destruction of Kairouan, the administrative centre of the state moved westward, at first to Qal'a Banī Hammād. One branch of the Banī Hammād succeeded in coming to an agreement with the Bedouin who had devastated Tunisia, and by means of an annual tribute protected its country from their incursions. During that period, the importance of the Qal'a Jewish community obviously increased, and a Jewish historian about a hundred years after the destruction of Kairouan notes that Qal'a shares Kairouan's spiritual heritage with Mahdiya.[9] The city of Majāna (north of Qal'a), with a district rich in natural resources, had also long had a large Jewish population, as evidenced by documents.[10]

In the late eleventh century, the Banū Hammād transferred their capital to Bajāya (now Bougie) on the Mediterranean, at about the longitude of Qal'a and Majāna, since it seemed safer to them from Bedouin raids. We may assume that Jews moved there together with the Sanhāja, although Jewish communities in Bajāya and Algiers are mentioned only in a list of places of Almohad days.[11]

THE ALMORAVIDS AND ALMOHADS; THE FIRST FORCED CONVERSIONS

In the very same period when Bedouin marauders descended upon the Banū Zīrī kingdom in the eastern part of the region (Tripolitania, Tunisia) and the Banū Hammād consolidated their position in the center (today Central Algeria), there arose in the west, among the Berbers in the Sūs and Dar'a valleys, the religious-social-military movement of the *murābitūn* (Almoravids), i.e., people of the *ribāt*, the strongholds of bands of defenders of Islam against enemies without and heretical views within. The people called those Berbers "veil-wearers" because they veiled their faces like women. The

Almoravids aimed at purifying Berber religious life in the spirit of traditional belief, as represented by the Malikite school, one of the four schools of orthodox [Sunni] Islam. They at first attacked the small Shi'ite principalities at Sijilmāsa and Taroudant. As they became more powerful, under the leadership of Yūsuf ibn Tāshfīn (1061–1106), the founder of Marrakesh (1062), they undertook large-scale conquests in Africa and Spain. After subduing Morocco, they turned eastward, captured Tlemcen, Wahrān (Oran), and Tenes, and advanced to east of Algiers, which fell to them (1082) after a siege. They thus reached the border of the Banū Hammād state.

We do not know whether the Jews suffered more by that fighting than the rest of the civilian population. This absence of information may indicate that they were not specially affected. Such an assumption may be strengthened by a report that the Jews of the Maghreb paid jizya (protection tax) under Yūsuf. The story of R. Isaac Alfasi, who fled from Fez to Cordova in 1088, contains no hint of religious persecution. One manuscript indeed has it that in 1071 Yūsuf ibn Tāshfīn imposed upon the Jews a *farīda* (compulsory levy), which yielded 100,000 dinars, a very considerable sum; this seems to have been a kind of property confiscation. Anyhow, it stands to reason that many Jews crossed to Spain in those days, which would account for the slackening intellectual activity and general quiescence we now find in Morocco. We know that the army of Alfonso VI of Castile, which fought the Almoravids in their drive into the Pyrenean Peninsula, included Jews, and it is also reported that the Muslim conquerors from Africa were helped by Jews who accompanied them or followed closely behind.[12]

After two generations, Almoravid power began to wane. There arose in that same South Moroccan region the new religious movement of the Almohads, i.e., upholders of unity (*muwahhidūn*), who proclaimed the absolute unity of God, maintaining that no physical or moral attributes must be ascribed to him.

This movement, too, whose founder was Muhammad ibn Tūmart, the Mahdi, i.e., the one guided by Allah, did not content itself with preaching, but sought to spread its ideas by the sword. At first, in the twenties of the twelfth century, Ibn Tūmart enlisted support among the Berbers of his country. He went to Fez, Meknes, and Salé, and also to Marrakesh, the capital of the Almoravids. Everywhere he debated with religious scholars, preached purity and staged demonstrations to stir up feelings against moral corruption. Eventually he settled in his home district, the Nefīs and Upper Sūs valleys. Here, in the wilderness of the High Atlas Mountains, he built the fortress of Tinmalal, whence he sent emissaries to organize his adherents and carry out purges (*tamyīz*) among those known or suspected to be unreliable. He died—according to most sources—in 1130, and the leadership passed to 'Abd al-Mu'min, his deputy, as directed in his will. The events and dates of his career are reported with great variations, but the general picture is clear.

'Abd al-Mu'min at first operated in the Atlas Mountains and the southern valleys; the Tāfilālet, i.e., the Southern Ziz Valley, and its capital, Sijilmāsa, yielded to him in 1140. But only in 1145 did he advance into the northern coastal plain. Here he captured Oran—at the defense of which Tāshfīn 'Ali, who had only recently succeeded to the Almoravid throne, was killed—and Tlemcen; Sijilmāsa sent a thanksgiving mission to erase the memory of insurrections against Almohad rule which had occurred there during the preceding years. Then the Almohads attacked Fez and Marrakesh (1146–47). In 1147, 'Abd al-Mu'min sent an army to Spain, where many important cities, including Seville, were conquered; others, such as Cordova, surrendered. The Banū Hammād state succumbed to the Almohads in 1152.[13]

The eastern parts of our region, Tripolitania and Cyrenaica, did not seem to interest the Almohad leader. Those countries had for a hundred years been a prey to nomad Arabs, the Banū Hilāl and Banū Sulaym, who turned fertile agricultural lands and thriving commercial cities into deserts. This situation had been taken advantage of by King Roger of Sicily, who during the years 1134 to 1148 captured the important seaports in that area, viz. (in geographical order): Jijilli (Algeria) Sousse, Mahdiya, Sfax, the Qerqina (Kerkenna) Islands, Qābes (1143–1148), the Jerba Peninsula (1134), and the Tripolitanian ports (1146).

In view of the threatening spread of Christian rule, the Muslims asked the Almohads for help, and the latter set out in 1159 from their Moroccan center to complete what they had begun fifteen years previously. In this campaign, the most difficult part of which was the capture of fortified Mahdiya, 'Abd al-Mu'min drove the Normans from Africa and shifted the boundary of his state to within the sphere of influence of Egypt, which was still under Fatimid rule.[14]

'Abd al-Mu'min died in 1163, a few years after completing his work—the union of the whole of North Africa under the Muminids, as the dynasty founded by Ibn Tūmart's deputy is called. But he himself had created the nucleus of the force which ultimately supplanted the Berbers in their own country. To prevent unrest in the newly conquered territories, and to resettle the Outermost Maghreb, depopulated by the mass extermination of opponents, he had brought Arab Bedouin to his homeland. This was the beginning of the end of the sovereignty of the Berber tribes.

MOSES DAR'I PREDICTS THE COMING OF THE MESSIAH

Arab historians completely ignore the sufferings of Jews and Christians in those days. Ibn al-Athīr reports that upon the capture of Tunis in 1159 'Abd al-Mu'min gave them the choice between conversion to Islam or death. Other sources say that the Almohad leader waived the jizya, and thus abrogated the protective relationship, and gave those who were not prepared to join him time to leave the country.[15]

These occurrences at the end of Almoravid rule, and particulars of the forced conversions are reflected in several Jewish sources, some of which are near to the events in place and time and may therefore be regarded as faithful first- and secondhand accounts, while others cast the available data into the mould of elegies, without aiming at order, historical correctness, or completeness of description.

Two versions of an epistle of Maimonides to Yemen contain a description of an event which deeply perturbed the Jews of Fez in the twenties of that [eleventh] century. After warning against the lure of self-proclaimed messiahs and telling about a "Messian" who had appeared in the East, he continues in the shorter version as follows:

There also arose a man in the west, in the city of Fez, eighteen years ago, saying that he was the harbinger and messenger of the Messiah, who would appear during that year. His prediction did not come true, and the Jews suffered fresh tribulations on his account. The story was told me by a person who was present at all those events.[16]

And here is the longer version:

And this I am reporting to you as something certain, knowing that it is true because of its nearness in time. For, fifty years ago or thereabouts, a devout, excellent man, a scholar in Israel by the name of Master Moses Dar'I, came from Dar'a to Spain to study the Law under Rabbi Joseph Halevi b. Megāsh, or blessed memory, of whom you have heard. Thereafter he came to the capital of the Maghreb, i.e., Fez, and the people of the place flocked to him because he was a devout, excellent and learned man. He said to them: Lo, the Messiah is coming, God has told me so in a dream. He did not, as that mad man had done, boast that he knew he was the Messiah; he only said he had been told that the Messiah had revealed himself. And the people were attracted to him and believed him. My father and teacher, may that righteous man's memory be blessed, would dissuade and prohibit the people from following him. But few listened to my father, their rabbi—in fact, all turned after R. Moses, may his soul rest in Paradise. Eventually, he would make predictions, which proved completely correct. If he said: it was revealed to me yesterday that such-and-such a thing would happen, it would be exactly as he had said. One day, he told them that on a certain Friday it would rain heavily, and the liquid that came down would be blood, and that would be the sign of which it is said "And I will shew wonders in the heaven and in the earth," etc. (Joel 3, 3). It was in the month of Marheshvan, and it rained hard and fast that Friday, and the water that came down was red and slimy, as if it had been mixed with clay. This was the sign by which he proved to all the people that he was undoubtedly a prophet; as I have told you, it is not impossible that prophesy will revive before the coming of the Messiah. And when most of the people believed him, he told them that the Messiah would come on Passover Eve of that year. And he ordered them to sell their property and to borrow money from the Muslims with the promise to pay ten dinars for every one, thus fulfilling the commandment of the Torah with regard to the Passover Festival, because they would never see them again; and they did so. And when Passover came and nothing happened, those people were ruined, for most of them lost all their property and were burdened with debts. The matter became known also among their Gentile neighbors and servants, and if he had been found he would have been killed. He could not remain in the lands of Islam after this, and he went to the Land of Israel and died there, may his memory be blessed.[17] On leaving, as I have been informed by all those who saw him, he foretold everything, great and small, that has happened in the Maghreb, in accordance with what God had announced to him.[18]

This long account, an enlargement of the first-quoted version, is important because of Maimonides' initial statement that he vouches for its truth as he heard the story from reliable persons who had known Moshe Dar' personally and whom he questioned about details. This emphatic affirmation, which Maimonides saw fit to place at the beginning of his report, undoubtedly deserves most serious notice. The discrepancy as to the date of the events—fifty years or forty-five years before the date of the letter (allegedly 1122 or 1127)—is not material to our subject; in any case, we do not know the exact date of the Epistle to Yemen in either redaction. The decisive fact is that Moses' Dar'i's prophecies were made after Muhammad ibn Tūmart had been in Fez. His visit took place before 1120. On that occasion, he debated with the tulabā, the scholars of Islam, on the principles of religion and went to the market with his disciples to smash musical instruments; according to one source, he was expelled from the city. From Fez, Ibn Tūmart went to Meknes and Marrakesh, and his appearance in these two places no doubt made a great impression and caused unrest not only among the Muslim population.[19]

In this general turmoil, Dar'i's prophecies of the coming of the Messiah on Passover Eve found willing ears, especially as they were accompanied by seemingly corroborating signs. Their nonfulfillment caused acute disappointment. The Muslims, too, must have heard of the episode, and the failure of the prophet surely was a trump card of the Almohads twenty years later in their attempts to convert the Jews.

In the early thirties of the century, we find at the court of the Almoravid ruler 'Alī ibn Yūsuf ibn Tāshfīn

(1106–1142) the physician Meir ben Qamniel and another Jewish physician Solomon b. al-Mu'allim, who had both been invited from Spain, the latter from Seville.[20] When at that time the local mosque, which had proved too small for the number of worshipers, was to be enlarged, it appeared that many Muslim endowment properties had passed into private hands and that most of the houses to the south were Jewish-owned. In accordance with religious law, the land necessary for the enlargement of the mosque was expropriated from both Muslims and Jews; this happened in the year 529 AH (1134–35). But the owners all received fair compensation, which may have been due to the influence of the two Jewish physicians who had access to the king; a sovereign's physicians in ordinary were always persons of consequence.[21]

However, the ban imposed by that ruler on the residence of Jews in the capital, Marrakesh, founded by his father, was a flagrant act of discrimination. Marrakesh was at first only a large encampment of Berber nomads, and the city of Aghmāt Wāylan, capital of the Banū Maghrāwa, the predecessors of the Almoravids, situated forty kilometers to the southeast in a grandiose landscape at the foot of the High Atlas, continued to be the administrative center of the country, although it remained unfortified.[22] We may assume that there were Jews at Marrakesh already in its early days, having come there in the course of their business, just as they came to other nomad encampments. In time, solid buildings were erected at Marrakesh, and 'Alī himself surrounded it with a wall—the hallmark of a royal city—and constructed a mosque which was subsequently destroyed by the Almohads because its mihrāb did not face south but east—in accordance with the Jewish custom of facing east in prayer, as noted by Ibn Tūmart's and 'Abd al-Mu'min's biographer. In those days began the decline of Aghmāt as the center of government, and many Jews apparently asked to settle in the new capital. This displeased 'Alī, who toward the end of his life shut himself up in his palace and harem and listened to religious scholars and his womenfolk. He demonstrated his Muslim zeal by building sumptuous mosques; besides erecting that of Marrakesh, he enlarged the Qarawiyīn (= people of Kairouan) Mosque in Fez and in 1136 constructed the Great Mosque in Tlemcen. He further decreed that any Jews found in Marrakesh at night should be killed and their property confiscated. They were only permitted to be in the capital in the daytime in the pursuit of their business or trade.[23]

THE ALMOHAD PERSECUTIONS

Abraham ibn Ezra's famous lament Ahā yārad (Oh, there descended) is our main source for that calamity, since it mentions several communities that were destroyed, describing the attendant events. First some in Spain: Seville, Cordova, Jaen, Almería. Then some in

Africa: Sijilmāsa, "city of the learned and wise"; Marrakesh, "the royal city"; Fez; Tlemcen; Ceuta; Meknes; Dar'a, "where the blood of sons and daughters was split on a Sabbath day." According to the poem, the persecution took place in the year 1070 or, if we follow the Tripoli MS, 1072 after the destruction of the Second Temple, i.e., 1138 or 1140 CE. The events are strung together without chronological or geographical order (those in Spain are placed first), so that we may assume that Ibn Ezra, who was roaming about Europe in those days, did not know their exact sequence. The lament must have been composed not later than the end of the fifties, i.e., before the news of the expulsion of the Normans from Africa and the conquests of 'Abd al-Mu'min in Tunisia and Tripolitania spread in Europe. It was very popular, and several additions and supplements to it have come down to us.[24]

Among the Geniza documents, Schirmann has discovered a fragment of this lament which differs in many points from the previously known version.[25] The main differences between the two versions concern the order in which the events are reported and the story of a disputation held in Dar'a between the Jews and the Muslim conquerors;[26] this story appears only in the Geniza fragment. We shall see below, in Solomon Cohen's letter, that a similar debate in Sijilmāsa lasted seven months. Such debates were fully in accordance with the spirit and methods of 'Abd al-Mu'min and his predecessor Ibn Tūmart. The Almohads at first tried to win over the population by debate and preaching, and only afterward resorted to more drastic means of persuasion.

An addition concerning Fez in the Geniza fragment describes that city as an important center of Jewish religious learning, but does not enrich our knowledge of historical events. The Geniza fragment makes no mention of Marrakesh. The above data as to 'Ali ibn Yūsuf's ban on Jewish settlement there make it likely that the verse about the "royal city," which appears in only one MS of the familiar version of the lament, is a late addition by a person who knew that Jews were harmed in that region also, but who knew no particulars. On the other hand, the Geniza fragment mentions Aghmāt and Sūs. This detail is important because it proves that the information given here is more exact than that contained in the familiar version.

Aghmāt is the name of the ancient settlement near Marrakesh where Jews lived because they had been forbidden to live in Marrakesh itself since the days of 'Alī ibn Yūsuf. It is not to be supposed that Jews moved to Marrakesh precisely during the three years of war and unrest between 'Alī's death and the capture of the city by the Almohads.[27]

In referring to the fate of Sūs, the poet meant the region south of Marrakesh and Aghmāt, which was the cradle of Almohadism. The Sūs Valley runs south from the Atlas Mountains and then turns toward the Atlantic coast; its mention in the Geniza fragment attests that it had a Jewish population. Hence all three South Moroccan valleys: the Ziz Valley, with Sijilmāsa, the Dar'a Valley, and the Sūs Valley, had Jewish populations.

Schirmann has published a fragment of yet another lament, which in his opinion likewise deals with North African events, but which mentions no place names. It begins with the words *Eykh neherāb* (Oh, there was devastated). Schirmann surmises that both fragments stem from Abraham ibn Ezra.[28] If this is correct, we must suppose that "Oh, there was devastated" is a later, amended version of "Oh, there descended," written when the poet had obtained more exact and detailed information, also as regards the chronological order of events.

Jewish historiography has preserved three short notes on the sufferings of African Jewry about the middle of the twelfth century. One is by Abraham ben David, who says: ". . . those were years of distress, oppression and persecution to Israel, and they were exiled from their localities: such as were for death, to death, and such as were for the sword, to the sword, and such as were for the famine, to the famine, and such as were for the captivity, to the captivity (Jer. 15:2). Jeremiah's prophecy was even added to: and such as were destined to leave the community left because of the sword of Ibn Tūmart, who went forth into the world in the year 4902 (1141–42)[29] and who had decided to eliminate Israel. They said, Come, and let us cut them off from being a nation; that the name of Israel may be no more in remembrance (Ps. 83:5). And so he left no name of them in the whole of his kingdom nor remnant in the city of Salé, from the end of the world to the city of al-Mahdiya."[30]

Abraham ben Daud wrote his book after North Africa had been conquered as far as the approaches of Egypt, but for some reason he did not specify all the places that suffered, but mentioned two typical localities, at either end of the region, to circumscribe the area of the disaster: the Atlantic port of Salé and Mahdiya on the Tunisian coast. Elsewhere he writes: "They did not leave a remnant of Israel from Tangiers to al-Mahdiya; turn back thine hand as a grapegatherer into the baskets (Jer. 6:9)."[31]

For an area to be defined by indicating two port cities at its western and eastern ends, respectively, was quite common. The settlements along the coast were close together and linked by a fixed caravan route in addition to the sea communication. It is reported that there was a signaling service by means of beacons all along the coast.[32] The reason why it is not Tripoli that is mentioned in the east will be given below.

The date of 4902 is absolutely exact, for it was in the year 536 (1141–42) that 'Abd al-Mu'min set out on his campaign to conquer areas outside its original territory in the Sūs Valley and the High Atlas.[33] From then onward, tribulations occurred which lasted many years—since there were intervals between one campaign and the next and attempts at persuasion and enticement.

Two other notes originate from R. Solomon ibn Verga.

(a) In connection with the fourth persecution, Ibn Verga reports that in 4872 (!) Ibn Tūmart threatened death to anyone who refused to embrace Islam. The Jews tried to ease their fate by discussion and the offer of their property, but did not succeed in influencing the king. Many communities thereupon foreswore Judaism. A month after the persecutions, however, the king died, and his son appeared to be more moderate, so that numerous converts returned to their former faith, while others, suspecting a trap, did not do so until much later.

(b) Elsewhere Ibn Verga says that a general severe persecution of the Jews for the purpose of conversion occurred in the whole of Barbary and the eastern lands in the year 4906 (1146).[34]

The year 4872 (1112) as the date of the persecution in the first note is clearly erroneous, and since the phrase "the sword of Ben Hūmard (!) went forth" points to influence of the *Sefer ha-Qabbala*, we should amend it to 4902, as there. The date in note (b), 4906 (1146), is correct, as in that year 'Abd al-Mu'min in fact began to conquer the important and populous cities.

The story of the debate between the king and the Jews is based on traditions that have some substance, as we have seen above. The dating of 'Abd al-Mu'min's death "one month after the persecution" is a literary exaggeration, but not far from the truth. He died in 1163, about a year after returning from his last campaign in Spain.

The dates so far reviewed show defects which detract from their value as historical material. They are extremely general and indefinite, replete with poetical flourishes and lacking the precision needed to determine facts.

SOLOMON COHEN'S LETTER

A detailed account of development is given in the letter of Solomon Cohen, a resident of Futstāt, who heard of the events from eyewitnesses, Jewish and Muslim refugees in Egypt, and reported them to his father, then in South Arabia (probably in Aden).[35] The father was eager for news of the Maghreb, since he was a native of Sijilmāsa and still had relatives in Moroccan cities. The letter, written in Judeo-Arabic, is dated of the month of Shebat in the year 1459 of the Seleucid era, i.e., January 1148 CE.

Here is the story of the persecutions, as told by Solomon Cohen:

'Abd al-Mu'min the Sūsi, (i.e., the one of the Sūs Valley), leader of the Almohads after the death of Muhammad ibn Tūmart the Mahdī, marched against the Emir Tāshfīn, who was in Oran, besieged and captured the city, killed Tāshfīn and crucified his body. Thereafter he captured Tlemcen and killed all those who were in it (i.e., including the Jews), except those who embraced Islam. At the news of these events, the Berbers in Sijilmāsa rose against the Almoravid governor and expelled him and his garrison force from the city. Some 200 Jews, sensing the impending trouble, fled Sijilmāsa at this juncture. They included two brothers of his father Yehuda, as well as Yehuda ben Farhōn, whom Solomon mentions specially, probably because he was a local notable and rabbinical scholar or a relative. They escaped to Dar'a, but it was not known what had happened to them afterwards. Following the expulsion of the Almoravid governor from Sijilmāsa, the inhabitants of the latter sent a surrender delegation to 'Abd al-Mu'min. On entering the city, the Almohads tried to convert the Jews to Islam by debate and persuasion, but after seven months of religious disputations, a new commander arrived in the city, who solved the problem by a more efficient method. One hundred and fifty persons were killed for clinging to their faith; the remainder converted. The first to adopt Islam was the *dayyan* (religious judge) of Sijilmāsa, Joseph ben'Amrān.[36] All the cities in the Almoravid state were conquered by the Almohads. One hundred thousand persons were killed in Fez on that occasion, and 120,000 in Marrakesh. Only Dar'a and Meknes had not been captured by the time of reporting. The Jews in all the localities from Bajāya (Bougie) westward groaned under the heavy yoke of the Almohads; many had been killed, many others converted, none were able to appear in public as Jews. The news of the capture of Bajāya reached Fustāt on the day the letter was written. Large areas between Seville and Tortosa had likewise fallen into Almohad hands.

This account tallies with the sequence of events as given by Arab historians, and in particular by Ibn Baydhaq, the biographer of Ibn Tūmart and 'Abd al-Mu'min, who were their contemporary and comrade-in-arms. This permits us to date the events as follows: Oran, 1145 or 1146; Tlemcen, Sijilmāsa, 1146; Fez, 1146–47; Marrakesh area, 1147; Bajāya, end of 1147 or beginning of 1148.

It should be noted that with regard to certain details Solomon's account clarifies some obscure passages in the Arab sources. This applies to his remark that Dar'a and Meknes had not yet surrendered to 'Abd al-Mu'min according to information available in Fustāt in January, 1148. This statement either disproves Ibn Ezra's lament for the murder of the Jews of Dar'a or postpones the event until at least 1148. The capture of Dar'a is in fact not mentioned in Arab sources as happening during that period. The date of the capture of Meknes is not clear;

Ibn Baydhaq and other authors are vague on this point: Solomon Cohen's information was probably correct.

The mention of the capture of Bajāya (Bougie), the capital of the Banū Hammād, at the end of 1147 or the beginning of 1148 is surprising. It is not a slip of the pen, for Solomon had already said that all the communities of the Maghreb, from Bajāya (in the eastern part of this region) onward, were under Almohad control. Upon examining Ibn Baydhaq and other sources, we find that on this point, too, our letter has preserved an important detail. The biographer of 'Abd al-Mu'min does not specify when the city was occupied, but notes that its inhabitants surrendered to the Almohads at the same time as the (Andalusian) admiral Ibn Maymūn. This, as he says elsewhere, was at the time of the fighting for Oran and Tlemcen. A year or more may have passed between the revolt of the people of Bajāya against their lawful Banū Hammād ruler and the entry of the Almohad garrison force, just as a considerable period elapsed between Ibn Maymūn's surrender and the establishment of control over Spain. It seems that Solomon knew of the coincidence of these dates, for he mentions the surrender of the Andalusians side by side with the conquest of Bajāya.

The private letter of a merchant of Fustāt, who had no pretensions of writing the history of the beginning of the persecutions that occurred in the Maghreb in the years 1145–61, is thus revealed as the only source for the sequence and dating of the events.

TUNISIA AND TRIPOLITANIA

We have already noted that several additions to Ibn Ezra's lament "Oh, there descended" have been preserved that refer to the fate of the eastern Maghrebi communities in the days of the Almohads. But before dealing with the information relating to that area during the period under discussion, we must briefly review the situation in Tripolitania and Cyrenaica in the preceding generations. While much material is found in responsa and the Geniza with regard to Tunisia, little information has reached us concerning other places whose names appear in the additions to Ibn Ezra's lament. However, the few Geniza documents, hints in Arab literature and the literature of the Gaonic period, and some contemporary epitaphs, will suffice—*faute de mieux*—to evoke a continuous chain of Jewish communities in Tripolitania and Tunisia, continuous both in space and time. It is, after all, inconceivable that all the communities mentioned in the laments should have sprung up during the period immediately prior to the Almohads; nor can we assume that only they were then in existence, while others, known from other sources, had completely disappeared—there were no doubt more.[37]

The reason why information concerning those Jews is so meager has in part already been given: those small communities had little religious learning and no rab-

binical scholars. Maimonides, in one of his responsa, exposes their ignorance in one sweeping, scathing sentence, . . .[38] Moreover, the political situation in the area was extremely precarious. Tripolitania was disputed by the rulers of Egypt and those of Tunisia, which later conquered it in 1022–23; the event is described in one of the Geniza letters. Even when the area was under one suzerainty, there were feuds between the emirs of the local dynasties and the Berber sheikhs. All this, in conjunction with nomad invasions, highway robbery, piracy, and general poverty—a land-starved, unproductive agriculture, no natural resources—results in a rather dismal picture of insecurity and economic instability.[39]

Most of the Jewish settlements in Cyrenaica, Tripolitania, and Tunisia were concentrated in the numerous port cities along the seacoast. Outstanding among the latter was Tripoli, an important commercial center in touch with its counterparts in Egypt, Syria, and Sicily. A query addressed to a Palestinian academy reveals that Tripoli had a rabbinical court not subject to the Rabbinical Grand Court of Palestine.[40]

An interesting letter fragment—the names of the writer and addresses are not preserved—reports, in an account of the writer's troubles during a journey to Spain, that a famous Jewish physician, by the name of Tubiya, was living in Tripoli. The "king" of Qābes, we are told, had revolted against the "king" of Mahdiya, and when he contracted the illness of which he was to die, he asked the sheikhs of the Banū Matrūh, the elders of Tripoli, to send him the Jewish physician from their city. He promised him a generous fee, part of which he paid in advance. But Tubiya did not want to go to Qābes, and he and his four sons went into hiding. Eventually, when the elders had seized all the Jewish notables of the city as hostages, he was compelled to come out of his hiding place and undertake the arduous journey.[41]

The letter is undated, but the story of the sheikhs of the Banū Matrūh and the enmity between Qābes and Mahdiya points to the time shortly before Roger's invasion of Africa. The disputes between the rulers of the two cities were one of the causes of that war.

From the frequency of the surname al-Lebdī, i.e., the one of Lebda (the Roman port of Leptis Magna), in the Geniza documents of the late eleventh until the middle of the twelfth century, and the fact that the bearers of this surname include important traders known beyond their own city, we may infer that Lebda had a sizable Jewish population.[42]

A Jew hailing from another coastal city, Barca, lived in Jerusalem in 1058.[43] On one occasion, Jewish captives were sent to Barca, probably in order that the local Jews should redeem them. Nearby was Ramāda, where, too, Arab pirates brought captives from Byzantium.[44] This area suffered greatly during invasions by nomad Arabs, of the Banū Sulaym and Banū Hilāl, who ruined harbors and fields, i.e., both commerce and agriculture.[45]

In the interior, there were several communities in the

Nafūsa Highlands in western Tripolitania. In the past century, Tripolitanian Jews believed that their community originated from that region, then known as Fassato.[46] The earliest news of Jews in Nafūsa occurs in a tenth-century responsum of the Gaon Hanināy of Pumbeditha.[47] From it, we learn incidentally that Nafūsa was devastated in a war, but it is not clear whether the reference is to a particular place in the area or to all inhabited localities. In the eleventh century and until the middle of the twelfth, the people of Nafūsa, Jādū and Mīsin are mentioned several times, and Arab geographers note that there are many Jews in the region. They seem to have engaged in trade and perhaps also in agriculture; we find a poet among them, as well as a rabbi who somehow got to Naples in the days of Benjamin of Tudela, and a scribe who copied the Tractate Gittin (Divorce) from the Babylonian Talumd.[48] Caravans traveling from the coastal cities to Tunisia passed through the Nafūsa Highlands; this route was very difficult, but apparently less dangerous than the storm- and pirate-infested sea route.[49]

At what is today the border between Tripolitania and Tunisia is the large oasis of Ghadāmes. It, too, had a Jewish population at that time, as appears from the surname of R. Moses Ghadāmsi.[50]

Let us now revert to the period of the Almohads and their conquest of Tunisia and Tripolitania. We have already mentioned that this event was preceded by attempts of the Norman king Roger of Sicily to subdue that coastal region. Their echo, as received in Aden in South Arabia, is contained in a letter of the merchant Abraham ben Perahya ben Yajū, a former inhabitant of Mahdiya, to his brother Mubashshir, who was still in that city.[51] Abraham has just returned to Aden (in the month of Tishri, 4910 [1149]) from a long trip to India and has heard what has happened to the communities on the African coast: Tripoli, Jerba, Kerkenna, Sfax, Mahdiya, and Sousse. To relieve his anxiety, he asks to be told who is dead and who has survived. The reports that have so far reached him are not clear; he intends to marry his daughter, who is with him, to the son of his (other) brother or his sister and considers the possibility of their settling in Mahdiya, Africa (!), Tunis, or Kairouan. By "Africa"—mentioned whereas Sousse and Sfax are omitted—Abraham probably means the narrow zone between Sousse and Sfax which had remained in Banū Zīrī hands.[52]

However, nothing is known from other sources of harm befalling Jews during the invasion of Africa by Roger's troops, and we are thus unable to gauge the measure of truth in the rumors current at Aden. We only know that the conquerors imposed the jizya, i.e., poll tax, on the inhabitants of the area;[53] but this was nothing new for the Jews, who had formerly paid it to the Muslims.

As stated, 'Abd al-Mu'min's drive into Africa at the head of the Almohad forces, which ended with the conquest of the territory from Tripolitania to Barca in Cyre-

naica, was induced by the victory of the Sicilian troops over the rebels in Mahdiya. During that campaign (1159–60), the Almohads, as already noted, encountered serious resistance only at the maritime fortress of Mahdiya; its siege lasted several months, and 'Abd al-Mu'min gained possession of it only after granting honorable terms of surrender to the Sicilian garrison. He deterred the rulers of provincial towns from fighting him by his harsh treatment of the people of Tunis, who had refused to surrender. Half the property of the Muslims of that city was confiscated for the Almohad treasury, and the Jews and Christians were faced with the choice between conversion and death; at the same time, 'Abd al-Mu'min spared the persons and property of families which had previously sent a peace delegation to him. So the other cities surrendered to 'Abd al-Mu'min; some of them did not even wait until the Almohad army reached them.[54]

It was a sacred tradition in Islam from the days of Muhammad and the first caliphs that populations which surrendered without a fight obtained much more favorable conditions than those worsted in battle, and the victors would honor their agreements with those who had yielded. So would 'Abd al-Mu'min. The rulers who had surrendered voluntarily were confirmed in their positions, although reliable men from 'Abd al-Mu'min's inner circle were attached to them; this implied no discrimination, since his extreme suspiciousness made him treat his own sons the same way. A sheikh of the Banū Matrūh tribe, who had revolted against the king of Sicily and hastened with a deputation of notables to occupied Mahdiya, remained in office in Tripolitania. He was readily accepted by 'Abd al-Mu'min and continued for many years as governor of the country. The prompt surrender of the city governors seems to be the main reason why the conquest of southern Tunisia and the areas east of Tunisia has not been much noted.

'Abd al-Mu'min's rule was severe. He divided the newly annexed areas, from Barca in Cyrenaica to Tlemcen, into administrative districts, ordered the lands throughout the state to be valued and imposed a tax payable in grain and money, from which only reliable Almohads were exempt, while other Muslims, including Almohads suspected of insincerity, had to pay it.[55]

Additions to Ibn Ezra's lament that have been preserved in the Tripolitanian MS (formerly in the possession of R. Abraham Khalfon) reflect with striking faithfulness the state of affairs as known from Arab sources.[56]

Here is a reference to the communities affected: "There is not a Jew, not a single one, in Dājayyā or al-Mahdiya, And for Sabrat and Tūrā my eye always weeps."

Dājayyā is corrupt for Bajāya, well known to us from Solomon Cohen's letter. The reading Sabrat for Kasbārā, a little town west of Tripoli which had a harbor already in Roman times, is very plausible.[57] Tūrā is difficult to locate; its identification with the Tripolitanian Plateau or the Nafūsa Highlands is mere guesswork. Another addition in the same MS mentions in correct geographical order Tunis, Sousse, Mahdiya (repeated for the sake of order), Qābes, and Tripoli.

There is a third addition.[58] Apostrophizing Ibn Ezra with the question why he had omitted certain places, an unknown poet who knew the particulars of events in that vicinity points out some other communities that suffered in those days: al-Hāma (near Qābes), Qafsā (in the interior of South Tunisia), the Isle of Jerba, Surmān (a seaport between Sabrat and Tripoli), Mesallāta (a highland in the interior between Tripoli and Homs), and Misurāta (a seaport east of Tripoli).

The poet especially bemoans the fate of the people of Misurāta, who were overburdened with taxes and part of whom had been exiled to Jerba, while others had migrated to Surmān. This means that even in this serious case, particularly dwelled on by the author, persecution was confined to monetary matters and exile. The passage relating to Tunis likewise mentions no forced conversions or killings. It therefore seems that Ibn al-Athīr (see page 133, note 1 [of original text]) mistakenly lumps the Jews together with the Christians, on whom 'Abd al-Mu'min wished to avenge the murder of Muslims by Roger's men. The Almohads apparently carried out no killings and demanded no conversions in this region. The local rulers, confirmed by them, were compelled to follow their example: worry the Jews, sometimes move them from one place to another, subject them to heavy taxes, all in accordance with 'Abd al-Mu'min's general policy; but they were not particularly active in this respect.

In Tripolitania and Libya, remains of Jewish tombstones and Hebrew inscriptions have been discovered which may perhaps be assigned to the period following the Almohad conquest, although the evidence is not sufficient.[59] The language of Maimonides' responsum on Reuben, who went "to Tripoli, where they seized him by order of the governor of the city for the ships (?), to have them (?) do war service," is too vague to prove the existence of a local Jewish population in Maimonides' time; on the contrary, it rather suggests that Reuben did not live in Tripoli.[60] Another version may indeed support the assumption of a Jewish population: "Our master has taught us concerning Reuben, who betrothed himself to Leah . . . and the marriage was to take place by a certain date. Then Reuben went to Tripoli in the Maghreb. And word came that the governor of the city had seized all the sailors of the ships and taken them to al-Mahdiya for war service. Reuben was delayed, and the stipulated time elapsed."[61]

It should be noted that a Jewish community certainly existed in Barca in the early thirteenth century, since the prayer book of R. Solomon bar Nathan Sijilmāsi was copied there in 1203.[62] T. Lewicki has established that the Ibādī sect survived in Tripolitania in the days of the Almohads; this means that Jewish communities were also able to exist.[63]

The Last Years of 'Abd al-Mu'min

The impression arises that in old age the Almohad ruler somewhat changed his attitude toward the Jews, becoming more moderate toward those who were living in the central, Moroccan part of his realm. Of course, those who had ostensibly recognized Muhammad's prophethood during the persecutions of the forties had to go on living outwardly as Muslims, but it seems that their faith was not inquired into and no strict observance of Muslim ritual was demanded of them. This is indicated by the fact that in 1159 or early in 1160 Maimon, the father of Maimonides, deemed it worthwhile to emigrate with his family from Spain to Morocco and settle in Fez. Here resided in those days R. Yehuda ha-Kohen ibn Sūsān, whose ancestors had come to Fez from 'Irāq and whose fame for learning and piety had spread to Spain. Maimonides, then twenty-five, studied under Yehuda. Also in Fez at the time was the poet Yehuda ibn 'Abbās, who had contacts with Yehuda Halevi and the Castilian poets. In Fez, Maimon wrote his *Epistle on Consolation*, and his son worked at his commentary on the Mishna and wrote the *Epistle on Forced Conversion*, also called the *Epistle on the Sanctification of the Divine Name* (or on *Martyrdom*). These two letters, as well as Maimonides' utterances after leaving Morocco, do not point to outrages and bloody persecution.[64]

Maimonides' remark to his son Abraham concerning the character of the Jews living in the Berber Mountains, the Isle of Jerba and generally in the area between Tunis and Alexandria, whom he describes as strong in faith but superstitious (see below pp. 165f [of original text]), permits the assumption that they were not in danger, for he would certainly not have talked about them in this way had their lives been threatened. In a letter to the community of Lunel, Maimonides deplores the decline of religious learning generally and in the Maghreb in particular, "it being known what persecutions that community has suffered." A similar sentiment is expressed by him in a letter to a disciple. The main trouble was the decline of religious learning.[65]

Nevertheless, although no immediate danger threatened the lives of North African Jewry, their residence in the area imperiled their Judaism and that of their children. This appears from the *Epistle on Forced Conversion*. Although, in the opening lines of that *Epistle*, Maimonides most strongly deprecates the condemnation of the forced converts by "the self-styled sage who has never experienced what so many Jewish communities experienced in the way of persecution," his conclusion is that a Jew must leave the country where he is forced to transgress the divine law: "He should not remain in the realm of that king; he should sit in his house until he emigrates, and if he must pursue any occupation he should do so secretly, until he emigrates." And once more, with greater insistence: "He should on no account remain in a place of forced conversion; whoever remains in such a place desecrates the divine name and is nearly as bad as a wilful sinner; as for those who beguile themselves, saying that they will remain until the messiah comes to the Maghreb and leads them to Jerusalem, I do not know how he is to cleanse them of the stigma of conversion."[66]

R. Maimon and his sons acted in accordance with that advice, and so did Yehuda ibn 'Abbās and the family of Joseph ben Yehuda 'Aqnīn, all admirers of Maimonides, and certainly many others. Maimonides' departure from the country of the Almohads is commonly assumed to have taken place in 1165; according to Saadia ibn Danān, it was prompted by the martyrdom of Yehuda ibn Sūsān, who had been called upon to forsake his religion and had preferred death to apostasy. R. Maimon's family tried to establish itself in Palestine, but after he had died in Jerusalem, his sons went to Egypt, where, in Saadia ibn Danān's words, Rabbenu Moshe became very great in wisdom, learning, and rank.[67]

The Maghreb was thus depleted of its last remaining scholars and of those who had come to it as refugees from Spain. Still, the Maghrebi communities continued to exist. This is evidenced by what Maimonides says about their sufferings in his above-mentioned letters. He also mentions the Fez community in a letter to the leadership of Marseilles Jewry, written after the *Epistle to Yemen* was published. That letter indicates that a missive attributed to him on messianic matters was circulating in Fez; he explains to the people of Marseilles that this is possibly the *Epistle to Yemen*. On the strength of this, it has lately been suggested that there may be some truth in an apocryphal pamphlet on the life of Maimonides at least insofar as it relates to an *Epistle on Appearance of the Messiah* circulated among the Jews of Fez.

In 1173, Maimonides appealed to some apparently North African Jewish communities to collect money for the redemption of captives. This suggests that their economic situation was by no means unfavorable. The geographer Yāqūt (1179–1229) reports that most of the merchants in the Dar'a Valley are Jews.[68]

'Abd al-Mu'min's reign brought a most serious crisis in the history of Maghrebi Jewry. Its life in the Almohad Empire becomes veiled in obscurity. Even Moroccan-Jewish popular tradition preserves no memory of these events. The author of a nineteenth-century historical work, who knows R. Yehuda ibn Sūsān from literature, merely adds: "For 'Abd al-Mu'min exerted heavy pressure on the Jews living in Fez to adopt Islam and resort to Muslim places of worship, and he closed all the synagogues; and R. Maimon and his two sons fled to Alexandria."[69] Little is known of what happened under the descendants and heirs of 'Abd al-Mu'min. And the little the historians deemed worthy of note is both sad and mortifying: discrimination was practiced only against Jews, for only they had remained of the country's non-

Muslim inhabitants. The remnants of Christian communities, insofar as still existing at the beginning of the Almohad conquest, had been completely wiped out. So the spite of the second Almohad generation was wreaked wholly upon the Jews. The Jews held out even under these circumstances, but the situation left its mark upon them. The particulars of these events, however, belong to a different chapter.

The refugees from the persecutions of those days scattered in all directions. We can trace them in their new places of residence, such as Genoa,[70] Sicily, Egypt, and Jerusalem. Part of them may have left the Maghreb before the Almohad period, e.g., the Tripolitanians in Sicily, which was under the rule of the Normans, the temporary conquerors of Tripolitania.[71] But the majority left the Maghreb in response to Maimonides' advice and example.[72] The presence of an "important and good community" of Maghrebis in Jerusalem at the time of Alharīzī's visit can only be explained as the result of immigration during the religious persecutions in Africa.[73] Surnames indicating Maghrebi origin were used for centuries.[74]

This, too, indicates that the Jewish quarter was still open to non-Jews, although the lease of dwellings to non-Jews in Jewish neighborhoods was not considered permissible. Nor had Jews misgivings about entering the Muslim quarter.

THE ALMOHAD REGULATIONS

A marked change for the worse in the situation of the Jews occurred in the days of 'Abd al-Mu'min's grandson, Abū Yūsuf Ya'qūb al-Mansūr (1184–99). The Arab historian 'Abd al-Wāhid al-Marrākeshi, a younger contemporary and countryman of al-Mansūr, reports that this ruler, toward the end of his life, ordered Muslims of Jewish origin to wear a dark blue robe with sleeves reaching to the feet, so as to distinguish them from the rest of the population. He also forbade them to wear a turban after the fashion of those days, and commanded them to don the qalansawa, a cap of strange and ugly shape which reached down to the ears. This dress was peculiar to Maghreb Jewry until the end of Abū 'Abdallah (1199–1214). Upon the entreaties of the Jews, supported by self-interested recommendations from veteran Muslims, that ruler consented to modify the regulations, permitting Jews to dress after the current fashion, but insisting that their robe and headgear must be yellow. Al-Marrākeshi adds that this has remained the Jewish garb until his own time (621/1224). According to him, the reason why Abū Yūsuf Ya'qūb compelled the new Muslims to wear distinctive clothing was a sneaking doubt as to the sincerity of their belief. "If I were sure," said Abū Yūsuf, "that these Jews have wholeheartedly embraced Islam, I should permit them to mix with the Muslims by marriage and in every other way. And if I were certain that they are infidels, I should put the men to death, sell their children into

slavery and confiscate their property in favour of the believers. But I am perplexed about the matter."[75]

Al-Marrākeshī's account indicates clearly that those converts were not permitted to marry the daughters of veteran Muslims because al-Mansūr was not sure whether to regard them as Jews or as true believers. On the other hand, R. Joseph ben Jehuda ibn 'Aqnīn, a contemporary of Abū Yūsuf, reproves those of his generation who contract marriage by means of the *sadāq*, i.e., the Muslim marriage contract dealing with the marriage settlement, rather than—at least in secret—by means of *huppah* and *qiddushīn* according to Jewish custom; he regards this as a grave offense. Those people apparently wished to convince the government of their adherence to Muslim law.[76]

Besides the *ghiyār* regulations, Ibn 'Aqnīn mentions several other discriminatory measures inflicted upon the pseudo-Muslim Jews.

Until the time of the Almohads, Maghreb Jewry had ramified business connections and played a significant part in intercontinental trade and in trade with the countries bordering on the Indian Ocean; no less important was its share in local trade and in peddling. But now the authorities ousted the Jews from these occupations and stripped them of their property. Moreover, they—i.e., the pseudo-Muslims—were forbidden to keep slaves. This disability, in addition to the social stigma it involved according to the concepts of the period, was a serious economic handicap.

Ibn 'Aqnīn further mentions the limitation of the capacity of those forced Muslims to be trustees and guardians. The Almohads deprived them of the right to bring up their children and ordered them to hand them over to trustworthy Muslims to be given a truly Muslim education. They were moreover disqualified for testamentary guardianship, although our author notes that the Muslim guardians were not very strict in the matter and left the minors to be cared for by their own families.

All these regulations were a logical consequence of the approach to Muslims of Jewish origin. According to Islamic law, a non-Muslim cannot be the natural or testamentary guardian of Muslim children. We have already seen, in connection with the question of marriage to Muslim women, that Abū Yūsuf did not regard the forced converts as full Muslims; he consequently denied them the guardianship of their children, who were considered Muslims from birth.[77]

After the Jews were permitted to revert openly to their religion, these regulations lapsed automatically. But the regulations concerning special clothing did not become void; they continued in full force, even though details as to color and cut were changed. In contrast to the pre-Almohad period, the *ghiyār* is now mentioned in Tunisia (1199) and Spain (end of the Middle Ages); at the instigation of Maghrebi fanatics, it was reintroduced in Egypt, where it had fallen into oblivion.[78] We possess a text on the duties of the *muhtasib*, the official—with judicial powers—in charge of markets, morals, and protected persons (*ahl al-dhimma*), by an author of African origin who lived in Spain at the end of the Middle Ages; here is what he says of the duties of the *muhtasib* with regard to protected persons:

He must prevent protected persons from looking down upon Muslims in their houses (i.e., from living in houses higher than those of Muslims); from wielding authority (over Muslims); from displaying wine and pork in Muslim markets; from riding saddled and decorated horses in Muslim streets, and other acts of ostentation. He must prescribe signs for them that enable them to be distinguished from Muslims, such as the *shikla*[79] for men and bells for women. He must prevent Muslims being asked to do anything degrading and offensive to them, such as removing refuse, transporting wine containers and tending pigs, or anything expressive of unbelief or superiority over Islam.[80]

The Jews eventually prevailed in this heavy struggle. The disabilities imposed upon them caused many descendants of forced converts to return wholeheartedly to Judaism. This process is particularly significant in view of developments in the case of the Christians, who vanished completely from North Africa although their social and political condition was more favorable than that of the Jews.[81] Most of the Maghreb rulers had Christian garrison troops whom they permitted to practice their religion and who had priests and churches and even church bells. If crypto-Christians had wished to return to their religion, they could have taken advantage of these facts. But, like the Christians in South Arabia, they assimilated to the Muslims.[82]

However, North African Jews paid a high price for their resistance and perseverance. Despised and vilified by the local Muslims—Arabs and Berbers—they lived under the most trying economic, social, and cultural conditions, segregated and cooped up in special quarters known as *mellāh* or *hāra*. Even the expellees from Spain, the Mediterranean islands and Portugal, who began to pour into the area, scorned the "residents," so different from them as to customs, manners, and livelihood. The merging of the two strata took centuries and is still not complete.

*For further clarification of any references, see original essay.

NOTES

1. Mann, *Jews* II, p. 163, 11. 27–29.

2. Arab sources are unanimous about the events, though divergent about dates; comp. Ibn 'Idhāri, pp. 263–95; Ibn Khaklūn 'Ibar VI, pp. 15–16, p. 158, I, pp. 34–38, II, pp. 20–22. Comp. Julien, *Histoire* II, pp. 74–75.

3. Mann, *Texts* I, pp. 244 and 246. This synagogue aroused the anger of a Muslim religious scholar, who regarded it as infringing Omar's Ordinance; comp. Idris, *Berbérie*, p. 768.

4. Goitein, *Zion* 27 (1962): 17–19.

5. Comp. The letter published by Braslavsky, *Zion* 7 (1942): 137, and p. 132 below.

6. Cazés, *Essai*, pp. 83–84.

7. Brunschvig, *Berbérie* I, p. 399.

8. *Dibrei ha-Yamim*, Amsterdam 1733, f. 114a. 'Ali of Heart (twelfth–thirteenth cent.; ed. Janine Sourdel-Thomine [Damascus, 1953], p. 53) knows that seven of the *tābi'in* (second generation of Muhammad's followers) are buried in Kairouan.

9. Comp. Ibn Daud, *SHQ* p. 58/78. Upon the expulsion of the Muslims from Sicily in 1061, a Jewish immigrant from Spain, Moses b. Joseph ibn Kashkil, left Sicily for Mahdiya, where in 1079 he wrote a commentary on a biblical story; comp. Mann, *Texts* I, pp. 386–93.

10. Comp. RA II, pp. 2 and 23, no. 69; Mann, *TI*, pp. 143, 1. 18, 344, 1. 17, and 362, 1. 7; Assaf, *Tarbiz* 20 (1950), pp. 179, 1. 3, and 181, n. 3; Goitein, *ibid.*, pp. 202 n. 38, and 203 n. 46.

11. Comp. p. 141 nn. 16, 17. A far echo about Kairouan in Eshtori ha-Farhi's, *Caftor wa-pherach* (fourteenth cent.) ed. A. Edelmann (Berlin, 1852), p. 26b.

12. Comp. Beaumier, *Roudh*, pp. 191 and 213; Ibn Daud, *SHQ*, p. 84; Hopkins, *Government*, p. 47.

13. Comp. Ibn al-Athīr X, pp. 401–402; Goldziher, *ZDMG* 41 (1887): 30–140; Marcais, *Berbérie*, pp. 245 and 253–75. The most important sources for this period are the biographies of Ibn Tūmart and 'Abd al-Mu'min by their contemporary, Abu Bekr al-Sinhājī, surnamed al-Baydhaq; comp. Lévi-Provençal, Documents. For the surrender of Sijilmāsa comp. Ibn Khaldūn, 'Ibar VI, p. 231 (II, p. 179).

14. Ibn 'Idhārī, pp. 313 and 316; Ibn al-Athīr XI, pp. 158–62; Beaumier, *Roudh*, pp. 279–81; Ibn Khaldūn, *'Ibar* VI, p. 337 (II, pp. 193–94).

15. Comp. Ibn al-Athīr XI, p. 160; Munk, *Notice*, pp. 40–45.

16. Halkin, *Maimonides' Ep. T.*, pp. 99 and 101–103.

17. For Moses' stay in Palestine comp. *Maimonides' Responsa*, ed. Freimann (1934), p. 9, 1. 7; also *Shebet Yehuda*, ed. Shohet, pp. 77 and 191. For Messianic movements in those days comp. Mann, *Hatekufa* 23 (1925): 243–61; 24 (1928): 335–58; Goitein, *JQR* 43 (1952–53): 57–76.

18. Halkin's view (introd., p. xxxii), that the longer version is the original one, is difficult to accept; its extant form, at any rate, is later than the extant form of the shorter version. According to the longer version, Moses Dar'i appeared fifty years previously, and according to the shorter version, forty-five years previously.

19. Comp. Lévi-Provençal, *Documents*, p. 63, and the notes to the translation, pp. 99ff.

20. Comp. Suesmann Muntner, ed., *Treatise on*

Asthma (by Maimonides) (Philadelphia, 1963), p. 94 (*Sefer ha-Qazeret* [Jerusalem, 1940], p. 43); Schirmann, *Tarbiz* 9 (1938): 52; Halkin, *Marx Jubilee Volume* (1950), English Section, p. 391.

21. Al-Jaznāi, *Zahrat al-Ās*, p. 57/125; Beaumier, *Roudh*, p. 75; comp. Also *ibid.*, p. 78.

22. For its importance in pre-Almoravid times comp. Ibn Hawqal, *BGA* II², p. 91; *Maqdisi, BGA* III, p. 227.

23. Comp. Lévi-Provençal, *Documents,* p. 105/174; Dozy-de Goeje, *Description,* p. 69/79–80 (see below, p. 125 n. 1); also Terrasse, *Histoire* I, p. 290.

24. The lament has been published many times; e.g., D. Kahana, *R. Abraham ibn Ezra* I, pp. 61–62, no. 1301. For the Tripolitanian MS. Comp. *Cazés, REJ* 20 (1890): 84; I. Loeb, *ibid.,* p. 316.

25. He published it in *Qobez al-Yad* 3, no. 13 (1939): 33–35.

26. Disputations were among the foremost activities of the Almohads; comp. Above p. 118, and Munk, *Notice,* pp. 42–44; Tritton, *Materials on Muslim Education in the Middle Ages* (1957), p. 84.

27. Idrīsi says of Aghmāt: "It is a pleasant prosperous place, inhabited only by Jews." Comp. ed. Dozy-de Goeje.

28. Comp. *Qobez* as quoted above.

29. Cohen, *SHQ*, pp. 66/88 and 141–42, explains the date (4) 873/1112–13 appearing in MS. De Rossi. But the "sword of Ibn Tūmart," i.e., the wars of his followers and their measures against the Jews began only in 536 H./1141. Comp. next page n. 3.

30. *SHQ* p. 66/88. Cohen reads (Hebrew word)= Silves (Portugal) rather than = salé; comp. next page n. 2.

31. *SHQ*, p. 70/96.

32. This is why [correctly reading the unvowelized Hebrew Ts-L-A] (or [S-L-A]) = salé seems more probable than [S-L-V] = Silves; against Cohen, *SHQ*, p. 142. Ibn Daud (p. 67/92) confirms that Salé had a Jewish community, but we have never heard of one at Silves.

33. Lévi-Provençal, *Documents*, p. 90/146.

34. *Shebet Yehuda*, pp. 21–22 and 74. Comp. also Kobak, *Jeschurun* 6 (1868): 1–34, and below, ch. VII n. 2.

35. It was published by J. M. Toledano, *HUCA* 4 (1927): 449–58, and a second time, with an introduction and translation into Hebrew, by the present writer, in *Y. F. Baer Jubilee Volume* (1960), pp. 134–53. We therefore content ourselves with a summary of the historical parts.

36. He was a friend of Abraham ibn Ezra; comp. N. Ben-Menahem, *H. Albeck Jubilee Volume* (1963), pp. 81–86. The *dayyān* subsequently reverted to Judaism; comp. below p. 352ff.

37. Comp. *Cazés, REJ* 20 (1890): 78ff.; also Slouschz, *Travels*, pp. 11 ff.

38. Comp. below p. 165.

39. Comp. Ibn 'Idhārī, pp. 265–69 and 357; Ibn al-

Athīr, IX, pp. 230–31, XI, pp. 79–80; Ibn-Khaldūn, VI, p. 159 (II, p. 22), pp. 166ff. (II, pp. 34ff.); *El s.v.* Tripoli.

40. *RA* III.

41. Assaf, *Sources*, pp. 130–34. Comp. also Braslavsky, *BJES* 9 (1942): 57.

42. Comp. Mann, *Jews* I, p. 23, n. 2; II, pp. 14–15, 78, n. 7; also B. Chapira, *REJ* 56 (1908): 233–34; Goitein, *Society* I, index.

43. Schechter, *Saadyana* (Cambridge, 1903), p. 114, 1.1.

44. Mann, *Jews* I, pp. 90–91, 123, n. 1; II, pp. 87–88; comp. Also Assaf, *Sefer ha-Shetaroth le-Rab Hay* (Jerusalem, 1930), p. 53; Braslavsky, *Tarbiz* 12 (1942): p. 44; Goitein, *Society* I, index.

45. There was a place named Yahudiyātayn between Surt and Barca; Maqdisī, p. 245.

46. Cazés, *REJ* 20 (1890): 79; Bartarelli, *Guida*, p. 333.

47. *RSh* 26b, no. 26; comp. Mann, *JQR* 7 (1916–17): 484.

48. Bekri, p. 9; Yāqūt s.v. Jādū; comp. Hirschberg, *Zion* 22 (1957): 16–17; Mann, *Texts* I, pp. 412–13; Poznanski, *REJ* 65 (1913): 42; N. Epstein, *MGWJ* 60 (1916): 112–13; Strauss, *Zion* 7 (1942): 142, 1. 25.

49. Assaf, *Sources*, pp. 130–34 (esp. letters 1, 11, 20, and 29).

50. Ibid., p. 141, 1. 8.

51. Published by Braslavsky, *Zion* 7 (1942). Abraham clearly was not, as assumed by Braslavsky, l.c., p. 136, referring to occurrences during the Almohad conquest. The Almohads did not arrive in the region until 1154–1160.

52. Comp. Ibn al-Athīr XI, p. 79; Brunschvig, *Berbérie* I, p. 3.

53. Comp. Ibn Khaldūn VI, p. 162 (II, p. 28); Marcais, *Berbérie*, p. 225.

54. Comp. Ibn al-AthIr XI, pp. 134–35 and 159–60; Ibn Khaldūn VI, p. 168 (II, p. 37); Brunschvig, *ibid.*, pp. 5–6.

55. Comp. Beaumier, *Roudh,* p. 281; Hopkins, *Government*, pp. 34–35.

56. Cazés, *REJ* 20 (1890): 85; Kahana, *Abraham ibn Ezra,* p. 250.

57. Comp. Yaqut *s.vv.* Sabrat, Sabra; Julien, *Histoire* I, 166–67 and 173–75; Bartarelli, *Guida* pp. 312–13. It seems unlikely that the reference is to Sabra, a suburb of Kairouan, also called Mansūriyya; comp. *Yāqūt, s.v.*

58. Comp. p. 133 n. 3 above.

59. Comp. Slouschz, *Azkara* IV, pp. 114–17; Gray, *Inscriptions*, pp. 56–57.

60. Comp. Maimonides, *Responsa,* ed. Freimann, p. 214 n. 225; also Slouschz, *Lub* II, p. 22.

61. Maimonides, *Responsa*, ed. Blau, I, pp. 138–39 n. 88.

62. Steinschneider, *Kerem Hemed* IX, p. 38.

63. Comp. *RO* 25, no. 2 (1961): 87–120; 26, no. 1 (1962): 97–123.

64. Saadia ibn Danān, *Seder ha-Doroth* (Edelmann), *Hemda Genūza*, 30b; Toledano, Ner, pp. 26 and 225; Ad. Neubauer, *REJ* 4 (1882): 173ff. Comp. also Baron, *PAAJR* 6 (1935): 83 and n. 164.

65. *Iggerot* (Amsterdam, 1712), pp. 10b–11a; *Responsa* (Leipzig, 1859), part 2 (Epistles), p. 44a.

66. Comp. Edelmann, *Hemda Genūza,* pp. 6a, 11b and 12 a–b.

67. Comp. Saadia ibn Danān, l.c. (see p. 137 n. 1 above).

68. Comp. *Iggerot*, p. 10a; *Responsa* II, p. 26b (for both sources see p. 137 n. 2 above); Halkin, *Ep. Y.*, p. 108f.; Margulies, *MGWJ* 44 (1900): 8–11; Yāqūt *s.v.* Dar'a.

69. MS. Sassoon 1007, pp. 12b–13a.

70. *The Itinerary of Benjamin of Tudela*, ed. Ascher, p. 6. Adler's edition, p. 5, reads: "R. Samuel, the son of the refugee, and his brother. They were dyers and came from Ceuta."

71. Comp. Roth, *JQR* 47 (1956–57): 322–23, 319 n. 8, 327 nn. 17, 24.

72. Comp. p. 114 (n. 136) above; Goitein, *Jewish Education in Muslim Countries* (Jerusalem, 1962), p. 117, tells of a silversmith of Ceuta, who left that city during the persecutions and settled in Egypt, where he lost his eyesight and became a teacher.

73. *Tahkemōni,* ed. Kaminka (Warsaw, 1899), p. 353; see also pp. 223–24.

74. Comp. e.g., A. Milano, *Storia degli Ebrei Italiani nel Levante* (Florence, 1949), p. 41; Sabatino Sigilmes.

75. R. Dozy, *The History of the Almohades by . . . al-Marrākoshi*[2] (Leyden, 1881), p. 223; al-Zarkashī, *Ta'rikh Dawlatayn*, p. 11; comp. E. Fagnan, *RAF,* 36, pp. 264–65; *REJ* 28 (1894): 294–98; Marcais, *Berbérie*, pp. 269–70; Hopkins, *Government*, pp. 61–62; for the *ghiyār* regulations in Iraq in the twelfth-century comp. KS 30 (1955), pp. 95–96. Comp. also *Shebet Yehuda*, p. 78.

76. Comp. Halkin, *Starr Memorial Volume*, p. 104 and n. 35; and comp. *RSh,* p. 8a, n. 54.

77. Comp. *K. al-Fiqh,* III, p. 486; IV, p. 26; Bergsträsser, *Grundzuge*, p. 45.

78. Comp. Zarkashī, *Ta'rīkh*, pp. 11, 25 (and Appendix Tunis); Pelissier et Remusat, *Histoire*, p. 224; Hopkins, *Government*, p. 62. For the *ghiyār* regulations in Egypt comp. L. A. Mayer, *Mamluke Costume*, p. 65.

79. The exact form of the *shikla* or *shakla* is not known. It seems to have been different in each Maghreb country.

80. Comp. Lévi-Provençal, *Traités*, p. 122.

81. Comp. Beaumier, *Roudh*, pp. 357–58, 372; Brunschvig, *Berbérie* I, pp. 499, 453 and 469; Hopkins, *Government*, pp. 69–70.

82. Comp. e.g., Budgett Meakin, *Empire*, pp. 239–50, 307–34; Le Tourneau, *Fez-Merinids*, p. 73; Corcos, *Jews*, I–II, pp. 284–85.

CHAPTER 43

The Pact of 'Umar in Morocco:
A Reappraisal of Muslim-Jewish Relations

Jane S. Gerber

An analysis of the history of the Jewish community of Fez prior to the advent of the French illustrates the extent of which the Pact of 'Umar was operative in a major center of Muslim and Jewish life in Morocco. As the imperial seat of Morocco under the Marinids, the Banu Wattas and the first Sa'adian Sherifs (thirteenth through sixteenth centuries), Fez could provide its Jews with a protective shield unavailable in many other Moroccan cities. Hence, even if conditions were atypical in Fez for Jews, they frequently displayed the optimal conditions which Jews could hope for in Morocco. Analysis of Muslim-Jewish relations in Fez in the late medieval period is particularly illuminating because of the variety of extant primary sources (in Hebrew, Arabic, and a number of European languages). In addition, the emergence of numerous court Jews in precisely the same period, usually interpreted as a symptom of Jewish integration, raises any fundamental questions about the legal status of the Jews in Morocco.

The pact of 'Umar is a theoretical formulation, or variant formulations, compiled in the early centuries of Islam concerning the limitations under which *dhimmis* (non-Muslims) were to be permitted to live in the world of Islam.[1] Although no single text has survived concerning Jewish disabilities, scholars have tended to accept the limitations placed upon the Christians as the model for Muslim-Jewish relations. Discriminatory regulations in the pact included the wearing of distinctive clothing to set off Muslim from *dhimmi*, e.g., special headwear surnames, riding on horses or bearing arms, the interdiction against erecting new synagogues or repairing old ones, as well as the stipulation that *dhimmis* not sell wine. In addition, the pact declared that non-Muslim religious symbols and festivals be as unobtrusive as possible. Although the pact emphasized the social and religious inferiority of the non-Muslim it did not mention any special discriminatory taxation. In Morocco, it should be noted, the economic and psychological effects of fiscal exploration played a major role in shaping the Jewish community into a beleaguered enclave in the Muslim *medina*.[2]

In order to ascertain what parts of this theoretical framework were operative, the historian must divest himself of such sweeping categories as "the Jews under Islam" and examine the history of each community within the context of the dynamics of life in that particular community. In the case of Fez, the first important fact about the pact which should be noted is that the Jews never refer to it by name. Yet, any stipulation regarding non-Muslims was intended solely for the Jews since they were basically the only non-Muslim group living in the city of Fez.[3]

In 1438 the Jews of Fez were consigned to a special quarter, the Mellah, which was to become the paradigm for the Moroccan ghetto. While the sultan at the time, 'Abd el-Haq ben Abu Said (1421–1465) intended this measure as a means of protecting the Jews of Fez from the growing antialien sentiment aroused by popular sheikhs, the Jews did not unanimously regard the move to the Mellah as a favorable turn of events.[4] Not only did the move entail economic hardship by removing the Jews from the commercially vibrant Kairouanian (Qayrawānian) Bank of the city, but it also left them in an extremely vulnerable position geographically, astride the ramparts of *Fez el-Jedid*, the imperial quarter of the city.[5] Although these measures were not intended as a form of discriminatory isolation, their net result was to remove the Jews from natural social and economic contacts with Muslims.[6]

In 1465 the Mellah was overwhelmed by an outburst of anti-Jewish as well as antidynastic agitation which resulted in the decimation of the Jewish community.[7] Apparently many Jews escaped the full wrath of the populace through flight or conversion to Islam. At this point one hears, for the first time since the Almohads, of discriminatory legislation. Forced converts, always the object of suspicion on the part of Muslims, were the subject of deliberation by merchants and the *'ulema* alike. The merchants attempted to isolate the new converts while the chief qaid, Ahmed el-Wancharisi (1475–1490), declared that forced converts could revert to Judaism provided that they adhered to the strictures of the Pact of

From *Muslim-Jewish Relations in North Africa* (New York: 1975), pp. 40–50.

'Umar.[8] Single statements of this sort, particularly when viewed in the context of an extreme situation of heightened religiosity and intolerance, cannot be regarded as indicative of a continuous state of affairs. Fortunately, many sources are available to test whether or not al-Wancharisi's views reflected the actual state of Muslim-Jewish relations.

During the sixteenth through the nineteenth centuries a number of European travelers visited Fez and remarked upon the situation of the Jews. Leo Africanus, a native of Fez who was captured by pirates, baptized in Rome and returned to Fez in the 1540s, noted that the Jews "are despised everywhere in Morocco" and were forced to wear sandals of straw in Fez.[9] According to Marmol, another visitor to Fez in the same decade, the Jews of Fez aren't permitted to wear shoes, except for the few who have entrée to the king and his officers. The rest wear sandals of straw.[10] An anonymous Portuguese traveler in Fez in the 1590s observed, "outside the *Juiverie* (the Mellah) the Jews don't wear their shoes but rather sandals of straw."[11] When the Jews had attempted to have this disability removed in the middle of the sixteenth century, the same informant relates, the king cynically forced them to pay a tribute for the "privilege" of wearing sandals outside the Mellah and shoes inside it. Le Père Mouëtte, a French missionary who proselytized in Fez at the end of the seventeenth century, observed the same phenomenon.[12]

Hebrew sources frequently provide important data on Muslim-Jewish relations inter alia. Jewish business contracts frequently made special provisions to meet the Jewish disability of distinctive clothing. For example, in a work contract from 1701, an employer agreed to provide a regular salary to his employee plus *taban* (straw shoes).[13] In another agreement an employer promised his worker two pairs of these straw shoes. The documents aren't explicit enough to ascertain whether the work involved was outside the Mellah except in one instance where this was clearly the case.[14] Apparently those Jews who worked outside the Mellah would as a matter of course accept the clothing distinctions demanded by the Muslims and expect their employers to furnish the necessary garb. A special branch of the Muslim cobblers' guild was devoted exclusively to the production of the Jewish sandals until modern times.[15] These comments span a period of over 150 years and are unrelated to any particularly noteworthy outbreaks of popular religious fanaticism.

The prohibition against using a horse, an animal of aristocratic and martial qualities in Arab tradition, was also applied during the period. One argument ex silencio in this regard is the absence of any reference to horses in the *Pinkas* (account book) of Fez although the document explicitly describes other animals used in service occupations. More positive proof of the application of the stricture can be found in a fascinating Arabic account of the 1465 pogrom. In Muslim eyes, one of the most infu-

riating actions precipitating the pogrom of 1465 was the fact that the Jewish vizier, Harous ben Battas, was wont to ride through the streets of Fez on a horse while carrying a sword containing a Qur'anic inscription.[16]

The stipulation of the Pact of 'Umar that the Jews refrain from wine production has left an echo in numerous Jewish sources. According to one garbled account of the foundation of the ghetto, the Mellah was founded after the Muslims discovered wine in a mosque, allegedly placed there by the Jews.[17] Although no other evidence supports this version, it serves to reveal Jewish fears and inhibitions projected upon a traumatic event in the life of the community. Given the xenophobic atmosphere in Fez from the fifteenth through the seventeenth centuries, Jewish leaders repeatedly promulgated ordinances (*Takkanot*) against the production and sale of wine. One such ordinance from 1602 prohibited the sale of wine by Jews to any Muslim, Berber, Christian (whether merchant or captive) or another Jew.[18] Only the *Nagid* (head of the Jewish community) or his deputies were exempted from this ordinance in order to pursue their diplomatic activities on the community's behalf.[19] The ban on wine production does not seem to have been successful despite the dangers. Jewish wine was noted by observers to be "absolutely perfect"[20] and wine and *mahia* (liquor) were conspicuously consumed at religious and social gatherings.[21] Generally the reiteration of *Takkanot* proves the pressing nature of the issue in question as well as the inability of the community to abide by its letter.

It is a well-known fact that the Muslim authorities generally ignored the provisions of the Pact of 'Umar relating to the construction and maintenance of synagogues. The degree of enforcement varied widely within the world of Islam as vividly illustrated by the proliferation of synagogues in new centers of urban life which followed the consolidation of the Arab conquests. Even within Fez, no rigid rule concerning synagogues construction can be formulated. While it appears that synagogues multiplied rapidly in the sixteenth century following the advent of the exiles from Spain to Fez, increasing in number from about five in 1497 to at least one dozen by the 1550s, these structures were generally modest and might have gone unnoticed by the Muslims.[22]

The presence of these new synagogues was a clear violation of the stipulations of the Pact of 'Umar. In general, legal guidelines of a discriminatory nature are more strictly adhered to in periods of political and economic instability. Given the chronic instability in Morocco, however, one cannot point to specific political catalysts which caused the destruction of almost all the synagogues in the Mellah. This destruction, recounted by the chroniclers of Fez in *Dibre ha-Yamim*, alludes to the fact that religious concepts of inferiority and superiority, built into the fabric of Islam, were the causal factors for the application of the Pact of 'Umar.[23] As Saul Serero relates:

On the 15th of Elul 5406 (August 1646) he (Muhammed el-Hajj) sent men to destroy the synagogues of the *Mellah*. On the 18th of Elul, because of our iniquities, the Great Synagogue of the Toshavim was destroyed; on the 23rd, it was the turn of the synagogue of the *Megorashim* and the community tried in vain to bribe them. All the sacred objects of the synagogue were destroyed except for the Torah scrolls which were saved through bribes. . . . Because of our iniquities . . . all the synagogues were closed by order of the head of the *zawiya* Muhammed el-Hajj. On Sunday, the 15th of Elul, the enemies penetrated our Temple, despoiled our sanctuary, demolished our synagogue. . . . On that day they left the ark and the women's gallery intact, but the following Thursday they destroyed these too. . . . The following week the Gentiles came to destroy the synagogue of the Tazans and caused enormous damage there. On the day of the Fast of Gedaliah, the enemies attacked the synagogue of the Talmud Torah and destroyed it. On the morrow, the synagogue of R. Isaac Abzardal met the same fate. . . . On the eve of Yom Kippur, they destroyed the old and the new houses of study. The synagogues of Saadiah Rabuah and Jacob Roti were spared by offering bribes. Between Yom Kippur and Succot, the synagogue of R. Chaim Uzziel was destroyed.

Thus, the destruction of the synagogues of Fez was not an isolated case of vandalism perpetrated by an unruly mob but rather concerted destructive effort initiated by a leading religious personality resident in the city. It is noteworthy that the destruction included the desecration of Jewish ritual objects.

For the Jews of Fez, the display of religious symbols and processionals weighed heavily on their security considerations. Some of the sumptuary legislation dating from this period reflects the Jewish realization that religious fanaticism, as embodied in the details of the pact, was prominent in Muslim-Jewish relations. For example, the rabbis of Fez attempted by decree to alter Jewish burial rites hallowed by custom for fear that a public procession to the cemetery, accompanied by holding the coffin aloft and blowing the *Shofar* (ram's horn), would incite the Muslims of Fez.[24] It is probably not accidental that Jewish attention focused on precisely those customs which echoed the prohibitions of the Pact of 'Umar.

Therefore the lack of reference to a particular document by Jew, Muslim, or Christian is not of major significance. In whatever fashion discriminatory regulations were identified and promulgated, they nonetheless conformed to many of the essential clauses of what is known as the Pact of 'Umar.

One of the fascinating questions about Jewish life in Fez during this period is that of interpreting the role of Jewish courtiers in the political life of the city. If the strictures of the pact were indeed in effect, how could Haroun ben Battas, a Jewish vizier in 1465, or Jacob Roti, the chief architect of diplomatic relations between Portugal and the kingdom of Fez, exercise their powers? It has been a popular notion in Jewish historiography to interpret the career of court Jews as symptomatic of Jewish integration in general society or as an indicator of Gentile tolerance toward Jews. A brief examination of the career of one of these courtiers in his political milieu, however, demonstrates that the dazzling political career of the courtier was also defined by the Pact of 'Umar and the realities of Moroccan political conditions.

Morocco is a profoundly divided country whose history has reflected her deep geographic and ethnic divisions. For most of her history she was not a political unit but rather a conglomeration of independent principalities with only limited areas contiguous to her few capital cities subject to any central control. Thus, one cannot accurately speak of a history of Morocco or her Jewish community: frequently in towns in such close proximity as Fez and Meknes conditions could be simultaneously favorable for the Jews in one city and dolorous in the other.[25]

Despite its progressive Arabization in the course of the Middle Ages, the Moroccan Berbers held tenaciously to their traditions of individualism and tribal loyalties. The dynamics of Moroccan history derive from her division into three main tribal groupings: the Masmouda, the Sanhaja and the Zenata. Morocco's seemingly anarchic history cannot be viewed simply as succession of hostile and rapacious dynasties but rather as an acting out on the stage of the Maghreb of deep-seated Berber antagonisms. The Almoravids (1062–1147) represent the domination of the Sanhaja, the Almohads (1147–1269) signalize the hegemony the triumph of the Zenata.[26] Those dynasties which lacked a strong tribal base, such as the Banu Wattas (1450–1550) and the Sa'adian Sherifs (1550–1650) were forced to seek alternate and far less reliable bases of support.

While all the main population groups of Morocco had the assurance of some protection through their legendary or biological links with some large tribal grouping, the Jews alone lacked support in the population. The comment of the chroniclers of the Jewish community of Fez that "the sultan is our salvation" indeed reflected Jewish dependency on the ruling dynasty.[27]

One group to which precarious dynasties would turn to form a *Makhzen* (a government) was the Jewish community. Observers noted and sources reveal the emergence of Jews in extremely crucial and delicate political positions. This apparent power bore no relation to their real power, as the Jews were often allied with dynasts [governors] who had no control over anyone but the Jews. In the period under discussion, the groups who represented popular feelings (such as the Marabouts or the qadis) harbored strong feelings of hostility toward all "infidels."[28] Thus we are dealing with a complex and paradoxical situation: Muslim-Jewish relations were not determined by ephemeral rulers in Fez, the "protectors" of the Jews, who could, at best, simply hold anti-Jewish passions in check and utilize the Jews out of considerations of expediency. The clearest example of such exploitation of Jewish skills as a result of the dynast's estrangement from his subjects can be seen in the career of Haroun.

In 1465 the last ruler of the tottering Marinid dynasty, 'Abd el-Haq ben Abou Said, decided to wrest control from his Wattasid regents and rule alone with the aid of his Jewish confidant Haroun ben Battas.[29] According to the most fulsome account of Haroun's career, that of 'Abd del-Basit ibn Khalil (1440–1514), Haroun rose to the position of vizier since "he was no threat to the sultan." Moreover, the sultan "rejoiced in the insult he could thus render to the Nabu Wattas" through the appointment of a Jew to this powerful office. This was not an insignificant achievement since, as 'Abd el-Basit reminds the reader, "'Abd el-Haq was on the throne of Fez for thirty years during which he was dominated by the Wattasid vizirs . . . such was the custom in the Maghreb . . . that the supreme authority was exercised by the vizirs who were the true masters of the people and the country."[30]

According to 'Abd el-Basit, Haroun used his position with an arrogance unacceptable for a Jew. When the preacher of the Kairouanian (Qayrawānian) mosque heard of the hubris of Haroun, he roused the populace with cries of "jihad." The excited crowd sought religious support from one of the leading sherifs of Fez. The latter refused to countenance rebellion, since the sultan was directly implicated, without receiving a fatwa from the 'Ulema. The 'Ulema finally consented and declared it licit to rise up against the Jews and the sultan. The crowd thereupon rushed to the Mellah and slaughtered countless Jews. Haroun and the sultan were caught in the carnage as were smaller Jewish communities within the jurisdiction of Fez.

The events of 1465 are instructive from a number of points of view. On the one hand, they reveal that the religious party in Fez was not unanimous but, rather, was divided between advocates of restraint and provocateurs. The conflict was enmeshed in political considerations. The Jewish position of identification with a floundering dynasty, while sparing the beleaguered Jews in 1438, could not help but overwhelm them when the dynasty was overthrown in 1465. On the other hand, a close reading of the career of Haroun also reveals that the assumptions of the Pact of 'Umar, i.e., the subordination of Jews to Muslims, were deeply embedded in the political life of Fez.

One important conclusion that should be drawn from an analysis of the dramatic career of Haroun is that the rise to political prominence of a Jew *should not* be constructed as evidence of Jewish security or acceptance in a given historical period. As Haroun's demise so graphically illustrates, the rise of a Jew to an important governmental post was symptomatic of the complete alienation of the dynasty from its subjects. The episode, furthermore, implies a consensus among wide sections of the Muslim population that Jews were expected to assume a low profile in the political life of the city.[31]

While the reconstruction of the life of the Jews in Morocco is still in its infancy, it is becoming increasingly apparent that the history of Jews in Muslim lands, for all its internal parallels, was not of one cloth. A close reading of the primary sources, particularly those in Hebrew, emphasizes the constant state of anxiety and vulnerability in which the Jews lived. Much of this precariousness stemmed directly from the acceptance and implementation by the Muslims of the letter as well as the spirit of the Pact of 'Umar. European records of diplomats, grain traders or sugar merchants notwithstanding, the Jews trod a very cautious path, constantly aware that their role in the *Dar ul-Islam* was carefully circumscribed by centuries of juridical precedents and attitudes of Muslim superiority vis-à-vis the Jews which have collectively become known as the Pact of 'Umar.

*For further clarification of any references, see original essay.

NOTES

1. Most of the literature on the Pact of 'Umar treats the question of its actual implementation in a cursory fashion. The two classical studies on the pact are Antoine Fattal, *Le Statut legal des non-musulmans en pays d'Islam* (Beirut, 1958), and A. S. Tritton, *The Caliphs and Their Non-Muslim Subjects* (London, 1930). Discussions of particular aspects of the pact are to be found in E. Ashtor (Strauss), "The Social Isolation of the Ahl ad-Dhimma," in *Études orientales à la memoire de Paul Hirschler* (Budapest, 1950); E. Fagnan, "Le signe distinctif des Juifs au Maghreb," *Rèvue des Études Juives* 28 (1894): 294–98; S. D. Goitein, *Jews and Arabs: Their Contacts through the Ages* (New York, 1955), 62–88; A. S. Tritton, "Islam and the Protected Religions," *Journal of the Royal Asiatic Society* 10 (1931): 34–38; Georges S. Vajda, "Juifs et musulmans selon le hadith," *Journal Asiatique* 229 (1937): 57–127. For the classical Muslim position see al-Mawardi, *Les statuts gouvernmentaux*, trans. E. Fagnan (Algiers, 1915). According to Claude Cahen the implementation of the pact is a moot point. See *Encyclopedia of Islam*, "Dhimma."

2. The constant fiscal oppression of the community is ubiquitous in the chronicles of Fez. The most important Hebrew chronicle is *Dibre ha-Yamim shel Fes*, Anonymous Collection, Library of the Jewish Theological Seminary of America. The text which will be cited is the French translation by Georges S. Vajda, "Un recueil de textes historiques judéomarocaines," *Hespéris* 12 (1951).

Chronicles drawing heavily upon the *Dibre ha-Yamim* are R. Elbaz, *Kisseh ha-Melakhim*, Sassoon Library, Letchworth, England, #1007, and Abner ha-Sarfati, *Yahas Fes*, Bibliothéque de l'Alliance Israélite Universelle, # H84A.

3. A small group of Christians, housed separately and represented by a Factor, did exist in Fez. Their situation bore no relationship to that of the Jews since they usually enjoyed the protection of some ecclesiastical or European political authority.

4. On the events of 1465 see 'Abd el-Basit ibn Khalil, *Deux récits de voyages inédits en Afrique du Nord au XVe siécle*, trans. Robert Brunschvig (Paris, 1936); H. Z. Hirschberg, *Toledot ha-Yehudim be-Afrika ha-sefonit*, 2 vols. (Jerusalem, 1965), 1: 297.

5. During this period the Jews frequently found themselves caught in the middle of antidynastic and sectional fights. See *Dibre h a-Yamim*, 24, 25, 26, 35, 36, 37.

6. Fez el-Jedid was a strongly fortified city containing the palaces of the Sultan, royal gardens, parade grounds and barracks for the troops. Economic institutions such as warehouses, bazaars or ateliers were only minimally developed. The move represented a genuine economic hardship for the Jews. The best description of the composition of the different quarters of Fez can be found in Roger le Tourneau, *Fès avant le pretectorat* (Casablanca, 1949).

7. See discussion below on the episode of Haroun.

8. Emile Amar, "La Pierre de touches des fetwas," *Archives Marocaines* 12 (1908): 231. The guild regulation pertaining to Jewish converts are contained in a fascinating manuscript from Rabat. See Louis Massignon, "L'Interdit corporatif à l'encontre des Juifs islamisés de Fès du XVIe au XVIIe siècle," *Révue du Monde Musulman* 58 (1924): 221–24.

9. Leo Africanus (Wazzan az-Zaiyati), *Description de l'Afrique*, trans. A. Epaulard (Paris, 1956), 61: 234.

10. Luis del Marmol Carvajal, *L'Afrique*, trans. d'Ablancourt, 2 vols. (Paris, 1661), 2: 168–70.

11. Henri de Castries, ed., *Une description du Maroc sous le Règne du Moulay Ahmed el-Mansour 1596* (Paris, 1909).

12. Père Mouëtte, *Sources inédits de l'histoire du Maroc: archives et bibliothèques de la France*, ed. Henri de Castries (Paris, 1918) vol. 2.

13. *Pinkas Maskeret Beth ha-Din,* Library of the Jewish Theological Seminary of America, Enelow Memorial Collection, #880, 22a. The word for straw in Arabic is *tibn*.

14. Ibid., 55a.

15. Roger le Tourneau and Louis Paye, "Les Cordonniers de Fès," *Hespéris* 22 (1936): 33.

16. 'Abd el-Basit, *Deux récits de voyages*, 113–14.

17. *Kisseh ha-Melakhim*, 22; *Yahas Fes*, 9b.

18. *Kerem Hemer*, II, #32, 7b; #93, 17b.

19. *Dibre ha-Yamim*, 73. In this account a tax collector arrived at the gate of the *Mellah* and demanded payment of an exorbitant levy by nightfall. The Jews finally obtained a reprieve through bribes and the expeditious use of wine.

20. Leo Africanus, *Description de l'Afrique*, 303.

21. *Kerem Hemer*, II, #92, 17b; #94, 18a.

22. The figure of five synagogues appears in the *Takkanot* of the Sephardim in *Kerem Hemer,* II, #2. By the 1540s the remarkable traveler and missionary Nicholas Clenardus noted eight or nine Sephardic synagogues. In addition, the indigenous Jews had their own communal institutions. Nicholas Clenardus, *Correspondance*, trans. Alphonse Roersch, 3 vols. (Brussels, 1941), 3: 104–55.

23. *Dibre ha-Yamim*, 46–47.

24. Cemeteries played an important part in the religious life of the community in North Africa. For specific burial customs in Morocco see Joseph Ben Naim, *Nohag be-Hokmah*, Library of the Jewish Theological Seminary of America, photocopy from anonymous collection, pp. 8ff.

25. This was the case in 1549 and again in 1701 when the Jews of Fez were forced to take refuge in Meknes. See *Les Sources inédits de l'histoire du Maroc: archives et bibliothèques de l'Espagne*, ed. Robert Ricard, 1: 133–39.

26. Roger le Tourneau, *Evolution politique de l'Afrique du Nord musulmane 1920–1961* (Paris, 1962), 11–41; Henri Terrasse, *Histoire du Maroc,* 2 vols. (Paris, 1949), 1: 25.

27. This dependency is apparent until modern times. The dichotomy in attitudes between ruler and ruled vis-à-vis the Jew is, of course, one fundamental characteristic of medieval Jewish history.

28. An important sheikh of the period, al-Maghili, exemplified this attitude. His biography provides much data on how the popular religious orders and charismatic leaders regarded Jews. Al-Maghili went so far as to declare that the Jews no longer deserved protection under Muslim law. See Ibn 'Askar, *The Sheikhs of Morocco,* trans. T. H. Weir (Edinburgh, 1904).

29. 'Abd el-Basit, *Deux récits de voyages*, 113–14.

30. Ibid.

31. When Jacob Roti guided and to a great extent formed the alliance between Fez and Portugal in the 1530s and 1540s his mission was presented to the 'Ulema of Fez in the most innocuous guise. Roti was merely serving as a translator in the company of Muslim diplomats. By assuming this low profile, he was able to pursue an effective political role without arousing the sensitivities of the religious party in Fez.

CHAPTER 44

New Documents regarding Attacks upon Jewish Religious Observance in Morocco during the Late Nineteenth Century

Eliezer Bashan

I. GENERAL INTRODUCTION

In exchange for Jews paying the poll tax and fulfilling the conditions of the Pact of Umar, Muslim governments were obligated to preserve their lives, property, religious liberty, and communal autonomy. Most scholars assume that this reciprocal commitment was observed.

In fact, several historians and anthropologists have idealized Jewish life in Islamic countries in general and in Morocco in particular. They support this claim by pointing out that Jewish life continued uninterrupted for generations. Furthermore, they argue that there were Jews who became wealthy, including several with close ties to the sultans, and that some held official positions. For example, Rabbi J. M. Toledano wrote that during the reign of Muhammad Ibn Abdallah (1757–1790), "the sun shone benevolently upon the Jews of Morocco." He even called him "a friend of the Jews" and described him as one who related to the Jews "with love." Rabbi Toledano based his arguments on the fact that Jews served as secretaries and interpreters at the court of Muhammad Ibn Abdallah and went on diplomatic missions. However, the sultan actually exploited them for his own purposes. While some Jews held certain privileges, the situation of the majority had not improved and most suffered from the same restrictions and humiliations that had always been their lot. For example, the fact that Jews were forced to relocate to the Mellah (a restricted area), beginning in Fez in 1438 and continuing subsequently throughout Morocco, has been interpreted both favorably and unfavorably. Some view this measure as protecting the Jews, while others, gleaning from Jewish sources, interpret it as part of the tendency of the authorities to isolate and humiliate them. Basing their conclusions upon personal memoirs from the period of the French protectorate in Morocco, several scholars view the status of the Jews in a positive light.[1]

The latter ignore the fate of the masses during the period prior to the protectorate, when Jews occasionally were subject to additional restrictions, along with those stipulated in the Pact of Umar, and suffered from harassment by governors and simple folk. Such maltreatment found expression in humiliation, attacks on persons, murders, false accusations, expulsions, robberies, and offenses against Jewish religious observance. From the 1860s, however, after the founding of the Alliance Israélite Universelle and a similar organization in England, the Anglo-Jewish Association, European Jews and foreign diplomats became aware of many such cases.[2]

Tourists, diplomats, and Christian missionaries wrote that although Moroccan Jews are not citizens who are equal to Muslims, the authorities do not attack their religious freedom and Muslims actually respect the Jewish religion.[3] Indeed, the Jewish community had the rights of freedom of religion and judicial autonomy, which included the means of administering punishments. In addition, religious services generally took place without the intervention of either local or central authorities.

Nevertheless, both Hebrew and foreign-language sources from the seventeenth to the early twentieth centuries recall attacks against Jewish religious observance in Morocco in the wake of disturbances, or at the instigation of local governors, who apparently acted with the approval of the sultan. As the Pact of Umar forbids construction of new synagogues or churches, both the buildings and their contents served as targets for attacks. Jews had to prove that a particular synagogue or at least its foundations were not new. In order to circumvent this restriction, Jews held services in private homes. For generations, synagogues were closed, desecrated or destroyed, or, in some cases, turned into mosques. Sources recall measures against teaching children, desecration and burning of Torah scrolls, prohibitions against blowing the shofar on the New Year or at funerals, or praying loudly.[4]

Occasionally, these were local events, however, at times, they originated in official circles. In 1611, fifteen Torah scrolls and many holy books were burned in the

Eliezer Bashan, *Pe'amim* (1995): 65–85. English translation by Rivkah Fishman.

town of Tadla by local hooligans. The following year, a synagogue in Fez was broken into and Torah scrolls were desecrated and sacred items stolen. And, as if that did not suffice, the thieves were known but "there was no trial because officials were involved."

Eleven years later, synagogues were destroyed and "Torah scrolls trampled upon" in the town of Tafilalet. In 1627, synagogues were closed and it was forbidden for the requisite quorum of ten men [minyan] to gather for prayer. The teaching of children was abolished in the towns of Tetuan, Fez, and Alqasar. In 1646, an order was issued in Fez to destroy the synagogues of the indigenous community and those of the descendants of Jews exiled from Spain. Sacred items were confiscated and the Torah scrolls were saved only because of a bribe. Only two private synagogues were not harmed. Five years later, synagogues again were destroyed in Fez, apparently even those which were built with the approval of the authorities and for a fee. In Tetuan, the great synagogue was confiscated in 1665.[5]

Under the son of Muhammad Ibn Abdallah, Yazid (1790–1792), hard times fell upon the Jews of Morocco. His anti-Jewish measures included an order to destroy synagogues or turn them into mosques.[6] Under his successor, Suleiman II (1792–1822) called "the Pious," new synagogues were burned down. Hence, in 1811, three synagogues, four Torah scrolls, and holy books were burned in Meknes.[7]

The governor of Tangier ordered the destruction of a synagogue in 1820 with the sultan's approval. Two years later, during the visit of Sultan Abd al-Rahman II (1822–1859), permission was granted for the renovation of two synagogues after the intervention of Judah Ben'uliel, a Jew who undertook diplomatic missions at the behest of the sultan and his predecessor.[8] During the reign of Sultan al-Hasan Ibn Muhammad (1873–1894), the synagogue of Chechuan was desecrated and its Torah scrolls torn apart.[9]

The death of a sultan was crucial for the fate of the Jews, for the period of transition between rulers often was a time when Jews were harassed. After the death of Sultan al-Hasan I Ibn Muhammad, in June 1894, synagogues were desecrated or destroyed in Marrakesh, Damnat, Amizmiz, and other locations in the Atlas Mountains. Torah scrolls and books were desecrated or sold by local tribesmen.[10] On July 12, 1908, the Jews of Wazzan (the holy city east of Fez) complained to the Alliance Israélite Universelle of the destruction of the synagogue along with other difficulties.[11] Among the descriptions of Jewish observance in Morocco, it is noteworthy to recall prohibitions against praying too loudly and blowing the shofar. Thus, for example, in 1767, the governor of Sefrou forbade the rabbis of the town to pray out loud.[12]

In 1840, during the funeral of the rabbi in Sefrou, shofars were blown in accordance with local custom. The qadi charged and fined the community. In 1898, the governor of the town of Tazza forbade blowing the shofar on Rosh Hashana (the Jewish New Year) as well. As the Jews did not obey, Muslims attacked the Mellah and plundered it. In Wazzan, Jews were forbidden to blow the shofar on Rosh Hashana. In July 1908, they wrote the Alliance, as follows: "Every year we are prevented from observing the commandment of blowing the shofar."[13]

A well-known anti-Jewish measure in Morocco involved forcing Jews to undertake tasks and perform services for the authorities. For example, Jewish women were forced to sew uniforms and tents for the army and to launder clothing.[14] Furthermore, Jews had to perform humiliating tasks such as cleaning public toilets, disposing carcasses of animals, and hanging the heads of criminals who had been beheaded. Jews first were required to salt these heads in order to prevent their decay.[15]

The sultans issued instructions for cancellation of these orders. For example, Muhammad XVIII (1859–1873) gave a royal decree, which he submitted to Sir Moses Montefiore on September 5, 1864, which stated that one is not allowed to force a merchant or a craftsman to work against his wishes.[16] On September 14, 1884, his successor, al Hasan I Ibn Muhammad, issued similar instructions to the governor of Damnat concerning the obligation of local Jews to act as workers, cleaners, and porters and allow the governor the use of their animals.[17]

II. COMPULSORY LABOR ON SABBATHS AND JEWISH FESTIVALS

Various sources, amongst them documents from the archive of the British Foreign Office, attest to imposition of compulsory labor on the Sabbath and the change of market days from a week day to the Sabbath for purposes of ending Jewish competition.

Our earliest source evidently is the statement of Rabbi Emanuel Mansano in 1739 that Jewish women in Fez were forced to work "day and night on the Sabbath and in general." Samuel Romanelli of Mantua who visited Morocco from 1787–1790, during the reign of Sultan Muhammad Ibn Abdallah, relates:

> I was extremely troubled and upset by what I saw. On the Sabbath, a caravan of Arab guards of the king came to synagogue with excessive destructiveness, took all the craftsmen and workers, and rushed to take them to engage in their specific tasks, according to their profession, for the king's service. Likewise, all the women who sew mittens and scarves were required to do so without pay. The taskmasters were quick to beat them with sticks, stones, or fists. They grabbed them by the corners of their clothing on their chests and dragged them mercilessly, and woe to those who tried to flee. These wicked men are called "Suhara." The Jews, who were still at prayer, had to leave the Torah and

desecrate the commandments, and as lambs led to slaughter, they left in order to perform their tasks at which they worked exceedingly hard until the evening.[18]

Similarly, according to reports of the Alliance Israélite Universelle and the Anglo-Jewish Association and from documents in the archives of the British Foreign Office, Jewish men and women were forced to work on the Sabbath and on festivals even in the nineteenth century.

According to a memorandum issued to the community of Tangier on April 25, 1864, the governor of Mogador demanded that Jewish women sew garments for the local governor, even on holidays. The governor did not accede to the request that the work be postponed until after the festivals. A similar notice from the 1870s recalls that Jewish men of Marrakesh were also obliged to work on holidays.[19]

Salting Decapitated Heads of Rebels on the Sabbath

In the 1870s, Jews were forced to salt the decapitated heads of rebels on the Sabbath. For example, Berber tribes frequently revolted against Sultan Muhammad XVIII. In order to force them to accept his authority, he would engage in punitive military campaigns. Among the tribes were the Musa, located south of Marrakesh. In 1872, the Sultan succeeded in quelling their revolt and forty-eight of their captives were condemned to death. In October 1872, on the order of the sultan, they were dispatched to Rabat for beheading. Their decapitated heads were to be exposed on the gates of the town for three days. Since the heads were to be sent to Fez, Jewish ritual slaughterers [*shohetim*] were forced to salt them and hang them for exposure on the Sabbath. Despite threats by the governor of Rabat, the Jews refused to do so. He then ordered soldiers to enter the homes of those who refused and drag them outside. After they were flogged, the Jews complied and performed the task and the heads of the rebels were exposed in public.

Knowledge of this affair reached the Alliance Israélite Universelle, and, on February 27, 1873, its president, A. Cremieux, requested that the British, French and Italian ambassadors in Morocco appeal to the sultan. The French and British officials, C. Tissot and J. Drummond Hay, respectively, replied on March 13, and the Italian, E. Scovasso, on April 21. They promised that they would discuss the matter at a meeting with the sultan with a request that he issue instructions to behave justly toward the Jews. It is noteworthy that the first letter only dealt with the attack on the Jews of Rabat and Meknes, while the second related mainly to the fact that the previous October, the Jews of Rabat were forced to salt the decapitated heads of rebels on the Sabbath. Both ambassadors were convinced that the sultan was neither aware of nor involved in this incident.[20]

The Anglo-Jewish Association was informed of these events only in May 1873, seven months after they occurred, and published a reaction in its annual report. According to the report, it was decided that the Association request that John Drummond Hay, who was in London at the time, bring the matter to the attention of the sultan and ask that the guilty parties be charged in order to prevent further incidents of a similar nature.

On 19 May, A. Benisch, vice president of the Anglo-Jewish Association, wrote to Drummond Hay that Jewish ritual slaughterers in Rabat, who were subjects of the sultan, were forced by the local governor to salt the heads of the rebels on the Sabbath. He even argued that this act violated the royal decree which the sultan had given Montefiore on February 5, 1864. The author of the letter stated that he was convinced that the sultan was not aware of the event, and therefore requested that as Britain's representative in Morocco, Drummond Hay would use his influence on the sultan in order to prevent further actions of this kind in the future.

In the meantime, Drummond Hay returned to Tangier and wrote his reply on May 30. He pointed out that in March (actually, in February), he had received a similar letter from Cremieux, the president of the Alliance, and that he and M. Tissot, brought the matter to the sultan's attention.

Their intervention was successful and the sultan issued strict orders to prevent similar acts.[21] At this point, let us add some information regarding the treatment of the different protagonists in this affair. The information from Rabat reached Paris before it reached London. For, as we have noted, as early as February 27, 1873, Cremieux requested that Drummond Hay intervene with the sultan regarding two matters: First, in August 1872, the governor forced the Jews of Meknes to work on Sabbaths and Jewish festivals. It was not reported in the publications of the Anglo-Jewish Association. Second, there was the issue of compelling Jewish ritual slaughterers in Rabat to salt the heads of the rebels on the Sabbath, despite the sultan's decree forbidding Jews to perform such despicable tasks.

Drummond Hay, the foreign secretary, and the sultan had corresponded until April 24, 1873, namely, before the Anglo-Jewish Association in London had become aware of the events in Meknes or had not yet dealt with them. On March 13, 1873, Drummond Hay passed the letter of Cremieux to the British Foreign Secretary, Lord Granville, along with a copy of Drummond Hay's reply to Cremieux. Drummond Hay does not seem to have been aware of what transpired in Meknes, whereas he read about the affair in Rabat in the *Gibraltar Chronicle* upon his return to Tangier. Afterward, he wrote his vice consul in Rabat requesting that he verify it and inform him of the results of his investigation. The vice consul, in turn, confirmed the truth of those events, but as the vizier in charge of foreign affairs was not present, Drummond Hay thought it would only be proper to wait until such news would reach the sultan's court. Then, in a private audience, he would raise the issue of the negative conduct of the local government. Similarly, he considered reminding the sultan that despite the fact that salting the heads of the rebels by Jews may have been done previously, it was the first time that he heard that Jews had to perform this disgusting task on the Sabbath.

On April 10, 1873, Drummond Hay and Tissot wrote a joint letter to the sultan as follows:

FO 99/154   April 10, 1873

The elders of the Hebrew communities in Europe have brought under the notice of the undersigned, acts of the Governors of Rabat and Mequinez [*sic*], which they are persuaded are in opposition to His Majesty's well-known justice towards subjects, whether Mohammedan or Jew. It is declared that the authorities have compelled the Jews to work on their Sabbath, and thus to disobey the laws of God as revealed to them through Seedna Moses. The Governor of Rabat has compelled certain Jews, to salt on their Sabbath the heads of some rebels sent to the town to be exposed.

His Majesty the Sultan, and His Majesty's ancestors, have always desired that the Jews should have full freedom in the exercise of their religion. This act of tyranny has been published in the journals throughout Europe, and has left a very unfavorable impression on the minds of Foreign Governments, as it is supposed that the Governor of Rabat acted under the authority of His Majesty. As the undersigned desire that their respective Governments should not alter, in any way, the opinion entertained of His Majesty's sentiments of justice towards his Hebrew subjects, they have thought it their duty to bring this fact under His Majesty's notice, and they are persuaded not only that a severe reprimand be given to the Governor of Rabat for his arbitrary conduct, but that orders will be given to all governors at the towns, not to compel the Jews to infringe the tenets of their religion.

It will be further satisfaction to the undersigned if the Sultan will cause a letter to be addressed severally to them, by one of His Majesty's Ministers, expressing His Majesty's disapproval of such acts, and stating that orders have been sent to His Majesty's authorities in the sense they have desired; as this communication would be transmitted to their respective Governments.

Morocco 10th April 1873
Signed C. Tissot & J. H. Drummond Hay

This letter contains several details typical of similar letters which Drummond Hay dispatched to this sultan and his successor relating to the maltreatment of Jews in Morocco, such as:

6. Recognition of the sultan's sense of justice and the fact that he desires the welfare of the Jews and only governors or those who were disrespectful of his authority harass the Jews.
7. The bad impression left by such acts on European governments, public opinion, and the press. The sultans were interested in trade with major European countries from which they purchased weapons and ammunition. The present sultan, like his predecessor, worked toward improving the army according to the European model, among other things, in order to overcome rebellious forces. Thus, the ambassadors took advantage of his weakness and expressed their apprehension, lest such cases harm the good name of the sultan and his good relations with European countries.

Two weeks later, Sid Deris ben Deris, secretary to the sultan, sent a reply to the two ambassadors in the sultan's name. He claimed that the sultan knew nothing at all about the actions of the governors of Rabat and Meknes. He further noted that if the Jews of Rabat and Meknes had submitted a complaint to the sultan, he would have straightened things out. He also added that the sultan had written the two governors involved, reprimanded them, and ordered them never to repeat such acts: "This decree is in accordance with repeated orders given to all governors, as we treat all human beings justly." As in similar cases, the gist of the sultan's statement emphasizes that he behaved justly towards all of his subjects regardless of their faith.

Drummond Hay reported to the foreign secretary on that day (April 24, 1893) and mentioned his reply to Cremieux of March 13 after the latter had called his attention to the cruel behavior towards the Jews on the part of several governors of Morocco. He even saw to the delivery of a copy of his and M. Tissot's joint memorandum to the sultan and copies of the identical reply of the sultan to this memorandum. As Drummond Hay assumed that Tissot would convey a report concerning their joint request to Cremieux via his government, he did think it was necessary to write to him. In another letter written by Drummond Hay to the foreign secretary on the same day, he expressed the hope that in several days, he could report that the sultan had taken measures to stop forcing Jews to work on the Sabbath.[22]

However, in 1888, prior to the meeting of the planning commission of the Protectorate, held in Madrid in 1890, the leaders of the Alliance again mentioned the decree forcing Jews to salt the decapitated heads of those who had been sentenced to death, on the Sabbath.[23]

In the early 1880s, the Jews of Damnat suffered from repressive measures on the part of the governor. Both men and women were forced to perform various services on the Sabbath and festivals. Whoever resisted immediately was incarcerated. This information was published in the daily *Le Reveil du Maroc* on September 2, 1884.[24]

The governor ordered that Jews be arrested arbitrarily, regardless of age or sex, for the purpose of labor for the army. In addition, they had to pay the soldiers who administered lashes. This information came from reports in a journal of the London-based Anglican Society for the Spread of Christianity among the Jews, which also was active in Morocco.[25]

After the sultan was informed, he responded by issuing seventeen articles of instruction including a prohibition against employing Jews on days when their religion forbids work.[26] Nevertheless, Jews were forced to desecrate the Sabbath in the coming years. In 1887, a Jew named Reuven Turgeman was arrested. On the order of the vizier, he was brought from Alqasar to Tangier, forced to travel on the Sabbath and not allowed to observe the Passover holiday.[27] According to the joint memorandum of the Anglo-Jewish Association and the Committee of Jewish Deputies to the Foreign Secretary on February 3, 1888, Jewish men and their wives and daughters were forced to work for government officials on the Sabbath and Jewish holidays. This point was included in the twenty-seven articles regarding humiliating measures and restrictions suffered by Moroccan Jews.

These practices continued into the 1890s as well, as confirmed by B. Meakin in the *Jewish Chronicle* on August 3, 1894. According to Meakin, one could only be released from such obligations by a payment.[28]

In the early 1890s, the Jews of Marrakesh suffered from the harsh policies of the governor and qadi of the town who cooperated with each other in harassing them. Information that reached Europe included details about Jews who were imprisoned and flogged to death for no reason. The sultan's intervention was of no help and the governor did not respect his order not to disturb the Jews. These tribulations even caused some Jews to convert to Islam. On October 8, 1893, Reuven Elmaliah, head of the Jewish community of Mogador, wrote a letter to Samuel Montagu (1832–1911), a member of Parliament and of the Committee of Deputies, in which he recounted the suffering of the Jews of his town in detail. He told of a Jewish woman whose husband converted to Islam while she remained a Jew. She was forcibly dragged from her home and forced to work on the Sabbath, thereby violating the commandments of her religion. The *Jewish Chronicle* published further details, including an item about the wives of two converts to Islam who refused to adopt their husbands' new faith. They angered the governor and the qadi, who ordered them to convert to Islam. One of the women was dragged from her home along with her infant on Yom Kippur (the Day of Atonement), transported to the Muslim quarter and forced to work on Sabbath. The other escaped with her children. But the elders of the community were forced to return her because of the government's threats of imprisonment, flogging, and desecrating the Jewish religion.[29]

Changing Market Day to the Sabbath

Market days were held on different days of the week, according to local customs. Some were held on Sunday and Thursday, and others, Monday and Thursday.[30] Changing market days to the Sabbath actually served as a means of Muslim economic competition against Jews. In 1861, G. Rohlfs, a German who visited Morocco, wrote that Jews were forbidden entry into the holy city of Tamgrut (located in Upper Wadi Dra'a) and prohibited from participating in the weekly market held outside the city. In order that they suffer from the severity of this restriction, market day was held on the Sabbath with the knowledge that Jews did not conduct business on that day.[31] Similarly, documents from the archive of the British Foreign Office show that the governor of Mazagan (some ninety kilometers from Casablanca) changed market day from Monday to Saturday. Upon hearing this, Drummond Hay and Tissot addressed the sultan in a letter dated April 10, 1873, entitled, "A Memorandum regarding the Said (Governor) Doo [?] and the Unfortunate Jews of Mazagan."

They asked the sultan to instruct the Said about reinstating Monday as market day, as it had been held on that day in the past. This subject appeared in Drummond Hay's report to the foreign secretary on April 24, 1873. The reply of the Sultan, written on April 25, reads as follows:

Regarding the complaint of the unfortunate Jews of Mazagan concerning the fact that market days were changed to Saturday, the Jewish Sabbath: this was done in order to help the tribes of the provinces. Therefore, it is justified that the governor choose a day which [is] most suitable for them. Moreover, in the past, it was reported to the Sultan, that market days were changed following requests by several local Jews who had received the protection of the United States of America and were not under the jurisdiction of Muslims. These were negative persons who acted in opposition to laws made by the governor.

Nevertheless, the Sultan would make sure that the matter would be investigated by disinterested parties who will examine the real reason for changing market day. If it becomes clear to the Sultan that the tribes have complained they have suffered damage, and therefore, have requested to change market day, then there is no reason to change it again. But if it becomes clear that this change is the whim of the governor, then market day will be restored to its previous day.

It is not clear what prompted Jews who had American protection to ask that market day be changed from Monday to Saturday, or if this indeed is correct. It is more likely that it was an unfounded accusation, circulated by people with vested interests for the purpose of emphasizing the distinctions between Jews with foreign protection and their local brethren who did not have foreign citizenship.

On July 28, Drummond Hay again wrote the vizier, as is evident from the latter's reply of August 13. The reply states that it was decided that market day be restored to its customary day (not Saturday) "for the sake of the Jews of Mazagan." This was the last letter which we found that dealt with this matter.[32] Therefore, based on available information, it is clear that market day was held on Saturday, not because of the tribes, as the sultan had assumed. For, the matter was concluded by restoring market day to a week day, when Jews could transact business.

Sometimes, changing market day to Saturday was a means of extortion on the part of governors. For example, in the wake of decrees and harassment by Muslims, the rabbis of Fez wrote to the Alliance on 11 Adar 5640 (March 12, 1880), as follows: "The official threatened us that he would change market day, when many Jews transact business, and would make it on the Sabbath."

It is not known if the official actually carried out his threat.[33] In any case, occasionally European tourists reported that this recurred in different places throughout Morocco in the early twentieth century.[34]

The fact remains that the during the late nineteenth century Jews were forced to desecrate the Sabbath and festivals by engaging in labor, performing services, and changing market day to Saturday. These measures were carried out on the initiatives of local governors, whereas the sultans wished to allow the Jews to live according to their faith. There was a gap between the orders of the sultans and facts on the ground. Governors occasionally ignored instructions and did not fear that their position would be endangered. The sultans had no control over what transpired in the provinces. Their orders regarding humane behavior toward Jews were not carried out consistently. The replies of the sultans to European ambassadors expressed their desire not to harm observance of the Jewish religion and to act kindly and justly toward the Jews. Such matters, however, were important only as far as they damaged their relations with Christian countries or affected their economic interests. Therefore, on occasion, the intervention of diplomats in reaction to requests by Jewish organizations in Paris and London met with success.

DOCUMENTS

Document 1

The letter of the British ambassador to Morocco to the foreign secretary concerning the compulsory salting of heads of rebels on the Sabbath by Jews in Rabat.

FO 99/154   Tangier 13 March 1873
The Right Honourable

The Earl Granville, K.G. [Knight of the Order of the Garter]
My Lord

I have the honour to transmit herewith the copies of a letter addressed to me by Mr. Cremieux President of l'Alliance Israelite at Paris requesting me to make a representation to the Moorish Authorities towards the Jews of Rabat and Mequinez and of the reply I have addressed to M. Cremieux under flying seal, which I request may be forwarded to that Gentleman, if Your Lordship sees no objection.

I had not received a report from any other quarter of the alleged arbitrary treatment of the Jews by the Moorish Authorities at Mequinez, but with reference to that part of M. Cremieux's letter in which he states that certain Jews at Rabat had been compelled by the Governor to salt the heads of rebels who had been killed when fighting against the Sultan's army in his progress from Fez to Morocco, I have to acquaint your Lordship, that the first notice I had of this proceeding, was from an article which appeared in the *Gibraltar Chronicle* shortly after my return to Tangier.

I then wrote to the Vice Consul at Rabat and requested him to inform me whether there was any foundation for this statement. The Vice Consul confirmed the report but as the Moorish Minister was absent, I thought it preferable to await until I arrived at the Court, before I interfered in this matter so that I may have with the Sultan, the conduct of his authorities. I should mention that it has been the custom from ancient times to compel the Jews to salt the decapitated heads of rebels, but this is the first time that I heard of Jews having required to perform this nauseous and horrible operation on their Sabbath.

I have the honour to be, with the highest respect,
My Lord
Your Lordship's most obedient humble servant
J. Drummond Hay

Document 2

The joint memorandum of the British and French ambassadors to Morocco to Sultan Muhammad XVIII, written in light of information which reached them from European Jews regarding compulsory work on the Sabbath required by the governors of Rabat and Meknes.

FO 99/154   10 April 1873
Memorandum of tyrannical acts towards the Jews of Rabat and Mequinez, by the Governors of those towns.

The elders of the Hebrew communities in Europe, have brought under the notice of the undersigned, acts of the Governors of Rabat and Mequinez, which they are persuaded are in opposition to His Majesty's well known justice towards subjects, whether Mohammedan or Jew. It is declared that the authorities have compelled the Jews to work on their Sabbath, and thus to disobey the laws of God as revealed to them through Seedna Moses. The Governor of Rabat has compelled certain Jews, to salt on their Sabbath the heads of some rebels sent to that town to be exposed.

His Majesty the Sultan, and His Majesty's ancestors, have always desired that the Jews should have full freedom in the exercise of their religion. This act of tyranny has been published in the journals throughout Europe, and has left a very unfavorable impression on the minds of Foreign Governments, as it is supposed that the Governor of Rabat acted under the authority of His Majesty. As the undersigned desire that their respective Governments should not alter, in any way, the opinion entertained of His Majesty's sentiments of justice towards his Hebrew subjects, they have thought it their duty to bring this fact under His Majesty's notice, and they are persuaded not only that a severe reprimand will be given to the Governor of Rabat for his arbitrary conduct, but that orders will be given to all governors at the towns, not to compel the Jews to infringe the tenets of their religion.

It will be a further satisfaction to the undersigned if the Sultan will cause a letter to be addressed severally to them, by one of His Majesty's Ministers, expressing His Majesty's disapproval of such acts, and stating that orders have been sent to His Majesty's authorities in the sense they have desired; as this communication would be transmitted to their respective Governments.

Morocco 10th April 1873

signed C. Tissot &
J. H. Drummond Hay

BIBLIOGRAPHICAL REFERENCES

Documents from the British Royal Archives, PRO:
CO (Colonial Office), FO (Foreign Office)
CO 91/52; FO 52/27, 28, 30, 59
FO 99/121, 154, 214,234, 235, 240, 259, 269, 302, 307
FO 413/4

L. Addison, *The Present State of the Jews* (London, 1675).
O. Agrell, *Neue Reise nach Marokos* (Nuremberg, 1798).
Alliance Israélite Universelle [Alliance].
Alliance, Bulletin, *Bulletin de l'Alliance Israélite Universelle*, Paris.
Alliance, Bulletin (German), *Bericht der Alliance Israélite Universelle (Allgemenen Israelitischen Allianz)*, Paris.
Alliance, Publication, *The Alliance Israélite Universelle:*
Publication of the Twenty-fifth Anniversary of Its Foundation (Paris, 1885).
Alliance, Twenty-five years, *Die Allgemeine israelitische Allianz. Bericht des Central-Comites ueber ersten Funfundzwanzig Jahre 1860–1885 Zweite deutsche Ausgabe* (Berlin, 1885).
Anglo-Jewish Association Report.
Ashmed Bartlett, *The Passing of the Shereefian Empire* (London, 1910).
N. Barbour, *Morocco* (London, 1965).
D. P. Barrows, *Berbers and Blacks* (New York, 1927).
E. Bashan, "Muslim Hatred of Jews in Morocco in the Nineteenth Century" [Hebrew], *Mahanaim* 1 (1992): 216–23.
———, "Sabbath Observance by Jews in the Maghreb and Its Economic Affects according to Christian Travelers" [Hebrew], in *Studies on the Jews of the Maghreb in Memory of R. Shaul Ziv*, ed. M. Amar (Jerusalem, 1983), 94–110.
Bat Ye'or, *The Dhimmi: Jews and Christians under Islam* [Hebrew] (Jerusalem, 1985).
T. Benady, "The Jewish Community of Gibraltar," in *The Sephardic Heritage*, ed. R. D. Barnett and W. M. Schwab, I2, 144–79.
M. Benayahu, ed., *History of Fez: Misfortunes and Events of Moroccan Jewry as Recorded by Ibn Danan's Family and Descendants* [Hebrew] (Tel Aviv, 1993).
H. Bentov, "Jewish Artisans in Fez during the 17th and 18th Centuries" [Hebrew], *Sefunot* 10 (1966): 414–81.
I. Brunot and E. Malka, *Textes Judeo-Arabes de Fes* (Paris, 1939).
C. E. Callwell and Count Gleichen, *Report on Morocco*, 1889, FO 99/269.
M. L. Chenier, *The Present State of the Empire of Morocco*, I–II (London, 1788).
J. J. Chetrit, "The Personal and Socio-Historical Poetry of R. Shelomo Halewa (Meknes, the XVIIIth Century) and the Tradition of the Hebrew Poetic Discourse in Morocco" [Hebrew] *Miqqedem Umiyyam* 4 (1991): 25–111.
N. M. Chetrit, *La Terreur du Reve: Recite epique sur l'Histoire Juive-Maroc* [Hebrew], ed. N. Yonatan (Tel Aviv, 1983).
A. Cohen, E. Simon-Pikali, and O. Salama, *Jews in the Moslem Religious Court: Society, Economy and Communal Organization in the Eighteenth Century: Documents from Ottoman Jerusalem* [Hebrew] (Jerusalem, 1996).
D. Corcos, *EJ* (2), IV, 543.
A. Cour, "Al-Hasan Mulay, Abu-'Ali-Al Hasan b. Muhammad Sultan of Morocco," *EI* (2), III, 275–76.
J. V. Crawford, *Morocco at a Glance* (Lymington, 1889).
E. F. Cruikshank, *Morocco at the Parting of the Ways: The Story of Native Protection to 1885* (Philadelphia, 1935).
J. Davidson, *Notes Taken during Travels in Africa 1835–1836* (London, 1839).

B. Dinur, *Yisrael ba-Golah* (2), I, 1 (Tel Aviv, 1959).

R. E. Dunn, *Resistance in the Desert, Morrocan Responses to French Imperialism 1881–1912* (Madison, 1977).

F. F. Ellingwood, *The Reaper* (1890), 235.

P. H. Emden, *Jews of Britain: A Series of Biographies* (London, 1922–1943).

J. Even Tsur, *Mishpat ve-Tsedek be-Ya'akov* 2, vol. 51 (1894–1903).

G. Gaskell, *Algeria as It Is* (London, 1875).

J. S. Gerber, *Jewish Society in Fez, 1450–1700: Studies in Communal and Economic Life* (Ann Arbor, 1975).

H. A. R. Gibb and H. Bowen, *Islamic Society and the West*, I/II (Oxford, 1957).

W. T. Gidney, *At Home and Abroad: A Description of the English and Continental Missions of the London Society for Promoting Christianity amongst the Jews* (London, 1900)

E. M. Grosvenor, *Narrative of a Yacht Voyage in the Mediterranean during the Years 1840–1841* (London, 1942).

J. Halfon, *Mishpatim Tsadikim* 28 (Jerusalem, 1935).

W. B. Harris, *Morocco That Was* (London, 1921).

J. Hassan, "The Treaty of Utrecht 1713 and the Jews of Gibraltar," *JHSET* 7 (1970): 1–16.

H. Z. Hirschberg, *A History of the Jews in North Africa: From Antiquity to Our Time* [Hebrew], I–II (Jerusalem, 1965).

H. Z. Hirschberg, "The 'Mellah' and the 'Masos' and the Jewish Quarter in Morocco," [Hebrew] *Eretz Israel* 4 (1957): 226–30.

———, *Land of the Setting Sun* [Hebrew] (Jerusalem, 1957).

G. Hoest, *Nachrichten von Marokos und Fes, Im Lande selbst gesammelt in den Jahren 1760 Bis 1768, aus dem daenischen uebersetzt* (Kopenhagen, 1781).

A. M. Hyamson, *A History of the Jews in England* (London, 1908); *The Sephardim in England 1492–1951* (London, 1951).

Saadia Ibn Danan, "Chronicle" [Hebrew], in *Fez and Its Sages*, ed. D. Obadia (Jerusalem, 1979), 1: 1–63.

I. Ibn Walid, *Va-Yomer Yitzhak* (Livorno [Leghorn], 1856).

J. G. Jackson, *An Account of the Empire of Morocco* (London, 1814). *The Jewish Chronicle.*

Jewish Missionary Intelligence.

R. L. N. Johnston, *Morocco, the Land of the Setting Sun* (London, 1902).

J. Jung, *Champions of Orthodoxy* (London, 1974).

D. Kaufmann, "Zu den marokkanischen Piutim," *ZDMG* 50 (1896): 234–40.

M. Keatinge, *Travels in Europe and Africa: Comprising a Journey through France, Spain and Portugal to Morocco, also a Second through France in 1814* (London, 1816).

R. Landau, *Portrait of Tangier* (London, 1952).

R. Landau and W. Swaan, *Morocco: Marrakesh, Fez, Rabat* (London, 1967).

M. M. Laskier, *The Alliance Israélite Universelle and the Jewish Communities of Morocco 1862–1962* (New York, 1983).

———, "Aspects of Change and Modernization: The Jewish Communities of Morocco's Bled," in *Communautes juives des marges sahariennes du Maghreb*, in ed. M. Abitbol (Jerusalem, 1982), 329–64.

———, "The Jews of Morocco and the Alliance Israélite Universelle: Selected Documents," *East and Magreb* 3 (1981): vii-xxiii.

A. Leard, *Morocco and the Moors, Being an Account of Travels, with a General Description of the Country and Its People*, 2nd ed., rev. and ed. R. Burton (London, 1891).

W. Lempriere, *A Tour through the Dominions of the Emperor of Morocco* (London, 1830).

N. Leven, *Cinquante ans d'histoire l'Alliance Israélite Universelle (1860–1910)*, I–II (Paris, 1911–1920).

V. D. Lipman, "Montagu," *EJ* (2), XII, 263

D. Littman, "Jews under Muslim Rule in the Late Nineteenth Century," *Wiener Library Bulletin* 28, nos. 35–36 (1975): 65–76.

D. Mackenzie, *The Khalifate of the West: Being a General Description of Morocco* (London, 1911).

E. R. Marciano, *Ir ha-Kohanim Debdou* (Jerusalem, 1987).

J. H. Mashash, *Otzar ha-Mikhtavim* (Jerusalem, 1968–1970).

G. Maxwell, *Lords of the Atlas: The Rise and Fall of the House of Glaova 1839–1956* (London, 1966).

L. A. Mayer, "The Status of the Jews under the Mamluks" [Hebrew] in *Magnes Anniversary Book* (Jerusalem, 1938), 161–66.

B. Meakin, "The Jews of Morocco," *JQR* 4 (1892): 369–96.

A. R. Meyers, "Patronage and Protection: The Status of Jews in Precolonial Morocco," in *Jewish Societies in the Middle East*, ed. S. Deshen and W. P. Zenner (Washington, 1982): 85–104.

L. H. Montagu, *Samuel Montagu, First Baron Swaythling: A Character Check* (London, 1913).

D. Obadia, *The Community of Sefrou* [Hebrew], I–V (Jerusalem, 1975–1992).

———, *Fez and Its Sages* [Hebrew] II (Jerusalem, 1979).

S. Ockley, *An Account of South West Barbary* (London, 1713).

F. V. Parsons, *The Origins of the Moroccan Question 1880–1900* (London, 1976).

I. O. Perdicaris, *American Claims and the Protection of Native Subjects in Morocco* (London, 1886).

F. Pulsky, *The Tricolor on the Atlas* (London, 1886).

Report, *London Committee of Deputies of the British Jews, Annual Report.*

W. Ridgeway, *Report on General Questions Connected with Morocco*, July 10, 1893, FO 99/302, 10–11.

F. G. Rohlfs, *Adventures in Morocco and Journeys*

through the Oases of Draa and Tafilet (London, 1874).

S. Romanelli, *Masa Ba-'Arav* (Cambridge, 1886).

C. B. Roth, "Samuel Sumbal, Forgotten Jewish Statesman" [Hebrew], *Ben Institute: Studies and Activities* 3 (1960): 13–17.

S. M. Samuel, *The History and Genealogy of the Jewish Families of Yates and Samuel of Liverpool, with Additions and Notes by L. Wolf* (London, 1901).

A. B. M. Serfaty, *The Jews of Gibraltar under British Rule* (Gibraltar, 1958).

M. M. Serels, *A History of the Jews of Tangier in the 19th and 20th Centuries* (New York, 1991).

A. Staehelin, *In Algerien, Marokko, Palaestina und am Roten Meere Reiseskizzen* (Basel, 1891).

N. A. Stillman, "The Moroccan Experience—A Revisionist View," *Association for Jewish Studies, Newsletter* 18 (1876): 13–14.

Taffiletta, *A Short and Strange Relation of Some Parts of the Life of Taffiletta* (London, 1669). *Times of Morocco.*

J. M. Toledano, *Ner Ha-Ma'arav: Hu Toledot Yisrael Be-Marokko* (Jerusalem, 1911).

R. N. Washington, "Geographical Notice of the Empire of Morocco," *Journal of the Royal Geographical Society* 1 (1832): 123–55.

R. S. Watson, *A Visit to Wazan: Sacred City of Morocco*, London, 1880.

J. Wolff, *Travels and Adventures of Joseph Wolff*, 2nd ed. (London, 1861).

A. Ya'ari, "Pinkas Shelihutam shel R. Yonah Moshe Navon u-R. Yona Saadia Navon," *Sinai* 25 (1949): 320–30.

G. Yver, "Morocco," *EI* (1), VI, 579–606.

NOTES

1. "Pact of Omar," according to Ibn Khaldun: Dinur, I,1, 66–67; according to Qalqashandi: Mayer, 162; Idealization: Landau, 1952, 179–81; Landau, 1967, 35; Dunn, 44–45. Contrary to the idyllic description of the reign of Muhammad Ibn Abdallah: Toledano, 164, there is information regarding restrictions on the Jews which began at that time, see: Hoest, 143–45; Chenier, I, 155–59, 352–54; Lempriere, 61, 154, 171, 180–83, 413, 436; Keatinge, 299–300, 304–305. On different approaches to compulsory residence in the Mellah, see: Laskier, 1983, 13. For an example of a conclusion based upon autobiographical memoirs, see the observation of: N. M. Chetrit, 1983, 184: "For many years, the Jews of Morocco lived without the experience of wars and enjoyed complete freedom of religion, wide-ranging social and cultural activities, and prosperous businesses."

2. For contemporary criticism of the idealization of Jewish life in Islamic countries, including Morocco, see: Stillman, 13–14. See also: Meyers, 86. For a selection of nineteenth-century sources on the humiliation of and restrictions upon Moroccan Jews see: Bat Ye'or, 252–70. On the twenty-seven articles of humiliation and restrictions upon Moroccan Jews according to the letter of the Anglo-Jewish Association and the Committee of Deputies of the Jewish Communities in London, on February 3, 1888, see: Anglo-Jewish Association Report, 1888, 24–26. Subsequent sources and literature repeat information about the humiliation and oppression of Moroccan Jews. Some consider the status of Moroccan Jews to be worse than that of Jews in other Muslim countries. See: Callwell, 64; Ellingwood, 235; Johnston, 9; Barrows, 67; Parsons, 4, 66. According to Benayahu's introduction, "there is no doubt that the decrees against Moroccan Jews were immeasurably worse that those regarding other communities," Benayahu, 9.

3. See Taffiletta, 34–35; Chenier, I, 159; Pulsky, II, 186–87. The British ambassador to Morocco, W. Ridgeway, mentions in his report of July 10, 1893, that while Jews enjoy religious freedom and their lives are run by rabbis according to the laws of their religion, they nonetheless suffer from limitations in other areas. See: Ridgeway, 11; Gibb and Bowen, I, 2,208; Barrows, 39; Cruikshank, 22. On Muslim respect for the Jewish religion, see Jewish Missionary Intelligence, 1844, 279.

4. On the prohibition against construction of new synagogues according to the Pact of Umar, see Mayer, 162, 165. On the implementation of this prohibition in Morocco, see Ockley, 100; Addison, 89. On privately owned synagogues: For Tangier, see: Halfon, I, no. 28, according to a source from 1778. In Tetuan, there were sixteen private synagogues: Report, 1877–1878, 119. On restrictions of Jewish religious observance in Jerusalem in the sixteenth century according to documents of the local Shari'a court, see: Cohen, nos. 138–40, 142, 147, 151.

5. See: Ibn Danan, 6, 37, 44, 89; Benayahu, 75, 89–90, 95, 98–99. Brunot, 198. In 1665 in Tetuan, see Ibn Walid, II, no. 105.

6. On the destruction of synagogues in Fez under Yazid, see Agrell, 177. On changing synagogues into mosques, as recalled in the poem of Shelomo Halewa, see J. Chetrit, 90–97; Mashash, II, 1262; Kaufmann, 239; Hirschberg, 1957, 75–76; Hirschberg, 1965, II, 295–301.

7. See Obadia, Fez, I, 76–77.

8. See Anglo-Jewish Association Report, 1877–1878, 113; Serfaty, 20; Serels, 267; Judah Ben'uliel, was born in Gibraltar in 1772, owned ships and a bank, was active in Jewish communal affairs in Gibraltar, and died in 1839. He is mentioned in documents of the British Colonial Office and the British Foreign Office from 1810–1830: CO 91/52; FO 52/27, 28. 30, 32, 59. In 1802, he signed in the ledger of Jewish contributors in Gibraltar to emissaries to the Land of Israel, see: Ya'ari, 336. The missionary Joseph Wolff met him in Gibraltar in 1821. According to Wolff, Ben'uliel was the richest Jew there. See Wolff, 95.

9. See: *Times of Morocco*, May 4, 11, 1889; Alliance, German, 1889, 62063. Jewish Missionary Intelligence, 68, 1890, 159. On the desecration of synagogues in the environs of Damnat, see: Jewish Missionary Intelligence, 68, 1894, 155.

10. For Marrakesh, see *Jewish Chronicle*, September 21, 1894, 9. For Damnat and environs, see *Jewish Chronicle*, September 7, 1894, 13. For Amizmiz, see Jewish Missionary Intelligence, 68, 1899, 153.

11. See Laskier, 1983, 54–56.

12. See: Obadia, Sefrou, I, no. 146; III, 144.

13. For Tazza, see Marciano, 52; for Wazzan, see Laskier, 1981, XVI; Laskier, 1983, 54–55.

14. See Even Tsur, II, No. 119; Jackson, 166–70; Davidson, 165; March 11, 1880, FO 413/4, 74, 93; 1884, FO 99/214, 149–50. Anglo-Jewish Association Report, 1885, 41; Littman, 73–74, published a document from the archive of the Alliance Israélite Universelle dated July 27, 1885, on Jews of Damnat who were flogged because they refused to work without pay. Meakin, 382; Harris, 311; Cruikshank, 21; Roth, 15; Hirschberg, 1965, II, 265; Bentov, 425; Gerber, 231.

15. See Washington, 143; Jewish Missionary Intelligence, 1841, 258; *Jewish Chronicle*, September 28, 1877, 7; *Jewish Chronicle*, June 11, 1880, 10–11; *Times of Morocco*, August 28, 1886; Report 1888, 25; Crawford, 11; FO 99/288; Jewish Missionary Intelligence, 1904, 176; Mackenzie, 62–63; Ashmed, 272; Barbour, 145; Maxwell, 27; Parsons, 6; Hirschberg, 1956, rejects the idea that the Jewish quarter was called the "Mellah" because of the salting (Hebrew, "meliha") of decapitated heads which was carried out by Jews.

16. See Cruikshank, 24–25; Hirschberg, 1965, II, 309–10.

17. Anglo-Jewish Association Report, 1885, 41.

18. Emanuel Mansano, in Benayahu, 136; Romanelli, 24–25.

19. See FO 99/121, 1864; *Jewish Chronicle*, September 28, 1877, 7; Anglo-Jewish Association Report, 1888, 25.

20. On Sultan Muhammad XVIII, see: Yver, 587; Cour, 275–76; Gaskell, 21; Bashan, 1983, 106. On the correspondence between the ambassadors and the Alliance Israélite Universelle, see Alliance, Bulletin, German, 1873, I, 143–45; Alliance, Publication, 53; Alliance, Twenty-five Years, 36.

21. Anglo-Jewish Assoc. Report, 1872–73, 36–38. On the royal decree, see: Hirschberg, 1965, II, 309–10.

22. FO 99/154 (n.p.).

23. Alliance, Bulletin, German, 1888, 38.

24. See FO 99/214, 150; Alliance Bulletin, Germany, 1884–1885, 32; Leven, I, 342–42; Laskier, 1982, 347–48.

25. Jewish Missionary Intelligence, 1885, 35.

26. Anglo-Jewish Association Report, 1885, 41; It is recorded in the archive of the Alliance Israélite Universelle as well, see Laskier, 1982, 346–48.

27. Reuven Turgeman was arrested because of a debt owed by his father to a Jew who held American citizenship. This information reached the Paris office of the Alliance, see: Alliance, Bulletin, German, 1887, 35–36. This affair was the subject of a correspondence between the Jewish associations in London and the British Foreign Office and the government in Morocco. For details, see FO 99/234, 235, 240. On the Committee of Deputies of the Jewish Communities, see: Report, 1887, 17–18, 22–23; Report, 1888, 31–32; Perdicaris, 51–54. Information regarding his desecration of the Sabbath and the fact that he could not celebrate Passover also appears in the *Times of Morocco*, April 21, 1887.

28. See Anglo-Jewish Association Report, 1888, 25; FO 99/259; Meakin, *Jewish Chronicle*, August 3, 1894, 8. On April 15, 1893, the *London Times* reported that a Jew in Tangier was kicked to death by a Muslim [for refusing] to sell him merchandise on the Sabbath. [In] *Jewish Chronicle*, April 28, 1893, 12.

29. FO 99/307, October 8, 1893. Samuel Montagu, banker and philanthropist, [Whitechapel] Member of Parliament (1885–1900), was active in Jewish communal affairs both in Britain and abroad. He visited the Land of Israel, Galicia, the United States, and Morocco. See Samuel, 59; L. Montagu; Emden, 228–36; Hyamson, 1908, 340–41; Hyamson, 1951, Index; Lipman, 263; Jung, 171–80; *Jewish Chronicle*, November 17, 1893, 10.

30. On Sunday: Ockley, 39. On Sunday in Damnat: *Times of Morocco*, May 26, 1887. On Sunday and Thursday in Tangier, see Grosvenor, 55; Watson, 37; *Jewish Chronicle*, April 9, 1880, 5; Leard, 13. On Thursday, in Wazzan: Martiniere, 126; in Fez, according to information from February 18, 1880; FO 413/4, 68. Regarding towns in the Atlas Mountains, see Jewish Missionary Intelligence, 1889, 68, 147; 68, 1892, 163; on Marrakesh, Jewish Missionary Intelligence, 1899, 187; Staehelin, 279. According to another report, there were two market days, and an additional slave market, three days a week: Jewish Missionary Intelligence, 1888, 161. The report of the Anti-Slave Trade Association states that there were four slave market days in Marrakesh: *Times of Morocco*, May 26, 1887. On Monday in the Atlas Mountains: Jewish Missionary Intelligence, 1907, 11.

31. Rohlfs, 349. See also Bashan, 1983, 104–105.

32. FO 99/154, no page given. On April 29, 1875, Drummond Hay wrote that it was the governor's wish that the Jews be prevented from going to the market, FO 99/170. For information about this affair, see Alliance, Bulletin, German, 1873, I, 178; II, 17–18.

33. Bashan, 1992, 220.

34. Bashan, 1983, 105.

CHAPTER 45

Jews under Muslim Rule—II: Morocco 1903–1912

David Littman

The historical framework for these letters, in the form of a short introduction, was to have been written by the late Professor H. Z. Hirschberg. Tragically, only four days after he received the 1976 Ben Zvi Award for his life's work on the history of Jews in Islamic lands, Professor Hirschberg passed away in Jerusalem. This documentation, based on letters relating to the first decade of the twentieth century in Morocco, from the Archives of the Alliance Israélite Universelle, is dedicated to the cherished memory of a highly esteemed scholar, teacher and friend.

The Alliance Israélite Universelle was founded in Paris in 1860. The principal objectives of its founders were to work everywhere for the emancipation and moral progress of the Jews, and assist those suffering from discrimination. By 1914, about fifty thousand boys and girls were receiving an education in its primary and vocational training schools dispersed throughout the Ottoman Empire, Persia, and the Maghreb.

Letters and reports flowed into the central office of the Alliance in Paris from the representatives of the regional Alliance communities and AIU school directors, from community leaders as well as individuals, and occasionally from French and foreign diplomats. These documents were generally written in French, although some are in other European languages or in Hebrew, Arabic, and Judeo-Arabic—often with an accompanying translation into French. The letters here published for the first time have all been specially translated into English.

This rarely used source material frequently portrays a dismal picture of the Jewish condition in the early part of the twentieth century, in what was generally a hostile environment. Hundreds of letters vividly authenticate the contemporary account of European travelers during the age of liberalism and emancipation, who almost unanimously agreed on "the degraded and precarious position of Jews in Muslim countries, and the dangers and humiliations to which they were subject."[1]

The material in the AIU archives from Morocco is probably the fullest from any Muslim country. Morocco had always retained its independence, but anarchy was frequent and the Jews suffered most from it, especially at the death, or change, of a sultan. Traditionally, nothing was easier for rebels or fanatics than to attack the feeblest and the most despised element of society.[2]

It is perfectly true that the Muslim Moroccan commoner also suffered during these periods of instability, but the degraded minority status of the Jews, as infidels and *dhimmis*, made them the most vulnerable victims of each and every brutal excess from a cruel *qa'id*, a ruthless mob, or tribesmen in revolt. From the time of the description of their wretched state by Addison in the seventeenth century, to Budgett Meakin's accounts at the turn of the twentieth century,[3] European travelers and diplomats rarely failed to note the abject condition of the Jews in the Sheriffian Empire.

The classical text on their condition in the late nineteenth century is that of Charles de Foucauld. Disguised as a Jerusalem rabbi in order to accomplish his "Reconnaissance au Maroc"[4] in 1883, this young French aristocrat and military officer was obliged to hear this gratuitous insult from each and every Muslim who passed him on the road to Chechuan: "*Que Dieu fasse brûler éternellement le père qui t'a engendré, Juif!*"[5] Thirty-one years later, describing the Jews of Arr'en in southern Morocco, Edmond Doutté wrote:

> *On rests confondu que sous une pareille tyrannie un people ait pu conserver intacte la foi qui lui valair ce martyre. On concoit encore la haine inspirée aux vainqueurs par la résistance de ces malheureux et les massacres périodiques qui les décimaient.*[6]

The letters and reports which follow, vividly illustrate the humiliation, misery, and exposure to physical violence which was still the lot of the ordinary Moroccan Jew in the first decade of the twentieth century.

CHRONICLE OF EVENTS

September 1902   Bu Himara (Jilali b. Idris al-Zarhuni) revolts against the Sultan 'Abdul-'Aziz.

From *The Wiener Library Bulletin* 1976, vol. 29, pp. 3–19.

April 1904	Franco-British Entente. France relinquishes all her rights and interests in Egypt, and Britain accepts a French protectorate in Morocco.
October 1904	Franco-Spanish agreement regarding their future respective zones of influence in Morocco. French bank consortium grants large loan to the sultan.
1905	Si Madani El Glaoui, a southern Berber chieftain, withdraws support from 'Abdul-'Aziz.
March 1905	Kaier William II visits Tangier with the aim of blocking French aspirations.
April 1906	The outcome of the Algeciras conference, called by Germany, was the Act of Algeciras, accepted by the sultan, which, due to British support, consolidated the 1904 Franco-Spanish agreement.
March 19, 1907	Dr. Mauchamp, French doctor and philanthropist murdered in Marrakesh. The French occupy Wajda on the Algerian frontier.
August 1, 1907	Nine Europeans killed in Casablanca. Jewish Mellah sacked and pillaged. Militarily, France intervenes throughout the Shawiyya region around Casablanca. 'Abdul-'Hafiz rebels successfully, with the help of El Glaoui, against his brother 'Abdul-'Aziz.
January 5, 1909	'Abdul-'Hafiz accepts the Act of Algeciras and is recognized by the French.
February 1909	Germany recognizes France's "special responsibility" in Morocco.
1909	Bu Himara captured by 'Abdul-'Hafiz.
1910	Tribes around Meknès rise in rebellion under new pretender; they are defeated by the French.
July 1, 1911	German gunboat *Panther* sent to Agadir, after which the French cede a crucial part of French Congo to Germany.
March 30, 1912	The Sultan 'Abdul-'Hafiz signs the treaty with France establishing the French protectorate over Morocco.
April 17–19, 1912	Uprising in Fez against the French, the Jewish Mellah sacked and pillaged.
11 August 1912	'Abdul-'Hafiz abdicated. Mouley Yusuf succeeds him.

DOCUMENTS

1903 Jizya (Poll Tax) Still Imposed on All Moroccan Jews

I have read with much pleasure the article in the *Journal des Débats* concerning the Jews in Morocco. Never before has such a precise and impartial study on our co-religionists in this country been published. There can be no doubt that the author of this article has lived in the country, that he has observed and judged what he has seen without allowing himself to be influenced by other publications or by diplomats in embryo who haunt the legations in Tangier. It is not surprising in a work of this scope and importance that the author has been guilty of some errors. This he states that the jizya or tribute paid by the Jewish communities to the sultan has been abolished in many cities. This tax is still in force and there is a tendency to increase it. Apart from this heavy tax burden, the Jews are obliged to give costly gifts to the *qā'id* and to important Muslims passing through the city; in time of war, which is the normal state of affairs in the country, they are forced to contribute toward the feeding and maintenance of the [tribal] chiefs and their soldiers. The Jews of the Riff and those subjected to the more or less independent Kabyles also have obligations to their lords and masters.

Moreover, it would be a mistake to generalize when speaking of the Jews of Morocco. Those from Tetuán are quite different from their co-religionists in Fez, and the Jews living in the towns have customs totally different from those living in the country who are, in essence, not to be distinguished from nomadic tribes. A few kilometers from Tetuán is the city of Chechuan where no European has ever penetrated and where two or three thousand of our co-religionists suffer the most dreadful persecution and harassment from the Muslims and from those in authority. . . .

Letter (12.6.1903) from E. Carmona, head of the Tetuán AIU Boys' School, to the President of the AIU, Paris (AIU MOROCCO I.C.1).

1903 Jews Assaulted in Rabat and Falsely Accused of Blaspheming Islam

. . . The events which for the last year are taking place in Morocco have had their repercussions on the Jews of Rabat . . . our redoubtable enemies the Zairs and the Zemmours [tribes] were preparing to erupt into the Mellah in order to pillage it. . . .

Mr. Méana, the Spanish consul and doyen of the diplomatic corps in Rabat, is a good and most charitable man, gifted with a modesty which enhances his fine character. He is the protector of the weak and hence a friend of the Jews, regarding whose fate he takes a heartfelt interest. . . . He immediately sent his emissary to the governor advising him to provide the necessary guards for the protection of our co-religionists and of those Spanish subjects residing in our quarter . . . later he made pressing requests through the Spanish legation in Tangier and the breaches in the exterior wall of the Mellah were repaired. Since then we have benefited from a little tranquility. Unfortunately it did not last.

A Jew named David Benzaquen, under Brazilian protection, was returning from Salé with his wife. In order to arrive earlier in the Mellah, the couple took a shortcut, when their way was barred by a group of tanners who worked in the area. When Benzaquen insisted on proceeding by that route, the fanatics rushed at him, beat him furiously with sticks, and swore to assassinate him in this isolated spot. He saved himself by taking flight.

To explain their behavior, the Arabs concocted a document, false in every respect, stating that our co-religionist had blasphemed the Muslim religion. The Cadi, who presided over the case, took the matter seriously and had the unfortunate man seized by his *shires* and, despite the strong protests of Mr. Benatar, the vice-consul of Brazil, the man was thrown in jail. Through a refinement of cruelty, the Cadi, in principle and by temperament an enemy of our race, placed a rigorous ban on access to the prison by the mother and brothers of Benzaquen, naturally anxious to do what they could to help this victim of Arab fanaticism. This incident had a sequel. Having seen that a protected Jew could be locked up with impunity, the Muslims assumed that anything was permissible against the Jews, and for several days they gave free rein to their hatred, striking them in the street, spitting in their faces, and inflicting upon them the most glaring injustices. If one of us raised a voice to protest against these abuses, a crowd of Arabs was always present and ready to testify in favor of the guilty ones and to make out that the intruder had committed blasphemy against the Muslim religion. The fact that Arab justice does not accept evidence by a Jew only made the situation more intolerable.

My intervention had become indispensable. On Saturday, June 12, I called on Mr. Méana (the Spanish consul) and then made a tour of all the other vice consulates, informing them of the situation and asking them for their cooperation, which they kindly agreed to give me. The following evening, accompanied by soldiers from the Spanish, French, British, German, Austrian, and Belgian embassies, I appeared before the governor to protest against the cruelties committed by the Arabs. My words were heard and on June 14, two soldiers went through the town from one end to the other urging all the shopkeepers and regional heads to protect the Jews and to seize and bring before the governor anyone who maltreated a Jew.

After this, the situation of the Jews in Rabat improved considerably. . . .

From an annual report (20.10.1903) to the AIU Central Committee, Paris, by J. Conquy, head of the newly founded Rabat Boys' school (AIU FRANCE XIV F 25).

1903 Jewish Population of Fez Demonstrated Loyalty to the Sultan

. . . The political situation of our brethren in Fez is neither good nor bad. So long as Morocco maintains the status quo, their situation will not improve. In the towns of the interior of Morocco, the condition of our brethren will not change until there is a European occupation. The Jews can hope for nothing from the present regime, which is unwilling to shake the Moroccans out of their inertia or eradicate their deep-seated ignorance, which holds anything European in horror. Any radical change in Morocco could only have favorable and beneficial effects for our co-religionists. . . .

. . . *Bu Himara.* An event which shook the whole of Morocco and for a while threatened to overthrow the present dynasty was the appearance of the only too notorious agitator Bu Himara.

We first heard of Bu Himara in September last year [1902], a year ago today. Not even his name, place of birth, or origin were known. There were vague stories that a saint, a messenger from God, one of those mystics who so often arise in the Sudan, the Sahara, and in North Africa, roused by the reforms which the Sultan 'Abdul-'Aziz wished to bring about in the country, was seeking, cunningly, to exploit the general discontent, and had put himself at the head of the discontented. To win over the ignorant and fanatical mountain people, he represented himself as a wizard, a magician—always mounted on a she-ass. For this reason, popular imagination gave him the name of Bu Himara (father of the she-ass). . . . Thus, it was from Taza, a small town situated two days' ride from Fez, a kind of Kiatha mountains, that Bu Himara raised the standard of revolt. . . .

Bu Himara is no more than a legendary figure like so many others who are depicted in popular stories and songs. The terror which he once inspired is gone. His name has given birth to a whole new literature which is much favored by the Arabs in Fez. The stories and songs composed in honor of Bu Himara are without number. This mysterious personality has, so to speak, fascinated and charmed most powerful Berber tribes with his persuasive words and great comprehension. In addition, his slightest expressions and gestures have been so magnified, his so-called miracles blown up into such stupid proportions, that he is already considered not as an impostor, but a revered saint in Morocco, particularly in the interior toward the mountains and wild regions that stretch from Taza to the Riff. . . .

In the eyes of these tribes, Bu Himara is a saint in a double sense because he fought for the Muslim faith, this following the example of Moulai Idris, the founder of Fez. Thus, it was for the good cause that he endangered his life; he merely wished to remove from the sacred soil of Fez a king with European tendencies—and the Europeans themselves.

As you can well imagine, the state of our co-religionists

during these woeful days was pitiful. We all know that Bu Himara would be fatal for the Jewish community of Fez. The *Makhzen* [government] itself did not conceal its fears on this subject. So, the Mellah had become a virtual barometer of the political temperature in Morocco. All the vicissitudes of the war, good or bad, had their repercussions in the Mellah. . . .

The panic and lamentations lasted until January 29 [4, 1903], the day when Bu Himara was defeated. From then on everything changed at the Mellah. Lamentation gave way to joy. The shouts and the din were again heard in the streets, but they were cries of rapture which became delirious when the cannon shots announced the news—false alas!—that Bu Himara had been captured.

I shall never forget the explosion of pure delight in the Mellah when the news was announced. Throughout the day, the streets of the Mellah were crammed with people. From the terraces could be seen the flood of people going from one end of the Mellah to the other, shouting their delight to the sky and chanting hymns and psalms. Thousands of lungs exhaled their praises to God, and their blessings on the Sultan 'Abdul-'Aziz.

The evening was even more colorful. The whole Jewish population proceeded with lanterns and lighted candles to the *Dar-El-Makhzen* [the sultan's palace], shouting hymns such as: *Adou Olam, Igdal, Az-Yashir Moshe*, and so on. There, for hours, they shouted, sang, laughed and cried, invoking blessings from the sky on the young sultan. And finally sacramental blessings were addressed to the sultan by everyone. *Allah-Harak-Amar-Sidi* (God bless the life of the sultan), repeated five, ten, even fifteen times by these thousands of Jews, men, women, and children. They were at a loss to know how to express their happiness that evening. This immense compact crowd, singing and shouting in the night, only a few steps from the sultan's palace, each with a lantern in his hand, created a fairy-like, thrilling effect. The *Makhzen* was not unmoved by these imposing demonstrations of loyalty by the Jews. To express its gratitude, a thousand fireworks were let off over the Mellah.

The parades recommenced in grand style the following day, but this time our brothers were bolder, observing a custom enshrined in centuries of tradition. They went into the Palace to express to the sultan himself their immense joy caused by the defeat of Bu Himara. More than three thousand Jews, among them many women and children, with musicians in the lead and banners displayed (banners consisting of large golden or silver sashes worn by women) offered their warmest congratulations to the sultan and Menebhi [his minister] for the brilliant victory of January 29.

Needless to say, our co-religionists were received with great kindness. El Menebhi himself, at the invitation of the sultan, condescended to make a short speech in which he encouraged his listeners to express their joy freely, to decorate and illuminate the Mellah, for, as he said, Bu Himara had a special hatred for the Jews. In fact, the Mellah was illuminated and decorated during two days and two nights.

Today [seven months later] all is relatively calm. No one speaks any longer of Bu Himara with fear. To see the tranquility that reigns in the city, it is hard to believe that there was ever any apprehension and that Bu Himara had ever represented any danger to our people.

May God grant that this calm[7] is of long duration and that there will be no recurrence of the horrors that caused ruin and desolation to the ill-fated community of Taza . . . [more than sixty Jews had been killed and many injured in Taza one year earlier].

From an annual report (1.9.1903) to the AIU Central Committee, Paris, by J. Valadji, head of the Fez Boys' School (AIU FRANCE XIV F 25).

1907 Cataclysmic Destruction and Pillage of Casablanca Mellah

On August 1, a band of about one hundred Kabyles, helped by some Arabs from the town, attacked the port dockyard, derailed a small train, killed nine Europeans, and destroyed a large part of the installations. An immediate panic spread in the town; it was a premonition of things to come. Tuesday and Wednesday were days of indescribable suspense. The Jewish population, anticipating the massacre and pillage, whoever should emerge as victors, rushed in despair to the merchant boats being laden with goods in the harbor. Almost all the rich and well-to-do families able to gather together specie and personal belongings went on board paying exorbitant sums either to the Kabyles who permitted them to embark, or for their journey to the boats. There were scenes of disorder and confusion: mothers who had mislaid their children, who disappeared; rich people who had put their entire fortune into a mattress, only to watch it disappear in the water.

The cruiser *Galilee* appeared offshore on Thursday, August 3. Its arrival spread a little calm in the town and until the following Tuesday, the situation seemed less alarming, despite the five to six thousand horsemen surrounding the town or because either the *Galilee* had received the order to bombard the town or Moulai-Ain, the uncle of the sultan, feeling overwhelmed, asked for protection from the French cruiser, the Europeans were warned at two in the morning to go in haste to their consulates. At 5:00 a.m. a picket of seventy-five sailors disembarked. You know the sequel: the *Makhzen*'s soldiers fired on them; they crossed the town leaving a number of corpses behind them, arrived at the French consulate, and gave the signal for the bombardment to commence.

With the first cannon shot, as if the Arabs were only waiting for this sign, the soldiers of the *Makhzen* rushed into the Mellah, followed by the whole population, and started the pillage. The five to six thousand men who were waiting at the gates penetrated the town, spread out through the Mellah and the *medina*, robbing, looting, raping, killing, and burning, and during three days, until the French troops disembarked, sowed terror throughout the town. Not a house, not a family, not a person was spared. There are only five to six Jewish houses that remained intact because they were situated near the consulates. The *Kaiseria*, the quarter of the Jewish merchants, with more than five hundred shops, was burned down; nothing but ruins remain. From one end to the other, without any exception, the Mellah was sacked: doors and windows smashed, furniture and contents gone; all has been cleaned out, demolished; our schools have been reduced to pieces; the benches and desks smashed, the equipment, the money stolen, the books burned. At the *Talmud-Torah*, where my assistant, Mr. Soussana, lived, everything was destroyed. Mr. Soussana was very ill: they took everything away from him, even his mattress and his nightshirt; he was left naked on his iron bedstead. . . . [A]ll the synagogues, except for two small oratories, have been sacked, the silver stolen and the *hekal* [altar] desecrated. To the honor of our co-religionists, the *sepharim* [scrolls of the law] were saved. Everywhere there is desolation and devastation. One wouldn't believe that men could have destroyed so much, rather that the city had been the victim of a cataclysm.

But the looting, the fire is nothing. Chased out of their homes, the Jews scattered in all directions, around the precincts of the consulates, particularly the French consulate. There were battles between the Arabs and Europeans besieged in their consulates. Suffering heavy losses, the Arabs fell on the weakest: the Jews. A veritable manhunt began. The Jews hid themselves in caves, under rubble, in empty tanks. Families lived for three days under straw, without food. The men were pursued and beaten with truncheons or stabbed; the women raped when there was time, or abducted with their children. Horrible scenes took place. The narrative from the mouths of the victims themselves is hair-raising. . . .

Following my three-day investigation, I have made the following estimate which the authorities consider is most probably correct: thirty dead; some sixty wounded, of which twenty seriously; an unlimited number of rapes (I dare not question the families nor would they dare admit it); more than 250 young women, girls, children abducted. . . .

Letter (15.8.1907) from Isaac Pisa, head of the Casablanca Boys' School to the president of the AIU, Paris (AIU MOROCCO II C 3).

1907 Starving Jewish Refugees from Casablanca

. . . But the most to be pitied are those who were made captive or were taken prisoner during their flight. Poor, sad, humanity! Many have had no food for four or five days. To return to the town, they are forced to use every imaginable kind of trick and deceit. Some have handed

over everything they happened to have with them; others escaped in the night: intercepted on the open road, they proclaimed they were Muslims on their way to fight a Holy War against the French. When they were released, they were sent back completely naked. They were gathered in the cap and given sacks to cover themselves, and later they came to see me. Two or three new families arrive each day: pale, emaciated, their bones showing, hollow-faced, sunken-eyed. I welcomed them at the *Talmud-Torah* and warmed them up with the rum I had with me. I had them washed and gave them food, and they returned into the town, swelling the numbers of the destitute—and my stocks of food were running out! By the middle of next week there will be nothing left. And then what will these wretches do?

There are at the moment 350 to 400 poverty-stricken families in town of which 5 families were once well-to-do but are now in misery and a hundred others who kept a little something which they will soon have consumed.

From a letter (23.8.1907) from Isaac Pisa, Casablanca, to the president of the AIU, Paris (AIU MOROCO II C 3).

1907 Four Hundred Destitute Refugees Arrive in Settat

This is to inform you that your family arrived here in good health, thanks be to God, but your sister died on arrival at Settat and was buried as a saint since she did not succumb on the way.

You will know from this letter that there are more than four hundred Jews from Casablanca here. They are all without clothing. I am doing everything possible to feed them, but I have nothing left. All the young girls were raped. You know the daughter of Israel, your neighbor, who is pretty; all the Arabs had her. Married women suffered the same fate; their husbands no longer wanted them and there is a great scandal. Everyone is dying from hunger. I beg you therefore to approach the notables in Casablanca and the teacher of the Alliance to do something for them, for otherwise they will all die of hunger and from their sufferings.

Letter in Judeo-Arab (22.8.1907) from David Amar, merchant of Settat, to Selam Edery, notable of Casablanca, translated and transmitted by Pisa to AIU Paris, registered 4.9.1907 (AIU MOROCCO II C3).

1907 Forced Conversion to Islam of Abducted Girls

Agury and the son [Dr. Henry] of the Baron de Rothschild.

I have to inform you that on the Thursday when you sent me into the interior, I spent the night with the *Oulad-Zyan*; I found no Jews there. On the Friday evening, I reached the territory of the *Mdakra*, in the abode of the *Ouled-Zidan*. There they wanted to kill me; the Arab you sent to accompany me saved my life. I found many young Jewish girls there: some have remained Jewish, others have been forcibly obliged to convert. Among those who were converted, there is a daughter of Mr. Benchimol who has been adopted by an Arab. On the Saturday, I arrived in Magouch amidst the Jews who inhabit that place. These poor people received me kindly and promised to help me to save all these young girls. I therefore beg you to go to Mr. Benaroche and ask him to prepare for you a letter of recommendation for the *Lfakra* (Sherifs) of Magouch who are his protégés. They have a lot of influence with the *Mdakra* tribes. Please send this letter to me at Joseph Benbaruh's with whom I am staying and who has paid the courier who will bring you this letter.

Letter in Judeo-Arab (29.9.1907) from Abraham Amstet at Margouch to Isaac Pisa, Casablanca, translated and transmitted AIU, Paris, registered there 8.10.1907. (AIU MOROCCO II C3).

1907 Settat Sacked, Jews in Headlong Flight

I have the honor to confirm to you my dispatch of today which red: "Settat sacked by Mzanza tribe. Jewish population has fled." A messenger brought me this sad news this morning. . . .

A few days ago, I gave you some information on Settat. With the astonishing vitality that is a sign of our race, the community had reorganized itself quickly after the pillage of four years ago. To give you an idea of the extent of the new calamity which has struck the Jewish population of this country: three hundred to four hundred families are again without shelter and without food, not counting the families from Casablanca who are still there and who have now suffered the horrors of a second pillage.

Letter (19.11.1907) from I. Pisa to the president of the AIU, Paris (AIU MOROCCO II C 3).

1908 Eyewitness Account of Destruction of Settat Mellah

Jews of Settat. Again the Jews of Settat! Yesterday evening I was urgently summoned by Mr. Malpertuy, the French Consul, who informed me of the following message from General d'Amade: "80 Jews from Settat having obtained French protection are proceeding to Casablanca; make arrangements to receive them.". . . This morning at 11 o'clock they arrived, under the guidance of the General staff, 135 of them in a most pathetic state. The men looked like ghosts, hair and beard disheveled, covered in stinking sacks, through which one could see their bare bodies, their feet swollen and covered with mud and sores. The women, hardly covered in a piece of colorless linen, revealing their phantom-like nudity, their emaciated features, most of whom were offering dried-up breasts to sickly infants and being followed by a swarm of noisy little brats. Impossible to tell the young from the old, so much their misery has given

them a uniform look. We fit them up on hay beds and serve them water, we give them bread and oranges and then listen to the story of their tribulations during the long months that the present situation has lasted.

"Do you know," a young woman told us "what we suffered four years ago? [For them, the pillaging of (December 27), 1903 is a date of ill-omen]. We had returned to our homes and our work, this one at growing cereals, that one cobbling. The following years were hard. There had been no rain and there was no harvest. For us it was hunger. But we were always able to save ourselves so long as we were left in peace in the Mellah. For six months we had known that things were going badly and that the Arabs were planning trouble. Then we heard about the pillage of Casablanca. The Jews who had fled from there had taken refuge with us. We received them all in our homes and our huts. Little by little they returned, some to Mazagan, some to Rabat. When we saw arriving the *mehalla* [army] of Mouley-Rachid, we had premonition of the pillage, for whether it was the *mehalla* or whether the tribes needed money, they would always fall on us.

"In fact, three months ago, the *Mzanza* [tribe] had plundered a section of the Mellah, taking advantage of the discord reigning between the tribes. They took all we had, which amounted to almost nothing, and we probably owe our lives merely to our misery. After they left, it was death by hunger for us. We could not go forward to Casablanca because the Arabs had barred the route; we could not go backward for fear of falling into the hands of the *hafidienne mehalla*, and we could not go and work in the deserted *douars*. Fortunately, a courier arrived from the school director of Casablanca with a letter for Sheik Ben-Omar in which we were recommended to him. This rich Arab received us all, gave us food for some weeks with such kindness that we could hardly believe he was an Arab.

"A month ago, the French arrived in Settat. All the Arabs fled and many Jews with them. Some three hundred of us remained in the town, hoping that the French would take it. But after staying only a few hours they left abruptly. They had only gone a few kilometers away— we could still see their lights—when the Arabs came back from the mountains. The two weeks that followed were horrible and I ask myself how we are still alive. . . . All the well-to-do people left the city and went behind the mountains to Rebi Ayouch-ben-Malca, who enjoys the respect of the Arabs. We remained in the town living in a state of continual trauma, constantly expecting to be pillaged.

"A few days later the French returned to the outskirts of Settat. Realizing that this time the French would stay, the Arabs plundered the city for the last time, taking some of us with them. Those who were left were picked up by the French troops who gave us food. They questioned us and we told them what we knew, that the *mehalla* no longer wanted to fight and that there was dissension between the tribes. We were finally taken to Ber-Rechid, slept a night at Medionna and here we find ourselves without any hope of returning to our homes."

"What has happened to the other Jews?" we asked anxiously. "For you are only fifteen, and in Settat and in the *douars* you were at least a thousand." "We do not know," was the reply, "many are at Casablanca with their parents; others are behind the mountains and many are probably among the Arabs."

All these refugees are *Chleuhs*. It is out of question to repatriate them. We are organizing aid to clothe and feed them, then we will find them housing and work, after which they will merge with the population.

Letter (9.2.1908) from I. Pisa, Casablanca, to the President of the AIU, Paris (AIU MOROCCO I B 2).

1908 Forty Settat Jews Killed, Remainder Courageously Protected by Arab Sheik

. . . Today I received a visit from Sheikh ben-Omar, who protected the Jews so effectively on my recommendation and that of Mr. Karl Tieke, the doyen of the German colony. He confirmed point by point the account that I sent you the day before yesterday, and added certain details which I have verified. When the French left after the first occupation of Settat, the Arabs threw themselves to the Mellah with the intention of exterminating them [the Jews] for having acclaimed the French troops. Some forty Jews were killed and the killing ceased only because Sheikh Omar in person went to protect the Mellah and killed with his own hand a pillager so as to show his determination to stop the looting. It was thanks to his action that the remainder were spared and survived until the French returned. He told me that many Jews remained behind at Settat and, according to him, they must have been killed after the second departure of the French.

Sheikh ben-Omar was taken prisoner by the French troops but was released because of his loyalty and is returning to Settat. He will write to let me know if it will be possible for the Jews to return.

Letter (13.2.1908) from I. Pisa to the president AIU, Paris (AIU MOROCCO I B 2).

1908 Jews of Fez Humiliated and Menaced with Pillage

I have the honor to inform you that following recent events in Morocco, and particularly at Fez, the situation of our unfortunate co-religionists in this town has become intolerable in all respects.

I will not speak of the terror and panic of each moment as well as the dangers with which we are constantly threatened. It is sufficient to tell you what you already know, that we live among savages who have already tried to satisfy their ferocious hatred by making

a carnage of all the Jews, and only await the first opportunity to try again. With each riot in town, there is talk of breaking into the Mellah and sacking it.

Other torments have now been added to this life of constant anxiety. Since the proclamation of Mouley Hafiz as sultan in this capital, our people have been forbidden to go into the *Medina*, the Muslim quarter, which is the business center—where both rich and poor Jews, artisans and businessmen, earn their living—under pain of being beaten and thoroughly ill-treated. The few heads of poor families, who risk their lives and go to the *Medina* to earn a few pence for food for their children, come back exhausted and desperate after their sufferings at the hands of the Muslims. They are subjected to all kinds of humiliations. They are forced to take off their shoes and walk barefoot. They are made to jump and dance, thus provoking the mirth of the Muslims and satisfying their scorn for the Jews. In fact all imaginable tortures are inflicted on them without any pity and anyone who dares to offer any resistance to these barbarous acts is beaten and maltreated. . . .

Letter (13.2.1908) from Rahamin Benzimra to the president of the AIU, Paris (AIU MOROCCO?).

1908 Mellah in Mzab Utterly Destroyed, Many Jews Massacred by Tribesmen

Jews of Mzab. Another disaster which I have the painful duty to communicate to you, concerning which our coreligionists of Mzab have been the victims. General d'Amade's column operating against the *Mdakras* [tribes] arrived on February 17 at the foot of the hills in the vicinity of Mzab. The *qā'di* of the Casbah Ben-Ahmed—the most populous of Mzab and the one which comprises the largest number of Jews—went to tender his submission to the French authorities. The next morning, in reprisal, the other Mzabis sacked the Casbah and destroyed stone by stone the two Mellahs, massacring a number of Jews and chasing the others like a herd of beasts across fields. This information has been confirmed to me officially.

From local sources, it appears that the Jews living in this Casbah—several hundred souls—are en route for Casablanca. A large number would have found refuge in the other Casbahs. Yesterday, I received a first contingent of ninety persons. . . .

Jews of Settat. A third contingent arrived on the February 16 bringing their number of 315. . . .

Mr. S. D. Levy from Mauricio informs me that it is not twelve thousand but twenty-nine thousand francs that the Jews of Buenos Aires have sent to Tangier "for the victims of Casablanca.". . .

Letter (25.2.1908) from I. Pisa to the president AIU, Paris (AIU MOROCCO I B 2).

1908 Description of Treatment of Meknès Jews by Rabbi Abraham Amar

Because I know of the greatness of the Alliance and its aim in coming to the aid of Jews, endeavoring to save them from oppression in all those countries where they are scattered, I have ventured to reveal to you something of the events which have befallen us recently and to inquire whether, in the name of the good and powerful Lord, you might intervene with the Jewish notables and members of the Alliance, for we are clumsy and gauche in expressing our feelings—the length and hardness of our captivity has stifled our spirit. This is why we ask you to be our interpreter and our worthy intermediary.

From the day when the revolution started in our city (the revolution which the Muslims of the city carry on against our good king, His Majesty 'Abdul-'Aziz) we have been in very great distress.

Our enemies started by making us eat the dust and by making us the objects of scorn and contempt. They forced us to walk barefoot and thus our standing has been completely destroyed. Several thousand are without food because our co-religionists were not willing to walk barefoot or submit to the shame and shocking treatment of these savages.

Moreover, they exact taxes from us daily which are hard to endure. On one occasion, we paid one thousand douros and not a day goes by without our miserable and anguished community being forced to pay a new tax to silence the mouths of thousands of our enemies and oppressors.

They have also been cunning enough to close any escape route—thus preventing us from finding salvation in flight—in order to oppress and exploit us until we are left naked. . . .

Hebrew letter (26.2.1908) from Abraham Amar, one of the Chief Rabbis of Meknès, to A. Ribbi, head of the Tangier AIU Boys' School; translated and transmitted to AIU, Paris, registered there 15.3.1908 (AIU MOROCCO IV C II).

1908 Confirmation of Rabbi Abraham Amar's Lament

I have the honor to enclose the original and the translation of a letter which I have just received from Meknès. The signatory, Mr. A. Amar, is one of the leading rabbis of the community. All that it says with regard to the exactions and profound misery suffered by our co-religionists is absolutely true. Our chief rabbi and various members of our community have received other letters which confirm what Mr. Amar writes. Jews from Meknès who live in Tangier say that they are receiving with every postal arrival identical news from their relatives and friends. . . .

Letter (10.3.1908) from A. Ribbi, Tangier, to the president AIU, Paris (AIU MOROCCO IV C II).

1908 Humiliation and Oppression of Jews in Wazzan

This is to inform you that news received this morning from Wazzan shows that the situation of our co-religionists from that town is desperate. Since Mouley-Hafiz's proclamation [as sultan] in that religion, the cycle of persecution began for these wretched people. They are exposed to the worst possible treatment and suffer the most irksome humiliations. Last Wednesday, three of the [Jewish] notables were arrested, stripped of all their possessions, and thrown into prison. Afterward, a mob of Arabs entered the Mellah, pillaged and sacked a synagogue, profaned sacred objects, lacerated the Scrolls of the Law, and threw them into the street. The frightened Jews barricaded themselves in their houses. They are in the greatest consternation. A meeting of *Ulemas* [doctors of Islamic law] is to be held to decree the conditions under which their lives may be spared and what will be their fate. As details on these distressing events are lacking, tomorrow's post is anxiously awaited.

Some merchants from her [Larache], being under European protection with interests in Wazzan, have given particulars of the situation to the [foreign] consuls, who have promised to refer the matter to their ministers [ambassadors] in Tangiers.

At Alcazar, too, the Jews are grossly misused. All kinds of persecution are inflicted upon them: They must take off their shoes in front of mosques, submit to all the humiliation of yesteryear, and even accept blows, without being able to complain to the authorities. The governor of the town, to whom they have paid one thousand pesetas for his protection, has told them that he is powerless before the fury of the populace and has advised them to avoid going out for fear they should be massacred. Great panic prevails within this ill-fated community. Some families have come to Larache to seek refuge.

To the Arabs of the interior, the arrival of Mouley-Hafiz represents a brilliant victory over the Europeans and must, as its immediate consequence, have given them the freedom of humiliating and ruthlessly oppressing the Jews—in the name of the liberator of Islam.

Letter (21.6.1908) from Bensimon, head of the Larache AIU Boys' School to the AIU, Paris.

1908 Houses of Wazzan Jews Confiscated, Windows Blocked Up

Subsequent to my letter of the 21st, I can give you some details on the events at Wazzan, taken from a letter received here yesterday by a [Jewish] notable.

After three days of indescribable fright, our co-religionists have been able to save their lives on the following conditions. Oppressive measures, revoltingly cruel, were decreed by the meeting of *Ulemas* and their application will render the situation of these wretches highly precarious. Judge for yourself:

First of all, they are forbidden to go about the streets with shoes on, to wear white clothes; they are even refused light and air—all windows opening to the streets must be blocked up. A synagogue in the neighborhood of [the] Sharif [noble, descendant of Muhammad] is closed. They are likewise forbidden to smoke, drink, or distil spirits. All stocks of tobacco and cigarettes found in their shops have been confiscated and burned. They would have accepted all these persecutions resignedly, if their houses had not been attacked. From one day to another, they found themselves dispossessed of their homes. Anyone having title to any kind of property must put it into the hands of the Sharifs. The three notables who were arrested obtained their freedom only by paying a ransom of fifteen hundred pesetas, an enormous amount given the poverty of this small community. What makes the situation of these unfortunate people even more wretched is that they are not allowed to leave the town either to attend to their business or to evade the cruelty of these fanatics. They cannot even hope to see their lot improve. To whom can they appeal, who will intervene on their behalf?

Letter (24.6.1908) from Bensimon to AIU, Paris.

1908 Benevolence Shown to Jews by Grand Vizier El Glaoui

I have the honour to acknowledge receipt of your letter of the 16th in which you have sent me through our faithful friend, M. Joshua Corcos.[8]

I have noted all that you have told me and have the pleasure, firstly, to inform you that I am no fanatic, as stated by the European newspapers. On the contrary, I maintain a genuine and fair equality toward all goodly men, without reference to their race or religion. You have no doubt been informed that, since my return to Marrakesh, I have taken all necessary precautions to abolish the recent vexatious measures taken against the Jews and, God be praised, have succeeded in this. They are at present quite as untroubled and highly respected in the *Medina* (the Arab quarter) as in their Mellah. They may wear their *baboush* [heavy slippers] in the *Medina* and may moreover even ride on animals outside the Mellah, that is, in the *Medina*. In short, they now have all freedom to do everything formerly forbidden to them. We hope that they will continue to be satisfied and we ask God Almighty to assist us for the general good.

As to reopening your schools here, you may rest assured that I shall give all assistance to the teachers you are to send, in order that they may open the schools without difficulty. So send the teachers, for they will be welcome. I should also inform you that I am very pleased with the schools you have in our empire and I have always esteemed the education given there to Jewish children. I know already that the sole object of your schools is the intellectual and moral elevation of all their pupils and that they maintain great respect for all religions. M. Corcos will undoubtedly inform you that, upon reading your letter, I summoned before me the two *Pashas* of the town and the *Pasha* for the outskirts of Marrakesh, where there are many Jews, and in the presence of M. Corcos enjoined them to do all they could to ensure that the Jews should not be mistreated and that no annoyance to them should occur at anytime. I also recommended the schools, teachers, and pupils to them.

I repeat that I love only the truth and the equality of all creatures. We remain staunch friends to all Europeans and in particular to our honorable neighbours, the French. I should also inform you that our revered sovereign, His Majesty the Sultan Mouley 'Abdul Hafiz, wishes well to everyone and desires the good of all, and that everything that the newspapers say about him is false.

Letter (26.10.1908) from Si Madani Elmezouar El Glaoui (Grand Vizier of His Sherifian Majesty, Mouley 'Abdul Hafiz, Sultan of Morocco) then in Marrakesh, to Narcisse Leven, president of the AIU, Paris.

1909 Sultan Promises Protection to Jews of Fez

This intervention and the steps taken could not have come at a more opportune moment. Amid the confusion of Moroccan politics, you were able to predict the moment when a détente was likely, so as to intercede appositely on behalf of our co-religionists in Fez. This is what happened: the sultan read most attentively the speeches on Morocco made in the Chambre [des Députés] in the last few days. As and when the newspapers arrived in Tangiers, special messengers brought him the translations. You will recall the report on the situation in the Mellah which I sent to M. Gaillard, the French consul in Fez, and which was forwarded to the minister for foreign affairs, and you saw how M. Pichon, when speaking in the Chambre on the situation of the Jews in Fez, was prompted by that report and quoted part of it. Furthermore, M. Pichon made representations on the subject to [Si Taïeb] El Mokhri [foreign minister], who passed them on to the sultan. Yesterday, El Glaoui, following these representations, convened the chief rabbis and the notables of our community, and, speaking in the name of his master, told him:

> It has come to our knowledge that the head of your school has on several occasions written on your behalf to the Alliance Israélite. I am instructed by my master to tell you that never again will you be obliged to submit to any injustice on the part of the *Makhzen* [government], that forced labor will no longer be imposed upon you, that your feasts and Sabbaths will henceforth be respected; I bring you the goodwill promises of the sultan, who loves you

as much as his most faithful subjects. The doors of *Dar el Makhzen* [the palace] are from this day forward wide open to you and you can always put your complaints and grievances before us; they will be equitably heard.

This is, more or less, what El Glaoui told the representatives of the Mellah. Shortly after the community leaders had left the grand vizier, I presented myself before him and handed him your letter, which made a considerable impression on him. El Glaoui was very flattered by your approach and showed it by the particularly charming manner in which he received me. After having renewed to me personally the promises made to the notables of the Mellah a few minutes previously, he rose to go in order to read to the sultan your letter, which I had taken the precaution of having translated beforehand into an elegant, literary Arabic.

Letter (7.12.1909) from Abraham Elmaleh, head of Fez AIU Boys' School, to AIU, Paris.

1911 Only the Alliance Is Able to Protect Marrakesh Jews

. . . The great majority of the people enjoy no protection except that of the Alliance. We are doing all we can for them. If Jews are unjustly imprisoned, molested and held ransom by the authorities or by fanatical Muslims, the representative of the Alliance makes it his duty to plead their case with the responsible authority and more often than not his efforts are crowned with success. We endeavor to maintain the best possible relations with the *Pashas* and the other local government authorities, and use these good relations to ease, as far as we can, the precarious situation of our co-religionists who are Moroccan subjects.

These relations are even more crucial to us since we have no right to interfere in the dealings between the *Makhzen* [government] and its own subjects. Thus, each time I have intervened on behalf of any Jew, it is on the basis of a *fabor* (grace, favor). One could not speak in terms of injustice or violence to these proud and arrogant men without the risk of being shown the door and forever barred access to the governor's house. . . .

Letter (27.9.1911) from Raphael Danon, head of the Marrakesh AIU Boys' School to the AIU, Paris (AIU FRANCE XIV F. 25).

1912 Improved Situation of Marrakesh Jews

One cannot fail to recognize the achievements accomplished so far by your schools in Marrakesh. If one were to remember for a moment the situation of the Jews in this city ten years ago, one is struck by the changes they have undergone in the material sense as well as from an intellectual and moral viewpoint.

Judging from conversations I have had with some Jews on the subject, it is clear that their situation was very precarious. With a deep sigh, they recall the painful moments which they experienced. Your eminent collaborators who have taught in your schools in Marrakesh have, no doubt, painted frequently for you a picture of the sad and heartbreaking situation of the Jewish community at that time. Nevertheless, I would like to add some details.

Confined to their somber ghettos, the Jews lived in unhealthy slums. Whole groups of people swarmed in one miserable room, heaped together, so to speak, on top of each other and breathing bad air. The shadows of ignorance and superstition had taken possession of almost all of them. Small wonder that in the streets, at almost every step, one could come across sickly people in tatters. Everything about them reeked of the most abject poverty and the crudest ignorance. . . .

Let us measure the progress made by the Jews in their relations with the Arabs since the period of the *Galut* [exile], which ended only with the assassination of Dr. Mauchamp [March 19, 1907]. A deep, unbridgeable gap separated the Muslims from the Jews. The latter were the object of torment, scorn, and ill-treatment. They were not allowed to leave the Mellah with shoes on their feet, with the exception of the president of the community, who was always escorted by the *pasha*'s soldiers. All were obliged to take off their *babouches* or leave them at home when they tried to enter the Arab quarter, no matter how prosperous their condition. The unfortunate ones who ran the risk of riding any sort of animal through the *Medina* (the Muslim quarter) were beaten with sticks or fists, and then forced to dismount in a trembling state. "Miserable Jew, how dare you ride an animal in the presence of your master?" "In the name of God have pity on me, I am dismounting." That is not all, in the *Medina*, the unfortunate Jews were the playthings of their tyrannical neighbors. The latter forced them to endure a thousand humiliations when they passed by, such as throwing their skull caps to the ground or filling them with urine and returning them. After which the Arabs spat in their faces, threw stones at them, or forced them to perform humiliating acts. Those who tried to defend themselves were knocked about without pity. Inured to the worst treatment, the poor Jews accepted with pious resignation all the repressive acts which their dangerous neighbors made them endure. In a word, the age for the *Galut* had been a period of suffering and endless torments for our unhappy brethren.

What a change has taken place! This sad and humiliating past is disappearing little by little before the path of light, of progress. Today, the Jews are treated almost as the equals of the Arabs and the Christians . . .

From a report (March 30, 1912) by L. Benoudiz, teacher at the AIU Boys' School, Marrakesh, to AIU, Paris (AIU MOROCCO II B. 9).

1912 Cataclysmic Destruction and Pillage of Fez Mellah

We are awakening from a horrible nightmare. I didn't feel able to describe it to you. The sack of the Mellah by the mutinous sherifian troops began on Wednesday, the seventeenth of this month at midday. I had just left the school and had sat down to lunch, when I was informed that shots were being exchanged at the gates of the Mellah. At first it was a quarrel of small importance. But, moment by moment, the news that came in was more and more alarming. I was told that the troops had massacred their instructors, that five thousand well-armed soldiers had revolted, and that there was a march on the Mellah and the European quarter. The doors of the Mellah were closed but unfortunately not guarded, for the Jews had no guns or munitions, and the attack was so sudden that it was impossible to organize a defense. Each tried to defend himself in his home near his family. Our schools were invaded by groups of women and children in tears seeking refuge, none of whom realized, unfortunately, as we understood later, that our presence was fatal for them, for the mutinous soldiers were out to massacre all the French of Fez. I tried to organize our group to defend itself in the best way, so that our lives would be sold dearly. We had only five guns for more than four hundred refugees. It was a desperate situation. About 2:00 p.m. I was told that the mob had burned the doors of the Mellah and penetrated the quarter. The sack began then and we could hear the cries of those who were being massacred and their screams of despair. I spared no effort to get news to the French minister and to the French camp in Dar Dbibagh about two kilometers from the Mellah, to obtain aid, but my letters never arrived.

I have set out this situation in a letter to the French minister of which I am sending you an enclosed copy. In any case, Mr. President, we Jews have been the innocent scapegoats for the anti-French movement that broke out in Fez. Many French have been killed and mutilated: officers, businessmen lost their lives that Wednesday. It is a cruel mourning for France and for us. I have lost dear friends whom I shall always remember. The tragedy that struck an entire community such as our Mellah was even more atrocious. From the whole city of Fez, we were the only ones to be attacked; how cruelly true it is that whenever popular anger explodes in Morocco, vengeance is wrecked on the Mellahs until hatred has been satiated.

The pillage that started at midday on the Wednesday continued without pause until Saturday morning. For three days, massacres, robbery, and conflagrations were accomplished in the Mellah without interruption. The night of Wednesday to Thursday was a night of hell. I shall never forget that night, guns in my hands, near my stricken family, hearing the shooting, the screams of the victims, in a district illuminated by the sinister light of the burning quarter, expecting at any moment to be attacked by the savage horde and massacred with my family. We passed through horrible moments. Around me, I had gathered my wife, my children, and my staff so that we might die together, for we would not have escaped death despite the desperate resistance we were prepared to offer; we knew this from the experience of several homes that had been defended with desperate resistance we were prepared to offer; we knew this from the experience of several homes that had been defended with desperate courage and which had finally yielded to the bullets and the flames. On the Thursday morning, because of the atrocities already committed and wishing to prevent further tragedies, I induced the people in the surrounding houses to leave. I myself left my house with my family and all the refugees and we fled to a garden adjacent to the sultan's palace. We passed the rest of the day there, tracked and pursued, from hedge to hedge and from one cottage to another!

Oh! That desperate flight in the garden, the cries of the women and children who clung to me, under the delusion that I had the means to save them. I will never be able to describe you the full horror of it. Deliverance came that evening. Filled with compassion, the sultan had all the Jews gathered together and opened the doors of his palace, those doors against which we had knocked in vain all that day. Nearly two thousand Jews took refuge that evening in one of the palace courtyards. We were among them. What had happened to the others? We shuddered to think of their fate. We spent that night in the courtyard under the rain, sick and starving (we had eaten nothing since Wednesday morning and it was not until Friday morning that we received a piece of bread). The following morning, Friday, the sultan sent for me with my family. We insisted that our staff should also gain entrance, to which he agreed. We were received in a house; the sultan came to see us and to talk with us, with simplicity and much kindness. At the palace we were given the utmost hospitality until the morning, when I left to go to the embassy in order to help the Jews. The other Jews were gathered together at the palace on Friday, and the sultan ordered a generous distribution of food to them. The military authorities, the embassy, and the British consul sent bread. . . .

The facades of the houses were ripped out, whole streets were piled with rubble from houses which had caved in, the doors of all the houses had been smashed; broken furniture and the remains of the pillaging carried out freely by several hundred looters during three days lay about. Fire everywhere, destruction, ruin, and desolation. The corpses which were piled up in the streets were removed, more than fifty of them, men, women, and children. How many more will be found under the rubble? I went into the school and into my apartment. There was nothing left. What could not be taken away had been broken, ripped up. What scenes of savagery have I reconstituted! . . .

Letter from Abrahama Elmaleh (22.4.1912), head of Fez AIU Boys' School to the president of the AIU, Paris (AIU MOROCCO).

1912 Report on the Massacre in Fez

The day after the April bloodbath which witnessed the complete plundering of the Mellah, a commission was named by special *dahir* of the Sultan Mouley Hafiz to redress the immense disaster which had struck the Jewish population.

Here is a translation of the imperial *dahir:*

Praise to the One God:

There is no strength or power except in God on High, the Sublime One. (Seal of S. M. Mouley 'Abdul Hafiz, Sultan of Morocco.)

This is to announce that with the aid of God we enjoin the setting up of a committee composed of fourteen members, under the chairmanship of our servant Tazi. We require this committee to examine ways of remedying the situation of the Jews of the Mellah in this city, and to take all steps necessary in this respect, therefore:

1. The committee will first concern itself with providing for the subsistence of the Jews.
2. It will then proceed to remove the rubble from those parts of the Mellah which have collapsed, and generally clean up the quarter.
3. It will choose an appropriate provisional encampment for the Jews.
4. It will take appropriate measures to protect the Jews and the Mellah.
5. The Committee will undertake these tasks with due solicitude and care in order to achieve the objectives outlined by the most practical means.

Greetings. This is our decree, may God prove it, the 5th Djoumada of the year 1330 (April 20, 1912). . . .

Following the looting, which had lasted nonstop for three days, the Mellah presented a picture of a city destroyed by some frightful cataclysm. All the part between the admission *bordj* and what had been a furnace was completely destroyed and at the mercy of the fire which had been started on the night of April 17 to 18. The streets which had previously been so gay, so full of life and movement were now just a mass of burned and smoking ruins. The rubble rose to a height of more than ten meters, reaching the top floors of the houses. Half of the area was in ruins, ravaged by fire and uninhabitable; sections of walls stood alone, gutted houses somehow held together by a miraculous balancing act; others which had been isolated by partial or total collapse of adjacent houses were dangerous to live in.

The whole Jewish population had fled and taken refuge in the courtyard of the sultan's palace. To the horror of destruction was added the horror of silence. The streets, encumbered with corpses, covered with blood-stains, varieties of debris, broken furniture, torn clothing, goods, and numerous other things, were proof of the violence of the destruction and also of the struggles between pillagers who robbed one another. A nauseating odor of decomposition, decay, and fire arose from this chaos, and the rain which had fallen hard for forty-eight hours had transformed the Mellah into a filthy cesspool.

More than sixty Jews dead, some five wounded, a third of the Mellah deliberately burned down, the complete sack of the quarter, a Jewish population of ten thousand people reduced, after the exodus, to eight thousand living on public charity, without shelter or clothing, neither with homes nor tools for work, stripped of all their possessions: that is the balance sheet of those tragic days and the situation which confronted the committee. . . .

The Jewish population remained at the palace from the April 19–28. At first squeezed in a narrow yard, they were later able to occupy the vast interior courtyards of the palace and the menagerie where the cages for wild beasts served as shelter. From the outset, the committee sent the necessary supplies to this population . . . .

The victims were able to return to the Mellah on the morning of April 28. It was time: they had suffered severely from the cold and humidity under their pathetic makeshift shelters which the rain penetrated. The return was heartbreaking. It was a pitiful column of men, women, and children, in rags, dirty, weeping with despair as they gazed at the mass of ruins. An immediate distribution of food was made and the Jewish population crowded itself together as best it could in their quarter, reduced in area by one-third. A large number of Jewish families emigrated at once to Meknés and the coast. I estimate that two thousand left of which a part returned to Fez because of the difficulties of subsistence.

All the Jews who came back to Mellah had need of aid, for no one any longer possessed anything. It was impossible to make a distinction between those who had been rich and comfortable and those who had been poor. Our task only began once the Jewish quarter was reestablished since some had to be provided with means of existence, others with working tools, and all with daily subsidies. . . .

From a report of A. Elmaleh (22.11.1912) published in Tangier (1913) (AIU MOROCCO).

1913 Jews of Fez Can Never Forget the Ghastly Bloodbath of 1912

It is perhaps useless to recall the bloody events which took place in Fez on April 17, 1912. However, what happened was so terrible that any recital would still fall short of the reality.

The Moroccans had been described as being sometimes sanguinary, but they carried out a crime of such infamy that day that the Jews of the Mellah will never be able to erase its evil memory.

Assassination, rape, fire, looting—nothing was spared this unfortunate Jewish community which was unable to defend itself since it had been completely disarmed a few days before by the Moroccan authorities under a futile pretext, which shows clearly that the revolution was organized and was not spontaneous as some have tried to pretend. . . .

On April 17, while the people of the Mellah went about their occupations as usual, a horde of Moroccans, amounting to thousands, rushed on the quarter and in cowardly fashion—while our wretched co-religionists begged for mercy, reminding them of past services— assassinated children, women, and old people under the eyes of their families who were powerless to help. These savages assuaged their passion on our wives and daughters, who were raped [before] their relatives with a brutality that defies description. The circumstances of these atrocities still make us tremble; they went beyond all that can be imagined. And when we say that some of these women and young girls, sullied in this manner, are dead and others will forever carry the traces of this violence, despite the care and attention of French doctors, the suffering which grips the Mellah can be understood.

While a part of the Moroccans brutally attacked us, others invaded our homes and after having carried off all of our possessions, they set fire to our houses, thus adding another element of horror to the situation. Our sufferings are not easy to describe for at that moment we had lost all sense of self: frightened, ready for certain death, separated from our loved ones, we awaited with anguish the moment of our deliverance.

However, the presence of the French soldiers had a salutary effect on Mouley Hafiz, who decided to save a population of about ten thousand people, which was wandering about the streets, most of them without clothing. The sultan's gardens were chosen as our refuge and there, without distinction of sex, we were herded into stables, into the cages of a menagerie, anywhere in fact where we could find shelter from the heavy rain that fell during those baneful days. There we remained for several days without covering and virtually without bread. The French soldiers freed us and, order having been reestablished, we were able to return to our homes. There we found another desolation since everything had been destroyed, and when we say that even the wood from our houses had been ripped off and carried away, the extent of the pillage can perhaps be imagined . . .

From a report (October 1913) probably prepared by A. Elmaleh for the French authorities in Paris (AIU MOROCCO).

NOTES

1. Bernard Lewis, "The Pro-Islamic Jews," *Judaism* 17, no. 4 (1968): p. 401.

2. George Vajda, "Un Recueil de texts historiques judéomarocains," *Hespéris* 12 (1951).

3. J. E. Budgett Meakin, "The Jews of Morocco," *JQR* 5 (1812); *The Moorish Empire* (1899); *The Land of the Moors* (1901); *The Moors* (1902).

4. Charles de Foucauld, *Reconnaissance au Maroc 1883–84* (Paris, 1888).

5. Michel Carrouges, *Foucauld: Devant l'Afrique du Nord* (Paris, 1961), p. 151.

6. Edmond Doutté, *Missions au Maroc: En Tribu* (Paris, 1914), p. 137.

7. See letters of 1912 on the pillage of Fez.

8. The letter of Leven to El Glaoui and his reply were inspired by Joshua Corcos, a Jewish merchant of Marrakesh, and banker to the Sultan.

CHAPTER 46

The Moroccan Jewish Experience: A Revisionist View

Norman A. Stillman

The historical experience of the Jews in Morocco—as elsewhere within the Islamic world—requires serious reassessment. In the last century there has been a tendency to idealize the history of the Jews under Islam generally. This tendency began to no small extent as an apologetic response to some of the painful failures of Jewish emancipation in Europe which were all too obvious during the last quarter of the nineteenth century. It was also greatly influenced by the romantic vision of Muslim Spain, which was then in vogue. By the twentieth century, the great tolerance of Islam toward the religious, cultural, and racial minorities within its midst had become the received wisdom. Few voices of any consequence have ever been raised to question it.[1]

It should be noted at this point that North African Jewish history—as Maghrebi history generally—has received far less treatment than has its Middle Eastern counterpart, an understandable case of periphery versus center.

The scholars who showed the most interest in the Muslim West for several generations were the French, whose work coincided with the colonial period and decreased thereafter. Most of their work regarding the Jews was either linguistic or ethnographic. Many of the pioneer Maghrebists were also colonial administrators or closely connected with the *mission civilisatrice*, which partly explains the descriptive and often utilitarian character of their research.

The first attempt to present Maghrebi Jewish history in a scholarly survey was the late H. Z. Hirschberg's *A History of the Jews in North Africa* (2 vols.). Since the appearance of the original Hebrew edition in 1965, Hirschberg's comprehensive history has been the standard reference work on the subject.

There exists no really comparable work for the Jewish histories of the three individual Maghrebi countries: Tunisia, Algeria, and Morocco. The single exception might be Rabbi Jacob Toledano's *Nèr ha-Ma'arāv* (Jerusalem, 1911), a history of Moroccan Jewry based primarily on traditional Jewish sources, but employing some Muslim and Western material as well. Toledano's book is particularly important not only for its use of manuscript sources, but also for reflecting how Moroccan Jews on the eve of the protectorate perceived their own past.

In recent years an increasing number of historical and anthropological studies have appeared, devoted to North African Jewry in general, and to Moroccan Jewry in particular. There has also been a rising interest in the Moroccan Jewish past by emigrès now settled in Israel, France, and North America. The recent founding of the Institute for the Study of North African Jewry in Jerusalem is indicative of this interest.

Among the more vocal members of some of the activist emigrè groups one frequently finds a rather idyllic view of their own Maghrebi past. This is in part due to a very natural human propensity for nostalgia (as in the popular romanticizing of the very unromantic *shtetl* life of Eastern Europe). This historical view *en rose* is in large measure an apologetic response to both real and imagined discrimination against North African immigrants in Israel (and, to some extent, France), as well as a rejection of the Zionist view of history. This theme has been taken up, quite understandably, by Arab polemicists in regard to the Arab-Israeli dispute and maintains, in brief, that Muslims and Jews in Morocco, as elsewhere in the Islamic world, enjoyed excellent relations until the coming of Zionism and the ensuing Middle East conflict spoiled things, much to the chagrin of both communities.[2]

Oddly enough, this tendency toward idealizing the Moroccan Jewish past has received aid from a most unexpected quarter, namely, in the work of American anthropologists such as Lawrence Rosen. Working in the Middle Atlas town of Sefrou during the 1960s, Rosen was struck by the vital economic and social interpersonal relationships which existed between Jews and Muslims in that community. This visible fact seemed to be in marked contrast to the observations made by travelers and historians of earlier periods who saw the Jews of Morocco in a state of abject degradation. This striking discrepancy led to a dismissal of much of the earlier evi-

Jerusalem Quarterly 9 (1978): 111–23.

dence rather than a reassessment. The case of Sefrou became the model for Muslim-Jewish relations in Morocco. So much so, in fact, that the name of the town is never even mentioned in Rosen's writings.[3] Next, the paradigm was projected back in time. It had become timeless.

Here we come to a serious methodological error. Societies—even highly traditional or conservative ones—do not exist in a historical vacuum. Although not a particularly profound observation, this is frequently ignored by historians and anthropologists alike.

Morocco during the 1960s was in many respects a very different country from that of the pre-protectorate period. The presence of the French brought about profound changes in many aspects of Moroccan social and political life. Not least among these was a change in the status of the Jewish subjects of the Sherifan Empire. Such a change could not help but affect, both for better and for worse, traditional Muslim-Jewish relations, especially in the major towns and cities where colonial administration was strongest. This fact is frequently forgotten in recent studies due to the disrepute into which colonialism has fallen.

Sefrou, furthermore, may be an inapt choice for the prototype of Muslim-Jewish relations in Morocco. It was in Sefrou that the Jews of neighboring Fez sought refuge during times of persecution, as, for example, at the accession of Mawlāy Yazīd to the throne in 1790.[4] Sefrou seems to have been somewhat insulated from the intense scholastic atmosphere of the ancient capital, and hence, from its intolerance. The demography of Sefrou also made it an unusual town. Nearly two-fifths of its inhabitants were Jews prior to the exodus of the early 1950s.[5] This proportion was considerably higher than that of most other Moroccan towns and cities.[6] The Vicomte de Foucauld, who reconnoitered the country for the French during the last century and who was generally a keen observer, noted that Sefrou and Demnate were the two places in Morocco where the Jews were happiest.[7] The case of Muslim-Jewish relations in Sefrou was clearly a notable exception to the rule even prior to the coming of the French.

Generalizations drawn from it, much less historical projections, must be approached with utmost caution.

HISTORY RECONSIDERED

What general observations can be made—if any—regarding the Moroccan Jewish experience? Actually, there are a number of significant ones. To be seen in perspective, a historical survey going back to the end of the Almohade period (mid-thirteenth century) is in order. Despite the fact that Jews have lived in Morocco since the days of Classical Antiquity, it is under the Almohades' successors that we see Jewish life in Morocco developing many of the characteristics which were to mark it until the beginning of the twentieth century.

The extent and severity of the Almohade persecution of Jews is still a matter for debate. One fact that is perfectly clear, however, is that Maghrebi Jewry was left spiritually and numerically impoverished in its wake.[8] The period is one of overall economic, social, and intellectual stagnation throughout the Islamic world. Entering a period of decline, the Muslim world began turning in on itself, and religious life became even more institutionalized and obscurantist. As a corollary, or perhaps concomitantly, so did intellectual and social life.

The position of the *ahl al-dhimma*, members of the tolerated non-Muslim populace, became ever more precarious. This was in a sense quite natural. *Dhimmis*, albeit protected subjects, were first and foremost humbled tribute bearers. During the earlier Middle Ages when Islam was much more a laissez-faire society economically and intellectually, the extreme implications of the *dhimmis'* status could be ignored more conveniently. But as Muslim society became more closed within religious brotherhoods (*tarīqāt*) and trade guilds (called *hanātī* in Morocco) the non-Muslim minorities became increasingly marginal. As Christian Europe increasingly rose into prominence, the believer could at least take comfort from the fact that within the *Dār al-Islām* the nonbeliever was still in his proper place in the natural order of things as *as asfal al-sāfilin* (the lowest of the lowly). In times of general social decay or instability it was frequently necessary to emphasize this lowliness.

In Morocco, indeed throughout the Maghreb, the Jew became the *dhimmi* par excellence, for no native Christian population seems to have survived the Almohade period. Jewish communities were openly reestablished in the major cities, including Fez, Marrakesh, Sijilmasa, Taza, and Cueta. The new Merinid dynasty was not at all ill disposed toward the Jews. They were nomadic Zenāta Berbers from the southeast (the name survives today in Merino sheep) and most probably felt themselves to be outsiders in the cities of Morocco. Their own alienation from the Arab bourgeoisie is apparent in their founding a new administrative quarter, *al-Madīna al-Baydā*, now called *Fās Jdīd*, outside of Old Fez in 1276.

The Merinids were not averse to appointing Jews to high positions within their administration. The Sultan Yūsuf b. Ya'qūb (1286–1307) had several Jewish courtiers from the Waqqāsa family, one of whom, Khalīfa the Elder, was his majordomo.[9] The latter's cousin, Khalīfa the Younger, served the Sultan Abu 'l-Rabī Sulaymān (1308–1310) in several unspecified offices.[10] The last Merinid sultan, 'Abd al-Haqq b. Abī Sa'īd (1421–1465), made a Jew, Hārūn b. Batash, his vizier during the final year of his reign.[11]

The presence of a few Jews in positions of authority ought not to be interpreted as indicating any widespread Jewish economic power in Morocco at the time, or any particular affinity between the Zenāta Berbers and the Jews. The Merinids employed Jews in their service because of the latter's extreme vulnerability, and hence, according to Islamic political psychology, dependability. It is for this same reason that Muslim rulers in the East had for centuries depended upon Turkish guards, black slaves, and eunuchs in a variety of hues. Since the Jews were a very marginal component of Moroccan society, they had no power base. They therefore offered no threat. Like aliens and slaves (both frequently employed in Islamic government and the military), the Jews were totally dependent.

Just how vulnerable the Jews actually were can be seen from their transferal to a special quarter next to the *Dār al-Makhzan* (the government administrative center) in Fās Jdīd. The Jews were brought to the Mellah, as such quarters came to be called in Morocco, in 1438. The removal of the Jews from Old Fez came in the wake of anti-Jewish disturbances which broke out when a rumor circulated that the Jews had poured wine into the lamp reservoirs of a mosque.[12] The accusation has its parallel in the Host desecration with which the Jews were frequently charged in Europe at that period. The unlikely nature of the crime was perfectly consistent with the negative stereotype of Jews common in Morocco, namely, that they were genuine ill wishers who sought to harm Islam and its faithful.[13]

This was not the first anti-Jewish riot in Merinid Fez. On March 10, 1276, a massacre began when it was rumored that a Jew had acted improperly toward a Muslim woman. The disorder was halted only by the appearance on the scene of the Sultan Ya'qūb b. Yūsuf. Once again, this was an offense completely in keeping with popular stereotypes.[14]

The eventual removal of the Jews to the Mellah was meant for their own protection. The *juderias* of medieval Aragon and Castile were similarly located near royal citadels and fulfilled much the same function. The Flemish priest and missionary Nicholas Clenardus, who spent a year in Fez between 1540 and 1541, wrote to a friend that he purposely chose to live in the Mellah rather than in the Christian *funduq* [inn] in Old Fez for reasons of security. As a priest, he was subject to all kinds of abuse in the Muslim streets. He added that the Jews detested Christians as much as the Muslims but were "less audacious."[15]

The Mellah of Fez became the prototype of the Moroccan ghetto. Despite the fact that it was founded for the protection of the Jews and not as a punishment, the Jewish sources make it quite clear that the Jews themselves viewed their confinement to the Mellah, as tragedy, "a sudden and bitter exile."[16] It only increased their sense of isolation and marginality. The Mellahs of the other towns of Morocco, all of which were established later under the Sa'adians (1550–1650) and the 'Alawids (1666–present), were founded with the express intent of ostracism rather than protection. The later legendary etymology of the word *Mellah* as a place where Jews originally salted the heads of executed criminals for public display emphasizes the outcast connotation which was attached to it.

The Fez Mellah did not always fulfill its protective function very well. On May 14, 1465, its inhabitants were almost entirely exterminated by the rebels who brought down the Merinid dynasty. The attack upon the Jews of Fez, according to a contemporary Egyptian traveler, 'Abd al-Bāsit, touched off a wave of similar massacres throughout the country.[17] The most immediate cause of this general uprising had been the appointment of the Jew Hārun b. Batash to the vizierate. Up until this time the Merinid sultans had always been able to stem any popular dissatisfaction with their having Jewish officials by the simple expedient of executing the official. The few Jewish courtiers who are known to us from the Muslim sources were, in fact, all put to death by the rulers they served—"and the dynasty was cleansed of their filth," as the chroniclers usually commented.[18] 'Abd al-Haqq tried this traditional method, but found it to no avail. He had gone beyond all acceptable bounds in appointing a *dhimmi* to such an office as the vizierate.

The Wattāsid sultans of Fez, who were cousins of the Merinids (1472–1554), continued to employ Jews in their *makhzan* (administration), but not in so sensitive and conspicuous a position as that of vizier with its definite Islamic connotations. All of the Jews who served the Wattāsids were of Spanish or Portugese origin; i.e., they were *megorāshīm* (exiles) and not *tōshāvīm* (indigenous residents). Invariably, they acted as commercial and diplomatic go-betweens because of their linguistic ability and their contacts with the Iberian Peninsula. Men such as Rabbi Abraham Ben Zamiro of Safi, Jacob Rosales, and Jacob Rute of Fez, were as much agents of the Portuguese crown as of the Wattāsids.[19]

The Sefardic exiles had come to Morocco in several waves in the fourteenth and fifteenth centuries. Many settled in the coastal towns under Portuguese control, such as Arzila, Azemmour, Safi, Magazan, and Santa Cruz (Agadir), to mention but a few. The newcomers were for the most part economically and culturally superior to the native Jewish population to whom they condescendingly referred as *forasteros* (strangers) or *berberiscos* (Berbers or natives). Those whom we see as intermediaries between the Wattāsids and Portugal—and to a lesser extent Spain—belong to the scholarly mercantile elite and were quick to dominate Jewish communal life in Morocco. Jacob Rute, for example, became the *Nāgīd* (secular head) of the Fāsi Jewish community. Many other refugees were members of the middle classes, including artisans and technicians with strategic military skills.[20]

Once again, one should not jump to hasty conclusions vis-à-vis the position of the Jews in Moroccan society at this time. With the exception of *conversos* who sought to return openly to their former faith, most of the newcomers seem to have preferred to live in the Portuguese-held coastal towns rather than the Islamic interior. They joined in the defense of these enclaves against Muslim attacks and sought to withdraw with the Christian colonists when the Portuguese had to withdraw.[21] The reasons for this interesting preference are both social and economic. The Portuguese were notably tolerant toward the Jews in their African possessions long after the issuance of the "Edict of Expulsion" of 1497 or the establishment of the Inquisition in 1540. Furthermore, the ports were probably the most active mercantile centers of the period, and artisans were not excluded by the Islamic guilds which existed in the major towns of the interior.

Those Jews who served the Wattāsids, various *qā'ids* (local rulers), and thereafter, the Sa'adians, were a privileged few. Like most men who moved in court circles, a considerable distance separated them from the rest of the populace. Some were concerned communal leaders whereas others were as oppressive and overbearing with their co-religionists as any courtier might be.[22] Life was probably not very easy for anyone outside the ruling elite in Morocco—an observation which to a great extent holds true to this day, even if we take into consideration the qualitative differences. For the average Jew, however, life was even more difficult, certainly more complex.

Throughout the later Middle Ages and into early modern times, the laws governing Jews in Morocco were among the most strictly applied in all the Arab world. By the end of the fifteenth century a considerable body of juridical opinion concerning the restrictive treatment of Jews had already built up, as can be seen from the *Kitāb al-Mi'yar al-Mughrib,* the great collection of Maghrebi fatwās (responsa) edited by Ahmad al-Wansharīsī (d. 1508).[23]

The discriminatory laws for non-Muslims were considerably harsher than most of those found in theoretical literature, which was not the case in the Middle East. Throughout the principal towns and orthodox religious centers of Morocco the Qur'anic injunction to humble the *dhimmi* was interpreted in the most literal sense. The sumptuary laws were generally enforced. In addition to the distinguishing garments and restrictions on mounts, Jews had to walk barefoot in the streets of some towns. In others, this applied only when a Jew passed by a mosque. The latter was the case in Sefrou, for example, up until the reign of Mawlāy al-Hasan (1873–1894), when this humiliating practice, which was a particularly Maghrebi innovation, was finally rescinded. Almost nowhere were Jews allowed to wear normal leather foot gear when walking outside the Mellah. In Fez from the early sixteenth century on, the prescribed shoes for Jews were sandals of straw.

The very strict application of the laws governing differentiation, or *shakla (ghiyār* in the Middle East), was most probably due to the rising sociopolitical importance of charismatic religious leaders throughout Morocco during the waning years of the Merinid dynasty. The inability of the Wattāsids to dislodge the Portuguese from the coast, and indeed their relatively close relations with them through Jewish intermediaries, only enhanced the prestige of the *Shorfa* (Classical Arabic, *shurafā*), the descendants of the Prophet, and the *Murabtīn* (Classical Arabic, *murābitūn*), Sufi holy men whom the Europeans called *marabouts*. The proliferation of these populist, charismatic figures, their rivalries and conflicts may have been a cause of severe political fragmentation in Morocco until the advent of the Alwid dynasty, but they nonetheless set the spiritual tone of the age, and it was a bellicose tone fired by the zeal of jihād (holy war) against the Christian incursions. Both the Sa'adians and the 'Alawids accepted the religious ideals and—no less important—the norms of this heroic, if anarchic age. Their legitimacy was based on their being both *Shorfa* and *Mjahdīn* (Classical Arabic, *mujāhidūn*), the Islamic equivalent of Crusaders. Such an atmosphere was understandably not very conducive to the lenient interpretation of the restrictive laws governing nonbelievers within the society.

Urban Jewish life, which is the only one really visible in the written sources, changed very little during the Sherifan period. The descriptions of Germain Mouette in the seventeenth, Georg Höst and Louis de Chènier in the eighteenth, and Charles de Foucauld in the nineteenth century are all basically in accord and bear ample witness to the contempt in which urban Jews were generally held.[24] Mouette, who spent eleven years in Morocco, offers a telling, though restrained, assessment of the social conditions of Moroccan Jewry:

> The Jews are very numerous in Barbary, and they are held in no more estimation than elsewhere; on the contrary, if there is any refuse to be thrown out, they are the first employed. They are obliged to work at their crafts for the King, when they are called, for their food alone. They are subject to suffering the blows and injuries of everyone, without daring to say a word even to a child of six who throws stones at them. If they pass before a mosque, no matter what the weather or season might be, they must remove their shoes, not even daring in the royal cities, such as Fez and Marrakesh, to wear them at all, under pain of five hundred lashes and being put into prison, from which they would be released only upon payment of a heavy fine.[25]

It ought to be kept in mind that much of this degradation described by Mouette and others, including the writers of the Jewish chronicles, was highly ritualized. Stoning by Muslim children was a time-honored custom in many parts of the Arab world, and though bothersome, was rarely dangerous, since there was usually no malicious intent. (I might add that I myself have seen youngsters throw stones at Jews even in Sefrou.) The harassment of Jewish funeral processions was also a widespread Muslim tradition to which Jews adapted themselves. On the whole, Jews accepted their enforced humility philosophically. It was, after all, natural for a people in exile.

This explains the strong currents in Morocco of Kabbalistic mysticism, messianism, and religious Zionism.

Moroccan Jewish men could also find refuge from the vicissitudes of their existence in *mahya*, their potent fig brandy. Like their Yemenite brethren, Moroccan Jews were hard drinkers.[26] Many travelers to both countries commented on the widespread alcoholism. The parallel is, I believe, not at all fortuitous. For these two countries were by far the strictest in the Arabic-speaking world in their interpretation and implementation of the laws pertaining to *dhimmis*, who in both instances were exclusively Jews.

The Jews' pariah status was not without some economic compensation. Excluded from many trades by the guilds, they were forced, or found their way, into a number of reprehensible (*makrūh*) occupations forbidden to Muslims. Thus, Jews had the virtual monopoly on jewelry smithing since in *Mālikī* eyes the fashioning of gold and silver objects for sale above the intrinsic value of the metal itself was akin to usury. Money lending was also a Jewish monopoly, but unlike the former, it was particularly despised. During the late nineteenth century Jewish moneylenders were the object of bitter Muslim resentment. As in medieval Europe, popular animus was frequently diffused against the entire group.[27] Naturally, the great majority of Jews were too poor to engage in such lucrative activities.

There was always a tiny percentage of Jews who were able to avoid many of the burdens inherent in *dhimmi*-hood. They were mostly members of the mercantile elite in the coastal towns, although some lived in the capitals of the interior, such as Fez, Meknes, and Marrakesh. As with the *megorashim* from whom most of them were descended, they maintained close familial and business contacts abroad and had a patina of European culture. At the very least they spoke Spanish or French. Foreign trade and service to the local European consuls were the surest means by which they could obtain the much desired status of protégés. This effectively removed them from the confines of the Moroccan legal system. Protection became increasingly more available in the late eighteenth century as European powers received, or took, extraterritorial rights within the weak Sherifan Empire. In the nineteenth century some Jewish merchants were able to acquire foreign citizenship by traveling abroad. This sometimes only entailed a short visit to neighboring French Algeria, where forged birth certificates were readily available.[28] Needless to say, the protégés and the foreign nationalized Jews comprised a very small minority—perhaps 1 percent of the total Jewish population at the end of the nineteenth century. They were frequently arrogant and heartily detested by the Muslim population. When the historian al-Nāsirī wishes to emphasize how unacceptable was the demeanor of the Jews after Sir Moses Montefiore's celebrated visit in 1864, he writes: "The Jews became arrogant and frivolous, *and not only the Jews of the port cities*."[29]

The same social and psychological factors that led so many members of the elite to seek protégé status or foreign citizenship later caused the overwhelming majority of urban Jews to associate themselves so closely with the protectorate and to embrace (I use here the rhetoric of the period) "the civilizing benefits of French culture."

This state of affairs was eminently suitable to the French and their policy of "divide and conquer." The educational activities of the Alliance Israélite Universelle (AIU) "produced a Jewish elite singularly versed in those fields most important to the Protectorate's undertakings."[30] Few Jews saw any reason to back the nationalist movement during its twenty years of development. However, since they did not have French citizenship as did their Algerian brethren, most kept their options open and remained on the sidelines.

The struggle for independence was relatively bloodless and did not engender the deep bitterness of the Algerian Revolution. Thus, Moroccan Jews did not find themselves in such an untenably compromised position as did Algerian Jewry.

Rising Islamic nationalism and impatience with what was perceived as *le nouveau colonialisme* (i.e., strong, continued French presence) made the weakened position of the remaining Jews more precarious, and it has led to the steady decline of the remaining Jewish population. To sum it up in John Waterbury's words: "Morocco's Jewish 'problem' is in the process of self-liquidation."

CONCLUSION

One might justifiably ask at this point whether this seemingly jaundiced perspective is all that there was to the Moroccan Jewish experience. It was, of course, not. Within this restrictive framework, which I have sketched only in brief, Moroccan Jewry created a rich cultural and spiritual life, a cultural life which deserves to be better known. The arrival of the *megorāshīm*, who came in several waves during the fourteenth and fifteenth centuries infused new cultural blood into Maghrebi Jewish society. To a great extent Moroccan Jewry preserved the Andalusian educational tradition which combined the study of practical jurisprudence (*halākhah le-ma'ase*) with Hebrew grammar and belles lettres. There is a very extensive and rich literature in both Hebrew and Judeo-Arabic. The very beautiful *piyyūtim* (religious poems) are perhaps the finest example of this literature. So too are the *qīnöt* (lamentations), which, I should note, are particularly ubiquitous.

All this, however, is a topic unto itself.

What I have tried to do here is to explain "the rules of the game" and the general perimeters within which Jewish life operated. Despite the restrictive nature of the system, it allowed a great deal of internal autonomy for the Jews. They had their own society within the confines of the Mellah. Their internal organization and care for their own poor were admired by Mouette and later Foucauld, neither of whom could be accused of being philo-

Semites. But once again, I must state that this is another topic. One ought not to confuse the internal life, which had elements of richness and beauty, with life within Moroccan society as a whole.

It would be an unfair distortion to depict Moroccan Jewish life as one of unrelenting and unmitigated persecution, just as it would be equally unjust to claim the opposite. Some periods were obviously better than others. In the early premodern period, in particular the nineteenth century, most town and city dwellers were frequently the victims of pillage and rapine at the hands of marauding tribesmen or rebellious troupes. But to suggest that the Jews were no worse off than anyone else is erroneous. The Mellah was usually looted before any other quarter of a city. To state that "[s]uch attacks were, however, invariably directed against the property of the Jews rather than against their person,"[31] is a sophistic distinction, to say the least. The Jewish chronicles, such as the *Yahas Fās* of Rabbi Avner ha-Sarfatī and the *Divré ha-Yāmīm* of the Ibn Danān family, as well as the records of the AIU, make it quite clear that lives were lost in considerable numbers.

Furthermore, there were periodic riots against Jews, as Jews, by fellow townsmen. These were usually inspired by populist religious reformers and frequently involved what were perceived to be violations of the *dhimmis'* contract with the Muslim community. The usual result was the destruction of a synagogue, since it was quite clear that all the houses of worship violated the code having been established after the advent of Islam. Some of these riots had socioeconomic causes as well.[32]

Seen historically, Moroccan Jews conducted their lives within the confines of their *dhimmi* status as perceived in its Moroccan form. The dynamics of the marketplace and personal face-to-face intercourse, where it existed, often had a localized mitigating effect, but it did not change the overall context in which the Jew was "the lowest of the lowly."

NOTES

1. Cf. Bernard Lewis, *Race and Color in Islam* (New York, 1971).

2. Cf. N. A. Stillman, "New Attitudes toward the Jew in the Arab World," *Jewish Social Studies* 37, nos. 3–4 (Summer–Fall 1975): 197 n. 1.

3. Lawrence Rosen, "A Moroccan Jewish Community during the Middle Eastern Crisis," *American Scholar* 37 (Summer 1968): 435–51, reprinted in *Peoples and Cultures of the Middle East* (Garden City, 1970); "Muslim-Jewish Relations in a Moroccan City," *International Journal of Middle Eastern Studies* (*IJMES*) 3, no. 4 (October 1972): 435–49.

4. Georges Vajda, ed. and trans., *Un recueil de textes historiques judéo-marocains,* Collection Hespéris, No. 12 (Paris, 1951), p. 87, translating Judah b. 'Ovēd Ibn 'Attār, *Zikkārōn li-Benē Yisrā'ēl.*

5. In 1936, Sefrou had a population of 7,298 Muslims and 4,382 Jews. In 1941, the figures for each group were 9,095 and 5,474, respectively; see *Initiation au Maroc,* 3rd ed. (Paris, 1945), pp. 255, 256. L. Rosen, "A Moroccan Jewish Community," *American Scholar* 37 (1968): 437, estimated the community to be approximately 650 (in 1967). By October 1972, the community had dwindled to 199—cf. N. A. Stillman, "The Sefrou Remnant," *Jewish Social Studies* 35, nos. 3–4 (July–October 1973): 255.

6. Compare the charts in *Initiation au Maroc,* pp. 255, 256.

7. Vicomte Charles de Foucauld, *Reconnaissance au Maroc* (Paris, 1939), p. 166.

8. The refugees who fled the Almohade Empire included much of the *intelligentsia.* Maimonides, the most famous of the refugees, on several occasions lamented the decline of Jewish learning in the Maghreb as a result of the persecutions. Cf. H. Z. Hirschberg, *Jews in North Africa,* 1: 100 (Hebrew); p. 137 (Eng. trans.) and the sources cited there.

9. Ibn Khaldūn, *Kitāb al-'Ibar* (Bulaq 1284 A.H.), 7: 232f; al-Nāsirī, *Kitāb al-Istiqsā* (Casablanca, 1954), 3: 80f; Ibn al-Ahmar, *Rawdat al-Nisrīn,* ed. and trans. C. Bou'ali and G. Marcais (Paris, 1917), p. 17 (text), p. 69 (trans.).

10. Ibn Khaldūn, *'Ibar,* 7, p. 239; al-Nāsirī, *Istiqsā',* 3: 100; Ibn al-Abmar, *Rawdat al-Nisrīn,* p. 19 (text), p. 71 (trans.).

11. See 'Abd al-Bāsit b. Khalīl's narrative in Robert Brunschvig, *Deux récits de voyage inédits en Afrique du Nord au Xve siècle* (Paris, 1936), pp. 50–55 (text), pp. 115–21 (trans.).

12. This is the reason given by Rabbi Abner ha-Sarfatī (nineteenth century) in his chronicle *Yahas Fās.* Cf. Y. D. Semach, "Une chronique juive de Fès: Le 'Yahas Fès' de Ribbi Abner Hassarfaty," *Hespéris* 19, fasc. 1–2 (1934): 91.

13. This image is discussed in some detail in Stillman, "Muslims and Jews in Morocco," *Jerusalem Quarterly* 5 (1977): 76–83.

14. Ibn Abī Zar', *Rawd al-Qirtās,* trans. A. Beaumier (Paris, 1860), p. 459.

15. Translated in R. Le Tourneau, "Notes sur les lettres latines de Nicolas Clénard, relatant son séjour dans le royaume de Fés (1540–1541)," *Hespéris* 19, fasc. 1–2 (1934): 51f.

16. Rabbi Abner Ha-Sarfatī, *Yahas Fās,* in Semach, "Une chronique juive," *Hespéris* 19, fasc. 1–2 (1934): 91; Toledano, *Nēr ha-Ma'arāv,* p. 44.

17. R. Brunschvig, *Deux récits de voyage,* pp. 53, 55 (text), pp. 118f, 121 (trans.).

18. *Wa-tuhhirat al-dawla min rijsihim*—Ibn Khaldūn, *'Ibar,* 7: 233.

19. A great deal of revealing documentation of their activities is to be found in P. de Cenival, David Lopes, and R. Ricard, eds., *Les sources inédites de l'histoire du Maroc: Archives et bibliothéques de Portugal,* 5 vols. (Paris, 1934–1951).

20. E.g., ibid., 3: 220–23; H. Z. Hirschberg, 1: 307f, 316 (Hebrew), and pp. 418f, 428f (Eng. trans.).

21. De Cenival, Lopes, and Ricard, *Les sources inédites* 3: 352–55.

22. Cf. Toldeano, *Nēr ha-Ma'ardv*, pp. 64f; also S. Romanelli, *Massā' ba-'Arav*, in *Ketavim-Nivharim* etc., ed. J. Schirman (Jerusalem, 1968), p. 110.

23. Partially translated by Emile Amar, "La pierre de touche," *Archives Marocaines*, 12–13 (Paris, 1908–1909), where the sections dealing with the treatment of *dhimmīs* are vol. 12, pp. 231–65 and vol. 13, pp. 30–36.

24. G. Mouette, *Histoire des conquestes de Mouley Archy* (Paris, 1683), reprinted in de Castries, ed., *Sources inédites-France*, II, 2nd ser. (Paris, 1924); G. Höst, *Nachrichten von Marokos und Fes* (Copenhagen, 1781); L. S. de Chénier, *The Present State of the Empire of Morocco* (London, 1788); Foucauld, *Reconnaissance au Manoc.*

25. G. Mouette, *Histoire in Sources inédites-France*, 2: 176f.

26. On alcoholism among the Yemenites, cf. Erich Brauer, *Ethnologie der Jemenitischen Juden* (Heidelberg, 1934), pp. 110–12; among the Moroccan, cf. Meakin, "Jews of Morocco," *Jewish Quarterly Review* 4 (1892): 390.

27. L. Bowie, "An Aspect of Muslim-Jewish Relations in Late 19th-Century Morocco: A European Diplomatic View," *IJMES* 7, no. 1 (January 1976): 14.

28. Ibid., pp. 5–7.

29. Al-Nāsirī, *Istiqsā'*, 9: 113f.

30. John Waterbury, *The Commander of the Faithful: The Moroccan Political Elite—A Study in Segmented Politics* (New York, 1970), p. 127.

31. Rosen, "Muslim-Jewish Relations," p. 447.

32. Bowie, "Muslim-Jewish Relations in Late 19th-Century Morocco," pp. 14–15.

CHAPTER 47

Excerpts from *The Israelites of Tunisia: Their Civil and Political Condition*

Jacques Chalom

AUTHORITY OF MUSLIM JURISDICTION AND ISLAMIC LAWS REGARDING ISRAELITES

Despite the ameliorations, timid as they are, that it has brought to the edifice of Muslim jurisdiction, the government of the protectorate has nevertheless elected to maintain the indigenous Israelites under the rule of Islamic law.

Tunisian Muslim Law

Muslim law is essentially religious, its source is in the revealed book (the *Qur'an*), the collection of traditions relating to the conduct of the Prophet Muhammad (hadiths) and the opinions given by his companions to the first caliphs (*Dejma*). On the four interpretations obtained by the procedure of legal analogy (*quias*) and forming the four orthodox [schools] of Islam, two rites, the *hanefite* and the *malikite* form the authority in Tunisia. Muslim legal scholars may comment on sacred tests in a more or less liberal way,[1] according to circumstances and their temperament; but the principles of Islamic law are intangible and the *bey* himself cannot depart from them; the legislative power of this prince has only two limits: the engagements taken with friendly powers, treaties, conventions and other contracts of the same kind, and the visa/imprimatur of the resident general. Regarding respect for the legal status of Europeans and Israelites on which the *bey* is prevented from legislating, it derives from the very principles of the religious law of Islam.[2]

The science of the law is part of theology,[3] but "if the legislative power of the Muslim sovereign cannot be substituted directly for traditional law, it can give the preponderance to one of the systems that share doctrine, and it can give the force of law to custom."[4]

A. The New Tunisian Code

The government of the protectorate is authorized by these principles to attempt to codify the civil commercial and penal legislation of Tunisia. The rules of this legislation are scattered among authors and jurisprudence in which contradictions abound, among customs and usages that offer no continuity. To put in the hands of Muslim magistrates the precise and ordered texts is to give those answerable to the law some guarantees against arbitrariness and inventions.

The Commission for Codification of Tunisian Laws, formed on 6 September 1896, had a dual task to perform. Its constituting act said it was intended firstly "to gather, classify and choose from within French legislation those materials capable of serving as the definitive volume of codification by leaving aside material relating either to personal legal status, or to the regime of property law. On the other hand, it had to search within Muslim jurisprudence for everything that might be utilized from the standpoint of either the principles of modern law or the actual conditions of the indigenous society."[5]

The resulting plan for a Tunisian civil and commercial code presented by a legal scholar, M. Santillana, was discussed and revised by a commission of eleven members, among whom figured Muslim doctors presided over by the Sheikh el Islam, chief of religious justice; it was promulgated under the name *Tunisian Code, Obligations and Contracts* by a decree from the *bey* bearing the stamp of the resident general, on 5 December 1906, to go into effect and be applied by Tunisian jurisdictions on 1 June 1907. This code, formed of 1,632 articles, is divided into two books, the first concerning obligations in general, and the second, contracts and quasicontracts.

This legislative work constitutes a highly laudable attempt to Islamicize European law, but does not appear to give satisfaction to the legitimate aspirations of indigenous Jews. They had hoped that Tunisia would reach uniformity of laws relative to commercial and exchange operations.

The indigenous Muslims of Algeria have been placed (for all matters not concerning personal status or non-French registered buildings) under the regime of French law.[6] This legal assimilation (against which the natives did not protest) has given excellent results. It brings the natives closer to the French, and responds to social and

---

From *Les Israélite de la Tunisie: Leur Condition Civil et Politique* (Paris: 1908), chs. 7 and 9. English translation by Susan Emanuel.

economic necessities. If Tunisia had proceeded in the same fashion, one would have avoided the reproach of having attempted the Islamicization of Tunisian Jews, who appear disposed to accept the French laws to which they were subject in their commercial relations with Europeans.

Indigenous Muslim Justice: Principles of Organization

We have seen what Tunisian law is like under the regime in which indigenous Jews live. The Muslim jurisdiction that applies this law has been organized according to the same rules. The *bey*, successor to the caliphs, holds in his hand legislative, executive, and judicial powers. He has delegated his judicial power, sometimes to *cadis*, religious magistrates (*chaara*) who deal with issues relative to the legal status of Muslims and real estate property, and sometimes to provincial tribunals.

Provincial tribunals[7] treat personal and movable property affairs as a last resort up to 200 francs, and appeals up to 1,200 francs; penal affairs as a last resort or on appeal; they apply penalties of fines and imprisonment. "It is the *cadi* who represents the public interest before provincial tribunals, under the supervision of the Director of Judicial Services, who is himself the agent of public action for the whole Regency by delegation from the Prime Minister."[8]

Justice administered by the *bey* still exists: "[T]he *bey* exercises his juridical powers in penal and civil law with the assistance of organized jurisdictions whose purely consultative role is to instruct proceedings and prepare draft judgments."[9] This administration of justice by the sovereign has the *Ouzara* as its organ. The Ouzara tribunal is composed of offices that hold public hearings for open debates/cross-examinations. These offices where draft judgments are prepared for presentation to the *bey* handle civil cases (civil section), criminal cases (penal section), and appeals from provincial tribunals.

The indigenous jurisdiction administered by Muslim personnel, at the head of which is the secretary general of the Tunisian government and a French magistrate, the regency's director of legal services, may enter into conflict with French jurisdiction. These conflicts, given the reciprocal independence of the two kinds of justice, are treated like any kind of legal difficulty between two states: the minister of foreign affairs represents the Tunisian government and the *Garde des Sceaux* [master of the seals] represents French justice.

The procedure followed before Muslim tribunals, apparently very simple, is in fact riddled with abuse. Thus the depositions of witnesses are received in civil or penal matters not by the magistrates, but by Muslim notaries.[10]

The oath is administered in the religious form, and the Israelite cannot attend the swearing of his Muslim adversary because it takes place in the mosque where he has no access!

No code of criminal directives protects the Tunisian subject against an abuse of authority.[11] Every latitude is left to indigenous repressive justice for case directives and the arrest of the accused.

ISRAELITES AND PUBLIC TUNISIAN RIGHTS

The administrative organization of the Tunisian Protectorate was founded on the following principle: "[T]he *bey* keeps his sovereignty, but France has the right of oversight of his actions."[12] The rights of the native, as well as the obligations which are its corollary, have their source not in French law, but in a combination of the Qur'an, custom, and the *bey*'s legislative acts.

Faithful guardian of religion, whose rules must direct the exercise of his sovereignty, the *bey* possessed the most extensive powers over the persons and goods of his subjects.[13]

Public Freedoms

The protectorate regime has maintained legislative, executive, and legal powers in the same hands, but one must recognize that France, having introduced into the functioning of the Tunisian state the rules of its public law, has granted all inhabitants of the regency public freedoms such as freedom of the press,[14] of association,[15] of assembly.[16] These freedoms have been the object of regulation[17] that limits their exercise, but gives them at the same time as civic rights, in a country where only the caprice of the sovereign ruled, whose arbitrary authority was manifested without any counterweight or oversight.

Inequalities between Jews and Muslims regarding the Exercise of Public Rights

The Islamic law that proclaims equality between Muslims does not grant the same treatment to Jews and to believers. The protectorate government, while trying to abolish these distinctions among Tunisian subjects, has taken account of custom and political necessities in a country where racial and religious conflicts are so strong. The situation of Israelites, from the standpoint of exercising public rights, can therefore not be identical to that of Muslims. We are going to indicate this difference in treatment.

Military Service

In the Muslim state, holy war[18] is considered as an obligation for all individuals comprising the nation: the Israelite subject cannot be part of the army. These principles admitted by all Muslim countries, including Turkey, have prevailed in Tunisia. The *bey*'s decrees on recruitment have always exonerated Jews from military service: the law of 12 January 1892 states that all "are subject without exception to the blood tax, *indigenous Muslims* of the territories of recruitment."

The protectorate government, by incorporating Tunisian contingents into the French army of occupation, has respected this rule. And still today the corps where Muslim natives may serve do not accept volunteers who are Israelites, who may only be accepted into the Foreign Legion.[19]

Public Functions/Civil Service

The religious supremacy of Islam, foundation of all institutions of the Muslim state, excludes Israelites from public/civil service functions. In addition, their participation in native administration,[20] which along with its hierarchy has been kept by a France that is respectful of traditions, is absolutely nil. Israelites are not even admitted into administrative offices requiring technical competence, like Finance, Public Works, Post & Telegraph, and Education where, alongside the French, the Muslims occupy the subordinate positions. Senator Pédebidou wrote on this subject: "We do not know that the Israelites are excluded from all public employment."[21] Interested parties pointed out the injustice of this situation: "Tunisian administrations," they say, "accept us rarely as civil servants, while a great number of places are reserved for Muslims . . . Israelites can be neither magistrates nor auxiliaries of indigenous justice."[22]

Very Reduced Participation in Public Power

Political rights properly speaking, by means of which individuals take part in the government of the country, are reduced for Israelites to very few things.

The participation of Tunisian subjects in the legislative power exercised by the sovereign and the French representative is limited to simple consultations on budgetary data. The decree of 2 February 1907, promulgated with the consent of the protectorate government, created a delegation of native notables designated by the resident general. The delegates gather in the month of November each year, with the elected from the three fractions of the French colony (farmers, tradesmen, and representatives of the third college) in an assembly or conference, giving opinions on parts of the budget put before them. Without entering into details of this organization,[23] which is modeled on the Algerian financial delegations, we would say that the constitutive decree summons, to sit in conference alongside the thirty-two French members and fifteen Muslim notables, *a single Israelite* to represent the whole Jewish population of all regions and classes, and does not take account of either special interests of the Israelites that were supposed to be represented *separately*, nor the important place that this people of shopkeepers and artisans occupy in the economic activity of the regency.

The protectorate government, in instituting in various localities of Tunisia some municipal councils, never wanted to admit into the composition of each assembly recruited under its auspices, more than one councillor to represent the Israelite element of the community.[24] The conclusion that may be drawn from this short exposition of the ensemble of political rights exercised by Tunisian Israelites is the rather inequitable way with which they have been treated. Either the Tunisian taxpayers should, without religious distinction, be represented in the same way in the meetings where their collective interests are discussed (then why limit the Israelites to a single delegate for each assembly?), or else the taxpayers might be grouped according to their origin and their social class (and then why not give the Jews representation corresponding to their number and their economic and regional importance?).

Despairing of ever being called to collaborate in the country's government in the same way as all other inhabitants, the Israelites see only one remedy for their situation: French naturalization alone would permit them to exercise all the political rights that are the guarantees of the freedoms of the civilized man.

CONCLUSION: THE ISRAELITES OF TUNISIA AND FRENCH COLONIZATION

French colonization has had the result not only of opening Tunisia to modern economic activity, but also of effecting changes in the patriarchal existence of the natives.

Living in urban agglomerations, the Israelite has felt, much more than his Muslim compatriot, the repercussions of the new situation. A deep sense of the realities have quickly made him glimpse the need to adopt the Western civilization that a French school had taught him to love. The young generation is the product of this effort to adapt by the Jewish race that has come spontaneously to increase the ranks of populations of various origins, on whom the work of France in Tunisia relies.

It is to the brave initiative of the Europeanized Israelites that are due the rapid progress of the Tunisian market, which offers the industry of metropolitan France increasingly extensive markets.[25]

Israelites artisans have learned to use the industrial tools introduced into Tunisia. Thanks to the efforts of associations for professional education, workshops are training artistic workers able to keep score with European manpower.[26]

Composed especially of small shopkeepers,[27] small manufacturers, and workers,[28] the Jewish population embraces the poorest proletariat of Tunisia. Six to seven thousand natives live in the poor quarters of Tunis, assisted by the charity of their co-religionists, among whom great fortunes are very rare.[29] The legend of the usurious and exploitative Jew would not find credence among those who have studied at close hand the material condition of the Tunisian Jew.

Very good minds have thought that in an essentially agricultural country like Tunisia, the Jews ought to spread out in the countryside and give themselves over to tilling the soil. The school of agriculture of Djedeïda (twenty kilometers from Tunis) founded by the Israelite Alliance Company, has proposed giving the Jews of the regency, whom the persecution of past times had confined to the cities, a taste for the farm and pastoral life that was that of their ancestors in Palestine. The number of Tunisians who follow the teaching of the farm school of Djedeïda is about thirty.

The success of this philanthropic work will never be complete until the day when students will be assured of finding use for the knowledge they have acquired. Belonging mostly to poor families, they do not possess the capital necessary to get established as colonists.

Still other difficulties oppose the development of their enterprises. Residing outside certain towns, they are subject to the *mejba*[30] or personal tax imposed on natives.

The security of their goods and their persons is threatened by ignorant and fanatical Arabs; the native authorities to which they turn are very little disposed to give them useful help or render justice to them.[31]

In many cases, the legal condition of Israelites explains their social condition. To relieve one is to improve the other. In Tunisia each ethnic and national group can put into movement, for the defense of particular or collective interests, one or several state organs. The rights of Europeans in Tunisia are guaranteed by treaties, respect for which is imposed on the protectorate government, those of Muslims have a safeguard in the institutions of the Muslim state that functions under the aegis of France. Placed between the European element to which they should be assimilated as a result of their tendencies and their degree of civilization, and the Muslim element to which their political status is compared,[32] the Israelites under the regency exist in a situation that calls for reform.

We believe that it is a duty of the government[33] to emancipate by accession to the title of Frenchmen the Israelites who were acquired for the work of colonization in Tunisia, of which they are by various standards the auxiliaries.

*For further clarification of any references, see original essay.

NOTES

1. See Ben Attar Sebai and Ettealbi, *L'Esprit liberal du Coran*. This 1905 study is an honorable attempt at liberal interpretation of sacred texts.

2. Conference on Tunisian administration. Padoux, secretary general of the Tunisian government, p. 304.

3. Religious law treats the believer and the infidel (*dhimmi*) differently: The testimony of a Jew is not accepted against a Muslim, a Jew cannot inherit from a Muslim, etc.

4. Proposal for a Tunisian civil and commercial code. Foreword by report author M. Santillana (Tunis, 1899).

5. Ibid.

6. Decrees of 10 September 1886 and 17 April 1889 relating to Muslim justice in Algeria.

7. See organic decree of 18 March 1896.

8. Lectures on Tunisian administration. S. Berge, *De la Juridiction Française en Tunisie* (1895), p. 180.

9. *La Tunisie: Histoire et description*, p. 43.

10. One cannot see that the native authority possesses any means of constraint to make witnesses testify, especially if they are of European nationality and thus not under its jurisdiction.

11. The verdicts rendered by Tunisian jurisdiction are executed by the *caïd/kaid* or the governor who represents the *bey*'s authority in his district.

12. De Dianous, *Notes de la Législation tunisiénne*, 1894.

13. See above (p. 124 [in original text]).

14. The decree of 14 October 1884 on the freedom of the press in Tunisia, whose main provisions are copied from the French law of 27 July 1881, contains certain restrictions aimed at Tunisian subjects. For example, "any newspaper or periodical writing published in a European language will have a *European editor*; any newspaper or periodical writing published in whole or in part in the *Arabic or Hebrew language* will have a *Tunisian editor*. The publication and circulation in Tunisia of newspapers or periodical writing in the *Arabic or Hebrew language* may be *banned* by a decision countersigned by the Resident General or the French Republic in Tunis."

15. The decree of 15 September 1888 states that no association can be constituted without the authorization of the government.

16. The decree of 13 May 1905 makes public meetings be declared to the regime, and an official must authorize those for the purpose of political or religious discussions.

17. Regulation is sometimes pushed to excess, even harming individual freedom: thus the Tunisian native cannot enjoy the liberty of coming and going, it is even forbidden to him to leave the territory of the regency without having a passport. The decree of 13 March 1897 fixes penalties of fines and imprisonment for those who contravene this. This passport is only delivered upon appearance before the Tunisian government and payment of a security deposit as guarantee of the applicant's civil and commercial engagements. Israelites constantly rail against these requirements by the administration; we possess a letter on this subject addressed to the president of the League for the Defense of the Rights of Man, with the following lines: "To have this very expensive document [the passport] there are formalities to complete: a certificate of good living and conduct, tax records, proof that one is not in bankruptcy or involved in a lawsuit—even all these do not suffice. The administration requires

a creditworthy deposit that would cover all debts. This requirement is so monstrous that it is not given to everybody to satisfy it. And yet a Tunisian cannot leave the territory if he does not fulfill it. Here lies an attack on individual freedom, and since these measures are not required of non-Tunisians, why subject only the children of this country to them?" (November 1906). It is to be hoped that travel for the purpose of trips abroad are not obligatorily preceded by such administrative formalities that constitute a useless hindrance to the freedom of Tunisian natives, since access to most countries is, by virtue of diplomatic arrangements, open to all.

18. The five fundamental principles of Islam are: 1. Zekat (debits that are both alms and tax); 2. Fasting; 3. Pilgrimage to Mecca; 4. Prayer; 5. Holy War (*Eldjehad*). See Abribat, *Receuil de notions de Droit musulman* (Tunis, 1896), p. 258.

19. The Foreign Legion is a special corps attached to the land army and open to any foreigner aged between eighteen and forty.

20. The *bey*'s finance receiver was in former times a Jew, but the state's need to call exceptionally on the talents of Israelites did not create in favor of the Jewish population any eligibility for other public functions.

21. Pédebidou, report on Tunisia presented to the Senate on 19 December 1906.

22. The number of Israelites who fill jobs in all Tunisian government offices does not exceed thirty. Smaja (Mardochée), *L'Extension de la juridiction et de la nationalité françaises en Tunisie* (Tunis, 1906).

23. The institution of the native delegation participating alongside those elected by the colony in examining the budget is too recent a creation for one to evaluate its results.

24. In Tunis, where the population is composed of 100,000 Muslims, 40,000 Israelites, 60,000 foreigners, and 18,626 Frenchmen, the composition of the municipal council is as follows: 6 French councillors, 9 Muslim councillors, 4 foreign councillors, and 1 native Israelite.

25. The general trend of imports and exports has gone from 76 million in 1802 to 170 million in 1906. Of this figure, exchanges between France and Tunisia count for 94 million. (Statistics on commerce of Tunisia in 1906.)

26. The Israelite element has always furnished local industry with intelligent manpower, and the guilds of tailors and jewelers were composed solely of Israelites. Apprenticeship schemes designed to direct the activity of Jewish Tunisians toward the manual professions are subsidized by the Société de l'Alliance Israélite of Paris. In 1906 there were sixty-five young male apprentices placed in the city's workshops who exercised the skills of blacksmiths, mechanics, electricians, sculp-

tors, engravers, etc., and thirty-one young women as seamstresses, milliners, laundrywomen, embroiderers, etc. (*Bulletin de l'Alliance Israélite* [1906]. Lecore-Carpentier, *Indicateur tunisien* [1907].)

27. Israelite shopkeepers are much too numerous in relation to the population of the country: the ratio is one Israelite shopkeeper to twenty natives. By comparison, in Algeria they are 1 percent of the indigenous population. (J. Saurin, *Manuel de l'émigrant en Tunisie* [brochure, 1896].)

28. Fifteen to twenty thousand Israelites are manual laborers.

29. The Israelites of the rich class generally belong to the European colonies. It is very difficult to find among official statistics (in which they are mixed with natives of whatever religion) any indications of the liquid and real estate holdings of Israelites. Nevertheless, the building census done with great care by the municipality of Tunis gives us for the year 1903 values for taxable real estate that are divided by nationality as follows: French, 34,859,000 francs (population 18,626); foreigners 26,890,000 francs (population 60,000); native Israelites 16,245,000 francs (population 40,000). Thus Israelites, who represent 25 percent of the Tunis population possess only 13 percent of the real estate capital.

30. The *mejba* only affects Tunisian subjects. This personal tax is fixed by the decree of 14 June 1902 at 23 francs. Natives residing in Tunis, Sousse, Monastir, Sfax, and Kairouan are exonerated from this tax. The number of Israelites established in these five privileged towns being fifty thousand souls, a good portion of the Israelite population (about two-thirds) escapes paying the *mejba*.

31. The caid of the territory may inflict up to fifteen days in prison for refusal to obey, constant bad behavior, etc.

32. Paying native personal taxes, contributing to the cost of religious teaching and welfare, Israelites who consume the same products as Europeans pay in indirect taxes in the same proportion as the latter. The Tunisian Israelite who belongs to the category of the most heavily burdened taxpayer is also the poorest.

33. Let us recognize, though, that the Tunisian Israelite problem has not failed to attract the attention of M. Stephen Pichon, the eminent statesman, today minister for foreign affairs, whose coming to head the protectorate government has been marked by promising reforms. We are convinced that thanks to his high influence, republican solutions will intervene to give satisfaction to the demands of Israelites. These demands, as we have demonstrated, are not incompatible with the interests of France in Tunisia or with the present form of the protectorate.

CHAPTER 48

"Outcaste": Shi'a Intolerance

Laurence Loeb

"PROTECTED" MINORITY

Proclaiming a spiritual debt to Judaism, the seventh-century Arab conquerors of Persia bestowed upon Jewry the title: "People of the Book." Together with Christians and Zoroastrians, Jews were henceforth to be considered *dhimmi*, a "protected minority." The concept of "protection" was an ideological rationale for permitting unbelievers to continue to live among the "faithful." In return for this privilege, *dhimmis* were obliged to pay a special poll tax, the *jizya*, and were denied some of the rights (and obligations) of full citizens. Provided the *dhimmis* lived up to their obligations, Islam offered to protect them from foes within the greater society and from without. The penalty paid for this guardianship was second-class citizenship, economic exploitation, and social discrimination.

INTIMIDATION

The incidence of Jewish persecution in the distant past is difficult to evaluate, due to the dearth of relevant accounts. But from the beginning of the seventeenth century, through 1925, Jewish survival was in constant danger, as Iranian hostility toward them increased. The harassment, intimidation, and restrictions directed toward the Jews seems sufficient cause for the development of certain Jewish behavior patterns and attitudes discussed later.

The proclamation of Shi'a Islam as the state religion has greatly contributed to the suffering of Iranian Jewry.[1] The Shi'a clergy has frequently led hostile action against the Jews. Today, the Shah's friendly policy toward Israel has engendered bitter opposition to his rule from the clergy (Iran Almanac, 1968: 532). During the June 1967 Six-Day War, the clergy was instrumental in effecting a boycott of Jewish business in Shiraz, Tehran, and elsewhere. In some cities the clergy prevented the sale of bread and other food to Jews for as long as three days, until the government intervened.

The restrictive code, *Jam Abbasi* (see appendices 1 and 2), decreed in the seventeenth century and based on the so-called Code of Omar, was the work of the clergy, as were later restrictive codes. These codes and the pogroms directed at the Jews were for the expressed purpose of converting them. Murder, expulsion, and robbery were only secondary considerations.

The type of restrictions placed on Jews and the methods of harassment have been numerous and varied (see appendix 2). They affected so many aspects of communal and personal living that they must be considered in some detail.

1. Forced Conversion

Forced conversion of Jews in Iran is known as early as the fifth century (see appendix 1). Since the period of Abbas I at the beginning of the seventeenth century, these have occurred regularly. In the reign of Abbas II (1642–1667), all the Jews of Iran were converted to Islam and many communities remained Muslim. All the Jews of Mashhad became *jadid al-islam* (new converts to Islam) in 1839 (Wolff, 1846: 395). Attempts were made to convert some of the smaller communities in Fars at the beginning of the twentieth century.

More often, individuals were singled out and forcibly converted. Usually it was a life-or-death choice given to those caught in a compromising situation (doctors were especially susceptible to such extortion), but sometimes victims were selectively kidnapped and tortured.

2. Law of Apostasy

In order to encourage Jews "voluntarily" to accept Islam, the Law of Apostasy was promulgated in the seventeenth century. It remained in effect officially until 1881, though it continued to be enforced unofficially until Reza Shah was induced to end the practice (Yishay, 1950: 70). This law stated that should a Jew convert to Islam he becomes the sole heir of all members of his family (lineage). This economic incentive was likely responsible for most of the "voluntary" conversion to Islam, which may have been considerable. A 1903 emis-

Laurence D. Loeb, ch. 2, appendices I–III in *Outcaste: Jewish Life in Southern Iran* (New York: 1977).

sary to Shiraz indicates that when he visited there was not a single Jewish family without a *jadid al-islam* waiting for a relative to die so that he might inherit from him (Alliance, 1903: 107).

3. Murder

Murders were commonly associated with riots and pogroms, but travelers and itinerant merchants were also frequent victims. Even when witnesses could be found, the murderer of a Jew was subject, in most cases, only to a *fine* (J. Benjamin, 1859: 259), or, at worst, a beating. The murder of Jews by unknown assailants, often without apparent motive, occasionally occurs in the present day. Due to improved communications, rumor of such murders now spreads quickly and widely throughout the country.

4. Beatings

Beatings and torture of Jews are often reported. Whereas prominent members of the community were often singled out for government-administered beatings, any Jew who ventured into the streets could be beaten and stoned by a mob. It is said that when a Jew was beaten he would immediately begin to scream and feign excruciating pain, claiming he had been wounded to death. Persians call this *jud baazi*, "Jew game."[2] The slowest, most painful and torturous death a Persian can conceive of is known as *jud kosht*, "Jew murder."

5. Kidnapping and Molestation of Jewish Women

The kidnapping of Jewish women, especially young virgins (married women were fair game too!), was frightening to Jews. Lotfali Khan-e Zand took girls from Isfahan and Shiraz for his harem (Levi, 1960, 3: 489), but lesser men too seized Jewish women for themselves. An informant told me that several years ago, a Muslim army officer was living in a Jewish home. A teenaged girl in the house was attractive and outgoing. One evening, he arranged for a jeep to come by and invited the girl for a drive. He made off with her, taking her from Shiraz to Ahwaz from where her parents received a letter stating that she had married him. The police did not interfere because she was sixteen and therefore of legal age.

Formerly, in contrast to the veiled Muslim woman, the Jewess was not permitted to cover her face in public. She was thus immediately identified as a Jew by Muslim men, who would then annoy her. An informant reported:

> Jewish women used to spin wool for carpets. When their spools were finished they would take them to the bazaar where they were told to put their heads against the wall while their work was inspected. Upon obeying this order, they would be hit over the head and stunned, while their wool was stolen.

When such incidents recurred, Jewish women stopped going to the bazaar.

Today, when even Muslim women are pinched and handled by Muslim men, Jewish women are singled out for special treatment because they are not protected by their kinsmen. The latter do not intervene for fear they will be beaten or even killed.

6. Blood Libel

Blood libel accusations, an idea probably imported from Europe, became common in Iran during the nineteenth century. The usual form was to accuse the Jews of ritually murdering a Muslim child. Sometimes a dead child would be placed in front of a Jewish home to support the accusation (Stuart, 1854: 325–26). The last major pogrom in Shiraz, in 1910, began as a blood libel (Alliance, 1910). As recently as 1945, Jews in Shiraz were accused of ritual murder (Yishay, 1950: 305).

A second sort of libel involves the profanation of Shi'a saints and imams. Informants confirm that during the nineteenth century Shirazi Jews were accused of representing Husseyn by a dog's head in the synagogue during Ashura, a day of Shi'a mourning. (See chapter 10 of original text.)

7. Expulsion, Living Restrictions, and Restricted Travel

Expulsion was an occasional alternative to conversion, but was dangerous because of hazardous travel. Fars at the beginning of the twentieth century was an area which saw a number of communities expelled, including Lar, Jahrom, Nobendigan and Darab. Periodically, Jews were forbidden to live in certain places or were permitted only with special restrictions. Thus fourteenth-century Abarquh (northern Fars) could not be settled by Jews (Mustawfi, 1919: 120) and in the twentieth century, only temporary residence was permitted. Jews were also prohibited from residing in Semnan (Curzon, 1892, 1: 291). In late nineteenth-century Qom, Jews could not sell wine or keep a shop (Bishop, 1891, 1: 170). Today there are no residence restrictions, but the twelve Jewish families in Mashhad and the seven in Tabriz are made to feel very unwelcome. Most interesting is the fact that in the nearly 450 kilometers between Zarqon (25 kilometers north of Shiraz) and Isfahan, there is not now, nor apparently was there previously, a town or village with permanent Jewish settlement. Jews were forced to get permission to move from one area to another, and this was only infrequently granted. This effectively prevented Jews from escaping especially difficult circumstances.

8. Ritual Pollution

The Jew is considered *najas*, "unclean." He is both ritually polluted and polluting, and the Shi'a Muslims in

Iran take numerous steps to avoid contact with him. Many of the traditional restrictions on the Jews were in support of this avoidance behavior.

The Mahalleh, a separate ghetto area to which Jews were restricted, was instituted in Iran long ago. In Shiraz, its size was very carefully regulated and a Jew's attempts to purchase property from Muslims, thereby extending the size of the Mahalleh, was firmly opposed by the Muslim clergy.

a) Physical contact with *dhimmis* generally was abhorred by the Muslim, but the Jew could understand this attitude as he had similar fear of pollution by the *"arelim"* or *"uncircumcised,"* i.e., Christians and Zoroastrians. Nevertheless:

> It is more easy to get the Mussulmans to eat food with the Parsis than with the Jews, whose religion ranks higher than Zoroastrianism in the popular regard. (Malcolm, 1905: 108)

A Jew who would enter the house of a Muslim would be expected to sit on a special rug. The water pipe, tea, or food would not be offered to him. Any object, especially food, touched by a Jew could not be used by a Muslim; thus animals slaughtered by Jews, if judged not ritually fit, could not then be sold to Muslims.[3]

A Jew planning on purchasing something could not handle or sort the merchandise, on penalty of being forced to purchase the entire lot at a price to be fixed by the Muslim merchant. This practice, now largely eliminated in Shiraz, is still observed in Burujerd, Hamadan, and elsewhere in the north of Iran.

b) Water was considered the most common agent of pollution, therefore Jews were not permitted to use the public baths. In recent years, they have been permitted to do so in Shiraz, but in Yazd, for example, they are restricted to their own bath or that of the Baha'is. The possibility that rainwater might splash off a Jew onto a Muslim led to the *prohibition of Jews walking in public during the rain*! One informant from Shiraz told the following anecdote:

> When I was a boy, I went with my father to the house of a non-Jew on business. When we were on our way home it started to rain. We stopped near a man who had apparently fallen and was bleeding. As we started to help him up, a Muslim *akhond* (theologian) stopped and asked me who I was and what I was doing. Upon discovering that I was a Jew, he reached for a stick to hit me for defiling him by being near him in the rain. My father ran to him and begged the *akhond* to hit him instead. The surprised *akhond* did not hit anyone and we were permitted to continue homeward.

Fear of pollution by Jews led to great excesses and peculiar behavior by Muslims. In nineteenth-century Qom,

> the few (Jews) who are allowed to reside here come from Koshan and Ispahan, and the ostentatious vocation which they pursue is peddling; but as the pious living in the religious atmosphere of so many descendants of the Prophet would be shocked at the idea of touching anything that has passed the hands of a defiled and impure Jew, they have had recourse to a more profitable traffic, the sale of spirituous liquors. (Stern, 1854: 184–85)

It was also reported that

> Christians and Jews according to Persian law are not subject to decapitation as they are considered unclean by the Mohammedans and not sufficiently worthy of this privilege. (Adams, 1900: 120)

In Barafarush on the Caspian Sea it was believed that disinterment and dispersion of the Jews' remains to the wind would be efficacious in obtaining rain. Jewish dead were burned and their ashes scattered by Muslims for this purpose. (Mounsey 1872: 274; Stern 1854: 264)

c) The badge of shame was an identifying symbol which marked someone as a *najas* Jew and thus to be avoided. From the reign of Abbas I until the 1920s,[4] all Jews were required to display a badge. The badge has been described as

> a little square piece of stuff; two or three fingers broad, sewed to their *Caba* or Gown in the middle of their Breasts, about two fingers above the Girdle, and it matters not what stuff the piece be of, provided the colour be different from that of the Cloaths to which it is sewed. (Thevenot, 1687, 2: 110)

Jews were sometimes required to wear a special hat such as the one prescribed by Abul Hassan Lari. In Teheran it was the practice for Jews to wear the traditional nightcap, *shubkolah*, all the time (Wills, 1887: 135). The Jews of Isfahan were "not permitted to wear the *kolah* or Persian head-dress" (Curzon, 1892, 1: 510). In about 1800, Jews in Bushehr were forced for a short time to wear the red Turkish Fez (Willis, 1887: 314). To this day, the head covering remains the Persian ethnic identification mark par excellence, although the Jew no longer wears a distinctive one.

Jewish women were required to wear a black chador, (an all-enveloping cloak), while exposing their faces (Benjamin, 1859: 230). This may explain the present-day Shirazi women's preference for a white chador.

9. Poll Tax

The *jizya* (poll tax) was universally applied to Jews in Muslim countries in return for their status as a *dhimmi* or "protected minority." The entire community shared the burden of its collection.

10. Name Calling

One of the great insults in Iran is to call someone a Jew or "Jud" (Fraser, 1825: 511). So low is the Jew thought, that the Turks once cursed Abbas I saying:

> I hope also from the divine Majesty, that in the Day of Judgement he will make you serve instead of Asses to the Jews, that that miserable Nation which is the Contempt of the World, may mount and trot with you to Hell. (Sykes, 1930, 1: 178–78)

11. Justice

It was mentioned previously that Jewish life was considered almost worthless by the courts. A Jew could never win a case in court against a Muslim, and, even today, a Jew will go to any length to avoid court action. Muslim-Jewish disputes used to be settled by an *akhond*, (Muslim theologian) with a fine or beating as the Jew's normal due. Children, too, were dragged before the *akhond* and beaten for alleged wrongdoing. The Shirazi Jewish mother still threatens her misbehaving child with the words: "The *akhond* will get you!"

Since Reza Shah, the courts have become more equitable. But only Muslims are permitted to practice law—perhaps because so much national law is based on Islamic law.

12. Public Degradation

The public greeting of the king or governor by the assembled population was described by Chardin in the seventeenth century (1923: 208). In Qajar times,

> at the arrival of a new provincial governor, the Jews are compelled to sacrifice an ox in his honour upon the high road at some distance from the town. The headman of the Hebrew community has to run with the bleeding head of the animal, imploring the governor's countenance and protection, until he is beaten off by the farrashes. (Wills, 1887: 231)

Morier witnessed the procession of the shah in early nineteenth-century Tehran, in which the minorities participated as follows:

> They (Armenians) all began to chant Psalms as His Majesty drew near and their zeal was only surpassed by that of the Jews, without also had col-

lected themselves into a body, conducted by their Rabbis who raised on a carved representation of the wood of the tabernacles, and made the most extravagant gestures of humiliation, determined that they at least should not pass unnoticed by the Monarch. (1818: 388)[5]

During the Qajar period, a very difficult time for all Iranian Jews, Shiraz was reputed to be the place where the Jews were most ill treated (Binning, 1857, 2: 120; Curzon, 1892, 1: 510–11). Harassment was a concomitant of living.

It was said that one religious fanatic, Sayid Sharif, upon catching a Jew, would cut off his side whiskers, shave part of his chin, make his hat into an ass's bonnet, tear his clothes into shreds, and send him away after having given him several blows on the head (Alliance, 1903: 110).

Muslims used to intrude into the houses of Jews, drink their wine and liquor, seize any household object to their liking and remove it to their homes without any overt objection of the Jewish owner. If a Muslim decided to sell a house to a Jew, he would demand a price five times its worth, and even after the transaction was completed the Muslim could find a way to reclaim his property (Alliance, 1903: 111).

> When a Jew marries, a rabble of the Mahommedan ruffians of the town invite themselves to the ceremony, and, after a scene of riot and intoxication, not infrequently beat their host and his relations and insult the women of the community; only leaving the Jewish quarter when they have slept off the drink they have swallowed at their unwilling host's expense. (Wills, 1887: 231)

Nearly as frightening as the actual physical harassment were the threats made daily against the Jew. Verbal abuse continues even to the present day. During World War II, Muslims used to tell Jews, "Hitler is in the cameo around my neck." They went around Shiraz selecting which houses they would take when Hitler took over Iran.

Although more subdued than in the past, verbal and physical abuse of the Jew still occurs in Shiraz during the month of Muharram and especially on Ashura, the day of mourning for Husseyn. Jews are very circumspect to avoid offending Muslims at this time. On Ashura itself, Jews pretended not to know the author in order that on this day, especially, he would not be identified with them. Nevertheless, rumor (untrue) spread through the city that the author had been jailed for three days for taking pictures of the Muslims' ritual pageant.

In the spring of 1968, Jews, who normally close their stores on Yom Ha'azma'ut (Israel Independence Day) in order to picnic in the gardens, remained open because the Muslim masses were upset about the military parade scheduled for that day in Jerusalem. Yom Ha'azma'ut eve, over five hundred men and women assembled in a Mahalleh synagogue to read psalms and penitential prayers—hoping for a peaceful parade.

Threats by the Muslim clergy kept the Jews at home during the 1967 Six-Day War. The synagogues were closed for nearly ten weeks until Tish'a B'av. Informants claimed that during the war the *goyim* tried to break into the Mahalleh, but were stopped by the police. Others said that some Jews were beaten up. One informant claimed that after several days, one member of the *Anjoman* (Central Committee) asked everyone to open his store and to keep it open on the Sabbath and on Shavu'ot to demonstrate that Shirazi Jews were *not* in sympathy with Israel. The same informant said that many Jews did as he asked.

The presence of SAVAK, the secret police, adds to the Jews' anxiety. There was an unconfirmed story that a Yeshiva student was arrested by them for publicly praising Israel after the Six-Day War. One student activist claimed that whenever Zionist programs take place, the secret police carefully questioned him about them.

It is readily apparent that Shi'a intolerance must have necessitated many adaptive responses on the part of Shirazi Jews. Choice of occupation, the nature of kin networks and political structures, self-perception, and worldview will be seen to have been pervasively affected by the passive strictures and active hostility of the dominant population and the authorities.

While *dhimmis* have been set apart in Iran as pariahs, generally without recourse to political power or influence, this is not to say that the *dhimmi* ethnicities were viewed by the populace as equivalent (cf. Fischer, 1973; Schwartz, 1973), although they were all "untouchable" outcastes, distinctive in their relative lack of esteem. Jews nevertheless believe themselves to have been singled out for special mistreatment by the Muslims. The Jew presumes that "the hand of God" has fated the Jew to be thus punished for his "sins": "This has truly been *galut* (exile)," say the Shirazis. "The *goyim* have severely oppressed the Jews and we have had no place to flee."

APPENDIX I

The Safavids

The Safavids ousted the latest of foreign conquerors, the Turkomans. For the first time in over eight hundred years, Persia was free of foreign domination. In a nativistic spirit, Shah Isma'il proclaimed the Twelver or Imami sect of Shi'a Islam as the state religion. In 1502 the capital was shifted from Tabriz to Qazvin, where its extensive commercial opportunities attracted many Jews. Shah Abbas I (1587–1629) later transferred the capital to Isfahan, which then became the main center of

Persian Jewish life. For economic reasons, Abbas settled Armenians in new Julfa outside of Isfahan, while Georgian Jews were established in Farahabad in Mazanderan. In the early years of his reign, other foreign Jews were attracted to Persia for trade and settlement.

The Jewish population of Persia was estimated at eight to ten thousand families during the reign of Abbas I (Teixeira, 1902: 252). During the reign of Abbas II, Chardin likewise estimated the Jewish population at nine to ten thousand families or thirty to thirty-five thousand people (Fischel, 1937a: 276). This Jewish population was widely dispersed throughout the country and included settlements at: Abarquh, Ardebil, Ashraf, Asterabad, Bandar [*sic*], Demavend, Farahabad, Gilar (Gilan?), Golpaygan, Hamadan, Hormuz, Isfahan, Jahrom, Kashan, Kerman, Kermanshah, Khonsar, Khorassan, Lar, Nahawand, Natanf (Natanz?), Qazvin, Qom, Shiraz, Shushtar, Tabriz, Tehran, and Yazd (Fischel, 1937a: 276–77). The above sites are documented but no doubt there were many other locations in which Jews resided.

The adoption of a strict, sectarian form of Islam as Persia's state religion had important economic and social consequences for the *dhimmi* population in general and for Jews in particular. On the one hand, more stringent interpretation of the laws of ritual purity prevented Jews from engaging in food production or sale, while on the other hand, more scrupulous adherence to religious law meant that Muslims could no longer manufacture liquor or wine, nor engage in music making or money lending. Competition between Jews and other minorities to fill such vacant occupational niches was intense.[6] Thus, at first, the Jews were the most important usurers (Chardin, 1735: 427), but Banians from India soon surpassed them (Tavernier, 1684: 202). A contemporary traveler also observed that

> the country trade is in the hands of the Persians and the Jews, [while] the foreign traffic is in the hands of the Armenians only. (Tavernier, 1684: 229)

Occupations associated with Jewish men of this period included: wine maker, silk farmer, druggist, doctor, magician, fortune-teller, tailor, miller, goldsmith, jeweler, musician, clown, funeral wailer, and dancer. Jews were also shopkeepers, money lenders, itinerant peddlers, peddlers of secondhand goods and of "produire des femmes" (Chardin, 1735: 427). Jewish women also engaged in commerce in order to service the confirmed Muslim women. Despite the variety of economic activity, Chardin considered their situation desperate:

> They are everywhere destitute. I have not seen a single family in the entire kingdom that one could call rich, and which, to the contrary, was not subsisting on the lowest of levels. (1735: 427, trans. mine)

The Safavid period was a time of great anxiety for the entire Persian Jewish community. It is not clear whether a decline in Jewish scholarship resulted from the stresses of the period or whether Persian Jews were, as Chardin claims, "the most ignorant in the whole world" (1735: 428). The Bible, *Siddur*, Mishna, Talmud, Shulkhan Arukh (code of Jewish law) and *Sefer Razim* (a kabbalistic work) were known and used (Bacher, 1906: 272), but scholarship was limited to biblical translation and chronicle poems such as the *Kitab-i Anusi* of Babay ibn Lutf. Centers of Jewish learning, such as there were, existed in Lar, Isfahan, and Kashan.

Ritual observance was not as it should have been either. Babay ibn Lutf chastises the Jews for numerous transgressions, such as eating bread without reciting a blessing, not fasting on appropriate occasions, not helping the poor, not assembling a *minyan* (quorum) for prayer and mourners *qaddish* and not properly observing the holidays (Fischel, 1937a: 288). But these oversights may have resulted from the zealous persecution of Jews under Abbas I and II.

In 1617, during the reign of Shah Abbas I, an intra-communal dispute occurred in the city of Isfahan. The community elders accused the *Nasi* (community leader), Siman Tov ben David, of cheating his customers by short-weighing their meat. When the elders appealed to the Shah to redress their wrong, Siman Tov converted to Islam and intimated to the Shah that the Jews were using a book of magic to work evil against the shah.[7] Elders of the community were brought before the *Diwan* (a government office for Jewish affairs) and asked to convert to Islam. Upon their refusal they were thrown to the dogs and killed. Thereupon all holy books in the community were thrown in a pile in the main square and the whole community was forced to convert. In 1622, several men who had been secretly practicing Judaism were executed. The community was finally permitted to return to Judaism by Shah Safi (1629–1642).

This happy occasion was named *Hag Habbsora,* "the holiday of good tidings" (Mizrahi, 1966: 37).

In 1622, a Jew from Lar, Abul Hassan Lari, was accused of selling improperly slaughtered meat. On Yom Kippur he converted to Islam and, to exact vengeance, enlisted the support of the Shi'a clergy to enforce restrictive measures against the Jews. In Lar, Isfahan, Kashan, and elsewhere, these restrictions were put into effect. Eventually, the strictures of Abul Hassan were incorporated into the *Jam Abbasi*, a more extensive code instituted by Abbas I (see appendix 2). From 1622 to 1925, Persian Jews were required to wear a special hat or piece of colored cloth as an identifying "badge of shame." A "Law of Apostasy" was promulgated permitting any Jewish convert to Islam to inherit all of the property of his relatives, even from those of distant degree.

In the reign of Shah Abbas II, from 1653 to 1666, almost all of the Jews of Persia were forced to become Muslims. According to Jewish sources, the cause of these persecutions was the theft of a silver dagger belonging to the shah by his gardener. One of the jewels from its handle was found in the possession of two Jewish merchants. On this evidence, the vizier attributed the crime to the Jews and received permission from the shah to convert all of the Jews of Isfahan as punishment. One Sabbath eve, the Jews fled from Isfahan and took refuge at the shrine of Serah bat Asher. Eventually, Jews in Lar, Shiraz, Kashan, Qom, Khonsar, Golpaygan, Hamadan, and elsewhere were compelled to convert. In the ensuing disorder, many Jews committed suicide or were killed or expelled. Jews fled from Hamadan to Kurdistan, Baghdad and even Palestine (Bacher, 1906: 247).

Jewish resistence to the decrees of Abbas II was mostly passive. The conversions were without conviction. Chardin tells us that a Jew questioned about his conversion replied:

I? A Muslim? Not at all. I am Jewish. It is true that they gave me two *Tomans* to swear a false oath. (1735: 427, translation mine)

Jewish sources say that soon after conversion to Islam, most Jews went back to observing the Sabbath; even the execution of those caught doing so did not deter the others. Finally, Abbas II relented and permitted Jews to return to their religion upon repayment of the bribe given them, renewed payment of the poll tax retroactive to the time they converted to Islam, and the donning anew the "badge of shame" (Fischel, 1937a: 287).

Their redemption from this oppression must have seemed nothing short of miraculous, as, indeed, the folklore bears out.[8] The Jews of Mazanderan must, therefore, have been particularly elated, in 1666, when word reached them of the coming of a new messiah, Shabbtay Zvi. The Jews of this region made swift preparations to go to Palestine, but were restrained by the pragmatic governor of the province, who requested payment of their unpaid taxes. The Jews agreed to wait three months for the messiah's arrival, at which time they would be free to go without payment. It was further stipulated that should the messiah fail to appear within that span, they would be obliged to pay a large penalty tax to the governor, and they never did go to Palestine (Chardin, 1735: 428).

Despite the government's permission to return to Judaism, many Jews must have remained converts to Islam. Muslim villagers in the Isfahan area are reputed to still light candles on Friday evening as is the Jewish custom. Lenjan, the village near the shrine of Serah bat Asher and site of the Isfahani Jewish cemetery, has no Jewish inhabitants, although it must be assumed to have had some earlier. Many of the Afghans claim that they were Jews until converted under Abbas II (Ben-Zvi, 1961: 188). There is also linguistic evidence to support the contention that some Iranian Muslims were Jews before the Safavid period.[9]

The later Safavids were nearly as cruel as the earlier ones. As an example, during the reign of Shah Suleyman, in 1678, Jewish notables of Isfahan were falsely accused and murdered, and their corpses thrown into the main square (Carmelite Chronicles, 1: 408)

The Afghan sacking of Isfahan (1722) marked the end of Safavid rule. Although one observer indicated that the Jews welcomed the new conqueror (Alexander, 1936: 648), a Jewish source claims:

> We have only fallen into the hands of new enemies, because at those times when Muslims kill, the lives of Jews are even less secure. (Fischel, 1937a: 293, translation mine)

In fact, there were new persecutions in Kashan in 1729 while the Jews of Golpaygan were fortunately able to buy off their enemies. Nevertheless, the Afghan period was, by comparison, something of a respite from the Safavid oppression.

Nadir Shah (1736–1747) was a Sunni and well disposed toward the Jews. For economic reasons he settled some forty Jewish families from Qazvin in the holy city of Mashhad in 1734 (Fischel, 1936: 52). A translation of the Torah and book of Psalms was undertaken at his direction by Babay ben Nuriel of Isfahan and completed in 1740 (Fischel, 1960: 1173). There is also a tradition that one day, when Nadir Shah was listening to the reading of the Torah, he was so moved by the story of Zalafhad's daughters (Num. 36) that he wished to further improve the lot of the Jew, but was prevented from doing so by his ministers and officers (Levi, 1960: 496).

Under the Zands (1750–1794) there was no reported violence against the Jews, despite considerable anti-Jewish propaganda in Shiraz, the capital. The only clear case of their exploitation was at the personal whim of Lotfali Khan, who abducted five Jewish girls from Isfahan and eight from Shiraz to be added to his harem (Levi, 1960: 496).

The Qajars

Under the Qajars (1796–1925) many of the restrictions of the Safavids were reimposed upon Iranian Jewry. Since the central government was usually weak and the provinces locally autonomous, the Jews of the outlying regions were often left to the mercy of the local population.[10] As has been shown elsewhere (Loeb, 1970: 424–30), this period could rightfully be characterized as "an uninterrupted sequence of persecution and oppression" (Fischel, 1950: 21).

The most significant development for Persian Jewry during this 130-year span was the reestablishment of communications with world Jewry. In 1858, Jewish organizations began to pressure the French and British ministers in Tehran to intervene on behalf to pressure the French and British ministers in Tehran to intervene on behalf of the Jews. In 1865, Sir Moses Montefiore considered making a personal visit to Persia, but was dissuaded from doing so by the British Foreign Office. After the famine of 1871, large sums of relief money were distributed among the Jews of Iran by representatives of the British government (Fischel 1950: 129). In 1873, when Nasser ad-Din Shah visited Europe, he was confronted everywhere by concerned Jewry. Adolphe Cremieux appealed to the shah on behalf of the Alliance Israélite Universelle to allow them to open schools in Iran and was given permission to do so (Fischel, 1950: 132).

Until the first Alliance school opened in Tehran in 1898, Jews either had no secular education or went to missionary schools. Missionary activity succeeded in converting small numbers of Jews to Christianity in Hamadan, Isfahan, and Tehran, while larger numbers became Baha'is. Jewish religious knowledge and literacy was very low despite occasional emissaries from Baghdad and Jerusalem, who had been coming to Persia since the early eighteenth century. The cities of Kashan, Shiraz, and Yazd[11] were the leading religious centers.

The 1906 constitutional movement did not bring any immediate benefits to Iranian Jewry, although eventually Jews were enabled to choose their own representative to *Majles* (parliament). Some of the official discriminatory regulations were removed, but such legislated improvement in conditions was too slow to practically affect the daily life of the Persian Jew.

The Pahlavis

The Pahlavi period, instituted by Reza Shah's seizure of power in 1925, has been the most favorable era for Persian Jews since Parthian rule. Jews have their own deputy in Majles who effectively serves the Jewish community *not* by active participation in public debate, but by means of personal influence with the shah. In this way the "Law of Apostasy" was abrogated about 1930. While Reza Shah did prohibit political Zionism and condoned the execution of the popular liberal Jewish reformer Hayyim Effendi, his rule was, on the whole, an era of new opportunity for the Persian Jew.

Hostile outbreaks against the Jews have been prevented by the government. Jews are no longer legally barred from any profession. They are required to serve in the army and pay the same taxes as Muslims. The elimination of the face-veil removed a source of insult to Jewish women, who had been previously required to have their faces uncovered; now all women are supposed to appear unveiled in public.

Although the Pahlavi government officially discouraged the spread of Alliance schools, ostensibly because of their emphasis on the French language, there were twenty-three of them serving eight thousand pupils in 1951 and thirty-four such schools by 1958 (Schechtman, 1961: 244). Secular educations were made available to Jewish girls as well as to boys, and, for the first time,

Jews could become government-licensed teachers. Otsar Hatorah eventually assumed responsibility for Jewish religious education in Iran, with apparent Pahlavi acquiescence.

Since the ascendance of Mohammad Reza Shah Aryamehr in 1941, the situation has further improved. In 1947, the American Joint Distribution Committee commenced operations in Iran through providing aid to education, medical services, feeding programs for the children, and sanitation programs to clean up the Mahalleh. Indeed, their efforts, together with the emigration impetus provided by the Jewish Agency, has raised the standard of living among the remaining Jews to a point where it is now substantially higher than that of the non-Jewish population. Not only has the number of poor been reduced, but a new bourgeoisie is emerging. There are even Jewish millionaires. For the first time Jews are spending their money on cars, carpets, houses, travel, and clothing. Tehran has attracted provincial Jews in large numbers and has become the center of Iranian Jewish life.

The Pahlavi era has seen vastly improved communications between Iranian Jewry and the rest of the world. Hundreds of boys and girls attend college and boarding school in the United States and Europe. Israeli emissaries come for periods of two years to teach in the Jewish schools. Improved roads, postal and telephone service have greatly increased contact between Jews in the provinces and those in Tehran. Rural Jews and small-town dwellers who only forty years ago may have constituted 25 percent or more of the total Jewish population are now less than 2 percent. Radio, TV, the phonograph, movies, and magazines are markedly affecting Iranian Jewish life.

A small Jewish publication industry has arisen since 1925. Religious texts in Judeo-Persian were edited and distributed in the 1920s by Hayyim More, originally of Kashan. Books on Jewish history, Zionism, the Hebrew language, and classroom texts have since been published. The Jewish newspapers *Ha-G'ula* and *Hahayyim* were sporadically issued for some years, and the Jewish Agency regularly distributes a newsletter.

On March 15, 1950, Iran extended de facto recognition to Israel. Relations with Israel are good and trade is growing. Israel provides Iran with technical aid and produce, such as eggs and foodstuffs: in return, Israel receives petroleum, landing rights for El Al, and, until recently, discrete unofficial sympathy from the Iranian government in its struggle against the Arabs.

Despite the favorable attitude of the government and the relative prosperity of the Jewish community, all Iranian Jews acknowledge the precarious nature of the present situation. There are still sporadic outbreaks against them, because the Muslim clergy constantly berates Jews, inciting the masses, who make no effort to hide their animosity toward the Jew. Most Jews express the belief that it is only the personal strength and good-

will of the shah that protects them: that plus God's intervention! If either should fail. . . .

APPENDIX 2

Restrictive Codes

Restrictions of the Safavid Period

Behavior Code of Abul Hassan Lari (1622)

1. Houses that are too high (higher than a Muslim's) must be lowered.
2. Jews may not circulate freely among the believers.
3. In their stores, Jews must sit on low stools, in order that they not see the purchaser's face.
4. Jews must wear a specially constructed hat of eleven colors.
5. Around this hat they must sew a yellow ribbon, three meters long.
6. Women must tie many little bells on their sandals.
7. Jewish women must also wear a black chador.
8. When a Jew speaks to a Muslim, he must humbly lower his head.

(Bacher, 1906, 52: 237)

The Jam Abbasi, *Instituted by Abbas I (C. 1618) and Administered in Some Measure until 1925*

1. Jews are not permitted to dress like Muslims.
2. A Jew must exhibit a yellow or red "badge of dishonor" on his chest.
3. A Jew is not permitted to ride on a horse.
4. When riding on an ass, he must hang both legs on one side.
5. He is not entitled to bear arms.
6. On the street and in the market, he must pass stealthily from a corner or from the side.
7. Jewish women are not permitted to cover their faces.
8. The Jew is restricted from establishing boundaries of private property.
9. A Jew who becomes a Muslim is forbidden to return to Judaism.
10. Upon disclosure of a disagreement between Jew and Muslim, the Jew's argument has no merit.
11. In Muslim cities, the Jew is forbidden to build a synagogue.
12. A Jew is not entitled to have his house built higher than a Muslim's.

(Mizrahi, 1966: 36)

Restrictions of the Nineteenth-Century Qajar Period

"Oppressions" Noted by a Jewish Traveler

1. Throughout Persia the Jews are obliged to live in a part of town separated from the other inhabitants; for they are regarded as unclean creatures who bring contamination with their intercourse and presence.
2. They have no right to carry on trade in stuff goods.
3. Even in the streets of their own quarter on the town they are not allowed to keep any open shop—they may only sell spices and drugs, or carry on the trade of a jeweler.
4. Under the pretext of their being unclean, they are treated with the greatest severity, and should they enter the street, inhabited by Mussulmen, they are pelted by the boys and mob with stones and dirt.
5. For the same reason they are forbidden to go out when it rains; for it is said the rain would wash dirt off them, which would dirty the feet of the Mussulmen.
6. If a Jew is recognized as such in the streets, he is subjected to the greatest insults. The passersby spit in his face, and sometimes beat him so cruelly that he falls to the ground, and is obliged to be carried home.
7. If a Persian kills a Jew, and the family of the deceased can bring forward two Mussulmen as witnesses to the fact, the murderer is punished by a fine of twelve tumauns (six hundred piastres), but if two such witnesses cannot be produced, the crime remains unpunished, even though it has been publicly committed, and is well known.
8. The flesh of animals killed according to Hebrew custom, but as *trefe* declared, must not be sold to any Mussulmen. The slaughters are compelled to bury the meat, for even the Christians do not dare to buy it, fearing the mockery and insult of the Persians.
9. If a Jew enters a shop to buy anything, he is forbidden to inspect the goods, but must stand at a respectful distance and ask the price. Should his hand by accident touch the goods, he must take them at any price the seller chooses to ask for them.
10. Sometimes the Persians intrude into the dwellings of the Jews and take possession of whatever pleases them. Should the owner make the least opposition in defense of his property, he runs the danger of atoning for it with his life.
11. Upon the least dispute between a Jew and a Persian, the former is immediately dragged before the Achund, and, if the complaint can bring forward two witnesses, the Jew is condemned to pay a heavy fine. If he is too poor to pay this penalty in money, he must pay it in his person. He is stripped to the waist, bound to a stake, and receives forty blows with a stick. Should the sufferer utter the least cry of pain during this proceeding, the blows already given are not reckoned, and the punishment is begun afresh.
12. In the same manner the Jewish children, when they get into a quarrel with those of the Mussulmen, are immediately led before the Achund, and punished with blows.
13. A Jew who travels in Persia is taxed at every inn and caravan-serai he enters.
14. If . . . a Jew shows himself in the street during the three days of the Katel ([mourning] feast . . . for . . . death of the [Shi'ite saint] Ali [probably *ashura*]) he is sure to be killed.

(Benjamin, 1859: 258–60)

APPENDIX 3

Judaism under Shi'a Islam

Jews survived under Islam with differential success, dependent on numerous sociohistorical factors. But, as Goitein (1955) pointed out in his comparative research of Jews and Arabs, the long-term survival of Jews in areas under the control of sectarian Islam presented a formidable challenge. Goitein focuses primarily on the Jews of Yemen, who responded with considerable ingenuity to the fanaticism of Shi'a Islam. Facing somewhat comparable circumstances, Iranian Jewry developed differently, with cultural attainments and social structures of a very different order than those of Yemen. A proper evaluation of these two adaptive strategies must await the availability of more complete historical and ethnographic materials from both societies (cf. Loeb, 1970).

Yet, the different cultural adaptations of Iranian and Yemenite Jews may be partially attributed, to the distinctive cultures of their respective dominant populations. Thus Yemenite Jews are like the Zayidi Shi'a Arabs in their predilection for a strong patrilineal kinship system and legal scholarship, whereas Iranian Jews are more bilateral in their kinship and stress epic poetry and mysticism as do the imami Shi'a. The relatively superior economic position of the Yemenite Jew and the wealth of his material culture may result from what Hitti (1960: 449) considers the more tolerant Sunni-like orthodoxy of the Zayidis.

The comparatively difficult situation of Jews under Shi'a rule as compared with Sunni rule may be explained in part by the nature of Shi'a Islam itself. Bernard Lewis (1960: 71) points out that Shi'a Islam was taken over soon after its inception by the discontents of the Mawali. Theoretically the equals of Arab Muslims, the Mawali Muslims, who were not full members by descent of an Arab tribe, were treated as social inferiors (B. Lewis,

1960: 70). The Mawali flocked to Shi'a Arab elite. Ivanow (1948: 12–20) indicates that Shi'a Islam arose as a class struggle between the lower-class village poor and upper-class town elite.

NOTES

1. See appendix 3 for an explanation of the unique circumstances of the *dhimmi* condition under Shi'a Islam.

2. See chapter 9 for another interpretation of *jud baazi*.

3. By contrast, in modern-day Shiraz, the hotels buy their beef from the Jewish butchers because it is fresher and cleaner and because Muslim butchers specialize in selling lamb.

4. The patch had to be worn in Shiraz until about 1920 according to informants and was required until the beginning of the twentieth century in Tehran (Alliance, 1898: 137), Yazd (Malcom, 1905: 51–52), and other places.

5. In 1975, upon the shah's proclamation of single "Resurrection" Party rule, the Tehrani Jewish establishment demonstrated its unquestioned support for the shah and his policies at a public ceremony, which by most accounts was both embarrassing and humiliating to Persian Jewry.

6. Refer to chapter 5 and Loeb (1976).

7. Abbas I may well have been a military genius, but descriptions of his religious fanaticism and brutality vis-à-vis his own sons, to me suggest a rather unstable personality. The events described occur late in his life while he suffered some painful disability which may well have clouded his judgment.

8. See chapter 10 and the discussion of the pilgrimage site of Serah bat Asher.

9. "It is interesting to note that in two of the villages (in the vicinity) of Isfahan, at Sedey and at G'ez, the Iranians call their language *zeboni ibri*, the Israelite tongue" (Abrahamian 1936: 2, translation mine).

10. After a pogrom in 1839, the entire surviving community or Mashhad was forcibly converted to Islam. They remained crypto-Jews until after World War II.

11. The latter was known as *Yrushalayim Haqqatan*, "little Jerusalem." Similar claims implying piety and scholarship were made by informants in Burujerd, Hamadan, and elsewhere, and, indeed, the claim of one's community being *Yrushalayim Haqqatan* was one of the most widespread initial statements made by informants upon making my acquaintance.

*For further clarification of any references, especially from appendices I–III, see original text.

CHAPTER 49

The Expulsion of Yemenite Jewry to Mawza' in 1679–80 in Light of Recently Discovered Sources

Yehuda Ratzaby

The expulsion of Yemenite Jewry to Mawza' in 1679–80 probably was the most difficult experience endured by Yemenite Jewry. The Jews regarded this catastrophe as an exile within an exile. The Imam al-Mahdi ordered the entire Jewish population of Yemen—men, women, and children—exiled to the plain of Tihama, known for its salty water and soil and generally unfavorable climate. In addition to the expulsion, there were destructions of synagogues, desecrations of the Torah scrolls, and inducements for conversion to Islam. Nevertheless, Yemenite Jewry remained faithful to Judaism and withstood the terrible challenge, despite enormous losses due to the intense heat and the spread of diseases and epidemics. Only one-quarter of those expelled returned to their homes; the rest perished. [Of the San'a community, for example, which had numbered about ten thousand, only about one-tenth—one thousand—returned from exile. Yehuda Ratzaby: "The Expulsion to the Desert," *Et-Mol* 9, 3 [53] (January 1984): 16–18. English translation by Rivkah Fishman.]

The expulsion to Mawza' remained alive in the collective memory of Yemenite Jews for many generations, in oral tradition and in written folk literature, both poetry and narrative. No other event in the history of Yemenite Jewry has been the subject of so many dirges, legends, and traditions. The poetry and dirges must be considered as authoritative and reliable sources because their authors actually experienced the expulsion. Poetry, however, is a medium which expresses emotions and, in this case, its major themes are feelings of pain and sorrow. Description of the events plays a minor role because the poets were familiar with the actual events. In the legends, fantasy and reality are intertwined and it is not easy to distinguish between the two. References to the expulsion in colophons, bills, and contracts, written at the time, are infrequent and not always clear.

Three chronicles written some time after the expulsion have survived. Rabbi Yahya Tsalah (the "Maharitz") wrote the earliest of these compositions, two generations after the event.[1] The two later chronicles, written in the nineteenth century, by Shalom Mantsura[2] and Hayyim Habshush,[3] respectively, were based mainly on legends. From my summary of the material on the Mawza' exile published in 1961 and based on the extant sources,[4] it is clear that important information was missing, particularly regarding the duration of the ordeal, life in Mawza', and the circumstances surrounding the end of the expulsion.[5] Despite the apparently abundant source material, the event was not described fully and several points remained obscure. The lack of sources of a chronological nature dating from the period of the expulsion which could have shed light on the events as they took place clearly affected my research.

All this changed when I happened to discover a letter of a chronological nature which had been used as the inner binding of a book brought from Yemen during the mass exodus of Yemenite Jewry to Israel in Operation Magic Carpet in 1949–50.[6] This newly discovered document sheds light on the Mawza' expulsion and fills in the missing facts. Furthermore, it enriches our knowledge of the history of the Jewish communities in the Land of Israel, namely, the Old Yishuv. For it includes information about a hitherto unknown emissary from the Jewish community of Hebron, who was active in Yemen at the time and was expelled to Mawza' together with his Yemenite brethren.[7] Along with the publication of this letter, I am including poetry and parts of poems written during the Mawza' expulsion from recently discovered manuscripts housed in the National Library in Jerusalem. The existence and publication of all of these sources call for a new study of the subject.

II

The chronological letter was sent by the residents of Dhuran[8] and its environs in 1684 after the expulsion had ended and the exiles had returned to their homes. It opens with a mention of the ancestral holiness of Hebron

Yehuda Ratzaby in *Zion* 37 (1972): 197–215. English translation by Rivkah Fishman.

and states that the righteousness and study and observance of Torah on the part of the Jews of Hebron protects
Jews dwelling outside the Land of Israel. The letter then
unfolds its main theme by describing the emissary,
Rabbi Amram the Hasid[9] from Hebron, who brought
lengthy letters concerning the plight of the Hebron community.[10] The authors of these letters expected that the
emissary would return with financial aid for the Jews of
Hebron. However, he found himself sharing the troubles
of the Yemenite community. The latter apologized for
not being able to help Rabbi Amran support the Jews of
Hebron properly because of the catastrophe in Yemen.[11]

According to this source, the order of expulsion was
accompanied by the destruction of synagogues[12] and
enticements to convert to Islam. The Muslims argued
that God had abandoned the Jews, and, therefore, they
should become Muslims. The devotion of the Jews to
their religion angered the Muslims, who reacted with
expressions of contempt, curses, insults, and verbal
abuse. Soldiers and policemen urged the Jews to leave
their homes quickly and those who delayed their departure were severely beaten. Their homes and property
were looted. Government officials ceased protecting
them and no one stood with them. The Jews tried to ame-
liorate their situation by offering a substantial sum of
money, to no avail. In their place of exile, they succumbed to the extreme heat and prevailing epidemics.
Seventy people who tried to escape died of heatstrokes.[13]
Others failed in their attempts to return to their homes
and were caught by guards who ambushed them. Community leaders, rabbis, and elders died during the
Mawza' expulsion.

Ultimately, the brother of al-Mahdi, a benevolent
ruler, came to the aid of the Jews.[14] He controlled eastern
Yemen and most of those who were expelled found their
way toward his kingdom,[15] which angered al-Mahdi. He
almost declared war upon his brother. The latter eventually convinced him to relax his hold on the Jews in order
that they recuperate. Later on, he could do what he
wished. Shortly afterward, al-Mahdi died suddenly[16] and
Muslims accused the Jews of rejoicing at his death and
levied a substantial fine on every town. In the meantime,
a revolt ensued which diverted the authorities' attention
from the Jews.[17] From the final passages of the letter, it
is evident that the order of expulsion was valid for less
than a year.[18] At the end of the letter, the Yemenite Jews
requested that their brethren in the Land of Israel pray
for them, asserting the efficacy of prayers at holy sites
such as . . . near the Temple Mount in Jerusalem, the
tombs of the patriarchs in Hebron, or the graves of holy
men throughout the land.[19]

The letter informs us of two additional measures
designed to humiliate and impoverish the Jews of
Yemen, namely, the orders to remove animal carcasses
from markets and public thoroughfares and to build low
and humble places of residence.[20] We may assume that
the letter was addressed to the community in Hebron

which sent the emissary to Yemen and that it represents
an apology of sorts on the part of its authors who could
not give the emissary proper treatment or relate to his
mission suitably. Apparently, the letter was given to the
emissary prior to his departure from Yemen. The document in our possession is a copy of the original text
given as a souvenir[21] and subsequently stored in a
Genizah. An adroit binder used it as the inner binding of
a book. There is no doubt that the emissary was active all
over Yemen as he was in Dhuran.[22] It is only by chance
that the letter of the community in Dhuran survived.
Rabbi Amram the Hasid was a diligent emissary. Unde-
terred by the catastrophe of Yemenite Jewry, he preferred
to stay with his people during the hard times and wander
with them during the expulsion.[23] Upon their return, he
waited for them to rebuild their communities and reha-
bilitate themselves. He then visited them again in order
to collect money for the Jews of Hebron and thereby
enable Yemenite Jews to participate in supporting the
Jewish communities in the Land of Israel.[24] Rabbi
Amram's mission to Yemen lasted four years, from
1679–83.

III

Several poems and poetic fragments convey additional
details about the expulsion. The leading poet of
Yemenite Jewry, Rabbi Shalem Shabbazi (1619–c. early
1700s)[25] wrote extensively about destruction of synagogues, cessation of services, removal of Torah scrolls,
and measures against communal prayer and public
[Torah] reading. He complained about the kidnapping of
orphans and young children and about the intermingling
of religions.[26] Hence, it appears that the Muslims acted
against the Jews and Judaism. Rabbi Shabbazi also states
that Jewish land owners had to abandon their fields and
that the Muslims who ruled the country harvested the
wheat.[27]

The supplements to the poems of Ibn al-Asbat[28] relate
that the authorities claimed that Jews, who permit the
drinking of wine, would urge Muslims to do so. Therefore, the Jews announced that they would give up
drinking wine. Ibn al-Asbat's words attest to the fact that
the Jews tried to get the authorities to rescind the order
of expulsion through various intercessors, letters, offers
of money, but to no avail. Eventually they gave up their
efforts and accepted their fate. The poems convey their
acceptance of the expulsion as a manifestation of divine
will and their view that the exile was punishment for
their sins.

Two factors worked in the Jews' favor: the rivalries
among the different rulers in Yemen and the sudden
death of al-Mahdi, which Jews regarded as a sign from
heaven. Muslim sources[29] relate that Yemen was divided
between five different rulers.[30] The Imam Muhammad b.
al-Mutawakkil 'Ali Allah Ismail succeeded al-Mahdi
with the agreement of the different rulers. However, he

ruled in name only. A benevolent figure, and not corrupt, he was called Abu 'Aafiyya ("The Father of Health"), because he never caused anyone bodily harm nor took [their] money.[31] Several of his brothers rebelled against him in 1686 and he was poisoned.[32] The period of his benevolent rule gave the Jews time to recuperate from the Mawza' exile. The letter of the Jews of Dhuran dates from his reign.[33]

The choice of the plain of Tihama as the destination for the expelled Jews indicates that al-Mahdi eventually planned to annihilate the Jews of Yemen, as local conditions contributed to much human suffering and heavy losses. For example, a twentieth-century German tourist described Tihama as follows:

Tihama is a dreadful place because of its terrible heat. Temperatures of fifty degrees centigrade in the shade last for several days. The Bedouins, who are used to a variety of climatic conditions, do not dare to cross the coastal strip between the Red Sea and the mountains of Yemen before sunset.... [T]he meager waters of the inner Tihama are salty and not potable, at least as far as Europeans are concerned. Therefore, for example, the drinking water for the port city Hudayda must be carried on the backs of donkeys from mountains as far as eighty miles away. The climate of Tihama is the most harmful to one's health in the entire Arabian peninsula. Harsh cases of malaria which gradually destroy the health of its inhabitants [occur commonly]. Even the Italian physicians in Hudayda [cannot] do much.[34]

IV

While the Mawza' exile was a local event, which involved only the Jewish community of Yemen, it must be considered within the broader context of the stormy history of world Jewry in the middle-late seventeenth century, in the wake of the appearance of the false messiah Shabbetai Zevi. Was there a link between the difficulties experienced by Yemenite Jewry and the messianic movement of Shabbetai Zevi? Rumors and messages concerning Shabbetai Zevi reached Yemen and profoundly affected many Jews, as in other Jewish communities. The apocalypse *Gai Hizayon* ("The Spectacular Valley"), written in Yemen in either 1666 or 1667, is replete with references to him and the events of his life.[35] The existence of this work proves that messianic ferment had reached its highest level in the Near East at that time.

It is noteworthy that there were harsh measures against Yemenite Jews prior to and during the activity of Shabbetai Zevi. Undoubtedly, some were linked directly to the appearance of Shabbetai Zevi. For example, in 1666, the imam ordered that the leader of Yemenite Jewry, R. Sulayman Jamal, be executed. Rabbi Hayyim Habshush definitely links this event with the Sabbatian movement[36] and the fervent hopes for redemption and the restoration of the Kingdom of Israel, which it aroused.[37] Likewise, the expulsion of Jewish leaders to the island of Kamran in the Red Sea in 1669[38] may have been associated with the Sabbatian movement. In contrast, a humiliating decree which forbade Jews from wearing turbans which dates from 1673 apparently is not related to the Shabbetai Zevi movement even though it was issued during his lifetime.

In conclusion, while there is much detailed information, none of the extant sources in our possession link the Mawza' expulsion directly to Shabbetai Zevi and his movement. Nevertheless, the expulsion should not be viewed simply as an isolated event, totally unrelated to the series of anti-Jewish measures which preceded it. In fact, somehow the Mawza' exile may have been an expression of the prevailing negative reactions on the part of the ruling circles in Yemen and in other Near Eastern countries to the appearance of Shabbetai Zevi and his message of national redemption for the Jewish people.

NOTES

1. Translator's note: This is a translation of the introduction to Yehuda Ratzaby's article in *Zion* 38 (1972). It includes three sets of newly discovered and published sources on the Mawza' exile of Yemenite Jews: the letter of the Dhuran Jews, written in verse and meter, in Hebrew, and constructed by string[s of] biblical phrases; the poetry of Rabbi Shalem Shabbazi, ... in the style of Hebrew liturgical poetry (piyyut), hitherto unnoticed by scholars; and various poems and poetic fragments in Hebrew and Judeo-Arabic, written by several Yemenite Jewish poets and found in manuscripts in the National Library of Jerusalem. This work was published by David Sasson in *Ha-Tsofeh le-Hokhmat Yisrael* 7 (1923): 1–14.

2. This work is included in: Yehuda Ratzaby, "The Mawza' Exile" [Hebrew], *Sefunot* 5 (1961): 383–90.

3. This work is edited by Joseph Kapah in *Sefunot* 2 (1959): 262–65.

4. Ratzaby, "The Mawza' Exile."

5. All of the extant dirges were composed at the beginning of the expulsion and do not recall details about conditions during the exile or its end.

6. The page was used for the book's inner binding. Other pages were glued onto it. It took much time and effort to separate the pages, remove the glue, and expose the written document.

7. It is surprising that this event did not receive attention in Jewish communities outside Yemen, despite the eyewitness account of the emissary, who obviously informed those who sent him about his experience. In contrast, the appearance of a false messiah in Yemen was treated at length in 1867. The emissary, Jacob Sapir, who visited Yemen in 1859, wrote about the latter in *Ha-Levanon* and in *The Second Epistle to Yemen* (1873), both in Hebrew. Rumors concerning that false messiah spread as far as Italy and Russia.

8. Dhuran [is today a village] southwest of San'a, three days' walking distance. In 1911–12, there were some twenty Jewish families, according to S. Yavnieli, *Mas'a le-Teiman* [Voyage to Yemen] (Tel Aviv, 1873), 88. Apparently at the time of the Mawza' exile, [Dhuran had] a large Jewish community. In one . . . [dirge], the poet Ibn al-Asbat refers to the Jews of Dhuran and its environs. [He] mentions the command to the messenger who visits the Jewish communities and announces the exile . . . : "All . . . communities of Hadhur remain! Go to Dhuran and count their inhabitants and their neighbors." In Ratzaby, "The Mawza' Exile," 359, l. 31.

9. Apparently other sources do not mention the emissary from Hebron.

10. Emissaries from the Jewish community of Hebron traveled extensively from 1650 to 1686. They visited Turkey, Italy, North Africa, London, Amsterdam, and Hamburg. See A. Ya'ari, *Sheluhei Eretz Yisrael* [Emissaries from the Land of Israel] (Jerusalem, 1951), 464–73.

11. This apology apparently was responsible for the substantial historical treatment of the Mawza' exile in the letter.

12. Accordingly, I correct the findings of my earlier study (Ratzaby, "The Mawza' Exile," 341–42) which stated that a decree of forced conversion to Islam was changed to exile.

13. Perhaps this fact resembles the account of the "Maharitz," which relates the rumor that eighty Jews died together prior to their arrival at Mawza', in *Megillat Teiman* [The Scroll of Yemen], *Ha-Tsofeh le-Hokhmat Yisrael* 7: 12.

14. See section III of this article.

15. According to Habshush (*Sefunot*, 2: 263), the local authorities in eastern Yemen did not comply with the royal order of expulsion and the Jews of Niham, Aljuf, and eastern Khulan did not leave their homes.

16. He died during the summer of 1681.

17. According to its authors, the revolt was in progress when the letter was written, in 1683–84.

18. The order was valid in 1679–80, namely, 5440 according to the Jewish calendar, before al-Mahdi's death in the summer of 1681. Other sources give different dates (Ratzaby, 1961, 343–44). As the letter was written in 1684, close to the time of the order of expulsion, it probably is most reliable.

19. They cite Rabbi Shimon bar Yohai in particular, thereby attesting their devotion to the Kabbalah.

20. The law prohibiting Jews from building structures taller than those of Muslims existed many years prior to this measure. It was confirmed again by the Imam Yahya in his writ of protection of the Jews of Yemen in 1896. See Rabbi Sulayman Habshush, *Eshkolot Merurot* [Bitter Clusters of Grapes], ed. S. D. Goitein, *Kovetz al Yad* 2, no. 12 (1938): 25.

21. It may be assumed because this copy does not have the signatures of the rabbis and elders of the Jewish community of Dhuran.

22. The letter states that "he [Rabbi Amram] did the same in every town."

23. This is proof that the Muslims destroyed the homes of the Jews after they had left their towns and villages.

24. It is to the credit of Yemenite Jewry that even in its most difficult times, it helped the emissaries from the Land of Israel.

25. These details may be found in Rabbi Shabbazi's poetic dirges.

26. It is noteworthy that the kidnapping of orphans and their forced conversion to Islam existed even then.

27. According to these poems, it appears that . . . Jews [then] engaged in agriculture, generally the work of Gentiles.

28. These details may be found in the poems by Ibn al-Asbat.

29. For example, Muhammad al-Shawkani, *Al-Badr al-Tali'* (Cairo, 1944), 2: 139.

30. The separation between the rulers is hinted by Rabbi Shabbazi: "My enemies dissolved their partnership; In His Anger, He [God] scattered their company" (Ratzaby, "The Mawza' Exile," 352, l. 15).

31. *Al-Badr al-Tali'*, 2: 139–40.

32. Al-Wasi'i, *Ta'arikh Aliman* (Cairo, 1928), 55.

33. He is buried in Dhuran (ibid.).

34. H. Helfritz, *Land ohne Schatten* (Leipzig, 1934), 212–13.

35. This text was published by Gershom Scholem, in *Kovets al Yad* 68, no. 4 (1946): 105–41.

36. *Sefunot* 2 (1958): 157–62.

37. Ibid., 162

38. Ibid., 290–93.

CHAPTER 50

Conversion to Islam among Yemenite Jews under Zaydi Rule: The Positions of Zaydi Law, the Imam, and Muslim Society

Yosef Tobi

INTRODUCTION

For the most part, Islam has followed the principle of no coercion in matters of religion, regardless of whether it pertains to Arabs, Jews, or Christians.[1] This idea appears in the Qur'an in the following passage: "There is no coercion in religion" (Arabic: *la ikrah fi al-din*) (Sura 2: "The Cow," 256).[1a] In fact, in 628, when Muhammad dispatched an officer of his army, Mu'adh b. Jabal, to conquer Yemen, he ordered him not to force Islam upon the Jews and neither to disturb their practice of their religion nor dissuade them from the observance of Judaism.[2] [According to the chronicle of the Muslim historian Ibn al-Atham (d. 926–27), however, during the brief caliphate of Ali b. Abi Talib (656–61), when one group of apostates in Yemen (Sanaa) adopted Judaism after becoming Muslims, "He (Ali) killed them and burned them with fire after the killing."][2a] Nevertheless, there were Jews who converted to Islam. Apparently, all of the Himyarites, whose descendants had converted to Judaism, abandoned the Jewish religion and accepted Islam.[3] Furthermore, three Jewish converts to Islam or of a Jewish origin—Ka'b al-Ahbar, 'Abdallah b. Saba, and Wahb b. Munabbih—were among the important figures of early Islam and played a significant role in transmitting Jewish traditions to their new religion.[4] Similarly, Rabbi Nathaniel ben Yesha (thirteenth–fourteenth centuries), Rabbi Yihye Qorah (d. 1881), and Rabbi Yihye Qafih (d. 1932) relate Jewish traditions which confirm the fact that Yemenite Jewry was not converted to Islam by force. On the contrary, they contend that Yemen served as a place of refuge for Jews escaping Muhammad's wars in northern Arabia or those waged by his cousin, the fourth caliph, 'Ali b. Abu Talib, who conquered Babylonia for Islam.[5] There is no extant information about Yemenite Jewry from the early Islamic period until the tenth century. Moreover, both letters discovered in the Cairo Geniza, which convey information from

rabbinic sources and works written by members of the Zaydi sect contain no evidence of Jewish conversions to Islam during that period. The rule of the Zaydi imams in Yemen was established at the end of the ninth century. Hayyim Hibshush (middle to late nineteenth century) argues that the founders of the ruling dynasty of Zaydi imams adopted a policy of destruction of all non-Muslim communities in Yemen. This subject shall be discussed at length later in this study. First, however, we shall treat the question of conversion to Islam among Yemenite Jews under the different dynasties which ruled Yemen from the twelfth to the sixteenth centuries, prior to the time when the Zaydis actually achieved stability and asserted their power throughout the country.

In the twelfth century, there were two attempts to convert Yemenite Jews to Islam by force. Both occurred during a time of exceptional outbursts of religious fervor. The first took place in the late 1160s, toward the end of the reign of the Hamdan dynasty, by the usurper 'Abd al-Nabi b. al-Mahdi. Maimonides mentions this event in his Epistle to Yemen (1172) as follows: "You have mentioned the affair of this rebel who has arisen in the land of Yemen and has decreed forced apostasy upon Israel, compelling people in all the places that have come under his sway to abandon the Faith."[6] 'Abd al-Nabi was a member of the radical sect of the Khawarij and sought to force his devout and strict beliefs upon all of the Muslims in Yemen. His attempt to forcibly convert the Jews to Islam must be considered against that background. This political pressure brought about two conflicting reactions among Yemenite Jews. On the one hand, there was a revival of messianism which was the major reason for the query to Maimonides by Rabbi Jacob b. Nathaniel, *Nagid* (official leader, literally "head") of Yemenite Jewry and the pretext for the Epistle to Yemen. On the other hand, a Yemenite Jew who had converted to Islam actively sought converts among the Jews. Two contemporary works show nega-

---

Yosef Tobi, *Pe'amim* 42 (1990): 105–26. English translation by Rivkah Fishman.

tive reactions both to messianism and to the presentation of Islam as the true faith and Muhammad as a messenger of God: *Bustan al-'Uqul* (The Garden of Intellects) by Rabbi Nathaniel Berav Fayyumi, father of Rabbi Jacob b. Nathaniel, mentioned above, and the anonymous *Kitab al-Maraqi* (Book of Degrees).[7] In 1173, the Jews were spared from forcible conversion to Islam when 'Abd al-Nabi was defeated by 'Ali b. Hatem, governor of San'a, and after the Ayyubid rulers of Egypt took control over all of Yemen. They restored the status quo ante as far as the Jews were concerned and Jews again were allowed to observe their religion in accordance with earlier Islamic tradition. The second, temporarily more successful, attempt at forcible conversion took place in 1198, under the Ayyubid sultan, Mu'izz al-Din Isma'il (1196–1201). Possibly mad, he viewed himself as the "caliph of the believers" and forced the Jews of Yemen to convert to Islam. He even ordered those who had converted outwardly and later openly returned to Judaism to be put to death. The sultan's death ended this sad episode. According to S. D. Goitein, "it was the act of a crazy ruler and contrary to the laws of Islam."[8]

Conversions to Islam by individual Jews under the Sunni Rasuli dynasty (1229–1454), who ruled from Ta'iz in southern Yemen, appear in a chronicle entitled *Al-'Uqud al-Lu'lu'iyyah* by al-Khazraji, which focuses mainly on the history of the dynasty. Such cases are not recorded in the context of direct coercion. There is no doubt, however, that the Rasuli dynasty encouraged Jews to convert to Islam, as is attested by the respect accorded to two Jewish converts who lived in Zabid. The two men adopted the Islamic religion on 25 Muharram 795 AH (November 1392) and on 4 Dhu Al-Hijjah 795 AH (October 1393), respectively. Both were given fancy clothes and permission to ride on a mule in a procession and were received by the authorities. In addition, the Shari'a court required the Jewish husband of a woman who had converted to Islam on 9 Ramadan 796 AH (July 1394) to pay her all that was coming to her and forbade him to have any contact with her unless he converted to Islam as well.[9]

In conclusion, conversions to Islam were not common among Yemenite Jews prior to the establishment of the rule of the Zaydi imams and the various dynasties maintained the earlier practice dating from the time of Muhammad, which frowned upon forcible conversions. The two episodes in the twelfth century were exceptional. The few extant Jewish sources corroborate this view regarding Yemen prior to the sixteenth century.

THE ZAYDI IMAMS OF YEMEN

Zaydi Rule

Zaydi imams began ruling Yemen in 897, when their founder Imam Yahya al-Hadi Ila al-Haqq (d. 910) took control over northern Yemen and made Sa'dah his capital. Until the sixteenth century, the Zaydis were not able to spread their influence in the central region and in other parts of Yemen. In effect, other dynasties ruled parts of the country. When the Turks took over much of Yemen (1546–1635), the Zaydi Yahya Sharaf al-Din (ruled 1507–1558) and his son, al-Mutahhar (1558–1573), held substantial political importance and even threatened Turkish rule. The Zaydis, who were descendants of Imam al-Qasim, leader of a revolt against the Turks in 1590, took all of Yemen in 1635. The new Zaydi state, which reached its largest size under Imam al-Mutawakkil Isma'il (1644–1676), had to maintain a continuous struggle in order to control the outlying areas of the country, especially to the south and the east. From the early eighteenth century on, different parts of the country were wrested from Zaydi control by local sheikhs and sultans, who declared their independence and ceased paying taxes to the imam who lived in San'a. The descendants of al-Qasim held on until the Turkish conquest of Yemen in 1872. In 1890, a new Zaydi dynasty, the Hamids, came to power. They led a revolt against the Turks and even reached an agreement with them, according to which Imam Yahya (ruled 1904–1948) would be granted authority over internal affairs, including the status of the Jews. In reality, the agreement took effect in 1913. With the departure of the Turks in 1918, Yahya became the sole ruler in Yemen, despite the fact that he had to subdue rebellious tribal leaders in the far corners of his country. He never extended his authority over southern Yemen, namely, the area of Aden and Hadramawt. After the revolution of 1962 and the establishment of a republic, the Hamid dynasty lost control of Yemen.[10]

The Arabs of Yemen are divided equally into two major religious groups: the Zaydis, located mainly in the northern and central regions and the Sunni Shafi'is in the south and west (Aden and Hadramawt). Conflicts between the groups continue owing to current political and social conditions. However, as far as the Jews were concerned, it made no difference whether they lived among Zaydis or Shafi'is. Several scholars have noted that it was better for the Jews under the Zaydis,[11] possibly because of the preservation of pre-Islamic traditions preserved by Zaydi tribes. In any case, as the most stable feature of Yemenite society for the past eleven hundred years, the Zaydi legal system was decisive regarding religious matters.

The Zaydi Sect and Its Law Books

The Zaydis are a Shi'ite Islamic sect named after Zayd b. 'Ali Zayn al-'Abidin b. Husayn b. 'Ali the caliph, the cousin of the Prophet Muhammad and the husband of his only daughter Fatimah. Zayd, therefore, was a fifth-generation descendant of Muhammad. He attempted to wrest the rights of authority from the Ummayads in the Islamic world. According to the Shi'ites, authority belongs only to the descendants of 'Ali. After Zayd fell in battle in 740, the Zaydis separated themselves from the major group of Shi'ites which recognized Muhammad al-Baqir, the brother of Zayd, as the imam who continued the Shi'ite dynasty. Of all the variations of Shi'a, the Zaydi branch is closest to Sunni orthodoxy and is regarded as such by Sunni thinkers. The Zaydi system is almost unique among the various Islamic sects in its adoption of the principles of the Mu'tazilah.[12] The latter emphatically rejects the Isma'ilis' approach, based on allegorical interpretation of the Qur'an and of the commandments of Islam and the preference for the hidden meaning (Arabic, *al-Batin*) over the revealed content (*al-Zahir*). While the Zaydis consistently maintain early Islamic tradition from the period of Muhammad and the early caliphs, they adhere to a gradual development characterized by synchronization with other Islamic systems.

Zaydi imams always regarded themselves as committed to the Zaydi legal system and tradition, especially in light of the fact that the imam served not only as the political and military head of state but also as its spiritual leader, chief justice, and highest religious authority.[13] Many imams also were legal experts and their works served the Zaydi theocracy. For example, the first Zaydi imam, Zayd Ibn 'Ali Zayn al-'Abidin, generally is regarded as the author of a great anthology of hadiths, entitled *Majmu' al-Fiqh* (Anthology of Laws) or *Al-Majmu' al-Kabir* (The Great Anthology).[14] The most important Zaydi authority of law and ideology and the founder of the dynasty in Yemen, Yahya al-Hadi Ila al-Haqq, wrote on numerous topics and is the subject of many works as well. Noteworthy is his fundamental book of Zaydi law, *Kitab al-Ahkam* (The Book of Laws).[15] A substantial part of subsequent Zaydi legal works simply consists of interpretations and commentary on the *Kitab al-Ahkam*.

Two additional important works served as sources for the legal status of Yemenite Jews under Zaydi rule: *Kitab al-Azhar* (The Book of Flowers) by Imam Ahmad b. Yahya al-Murtada (1373–1436) and *Kitab al-Sayl al-Jarrar al-Mutadafiq 'ala Hadai'q al- Azhar* (The Book of the Abundant Spring which Flows from the Flower Gardens), a commentary on al-Murtada by Muhammad b. 'Ali al-Shawkani (1759–1834).[16] Furthermore, *fatawa* (legal opinions) also serve as an important source for the position of Zaydi law to the legal status of the Jews. Zaydi authorities issued *fatawa* in response to practical questions, such as matters of places of residence of Yemenite Jews in the sixteenth and seventeenth centuries. In the eighteenth and nineteenth centuries, some of the subjects included the religion of a Jewish minor whose parents had died and issues regarding menial work and garbage collection for Jews. While several *fatawa* have been published, most are extant only in unpublished manuscripts.[17]

This study will examine the question of conversion to Islam among Yemenite Jews under Zaydi rule, while exposing the tension between the laws in the works of Zaydi scholarly authorities and the reality which was influenced by both society and government officials.

The Relationship between Law and Conversion to Islam

The earliest Zaydi sources, *Majmu' al-Fiqh* by Zayd b. 'Ali and the works of al-Hadi, exhibit a fair attitude toward the Jews, in accordance with the pattern determined by Muhammad. There is no reference to the body of laws characterized by discriminatory humiliation and isolation, known in the Sunni tradition, as *Ghiyar*. While Jews were required to pay the tax (*jizya*) in exchange for protected status (*dhimma*),[18] there are no indications of forcible conversion to Islam and no information about voluntary conversions to Islam. However, there are reports of destructions of synagogues, which allegedly were built illegally and after the Islamic conquest. Similarly, the authorities sought to free Muslim slaves owned by Jews. Nonetheless, Jews were permitted to live according to their religion and even to retain possession of land which they had owned prior to the arrival of the Muslims in Yemen. They also were allowed to hold on to land which they had purchased after the Muslim conquest. Jews had to pay approximately one-ninth of the produce of land which they had not owned before the Muslim conquest as a compensatory tax for the loss of the income to the Zaydi state which resulted from not paying the compulsory tithes which Muslims paid the government for their property.[19]

From the fifteenth century, however, legal works show greater strictness in applying discriminatory legislation against non-Muslims. Such legislation in Yemen, in effect, was directed only against the Jews, as there were no other religious minorities. The *dhimmi* agreement of protection was maintained. For example, in *Kitab al-Siyar*, al-Murtada, the first Zaydi legalist who imposed the *Ghiyar* laws upon the Jews, wrote as follows:

And it is right to uphold the agreement[20] with the Persians or the *Kitabi* ("peoples of the book"),[21] by means of the *jizya*; and those who live in *Dar al-Harb* ("the Land of War") who have converted to Islam should not return to their [original] religion. They shall be required to wear clothing which distinguishes them and shows their subjugation, such as a belt, or wear a discriminatory sign. They shall cut the forelocks of the hair in the center and shall not ride on saddles, but ride side-saddle.[22] They shall display banners only in their houses of worship (literally, churches) and shall not build new houses of worship; but they are permitted to rebuild what has been destroyed. They are not allowed to live outside their own quarters and [may leave them] only with the permission of the Muslims and for a specific purpose. They shall not display crosses on their holidays or in their houses of worship, not ride a horse nor build their houses higher than those of Muslims. They shall sell the Muslim slaves whom they have purchased or acquired by any other means and they shall be forced to free them upon entry into *Dar al-Harb*.[23]

Our study will not treat Murtada's text in detail. It is clear that the statements presented above were influenced by the false *'Ahd 'Umar* (Pact of Umar) and by Mamluk ordinances which relate to *dhimmi*, namely, Christians and Jews.[24] They certainly did not intend to impose Islam upon the Jews. In principle, they preserved the earlier framework of the status of protected peoples, which did not undergo substantive changes in the works of Zaydi scholars of law in the eighteenth century, such as Shawkani, whom we have mentioned above.

Moreover, there is evidence that such attitudes influenced the legal decisions of Zaydi courts in 1877 under Turkish rule. For example, a Jewish lad who had converted to Islam in order to evade punishment for a false accusation was brought before the Zaydi court. According to a Turkish physician whom the boy's relatives sent in order to examine him, and in the name of the Turkish pasha, the lad argued that he unwillingly had converted to Islam. The Zaydi judges had no choice but to answer that they would not force him to convert to Islam. They brought the boy before the court in the presence of the *Hakham Bashi* (chief rabbi), in order that he accept Islam on his own volition. However, as he had stated previously that he did not want to change his religion, the judges released him.[25] Nevertheless, there is no doubt that Zaydi law looked favorably upon the conversion of Jews to Islam and even encouraged it, as will be shown in the description of their official policy.

THE POLICY OF ZAYDI RULERS: INDIRECT COERCION

Generally speaking, the policy of Zaydi authorities may be regarded as "indirect coercion," namely, the application of continuous pressure upon the Jews to convert to Islam in a variety of ways. Direct coercion was used as well, as will be explained later in this study.

Restrictions regarding Residence and Orders of Expulsion

It is common knowledge that Jews lived in the western part of the Arabian Peninsula from the north near the southernmost town of Eilat in Israel today, to the south of which at present is the country of South Yemen. Jews did not reside in the villages in the center of the peninsula, with the exception of Khaybar. From the time of Muhammad, who annihilated the Jewish communities in the region of Medina, the area of Jewish habitation continuously was diminished. It is clear that the Muslim attitude toward the Jews was formed in the generation after Muhammad. The followers of Muhammad held that before his death, their Prophet had commanded that "there should not be two religions in the Hijaz." In fact, there was a fairly systematic policy of eliminating Jewish communities in that region. From the eleventh century, Jews remained only in the southern part of the peninsula.

But even in that area, the Jewish population dwindled, when the communities in Hadramawt were wiped out in the wake of the appearance of the false messiah from Bayhan in 1495, during the reign of Al-Zafar Salah al-Din 'Amr (ruled 1488–1517), the last member of the Shafi'i Tahirid dynasty.[26] Our sources do not indicate the actual reason for the elimination of the Jews of Hadramawt or whether it was accomplished by physical annihilation, expulsion, or forcible conversion to Islam. Later sources indicate that the land of Hadramawt was considered holy even from the time of the *jahiliyyah* (pre-Muslim period) because the prophet Hud was active there. Therefore, non-Muslims were forbidden to live there.[27] In fact, in Hadramawt, there were only a few places where Jews lived, mainly in Habban. Even there, the sparsely populated communities developed relatively late.[28]

For our purposes, what is important is the idea that parts of the Arabian Peninsula were considered holy to Islam and non-Muslims were prevented from living there. This restriction first emerges in connection with Yemen under the Zaydi imam, Al-Mutawakkil Yahya Sharaf al-Din (1507–1558). The question remains as to whether Muhammad's dictum that there cannot be two religions in the Hijaz applies only to the Hijaz or to the entire Arabian Peninsula. The Zaydi imam and his *qadi* Muhammad b. 'Abdallah Dawwa' issued an order based on the opinion of Zaydi and Shafi'i legal experts that the holiness of Arabia applies only to the Hijaz and not to Yemen.[29] It is important because if Yemen were to be included in the area holy to Islam, Yemenite Jews would have had to face a difficult choice: expulsion, death, or conversion to Islam.

In 1667, the legal status of Yemenite Jewry was undermined as a consequence of messianic ferment, which was linked to the Sabbatian movement. The Jews were regarded as breaking their agreement of protection (*dhimma*). Therefore, according to Islamic views, messianic activities constituted an act which removed governmental protection.[30] Moreover, the question of the holiness of Yemen resurfaced along with issue of the right of Jews to live there. The imam, Al-Mutawakkil Isma'il (1644–1676), in whose time the Sabbatian agitation took place, consulted with legal experts from both of the sects in Yemen. He received different assessments and could not make a definitive decision. Close to his death, the view that Yemen was as holy as Hijaz prevailed and, hence, he deemed it necessary to expel the Jews. The decision of the imam derived from his position in the Zaydi Shi'ite tradition, as one who held the authority of the *'ismah*, namely, the right to interpret law (*fiqh*) and was immune from error. However, he could not carry out his decision and left it to his successor, Al-Mahdi Ahmad, the son of his brother Husayn (ruled 1676–1681). In 1679, the Jews of Yemen were given the choice of death, Islam, or expulsion. They preferred expulsion, whose destination at first was the African shore of the Red Sea. After the intercession of several Muslim dignitaries, the imam acquiesced in exiling the Jews to the environs of Mawza' in western Yemen, east of Mokha. Probably, permission was granted because the area of Mawza' was not considered part of Yemen and representatives of European powers and companies were located there as they were forbidden from entering San'a. The well-known affair of the exile of Mawza' lasted for about a year and a half.

Therefore, even though Islam was not forced upon the Jews of Yemen, this sad episode demonstrated that the Zaydi rulers, with the support of the religious figures, indeed threatened to kill or exile the Jews if they did not convert to Islam. When the Jews rejected conversion to Islam, the government tried to limit their places of residence. When, for economic reasons, the authorities overlooked their return from Mawza', they did not permit the Jews to return to their former neighborhoods within the walls of the cities and near the dwellings of Muslims either in villages or towns. They were confined to their own neighborhoods, outside the walls of towns and on the outskirts of villages.[31]

Conversion to Islam in Exchange for Release from Punishment

According to Zaydi religious leaders, conversion to Islam releases a Jew from punishment for an offense committed while he was a Jew, even in the case of a serious crime punishable by a death penalty, or an offense punishable by imprisonment, fines, or the like. Such views contradict Muslim jurists of other sects such as the Hanbalites.[32] Naturally, this law intended to encourage Jews to convert to Islam. In fact, when they stood trial, Jews, even those facing a death sentence, usually rejected the offer of release via conversion. Some, however, succumbed. For example, Rabbi Solomon Jamal of San'a (seventeenth century), a leading figure of the messianic movement in 1667, was sentenced to death by Imam Isma'il. Before the sentence was carried out, he was offered conversion to Islam in order to spare his life. The rabbi refused and, therefore, he was beheaded by the sword, the punishment for rebels. The opposite occurred in 1846, when a Jew named Joseph Alshaikh, who, like other members of his family, minted coins for the imam, was charged with embezzlement. Brought before the Muslim court, he converted to Islam. According to Rabbi Jacob Sappir, he was released. In contrast, in 1862, a member of the same family, Rabbi Shalom Alshaikh, whom an official falsely accused of minting counterfeit coins, rejected the offer of conversion and suffered the death penalty.[33]

CONVERSION TO ISLAM IN EXCHANGE FOR RECEIVING FOOD FROM THE IMAM'S SUPPLIES DURING PERIODS OF FAMINE

According to Zaydi tradition, one of the tasks of the imam was collecting the *zakat* (alms tax) from his Muslim subjects in order to provide funds for welfare and social services, mainly charity for the poor. Non-Muslims were not obliged to pay the *zakat*, whose purpose was to purify its donors and thereby enable them to receive eternal life. The non-Muslim poor are forbidden from benefiting from the income of the *zakat*.[34] Hence, the imams took advantage of this Zaydi tradition. When they distributed wheat and other staples from their storehouses to starving Muslims in times of famine, they prevented Jews from sharing in their food supply unless they converted to Islam beforehand.

Several works attest to the existence of this practice. Rabbi Sa'id Sa'di describes the famine of 1724 in his Hebrew chronicle *Dofi ha-Zeman* (Faults of the Times), as follows:

> Because of our many sins, the famine has become more severe in the month of Tammuz (July). Four or five Jews in this area [San'a] are converting to Islam every day; sometimes as many as ten or more—women, men, and children. The king supplies them with their needs. They number some 750, including accursed women and precious children. Likewise, in the villages, they have become wicked before God [have converted to Islam]. Last but not least, there are the informers [to the authorities], both men and women who show no mercy. For they do not know and do not understand that it is a matter of life and death. Even though they have sinned [converted to Islam], they remain Israelites [Jews]. And, in the future, they will descend to the lowest level of hell and will receive judgment for generations.[35]

This Zaydi practice may explain why there were many Jewish converts to Islam during periods of famine. According to the chronicle of Rabbi Sa'adiah Halevi, written in 1669, such an event took place in 1668: "And there was a severe drought throughout the entire world—east and west, north and south—from one end to the other. Even the wild beasts and domesticated animals and the reptiles which crawl the earth [were affected]. And many Jews converted [to Islam], nearly five hundred or more. It was like the times of forcible conversion, because of the poverty which was present from the outset and because of the starvation which had come upon the world."[36]

Continuous Social Pressure for Conversion

Like other Islamic sects, the Zaydis regarded the conversion of Jews to Islam as a definite sign of the superiority and triumph of their religion. They claimed that, as far as the Jews were concerned, their conversion would serve them well both in this world and in the next.[37] Therefore, they tried to encourage conversion in many ways. There are no accurate statistics regarding the number of converts to Islam among Yemenite Jews. Apparently, however, social pressure was a successful means of bringing Jews to Islam. Such pressures included seduction and enticements, religious polemics, and discriminatory and humiliating legislation.

Seduction

Both government and clerical elements encouraged enticing children, and particularly young and naive girls for the purpose of marriage [which involved acceptance of Islam].[38] Muslims honored a Jew who had converted to Islam by arranging a lavish procession, during which they would shout out loud, "*Zad allah fi din al-Islam*" ("May God enlarge the religion of Islam"). The attitude towards the convert upon his acceptance of Islam was warm and sympathetic. However, owing to importance of the family and tribal relations in Yemen, Jewish converts to Islam usually came from the lower classes of Jewish society.[39] Nevertheless, a Muslim family in San'a, called *muhtadi*, the commonly used epithet for a Jewish convert to Islam, boasted several members who held prominent positions in the government.[40]

Religious Polemics

The purposes of religious polemics were to cause the Jews, by a slip of the tongue, either to acknowledge the truth of Islam or to slander and deny Muhammad and the Qur'an. For example, in his poem "*Ayyahu al-Qasr al-Yamani*," the poet Rabbi Shalom (Salem) Shabazi (seventeenth century) refers to Imam Ahmad al-Mahdi, who ordered the expulsion of the Jews to Mawza', as follows: "And an old fool desired to change the religion of the remnants [Jews]; he wished that my tongue would slip and I would abandon the religion of my Creator."[41] Offending the principles of Islam was considered breaking the agreement of protection (*dhimma*) and would release the imam from his obligation to protect Jewish lives, property, and religion. Moreover, it entailed a severe punishment, occasionally the death penalty. Hence, extremely intense pressure for conversion to Islam was applied.[42] Yemenite Jewish sages, therefore, deemed it necessary to encourage the Jews and teach them proper responses to Muslims arguing against the validity of the Jewish religion. For example, Rabbi Nathaniel Berav Fayyumi's *Gan ha-Sekhalim* (The Garden of the Intellects), the anonymous *Kitab al-Maraqi*, and R. Israel b. Samuel's *Riasalah fi Ibtal al-Diyanah al-Yahudiyyah* (Epistle concerning the Abrogation of the Jewish Religion), all of which were written in the twelfth or thirteenth century, constituted such arguments. Rabbi Abraham Harazi's *Netivot ha-Emunah* (The Paths of Faith), written in the eighteenth century, resembles the earlier works.[43]

Despite the existence of these treatises, Yemenite rabbis warned their communities against being drawn into such disputations.

Discriminatory and Humiliating Legislation

This study will not present a detailed discussion of the discriminatory laws against the Jews of Yemen included in the works of Zaydi scholars and legal authorities from the fifteenth century on. In any case, systematic discrimination increased over time and included laws, which Jews called "the decree of the orphans," and additional restrictions, which were not issued in other Islamic countries.[44] This systematic discrimination served as a means of pressure upon Jews and occasionally succeeded in getting Jews to accept Islam. Rabbi Shabazi's poems, which recall the destruction of synagogues in 1677, refer to such matters. In his poem "*Masa'un fi Rada al-Rahman*" (An Evening of Pleasing of the Merciful One), he writes as follows: "And a savage came with grief and destroyed the synagogues which were built magnificently and he mixed up the religions." In another poem, entitled "*Tair al-Hamam Sharrad li-A'yani*" (The Dove Bird Drove Away Sleep from my Eyes), Rabbi Shabazi states: "Look how the evil of the savage has dispersed me; he has taken my beloved; he rushed me out of the synagogues; I have walked alone; he came to advise me to turn to his religion; because he exulted in my revolt. How can I leave the One [God] the Rock of my Creation, Who guards my path; And desire the despicable religion [Islam], to which he incites me, and forsake my Praised One."[45]

While conversion to Islam was not unusual among the Yemenite Jewish public, as a result of spiritual and psychological collapse caused by despair, occasionally even leading figures in the community abandoned their people and joined the ruling majority.[46] While, according to the Muslims, such cases may have offended Islam by bringing about the abrogation of the agreement of protection, they actually served to encourage the Jews to convert to Islam. Al-Murtada refers to the cancellation of the agreements of protection as follows: "The agreement will be cancelled if all or some of them break it, and if they do not separate themselves from those who remain [Jews] in word and in deed, and likewise, [the agreement] is cancelled with one who refrains from paying the *jizya*, if one is not able to force him [to do so]. We shall say: 'Either he [a Jew] has taken the virginity of or has fornicated with a Muslim woman or killed or seduced or exposed the nakedness or robbed a Muslim on the highway.'"[47] Al-Shawkani comments on these issues, as follows: "If their [the Jews'] obligations are not fulfilled, they revert to the situation in which their persons and property are no longer protected by the agreement, namely to the state of affairs prior to the agreement of protection."[48]

Therefore, Yemenite Jewish leaders and sages constantly repeated their warnings that Jews should not do anything which may be interpreted as offensive to the Islamic religion or encourage jealousy on the part of the Muslims.[49]

THE POLICY OF THE ZAYDI AUTHORITIES: DIRECT COERCION

The Decree of the Orphans

A unique law of the Zaydi authorities of Yemen determined that a boy or girl of protected peoples whose parents died before they had reached maturity had to be raised as Muslims. Scholars have deliberated about the source of this law. In 1938, Professor S. D. Goitein wrote that there was no reference to such a law in any of the Zaydi law books and that such a practice went against accepted Islamic legislation. Goitein stated that "this decree was based on the famous hadith: Everyone was born into the natural religion (namely, Islam). Only one's ancestors made one into a Jew or a Christian (Al-Bukhari, Book 82, Item 3). Therefore, one may conclude that if one's father died before managing to judaize his son, the child must return to and be raised in the midst of the natural religion [Islam]."[50]

In fact, there is evidence that this practice existed in the twelfth century in a work entitled *Tib al-Nufus* (The Healing of the Soul) by Joseph b. 'Aknin, a disciple of Maimonides, as follows:

> There is a new decree, more bitter than the previous one, and it denies our right to inherit and raise our children, and gives them to the Muslims. . . . Thus they seek to have us assimilate among the Muslim community. For the [Muslim] guardians can do with our children and their possessions whatever they wish. . . . For one of their principles is that all children are really born as Muslims, and only their parents will bring them up as Jews, Christians or Zoroastrians. Therefore, if one will raise them in their true religion [Islam] and not allow them to fall into the hands of those [the Jews] who wish to kidnap them [from Islam], Allah will reward him amply. However, if he is evil . . . he is only concerned with money.[51]

However, Jewish orphans are neither the subject of the hadith of al-Bukhari nor that of the testimony of Ibn 'Aknin. The Decree of the Orphans was unique to the Zaydis of Yemen. Many Zaydi legal tracts have been published since the appearance of Goitein's article, and even more recently. For example, a treatise by Ibn Qayyim al-Jawziyya (early fourteenth century), who was not a Zaydi, provides the source of this practice. It presents the most extreme views expressed by the head of the Sunni schools of legal thought (*madhahib*), Ahmad Ibn Hanbal (d. 855). The full text on laws relating to children of protected peoples appears as follows:

Because a child is not independent, there is no escaping the necessity for [appointing] a guardian who will take care of his interests and will be attached to him. It is most proper that the parents determine [the matter] because they are the reason for his existence and he [the child] is part of them. Therefore, they have rights over him which others do not have. They are his closest relations and are the most obligated as far as responsibility for him and his education are concerned. And therefore, it is necessary that he be brought up in their religion and language. Their ancestors made him a Jew, Christian or Zoroastrian. Had they been Muslims, true monotheists, who believed in the one God, they would have raised and educated him in that way and the natural character and education of his parents would have been absorbed by him. However, had they been infidels, they would have removed him from the natural character which God had imprinted upon him, by teaching him polytheism and educating him in that way. . . . And if the child would have grown up with his parents he would have become an adherent of their religion. If he cannot be joined to his parents because of death or by an end to the relationship, as in the case of a child born of an illicit sexual relationship, or born to parents who were separated after a *li'an*[52] or in the case of a foundling, captive or Mamluk, the legal authorities must decide the fate of each child individually.

But as for the first matter, namely, the case of the death of both or of one of the parents, there are three opinions: First, the child will not be converted to Islam, but will remain in his own religion. It is the opinion of the majority and often it is argued that it is the generally accepted practice. For we know that the protected peoples have not ceased dying and leaving orphans. And we do not have any indication that the Messenger of God [Muhammad], the pious caliphs after him, or one of the imams after them commanded that these children of infidels be converted to Islam after the death of their parents. And we know of no such cases in Islam. That is the way of Malik and Abu Hanifah and al-Shafi'i and Ahmad [Ibn Hanbal] in one version of their work. The second view is to instruct that upon the deaths of one or both of their parents, such children be converted to Islam, regardless of whether they died in *Dar al-Harb* or *Dar al-Islam*. This opinion of the school of Ahmad [Ibn Hanbal] is preferred by several of its adherents. It is considered incorrect because of several points, listed below. . . . The third opinion is that the child be converted to Islam if both parents died in *Dar al-Islam* but not in *Dar al-Harb*. It is mentioned explicitly by Ahmad [Ibn Hanbal] and was preferred by most of his colleagues. And they brought proof [of its validity] from the words of the prophet [Muhammad] . . . "Everyone who is born, is born in his natural character [namely, is a Muslim], it is his father who makes him into a Jew, Christian or Zoroastrian."[53]

There is no doubt that the writings of Ibn Qayyim al-Jawziyya influenced Imam Abdallah Ibn Abi al-Qasim, known as Ibn Muftah (d. 1472–73), the first Zaydi legal authority who dealt with the question of the religious status of orphan children of protected peoples. In *Sharh al-Azhar*, a commentary of the work of al-Murtada, Ibn Muftah wrote that in the absence of parents of a *dhimmi* child, living in Dar al-Islam, the child is considered a Muslim, as follows: "Every Muslim child knows that he is bound by the laws of Islam, if one of his parents converts to Islam, even if the other remains a non-Muslim. Therefore, if he is without parents, the child should be a Muslim, when he is in our land, without both of his parents."[54] Apparently, the inclusion of this law in Ibn Muftah's commentary on al-Murtada was not sufficient in convincing all of the Zaydi religious authorities. While it may have been valid for some, two leading figures of the late nineteenth century were obliged to write lengthy and reasoned legal decisions on the subject: *Fi Intiza' Atfal Ahl al-Dhimmah 'ind Mawt al-Aabawayni* (On Confiscating Children of the Protected Peoples upon the Death of their Parents) by Yahya al-Sahuli (1722–1795) and *Risalah fi Hukm Sibyan al-Dhimmiyyin idha Mat Abawahum* (On the Law regarding Children of Protected Peoples upon the Death of their Fathers) by Muhammad al-Shawkani.[55]

There is no proof of Rabbi Amram Qorah's argument that the Decree of the Orphans existed before the first Turkish conquest in the sixteenth century.[56] The earliest evidence comes from the poem by Shabazi entitled "*Masa'un fi Rada al-Rahman*," which mentions that the imam who ordered the expulsion of the Jews to Mawza' "stole the orphans from their families."[57] Other documents dating from that period do not mention this practice. In any case, apparently the legal opinions of al-Sahuli and al-Shawkani in the late eighteenth century have dispelled any doubts regarding the question of the orphans' conversion to Islam. According to Hayyim Hibshush, the Decree of the Orphans was enforced toward the end the eighteenth century during the reign of Imam al-Mansur 'Ali (1775–1809),[58] and throughout the nineteenth century until the Turkish conquest of 1872. Conversions of Jewish orphans were widespread and difficult for Yemenite Jewry. Referring to those times, Rabbi Amram Qorah related that "old men of the previous generation assumed that some ten Jews converted to Islam every week. They included orphans and others who became Muslims because of the pressure of poverty and hard times."[59]

The Decree of the Orphans was not enforced during the Turkish period (1872–1918). However, Imam Yahya enforced it vigorously, despite Rabbi Qorah's claim that the imam encouraged "perfunctory, correct behavior, no searches or scrutiny . . . but, whoever is caught, we shall

hunt down, particularly, a pretty orphan girl."[59a] This study will not elaborate upon the prevalence and consequences of the Decree of the Orphans in the different parts of Yemen during the reign of Imam Yahya (1918–1948) or the determined efforts on the part of the leadership of the Jewish community of San'a and elsewhere in smuggling orphans to areas where they could live clandestinely, even outside Yemen, in Palestine. At all events, the law forcing conversion of orphans to Islam became a salient feature of Jewish life in Yemen. It caused Jews to feel the lowliness of their lives under Zaydi rule and provided motivation for immigration to Israel.[60]

Forced Conversions to Islam by Claimants to the Throne, Seers, and Messianic Figures

Among the Muslim population of Yemen, even during the centuries of Zaydi rule, there were many claimants to the throne, seers, and messianic figures who wished to bring about a new order, based on a stricter version of Islam. Such men emerged particularly in the wake of the increasing influence of foreign political elements, such as the British or the Turks. Like the Almohads of North Africa during the twelfth century, one of their goals was the eradication of other religions in Yemen. It is noteworthy that the Zaydi imams who took power as legal heirs to the throne did not force non-Muslims to convert to Islam.

For example, in 1700, many Jewish communities north of San'a, from the regions of Hajjah to Sudan and Khamir, were forced to convert to Islam by a claimant to the throne in western Yemen. Extremely charismatic, he instigated against the Jews and listened to the advice of the peoples of western Yemen. Under his influence, a substantial number of Jews converted to Islam. Some, however, chose to die as martyrs or escaped and later returned to Judaism after the claimant was killed.[61] Similarly, Faqih Sa'id, who regarded himself as the messiah (the Islamic *al-Mahdi al-Muntazar*, the longed-for messiah) and was active in southern Yemen in 1840 and Sharif Isma'il, who ruled from Mecca and was active in southern Yemen in 1847, sought to annihilate Yemenite Jewry along with other non-Muslims, namely, the British, or to convert them to Islam. Their efforts met with failure.[62]

Kidnapping Young Jewish Girls for the Purpose of Marriage

While this practice was not widespread, it exerted substantial influence upon the Jews of Yemen. Legends of dubious veracity spread through various parts of the country at different times. For example, it was related that a Muslim governor had kidnapped the daughter of the seventeenth-century poet Rabbi Shalom (Salem) Shabazi, in order to marry her. She died before reaching his home. And there was a rumor that one of the wives of Imam Yahya was a kidnapped Jewess.[63]

CONCLUDING REMARKS

In Yemen, the early Islamic tradition of not forcing Jews to convert to Islam was maintained. However, the authorities, the *Sada* (notables), religious figures, and Muslim society generally regarded the existence of Jews as Jews as an anomaly that must be changed via constant pressure. In different ways, this pressure was highly successful in converting Jews to Islam, despite the fact that direct forced conversions were the exception in Yemen. In contrast, conversion as a result of indirect pressure deriving from humiliation or denial of various benefits was rather prevalent. Both written and oral Jewish sources, of course, tried to conceal this embarrassing phenomenon.

Muslim law and the teachings of early authorities which nullified conversions by force or seduction were preserved formally, but in spirit, Yemenite Jews lived under constant pressure to covert to Islam.

NOTES

1. On the attitude of Islam to Zoroastrians, see Ibn Qayyim al-Jawziyyah, Index to v. 2, 988, "al-Majus." Despite the fact that the Zoroastrians were pagans, they were not forced to convert to Islam. (After the Muslim conquest, the Zoroastrian religion had ceased to be the official religion of Persia.)

1a. *Editor's note*: Rudi Paret, however (in "Sura 2,256: la ikraha fi d-dini. Toleranz oder Resignation?" *Der Islam* 45 [1969]: 299–300) argued that 2:256 is not an endorsement of tolerance, but an acknowledgment of resignation. The verse is not a prohibition of intolerance—since the pagan Arabs were forced to embrace Islam or be killed—but a statement that it is impossible to compel one to accept the true faith, i.e., Islam:

[T]he pagan Arabs were forcefully compelled to accept Islam; stated more accurately, they had to choose either to accept Islam or death in battle against the superior power of the Muslims (cf. suras 8:12; 47:4). This regulation was later sanctioned in Islamic law. All this stands in open contradiction to the alleged meaning of the Qur'anic statement, [noted above]: *la ikraha fi d-dini.* The idolaters (mushrikun) were clearly compelled to accept Islam—unless they preferred to let themselves be killed. In view of these circumstances it makes sense to consider another meaning. Perhaps originally the statement *la ikraha fi d-dini* did not mean that in matters of religion one ought not to use compulsion against another but that one could not use compulsion against another (through the simple proclamation of religious truth). . . . The statement of the Qur'an, then, would be not a proclamation of tolerance, but much more an expression of resignation.

2. Azhari, 68–70, 74, 79; Baldhari, 71; Dinur, 13.

2a. *Editor's note:* Ibn al-Atham, *Kitab al-Futuh* (Hyderabad, 1968–1975), 2: 71, quoted in Parfitt, *The Road to Redemption*, p. 18.

3. Regarding the fact that the Himyarites had not really become Jews and that, as far as we know, the Yemenite Jews were not descendants of the Himyarites, see Goitein, *Yemenites*, 4: 344; Qafih, *Links*, 31.

4. On Ka'b al-Ahbar, see Wolfensohn; Schmitz; on Ibn Saba, see Hodgson; on Ibn Munabbih, see Horovitz. Recently there has been a sharp trend among scholars of Islam to minimize the role of these converts in the Islamic tradition. For example, see Juynboll, 121–38.

5. Tobi, *Studies,* 58–61.

6. Translation of the Epistle to Yemen, in Stillman, 234; Maimonides, *Epistle to Yemen*, 4–5; and introduction by A. Halkin, v–vii.

7. Nathaniel Berav Fayyumi; *Kitab al-Maraqi.*

8. Goitein, "India," 63–66, 64 n. 4. This affair was known only from the letter of the Jewish woman from Aden preserved in the Genizah. There is no reference to this in the biography of Mu'izz al-Din Isma'il which is included in the book by Hamdani, part 1, 43–83, although his pretensions of being a caliph are mentioned there in detail, 81ff.

9. Khazraji, 2: 200, 218.

10. For a general survey of the history of the rule of the Zaydi imams in Yemen, see Stookcy, 79–99, 127.

11. For example, O'Ballance, 21.

12. Madelung; Zir.

13. Abrahamov.

14. Zayd Ibn 'Ali. This edition includes an important introduction on Zaydi history and personalities along with detailed indices. For a French translation of selections from *Majmu'*, see Bousquet and Berque.

15. For a list of his works, see Arendonk, 250–305; Wasi'i, 40–44; Zir, 193; on the many manuscripts of *Kitab al-Ahkam*, see: Arendonk, 299–300 n. 8. The major work about al-Hadi, *Sirat al-Hadi*, dates from the first half of the tenth century. See 'Alawi; Abu Zuhra. Arendonk's study is based on this work. For a recently published anthology of the new hadiths of al-Hadi, see Sa'di, Durar.

16. Murtada; Shawkani. For the history of Murtada and a list of his works, see Wasi'i, 40–44; for Shawkani, see Zubara, 2: 297–302; for a list of his works, see Hibshi.

17. Regarding a fatwa that has been published, see: Tazi; for *fatawa* which have not been published and may be found in manuscripts in San'a and Cairo, see Zabarah, 2, 94, and Qorah, 26, notes. Israeli scholars have made extensive efforts to acquire copies of the *fatawa*, without success.

18. On the various *Ghiyar* laws and their application in different countries and in different periods, see Ibn Qayyim al-Jawziyyah, Bat Ye'or, Tritton, Stillman, Fattal.

19. For details, see Tobi, Al-Hadi.

20. It is a well-known term used only in the Zaydi tradition. Al-Hadi mentioned it regarding an agreement which he made with the *ahl al-dhimmah* in Najran. See Tobi, Al-Hadi, 70, 78.

21. One of the *ahl al-kitab* ("Peoples of the Book"), namely, a Jew or a Christian.

22. This means riding with both legs on one side of the animal, like a woman. It is clearly a sign of humiliation.

23. The original Arabic source may be found in Murtada, 322. It comes from the section entitled *Kitab al-Siyar* (Book of Conduct) which is part of *Kitab al-Azhar*. This section may be found in nearly all of the Zaydi law books, such as al-Hadi's *Kitab al-Akham*. It treats the range of laws which govern the relations of the imam with non-Muslims in his land (*Dar al-Islam*) and elsewhere (*Dar al-Harb*). For further details, see: Murtada, 313–15, and the editor's comments in the second edition, 517.

24. On the Pact of 'Umar, see Stillman, 157; on Mamluk decrees, see Mayer.

25. Karasso, 163–65. At that time, the author lived in San'a.

26. For a description of this affair, see Goitein, *Yemenites*, 135–38.

27. The legendary prophet Hud is mentioned in the Qur'an 11: 49–59, hence, the sura is called "Hud." See Wenner, 29 n. 4; Ma'tuf, 8. On pilgrimage to the grave of the prophet Hud and the ceremonies performed there, see Serjeant.

28. Rabbi Zechariah Al-Zahiri, who visited Hadramawt in the sixteenth century states that there were no Jews. Zahiri, 220–27.

29. Ghayat al-Amani, 685.

30. Murtada, 322–23. For a detailed description of Sabbatian events in Yemen, see: Tobi, *Studies*, 82–150.

31. The practice of isolating protected peoples in separate residential areas dates from the classical period of Islamic history. See Strauss (Ashtor).

32. For the opinions of Zaydi legal authorities, see Sappir, 2: 147–48; for the views of the Hanbalite school, see Ibn Qayyim al-Jawziyyah, 2:792.

33. On Rabbi Slyman Jamal, see Tobi, *Studies*, 107; on Joseph Alshaikh, see Tobi, *Nineteenth Century*, 38–39; on Rabbi Shalom Alshaikh, ibid., 58ff.

34. On the *zakat*, see Qur'an 9:60; on the recipients of the *zakat*: 9:104. See also Tobi, Al-Hadi, 62, 79; Murtada, 67–70.

35. Sa'di, *Dofi*, 205.

36. Tobi, *Studies*, 123–24; for similar cases, ibid., n. 60.

37. For example, see Shemen, 130.

38. For example, see Sabari, 136; Ovadia, 40; on young girls, see: Gamliel, *Jews*, 1: 409–15.

39. On giving gifts and honoring Jews who converted to Islam under the Rasuli rulers, see Gamliel, *Jews*, vol. 1, chap. 1, the section before n. 9. For an early twentieth-century example, see Gamlieli, *Hevion*, 86–87. On tribal

and family attitudes: Gamlieli, *Sects*. On mass conversion to Islam in the Damt region in the nineteenth (?) century and the negative attitude toward the Jewish converts on the part of the Muslims, see Gamlieli, *Geulah*, 68–70.

40. On Muslims in San'a who are called al-Muhtadi, see Gamliel, *Jizyah*, 97, 106 and Gamliel, Jews, 1: 216.

41. Hafetz Hayyim, 137.

42. For more recent examples, see Qafih, introduction to Rabbi Nathaniel Berav Fayummi, 10–12.

43. The statements of R. Nathaniel and R. Israel appear in Rabbi Nathaniel Berav Fayummi, 12. On Rabbi A. Harazi, see Nahum, 173–75, and additional material in Ahroni and Halevi.

44. On the decree of the orphans and the restrictive decrees, see Tobi and Tsur, 30–32.

45. Hafetz Hayyim, 460, 328; Seri and Tobi, 10–11.

46. Tobi, *Legacy*, 65–117.

47. For the original Arabic source, see Murtada, 322–23.

48. For the original Arabic source, see Shawkani, 4, 574.

49. For the warning against selling wine to Muslims, see Tobi, *Nineteenth Century*, 197–204; and the warning against wearing fancy clothes in the company of Muslims, see Mahris, end.

50. Goitein, Hibshush, 91 n. 11.

51. Bat Ye'or, 287. On the validity of this hadith regarding Christian children in Syria in 1860, see Bat Ye'or, 224.

52. *Li'an* is a ceremony like that which relates to a woman suspected of adultery in the Bible; see "Li'an," *Encyclopedia of Islam*.

53. Ibn Qayyim al-Jawziyyah, 490–92.

54. Zaydan, 350 n. 4.

55. For al-Sahuli's statements, see Zabarah, 387; for Shawkani, see Hibshi, no. 163. The two treatises exist only in manuscript form and have not been published. Israeli scholars have not seen them. See also: Ratzaby, 130.

56. Qorah, 157.

57. Hafetz Hayyim, 137.

58. Hibshush, History, 166.

59. Qorah, 157. The document was published in: Gamliel, *Jews*, I, 214–16.

59a. It is doubtful whether one can find information concerning the conversion of an orphan in that document, despite the latter's arguments.

60. Shemen, 130–31; Yesha'yahu, 16. On activities relating to bringing the orphans to Israel, see: Klein-Franke.

61. A brief history of this subject by Rabbi Joseph b. Said Halevi Mu'allim of Khamir was first published by Sassoon, 25. See also: Greidi, 111–12; Hibshush, History, 265–66; Goitein, *Yemenites,* 169.

62. Tobi, *Nineteenth Century*, 34–37.

63. On the daughter of Rabbi Shabazi, see Naddaf, 4:1. For a literary version of the story of the imam's Jewish wife, see Amir. See also Gamliel, *Jews*, 1:409–15.

BIBLIOGRAPHY: WORKS IN ARABIC

Abu Zuhra Abu Zuhra, *Al-Imam Zayd* ('Abidin, 1959).

'Alawi 'Ali b. Muhammad b. 'Ubayd Allah al-'Alawi, *Sirat al-Hadi*, ed. Suhayl Zakkar ('Abidin, 1972).

Azhari Muhammad b. 'Ali al-Ahdali al-Husayni al-Yamani al-Azhar, *Bir al-Dar al-Maknun Min Fadail al-Yaman al-Maymun* (Cairo, 1944).

Baladhuri Ahmad b. Yahya al-Baladhuri, *Kitab Futuh al-Buldan*, ed. De Goeye (Leiden, 1866).

Ghayat al-Amani Yahya b. al-Husayn b. al-Qasim, *Ghayat al-Amani fi Akhbar al-Qutr al-Yamani* (Cairo, 1968 [1388 AH]).

Hamdani Al-Amir Badr al-Din Muhammad [. . .] al-Yami al-Hamdani, *Kitab al-Simt al-Ghali al-Thaman fi Akhbar al-Muluk min al-Ghuz bi-al-Yaman*, v. A-B, ed. G. R. Smith (London, 1974–78).

Hibshi 'Ayn al-Hibshi, *Thabt bi-Muallafat al-Allamah Muhammad b. 'Ali al-Shawkani* (n.p., n.d.).

Ibn Qayyim al-Jawziyyah Shams al-Din b. 'Abdullah Muhammad b. Abu Bakir Ibn Qayyim al-Jawziyyah, *Ahkam Ahl al-Dhimmah*, ed. Subhi Salih, v. A-B (Beirut, 1961).

Khazraji 'Ali b. al-Hasan al-Khazraji, *al-'Uqud al-Lu'lu'iyyah Ta'rikh al-Dawluh al-Rasuliyyah*, v. A-B, ed. Muhammad al-Akwa' al-Hawali (San'a\Beirut, 1983).

Kitab al-Maraqi S. Greidi, ed., *Kitab al-Maraqi*, in *Revelation of Yemenite Treasures*, ed. Y. L. Nahum, (Hebrew, Holon, 1971), 288–321; trans. and ed. J. Qafih (Jerusalem, 1944).

Murtada Ahmad b.Yahya al-Murtada, *Kitab al-Azhar fi Fiqh al-A'immah al-Athar* (Beirut, 1972); also published as *'Uyun al-Azhar* (Beirut, 1944).

Nathaniel Berav Fayyumi, *Sefer Bustan al-'Uqul* (Hebrew: *Gan Ha-Sekhalim*) (2), trans. and ed. Y. Qafih (Jerusalem, 1984).

Sa'adi, Darar 'Abd Allah Muhammad b. Hamzah b. Abu al-Najm al-Sa'di, *Durar al-Ahadith al-Nabawiyya bi-al-Asanid al-Yahyawiyya li-al-Hadi Ila al-Haqq Yahya b. Husayn*, ed. Yahya 'Abd al-Karim al-Fudayl (Beirut, 1979).

Shawkani Muhammad b. 'Ali al-Shawkani, *Kitab al-Sayl al-Jarrar al-Mutadafiq 'ala Hada'iq al-Azhar*, v. A-D (Beirut, 1985).

Tazi 'Abd al-Hadi al-Tazi, *Al-Nusus al-Zahirah fi Ijlaa al-Yahud al-Fajirah*, *Dirasat Yamaniyyah*, 123–48.

Wasi'i 'Abd al-Wasi' al-Wasi'i, *Ta'rikh al-Yaman* (Cairo, 1927–28 [1346 AH]).

Zaydan 'Abd al-Karim Zaydan, *Ahkam al-Dhimiyyin wal-Musta'minin* (Baghdad, 1964).

Zir 'Ali Muhammad Zir, *Mu'tazilat al-Yaman: Dawlat al-Hadi wa-Fikruhu* (San'a\Beirut, 1981).

Zubara Muhammad b. Muhammad Zabarah al-San'ani, *Nayl al-Watar* (Cairo, 1931 [1350 AH]).

BIBLIOGRAPHY

B. Abrahamov, "Al-Kasim Ibn Ibrahim's Theory of the Imamate," *Arabica* 34 (1987): 80–105.

R. Ahroni, "From Bustan al-uqul to Qissat Al-batul: Some Aspects of Jewish-Muslim Religious Polemics in Yemen," *HUCA* 52 (1981): 331–60.

Y. Amir Wahab Levi, Kadiya (Jerusalem, 1989).

C. V. Arendonk, *Les debuts de l'imamat zaydite au Yemen*, trans. J. Ryckmans (Leiden, 1960).

Bat Ye'or, *The Dhimmi: Jews and Christians under Islam* [Hebrew] (Jerusalem, 1986).

G. H. Bousquet-J. Berque, *Recueil de la loi musulmane de Zayd Ben 'Ali* (Algiers, 1941).

D. Karasso, "Masa' Teman," in *The Jews of Yemen in the Nineteenth Century*, ed. Y. Tobi (Tel Aviv), 121–90.

Z. Al-Zaihri, *Sefer Hammusar*, ed. Y. Ratzabi (Jerusalem, 1965).

B. Z. Dinur, ed., *Yisra'el Ba-Golah*, v. 1, 1 (Jerusalem, 1926).

A. Fattal, *Le statut legal des non-musulmans en pays d'Islam* (Beirut, 1958).

S. Gamliel, (*Jews*) *Ha-Yehudim ve-Ha-Melech be-Teman*, 1–2 (Jerusalem, 1986–1987).

———, (*Jizyah*) *The Jizyah-Poll Tax in Yemen* [Hebrew], ed. M. M. Caspi (Jerusalem, 1982).

N. B. Gamlieli (*Geulah*) *Teman u-Mahane Geulah* (Tel Aviv, 1966).

———, (Hevion) *Hevion Teman: From the Depth of Yemen: Memories, Folktales and Legends* [Hebrew], (Ramla, 1983).

———, (*Sects*) "The Arabs amongst whom the Yemenite Jews lived: Islamic Sects, their Inter-Relationships and Relations with the Jews" [Hebrew] in *The Jews of Yemen: Studies and Researches*, eds. Y. Yesha'yahu and Y. Tobi (Jerusalem, 1975), 47–69.

S. D. Goitein (*Hibshush*) "An Arabic-Hebrew Book on a Tour in Yemen in 1870" [Hebrew], in *Magnes Anniversary Book*, ed. I. F. Baer et al. (Jerusalem, 1938), 89–96.

———, (*India*) "Yemenite Jewry and the India Trade" [Hebrew], in *The Jews of Yemen: Studies and Researches*, ed. Y. Yesha'yahu and Y. Tobi (Jerusalem, 1975), 47–69.

———, (*Yemenites*) *The Yemenites: History, Communal Organization, Spiritual Life: Selected Studies* [Hebrew], ed. M. Ben Sasson (Jerusalem, 1983).

S. Greidi, "Kavim le-Toledot Yehude Teman be-Meah ha-Shemoneh Esreh," in *Mi Teman le-Zion*, ed. Y. Yesha'yahu and S. Greidi (Tel Aviv, 1938), 106–38.

H. Hibshush, (*History*) "Hayyim Hibshush's 'History of the Jews in Yemen'" [Hebrew], ed. J. Qafih, *Sefunot* 2 (1958): 246–86.

———, (*Travels*) "Travels in Yemen [Joseph Halevy's Journey to Najran in the Year 1870 as related by Hayyim Hibshush's Original Judaeo-Arabic Text and

Translated into Hebrew]," trans. and ed. S. D. Goitein (Tel Aviv, 1939).

Hafetz Hayyim, *Hafetz Hayyim—Shire Rabbenu Shalom Shabazi . . . u-Meshorere Teman* (Jerusalem, 1966).

R. Halevi, "Sippur ha-Ikar Hibbur Abba Shalem Shabbazi," *Afikim* 79 (1989): 12–13.

M. G. S. Hodgson, "'Abd Allah B. Saba," *EI* (2), v. 1 (Leiden, 1960).

J. Horovitz, "Wahb B. Munabbih," *EI* (1), v. 4 (Leiden, 1960) 1084–85.

G. H. A. Juynboll, *The Authenticity of the Tradition Literature: Discussions in Modern Egypt* (Leiden, 1969).

J. Qafih, (*Links*) "Keshareha shel Yahadut Teman Im Merkaze ha-Yahadut," in *Yahudut Teman* (Jerusalem, 1976), 29–46.

J. Qafih, (*Writings*) "Ketavim: Halakhah, Mahshavah, Divre Rishonim, Mishnat Ha-Rambam," in *Yehude Teman*, I–II (Jerusalem, 1989).

A. Klein-Franke, "The Orphans: Their Flight and Their Immigration to Eretz Israel: A Study of a Rescue Operation" [Hebrew], in *Yemenite Paths*, ed. S. Gamliel, M. Caspi, S. Avizemer (Jerusalem, 1984), 85–111.

A. Qorah, *Sa'arat Teman*, ed. S. Greidi (Jerusalem, 1954).

S. Ma'atuf, *Habban (Hadramaut) Jewry in the Last Generations* [Hebrew] (Tel Aviv, 1987).

W. Madelung, "Imam Al-Qasim Ibn Ibrahim and Mu'tazilism," in: *On Both Sides of Al-Mandab: Ethiopian, South-Arabic, and Islamic Studies Presented to Oscar Lofgren* (Stockholm, 1989), 39–48.

Maharitz, "Letter of the 'Mahris' (Rabbi Yihye Salih)" [Hebrew], in *Tiklal Shivat Zion*, ed. J. Qafih (Jerusalem, 1952).

Maimonides, *Epistle to Yemen*, ed. A. Halkin (New York, 1952).

L. A. Mayer, "The Status of the Jews under the Mamluks" [Hebrew], *Magnes Anniversary Book*, ed. I. F. Baer et al. (Jerusalem, 1938), 161–67.

A. Nadaf, *Hoveret Seride Teman* (Jerusalem, 1938).

Y. L. Nahum, *Revelation of Yemenite Treasures* [Hebrew] (Holon, 1971).

E. O'Ballance, *War in Yemen* (London, 1971).

A. Ovadia, *In the Paths of Yemen and Zion* [Hebrew], ed. Y. Tobi (Tel Aviv, 1985).

Y. Ratzaby, "Urban Jewish Life in Central Yemen" [Hebrew], *Sefunot* 19 (1989): 123–64.

Sa'adi, "The Book *Dofi Ha-Zeman* ('The Chastisements of Time') of Rabbi Sa'id Sa'di: Events Befalling the Jews of Yemen during the years 1717–1726" [Hebrew], ed. J. Qafih, *Sefunot* 1 (1956): 185–243.

Yihye Sabari, *Through the Paths of Yemen: The Memoirs of Yihye Sabari* [Hebrew], ed. Y. Tobi (Tel Aviv, 1990).

J. Safir, *Even Sappir*, vol. 1 (Lyck, 1866); vol. 2 (Mainz, 1874).

D. Sassoon, "Le-Korot ha-Yehudim be-Teman"

[Hebrew], in *Ha-Tsofeh le-Hokhmat Yisrael* 15 (1931): 1–26.

H. Schmitz, "Ka'b Al-Ahbar," *EI* (2), vol. 4 (Leiden, 1978), 316–17.

S. Seri and Y. Tobi, *New Poems of Rabbi Shalom Shabazi* [Hebrew] (Jerusalem, 1976).

R. B. Serjeant, "Hud and Other South Arabian Prophets," *Le Museon* 24 (1953): 121–79.

Shemen, "Rabbi Yosef Shemen's Pamphlet, *Haye ha-Temanim* (On the Distress of Yemenite Jewry in the Twentieth Century), by Y. L. Nahum and Y. Tobi [Hebrew], in *The Jews of Yemen: Studies and Researches*, ed. Y. Yesha'yahu and Y. Tobi (Jerusalem, 1975), 95–113.

N. A. Stillman, *The Jews of Arab Lands* (Philadelphia, 1979).

R. W. Stookey, *Yemen: The Politics of the Yemen Arab Republic* (Boulder, Colorado, 1978).

E. Strauss (Ashtor), "The Social Isolation of Ahl adh-Dhimma," in *Études orientales a la memoire de Paul Hirschler*, ed. O. Komlos (Budapest, 1950), 73–94.

Al-Hadi Tobi, "The Attitude of Imam al-Hadi, the Founder of the Zaydi Kingdom to the Jews of Yemen" [Hebrew], in *The Culture and Society of Medieval Jews: Studies dedicated to the Memory of Haim Hillel Ben-Sasson*, ed. M. Ben-Sasson et al. (Jerusalem, 1989), 53–82.

Y. Tobi, (*Legacy*) "The Jewish Community in Yemen" [Hebrew], in *Legacy of the Jews of Yemen: Studies and Researches* (Jerusalem, 1976), 65–117.

———, (*Nineteenth*) *The Jews of Yemen in the Nineteenth Century* [Hebrew] (Tel Aviv, 1976).

———, (*Studies*) *Studies in 'Megillat Teman': Community of San'a, Shabbateanism, Iraqi Family, Mahris* [Hebrew] (Jerusalem, 1986).

Y. Tobi, ed., (*History*) *The History of the Jews of Yemen from Their Own Chronicles* [Hebrew] (Jerusalem, 1979).

Y. Tobi and Y. Tzur, *The Zaydi Sect and the Imams: The Foundations of Their Attitude to the Jews, Unit Two: The Jews of Yemen: Chapters in Their History and Culture* (Tel Aviv, 1985).

A. S. Tritton, *The Caliphs and Their Non-Muslim Subjects: A Critical Study of the 'Umar Covenant* (London, 1930).

M. Wenner, *Modern Yemen, 1918–1966* (Baltimore, 1967).

I. Wolfensohn, *Ka'b Al-Ahbar und seine Stellung im Hadith und in der islamischen Legendliteratur* (Gelnhausen, 1933).

Y. Yesha'yahu, "Pne Teman," in *Mi-Teman le-Zion*, ed. Y. Yesha'yahu and S. Greidi (Tel Aviv, 1938), 5–32.

Y. Yesha'yahu and S. Greidi, eds., *Mi-Teman le-Zion* (Tel Aviv, 1938).

Y. Yesha'yahu and Y. Tobi, eds., *The Jews of Yemen: Studies and Researches* [Hebrew] (Jerusalem, 1975).

Zayd b. 'Ali, *Corpus iuris di Zayd ibn 'Ali, testo arabo . . . con introduzione . . . da eugenio griffini* (Milano, 1919).

CHAPTER 51

The Sephardim in Bosnia: A Contribution to the History of the Jews in the Balkans

Moritz Levy

Our community records provide some further interesting information on special laws applicable to Jews, or, more accurately, to non-Muslims.

Following their arrival in Turkey, the first concern of the Jews expelled from Spain was to adapt their dress to local customs so as to render themselves inconspicuous to the Muslims. They exchanged the three-cornered hat, long skirt, short trousers, and knee-length stockings for the local garb of long and short breeches (*Šalvare* and *Čakšire*) and other garments. However, they were not for long permitted to resemble the Muslims in external appearance, since in 1579 Sultan Murad issued a *firman* [sovereign decree] prohibiting both Jews and Christians from wearing the same apparel as Turks. They were not permitted to wear silk robes in public, and turbans had to be replaced by distinctive caps, which would make the wearer instantly recognizable.[1] My sources are silent on how long this *firman* applied or whether it was valid in all parts of the empire.[2] We learn from the previously mentioned document "Hazad Zewi" by Neshemia Shajon that as late as 1714 the Ottoman authorities were taking strict measures to ensure that Jews and Christians did not wear the same apparel as Turks.[3]

So what were the differences in dress? The authorities do not seem to have paid much attention to enforcing the ban on Jews wearing silk, so that the differences were essentially restricted to head- and footwear. As regards headwear, it should be noted that, for Christians and Jews, not only turbans, but any headwear that was the same or similar to that of Muslims was forbidden. In Bosnia, Jews and Christians had to wear special black caps, known locally as *čita*, similar to those worn by the Capuchins and Franciscans except for the fact they sat lower on the head. The turbans that rabbis were accustomed to wearing as a sign of their status must not be made of white wool or linen. Some other colored material (except green) had to be used, and they must not be too high or wide. As a result, the rabbis wore only a narrow strip of material around their black headdress.

As far as footwear was concerned, the differences lay solely in the color, not in the style. In this respect, women were in the same position as men. Muslim men wore black shoes known as *mestve* with red overshoes (*firale*); for Christians and Jews, the *firale* had to be black. Turkish women wore tall yellow boots with overshoes (*papuče*), while their Jewish counterparts could only wear black footwear of this kind. It is to some extent understandable why the women were dismayed by this restriction, since boots were considered genteel and fashionable. The rich and proud *hanumen*[4] sported them and took it amiss when their Jewish counterparts took to wearing them too, even in concealed form.

The watchful eyes of the authorities did not fail to notice the boots, even when the feet were concealed beneath long outer garments. The authorities were strict on this point and it is therefore not surprising that people felt virtually obliged to resort to means of appeasement. Thus, we find the following entries in the records:

- *1754:* 480 pul (2 groschen, 32 heller), to the captain of the Guard regarding the wearing of yellow boots.
- *1769:* 40 groschen to the Qadi regarding footwear; 13 groschen to the Mutessellim so that he should not pay attention to women's footwear; 16 groschen to the Aga and Treasurer (Haznadar) regarding footwear.
- *1778:* 21 groschen to the Aga regarding footwear.
- *1779:* 5 groschen to the Qadi from Jakob Eskenazi regarding footwear; 1 groschen to the Buljukbaša (captain) so that he should overlook women's footwear; 2 groschen to the Qadi's servant for the same reason; 8 groschen to the Mutessellim for the same reason; 13 groschen to Himzo[5] for the same reason; 2½ groschen for a courier to Travnik with respect to footwear; 18 groschen in fees, sent to Travnik for a letter on the subject of footwear; 80 groschen to the

Moritz Levy, ch. 9 in *The Sephardim in Bosnia: A Contribution to the History of the Jews in the Balkans* (Sarajevo: 1911).

Bašiskije,[6] to annul the footwear decision; 26½ groschen for coffee cups, cupholders (*zarfe*) and confectionery as a present for the Qadi in respect of footwear.

- *1789:* 5 groschen to the Mutessellim regarding footwear.
- *1790*: 21 groschen to the Mutessellim regarding footwear.
- *1794*: 150 groschen to the Mutessellim regarding footwear.
- *1801*: 183 groschen for footwear permits.
- *1804*: 45 groschen to the Qadi and Captain of the Guard for footwear permits.

There is no further mention of footwear matters after 1804.

On top of these restrictions, both Jews and Christians were forbidden to ride horses in towns and their precincts. When Christians or Jews set out on a journey, they had to wait until they were outside the town before mounting their horses. Even outside the town, non-Muslims must not be ostentatious or conspicuous. The harness must be cheap and simple. The saddle must not have fittings of silver or any other metal, or have fringes or any other decoration. The reins must be made exclusively of black leather (not red, white, or yellow) and be without tassels or other appendages on the horse's head, neck, or mane, as was customary among the Turks of Bosnia. There is only one brief mention of these matters in the records, from 1804, which states: "22 groschen to the Qadi and Mutessellim, for permission to ride horses at the funeral of the Shasham David."[7]

It will come as no surprise in the light of the above that Jews and Christians were forbidden to carry guns, sabers, and other prestigious weapons.[8] For their protection they could carry only a short knife in the belt and perhaps a pistol, as long as the butt was undecorated. Mosaic purity laws stipulate that women must bathe in living (flowing) water after each menstruation; otherwise sexual relations are strictly forbidden. For this purpose, the Jews of Sarajevo had paid out of their own funds for the construction of a pool meeting rabbinical standards in the public baths[9] in the Čaršije (market), for which, in addition to the fee for every individual bather, they paid an annual rent of ten groschen a year to the owner of the baths. For unknown reasons, however, the Qadi forbade Jewish women from visiting the baths after the second hour before sunset, i.e., at precisely the time when Jewish law prescribes the aforementioned ablutions. In this respect we find in the records: "*1767*: 53 groschen to the Qadi for permission for women to visit the baths after the Ikindi."[10]

The same point appears in the records for 1769 and 1778.

An interesting curiosity is a plan to carry out death sentences by hanging at the Jewish ghetto gates. In this respect, we learn the following from the records: In 1748 a Turkish woman was sentenced to death by hanging. The Buljukbaša, who also seems to have been the public executioner, wanted to hang the criminal—apparently in order to subject her to the scorn and derision of the populace—at the Jewish ghetto gates. The Jews, in order to avoid this ridicule, which was indirectly aimed at them, offered four thousand pul (about sixteen groschen) to the Buljukbaša, who, following receipt of the money, carried out the hanging somewhere else. In the entry for 1747 we read in so many words: "4,000 pul to the Buljukbaša so that he does not hang the Turkish woman at the ghetto gates." So a pretext was found for using the ghetto gates as a place of execution; the Buljukbaša apparently derived pleasure from this, while knowing full well that the Jews would pay him to abandon the plan. And we do indeed find payments to the same official recorded almost every year until 1802, "so that he should not hang Christians on the ghetto gates." At first the price fluctuated, but later on it seems to have stabilized at one groschen to the Buljukbaša for each hanging. Entries in the records inform us:

- *1753*: 660 pul to the Buljukbaša so that he should not hang a Christian at the ghetto gates.
- *1754*: 1,260 pul to the Buljukbaša to prevent 3 hangings at the ghetto gates.
- *1766*: two groschen for one hanging.
- *1779*: one groschen for one hanging.
- *1785* and *1787*: one hanging each, two groschen.

And so it goes on until 1802—twenty-two hangings at a rate of one groschen apiece. Were it not for the fact that some of the annual accounts have not been entered into the records, one could have established the total number of hangings in Sarajevo over a fifty-five-year period.[11]

Also of interest are the entries concerning "loans" contracted by the town from the Jews. So our proud Sarajevo community was paying such loans 170 [years] ago. These did not amount to millions, since in those days people were more modest and were satisfied with a few thousand pul. The citizens did not make special demands on the esteemed City Council. According to the records: in 1738, 12,000 pul (about 9 crowns) borrowed by the town; in 1742, another 12,000 pul; and so on and so forth until 1777. In 1766 the debt reached its highest level at 55,890 pul (some 39 crowns).

*For further clarification of any references, see original essay.

NOTES

1. Grätz, *Geschichte der Juden*, vol. 9, p. 409. From a report by the Venetian ambassador Maffeo Venier.

2. From the sources consulted, it appears probable that these measures were aimed exclusively at the Jews of Constantinople.

3. See also Novakovič, *Geschichte*, p. 75.

4. Respectable Turkish women.

5. Turkish proper name.

6. The population of Bosnia and Herzegovina was divided into different local groups known as Jemat. At the head of each Jemat stood a Bašiskija. (It corresponds roughly to the still existing institutions of the Jematbaša and Bašmuktar, which derive from Turkish times.) This was a prestigious position; there were five such Jemat in Sarajevo.

7. The Jewish cemetery is located on a rather steep hill, at that time some distance away from the city, presenting a difficult climb in winter. This burial must have taken place in winter.

8. See Novakovič, *Geschichte*, p. 75.

9. The ruins of these baths can still be found today in the little street of Čulhan. Jews and Christians were not allowed to use the other two baths, Isa-Bey and Ghazi Husrev-Bey.

10. The third daily prayer—two to three hours before sunset—of the five daily prayers that the Prophet Muhammad prescribed for Muslims. The people measured the day by these prayers.

11. Apart from in the initial case, all the condemned were Christians.

CHAPTER 52

Palestine under the Rule of Ibrahim Pasha

E. R. Malachi

I

... In the late 1820s, Turkish Palestine was conquered by the Egyptians and its governor was Ibrahim Pasha.[1] An enlightened and admired figure, Ibrahim Pasha made changes in law and administration in the country. One of his new laws was military conscription of both the rural and urban Arab residents, who, in the past, were released from military service under the Turks by paying a tax. The Arabs rejected the new law and decided to resist conscription. However, Ibrahim Pasha was determined to carry out his program and threatened punitive measures, while enforcing the draft. The city dwellers exploited the resentment of the fellahin (peasants) and incited them against Ibrahim Pasha by branding him a heretic or a Christian disguised as a Muslim, thereby preaching a holy war against him.

Even before the outbreak of a full-scale, organized rebellion, riots occurred throughout the land. The Bedouins and fellahin began by ambushing and robbing those who traveled on the roads. Ibrahim Pasha, who learned of the planned rebellion while in Alexandria quickly dispatched troops to Palestine. He tried to quell the outbreak of violence in a piecemeal fashion. For example, upon hearing that Nablus (Shechem) was a hotbed of sedition, he went there. On his arrival in Nablus, he was honored by the mayor and the notables. Even the heads of the tribes of fellahin came to pledge their loyalty to him. But Ibrahim Pasha did not trust them and learned of a plot to assassinate him at the local soap factory from one Hasin. The two fled Nablus in the darkness of night. The Nablus encounter served to ignite the flames of revolt everywhere. While Ibrahim Pasha gathered his forces in order to subdue Nablus, he heard that the revolt had spread and that an army of Bedouins and fellahin, along with residents of Nablus area were on their way to Jerusalem.

II

Early nineteenth-century Jerusalem was a city surrounded by strong walls and iron gates. The governor of the city would close the gates and refuse permission to those who wished to enter or leave it. The fact that a company of soldiers loyal to Ibrahim Pasha was stationed there encouraged those who entertained hopes that the fellahin would not launch an attack on the city. These hopes, however, were dashed when forty fellahin from Bethlehem took the city stealthily by sneaking into Jerusalem through the sewage canals of the village of Silwan at midnight. At that point, a large group of riffraff joined the invaders and opened the gates of the city and "at once thousands [of fellahin and Bedouins] entered."[1a] The soldiers tried to fight against the rebels, but when they saw the increasing number of riffraff they came to the conclusion that they could not win and ran away, seeking refuge in their barracks in the Tower of David.

A riot broke out and the rabble began attacking the Jews, plundering their property and even murdering them. Many Jews hid in their homes or in the caves and crevices in the rocky hills surrounding Jerusalem. Rabbi Jehoseph Schwarz described the situation in Jerusalem on the night of the attack on May 31 (22 Iyar) as follows:

> The savage victors, men, women and children surrounded the markets and the streets and cheered and shouted the strange catcall, "loo, loo, loo" [ululated]. Their savagery mingled with the noise of the soldiers and cries of the unfortunate inhabitants of the city, which had become a scene of terrible fear. And at dawn, we looked through our windows and saw that the city was full of wild and cruel Bedouins. We assumed that all was lost, as several homes had been devastated.[2]

While all this was going on and the rabble had decided to take the Tower of David, rumor had spread that Ibrahim Pasha was advancing on Jerusalem. The very

This article, originally published in *Ha-Doar* 14 (1935), 28–31, was translated by Rivkah Fishman from A.[*sic*] E. R. Malachi, *Studies in the History of the Old Yishuv* (Tel Aviv, Israel: 1971), pp. 65–78.

sound of the name "Ibrahim Pasha" inspired fear in the hearts of the rebels, and they hastened to flee the city. When Ibrahim Pasha arrived, the Jews were relieved and returned to their destroyed and plundered homes. To their joy, Ibrahim Pasha had subdued the rebels, but only temporarily. One of their leaders, Qasim al-Ahmar, assembled a large force and again attacked Jerusalem. Ibrahim Pasha lost this battle and had to leave Jerusalem quietly for Jaffa. In Jaffa, he met his father Muhammad 'Ali, the governor of Egypt, who hastened to help him with substantial naval and ground forces. The rebels in Jaffa and the neighboring villages surrendered to Ibrahim Pasha, who hanged them and punished the people by levying taxes and ordering military service. That first conscription only affected Muslims, but later Christian Arabs as well because a Christian had killed a soldier. Despite his victory in Jaffa, however, he could not suppress the revolt and bring calm to the country. The rebels were prevailing in Safed, Tiberias, and Hebron.

III

The revolt in Safed began on June 14 (7 Sivan), the day after the Jewish festival of Shavuot (Pentecost). The governor tried to put it down, but when he realized that he could not, he handed the city to the enemy and escaped. At the time, Safed was the most important Jewish community in the country and numbered some "two thousand households."[3] It was divided into three groups: Sephardim, Perushim [disciples of Rabbi Elijah, the Gaon of Vilna], and Hasidim. Most Hasidic and non-Hasidic immigrants from eastern Europe chose Safed as their place of residence. The leaders of the Ashkenaznic communities were: Rabbi Israel Porush of Shklov, a disciple of the Gaon of Vilna and author of the halakhic tracts, *Thaklin Hadathin* (New Shekels) and *Peat Ha-Shulhan* (The Corner of the Table); Rabbi Gershon Margolis; and the Hasidic rabbi Abraham Dov Baer of Ovruch, author of *Bat 'Ayin* (Pupil of the Eye). They were respected by the authorities and by Muslim religious leaders and Jews generally lived peacefully with the Arabs and often were partners in business. Arabs often used the services of Jewish craftsmen.[4]

When the riots broke out, at first the Jews did not know whether to remain in Safed and guard their property and their homes or to hide until the situation improved. In the meantime, the pogroms had started. Arabs had begun to attack Jews physically and to rob their homes. Several soldiers, loyal to Ibrahim Pasha, remained in the town and tried to protect the Jews, but the rebel forces numbered several thousand because residents of surrounding villages had joined them.[5]

Therefore, the Jews were defenseless and their situation continuously worsened. Furthermore, as many were newcomers to Safed, they knew neither Arabic nor local customs. They did not even know where to flee or hide. Those who could sought refuge in villages near Safed,

such as 'Ayn Zaytun, Biriyah, and Meron where they had Arab acquaintances who had promised to protect them for a substantial payment. However, while en route to their destinations, other Arabs attacked them and stripped them of their clothing, so they arrived naked and barefoot. In his work, *Iben Safir* (1: 1–2), the traveler Jacob Safir describes the condition of the refugees of Safed in 'Ayn Zaytun, as follows:

> For three days we did not eat a thing. Afterwards they gave us a small cake for a whole day's sustenance. We stayed there for forty days in fear of death by the robbers. Our property was taken by strangers and we were not certain that we would survive. We appeared naked, for they had stripped us of our clothing and emptied our homes of everything we owned. They did not leave small items, a door or a window.

Several Jews had escaped to an ancient fortress near Safed which they called "the palace of Joseph b. Gorion, the *kohen* (priest)."[6] Sequestered there for four weeks, they were surrounded by bandits who attempted to demolish and break through the building. But the fortress was sufficiently strong and their tools could not destroy it. Therefore, it was abandoned after the rioters demanded that the Jews give them their money. The Arabs slaughtered the Jews who could not flee Safed. Many who hid in caves and graveyards were found out by the vandals and killed in their hiding places. Among the wounded, who hid in a grave, was Rabbi Nathan Neta', the son of Rabbi Mendel Porush of Shklov, whose eye was gouged out by the bandits. However, most found refuge in synagogues and houses of study, where entire families were sheltered, who were "full of wounds and bruises."[7] There they wept, prayed, and pleaded with God to save them from danger. They fasted, blew the shofar and awaited their death.

The savage crowd then launched attacks on synagogues and on all the Jews. They did not show compassion toward the elderly or the young, children or pregnant women. They burned Torah scrolls and tore holy books, ripped prayer shawls and phylacteries (*tefillin*). Over five hundred Torah scrolls were burned, among them the scroll of Rabbi Isaac Aboab, the prized possession of the community of Safed, viewed as a source of miracles and legends for the faithful. In addition, the Torah scroll of Rabbi Isaac Luria, the famous kabbalist of the sixteenth century, which had been placed on top of the grave of the second-century sage Rabbi Simon Bar Yohai, in Meron, was torn to shreds. For several weeks, pieces of that Torah scroll were to be found in the streets of the city. In the introduction to *Peat ha-Shulhan* (Safed, 1836), Rabbi Israel Porush of Shklov wrote that "they [the Arabs] looted and discarded all of the holy phylacteries and the mezuzahs of our homes and they took [parts] from the Torah scrolls and made reins for their horses and shoes for their feet." Rabbi Menahem Mendel of Kamenitz wrote in a similar vein, as follows: "They made shoes and aprons for blacksmiths from Torah scrolls. They ripped phylacteries and took the straps for tying sacks and made sashes for their bodies from prayer shawls and they tore volumes of the Talmud to shreds."[8] The rioters tortured women and children in the synagogues and "defiled gentle women on parchment scrolls of the Torah"[9] in front of their husbands and their children. Those who tried to protect their wives and courageously defend their honor were murdered by the bandits.

IV

Several historians have tried to defend the actions of the rioters somewhat by claiming that neither a desire for removal of the Jews nor bloodthirstiness motivated their attacks, but rather their passion for taking the Jews' possessions. The impoverished Arab masses believed that the Jews were extremely wealthy and had hidden stores of gold in their homes. Therefore, the rioters simply were after money and booty, which they could extract from the Jews by threats. They killed the Jews for their property. In any case, the lives of the Jews were dependent upon them. When the Arabs attacked, they demanded payment for sparing their lives, but when they received the money, they resumed the attacks and demanded more. A particular target was the Gaon Rabbi Israel Porush, leader of the Perushim, who suffered terrible torture in his house of study. The attackers threatened to kill him, placing a sword upon his neck, if he did not give them all of the money of his community, of which he was in charge. After pleading with the rioters, Rabbi Israel was able to save himself by paying them his last seven gold rubles. Aware of imminent danger to his community, he ordered them to flee the city. However, among them were many sick, elderly, and weak people who could not undertake such a journey. Rabbi Israel found shelter for them in the vineyard of an Arab. Those who did not flee were murdered. Meanwhile, the refugees in 'Ayn Zaytun learned that Rabbi Israel was in danger and they paid several Arabs to proceed to Safed in order to bring the rabbi 'Ayn Zaytun. When the Arabs came for Rabbi Israel, the Jews thought they had come to kill them and burst into tears. However, the Arabs calmed them and on Rabbi Israel's request, took all the Jews with them.[10]

Many Hasidim found shelter in the house of the *qadi*, who promised to protect them for a fee paid from the community fund by their leader Rabbi Gershon Margolis. The rest, about six hundred people, among them Rabbi Abraham Dov Baer of Ovruch, fled to one of the ruined houses on top of a mountain near Safed. They remained there for several weeks, suffered terribly, and were extremely distressed about their fate and that of their brethren who had been scattered in these weeks of

riots: "No one knew where they were and they did not know where their husbands, wives or children had gone."[11] In addition, they were sad "when they heard about the glee of the looters in the city who had plundered the Jews and whose shouts of joy were heard from afar."[12]

Even those who found refuge in 'Ayn Zaytun were fearful and shuddered at the slightest noise. Although they were hungry and thirsty, they were afraid of leaving their hiding place until they heard that the riots had ceased. Some disguised themselves as Arabs and returned to Safed in order to save their property and the money of the community and remove the sick and the wounded. Several Jews saved some of their property after coming to terms with the robbers and dividing it.

When the riots first broke out, there were Jews who gallantly and courageously defended themselves, their families and their property. The Hebrew account, *Korot ha-'Itim* (Events of the Times, 4:2, 5:1) by Rabbi Menahem Mendel of Kamenitz mentions two who acted honorably in order to protect their families and property, as follows:

And behold, Rabbi Jacob Hirsch of Moghilev and a Sephardic rabbi closed the entrance to their front yard and brought many stones to the roof of their houses. They went up to the roof in order to throw the stones at anyone approaching their yard. The looters became angry and shot and killed the Sephardic rabbi and wounded Rabbi Hirsch. Afterwards they entered the yard and plundered the premises, stealing everything, even stripping the clothes from the dead bodies and defiling the women who were in the yard.

When they finished dividing the loot among themselves, the robbers took a short break and declared, *Thaman*, in Arabic, thereby calling an end to the violence and allowing the Jews to return to their homes. However, the Jews had barely managed to leave their hiding places when the riots resumed. When there were no Jews on whom to take vengeance, the rioters vented their anger in random violence, burning houses, shattering furniture and household goods which they could not take. In *Das Heilige Land* (The Holy Land [Frankfurt, 1852], p. 253), Rabbi Jehoseph Schwarz relates that one of the Arabs stole a large wooden crate full of clothing and dishes, which was so heavy that when he bent down, it fell on his head and he died. Another robber was reprimanded by his mother, who did not allow him to join the rioters and leave his home in order to attack the Jews. His anger was so intense that he stabbed her with his dagger, and as she was dying he hurried to loot Jewish homes. During the riots, the robbers totally destroyed the printing house established by Rabbi Israel Bak[13] and beat him, permanently injuring his legs.[14]

Drunk with their victory over the Jews, the Arabs apparently forgot their main objective: their revolt against the government. All their anger and frustration had been focused on the Jews. Their good fortune was that Ibrahim Pasha was in Hebron and therefore, no one could stop their violence. Safed was isolated from the world. In order to see to it that reports of the violence would not reach the consuls of European countries who were stationed in Beirut, the rioters placed sentries on the roads. Thus, they could ambush the Jews, most of whom were subjects of the various European states, when they attempted to leave Safed. According to *Korot ha-'Itim* (5, 2), there was careful Arab surveillance:

While we were in the courtyard . . . , Rabbi Abraham Baruch approached us and informed us that when the looters heard that three Jews, namely, Shemaiah and two Ashkenazic men, had gone to inform the consul about what had been done to the Jews, they [the looters] told them [the Jews] to hand those men over to them. If not, they would kill all the Jews in the town.

Similarly, Rabbi Israel Porush relates that "at that time, all the roads were blocked. One could neither enter nor leave Safed in order to inform representatives of the [foreign] governments in the ports near the Land of Israel." By chance, a Jew from Beirut who happened to meet Rabbi Israel informed the consuls about the imminent danger to the Jews.[15] When the consuls were told of the events, they immediately turned to Ibrahim Pasha, who hastened to put an end to the uprising by sending a large force headed by Bashir, the Druze emir in Lebanon. The news that Bashir was about to invade Safed terrified the rebels. Some, however, tried to resist him and even forced the Jews to transport their weapons to the battle field. Among them, according to *Korot ha-'Itim*, was Rabbi Mordecai of Pinsk. But the rebels quickly understood that it would be better for them either to escape or to surrender to Bashir.

Bashir entered Safed on July 17, 1834 (10 Tammuz 5594), and the riots ceased immediately. He placed guards in the Jewish quarter and proclaimed that anyone causing bodily harm to a Jew would not be exonerated. The Jews slowly returned to their gutted and looted homes.

The violence lasted thirty-three days,[16] during which the town nearly was destroyed. Many Jews were killed and hundreds were wounded. The estimated damage to property was extremely high. However, Bashir avenged the Jews and punished the leaders of the rebels very severely. Thirteen of them, including the governor of Safed, were brought to Acre, where they were put to death in a cruel manner. Furthermore, Ibrahim Pasha levied a heavy tax on the Arabs in order to pay the Jews for damage to their property. However, because of the riots of 1838, the Jews received only a small amount of this money.[17]

The Jews of Tiberias were left alone. The Arabs were planning to attack them, but at the last minute they decided not to harm the Jews, but simply to take ransom from them. They demanded a huge sum of money and the Jews were in danger until they paid in full. They painstakingly collected an enormous amount (one hundred purses, the equivalent of five hundred pounds sterling) after selling all their belongings. In *Giv'at Shaul* (p. 83), Shaul Hornstein recalls the situation of the Jews of Tiberias, as follows:

And the enemy did not enter the holy city of Tiberias because a man named Anul al-Agar who was known among the Arabs for his heroism, and therefore, was given the position of governor. All the Bedouins and Arabs obeyed him. His word spelled life or death for them. And a Jew from the holy city of Tiberias, Uri Leib Consantiner who is still alive, was his assistant. Therefore, he liked the Jews of the holy city of Tiberias and helped and supported them and preserved the town and did not allow the enemy to enter.

However, the latter apparently is an apocryphal tale reported by a Dr. Sfati. For historical sources indicate that the governor collaborated with the rioters in order to compel the Jews to pay ransom. In his introduction to *Peat ha-Shulhan*, Rabbi Israel Porush recalls: "And in Tiberias, may it be finished and completed, the Jews were surrounded and were forced to pay ransom to the Gentiles in the town." And in *Korot ha-'Itim* (6, 2), Rabbi Menahem Mendel of Kaminetz notes:

When the Jews of Tiberias heard what the rioters had done in Safed and that they also wanted to destroy the Jews in Tiberias, they agreed to give them 100 purses, the equivalent of 500 Pounds Sterling in gold coins. Despite this, they reneged and wanted to rule over them for the period of 33 days when the Philistines [rioters] had come to both Safed and Tiberias. However, Ibrahim Pasha ordered that the ransom money be returned to the Jews.

The Jews of Hebron suffered terribly during the riots. They were victims of both the rioters and the army of Ibrahim Pasha. It was with great effort that Ibrahim Pasha conquered Hebron because the rebels from Shechem and Jerusalem took refuge there and it was the scene of a major battle. When he took Hebron, he gave the soldiers permission to control the city for six hours and to loot and destroy it. The Jews were victims because the soldiers did not distinguish between the rioters and the Jews. They raided their homes and defiled any women whom they found. Had Ibrahim Pasha not hastened to come to their aid, there would not have remained a single Jew left in Hebron. The pogroms in

Hebron took place on July 24 (17 Tammuz, a Jewish fast day). When the rumor of attacks reached Safed, Rabbi Israel Porush composed a prayer of lamentation for the martyrs of Hebron.

No harm came to the Jews of Jerusalem. During the suppression of the revolt, however, Rabbi Joseph of Lyadi was killed by one of Ibrahim Pasha's troops. The soldier knocked on the door of the rabbi's home and when he opened the door, the soldier killed him.[18]

V

The Jews of Safed had not yet recovered when another calamity struck them. In 1838, the Druze rebelled against Ibrahim Pasha. As in the previous revolt, the rebels used the occasion in order to attack and murder the Jews and loot their property. In late June–July (Tammuz),[19] they tried to take Safed. The governor of the town immediately gathered his forces and sent his brother 'Abd al-Kader to fight against the Druze. He also requested that the Jews assemble in their synagogues and houses of study in order to pray for his victory.

At that time, the distinguished linguist Dr. Louis Loewe (Hebrew, Eliezer Ha-Levi), the secretary of Sir Moses Montefiore, was in Safed. He sent a request to the local authorities to protect Jewish lives and property. The governor pacified him and promised him that the Jews would not suffer from the rebels. In order to prove his point, he sent several soldiers to protect the Jewish neighborhood. However, the town came under siege and the Jews began to fear imminent pogroms. The Arabs began to whisper in public that they intended to attack the Jews tomorrow or the day after.

Many waited impatiently for the Druze onslaught and joined them in order to plunder the Jews. Fearing the worst, most of the Jews left their homes and gathered at the residence of their leader, Rabbi Abraham Dov Baer of Ovruch. That night, the Arabs surrounded the rabbi's house and scared the Jews by making strange and loud noises. At midnight, the Jews summoned Dr. Loewe to come quickly to the house of the rabbi, as they sensed that they were in mortal danger. When Dr. Loewe arrived, he found the house full of men, women, and children of all ages who were weeping and wailing. They congregated around him, kissing his hands and pleading with him: "Save us from this horrible death." Dr. Loewe hastened to the governor and again was promised that no harm would come to the Jews.[20]

Later, rumors had spread throughout Safed that the Druze had entered the town. The rabbi again sent for Dr. Loewe and asked him to accompany him to plead with the rebels to show mercy to his people. They had barely managed to leave the house when the Druze suddenly emerged. The rabbi addressed him tearfully, saying: "We are ready to pay any amount of money in order to save our lives. Do not harm any of the poor Jews." The Druze replied that they would discuss this matter later but first they demanded the money. One of them approached Dr. Loewe and stripped him of his clothing. He took his money and then gave the signal for all of the Druze to enter the house.

When the Druze rebels entered Safed, the governor did not try to fight against them but ran away in order to save his life and fled the town. The Druze then joined the Arabs and attacked the Jews, the purpose of which was to annihilate and plunder them. The Jews began to flee but the Druze pursued them, surrounding them on all sides and assaulting them.[21] Afterward, they stripped them of their clothing and permitted them to escape. The departure of the governor also encouraged the Arabs who had lived peacefully with the Jews to join the rabble when the attacks began. Together, the Druze and the Arabs raided all of the homes belonging to the Jews and plundered their property. What they could not take with them, they burned or destroyed. Then they proceeded to the synagogues and houses of study, where many Jews had assembled. After they burned the Torah scrolls, they forced them at sword's point to hand over their money and stabbed those who refused to do so.

Several Jews managed to escape. They hid in the cemetery, where they lay for three days, pretending that they were dead, until the Druze left the town. Many Jews fled to 'Ayn Zaytun, but the Druze overtook them and tortured them brutally. Five Druze armed with knives, pistols, axes, and clubs, broke into a house where many Jews were hidden and beat them cruelly until blood flowed. They then took them out and placed a sword on their necks in order to scare them into giving them money. When they learned that the Jews had no money in their bags, they stripped them naked and left them. But straight away, another group of Druze arrived and began to molest them. The unfortunate Jews begged to be killed rather than be tortured by them, but the rioters closed their ears and continued their fiendish games until several Jews died out of fear and terror. Dr. Loewe, who was among the Jews who had fled to 'Ayn Zaytun, describes his predicament as follows:

> After they stripped me of my clothes and took my money . . . I stood up and looked calmly behind me, for now I had nothing to worry about except my life. And what value is one's life after seeing the destruction of several thousand innocent souls of my people. That is why I did not care to escape, and what is more, I knew of no place for refuge for me anyway. My feet naively carried me to one of the villages, called 'Ayn Zaytun, so at least I should not see the misery befalling thousands of my people. The Enemy showered me with a rain of stones and bullets. There too, I was encircled by old men, women, and children, all bemoaning their calamity. The local people of this village, who are also Druze, hurried us into one place and locked us in a small synagogue.[22]

The Druze then poured out their wrath upon the Jews who remained in Safed. As we have noted above, they had assembled at the home of Rabbi Abraham Dov of Ovruch and were prepared to die. The rioters tortured them cruelly and asked them to hand over their money. The rabbi had given them a sum of seventy-five thousand piasters from the treasury of the community when the attacks had begun. But they were not satisfied with this amount and demanded more, as they believed that the Jews had silver and gold and silver jewelry hidden in their homes. In order to terrorize the Jews, they took the rabbi prisoner and began to torture him brutally, preparing to kill him. But the rabbi remained calm and accepted his fate, saying: "My sons, allow me to entreat God and bless him for the sentence he has granted me today."[23]Afterward, he asked for water to wash his hands and, lifting his eyes toward heaven, he pronounced the prayer recited at death: "You are a righteous God and faithful in judgment." He then requested that the Druze allow him to recite the afternoon service. The rioters granted him his request and while he poured out his heart, they sat and ate their meal.[24]

Then miraculously, Ibrahim Pasha suddenly arrived in Safed. While they were eating and tormenting their victims, an elderly Arab entered the house and shouted to them: "Why are you sitting here so calmly? Ibrahim Pasha and his army are now in the city." The Druze quickly fled, leaving all the items they had stolen. Ibrahim Pasha took revenge upon them cruelly. Many were put to death and he taxed them heavily.

The riots lasted for three days, but the Druze had caused such great devastation that a long time passed before the Jews could rebuild their ruined homes. When they returned, they found that their homes were empty and there were "scattered feathers and broken vessels and ripped books."[25] They were naked and penniless. Fortunately, an Arab friend of the Jews by the name of Mustapha Muhammad, who had tried to protect them during the riots, lent them some money and provided them with food and clothing.

Fearing the punishment of Ibrahim Pasha for not stopping the riots, the authorities in Safed demanded that the Jews give them a certificate stating that they tried to protect them. When the Jews refused, they threatened that if they would not sign, they would set the Arabs of the local villages against them. However, in any case, Ibrahim Pasha did not pay attention to this document and blamed the government officials and punished them.

When the riots had ceased, Ibrahim Pasha ordered the Jews to make an inventory of their belongings which had been plundered. The streets were full of gold and silver vessels, copper pans and kettles, clothing, and "many other household items,"[26] which the Arabs had hurriedly brought forth when they feared that they would be punished lest the stolen goods be found in their possession. The soldiers of Ibrahim Pasha searched the Arabs' homes, collected all the belongings of the Jews, and returned all that had been stolen. Ibrahim Pasha also levied a tax upon all those involved in the rioting as compensation for the Jews. However, as in 1834, only a few actually paid.[27] In order to atone for the damage done to the Jews, Ibrahim Pasha proposed giving them estates and villages. However, fear of the Arabs rendered implementation of this plan virtually impossible. Only the printer Israel Bak received the large village of Jermaq, where he and his people lived and engaged in agriculture for several years.

Jews who lived in other parts of the country were spared. Although the Arabs had rioted, Ibrahim Pasha quelled the revolt on time. For example, in Hebron, there were plans to attack the Jews, but the governor of the town put a stop to them by proposing that the attackers wait three days. In the meantime, he left for Jerusalem in order to see whether Ibrahim Pasha had been defeated. If that were the case, he would join the mob. But upon his arrival, he found the city calm and quiet because Ibrahim Pasha had put down the rebellion in a single day. His soldiers had proclaimed his victory throughout all of the villages. Henceforth, the Arabs did not dare to harm the Jews because they feared Ibrahim Pasha and always recalled the punishment which he dealt the Arabs of Safed.

Although the Jews of Safed were safe, the riots, along with the earthquake of 1837, brought about the depletion of the community. By the early 1840s, Jerusalem had become the center of the Jewish population in the Land of Israel.

NOTES

1. "Ibrahim Pasha," *Encyclopædia Britannica* (2007), http://www.britannica.com/eb/article-9041946/Ibrahim -Pasha. Ibrahim Pasha was born 1789 in Kavalla, Rumelia, and died November 10, 1848, in Cairo, Egypt. A son, or adopted son, of the famous vali Muhammad 'Ali, in 1805 Ibrahim joined his father in Egypt, where he was made governor of Cairo. During 1816–18 he successfully commanded an army against the Wahhabite rebels in Arabia. Muhammad 'Ali sent him on a mission to the Sudan in 1821–22, and on his return he helped train the new Egyptian army on European lines. When the Ottoman sultan Mahmud II asked for Egyptian assistance to crush the Greek revolt, an expedition commanded by Ibrahim landed in Greece in 1824 and subdued the Morea (Peloponnese), but a combined British, French, and Russian squadron eventually compelled the Egyptian force to withdraw. It was in Syria that Ibrahim and his French chief of staff, O. J. A. Sève (Suleiman Pasha al-Faransawi), won military fame. In 1831–32, after a disagreement between Muhammad 'Ali and the Ottoman sultan, Ibrahim led an Egyptian army through Palestine and defeated an Ottoman army at Homs. He then forged the Bailan Pass and crossed the Taurus, gaining a final victory at Konya on December 21, 1832.

By the Convention of Kütahya, signed on May 4, 1833, Syria and Adana were ceded to Egypt, and Ibrahim became governor general of the two provinces. Ibrahim's administration was relatively enlightened. At Damascus he created a consultative council of notables and suppressed the feudal regime. But his measures were harshly applied and roused sectarian opposition. Sultan Mahmud resented the Egyptian occupation, and in 1839 an Ottoman army invaded Syria. At Nizip on June 24 Ibrahim won his last and greatest victory; the Ottoman fleet deserted to Egypt. Fearing the disintegration of the Ottoman Empire, the European powers negotiated the Treaty of London in July 1840, by which Muhammad 'Ali forfeited Syria and Adana in return for the hereditary rule of Egypt. British naval forces threatened the Egyptians, who evacuated the occupied territories in the winter of 1840–41. By 1848 Muhammad 'Ali had become senile, and Ibrahim was appointed viceroy but ruled for only forty days before his death.

1a. "Memoirs of Rabbi Jacob Saul Elyashar," in *Luah Eretz Yisrael: 5661 (Calendar)*, ed. A. M. Luncz (Jerusalem, 1900–1901). Luncz's calendar actually is a literary almanac.

2. Jehoseph Schwarz, *Tevuot ha-Aretz* [Crops of the Land] (Jerusalem, 1901), 483–84. See also n. 1, and S. Rafaeli, "Matzor Yerushalayim be-Yemei Ibrahim Pasha" [The Siege of Jerusalem under Ibrahim Pasha: Chronicle of an English Family in Jerusalem], in Luah Eretz Yisrael: 5672 (*Calendar*), ed. A. M. Luncz (Jerusalem, 1911–12). According to Rabbi Menaham Mendel of Kaminetz, Jerusalem was taken the day before the Festival of Shavuot. He writes as follows: "And they came to Jerusalem on Friday night (the Sabbath), before the Festival of Shavuot. There were only a few soldiers in the city because they had gone into hiding. And those who came looted and plundered the city. And the shortage of water was so acute that a waterskin cost six thalers. And the Jews were in great danger." *Korot ha-'Itim* [Events of the Times] (Vilna, 1840), 4.

3. *Korot ha-Itim*, 10, 1.

4. Ibid., 5: "And we chose Rabbi Leib Cohen and Rabbi Shalom Hayyat because they understood their language [Arabic] and also could speak it well. And they had acquaintances among the Arabs who would sew clothes for them."

5. Ibid.: "The riots took place with the advice and agreement of the governor of Safed. When the residents of Safed heard what the people of Shechem had done in Jerusalem, all of them came to the governor and asked him what they could do in accordance with the law. He advised them to do what the people of Shechem had done in Jerusalem and take over the Jews."

6. This fortress dates from the period of the Crusades (twelfth century). The Jews, however, mistook it for the fortress of Jotapata in the Galilee, where Josephus Flavius was besieged by the Romans during the Great Jewish Revolt against Rome in 67 CE. The name

"Joseph ben Gorion the *kohen* (priest)" comes from the widely circulated *Sefer Yosippon, The Hebrew Adaptation of Josephus Flavius' Classic Work, The Jewish War.*

7. *Korot ha-Itim.*

8. Ibid., 6, 2.

9. Rabbi Israel Porush, introduction to *Peat ha-Shulhan* (Safed, 1836). See also Dr. Louis Loewe (Eliezer Ha-Levi), in *Devir*, ed. Rabbi M. A. Guenzburg (Vilna, 1865), 12. According to *Korot ha-Itim*, a wealthy woman offered a substantial bribe to one of the robbers not to touch her and the wife of Rabbi Joshua of Pinsk. He agreed and hid them both in his house. But later on, he disavowed them and wanted to rape them. The Jews who found refuge in the house of the *qadi* ransomed them with great effort, for the price of four rubles.

10. Jacob Safir, *Iben Safir* (Lyck, 1866), 1: 1: "And the exalted Rabbi Israel, may the memory of the righteous be blessed, pleased the sheikh (the elder of the village) all who fled with him lived under his protection."

11. *Korot ha-Itim.*

12. Ibid.

13. Introduction to *Peat ha-Shulhan.*

14. *Korot ha-Itim*, 5, 1.

15. In his introduction to *Peat ha-Shulhan*, Rabbi Porush writes: "And the Merciful One [God] had mercy upon the land and . . . a man went before us, running from the port city of Beirut, and through him, I related the entire event to all the officials of the kings and the ministers of greater Aleppo and the minister of state and [informed them] that we were in mortal danger. When all this became known to the evil men, God rescued us from them." In *Giv'at Shaul* [The Hill of Saul] (Vienna, 1893), 82, Rabbi Shaul Hornstein states: "And they assembled at the wall of Jotapata (see n. 6) and took counsel regarding what course of action to take and how we could inform Ibrahim Pasha. And God gave them sound advice. They chose two men, Tzvi the son of Rabbi Sender and Ira Pahami who knew how to speak Arabic well. And they dressed like Arabs and left the walls of the city. When the guards heard them speaking Arabic with each other, they thought they were either Druze or Arabs and let them continue on their way. And they came to Acre where Ibrahim Pasha was staying. The two implored him to save them and their brethren who were in a sorry state. And Ibrahim Pasha, a kind man and a friend of the Jews, had mercy on them and told them not to be afraid and to return to their brethren and tell them that within three days he would come to help them. They returned joyfully." This account is fanciful and apocryphal and without any historical basis. The author was not in the Land of Israel at the time and it is not clear where he derived this information. In fact, the rioters left the fortress of Jotapata when they could not enter it.

16. In his introduction, Rabbi Porush indicates the number of days after the sentence ending "until this round [of violence]."

17. In his letters, Dr. Louis Loewe presents a list "of

money which was looted from the Jews on that day of rage in 1834," which he copied from the memorandum of the Russian consul in Acre. The number of families which were subjects of European countries and suffered during the riots reached 745 (M. A. Guenzburg, *Devir*, I).

18. *Korot ha-Itim*, 7, 2.

19. Rabbi Moshe Reisser, *Sha'arei Yerushalayim* [The Gates of Jerusalem] (Lwow, 1879), sec. 4, dates the events in the Hebrew month of Sivan (May 25–24, June 1838), as follow: "On 14 Sivan (June 7) God struck the Jewish residents of Safed, may it be rebuilt, when the Philistines rebelled against Ibrahim Pasha, governor of Egypt and Syria, and freed themselves from his subjugation." The eyewitness, Dr. Loewe, however writes that the riots began "on 12 Tammuz (July 5)." Similarly, Jehoseph Schwarz notes that "in the month of Tammuz 5598 (24 June 22–22, July 1838), while Ibrahim Pasha fought against the Druze of the Lebanon, suddenly a large camp of Druze entered Safed and looted the entire town. There was no one to deliver them and they left Safed and Israel became impoverished" (*Tevuot Ha-Aretz*, 479–80).

20. *Sha'arei Yerushalayim*, sec. 4.

21. According to Reisser, his father-in-law also sought the protection of the governor, in the name of Rabbi Abraham Dov of Ovruch. In *Sha'arei Yerushalayim*, he writes as follows: "And my father-in-law also was there. For he served as an intercessor and a translator of Arabic when it was necessary to speak before the officials. He was a native of the holy city of Tiberias, 'may it be completed and rebuilt,' and was known for his fluent and clear Arabic. And the rabbi asked him to go to the city official and possibly try to save the Jews. He prepared a purse of money for him and many other gifts. And he went to the official's home and blessed him in Arabic and pleased him and even received a gift from him. The latter promised to protect the city and its Jews so that they would live without fear of enemies. And he returned to the rabbi and reported the conciliatory words of the official. The rabbi and his people were very happy. But their happiness was in vain."

22. *Devir* (Vilna, 1865), 1, 16–17. A fine English translation of Dr. Louis Loewe's account of events in Safed in 1838 may be found in N. Stillman, *The Jews of Arab Lands: A History and Source Book* (Philadelphia, 1979), 342–46. This text comes from Stillman, 344.

23. According to Reisser, *Sha'arei Yerushalayim*, these events took place in the "palace of Joseph ben Gorion," and not at the home of Rabbi Abraham Dov. He relates: "The evil Philistines came to the home of the rabbi, may the memory of the righteous be blessed. They seized and bound his hands with ropes, along with many other Jews. They took the Jews as captives to the palace of Joseph ben Gorion there, and they were prepared to die." Dr. Loewe's letter (see n. 22), however, does not mention this episode at all. Other sources also indicate that Rabbi Abraham Dov did not want to leave Safed, despite entreaties to do so by those who warned him that "the Galilee will be destroyed." He, however, replied that he would stay in the town until he died.

24. Dr. Loewe.

25. *Sha'arei Yerushalayim*.

26. Ibid.

27. According to A. M. Luncz, "Ha-Yehudim be-Eretz ha-Tzvi" [The Jews in the Holy Land], 6: 310–11: "In 1840, Rabbi Israel Bak was sent to Cairo by the Jews of Safed and Tiberias in order to intercede on their behalf in obtaining the payment for damages owed them. He spent several months there regarding this issue, but he could not do much. In the meantime, the Damascus blood libel occurred. Therefore, he ceased dealing with the damage suits and began to work for the release of the prisoners in Damascus. He sent letters to Sir Moses Montefiore concerning the latter and therefore, the payments for damages were forgotten."

CHAPTER 53

The *Dhimmi* Factor in the Exodus of Jews from Arab Countries

Bat Ye'or

The *dhimmi* condition can only be understood in the context of jihad because it originates from this ideology. From the eighth and ninth centuries, Muslim theologians and jurists had endeavored to give to the jihad (war of conquest) a religious and legal structure. Living during and after the great wave of Arab-Muslim expansion on mainly Christian lands, they based themselves on the Qur'an and the hadith (the words and acts attributed to the Prophet Muhammad). Thus they elaborated the concept and doctrine of jihad that established the relationship between Muslims and non-Muslims in terms of belligerency, hostility, or submission. The aims, tactics, and strategies of jihad were defined, as well as the rules concerning the troops, the compulsory conditions for treaties, the treatment of prisoners, and the apportionment of the booty. This conceptualization of war led to a considerable literature that constituted the classical doctrine of jihad which was fixed, from the mid-eighth century onward, in comprehensive theological and legal treatises.

According to this doctrine, the right to rule the world belongs only to the *umma* (the Islamic community of Allah) because it is elected above all others (Qur'an 3: 106: "You are the best nation ever brought forth to men"). It allows what is good, forbids what is wrong, and possesses the divine revelation transmitted by Muhammad, the Apostle of God and his last messenger. Islam is Allah's religion (Qur'an 3:17). Muslim theologians expounded that jihad is a collective, religious obligation (*fard 'ala al-kifaya*) binding the community and each individual (*fard 'ala al-ayn*) in different ways according to situations and circumstances.

Here are two definitions of jihad by recognized authorities: Abu Muhammad Abdallah Ibn Abi Zayd al-Qayrawani (d. 966) and Ibn Khaldun (d. 1406).

> Jihad is a precept of divine institution. Its performance by certain individuals may dispense others from it. We Malikis [one of the four schools of Muslim jurisprudence] maintain that it is prefer-

able not to begin hostilities with the enemy before having invited the latter to embrace the religion of Allah except where the enemy attacks first. They have the alternative of either converting to Islam or paying the poll tax (*jizya*), short of which war will be declared against them.[1]

> In the Muslim community, the holy war is a religious duty, because of the universalism of the (Muslim) mission and (the obligation to) convert everybody to Islam either by persuasion or by force. Therefore, caliphate and royal authority are united (in Islam), so that the person in charge can devote the available strength to both of them (religion and politics) at the same time.[2]

> Jihad may be exercised by pen or speech (propaganda): at other times by money (corruption); and, whenever possible, by arms: terrorism, guerilla and open warfare.

According to the jihad doctrine, the "enemies" are those who oppose the establishment of Islamic law and its sovereignty over the non-Muslim world—that is, all the infidels who constitute the world of unbelief. This world is considered as one entity, as is stressed in article 22 of the 1988 Charter of the Islamic Palestinian Movement, Hamas. The whole region of infidelity is called the *dar al-Harb* (region of war), because all acts of war are allowed there until, through jihad, it will come under Islamic rule. The war between the region of Islam (*dar al-Islam*) and the region of war is supposed to be an eternal one, so long as unbelief prevails (Qur'an 3:189). There can be peace treaties extending for up to ten years. There can also be a situation of no peace, no war, allowing coexistence in cases where Muslim victory through warfare is doubtful, but this situation is temporary and is usually accepted in exchange for the payment of a tribute. In fact, it is the situation of war that is normal, and the peace situation is only brought on by conjunctural necessities.[3]

Among the infidel peoples there are differences.

Bat Ye'or in *The Forgotten Millions: The Modern Jewish Exodus from Arab Lands*, edited by Malka H. Shulewitz (New York: Cassell, 1999), pp. 33–51.

Those who do not possess Revealed Scriptures have, in theory, the choice between Islam or death. The others—principally the Jews and Christians—are granted protection status, according to the modalities of the conquest, henceforth becoming *dhimmis*—people protected by the law of Islam.

In fact, the jurists leave the freedom of decision to the ruling imam or caliph:

1. He can kill all the vanquished males, whatever their religion, and enslave their women and children.
2. He can also enslave the males if he so chooses.
3. He can grant the *dhimmi* status to all those in possession of Revealed Scriptures.[4]

It is a historical fact that all the Muslim countries around the southern and eastern Mediterranean were Christian lands before being conquered by jihad during a millennium. The vanquished populations were then "protected," providing they submitted to the Muslim ruler's conditions. Therefore, in the context of a conquest, "protection" results from a war and this situation determines specific consequences. The main characteristics of the *dhimmi* condition which developed from this situation are: in the legal domain—the Islamic concept of protection/submission; in the economic domain—the concept of *fay* (booty); in the social domain—the concept of vilification. All three characteristics are integrated into the doctrine of jihad that encompasses the world.

THE SYSTEM OF DHIMMITUDE

Political Aspects

The concepts of protection and toleration are linked: he who protects also tolerates, and toleration depends on the rules laid down by the protector for conceding his protection. In the context of jihad, the non-Muslim living in the region of war (a *harbi*) has no rights; his life and goods are at the mercy of any Muslim because of the situation of war between his land (the *dar al-harb*) and the land of Islam.[5] He obtains rights only if he submits to the Muslim ruler without fighting. It is therefore in a context of war—where there is a total negation of rights—that "rights" are conceded to Jews and Christians by the Muslim community (*umma*) as defined by it.

On an individual base, security is granted on special conditions to a foreigner (*harbi*) coming to a Muslim land. Any Muslim can give him this protection (*aman*), which cannot exceed one year unless the *harbi* becomes a *dhimmi* by paying the *jizya*, a Qur'anic poll tax. In both cases, it is the Muslim community that concedes rights to the non-Muslim.

Protection status is provided through the Islamization of conquered lands. The vanquished scriptural peoples are granted security for their life and possessions by the Muslim authority, as well as a relative self-autonomous administration and permission to worship according to the modalities of the conquest. These rights are subject to two conditions: the payment of the *jizya*, and submission to the provisions of the Islamic law. On these conditions—and only on these conditions—Jews and Christians were tolerated and were relatively secure in their native countries, now conquered by jihad and governed by Islamic law. Their acceptance of Muslim toleration guaranteed safety to them. This status is still clearly expressed in the Palestinian Hamas Charter (articles 6 and 31) and by other Islamist movements that base themselves on similar traditional doctrines.

In the jihad doctrine, the Muslim community is the only source and guarantor for the legitimacy of the *dhimmis'* rights. Christians and Jews share the same Islamic theological and legal category, referred to in the Qur'an as the "People of the Book." The legal status common to the Jewish and Christian indigenous populations in the lands conquered by jihad and subjected to Islamic law I have called the "regime of *dhimmitude*," the "laws of *dhimmitude*," the "world of *dhimmitude*," the "mentality of *dhimmitude*," and the "policy of *dhimmitude*."

It is important to stress, however, that these concepts of warfare and protection were common in the socio-political context and mentalities of pre-Islamic Arabia. This conception of pagan intertribal relationship was enlarged after the seventh- to eighth-century Arab conquests into a universal political ideology expressed in a religious framework.

The first "right" is the right to life, which was conceded on payment of the *jizya* (Qur'an 9:29). Life is not considered a natural right. It is a right which each Jew and Christian must repurchase annually by paying the poll tax with humility to the *umma*. Only then are their lives "protected." The concept of toleration is linked to a number of discriminatory obligations in the economic, religious, and social fields, imposed by Islamic law on the *dhimmis*. There are different opinions among the jurists concerning which transgression of these obligations can be considered as breaking the protection pact (*dhimmi*), and which sanctions should be applied. Usually the refusal to pay the *jizya* is considered by all jurists as a rupture of the *dhimmi*, which automatically restitutes to the *umma* its initial rights of war—to kill and to dispossess the *dhimmi* because he has returned to his former status of being a *harbi*, an unsubjected infidel. The renowned eighth-century jurist Abu Yusuf Ya'qub wrote:

> The wali [governor of a province] is not allowed to exempt any Christian, Jew, Magean, Sabaen, or Samaritan from paying the tax, and no one can obtain a partial reduction. It is illegal for one to be

exempted and another not, for their lives and belongings are spared only because of payment of the poll tax.[6]

In a few regions—for instance, in Iran at some periods—one finds the concept of collective responsibility applied to an individual act. This meant that the whole Jewish or Christian community could be made responsible for the alleged misbehavior of one of its members, and would suffer the abrogation of the community's protection.

Protection is abolished if the *dhimmis* rebel against Islamic law, give allegiance to a non-Muslim power, refuse to pay the *jizya*, entice a Muslim from his faith, harm a Muslim or his property, or commit blasphemy. Blasphemy includes denigration of the Prophet Muhammad, the Qur'an, the Muslim faith, the shari'a by suggesting that it has a defect and by refusing the decision of the *ijma*, which was the consensus of the Islamic community (Qur'an 3:106), and later of its scholars. The moment the "pact of protection" is abolished the jihad resumes, which means that the lives of the *dhimmis* and their property are forfeited. Today, some Islamists in Upper Egypt who kill and pillage Copts consider that these *dhimmis* have forfeited their "protection" because they no longer pay the *jizya.*

Clearly, this notion of protection is different from the concept of individual rights. Islamic protection established a bilateral relationship between the Muslim conqueror who concedes rights defined by him to the subjected dhimmi. This means that rights have a beginning— the moment the protection is given—and, consequently, they can have an end—the eventual abolition of the protection. It is therefore a hierarchic relationship between a superior, who grants rights to an inferior, who is grateful to receive them. On the other hand, the concept of human rights implies that all human beings are born with fundamental and inalienable rights. The opposition between these two concepts appears very clearly in the situation of the Baha'i religion, which is not a protected religion in Iran. In 1994 two Muslims kidnapped and killed a Baha'i. The Islamic court held that as the Baha'is were "unprotected infidels . . . the issue of retribution is null and void."[7] This means that an infidel has no human rights whatsoever, unless he is protected by the provision of Islamic law. Islam, in this context, is conceived as the only theological and juridical source that rules, legitimizes, and guarantees the rights of non-Muslims.

In the context of its time, the protection system presented both positive and negative aspects. It provided security and a measure of religious autonomy, but *dhimmis* suffered many legal disabilities intended to reduce them to a condition of humiliation, segregation, and discrimination. These rules, established from the eighth to ninth centuries by the founders of the four schools of Islamic law, set the pattern of the Muslim community's social behavior toward *dhimmis.*

The Economic Aspects

In the economic domain, there is a somewhat contradictory attitude concerning the *dhimmis*. All the jurists state that they should be treated according to the conditions stipulated in their treaty of submission, that their lives and possessions should be respected and protected against looting and expropriation. Several Qur'anic verses and many hadith are invoked to implement this peaceful policy that was in theory the norm. However, another interpretation was expressed after the conquests—this is the theory of *fay*, specified in the jihad doctrine. *Fay* is the collective booty acquired through *jihad* and kept as a *waqf* (holy endowment) for the *umma*. This point is well explained by the second caliph. Umar Ibn al-Khattab, in his replies to the Muslims who demanded the sharing of the lands of Iraq, Syria, and Palestine among the conquerors.

But I thought that we had nothing more to conquer after the land of Kesra [Persia], whose riches, land, and people Allah has given us. I have divided the personal possessions among those that conquered them after having subtracted a fifth, which under my supervision was used for the purpose for which it was intended. I thought it necessary to reserve the land and its inhabitants, and levy from the latter the *kharaj* by virtue of their land, and the capitation [*jizya*] as a personal tax on every head, this poll tax constituting a *fay* in favor of the Muslims who have fought there of their children and of their heirs.[8]

Dhimmis should not be reduced to slavery which would disperse them, but should be considered as an economic asset, used to increase the welfare and the strength of the *umma*—and to advance the interests of Islam. This is their "service," a service which is due to the *umma*. We read in the *History of the Patriarchs of the Coptic Church of Alexandria* that

'Omar [the caliph 'Umar b. Abd al-Aziz (717–720)] *commands, saying: Those who wish to remain as they are, and in their own country, must follow the religion of Muhammad as I do; but let those who do not wish to do so, go forth from my dominions.* Then the Christians gave him all the money that they could, and trusted in God and rendered service to the Muslims, and became an example to many. For the Christians were oppressed by the governors and the local authorities and the Muslims in every place, the old and the young, the rich and the poor among them: and Omar commanded that the poll-tax should be taken from all men who would not become Muslims, even in cases where it was not customary to take it. But God did not long respite him, but destroyed him swiftly, and granted him the government no longer, because he was like

Antichrist. Then Yezid reigned after him; but we have no wish to relate nor describe what happened in his days, on account of the miseries and trials: for he walked in the path of Satan, and deviated from the paths of God.[9]

I give this example because the idea of rendering services to the Islamic cause should not be viewed as a past condition of the *dhimmis'* existence, as even today it is still a basic principle of the Eastern *dhimmi* churches and of Eastern Christians in general. Since 1993, some Israeli politicians have also invoked "services" that Israel could provide (medical, economical, technological) as a means to facilitate its integration into the Arab-Muslim world. From this viewpoint, Israel's acceptance is not to be achieved by the recognition of its legitimacy, but by the "services" it can grant to the *umma* in exchange for the latter's toleration. Conversely, the notion of rendering service to other nations in order to obtain recognition of rights of existence is never expressed by the *umma*. The "service syndrome" has grown out of an asymmetrical relationship and a situation of vulnerability, both of which are typical of the status of *dhimmitude*.

The third domain of the *dhimmi* legal status is social and religious, and here we find an infinite and extremely minute set of regulations, whose aim was to reduce the *dhimmi* to a state of vilification and vulnerability hardly imaginable today. Here are only two examples: a *dhimmi* had no right to defend himself if he was physically assaulted by a Muslim; he could only beg for pardon. A *dhimmi* could not testify against a Muslim in a law court as his testimony was refused. These interdictions stripped him of two fundamental rights: the right of self-defense against physical aggression and the right to defend himself under the law.

It should be stressed that none of these regulations are mentioned in the Qur'an. The codification and institutionalization of jihad were carried out by medieval jurists. Likewise, the numerous humiliatory rules and discriminations developed later in the course of history. In this complex picture, one may distinguish a classical pattern common to the whole of the *dar al-Islam*, as well as regional rules emerging from specific geographical or political contexts, such as the extremely severe conditions of Jews, bordering on slavery, in isolated Yemen and semi-desert areas of North Africa.

Whereas "toleration" and *dhimmitude* refer to the same historical domain, they express two different views on history. The first is of a theological nature: static and monolithic, affirming the point of view of the *umma*, which embodied the ideological and juridical source of tolerance for Jews and Christians. Rights which do not conform to the Islamic system of toleration are considered illegal, as being against Allah's will, and should therefore be suppressed. The second (*dhimmitude*) is an analytical concept, referring to the historical experience of the *dhimmi*

peoples, those who incarnated the human material of *dhimmitude* throughout the centuries. Therefore, each represents a different perception of history due to different sensibilities. The *umma* considers that its toleration was "just" according to its own Islamic values—and this justice is only conceived in terms of Islamic justice.

Dhimmitude is, in effect, a study of the ideology of jihad and of the jurisdiction that was imposed on the vanquished peoples on the bases of the modalities of battles and conquests. For traditional Muslim jurists, the modalities of conquest of each land or city will determine for all time the jurisdiction to be applied there. Here are two examples.

In the early fourteenth century, churches and synagogues were closed in Cairo and a legal opinion on this matter was requested from Ibn Taymiya, a renowned Hanbali jurist from Damascus. He confirmed the legality of the closure by referring to the conditions of Egypt's conquest in the seventh century by the Muslim army.[10] Another example comes from Morocco five centuries later. In 1836 to 1837, the Jews of Fez had asked the Sultan Abd ar-Rahman for permission to build a *hammam* (public bath) in their quarter. The most learned judges (*qadis*) were consulted; they produced twelve fatwas on the subject, going back to ancient chronicles that described the conditions of the Islamic conquest of the Maghreb more than a thousand years earlier. All of them—with one exception, who was called a donkey by his colleagues—ruled that Jews could not be granted the right to build a *hammam* because of the manner in which the conquest of the Maghreb had taken place in the seventh century. As late as 1898, the same request was again refused to the Jews.[11]

So one sees that, throughout the ebb and flow of history, *dhimmitude* is composed of a fixed structure—either ideological or legal—and of circumstantial, transient factors. *Dhimmitude* encompasses various types of relationships on all levels between the Muslim ruler and the dominated and tolerated *dhimmis*. Since the status of *dhimmitude* lasted from a period of five hundred years to thirteen centuries, dependent on regions, it allows one to study the cases of many peoples, all theoretically subjected to the same Islamic jurisdiction, with some differences here and there.

In those Islamic lands where Muslims were in a minority among the native *dhimmis* (Spain and European Turkey), the laws of *dhimmitude* were less severe. The worst oppression developed in rural areas, causing the flight, extermination, or expropriation of the numerous Jewish and Christian peasantry of the Middle East. Likewise, in the provinces, which were barely controlled by the central Islamic power and where anarchy was endemic, *dhimmis* were subjected to continual extortion and survived only by paying ransom money to tribal chieftains, as in Kurdistan, the Levant, and especially Palestine and some regions of the Maghreb until the twentieth century. In Palestine, Jews could barely survive in their homeland, but conditions improved from the 1840s after European consuls were allowed to reside in Jerusalem, and during the 1860s reported to their ambassadors in Constantinople on the infringements of the sultan's religious reforms, guaranteed by treaty. *Dhimmis* preferred large towns where Islamic protection could be more effective, as they could appeal to honest and learned Muslim judges and to the central authorities for redress.

The system of *dhimmitude* is composed of theological framework, economic factors, and political contexts. The three domains interrelate and interact with one another in the dynamic of history, but each played a dominant role in circumstantial contexts. In relation to the theological frame, one should stress that religious prejudices and oppression were current in all societies and were not limited to Islam. Over the centuries and up to the present there were constant borrowings, interactions, and a mutual influence of Islamic and Christian religious intolerance, either in military confrontation—jihad from the seventh century for a millennium; and its Christian reaction, the crusades from 1096 for two centuries—or joined in a united alliance against dissident churches or later against Zionism.

Reading through the sources from various periods provides interesting information on the *dhimmi* mentality and the psychological distortion brought about by oppression. It also reveals opinions held by others on the *dhimmis*. Here are two noteworthy examples.

In rural Yemen, before their mass exodus to Israel in 1948, Jews were protected only if they belonged to Arab tribes, in conformity with the pre-Islamic Arabian custom of *jiwar*. Here it is clear that "protection" is linked with the suppression of rights. Rights to life and to security are only guaranteed to a Jew who is under "protection." If a Muslim killed a Jew, the criminal would not be brought to trial because Muslim blood was considered superior to Jewish blood. Hence, the *lex talionis* practiced by Islam could only be applied between equals—that is to say, between Muslims—but not between a Muslim and a *dhimmi*, whether Jew or Christian, whereas the *talion* would be applied between these two non-Muslim groups. Thus, if a Jew belonging to tribe A is killed by a Muslim from tribe B, then a Jew from tribe B would be killed by a Muslim from tribe A. So two Jews are killed without the Muslim murderer being arrested, a game that could go on for generations as a form of retaliation. In this legal system the Jew, like an object or a camel, is excluded from human justice. His disappearance is felt as a deprivation for his Arab master, who obtains retribution by depriving another Arab of his Jewish asset. What is doubly interesting is that this information is provided in an article published in 1953 by a distinguished Cambridge University scholar, the late Professor Robert Serjeant, as an example of and a testimony to Islamic justice and tolerance.[12] This means that he himself accepted the concept that a person, because he is a Jew, can be deprived of all his rights in a system that reduces his life to "protection" and "services."

Jewish life in the Djabal Nefusa in Tripolitania provides a related example. Jews there were treated as serfs or slaves belonging to their master. When the Arab or Berber master died, his heirs inherited their Jews. If there was only one Jew and several heirs, each person would inherit a part of the Jew. The Ottomans liberated the Jews from this condition when they took control of Libya in 1858.[13]

The world of the *dhimmi* is one of silence, as Islamic law refuses his testimony against a Muslim. Likewise, confronted with the Islamic historical version of tolerance, the *dhimmi*'s historical testimony of *dhimmitude* is refused. Moreover, since religion, law, and politics are all bound together in Islam, any criticism of Muslim law or Islamic politics is considered blasphemous. The *dhimmi* mentality is characterized by a feeling of gratefulness toward the power that tolerated this humiliated and threatened existence, what I have called the "*dhimmi* syndrome." Hence, vulnerability led to a lack of revendication against injustice, a hapless state that caused resignation. Jews would say: "We are in *galut* [exile]; we have to suffer." They, like the Monophysite Christians, lived their trials through the spiritual world of the Bible.

Sources on *dhimmitude* abound. First, there are the Islamic sources: legal, religious, and historical. The literature of jihad by Muslim historians is quite extensive. It describes the conquest and the process of Islamization of Christian lands. Then there are the *dhimmi* sources: Jewish, Christian, Coptic, Syriac, Nestorian, Armenian, Greek, and Slav. These sources are not uniform: Some are very meagre because of the utter destruction of its peoples, while some are more abundant.

PATTERN OF *DHIMMITUDE*

Dhimmitude covers more than a millennium of Christian and Jewish history, and is a comprehensive civilization encompassing customs, legislation, social behavior and prejudices. Numerous laws were enacted over the centuries in order to implement its principles. The geographical panorama of *dhimmitude* shows two aspects: one displays a permanent and uniform structure in the economic, religious, social, and legal domains: the other discloses regional practices resulting from specific local conditions. The former constituted the classical legal status of *dhimmis*, prescribed by all jurists at different periods, and obligatory throughout the lands of Islam. Its various constituents were constantly imposed with lesser or greater severity depending on circumstances—they may be found as much in the Balkans, in Anatolia, and further afield, in the Levant, Persia, Yemen, and the Maghreb.

Classical Clements

The first major achievement of jihad was a territorial expropriation of the native people by transferring possession of the conquered lands to the conqueror. The *jizya* was mandatory under threat of jail, conversion, slavery, the abduction of *dhimmi* children, or death. *Dhimmis* paid double the taxes of the Muslims and were subjected to the most degrading corvées. In North Africa and Yemen, repugnant obligations, such as executioner, gravedigger, cleaner of public latrines, and the like were forced on Jews, even on Saturdays and holy days. In 1894 to 1896, in Mesopotamia, after the first genocidal massacres of Armenians, Jews were often obliged in many places to bury the corpses. Religious restrictions were numerous, ranging from prohibitions in building, repair, and enlargement of synagogues and churches to regulations imposing humility, silence, and secrecy in prayer. The takeover and Islamization of synagogues, and more often churches, was common.

In the legal sphere, the law ordained permanent inferiority and humiliation for *dhimmis*. As their blood was valued at half that of a Muslim, contempt for their life was expressed through inequality of punishments for the same offense. The penalty for murder was much lighter if the *dhimmi* was the victim. The murderer of a *dhimmi* was rarely punished, as he could justify his act by accusing his victim of blasphemy against Islam or having assaulted a Muslim. The *dhimmi* could hardly defend himself since *qadis* accepted only a Muslim's testimony. *Dhimmis* were forbidden to possess or carry arms, to have authority over Muslims, to possess or buy land, to marry Muslim women, to have Muslim slaves or servants, and, in theory, to write in Arabic.

In the social domain *dhimmis* had to be recognized by their discriminatory clothes whose shape, color and texture were prescribed from head to foot; likewise their houses (color and size) and their separate living quarters. *Dhimmis* were forbidden to ride a horse or a camel, since these animals were considered too noble. A donkey could be ridden outside towns but only on a pack-saddle, the *dhimmi* sitting with both legs on one side and dismounting on sight of a Muslim. A *dhimmi* had to hurry through the streets, always passing to the left (impure) side of a Muslim, who was expected to force him to the narrow side or into the gutter. He had to walk humbly with lowered eyes, to accept insults without replying, to remain standing in a meek and respectful attitude in the presence of a Muslim, and to leave him the best place. If he was admitted to a public bath, he had to wear bells to signal his presence. Stoning Jews and Christians—especially in Arab-populated regions—was not unusual; likewise disdain, insults, and disrespectful attitudes toward them were customary. Some regional rules represent an aggravation of this pattern. In Morocco and Yemen, Jews were forbidden footwear outside their segregated quarter. In Yemen, a Jewish child whose father had died was taken from its family and placed with Muslim foster parents or in an orphanage. The profanation of the tombs of *dhimmis*, especially in North Africa, was common.

In their struggles to regain their liberty and dignity, *dhimmi* nations were compelled, by history or geography, to adopt different paths. Christians from the European provinces of the Ottoman Empire fought for national goals; this policy was also chosen later by the Armenians and the Jews. The eastern Arab Christians, however, chose assimilation in an alleged secularized Arab society. The national liberation of *dhimmi* peoples meant that the jurisdiction of *dhimmitude* imposed by jihad was abolished. Their land and they themselves were no longer considered as booty (*fay*), nor as a *waqf* landed at the disposal of the Muslim community. They were no longer forbidden to have positions that might give them equality or superiority over a Muslim. They could revive their prohibited language, as well as their history and their culture. They were no longer dehumanized *dhimmis*, deprived of the right to speak, to defend themselves, and to preserve their own history. The national liberation of a *dhimmi* people meant the abolishment of the laws of *dhimmitude* for native populations on their historical homelands.

These laws are the basic regulations set down in the classical texts on *dhimmis* and they had to be enforced throughout the lands of *dhimmitude*. Jurists strongly condemned the alleviation of these measures when it temporarily occurred. This comprehensive system lasted for over thirteen centuries in some regions. Its archetype—the dehumanized *dhimmi*—has permeated Islamic civilization and culture and is being revived in some aspects today through the Islamist resurgence and the return of the shari'a in some countries. *Dhimmitude* constitutes an ideological, sociological, and political reality. This is proved by its geographical development, its historical perenniality, and its present resurgence.

In the nineteenth century, the world of *dhimmitude* (Islamic supremacy) was shaken by three political movements: territorial independence for some ethnic *dhimmi* peoples (Greeks and Slavs); the theoretical emancipation of the *dhimmis* imposed by Europe (Ottoman Empire); and colonialism (Maghreb and Levant). In the last two cases, the shari'a law was replaced by European jurisdiction. The abolition of discrimination against Christians and Jews by secular, non-Islamic rules introduced by Europeans increased Muslim frustration and hatred against their former *dhimmis*. Christian independence and emancipation from the rules of *dhimmitude* led, during the whole of the nineteenth century and later, to bloody reprisals by the *umma*. Jews, too fearful to take advantage of their new rights, were spared.

The nineteenth-century Christian wars of national liberation and the later Arab-Israeli wars fit into the same pattern of *dhimmi* rebellions. *Dhimmi* lands, conquered by jihad, belonged to the *umma* as *fay* land (i.e., the collective booty of the *umma*, as reiterated in the 1988

Palestinian Hamas Charter). Regarding rebellious *dhimmis*, according to Muslim jurisconsults, the ruler was duty-bound to execute the males, reduce their women and children to slavery, and appropriate their possessions.[14]

Muslim reprisals against Christians in distant provinces far from the military fronts—who had not participated in the Christian rebellions—were motivated by many factors. Two are relevant here: Christian *dhimmis* were accused of having appealed to foreign powers for help; Christians in the Ottoman Empire were suspected of sympathizing with the rebels.

For Muslim jurists, these two reasons justified the expulsion or the execution of the *dhimmis*. The accusation of collusion with the infidels abolished the protection of their life and goods. Thus, during the Balkan wars in the nineteenth century until the genocide of the Armenians during the First World War, Christian *dhimmi* communities were terrorized and hence were hostile to the Christian rebels. The Muslim hostility toward them was similar to modern Arab anti-Israeli and anti-Jewish prejudices.

In the context of Zionism, Jews from Arab countries suffered reprisals for the same reasons. Palestinian emissaries traveled through Muslim lands to arouse anti-Jewish fanaticism. Their propaganda of hate relied on terror as a deterrent. In distant Yemen, for instance, the influence of Palestinian emissaries in the 1920s was responsible for the severe deterioration of Jewish life, especially regarding the law obliging the abduction of orphans of a Jewish father. As Jews did not rebel against the Arab regimes, nor attack Muslims, they were now accused of harboring sympathy for the Jewish struggle in Palestine. It is under this accusation that Jews, as *dhimmis*, suffered extortion, imprisonment, rape, expropriation, and massacre in Arab countries, although some Arab rulers—especially Muhammad V of Morocco—endeavored to protect them.

The validity of the *dhimmi* status in modern times was acknowledged at the Fourth Conference of the Academy for Islamic Research, held in September 1968 at Al-Azhar University in Cairo, when Egyptian Sheikh Muhammad Abu Zahra stated:

It may be said that they (the unbelievers) are non-Muslim subjects, living in our midst, and therefore we have to take care of them. Within this group are cited the Jews, residing in certain Muslim states, the head of which, together with men in authority, favor them with amity and shield them from the masses, adenopathy or thyromegaly of Muslims. But we say to those who patronize the Jews that the latter are "*dhimmis*," people of obligation, who have betrayed the covenant in conformity with which they have been accorded protection. . . . These people have broken their covenant and violated their pledges: how, then, are we going to retain our obligation to protect them?[15]

This quotation illustrates the conflict between a rigorist interpretation of the law and the more liberal policy of some Muslim governments. It should be stressed that secular Turkey dissociated itself from the Arab League's jihad against Israel. Likewise, under the last shah of Iran, religious prejudices against non-Muslims were strongly condemned and minorities were protected against fanaticism.

The Charter of Hamas states in its articles 6 and 31 that peace for Jews and Christians is only possible if they are under the rule of Islam. Independence and nationhood are denied them:

Under the shadow of Islam, it is possible for the members of the three religions—Islam, Christianity and Judaism—to coexist in safety and security. Safety and security can only prevail under the shadow of Islam, and recent and ancient history is the best witness to that effect. (Article 31)

Thus, in some Arab countries which had just obtained their independence, Jews were considered as *dhimmis* in conformity with tradition. Discrimination and insecurity prompted them to leave in tragic circumstances from 1945 to 1975, stripped of all their belongings, while suffering brutality and humiliation. In other countries like Syria, thousands were kept until recently as a hostage population.

The Return of Dhimmitude

Today, all the aspects of *dhimmitude* mentioned above are still active or potential political forces. It is therefore important to know these aspects in order to recognize them and thus to realize that the situation of Jewish *dhimmis* and of the state of Israel is not exceptional. It belongs to a fixed, political, Islamic constellation that includes many nations and peoples and whose evolution affects its components altogether, as can be seen in the Islamist ideology. Thus each *dhimmi* community can learn from the other. For Israel, the study of jihad, and particularly of Christian *dhimmitude*—the mechanism for transforming a national entity into a *dhimmi* minority—is essential.

Although the Jewish *dhimmi* condition is not exceptional, having been shared by millions of Christians and others over the centuries, nonetheless Israel's fight for survival as a sovereign state in its ancestral homeland is unique. This struggle implies overcoming not only traditional Islamic prejudices—the jihad and *dhimmi* concepts concerning Jews—but also European and Eastern Christian Judeophobia, which led to a policy of Jewish territorial dispossession and debasement in exile. Israel's legitimacy has not yet been fully acknowledged by the World Council of Churches, while the Vatican has adopted an ambiguous position, balancing its recognition of Israel in 1993 by a similar attitude toward the

Palestinians. However, there is no relationship between the church's policy toward the Jews during sixteen centuries and its support for Arab Palestinians, since Palestine is a geographical entity created in its modern boundaries by Britain in 1923 under its League of Nations Mandate.

The rules concerning Christians in modern Muslim states are inspired by the traditional rules of dhimmitude relating to the laws of blasphemy, mixed marriage, and apostasy; those concerning the building and repairing of churches and for religious processions; discrimination in employment, in education, as well as in penal cases which exclude the testimony of a non-Muslim when an Islamic punishment is applicable (Pakistan). Muslim criminals pay half of the compensation stipulated by law when the victim is a non-Muslim (as in Pakistan). In Iran, the financial reparation for injury and crimes is less severe if the victim is a non-Muslim, while the punishment for any crime is stricter.[16]

The study of *dhimmitude* necessitates an examination of the joint condition of both Jews and Christians because they form a single category under Islam, the People of the Book. They are complementary: the rules concerning one also concern the other. However much Christians object to this common destiny, Muslim doctrine has linked them to the Jews.

Zionism, however, was different from the struggle by Christian peoples for national liberation from *dhimmitude*, because on theological grounds the church had condemned the Jewish people—and only them—to abasement in their ancestral homeland and exile from Jerusalem. This exceptional policy placed the Jews in a unique category in their own country. Early Christian doctrine professed that the Jews were a deicidal people, condemned by God to dispersion and suffering. Church Fathers had considered it a pious act to defile their religious shrines and humiliate them in the Land of Israel, as "proof" of their rejection by God. This Christian doctrine prevailed until the 1965 *Nostra Aetate* statement of the Ecumenical Council of Vatican II.

For a century, Arab Christians—foremost among them the Palestinian clergy—were in the vanguard of anti-Zionism and theological Judeophobia. When after the Holocaust, some European Christian theologians fought within the church to suppress the deicidal accusation, they were strongly opposed by the Eastern churches and Islamic-Arab pressures. Later, these Eastern bishops attempted to block the Vatican's efforts of reconciliation before and after Vatican II (1962–1965) and fought to retain the deicidal accusation.[17] George Habash, Nayef Hawatmeh, Wadi Haddad, Kamal Nasser, Father Sakkab, the Syrian Melkite Bishop Hilarion Capucci, and others militated in the most extreme PLO terrorist movements. The killing of Jews was their sacred Christian "service" to the *umma*.[18] Some of them collaborate now with the Islamist movements.

Consequently, Christian anti-Jewish theology and the Islamic policy of dhimmitude constituted a solid common ground that cemented the Islamic-Christian alliance against Zionism from its beginning.[19] This war against the Jews and Zionism throughout the twentieth century adopted multifaceted aspects: from a policy of mass extermination and pillage to camouflaged tactics behind the Palestinian cause, with media support. Commenting on the restoration of the new state of Israel and its secularist basis, the Vatican newspaper, *Osservatore Romano*, declared in 1948: "For this reason the Holy Land and its sacred places belong to Christendom, the true Israel."[20] Among other calumnies against the new state, the official bulletin of the French Catholic Church, *La Documentation Catholique*, proclaimed in 1949 that it could only agree "that Zionism is Nazism in a new guise"—a cynical defamation later used by Arab propaganda and recently by the Palestinian Hamas movement.[21]

It is the *dhimmi* condition of total insecurity that motivated Eastern Christians to promote a secular society (Arab nationalism) in which they would feel integrated. They saw in anti-Zionism a tool to cement an Islamic-Christian solidarity in a common war against Israel. Arab Christians were afraid—and still are—that a Jewish-Christian reconciliation would endanger them and provoke Muslim retaliations. In this context, the interference from Islamic powers have kept alive conflictual issues between Jews and Christians by using Eastern Christians as hostages.[22] This is not the only example and it explains the general taboo which the Eastern churches tried to impose in order to conceal *dhimmi* history, thereby separating themselves from any ties with the Jews.[23] But this silence contributed to the return of religious intolerance and the jihad mentality, expounded by Islamists, whose victims today are the Eastern Christians and reformist Muslims.

One may contrast the Palestinian churches' opposition to Israel, rooted in the deepest prejudices against the alleged deicidal people, with the pro-Zionist Christian Lebanese trend. Indeed, Zionism has deep roots also in some Christian movements. The Lebanese current, represented by Maronite patriarch Antun Arida and Archbishop Ignace Mubarak in the 1930s and 1940s, fully understood the common fate of Jews and Christians in relation to Islam. It therefore claimed from the international community the recognition of two independent states liberated from *dhimmitude*: a Christian state in Lebanon and a Jewish state in Palestine.

In his powerful plea to the 1947 UNSCOP Committee of Enquiry, Archbishop Mubarak clearly exposed the problematics of *dhimmitude* for Jews and Christians, and their intrinsic solidarity to face it. The pro-Zionist Catholic trend in Lebanon was smothered by the Vatican and strongly opposed by the Arab churches, especially the Palestinian churches allied with the PLO. This internecine Christian war continued until the destruction of the Christian Lebanese political power by the PLO and its Muslim and Christian allies.[24] It is not the only example where a Christian anti-Jewish policy is diverted from its target, harming Christians themselves.

The recognition of Israel by the Vatican in December 1993 came too late for those Lebanese Christians who were pleading for a strong alliance of the People of the Book against the rules of *dhimmitude*. As for Europe, it supported the Arab jihad in its Palestinian garb. As Bechir Gemayel affirmed in his last speech just before his assassination: "Europe, driven by its antisemitism, preferred to mutilate itself by sacrificing the ancient Lebanese church rather than supporting Israel."[25] European backing for the Palestinians against the Lebanese-Israeli alliance was intended to strengthen Eastern Christians, as well as buttressing an Islamic-European-Christian solidarity against Israel. Toward this goal, Europe and the Arab Palestinian churches provided strong anti-Israeli propaganda on an international level.

In the context of *dhimmitude*, the position of the Israelis—a people liberating its land from the laws of *dhimmitude*—differs from similar Christian movements. Israel had to struggle against the Christian theological curse that led to the Holocaust, and also against *dhimmitude*.

The history of *dhimmitude* has yet to be accepted by the Muslim intelligentsia, although they should acknowledge that the peoples whom they subjugated in their imperial onslaught on three continents have the right to evaluate their own history from their sources, their viewpoint and their values. Indeed, many Qur'anic verses recommend tolerance, and Muslim rule over a vast multireligious and multiethnic empire, when Muslims were a minority, could only be maintained by a degree of political tolerance. But this tolerance was contingent on political, economic, and social factors. The principle of religious tolerance is enshrined in the Muslim Revelation and is a well-known fact. However, it is not this principle that Muslim theologians and political leaders are discussing even today, but its limitations.

Dhimmitude should be recognized not only on a human and moral level, but also as a grave modern political problem. As long as the prejudices and the ideologies that have justified *dhimmitude* for Jews, Christians, and other religious groups are not clearly denounced in the Muslim world, they will continue to influence Muslim politics and perceptions of these peoples. The reactions will be more detrimental to the Muslims themselves, especially those living in the Western countries. It is therefore important that Muslim religious and political leaders denounce the sources of intolerance in their own culture, in order to build the bridges of a universal reconciliation. The study of *dhimmitude*—and especially its Jewish aspect, because it also involves Christian Judeophobia—is essential, so as to eliminate religious prejudices in the triangular relationship of the three monotheistic faiths.

NOTES

1. Ibn Abi Zayd al-Qayrawani (d. 966), *La Risála* [*Epitre sur les Eléments du dogme et de la loi de l'Islam selon le rite málikite*], trans. L. Bercher, 5th ed. (Algiers: 1960), p. 163; English version, in Bat Ye'or, *The Dhimmi: Jews and Christians under Islam* (London: Associated University Presses, 1985), p. 161.

2. Ibn Khaldun, *The Muqaddimah: An Introduction to History*, trans. F. Rosenthal (New York: Pantheon Books, 1958), 1: 473. Quoted in Bat Ye'or, *The Dhimmi*, p. 162.

3. The institutionalization of jihad as a religious injunction has produced an extensive juridical literature. For references, see Bat Ye'or, *The Decline of Eastern Christianity under Islam: From Jihad to Dhimmitude: 7th to 20th Century* (London: Associated University Presses, 1996), p. 455 n. 10; *Juifs et Chrétiens sous l'Islam: les dhimmis face au défi intégriste* (Paris: Berg, 1994), p. 24 n. 33; Rudolph Peters, *Jihad in Classical and Modern Islam: A Reader* (Princeton, NJ: Markus Wiener, 1996); Al-Azhar University, *The Fourth Conference of the Academy of Islamic Research, 1968* (Cairo: Government Printing Offices, 1970).

4. See Ibn Taimiyya (d. 1328), in Henri Laoust, *Le Traité de Droit Public d'Ibn Taimiya*, French trans. of *Slyasa Šar'iya* (Beirut: Institut Français de Damas, 1948); an-Nawawi, *MinhâdjAt-Tâlibin* [*Le Guide des Zélés Croyants. Manuel de Jurisprudence musulmane selon le rite de Châfi'š*], trans. L. W. C. van den Berg (Batavia: Imprimerie du Gouvernement, 1883), 3: 255, 264–65. For English quotations from Abu Yusuf Ya'qub, Ibn Taimiyya and al-Mawardi, see Bat Ye'or, *The Dhimmi*, pp. 165–80.

5. Abu Yusuf Ya'qub, *Le livre de l'impôt foncier* [*Kitâb al-Kharâdj*], trans. E. Fagnan (Paris: Geuthner, 1921), p. 293; see Bat Ye'or, *Juifs et Chrétiens*, p. 40 n. 13; Peters, *Jihad*, pp. 30–31; Alfred Morabia, *Le Gihad dans l'Islam Médiéval, Le 'Combat Sacré' des origines au Xe siècle*, preface by Roger Arnaldez (Paris: Albin Michel, 1993).

6. Abu Yusuf Ya'qub, *Le livre*, p. 189. For text in English, see Bat Ye'or, *The Dhimmi*, p. 168 n. 1.

7. Pedro C. Moreno, ed., *Handbook on Religious Liberty around the World* (Charlottesville, VA: Rutherford Institute, 1996), p. 277.

8. Abu Yusuf Ya'qub, *Le livre*, p. 40. English translation (excerpts) in Bat Ye'or, *The Dhimmi*, p. 165; Ibn Taimiyya, *Le Traité*, pp. 35–36. For the goods of the infidels destined to become "booty," see the opinion of the Andalusian jurist Ibn Hazm (eleventh century) in Roger Arnaldez, "La Guerre Sainte, selon Ibn Hazm de Cordoue," in *Études d'Orientalisme dédiées à la mémoire de Lévi-Provençal* (Paris: Maisonneuve et Larose, 1962), 2; 457: "God has established an ownership for infidels over their possessions, only for the institution of booty for the Muslims." See Bat Ye'or, *Juifs*, p. 46 n. 30 (English trans.).

9. Patrologia, *History of the Patriarchs of the Coptic Church of Alexandria, III: Agathon to Michael I* (766); English translation by B. Evetts in *Patrologia Orientalis* (Paris: Firmin-Didot, 1910), vol. 5., facs. 1, p. 72.

10. M. Schreiner, "*Contribution à l'histoire des Juifs en Egypte*," *Revue des Études Juives* 31 (1895): 9–10; English translation in Bat Ye'or, *The Dhimmi*, pp. 194–96.

11. Paul Paquignon, "Quelques Documents sur la condition des *Juifs* au Maroc." *Revue du Monde Musulman* 9 (1909): 112–19. The fatwas mention all the humiliations imposed on the tributaries: for the interdiction to wear shoes outside the Mellah, ibid., pp. 119–23. See Bat Ye'or, *Juifs*, p. 106.

12. Robert B. Serjeant, "A Judeo-Arab House-Deed from Habbán (with notes on the former Jewish communities of the Wahidi Sultanate)," *Journal of the Royal Asiatic Society* (October 1953), reprinted in ibid., *Customary and Shariah Law in Arabian Society* (London: Variorum Reprints, 1991), 8: 113. See Bat Ye'or, *Juifs*, pp. 74–75. For the condition of the Jews of Yemen in the first half of the nineteenth century, see Tudor Parfitt, *The Road to Redemption: The Jews of the Yemen 1900–1950* (Leiden: Brill, 1996).

13. Harvey E. Goldberg, *The Book of Mordechai: A Study of the Jews of Libya* (Philadelphia: Institute for the Study of Human Issues, 1980), p. 74.

14. An-Nawawi, *Le Guide*, 3: 287; Abu Yusuf Ya'qub, *Le livre*, pp. 329–31; see also Bat Ye'or, *Juifs*, p. 54.

15. Muhammad Abu Zahra, "*The Jihad*," in Al-Azhar, *The Fourth Conference*, p. 59; reprinted in D. F. Green, ed., *Arab Theologians on Jews and Israel: Extracts from the Proceedings of the Fourth Conference of the Academy of Islamic Research*, 3rd ed. (Geneva: Editions de l'Avenir, 1976), p. 61.

16. Moreno, "Pakistan," in *Handbook*, pp. 95–104; "Iran," in ibid., pp. 276–83; Nina Shea, ed., *In the Lion's Den: A Shocking Account of Persecution and Martyrdom of Christians Today and How We Should Respond: Based on Eyewitness Accounts!* (Nashville: Broadman & Holman, 1997).

17. Henri Tincq, *L'Etoile et la Croix. Jean-Paul II-Israël: L'explication* (Paris: Lattès, 1993), pp. 31–41; William Nicholls, *Christian Antisemitism. A History of Hate* (Northvale, NJ/London: Jason Aronson, 1993).

18. Christian obligation to serve Muslim interests was vigorously expounded by Christian Arab nationalists, especially by Michel Aflak, cofounder of the Ba'ath Party, and by Christian Palestinians. It was strongly affirmed as a sacred duty in the writings of Father Yoakim Boubarak.

19. Negib Azoury, *Le Rèveil de la Nation Arabe dans l'Asie Turque. En Prèsence des Intèrēts et des Rivalitiès des Puissances Etrangères, de la Curie Romaine et du Patriarcat oecumènique: Partie Asiatique de la Question d'Orient et Programme de la Ligue de la Patrie Arabe* (Paris: Plon, 1905). In his book, Azoury outlined the ideological and political bases of Arab nationalism "from a triple point of view: diplomatic, political and economical" will be completed by a complementary study called *Le Péril Juif Universel: Révélations et études politiques*. This work never appeared, but its title resembles what was soon to become known as *The Protocols of the Learned Elders of Zion*, first published in a Russian edition in 1905.

20. Friedrich Herr, "The Catholic Church and the Jews Today," in *Midstream* (New York: Theodor Herzl Foundation, 1971), p. 22.

21. Ibid., p. 23.

22. Tincq, *L'Etotle*, p. 40; George Emile Irani, *Le Saint-Siége et le Conflit du Proche-Orient* (Paris: Desclée de Brouwer, 1991), pp. 30–31.

23. See the lecture by Father Michel Hayek given on March 6, 1967, "Nouvelles approches de l'islam," *Les Conférences du Cénacle* (Beirut, 1968), nos. 9–10, 22 année, p. 11: "Why not admit it clearly, so as to break a taboo and a political interdict, which is felt in the flesh and the Christian conscience—that Islam has been the most appalling torment that ever struck the Church. Christian sensibility has remained traumatised until now." Quoted in Bat Ye'or, *Juifs*, p. 309 n. 45 (English trans.). See also "*Actes du Colloque des Chrétiens du monde arabe (CMA) à Paris*," in *Les Chrétiens du Monde Arabe: Problématiques Actuelles et Enjeux*, preface by Rondot (Paris: Maisonneuve & Larose, 1989).

24. See Walid Phares, *Lebanese Christian Nationalism: The Rise and Fall of an Ethnic Resistance* (Boulder, CO/London: Lynne Rienner, 1995).

25. Quoted in Bat Ye'or, *Juifs*, p. 252.

CHAPTER 54

Endowing Denial

Andrew G. Bostom

The Harvard Divinity School may return a $2.5 million donation from the United Arab Emirates ruler, Sheikh Zayed Bin Sultan Al Nahyan, earmarked to fund a professorship in Islamic studies. Why? As reported in the *Boston Globe* by Jenna Russell,[1] the benevolent sheikh openly espouses a virulent Judenhass. Moreover, his Zayed Center funds lectureships for noble, learned figures like perennial presidential candidate Lyndon LaRouche, who opines on international Jewish conspiracies; Roger Garaudy, an "expert" Holocaust denier; Umayma Jalahma, a Saudi blood libel "scholar" esteemed for her authoritative claim that Purim pastries contain Gentile blood; and Thierry Massan, author of a runaway best-seller in France maintaining that the US government orchestrated the September 11, 2001, attacks on the World Trade Center.

The *Globe* report, however, completely missed a less sensational but equally insidious thread related to this story: the attempt by the Zayed Center to negate and rewrite the millennial history of brutal oppression of Mizrachi (Oriental) Jews under Arab Muslim rule. A June 2002 report[2] in the *Gulf News* highlighted the "findings" from a symposium sponsored by the Zayed Center, entitled *The Jews in the Arab World*. The Goebbels–like summary communique included such frank howlers as:

"[The Oriental Jews'] situation in the Arab countries throughout the history of the Arab Islamic civilization . . . rendered an exemplary model of tolerance, understanding, peaceful living, religious and sectarian freedom, in addition to preservation of the rights to privacy."

"[The present] peaceful co-existence of Muslims and Jews in Arab Muslim countries, where Jews are treated equally and enjoy their fundamental rights and freedom, which they cannot under Israeli regimes. . . . Arab Jews have always been denied their fundamental rights and freedom under Israeli regimes."

Even more disturbing was the openly proclaimed agenda, based upon this obscene historical negationism:

The participants also called upon Arab research centers to conduct studies and research focusing on the fact that the Jews have never enjoyed freedom and good treatment such as that provided under the Arab Islamic rule.

Primary source documents compiled by a serious, objective Middle East Studies scholar, Dr. Tudor Parfitt, characterize the plight (which had persisted for over a millennium) of three hundred thousand Moroccan Jews, until Morocco became a French protectorate in 1912. Only then, in the early twentieth century, was the discriminatory treatment of Jews under the Shari'a (Islamic holy law) abrogated by direct French control. Jews throughout North Africa, as well as in Yemen and Palestine, shared a similarly bleak fate under the Shari'a.

Professor Parfitt's essay, "Dhimma versus Protection in Nineteenth-Century Morocco," contains a written appeal from the president and vice president of the Anglo-Jewish Association in February 1888 to Lord Salisbury, elucidating the horrific persecution of the Jews of Morocco.[3] Their basic desire was abolition of the *dhimma* imposed on their Moroccan co-religionists. This pact (*dhimma*) by which Jews (and other non-Muslims) conquered by jihad wars were afforded their lives and some limited autonomy, in exchange for payment of the blood ransom poll tax (*jizya*), also entailed a host of discriminatory and humiliating regulations. These regulations created long-standing, serious disabilities for Moroccan Jews, twenty-seven examples of which were enumerated in this 1888 appeal:

- Jews are compelled to live in the ghetto.
- Jews are not allowed to ride outside the ghetto.
- On leaving the ghetto, they are compelled to remove their footwear and remove their head covering. They are not allowed to use a walking stick although the old and sick are permitted to use a reed.
- Moors frequently amuse themselves by throwing live coals, broken glass, old tinware, and such things in thoroughfares traversed by Jews and

Andrew G. Bostom, "Endowing Denial," FrontPageMagazine.com, May 13, 2003, http://www.frontpagemag.com/Articles/Read.aspx?GUID=A30735FB-CC15-4672-B43E-D9C80A526E43.

enjoy the fun of seeing the latter smart under the burn or wound inflicted on their bare feet.

- Jews are not permitted to build their houses above a certain height.
- Jews are debarred from having stores or shops in the Muslim quarter.
- The Jew is bound to pass the Moor on the left side and if he fails so to do he must retrace his steps.
- Jews are forced to buy damaged government property such as grain, or overstocked provisions or poor items, at the normal price of undamaged goods.
- Jews with their wives and daughters are compelled to undertake work for any government official at all times (even on the Sabbath and on sacred festivals) and to receive payment far below the market rate of wages.
- They are compelled to undertake work such as a Moor would consider degrading, e.g., the cleaning of sewers, carrying away carcasses of dead animals from government stables, etc. When the head of rebels or of criminals are sent to a town to be exposed at the town gate the Jews are made to salt them before they are exhibited.
- Jews pay capitation tax to be exempt from military service but in paying this "they submit to the humiliation of receiving a slap on the head."
- Jewish purveyors (butchers, grocers, bakers, etc.) are bound to supply gratis all the requirements of various functionaries, otherwise their trade is cut off.
- A Jew cannot appoint a Jewish attorney to plead before the Kadi against a Moor. Thus he must either conduct his case in person, or must appoint a Moorish attorney, or suffer his case to pass undefended.
- Jews are barred from the liberal professions.
- Jews are disqualified from public office.
- Jews are required to wear a special costume consisting of a black skullcap and black shoes.
- Jews are not allowed to use public baths and "are even denied the use of baths in the ghetto."
- Jews "are not allowed to drink from the public fountains in the Moorish quarter nor to take water therefrom" as the Jews are considered unclean.
- Jews are obligated to give gifts to public functionaries on special occasions—births, marriages and deaths—as well as on Jewish festivals.
- Jews are not allowed to carry arms.

- Jewish life is compensated for by the payment of forty pounds: there is no other punishment of the murderer. Of this sum the authorities deduct a substantial proportion.
- Jewish evidence is not heard (in courts of law, where a Muslim is a party).
- A Muslim can always denounce a Jew, "a thousand Jews" will fail to indict a Muslim.
- A Jew condemned to imprisonment or flogging has to pay the fees of all officials engaged in his punishment. If he is without funds he stays in prison until such time as they are paid.
- Jews are denied access to common quarters in the prisons.
- If a Jew is suspected of immoral intercourse with a Moorish woman (though she be a prostitute) he is liable to imprisonment for an indefinite period. If he confesses, death is his punishment.
- If a Moor chooses to assert that a Jew has abjured his faith he is compelled to become a Muslim "and should he afterwards attempt to conform to the Jewish ritual, he would be liable to be stoned or burned to death."

Well-heeled, oil-money-supported, pseudoacademic "think tanks" such as the Zayed Foundation should not be allowed to promote their warped historiography, which negates the suffering of Oriental Jews, in Islamic studies and/or Middle East studies programs. Under the Shari'a in Morocco, into the early twentieth century, the murder of a Jew by a Muslim could be "compensated" for by the payment of forty pounds. At the beginning of the twenty-first century, in a free and decent society like the United States, we must make clear to our academic institutions that no donation, whatever its sum, will permit the suppression of this sad, brutal historical legacy.

NOTES

1. Jenna Russell, "Harvard Is Pressured to Return $2.5M Gift," *Boston Globe*, May 11, 2003. The funds were in fact eventually returned. See Ralph Ranalli, "Harvard to Return $2.5M Given by Arab President," *Boston Globe*, July 28, 2004.

2. *Gulf News*, June 20, 2002.

3. In Tudor Parfitt, ed., *Israel and Ishmael: Studies in Muslim Jewish Relations* (New York: St. Martin's Press, 2000), pp. 142–66.

CHAPTER 55

Modern Egyptian Jew Hatred: Indigenous Elements and Foreign Influences

Bat Ye'or

Starting in 1955–56 one noticed in Egypt an enormous expansion in anti-Jewish literature. This genre issues from a long tradition, going back to Manethon, Apion, the Acts of the Pagan Martyrs, and Origen—to cite only the most illustrious of Classical Antiquity—as well as to the Qur'an and hadiths in the Arab period. The themes are indeed by no means new—or "far from it!" Thus the fable of the lepers is applied by Fathī 'Uthman al-Mahlāwī to the Zionists: "And thus Britain wanted to exhaust the strength of the Arabs and divide them, and at one and the same time to get rid of the Zionist plague in her country: she assembled these thousands of vagabonds and aliens, blood-suckers and pimps and said to them: 'Take for yourselves a national home called Israel.' Thus the dregs of the nations were collected in the Holy Land."[1]

I cannot analyze here all the Egyptian anti-Jewish literary production, to which special studies have been devoted. I will confine myself to indicating the essential themes, coming respectively from Islamic culture properly speaking, from Pan-Arabism, and from Nazi antisemitism. (The latter has negligible direct influence but supplied a technique.) Arab anti-Judaism currently presents a theological and political ideology that is imposed by a technique that perfectly exploits the procedures of mental alienation of the masses.

The proceedings of the Fourth Conference of the Academy of Islamic Research[2] give a full insight into the theological anti-Jewish themes that have spread in all eras in the Arab world. It would be a mistake to underestimate the importance of this conference, which took place under the patronage of Nasser, that gathered in Azhar, the center of the Islamic world, the most prestigious religious leaders of Islam.

It is interesting to note that the theological university Al Azhar was affiliated with the Egyptian presidency on June 23, 1961, by a resolution voted in the National Assembly. This meant that religion was now at the service of state policy and would support it. In fact, religion became a political instrument and an essential element in government.

The Judeophobic themes enunciated at Al Azhar highlight the religious roots of Arab anti-Judaism. What arises from the evidence of these conference lectures is the irrationality of intolerant and even racist prejudices that oppose the incontestable superiority of the Muslim and the Arab, on the one hand, to the villainy and abjection of the Jews on the other.

Jews are bad because the Qur'an says so. The Qur'an is a divine book whose teachings cannot be contested. Consequently, Jews have a theological perversity, meaning diabolical: they incarnate metaphysical evil. They are Satan.

This religious dimension of the Jewish evil as it is enunciated by the lecturers at Azhar is manifested under two aspects: its permanence, which classifies it in a certain fashion as outside time (eternal as the devil) and then its very quality (evil is consubstantial with Jewish nature). Over and over the theologians stress these two essential characteristics of Judaism.

While in these lectures the theological foundation is primary, the Pan-Arab and Nazi elements are no less interesting. I shall cite briefly the principal accusations of the anti-Jewish theological polemic.

THE MISFORTUNES AND DISPERSAL OF THE JEWISH PEOPLE ARE WILLED BY GOD.

In his inaugural speech, the rector of Al Azhar, the Grand Imam Sheikh Hassan Mahmoud declares that the war of 1967 took the Arabs and Muslims by surprise, for the deceitful Zionists are "destined to dispersion by the Deity."[3]

The same opinion is shared by Kamal Ahmad Own, vice principal of the Tanta Institute, who refers to the Qur'an in predicting that the Jews will suffer until the end of time torments and persecutions from the peoples

---

Bat Ye'or in *Yehudi Mitzraim* (*Jews in Egypt*) (Tel Aviv: 1974), 140–41. English translation from the original French by Susan Emanuel.

who will disperse them. The Qur'an also reveals how the *"wicked nature"* of Jews led them to falsify the word of Allah, to kill the prophets, to deny the divine mission of Muhammad, and to commit sins. There is no doubt that *"evil, envy, hatred and cruelty"* are inherent in the Jews, since the Qur'an affirms this and it is the word of Allah.[4]

After having discoursed at length about the deceitfulness and malfeasance of the Jews and the legitimate hatred in which humanity holds them, Azzah Darwaza states that *"the conduct and instincts of Jews . . . suffices to prove the justification of the punishment that is everywhere and in all circumstances inflicted on them."*[5] According to Sheikh Abdul-Hamid 'Attiyah al-Dibani of Libya, *"God has also made it clear that they will be marked by humiliation, misery and submission, and that they will suffer dispersal and torment until the Day of Judgment."*[6]

Professor Abdul Sattar El-Sayed of Syria writes:

It is for this reason that God has decreed that they are scattered all over the globe and that no nation will be composed of them. Instead they will live as an evil on the land, like sickness and pestilential germs. And thus their malfeasance is not confined to one people or to one nation.[7]

THE JEWS HATE THE MUSLIMS. THE SCHEMING, CORRUPT, SEDITIOUS AND COWARDLY NATURE OF JEWS. FALSIFICATION OF SCRIPTURE.

Mohammed Taha Yahia has drawn from his historical and comparative study of the Qur'an and the Old and New Testaments the following conclusions: Jews are congenitally ambitious, obstinate, cruel, aggressive, arrogant, harmful, inhuman, avaricious, ruthless, hypocritical, and revengeful: *"From the very beginning Jews declared their hostility to Islam and even to all the other religions. [. . .] They always try to seize any opportunity to take revenge on Islam and Muslims."*[8]

In his study of the attitude of Jews toward the Arabs and Muslims in Muhammad's time, Sheikh Abd Allah al Meshad states that in Medina the Jews controlled the economy, practiced usury, and monopolized food. They were characterized by *"avarice, as well as numerous other vices."* They were hypocrites, perfidious, and corrupted Islamic society.

The Jews colluded with every hostile movement against the Islamic Call and the Muslims. Those are some aspects of the enmity displayed by the Jews toward the Muslims. It is due to dangerous psychological factors symbolized in the scorn of Arabs and the rejection of the idea of the last Apostle to be from them. . . . That scorn was an aspect of envy rooted in them.

The Jews merit the description "worst of beasts" applied to them in the Qur'an. Cowardly and fearful, perfidious and resentful, the Jews plot to take vengeance on Muslims. *"Their methods in attacking the Faith were conspiracies, plots, intrigues, seditions, separation for the believers, distortion of the Call, and attempts to drive the Muslims out of their purified Creed."*[9] Jews represent a great peril, for they never lose hope of spreading their corruption, they are everywhere and always instigators of sedition. In chasing them out of Arabia, Omar *"purged"* the peninsula *"of their pollution."* After having described the Jews' conspiracies, the author cites *"the perverse attributes that are inherent in them,"* invoking passages from the Qur'an. I will mention only the subtitles of this exposition.

Telling lies about God . . . Their fondness for listening to falsehood . . . Disobedience against Allah. . . . Mutiny against His Messengers . . . Facility of assassination . . . Perjury . . . Hardheartedness . . . Argumentativeness and two-facedness . . . Suppression of truth and Misguidance . . . Hypocrisy . . . Egoism . . . Desire for corrupting people . . . Lack of conscience . . . Loving malignancy . . . Their resentment against the blessings granted to others . . . Hastening to commit sins and to disobey Allah's injunctions . . . Self-conceit and haughtiness. . . . Opportunism and exploitation . . . Trickery for transgression . . . Cowardice . . . Indecency of speech . . . Miserliness . . . Excessive selfishness . . . Fear of death . . . Garbling of the sacred Books.[10]

Muhammad Azzah Darwaza refers to the Qur'an to prove that at the time of Muhammad, the Jews were falsifying Scripture, contradicting the truth, were hedonists and hypocrites. They gathered together to deceive people secretly, betraying their promises and *"delivering themselves to malign and harmful practices against the people."* They led people into error, swindling their money; they were seditious and corrupters. Greedy, avid and concupiscent, they practiced idolatry, committed *"crimes against law and morality."* Allah had marked them with *"stigmata of humiliation and pettiness"* and will continue to persecute them until the final day. And, says the author, the Jews of today are exactly like those described by the Qur'an, as noxious to Muslim society as were their ancestors.[11]

Sheikh Abdul-Hamid Attiyah al'Dibani, taking up all the accusations enumerated above, states that according to the Qur'an the worst enemies of Muslims are the Jews. For this reason, Muslims should never make peace with the Jews, *"who are only a band of thieves and criminals."*[12]

This opinion is confirmed by Professor Muhammad Él-Sayed Hussein al-Dahabi along with all the previously cited accusations. The Jews *"are known for being a mendacious and lying people. Their hatred of Islam and Muslims goes beyond all bounds."*[13] Scheming and unctuous, they try by all means to corrupt the faith of Muslims.

JEWS ARE THE ENEMIES OF HUMANKIND.

According to Kamal Ahmad Own, the pernicious nature of Jews never changes:

> Brief as this treatise is, it illustrates that the Jews as represented by their Holy Book are hostile to all human values in this life, that their evil nature is not to be easily cured through temporary or half-measures. . . . Vice, perversity, perjury, and idolizing money are the inherent characteristics of the Jews.

The misfortunes that have devastated the Jews are justified by the fact of *"their vicious nature, which has always alienated them from humanity."*[14] This opinion is repeated in the speeches of many theologians, in particular that of Mohammed Taha Yahia.

THE DUTY OF MUSLIMS IS TO MAKE HOLY WAR AGAINST THE JEWS.

In a speech titled "Jihad in the Cause of Allah," Hassan Khaled declares:

> This battle is not a mere combat between two parties but it is a battle between two religions (namely, it is a religious war). Zionism in fact represents a very perilous cancer, aiming at dominating the Arab countries and the whole Islamic World.[15]

According to Sheikh Abu Zahra,

> All Muslims should rise in arms as one man and start a violent, irresistible onward onslaught to deliver the Holy Land that has been desecrated by the sworn enemies of humanity.[16]

Jihad against Israel and the Jews is ardently encouraged by all the lecturers, in often very violent terms.

Political and Economic Factors in Egyptian Anti-Judaism

We have seen that at the end of the nineteenth century, an ambivalent feeling of admiration and hatred toward the Christian West and its industrial and technological civilization was developing in the colonized Arab countries. After the defeat of 1948 and the accusations of collusion between the Israelis and the West raised by Arab potentates, the animosity against Western industrial society crystallized on Israel, symbol of this hated modern civilization, inaccessible and ardently coveted. For the inaugural address:

> We, 'Ulemas, have also to make clear to the Arab nation and Islamic peoples that the lingering spirit of the Crusades of the past that had been utterly routed by the feats of valor and heroic resistance of

our forefathers, had made of the present day Zionism a spear-head launched (against Arabs and Muslims) by the enemies of humanity and advocates of imperialism (and colonialism).[17]

> The enemies of Islam have thrown in the backs of the Muslims and Arabs a poisonous dagger by allowing Zionists to settle in Palestine and to occupy its lands and appropriate Jerusalem for themselves.[18]

> Imperialism creates in Palestine a state of conspiracies to disunite and crush the unity of the Arab and Islamic world and divide it into two distinct parts, African and Asian.[19]

Studying the problem of Palestine, Abdullah Kannoun declares that it concerns all Muslims and not only Arabs, due to the Crusades that the West is leading against Islam.

> The attitude of flagrant challenge taken up by the Western powers towards the cause of Palestine [. . .] has as its only explanation the hatred of such powers for Islam and the rancor they harbor toward Muslims, especially at a time when Muslims contemplate closing their ranks in a bid to establish a Muslim League which, in the Western view, would be more threatening to their interests than the danger of the yellow peril.

He continues: The Arab-Israeli conflict is not a political conflict but a religious conflict of all Muslims against Zionism, an offshoot of Imperialism that is only a disguised form of the crusade launched by the Christian West against the Muslim East in the Middle Ages to subjugate Muslims and bring them under Western domination. [. . .] The cursed imperialists had no alternative—after full calculation and deliberation—but to drive the rotten wedge of Zionism in the heart of the Muslim world. This is an endeavor to impede Muslim unity, hinder the process of independence of Muslim states, and humiliate Muslims by having them subjugated by the basest race and people for imperialist ends, while at the same time satisfying the grudge of remnants of the crusaders, whom nothing could satisfy but to see the Muslims attacked in the main part of their countries.

On the theme of a religious war between Islam and Christianity, Kannoun concludes that

> we the scholars of Islam [are allowed] to declare far and wide that a crusade is being launched against us, and the hatred our enemies feel towards us drives them to take revenge on us with such ferocity, pushing the dregs of peoples and of countries from among brutal Zionists to punish our brethren in Palestine.[20]

On December 13, 1953, Egyptian president Nasser declared:

Israel, which is supported by imperialism that does not want liberty in this area, which considers us as a chattel for its own advantage, as it is always the imperialist plan to put an end to all the Arab nations. This is not a short-term plan but a long-term plan, whose aim is to put an end to the whole of Arabism.

And eight years later:

Israel, which imperialism established in the heart of the Arab world to give a death-blow to Arab nationalism, to strike at the Arab nation in order to prevent [its] awakening and building itself from the social, economic and political points of view . . . (July 22, 1961).[21]

All the arguments cited above are enunciated in a condensed form in a speech by the president of Egypt, Anwar Sadat, given at the Mosque of El Hussein in Cairo on April 25, 1972.[22] The Qur'an, which expresses divine will, has doomed the Jews to diaspora, misery, and humiliation. It describes them as liars and traitors who attacked the Prophet. Basing himself on the Qur'an, Sadat declares that the Jews "*are a nation of liars and traitors, hatching plots, a people born for acts of perfidy.*" Moreover, Israel is only the offshoot of imperialism (the United States). The goal they pursue is to sap the faith of true believers. Consequently, there can be no negotiation, no contact, between Israel and an Egypt whose duty is to pursue the war until it imposes on Jews the condition of misery and humiliation that the Qur'an has assigned them.

There is nothing original about this view. It merely continues the segregationist and discriminatory practice that Islam has applied obstinately and for centuries to *dhimmis*, whether Jews or Christians.

In effect, the Qur'an recommends that Muslims have no relations whatever with the infidels, from fear that the latter might sap their faith.[23] The traditional distinctive and obligatory signs of Islam [for non-Muslims], worn even in public baths, aim not only to throw opprobrium on the *dhimmis*, but also to mark their estrangement, their isolation, their exclusion from the ensemble of believers. Just as the Muslim, permeated by his superiority (especially if he is Arab), has no relations with the *dhimmi* whom he despises, so the Arab countries establish no contact with the *dhimmi* state of Israel and seek to expel it from the community of nation-states.

Nazi Antisemitic Elements

Arabs borrowed from Nazi antisemitism the concepts of race and of contamination. Jews corrupt the purity of the Arab race and the Jewish cancer infects the world, although the theme of the impure is precisely the theory that had been advanced by Manethon.

Jews, in no matter which community, have always been a factor for sedition. Moreover, they have constituted a curse spreading among people, engendering corruption, sowing seeds of enmity and hatred and breaking the ties of fraternity among people who as a result were engaged in endless conflicts. . . . For the Jews are similar to those evils that have the same effect whatever their quantity, like those germs of malignant illnesses of which only one suffices to exterminate an entire nation.[24]

The author notes the harmful effect of the Jews: "*Spread across the whole world*," they bring to every people evils and catastrophes: They are "*a sore that humanity must tolerate, which it must accommodate like other calamities of life and other diseases.*"

The Jews are a blight more generally. The Holy Qur'an reveals the congenital poison of Jews "*and constitutes the microscope through which we may observe the monsters and poisons that reside in their minds and hearts.*" The testimony of prophets proves that the Jews are "*of a nature different from human nature, bearers of disease and harmful germs.*" The prophets tried to treat these diseases and to prevent the germs from infecting the whole world. The Qur'an describes "*the ancient vice transmitted through the ages from one generation of Jews to another.*" Not only do the Jews hate humanity, but they have the effect of "*poisonous needles and chronic illnesses that corrupt human kind and continue their harmful effect as long as the needle, the illness, [the Jews] is not suppressed.*" Developing his obsession with illness and blight, the author concludes:

Here is our enemy, and the sickness that has ravaged our lands. According to the descriptions of Jews in the Koran, they are an enemy devoid of any human sentiment, like a harmful germ, a cursed plague, as Satan was, chased by God from the Kingdom of his Grace. This enemy also has the mission of unleashing war on the peoples, exactly like Satan. God has warned us against Satan by saying: "Satan is our enemy, and consider him as such." God has also warned us against the Jews by saying: "The most violent enemies of believers are the Jews and unbelievers. . . . They are the enemy. So beware of them! May Allah kill them! How far they are from the Way!" [63:4][25]

The Protocols of the Elders of Zion has also profoundly influenced contemporary Arab anti-Judaism. The sexual accusations against the Jews that one finds in Arab literature reveals a frustration and a profound social disequilibrium in modern Egyptian society. All the racist themes and conclusions of the *Protocols* are coordinated in a pseudoscientific form in this book, supposedly by a Copt.[26] The book is remarkable for its confusion of historical texts, its erroneous interpretation of them, references of a veracity that is doubtful at the very least, as well as anachronistic statements. This work illustrates the Nazi pseudoscientific technique adopted by Arab anti-Jewish literature, in which the noxious characteristics of the Jews are applied to the Zionists.

We may definitively recognize that properly Islamic elements essentially contribute to feeding contemporary Egyptian anti-Judaism. The pejorative characteristics of Jews as they are described in Muslim religious texts are applied to modern Jews. Anti-Judaism and anti-Zionism are equivalent, for due to the inferior status of the Jew in Islam, and because divine will dooms him to wandering and misery, the Jewish state appears to Muslims as an unbearable affront and a sin against God. Therefore it must be destroyed by jihad. Here the Pan-Arab and anti-Western theses that consider Israel as an advanced instrument of the West in the Islamic world come to reinforce religious anti-Judaism. The religious and the political fuse in a purely Islamic context onto which are grafted foreign elements. If, on the doctrinal level, Nazi influence is secondary to the Islamic base, the technique with which the antisemitic material has been reworked, and the political purposes being pursued, present striking similarities with Hitler's Germany.

Nasserian antisemitism makes concrete and coordinates into one coherent policy both the theological and Pan-Arab elements of anti-Jewishness. Hence an evolution has taken place in Egypt that is similar to Hitler's Germany. The same situation of crisis that in Europe crystallized antisemitism is being reproduced in Egypt, where the penetration of Western values and industrial and technological civilization had profoundly upset the mental and socioeconomic structures of a feudal society.

The essential similarities have been noted.[27] As in Nazi Germany, latent antisemitism spreads and strengthens in intellectual circles and among the petite bourgeoisie that accedes to power with the advent of military dictatorship. Onto the demeaning theological image is grafted a social and political animosity that is also expressed against all foreigners, but that is particularly virulent against Jews, behind whom is profiled the baleful power of Zionists. Just as in Nazi Germany, so in Egypt, Jews and Israel are represented as a monstrous danger threatening the whole Arab nation. Nasser and Sadat declared several times, that Israel wanted to establish itself from the Nile to the Euphrates. Israel

is one of the most dangerous pockets of imperialist resistance. . . . Our struggle against the Israeli policy of infiltration in Africa is only an attempt to limit the spread of a destructive imperialist cancer.[28]

Hence the problem of Israel is not only the problem of Palestine but has dangerous results apart

from Palestine, for Israel is a real expansionist danger with wise and perilous possibilities, since [she] is working for the day when the Arab peoples between the Nile and the Euphrates will be a horde of refugees.[29]

All political initiatives are presented as measures of defense against the expansionist aggression of Israel. The struggle against the enemy and the fear of this danger serve to consolidate military power. And as in Nazi Germany, the common hatred is used to cement the union of Arabs and to forge an identity in a society dislocated by the twentieth century. A common hatred and aggressiveness reinforce national unity and identification.

Apart from its function of political identification, common hatred also fulfills a social function by steering toward the exterior any popular discontent caused by poverty and internal problems. The struggle between the Arabs and Jews takes on the proportions of a battle between the forces of good and evil, it is on a universal scale. Egyptian soldiers are the soldiers of Allah.[30] Like Hitler, Nasser felt invested in a divine mission to save the Arabs and the purity of their race from Jewish corruption, and as in Nazi Germany, the religious overlaid the political.

The predestined hero of the Arab nation, Nasser felt called to enlighten the nations.[31]

My duty is to deliver the Arab world from the destruction caused by the Zionist intrigues that have their roots in the United States.[32]

The battle in which we are now engaged . . . is against Israel, the instrument of imperialism created at the heart of the Arab world to deflect our nationalism. We will all defend our freedom and Arabism and we will fight to see the Arab Nation extend from the Atlantic Ocean to the Persian Gulf.[33]

Sadat and Egypt carry the Prophet's banner and pursue his mission. They fight for Allah, who has made them "*a nation elected above all nations.*"[34]

As happened in Germany, Arab religious leaders encourage the anti-Jewish campaign. To the Aryan myth corresponds the myth of Arab glorification. Like Hitler, Nasser propagated his ideas through an intensive campaign disseminated through the press, radio, mass meetings, and speeches in mosques. This intoxication on a national level produces monstrous psychosocial distortions that no longer have any relation with reality.

These comparisons by no means signify that Egyptian anti-Judaism is imported from the West, but that similar political, social, and ideological factors reproduce similar situations. Like Nazi ideology,[35] religious Pan-Arabism in Muslim societies in crisis must endeavor to elaborate a new national identity.

That anti-Jewish opinions have been widely spread in Arab nationalist circles since the 1930s is not in doubt. But their confirmation at Azhar by the most important authorities of Islam enabled them to be definitively imposed, with the cachet of infallible authenticity, upon illiterate masses that were strongly attached to religious traditions.

One cannot deny the extremely harmful effect on Jewish youth of governmental anti-Judaism erected into a national policy and constantly used as an instrument for exasperating the masses. As we know, in 1948 censorship and espionage had begun isolating Egyptian Judaism from foreign Jewish cultural life. Any information concerning the state of Israel was rigorously prohibited in Egypt. The dissolution of communities, the emigration of their best elements, the aggressiveness of propaganda and social hostility combined to produce among Jews an alienation all the more profound in that it was unconscious. They lived huddled among themselves in fear and distrust, having renounced in all manifestations of social and professional life any assertion or demonstration of their religious identity.

In Egypt the last vestiges of Judaism that are still retained are of an economic order, but they are also psychological, like emotional attachment to the country and apprehension about the difficulties of assimilating into a foreign and technological society. For youth growing up in the 1950s and 1960s, the alienation was total. An exodus that opened up horizons of freedom also led it to discover Judaism itself. Today, émigrés from Egypt who opted for diaspora are disseminated through the world, nourishing a vague nostalgia, keeping the indelible mark of refugees in search of an identity, tormented internally by the concern to pass on to their children their own destiny.

The Jews who have emigrated from Egypt to Israel would seem the ones most able to work effectively for better understanding between those two countries. In effect, similar in their common customs and traditions (the primordial vehicle for emotional and intellectual exchanges), Jewish refugees from Egypt, so intimately linked to Islamic civilization, might aid the Arab peoples to accede to political maturity by struggling against the fanatic ideologies, catalysts of hate, of which they were once the most vulnerable victims.

It was a policy that determined the persecutions (we have briefly discussed that policy's substance, theological structure, genesis, motivations, and growing influence)—of which the people, due to the conditions of alienation of poverty and modern propaganda, then became the irresponsible instrument.

NOTES

1. "A Spearhead against Arab Nationalism," in a special issue of the *Journal of Arab Nationalism* (January–March 1959), quoted in Yehoshaphat Harkabi, *Arab Attitudes to Israel* (Jerusalem: Israel University Press, 1971), p. 130.

2. Al Azhar, *Fourth Conference of the Academy of Islamic Research* (Cairo: General Organization for Government Printing Offices, 1970); 1 volume in English, 3 volumes in Arabic. Extracts were published in English with an introduction by D. F. Green in *Arab Theologians on Jews and Israel* (Geneva: Editions de l'Avenir, 1971), and in French as *Les Juifs et Israel vus par les Théologiens arabes* (Geneva: Editions de l'Avenir, 1972). All the quotations below were taken from the Geneva publication in English.

3. Ibid., p. 15.

4. Ibid.

5. Ibid., pp. 33–38.

6. Ibid., pp. 38–41.

7. Ibid., pp. 41–45.

8. Ibid., p. 25.

9. Ibid., pp. 27–28.

10. Ibid., pp. 29–32.

11. Ibid., pp. 33–38.

12. Ibid., pp. 38–41.

13. Ibid., pp. 41–45.

14. Ibid., pp. 19–20.

15. Ibid., p. 66.

16. Ibid., p. 62.

17. Ibid., pp. 15–16. Speech by the Grand Imam Sheikh Hassan Mahmoud.

18. Ibid., p. 18. Speech by Dr. Mahmoud Hobbalah.

19. Ibid., p. 26. "Jewish Role in Aggression on the Islamic Base in Medina," by Dr. Abdel Aziz Kamil.

20. Ibid., pp. 55–56. "Muslims and the Problem of Palestine," by Abdullah Kannoun.

21. Harkabi, *Arab Attitudes to Israel*, p. 159.

22. Cairo Radio.

23. Qur'an 3:28.

24. Al Azhar, *Fourth Conference*, Prof. Abdul Sattar Él-Sayed, p. 527.

25. Ibid., by Prof. Abdul Sattar Él-Sayed, pp. 527–33.

26. Ibrahim Amin Ghali, *L'Egypte et les Juifs dans l'antiquité* and *L'Oriente Chrétien et les Juifs (70–632),* (Paris: Cujas, 1969, 1970).

27. Saul Friedlander, *L'Antisémitisme Nazi: Histoire d'une psychose collective* (Paris: Seuil, 1971).

28. Egyptian National Charter, chapter 10, quoted by Harkabi, *Arab Attitudes to Israel*, p. 71.

29. Nasser's speech to the National Council, March 26, 1964, quoted by Harkabi, *Arab Attitudes to Israel,* p. 73.

30. Sadat, Cairo Radio, February 4, 1971.

31. Rony E. Gabbay, *A Political Study of the Arab-Jewish Conflict. The Arab Refugee Problem (A Case Study),* Études d'Histoire Economique, Politique et Sociale sous la direction de Jacques Freymond et Jaques L'Huillier, vol. 29 (Genève: Librairie E. Droz, 1959); p. 510/Look for corrections on p. 10.

32. Nasser in *Al-Ahram*, Cairo, October 15, 1955.

33. Nasser, July 26, 1956.

34. Sadat, speech of April 25, 1972.

35. Saul Friedlander, *L'Antisémitisme Nazi.*

CHAPTER 56

Judaism and Islam as Opposites

Johann von Leers

It is of some interest to read Jewish historians from time to time, not because we can find truth in them, but in order to gain insight into the psychology of Jews. Here we are concerned with one such case that is highly unique— whenever the Jews happen to discuss Muhammad and Islam, they are exceptionally hostile, indeed hateful. For example, Simon Dubnow, in his *General History of the Jewish People* (Berlin, 3: 282 ff.)[1] describes Muhammad, but does not fail to note that he was not able to read, and then adds the following:

Thus in the mind of this half-Bedouin there ripened the idea of monotheism, which in him became a fiery passion that drove him to engage in a "holy war" in which any means was permissible. For Muhammad, the knowledge of God was in no way connected with the sublime ethical consciousness that makes the ethical monotheism of the biblical prophets and the one-sided evangelical doctrine of "not of this world" so attractive. The life of Muhammad reveals neither an enchanting personality nor an embodiment of the highest ethical principles capable, even more than the abstract idea, of captivating pious souls. The life of the "Emissary of Allah" and the Qur'an itself are full of examples of how the founder of a religion should not speak and behave. Behind the mask of a prophet we find only too often the eye of a half-savage; the Prophet's inspiration is overshadowed by the crude passion of the Bedouin who ruthlessly murders in war and does not hesitate to carry off the wives or daughters of the men he murders in order to add them to his harem. All these character traits of Muhammad are particularly clear in his behavior with regard to Jews in Arabia.

This is not historical writing, but rather a campaign of hatred and libel.[2] First of all, Muhammad was neither a Bedouin nor a half-Bedouin; instead, he was a member of the old family of urban nobility in Mecca, the Quraysh, so the Jewish critic Dubnow obviously has not read the Qur'an, since he makes such an egregious error.

But one thing this passage surely betrays—the Jews' mortal hatred, fourteen hundred years later, for the man who gave birth to the most recent and, in many respects, the most successful of the world religions.

The clash between Muhammad and Jewry is not well known, but is actually very interesting. Even before Emperor Titus's destruction of Jerusalem (70 CE) there were already a few Jews in Arabia, and after the destruction of Jerusalem large groups emigrated to Arabia, settled in Arabian cities, and there carried on active agitation on behalf of Judaism. The three tribes, Banu Qaynuqa, Banu Nadir, and Banu Qurayza, took up residence especially in the city of Yathrib, while other Jews settled in Khaybar, Fadak, Taima, and Wadi-el-Kura— cities that were in fact fully under their control. There were also Jewish groups in southern Arabia, as far south as Aden. The Jews consciously pursued their mission; if many Jewish tribes had the same particularist spirit, the same tribal feuds, and the same customs of blood revenge as the Arabs, this was frequently not because the Jews were becoming Arabized, but on the contrary because in these Jewish tribes there were many converted Arabs. However, the headquarters of the area taken over by the Jews was Yathrib, from which emanated Jewish agitation; there, the three previously mentioned Jewish tribes had intervened in the conflicts between the two largest Arab tribes, the Aws and the Khazraj [sometimes referred to collectively as Banu Qayla],[3] which they incited against each other and in this way took control over the city. This penetration was achieved by means of economic activity, settlement, and trade, but above all by the Jews' spiritual influence. To be sure, Christian influences from Byzantium and Abyssinia were also involved, but of the foreign religious creeds Judaism was the most widespread, active, and successful.

The Jews later sought to prove how much Islam had borrowed from Judaism. It is characteristic of Judaism's vanity that it always sees itself as the origin of all new knowledge. In reality some external respects in which Islam and Judaism agree were borrowed not from Judaism but rather from ancient Oriental folk customs.

Johann von Leers, "Judentum und Islam als Gegensatze," *Die Judenfrage in Politik, Recht, and Wirtschaft* 6, no. 24 (December 24, 1942): 275–78; translated by Steven Rendall.

The prohibition on pork corresponds to very ancient hygienic experiences in the Orient, because in that region's climate this fatty meat is not easily digestible; in addition there is the danger of trichinosis. If the Qur'an occasionally refers to Jewish matters, the reason for this is not that Muhammad learned from Judaism, but rather that energetic Jewish missionary work had introduced many Jewish legends and ideas among the Arabs. Had the development of this Jewish penetration continued undisturbed, large numbers of the Arab people might have become Judaized—just as they later adopted Islam. Judaism would thereby have gained an enormous increase in power. Jews would have been able to unleash to their own ends all the natural warlike and political forces of the Arab people. The swarms of horsemen that under 'Umar later conquered Egypt and Persia, and pushed as far as Spain and India, would have entered the field on behalf of the Talmud. This would have resulted in a cruel catastrophe for the whole of cultured humanity.

The Arab peoples of the pre-Islamic era had little to oppose to the Jewish mission. The belief in their old local and nature gods was undermined and dissolved because it no longer corresponded to the sober, clear, comprehensible thought of the people. We hear about persons of that time who tried out various religions, "Hanifs" or meditative individuals who sought religious clarity. In the Arab world of that time there was certainly a search for religious truth, for a healthy, clear way of life in accord with God's will. The people was in a religious crisis and was looking for a way out of it.

While still a child, Muhammad ibn Abdallah is supposed to have encountered a Christian monk who saw in him a future bearer of religious knowledge and warned his escort to protect him against the Jews, who would bedevil him all during his life. It is possible that the boy Muhammad at that time already said something about the Jews that revealed his quick-wittedness to the monk, who may have been well versed in psychology. But it was not until he reached forty, after a highly successful career as a businessman, that Muhammad was first deeply gripped and shaken by the religious question. Enlightenment came to him in the loneliness of the mountains above Mecca. The German scholar Müller[4] rightly says (in "*Der Islam im Morgen- und Abendlande*," 1:57)—and this statement made by an objective German clearly contrasts with the hateful outburst of a man like Dubnow—"Those who mocked him called him mad, a dreamer, a swindler—but the consistent sureness of his behavior, the integrity of his whole being was never criticized, and still today emerges clearly from the Qur'an. . . . His perfect nobility in the Meccan period is still less subject to doubt. The conditions of despairing fear that emerged from the decisive vision, the truly admirable persistence with which this by no means courageous man continued his preaching for a decade under the most severe persecution, and finally under a serious threat to his life, without the slightest prospect of ultimate success, bears clear testimony to the overwhelming power of the idea that had taken hold of him and that brought him, independently of his own will, to the firm conviction that the inspiration that impressed itself on his thought was revealed by God himself. Thus we have the portrait of a true prophet."

For years Muhammad sought in Mecca to succeed with his preaching that there was only one God, the sole, all-merciful king of Judgment Day. He opposed to the Christian Trinity the unity of God, rejected the Christian doctrine of original sin and salvation, and instead gave every believer as a guiding principle the complete fulfillment of the commands of the righteous, given by a compassionate and just God, before whom every individual person had to account for his acts. As a result of the close connection between the ruling class in Mecca and previous religious practices, he was able to find believers in his message only in a small contingent of his own family. Then he came into contact with men from Yathrib [Medina], Arabs who had moreover heard of the Jews' promise of the Messiah. He brought these men together and converted them to Islam. Through very clever maneuvering, he was able to reconcile the two opposing Arab tribes, the Aws and the Khazraj, so that he had already created a political base for himself when on September 20, 622, he left Mecca for Medina, where he took up residence. Here he encountered the Jewish problem for the first time. He believed in the victorious power of good in the world, he was firmly convinced that the religion of the one and only God, with its easy, practical, reasonable, basic laws for human life, was nothing other than the original religion. He wanted to take humankind out of the current turmoil and lead it toward the original, clear vision of God. But since he had to deal with people who had been influenced by both Christianity and Judaism, he said that it was the religion in which Abraham (Ibrahim) had already believed, and which Christ and Moses had proclaimed, only each time it had been distorted by human beings. He said that this had been revealed anew to him by God. He wanted to make the path easy to follow for both Christians and Jews; thus at first he allowed his followers to pray facing toward Jerusalem. He repeatedly emphasized that he only wanted to purify the existing religions, to establish the restored, newly revealed faith. At the same time he was a skilled statesman. When the Arab tribes were unified, the Jews became a minority in Medina. Muhammad provided them with a kind of protectorate agreement: They were to retain their administration and their forms of worship, help the faithful defend the city, not ally themselves with Muhammad's opponents, and contribute to the faithful's wars.[5] The Jews could have been satisfied with this. But they began a general hate campaign against Islam, which proclaimed a pure conception of God and rejected the worldwide reign of Jehovah promised to the Jews. The Jews took pleasure in driving Muhammad into a corner with their mockery and underhanded questions, using the indecent and crafty methods of Talmudic dialectics in order to destroy the faith he proclaimed. They engaged in both open and secret subversive activities against him. Muhammad lost patience and complained: "Those to whom we gave the scripture rejoice in what is revealed unto thee. And of the clans there are who deny some of it" (Qur'an 13:36). Then he changed the direction of prayer toward Mecca, canceled fasting on days of atonement that coincided with the Jewish holiday of the same name and replaced it by the Ramadan fast, and to the shofar, the horn of the Jewish synagogue, opposed the muezzin's call to prayer. When the people of Mecca attacked him and were defeated in the victorious Battle of Badr, at which the triumphant cry "There is no God but God!" rang out for the first time, the Jews showed their deep hostility to Islam. The Jew Ibn al Ashraf wrote a lament for the fallen Meccans and explained that he preferred the Arabs' old idols to Muhammad's religion. In an infamous satirical poem the Jew Abu Afak called upon the Arabs of Medina to drive Muhammad away. It had become very clear that the Jews were fighting to keep the Arabian peoples from being united through Islam. Then the Prophet struck back:

Lo! the worst of beasts in Allah's sight are the ungrateful who will not believe;

Those of them with whom thou madest a treaty, and then at every opportunity they break their treaty, and they keep not duty (to Allah).

If thou comest on them in the wear, deal with them so as to strike fear in those who are behind them, that haply they may remember.

And if thou fearest treachery from any folk, then throw back to them (their treaty) fairly. Lo! Allah loveth not the treacherous. (Qur'an 8:55–58)

When the Jewish tribe Banu Qaynuqa indecently assaulted an Islamic woman, he caused its neighborhood to be besieged and forced it to surrender. Only the support of the influential Abdullah ibn Ubayy saved the Jews from being punished. The Prophet granted them their lives and only forced them to leave the city, but on his deathbed he still said to Abdullah, "O, Abdullah, did I not warn you against your love for the Jews? But you would not listen to me." However, the other Jewish tribes were no better. A Jewish versifier who wrote hate poems, Ka'b ibn Ashraf, was killed by a Muslim because he publicly abused Muhammad. The Banu Nadir tribe, with whom a new agreement had been concluded, immediately used the Muslims' lack of success at the Battle of Uhud to renew its hostility. From that time, his Eminence the Great Mufti of Jerusalem, Haj Emin El-Husseini, reports (in Muhammad Sabri's outstanding work "Islam, Judentum, und Bolschewismus") the following authenticated tradition:

While Muhammad was engaged in friendly discussion with one group of Jews, another group was preparing an attack on his life. They persuaded a man that he should hurl a heavy block of stone at Muhammad's head. Muhammad would have been lost had God not granted him a warning. An inner voice told him that he should leave the place, and thus the treacherous Jews were unable to carry out their plan. Muhammad sent one of his prosecutors to the Jews and to tell them that they had to leave the city within ten days. They had, he said, broken the agreement that they had concluded with him, since they had tried to kill him. Every Jew found to be still in the city after ten days would be put to death.

As soon as he had repelled the Meccans' attack, Muhammad immediately moved against them and forced them to emigrate. Despite their strong fortifications, the Jews had to leave. In the fifty-ninth sura Muhammad recalls this event: "All that is in the heavens and all that is in the earth glorifieth Allah, and he is the Mighty, the Wise./He it is who hath caused those of the People of the Scripture who disbelieved to go forth from their homes unto the first exile. Ye deemed not that they would go forth, while they deemed that their strongholds would protect them from Allah. But Allah reached them from a place whereof they wrecked not, and cast terror in their hearts so that they ruined their houses with their own hands and the hands of the believers. . . . On the likeness of those (who suffered) a short time before them, they taste the ill effects of their conduct, and theirs is painful punishment" (Qur'an 59:1–2, 15). But even the last Jewish tribe, the Banu Quyraza, broke its word and agreement. When a large army of Muhammad's enemies approached, they contacted the chieftain of the exiled Banu Nadir, the Jew Choniben Akhtab, and asked him to hand the city over to them. However, through an extremely clever ploy—he had a deep ditch dug that hindered the enemy's cavalry's attack—Muhammad was able to force the besieging army to withdraw. Then he acted against the Banu Qurayza, surrounded their neighborhood and forced them to surrender. The Jews probably thought that they too would just be forced to emigrate, but Muhammad entrusted the decision regarding their fate to the sheikh of the Aws tribe, who had been wounded by them, and he demanded that the Jews be executed. This was the only mass execution that the lenient Muhammad ever allowed to take place, and it was entirely permissible according to the law of war, because the Jews had committed treason by bearing arms as allies of the enemy. The Banu Qurayza tribe was therefore annihilated, but remnants of it fled to Khaybar. Muhammad besieged this city. He forced it to surrender in 628. An old Islamic legend reports that after the very lenient terms of the city's capitulation were agreed upon, the Jewess Zainab invited Muhammad to dinner. She set before him spicy roast meat. Muhammad's weapons bearer, Beshr-ibn al Baraa, rashly ate a piece of it, but Muhammad did not swallow his first bite because it seemed to him to have a strangely bad taste, and he immediately said that the meat had been poisoned. The weapons bearer subsequently died of poisoning. However, Muhammad is supposed to have been ailing ever after.

It is little known that the Jews still scornfully boast that they poisoned Muhammad. Dubnow[6] (3: 403) writes with unconcealed joy:

A courageous Jewess was found who tried to take revenge on the enemy of her people for all the sufferings inflicted on the Jews. The young Zainab, the wife of a hero who fell at Khaybar, prepared his favorite meal for Muhammad, roast mutton, and set it before him. However, she had previously poisoned the meat, so that one of the men dining with the Prophet who had eaten of the roast died. However, Muhammad spit the poisoned morsel out and thus escaped certain death. When he asked Zainab why she had done this, she said: "You have inflicted unspeakable sufferings on my people, and now I thought: if you are only an ordinary conqueror, then by poisoning you I will give my people peace; but if you are a prophet, then God will warn you of my intention, and you will remain unharmed." Muhammad immediately decided that she would die. For a long time afterward he felt the effects of the poison and on his deathbed believed that even his mortal illness should be attributed to this poisoning.

Thus still today the Jews rejoice in this crime! Even in Medina they sought again to divide the local Arab tribes and to turn them away from Islam. They sang again the tribes' old battle and camp songs from the time when the tribes were fighting each other, and Muhammad had to travel to Medina himself and put things in order again. In accord with his plan, while he was in his thirties Muhammad fought the Jews, drove them out of Taima and Wadi-el-Kura or at most allowed them to remain in certain places if they paid a poll tax. The Qur'an is full of warnings about the Jews, who are bluntly called "Satans."[7] Muhammad also observed how many people were constantly being turned away again from right knowledge. "And when they fall in with those who believe, they say: 'We believe; but when they go apart to their devils they declare: Lo! we are with you; verily we did but mock'" (Qur'an 2:14). Ibn Huraira even communicates to us the following assertion of the great man of God: "Judgment Day will come only when the Muslims have inflicted an annihilating defeat on the Jews, when every stone and every tree behind which a Jew has hidden says to believers: 'Behind me stands a Jew, smite him.'"[8] On his deathbed Muhammad is supposed to have

said: "There must not be two religions in Arabia."[9] One of his successors, the caliph 'Umar, resolutely drove the Jews out of Arabia. They were subjected to a very restrictive and oppressive special regulation that completely crippled Jewish activities. All reporters of the time when the Islamic lands still completely obeyed their own laws agree that the Jews were particularly despised. On the other hand, the Jews hated Islam to the depths of their hearts. We may note here that Jewish agitation played a not insignificant role in launching the Crusades, since the "refutation" of Islam written by the baptized Jew Petrus Alfonsus was literally the single literary source of agitation[10] for the First Crusade of 1096–1099. The wicked distortion of Muhammad's teaching and the criticism of his personality hatched by this Jew were taken over in ecclesiastical writings against Islam and are found in the monks Petrus Reverendus and Gualterus de Sens, in Guibert de Nogent-sous-Coucy, in Bishop Hildebert of Le Mans, and in other, mostly French writers who through a planned distortion of Islam that was nonetheless always based on the poisonous work of the Jew Petrus Alfonsus, unleashed the crusading fever in Europe.

Muhammad's opposition to the Jews undoubtedly had an effect—Oriental Jewry was completely paralyzed by Islam. Its back was broken. Oriental Jewry has played almost no role in Judaism's massive rise to power over the last two centuries. Scorned, the Jews vegetated in the dirty alleys of the Mellah, and were subject to a special regulation that did not allow them to profiteer, as they did in Europe, or even to receive stolen goods, but instead kept them fearful and under pressure. Had the rest of the world adopted a similar method, today we would have no Jewish question—and here we must absolutely note that there were also Islamic rulers, among them especially the Spanish caliphs of the House of Mu'awiya, who did not adhere to Islam's traditional hostility to Jews—to their own disadvantage. However, as a religion Islam has performed the immortal service of preventing the Jews from carrying out their threatened conquest of Arabia and of defeating the dreadful doctrine of Jehovah through a pure faith that opened the way to higher culture for many peoples and gave them an education and humane training, so that still today a Muslim who takes his religion seriously is one of the most worthy phenomena in this world in turmoil.

NOTES

1. "Dubnow, Simon Markovich." *Encyclopædia Britannica*, 2007, http://www.britannica.com/eb/article–9031329/Simon-Markovich–Dubnow. Simon Markovich Dubnow (1860–1941) was a Russian Jewish historian born in what is now Belarus. Dubnow is credited with introducing a sociological emphasis into the study of Jewish history, particularly that of eastern Europe. He was one of the initial scholars to subject Hasidism to systematic and unbiased

study based upon laboriously collected source materials from both the Hasidim and their sundry opponents. Dubnow's historical magnum opus was the monumental *Istoriia evreiskogo naroda na Vostovka* (*History of the Jews*), which was translated into several languages. According to the *Encyclopedia Britannica* entry, "The work is notable for its scholarship, impartiality, and cognizance of social and economic currents in Jewish history. According to Dubnow, the Jews not only are a religious community but also possess the distinctive characteristics of a cultural nationality and as such create their own forms of autonomous social and cultural life. He viewed the history of the Jews as a succession of large autonomous communities, or centers." As a cultural nationalist Dubnow rejected Jewish assimilation but at the same time believed that political Zionism was messianic and unrealistic. He left Russia in 1922 because of his hatred for Bolshevism and settled in Berlin. In 1933 he fled Germany because of the anti-Jewish policies of the Nazi government, seeking refuge in Riga, Latvia. Dubnow was murdered by the Nazis during the deportation of most of Riga's Jewish population to extermination camps.

A contemporary English translation from the Russian by Moshe Spiegel (which includes volumes 3 and 4 of the German edition cited by von Leers), *History of the Jews—From the Roman Empire to the Early Medieval Period* (New York, 1968), states, on pp. 312–13,

> Thus the elementary idea of monotheism matured in the soul of this semi-Bedouin, and was transformed into a flaming passion that impelled him toward savage, barbaric holy wars. The knowledge of God did not harmonize in Muhammad's mind with the higher ethical conscience, which adds such charm to the ethical monotheism of the biblical prophets, and even to the one-sided evangelical teaching ("not of this world"). The biography of "Allah's Messenger" and the Qur'an itself are replete with examples of what a teacher of religion must not say or do. The semibarbarian hero frequently peeps out of the mask of the clairvoyant prophet. The ecstasy of the clairvoyant is stigmatized by the brutal passion of the Bedouin, who kills his enemy and forthwith takes the latter's wife or daughter into his harem. These features of Muhammad's character manifested themselves particularly in his relations with the Arabian Jews.

2. Von Leers adopts uncritically the pious, apologetic Muslim narrative of Muhammad's career perhaps auguring his later conversion to Islam. His very favorable disposition toward Islam on the one hand, and inveterate Jew hatred on the other, causes von Leers to take great umbrage at Dubnow's negative characterization of the Muslim prophet. For a balanced early twentieth-century perspective on Muhammad, which eschews apologetics, it is useful to compare the assessment of the

great scholar of Islam's origins (and devout Christian), David S. Margoliouth (1858–1940). Margoliouth's biography (*Muhammad and the Rise of Islam* [London, 1905; reprinted, New Delhi, 1985], preface, vi–vii) recognized Muhammad as "a great man, who solved a political problem of appalling difficulty—the construction of a state and empire out of the Arab tribes." Dr. Margoliouth recounted this accomplishment without "apology," or "indictment." Summarizing faithfully (in "Muhammad," *Encyclopedia of Religion and Ethics* [1908–1927], 8: 878) the full picture of Muhammad that emerges in Ibn Ishaq's biography, Margoliouth also observes:

> In order to gain his ends he recoils from no expedient, and he approves of similar unscrupulousness on the part of his adherents, when exercised in his interest. He profits to the utmost from the chivalry of the Meccans, but rarely requites it with the like. He organizes assassinations and wholesale massacres. His career as tyrant of Medina is that of a robber chief, whose political economy consists in securing and dividing plunder. . . . He is himself an unbridled libertine and encourages the same passion in his followers. For whatever he does he is prepared to plead the express authorization of the deity. It is, however, impossible to find any doctrine which he is not prepared to abandon in order to secure a political end. . . . This is a disagreeable picture for the founder of a religion, and it cannot be pleaded that it is a picture drawn by an enemy.

Thus in accord with what has been described at great length earlier (see especially "Antisemitism in the Hadith and Early Muslim Biographies of Muhammad," pp. 63–91), notwithstanding von Leers's recapitulation of the standard Muslim apologetic characterization of the actual contents of the hadith and sira, in particular Ibn Ishaq's biography of Muhammad, Dubnow offers this accurate assessment (p. 317, from the Siegel translation *History of the Jews—From the Roman Empire to the Early Medieval Period*):

> After Muhammad had defeated the pagans of Mecca at the battle of Badr (624), he intensified his campaign against the Jews. He had already begun to propagate his religion by means of the "sword of Allah" and he resolved to apply this also toward the recalcitrant "possessors of the Scriptures," who refused to sanctify Islam with their authority. Since the behavior of the Jews remained belligerent after the victory of the Muslims, Muhammad desired vengeance upon them. Ka'ab Ibn Ashraf, the Jewish poet, had composed an elegy to the memory of the heroes of Mecca—the Qurayrshites who fell in battle at Badr. Asma the poetess, also of Jewish descent, composed a satire about the false messiah, for which she paid with her life. In the circle of his

associates (*ansars*) Muhammad expressed a wish "to be rid of that woman," and on the following night a fanatical Muslim entered her bedroom and killed her while she suckled her infant. In the same manner perished the venerated Jewish elder, Abu Afak, who in a letter to the inhabitants of Medina reproached them for heeding the alien Muhammad. Some time later, Ibn Ashraf met the same fate. Before long, the vindictive prophet passed on from individual acts of revenge to mass murder.

And Richard Bell (*The Origin of Islam in its Christian Environment* [London, 1926], pp. 134–35, 151, 159 ff.) summarized Muhammad's final interactions with the Christians of northern Arabia, which were comparable to his campaigns to subjugate the Jews. He noted that "Muhammad complains (Qur'an 2:113–114) that neither Jews nor Christians will be satisfied with him until he follows their milla or type of religion. It was just as impossible for him to make concessions. . . . Thus the relationship with the Christians ended as that with the Jews ended—in war." Bell's analyses, based upon the sacred Muslim texts and authoritative Qur'anic commentaries, conclude:

[B]efore the end of his life Muhammad was in conflict with Christian populations in the north of Arabia, and even within the confines of the Roman [Byzantine] Empire. What would have happened if he had lived we do not know. But probably the policy which Abu Bakr [the first caliph, who "succeeded" Muhammad] carried on was the policy of Muhammad himself. There could have been no real compromise. He regarded himself as vicegerent of God upon earth. The true religion could only be Islam as he laid it down, and acceptance of it meant acceptance of his divinely inspired authority. . . . The Hijra and the execution of the Divine vengeance upon the unbelievers of Mecca had given the immediate occasion for the organization of such a warlike community. The victory of Badr confirmed it. This is what it had grown to, a menace to whatever came in its way. Muhammad could bide his time, but he was not the man to depart from a project which had once taken hold of his mind as involved in his prophetic mission and authority. He might look with favor upon much in Christianity, but unless Christians were prepared to accept his dictation as to what the true religion was, conflict was inevitable, and there could have been no real peace while he lived.

3. W. Montgomery Watt, "Al Ansar," *Encyclopedia of Islam.*

4. Müller, (Friedrich) August, 1848–1892. Müller who was successively a professor at Konigsberg and Halle, is best known for his writings on Hebrew grammar (1878),

and the work cited by von Leers, *Der Islam im Morgen- und Abendland* (Berlin, 1885).

5. Von Leers does not refer to serious scholarship available to him on this so-called Constitution of Medina, i.e., the German scholar Julius Wellhausen's (1844–1918) *Muhammads Gemeindeordnung von Medina* (published in 1889) and *Mohammed en de Joden te Medina* (published in 1908) by the Dutch scholar Jan Arent Wensinck (1882–1939). [See notes 292 and 294, earlier in the opening survey.]

I doubt that there was indeed a written agreement of which both parties had a copy. The Jews never referred to their document. . . . In any case, there cannot have been a general agreement with the Jews, but only special arrangements with individual clans, for the Jews were no political unit, rather each of their clans formed a confederation with the neighboring Arab clan . . . the constitution as transmitted by Ibn Ishāq . . . did not represent an agreement with the Jews. . . . [Islamic] Tradition has a simple explanation why Muhammad's relation with the Jews was so little affected by the agreement: Every hostile act of Muhammad was precipitated by the Jews and justified by planned or accomplished treachery, even though they had no intention openly to break the agreement. . . . We, however, will find that it was Muhammad who committed the perfidy. He gladly used every chance to punish the Jews, and contrived to create reasons if there were none. (Wellhausen)

The constitution was no treaty concluded between muhājirūn, ansār, and the Jews. It was an edict defining the relation of the three parties; above them was Allah, i.e., Muhammad. It was evidence of his great authority that, after a short stay in Medina, he, the stranger, could lay down the law for all segments of the population. In religious matters the break with the Jews was irreconcilable. Muhammad did not express his annoyance over this. For the time being, he needed the Jews and included them in the ummah. His first plan failed; he had come to Medina hoping the town would soon be a religious unity as a theocratic monarchy under his leadership. If the Jews would have recognized him, this hope might have been realized. . . . But the Jews showed no such inclination. What to do? They could not be attacked openly because Muhammad's position was still insufficiently established. All he could do was to use them in his plans, or in any case, neutralize them. (Wensinck)

And Moshe Gil's contemporary assessment from 1974 [see earlier note 295] concurs with the previous judgments of Wellhausen and Wensinck:

The document is better understood as an act of preparation for war, and not as its result. Through his alliance with the Arab tribes of Medina the Prophet gained enough strength to achieve a gradual anti-Jewish policy, despite the reluctance of his Medinese allies, who had formerly been those of the Jews. . . . It is therefore an obvious alibi that Muslim sources have developed a tradition about a treaty between Muhammad and the Jews, be it this document or a lost one, as presumed by some modern scholars. . . . The document therefore, was not a covenant with the Jews. On the contrary, it was a formal statement of intent to disengage the Arab clans of Medina from the Jewish neighbors they had been allied with up to that time.

6. Von Leers omits Dubnow's accurate characterization (from the Siegel translation *History of the Jews*, p. 321) of the events which just transpired *right before* Muhammad's poisoning by the Khaybar Jewess Zainab, in the paragraph immediately prior to the one he quotes:

Having occupied the city [i.e., Khaybar], the victors took to plundering. Muhammad ordered the Jews to hand over all their personal property. In order to force him to reveal the hideout of the treasures, Kinana, the Jewish leader, was at first tortured, and then killed. This execution was carried out to gratify Muhammad, who became infatuated with Safiyya, the beautiful wife of the Jewish military leader. After the execution of her husband, Muhammad took her into his harem. This time the leader of the Muslims did not slay all the vanquished. He permitted the Jews to remain in Khaybar and obligated them to till their plantations, and to give half their crop to the Muslim rulers. The defeated inhabitants of the neighboring Jewish settlements, Fadak, and Wadi-el-Kura, were subject to the same harsh taxes. Even the community of the remote Taima had to accept the same conditions. (628)

7. I.e., the Jews being associated with Satan, and consigned to hell (see Qur'an 4:60, 4:55, 58:14–19, and 98:6).

8. Sahih Muslim, bk. 41, no. 6985; Sahih Bukhari, vol. 4, bk. 52, no. 177.

9. Sahih Muslim, bk. 10, no. 3763; Sahih Bukhari, vol. 3, bk. 39, no. 531.

10. Petrus Alfonsus, born Moses Sephardi at Huesca, Aragon, in 1062, was a physician to King Alfonso VI of Castile, who died in 1110 at the age of forty-eight. He apostasized from Judaism and embraced Christianity at age forty-four, being baptized at Huesca on St. Peter's Day, June 29, 1106. In honor of the saint and of his royal patron and godfather, he took the name of Petrus Alfonsus (Alfonso's Peter). Despite von Leers's unsupported statement that Petrus Alfonsus, "was literally the single literary source of agitation for the first Crusade of 1096–1099," this bizarre claim ignores the fact that Alfonsus, like all the apostates from Judaism of his time, sought to show his zeal for the new faith *by attacking first and foremost Judaism, and defending the truths of the Christian faith.* Alfonsus composed a series of twelve *dialogues against the Jews*, the supposed disputants being Mose and Pedro (= Moses Sephardi and Petrus Alfonsi, i.e., himself before and after conversion). According to the rabbi and scholar George Alexander Kohut (1874–1933), [JewishEncyclopedia.com, "Alfonsi, Petrus"], "the work is . . . little known today; and . . . fully merits the oblivion into which it has fallen."

Islamic Fundamentalism, Antisemitism, and Anti-Zionism

Emmanuel Sivan

The resurgence of Islamic fundamentalism is the most important development that has taken place in the Muslim world over the last fifteen years. It spread from Pakistan to Morocco, seeping into every corner of society, especially in towns but increasingly also into the countryside. It is particularly felt among those social strata which are in part modernized, but traditionalists are also being swept up in its wake. While this movement seized power in only a number of countries (Pakistan, Iran, Sudan) it holds cultural hegemony almost everywhere else. It sets the tone of the debate over public affairs, the terms and concepts according to which they are conducted, and exerts strong influence over the order of priorities in Muslim societies. This begins to be true even in faraway Islamic lands such as Malaysia (as proved by the incident with the New York Philharmonic Orchestra about playing works by Jewish composers). The fundamentalist attitude toward Jews, Israel, and Zionism is thus of vital import.

"WESTOXICATION" AND AUTHENTICITY

This attitude is characterized by a sort of seesaw movement—between disdainful disregard and obsessive hatred—with a whole gamut of shades and nuances in between. The two major characteristics of this movement since its inception in the late 1950s are the cause of this "seesaw syndrome." On the one hand this is a movement almost totally concerned with internal problems, not with outside enemies. The fundamentalists consider that Islam is now facing a mortal danger, which in scope and nature is quite unlike anything it has ever faced before. In this day and age the danger comes from within, from secularist-minded Muslim movements, which, though sincere in their concern for the welfare of their peoples, are nonetheless voluntary prisoners of "poisonous" Western ideas, be they nationalism, socialism, liberalism, democracy, economic development at any price, and so on. This "Westoxication" (as Khomeini has called it) is greatly encouraged by the insidious impact of the audiovisual media, which creep subliminally into the hearts and minds of Muslims and enhance their infatuation with modernity and its alleged "good life." The modern state in Islamic lands, as purveyor of these values, is thus the ultimate danger. Speedy reform must be attempted, but failing that, power must be seized. As against this background foreign forces are deemed much less important than they used to be in the days of the anticolonialist struggle; the postcolonial Muslim state is enemy number one. As Israel was (at least prior to 1977) very rarely the ally of such Muslim states—the shah's Iran being, of course, a notable exception—such a frame of mind is certainly not one which should lead to obsession with it. Israel is an execrable force, no doubt, but one which should be dealt with only at a much later stage, well after Islam is purified from within and regimes based on Muslim law are instituted everywhere.

On the other hand Islamic fundamentalism espouses the quest for authenticity—namely, a return to the pristine verities of Islam—as its positive response to modernity (mere rejection and expurgation not being enough). This means that the program it sets forth is to be predicted upon vigorously pure Islamic answers to today's problems; outside (usually Western) criteria are spurned as apologetic. As the Pakistani thinker Maudoodi put it, instead of endeavoring to "prove" that Islam is truly compatible with reason and science—as the "Westoxicated" try to do—one should simply say that true reason (and "true science") is inevitably Islamic. Instead of trying to show that Islam is democratic, the fundamentalists claim that since Islam is theocratic, democracy is simply out of the question for a Muslim regime. The same holds true for tolerance. Modern-style tolerance predicated as it is on the relativity and fallibility of all human beliefs is incompatible with the Islamic dogma that Islam is the "pinnacle of all revelation," the perfect truth, superior to all other partly true revelations (Judaism, Christianity) and other, totally false, religions and creeds.

It follows from this last facet of Islamic authenticity, as interpreted by the fundamentalists, that there is no point (indeed it is a grave sin) in arguing—with the

Emmanuel Sivan in *Anti-Zionism and Antisemitism in the Contemporary World*, edited by Robert Wistrich (New York: 1990), pp. 74–82.

"Westoxicated"—that Islam accepts this kind of tolerance. At most Islam can live with medieval-type tolerance, that is a state of affairs where one religion holds a
monopoly of truth and power, yet deigns to grant partial
rights to some other religions, on sufferance and not
based on equality.

There are, it should be pointed out, three major lines
of discrimination in classical Islam: male/female,
Muslim/non-Muslim, free man/slave. The first two are
now openly espoused by the fundamentalists, and
unashamedly so. They no longer feel the need to discul-
pate Islam from male chauvinism and from discrimination of non-Muslim religions, as long as Jews and
Christians know their place and are content to accept the
position of inferiors—with guarantee of rights of worship and internal autonomy—they can be left alone.
When they break the sacred hierarchy and "arrogantly"
ask for equality, let alone when they become superior to
Muslims (Jews in Israel, Baha'is in Iran, Christians in
southern Sudan), they should be fought as dire enemies.

The quest for authenticity—i.e., redefinition of the
bounds of Muslim identity—has yet other consequences
in this context. It has put an end to all attempts designed
to nurture "ecumenic dialogue" with other religions
(especially Christianity and Hinduism; Judaism was
never considered a likely candidate). It even revived past
diatribes, long-held "historical accounts" to be settled
with other creeds, especially with Islam's two early competitors, Judaism and Christianity. Medieval polemical
tracts were thus dug out. The "sins" of non-Muslims
against nascent Islam (for example, the struggle of the
Jews of Arabia against Muhammad) tend to be stressed,
if for no other reason (and there are, as we shall see, such
reasons), than as part and parcel of a renewed fundamentalist and literalist interest in Muslim history. A good
example is the resuscitation of the partly forgotten
Karamic image of Judaism as the "angry and pedantic
religion," the mirror image of a supposedly tolerant and
lenient Islam. Muslims thus learn to redefine their true
identity by looking at others.

DISDAINFUL DISREGARD

The combination of these two forces—internal jihad
(holy war) and authenticity—gave birth in the early days
of the movement (before 1967) to a sort of disdainful
disregard for Jews and Israel. There were almost no Jews
left in Islamic lands (Iran excepted) when the movement
arose in the late 1950s and thus non-Muslim native col-
laborationists with the "Westoxication campaign" were
mostly Christians, usually lumped together with heterodox Muslims (such as the Alawites). Israel was excoriated as an extension of Judaism in the Middle East, but
being a factor operating outside Muslim society (unlike
local Christians and Alawites) was certainly a secondary,
perhaps even marginal, factor, to be tackled at some
later, indeterminate date.

Thus Sayyid Qutb, the founder of fundamentalism in
Egypt, did consecrate hostile commentaries to the Jews
(who rejected Muhammad out of hand) in his famous
exegesis of the Qur'an, written in Nasser's prisons
during the 1950s. He gives voice there to the traditional
themes of Islamic antisemitism and links them to
present-day Israel as their ineluctable extension (Jewish
wrath and fastidiousness, will for power and domination,
exclusivity, etc.). Yet once out of prison in the early
1960s his actual activity concentrated on Nasser's so-
called paganism as the overwhelming danger to Islam.
This disregard (hateful, not lenient) of Israel was of
course helped by the relative lull in the Arab-Israeli conflict in those days. Yet from time to time an anti-Israel
obsession surfaces in Qutb's action, a manifestation of
that "seesaw syndrome" referred to earlier. While
preparing, for instance, a series of terrorist attacks
against government installations in 1965, Qutb's aides
planned to hit power stations and communication centers
all over Egypt. Qutb himself long opposed this plan for
it "might enfeeble Egypt vis-à-vis the ever alert Israeli
enemy." Yet finally he was prevailed upon: striking
Nasser's regime was the overriding goal (the plan itself
failed and led to the arrest of the ringleaders, including
Qutb, and their execution a year later).

The Syrian movement, led in those days by Marwen
Hadid, paid even less attention to Israel, focusing on the
struggle for the liberty of religion and against Ba'ath
atheism and nationalization policies (1964–67). The
same holds true of Lebanon, Pakistan, and Maghreb.
Iran, on the other hand, had a large, prosperous, and
modernized Jewish community as well as a conspicuous
Israeli presence in close alliance with the shah. This is
why Khomeini from the early days of his preaching
(1963) put Israel on a par with that other "Great Satan,"
the United States, harping on this theme continuously
with frequent references to Qur'anic anti-Jewish lore.
Yet even there, interest in Israel and Zionism knew many
ups and downs (depending on the particular facet of
"Westoxication" discussed and whether Jews or Israel
had much to do with it). Moreover never were the
"external Satans" anything more than a secondary
danger, an auxiliary of the enemy within, that is the
shah's white revolution with its reliance on modern technology and a return to a pre-Islamic Persian identity.
Even the Baha'is, relatively richer and more conspicuous, scored better than the Jews as a scapegoat for popular hostility, and one should also remember that the
Israeli presence in Iran was then just beginning to
expand.

THE 1967 SHOCK

Disdainful disregard characterized the fundamentalist
attitude to the 1967 war. It is quite symptomatic that in
the very days preceding the war, in late May 1967, when
Islamic militant inmates in Nasser's prison camps were

called upon to support the war effort, a hard-core group refused to have anything to do with the "tyrant's war," arguing that toppling Nasser was more important than fighting outside enemies. No doubt hatred of the Egyptian rule born out of the torture sessions in his prisons was so powerful as to rule out any collaboration with him even in an emergency. The hard core held out except for those who gave way under the pressures and supplementary tortures. It is from this hard core of the "prison generation"—whose traumatic experience was persecution by the modern Middle Eastern state—that the leaders of the Islamic groups of the 1970s would come.

However, the 1967 debacle was a shock even to these inmates. Their joy at the "defeat of the tyrant" was mingled with a sense of humiliation [demeaning of the Abode of Islam], the loss of honor and Islamic territory, all the more devastating in that it came at the hands of Jews, a despised minority and one not traditionally known for military valor but rather for meekness and timidity. The oft-recurring argument as to the new-fangled Jewish "arrogance" (that is, not knowing their true place) exemplified this sense of a world order turned upside down.

The shock was even stronger among fundamentalist sympathizers outside prisons, especially in the young age group. Many of the youngsters who formed the Islamic groups in high schools and universities in the late 1960s were motivated by a sense of confusion and utter despair bred out of the war. Many passed through a long period of wailing and brooding, till they found (thanks to some friend or older mentor) their way to the Muslim Association (*jama'at*). This creed offered them a reasonable explanation for the debacle—the "paganism" of Nasserism and the Ba'ath—and channeled their energies into a struggle for the revamping of society. It gave them faith that their enemies (first internal, then external) could be overcome and that an Islamic world order could be restored.

The fall of Jerusalem—the third most sacred city of Islam—and the attempted arson of the El-Aqsa mosque in 1969, spread the shock waves further afield to Iraq (where Khomeini had been in exile since 1965), Iran and Pakistan. There were even cases of Muslim militants beginning to pray in the direction of Jerusalem. This had been the custom in the early days of Islam, 622–624, before Muhammad, disenchanted with his erstwhile Jewish allies, instituted the Blackstone of Mecca as *qibla* or direction of prayer.

The upshot of all this was a generational split in the fast spread of the fundamentalist movement of the 1970s. Among the rank and file, particularly those in their twenties, members of the post-1967 generation, hatred of Israel and the demonology of Zionism—a twentieth-century reincarnation of the insidious and cunning spirit of Judaism—was rampant. It is quite symptomatic that Jerusalem as *qibla* was a practice in this age

group. They were also the most avid readers of the anti-Jewish literature put out by fundamentalist publishing houses as part and parcel of the "authenticity drive" discussed above. Muslim student associations even republished many such medieval treatises and anti-Jewish disputations on their own with introductions linking the "rotten essence" of Judaism to the misdeeds of Zionism. The defeats of the military regimes at the hands of Israel were not only taken as proof of their overall failure and bankruptcy but sometimes also as the result of outright conspiracy (subjective and not only objective alliance) with Israel. Assad in particular was taken to task by the Syrian Muslim Brethren for failing to use the air force against Israel in 1967 (he was the air force commander then) thus leading to the loss of the Golan Heights.

The leaders of the Islamic resurgence were recruited, however, from the "prison generation" whose almost exclusive fixation was the "terror state regimes'" as harbingers of secularism. Even superpower allies (the United States in the case of Tunisia, Lebanon, and Egypt, the USSR in that of Syria and Iraq) were still not getting much attention, let alone their so-called lackey, Israel. An Islamic militant group such as the Muslim Liberation Party (which tried to seize power in Egypt in 1974) although led by a Palestinian, Salah Siriya, a former inmate of Nasser's prison, set as its goal the restoration of the Caliphate and had little to say on Zionism, at least in official declarations. Another major terrorist group, the Takfirwa-Hijra (which kidnapped and assassinated a former minister in 1977) said that Egyptian soldiers killed in the 1973 war were not martyrs of the faith for this was not a jihad. The real holy war had to be fought against Sadat himself and his ilk; the "new Pharaoh" should not be let off the hook and be able to present himself as the paragon of religion. The leader of this group, Shukri Mustafa, as well as his aides, were again men in their thirties whose formative experience had been acquired in Nasser's prisons. Nevertheless among the people there was a greater though somewhat fitful interest in the Israeli danger, when compared to positions taken by the movement in the 1960s. Israel was the close ally of the West which now tried to sell to the Arabs the notion of peaceful coexistence as a precondition for economic development and modern consumption patterns; the latter being the new carrot with which the Middle East was to be further lured into relinquishing its heritage.

The generational split brought about an intense internal debate within the movement, evidenced at times in outbursts of interest in Zionist danger followed by quick decline. One catches a glimpse of that debate in a samizdat work, "The Absent Precept," written by Abd Al-Salam Faraj, leader of the Jihad Organization (who was to be executed for his role in the assassination of Sadat):

There are some who say that the Jihad effort should

concentrate nowadays on the liberation of Jerusalem. It is true that the liberation of the Holy Land is a legal precept binding upon every Muslim . . . but let us emphasize that the fight against the enemy nearest to you has precedence over the fight against the enemy further away. All the more so as the former is not only corrupted but a lackey of imperialism as well. . . . In all Muslim countries the enemy has the reins of power. The enemy is the present rulers. It is hence, a most imperative obligation to fight these rulers. This Islamic Jihad required today the blood and sweat of each Muslim.

Roughly the same position was taken by the leadership of the Muslim Brethren as against impatient young followers still smarting under the "shameful blow" of the 1967 defeat. The order of priorities set by the older generation was explicitly formulated by the Brethren. The military commander in Aleppo, Husni Abbu, during an exchange with the tribunal in his trial, answered as follows:

Don't your terrorist actions serve Israel?
They serve Islam and the Muslims and not Israel. What we want is to rid this country of impiety.
Why don't you fight against Israel?
Only when we shall have finished purging our country of godlessness shall we turn against Israel.

This was no different from the way Shukri Mustafa (of the Takfir group) responded to his judge's question as to what his followers would do if Israel attacked Egypt: "If the Jews or others come, our movement would not take part in combat in the ranks of the Egyptian army. We would rather escape to a safe place. . . . For by no means can the Arab-Jewish conflict be considered an Islamic warfare."

Yet at one and the same time, the Islamic fundamentalist press—in these core countries but also in peripheral ones such as the Maghreb and Sudan—tended to use racialist, Stürmer-style caricatures of Jews and of Israel's leader. They gave more space to recounting the historical misdeeds of Jews against Islam (linking them, among others, with the Crusaders, that medieval prefiguration of the state of Israel), resuscitated the blood libel and its "Talmudic origins" and gave vent to the arguments of *The Protocols of the Elders of Zion.* Whether this was done by the leadership out of conviction (bred out of the post-1967 escalation of the Israeli-Arab conflict) or just in order to placate young hothead militants cannot be determined. Still, the anti-Zionist issue could no more be said to be marginal; it was now significantly growing in strength.

THE WATERSHED

The years 1977–1978 constitute a watershed in the evolution of fundamentalists thought on the Arab-Israeli conflict. This was due to the convergence of two events: the Sadat peace initiative and the Iranian revolution. Both events took place against the background of the rise to prominence (and subsequent leadership) of the post-1967 generation (now in its thirties) who had always been particularly sensitive to anti-Zionist themes.

The Sadat initiative, in breaking a long-held taboo, dealt yet another shock, comparable to that of the Six-Day War, to this generation now coming to revolutionary maturity. It further highlighted what was only vaguely perceived till then—the intricate relationship between domestic and foreign policy. The "Coca-Cola, Dallas, and Love-Boat invasion" was linked to the pro-American orientation (not merely in Egypt but in other Middle Eastern countries as well) and this in turn required the price tag of peace with Israel. To fight the one ("Open Door" economic policy, advertising which encouraged consumption), the others must be fought too. Even certain members of the older generation such as the widely popular preachers sheikhs Kishk and Sharawi came to that conclusion. Their deep antipathy to Judaism as the most ancient foe of Islam, a product of the attachment to authenticity, was reactivated and came to the fore. That Sadat made the particular gesture of a visit to Jerusalem only made things worse. Belief in the sanctity of Jerusalem and the notion of the shame of its fall—an emblematic symbol of the decline of Islam—has long been powerful among fundamentalists. This is despite the fact that the Islamic school from which it borrowed many of its ideas, the neo-Hanbalism (founded in the fourteenth century by the theologian Ibn Taymiyya) had always been skeptical about the sanctity of Jerusalem, as a sort of "innovation" which might eclipse Mecca and Medina. Jerusalem was indeed one of the very points on which twentieth-century fundamentalists deviated from the dictum of their medieval precursors, a concession no doubt to contemporary sensitivity.

The Iranian revolution fired the imagination of the Arab fundamentalists, even though—as we shall later see—they did not accept its direct authority, the revolution being Shi'ite and they Sunnis. The revolution seemed to prove that the unthinkable can happen—an upheaval may be mustered and a "pseudo-Muslim" tyrant toppled. The methods and beliefs of the Khomeini movement came to serve as a model to be studied, except, of course, on points, which were too evidently Shi'ite. One of the major characteristics of the Khomeini gospel, at least in the years immediately preceding the revolution, was the insistence on the relationship between domestic and foreign policy and particularly on "the American-Israel satanic connection" as a safety net of the regime. Insistence on Israel's role in Iran grew as it became increasingly prominent in the 1970s, all the more so with regard to its help to the execrated SAVAK security services. Iranian revolutionary anti-Israel propaganda and the flaunting of its alliance with the PLO thus did not fall on deaf ears in the Arab fundamentalist circles which were already sensitized to these issues by Sadat's initiative and the rise to the top of the post-1967 generation.

Anti-Zionism came to take pride of place, presented as the modern-day incarnation of the authentically Islamic hostility to the Jews. The alliance between the powers that be (open in the case of Egypt and Lebanon, tacit in the case of Syria and Saudi Arabia) was yet another manifestation of Jewish deviousness and the incessant craving for dominance.

The combined impact of the Israeli-Arab conflict and the Iranian revolution propelled the anti-Zionist theme into greater prominence among the fundamentalists in the early 1980s. Exasperation with the solidity of the Egyptian-Israeli peace treaty and with that of the Sadat-Mubarak regime (despite the October 6, 1981, assassination) brought about stronger verbal violence and a growing tendency to see the foreign supporters of the present Arab regimes (United States, Israel) as perhaps no less important enemies than the internal foes of fundamentalism. The Israeli invasion of Lebanon, dubbed by the fundamentalists the "Tenth Crusade against Islam" with its shocking climax—the first siege of an Arab capital by the Jewish army—had shaken the Islamic militants almost as severely as 1967, especially as most Arab states stood idly by, launching empty protests and threats. The shock was much greater than that occasioned by the Russian invasion of Afghanistan. In both cases infidels conquered parts of the land of Islam, but Afghanistan was peripheral while Lebanon lay in the core areas; Russia was a superpower and hence its victory understandable, while Israel was tiny and inexplicably strong. The "cognitive dissonance" involved in this latter phenomenon was, as one could expect, bridged over by conspiratorial explanations—

Israel manipulating the United States, Israel an ally of the Maronites, and so on.

Conspiratorial explanation, borrowing heavily from Qur'anic vituperations against Jewish crookedness and infidelity, were combined—very early in the summer of 1982—with the demonic image of the "Zionist entity": powerful, ruthless, barbarian, albeit technologically advanced. This of course is not a new theme in the annals of the Arab-Israeli conflict, but it was coined here anew in a particularly fundamentalist mold—the image of Israelis as new Mongols. The Mongol theme is a central one in fundamentalist mythology and demonology; the state of Islam is now assumed to be as critical as it was in the wake of the destruction of caliphate by the Mongol hordes in 1258. Thus Assad, Sadat, and Saddam Hussein were always defined as new Mongols, this time doing the work of destruction from within. It was no mere chance that the fundamentalists justified their recourse to violence against the powers that be by referring to the fourteenth-century neo-Hanbalites. The neo-Hanbalites had pondered the situation of Islam after the fall of the caliphate and had recognized the need to fight even so-called Muslim rulers, as the Mongols had become in the late thirteenth century. Regarding the Jews (or Israelis) as Mongols was thus a way of putting the outside danger almost on a par with the internal danger. It was not only a matter of theology—at the popular experiential level the Mongols (Tartars) always stood for the utmost cruelty and humiliation. Thus the term "Tartar" was a potent, emotionally charged one of vilification, almost dehumanization. The Sabra and Shatila massacre, which took place after this evolution in fundamentalist thought had occurred, powerfully vindicated this new image.

CHAPTER 58

Based on Qur'anic Verses, Interpretations, and Traditions, Muslim Clerics State: The Jews Are the Descendants of Apes, Pigs, and Other Animals

Aluma Solnick

INTRODUCTION

Depicting Jews—and sometimes also Zionists—as "the descendants of apes and pigs" is extremely widespread today in public discourse in the Arab and Islamic worlds.

For example, in a weekly sermon in April 2002, Al-Azhar Sheikh Muhammad Sayyid Tantawi, the highest-ranking cleric in the Sunni Muslim world, called the Jews "the enemies of Allah, descendants of apes and pigs."[1]

In one of his sermons, Saudi sheikh Abd Al-Rahman Al-Sudayyis, imam and preacher at the Al-Haraam mosque—the most important mosque in Mecca—beseeched Allah to annihilate the Jews. He also urged the Arabs to give up peace initiatives with them because they are "the scum of the human race, the rats of the world, the violators of pacts and agreements, the murderers of the prophets, and the offspring of apes and pigs."[2]

"Read history," called Al-Sudayyis in another sermon, "and you will understand that the Jews of yesterday are the evil fathers of the Jews of today, who are evil offspring, infidels, distorters of [others'] words, calf-worshippers, prophet-murderers, prophecy-deniers . . . the scum of the human race 'whom Allah cursed and turned into apes and pigs. . . .' These are the Jews, an ongoing continuum of deceit, obstinacy, licentiousness, evil, and corruption."[3]

In a sermon at the Said Al-Jandoul mosque in Al-Taif, Saudi sheikh Ba'd bin Abdallah Al-Ajameh Al-Ghamidi explained that "the qualities of the Jews" were present at all times and in all places: "The current behavior of the brothers of apes and pigs, their treachery, violation of agreements, and defiling of holy places . . . is connected with the deeds of their forefathers during the early period of Islam—which proves the great similarity between all the Jews living today and the Jews who lived at the dawn of Islam."[4]

In an August 2001 sermon, Sheikh Ibrahim Madhi, Palestinian Authority official and imam of the Sheikh Ijlin mosque, Gaza City's main mosque, called on the Palestinian people to forget their internal disagreements and turn all weapons against Jews: "[L]ances must be directed at the Jews, the enemies of Allah, the nation accursed in Allah's book. Allah described [them] as apes and pigs, calf-worshipers, idol-worshippers."[5]

Seeing Jews as "descendants of apes and pigs" is common also in Shi'ite Islam. Such statements appear, for instance, in a 1998 speech by Hezbollah secretary-general Hassan Nasrallah on the occasion of the Shi'ite 'Ashoura holiday. Nasrallah regretted that the holiday fell "on the 50th anniversary of the bitter and distressing historical catastrophe of the establishment of the state of the grandsons of apes and pigs—the Zionist Jews—on the land of Palestine and Jerusalem." He closed his speech with these words: "We reaffirm the slogan of the struggle against the Great Satan and call, like last year: 'Death to America. To the murderers of the prophets, the grandsons of apes and pigs,' we say: . . . 'Death to Israel.'"[6]

These statements are made not only by clerics and preachers. Following their lead, public opinion leaders in the Arab world also call the Jews "the descendants of apes and pigs." The image has pervaded the public consciousness, even in child-rearing. In May 2002, Iqra, the Saudi-Egyptian satellite television station, which according to its Web site[7] sets for itself the goals of "highlighting aspects of Arab Islamic culture that inspire

Aluma Solnick, "Based on Qur'anic Verses, Interpretations, and Traditions, Muslim Clerics States: The Jews Are the Descendants of Apes, Pigs, and Other Animals," Middle East Media Research Institute, Report #1, November 1, 2002, http://memri.org/bin/articles.cgi?Page=archives&Area=sr&ID=SR01102.

respect," "highlighting the true and tolerant picture of Islam and refuting the accusations directed against Islam," and "planting a spirit of mutual understanding and dialogue among members of the nation and opening channels of cultural connection with the cultures of other nations," interviewed a three-and-a-half-year-old "real Muslim girl" about Jews. On *The Muslim Woman Magazine* program, the girl was asked whether she liked Jews; she answered, "No." When asked why she didn't like them, she said that Jews were "apes and pigs." "Who said this?" the moderator asked. The girl answered, "Our God." "Where did He say this?" "In the Qur'an." At the end of the interview, the pleased moderator said: "No [parents] could wish for Allah to give them a more believing girl than she. . . . May Allah bless her, her father and mother. The next generation of children must be true Muslims. We must educate them now while they are children, so that they will be true Muslims."[8]

In April 2002, a weekly talk show on the Al-Jazeera satellite television station, *The Opposite Direction*, which claims to have tens of millions of viewers across the world, addressed the question "Is Zionism worse than Nazism?" The moderator, Dr. Faisal Al-Qassam, included in the discussion the opinion of a viewer who wrote in from the station's Web site: "The sons of Zion, whom our God described as the sons of apes and pigs, will not be deterred unless there is a real holocaust, that will destroy all of them at once, together with the traitors—those who collaborate with them, the scum of this [Islamic] nation."[9]

Salim 'Azzouz, columnist for the Al-Ahrar Egyptian opposition daily, affiliated with the religious Liberal Party, described Israel's May 2000 withdrawal from Lebanon: "They fled with only the skin on their bodies, like pigs flee. And why say 'like,' when they actually are pigs and apes?"[10]

This paper aims to place these references to Jews as apes and pigs in their religious and historical context and show their roots in Muslim religious sources.

CHAPTER ONE: ISLAMIC RELIGIOUS SOURCES ON THE JEWS—THE "DESCENDANTS OF APES AND PIGS"

According to Islam, the ancient Jews were turned into animals for transgressing the word of God.[11] This divine punishment is mentioned in the most important sources of Islamic religious law, in both the Qur'an's recounting of the divine revelation, and in the extremely reliable hadiths (traditions of the Prophet Muhammad) compiled by the leading ninth-century sages Muslim and Al-Bukhari,[12] which mention also mice, lizards, and other animals in the same context.

The divine punishment of Jews is mentioned in three Qur'anic verses: "They are those whom Allah has cast aside and on whom His wrath has fallen and of whom He has made some as apes and swine" (5:60); "You have

surely known the end of those from amongst you who transgressed in the matter of the Sabbath, in consequence of which we condemned them: Be ye like apes, despised" (2:65);[13] and "when, instead of amending, they became more persistent in the pursuit of that which they were forbidden, we condemned them: Be ye as apes, despised" (7:166).[14]

Arab literature (Adab) also discussed Jews' transformation into animals. In his ninth-century treatise *The Book of Animals*, the greatest of these authors, Al-Jahiz,[15] mentions that it is generally thought that the cheetah, eel, white ant, mouse, and lizard were originally Jews. He mentions the tradition telling how a sage saw a man eating a lizard and said to him: "Know that you have eaten one of the sheikhs of the sons of Israel." He does not mention why they were changed into animals, but does say that proof of this is that "the lizard's foot resembles the human hand."[16]

CHAPTER TWO: QUR'ANIC COMMENTARY: CHRISTIAN AND MUSLIM SINNERS WERE ALSO TRANSFORMED INTO APES AND PIGS

Although in the Qur'an, transformation into apes and pigs is connected only with Jews, Qur'anic commentary links transformation into apes and pigs with Christians as well. Verse 5:112–15 relates that the Apostles wanted to know whether God could bring down a table laden with food from the heavens. Jesus directed this request to God, and it was answered. However, God warned him that anyone who ate at the table and would then commit blasphemy would be punished in a way that no one had yet been punished. In his commentary on this verse, the renowned tenth-century commentator Al-Tabari[17] says, that despite God's warning, some did commit blasphemy and were punished by being turned into apes and pigs—or, in another version, only into pigs.[18]

Another verse linking Christians with apes and pigs is 3:61; according to the commentary on this verse, a deputation of Christians from Najran came to Al-Madina to debate the Prophet about the question: Was Jesus the son of God, as the Christians claimed, or flesh and blood, with no mother or father, like the first man, as the Muslims claimed? After finding that they could not agree, they decided to meet again and curse each other, thinking that God's curse would apply to whichever of them was lying. When the Christian deputation saw that the Prophet brought with him his relatives from the 'Ali bin Abu Taleb family, they were frightened, and acknowledged his prophetic mission and decided to make peace with him, recognize his rule, and pay *jizya* [poll tax on non-Muslims]. According to a hadith of the Prophet, cited mostly in Shi'ite sources, had they instead cursed him they would have been turned into apes and pigs.[19]

In the Islamic traditions, Muslims too were threatened with being turned into apes and pigs. However, for Jews and Christians this punishment was a thing of the past, for Muslims it would be meted out on Judgment Day. In his article "Apes, Pigs, and the Islamic Identity," the researcher U. Rubin indicates that the Muslims threatened with being turned into animals were not ordinary sinners, but those whose sin had a Jewish or Christian nature. The use of a punishment connected to Jews and Christians was aimed at fighting Jewish and Christian influence in Islamic society that threatened the unique Islamic identity. Islamic identity was supposed to be based on unity and morality; thus, any Muslims imitating Jews or Christians constituted a threat to it.

Muslim unity was threatened by Muslims who had rejected orthodox ideas and were suspected of following the Judeo-Christian example. Thus, most traditions on Muslims who were to be punished on Judgment Day by being transformed into animals related to the Qadaris. The Qadaris rejected the idea of predestination (Qadar) and their views were perceived by those who opposed them to be of Judeo-Christian origin; thus, they were stigmatized in the way highly typical for Jews and Christians by being associated with transformation into apes and pigs. Moreover, the ideas of the Qadaris were significantly widespread in the city of Basra; thus, Basra is described in the traditions as the place where such transformation was particularly likely to come about.

Danger to Muslim morality came from Muslims who adopted profane aspects of Judeo-Christian culture. Thus, eschatological transformation into apes and pigs was associated also with Muslims who committed sins such as drinking wine, playing instruments in the company of singing slave girls, and sometimes wearing silk; other sins were giving false testimony, usury, and homosexuality. Some of these sins were linked with Jews and Christians (usury, wine, music); others were connected with all non-Arabs (silken garments). These deeds were thought to pose a threat to Islamic identity; thus transgressors were threatened with this classical Judeo-Christian punishment.[20]

The idea of transformation into animals was also used by both of Islam's two major factions, the Sunnis and Shi'ites, in their claims against each other. According to Shi'ite tradition, the second Muslim Khalifah, Omar bin Al-Khattab, who is particularly admired by the Sunnis, wanders the earth in the form of an owl. Another Shi'ite tradition is that the murderer of the Prophet's grandson Hussein bin 'Ali, admired by the Shi'ites, was punished by being turned into a four-eyed dog. The murderer was also sentenced to desperately seek water and not be able to get to it even when he found it, because he had prevented Hussein's family from reaching a water source at the Battle of Karbala.[21]

In contrast, Sunni tradition has it that some of the Shi'ites in Al-Madina and other places were turned into apes and pigs, and that their hearts and faces would change their form at the time of their death. This is in the context of the charge that the Shi'ites greatly resemble Jews, "which should not be wondered at," as Dr. Abu

Muntasir Al-Baloushi explains on a Sunni Web site,[22] "because the Jews invented the Shi'a [the Shi'ite religion] and [the Shi'a] is pervaded by [the Jews'] beliefs and principles, from the day it was created."

CHAPTER THREE: THE HISTORICAL ROOTS OF THE PUNISHMENT

The belief that people were transformed by supernatural intervention—usually divine punishment—into animals, statues, or stars was common among the Arabs and other peoples before Islam.

In the Jewish and Christian sources (Gen. 19:26) Lot's wife was turned into a pillar of salt when she violated the divine prohibition against looking back at Sodom.[23] Another familiar story from the pre-Islamic period is that of Isaf and Na'ila—two lovers who made a pilgrimage to Mecca. When they found themselves alone in the Ka'abah, they fornicated, and were immediately turned into stone. Al-Jahiz said that the shrimp was originally a dressmaker who stole thread and was turned into a threaded creature, to remind her of her crime. Al-Jahiz also said that the snake once had the form of a camel, but God punished it by forcing it to crawl on the earth. Iranian legends link some animals—bears, elephants, tortoises, vultures, crows, owls, hornets, hoopoes, apes, pigs, dogs, and lizards—with transformations that occurred after Islam began. The planet Venus was purportedly a prostitute who ascended to the heavens and became a star by virtue of her knowledge of the greatest name of Allah. In *The Thousand and One Nights*, people are frequently changed into animals and back again, usually by having water sprinkled on them.[24]

Various researchers have attempted to explain the origin of the punishment of transformation mentioned in the Qur'an. The researcher F. Viré maintains that the Qur'anic punishment originates from the well-known legend mentioned in the Talmud, that some of the builders of the Tower of Babel were cursed by God and turned into apes. He bases this story on a Talmudic tractate of Sanhedrin,[25] in which the builders who sought to reach the sky "were divided into three groups. One said, 'Let us ascend and dwell there'; one said, 'Let us ascend and worship the stars'; and one said, 'Let us ascend and make war.' The ones who said: 'Let us ascend and dwell there,' God dispersed. The ones who said: 'Let us ascend and make war,' were turned into apes and ghosts and demons and evil spirits. And the ones who said: 'Let us ascend and worship the stars,' for them God confused the languages of all the earth."[26]

Ilse Lichtenstadter explains that these verses were part of Prophet Muhammad's attempt to gain the support of the Jews of Medina, by threatening with severe punishment if they persisted in refusing to join him. She identifies two ancient sources for the punishment of transformation into apes mentioned in the Qur'an. Apes played a role in legend or ritual in two ancient cultures. In India, the monkey-god Hanuman was widely known, and tales about him reached the Arabian Peninsula via the spice trade between India and southern Arabia. The ancient Egyptians had the baboon god Thoth, usually depicted as a monkey with a dog's head. The stories of a race of people with dogs' heads, associated with the baboon, also reached Christianity. According to a Greek legend, St. Christopher had once belonged to a race of dog-headed people, and upon his conversion to Christianity he was given the ability to speak like a human instead of barking. He was martyred, (possibly) during the rule of the Roman Emperor Decius, in the third century; his symbol is a dog's head. The influence of Christian-Syrian culture reached the Arabian Peninsula; the legends of men with animals' heads could have reached the Prophet.

Lichtenstadter also describes the attitude toward the animals connected to the punishment. Pigs are linked with idol worship, as they were offered as idolatrous sacrifices; therefore the Qur'an prohibits eating them. The ape is identified in ancient sources with evil, demons, and the devil; thus, those who were transformed into apes were banished from human society and thrust into the sphere of the devil.[27]

The influence of the idea of transformation into animals on the Muslim consciousness is marked throughout history. In Spain, for example, during periods of friction between the various religious communities Muslims called Jews "apes" and Christians "pigs and dogs." In North Africa under the Muslim Aghlabid dynasty (ninth through eleventh centuries), Jews were forced to wear a shoulder patch with a picture of a monkey and Christians had to wear a patch with a picture of a pig. These images also had to be affixed to the doors of their respective homes.[28] Furthermore, the concept of transformation influenced Islamic dietary law. Generally speaking, Shi'ites enlarged the number of animals thought to be of human origin and forbade their consumption. Thus, for example, the hare was also included in this list. In contrast, the Sunnis tended to cut down the list; although there are Sunni traditions on people being transformed into animals, they are not commonly cited by Sunni jurists when they determine dietary laws.[29]

CHAPTER FOUR: ISLAMIC COMMENTARY ON THE TRANSFORMATION OF THE JEWS INTO APES AND PIGS

A. The Circumstances of the Punishment

In his comprehensive treatise on the Qur'an, tenth-century commentator Al-Tabari explains that Jews were transformed into animals because they refused to accept Friday as the day of rest. Jews, he said, like the other nations, were ordered to consider Friday their holiday "because of its virtues, and its importance in the heavens and in the eyes of the angels, and because Judgment Day would come on Friday." The Muslims agreed to accept Friday as

the most important day, while the Jews refused, claiming that Saturday was the best day, as Allah created the heavens, the earth and everything else in six days and rested on the seventh. The Christians, too, refused to follow God's command to honor the sixth day, saying that Sunday was the best day. Allah instructed Jesus to allow them to take Sunday as their day of rest, provided that they did so according to certain precepts; however, the Christians did not follow these precepts and their insubordination is mentioned in the Qur'an. Allah also told Moses to allow the Jews to take Saturday as their day of rest, upon the condition that during it they would refrain from fishing and from all work permitted on weekdays. However, the Jews did not meet these conditions, and therefore, they were punished.

Jews who were transformed into animals are largely identified by Qur'anic commentary as residents of the village of Iliya,[30] situated on the Red Sea coast. The Qur'anic commentary tells the story of how Allah made great schools of fish appear on Saturday and disappear before nightfall, to test the Jews' faith and obedience to his commandments. This was too much to bear for the Jews, and they found ways of getting around the divine prohibition against fishing on Saturday. Ibn Abbas, a cousin of the Prophet Muhammad and one of the first Qur'an commentators, wrote that one Jew secretly caught a fish on Saturday, tied it with a string, and threw it back into the water after tying the string to a stake in the ground. The next day, he pulled the fish in and ate it. When he saw that he was not punished, he repeated his actions on the following Saturday, and on the Saturday after that. Eventually, the neighbors noticed the smell of the fish from his cooking, and began following his example. For a long time they ate in secret, and Allah did not hasten to punish them, but when they began to fish openly and sell their prohibited catches in the markets, they were punished.

Al-Tabari mentions another tactic used by Jews to circumvent the prohibition. One Jew who craved fish dug a pit with a channel leading from it to the sea. On Saturday, he opened the channel so the waves would wash the fish into the pit. On Sunday, the man cooked the fish. The aroma of the cooking fish reached the neighbors, who followed his example, and it soon became common for the Jews to eat fish caught on Saturday. When the sages warned them, they claimed they were fishing on Sunday, when they removed the fish from the pit, and not on Saturday, when they opened the channel.[31]

Not all the Jews acted in the same way. The Qur'an commentators identify three groups in this context: some of the Jews sinned and violated the divine precept not to fish on Saturday; some warned the sinners of Allah's punishment and forbade them from continuing to do so. The others held their tongues; although they did not eat the fish that the sinners caught on Saturday, they also did not forbid the sinners from sinning.[32]

In such a situation, when the sinners refused to stop sinning, those who followed the divine precept decided that they were unwilling to live in the same village with the sinners and built a wall between them. One day, the sinners were not seen leaving their gate. Those who observed the divine precept climbed the wall and went to check the houses, and found them locked. When they opened the doors, they found that everyone—men, women, and children—were turned into apes. "They locked their houses at night, when people lock themselves in, and awoke as apes."[33] The thirteenth-century Andalusian Qur'an commentator Al-Qurtubi[34] said that the apes identified their human relatives, approached them, smelled their clothes, and cried. The humans, in contrast, could not identify their relatives, but told them: "'Didn't we forbid you [from violating the word of God]?' The apes nodded their heads in assent." According to some commentators, the young people of the village became apes while the elderly became pigs.[35]

In his doctoral dissertation "The Sons of Israel in the Koran and in the Muslim Hadith Tradition," Al-Azhar Sheikh Muhammad Sayyid Tantawi explains the Jews' transformation into apes and pigs in the Qur'an in another way. Tantawi devotes a chapter to the various ways in which Allah punished the sons of Israel, among them changing their form. In explaining Qur'an verse 5:60, Tantawi says that the Jews asked the Prophet Muhammad what prophets he believed in. The Prophet enumerated Abraham, Ishmail, Isaac, Jacob, the tribes [sic], Moses, and Jesus, and said that he did not differentiate between them. At the mention of Jesus, the Jews denied his prophecy, saying: "We do not believe in Jesus or anyone who believes in Him [that is, Muhammad himself], and we do not think our religion is worse than yours." Against this backdrop, the Qur'an clarified the evil of the religion of the Jews, whom "Allah cursed and against whom He was wroth, and He turned some of them into apes and pigs."[36]

In his treatise *The Life of Animals*, the fifteenth-century Egyptian scholar Al-Damiri[37] mentions another tradition linking Jews' attitude toward Jesus and the punishment meted out to them. According to this commentary tradition, Jesus encountered a group of Jews who slandered him and his mother, saying, "Here comes the magician, son of the sorceress." When Jesus heard them he cursed them, and then Allah turned them into pigs.[38] Al-Tabari also presents the Qur'anic story about Jesus's cursing Jews[39] as explanation for the punishment of turning them into apes.

In his commentary, Al-Tabari provides another explanation for why Jews were turned into pigs. He describes a woman from among the sons of Israel who believed in Allah and fought a holy war against the king of the sons of Israel "for the religion of Allah." Three times she waged war, with people who believed in her and followed her, and three times she was defeated. Her men were wounded and killed, but she managed to escape. After the third attempt, she despaired, and called to Allah: "Had this religion a shield and a savior, You would have

already revealed him." It is said that the woman fell asleep in sadness, and that during the night Allah answered her pleas and turned the villagers into pigs.[40]

B. The Punishment in Practical Terms

Most of the commentators take the writings literally and maintain that the Jews were physically changed into apes and pigs, as explicitly stated in the Qur'an. Only one Qur'an commentator, Mujahid,[41] cited by various other interpreters, wrote that the Jews were not physically transformed, but that change was metaphoric, as in the Qur'anic adage about the Jews being like "an ass carrying books"[42] (62:5). According to Mujahid, it was not their external form that was changed; rather their hearts were changed [and their souls came to resemble those of apes]. However, according to the commentators, Mujahid is alone in this view.[43]

Recently, the Hamas monthly *Falastin Al-Muslima* published a series of articles on how Allah punished Jews. One chapter was devoted to the punishment of transforming them into animals. Series author Ibrahim Al-'Ali takes the approach of most Qur'an commentators, explaining that the change was actually physical. He writes: "Allah did not mete out the punishment of transformation on any nation besides the Jews. The significance of the punishment is actual change in the image of the Jew, and the perfect transformation from a human condition to a bestial condition—an actual change from human appearance to the form of genuine apes, pigs, mice, and lizards. . . . The transformation was actual, as it is not impossible that the omnipotent Allah, who created man in his human form, would not be capable of changing the Jew from human into animal."

Al-'Ali cites the tradition in which the Prophet's wife 'Aisha called the Jews "the brothers of apes and pigs." As the tradition goes, "the Jews came to the Prophet and said to him, 'Poison be upon you' [which in Arabic sounds close to 'Peace be upon you']. The Prophet answered, 'Poison be upon you,' and 'Aisha added, 'Poison be upon you, brothers of apes and pigs, and the curse of Allah and his wrath too be upon you.'"[44]

C. The Logic behind the Punishment

As the fourteenth-century Qur'an commentator Ibn Kathir[45] says, every deed has its appropriate recompense. He goes on to explain why Jews were punished by being transformed into apes and pigs: the Jews conspired to fish on Saturday, preparing hooks, nets, and poles ahead of time. When the schools of fish appeared near the shore on Saturday, they were caught by the nets, which the Jews had cleverly devised so that they could not escape that day. In the evening, the Jews came to collect the fish; when they did, Allah turned them into apes, which most closely resemble humans but are not really human. The Jews' actions and subterfuges were outwardly like the truth, but in essence opposed to it—and their reward was thus suited to their deeds.[46]

In a chapter of the Hamas monthly *Falastin Al-Muslima* that discusses the punishment of turning the Jews into animals, Jordanian researcher Dr. Sallah Al-Khaledi explains:

Perhaps the logic of this transformation is that Allah wanted them to be humans who would live as real people and actualize their humanity in the best possible way. But when they rebelled against Allah's laws, they rejected the divine grace, and thus relinquished their humanity and honor and turned spiritually into animals. Then Allah [also] changed their form into apes, and turned them into real animals, [thus] creating a correlation between the spiritual and physical images. . . .

Adherence to divine law is one of man's dignified qualities, while rebellion against divine law is the abolition of man's human qualities. . . . Accordingly, an aggressive, oppressing and sinning man relinquishes human qualities in favor of the bestial qualities [within him], and he [becomes] an animal in his soul, in his emotions, and in his traits, even if he is human in his external form. . . . The aggressive and rebellious Jews were apes spiritually and emotionally, in their souls, in their behavior, and in their traits. They are not part of the human race except in their external form, body, senses, and voices. Their transformation by Allah into apes created a correspondence between their real essence and their form.[47]

D. Did the Jews Who Were Transformed Have Offspring?

Another issue on which the Qur'an commentators and authors of the Adab prose literature focused was whether the Jews who were changed into animals had offspring. Al-Qurtubi explains that two approaches developed among clerics on this matter. According to the first, all apes today are the offspring of the sons of Israel. This was also the view of Ibn Qutaiba,[48] the important ninth-century scholar and author of famous Adab works, who thought that apes who were originally Jews do reproduce.[49]

According to the second approach, the apes who used to be Jews left no offspring. Therefore, today's apes, pigs, and other animals are the offspring of animals in existence before the divine punishment. Ibn Abbas, for example, maintained that anyone whose form was changed lived for no more than three days and did not eat, drink, or propagate.

Those who believe that today's animals are the offspring of the sons of Israel base their belief on some reliable traditions from the Prophet Muhammad, in which he warned against eating particular animals out of fear that they were originally the sons of Israel. In the tradition in the reliable compilations of Muslim and Al-Bukhari, the following is attributed to the Prophet Muhammad: "A group of the sons of Israel, and it is not

known what they did, was lost, and I fear that they are mice. Don't you see that when mice are given camel's milk they don't drink it, and when they are given sheep's milk they drink it?" As the thirteenth-century hadith commentator Al-Nawawi[50] explains, "The flesh and milk of camels are forbidden to the sons of Israel, while the flesh and milk of sheep are not. Therefore, the mice's refraining from drinking camel's milk and their not refraining from drinking sheep's milk proves that they are the sons of Israel in animal form."[51]

Al-Qurtubi also mentions the tradition in Muslim's compilation, according to which a lizard was brought to the Prophet but he refused to eat it, saying, "Perhaps it is of the [people] of the generations whose form was changed." In *Falastin Al-Muslima*, Ibrahim Al-'Ali also cites traditions in which the Prophet is wary of eating lizards. According to one of the traditions, for example, in the compilation of traditions accepted as reliable by the ninth-century sage Abu Daoud,[52] people in the company of the Prophet caught lizards, roasted them and ate them. One of the roasted lizards was offered to the Prophet, who took a palm frond and with it counted the fingers of the lizard [which looked like a human hand], saying: "A group from among the sons of Israel turned into reptiles, and I do not know, perhaps the [lizard] is of this group." In the tradition appearing in Muslim's compilation, the Prophet was firmer about the origin of lizards. It is said that a Bedouin entreated the Prophet to clarify his position on eating lizards, and the Prophet said: "Allah was angry at one of the tribes of the sons of Israel and turned them into reptiles crawling on the earth. I think that these are them [the lizards]; I don't eat them and I don't prohibit it."

Al-Qurtubi notes that the twelfth-century Andalusian judge Ibn Al-Arabi[53] adopted the approach that today's animals are the offspring of the sons of Israel, and mentions another tradition underpinning Ibn Al-Arabi's opinion. Some of the versions of Al-Bukhari's compilation of traditions mention the words of Amer bin Maimoun:[54] "During the Jahiliya [pre-Islamic period] I saw a female ape who had committed adultery, and [apes around her] stoning her and I joined them and stoned her too." In Ibn Al-Arabi's view, the animals passed the knowledge of the religious laws [including the law about stoning adulterers] from generation to generation, down to the time of bin Maimoun. He adds that the Jews changed the [law] of stoning and Allah wanted them to uphold it while they were in a different form [i.e., apes].[55]

The Prophet's fear, in various traditions, that mice, lizards, and other animals are humans who were transformed, is explained by Al-Qurtubi: This was a hypothesis raised by the Prophet before he received the divine inspiration that made it clear to him that Allah did not give offspring to such humans in changed form. After he got this inspiration, he was no longer fearful, and stated: "Allah did not destroy people or torment them [and at the same time] give them offspring. The apes and the pigs [we see today] existed before." According to Al-Qurtubi, this tradition is most reliable, and it appears in Muslim's compilation of traditions. He adds that the tradition about eating lizards in the Prophet's presence and at his table without [the Prophet's] condemnation proves that they are not the offspring of the sons of Israel.[56]

Like Al-Qurtubi, Ibrahim Al-'Ali prefers the approach according to which Jews punished by transformation to animals had no offspring. In *Falastin Al-Muslima*, he writes that Jews who were turned into apes, pigs, lizards, and mice were also punished by not being able to reproduce: "They existed in the world for as long as Allah wanted, and then he made them extinct without their leaving offspring. Remaining [in the world] were the apes, pigs, and other animals which had existed before [the divine punishment] . . . and it is they who propagated and left offspring."

But, Al-'Ali goes on to explain, "the extinction of Jews punished with transformation does not mean that their punishment had ended. The punishment left its impression in the souls of the Jews who came after them: their spirit, their opinions, their feelings, and their ways of thought—which are reflected in face and external appearance—became like their nature and like the appearance of apes and pigs, and this profoundly affected their ways of behavior."

In *Falastin Al-Muslima*, Ibrahim Al-'Ali presents "scientific" proof for the claim that Jews were punished in this way by Allah. He states that Jews invented the theory of evolution in order to rid themselves of the shame of the ancient punishment: "Since Jews felt disgrace and shame because of this special punishment, that changed them into the brothers of apes and pigs, they attempted to dispel this accusation from themselves, with the help of the satanic thought that guided them in despising the entire human race by saying that [man's] origin was in animals, and that it developed over time from an ape to human form, by means of the theory . . . of the Jewish ape Darwin."[57]

CONCLUSION

Associating Jews with apes, pigs, and other animals, which is widespread in the Arab and Muslim world among both Shi'ites and Sunnis, is firmly grounded in the most important Islamic religious sources, and also has roots in the folklore of other ancient peoples. This idea has been used not only in religious writings but also in prose and fiction, both in the past and today.

NOTES

All links provided worked upon original publication, November 1, 2002, but may no longer.

1. http://www.palestine.info/arabic/palestoday/readers/mashhoor/22_4_01.htm.

2. http://www.alraialaam.com/20-04-2002/ie5/ frontpage.htm#03;http://www.palestine.info.info/arabic/palestoday/dailynews/ 2002/apr02/20_4/ detail1.htm.

3. http://www.alminbar.cc/alkhutab/khutbaa.asp ?mediaURL=5544, April 19, 2002.

4. http://www.alminbar.cc/alkhutab/khutbaa.asp ?mediaURL=4331, undated.

5. Palestine Television, Palestinian Authority, August 3, 2001.

6. http://www.nasrollah.org/arabic/hassan/khitabat/ khitabat08.htm.

7. See http://www.iqraatv.com.

8. Iqra Television, Saudi Arabia/Egypt, May 7, 2002.

9. From official transcript, Al-Jazeera TV, Qatar, May 15, 2001.

10. *Al-Ahrar* (Egypt), May 30, 2000.

11. The Arab term for this kind of physical transformation is *maskh*, meaning "change of external form to a more abhorrent form." See Lissan Al-Arab, "Maskh."

12. Muslim bin Al-Hajjaj (died 875) and Muhammad bin Isma'il Al-Bukhari (died 870).

13. According to Qur'an commentators, this is a reference to the punishment of transformation into apes banished [from the divine] good, humiliated and despised.

14. Elsewhere, the Qur'an speaks in general of the transformation of the infidels (non-Muslims): "If we so will, we may change them (*la masakhnhum*) where they are . . ." (36:67). It should be noted that this is the only place in the Qur'an where the term *maskh* is used, and that this term refers to a change in form that takes place on Judgment Day. This concept was not always linked to the idea of punishment by transformation into apes and pigs. The first Qur'an commentators were divided regarding the *maskh* awaiting sinners, offering a number of possibilities such as transformation into stones, laming, or crippling in the legs and arms. In the hadith literature, too, there is a tradition depicting an eschatological *maskh* with no mention of apes and pigs. Most of the traditions concerning future *maskh* describe a threefold catastrophe heralding Judgment Day: the earth will split open and swallow the sinners (*hasf*), [rocks] will be thrown [from the sky] (*qadhf*), and there will be transformation into a lower life form (*maskh*). Sometimes there are also mentions of an earthquake (*rajf*) in this context. An examination of the historical background of the appearance of these traditions shows that they emerged during the civil wars among the Muslims in the Umayyad period. The great distress of that time cultivated a sense of impending apocalypse, which in turn gave rise to traditions that anticipated the end of the world and Judgment Day. See Uri Rubin, "Apes, Pigs, and the Islamic Identity," *Israel Oriental Studies* 17 (1997): 89–93.

15. Omar bin Bahar Al-Jahiz (d. 869).

16. Al-Jahiz, Omar bin Bahar, Kitab Al-Hayawan.

17. Muhammad bin Jarir Al-Tabari (d. 923).

18. Al-Tabari, 5:115. Other sources tell that an Israelite tribe that manifested undue skepticism when the miracle of the table was vouchsafed to Jesus, was turned into lizards.

See M. Cook, "Early Islamic Dietary Law," *Jerusalem Studies in Arabic and Islam (JSAI)* 7 (1986): 223.

19. A tradition mentioned, for example, in the book by Fakhr Al-Din bin Muhammad Al-Tarihi (d. 1087) Majma' Al-Bahrain. See http://www.islam4u.com/almojib/4/0/4.0.2.htm.

20. Rubin, "Apes, Pigs, and the Islamic Identity," pp. 93–102. It should be noted that even today, Islamic preachers deter their congregations from transgressions such as drinking wine, singing, and playing music with hadiths threatening the sinners that they will be transformed into apes and pigs. [Such] sermons of are not as common as sermons mentioning Jews as the offspring of these animals, but are more common than sermons referring to Christians in this context. See, for example, the sermon of the Sudanese preacher Muhammad Abd Al-Karim on singing, http://www.alminbar.net/alkhutab/khutbaa.asp?mediaURL=3124.

21. At the Battle of Karbala (680), the grandson of the Prophet and his men were murdered. This gave the Shi'ite movement its aura of martyrdom. The tradition of the four-eyed dog is taken from Charles Pellat, "Maskh," *Encyclopedia of Islam*, 2nd ed., 737.

22. See the Web site of the Iranian Sunni League, http://www.isl.org.uk/article.php?sid=11.

23. It is interesting that the case of Lot's wife's transformation is not mentioned in the Qur'an's version of the story of Lot (Qur'an 11:81).

24. See Pellat, "Maskh," 736–38.

25. Sandedrin tractate, 11:109a.

26. See F. Viré, "Kird," *Encyclopedia of Islam*, 2nd ed.

27. Ilse Lichtenstadter, "And Become Ye Accursed Apes," *JSAI*, 14 (1991): 162–75.

28. Viré, "Kird."

29. Cook, "Early Islamic Dietary Law," 223–33.

30. Ibn Kathir (7:166) explains that Iliya is situated on the coast between Egypt and Al-Madina. According to Al-Damiri, Iliya is between Midian and Al-Tur. Other places identified in the commentary with "the village on the coast" are "Median" situated between Iliya and Al-Tur (see Al-Tabari 2:65, Ibn Kathir, 2:65 or Tiberias).

31. Ilse Lichtenstadter identifies two Jewish folklore motifs that apparently influenced Al-Tabari's explanation of the punishment. One is the legend of the Leviathan and the Sambation River: In the Torah, God uses the Leviathan to defeat the enemies of his people, and in the Talmud, the Baba Batra tractate (746) tells how the Leviathan was slaughtered by God for food for the righteous in the Hereafter. With regard to the Sambation River, it is told that it is a river full of sand and rocks that rushes and surges during the week but is quiet on Saturday. According to another version, the river is quiet during the week and rises on Saturday. It would seem that it is the version in which the river rises on Saturday which underpins Al-Tabari's commentary, because the schools of fish arrived on Saturday but not during the week. See Lichtenstadter, "And Become Ye Accursed Apes," 159–61.

32. Two commentator positions emerged on the matter of what happened to the Jews who neither fished nor prevented the others from fishing. According to one view, only the actual sinners were changed into animals, and they were then destroyed; the other two groups that did not sin, whether actively or passively, were not. According to the second view, only those who explicitly spoke out against and forbade the sin were saved, and those who remained passive were also transformed. See, for example, 7:166.

33. Al-Tabari 2:65, Ibn Kathir 2:65.

34. Ibn Farrah Al-Qurtubi (b. 1273).

35. Al-Qurtubi 2:65.

36. Muhammad Sayyid Tantawi, "The Sons of Israel in the Koran and Muslim Tradition," *Cairo: Dar Al-Shurouq*, 2nd ed. (2000), 695–97.

37. Kamal Al-Din Al-Damiri (b. 1405).

38. Al-Damiri, Kamal Al-Din, Hayat Al-Hayawan, vol. 1, 386.

39. According to Al-Tabari's commentary on 5:78: "Those of the children of Israel who disbelieved were cursed by David and by Jesus, son of Mary; that was because they disobeyed and were given to transgression." See Al-Tabari 2:65.

40. Al-Tabari 5:60.

41. Mujahid bin Jaber Al-Maki (d. c. 718–22).

42. "The case of those who were made subject to the Law of the Torah, but did not carry out their obligations under it, is like that of a donkey carrying a load of books. Evil is the case of the people who reject the Signs of Allah, and Allah guides not the wrongdoing people" (62:5).

43. Al-Tabari, 2:65, Ibn Kathir, 2:65, Al-Qurtubi 2:65.

44. *Falastin Al-Muslima* (London), September 1996, 54–55.

45. Isma'il bin Amer Ibn Kathir (d. 1373).

46. Ibn Kathir, 2:65.

47. *Falastin Al-Muslima*, September 1996, pp. 54–55.

48. Muhammad bin Abdallah Ibn Qutaiba (b. 889).

49. Pellat, "Maskh," 737.

50. Yahyah Al-Nawawi (b. 1277).

51. This interpretation appears in Ibrahim Al-'Ali's article in *Falastin Al-Muslima*, September 1996, pp. 54–55.

52. Abu Daoud Al-Sijistani (b. 889).

53. Abu Bakr Ibn Al-Arabi (b. 1148).

54. One of the important men of the second generation of supporters of the Prophet in the city of Kufa.

55. Al-Qurtubi expresses reservations about this tradition, claiming that perhaps it "is one of the things that was attributed forcibly to Al-Bukhari." He says that some scholars doubt that anyone not obligated by the religious precepts can commit adultery [that is, apes], and thus God's punishments apply also to animals. He adds that "If this is true, [and the female ape was stoned by the other apes], she was from among the demons [*Jinn*], because the ritual precepts apply to man and *Jinn* alone."

56. Al-Qurtubi, 2:65.

57. *Falastin Al-Muslima*, September 1996, pp. 54–55.

CHAPTER 59

Jews as "Christ-Killers" in Islam

Andrew G. Bostom

Lenny Bruce often confronted the deicide or "Christ-killer" allegation in his bold pre–Vatican II act. The comedian would relate how a beleaguered Jew put a note in his cellar, where it could easily be found, to absolve all other Jews. It said: "I did it. Morty." For weeks, the American media has been inundated with apoplectic diatribes surrounding the unproven (soon to be disproven?) potential impact of Mel Gibson's recently released *The Passion of the Christ* on reviving this now heretical allegation, forty years after Vatican II.

Curiously ignored in this overheated discussion is the openly professed, orthodox theological view of Islam and Muslims that the Jews themselves (à la Morty?), claimed to have killed Christ. Specifically, Qur'an 4:157–58 iterates,

> That they [i.e., the Jews] said in boast, "We killed Christ Jesus the son of Mary, the Messenger of Allah";—but they killed him not, nor crucified him, but so it was made to appear to them, and those who differ therein are full of doubts, with no (certain) knowledge, but only conjecture to follow, for of a surety they killed him not. . . . Nay, Allah raised him up unto Himself; and Allah is Exalted in Power, Wise . . .

Ibn Kathir (d. 1373), a preeminent Muslim historian, theologian, and Qur'anic commentator, provides this elaboration of Qur'an 4:157–58, which emphasizes the Jews' overall perfidy, especially their gloating (but unknowingly "false") claim to have killed Jesus:

> When Allah sent Isa (Jesus) with proofs and guidance, the Jews—may Allah's curses, anger, torment, and punishment be upon them—envied him because of his prophethood and obvious miracles. . . . [T]he Jews defied him . . . and tried their best to harm him. Allah's Prophet Isa (Jesus) could not live in any one city for long and he had to travel often with his mother. . . . Even so, the Jews were not satisfied, and they went to the King of Damascus at that time a Greek polytheist who worshipped stars. They told him there was a man . . . misguiding and dividing the people in Jerusalem and stirring unrest among the king's subjects. The king became angry and wrote to his deputy in Jerusalem to arrest the rebel leader, stop him from causing unrest, crucify him and make him wear a crown of thorns. When the king's deputy in Jerusalem received these orders, he went with some Jews to the house that Isa (Jesus) was residing in, and he was with twelve, thirteen, or seventeen of his companions. That day was a Friday, in the evening. They surrounded Isa (Jesus) in the house, and when he felt that they would soon enter the house or that he would sooner or later have to leave it, he said to his companions, "Who volunteers to be made to look like me, for which he will be my companion in Paradise?" A young man volunteered, but Isa (Jesus) thought that he was too young. He asked the question a second time and third time, each time the young man volunteering, prompting Isa (Jesus) to say, "Well, then you will be that man." Allah made the young man look exactly like Isa (Jesus), while a hole opened in the roof of the house, and Isa (Jesus) was made to sleep and ascended to heaven while asleep. . . . When Isa (Jesus) ascended, those who were in the house came out. When those surrounding the house saw the man who looked like Isa (Jesus), they thought that he was Isa (Jesus). So they took him at night, crucified him and placed a crown of thorns on his head. The Jews boasted that they killed Isa (Jesus) and some Christians accepted their false claim due to their ignorance and lack of reason.[1]

In his commentary on the related Qur'anic verse 4:159, "And there is none of the People of the Book but must believe in him before his death; and on the Day of Judgment he will be a witness against them,"[2] Ibn Kathir elucidates the Islamic version of the "Resurrection" from the hadith (oral tradition recording Muhammad's words and actions) in which Isa (Jesus), who is merely a Muslim prophet preaching Islam, returns to "break the

---

Andrew G. Bostom, "Jews as 'Christ-Killers' in Islam," FrontPageMagazine.com, March 3, 2004, http://www.frontpagemag.com/Articles/Read.aspx?GUID={7D37FB0D–0331–41B6–9E31–D807A55D1308}.

cross, kill the pig, and banish the *jizya* [Qur'anic poll tax signifying non-Muslim subjugation by Islam] and call all the people to Islam."

Ibn Kathir's commentary on Qur'an 4:155–59 also discusses Isa's role in defeating the Dajjal (i.e., the Muslim Antichrist), and his Jewish minions,[2a] invoking the apocalyptic canonical hadith of Jew annihilation (*Sahih Muslim* bk. 41, no. 6985), which was incorporated into the 1988 Hamas Charter.[2b] The invocation of *Sahih Muslim* bk. 41, no. 6985, by Ibn Kathir—a seminal fourteenth-century Qur'anic exegete, and Muslim historian—debunks the recently espoused, spurious contention that this prominent apocalyptic motif from the canonical hadith somehow received "no mention" in Arabic literature until "after at least 1870."[2c]

It is critically important to understand that all the essential themes of Ibn Kathir's narrative regarding the Crucifixion are reiterated in the authoritative contemporary manual of Islamic law *'Umdat al-salik wa'uddat al-nasik* (*Reliance of the Traveler*), which is certified by Cairo's distinguished Al-Azhar University. In addition, *Reliance of the Traveler* reaffirms the accepted interpretation of Isa's (Jesus's) return as described in the Qur'an and hadith:

> (T)he time and place for [the poll tax] is before the final descent of Jesus. . . . After his final coming, nothing but Islam will be accepted from them, for taking the poll tax is only effective until Jesus' descent.[3]

The modern pronouncements and teachings of the Roman Catholic Church stand in stark relief. For example, Professor Phillip Cunningham summarized the principal features of the Second Vatican Council's "Declaration of the Relationship of the Church to Non-Christian Religions" (*Nostre Aetate*), issued in 1965, as follows:

> *Nostre Aetate* rejected key elements of the ancient anti-Jewish tradition. "The Jews" were not guilty of the crucifixion, had not been renounced by God, were not under a wandering curse, and their covenantal bond with God endured.[4]

Furthermore, despite the fact that Islam categorically rejects the Gospels' account of the Crucifixion, large segments of the Muslim intelligentsia were infuriated by the *Nostre Aetate* declaration rejecting the charge of deicide against the Jewish people. According to prominent *dhimmi* cleric advocates of the Islamic viewpoint, such as Youakim Moubarac, Muslim protestations "against the disculpation of the Jewish people" were lodged in "a perfectly authentic pursuit" of the Qur'an "for the honor of God and the Virgin."[5] Moubarac added that Jews were "the principal agent of an entire sinful mankind [and] . . . blame cannot be placed on this mankind for a deed for

which its prime author is absolved." The historian Bat Ye'or has noted bluntly that the sentiments expressed by Moubarac and his ilk reflect an "Islamic and Christian anti-Judaism [which] mutually strengthened each other in order to torpedo Judeo-Christian rapprochement."[6]

As a Jew, even an admittedly very secular one, it has been quite reassuring to see the preponderance of devout American Christians fully prepared and willing to mollify any potentially antisemitic (especially deicidal) motifs in *The Passion of the Christ*, due in no small part to the church's sincere modern teachings. There is no remotely comparable progressive strain evident in the Islamic world. Muslim clerics and regimes, especially in the Near East, vehemently opposed, and continue to oppose, the Vatican II/*Nostre Aetate* renunciation of the deicide allegation against Jews.[7] Moreover, basic Islamic theology regarding the deicide allegation, and its ugly related politics, are barely known in the West, due to a combination of profound ignorance and deliberate, cynical obfuscation. The chasm between modern Muslim and Christian teachings with regard to the "deicide/Christ-killer" allegation against the Jews, as well as the overall conception of Jesus, couldn't be wider. Religious leaders, as well as elites in government policy, academia, and the media must begin to discuss this asymmetry candidly, as well as its implications for serious, meaningful interfaith "dialogue" between Jews, Christians, and Muslims.

NOTES

1. Tafsir Ibn Kathir, vol. 3 (Riyadh: 2000), pp. 23–43.

2. Ibid., pp. 26–27.

2a. Ibid., pp. 33–34.

2b. The Covenant of the Islamic Movement—Hamas," *Middle East Media Research Institute*, Special Dispatch Series, no. 1092, February 14, 2006.

2c. Debating the Islamist-Nazi Connection," *Front PageMagazine.com*, January 2, 2008.

3. *'Umdat al-salik wa'uddat al-nasik* [*Reliance of the Traveler*] (Cairo, 1991), pp. 602–603.

4. Phillip Cunningham, *Education for Shalom: Religion Textbooks and the Enhancement of the Catholic-Jewish Relationship* (1995), p. 39.

5. Youakim Moubarac, *L'Islam et le Dialogue Islamo-Chretien, Pentalogie Islamo-Chretienne* (1972–1973), p. 158, 169, 172; cited in Bat Ye'or, *Islam and Dhimmitude: Where Civilizations Collide* (Cranberry, NJ: 2001), pp. 272–73.

6. Bat Ye'or, *Islam and Dhimmitude*, p.

7. See, for example, Middle East Media Research Institute, "Sheik Yousef Al-Qaradhawi: The Jews of Today Bear Responsibility for Their Forefathers' Crime against Jesus, " August 26, 2006, clip #1249, from Qatar Television.

CHAPTER 60

Antisemitism in (Contemporary) Islam: Europe in the Conflict between Tolerance and Ideology

Hans-Peter Raddatz

1. MUSLIM LIFE—ON WHAT TERMS?

Islam is not only a political religion that combines faith and state. In discussing this subject we must also take into account the fact that this religion is also a trans-temporal phenomenon that draws its strength from sources in the distant past that are nevertheless part of a present-day consciousness. The Qur'an and the associated tradition are alive today in much the same way as they were in the days of their founder Muhammad and in the early period of Islam; the teachings and practices handed down from those times have been cited continually by the theologians as exemplary and have been further developed as a binding doctrine of faith. Since the religion encompasses man, the family, society, and the state, it also provides a model for explaining Islamist movements [*Islamismus*], which are conservators today of a premodern worldview that increasingly brings the great majority of Muslims into political and legal conflicts with the present.

In an age of Islamic migration and its intercultural confrontation with the non-Islamic world, it would of course be disastrous to assume that the West can deny these fundamental differences and genuinely incorporate the Muslim diaspora in a sort of "splendid isolation." Contemporary Islam is unthinkable without its prophetic primordial model, nor can any "dialogue" overlook its foundations, some of which—especially in the legal-political realm—are controversial. The universal and timeless structure of this political religion obliges its adherents to maintain its traditions and customs unaltered and also, whenever possible, to impose them on a non-Islamic milieu. It should therefore come as no surprise to the reader if facts are presented in the following pages which seem to have no immediate connection with the contemporary Islamic scene.

Inasmuch as the majority of Muslims, today as in the past, equate religion and politics and thus equate their whole existence with truth itself, one of their most important dogmas is their self-definition, which contrasts them to the non-Islamic religions and systems of government that they have conquered over the course of history. Although this expansion continues today in the form of modern migration, that does not mean that they have also adopted the methods of liberalism and acculturation.

History and current events show, rather, that [Islam's] guiding force in this intercultural encounter is a historical, deep-rooted, aggressive, and discriminatory set of rules that makes its own continuation the top priority. Termed Shari'a (Arabic for "the way"), it has been for half a millennium now the official, unchangeable substance of Islamic theology. It is the integral basis for Muslim life, belief, and politics, and, according to the Cairo Commission, for a comprehensive edition of the Muhammad tradition, it is "the royal road bestowed by Allah . . . which includes all the concerns and departments of life."[1] Since Western pluralism often does not appreciate this all-encompassing context, it misses an important distinctive feature of the Islamic worldview, wherein it is an integral component of *spirituality* to fend off or, if possible, to conquer the non-Islamic world *politically*.

2. JIHAD AGAINST JEWS, CHRISTIANS, AND WOMEN

Since Jews and Christians are regarded as "falsifiers of Scripture" (as the Qur'an itself attests) and today are viewed essentially as the originators of modernity, they—together with women—play the traditional role of antagonists in Islamic ideology. They represent and embody intellectual principles that could call into question the continued existence of Islam: the Judeo-Christian ethical system, on the spiritual level, and the autonomy [*Selbständigkeit*] of women, on the biological level. Within the Islamic world there is no free discussion about the ethical self-discovery of the Jews in the Decalogue [i.e., the fact that by receiving the law they were constituted as a

English translation by Michael J. Miller.

covenant people], nor about the (theoretical) self-restraint of Christians in renouncing power, nor about the sexual or intellectual self-determination of women; consequently, these ideas have been and still are strictly regulated as "controlled substances."

This control is carried out through the rules of Shari'a; the conformity imposed by Islamic law gives rise in turn to a "charismatic competition" to fulfill this law as perfectly as possible. Like all ideologies that lay claim to the consciousness of its adherents, it confers power and hence has not failed to have an effect on Western elite groups as well. This has given rise to the tendency to separate Islamist movements from Islam, resulting in an increasing acceptance by those elites of Shari'a as a substitute political system [Stellvertreter-politik, that is, for Muslim minorities in Western countries]. At the same time, the slogan of "tolerance," whether deliberately or not, is used to leverage the curtailment of the deep-rooted rights of the general population.

Since there is no true nature [kein Sein] and thus no freedom of choice outside of Islam, the rejection of the non-Islamic world is not just a part of Muslim life, but rather its indispensable vital core. Therefore those who oppose concepts such as Judeo-Christian civilization and/or the autonomy of women proclaim their faith in a particularly convincing way. Within the context of "proxy politics" [Stellvertreter-politik], the Western "dialogue with Islam," too, has adopted this view, and it conducts its intercultural discussions more and more along the lines of protecting Islamic interests.

This Islamic dynamic, which finds alternative worldviews acceptable only under certain very narrow conditions, has meanwhile become known to a wider public as "jihad." The term includes various nuances of "striving" or "effort," a broad spectrum of meanings which motivate the "charismatic competition" and make it possible for the individual Muslim to fulfill himself as a useful part of the Islamic community. As the connecting link between Islam and Islamist movements [Islamismus], this "striving" ranges from spiritual endeavors on behalf of the faith through attempts to control women, to the most extreme efforts to destroy one's political opponent physically, including even suicide.

In this [polyvalent] modality, the oft-cited formula stating that there is "no compulsion in faith" (Qur'an 2:256) takes on its actual meaning. It describes Islamic freedom, which knows no restrictions when the continuation and expansion of the Umma (Muslim unity and community) is concerned. The Umma is understood as "the best of all societies that have ever developed" (3:106), and in order to defend itself it even embraces violence. In a worldview that is thus limited to Islam, the prohibition against killing must also be limited to Muslims. In contrast, with regard to non-Muslims or disobedient women, this prohibition is not only annulled but transformed into a commandment to kill, which is attested in many places in the Qur'an and the tradition.

The degree to which it is binding depends, on the other hand, upon the accompanying circumstances of the "charismatic competition" as put into practice concretely at any given time. With regard to unbelief, this "freedom" is expressed in propaganda against Jews and in the battle against Israel; with regard to women, it is expressed in the rights [of Muslim men] to beat or rape them or to carry out "honor killings."

3. THE BATTLE OF EUROPEAN ISLAM AGAINST THE JEWS

As a result, the more this "charismatic competition" on behalf of the overarching Islamic cause [Verdienste] produces concrete, practical advantages, the nearer one comes to legitimizing violence. The Muslim entity not only considers itself superior to all the other alternatives, but also differentiates itself from them quite graphically in a derogatory, Darwinian manner. Thus Jews are compared with apes, Christians with pigs, and women with dogs; they are devalued to such a degree that Islamic theology makes it a "natural" duty to impose strict limits on their living conditions, to keep constant watch over them, and, on occasion, to destroy them.

Thus to any Muslim believer, even the leading authorities of Islam worldwide, it seems absurd to recognize those life forms that are found outside of Islam or that potentially threaten its own continued existence—to say nothing of abrogating, in their favor, the principles underlying their own claim to dominion. Hence Islamic morality aims in the first place to safeguard this claim, the vital core of which, in turn, consists in the dominance of Islamic law, of Allah's Shari'a.

Within this framework, one important point of reference is the battle against the Jews, which got under way thanks to the efforts of the Prophet himself, when he had one of the Jewish tribes of Medina exterminated. This measure acquired a downright metaphysical significance, which looms much larger than the political arena. Only in this way can we explain the persistence of Islamic pressure on the Jewish diaspora, which has lasted more than a millennium and continues in our days in the battle against Israel.

The leading part played by this goal requires the authorities of Islam to repeat and confirm it again and again in public. For Muhammad Tantawi, chief mufti of Egypt, and Azhar-[Sheikh] there is no doubt "that we must return to the teachings of Islam in order to fight against Allah's enemy and to cleanse the sacred ground from the Jews."[2] He issued a religious ruling (fatwa) stating that assassins should be considered martyrs even and especially if Jewish women and children—and thus the future of Israel—are killed in their attacks.[3] He cites as his forerunner and authority no less a figure than Adolf Hitler, who for his part invoked a deity that mediated violence: "By resisting the Jews, I fight for the cause of the Lord."[4]

This "Lord" speaks in a very similar way in the Qur'an as well:

> And because they broke their pledge, we have cursed them. . . . And again and again you will see that they produce falsehood. (5:13)

> And you will surely find that the people who prove to be most hostile to the believers are the Jews and the pagans. (2:96)

> And this is to punish them because they did not believe Allah's signs and unjustly killed the prophets. (3:112)

> O you who believe, protect yourselves and your relatives from a fire that is fueled by men and stones. (66:6)

So it is not surprising that Arabic literature is so full of references to a repressive practice called *dhimma*, "a security agreement" that regulates dealings with the "People of the Book"—Jews and Christians. Although according to the Qur'an these groups are assured of special treatment, this precept was regularly honored in the breach. There is no lack of reports that give the same evidence of the oppression under which the Jews lived, whether in Yemen or Egypt, in Syria, Iraq, or North Africa.[5] "In the long run the result of it was that the indigenous agrarian population of believing Jews and Christians disappeared."[6]

A secularized form of antisemitism asserted itself in colonialism. It continued the tradition of ecclesial hostility toward the Jews, which was essentially unaffected by either the Reformation or the Enlightenment. Inasmuch as the Jews, for their part, kept themselves separate in their Zionist aspirations [*Zionismus*], they involuntarily contributed to the rapprochement of European antisemites and Islamic Jew-haters. Routine slanders, such as charges of the ritual murder of children and of a "Jewish conspiracy," which were and are alleged in *The Protocols of the Elders of Zion*, helped considerably to confirm Muslims in their anti-Jewish tradition and to make the Jews the universal scapegoat for the outrages of colonial occupation.

It seems then to be no coincidence that the same great minds that are presented as harbingers of a tolerance that comes from the East were to some extent also great anti-Semites. Besides Voltaire, who saw the Jews as a "degenerate and inferior race," Immanuel Kant considered them completely incapable of benefiting society: "Nothing will come of it as long as they are Jews. . . . Now they are the vampires of society."[7]

A late eighteenth-century German philosopher, Johann Gottlieb Fichte, came close to this opinion in advocating a selective tolerance for certain religions. He scoffed at Lessing's efforts for the [political] emancipation of the Jews; to integrate them as a "state within a state" seemed to him impossible: "But I, at least, see no other way of giving them the rights of citizens than to cut off all their heads some night and to replace them with others in which there is not a single Jewish idea. In order to protect ourselves from them, again, I see no other way than to conquer their holy land for them and to send them all there."[8]

Fichte had intuitions of a gnostic, self-deifying consciousness, a "primordial German people" [*deutsches Urvolk*] in a unified national [i.e., ethnically German] state, which became an important foundation stone for modern antisemitism of the German variety. According to him, Christianity and Judaism, as concepts that were ultimately "Asiatic" and "held by blind faith," had no business being in Europe, unless they allowed themselves, as he envisioned it, to take "the spirit of the Germanic tribes" as their inspiration.

As the precursor of the ideologies that are behind uncritical dialogue with Islam and also New Age thinking, which advocate "genuine" Islam—that is, Islam as a homogeneous legal entity—Friedrich Schleiermacher wanted to save the German "national organism," as a racially homogeneous social unit, from integration with German Jewry. He thought that the Jews should reach a settlement with the German nation so as not to run the risk of being dehumanized and, as he put it, being "thrown out." Judaism seemed to him to be a defective husk of Christianity to which a place in the German nation should be allotted, at least for its elite.

Finally, G. W. F. Hegel saw Christianity as a summons to renounce the world, a demanding religion which, having been influenced by nonsensical Jewish morality [*jüdische Unmoral*] and Roman syncretism, left room for practically nothing but a completely ahistorical slave mentality. And yet he marveled at the mysterious escape hatch out of this dilemma that the combination of Christ's teaching and person seemed to provide. He admitted reluctantly that, despite the alienation of the clergy, Christianity had managed to arrive at a distinctive freedom of choice, which made possible the emancipation of the individual, as well as science and the secularizing trend. In order to ensure that this freedom would last, however, he demanded a complete break with Judaism, which, with its mechanized behavior, appeared to him as the very antithesis of that freedom and thus as a danger to enlightened society.

It is no accident that this [rationalistic] view of a Christianity that is subject to every [governmental] authority and thus distances itself from Judaism displays obvious parallels to the ideology of orthodox Islam concerning *dhimmitude*, which has remained in force to this day. This ideology, in turn, is just as obviously in agreement with the Marxist teaching which declares that all human salvation must fail as long as Judaism continues to exist.[9] Anyone who wants to make secular and in particular financial progress must therefore detach himself from Judeo-Christian civilization.

This results in an important interface for the political strategy of Islam worldwide, especially of the Islamic Conference, which is striving for a "joint proprietorship of Europe" and is contributing to a division in the European Union. After all, besides the office [in Brussels] that monitors antisemitic activities in Europe, there is a Parliamentary Association for European-Arab Cooperation (PAEAC), which lobbies more and more openly against the interests of Israel.[10]

As the European Constitution and Islamic Shari'a law gradually come to resemble each other, the Europeans can also move closer to the alternative Islamist model and become America's competitors. Historically they stand in the tradition of their great intellectual precursors like Kant, Fichte, Hegel and Marx, whose ideas prepared the way also for the myths of Islamic peace and of Palestine as an Arab homeland and, to use Schleiermacher's language, for "throwing out" Judeo-Christian civilization.

4. "DIALOGUE" COUNTERPRODUCTIVE FOR JUDAISM

In dealing with the Jewish question in Islam, it becomes apparent how resolutely people in Europe disregard all ideological misgivings and the historical evidence for them. Meanwhile almost all representatives of the most important institutions have adopted an ambivalent and uncritical interpretation of the Muslim worldview. As a typical example, illustrating the views of many others, we can mention the sociologist Bassam Tibi, who subscribes to the historically unprovable thesis of the historian Bernard Lewis. According to this thesis, "neither hatred of the Jews nor antisemitism has any roots at all in Islamic history."[11] At the same time Tibi reveals the objective dilemma that proponents of this view find themselves in when he admits that this hatred of the Jews has existed even without [i.e., before] the founding of the state of Israel.[12]

If these facts are suppressed and replaced with fictions, then we will surely see the acceptance of a worldview that tries to legitimize violence, and not just Muslim violence. Tibi provides evidence which graphically proves that a paradigm shift is taking place. On the one hand he criticizes the wishful thinking of the Europeans with regard to Islam; on the other hand he proposes an Islamic vision of peace, which allegedly counterbalances the reality of Islamist movements. Still, he mentions also in passing that within the framework of this transformation, the European elites infringe on democratic rights and responsibilities.

Tibi's overly optimistic and self-contradictory version of the story is essentially based on three fictions. First, he thinks that the Islamic expansion in late antiquity was a blessing for Europe, because it cut the continent off from the Orient and forced it to concentrate on its own territory and spiritual and intellectual potential.[13] What

this activity consisted of, concretely, is never explained, whereas the Orient is portrayed as the master key which, whether united with the West or separated from it, constitutes a universal source of culture. Its mere existence—for example, in the well-known myth of Cordoba—becomes the prerequisite for a cultured West.

As a consequence of this, secondly, Muslim migrants take on the role of the European *citoyen* (the idealized citizen of the French Revolution) and become so-called Euro-Muslims. Muslims are supposedly able to accomplish this in a way that is different from that of the Islamists, even though they form an Islamic collective group and experience no individual acculturation. Tibi does not hide the fact that he is familiar with this dilemma, too; in fact he warns against becoming naturalized citizens in Germany. From his point of view, naturalization is based on a "racist, pre-modern, ethnically grounded law," which would be "extremely problematic" for Muslims to accept.[14]

The theory of the Orient as the master key to civilization demands powerful image-enhancement software that filters out historical analyses that run contrary to it. Thus the Crusades must be seen against the backdrop of Western violence [and expansionism], while the anti-Crusade campaigns conducted by Saladin, Lessing's poster boy for tolerance, are to be framed in terms of Islamic peace as "the beginnings of present-day precepts of international law."[15] For our topic specifically, this leads to a third fiction: There is supposed to have been a universal "Jewish-Islamic symbiosis" (a notion that Tibi borrows from Lewis), which ended only with the Islamist extremism of the Muslim Brotherhood and the antisemitism that it imported from the West.[16]

We don't get to hear [from Tibi] another interpretation by his authority, Lewis, who alternatively sees this occurrence as "the historical, perhaps irrational reaction of an old rival against our Judeo-Christian heritage, our secular contemporary society and the worldwide expansion of both." Lewis dismantles the ethical guardrails and adopts the elitist strategy, in which power can attain a rationality and legitimacy that is scruple free. According to this mentality, the Jewish claim to the right to live [*Lebensrecht*, i.e., in freedom in a homeland of their own] has itself provoked the forces bent on its destruction, inasmuch as "oppression by a Muslim mob or state is the price for the disloyal behavior of subjugated groups."[17]

5. ISLAMIC ANTISEMITISM AND THE PALESTINE MYTH

Like Tibi, many ambivalent mountain climbers who scale the perilous cliffs of "dialogue" cite as their authority for the alleged intercultural harmony Maimonides, of all people: the greatest Jew of the Islamic Middle Ages. On the other hand, he is hardly ever taken into account as a harsh critic of Islamic despotism. "No people has ever caused Israel more suffering. No people ever did as much [as the Muslims] to degrade and humiliate us. No people has even been able to subjugate us as they have done."[18]

Despite this and other contemporary testimonies, the Muslims are supposed to have established universal peace in the East and to have maintained over the course of many centuries a symbiosis with the Jews, which ended only through the violence of European antisemitism. The proponents of this thesis are faced with a twofold dilemma. First, for them any commentary on the Qur'an as a source of anti-Jewish ideology is forbidden; second, they conjure up a fictitious peaceful Islam but do not specify how such a system looks in practice. For they will not admit historical data that do not correspond to their view. As a logical consequence, the result is a quasi-Islamic approach that rejects Western concepts and also makes antisemitism presentable again in fashionable society.

Whether consciously or not, they become fellow travelers with radical Islamic propaganda, which portrays the Jewish state as the spearhead of a twofold challenge. Among the unreasonable demands being made on Islamic culture, which is now exposed to Western economic superiority, liberalism, film and television, feminism, music, pornography, and so on, the ultimate outrages are "global Jewry" [*Weltjudentum*] and Israel. Whereas the Christians in the region have been almost noiselessly decimated over the years and offer no resistance to Allah's claim, the unity of the *Umma* is divided by an Israel which, for its part, has a historically rooted claim to live in the land of its forefathers.

In the semitotalitarian systems of the territory dominated by Islam, a seamless syndicate of anti-Jewish indoctrination has been built up in the mosques and the media. Unremittingly *Al-Akhbar*, Egypt's largest newspaper, calls for the eradication of the "curse of the Jews" that weighs upon this world. "I want you dead; that's what I call peace," adds *Al-Ahram*, the mouthpiece of the Egyptian government, a sentiment that is echoed by *Akil*, the organ of the Turkish Islamist Party. "If every Arab kills one Jew, there will be no Jews left," is a central and recurring theme for the television, film, and print media. In the same way, countless papers, especially in Saudi Arabia, perpetuate horror stories about Jewish ritual killings, which are supposed to justify the killing of the Jews by the Nazis. Their connections with the Muslim Brotherhood are considered proof, and Hitler's statement that he "could win the war as a Mohammedan" has suggested to Arabs since that time that the Holocaust is a duty—a duty that has been reiterated sensationally by the Iranian president.

For a long time the supposed "peace process" in Israel and Islamic antisemitism have joined forces to create a catalog of propaganda for violence. Journalists who call for moderation in dealing with the Jews are branded as "Western agents," and are threatened with imprisonment

and torture or else the loss of their lives. The radical mainstream makes sure that there is a constant supply of destruction, violence, and suicide bombings. Since arguments justifying these measures are found even in the school textbooks that are "financed in part by the West," it is almost impossible to tell whether there is any serious hope for peace at all, or where a willingness to make peace should begin, if not with young people.

Since September 11, aspiring suicide bombers have learned that detonating themselves guarantees them entrance into "Paradise." Mosques, newspapers, radio, and television carry on an endless, high-powered advertising campaign with "legal opinions" in favor of meritorious suicide. "Even in a completely lacerated state, as collections of bits of limbs and organs scattered all over," so the readers and listeners are assured, "the martyrs and their loyalty will be accepted by Allah in good faith. For it is Allah himself who selects them for the war against the Jews and out of their sacrifice accomplishes our victory."

It is not difficult to see that this type of hostility toward the Jews has little to do with European antisemitism. The Arab variety, which has instead a metaphysical character, is free of secular elements, just as Islam itself is opposed to modernization. And it makes something else clear which often meets with a lack of understanding in the pluralistic West: Islamic violence as a function of [the duty to offer] sacrifice. Since the principle of free will is unknown to Islamic theology, it knows nothing about guilt either, and there are no conceptual foundations upon which a sublimation of violence could be developed, much less a "salvation."

Thus the rejection of Western freedom is understandable, along with the enthusiasm of young Palestinian women, who would rather be blown up today than tomorrow, whereas such a longing for death is relatively foreign to Judeo-Christian civilization.[19] Accordingly, the sacrifice is still, in the first place, the non-Islamic Other, upon whom everything negative is projected—a vicious circle fraught with stereotypes, which makes it hard for Islam to become an "Abrahamitic" religion, because the God of the Jews put an end to human sacrifice. As long as modernization is rejected, the privatization of the [Islamic] faith and the sublimation of the [requisite] sacrifice remain a mere theory that aids and abets the bloody praxis.

Since the twofold offense [to Islamic sensibilities] by Israel is ongoing as well—worse yet, with the support of the United States—the Islamists have seized Islam's metaphysical claim to authority and have occupied it politically. From the Muslim Brotherhood to Jihad Islami, from Hamas to Hezbollah, the sovereign interpretation within Islam includes the anti-Western strategy, which not only exerts pressure on the liberal sector of the Islamic elite, but has also taken in Europe. Of course, however radically these organizations behave, to the European elites they appear so "moderate" that for quite some time now they have been promoting them through both propaganda and financial support. Arafat was not only a terrorist and a Nobel Peace Prize winner, but also a long-term beneficiary of this collaboration, in which Europe has gradually been assuming the features of a "charismatic competitor" with America in the battle for Islamic goodwill.

As we have seen, this development, for its part, did not just fall from the sky, but in fact has its roots in recent European history—not exclusively, but additionally. Corresponding to the "twofold offense" against Islam, Europe pays its tribute in the form of a twofold myth. On one side of the coin, the myth of Islam as a model of peace was cultivated; in the twentieth century the other side was added: the myth of Palestine as a lost homeland. According to the latter, the Arabs were driven out of flourishing countrysides, the victims of an insidious and chiefly American neocolonialism.

Anyone who investigates the historical sources (which understandably are appreciated neither in Islam nor in the "dialogue" with it) will come up just as short of facts concerning the Palestinian ideal as in the case of the "Jewish-Islamic symbiosis." Palestine plays no role whatsoever in either the Old or the New Testament, much less in Islam. The name was coined by the Romans, and it replaced the old designation "Judea" over the course of the Jewish uprising, the destruction of the temple in 70 CE and the following "pacification."

This region was not a territorial unit, nor have the Arabs ever in their history made a claim to it. Contrary to the myth that is repeated today so incessantly yet without evidence, we are talking about a region that for much more than a millennium was ruled, exploited, and devastated by alternating tribal chiefs, who were often of Turkish descent. The unbearable living conditions drove people out and made Palestine an almost empty, ruined land as the logical result of the Islamic system.

For this land, ultimately, cannot have been cultivated by Arabs, at least not by Muslim Arabs, because farming itself is not among the priorities of Islam, but only the exploitation of agriculture through taxation. Thus numerous accounts of travel in Palestine from the modern [i.e. post-Renaissance] period depict the details of *dhimmi* life, namely, the cultivation of the poor land, along with the practice of trades and the running of small businesses by Jews and Christians, and their exploitation by local potentates.[20]

Repeated often enough, the myth has become accepted as history: according to it, "millions of Arabs" were driven out of Palestine, that land which for thousands of years (or, as the official version goes, "from time immemorial") was their home. This view found its logical continuation in the subsequent refugee policies. With England's support, an illegal yet officially tolerated immigration of Arabs was developing already during World War II, while an attempt was made by all means to prevent the immigration of Jews, who were often stopped at the borders; some of them were even sent back to Europe, where they perished in the Nazi gas chambers.

6. THE WESTERN-ISLAMIC ANTISEMITIC ALLIANCE

After the founding of Israel and the loss of the war waged by the Arabs in 1948, the refugee camps were preserved as human rights monuments, which commemorated the Arab claim to Palestine; meanwhile every constructive solution to the situation was refused. The British foreign minister at that time, E. Bevin, suggested one reason why no one was interested in a solution from the very start, and it is still valid today: "The price of friendship with Israel would be too high, namely, endangering relations with the Arabs, whether the base of operations [*die Basis*] in Egypt or Near-Eastern oil."[21]

Within the context of today's political constellations, with new players in the Balkans, the Caucasus and Iran, and also with Hamas, al-Qaeda and other terrorist groups, a peaceful solution is becoming more unlikely than ever. It would merely weaken the influence of the old "protecting powers," especially America and Great Britain, and run counter to Islam's claim to authority, which is steadily gaining strength, whereas the Europeans think that if this claim were to be fulfilled, they could develop an independent position vis-à-vis America.

Accordingly, it seems that the antisemitism of the Islamic region is not only an indigenous variety, but has also been affected by European radicalization. For many years the European Union has been subsidizing a massive mosque-building campaign, while at the same time making it more difficult for immigrant Muslims to be integrated into society. There are increasing symptoms of Americo- and Judeophobia, and in a parallel development the Eurocrats are gradually being won over to the notion that Islam is "part of the Western system of values," and thus, as the saying goes, "has a claim to joint ownership of Europe."[22] As we have mentioned, the EU even appears in the role of financier for the Islamists, who are the driving force of anti-Jewish propaganda within the Islamic community. Through this sort of triangulaton [*Über diesen Hebel*], Europe has developed a case of Islam-induced antisemitism, which unites the two sides, including the Far Left, and seems to be on the way to subscribing to the "old" fascist variety of hatred for the Jews.

Therefore when we speak about antisemitism in (contemporary) Islam, it is difficult, within the global context, to separate Europe's commercial interests from the ideological blockades set up in the "dialogue with Islam," just as the competition within the West to become a world power is connected with the Muslims' interests in expanding. Once again the "charismatic competition" is at work, which, of course, fights for its commercial and ideological market share, ultimately at Israel's expense. For if it is true that history is written by the victors, and furthermore that the elites, as Michel Foucault once put it, "see to it that new truths replace the old," then we can continue to forecast favorable weather for the twofold myth of peace from Islam and its claim to Palestine.

Accordingly, not only commercial reasons related to the politics of natural resources and exports, but also and in particular ideologies which have developed in a shared historical hostility to the Jews, are drawing the Western and Islamic partners even closer together. Precisely in the global context, the age-old problem of antisemitism can hardly be isolated in years to come, because it is, last but not least, also a totalitarian phenomenon.[23] Not a few proponents of the "dialogue with Islam" have already begun to weaken the scruples caused by the memory of the Shoah [Holocaust] and to make the hostility to the Jews exhibited by Muslims in Europe acceptable by imputing it to "provocation by Israel."

As early as 1974 the United Nations spoke about the head of the PLO [Palestine Liberation Organization] as "the leader of the Palestinian nation," and Pope John Paul II received him in audience more often than any other world "leader." Ever since the UN conference in Durban, people have been talking about the "terrorist state of Israel" and have suggested that its battle for its continued existence is comparable to the Holocaust. Under the impression of the especially pronounced antisemitism in France, the former prime minister Rocard viewed the founding of the Jewish state as a "historical mistake."

Islamists and their Western sympathizers are unmistakably acting in concert. Under the old rubric of "dialogue" and the newer pretext of the PAEAC [Parliamentary Association for European-Arab Cooperation], a European Union–wide lobby is becoming established, which not only shapes pro-Islamic opinions, but increasingly imposes them by force. Sociologists call such post-democratic structures "neoinstitutions," because they encroach upon the old institutions in government and society and conform them to a pro-Islamic program. As a logical consequence, important political and legal questions concerning the future are more and more often construed to the detriment of the majority, which for its part is less and less able to articulate its views in a democratic way. Hence many representatives in government ministries, political parties, the justice department, foundations, and the like, consider it legitimate to consult with the terrorists of Hamas and Hezbollah and to lend an air of gravitas [*Nachdruck*] to their antisemitic demonstrations.

Sooner or later this lobby will confer on the Islamists their seal of approval, the title of "moderate Islamists,"

or else "fledgling democratic forces." The fact that the Federal Office for the Protection of the Constitution [Germany's extremist investigation bureau] at the same time classifies them [whether leftist, rightist, or Islamist] as security risks illustrates the upheavals in the EU countries and the revolutionary contradictions between their respective national constitutions and the worldview that is coming to dominate their societies. The surest indicator for the continued de-democratization of Europe, however, is the extent to which it could also strengthen its tendency toward antisemitism in the future. On the other hand, it appears that Pope Benedict XVI wants to counteract that trend. Not only in contrast to his predecessor, but also with a view to Poland, the most Catholic and at the same time the most antisemitic country in the European Union, he is pleading for the integration of the Jews into the dialogue about the future.

*For further clarification of any references, see original text.

NOTES

1. Nagel, *Islamisches Recht* (Westhofen, 2001), 3.

2. Tantawi, *Das Volk Israels in Koran und Sunna* (Cairo, 1966), 161 f.

3. *Hannoversche Allgemeine*, April 18, 2002.

4. Jochmann, *Adolf Hitler—Monologe im Hauptquartier* (Frankfurt/Berlin, 1999), 301 f.

5. Peters, *From Time Immemorial* (Chicago, 1984), 33–73.

6. Bat Ye'or, *Decline of Eastern Christianity under Islam* (London, 1996), 73.

7. Brumlik, *Deutscher Geist und Judenhass* (München, 2000), 35.

8. Ibid., 90.

9. Ibid., 286.

10. Bat Ye'or, *Eurabia* (Cranbury, NJ, 2005), 141.

11. Schoeps et al., *Judenhass* (Berlin, 2006), 179.

12. Ibid., 182.

13. Tibi, *Kreuzzug und Djihad* (München, 1999), 93 f.

14. Tibi, *Schatten Allahs* (München, 1996), 309 f.

15. Ibid., 125.

16. Schoeps et al., *Judenhass* (Berlin, 2006), 187.

17. Kieser, *Der verpasste Friede* (Zürich, 2000), 17.

18. Lewis, *Die Juden in der islamischen Welt* (München, 1987), 97.

19. *Israel heute* 6 (2006).

20. Peters, *From Time Immemorial*, 145 f (Chicago, 1984)

21. Ibid., 357.

22. Bat Ye'or, *Eurabia*, 141.

23. Grunberger, Dessuant, *Narzissmus, Christentum, Antisemitismus* (Stuttgart, 2000), 360 f.

PART 9

Documents and
Eyewitness Accounts

CHAPTER 61
Decrees of *Dhimmitude*, 850–1905

DECREE OF CALIPH-AL-MUTAWAKKIL (850)

In that year (235/850), al-Mutawakkil ordered that the Christians and all the rest of the *ahl al-dhimma* be made to wear honey-colored *taylasans* (hoods) and the *zunnar* belts. They were to ride on saddles with wooden stirrups, and two balls were to be attached to the rear of their saddles. He required them to attach two buttons on their *qalansuwas* (conical caps)—those of them that wore this cap. And it was to be of a different color from the *qalansuwa* worn by Muslims. He further required them to affix two patches on the exterior of their slaves' garments. The color of these patches had to be different from that of the garment. One of the patches was to be worn in front on the breast and the other on the back. Each of the patches should measure four fingers in diameter. They too were to be honey-colored. Whosoever of them wears a turban, its color was likewise to be honey-colored. If any of their women went out veiled, they had to be enveloped in a honey-colored *izar* (large wrap). He further commanded that their slaves be made to wear the *zunnar* and be forbidden to wear the *mintaqa* (Arab military belt).

He gave orders that any of their houses of worship built after the advent of Islam were to be destroyed and that one-tenth of their homes be confiscated. If the place was spacious enough, it was to be converted into a mosque. If it was not suitable for a mosque, it was to be made an open space. He commanded that wooden images of devils be nailed to the doors of their homes to distinguish them from the homes of Muslims.

He forbade their being employed in the government offices or in any official business whereby they might have authority over Muslims. He prohibited their children [from] studying in Muslim schools. Nor was any Muslim permitted to teach them. He forbade them to display crosses on their Palm Sundays, and he prohibited any Jewish chanting in the streets. He gave orders that their graves should be made level with the ground so as not to resemble the graves of Muslims. And he wrote to all his governors regarding this.

Al-Tabari (d. 923), *Ta'rikh al-Rusul wa'l-Muluk,* in *The Jews of Arab Lands—A History and Sourcebook,* ed. Norman Stillman (Philadelphia, 1979), pp. 167–68.

THE *JIZYA*'S MEANING: EDICT OF CALIPH AL-AMIR BI-AHKAM ILLAH (1101–1130)

Now, the prior degradation of the infidels in this world before the life to come—where it is their lot—is considered an act of piety; and the imposition of their poll tax, *jizya*], "until they pay the tribute out of hand and have been humbled" (Koran 9:29) is a divinely ordained obligation. As for the religious law, it enjoins the inclusion of all the infidels in the payment of the *jizya*, with the exception, however, of those upon whom it cannot be imposed; and it is obligatory to follow in this respect the line laid down by Islamic tradition.

In accordance with the above, the governors of the provinces in their administration must not exempt from the *jizya* a single *dhimmi*, even if he be a distinguished member of his community; they must not, moreover, allow any of them to send the amount by a third party, even if the former is one of the personalities or leaders of their community. The *dhimmi*'s payment of his dues by a bill drawn on a Muslim, or by delegating a real believer to pay it in his name will not be tolerated. It must be exacted from him directly in order to vilify and humiliate him, so that Islam and its people may be exalted and the race of infidels brought low. The *jizya* is to be imposed on all of them in full, without exception.

The [Jewish] inhabitants of Khaybar and others, in this respect, are on equal terms. The Khaybaris [inhabitants of Khaybar] had pretended that they were not to be subjected to the *jizya*, in consequence of an agreement concluded between themselves and the Prophet; but that is nothing but a deceit, an invention, and a lie, which men of religion and instruction will recognize without difficulty. These imposters have invented this tale, they have fabricated it; then they spread it abroad, thinking that the men of learning would not discern it and that it would be acknowledged by the Muslim *ulama*, but Allah allowed us to expose the absurdities and fraud of these imposters.

Now the traditions are in agreement, and it is authentic, that Khaybar was taken by force, and that the Prophet was resolved to expel the Khaybaris, just as he had done in other localities to the brethren-in-belief of their Scriptures. But they having conveyed to Muhammad that they were the only ones who knew how to irrigate the palm groves properly and till the soil of the region, the Prophet let them remain as tenants; he accorded them half of the harvest and this condition was expressly stipulated, for he told them: "We will allow you to remain in this land as long as it pleases us." He thus placed the Khaybaris in a state of abasement; they remained in the land, working on these conditions; and they were given neither any privileges, nor distinction, that might exempt them from the *jizya* and make an exception between them and the other *dhimmis*. . . .

In this same document, one also learns: "We have exempted them from taxes and corvées." Now, during the Prophet's lifetime, there was nothing of the sort, nor for that matter in the time of the caliphs, who distinguished themselves by outstanding piety. When the Muslim territory grew and the bulk of the people converted to the faith and there were among the Muslims men capable of tilling the soil and irrigating the palm trees, Umar b. al-Khattab drove the Khaybari Jews out of the isle of the Arabs [Arabia] with the words: "If Allah prolongs my life, I shall certainly chase all the Jews and Christians from Arabia and will leave only Muslims" (18:475–78).

Ibn Naqqash (d. 1362) was an Egyptian preacher and author of an important fatwa on the *dhimmis*. Excerpts from Bat Ye'or *The Dhimmi: Jews and Christians under Islam* (Cranbury, NJ, 1985), pp. 188–89.

A TWENTIETH-CENTURY YEMENITE VERSION OF THE PACT OF 'UMAR,[1] FOR JEWISH DHIMMIS (1905)

In the Name of Allah, the Merciful, the Beneficent
This is a decree which the Jews must obey as
   commanded.
They are obliged to observe everything in it.
   They are forbidden to disobey it.

That is that these Jews are guaranteed protection upon payment of the *jizya* by each adult male: from the rich, 48 silver qafla, which is equivalent to 3 3/4 riyal; from the middle class, 24 qafla, or 2 7/8 riyal; from the poor, 12 qafla, or 16/17 riyal. In this way, their blood is spared, and they are brought into the pact of protection. They may not avoid it. It is incumbent upon each individual to pay it prior to the year's end into the hand of the person whom we have commended to receive it from them. This is religious law revealed by Allah unambiguously in His Scripture.

Furthermore, they are not to assist each other against a Muslim. They may not build their houses higher than Muslim homes. They shall not crowd them in their streets. They may not turn them away from their watering places. They may not belittle the Islamic religion, nor curse any of the prophets. They shall not mislead a Muslim in matters pertaining to his religion. They may not ride on saddles, but only sit sidesaddle. They may not wink or point to the nakedness of a Muslim. They may not display their Torah except in their synagogues. Neither shall they raise their voices when reading, nor blow their shofars loudly. Rather, a muffled voice will suffice. They are forbidden from engaging in reprehensible relations[2] which bring down the wrath of Heaven. It is their duty to recognize the superiority of the Muslim and to accord him honor.

The Jews of San'a have chosen the *dhimmis* Aaron Al-Kīhūn, Yihya Qāfih, Yihya Isaac, and Yhiya al-Abyad to correct any of their misdeeds and to conduct their affairs according to rules of their religious law. The Jews are hereby ordered to obey them and to comply with their directives. It is incumbent upon those leaders not to let them deviate from the right path.

They are not to change anything from their religious law. They shall not make themselves aloof from them out of greed, so that the weak will not be destroyed by the strong. They may not prevent any of their people who wishes to seek justice according to Muhammad's religious law.

We have appointed Yihya Danokh to be Shaykh[3] over them. He shall act in accordance with the commands that we issue for San'a. The Jews shall conduct themselves as is required. They shall live in their homes and shall refrain from whatever is to be avoided. He is to carry this out and to conduct wisely the affairs of all who are under the Prophet's pact of protection and under ours.

Sulaymān b. Yihya Habshūsh, *Eshkōlōt Merōrōt*, in *The Yemenites*, ed. S. D. Goitein (Jerusalem, 1983), pp. 190–91, reproduced from *The Jews of Arab Lands in Modern Times*, ed., Norman Stillman (Philadelphia, 1991), pp. 225–26.

NOTES

1. The classic study of this pact is Arthur S. Tritton's *The Caliphs and Their Non-Muslim Subjects—A Critical Study of the Covenant of 'Umar* (Oxford, 1930).

2. The reference is to prostitution.

3. The Yemenite Arabic term used here is 'āqil. The person referred to is the secular head of the community who bears the parallel Hebrew title of nāsī. Concerning this office, see Erich Brauer, *Ethnologie der jemenitischen Juden* (Heidelberg, 1934), pp. 281–83; also Yehuda Nini, *Yemen and Zion: The Jews of Yemen, 1800–1914* [Hebrew] (Jerusalem, 1982), pp. 103–109.

CHAPTER 62

Jews as *Dhimmis* and Muslim Chattel, 1790–1949

REIGN OF TERROR IN FEZ (1790–1792)

Thereafter the Malicious One [Mulay Yazid] came to Fez, and the whole community went forth from al-Harumat,[1] where they were, with presents in their hands in order to receive him. But he paid no attention and did not accept the presents from them, and they returned disappointed. And the Malicious One asked the Chief whether the Jews had paid the tax, and he told him that they had given only twelve talents. And on Sunday, the 24th Sivan of the year [May 26–June 6, 1790], in the early morning, the Malicious One sent a man, and he came to us and assembled the Jews and said to them: Give me a note for one thousand mithqals, for the Malicious One has forgiven you. And they gave him their hand-writing, and he at once told them: The forgiveness he grants them relates to your persons and money, that you will not be hurt, but he had decreed that you shall leave the city [Mellah] and dwell in al-Qasba de-Zirara [Shrarda].[2] And when we heard this, we were seized with trembling, with pangs as a woman in travail, for the King's [sultan's] order required haste, saying: Arise, depart from this place; and at once some chiefs and slaves came and urged us to depart from the city, and we began to depart. And if I said: I will report all the occurrences and happenings that happened to us, time would run out but they would not run out, for on that day we were very hot, because the sun had come out of its sheath in the Tammuz season, and we walked barefoot to the said al-Qasba with the donkey drivers and porters who carried our belongings and put them in the street there. And the way was long, and on the same day the slaves who were among us went to live in Meknes, they and their wives and children, and the Wadaya[3] who lived in Meknes, about 3,000 came to live here in Fez, they and their wives and children; the former left and we left and the latter came in. And there was a great throng and much dust and an intense heat, so that we were bathed in sweat; and we kissed the walls of the synagogues, as it is written: For their servants take pleasure in their stones (Ps. 102:15), and we wept and wept for others, because of all the tribulation that had befallen us. And he decreed

that if anyone remained until evening his blood would be upon his head. And there were many thieves and robbers on the way, and they despoiled us until nothing was left us; several householders, poor people, rabbis, and invalids had left all their possessions in the city for fear. And there was fulfilled in us the passage: I will send a faintness into their hearts (Lev. 26:36).

. . . And the Gentiles entered our houses and took away all the locks and doors of the houses and courtyards. And they entered all the synagogues and houses of study and took from them all the benches and arks and lecterns, and several Torah scrolls were stolen and it was just like the Destruction of the Temple; and the meeting-house was converted into a place of idolatry and prostitution. And they devastated them and distilled liquor in them, and all the majesty of the community of Fez departed from it.

. . . And our faces became like the underside of a pot because the sun looked upon us; and we lived in tents like the sons of Kedar and Arabia and we were left without knowledge and understanding, without worship, prayer, and Torah, because our minds had become disordered with sorrow and grief. We found no rest, for there was so much dirt that we did not even find a place wherin to put the Torah scrolls; everybody voided or threw his excrement in the streets of al-Qasba, and an evil stench pervaded the whole of that locality. And we were in great trouble concerning the times of the sanctification of the Sabbath, and of prayer, for every place was full of excrement so that there was no room. And dainty women drew water, and we paid money for the water we drank, and poor Jews bought water every week at the price of one-and-a-half okiya. And that summer, there were many flies, fleas, vermin, scorpions, mice, and snakes, and we did not sleep, until we were tired of life; and a number of little children died of the heat. And every day, a strong wind came, rending mountains, breaking rocks, and upsetting all the tents, so that our eyes and ears filled with dust and sand, and it put out all the candles at night, so that we sat in darkness as they that be dead of old (Lam. 3:6). And on every Sabbath night we ate in the dark, and the Malicious One decreed that the whole of our cemetery be dug up and that the dust of the dead and the stones on the graves be taken and a *jami'a* in a place called Arsif;[6] for the graveyard was very large, and gangs of Gentiles dug in all its different corners, and a number of beasts and donkeys carried the dust and stones to build also the new wall of Asluqiya,[7] and they dug up the old graves, of the past three centuries, bottom layer, second layer and third layer, and they found courtyards and wells and walls—a world of former generations. And the workers took the shrouds of the dead in which there was silver and gold, and some became rich thereby. And they also dug up the cave of the Castilian rabbis, may their memory be blessed in heaven, and, may the Lord cause their light to shine, and the graves of a number of just men and of countless pious men, and our eyes saw it and failed, but we were powerless, for our sins were too many, and we went to the cemetery, with the chief of al-Qasba who sat at the gate, every second week and every month, and we gathered the bones, skulls, arms, and legs of the dead which were scattered there, and we dug a great ditch at the place called al-Gisa[8] and buried those bones there; and they threw stones and sticks at us and said to us: Get you out of our city! The Malicious One has taken it from you and given it to us. And they gnashed upon us with their teeth. And we recognized the justice of the judgment inflicted upon us. . . .

. . . And the Malicious One decreed that no Jew or Jewess was to wear vetch green at all or a vetch green garment, and the chief came to al-Qasba and they issued a proclamation to this effect in the name of the Malicious One. And he enacted the same decree in all the cities of the Maghreb, and the Jews lost much money and the scarlet garments they had. Most of them put them into a dye vat to dye them a different colour, and the garment was eaten away. And after a year, they had no festive clothes left because they were all spoilt, and they had to buy new ones. . . . And that King resolved that he would not see or talk to any Jew, and everyone that was called Hebrew was utterly despised. And all the Jews who had served his father—may God have mercy upon him—in high positions were killed by him either by the sword or by hanging. And His Honour, our teacher, Rabbi Mas'ud ben Zikri and others, were hanged by their feet at the gate of the city Meknes, and remained hanging there alive for about fifteen days and then died. . . .

It so befell that we stayed in exile at al-Qasba for twenty-two months—representing the twenty-two letters of the Torah—to make expiation (2:296–99).

Yehudah b. Obed Ibn Attar (1725–1812), *Zikkaron li-benei Yisrael* [In Memory of the Sons of Israel], in *A History of the Jews of North Africa, Volume II: From the Ottoman Conquests to the Present Time*, ed. H. Z. Hirschberg (Leiden, 1981), pp. 296–99.

Ibn Attar was *dayyan* (rabbinical judge) at Fez. On one occasion he and the scholars of the city were incarcerated by Mulay Yazid for many days in an underground prison.

Notes

1. Possibly the name of a district within the city.
2. A fort on the northern wall of the city between Fas Jadid and the Medina.
3. An Arab tribe, part of which was encamped in Fez as a police force, formed by Mulay Isma'il.
4. Perhaps a deformation of Tala, the central avenue of Fas al-Bali.
5. Bu Jalud, area between the Medina and Fas Jadid.
6. "The pavement" in the Kairuwan quarter.
7. Unknown.
8. Bab Gisa, entrance to the Medina, which led to the city's cemetery.

JEWS OF ALGIERS BEFORE THE FRENCH CONQUEST (1825)

The Jews, of whom there are about five thousand in this city, have the free exercise of their religion secured; they are governed by their own laws in civil cases, administered by a chief of their own nation, who is appointed by the Bashaw; as Algerine subjects they may circulate freely, establish themselves where they please, and exercise any lawful calling throughout the kingdom; and they cannot be reduced to slavery. They pay a capitation tax, and double duties on every species of merchandise imported from abroad; as elsewhere, they practise trade in all its branches, and are here the only brokers, and dealers in money and exchanges; there are many gold and silversmiths amongst them, and they are the only artificers employed in the mint.

Independent of the legal disabilities of the Jews, they are in Algiers a most oppressed people; they are not permitted to resist any personal violence of whatever nature, from a Mussulman; they are compelled to wear clothing of a black or dark colour; they cannot ride on horseback, or wear arms of any sort, not even a cane; they are permited only on Saturdays and Wednesdays to pass out of the gates of the city without permission; and on any unexpected call for hard labour, the Jews are turned out to execute it. In the summer of 1815, this country was visited by incredible swarms of locusts, which destroyed every green thing before them; when several hundred Jews were ordered out to protect the Bashaw's gardens, where they were obliged to watch and toil day and night, as long as these insects continued to infest the country.

On several occasions of sedition amongst the Janissaries, the Jews have been indiscriminately plundered, and they lived in the perpetual fear of a renewal of such scenes; they are pelted in the streets even by children, and in short, the whole course of their existence here, is a state of the most abject oppression and contumely. The children of Jacob bear these indignities with wonderful patience; they learn submission from infancy, and practise it throughout their lives, without ever daring to murmur at their hard lot. Notwithstanding these discouraging circumstances in their condition, the Jews, who through their correspondence with foreign countries are the only class of Algerine society possessing any accurate knowledge of external affairs, meddle with all sorts of intrigue, even at the risk of their lives, which are not unfrequently forfeited in consequence. The post of chief of the Jews is procured and held through bribery and intrigue, and is exercised with a tyranny and oppression corresponding to the tenure by which it is retained. During the times of prosperity of the Regency, several Jewish houses of trade rose here to great opulence, but of late years, through the intolerable oppression under which they live, many wealthy individuals have been ruined, others have found means to emigrate, and the Moors, who have a singular aptness for trade, are daily supplanting them in the different branches of commerce practicable in this country; so that they appear now to be on a rapid decline even as to their numbers. It appears to me that the Jews at this day in Algiers, constitute one of the least fortunate remnants of Israel existing.

In respect of manners, habits, and modes of living, with the above exceptions, the Jews in Algiers differ so little from the other corresponding classes of society that they are not worth describing. The Jews of Algiers are a fine robust race, with good complexions, but the effects of the abject state in which they are born and live, are imprinted on their countenances; nothing is more rare than to discover a distinguished trait in the physiognomy of an Algerine Jew, whether male or female. There is a very affecting practice here with these people, which cannot be contemplated without feelings of respect, and even of tenderness, for this miraculous race. Many aged and infirm Jews, sensible that all their temporal concerns are drawing to a close, die as it were a civil death, investing their heirs with all their worldly substance, with the reserve of only the small pittance necessary to support the lingering remnant of their days in Jerusalem, where they go to die. In the year 1816, I witnessed the embarkation of a number of ancient Hebrews, on this last earthly pilgrimage, on board of a vessel chartered expressly for the purpose of transporting them to the coast of Syria. The number of Jews in the kingdom of Algiers is computed at about thirty thousand.

William Shaler, American Consul General in Algiers (1816–1828), from his *Sketches of Algiers, Political, Historical, and Civil* (Boston, 1826), pp. 65–68.

PLIGHT OF BOKHARAN[1] JEWS, 1863 AND 1898

[1863][2] The Jews in the Khanate are about 10,000 in number, dwelling for the most part in Bokhara, Samarkand, and Karshi, and occupying themselves rather with handicrafts than with commerce. In their origin they are Jews from Persia, and have wandered hither from Kazvin and Merv, about 150 years ago. They live here under the greatest oppression, and exposed to the greatest contempt. They only dare to show themselves on the threshold when they pay a visit to a "believer" [a Muslim]; and again when they receive visitors, they are bound in all haste to quit their own houses, and station themselves before their doors. In the city of Bokhara, they yield yearly 2,000 Tilla Djizie [the *jizya* tribute],[3] which the chief of their whole community pays in, receiving as he does so, two slight blows on the cheek, prescribed by the Koran as a sign of submission. The rumor of the privileges accorded to the Jews in Turkey has attracted some to Damascus and other places in Syria; but this emigration can only occur secretly otherwise they would have to atone for the very wish by confiscation or death.

[1898][4] At the opposite pole [i.e., from "the reigning dynasty" of Uzbeks] stand the Jewish community, which is traditionally believed to have migrated hither from Baghdad. Half a century ago they numbered 10,000, but they have dwindled to perhaps half as many under the grinding persecution to which they have been subjected. Bokhara is not a whit in advance of medieval Europe in its treatment of this forlorn colony. The time, indeed, has gone by when Jews might be savagely assaulted by a true believer, and even killed with impunity. But they are still relegated to a filthy and crowded Ghetto. They are forbidden to ride in the streets, and must wear a distinctive costume, a small black cap edged with two fingers' breadth of sheep-skin, a dark dressing-gown of camels' hair, and a rope girdle, a survival of a time when it might at any moment be required for its wearer's execution.

Notes

1. Bokhara refers to the former khanate occupying region around the city of the same name, in western Asia, which later became a protectorate in Russian Central Asia, and subsequently a part of Soviet Uzbekistan.
2. Arminius Vambery, *Travels in Central Asia* (London, 1864), pp. 372–73.
3. Skrine and Ross report that the *jizya*, "or infidel tax," was still being collected in Bokhara through the mid-1890s. In Francis Henry Skrine and Edward Denison Ross, *The Heart of Asia: A History of Russian Turkestan and the Central Asian Khanates from the Earliest Times* (London, 1899), p. 380.
4. Ibid., pp. 365–66.

MID-NINETEENTH-CENTURY KURDISTAN

The Jews scattered here and there [in Kurdistan], and forced to remain at the places assigned to them, are in the true sense of the word, surrounded by tribes of savages. One often finds five, ten, or even twenty Jewish families the property of one Kurd, by whom they are burdened with imposts, and subject to ill treatment. Heavy taxes are imposed upon them, which for the poorest, amount annually to 500 piastres. Finally, they are compelled at different periods of the year to perform serf-service, to cultivate their master's field, without receiving or being entitled to demand the smallest compensation for their labor. This is really an awful state of affairs and with heart and soul do we sympathize with our distressed co-religionists and we felt deeply grieved that it was not in our power to help them. . . . The [Kurdish] master has absolute power of life and death over his [Jewish] slaves; at his will he can sell them to another master, either in whole families or individually. [1]

Excerpt from J. J. Binyamin, *Eight Years in Asia and Africa, from 1846–1855* (Hanover, Germany) p. 126.

MID-NINETEENTH-CENTURY ATLAS MOUNTAINS, LIBYA

The Berber [Muslim] lord passed his Hebrew slave down to his children as an inheritance. If the Berber lord had many sons, each inherited a share in the slave. Each could also sell his share in the slave . . . if the Hebrew slave met his obligation in giving homage to his lord and was able to acquire money, he could redeem himself by paying a sum agreeable to both parties. With this deed he could acquire a deed of manumission for that portion of the rights held by the seller.[1]

. . . [T]o this very day [1865] . . . there is no Israelite family without an Ishmaelite master to whom the Israelite must make a token payment every year. The Ishmaelite may sell him to another, and this arrangement persisted until only six or seven years ago.[2]

Notes

1. *The Book of Mordechai* [Selections from the *Highid Mordekhai* of Mordechai Hakohen]—*A Study of the Jews of Libya*, ed., trans., and ann. Harvey E. Goldberg (London, 1993), p. 74. An accompanying note 2, on p. 76 indicates that Hakohen used the word *'eved* which may be translated as "slave" or "servant."

2. Ibid., p. 76n4, referring to this extract from A. Adadi.

"PROTECTION"/OWNERSHIP OF JEWS BY RURAL YEMENITE MUSLIMS (THROUGH THE EARLY TWENTIETH CENTURY)

. . . Judging by Arabic sources, the Jews of South Arabia were . . . dealt with . . . in fairly strict accordance with the shariah relating to the protected faiths . . . [for example] Outside the centralized Yemenite administration the Jew was protected by the Sultan, or even by the individual tribe; such was the case on the Habbanis. The protector would of course, be of the arms-bearing[1] classes or perhaps of the religious aristocracy. In South Arabia it is shameful to kill a Jew, as it would be to kill a woman. *An excellent example* (emphasis added) of this form of protection . . . is to be found in a passage from the Fakhir of al-Mufaddal b. Salamah. A protected Jew of al-Husain, the Sayid of the Banu Sahm, was murdered by the Banu Sirmah, so the Sahm in turn slew a protected Jew of the Sirmah . . . the Sirmah came to al-Husain to discuss the matter. Al-Husain replied, "You killed *our* Jew, so we killed *your* Jew," adding that it would be a pity if two tribes closely related should actually engage each other in war.[2]

Notes

1. Jews as subjugated and humiliated *dhimmis* could not bear arms, one of the many restrictions they endured vis-à-vis the Pact of 'Umar, which afforded their "protection," first and foremost, from the resumption of jihad war against them.

2. The entire passage is taken from R. B. Serjeant's "A Judeo Arab House Deed from Habban," published in the *Journal of the Royal Asiatic Society* (of Great Britain and Ireland), 3 and 4 (1953): 117–31, specifically, pp. 118–19. Robert Bertram Serjeant (1915–1993) was appointed reader, and then professor of Arabic at the School of Oriental and African Studies. He moved to the Middle East Centre, University of Cambridge, in 1964, eventually retiring as director, and as professor of Arabic, in 1982. Serjeant was a prolific author and editor of publications on a wide range of Middle Eastern subjects. Bat Ye'or has written a commentary on this particular analysis by Professor Serjeant. The key excerpts from her commentary are quoted below. [From "The Dhimmi Factor in the Exodus of Jews Arab Countries," in *The Forgotten Millions*, ed. M. Shulewitz (London/New York, 1999), p. 41. The complete essay is reproduced in this collection.] Noting that such a system of "protection" existed in rural Yemen through at least the early twentieth century, and may have persisted until the mass exodus of Yemenite Jews to Israel in the mid-twentieth century, Bat Ye'or continues,

Here it is clear that "protection" is linked with the suppression of rights. Rights to life and to security are only guaranteed to a Jew who is under "protection." If a Muslim killed a Jew, the criminal would not be brought to trial because Muslim blood was considered superior to Jewish blood. Hence the *lex talionis* practiced by Islam could only be applied between equals—that is to say between Muslims—but not between a Muslim and a *dhimmi*, whether Jew or Christian, whereas the *talion* would be applied between these two non-Muslim groups. Thus if a Jew belonging to tribe A is killed by a Muslim from tribe B, then a Jew from tribe B would be killed by a Muslim from tribe A. So two Jews are killed without the Muslim murderer being arrested, a game that could go on for generations as a form of retaliation. In this legal system, the Jew, like an object or a camel, is excluded from human justice. His disappearance is felt as a deprivation for his Arab master, who obtains retribution by depriving another Arab of his Jewish asset. What is doubly interesting is that this information is provided in an article published in 1953 by a distinguished Cambridge University scholar, the late Professor Robert Serjeant, as an example of and a testimony to Islamic justice and tolerance. This means that he himself accepted the concept that a person, because he is a Jew, can be deprived of all his rights in a system that reduces his life to "protection" and "services."

JEWS OF BAGHDAD (1877)

. . . The anguish of our hearts has brought us to make our suffering public to our people. Indeed, our brethren in Baghdad still dwell in humiliation and turn their cheek to the hand of those that smite them. They are satiated with scorn and the oppression of the Muslims who inhabit the city and continue to accost us with the words "turn aside, you impure (one)"; and they greet us with reproach and spit in our faces. Whenever a Jew passes in the street, "wolves" gather around him to hail him with pieces of refuse and cover his head with dirt. If he be an important person wearing a smart turban, then they scheme in their jealousy to downgrade his elegance and knock off his headgear so that it rolls in the mud and dirt. Once this happened to one of our most distinguished merchants while he was sitting among other [Muslim] traders. They threw his turban onto the ground. He, however, remained as silent as one who is dumb in order not to attract attention to his humiliation in public, so that he should not become the subject of scorn and derision. Were I to recount all the many and terrible tribulations that daily fall to our lot, all my paper would be used up and I still would not have related enough. So I will recount only one incident that is indicative of all the rest, that you may grasp the situation that we have to endure from the inhabitants of this country. It happened that one of our brethren had lent some money to a Muslim. When the appointed date was due he went to claim his loan. The

Muslim impudently replied that he could not return the money at present and that the Jew was not the Angel of Death to claim money from him immediately. In his great disappointment the Jew cursed the Angel of Death, at which the Muslim rejoiced exceedingly as one who had found a great booty. For, in order to evade his debt he began to shout out to the Muslim bystanders: "Did you not hear how the Jew has cursed our faith and is deserving of the death penalty in accordance with Islamic law?" The Muslim passers-by surrounded the Jew on all sides and began to smite him until blood poured from him. Everyone passing by, seeing them hitting him so, joined in to strike the unfortunate Jew. Their anger was not appeased until they had dragged him to the prison house known as the *Saray*, where he was remanded into custody impending the decision as to what was to be done with him according to Islamic law. So we beseech our brethren, guardians of our deliverance, especially the representatives of the Alliance Israélite, to watch over their brethren in Baghdad and to inform their honorable governments of the terrible sufferings that have befallen us and to plead on behalf of their brethren that they should look kindly upon us to put an end to the beatings and persecutions from these savages, for we have heard that your government protects all those who seek refuge beneath its wings. The Master of retribution will surely reward your kindness.

Account of Rabbi Solomon Bekhor-Husayn (1842–1892), who was a celebrated printer, community leader, and journalist of nineteenth-century Baghdad. Reproduced from Bat Ye'or, *The Dhimmi*, pp. 372–73.

THE JEWISH COMMUNITY OF SIDON, LEBANON, AT THE TURN OF THE CENTURY (1902)

Formerly queen of the seas, Sidon, the flourishing city of the Phoenicians, is today nothing but a somber little town of 15,000 to 18,000 souls, a big village without commerce or industry. The great bulk of the population lives almost exclusively from the revenues of the numerous gardens that surround the town, from which the produce is exported to either Egypt or England, where the oranges of Saida[1] are, apparently, particularly in demand. The inhabitants are crammed pell-mell into tiny houses, which could not be more dilapidated, made of stones gathered from the fields that it was not even necessary to quarry.

I shall not even try to describe the maze of narrow streets, congested at practically every step by vaults supporting the houses, which are as if perched in the air, and where—without exaggeration—it is gloomy even at the height of noon. I have visited the oldest quarters of Jerusalem and Damascus, but I have never seen anything resembling the picture of desolate decay presented by Saida, a small town that knows no tourism and is still untouched by modern civilization.

It is one of the most somber of these alleys that leads into the Jewish quarter via a low, narrow, little gate. Passing through this portal, we are in the ghetto. Imagine a long courtyard, narrow and dark, a sort of corridor, as sinuous as can be, whose width is never more than two meters. On either side are two- and three-story houses— or rather cells cut into the walls, not receiving even a little of the dim light from the side of the narrow passage that forms the street. I asked myself more than once during my visits to the quarter whether people in Europe would be content to keep convicts in such a frightful prison where poverty is keeping a thousand of our co-religionists. . . . But continuing on our way, let us go further down this single street, which is not even paved. The unfortunate individuals who live there and to whom the street belongs (like the courtyard of a house) have asked in vain for the authorities to pave it at their own expense. The authorities are opposed to it! All the way at the end, we finally reach a small square of approximately 150 to 200 square meters, where the gay rays of sunlight are able to penetrate and where one can breathe a little more easily. it is on this square that the synagogue and Talmud Torah are to be found at the far end.

I had just said that Saida is a town without commerce. The gardens which feed the great majority of the people belong almost exclusively to the Muslims who comprise about nine-tenths of the population of Saida. The Christians, who are well protected by the consuls and by their priests who have influence with the authorities, enjoy a certain degree of ease and consideration. Only the Jews, left to themselves, stagnate in dark poverty in which the others have little share, and they are the object of contempt and disdain in the eyes of their neighbors of other faiths. Peddling is practically the only way of making a living. Saturday night, they leave their ghetto and disperse left and right throughout the countryside painfully struggling to earn a few miserable piastres, which they leave at home when they return on Friday. This occupation is certainly arduous, at times humiliating, and always thankless. It does not feed its man—as they say. But can they do any better? They know nothing else. The few Jewish carders who work at Saida do not always even earn their daily keep, which is about two piastres, or 0.35 francs! What misery for a man who has a family to feed.

I stopped for a bit in each of the little shops maintained by those of our co-religionists who do business in town. I interrogated them one after the other. It was always the same sorry response: they are poor and they are unhappy.

The richest among them considers himself fortunate when on the most fruitful day he realizes an earning of ten piastres, barely two francs!

Report by M. Angel, Beirut, May 1902. AIU Archives (Paris) Liban I.C.2. Reproduced from Stillman, *The Jews of Arab Lands in Modern Times*, pp. 197–98.

Note

1. The Arabic name of Sidon.

JEWS, BERBERS, AND ARABS (LIBYA, 1906)

The relationship between Jew and Berber is better than that between Jew and Arab. Until the middle of the last century, the Jews were treated as the serfs of the Berber lords. While abolishing this humiliating institution, Turkey has not yet had the time to curb the moral vexations that the Muslims inflict on their Jewish neighbors. One example out of a hundred: the rabbi of the region [Djebel Nefussi], having journeyed to Nalut, was attacked by local inhabitants who ordered him to get down from his mule, since a Jew may not straddle a mount in the presence of Muslims. Should he dare to complain, he would run the risk of seeing his family massacred by the Arabs.

The most venerated places of worship, the most ancient cemeteries are desecrated by the Muslims and as for agriculture, their Arab neighbors have no qualms in seizing the products of the Jews' harvest. In spite of the goodwill of the ruling authorities [the Turks], these matters often escape their control.

For example, is it known in Tripoli that the Jewish inhabitants of a village called Al Qsar, who possess about fifty acres of arable land and several hundred olive trees, were forced last year to pay 1,600 francs for their tithe and, moreover, that many a Jew, after having been molested by the local inhabitants, would not dare to lodge a complaint for justice with the authorities (pp. 107–108).

N. Slouschz, "Israélites de Tripolitaine," *Bulletin Alliance Israélite Universelle* (1906): 107–108; English translation reproduced from Bat Ye'or, *The Dhimmi*, pp. 328–29.

EXPROPRIATION IN TRIPOLITANIA (LIBYA, 1908)

Yehud Beni-Abbes is on the very margin of the desert which lies between the oasis and Tripoli; the village comprises two hundred and forty inhabitants, who take up six underground courts. At one time the Jews were very numerous in this country, holding most of the land and defending it successfully against all invaders. We were shown the fertile ravine, which ends in a well-watered valley and which commands the approach of the region towards Tripoli. Here, on the slopes, we found grottoes and traces of mines of an ancient civilization.

We were led across spaced-out fields, and were told that all of this splendid country belonged at one time to the Jews. But towards 1840 the plague ravaged the Jewish population; the only survivors were four families of Beni-Abbes, while many of the neighboring villages were completely wiped out.

The Ulad Beni-Abbes Arabs took advantage of the unhappy plight of the Jews to deprive them of their lands; the rightful owners kept on struggling against the invaders, but to no purpose; besides this, the Arabs, with the meanness characteristic of the servile *fellah*, took possession of the cemetery, the resting place of a whole line of ancestors, and ploughed it up. They could not have conceived a more malignant act, nor one which would have wounded so deeply the "infidels," who now, with tears in their eyes, led us across this field which contained the desecrated remains of their ancestors and their rabbis.

The Arabs, however, had not dared to dispossess the last native Jews entirely; they managed, instead, to force them into a collective ownership of the whole village, so that the Jews, having no distinctive property of their own, are yet forced to till fields and cultivate fruit trees belonging exclusively to the Mussulmans, and at a distance from their homes. The outcome is that the Jewish farmer must look on, without daring to protest, while his Arab neighbor appropriates the first-fruits of his olive-groves and the best produce of his own plot of land, which is swallowed up in the vast Arab fields.

Even this did not satisfy the oppressors. There is in the village an ancient synagogue, a sanctuary held in deep veneration. It is situated in a hollow surrounded by an open court, and its roof is colored like the soil in order to conceal it from view. This spot affords them the only moral gratification they have; it is the one meeting place where they can offer up their prayers or pour out the plaints of the Piyyutim [liturgical compositions], which mourn the sorrows and proclaim the hopes of Israel.

The fanatic Mussulmans, jealous of this sanctuary, planned, after the desecration of the cemetery, the ruin of the synagogue, on the pretext that the neighboring mosque would, according to Mohammedan law, be profaned by its proximity.

Fortunately, there were judges in Tripoli and money in the hands of the Jews. By a happy chance the Jews have in their possession a document which proves that the synagogue was in existence on its present site five hundred years before the foundations of the mosque were laid, that is to say, seven or eight centuries ago. The administration, basing its decision on the right of priority, was able to rescue the synagogue, to the unbounded joy of the Jews. Looking through the Geniza of this sanctuary we found, among other things a tablet dating from 5359—that is, 348 years old. Surely these Jews, swallowed up in the Sahara, have deserved a better fate.

N. Slouschz, *Travels in North Africa* (Philadelphia, 1927), pp. 127–29.

BEHAVIORAL DISTORTIONS RESULTING FROM OPPRESSION (YEMEN, 1910)

Here is a handsome robust fellow, his face well defined, a pointed nose, an intelligent countenance: Aaron Hayyim Uzayri from Malhan. . . . I tell him that I intend visiting him in his workshop in Malhan. What a look of terror appears on his face upon hearing my words: "Don't do that, Rabbi," he trembles, pleadingly, "they will kill you"; and he throws himself down at my knees and starts kissing my feet, so that I promise him I will not go to Malhan. "But you," I ask him, "how do you live there?" "We are in *jalut* [exile], we are accustomed to suffering, we are not humans, we are beasts." It was said in such a tone of despair that I was deeply overcome with emotion. This human being, whom I saw for the first time, so different from myself by his dress, his thoughts, his manners, I felt to be a brother, a Jew like myself. He bowed his head before an unavoidable fate, but one sensed within him a great courage, a suppressed energy, a tenacious hope for the end of the *jalut*, the future redemption; and I thought to myself that, whatever the cost, this man must be delivered from his misery, his disgrace, as well as his brethren, who are as wretched as he.

Everyone is happy to see the representative of the Alliance, and all bid me welcome, voicing their hopes that I will improve their situation and that a new era is about to commence for them. They keep repeating to me; "We are ignorant and know nothing, we are uncivilized and want to become men. We have written so much, prayed so much and cried so much, but our voice has not been heard. Now at last God has had pity upon us." In fact, no, on the contrary, despite their miserable appearance, I do not find them so uncivilized; in discussion they make an excellent impression. They are ignorant of many things, which is not their fault, but they have an intelligent air about them; what they need is order, method, and manners. They lack confidence in themselves, and beneath the weight of Arab oppression they cower and crawl in the dust. They are despised and they seem despicable. Yet their spirit is not destroyed . . . they have had the time to devote themselves to intellectual pursuits. A large part of the day and night is devoted to prayer and pious reading, and their eyes sparkle with the light of wisdom. When conversing with them, I do not perceive their ludicrous appearance; rather, I reflect on the vivacity of intellect, which has been preserved despite ten centuries of ignorance and degradation.

The Jew is not allowed to wear white or colored garments outside his quarter. . . . [H]e must wear a ridiculously short garment that does not cover his legs, and he must walk barefooted and wear on his head a little black cap. . . . The Jew cannot ride within the town on a donkey and morning and evening he must walk on foot the two miles that separate his quarter from the market-place. Recently, the chief Arab sheikh said to the chief

662   Part 9: Documents and Eyewitness Accounts

rabbi, "It is rumored that you would like to ride on a donkey, even on a horse. Beware." The rabbi hasn't forgotten this warning and whenever I invite him to ride with me in the carriage he always refuses and sadly replies: "Do you want me to be stoned? If I were not in your company, I would never have ventured down the main street on a Friday." So we went on foot and his dragging steps raised clouds of dust that whitened his thin legs. Last year a Jew from Tiberias, on a fund-raising mission, was nearly knocked unconscious because he had walked through the town clad in a long cloak. The Arab children spat at him and covered him with garbage and he was saved only by the arrival of a *mullah* who knew him from Palestine. Every day young Arabs found amusement in throwing stones at passing Jews while they, pretending not to notice, would hasten their stride. If one spits in their face, they turn their heads. A high-ranking [Turkish] officer described to me a scene that he had witnessed more than once: some youths had caught hold of an elderly Jew and amused themselves by pulling his sidelocks, while their victim grinned and simpered stupidly. Constantly obliged to bear these insults, the Jew has lost all sense of dignity, and has come to accept his fate; instead of fighting back, he smiles. What else can he do? A revolt would bring even more trouble. Every day our co-religionists suffer all kinds of humiliations and violence. They do not even complain: for them there is no justice, there cannot be. The Yemenite courts are all religious courts and the testimony of Jews is not accepted. A Muslim can knock down a Jew in front of fifty witnesses, yet he need only deny it to be acquitted; no Muslim would want to lodge a complaint against a brother for the sake of an infidel.

Y. D. Sémach, *Une Mission de l'Alliance au Yémen* (Paris, 1910), pp. 72–73; English translation reproduced from Bat Ye'or, *The Dhimmi*, pp. 341–43.

THE *DHIMMI* EXPERIENCE IN YEMEN, THROUGH 1949

Until our departure from Yemen in 1949, it was forbidden for a Jew to write in Arabic, to possess arms, or to ride on a horse or camel. The Jews could only ride on donkeys, both legs on one side [sidesaddle] and were obliged to jump to the ground when passing a Muslim, and had to make detours. Pedestrians went on the left of Muslims. It was forbidden for Jews to enter mosques, but the Muslims couldn't enter synagogues either. The Arabs forbade us to wear shoes, so that we hid them when, as children, we went searching for wood for cooking. When we were far enough away, we put on our shoes; on returning, we took them off and hid them in the branches. The Arabs frequently searched us, and if they found them, they punished us and forbade us to collect wood. We had to lower our head, accepting insults and humiliations. The Arabs called us "stinking dogs."

Jewish children who became orphans before they were fifteen were forcibly converted to Islam. The families tried to save them by hiding them in bundles of hay. Afterward, the children were sent to other villages where they hid with another family and were given other names. Sometimes the children were put into coffins and the Arabs were told that they had died with their parents. Then they were helped to escape.

One of my brothers [Hannah is speaking] went to work as usual at the house of Arabs, friends of my mother. One day we heard a lot of noise. My brother had been dressed in a fine costume and had been put on a horse. He was happy . . . he was five years old. An Arab woman came secretly to inform us that they wanted to make him a Muslim. My mother was working outside of the village, my father was dead. My uncle went and took my brother, locked him up, and punished him severely.

One of my uncles worked for Arabs. Although he was quite young, he was married and a father of four children. One day the Arabs wanted to convert him and locked him in a room; they tied him up and wanted to force him to swallow a soup with meat, which is forbidden in our religion [probably camel meat]. They beat him terribly, then they went to sleep. My uncle was able to free himself from his bonds and escape. He returned home and cried continuously and didn't speak a word. He was questioned, but didn't reply, and tears flowed all the time. He refused to eat or drink. He died two days later. When he had been prepared for burial, one saw that his body was covered with wounds. We learned the whole story later because the Arabs told it to us secretly.

I had cousins who became orphans. One of my uncles escaped with them from the village. He hid them for five years. The Arabs searched for him everywhere. Finally, they found him. The head of the village told him, "If I didn't know you as well as I do, I would have killed you for what you have done."

The Jews worked in all occupations except agriculture. They made shoes for the Arabs, but they themselves were not allowed to wear them. We liked the Imam Yahya [assassinated on February 17, 1948]; he was good to us. He protected us, he was just. . . . [This statement has been made frequently to the author by many Jews from Yemen. Yahya was succeeded by his son, Ahmad, who allowed forty-four thousand Jews to emigrate to Israel in 1949–50].

Bat Ye'or's interview (October 8, 1983) with Hannah [Lolou] and Sa'adya b. Shelomo Akiva [Aqua], born respectively at Dhamar and Menakha (Yemen). Since 1949 they have been citizens of Israel and live in Nes Ziyyona. Reproduced from Bat Ye'or, *The Dhimmi*, pp. 380–82.

CHAPTER 63

Two Anti-Jewish Pogroms in the Modern Era before the Creation of Israel: Baghdad (1941) and Tripolitania (1945)

MEMORIES

Every Jew of our community well remembers these two sorrowful days during which cruel killings took place instead of seeing our way to enjoy them as they were the days of "visits festivals" . . . which turned to be days of sadness and terror.

Every child remembers these two frightful days which turned to be days of weeping and appeals for help. . . . We should hear the appeal for help of those girls and women who were touched by the dirty hands. We should share with those children their feelings of terror when they saw with their own eyes their fathers and mothers being killed and dishonored.

We should look upon the memory of those days as a guiding light that will show us our way in the dark of the future.

We tell every man, woman, young man, and girl, and children too, in this day. "Slavery will not save us from being looted, disdain will not prevent us being annihilated, and caring not for ourselves will not guarantee our lives, so you should beware companions, because the day is today."

We have decided not to keep quiet and not to forget our sorrows until the day will come when Israel and its lost people get back to rescue the land of their forefathers.

We shall remember . . .

What Happened in Baghdad

The disturbances of Rashīd ʿAlī were over within a month of commencement, after which the Jews felt free again, and they began to show themselves out in the city with gay appearances. This might have increased the hatred of their enemies to them. So it might have been better for the Jews to have been wiser in the manner of showing themselves out again after the disturbances.

It was on the first day of the "Jewish Festival of Visits" when a Jew was wounded in Ghazi Street. The effect of this event was dreadful among the Jews in general, and they began to run to their homes. They all disappeared after a few minutes of the event, and their enemies, seeing this, were encouraged to treat them with killings, especially when no sign of defense was seen from them. The mob attacked the houses of the Jews and looted them, treating their inhabitants in the way they desired. Jewish men were afraid and were looking for escape from death. Their cries and appeals filled the air, and many of them did actually run away, leaving their women and children struggling in the hands of the enemies.

Bands of enemies were wandering inside the Jewish quarters and were killing and looting. Such events lasted until midnight, and many were killed. Heads of children were cut off like sheep, old men were killed, while women were disgraced. . . . This was how the night passed. In the morning the Jews did not know what had happened to their brothers during the night, and they went out for work as usual, but it was only a short interval given by the killers, after which they resumed their terrorism under the management of policemen and ex-soldiers. They began at 9:30 a.m., completing their pogrom of the night before. Their action was begun in Rashid Street and Shorja, where they broke into the shops and commercial stores belonging to the Jews and looted all they could find in them. They moved thereafter to the neighboring Jewish houses and did similarly in them. Ghazi Street found trouble again that day, later on Amīn Street, as well as the Jewish quarters of Abū Seifayn, ʿAbbās Effendī, Aqūliyya, and other far and nearby quarters.

Killing and looting lasted until 11 a.m. that day. . . . Bodies of the dead were thrown on pavements on both sides of the street, and this drama did not stop until its conductors wished it off, i.e., some units of the Kurdish Iraqi soldiers gave a hand and all trouble was over within a few minutes.

Every Jewish house sustained the loss of one of its members, or it had at least had one of them wounded. The remaining people lived in terror.

What Do We Learn from the Massacre of Baghdad?

What was it that the Baghdad Jews did not to be trusted by the Arabs? They gave up their Hebrew language. Did they not stop giving money for the sake of the Land of Israel?[1] They accepted participating with the Arabs in every activity that was in the interests of the country. They were always the first in giving money to help achieving any national scheme in Iraq and especially in Baghdad. Some of the rich Jews have generously contributed to the funds gathered for the followers of the Mufti, who were called the Palestinian Patriot Fighters.

The Jews in Baghdad, for the sake of buying safety for themselves and a comfortable life for their families, abandoned their human dignity and their liberty. Their rich families in Baghdad lived comfortably, but with fear and disdain, while they forgot their brothers who were astray in Europe and who are working hard in the land of Israel. But did they gain any benefit from all this during the days of slaughter? Could they buy their lives with their dignity, or have they found safety for themselves after having so heavily sacrificed? Never. They never did gain any benefit from all this, as slavery will never make them free from being looted and disdained, or from being annihilated.

Death is the result of giving up our rights and all efforts to show the others that we do not cling to Judaism and awakens hatred in the hearts of our enemies. Every endeavor on the part of the Jews to mix with others and do as the others do leads to butchery. Iraq is just like Yemen. Our luck is the same in all the Eastern countries. It is not enough for the Jews to experience such difficulties. Does our history, which is full of news of killings, teach us nothing of the past? Are our memories so feeble that we forget all that has been done against us so long as we gain profits?[2]

Our aim is a Hebrew National State with Hebrew Power, and our hope lies in defending ourselves and our dignities in life.

PRO (London) FO 624/38/502 *Translated Extracts from "The Tragedy of 1st and 2nd June, 1941 in the Capital of Iraq"* (Arabic or Hebrew original not in file); reproduced from Stillman, *The Jews of Arab Lands in Modern Times*, pp. 457–59.

Notes

1. The translator's typescript reads: "They did not stop giving money for the sake of the future of the Israel Land." This, however, seems to be at variance with the gist of the paragraph.

2. Stillman believes this statement was prepared by members of a Zionist Socialist movement.

A BRITISH MILITARY INTELLIGENCE REPORT ON JEWISH ATTEMPTS TO LEAVE IRAQ FOR PALESTINE AND ELSEWHERE AFTER THE FARHUD (1942)

To: HBM Embassy, BD CICI, BD
Subject: *POLITICAL-IRAQ.*
Ref. telegram (M) 903 27 Apr 42.

The following information has been obtained from a reliable Jewish source:

The emigration from Iraq is taking place under two classes:

a) poor Jews who either have no money, or were looted last May–June, are paying money to friendly Jewish lorry drivers and in some cases soldiers of H.M. Forces, to take them over the frontier into Palestine. Most of these Jews are joining or intend to join Jewish forces in Palestine i.e., the Buffs.[1] The Jews usually contact drivers at Rutba;[2]

b) rich Jews who have listened to bazaar rumors and are apprehensive about their future. they feel that whatever the outcome of the area that the Iraqis will punish the Jews eventually. Some rumors are to the effect those Jews who escaped last June will not escape the anti-Jewish riots that will coincide with Hitler's Spring Offensive. It is stated that these Jews are willing to pay large sums for visas to the passport authorities, and actually do have to pay before they can obtain the necessary visa.

No organized movement is in force but the emigration is the result of fear inspired by Moslem threats.

(signed) T. W. Boyd
Lieut-Col
GSI.

WHM. 29.4 PRO (London) FO 624/29/374, facsimile published in Yoav Gelber, *Tōldōt ha-Hitnaddevūt*, vol. 3: *Nōs'é ha-Degel* (Jerusalem, 1983), p. 21; English translation reproduced from Stillman, *The Jews of Arab Lands in Modern Times*, p. 418.

Notes

1. Apparently a sobriquet for the Palestinian Jewish units in the British army.

2. A small town approximately two hundred miles east of Baghdad, just before the cross-desert highway forks northwest to Syria and southwest to Transjordan and Palestine.

THE JEWISH COMMUNITY'S OFFICIAL REPORT ON THE ANTI-JEWISH RIOTING IN TRIPOLITANIA (1945)

1. General Survey

From the 4th to the 7th of November, 1945, mobs of Arabs, old and young, made a vicious and sudden attack on the Jews in different parts of Tripolitania. Never in the history of Tripolitanian Jewry, not even in the darkest periods of their existence, has such a pogrom been launched against them.

In Tripoli and the smaller provincial centers of Suk el Jouma, Tagiura, Kussabat, Zanzur, and Zavia, more than 100 Jews, law-abiding and unarmed (including a large percentage of women, old people, and children), were savagely massacred, some after cruel torture, others by being burned alive. A great number of houses, shops, and stores were plundered and set alight, five synagogues in Tripoli, two in Amrus (Suk el Jouma), one in Tagiura, one in Zanzur were profaned, plundered, and fired, together with the Scrolls of the Law, all equipment and the sacred books. Well-to-do families were reduced to abject poverty overnight. Scores of widows, orphans, and others who lost relatives who had supported them now swelled the ranks of the already numerous poor Jews.

2. Outbreak and Development of Riots

In the later afternoon on Sunday, the 4th of November, the President of the Jewish community received news of the first serious attacks, which occurred simultaneously, as if by a prearranged signal, in different parts of Tripoli. He rushed to police headquarters to report the attacks and urged that immediate measures be taken to prevent further trouble.

No police officer, however, was to be found at headquarters, and it was also impossible to trace them elsewhere. Noncommissioned police officers who were at the station confined themselves to assuring the President that all the police were on duty. It seemed that order would be promptly reestablished. Though the reports on 4th November had been numerous and simultaneous, they did not last so long, nor were they so extensive as to give reason for the belief that they would increase with greater severity on the two successive days.

On Monday morning the riots broke out afresh. (The rioters in the town were joined meanwhile by several thousand Arab villagers.) The heads of the Jewish community proceeded early in the morning to report to Headquarters of the Senior Civil Affairs Officer of the Province, Lieutenant-Colonel Oulten. This officer, who had been out of Tripoli, returned to Headquarters at about 9 that morning. He was immediately informed of the gravity of the situation and urged to take steps at once to quell the disorders with the aid of British troops,

since the civil police had revealed their inability to keep the situation under control. Lieutenant-Colonel Oulten promised that he would give his immediate attention to the matter. Unfortunately, however, the British Forces were not actually called upon to intervene until more than forty-eight hours after the outbreak of the riots, despite the fact that on the same day, Monday, both the Chief of the Tripolitania Police and Colonel Mercer, Chief Secretary to the British Military Administration (since the Chief Administrator, Brigadier Blackely, had been out of town for some days), were also informed by Jews and Arabs of the increasing severity of the riots and exhorted to take energetic and proper measures against them. Indeed, notwithstanding the curfew imposed of the Monday, that same evening, and on the following Tuesday, the 6th of November, large-scale, renewed attacks, plundering, and firing of Jewish homes occurred. On Monday evening the few troops that began to appear on the streets took no action against the mob or used their arms to repress the rioting.

Only on Tuesday evening (the 6th of November) and on Wednesday (the 7th of November), did the Military Commander finally take action. At first he prohibited the assembly of crowds and the carrying of sticks and other offensive articles, and later he proclaimed a State of Emergency. British patrols began to patrol the streets and to search passersby and Arab houses.

In Tripoli this firm stand on the part of the authorities was sufficient to diminish the disorders considerably, without resorting to arms, as from Tuesday night. The arrest of Arabs guilty of acts of plundering and aggression did not, however, take place until Wednesday. The Jewish quarter of Hara had been previously attacked by bands of Arabs at different external points, but they did not succeed in penetrating the quarter, owing to active defense measures taken by the Jewish inhabitants. Meanwhile thousands of Jews swarmed from the more exposed places to take refuge there.

In other places, at Zanzur and Zavia, for instance, the mass slaughter of Jews occurred on Tuesday night.

In Tripoli, the most serious attacks occurred in the streets of the old city, where there was a mixed population, and the busy parts of the new town, where the Jews lived in isolated houses and were therefore unable to resist the attackers to any appreciable extent. And indeed the rioters could make no mistake, since some mysterious band had previously marked the doors of houses and shops of non-Jews with suitable signs. During the riots only one Arab was killed, presumably by one of those attacked in self-defense.

On Wednesday, the 7th of November, and Thursday, the 8th of November, it was possible to provide for the burial of the victims of Tripoli and Zanzur. The funeral, directed by the President of the community, aided by the personnel of the Burial Society, took place at the beginning of the curfew, following a route largely patrolled by armed troops but, as a sign of protest, unaccompanied by relatives or co-religionists. Administrative and military authorities, however, were represented at the funeral. The other communities arranged the burial of their dead on the spot. British officials inspected and photographed some bodies, especially those on which signs of the attackers' cruelty were more evident. With the exception of two (Rabbi Saul Dabuse and Rabbi Abraham Tesciuba), the victims were buried in only one section of the Jewish Cemetery of Tripoli (Kever Ahim).

3. Arms and Methods

In order to carry out the slaughter, the attackers used various weapons: knives, daggers, sticks, clubs, iron bars, revolvers, and even hand grenades. Generally, the victim was first struck on the head with a solid, blunt instrument and, after being knocked down, was finished off with a knife, dagger, or, in some cases, by having his throat cut.

In Zanzur and Amrus (Suk el Jouma) in particular, after having killed or injured their victims, the attackers poured benzine or petroleum over them and set them on fire, and ultimately those killed were so charred as to be unrecognizable. Grenades were used especially at Amrus (Suk el Jouma) against the synagogue as well as the houses. On some of the bodies signs of unimaginable cruelty could be discerned.

4. Direct and Indirect Victims

Up to December 31, 1945, the number of killed (increased by the number who had succumbed to their injuries) amounted to 130, divided as follows (see Appendix A):[1]

Tripoli	35, of whom 31 were killed in the riots, 3 succumbed to their injuries, and 1 was unaccounted for.
Armus (Suk el Jouma):	38, all killed in the riots (buried on the spot).
Tagiura:	7, of whom 6 were killed in the riots (buried on the spot) and 1 succumbed to injuries (buried in Tripoli).
Kussabat:	3, all killed in the riots (buried on the spot).
Zanzur:	34, of whom 33 were killed in the riots and 1 succumbed to injuries (all buried in Tripoli).
Zavia:	13, of whom 8 were killed in the riots (buried on the spot) and 5 succumbed to injuries (buried in Tripoli).

In consequence of the slaughter, 30 widows and 93 orphans have been registered. (See Appendix B.)[2]

In certain cases whole families were exterminated; others have lost a great part of their members.

There were other crimes, not less painful to record, even though the facts cannot be ascertained fully. In Kussabat, many of our women and girls were violated under the eyes of their own relatives; and many men and women, in order to save their lives, were compelled to abjure their faith and to embrace Islam.

5. Material Damage

The damage caused in the riots was various: plunder, rape, fire, etc.

The most affected areas in Tripoli were Suk el Turk (variety shops, modes, mercery shops, ironmongeries, tailor shops, shoe shops, goldsmith shops, household articles, etc.), Suk el Siaga (silverware market), Suk el Attara (grocery market), Suk el Harrara (imported textile and locally made silk shops), Suk el Muscir (mercers and ironmongeries), Suk el Naggiara (where the shops are wholly of Jewish ownership or in overwhelming majority).

Nothing was spared by the attackers; whatever they did not want or could not carry away owing to bulk or weight was damaged, destroyed, or set on fire. Massive safes were demolished; pieces of furniture destroyed, or set aflame; glasses and mirrors, even the smallest, were smashed to pieces. It was real vandalism. After the removal of the military cordons (which took place on December 16th), Suk el Turk in particular was a scene of desolation.

Besides shops, many homes, stores, and factories were plundered or damaged. Most of the houses were wholly emptied, and therefore the families who occupied them now find themselves without even personal effects.

The Jewish community, as a body, also suffered a conspicuous part of the damage. In the nine synagogues attacked in Tripoli and in the other minor communities the furnishings, household goods, and furniture were destroyed by fire or damaged; 35 Scrolls of the Law, 2,084 Sacred Books, and 89,086 kg. of silver (sacred ornaments) were plundered.

Those who suffered most were the small merchants, shopmen, and artisans. Nearly all were reduced literally to penury, and they are still inactive awaiting rehabilitation.

Appendix C contains a statistical summary of the claims lodged directly with the police by the interested parties, a copy of which was submitted to the Jewish community. Appendix D gives a classification of 813 claims for plunder and damage to shops, stores, factories, etc. (excluding homes).[3]

Up to December 31, 1945, the claims reached the number of 1,435 for a sum of 268,231,752 = Military Authority Lire (Official exchange rate M.A.L. 480 = L1).

There is reason to believe that other damage inflicted, especially in the minor communities of Tripolitania, has not been brought to the notice of the police or of the Jewish community and it may therefore be reasonably assumed that the amount of the damage inflicted on the Jews of Tripolitania is about 300 million M.A.L. and this without bringing into account the indirect damage caused by the idleness forced upon many shopkeepers, factory owners, or ordinary shop clerks, who until now have been unable to resume their work.

CZA (Jerusalem) S 25/5219, "Anti-Jewish Riots in Tripolitania," pp. 1–6[4]; reproduced from Stillman, *The Jews of Arab Lands in Modern Times*, pp. 461–65.

Notes

1. Pages 8–12 of the report, giving the names and statistical data of Jews killed in the riots; not included here.

2. Pages 13–16 of the report, giving the names and ages of widows, and orphans; not included here.

3. Pages 17–18 of the report; not included here. These appendices are reproduced in reverse order (i.e., D, C) in Renzo de Felice, *Jews in an Arab Land: Libya, 1835–1970*, trans. Judith Roumani (Austin, 1985), pp. 367–68, table N-7 and 8.

4. Sec. 2 of this report is also published in ibid., pp. 193–94, using a copy in CZA (Jerusalem) S 25/6457.

CHAPTER 64

Light-Skinned Egyptian Muslim Repeatedly Beaten by His Co-religionists for "Looking Jewish" (1948)

From a letter to the editor published in the newspaper Akhir Sa'a *and translated into French in a survey of newspapers that appeared in La Bourse egyptienne:*

It would seem that most people in Egypt are unaware of the fact that among Egyptian Muslims there are some who have white skin. Every time I board a tram I see people pointing at me saying, "Jew, Jew!" I have been beaten more than once because of this. For that reason I humbly beg that my picture (enclosed) be published with an explanation that I am *not* Jewish and that my name is Adham Mustafa Galeb.[1]

NOTE

1. From *La Bourse egyptienne*, July 22, 1948. Cited in Yehudiya Masriya, *Les Juifs en Egypte* (Geneva, 1971), p. 54; English translation in Ya'akov Meron, "The Expulsion of the the Jews from the Arab Countries: The Palestinians' Attitude towards It and Their Claims," in *The Forgotten Millions—The Modern Exodus of Jews from Arab Lands*, ed. Malka Shulewitz (London, 1999), p. 92.

CHAPTER 65

"Jews in Grave Danger in All Moslem Lands"

NINE HUNDRED THOUSAND IN AFRICA AND ASIA FACE WRATH OF THEIR FOES

For nearly four months, the United Nations has had before it an appeal for "immediate and urgent" consideration of the case of the Jewish populations in Arab and Moslem countries stretching from Morocco to India.

Even four months ago, it was the Zionist view that Jews residing in the Near and Middle East were in extreme and imminent danger. Now that the end of the mandate has precipitated civil war or even worse developments in Palestine, it is feared that the repercussions of this in Moslem countries will put the Jewish populations in many of these states in mortal peril.

Reports from the Middle East make it clear that there is serious tension in all Arab countries. The Jewish populations there are gravely worried at the prospect that an Arab-Jewish war may break out suddenly at any moment.

FEELING RUNS HIGH

Already in some Moslem states such as Syria and Lebanon there is a tendency to regard all Jews as Zionist agents and "fifth columnists." There have been violent incidents with feeling running high. There are indications that the stage is being set for a tragedy of incalculable proportions. Nearly 900,000 Jews live in these Moslem and Arab countries stretching from the Atlantic along the Mediterranean to the Indian Ocean. Zionist leaders today are convinced that their position is perilous in the extreme.

When the Economic and Social Council of the United Nations meets in Geneva next July, this matter will come before it.

On January 19, 1948, the World Jewish Congress submitted a memorandum on the whole problem to the Economic and Social Council, asking for urgent action during the spring session of the Council.

This plea arose to some extent from statements, made by Arab spokesmen during the General Assembly session last autumn to the effect that if the partition resolu-

tion was put into effect, they would not be able to guarantee the safety of the Jews in any Arab land.

The memorandum of the World Jewish Congress went into considerable detail on this danger. It cited the text of a law drafted by the Political Committee of the Arab League which was intended to govern the legal status of Jewish residents in all Arab League countries.

It provides that beginning on an unspecified date all Jews except citizens of non-Arab states, would be considered "members of the Jewish minority state of Palestine." Their bank accounts would be frozen and used to finance resistance to "Zionist ambitions in Palestine." Jews believed to be active Zionists would be interned and their assets confiscated.

The memorandum gave many details of instances of persecution of Jewish individuals and whole communities. It is listed the following tabulation of the Jewish residents in Arab countries:

French Morocco	190,000
Iraq	130,000
Algeria	120,000
Iran	90,000
Egypt	80,000
Tunisia	80,000
Turkey	75,000
Yemen	40,000
Libya	30,000
Spanish Morocco and Tangier	30,000
Syria	11,000
Lebanon	7,000
Aden (including refugees from Yemen)	8,000
Afghanistan (including refugees in India)	5,000
Other countries (Hadramuth, Sudan, Bahrein)	3,000
Total	**889,000**

Later information submitted to the Economic and Social Council was to the effect that:

From the *New York Times*, May 16, 1948. Used by permission.

In Syria a policy of economic discrimination is in effect against Jews. "Virtually all" Jewish civil servants in the employ of the Syrian Government have been discharged. Freedom of movement has been "practically abolished." Special frontier posts have been established to control movements of Jews.

In Iraq no Jew is permitted to leave the country unless he deposits £5,000 ($20,000) with the Government to guarantee his return. No foreign Jew is allowed to enter Iraq even in transit.

In Lebanon Jews have been forced to contribute financially to the fight against the United Nations partition resolution on Palestine. Acts of violence against Jews are openly admitted by the press, which accuses Jews of "poisoning wells," etc.

DANGER EMPHASIZED

Giving many other details of persecution, this report declares that "the very survival of the Jewish communities in certain Arab and Moslem countries is in serious danger unless preventative action is taken without delay."

Today, with a Jewish State an established fact, Jewish spokesmen at Lake Success do not conceal their anxiety that this danger to the survival of the Jewish populations of the Arab countries is even more imminent, and that the only effective solution would be to facilitate their quick transfer in so far as is possible and practicable, to the new Jewish State.

Conditions vary in the Moslem countries. They are worst in Yemen and Afghanistan, whence many Jews have fled in terror to India. Conditions in most of the countries have deteriorated in recent months, this being particularly true of Lebanon, Iran, and Egypt. In the countries farther west along the Mediterranean coast conditions are not so bad. It is feared, however, that if a full-scale war breaks out, the repercussions will be grave for Jews all the way from Casablanca to Karachi.

Mallory Browne, "Jews in Grave Danger in All Moslem Lands," *New York Times*, May 16, 1948.

CHAPTER 66

New York Times Reports on the Exodus of Jews from the Arab Muslim Middle East, 1955–1962

"JEWS SHOW DROP IN ARAB REGIONS," JULY 4, 1959

More than 200,000 Jews have been driven from Iraq, Egypt, and Syria in the last 25 years according to a report, "Jews in Moslem Lands," issued yesterday by the World Jewish Congress. The report also says that 100,000 Jews have fled from other Arab lands including Yemen and Libya [note: ~ 300,000 refugees, combined]. . . . In parts of the Middle East, the report asserts, only small groups of elderly Jews remain where there were once considerable communities.

"JEWS IN MOROCCO FRANTIC TO LEAVE," MARCH 12, 1956

The advent of Moroccan independence and the uncertainties of Arab rule are turning latent apprehensions into near panic. Instances of this were reported here today by Ira Hirschmann, a New York businessman who is on an unofficial mission of inquiry in Morocco. . . . The upward spiral of Jewish emigration to Israel was cited as evidence of the anxiety that has seized Moroccan Jews. *The trickle of emigration began to swell after the massacre of twelve Jews in the little town of Petitjean on August 3, 1954* [emphasis added]. In 1954 10,500 Jews left the country. In 1955 the figure jumped to 28,761. It is estimated that a total of 45,000 will depart this year. The figure for one recent month alone was 3,338. The number of departures would be infinitely greater if the necessary funds and ships were available. More than a fourth of Morocco's 210,000 Jews already are registered for emigration to Israel and more are coming forward all the time. *Several small Jewish communities in the interior have vanished entirely and the institutional structure of the Moroccan Jewish community is threatened* [emphasis added].

"EXODUS IS RESUMED BY MOROCCAN JEWS," FEBRUARY 8, 1962

The collective emigration of Moroccan Jews has been resumed after a month's suspension. The departures of Jews are now less frequent and more discreet, however, apparently to avoid provoking a renewal of attacks against the Moroccan Government for condoning group emigration. A French ship sailed from Casablanca for Marseilles more than two weeks ago with about 250 Moroccan Jews aboard. On Monday 450 more Jews left on the same ship. A total of 2,000 Jews, most of modest means, left Morocco in December by ship and plane. Air emigration is believed to have been ruled out now because it draws public attention. The suspicion of Jewish emigration contributed to a violent press campaign against an exodus of Jews allegedly going to Israel. The renewed departure of Moroccan Jews results from continued poverty and *the racist attitudes of the predominantly Moslem political parties here, according to* The Voice of the Communities, *the organ of the Jewish communities of Morocco* [emphasis added].

"500 JEWS LEAVING TUNISIA IN MONTH," MARCH 25, 1956

Twenty-seven thousand five hundred Jews have left the country since the beginning of 1947, according to the 1956 census. Jews of French and Italian citizenship, of whom there are nearly 25,000 in Tunisia, are not included in the figures. Tunisian Jews are now emigrating to Israel at the rate of about 500 a month, financed by the Jewish Agency for Palestine. Last year 6,000 Jews quit the country; 6,000 more are expected to go this year. There are 10,000 on the waiting list. Of these, 3,500 have been screened by the agency, and they have received medical examinations to qualify them for Israeli entrance visas. . . . [T]he major reason for the emigration, despite the fraternal overtures of the Neo-Destour [Tunisian Nationalist Party], is about the future in a Moslem nation* [emphasis added]. This is demonstrated by the figures . . . On July 31, 1954 Pierre Mendes-France, then Premier of France, promised internal autonomy to Tunisia. In August the emigration jumped to 320. The total emigration for the last five months of 1954 reached 2,600. In the nineteen months between M. Mendes-France's promise and March 1, 1956, 9,250 Jews emigrated with the assistance of the Jewish Agency.

CHAPTER 67

An Eyewitness Account of the Anti-Jewish Riots in Tunis at the Outbreak of the Six-Day War (1967)

This is a first report on the events of June 5th as they affected Tunisia written by an eyewitness. This report is not intended for publication but only for information.

The outbreak of hostilities in the Middle East on June 5 saw a major outburst of anti-Jewish demonstrations in Tunis. Shortly before noon a crowd arrived at the British Embassy and in short order the entire building was sacked and the library on the ground floor completely burned out. As the afternoon wore on, the crowd grew larger and different bands attacked the American library, the offices of TWA, and the American Embassy. . . . But by far the heaviest damage was done to Jewish retail establishments throughout the city. The gangs came prepared with gasoline as well as heavy metal cutters with which to open iron shutters. Jewish shops were systematically looted and burned. Over 100 shops were affected, this representing the major part of the shops that were in existence. Little attempt was made by the police to stop the looting and pillage. In most instances police calmly continued to direct traffic while the mobs were running riot in their immediate vicinity. Cars belonging to Jews were identified by the mobs, turned over, and set ablaze. During the course of the afternoon the mobs penetrated into the main synagogue, pulled out some 40 Torah Scrolls, urinated on them, and set them ablaze. Memorial plaques were ripped off the walls and the benches set fire with gasoline. A number of smaller synagogues around town were similarly dealt with. The Tunis Community flour distribution center was completely destroyed and the book distribution center as well. During the course of the afternoon a group of 30 arrived at the JDC offices, threw gasoline under the door, and set it ablaze. They did not get inside, and the office staff extinguished the fire after they had left.

By 1:30 p.m. Tunis looked like it had been bombed. Smoke was pouring out of scores of Jewish establishments, and the mobs continued to dominate the streets. Tunisian troops, who are quartered in barracks within ten minutes of the center of the city, did not arrive until four in the afternoon and then quickly drove the mobs off the streets. The mobs consisted mostly of youngsters between fourteen and twenty years of age, but I saw as

well a considerable number of young men in their twenties who were haranguing and leading them on.

There is no question in the mind of anyone that these demonstrations were organized. The Tunisian Government talks about Algerian troublemakers, but it is likely that certain activist members of the Destourian party were involved as well. The mobs came prepared with gasoline. The pillaging was systematic, and what is more significant, no one at all was hurt during the course of a five-hour riot of major proportions. An eyewitness reported seeing a Jew who had lost his nerve as his establishment was being pillaged, begging the mob not to hurt him. He was told that no one had any intention of hurting him, he was simply to go home! The police reacted feebly when they reacted at all, and it took five hours to get troops into the city.

These demonstrations were stopped when President Bourguiba addressed the country over the radio and television later in the afternoon. He is reported to have wept, but in any case, he roundly denounced the rioters and insisted that they cease immediately. It is probable that a major tragedy for the Jews living in the small towns in the interior of the country was averted as a result of the stand Bourguiba took. No attacks on Jews in the South were made during the week of hostilities except in one small town where stones were thrown. Bourguiba found himself in a very difficult position in the weeks that ensued. Although the troops were withdrawn from the Jewish sections of the town within a few days, they remained in the nerve centers of the city for several weeks. Armored cars were placed at several points and the radio-broadcasting station as well as other crucial locations were completely surrounded by armed troops. Despite the fact that a contingent of troops was sent to the "front" (incidentally, reaching the Libyan border after a leisurely three-day voyage just in time to turn right around at the end of hostilities), cries of "Bourguiba yahoud" (Jew Bourguiba) were heard in the streets. There was considerable question regarding the stability of the government for a few weeks, but by now the situation seems well in hand.

On Tuesday morning the Tunis Jewish Community

From Norman Stillman, *The Jews of Arab Lands in Modern Times*.

Council was convoked to the steps of the gutted main synagogue and four government ministers came to express their regrets and promised that the rioters would be punished and restitution made for all damages. Since then the government has repaired all store fronts and has repainted the outside of the synagogue and all visible evidence of the riots has been removed. Although a commission has been created to reimburse spoliated Jewish businessmen, no one has received anything yet, and it is likely that no one ever will. A goodly number of the rioters, however, have received prison sentences.

The immediate result of the riots was a heavy exodus of Jews from Tunisia to France. Our best estimates indicate that within the month following the riots, some 2,500 people left. Many of those were women and children sent ahead. By now some of these have returned, presumably to prepare for definite departure. Passports continue to be issued in Tunis, although in the interior great difficulties are encountered, as heretofore.

As for those who did not leave immediately following the riots, a large proportion say that they will be leaving in the months that come. This tendency is particularly evident in the different community institutions, which have already lost considerable personnel and will continue to do so. The total destruction of the Bokobza Boukha[1] and Kosher Wine Factory will create a heavy loss of community income, and major reductions in revenue from meat taxes are expected as well.

It is the unanimous opinion of Jews one talks to that if there was any doubt about the question previously, it is quite clear now that there is no future for them in Tunisia. Although it is impossible to make firm predictions, many people feel that of the roughly 23,000 Jews who were in Tunisia in early June, at least 5,000 to 6,000 will have left the country by the end of the year.

AJDC (Jerusalem) 245A.13, confidential memo from Henri Elfen (Geneva) to members of the Standing Conference of European Jewish Community Services, August 16, 1968; reproduced from Stillman, *The Jews of Arab Lands in Modern Times*, pp. 550–51.

NOTE

1. Boukha is the Tunisian Jewish eau-de-vie. The Bokobza company mentioned here is now one of the leading producers of kosher wine in France.

CHAPTER 68

A Libyan Jew Breaks Her Silence Thirty-six Years after Surviving the 1967 Tripolitan Pogrom

This is the first time I have ever written about my experience as a Jew from Libya. It's not easy for me. The memories are still painful. Jews had a continual presence in Libya for over two thousand years, predating the Arab conquest and occupation by centuries. My own family had lived on Libyan soil for hundreds of years, if not longer. I was born in Libya in 1951, the year of the country's independence. Most of the nearly 40,000 Jews left Libya between 1948 and 1951 because of a wave of anti-Jewish rioting, beginning in 1945, that left hundreds dead and injured and thousands homeless. My family, however, decided to stay and see if things would improve. After all, it was our home, it was our language, and it was the land of our ancestors. And the new Libyan constitution offered guarantees that gave us hope. We were wrong. The hope was misplaced. The guarantees were absolutely worthless. By 1961, Jews could not vote, hold public office, obtain Libyan passports, buy new property, or supervise our own communal affairs. In other words, at best we were second-class residents—I can't even say citizens—though this was our birthplace and home. Our fate was sealed six years later. In June 1967, the anti-Jewish atmosphere in the streets became terrifying, so much so that my family could not leave our house in Tripoli. My parents and I, along with my seven brothers and sisters, sat frightened at home for days. And then the mob came for us. I can't even begin to describe the scene. It seemed there were a thousand men chanting "Death to the Jews." Some had jars of gasoline which they began to empty on our house. They were about to strike a match. We were near hysteria. But then one man from the mob courageously spoke up. He said he knew us and we should be left alone. Amazingly, the mob complied and moved elsewhere. Other Jews, however, were not as lucky. Some, including close friends of ours,

were killed, and property damage was estimated in the millions of dollars. Our family went into hiding for several weeks before we were finally able to leave the country and reach Italy. We arrived with barely a suitcase each. Today, to the best of my knowledge, there is not a single Jew left in Libya, not one. An ancient community has come to a complete end. My family had to start from scratch in Italy. We had nothing and no one. But we persevered. We knew that we weren't the world's first Jewish refugees, or the last, and that we would just have to make the best of a difficult situation. And that's exactly what we did. We did not wallow in self-pity. We did not seek to make ourselves wards of the international community. And we didn't plot revenge against Libya. We simply picked up the pieces of our lives and moved on. The more I think about what befell us, though, the angrier I become. In effect, we were triple victims. First, we were uprooted and compelled to leave our home for ever solely because we were Jews. Second, our plight was largely ignored by the international community, the UN and the media. Do a search and you'll be shocked at how little was written or said about this tragedy. And third, Libya erased any trace of our existence in the country. Even the Jewish cemeteries were destroyed and the headstones used in the building of roads. In other words, first our homeland was taken away from us, then our history as well. I can no longer be a Jew of silence, nor can I allow myself to become a forgotten Jew. It is time to reclaim my history. It is time to demand accountability for the massive human rights violations that occurred to us in Libya. That's why, after 36 years, I've chosen to speak out today.

Giulia Boukhobza, "Justice for Jews from Arab Nations," *International Herald Tribune*, July 1, 2003.

CHAPTER 69

The Modern Rhetoric of Antisemitic Jihad Genocide

THE PROTOTYPE: *HAJJ AMIN EL-HUSSEINI*

November 2, 1943, the 26th Anniversary of the Balfour Declaration, at Luftwaffe Hall in Berlin (from Maurice Pearlman, *The Story of Haj Amin El Husseni* [London: 1947], p. 49):

> The Treaty of Versailles was a disaster for the Germans as well as for the Arabs. *But the Germans know how to get rid of the Jews* [emphasis added]. That which brings us close to the Germans and sets us in their camp is that up to today, the Germans have never harmed any Moslem, and they are again fighting our common enemy (applause) who persecuted Arabs and Moslems. *But most of all they have definitely solved the Jewish problem. These ties and especially the last* [emphasis added], make our friendship with Germany not a provisional one, but a permanent and lasting friendship based on mutual interests.

Radio broadcast from Berlin on March 1, 1944, when the pro-Zionist Wright-Compton and Wagner-Taft resolutions were before the US Congress (from Joseph B. Schechtman, *The Mufti and the Feuhrer* [New York: 1965], pp. 150–51):

> No one ever thought that 140 million Americans would become tools in Jewish hands. . . . How would the Americans dare to judaize Palestine while Arabs are still alive? . . . The wicked American intentions are now clear, and there remain no doubts that they are endeavoring to establish a Jewish empire in the Arab world. More than 400 million Arabs [Muslims?] oppose this criminal movement. . . . Arabs! Rise as one and fight for your sacred rights. *Kill the Jews wherever you find them. This pleases God, history and religion. This saves your honor. God is with you* [emphasis added].

SHEIKH MUHAMMAD SAYYED TANTAWI, THE TOP EGYPTIAN CLERIC OF AL-AZHAR UNIVERSITY

According to the Middle East Media Research Institute, a Web site associated with Al-Azhar University recently reported in early 2002: "The great Imam of Al-Azhar

Sheikh Muhammad Sayyed Tantawi, demanded that the Palestinian people, of all factions, intensify the martyrdom operations [i.e., suicide attacks] against the Zionist enemy, and described the martyrdom operations as the highest form of Jihad operations. He says that the young people executing them have sold Allah the most precious thing of all. [Sheikh Tantawi] emphasized that every martyrdom operation against any Israeli, including children, women, and teenagers, is a legitimate act according to [Islamic] religious law, and an Islamic commandment, until the people of Palestine regain their land and cause the cruel Israeli aggression to retreat . . . "[1]

SHEIKH DR. AHMAD AL TAYYEB, EGYPTIAN MUFTI

The solution to the Israeli terror lies in a proliferation of *Fidai* [martyrdom] attacks that strike horror into the hearts of the enemies of Allah. The Islamic countries, peoples and rulers alike, must support these martyrdom attacks."[2]

SHEIKH YOUSEF AL-QARADHAWI, HEAD OF THE EUROPEAN COUNCIL FOR FATWA AND RESEARCH, PRESIDENT OF THE INTERNATIONAL ASSOCIATION OF MUSLIM SCHOLARS (IAMS), AND SPRITUAL GUIDE FOR THE MUSLIM BROTHERHOOD

"We are fighting them in the name of Islam, because Islam commands us to fight whoever plunders our land, and occupies our country. All the school of Islamic jurisprudence—the Sunni, the Shi'ite, the Ibadhiya, and all the ancient and modern schools of jurisprudence—agree that any invader who occupies even an inch of land of the Muslims must face resistance. The Muslims of that country must carry out the resistance, and the rest of the Muslims must help them. If the people of that country are incapable or reluctant, we must fight to defend the land of Islam, even if the local [Muslims] give it up."[3]

"We do not disassociate Islam from the war. On the contrary, disassociating Islam from the war is the reason for our defeat. We are fighting in the name of Islam."

"They fight us with Judaism, so we should fight them with Islam. They fight us with the Torah, so we should fight them with the Koran. If they say 'the Temple,' we should say 'the Al-Aqsa Mosque.' If they say: 'We glorify the Sabbath,' we should say: 'We glorify the Friday.' This is how it should be. Religion must lead the war. This is the only way we can win."

"Everything will be on our side and against Jews on [Judgment Day]; at that time, even the stones and the trees will speak, with or without words, and say: 'Oh servant of Allah, oh Muslim, there's a Jew behind me, come and kill him.' They will point to the Jews. It says 'servant of Allah,' not 'servant of desires,' 'servant of women,' 'servant of the bottle,' 'servant of Marxism,' or 'servant of liberalism' . . . It said 'servant of Allah.'"

"There is no dialogue between us [Muslims and Jews] except by the sword and the rifle."[4]

HEZBOLLAH, MUSLIM TERRORIST ORGANIZATION

- In a 1992 statement, Hezbollah vowed, "It is an open war until the elimination of Israel and until the death of the last Jew on earth."[5]
- The Hezbollah Founding Statement reads:"We are the sons of the *umma* [Muslim community]—the party of God . . . the vanguard of which was made victorious by God in Iran. . . . We obey the orders of one leader, wise and just, that of our tutor and *faqih* (jurist) who fulfills all the necessary conditions: Ruhollah Musawi Khomeini. . . . Our culture is crystal clear. It is not complicated and is accessible to all. No one can imagine the importance of our military potential as our military apparatus is not separate from our overall social fabric. Each of us is a fighting soldier. And when it becomes necessary to carry out the Holy War, each of us takes up his assignment in the fight in accordance with the injunctions of the Law, and that in the framework of the mission carried out under the tutelage of the Commanding Jurist. . . . We combat abomination and we shall tear out its very roots, its primary roots, which are the U.S. All attempts made to drive us into marginal actions will fail, especially as our determination to fight the U.S. is solid."

In a section entitled "The Necessity for the Destruction of Israel," the Hezbollah Founding Statement says:

We see in Israel the vanguard of the United States in our Islamic world. . . .This enemy is the greatest danger to our future generations and to the destiny of our lands . . . from the Euphrates to the Nile. Our primary assumption in our fight against Israel states

that the Zionist entity is aggressive from its inception, and built on lands wrested from their owners, at the expense of the rights of the Muslim people. Therefore our struggle will end only when this entity is obliterated.We recognize no treaty with it, no cease fire, and no peace agreements, whether separate or consolidated.[6]

KHALID MASHAL, MEMBER OF THE HAMAS POLITICAL BUREAU

"You [Jews] will be defeated with God's help. Victory's day is approaching with God's help. Before Israel dies, it will not escape humiliation and surrender. Before they die, with God's help they will witness humiliation and surrendering. And America will not be there to help; nor will their generals. The last general is forgotten. God made Sharon disappear and he was departed from them. . . . We forced a new equation in this battle. The new equation plays to our hands. We will defeat them [the Israelis]. We will defeat them emotionally and mentally before we defeat them in the field of battle. Gaza is the victory's bed. . . . Victory in these elections sends a message to Israel and America and all the abusers of this world. With us you will never succeed and you will always lose. If you want war, we are ready for war. . . . The days of defeat within six days with hours are over. Today you are fighting against the army of Allah. Today you are fighting against people who care for dying for Allah, dying for honor and prestige more than they care for life itself." [7]

EXCERPTS FROM PALESTINIAN AUTHORITY SERMONS

"We the Palestinian nation, our fate from Allah is to be the vanguard in the war against the Jews until the resurrection of the dead, as the prophet Mohammed said: 'The resurrection of the dead will not arrive until you will fight the Jews and kill them . . .' We the Palestinians are the vanguard in this undertaking and in this campaign, whether or not we want this." (Palestinian TV, July 28, 2000)

"Blessed is he who fights *jihad* in the name of Allah, blessed is he who [goes on] raids in the name of Allah, blessed is he who dons a vest of explosives on himself or on his children and goes in to the depth of the Jews and says: 'Allahu Akbar, blessed be Allah.' Like the collapse of the building upon the heads of the Jews in their sinful dance-hall, I ask of Allah that we see the Knesset collapsing on the heads of the Jews." (Palestinian TV, June 8, 2001)

"The battle with the Jews will surely come . . . the decisive Moslem victory is coming without a doubt, and the prophet spoke about in more than one *Hadith*. And the day of resurrection will not come without the victory of the believers [the Moslems] over the descendents of the monkeys and pigs [the Jews] and with their annihilation." (*Al-Hayat Al-Jadida*, May 18, 2001)

"The Jews are the Jews. There never was among them a supporter of peace. They are all liars . . . the true criminals, the Jewish terrorists, that slaughtered our children, that turned our wives into widows and our children into orphans, and desecrated our holy places. They are terrorists. Therefore it is necessary to slaughter them and murder them, according to the words of Allah . . . it is forbidden to have mercy in your hearts for the Jews in any place and in any land. Make war on them anyplace that you find yourself. Any place that you encounter them—kill them. Kill the Jews and those among the Americans that are like them. . . . Have no mercy on the Jews, murder them everywhere." (Palestinian TV, October 13, 2000)

"O Allah, destroy America as it is controlled by Zionist Jews. . . . Allah will avenge, in the name of His Prophet, the colonialist settlers who are the descendents of monkeys and pigs." (Ikrime Sabri, Mufti of the Palestinian Authority [from weekly sermon in the Al-Aqsa Mosque in Jerusalem], *Voice of Palestine*, July 11, 1997)[8]

FATAH, TERRORIST FACTION HEADED BY THE LATE YASSER ARAFAT

Article 9 of the "Essential Principles" of Fatah's Constitution state: "Liberating Palestine and protecting its holy places is an Arab, religious, and human obligation."[9]

AL-QAEDA, MUSLIM TERRORIST ORGANIZATION

In 1998, al-Qaeda issued a statement of its ideals and worldviews in a document entitled "Jihad Against Jews and Crusaders," which Osama bin Laden coauthored with, among others, Ayman al-Zawahiri. The document reads: ". . . [I]n compliance with God's order, we issue the following *fatwah* [ruling on Islamic law] to all Muslims: The ruling to kill the Americans and their allies—civilians and military—is an individual duty for every Muslim who can do it in any country in which it is possible to do it . . . to comply with God's order to kill the Americans and plunder their money wherever and whenever they find it. We also call on Muslim *ulema*, leaders, youths, and soldiers to launch the raid on Satan's U.S. troops and the devil's supporters allying with them, and to displace those who are behind them so that they may learn a lesson."[10]

The terror organization further details its objectives, motives, and strategies in an al-Qaeda training manual, discovered in 2001 in a UK house search by the Manchester Metropolitan Police, instructs terrorists how to murder infidels. It states, "Islamic governments have never and will never be established through peaceful solutions and cooperative councils. They are established as they [always] have been by pen and gun, by word and bullet, by tongue and teeth."

The manual also requires jihadists to "pledge . . . to make their [the infidels'] women widows and their children orphans . . . to slaughter them like lambs and let the Nile, al-Asi, and Euphrates rivers flow with their blood . . . to be a pick of destruction for every godless and apostate regime." The manual begins with an invocation "In the name of Allah, the merciful and compassionate," and it states that al-Qaeda's "long-term goals" include "establishment of an Islamic state," but with the significant qualifier that an "Islamic government would never be established except by the bomb and rifle. . . . Islam does not coincide or make a truce with unbelief, but rather confronts it. The confrontation that Islam calls for with these godless and apostate regimes, does not know Socratic debates, Platonic ideals nor Aristotelian diplomacy. But it knows the dialogue of bullets, the ideals of assassination, bombing, and destruction, and the diplomacy of the cannon and machine-gun."[11]

YAHYA RAHEEM SAFAVI, IRANIAN REVOLUTIONARY GUARDS COMMANDER (JULY 30, 2006)

"We Must Keep the Hatred of America Burning in Our Hearts Until the Moment of Revenge Arrives."

"I hope that our courageous and great nation will succeed one day in taking revenge against Israel and America, avenging the blood of the oppressed Muslims and the martyrs."

"We see America as also being the cause of the death of the 200,000 martyrs in the war that was forced upon us [i.e. the Iran-Iraq war], since it urged Saddam [Hussein] to attack Iran. We must keep the holy hatred burning in our hearts until the moment of revenge arrives."

"In light of the Zionists' crimes and oppression, I ask God to hasten the years when this regime will no longer exist. . . . The Zionists are hastening their own death through their foul deeds, since Hizbullah and the Lebanese people are undefeated. There is a need to topple the phony Zionist regime, this cancerous growth [called] Israel, which was founded in order to plunder the Muslims' resources and wealth."[12]

AYMAN AL-ZAWAHIRI, CHIEF LIEUTENANT TO OSAMA BIN LADEN

On July 27, 2006, Al Jazeera broadcast a videotape of Al-Zawahiri exhorting Muslims to wage jihad against Israel by joining the ongoing military conflicts in Lebanon and Gaza. He stated that he sees "all the world as a battlefield open in front of us," and that the Israeli-Hezbollah war would not be ended with "cease-fires or agreements." Zawahiri added: "It is a *jihad* for the sake of God and will last until [our] religion prevails . . . from Spain to Iraq. We will attack everywhere." "My fellow Muslims," he added, "it is obvious that Arab and Islamic governments are not only impotent but also complicit . . . and you are alone on the battlefield. Rely on God and fight your enemies . . . make yourselves martyrs. . . . The shells and rockets ripping apart Muslim bodies in Gaza and Lebanon are not only Israeli [weapons], but are supplied by all the countries of the crusader coalition. Therefore, every participant in the crime will pay the price. We cannot just watch these shells as they burn our brothers in Gaza and Lebanon and stand by idly, humiliated." Al-Zawahiri also instructed Muslims to attack "crusaders and Zionists" and to support jihad "until American troops are chased from Afghanistan and Iraq, paralyzed and impotent . . . having paid the price for aggression against Muslims and support for Israel."[13]

YASSER ARAFAT

"Peace for us means the destruction of Israel. We are preparing for an all-out war, a war which will last for generations."[14]

"Continue to press on soldiers of freedom! We will not bend or fail until the blood of every last Jew from the youngest child to the oldest elder is spilt to redeem our land!"[15]

THE CHARTER OF HAMAS (1988)

The Charter of Hamas puts forth "The Slogan of the Hamas," which reads as follows: "Allah is its goal, the Prophet its model, the Qur'an its Constitution, Jihad its path, and death for the case of Allah its most sublime belief." The charter says that jihad, or holy war, "becomes an individual duty binding on every Muslim man and woman; a woman must go out and fight the enemy even without her husband's authorization, and a slave without his master's permission." The Hamas Charter explicitly abjures negotiated settlements as mechanisms for peaceful coexistence: "There is no other solution for the Palestinian problem other than jihad. All the initiatives and international conferences are a waste of time and a futile game." According to the charter, those against whom jihad is to be directed are the Jews. "The Nazism of the Jews," it says, "does not skip women and children, it scares everyone.

They make war against people's livelihood, plunder their moneys and threaten their honor." Hamas seeks to fulfill the Qur'anic scripture which reads: "The prophet, prayer and peace be upon him, said: The time will not come until Muslims will fight the Jews (and kill them); until the Jews hide behind rocks and trees, which will cry: O Muslim! There is a Jew hiding behind me, come on and kill him!" The Hamas Charter further states: "Israel will exist and will continue to exist until Islam will obliterate it, just as it obliterated others before it"; "The day the enemies usurp part of Moslem land, Jihad becomes the individual duty of every Moslem. In the face of the Jews' usurpation, it is compulsory that the banner of Jihad be raised"; "Ranks will close, fighters joining other fighters, and masses everywhere in the Islamic world will come forward in response to the call of duty, loudly proclaiming: 'Hail to Jihad!' This cry will reach the heavens and will go on being resounded until liberation is achieved, the invaders vanquished and Allah's victory comes about."[16]

HASSAN NASRALLAH, LEADER OF HEZBOLLAH

"Anyone who reads the Koran and the holy writings of the monotheistic religions sees what they did to the prophets, and what acts of madness and slaughter the Jews carried out throughout history. . . . Anyone who reads these texts cannot think of co-existence with them, of peace with them, or about accepting their presence, not only in Palestine of 1948 but even in a small village in Palestine, because they are a cancer which is liable to spread again at any moment."[17]

"One of the central reasons for creating Hizbullah was to challenge the Zionist program in the region. Hizbullah still preserves this principle, and when an Egyptian journalist visited me after the liberation and asked me if the destruction of Israel and the liberation of Palestine and Jerusalem were Hizbullah's goal, I replied: 'That is the principal objective of Hizbullah, and it is no less sacred than our [ultimate] goal.' We face an entity that conquered the land of another people, drove them out of their land, and committed horrendous massacres. As we see, this is an illegal state; it is a cancerous entity and the root of all the crises and wars and cannot be a factor in bringing about a true and just peace in this region. Therefore, we cannot acknowledge the existence of a state called Israel, not even far in the future, as some people have tried to suggest. Time does not cancel the legitimacy of the Palestinian claim."[18]

"If we searched the entire world for a person more cowardly, despicable, weak and feeble in psyche, mind, ideology and religion, we would not find anyone like the Jew. Notice, I do not say the Israeli."[19]

Nasrallah has characterized Jews as the "grandsons of apes and pigs," and as "Allah's most cowardly and greedy creatures."[20]

MAHMOUD AHMADINEJAD, PRESIDENT OF IRAN[21]

"The skirmishes in the occupied land are part of a war of destiny. The outcome of hundreds of years of war will be defined in Palestinian land."

"As the Imam [Ayatollah Khomeini] said, Israel must be wiped off the map."

". . . the annihilation of the Zionist regime will come."

"The Islamic *umma* [community] will not allow its historic enemy [Israel] to live in its heartland."

"Any leaders in the Islamic *umma* who recognize Israel face the wrath of their own people."

"There is no doubt that the new wave [of attacks] in Palestine will soon wipe off this disgraceful blot [Israel] from the face of the Islamic world."

"The creation of the occupying regime in [Israel] is a strong action by the ruling arrogant [American imperialist] world order against the world of Islam. There continues a historic war between the World Arrogance and the Islamic world, the roots of which go back hundreds of years ago. . . . The World Arrogance turned the Zionist regime occupying Jerusalem into a staging-ground to dominate the Islamic world. This occupying country is in reality the staging-ground of the World Arrogance in the heart of the Islamic world. They have created a base, from where they can expand their rule over the entire Islamic world; it has no other purpose other than this."

"The war that is presently going on in Palestine is the frontline of the war of destiny between the Islamic world and the World Arrogance, which will determine the outcome of hundreds of years [of war] in Palestine."

"Our dear Imam [Ayatollah Khomeini] ordered that the occupying regime in Jerusalem be wiped off the face of the earth. This was a very wise statement. The issue of Palestine is not one which we could compromise on. . . . This would mean the defeat of the Islamic world."

"The issue in Palestine is by no means finished. The Palestinian issue will only be resolved when all of Palestine comes under stringent Palestinian rule."

"I am hopeful that just as the Palestinian nation continued its struggle for the past ten years, they will continue to keep their awareness and vigilance. This period is going to be short-lived. If we put it behind us successfully, god willing, it will pave the way for the destruction and the downfall of the Zionist regime."

Ahmadinejad has called Israel a "tumor" that should be "wiped off the map" or moved out of the Middle East, perhaps to Alaska.

"Zionists have launched their own destruction by attacking Lebanon." (July 23, 2006)

"Their [Israelis'] methods resemble Hitler's. When Hitler wanted to launch an attack, he came up with a pretext. Zionists say they are Hitler's victims, but they have the same nature as Hitler."

"The Zionist regime is counterfeit and illegitimate and cannot survive. . . . The big powers have created this fraud regime and allowed it to commit all kind of crimes to guarantee their interests."

"They [the Jews] have no boundaries, limits, or taboos when it comes to killing human beings. Who are they? Where did they come from? Are they human beings? 'They are like cattle, nay, more misguided.' A bunch of bloodthirsty barbarians. Next to them, all the criminals of the world seem righteous."

"When I see the behavior of America, England, and their other accomplices in recent days, I get the impression that they are preparing even greater crimes. I warn them: Know that the fire of the wrath of the peoples is about to erupt and overflow. If you do not put an end to your crimes, know that the ocean of the peoples will soon rage. When the peoples begin to move, they will drag everybody to the defendant's bench, and will remove them from the throne of power."

"Today, the Iranian people is the owner of nuclear technology. Those who want to talk with our people should know what people they are talking to. If some believe they can keep talking to the Iranian people in the language of threats and aggressiveness, they should know that they are making a bitter mistake. If they have not realized this by now, they soon will, but then it will be too late. Then they will realize that they are facing a vigilant, proud people."

NOTES

1. "Leading Egyptian Government Cleric Calls For: 'Martyrdom Attacks that Strike Horror into the Hearts of the Enemies of Allah," Middle East Media Research Institute (MEMRI), April 7, 2002, http://memri.org/bin/articles.cgi?Page=archives&Area=sd&ID=SP36302.

2. "Leading Egyptian Government Cleric Calls For: Martyrdom Attacks that Strike Horror into the Hearts of

the Enemies of Allah," Middle East Media Research Institute MEMRI, April 7, 2002, http://memri.org/bin/articles.cgi?Page=archives&Area=sd&ID=SP36302.

3. "Leading Islamist Sheikh Yousef Al-Qaradhawi: We Are Fighting in the Name of Islam . . . This Jihad Is an Individual Duty of the Entire Muslim Nation . . . They Fight Us with the Torah . . . We Should Fight Them with the Koran: 'There Is a Jew behind Me, Come and Kill Him,'" MEMRI, February 28, 2006, http://memri.org/bin/articles.cgi?Page=archives&Area=sd&ID=SP110206.

4. "Sheikh Yousef Al-Qaradhawi: 'There Is No Dialogue between Us and the Jews Except by the Sword and the Rifle,'" MEMRI, July 27, 2004, http://memri.org/bin/articles.cgi?Page=archives&Area=sd&ID=SP7530.

5. 1992 Hezbollah statement, cited in "Nasrallah's Nonsense," *New York Sun*, March 11, 2005, http://www.nysun.com/article/10439; and Badih Chayban, "Nasrallah Alleges 'Christian Zionist' Plot," *Daily Star*, c. October 23, 2002, http://web.archive.org/web/20021024133755/http://www.dailystar.com.lb/23_10_02/art5.asp.

6. "An Open Letter: The Hizballah Program," [abridged], issued Beirut, February 16, 1985 [never published fully by any Hezbollah Web site], cited in *Jerusalem Quarterly* 48 (Fall 1988), http://www.standwithus.com/pdfs/flyers/hezbollah_program.pdf.

7. Khalid Masha'al, video, February 2006, http://switch3.castup.net/cunet/gm.asp?ClipMediaID=123232&ak=null, see also videotaped statement, March 17, 2006, http://switch3.castup.net/cunet/gm.asp?ClipMediaID=120176&ak=null.

8. Fateh Constitution, Fateh Online, http://www.fateh.net/e_public/constitution.htm#Introduction%20to%20the.

9. Itamar Marcus, "Palestinian TV, Radio, Newspapers and Textbooks—in Teaching the Islamic Attitude toward Jews—Have Fueled an Intense Hatred for Israel and Promoted Violent Jihad," July 21, 2001, http://www.aish.com/jewishissues/middleeast/Islams_War_Against_the_Jews_Quotes_from_the_Palestinian_Authority.asp; Ahmad Abu Halabiya, "Murder of Jews Is Allah's Will," Palestinian Authority TV, October 13, 2000, http://pmw.org.il/asx/PMW_Halabiya_kill_7.asx; see also Steven Stalinsky, "Palestinian Authority Sermons, 2000–2003," MEMRI, Special Report No. 24, December 26, 2003, http://www.memri.org/bin/articles.cgi?Page=archives&Area=sr&ID=SR2403.

10. Al-Qaeda fatwa, "Jihad against Jews and Crusaders," February 23, 1998, http://www.fas.org/irp/world/para/docs/980223-fatwa.htm.

11. "Al-Qaeda Training Manual," discovered 2001, http://www.fas.org/irp/world/para/manualpart1.html and http://www.fas.org/irp/world/para/manualpart1_1.pdf; see also Roy Gutman, "Training in Terror," *Newsweek*, October 26, 2001, http://www.msnbc.msn.com/id/3067505/site/newsweek/ from/RL.2/.

12. "Iran and Syria Beat the Drums of War," MEMRI, Special Dispatch No. 1225, August 2, 2006, http://memri.org/bin/articles.cgi?Page=archives&Area=sd&ID=SP122506.

13. "Al-Qaeda Vows Reprisal for Israeli Attacks," July 27, 2006, cited in Rantburg from Associated Press, http://rantburg.com/index.php?D=2006-07-27&HC=1; Statement of US Rep. John Shadegg, floor of the US House of Representatives, February 13, 2007, http://johnshadegg.house.gov/News/DocumentSingle.aspx?DocumentID=58442

14. Ben Lynfield, "Palestinian Faction-Fighting Drifting into War," *Scotsman*, December 20, 2006, http://news.scotsman.com/topics.cfm?tid=1260&id=1886222006.

15. CNN Late Edition with Wolf Blizter, July 30, 2006, http://transcripts.cnn.com/TRANSCRIPTS/0607/30/le.01.html; Dan Schuster, "Roadblocks to Peace," *Michgan Daily*, April 6, 2005, http://www.michigandaily.com/home/index.cfm?event=displayArticlePrinterFriendly&uStory_id=373a012e-4fe2-4373-b917-6f8caeae027a.

16. "Charter of Allah: The Platform of the Islamic Resistance Movement," August 18, 1988, http://www.palestinecenter.org/cpap/documents/charter.html; see also http://www.yale.edu/lawweb/avalon/mideast/hamas.htm.

17. Hassan Nasrallah, April 9, 2000, cited in Roy Holladay, "Where Are We in Prophecy," August 12, 2006, http://www.ucg.org/sermons/transcripts/200608prophecy.htm http://www.mfa.gov.il/MFA/MFAArchive/2000_2009/2000/4/Excerpts%20from%20Speech%20by%20Hizbullah%20Secretary-Genera.

18. Hasan Nasrallah, interview, Egyptian television, June 2, 2000, cited in Eyal Zisser, "The Return of Hizbullah," *Middle East Quarterly* (Fall 2002), http://www.meforum.org/article/499#_ftnref26.

19. Hasan Nasrallah, cited in Jeffrey Goldberg, "In the Party of God, Part I," October 14, 2002, *New Yorker*, http://www.jeffreygoldberg.net/articles/tny/a_reporter_at_large_in_the_par.php.

20. Aluma Solnick, "Based on Koranic Verses, Interpretations, and Traditions, Muslim Clerics State: The Jews Are the Descendants of Apes, Pigs, and Other Animals," November 1, 2002, citing Nasrallah's Arabic Web site at www.nasrollah.org/arabic/hassan/khitabat/khitabat08.htm.

21. "Iran's President Says Israel Must Be Wiped Off the Map," *New Tork Times*, October 26, 2005; "Ahmadinejad on Israel, Again" Al Jazeera Online, January 3, 2006, http://english.aljazeera.net/English/archive/archive?ArchiveId=17547; Justus Reid Wiener et al., "Referral of Iranian President Ahmadinejad on the Charge of Incitement to Commit Genocide," Jerusalem Center for Public Affairs, 2006; "The Islamic Genocide Plan," *FrontPageMagazine*, December 1, 2006, http://www.front pagemag.com/articles/read.aspx?GUID={791FAE48-6A36-47B6-BBD3-ED9C81EFC775; Matthias Kuntzel, "Iran's Obsession with the Jews," *Weekly Standard*, February 19, 2007.

Major Contributors

Eliezer Bashan is an associate professor in the Department of Jewish History at Bar Ilan University in Israel. His major academic interest is the history of the Jews in the Middle East and North Africa during the period of Ottoman rule. He has written *Yahadut Maroko: `avarah ve-tarbutah* [Jews of Morocco] (2000) and *Nashim Yehudiyot be-Maroko: demutan be-rei mikhtavim min ha-shanim 1733–1905* [Jewish Women in Morocco: Seen through Letters from 1733–1905] (2005), in addition to editing H. Z. Hirschberg's *A History of the Jews in North Africa, vol. 2: From the Ottoman Conquests to the Present Time (1974–1981)*, and publishing some 120 scholarly papers.

Bat Ye'or (pseudonym), born in Cairo, has written four books and numerous articles on the condition of non-Muslim populations vanquished by jihad, and on living as tributary *dhimmis* under Islamic law. Her *Les Juifs en Egypte* (French, 1971; Hebrew, 1974), *Le Dhimmi* (Paris, 1980; expanded English translation, 1985), and *The Decline of Eastern Christianity under Islam: From Jihad to Dhimmitude* (French, 1991; English, 1996), in particular the latter two works, elucidate what she has termed the "civilization of *dhimmitude*." *Islam and Dhimmitude: Where Civilizations Collide* (2001) highlighted the recrudescence of *dhimmitude* in the Muslim world during the twentieth century. Her fifth and most recent book, *Eurabia: The Euro-Arab Axis* (2005), is an examination of *dhimmitude* as a living historical force in western Europe and its role in the transformation of the continent into a cultural and political appendage of the Arab Muslim world.

Haggai Ben-Shammai is chairman of the Ben-Zvi Institute, and he teaches in the Department of Arabic Language and Literature at the Hebrew University of Jerusalem. Professor Ben-Shammai specializes in the study of Karaite Jewry. Among his publications is the essay "The Attitude of Some Early Karaites towards Islam," which appeared in vol. 2 of Isadore Twersky's *Studies in Medieval Jewish History and Literature* (1984).

Jacques Chalom (fl. early twentieth century) was author of a doctoral dissertation, *Les Israélites de la Tunisie: leur condition civile & politique*, published as book in 1908. Chalom analyzed the impact on Tunisian Jewry of late nineteenth- and early twentieth-century French attempts to reform the existing Shari'a-based system of law.

Abdul-Hamid 'Attiyah al-Dibani (fl. 1968) was rector of the Libyan Islamic University when he presented "The Jewish Attitude towards Islam and Muslims in Early Islam" at the Fourth Conference of the Academy of Islamic Research, Cairo, 1968.

Edmond Fagnan (1846–1931) earned a doctorate in law from the Universite de Liege and later obtained a diploma in Arabic, Persian, Turkish, and Hebrew from the Écoles des Langues Orientales Vivantes, Paris. In 1873 he joined the Department des Manuscrits of the Bibliotheque Nationale, where he collaborated in the production of Oriental historians in the Persian l'École des Lettres d'Alger, a post he held until his retirement in 1919. Fagnan translated and annotated the classical Arabic histories of Maghreb and Spain by Ibn al-Athir (published in 1898 as *Annales du Maghreb et de l'Espagne*), and Ibn 'Adari, al-Marrakushi (published between 1901 and 1904 as *Histoire de l'Afrique et de l'Espagne, intitulée al-Bayano'l-Mogrib*). His own writings include *Concordance du Manuel de Droit de Sidi Khalil* (1889) and *Additions aux Dictionnaires Arabes* (1923).

Jane Gerber is a prominent scholar in Judaic studies and is the director of the Institute for Sephardic Studies at the City University of New York Graduate Center. Her major books include *Jewish Society in Fez: 1450–1700* (1980), and *The Jews of Spain* (1992). She also edited *Sephardic Studies in the University* (1994). Among her many review essays Dr. Gerber has written "Toward an Understanding of the Term: 'The Golden Age' as an Historical Reality" in *The Culture of Spanish Jewry* (ed. Aviva Doron, 1994), and "The Jews of North Africa and the Middle East," in *The Modern Jewish Experience* (ed. J. Wertheimer, 1993).

Shlomo Dov [S. D.] Goitein (1900–1985) was a historian of Muslim-Jewish relations and a Jewish ethnographer, renowned for his expositions of Jewish life in the High Middle Ages (c. 950–1250 CE), based on the careful analysis of thousands of Geniza documents, an accumulation of almost two hundred thousand Jewish manuscripts that were found in the "geniza," or storeroom depository of the Ben Ezra synagogue (built 882) of Fostat, Egypt (now Old Cairo), the Basatin cemetery east of Old Cairo, and a number of old documents that were brought to Cairo in the latter part of the nineteenth century. Goitein's seminal research findings were widely published, most notably in the monumental five-volume work *A Mediterranean Society: The Jewish Communities of the Arab World as Portrayed in the Documents of the Cairo Geniza (1967–1993)*.

Yehoshafat Harkabi (d. 1994) received academic degrees from the Hebrew University of Jerusalem and Harvard, becoming a guest scholar at Princeton and at the Brookings Institute, and later director of the Leonard Davis Institute of International Relations and Middle East Studies at the Hebrew University. His first major study, *Arab Attitudes to Israel* (Hebrew, 1967), was published in English in 1971; then *Palestinians and Israel* in 1974 (French, 1972). Several books and articles followed, the last being *Israel's Fateful Hour* (1989). D. F. Green was the joint pseudonym of David G. Littman [D.] and Yehoshafat (Fati) Harkabi [F.], which was used to publish *Arab Theologians on Jews and Israel* (English, 3 eds., 1971–76; French, 2 eds., 1972–74; and German, 1976).

H. Z. Hirschberg (1903–1976) was born in Tarnopol, Austrian Galicia, and educated in Wien, where he also eventually received a DPhil in 1935 at the Universität for his study *Judisches und Christliches im Vorislamischen Altertum; Ein Beitrg zur Entstehungeschichte des Islams*. He emigrated to Palestine in 1943, where he became a professor of Jewish history and then head of the department at Bar Ilan University. His major writings include *A History of the Jews of North Africa* (1974–1981), and the translation *Der Diwan des as-Samaui ibn Adija und die unter seinem Namen Gedichtefragmente* (1939).

Hartwig Hirschfeld (1854–1934), born in Thorn, Germany (now Torun, in Poland), received his doctorate in Strasbourg, France (then in Germany), and moved to England in 1889. Hirschfeld taught initially at Montefiore College, Ramsgate, and in 1901 was appointed librarian and professor of Semitic languages at Jews' College, London. He also taught Hebrew, Semitic epigraphy, and Ethiopian at University College. His major work was on the interaction between Jewish and Arabic cultures as well as the Arabic literature of the Jews. Hirschfeld published Judah Halevi's *Kuzari* in its original Judeo-Arabic and in Hebrew, German, and English translations. Among his many other works is a series of essays on Arabic frag-

ments in the Cairo Geniza, and his analysis of the Jews of Medina, included in this collection.

Salah al-Khalidi (fl. late twentieth century) is known for his major work *Haqa'iq Qur'aniyya al Qadiyya al-Filastinniya* [Qur'anic Facts regarding the Palestinian Issue], which was first published in 1991 by the Hamas Publishing House Manshūrāt Filastin al-Muslima and translated into Urdu, Hindi, Turkish, Russian, and English (formerly available online at www.assabeel.com) due to its international popularity. He is also the author of *Amrika min al-Dakhil bi-minzar Sayyid Qutb* [Inside America in the Eyes of Sayyid Qutb].

Johann von Leers (1902–1965) studied history, economics, and law, completing his degree in the latter in 1925. He then mastered Japanese, which helped him gain a post as a cultural attaché in the foreign ministry from 1926 to 1928. By August 1929, Leers joined the National Socialist German Worker's Party, thus identifying himself as an "old fighter" of the Nazi movement. His devoted efforts caught the attention of Joseph Goebbels, who appointed Leers as associate editor of the propaganda ministry's journal (*Auf Wille und Weg*), as well as contributing author for the weekly newspaper (*Der Angriff*). Subsequently Goebbels appointed Leers to teach and assist in the planning of academic seminars in Berlin (1933–1935), which in turn enabled him to secure a special teaching post at the University of Jena by the fall of 1936. Through these editorial and academic appointments Leers emerged as one of the most prolific and virulently antisemitic Nazi-era propagandists. Leers's writings and personal career trajectory—as a favored contributor in Goebbels's propaganda ministry, to his eventual adoption of Islam as Omar Amin von Leers while working as an anti-Western and antisemitic/anti-Zionist propagandist under Nasser's regime from the mid-1950s through 1965—epitomizes the convergence of Islamic antisemitism and racist Nazi antisemitism. Indeed, two decades before his conversion to Islam, Leers, in *Blut und Rasse in der Gesetzgebung* [Blood and Race in Legislation (1936)], expressed his admiration for "the imperious and warlike Islam [of the peoples] who still had a clear Nordic racial component," while also extolling, in *Der Kardinal und die Germanen* [The Cardinal and the Germans (1934)] Islam's ecumenical "tolerance." Until his death in 1965, Leers was unrepentant about the policies toward the Jews he helped advance as a propagandist of extermination, serving Hitler's Reich. He remained convinced of the righteousness of the Nazi war against the Jews, and, as a pious Muslim convert, Leers viewed the Middle East as the succeeding battleground to seal the fate of world Jewry.

Moritz Levy (fl. early twentieth century) was author of *Die Sephardim in Bosnien*, a study of Bosnian Jewry under Ottoman rule published in 1911.

David Gerald Littman was born in London and received his BA (with Honors) and MA degrees in modern history and political science at Trinity College Dublin, followed by postgraduate studies at the Institute of Archaeology in London—interrupted in 1960 after his marriage, when he moved to Switzerland with his wife. In 1970 they and others founded the Centre d'Information et de Documentation sur le Moyen-Orient (CID) in Geneva, which he supervised for four years; dozens of CID articles on the Middle East (French and English) were published and widely circulated for two decades. Since the 1970s he has authored many articles on Jews and Christians (*dhimmis*) under Islam, while translating into English articles—and cotranslating three books—by Bat Ye'or. He has been highly active for several NGOs on human rights issues at the UN Commission (now "Council") on Human Rights since 1986. In 1971 he coedited with Yehoshafat Harkabi a landmark study, *Arab Theologians on Jews and Israel*, followed by several articles in the *Wiener Library Bulletin* (London), *Les Temps Modernes* (Paris), and *Yod* (Publications Orientalistes de France) on Jews in nineteenth-century Persia and in North Africa, and a monograph, "Mission to Morocco (1863–64)" in *The Century of Moses Montefiore* (1985). A dozen articles, old and recent, with several UN written and oral statements were edited by him under the title "Human Rights and Human Wrongs at the United Nations" in *The Myth of Islamic Tolerance: How Islamic Law Treats Non-Muslims* (ed. Robert Spencer, 2005).

Laurence Loeb is an associate professor of anthropology at the University of Utah who specializes in Middle East ethnology, social organization, and religion. He received his PhD from Columbia University in 1970 for a thesis entitled "The Jews in Southwest Iran: A Study of Cultural Persistence." In 1976 Loeb published the research paper "*Dhimmi* Status and Jewish Roles in Iranian Society" in *Ethnic Groups*. His major work is the book *Outcaste: Jewish Life in Southern Iran* (1977).

Eliezer Raphael [A. R.] Malachi (1895–1980) was born in Jerusalem to a Lithuanian rabbinical family of the Old Yishuv (pre-Zionist Jewish community). He studied in yeshivas (Talmudical academies) and had no formal secular education. Largely self-taught, as a teenager he began writing and publishing his own short stories and articles in Hebrew and in Yiddish in the nascent local Hebrew press in Jerusalem. At the age of seventeen, he moved to New York, returning to Jerusalem briefly for several years after World War I. Malachi was a prominent Hebrew writer in the United States. His articles appeared regularly in *Ha-Doar*, the leading American Hebrew periodical. In addition to fiction and literary criticism, he wrote about the history of the Hebrew press and of the Old Yishuv in Jerusalem, Hebron, Safed, and Tiberias in the nineteenth and twentieth centuries. Malachi is considered a pioneer of the genre of local historiography. Through his studies, the importance, sources, and narratives of the Jewish communities in the Land of Israel have become known to the wider public. His major historical studies of the Old Yishuv appeared in the Hebrew volume entitled *Studies in the History of the Old Yishuv*, ed. G. Yardeni-Agmon and Shlomo Derech (1971). Malachi's correspondence, articles on the Hebrew press, and hitherto-unpublished historical and literary studies have been published in the Hebrew volume *Mi-Neged Tireh* [View the Land from a Distance], ed. Elhanan Reiner and Haggai Ben Shammai (2001).

Jacob Mann (1888–1940) was born in Przemysi, Austria, and received his PhD in 1920 from the University of London for his pioneering analysis based on the Geniza documentary record entitled *The Jews of Egypt and in Palestine under the Fatimid Caliphs*. Mann became a professor of Jewish studies at Hebrew Union College in Cincinnati, Ohio. In addition to numerous scholarly essays, Mann's major published works were *Text and Studies in Jewish History and Literature* (1931–35) and *The Bible as Read and Preached in the Old Synagogue* (1946–66).

Moshe Perlmann (1905–2001) was born in Odessa. The family spent a few years in Budapest and returned to Odessa at the outbreak of World War I. Perlmann studied at the University of Odessa but he was arrested for Jewish Socialist activity and expelled from the country in 1924. He lived in Palestine from 1924 to 1937, studying Arabic and Islamic history at the Hebrew University, and completing his PhD (entitled *Muslim Polemics against Jews and Judaism*, published in 1941) at the University of London, School of Oriental and Asiatic Studies, under the aegis of Arthur S. Tritton. Perlmann came to the United States in 1940, and from 1941 to 1955 he taught at Herzelia in New York, and also had part-time appointments at the New School and Dropsie College. From 1955 until 1961, he held the position of lecturer in Israeli studies at Harvard University. In 1961 he was appointed professor of Arabic at the University of California, Los Angeles, and he retired in 1973. Perlmann's scholarship was focused on Islamic-Jewish-Christian polemics, and he produced critical editions and translations of three significant Arabic texts, Samau'al al-Maghribī's *Ifḥām al-Yahūd* [Silencing the Jews] (1964), Ibn Kammūna's *Examination of the Three Faiths; A Thirteenth-Century Essay in the Comparative Study of Religion* (1971), and *Shaykh Damanhūrī on the Churches of Cairo, 1739* (1975). His writings also included a translation from al-Tabari's history, *The Ancient Kingdoms* (1987).

Yusuf Qaradawi is a modern Muslim scholar and preacher best known for his popular Al Jazeera program "ash-Shari'a wal-Hayat" [Shari'a and Life], and his Web site IslamOnline. He has also published some fifty books, including *The Lawful and the Prohibited in Islam* and *Islam: The Future Civilization*. Al-Qaradawi was born in Egypt, and attended the Al-Azhar Theological Seminary. Qaradawi was a follower of Muslim Brotherhood founder Hasan al-Banna during his youth, and was imprisoned first under the monarchy in 1949, then three times after the release of his *Tyrant and the Scholar*, poetic Islamic plays expressing political messages. He has also worked in the Egyptian Ministry of Religious Endowments, has been the dean of the Islamic Department at the Faculties of Shari'a and Education in Qatar, and has been chairman of the Islamic Scientific Councils of Algerian Universities and Institutions. Qaradawi is a member of the Muslim Brotherhood, and the head of the European Council for Fatwa and Research.

Sayyid Qutb (1906–1966) was one of the greatest Islamic scholars of the twentieth century. Qutb served a long sentence in prison for his Islamic and political opinions and was sentenced to death in Nasser's Egypt in 1966. Posthumously he has remained an immensely popular Islamic spiritual guide. Qutb's conception of religion and its relation to secular modernity has had a pervasive influence throughout the Muslim world, particularly in Egypt and other Arab countries. He wrote the extensive Qur'anic commentaries *In the Shade of the Qur'an*, and is also remembered for his work on Islam's socioeconomic aspects, *'Adalah fi al-ijtimaiyah al-Islam* (1949) and its translation, *Social Justice in Islam* (1953).

Hans-Peter Raddatz received his MA and PhD in Islamic science and economics at Bonn University. His 1967 thesis was entitled *Die Stellung und Bedetung des Sufyan at-Tauri; ein Beitrag zur Gesitesgeschichte des fruhen Islam*. Raddatz wrote the essay in the *Encyclopedia of Islam* on the prominent representative of early Islamic law, tradition, and Qur'an interpretation Sufyan al-Thawri, in follow-up to his PhD research. He is the author of six books since 2001, including *From God to Allah* (2001), *From Allah to Terror—Djihad and the Deformation of the West* (2002), *Allah's Veil—The Woman in the Clash of Civilizations* (2003), *Iran—Descent from High Culture to Irrational Violence* (2006). Raddatz is currently writing the book *Allah and the Jews—The Islamic Renaissance of Antisemitism*, which is slated for publication in April 2008.

Yehudah Ratzaby is a professor emeritus at the Hebrew University of Jerusalem and a prolific scholar specializing in Judeo-Arabic literature and criticism. He completed seminal analyses of the late seventeenth-century Mawza exile of Yemenite Jewry in the 1960s and 1970s, and in 1976 published *The Yemenite Jews: Literature and Studies: Bibliography 1935–1975*. More recently Professor Ratzaby published a study entitled "Yemenite Jewry in Non-Jewish Courts: Eleven New Court Documents" [Hebrew], in *East and Maghreb* 6 (1995).

Abdul Sattar El Sayed (fl. 1968) was the mufti of Tursos Syria when he presented "The Jews in the Qur'an" at the Fourth Conference of the Academy of Islamic Research, Cairo, 1968.

Alexander Scheiber (1913–1985) was born in Budapest. He was educated in Hungary and the United Kingdom, obtained a doctorate, and was ordained a rabbi. Scheiber was a professor in Budapest and Szeged. His writings include *Geniza Studies* (1981), and he also edited Ignaz Goldziher's *Tagebuch* (1977).

Emmanuel Sivan is professor emeritus of Islamic history at the Hebrew University in Jerusalem. In the late 1980s he was among the first scholars to evaluate Islamic movements emerging after the 1979 Iranian Revolution. His books include *L'Islam et La Croisade* (1968), *Islamic Fundamentalism and Antisemitism* (1985), *Interpretations of Islam, Past and Present* (1985), and *Radical Islam: Medieval Theology and Modern Politics* (1990). Professor Sivan has also written more than 150 articles and book chapters.

Aluma Solnick-Dankowitz is a research associate with the Middle East Media Research Institute. She was born in Jerusalem and earned a BA in Arabic language and the history of the Middle East from the Hebrew University in Jerusalem. She is presently completing her MA in Arab language and literature from the Hebrew University.

Norman Arthur Stillman is the Schusterman-Josey professor and chair of Judaic history at the University of Oklahoma. Stillman studied at the University of Pennsylvania, receiving a BA (magna cum laude) in 1967 and PhD in Oriental studies in 1970, under the tutelage of Shlomo Dov Goitein. He was a postdoctoral fellow at the Jewish Theological Seminary of America. His work has focused on the sociopolitical history of Jews living under Islamic suzerainty, in particular, the Jewish communities of North Africa. Professor Stillman's major publications include *The Jews of Arab Lands: A History and Source Book* (1979), *Samuel Romanell's Travail in an Arab Land* (1989, in collaboration with his wife, the late Yedida Kalfon Stillman), *The Jews of Arab Lands in Modern Times* (1991), and *Sephardi Religious Responses to Modernity* (1995).

Afif Abd al-Fattah Tabbara (fl. late twentieth century) was a prolific Qur'anic commentator and writer best known for his *al-Yahud fi al-Qur'an* [Jews in the Qur'an], originally published in 1966, which has also been translated into Turkish.

Muhammad Sayyid Tantawi has been the Grand Imam of Al-Azhar University in Cairo, Egypt, since 1996. He graduated from Al-Azhar University's Faculty of Religious Studies in 1958, and received his PhD in 1966. His

PhD thesis, *Banu Israil fi al-Quran wa-al-Sunnah* [Jews in the Qur'an and the Traditions], was published in 1968–69, and republished in 1986. Two years after earning his PhD, Sheikh Tantawi began teaching at Al-Azhar. In 1980 he became the head of the Tafsir Department of the University of Medina, Saudi Arabia, a position he held until 1984. Sheikh Tantawi became Grand Mufti of Egypt in 1986, a position he was to hold for a decade before taking on his current post.

Yosef Tobi is an associate professor of Hebrew and comparative literature at the University of Haifa. Tobi has written on medieval Hebrew and Arabic poetry, and is a leading authority on the history of Yemenite Jewry, about which he has written and edited many important studies. He was named 1999 winner of the prestigious Jerusalem Prize for outstanding studies of Jewish ethnic groups. His most recent book, *Acceptance and Rejection: The Relationship of Hebrew and Arabic Poetry in the Middle Ages*, shared one of the 1998 Bahat Prizes awarded by the University of Haifa Press in conjunction with the prestigious Israeli publisher Zmora-Bitan for belles lettres in Hebrew.

Georges Vajda (1908–1981) was born in Budapest and educated in the local rabbinical seminary. He moved to Paris in 1928, where he resided until his death. In 1931 Vajda began his teaching career as a lecturer at the Seminaire Israelite de France. He gained a faculty appointment in 1937 at the École Pratique des Hautes Études, Paris. After escaping the German occupation by hiding in Haute-Loire, Vajda resumed his work with unparalleled vigor, rising to Direçteur D'Études in 1954, and professor at the Sorbonne. His seminal 1937 analysis of the characterization of the Jews in the hadith ("Juifs et Musulmans selon le Hadit") is featured herein. Vajda's major studies include *Introduction a la Pensee Juive du Moyen Age* (1947), *Repertoire de Catalogues et Inventaires de Manuscrits Arabes* (1949), and *Judische Philosophie* (1950).

APPENDIX B
Muslim Jurists, Theologians, and Historians

Abd al-Wahid Al-Marrakushi [Merrakechi] (d. 1224). North African historian of the Almohads.

Abu Bakr Abd Allah Al-Maliki (eleventh century). Tunisian historian; author of a famous chronicle, *Riyad an-Nufus*.

Abu Hanifa (d. 767). An-Nu'man b. Thabit b. Zuta abu Hanifa; theologian and jurisconsult, founder of the Hanafi school of jurisprudence. He died in Baghdad.

Abu Yusuf Ya'qub (731–98). A renowned jurist of the Hanafi school of law; author of a basic treatise on public finance.

Al-Amili (1547–1621). Born in Syria, he emigrated to Persia, eventually obtained an honored position at the court of Shah Abbas I, and wrote an important exposition of Shi'ite jurisprudence, in Persian, the *Jami-i-Abbasi*.

Al-Baghawi (d. 1117/1122?). A legist of the Shāfi'ī school, traditionist, and commentator on the Qur'an. Although he wrote on various subjects, the work for which he is most famous is his *Mishkat Al-Masabih* (i.e., the edition of his work arranged by Walī al-Dīn [d. 1342], an Urdu poet), which consists of a collection of traditions arranged according to their subject matter.

Al-Baladhuri (d. 892). Eminent Persian historian who lived at the caliphs' court from 847 to 892; author of *Book of Conquests*.

Al-Baydawi (d. 1286–1316?). A Shafi'ite jurist of the thirteenth to early fourteenth century who attained the position of chief kadi of Shiraz. He had a reputation for wide learning and wrote on a number of subjects, most notably Qur'anic exegesis and jurisprudence. His most famous work is a Qur'anic commentary that is largely a condensed and amended edition of Al-Zamakshari's *al-Kashaf*.

Al-Bukhari (810–870). Born in Bukhara and died in Samarkand. His most famous work is the Sahih, which took him sixteen years to compile. It is said that he selected his traditions from a mass of six hundred thousand. This famous collection of traditions is arranged in 97 books with 3,450 chapters. There are 7,397 traditions with full *isnād*s (documented chains of transmission), but if repetitions are omitted the total is 2,762. This work, which claims to contain only traditions of the highest authority, is classified according to subject matter.

Al-Ghazali (1058–1111). Born at Tus in Khurasan, near modern Meshed, and became a renowned theologian, jurist, and mystic. Al-Ghazali's early training was as a jurist, and he continued to have an interest in jurisprudence throughout his career, writing a work, the *Wadjiz*, dated 1101, that is, in the last decade of his life. W. M. Watt wrote of Al-Ghazali, *"acclaimed in both the East and West as the greatest Muslim after Muhammad, and he is by no means unworthy of that dignity. . . . He brought orthodoxy and mysticism into closer contact . . . the theologians became more ready to accept the mystics as respectable, while the mystics were more careful to remain within the bounds of orthodoxy."*

Al-Jahiz (776–868/869). Born in Basra, Iraq, Al-Jahiz was a prolific Arabic prose writer, historian, and author of works of literature, theology, and politico-religious polemics. He authored two hundred books throughout his lifetime that discuss a variety of subjects, including Arabic grammar, zoology, poetry, lexicography, and rhetoric.

Al-Jaubari (d. 1222). A dervish and alchemist from Damascus who traveled and wrote in the first half of the seventh/thirteenth century. He authored *al-Mukhtar fi kashf al-asrar* [The Chosen One's Unmasking/Clarification of Divine Mysteries].

Al-Maghili (1440–1503/1505). A theologian/jurist of Tlemcen, known for his persecution of the Jewish community of Tuwāt [Touat] in the Algerian Sahara and for the advice he gave to Sudanic rulers. He wrote a treatise that maintained the Jews of Tuwāt had broken their pact with the Muslims, and thus forfeited their protection, by not paying *jizya* regularly in a state of "abasement and humiliation" and by "rebelling against Islamic laws" through too close an association with their Muslim overlords. He also claimed that the existence of the Tuwāt synagogue was contrary to Islamic law and demanded its destruction. Al-Maghili's writings were widely circulated in Morocco and continued to influence the treatment of Moroccan Jewry through the early twentieth century.

Al-Maqrizi [Makrizi] (1364–1442). Renowned historian, born in Cairo; author of several works, particularly on the Mamluk sultans of Egypt.

Al-Mawardi [Mawerdi] (d. 1058). Famous Shafi'i jurist of Baghdad; author of an important law treatise, *Al-ahkam as-Sultaniyya*, and a treatise on morality.

Al-Nasai (830–915). Author of one of the six canonical collections of traditions of hadith. Very little is known about him. He is said to have made extensive travels in order to hear traditions, to have settled in Egypt, afterward in Damascus, and to have died as a consequence of ill treatment to which he was exposed at Damascus, or, according to others, at Ramla, in consequence of his feelings in favor of Ali and against the Umayyads. On account of this unnatural death he is called a martyr. His tomb is at Mecca.

Al-Shafi'i (d. 820). Born in Gaza; theologian and jurisconsult, disciple of Malik, founder of the Shafi'i school of jurisprudence.

Al-Shaybani (d. 805). Jurist of the Hanafi school of jurisprudence, disciple of Abu Yusuf; author of several authoritative works, particularly an important work on jihad, *The Islamic Law of Nations*.

Al-Suyuti (1445–1505). Born in Cairo, where his father taught Shafi'i law and acted as a substitute kadi. Al-Suyuti is presently recognized as the most prolific author in the realm of Islamic literature. A brilliant multidisciplinary scholar, Al-Suyuti was a learned jurist, historian, and biographer. Among his many scholarly contributions are about twenty works of Qur'anic studies, including seminal Qur'anic commentaries.

Al-Tabari (838–923). Born in Tabaristan, died in Baghdad; historian, theologian, and jurisconsult; author of a monumental commentary on the Qur'an and a universal history, *Annals*, and *Kitab al-Jihad* [Book of the Holy War].

Al-Wakidi [Waqidi] (747/8–822). From Medina; was an often-quoted authority on early Islamic history, in particular the expeditions and raids organized by Muhammad in the Medinan period, recorded in his *Kitāb al-Maghazi*. Wakidi was also an expert in Islamic law.

Al-Wansharīsī (1431–1508). Known for his profound knowledge of Mālikī fiqh, which made him the flag-bearer of the school of Islamic law at the end of the ninth/fifteenth century. The principal work of al-Wansharīsī is a vast compilation of Andalusian and North African fatwas from the third/ninth to the ninth/fifteenth centuries. He wrote some thirty books in all.

Al-Zamakhshari (1070?–1143). A Persian scholar who was born at Zamakhshar, a village of Khwarizm, studied at Bukhara and Samarkand, and enjoyed the fellowship of the jurists of Baghdad. He stayed at Mecca for many years, becoming known as Jar-idlah ("God's client"). Later he returned to Khwarizm, where he died at the capital, Jurjaniyya. Zamakhshari's fame as a scholar rests upon his commentary on the Qur'an, called *al-Kashaf* [The Revealer], which was the basis of the widely read commentary of Baidhawi.

Burhanuddin Ali, (Shaikh), of Marghinan (1135–1183). Born in Transoxiana, he composed the important Sunni text of Islamic law the *Hidayah*, which was translated into English in 1791 by Charles Hamilton.

Ghazi Al-Wasiti (fl. 1292). A native of the town of Wasit on the Tigris (in Iraq); the author of a well-known treatise on the *dhimmis*.

Ibn Abdun, Muhammad b. Ahmad (d. 1134). Andalusian author of an authoritative legal treatise on Seville.

Ibn Abi Zayd Al-Qayrawani (922–996). Head of the North African Maliki school of Qairuan; author of several legal works and of a compendium that ensured the triumph of the Maliki school of jurisprudence.

Ibn al-Athir (1160–1233). Born in Jazirat Ibn Umar on the Tigris (Iraq), lived in Mesopotamia and Palestine; author of historical works on the Zangrid dynasty of Mosul (al-Bahir) and of a vast corpus of chronicles (*al-Kamil fi't-tarikh*).

Ibn al-Fuwati (1244–1323). Born in Baghdad; historian and librarian in Maragha and Baghdad; author of several historical works and bibliographies.

Ibn Battuta (1304–c. 1368). Born and died in Tangiers; author of accounts describing places visited in the course of several lengthy travels throughout the Islamic world, including India and China.

Ibn Hanbal (d. 855). Theologian and jurisconsult, editor of a corpus of traditions, and founder of the Hanbali school of jurisprudence.

Ibn Hazm (994–1064). Born in Cordoba; a poet, historian, jurist, and theologian, considered to be one of the seminal thinkers in Arab-Muslim civilization. Ibn Hazm codified the literalist Zahiri doctrine, and, according to Roger Arnaldez, "applied himself to reconstructing a legal system stripped of all that he considered to be additions made by the jurists who came after the Prophet and the Companions."

Ibn Hisham (d. 813). Born and died in Egypt; grammarian and genealogist, famous for his recension of Ibn Ishaq's biography of Muhammad.

Ibn Ishaq (d. 761). Author of the most famous biography of Muhammad.

Ibn Kathir (1300–1373). Born in Basrah in 1300, Ibn Kathir died in Damascus in 1373. He was one of the best-known historians and traditionalists of Syria during the reign of the Bahri Mamluks, compiling an important history of Islam, as well as a Qur'anic commentary that foreshadows in its style the commentary of Al-Suyuti.

Ibn Khaldun (1332–1406). Born in Tunis, died in Cairo; jurist, qadi (Maliki), renowned philosopher, historian, and sociologist. Author of a history of the Berbers and a universal history, preceded by an introduction to history (*al-Muqqddima*).

Ibn Maja (824–887). Compiled the last of the six canonical hadith collections, *Sunan Ibn Maja*. He was born in the modern Iranian province of Qazvin in 824. According to Ibn Kathir, he also wrote a *tafsir* (commentary on the Qur'an) and a book on history, but neither survives. Other authors began to add him to the canonical five hadith collectors beginning in the thirteenth century, but his position remained controversial as late as the eighteenth century.

Ibn Rushd (1126–1198). Known as Averröes in the medieval West, Ibn Rushd was a scholar of the Qur'anic sciences and natural sciences (physics, medicine, biology, astronomy), theologian, and philosopher. Between 1153–1195, under the Almohad caliphs 'Abd al-Mu'min, Abu Ya'kub Yusuf, and Ya'kub al-Mansur, he served as either a kadi or a physician in both North Africa (Marrakesh) and Andalusia (Seville and Cordoba).

Ibn Sa'd (784–845). A traditionist, born in Basra, whose fame rests on his *Kitab al-Tabakat al-kabir*, which provided information on some 4,250 persons (including about 600 women) who, from the beginning of Islam down to the author's time, had played a role as narrators or transmitters of traditions about the Prophet's sayings and doings. Ibn Sa'd opens his work with a biography of the Prophet; the subsequent articles on the companions of the Prophet are often extensive. He traveled in search of traditions and studied under many authorities. Later Ibn Sa'd settled in Baghdad and attached himself to al-Wakidi, became his secretary, and transmitted his works.

Mulla Muhammad Bakr Majlisi (1627–1698). An authoritative jurist and prolific hadith collector, Majlisi was also well educated in Islamic philosophy and mysticism. During the late Safavid period, he became a dominant authority in politics, and social and judicial matters. Majlisi's professed goal in his Persian writings was to disseminate the Shi'a ethos to "the masses of believers and common Shi'a" who had "no familiarity with the Arabic language." Majlisi had very close relationships with at least two of the Safavid monarchs, Shah Sulayman (d. 1694) and Shah Sultan Husayn (d. 1713). In 1686 he was appointed the Shaykh al-Islam by Shah Sulyman. Upon Shah Husayn's accession to the throne in 1694, his title was changed to Mullabashi. Majlisi personally undertook legal matters and proceedings while holding these supreme institutionalized clerical offices. During the last four years in this official state office under Shah Sultan Husayn, Majlisi was the de facto ruler of Iran.

Malik b. Anas (710–795). Theologian and jurisconsult from Medina, founder of the Maliki school of jurisprudence; author of *al-Muwatta*, the oldest extant treatise of Islamic law, as practiced in the Hijaz.

Sayyid Abul A'la Mawdudi (1903–1979). A journalist, fundamentalist theologian, major influence in the politics of Pakistan, and one of the leading interpreters of Islam in the twentieth century. Mawdudi's academic output was voluminous: tradition, law, philosophy, history, politics, economics, sociology, and theology being among the subjects covered. Many of his works have been translated, some into over a dozen languages. His masterwork is his Qur'an commentary, *Tafhīm al-Qur'an*, which took him thirty years to finish.

Muslim (d. 874). Disciple of al-Bukhari and one of Islam's outstanding early collectors of prophetic traditions (hadith). Muslim is associated in the first place with this collection of prophetic hadith, usually called Sahih (sound) for short. According to the consensus of Sunni Muslim tradition experts, it forms together with the Sahih of Bukhari, the most reliable collection of prophetic traditions of all time.

Shaykh Ahmad Sirhindi (1564–1624). Sirhindi was an eminent Sufi mystic, connected with several Sufi orders (including the Naqshbandi order), who contributed considerably toward the revival of orthodox Islam following the heterodox experiments of Akbar's reign (1556–1605). He published a number of tracts and letters promoting these views.

Sources and Credits

Excerpts from Marmaduke William Pickthall, *The Glorious Qur'an* (Elmherst, NY: 2001); M. H. Shakir, *The Qur'an Translation* (Elmherst, NY: 1999); A. J. Arberry, *The Koran Interpreted: A Translation* (New York: 1996).

Haggai Ben-Shammai, "Jew-Hatred in the Islamic Tradition and the Koranic Exegesis" in *Antisemitism through the Ages*, ed. Shmuel Almog (Oxford: Pergamon, 1988).

Excerpts from the Canonical Hadith Collections: M. Muhsin Khair, "Translation of Sahih Bukhari"; Abdul Hamid Siddiqi, "Translation of Sahih Muslim"; Ahwad Hasan, "Partial Translation of Sunan Abu Dawud"; Muslim Students Association, University of Southern California. "Hadith by Tirmidhi and Muslim from the al-Baghawi Complication," English translation by James Robson (Lahore: 1963), vol. 3.

Georges Vajda, "Juifs et Musulmans selon le Hadit" (Jews and Muslims according to the Hadith), *Journal Asiatique* 229 (1937): 57–129. Translated by Susan Emanuel.

Ibn Ishāq/Ibn Hashām, "Muhammad's Jewish Adversaries in Medina," in Norman Stillman, ed., *The Jews of Arab Lands: A History and Source Book* (Philadelphia: Jewish Publication Society of America, 1979). Reprinted from *The Jews of Arab Lands: A History and Source Book*, © 1979 by Norman Stillman, published by the Jewish Publication Society, with the permission of the publisher.

Ibn Ishāq/Ibn Hashām, "The Affair of the Banu Qaynūqāᶜ," in Norman Stillman, ed., *The Jews of Arab Lands: A History and Source Book* (Philadelphia: Jewish Publication Society of America, 1979). Reprinted from *The Jews of Arab Lands: A History and Source Book*, © 1979 by Norman Stillman, published by the Jewish Publication Society, with the permission of the publisher.

Ibn Ishāq/Ibn Hashām, "The Assassination of the Kab b. al-Ashrafᶜ," in Norman Stillman, ed., *The Jews of Arab Lands: A History and Source Book* (Philadelphia: Jewish Publication Society of America, 1979). Reprinted from *The Jews of Arab Lands: A History and Source Book*, © 1979 by Norman Stillman, published by the Jewish Publication Society, with the permission of the publisher.

Ibn Ishaq/Ibn Hashām, "The Brothers Muhayyisa and Huwayyisa," in Norman Stillman, ed., *The Jews of Arab Lands: A History and Source Book* (Philadelphia: Jewish Publication Society of America, 1979). Reprinted from *The Jews of Arab Lands: A History and Source Book*, © 1979 by Norman Stillman, published by the Jewish Publication Society, with the permission of the publisher.

Al-Wakidi, "The Raid against the Banu Nadir," in Norman Stillman, ed., *The Jews of Arab Lands: A History and Source Book* (Philadelphia: Jewish Publication Society of America, 1979). Reprinted from *The Jews of Arab Lands: A History and Source Book*, © 1979 by Norman Stillman, published by the Jewish Publication Society, with the permission of the publisher.

Ibn Ishāq/Ibn Hashām, "The Extermination of the Banū Qurayza," in Norman Stillman, ed., *The Jews of Arab Lands: A History and Source Book* (Philadelphia: Jewish Publication Society of America, 1979). Reprinted from *The Jews of Arab Lands: A History and Source Book*, © 1979 by Norman Stillman, published by the Jewish Publication Society, with the permission of the publisher.

Ibn Ishāq/Ibn Hashām, "Muhammad and the Jews of Khaybar," in Norman Stillman, ed., *The Jews of Arab Lands: A History and Source Book* (Philadelphia: Jewish Publication Society of America, 1979). Reprinted from *The Jews of Arab Lands: A History and Source Book*, © 1979 by Norman Stillman, published by the Jewish Publication Society, with the permission of the publisher.

Excerpts from the Sira of Ibn Sa'd. English translation by S. Moinul Haq and H. K. Ghazanfar.

Al-Tabari, "The Victory of Islam," in Michael Fishbein, *The History of al-Tabari*, vol. 8 (New York: State University of New York Press, 1997).

Hartwig Hirschfeld, "Essai sur l'Histoire des Juifs de Medina" (History of the Jews of Medina), *Revue des Études Juives* 7 (1883); 10 (1885). English translation by Michael J. Miller.

Al-Qalqashandi, "The First Jews' Oath in Islam," in Norman Stillman, ed., *The Jews of Arab Lands: A History and Source Book* (Philadelphia: Jewish Publication Society of America, 1979). Reprinted from *The Jews of Arab Lands: A History and Source Book*, © 1979 by Norman Stillman, published by the Jewish Publication Society, with the permission of the publisher.

Excerpts from Joshua Finkel, trans., "Why the Muslims Prefer the Christians to the Jews," in "A Risāla of Al-Jāhiz," *Journal of the American Oriental Society* 47 (1927). Reprinted by permission of the publisher.

Al-Tabari, "A Renegade Jew as the Source of the Shi'ite 'Heresy' and the 'Conspiracy' to Destroy the Early Islamic Caliphate," English translation in Ronald M. Nettler, "Islamic Archetypes of the Jews: Then and Now," in *Anti-Zionism in the Contemporary World*, ed. Robert Wistrich (New York: New York University Press, 1990).

Al-Jaubari, "To Disclose the Fraudulence of the Jewish Men of Learning," from "Notes on the Position of Jewish Physicians in Medieval Muslim Countries," *Israel Oriental Studies* 2 (1972), translated by Moshe Perlmann. © 1972. Reprinted with permission from Brill Academic Publishers.

Al-Wansharisi, "A Collection of Legal Opinions Demonstrating the Attitudes of Muslim Jurists and Citizens toward the Jews of Muslim Spain and North Africa, Ninth–Fifteenth Centuries," in "Tributaries in the Medieval Muslim West, according to the *Mi'yar* of al-Wansharisi," English translation by Michael J. Miller. © Brill Academic Publishers. Translation rights by permission of the publisher. Reprinted with permission.

Ghazi al-Wasiti, "Anti-Jewish Anecdotes from an Anti-Dhimmi Treatise," in Norman Stillman, ed., *The Jews of Arab Lands: A History and Source Book* (Philadelphia: Jewish Publication Society of America, 1979). Reprinted from *The Jews of Arab Lands: A History and Source Book*, © 1979 by Norman Stillman, published by the Jewish Publication Society, with the permission of the publisher.

Sirhindi, "On Killing a Jew," in Yohanan Friedmann, *Shaykh Ahmad Sirhindi: An Outline of His Thought and a Study of His Image in the Eyes of Posterity* (Montreal: McGill University, Institute of Islamic Studies, 1971).

Muhammad Al-Majlisi, "Lightning Bolts against the Jews," *Die Welt des Islams* 32 (1992). English translation by V. B. Moreen. © 1992. Reprinted with permission by Brill Academic Publishers.

Moshe Perlmann, "Eleventh-Century Andalusian Authors on the Jews of Granada," *Proceedings of the American Academy of Jewish Research* 18 (1948–49). Reprinted by permission.

Georges Vajda, "'*Adversos Judaeos*': A Treatise from Maghrib—'*Ahkam ahl al-Dhimma*' by Sayh Muhammad ben 'Abd al Karim al-Magili," in *Études d'Orientalisme dédiées à la mémoire de Lévi-Provençal* (Paris: G.-P. Maisonneuve et Larose, 1962). English translation by Michael J. Miller. Reprinted with permission by Brill Academic Publishers.

Sayyid Qutb, "Our Struggle with the Jews," in *A Muslim Fundamentalist's View of the Jews* (Oxford: Pergamon, 1987).

Abdul Sattar El Sayed, "The Jews in the Qur'an," from the *Fourth Conference of the Academy of Islamic Research* (Cairo: 1970).

Abdul-Hamid 'Attiyah al-Dibani, "The Jewish Attitude toward Islam and Muslims in Early Islam," from the *Fourth Conference of the Academy of Islamic Research* (Cairo: 1970).

D. F. Green (David Littman and Yehoshafat Harkabi), eds., "Arab Theologians on the Jews and Israel," extracts from the *Fourth Conference of the Academy of Islamic Research* (Cairo: 1970).

Muhammad Sayyid Tantawi, extracts from "The Children of Israel in the Qur'an and the Sunna" (Cairo: Zahraa' lil-I'laam al-'Arabi, 1986–87).

'Afiif 'Abd al-Fattah Tabbara, extracts from *The Jews in the Qur'an* (Beirut: Publishing House of Knowledge for the Millions, 1980).

Salāh 'Abd al-Fattāh al-Khālidī, extracts from "Qur'anic Truths regarding the Palestinian Issue" (London: Muslim Palestinian Publications, 1994).

Yusuf Al-Qaradawi, excerpts from "Our War with the Jews Is in the Name of Islam" (February 25, 2006), Clip #1052 from Qatar Television. Reprinted by permission from the Washington-based Middle East Media Research Institute.

Yusuf Al-Qaradawi, excerpts from "The Jews of Today Bear Responsibility for Their Forefathers' Crime against Jesus" (August 26, 2006), Clip #1249 from Qatar Television. Reprinted by permission from the Washington-based Middle East Media Research Institute.

Sheikh 'Atiyyah Saqr, excerpts from "The Jews' Twenty Bad Traits as Described in the Qur'an" (April 6, 2004), Special Dispatch series #691. Reprinted by permission from the Washington-based Middle East Media Research Institute.

Shlomo Dov Goitein, "Evidence on the Muslim Poll Tax from Non-Muslim Sources: A Geniza Study," *Journal of the Economic and Social History of the Orient* 6 (1963). © 1963. Reprinted by permission of Brill Academic Publishers.

Georges Vajda, "À propos de la situation des Juifs et des Chrétiens à Séville au début du XIIe siècle" (Concerning the Situation of the Jews and Christians in Seville at the Beginning of the Twelfth Century), *Revue des Études Juives* 99 (1935). English translation by Michael J. Miller. Reprinted by permission of the publisher.

Edmond Fagnan, "Le sign distinctif des Juifs au Maghreb" (The Distinctive Sign of the Jews in Maghreb), *Revue des Études Juives* 28 (1894). Translated by Michael J. Miller.

Alexander Scheiber, from "The Origins of 'Obadyah, the Norman Proselyte—'Obadyah's Experiences in Baghdad, Early Twelfth Century," *Journal of Jewish Studies* 5 (1954). Reprinted by permission of the publisher.

Jacob Mann, "Moses b. Samuel, a Jewish Katib in Damascus, and His Pilgrimage to Medina and Mecca,"

Journal of the Royal Asiatic Society (1919). Reprinted in *The Collected Articles of Jacob Mann* (Gedera, Israel: 1971).

H. Z. Hirschberg, "The Destruction of the Kairouan, and the Almoravid and Almohad Persecutions," in *A History of the Jews of North Africa* (Leiden: Brill, 1974). © 1974. Reprinted with permission from Brill Academic Publishers.

Jane S. Gerber, "The Pact of 'Umar in Morocco: A Reappraisal of Muslim-Jewish Relations," in *Muslim-Jewish Relations in North Africa* (New York: Jewish World Congress, American division, 1975).

Eliezer Bashan, "New Documents regarding Attacks upon Jewish Religious Observance in Morocco during the Late Nineteenth Century," *Pe'amim* (1995). English translation by Rivkah Fishman.

David Littman, "Jews under Muslim Rule—II: Morocco 1903–1912," *Wiener Library Bulletin* (London) 29, nos. 37, 38 (1976). Reprinted with permission.

Norman Stillman, "The Moroccan Jewish Experience: A Revisionist View," *Jewish Quarterly* 9 (1978).

Jacques Chalom, excerpts from *Les Israélites da la Tunisie: Leur condition civil et politique* (The Israelites of Tunisia: Their Civil and Political Condition) (Paris: 1908). English translation by Susan Emanuel.

Laurence D. Loeb, "'Outcaste': Shi'a Intolerance," selections from *Outcaste: Jewish Life in Southern Iran* (New York: Routledge, 1977).

Yehuda Ratzaby, "The Expulsion of Yemenite Jewry to Mawza' in 1679–80 in Light of Recently Discovered Sources," *Zion* 37 (1972). English translation by Rivkah Fishman.

Yosef Tobi, "Conversion to Islam among Yemenite Jew under Zaydi Rule: The Positions of Zaydi Law, the Imam, and Muslim Society," *Pe'amim* (1990). English translation by Rivkah Fishman.

A. [sic] E. R. Malachi, "Palestine under the Rule of Ibrahim Pasha," *Ha-Doar* 14 (1935). English translation by Rivkah Fishman from Malachi, *Studies in the History of the Old Yishuv* (Tel Aviv: 1971).

Bat Ye'or, "The *Dhimmi* Factor in the Exodus of Jews from Arab Countries," ed. Malka H. Shulewitz (New York: Cassell, 1999).

Andrew G. Bostom, "Endowing Denial," *FrontPageMagazine.com*, May 13, 2003.

Bat Ye'or, "Modern Egyptian Jew Hatred: Indigenous Elements and Foreign Influences," in *Yehudi Mitzraim* (Jews in Egypt) (Tel Aviv: 1974). English translation from the original French by Susan Emanuel.

Johann von Leers, "Judentum und Islam als Gegensatze" (Judaism and Islam as Opposites), *Die Judenfrage in Politik, Recht, und Wirtschaft* 6, no. 24 (December 24, 1942). English translation by Steven Rendall.

Emmanuel Sivan, "Islamic Fundamentalism, Anti-semitism, and Anti-Zionism," in *Anti-Zionism and Anti-semitism in the Contemporary World*, ed. Robert Wistrich (New York: New York University Press, 1990).

Aluma Solnick, "Based on Koranic Verses, Interpretations, and Traditions, Muslim Clerics State: The Jews Are the Descendants of Apes, Pigs, and Other Animals" Middle East Media Research Institute, report #1, November 1, 2002. Reprinted by permission from the Washington-based Middle East Media Research Institute.

Andrew G. Bostom, "Jews as 'Christ-Killers' in Islam," *FrontPageMagazine.com*, March 3, 2004.

Hans-Peter Raddatz, "Antisemitism in (Contemporary) Islam: Europe in the Conflict between Tolerance and Ideology," originally published as "Antisemitismus in (Gegenwarts-)Islam: Europa em konfliltzwischen toleranz and ideologie." Reprinted by permission of the author.

Al-Tabari, "Decree of Caliph al-Mutawakkil," in *The Jews of Arab Lands: A History and Source Book*, ed. Norman Stillman (Philadelphia: Jewish Publication Society of America, 1979). Reprinted from *The Jews of Arab Lands: A History and Source Book*, © 1979 by Norman Stillman, published by the Jewish Publication Society, with the permission of the publisher.

Ibn Naqqash, from Bat Ye'or, "The Jizya's Meaning: Edict of Caliph al-Amir Bi-Ahkam Illah (1101–1130)" in *The Dhimmi: Jews and Christians under Islam* (Madison, NJ: Fairleigh Dickinson University Press, 1985). © 1985. Reprinted by permission of the Associated University Presses.

Sulaymān b. Yihya Habshūsh, *Eshkōlōt Merōrōt*, in *The Jews of Arab Lands: A History and Source Book*, ed. Norman Stillman (Philadelphia: Jewish Publication Society of America, 1979). Reprinted from *The Jews of Arab Lands: A History and Source Book*, © 1979 by Norman Stillman, published by the Jewish Publication Society, with the permission of the publisher.

Yehudah b. Obed Ibn Attar, from *Zikkaron libenei Yisrael* (In Memory of the Sons of Israel), in *A History of the Jews of North Africa, Vol. 2: From the Ottoman Conquests to the Present Time*, ed. H. Z. Hirschberg (n.p.: Brill Academic Publishers, 1997). © 1997. Reprinted by permission of the publisher.

Account of Rabbi Solomon Bekhor-Husayn, "Jews of Baghdad," in Bat Ye'or, *The Dhimmi: Jews and Christians under Islam* (Madison, NJ: Fairleigh Dickinson University Press, 1985). © 1985. Reprinted by permission of the Associated University Presses.

N. Slouschz, "Israélites de Tripolitaine," *Bulletin Alliance Israélite Universelle* (1906) in Bat Ye'or, *The Dhimmi: Jews and Christians under Islam* (Madison, NJ: Fairleigh Dickinson University Press, 1985). © 1985. Reprinted by permission of the Associated University Presses.

Y. D. Sémach, *Une mission de l'alliance au Yémen* (1910) in Bat Ye'or, *The Dhimmi: Jews and Christians under Islam* (Madison, NJ: Fairleigh Dickinson University Press, 1985). © 1985. Reprinted by permission of the Associated University Presses.

BIBLIOGRAPHY

Books, Articles and Sites Mentioned in Text, Notes, and Documents

COMPILER'S REMARKS

"Herein" refers to the present publication.

For consistency,

—most diacritics and pronunciation marks are removed from transliterated names and titles;
—in alphabetizing entries, most name prefixes (Abu, al-, de, Father, Ibn, von, etc.) are ignored;
—inconsistencies in the names and text are not necessarily reproduced in the bibliography and indices.

Often, more recent editions are included, besides those given by authors herein.

ABBREVIATIONS USED BY THE COMPILER:

an.	annotations / annotated by
ed.	editor(s) / edited by / edition
H	Muslim year
introd.	introduction
pub.	publication
trans.	translation / translator
Ar.	Arabic
Eng.	English
Fr.	French
Heb.	Hebrew
AIU	Alliance Israélite Universelle (Paris)
British Royal Archives (London)	
CO	British Colonial Office
FO	British Foreign Office
EI1, 2, 3, -S, -O	*The Encyclopedia of Islam (1st–3rd, Shorter, Online eds.)*
HUCA	*Hebrew Union College Annual*

IJMES	*International Journal of Middle Eastern Studies*
JAOS	*Journal of the American Oriental Society* (New Haven, CT)
JESHO	*Journal of the Economic and Social History of the Orient* (Leyden)
JQR	*Jewish Quarterly Review* (Jerusalem)
JQ	*Jerusalem Quarterly*
JRAS	*Journal of the Royal Asiatic Society* (London)
JSAI	*Jerusalem Studies in Arabic and Islam* (Jerusalem)
JSS	*Jewish Social Studies* (New York, 1939–1988/1993)
MEMRI	Middle East Media Research Institute (http://memri.org/archives.html, accessed October 1, 2007)
SDS	*Special Dispatch Series*
SR	*Special Report*
TVM	*TV Monitor Project Clip*
PAAJR	*Proceedings of the American Academy for Jewish Research* (New York)
REJ	*Revue des Études Juives* [Review of Jewish Studies] (Paris)
WLB	*The Wiener Library Bulletin*, New series (Vienna)
ZDMG	*Zeitschrift der Deutschen Morgenländischen Gesellschaft* [Journal, German Oriental Society] (Leipzig)

Abu. . . . *See* Dawud, Halabiya, Makki, etc.

Abd al-Basit. *Rawd al-basim.* Biblioteca Apostolica Vaticana mss. 728–29 [728 covers 844–50 H, 729 covers 865–74 H]. Vatican. Fr. trans. in Brunschvig, *Deux récits.*

Abd Allah of Granada. *Kitab al-Tibyan.* Trans. by Bernard Lewis. N.d. or p. Extracts reproduced in Stillman, *The Jews . . . Source Book*: 224–25.

Abitbol, Michel, ed. *Communautés juives des marges sahariennes du Maghreb.* Jerusalem, 1982.

Abrahamian, Roubène. *Dialectes des Israélites de Hamadan et d'Ispahan et dialecte de Baba Tahir.* Paris, 1936.

Abrahamov, B. "Al-Kasim Ibn Ibrahim's Theory of the Imamate." *Arabica* 34 (1987): 80–105.

Abribat, Jules, trans., an. *Receuil de notions de droit musulman et d'actes notariés, judiciaires et extrajudiciaires.* Tunis, 1896.

Abulfeda. *An Abridgment of the History of the Human Race, in the Form of Annals Extending from the Creation of the World to the Year 1329.* 2 vols. Constantinople, 1869. Vol. 1 (Pre-Islamic history) in Latin trans. by Fleischer, Leipzig, 1834. *See also* Wüstenfeld, *Die Geschichtschreiber.*

Adams, Isaac. *Persia by a Persian; Personal Experiences, Manners, Customs, Habits, Religious and Social Life in Persia.* Washington, DC, and Chicago, 1900. London, 1906.

Addison, L. *The Present State of the Jews.* London, 1675.

Adler [E. N.] Collection (New York): 4020, f. 30.

Adler, E. N. Article on Obadyah fragment. *REJ* 69 (1919): 129–34.

Adler, Marcus N., ed. *The Itinerary of Benjamin of Tudela; Critical Text, Translation and Commentary.* New York and London, 1907. New York, ca. 1975.

al-Afghani, Sa'id. *Ibn Hazm al-andalusi wa-risala fi-l-mufadala bayna-s-sahaba.* Damascus, 1940.

Afshari, Reza. *Human Rights in Iran: The Abuse of Cultural Relativism.* Philadelphia, 2001.

Age, The. "Howard Compares Iran to Nazi Germany." *Theage.com.au,* May 20, 2006. http://www.theage.com.au/news/world/howard-compares-iran-to-nazi-germany/2006/05/20/1147545564528.html (last accessed November 16, 2007).

Agrell, O. *Neue Reise nach Marokos.* Nuremberg, 1798.

Ahmad, Ahmad Yusuf. *Al-Sh'b al-Dalil Isra'il* [Israel—the Misled People]. Cairo, 1962. Cited in Harkabi, *Arab Attitudes*: 92.

Ibn al-Ahmar. *Rawdat al-Nisrin.* Ed. and trans. by C. Bou'ali and G. Marçais. Paris, 1917.

Ahmed b. Hanbal. *Musnad Ahmed.* Cairo, 1313 H.

Ahroni, R. "From Bustan al-uqul to Qissat Al-batul: Some Aspects of Jewish-Muslim Religious Polemics in Yemen." *HUCA* 52 (1981): 331–60.

Ajami, Fouad. "Enemies, a Love Story. A Nobel Laureate Argues that Civilizations Are Not Clashing." *Washington Post,* April 2, 2006.

al-. . . . *See* Afghan, Alawi, Azhar, etc.

al-Alawi, Ali b. Muhammad b. Ubayd Allah. *Sirat al-Hadi.* Ed. by Suhayl Zakkar. Abidin, 1972.

Albeck, Hanoch. *Sefer ha-Yovel—Albeck Jubilee Volume* (Heb.). Jerusalem, 1963.

Alexandrescu-Dersca Bulgaru, M. M. "The Roles of Slaves in Fifteenth-Century Turkish Romania." *Byzantinische Forschungen* 11 (1987): 15–22. Eng. trans. in Bostom, *The Legacy of Jihad*: 566–72.

Alexandris, Alexis. *Greek Minority of Istanbul and Greek-Turkish Relations, 1918–1974.* Athens, 1983/1992.

Algermissen, E. *Die Pentateuchzitate Ibn Hazms. Ein Beitrag zur Geschichte der arabischen Bibelübersetzungen.* Inaugural dissertation. Münster, 1933.

Ali, Abdallah Yusuf. *The Holy Qur'an. Text, Translation, and Commentary.* Reprint of the 1934 ed. Elmhurst, NY, 2001.

Ali b. Ahmad. *See under* Asin Palacios (1927).

al-Ali, Ibrahim. Series article. *Falastin Al-Muslima* (London, September 1996): 54–55.

Ali, Jawad. *Ta'riikh al-Arab qabla al-Islaam* [History of the Arabs before Islam]. 8 vols. Baghdad, 1950–59.

Alliance Israélite Universelle. *Die Allgemeine israelitische Allianz. Bericht des Central-Comites ueber ersten Funfundzwanzig Jahre 1860–1885.* 2nd ed. Berlin, 1885.

———. Archive document dated July 27, 1885. *See* in Littman, "Jews under Muslim Rule" (1975): 73–74.

———. *Bericht der Alliance Israélite Universelle (Allgemenen Israelitischen Allianz).* Reports (Paris): 1873, I, II; 1884–1885; 1887; 1888; 1889.

———. *The Alliance Israélite Universelle: Publication of the Twenty-fifth Anniversary of Its Foundation.* Paris, 1885.

———. *Bulletin de l'Alliance Israélite Universelle*: 1898, 1903, 1906.

Allouche-Regragui. *Catalogue des Manuscrits Arabes de Rabat.* N.p., 1954.

Almog, Shmuel. *Antisemitism through the Ages.* Oxford, 1988.

———. "What's in a Hyphen?" *SICSA Report* (Summer 1989). http://sicsa.huji.ac.il/hyphen.htm (accessed October 1, 2007).

Aluma, Solnick. "Based on Qur'anic Verses, Interpretations, and Traditions, Muslim Clerics State: The Jews Are the Descendants of Apes, Pigs, and Other Animals." MEMRI, SR 11 (2002). http://memri.org/bin/articles.cgi?Page=archives&Area=sr&ID=SR01102 (accessed October 1, 2007).

Amar, Abraham. Letter to A. Ribbi (Tangier, February 26, 1908) (Heb.). Trans. and transmitted to AIU, Paris (registered March 15, 1908). AIU Archives: MOROCCO IV C II.

Amar, David. Letter (Settat, August 22, 1907) to Selam Edery, Casablanca (Judeo-Arab). Trans. and transmitted by Pisa. AIU Archives: MOROCCO II C3.

Amar, Emile. "La Pierre de touches des fetwas." *Archives Marocaines* 12–13 (Paris, 1908–1909) [12: 231–65; 13: 30–36].

Amar, M., ed. *Studies on the Jews of the Maghreb in Memory of R. Shaul Ziv* (Heb.). Jerusalem, 1983.

al-Amili. *Jami-i-Abbasi* (Persian). Tehran, 1942. Eng. trans. of excerpts in Bostom, *The Legacy*: 213–15.

Amir Wahab Levi, Y. *Kadiya* (Heb.). Jerusalem, 1989.

Amstet, Abraham. Letter (Margouch, September 29, 1907) to Isaac Pisa, Casablanca (Judeo-Arab). Trans. and transmitted by Pisa to AIU Paris (registered October 8, 1907). AIU Archives: MOROCCO II C3.

Anawati, Georges. *See under* Gardet, *Introduction*.

Anderson, Sonia. *An English Consul in Turkey: Paul Rycaut at Smyrna, 1667–1678*. Oxford, 1989.

Andric, Ivo. *The Development of Spiritual Life in Bosnia under the Influence of Turkish Rule* (1924). Eng. trans. by Zelimir B. Juricic and John F. Loud. Durham, NC, 1990.

Angel, M. Report from Beirut, May 1902. AIU Archives: Liban I.C.2. In Stillman, *The Jews . . . Modern Times*: 197–98.

Angelov, Dimitar. *Les Balkans au moyen age. La Bulgarie des Bogomils aux Turcs*. London, 1978. Eng. trans. of the chapter "Certain Phases of the Conquest of the Balkan Peoples by the Turks" in Bostom, *The Legacy*: 462–517.

Anglo-Jewish Association. Reports. 1872–73; 1877–1878; 1885; 1888.

Ankawa, Abraham ben Mordecai. *Kerem hemed*. 2 vols. Ashdod, 1997.

Anonymous. *Kitab al-Maraqi (Book of Degrees)*. In Greidi, *Kitab al-Maraqi*.

——— Collection. *Dibre ha-Yamim shel Fes*. Library of the Jewish Theological Seminary of America. Fr. trans. by Vajda in his "Un recueil de texts" (1951).

Ibn Aqnin. *Tibb al-nufus* [Therapy of the Soul]. Written in Judeo-Arab. Bodleian ms Neubauer 1273 (Oxford).

Arberry, A. J. *The Koran Interpreted*. Oxford, 1964.

———. *The Koran Interpreted: A Translation*. New York, 1996.

van Arendonk, C. *Les debuts de l'imamat zaydite au Yemen*. Trans. by J. Ryckmans. Leyden, 1960.

———. "Ibn Hazm." *EI*.

Aribas Palau, Mariano. "Los comunidades Israelitas bajo los primeros sa'diés." In *Homenaje a Millás Vallicrosa*, Vol. I, Barcelona, 1954.

Arnaldez, Roger. "al-Muhasibi." *EI2*.

———. "La guerre sainte selon Ibn Hazm de Courdoue." In *Études d'Orientalism*, Vol. 2: 445–59. Eng. trans. in Bostom, *The Legacy*: 267–81.

———. Preface in Morabia, *Le Gihad* (1993).

Arnoni, M. S. *Le Nationalisme Arabe et les Nazis*. Tel Aviv, 1970.

Ibn al-Asbat. Poems. *See* Ratzaby, "The Mawza": 352.

Ashmead-Bartlett, Ellis. *The Passing of the Shereefian Empire*. London, 1910.

Ashour, Said Abdel Fattah. "Jews in the Middle Ages: Comparative Study of East and West." In Al-Azhar, *Fourth Conference*: 497–505; Green, *Arab Theologians*.

Ashtor, E. *See* Strauss.

Asia News. "Islamic Groups Impose Tax on Christian 'Subjects.'" March 19, 2007. http://www.asianews.it/index.php?l=en&art=8773&size=A# (accessed October 1, 2007).

Asin Palacios, Miguel. *La indiferencia religiosa en la Espana musulmana segun Abenhazam, historiador de las religiones y las sectas*. Madrid, 1907.

———, Ibn Hazm, and Ali b. Ahmad. *Abenhazam de Cordoba y su Historia critica de las ideas religiosas*. Madrid, 1927.

Ibn al-Asir. *Usd al-Gaba* [Lions of the Thicket]. Cairo, 1970.

Ibn Askar. *Dawhat al-nashir li-mahasin man kana bi 'l-maghrib min mashayikh al-qarn al-'ashir*. Fez, 1891/92. Eng. trans. in Hunwick, "Al-Maghili": 161. Fr. trans. in A. Graulle, *Archives Marocaines* 19 (1913): 224–25.

———. *The Sheikhs of Morocco*. Trans. by T. H. Weir. Edinburgh, 1904.

Assaf, S. *Sefer ha-Shetaroth le-Rab Hay* (Heb.). Jerusalem, 1930.

———. *Gaonica; Gaonic responsa and fragments of halachic literature from the Geniza and other sources*. Jerusalem, 1933.

———. *Texts and Studies in Jewish History* (Heb.). Jerusalem, 1946.

———, and Shmuel Glick. *Mekorot le-toldhot ha-hinukh be-Yisrael—Sources for the history of Jewish education*. Jerusalem, 2004.

Association Française pour l'Avancement des Sciences. *La Tunisie. Histoire Et Description. Agriculture, Industrie, Commerce*. 4 vols. Paris, Nancy, 1896.

Assyrian International News Agency. "Muslims Forcing Christian Assyrians in Baghdad Neighborhoods to Pay 'Protection Tax.'" March 18, 2007.

Ibn al-Atham. *Kitab al-Futuh*. 8 vols. Hyderabad, 1968–1975.

Ibn al-Athir. *Annales du Maghreb et de l'Espagne (al-Kamil fi't-tarikh)*. Trans. and an. by E. Fagnan. Alger, 1898.

Ibn Attar, Yehudah b. Obed. *Zikkaron li-benei Yisrael* [In Memory of the Sons of Israel]. In Hirschberg, *A History*, 2: 296–99.

Auron, Yair. *The Banality of Indifference*. New Brunswick, NJ, 2000.

Avi-Yonah, Michael, ed. *A History of the Holy Land*. New York, 2001.

Avizemer, S. *See under* Gamliel et al., *Yemenite Paths*.

Al-Azhar (Academy of Islamic Research). *The Fourth Conference of the Academy of Islamic Research*. Cairo, 1970. Extracts in Green, *Arab Theologians*.

———. *Al-Muntakhab fii Tafsiir al-Qur'aan al-Kariim*. 11th ed. Cairo, 1406 H (1985).

al-Azhar [Azhari], Muhammad b. Ali al-Ahdali al-Husayni al-Yamani. *Bir al-Dar al-Maknun Min Fadail al-Yaman al-Maymun*. Cairo, 1944.

Azoury, Negib. *Le Réveil de la Nation Arabe dans l'Asie Turque. En Présence des Intérêts et des Rivalités des Puissances Etrangères, de la Curie Romaine et du Patriarcat oecuménique: Partie Asiatique de la Question d'Orient et Programme de la Ligue de la Patrie Arabe*. Paris, 1905.

Azzouz, Salim. Article in *Al-Ahrar* (Egypt), May 30, 2000.

Baba, Ahmad. *Nayl al-ibithag*. Cairo, 1351 H [1932]. Copied in Maryam, *Bustan*: 288–93.

Babinger, Fr. "Khosrew, Molla." *EI3*.

Bacher, Wilhelm. "Der arab. Titel d. religionsphil. Werkes Abr. B. Dauds." *ZDMG* 42.

———. *See under* Gottheil, "Benjamin of Tudela."

Baer, I. F. *A History of the Jews in Christian Spain* (Heb.). Tel Aviv, 1945.

———, ed., et al. *Magnes Anniversary Book*. Jerusalem, 1938.

al-Baghawi, al-Baghdadi, and Nasafi. *Tafsir al-Qur'an an Jalil*. 4 vols. N.p., 1883.

———. *Mishkat Al-Masabih*. 4 vols. Eng. trans. by James Robson. Lahore, 1963. Repr. 1994.

al-Baladhuri, Ahmad b. Yahya. *Kitab Futuh al-Buldan* [Book of the Conquests of Lands]. Leyden, 1866. Trans. by Philip K. Hitti as *The Origins of the Islamic State . . . Kitab Futuh al-Buldan*, New York, 1916; repub. Piscataway, NJ, 2006.

Bali, Rifat. "Stereoytpe du Juif dans le Folklore Turc." In *Relations Entre Turcs et Juifs*, Istanbul, 2001.

Barbour, N. *Morocco*. London, 1965.

Barges, J. J. L. *Complément de l'Histoire des Beni Zeiyan*. Paris, 1887.

Barnett, Richard David, and W. M. Schwab, eds. *The Sephardi Heritage: Essays on the Historical and Cultural Contribution of the Jews of Spain and Portugal*. London, 1971.

Baron, Salo W. "The Historical Outlook of Maimonides." *PAAJR* 6 (1934–1935): 5–113.

———. *See in PAAJR* (1936): 83 and n. 164.

———. *A Social and Religious History of the Jews*. Vol. 3 of 18: *Heirs of Rome and Persia*. New York, 1957.

Barrois, A. G. *Précis d'archéologie biblique*. Paris, 1935.

Barrows, D. P. *Berbers and Blacks*. New York, 1927.

al-Basit, Abd. *Rawd al-basim*. Biblioteca Apostolica Vaticana mss. 728–29 [728 covers 844–50 H, 729 covers 865–74 H]. Vatican. Fr. trans. in Brunschvig, *Deux récits*.

Bashan, Eliezer, ed. *See under* Hirschberg. *A History of the Jews in North Africa*, vol. 2 (1981).

———. "Sabbath Observance by Jews in the Maghreb and Its Economic Effects according to Christian Travelers." In M. Amar, ed., *Studies on the Jews* (1983).

———. "Muslim Hatred of Jews in Morocco in the 19th Century (Heb.)." *Mahanaim* 1 (1992): 216–23.

———. "New Documents regarding Attacks upon Jewish Religious Observance in Morocco during the Late Nineteenth Century (Heb.)." *Pe'amim* (1995): 65–85. Herein, Eng. trans. by Rivkah Fishman.

———. "The Prohibition on Non-Muslims Entering Mosques in the Ottoman Empire as Reflected in European Sources." *Shofar* (Winter 1997): 63.

———. *Yahadut Maroko: `avarah ve-tarbutah* [Jews of Morocco]. Tel Aviv, 2000.

———. *Nashim Yehudiyot be-Maroko: demutan be-rei mikhtavim min ha-shanim 1733–1905* [Jewish women in Morocco: seen through letters from 1733–1905]. Ramat-Gan, 2005.

al-Bashir, Omar. Radio Monte Carlo broadcast, April 5, 2002. *See in* Intelligence and Terrorism, "Islamic Antisemitism."

Bat Ye'or. *Yehudi Mizraim (Jews in Egypt)*. Enlarged ed., trans. from Fr. to Heb. by Aharon Amir. Foreword by Hayyim Ze'ev Hirschberg. Tel Aviv, 1974. *See* Masriya, *Les Juifs*.

———. "Aspects of the Arab-Israeli Conflict." *WLB* 32 (1979): 68.

———. *Le Dhimmi. Profil de l'opprimé en Orient et en Afrique de Nord depuis la conquête arabe*. Paris, 1980.

———. *The Dhimmi: Jews and Christians under Islam* (Heb.). Jerusalem, 1985. 6th printing, 2003.

———. *The Dhimmi: Jews and Christians under Islam*. Trans. from Fr. by David Maisel, Paul Fenton and David Littman. Preface by Jacques Ellul. Revised and enlarged English edition. Cranbury, NJ, 1985.

———. *Ha-Dhimmim: B'nai Hasoot*. Enlarged Heb. ed. of *The Dhimmi*. Trans. by Aharon Amir, with a preface by Jacques Ellul, and an introduction by Moshe Sharon. Jerusalem, 1986.

———. "Islam and the Dhimmis: Rejoinder [to Mark Cohen, *JQ* 38 (1986): 125–37]." *JQ* 42 (1987): 85.

———. *The Decline of Eastern Christianity under Islam. From Jihad to Dhimmitude: Seventh–Twentieth Century*. Transl. from Fr. ed. of 1991 by Miriam Kochan and David Littman. Foreword by Jacques Ellul. Madison, NJ, 1996.

———. "The *Dhimmi* Factor in the Exodus of Jews from Arab Countries." In Shulewitz, ed., *The Forgotten* (1999): 41. Trans. from Fr. by Miriam Korach and David Littman. Madison/Teaneck, NJ, 2002. 2nd printing, 2003.

———. *Islam and Dhimmitude. Where Civilizations Collide*. Cranbury, NJ, 2001.

———. "Juifs et Chrétiens sous l'Islam. Dhimmitude et Marcionisme." In *Commentaire* 25, no. 97 (Spring 2002). Eng. trans., "Jews and Christians under Islam. Dhimmitude and Marcionism," at http://www.dhimmitude.org/archive/by_dhimmitude_marcionism_en.pdf (accessed October 4, 2007).

———. *Eurabia: The Euro-Arab Axis*. Madison/Teaneck, NJ, 2005.

————. *See under* Littman, "Protected Peoples" (2005).

Baumstark, A. "Das Problem eines vorislamischen christlich-kirschkichen; Schrifttums in arabischer Sprache" [A Problem of the Pre-Islamic Christian Church: Texts in the Arabic Language]. *Islamica* 4 (1931): 562–75.

Baydawi. *Commentaius in Coranum. Anwaar al-Tanziil Wa-Asraar al-Ta'wiil.* Ed. by H. O. Fleischer, 1846–48. Reprint Osnabrück, 1968.

Bayraktar, Hatrice. "The anti-Jewish Pogrom in Eastern Thrace in 1934: New Evidence for the Responsibility of the Turkish Government." *Patterns of Prejudice* 40 (2006): 95–96.

Beaumier, A. *Rawd [Roudh] al Kirtas. Histoire des Souverains du Maghreb et Annales de la Ville de Fes.* Paris, 1860. Rabbat and Paris, 1999.

Beaussier, Marcelin, and Mohammed Ben Cheneb. *Dictionnaire pratique arabe-français : contenant tous les mots employés dans l'arabe parlé en Algérie et en Tunisie, ainsi que dans le style épistolaire, les pièces usuelles et les actes judiciaires.* Alger, 1958.

Bedein, David. "A Not So Merry Christmas in the Holy Land." *FrontPageMagazine.com* (December 26, 2003). http://www.frontpagemag.com/Articles/Read .aspx? GUID={022F7397-9DF7-4C0A-8DAF-12E4 B56221F1} (accessed October 1, 2007).

Behn, Wolfgang, trans. *See under* Wellhausen, "Muhammads Gemcindcordnung;" and Wensinck, *Muhammad* (1982).

————. *Concise Biographical Companion to Index Islamicus.* 3 vols. Leyden and Boston, 2004.

Bekhor-Husayn, Solomon. *ha-Zefirah* [Letter on Jews of Baghdad]. Warsaw, 1877. Eng. tr. in Bat Ye'or, *The Dhimmi* (1985): 372–73.

Bell, Richard. *The Origin of Islam in Its Christian Environment.* London, 1926.

Ben Cheneb, M. *See under* Beaussier, *Dictionnaire pratique arabe-français* (1958).

————, ed. *See under* Maryam, *Bustan.*

Ben Naim, Joseph. *Nohag be-Hokmah.* Library of the Jewish Theological Seminary of America. N.p., n.d.

Benady, T. "The Jewish Community of Gibraltar." In Barnett and Schwab, *The Sephardic Heritage* 2: 144–79.

Benattar, César, El Habi Sebai, and Abdelaziz Ettealbi. *L'Esprit Libéral et le Coran.* Paris, 1905.

Benayahu, M., ed. *History of Fez: Misfortunes and Events of Moroccan Jewry as Recorded by Ibn Danan's Family and Descendants* (Heb.). Tel Aviv, 1993.

Benjamin, J. J. *See* Binjamin.

Benoudiz, L. Report (Marrakesh, March 30, 1912) to AIU, Paris. AIU Archives: MOROCCO II B. 9.

Ben-Sasson, M., ed., et al. *The Culture and Society of Medieval Jews: Studies Dedicated to the Memory of Haim Hillel Ben-Sasson* (Heb.). Jerusalem, 1989.

Ben-Shammai, Haggai. "The Attitude of Some Early Karaites towards Islam." In Twersky, *Studies* (1984): vol. 2.

————. "Jew-Hatred in the Islamic Tradition and Qur'anic Exegesis." In Almog, *Antisemitism* (1988): 161–69.

————, ed. *See under* Malachi, *Mi-Neged Tireh* (2001).

Bentov, H. "Jewish Artisans in Fez During The 17th and 18th Centuries (Heb.)." *Sefunot* X (1966): 414–81.

Ben-Ze'ev, Yisra'el. *Ha-Yehudim ba-'Arav.* Jerusalem, 1957.

————. *See also* Wolfson.

Ben-Zvi, Itzhak. *The Exiled and the Redeemed.* Philadelphia, 1961.

Benzimra, Rahamin. Letter (February 13, 1908) to AIU President, Paris. AIU Archives: MOROCCO.

Berge, S. *De la Juridiction Française en Tunisie.* N.p., 1895.

Bergsträsser, Gotthelf. *Grundzüge des islamischen Rechts: Bearb. u. hrsg. v. Joseph Schacht.* Berlin and Leipzig, 1935.

Berque, J. *See under* Bousquet, *Recueil de la loi musulmane.*

d'Beth Hillel, David. *The Travels of Rabbi David d'Beth Hillel: From Jerusalem, through Arabia, Koordistan, Part of Persia, and India to Madras.* Madras, 1832.

Bialoblocki, M. S. *Materialien zum islamischen und jüdischen Eherecht* [Materials for the Study of Islamic and Jewish Marriage Laws]. Giessen, 1928.

Bibliothèque nationale de France. Archive ms 5452.

Bikhazi, Ramzi Jibran, ed. *See under* Gervers, *Conversion.*

Binjamin, J. J., II. *Eight Years in Asia and Africa. From 1846 to 1855.* Hanover, 1863.

Binning, Robert B. M. *A Journal of Two Years' Travel in Persia, Ceylon, Etc.* London, 1857.

Blachère, M. R. *Le Coran.* Paris, 1957.

Blizter, Wolf. *CNN Late Edition* (July 30, 2006).

Bodansky, Yossef. *Islamic Antisemitism as a Political Instrument.* Houston, 1999.

Bodleian Library. Oxford, mss. Heb.: c 28 (2876), f. 65; d 66 (2878), f. 135; f. 56 (2821), f. 19, see in *JQR* 43 (1952): 76.

Bonar, A. A. and R. M. McCheyne. *A Narrative of a Mission of Inquiry to the Jews from the Church of Scotland in 1839.* Edinburgh, 1842.

Bostom, Andrew G. "Endowing Denial." *FrontPageMagazine.com*, May 13, 2003. http://www.front pagemag.com/Articles/Read.aspx?GUID=A30735FB -CC15-4672-B43E-D9C80A526E43 (accessed November 19, 2007).

————. "Jews as 'Christ-Killers' in Islam." *FrontPageMagazine.com*, March 3, 2004. http://www.front pagemag.com/Articles/Read.aspx?GUID=7D37FB0 D-D331-41B6-9E31-D807A55D1308 (accessed November 19, 2007)

————, ed. *The Legacy of Jihad: Islamic Holy War and the Fate of Non-Muslims.* Foreword by Ibn Warraq. Amherst, NY, 2005.

———. "The Yellow Badge of Denial." *American Thinker*, May 23, 2006. http://www.americanthinker.com/2006/05/the_yellow_badge_of_denial.html (accessed November 19, 2007).

Bosworth, C. E. "Bu'ath." *EI2*, vol. 1: 283.

———. "Christian and Jewish Dignitaries in Mamluk Egypt and Syria: Qalqashandi's Information on Their Hierarchy, Titulature, and Appointment (I)." *IJMES* 3 (1972): 65–66.

Boukhobza, Giulia. "Justice for Jews from Arab Nations." *International Herald Tribune*, July 1, 2003.

Bousquet, G. H. *Khalil ben Ish'aq, Abrégé de la Loi Musulmane selon le rite de l'Imam Malek.* Vol. 1. Alger, 1956.

———, and J. Berque. *Recueil de la loi musulmane de Zayd Ben 'Ali.* Alger, 1941.

Bowen, H. *See under* Gibb, *Islamic Society.*

Bowie, L. "An Aspect of Muslim-Jewish Relations in Late 19th Century Morocco: A European Diplomatic View." *IJMES* 7, no. 1 (January 1976): 14.

Boyd, T. W. "POLITICAL-IRAQ." Letter to HBM Embassy (1942). WHM. 29.4 PRO (London) FO 624/29/374. See facsimile in Gelber, *Tōldōt* 3: 21; and in Stillman. *The Jews . . . Modern Times*: 418.

Braude, Benjamin, and Bernard Lewis, eds. *Christians and Jews in the Ottoman Empire: The Functioning of a Plural Society.* New York, 1982.

Brauer, Erich. *Ethnologie der Jemenitischen Juden.* Heidelberg, 1934.

Brecher, G. *Das Transcendentale Magie und magische Heilarten.* Vienna, 1850.

British Royal Archives. CO 91/52.

———. FO 413/4 (March 1880).

———. FO 52/27, 28. 30, 32, 59.

———. FO 624/38/502. *Translated Extracts from "The Tragedy of 1st and 2nd June, 1941 in the Capital of Iraq"* (Ar. or Heb. original [1944] Zionist pamphlet not in file). Reproduced herein from Stillman. *The Jews . . . Modern Times*: 457–59.

———. FO 99/121 (1864), 150, 154, 170, 214 (1884), 234, 235, 240, 259, 269, 288, 302, 307 (Oct. 1893).

Brockelmann, Carl. *Geschichte der arabischen Literatur.* 2nd ed. with supplement. Leyden, 1937–49.

Browne, E. G. *A Literary History of Persia.* 4 vols. Cambridge, 1902–1924. With a new introduction by J. T. P. de Bruijn, 4 vols., Bethesda, 1997.

Browne, Mallory. "Jews in Grave Danger in All Moslem Lands." *New York Times*, May 16, 1948.

Broydé, Isaac. *See under* Jacobs, "Samuel Ha-Nagid."

———. *See under* Kohler, "Solomon ben Jeroham."

Brumlik, Micha. *Deutscher Geist und Judenhass.* Munich, 2000.

Brunot, I., and E. Malka, *Textes Judeo-Arabes de Fes.* Paris, 1939.

Brunschvig, Robert, ed. *Deux récits de voyages inédits en Afrique du Nord au XVe siécle.* Paris, 1936.

———. *La Berberie Orientale sous les Hafsides des Origines à la Fin du XV Siecle.* Paris, 1940.

Buber, Salomon. *Midrash Tanhuma . . . alHamishah Humshe Torah* (Heb.). Vilna, 1885.

al-Bukhari. *Sahih.* Eds. Krehl-Juynboll. Leyden, 1862–8; 1907–8.

———. *Al-Sahih (sometimes called Al-Jaami` al-Sahih).* 10 vols. Cairo, 1303 H [1885–86].

———. *Irsad as-sari ila sarh sahih al-Buhari.* Ed., with commentary, by al-Kastalani. Bulak, 1868.

———. *Sahih Bukhari: Translation of the meanings of Sahih al-Bukhari.* Trans. by M. Muhsin Khan. 9 vols. New Delhi, 1987.

———. *Translation of Sahih Bukhari.* Trans. M. Muhsin Khan. USC-MSA Compendium of Muslim Texts. http://www.usc.edu/dept/MSA/fundamentals/hadithsunnah/bukhari/ (accessed October 1, 2007).

Burhanuddin Ali of Marghinan. *The Hidayah or Guide: A Commentary on the Mussulman Laws.* Trans. into Eng. by Charles Hamilton. 4 vols. London, 1791. 2nd rev. ed., Kitab Bhavan, India, 1994.

Byers, David. "Report: London Mosque's DVDs Predict Mass Extermination of Jews." *European Jewish Press,* January 11, 2007.

Caetani, Leone. *Annali dell' Islam compilati de Leone Caetani, Principe de Teano.* 10 vols. Milan, 1905–26.

Cahen, Claude. "Le régime des impôts dans le Fayyum ayyubide." *Arabica* 3 (1956).

———. "Histoires Coptes." *Bull. de l'inst. français d'archéologie orientale (1960).*

———. "Djizya." *EI2.*

———. "Dhimma." *EI.*

Callwell, C. E., and Count Gleichen. *Report on Morocco* (1889). FO 99/269.

Cambridge University, Westminster College. [Geniza ms] 43.

Cambridge University Library. [Geniza mss] 1080 J 80, J 258; 1081 J 13, J 61.

———. *See also* Taylor-Schechter Collection.

Carette, E., et al. *Exploration scientifique de l'Algerie . . . Sciences historiques et geographiques.* 16 vols. Paris, 1844–53.

Carmona, E. Letter (Tetuán, June 12, 1903) to the AIU, Paris. AIU Archives: MOROCCO: I.C.1.

Carolyn, Glick. "Let's Ignore Hamas." *Jerusalem Post,* April 3, 2006. http://www.jpost.com/servlet/Satellite?cid=1143498792670&pagename=JPost%2FJPArticle%2FPrinter (accessed October 1, 2007).

Carrouges, Michel. *Foucauld: Devant l'Afrique du Nord.* Paris, 1961.

Caspi, M. *See under* Gamliel et al., *Yemenite Paths.*

———, ed. *See under* Gamliel, *The Jizyah.*

de Castries, Henri, ed. *Une description du Maroc sous le Règne du Moulay Ahmed el-Mansour (1596) d'après un manuscrit portugais de la Bibliothèque nationale : texte portugais et traduction française.* Paris, 1909.

———, et al., eds. *Les sources inédites de l'histoire du Maroc.* 22 vols. Paris, 1918–61.

Catalogue of Hebrew Manuscripts in the Collection of Elkan Nathan Adler. Cambridge, 1921.

Caussin de Perceval, A. P. *Essai sur l'histoire des Arabes avant l'islamisme, pendant l'époque de Mahomet, et jusqu'à la réduction de toutes les tribus sous la loi musulmane.* 3 vols. Paris, 1847.

Cazes, David. *Essai sur l'histoire des Israélites de Tunisie: depuis les temps les plus reculés jusqu'a l'établissement du protectorat de la France en Tunisie.* Paris, 1882.

de Cenival, P., David Lopes, and R. Ricard, eds. *Les sources inédites de l'histoire du Maroc: Archives et bibliothèques de Portugal.* 5 vols. Paris 1934–1951. A series in, de Castries, *Les sources inédites.*

Central Zionist Archives (CZA, Jerusalem). S 25/5219. "Anti-Jewish Riots in Tripolitania [Sec. 1]." Report, pp. 1–6. In Stillman, *The Jews . . . Modern Times:* 461–65.

———. S 25/6457. "Anti-Jewish Riots in Tripolitania [Sec. 2]." In de Felice, *Jews:* 193–94.

Chalom, Jacques. *Les Israelites de la Tunisie: Leur condition civile et politique.* Paris, 1908.

Chardin, John. *Voyages du chevalier Chardin, en Perse, et autres lieux de l'Orient.* Amsterdam, 1735.

Chayban, Badih. "Nasrallah Alleges 'Christian Zionist' Plot." *Daily Star,* October [23], 2002. http://web.archive.org/web/20021024133755/http://www.dailystar.com.lb/23_10_02/art5.asp (accessed October 1, 2007).

de Chénier, L. S. *The Present State of the Empire of Morocco.* London, 1788.

Chetrit, J. J. "The Personal and Socio-Historical Poetry of R. Shelomo Halewa (Meknes, the XVIIIth Century) and the Tradition of the Hebrew Poetic Discourse in Morocco (Heb.)." *Miqqedem Umiyyam* 4 (1991): 25–111.

Chetrit, N. M. *La Terreur du Rêve: Récit épique sur l'Histoire Juive—Maroc* (Heb.). Ed. by N. Yonatan. Tel Aviv, 1983.

Chew, Samuel C. *The Crescent and the Rose.* New York, 1937.

Chouraqui, Andrew. *La Condition Juridique de L'Israélite Marocain.* Paris, 1950.

Christian Science Monitor. "The Position of the Jewish Communities in Oriental Countries." March, 1946: 16–17.

A Chronicle of the Carmelites in Persia and the Papal Mission of the 17th and 18th Centuries. London, 1939.

Clark, Edward. "The Turkish Varlik Vergisi Reconsidered." *Middle East Studies* 8 (1972): 208–209.

Clenardus, Nicholas. *Correspondance.* Trans. Alphonse Roersch. 3 vols. Brussels, 1941.

Clot-Bey, A. B. *Aperçu general sur l'Egypte.* 2 vols. Paris, 1840. Excerpts trans. by Martine Chauvet in Landau, *Jews in Nineteenth-Century Egypt,* Document XII: 152–54.

CNN.com. "Two Men Convicted in Tunisia Bombing." May 10, 2006. http://www.cnn.com/2006/WORLD/europe/05/10/spain.tunisia.bombing/ (accessed October 1, 2007).

Cohen, A., E. Simon-Pikali, and O. Salama. *Jews in the Moslem Religious Court: Society, Economy and Communal Organization in the Eighteenth Century: Documents from Ottoman Jerusalem* (Heb.). Jerusalem, 1996.

Cohen, Gerson D. *See under* Ibn Daud, *A Critical Edition.*

Cohen, M. A. "Les Juifs dans l'Afrique septentrionale [Jews of Northern Africa]." *Recueil des notices de la Société archéologique de Constantine,* 1867.

Cohen, Solomon. Letter. Published in Toledano, *HUCA* 4 (1927): 449–58; and in Hirschberg, *Y. F. Baer Jubilee:* 134–53.

Colin, G. S., and E. Lévi-Provençal: *Un manuel hispanique de hisba: traité d'al-Saqati sur la surveillance des corporations et la répression des fraudes en Espagne Musulmane.* Ar. text with introduction, notes and glossary. Paris, 1931.

Conger, George. "UK MPs Find Leap in Antisemitism." *Jerusalem Post,* September 5, 2006.

Connolly, Kate. "Letter Proves Speer Knew of Holocaust Plan." *Guardian,* March 13, 2007.

Conquy, J. Annual report (Rabat, October 20, 1903) to AIU Central Committee, Paris. AIU Archives: FRANCE XIV F 25.

Cook, David. "Muslim Fears of the Year 2000." *Middle East Quarterly* 5, no. 2 (June 1998): 51–62.

Cook, Michael. *Muhammad.* Oxford, 1983, 1996.

———. "Early Islamic Dietary Law." *JSAI* 7 (1986): 223–33.

Corcos, David. *Studies in the History of the Jews of Morocco / Prof. E. Ashtor.* Jerusalem, 1976.

Cour, A. *L'établissement des dynasties des Chérifs au Maroc.* Paris, 1904.

———. "Al-Hasan Mulay, Abu-'Ali-Al Hasan b. Muhammad Sultan of Morocco." *EI2* 3: 275–76.

Crawford, J. V. *Morocco at a Glance.* Lymington, 1889.

Creswell, K. A. C. "Architecture." *EI2* 1: 609.

Cruikshank, E. F. *Morocco at the Parting of the Ways. The Story of Native Protection to 1885.* Philadelphia, 1935.

Cunningham, Phillip. *Education for Shalom: Religion Textbooks and the Enhancement of the Catholic-Jewish Relationship.* Collegeville, MN, 1995.

Curzon, G. N. *Persia and the Persian Question.* 2 vols. London, 1892. London and New York, 1966.

Cvijic, Jovan. *La Péninsule Balkanique.* Paris, 1918.

Dadrian, Vahakn. "The Role of Turkish Physicians in the World War I Genocide of Ottoman Armenians." *Holocaust and Genocide Studies* 1 (1986): 169–92, note 44.

———. *The History of the Armenian Genocide.* Providence, Rhode Island, 1995. 6th rev. ed. New York and Oxford, 2003.

————. *Warrant for Genocide*. New Brunswick and London, 2003.

al-Dahabi. *See* Husein al-Dahabi.

al-Damiri, Kamal al-Din. *Hayat Al-Hayawan "A Zoological Lexicon."* Trans. from the Ar. by Lt-Col Jayakar. 2 vols. London and Bombay, 1906–1908.

Ibn Danan, Saadia. Chronicle. *See in* Obadia, ed. *Fez and Its Sages*: 1–63.

————. *Seder ha-Doroth. See under* Edelmann, *Hemda Genuza*: 30b.

Danon, Raphael. Letter (Marrakesh, September 27, 1911) to AIU, Paris. AIU Archives: FRANCE XIV F. 25.

Darwaza, Muhammad Azzah. "The Attitude of the Jews toward Islam, Muslims, and the Prophet of Islam at the Time of His Honourable Prophethood." In Al-Azhar, *Fourth Conference*: 467–96; extracts herein from Green, *Arab Theologians*: 33–38.

Ibn Daud, Abraham. *A Critical Edition with a Translation and Notes of the Book of Tradition (Sefer ha-qabbalah)* Trans. and ed. by Gerson D. Cohen. Philadelphia, 1967.

————. *Sefer Seder ha-Kabbalah* [The Line of Tradition]. Written in 1161. For Samuel Ha-Nagid, *see* http://www.fordham.edu/halsall/source/ha-nagid.html (accessed September 27, 2007).

Davidson, J. *Notes Taken during Travels in Africa 1835–1836*. London, 1839.

Davison, Roderick. "The Armenian Crisis, 1912–1914." *American Historical Review* 53 (1948): 482–83.

————. "Turkish Attitudes concerning Christian-Muslim Equality in the Nineteenth Century." *American Historical Review* 59 (1954): 848.

Dawood, N. J. *The Koran*. Harmondsworth, UK, 1956.

Abu Dawud. *Sunan*. Cairo, 1280 H. 3 vols. New Delhi, 1997. Partial translation by Ahmad Hasan at http://www.usc.edu/dept/MSA/fundamentals/hadithsunnah/abudawud/ (accessed October 1, 2007).

Dayanim, Pooya. "Imagine Being a Jew in Iran." *Iranian,* March 12, 2003.

Denys de Tell-Mahre, *Chronique de Denys de Tell-Mahre*, Trans. from the Syriac and ed. by Jean-Baptiste Chabot. Paris, 1895. Eng. trans. in Bat Ye'or, *The Decline* (1996): 74.

Deshen, Shlomo, and Walter P. Zenner, eds. *Jewish Societies in the Middle East*. Washington, 1982.

————, and idem, eds. *Jews among Muslims, Communities in the Precolonial Middle East*. Basingstoke, 1996.

Deverdun, G. "Ibn 'Askar." *EI2*.

Diab, Zuhair, ed. *International Documents on Palestine, 1968*. Beirut, 1971.

de Dianous, P. *Notes de la Législation tunisiénne*. Paris, 1894.

al-Dibani, Abdul-Hamid Attiyah. "The Jewish Attitude towards Islam and Muslims in the Early Islam." In Al-Azhar, *Fourth Conference*: 507–26. Extracts herein from Green, *Arab Theologians*: 38–41.

Dictionnaire Beaussier. See under Beaussier.

Ibn Abu Dinar Kayrawani. *Kitâb el-mou'nis fi akhbâr ifrik'iyya wa-tounis* [The Pleasant Book about the History of Africa and Tunis(ia)]. Tunis, n.d. Fr. trans. in Carette, *Exploration scientifique de l'Algérie*.

Dinur, B. Z., ed. *Yisra'el Ba-Golah* (Heb.). Jerusalem, 1926. Tel Aviv, 1959.

Disraeli, Benjamin. *Coningsby*. London and New York, 1911. Quoted in B. Lewis, *Islam in History*: 317 n.15.

Diwân el-inchâ [inshaa' coming into being] (Ar.). Académie Française, ms no. 1573: folios 140 and 303.

al-Diyarbakri, Husayn ibn Muhammad. *Ta'rikh al-Khamis fi ahwal anfas nafis*. 2 vols. Cairo, 1302 H [1885].

Doron, Aviva, ed. *The Culture of Spanish Jewry* [The Heritage of the Jews of Spain] (Heb.). Tel Aviv, 1994.

Doukas. *Decline and Fall of Byzantium to the Ottoman Turks*. An. trans. of *Historia Turco-Byzantina* by Harry J. Magoulias. Detroit, 1975.

Doutté, Edmond, *Missions au Maroc: En Tribu*. Paris, 1914.

Dozy, Reinhardt. *Dictionnaire détaillé des noms des vêtements chez les Arabes* [Detailed dictionary of the names of Arab clothes]. Amsterdam, 1845; Beirut, [1969].

————. *Recherches sur l'histoire et la littérature de l'Espagne pendant le moyen âge* [Research on the history and literature of Spain during the Middle Ages]. 2 vols. Leyden, 1849.

————, ed. *See under* Maqqari, *Analectes* (1855).

————, and M. J. de Goeje, trs., eds. *Description de l'Afrique et de l'Espagne par Edrisi* [Description of Africa and Spain by Edrisi]. Leyden, 1866.

————. *The history of the Almohades by Abdo-'l-wahid al-Marrekoshi*. Leyden, 1881.

————. *Supplément aux dictionnaires Arabes* [Supplement to Arab dictionaries]. Leyden, 1881.

————. *Spanish Islam: A History of the Muslims in Spain*. Trans. by Francis Griffin Stokes, London, 1915. Reissued Whitefish, Mont., n.d.

————. *Histoire des Musulmans d'Espagne*. 2nd ed. of E. Lévi-Provençal. Leyden, 1932.

Dropsie College (Philadelphia). [Geniza mss] 358, 379, 392, 393, 398, 410 (loan).

Drummond-Hay, J. *Western Barbary: Its Wild Tribes and Savage Animals*. London, 1844.

————. Letter. Tangier, March 13, 1873. FO 99/154.

————, and C. Tissot. *Memorandum of Tyrannical Acts towards the Jews of Rabat and Mequinez, by the Governors of Those Towns*. Joint letter to the sultan, April 10, 1873. FO 99/154.

————. Letter, April 29, 1875. FO 99/170.

Dubnow, Simon. *Divrei Yemei Am Olam* [General History of the Jewish People]. Trans. to Heb. by Barukh Krupnik. 11 vols. Berlin and Tel Aviv, 1923-1940.

————. *History of the Jews*. Trans. from the Russian by Moshe Spiegel. 5 vols. South Brunswick, NJ, 1967.

Dufourcq, C. E. "Les Mozarabes du XIIe siècle et le prétendu 'Evêque' de Lisbonne [12th-century Mozarabs and the So-called 'Bishop' of Lisbon]." *Revue d'Histoire et de Civilisation du Maghreb* 5 (1968): 125–26.

———. *La Vie Quotidienne dans l'Europe Médiévale sous Domination Arabe.* Paris, 1978. Eng. trans. of citations herein in Bostom, *The Legacy*: 40, 56–57, 419–32.

Dumont, Paul. "Jewish Communities in Turkey during the Last Decades of the Nineteenth Century in Light of the Archives of the Alliance Israelite Universelle." In Braude and Lewis, *Christians and Jews* 1: 209–42.

Dunn, R. E. *Resistance in the Desert, Morrocan Responses to French Imperialism 1881–1912.* Madison, 1977.

Durant, Will, and Ariel Durant. *The Story of Civilization.* 7 vols. New York, 1935.

Durie, H. *Land ohne Schatten.* Leipzig, 1934.

Durie, Mark. "Isa, the Muslim Jesus." In Robert Spencer, *The Myth* (2005): 541–55.

Edelmann, Zvi Hirsch ben Mordechai. *Hemda Genuza.* N.p., 1971.

Egyptian Gazette. "The Minority Policy in Turkey." Cairo, January 4, 1946.

Egyptian National Charter. Quoted in Harkabi, *Arab Attitudes*: 71.

Ehrensvärd, Ulla, Christopher Toll, and Oscar Löfgren. *On Both Sides of Al-Mandab: Ethiopian, South-Arabic and Islamic Studies Presented to Oscar Löfgren on His Ninetieth Birthday, 13 May 1988.* Stockholm, 1989.

Elbaz, R. *Kisseh ha-Melakhim.* Sassoon Library (Letchworth, UK): no. 1007.

Elfen, Henri. Confidential memo to members of the Standing Conference of European Jewish Community Services. Geneva, August 16, 1968. AJDC (Jerusalem): 245A.13. In Stillman, *The Jews . . . Modern Times*: 550–51.

Ellingwood, F. F. *The Reaper.* N.p., 1890.

Elmaleh, Abraham. Letter (Fez, December 7, 1909) to AIU, Paris. AIU Archives.

———. Letter (Fez, April 22, 1912) to AIU President, Paris. AIU Archives: MOROCCO.

———. Report (November 22, 1912). Tangier, 1913. AIU Archives: MOROCCO.

———. Report (October 1913). AIU Archives: MOROCCO.

Elpeleg, Zvi. *The Grand Mufti Haj Amin Al-Hussaini.* Trans. by David Harvey. Portland, OR, 1993.

Emden, P. H. *Jews of Britain: A Series of Biographies.* London, 1922–43.

Encyclopedia Britannica Online. http://www.britannica.com/ (accessed October 1, 2007).

———. "Dubnow, Simon Markovich." (2007).

Encyclopedia of Islam. A Dictionary of the Geography, Ethnography and Biography of the Muhammadan Peoples. 1st ed., 9 vols. Ed. by M. Th. Houtsma, et al. Leyden, 1913–1938.

Encyclopedia of Islam. 2nd ["New"] ed. 12 vols., Indices, An Historical Atlas. Ed. by P. J. Bearman, et al. Leyden, 1960–2005.

———. 3rd ed. Leyden, 2005–.

Encyclopedia of IslamOnline. Includes all material from 2nd and 3rd eds. 2005–. http://www.brill.nl/default.aspx?partid=17&pid=27684 (accessed October 1, 2007).

Encyclopedia Judaica. Jerusalem, 1972.

Encyclopedia of Religion and Ethics. Ed. by J. Hastings, et al. 13 vols. New York and Edinburgh, 1908–27.

Engelhardt, Edouard. *La Turquie et La Tanzimat.* 2 vols. Paris, 1882.

Etudes d'orientalisme dédiées à la mémoire de Levi-Provençal. 2 vols. Paris, 1962.

Even Tsur, J., *Mishpat ve-Tsedek be-Ya'akov* (Heb.). N.p., 1894–1903.

Ibn Ezra, Abraham. *Ahah Yarad Al Sefarad* [Poem: "O, there descended . . . "]. *See in* Hirschberg, *A History.*

Faber, Klaus, Julius H. Schoeps, and Sacha Stawski. *Neu-alter Judenhass: Antisemitismus, arabisch-israelischer Konflikt und europaïsche Politik.* Berlin, 2006.

Fagnan, Edmond. "Le signe distinctif des Juifs au Maghreb" [The Distinctive Sign of the Jews in the Maghreb]. *REJ* 28 (1894): 294–98. Herein, trans. by Michael J. Miller.

———. *Concordance du Manuel de Droit de Sidi Khalil.* Alger, 1889.

———, trans., an. *See under* Ibn al Athir, *Annales du Maghreb et de l'Espagne* (1898).

———, trans., an. *See under* Idhari, *Histoire de l'Afrique et de l'Espagne* (1901–1904).

———, trans. *See under* Mawardi, *Les statuts gouvernementaux* (1915).

———, trans. *See under* Ya'qub, *Le livre de l'impôt foncier* (1921).

———. *Additions aux Dictionnaires Arabes.* Alger, 1923; Beirut, 1974?.

Ha-Farhi, Eshtori. *Caftor wa-pherach.* Ed. by A. Edelmann. Berlin, 1852.

Fathi, Nazila. "Iran's President Says Israel Must Be Wiped Off the Map." *New Tork Times.com*, October 26, 2005.

Fattal, Antoine, *Le statut legal des non-musulmans en pays d'Islam.* Beirut, 1958.

Fayyumi, Nathaniel Berav. *Sefer Bustan al-'Uqul (Gan Ha-Sekhalim)* 2. Introd., trans. to Heb., and ed. by Y. Qafih. Jerusalem, 1984.

de Felice, Renzo. *Jews in an Arab Land: Libya, 1835–1970.* Trans. from Italian by Judith Roumani. Austin, 1985.

Feuerstein, Salomon. *Der Commentar des Karäers Salmon ben Jerucham zu den Klageliedern: Zum ersten Male nach der Pariser Handschrift edirt.* Krakau, 1898. Eng. trans. by Ben-Shammai, "The Attitude."

Finkel, Joshua, trans. "A Risala of Al-Jahiz." *JAOS* 47 (1927): 311–34.

Fischel, W. J. *Jews in the Economic and Political Life of Medieval Islam.* London, 1937.

———. *The Jews of Kurdistan a Hundred Years Ago.* New York, 1944. Reprinted from *JSS* 6, 3: 223.

———. "Secret Jews of Persia." *Commentary* (January 1949): 29.

———. "The Jews of Persia, 1795–1940." *JSS* 12 (1950): 121.

———. "Isfahan—The Story of a Jewish Community in Persia." In Starr, *Joshua Starr* (1953): 122–23.

———. "The Jews in Medieval Iran from the 16th to the 18th Centuries: Political, Economic, and Communal Aspects." *Irano-Judaica* (Jerusalem, 1982): 266.

Fishman, Joel. "The Big Lie and the Media War against Israel: From Inversion of the Truth to Inversion of Reality." *Jerusalem Center for Public Affairs*, July 29, 2007. http://www.jcpa.org/JCPA/Templates/Show-Page.asp?DBID=1&TMID=111&LNGID=1&FID=388&PID=0&IID=1704 (accessed October 4, 2007).

Fleischer, H. O., ed. *See under* al-Baydawi, *Commentaius in Coranum.*

Fletcher, Richard. *Moorish Spain.* Berkeley, CA, 1993.

de Foucauld, Charles. *Reconnaissance au Maroc 1883–84.* Paris, 1888. Paris, 1939.

Franco, M. *See under* Jacobs, "Joseph Ben Isaac Sambari."

Frankfurter Illustrierte, August 25, 1957. Cited in Bat Ye'or. *Eurabia*: 328, note 9.

Fraser, James B. *Narrative of a Journey into Khorasan in the Years 1821 and 1822.* London, 1825.

Friedländer, Israel. "Zur Komposition von Ibn Hazm's Milal wa'n-Nihal." In *Orientalische Studien Th. Nöldeke gewidmet* I, Giessen, 1906: 267.

———. "Ibn Saba." *Zeitschr. F. Assyr.* 23 (1909).

Friedlander, Saul. *L'Antisémitisme Nazi: Histoire d'une psychose collective* [Nazi antisemitism: History of a collective psychosis]. Paris, 1971.

Friedman, Matti. "Khaled Abdelwahhab of Tunisia First Arab Nominated for the 'Righteous among Nations' Holocaust Honor." *Associated Press*, January 30, 2007.

Friedman, Saul S. *Without Future. The Plight of Syrian Jewry.* New York, 1989.

Friedmann, Yohanan. *Shaykh Ahmad Sirhindi: An Outline of His Thought and a Study of His Image in the Eyes of Posterity.* Montreal, 1971.

Fritsch, Erdmann. *Islam und Christentum im Mittelalter; Beitrage zur Geschichte der muslimischen Polemik gegen das Christentum in arabischer Sprache.* Breslauer Studien zur historischen Theologie, Bd. 17. Breslau, 1930.

FrontPageMagazine.com. "The Islamic Genocide Plan." December 1, 2006.

Fück, J. W. "Ibn Sa'd, Abu 'Abd Allah Muhammad b. Sa'd b. Mani c al-Basri al-Hashimi Katib al-Wakidi." *EI.*

al-Fudayl, Yahya Abd al-Karim, ed. *See under* al-Sa'di, *Durar al-Ahadith.*

Gabbay, Rony E. *A Political Study of the Arab-Jewish Conflict. The Arab Refugee Problem (A Case Study).* Études d'Histoire Economique, Politique et Sociale sous la Direction de Jacques Freymond et Jaques L'Huillier, 29. Geneva, 1959.

Gairdner, W. H. T. "Muhammad without Camouflage." *Moslem World* 9 (1919): 36.

Galeb, Adham Mustafa. Letter published in *Akhir Sa'a* (1948). Fr. trans. in *La Bourse egyptienne,* July 22, 1948. Cited in Masriya, *Les Juifs*: 54. Eng. trans. in Meron, "The Expulsion": 92.

Gamliel, S. *The Jizyah—Poll Tax in Yemen* (Heb.). Ed. by M. M. Caspi. Jerusalem, 1982.

———, M. Caspi, and S. Avizemer, eds. *Yemenite Paths.* Jerusalem, 1984.

———. *Ha-Yehudim ve-Ha-Melech be-Teman* (Heb.), 1–2. Jerusalem, 1986–1987.

Gamlieli, N. B. *Teman u-Mahane Geulah.* Tel Aviv, 1966.

———. "The Arabs amongst Whom the Yemenite Jews Lived: Islamic Sects, Their Inter-Relationships and Relations with the Jews (Heb.)." In Yesha'yahu and Tobi, *The Jews of Yemen* (1975): 47–69.

———. *Hevion Teman: From the Depth of Yemen: Memories, Folktales and Legends* (Heb.). Ramla, 1983.

Gams, Bonifacus. *Series Episcoporum Ecclesiæ Catholicæ.* Ratisbonæ, 1873.

Garcia Gómez, E. *Polemica religiosa entre Ibn Hazm e Ibn al-Nagrila. al-Andalus,* 4. N.p., 1936.

———. *Un alfaqui español Abu Ishaq de Elvira.* Madrid and Granada, 1944.

Garcia-Arenal, M. "Jewish Converts to Islam in the Muslim West." *Israel Oriental Studies* 17 (1997): 239.

Gardet, L., and G. Anawati. *Introduction à la théologie musulmane.* Paris, 1948.

Gardner, W. R. W. "Jihad." *Moslem World* 2 (1912): 347–57. Reprod. in Bostom, *The Legacy*: 293–300.

Gaskell, G. *Algeria as It Is.* London, 1875.

Gatje, Helmut. *The Qur'an and Its Exegesis.* Berkeley, CA, 1976.

Gaudefroy-Demombynes, M. "Marocain Mellah." *Journal Asiatique* 3 (1914): 651.

Gedaliah of Siemiatyce. *Sha'alu Shelom Yerushalayim (Pray for the Peace of Jerusalem).* Berlin, 1716. Eng. trans. in Bat Ye'or, *Decline*: 377–80.

Geiger, A. *Was hat Mohammad aus dem Judenthume aufgenommen* [What did Muhammad borrow from Judaism]. Bonn, 1833. For Eng. trans., *see under* Perlmann, *Judaism and Islam* (1970).

Gelber, Yoav. *Tōldōt ha-Hitnaddevūt.* Vol. 3: *Nōs'é ha-Degel.* Jerusalem, 1983.

Gerber, Jane S. "The Pact of Umar in North Africa: A Reappraisal of Muslim-Jewish Relations." In *Proceedings* (1974): 40–50.

———. *Jewish Society in Fez 1450–1700: Studies in*

Communal and Economic Life. Ann Arbor, 1975. Leyden, 1980.

———. *The Jews of Spain: A History of the Sephardic Experience.* New York, 1992.

———. "The Jews of North Africa and the Middle East." In Wertheimer, *The Modern* (1993).

———. "Towards an Understanding of the Term: 'The Golden Age' as an Historical Reality." In Doron, *The Heritage* (1994): 15.

———, ed. *Sephardic Studies in the University.* Cranbury, NJ, and London, 1995.

Gervers, Michael, and Ramzi Jibran Bikhazi, eds. *Conversion and Continuity: Indigenous Christian Communities in Islamic Lands, Eighth to Eighteenth Centuries.* Toronto, 1990.

Ghali, Ibrahim Amin. *L'Egypte et les Juifs dans l'antiquité.* Paris, 1969.

———. *L'Orient Chrétien et les Juifs (70–632).* Paris, 1970.

Ghallab, Said. "Les juifs sont en enfer." *Temps Modernes* 277 (1965): 2247. Eng. trans. in Spencer, *The Myth*: 95.

al-Ghazali. *Kitab al-Wagiz fi fiqh madhab al-imam al-Safi'i.* Beirut, 1979. Excerpts in Bostom, *Legacy*: 199.

Gibb, H. A. R., and H. Bowen, *Islamic Society and the West.* Vol. 1, parts I/II. London, 1950/1957.

Gidney, W. T. *At Home and Abroad: A Description of the English and Continental Missions of the London Society for Promoting Christianity amongst the Jews.* London, 1900.

Gil, Moshe. "The Constitution of Medina: A Reconsideration." *Israel Oriental Studies* 4 (1974): 64–65.

———. "Dhimmi Donations and Foundations for Jerusalem (638–1099)." *JESHO* 37 (1984): 166–67.

———. *A History of Palestine, 634–1099.* Trans. by Ethel Broido. Cambridge and New York, 1992.

Gilbert, Martin. *The Jews of Arab Lands. Their History in Maps.* London, 1976.

Ginsberg, Louis. "Capsali." http://www.jewishencyclopedia.com/view.jsp?artid=132&letter=C (accessed October 1, 2007).

Ginsbury, N. *See under* Goitein, "Jerusalem in the Arab Period" (1982).

El Glaoui, Si Madani Elmezouar. Letter (Marrakesh, October 26, 1908) to Narcisse Leven, AIU President. AIU Archives.

Gleichen, Count. *See under* Callwell.

Godard, Leon N. *Description et histoire du Maroc.* Paris, 1860.

de Goeje, M. J., trans., ed. *See under* Dozy, *Description de l'Afrique* (1866).

———, ed. *See under* Tabari, *Ta'rikh al-Rusul* (1879).

———, ed. *See under* Tabari, *Selections* (1902).

Goitein, S. D. "An Arabic-Hebrew Book on a Tour in Yemen in 1870 (Heb.)" In Baer, *Magnes* (1938): 89.

———, trans., ed. *See under* Hibshush, *Travels in Yemen* (1939).

———. "Ibn 'Ubayya's Book on the Destruction of the Synagogue of the Jews in Jerusalem in 1474 (Heb.)." *Zion* 13–14 (1948–49): 18–32.

———. *Jews and Arabs: Their Contacts through the Ages.* New York, 1955.

———. "Readings in Mediterranean Social History." *JESHO* 5 (1957): 278.

———. "The Main Industries of the Mediterranean Area as Reflected in the Records of the Cairo Geniza." *JESHO* 4 (1961): 168.

———. *Jewish Education in Muslim Countries.* Jerusalem, 1962.

———. "Evidence on the Muslim Poll Tax from Non-Muslim Sources: A Geniza Study." *JESHO* 6, no. 3 (December 1963): 278–95.

———. "The Social Services of the Jewish Community." *JSS* 26 (1964).

———. *Jews and Arabs.* New York, 1967.

———. *A Mediterranean Society: The Jewish Communities of the Arab World as Portrayed in the Documents of the Cairo Geniza.* 6 vols. Vols. 1–3. Berkeley, CA, 1967–1978; 6 vols., London, 1967–1993.

———, ed. *See under* Mann, *The Jews in Egypt* (1970).

———. "Minority Self-Rule and Government Control in Islam." *Studia Islamica* 31 (1970): 101, 104–06.

———. "Origin and Significance of North African Jewry." In *Proceedings* (1974): 12.

———, ed. *Religion in a Religious Age.* Cambridge, MA, 1974.

———. "Yemenite Jewry and the India Trade (Heb.)." In Yesha'yahu and Tobi: *The Jews* (1975): 47–69.

———, and N. Ginsbury. "Jerusalem in the Arab Period (638–1099)." *Jerusalem Cathdera* 2 (1982): 170.

———. *The Yemenites: History, Communal Organization, Spiritual Life: Selected Studies* (Heb.). Jerusalem, 1983.

———. "Jewish Elements in the K. Ansab al-Asraf de Baladuri (Heb.)." *Siyôn*, 1: 75–81.

Gökalp, Ziya. *The Principles of Turkism.* Trans. and edited by R. Devereux. Leyden, 1968.

Goldberg, Harvey E., ed., trans., an. *The Book of Mordechai: A Study of the Jews of Libya—Selections from the "Highid Mordekhai" of Mordechai Hakohen.* Philadelphia, 1980. London, 1993.

Goldberg, Jeffrey. "A Reporter at Large: In the Party of God, Part I." *New Yorker*, October 14, 2002. http://www.jeffreygoldberg.net/articles/tny/a_reporter_at_large_in_the_par.php (accessed October 1, 2007).

Goldhagen, D. J. *Hitler's Willing Executioners—Ordinary Germans and the Holocaust.* New York, 1996.

———. "Iran Bares 'Genocidal Intent.'" *New York Sun*, November 3, 2005.

———. "The New Threat—The Radical Politics of Islamic Fundamentalism." *New Republic Online.* March 13, 2006.

Goldziher [Goldhizer], Ignac. "Arabische Aeußerungen über Gebräuche der Juden beim Gebet und Studium." *MGWJ* 4 (1871): 178–83.

———. "Proben Muhammedanischer Polemik Gegen den Talmud." In Kobak, *Jeschurun* 8 (1873).

———. "Über jüdische Sitten und Gebräuche aus muhammedanischen Schriften." *MGWJ* 8 (1880): 355–65.

———. *Die Zâhiriten, Ihr Lehrsystem und Ihre Geschichte.* Leipzig, 1884.

———. "Materialien zur Kenntnis der Almohadenbewegung in Nord-afrika." *ZDMG* 41 (1887): 30–140.

———. "Le Dénombrement des Sectes Mohamétanes." *Rev. de l'Histoire des Religions* 26 (1892): 129–37.

———. *Die Sabbathinstitution im Islam (Gedenkbuch . . . Kaufmann).* Breslau, 1900.

———. *Translation of the Chapter on Hadith and the New Testament from Muhammadanische Studien, Vol. II.* London, 1902.

———. "Kämpfe um die Stelhung des Hadit im Islam." *ZDMG* 61 (1907): 860–72.

———. *Vorlesungen über den Islam.* Heidelberg, 1910; 1925.

———. *Muslim Studies.* 2 vols. Trans. by C. R. Barber and S. M. Stern. London, 1967–1971.

———. *Die Richtungen der islamischen Koranauslegung, an der Universitaet Upsala gehaltene Olaus-Petri-Vorlesungen von Ignaz Goldziher.* 2nd photomechanical reprint. Leyden, 1970.

———. *Tagebuch.* Ed. by Alexander Scheiber. Leyden, 1978.

———. *Introduction to Islamic Theology and Law.* Princeton, NJ, 1981.

———. "'ahd 'Omar."

———. "*Milal Literature.*" *ZDMG* 65: 349.

Goodenough, Stan. "Nazis, Arabs Planned Final Solution for Pre-state Israel." *Jerusalem Newswire,* April 10, 2006.

Gottheil, Richard, ed. *See under* al-Wasiti, "An Answer to the Dhimmis," and *Kitab Radd* (1921).

———, and Wilhelm Bacher. "Benjamin of Tudela." JewishEncyclopedia.com. http://www.jewish encyclopedia.com/view.jsp?artid=754&letter=B (accessed October 1, 2007).

———, and Joseph Jacobs. "The Crusades." Jewish Encyclopedia.com. http://www.jewishencyclopedia .com/view_friendly.jsp?artid=908&letter=C (accessed October 1, 2007).

———, and Meyer Kayserling. "Cordova." Jewish Encyclopedia.com. http://www.jewishencyclopedia .com/view.jsp?artid=771&letter=C (accessed October 1, 2007).

———, and Meyer Kayserling. "Ephraim B. Gershon." JewishEncyclopedia.com. http://www.jewish ency-clopedia.com/view.jsp?artid=407&letter=E (accessed October 1, 2007).

Graetz, Heinrich. *History of the Jews from the Earliest Times to the Present Day.* 5 vols; ed. and in part trans. by Bella Löwy. London, 1891–92. Philadelphia, 1891–1898.

———. *Geschichte der Juden: von den ältesten Zeiten bis zur Mitte des 19. Jahrhunderts.* Berlin, 2004 [Electronic Resource].

Grandquist, H. *Marriage Conditions in a Palestinian Village,* II. Helsingfors, 1935.

Grant, A. *The Nestorians.* New York, 1841.

Graulle, A. *See under* Askar, *Da'wat al-nasir.*

Gray, John. "The Jewish Inscriptions in Greek and Hebrew at Tocra, Cyrene and Barce." In *Cyrenaican Expedition of the University of Manchester, 1952, . . .* Manchester, UK, 1956: 43–59; with map, plates, plans.

Green, D. F. [compound pseudonym for D. G. Littman and Y. Harkabi]. *Arab Theologians on Jews and Israel. Extracts from the Proceedings of the Fourth Conference of the Academy of Islamic Research (1968).* Geneva, 1971; 1976. Published in French as, idem, *Les Juifs et Israël vus par les Théologiens arabes.* Geneva, 1972.

Greenberg, Harold. *See under* Sedar.

Greenstone, Julius. "The Turcoman Defeat at Cairo." *American Journal of Semitic Languages and Literatures* 22 (1906): 144–75.

Greidi, S. "Kavim le-Toledot Yehude Teman be-Meah ha-Shemoneh Esreh." In Yesha'yahu and Greidi, *Mi-Teman* (1938): 106–38.

———, ed. *Kitab al-Maraqi.* In Nahum, *Revelation of Yemenite Treasures* (1971): 288–321.

Grohmann, Avraham. *Die Arabischen Papyri aus der Giessener Universitaetsbibliotbek.* Giessen, 1960.

———. "The Economic and Social Background of Hostile Attitudes toward the Jews in the Ninth- and Tenth-Century Muslim Caliphate." In Almog, *Antisemitism* (1988): 178.

Grosvenor, Elizabeth Mary. *Narrative of a Yacht Voyage in the Mediterranean during the Years 1840–1841.* London, 1842.

Grunberger, Béla, and Pierre Dessuant. *Narzissmus, Christentum, Antisemitismus: eine psychoanalytische Untersuchung.* Stuttgart, 2000.

von Grunebaum, G. *Medieval Islam.* Chicago, 1946.

Guenzburg, M. A. *Devir* (Heb.). Vilna, 1865.

Guidi, I. *Il Muhtasar o Sommario del Diritto Malechita . . . 1.* Milan, 1919.

Guillaume, A., trans. *The Life of Muhammad, A Translation of Ishaq's "Sirat Rasul Allah."* Karachi and London, 1955. Karachi, 2003. New Delhi, 2004.

Gulf News. [Abu Dhabi symposium *The Jews in the Arab World* at the Zayed Center] June 20, 2002.

Gutman, Roy. "Training in Terror." *Newsweek,* October 26, 2001. http://www.msnbc.msn.com/id/3067505/ site/newsweek/from/RL.2/ (accessed October 1, 2007).

Gwarzo, H. I. "The Life and Teachings of al-Maghili with Particular Reference to the Saharan Jewish Community." Unpubl. doctoral diss., University of London, 1972. (Microfilm copy, 1985).

Ha- . . . . *See* Farhi, Kohen, Levi.

Haaretz. "Moroccan Jews Ask Court to Try Amir Peretz for War Crimes." August 3, 2006.

Habshush, Sulayman. *Eshkolot Merurot (Bitter Clusters of Grapes).* Ed. by S. D. Goitein. *Kovetz al Yad* 2, no. 12 (1938): 25.

———. *Eshkōlōtt Merōrōt* (Ar.). In Goitein, *The Yemenites* (1983): 190–91, reprod. from Stillman, *The Jews . . . Modern Times*: 225–26.

Hacker, Joseph. "Ottoman Policy toward the Jews and Jewish Attitudes toward the Ottomans during the Fifteenth Century." In Braude and Lewis, *Christians* (1982): 117–26.

———. "The Sürgün System and Jewish Society in the Ottoman Empire during the 15th–17th Centuries (Heb.)." *Zion* 55 (1990): 27–82. Republished in Eng. trans. in Rodrigue, ed., *Ottoman*: 1–65.

al-Hadi. *See* al-Haqq.

Haim, Sylvia. "Islam and the Theory of Arab Nationalism." *Die Welt Des Islams* 2 (1955): 124–49.

———. *Arab Nationalism—An Anthology.* Berkeley, CA, 1962.

———, ed. *See under* Kedourie, *Zionism and Arabism* (1982).

Abu Halabiya, Ahmad. "Murder of Jews Is Allah's Will." Palestinian Authority TV, October 13, 2000. http://pmw.org.il/asx/PMW_Halabiya_kill_7.asx (accessed October 1, 2007).

Halevi, R. "Sippur ha-Ikar Hibbur Abba Shalem Shabbazi." *Afikim* 79 (1989): 12–13.

Halevi, Sa'adiah. "Chronicle of 1669." In Tobi, *Studies*: 123–24.

Halil. *Muhtasar* (Ar.). Paris, 1900. Italian trans. by Guidi, *Il Muhtasar*: 412–19. Fr. trans. by Bousquet, *Khalil*: 215–16.

Halkin, Abraham. See in *Marx Jubilee Volume* (1950): 389.

———, ed. *See under* Maimonides, *Iggeret* (1952).

Hallevi, Judah. *Kitab al Khazari.* Trans. Hartwig Hirschfeld. New York, 1905.

Hamas. "Charter of Allah: The Platform of the Islamic Resistance Movement." August 18, 1988. http://www.palestinecenter.org/cpap/documents/charter.html (accessed October 1, 2007). See also http://www.yale.edu/lawweb/avalon/mideast/hamas.htm (accessed October 1, 2007).

———. *The Charter of Hamas.* http://64.233.161.104/search?q=cache:T-e99pjS9VoJ:www.palestinecenter.org/cpap/documents/charter.html+ (accessed October 1, 2007).

Hamdani, Muhammad ibn Hatim. *A Critical Edition of Kitab al-Simt al-ghali al-thaman fi akhbar al-muluk min al-Dhuzz bi-al-Yaman* (Ar.). Ed. by G. R. Smith. London, 1974–78.

Hannaghid, Shemuel. *See under* Sassoon, *Diwan.*

al-Haqq, Yahya al-Hadi Ila. *Kitab al-Ahkam* [The Book of Laws]. San'a, 1990.

Harkabi, Yehoshafat. *The Arabs Position in Their Conflict with Israel* (Heb.). Tel Aviv, 1968.

———. *Arab Attitudes to Israel.* Trans. by Misha Louvish. Jerusalem, 1972.

———. *Palestinians and Israel.* New York, 1975.

———. *Israel's Fateful Hour.* New York, 1989.

———, and David G. Littman. *See* Green, D. F. (pseud.).

Harkavy, A. *Berliner-Festschrift,* Frankfurt a. M., 1903.

Harris, W. B. *Morocco That Was.* London, 1921.

Hassan b. Thabit, *The Diwan of Hassan b. Thabit (ob. A.H. 54)* (Ar.). Leyden and London, 1910.

Hassan, J. "The Treaty of Utrecht 1713 and the Jews of Gibraltar." *Transactions (Jewish Historical Society of England)* 7 (1970): 1–16.

Hathaway, Jane. "The Grand Vizier and the False Messiah: The Sabbatai Sevi Controversy and the Ottoman Reform in Egypt." *JAOS* 117 (1997): 665–71.

Al-Hayat Al-Jadida. Sermon, May 18, 2001.

Hayek, Michel. "Nouvelles approches de l'islam." Lecture, March 6, 1967. *Les Conférences du Cénacle* 22, nos. 9–10. Beirut, 1968.

Hayyim, Hafetz. *Hafetz Hayyim—Shire Rabbenu Shalom Shabazi . . . u-Meshorere Teman.* Jerusalem, 1966.

Ibn Hazm. *Izhar tabdil alyahud wa-n-nasara li-t-taurat wa-l-injil.* In idem, *K. al-Fisal* 1. Quotations herein trans. in vols. 2–5 of Palacios, *Abenházam.*

———. *K. al-Fisal (al-fasl) fi-l-milal wa-l-ahwa' wa-n-nihal.* 5 vols. Cairo, 1317–21 H.

———. *Ta'rikh Yusifus al-Yahudi.* Beirut, 1872.

Hebraeus. *The Chronography of Bar Hebraeus.* Trans. by E. A. W. Budge. London, 1932.

Helfritz, H. *Land ohne Schatten.* Leipzig, 1934.

Herf, Jeffrey. *The Jewish Enemy—Nazi Propaganda during World War II and the Holocaust.* Cambridge, MA, 2006.

Herr, Friedrich. "The Catholic Church and the Jews Today." *Midstream* (May 1971): 22.

Hezbollah. "Nass al-Risala al-Maftuha allati wajahaha Hizballah ila-l-Mustad'afin fi Lubnan wa-l-Alam" [An open letter: The Hizballah program . . . to all the oppressed in Lebanon and the world]. *al-Safir* (Beirut) February 16, 1985. Abridged citation in *JQ* 48 (Fall 1988). http://www.standwithus.com/pdfs/flyers/hezbollah_program.pdf (accessed October 1, 2007).

———. 1992 statement, cited in *New York Sun,* "Nasrallah's Nonsense." *See also* Chayban, Badih, "Nasrallah Alleges."

al-Hibshi, Ayn. *Thabt bi-Muallafat al-Allamah Muhammad b. Ali al-Shawkani.* N.p., n.d.

Hibshush, H. *Travels in Yemen [Joseph Halevy's Journey to Najran in the Year 1870 as Related by Hayyim Hibshush's Original Judaeo-Arabic Text and Trans. into Heb.].* Trans., and ed., S. D. Goitein. Tel Aviv, 1939.

———. "Hayyim Hibshush's 'History of the Jews in

Yemen' (Heb.)." Ed. by J. Qafih. *Sefunot* 2 (1958): 246–86.

Higger, M. "The Formation of the Child." *Gaster Anniversary Volume* (1936): 250–59.

Hilberg, Raul. "The Goldhagen Phenomenon." *Critical Inquiry* 23 (1997): 721–28.

———. *The Destruction of the European Jews*. 3rd ed. New Haven, CT, 2003.

Hirsch, Emil G., M. Selighson, and Solomon Schechter. "Machpelah." JewishEncyclopedia.com. http://www.jewishencyclopedia.com/view.jsp?artid=29&letter=M (accessed October 1, 2007).

Hirschberg, Haim Z., trans. *Der Diwan des as-Samaui ibn Adija und die unter seinem Namen Gedichtefragmente*. Crakow, 1931.

———. *Judisches und Christliches im Vorislamischen Altertum; Ein Beitrg zur Entstehungeschichte des Islams*. Crakow, 1939.

———. "The 'Mellah' and the 'Masos' and the Jewish Quarter in Morocco" (Heb.). *Eretz Israel* 4 (1957): 226–30.

———. *Land of the Setting Sun* (Heb.). Jerusalem, 1957.

———. *Toledot ha-Yehudim be-Afrika ha-sefonit* (Heb.). 2 vols. Jerusalem, 1965.

———. *A History of the Jews of North Africa*. Vol. 1. Leyden, 1974.

———, with Eliezer Bashan, and Robert Attal, eds. *History of the Jews in North Africa. Volume 2, From the Ottoman Conquests to the Present Time*. Leyden, 1981.

Hirschfeld, Hartwig. *Jüdische Elemente im Koran. Ein beitrag zur Koranforschung*. Berlin, 1878.

———. "Essai sur l'histoire des Juifs de Medine [The History of the Jews of Medina]." *REJ* 7 (1883): 167–93; 10 (1885): 10–31.

———. "Historical and Legendary Controversies between Muhammed and the Rabbis." *JQR* 10 (1898).

———. "Mohammedan Criticism of the Bible." *JQR* 13, no. 2 (January 1901): 222–40.

———. *New Researches into the Composition and Exegesis of the Quran*. London, 1902.

———. "The Arabic Portion of the Cairo Genizah at Cambridge." *JQR* 15 (1905): 170–74.

———, trans. *See under* Hallevi, *Kitab al Khazari* (1905).

———. "The Annals of Islam." *JQR* 20 (1908): 876.

———. "Abdallah Ibn Saba." JewishEncyclopedia.com. http://www.jewishencyclopedia.com/view.jsp?artid=189&letter=A (accessed October 1, 2007).

Hirszowicz, Lukasz. *The Third Reich and the Arab East*. London, 1966.

Ibn Hisham. *al-Sira al-Nabawiyya*. 2 vols. Cairo, 1955. Eng. trans. and an. in Stillman, *The Jews . . . Source Book*. See also Guillaume, *The Life of Muhammad*.

———. *Siira*. Al-Halabi Publishers. N.p., 1955.

———. *Sirat Rasul Allah: das Leben Muhammed's*. Compiled by F. Wüstenfeld. Frankfurt a.M., n.d.

Hitler, Adolf. *Mein Kampf*. http://www.crusader.net/texts/mk/ (accessed October 1, 2007).

Hitti, Philip K., trans. *See under* al-Baladhuri, *The Origins of the Islamic State*.

Hobbalah, Mahmoud. Speech at Fourth Conference, Al-Azhar, 1969. In Al-Azhar, *Fourth Conference*; extracts herein from Green, *Arab Theologians*: 18.

Hodgson, M. G. S. "'Abd Allah B. Saba." *EI2* 1.

Hoest, G. *Nachrichten von Marokos und Fes, Im Lande selbst gesammelt in den Jahren 1760 Bis 1768, aus dem daenischen uebersetzt*. Kopenhagen, 1781.

Holladay, Roy. "Where Are We in Prophecy." August 12, 2006. http://www.ucg.org/sermons/transcripts/200608 prophecy.htm (accessed October 1, 2007).

Hopkins, J. F. P. *Medieval Muslim Government in Barbary until the Sixth Century of the Hijra*. London, 1958.

———. "Ibn Tumart." *EI2*.

Hornstein, Shaul. *Giv'at Shaul* [The Hill of Saul]. Vienna, 1893.

Horovitz, Josef. Ms. Frankfurt, publ. in *Zeitschrift f. Hebr. Bibliogr.* 4 (1900): 155–58.

———. *Koranische Untersuchungen*. Berlin, 1926.

———. "Wahb B. Munabbih." *EI1* 4: 1084–85

Horovitz, S. *Sifre zuta—Der Sifre Sutta, nach dem Jalkut und anderen Quellen*. Breslau, 1910.

Houdas, O. *See under* Ufrani, *Nuzhat*.

Huici-Miranda, A. "Ibn Habib, Abu Marwan 'Abd al-Malik b. Habib al-Sulami." *EI3*.

Hunwick, John O. "Al-Maghili and the Jews of Tuwat: The Demise of a Community." *Studia Islamica* 61 (1985): 155–83.

Husein Al-Dahabi, Muhammad El-Sayyid. "Israelite Narratives in Exegesis and Tradition." In Al-Azhar, *The Fourth Conference*: 579–735; extracts herein from Green, *Arab Theologians*: 41–45.

el-Husseini, Musa Kazem. Formal request (December 10, 1920) to High Commissioner for Palestine (trans. January 2, 1921). Israel State Archives, R.G. 2, Box 10, File 244.

Hyamson, Albert M. *A History of the Jews in England*. London, 1908.

———, ed. *The British Consulate in Jerusalem (in relation to the Jews of Palestine, 1838–1914), Part I, 1838–1861*. London, 1939.

———. *The Sephardim in England 1492–1951*. London, 1951.

Ibn . . . *See* Aqnin, Hazm, etc.

Ibn Idhari, Muhammad. *Histoire de l'Afrique et de l'Espagne, intitulée al-Bayano'l-Mogrib*. Trans. and an. by Edmond Fagnan. Alger, 1901–1904.

Idris, H. R. "Contributions à histoire de l'Ifriqiya" (Riyad an Nufus d'Al-Maliki). *Revue des Études Islamiques*, 1935. Eng. trans. in Bat Ye'or, *The Dhimmi* (1985): 186.

————. *La Berbérie orientale sous les Zirides Xe–XIIe siècles*. 2 vols. Paris, 1962.

————. "Les tributaires en Occident Musulman médiéval d'apres *Mi'yar* d'al-Wansarisi." In Salmon, *Mélanges d'islamologie* (1974): 172–96. Eng trans. of extracts herein by Michael J. Miller.

Inalcik, Halil. *The Ottoman Empire—The Classical Age, 1300–1600*. London, 1973.

Initiation au Maroc. 3rd ed. Paris, 1945.

Intelligence and Terrorism Information Center. "Islamic Antisemitism: The Jews Depicted as Apes and Pigs." *Bulletin* 5 (October 2002): Chap. 3.

Iqraa. TV interview on *Muslim Woman Magazine* program, May 7, 2002. http://www.afsi.org/MEDIA/ news Links/shockers/toddler.htm (accessed October 1, 2007).

Irani, George Emile. *Le Saint-Siége et le Conflit du Proche-Orient*. Paris, 1991.

Isaac b. Samuel of Acre. *Osar Hayyim* [Treasure Store of Life] (Heb.). Moscow. *Russian State Library*: Ms. Gunzburg 775 fol. 27b. Eng. trans. in Bat Ye'or, *The Dhimmi* (1985): 352–54.

al-Isbahani, Abu Nu'aym. *Hilyat al-awliya' wa-tabaqat al-asfiya'*. 10 vols. Cairo, 1932–38.

————. *Taqrib al-bughyah bi-tartib ahadith al-Hilyah*. 3 vols. Beirut, 1999.

Israeli, Raphael. "Anti-Jewish Attitudes in the Arabic Media, 1975–1981." In Wistrich, *Anti-Zionism* (1990): 103.

————. *Islamikaze—Manifestations of Islamic Martyrology*. London, 2003.

Issacharoff, Avi. "Haniyeh in Tehran: Iran Gives Us 'Strategic Depth.'" *Haaretz*, December 10, 2006.

————. "Hamas Minister Target of Attempted Assassination in Gaza." *Haaretz*, December 12, 2006.

Ivanow, Wladimir. *Studies in Early Persian Ismailism*. Leyden, 1948.

Jabré, F. *La notion de certitude selon Ghazali*. Paris, 1958.

Jackson, J. G. *An Account of the Empire of Morocco*. London, 1814.

Jackson, P. "Wassaf—The Court Panegyrist." *EI-O*.

Jacobs, Joseph. *See under* Gottheil, "The Crusades."

————, and M. Franco. "Joseph Ben Isaac Sambari." JewishEncyclopedia.com. http://www.jewish encyclopedia.com/view.jsp?artid=112&letter=S (accessed October 1, 2007).

————, and Isaac Broyde. "Samuel Ha-Nagid (Samuel Halevi Ben Joseph Ibn Nagdela [Naghrela])." JewishEncyclopedia.com. http://www.jewishencyclopedia.com/view.jsp?artid=183&letter=S (accessed October 1, 2007).

————, and M. Seligsohn. "Michael Ben Shabbethai Cohen Balbo" JewishEncyclopedia.com. http://www.jewishencyclopedia.com/view.jsp?artid=569&letter=M (accessed October 1, 2007).

Jacques-Meunié, Dj. "Les Oasis des Lektaoua et des Mahamid." *Hespéris* 34 (1947): 397–429.

————. "Hiérarchie sociale au Maroc pré-saharien." *Hespéris* 45 (1958): 239–69.

al-Jahiz. *Kitab al-Hayawan* [Book of animals]. Cairo, 1906.

————. "A Reply to the Christians." Trans. by Finkel in "A Risala of Al-Jahiz." (1927): 311–34.

al-Jaubari. *al-Mukhtar fi kashf al-asrar* [The Chosen One's Unmasking/Clarification of Divine Mysteries]. Egypt, 19—. Excerpt herein, "To Disclose the Fraudulence of the Jewish Men of Learning," from chap. 5 in Eng. trans. by Moshe Perlmann in "Notes on the Position of Jewish Physicians": 316–17.

al-Jawziyyah, Ibn Qayyim. *Ahkam Ahl al-Dhimmah*. Ed. by Subhi Salih. Beirut, 1961.

Al Jazeera Online. "Ahmadinejad on Israel, Again." January 3, 2006. http://english.aljazeera.net/English/archive/archive?ArchiveId=17547 (accessed October 1, 2007).

al-Jaznai. *Zanat zahrat al-as fi bina madinat Fas*. Al-Jaza'ir, 1922.

Jerusalem Post. "Hamas Discusses Forming Government." January 7, 2006.

————. "Hamas Head: We Will Never Recognize Israel." February 3, 2006.

Jewish Agency for Palestine. *The Position of the Jewish Communities in Oriental Countries*. Submitted March 1946 to the Anglo-American Committee of Inquiry. Jerusalem, 1947.

Jewish Chronicle. September 28, 1877: 7; April 9, 1880: 5; June 11, 1880: 10–11; April 28, 1893; November 17, 1893: 10; August 3, 1894: 8; September 7, 1894: 13; and September 21, 1894: 9.

JewishEncyclopedia.com. http://www.jewishencyclopedia.com/index.jsp (accessed October 1, 2007).

Jewish Missionary Intelligence. (1841): 258; (1885): 35; (1888): 161; (1890): 159; (1894): 155; (1899): 153; (1904): 176; and (1907): 11.

Jochmann, Werner. *Monologe im Führer-Hauptquartier 1941–1944*. Munich, 2000.

Johnston, R. L. N. *Morocco, the Land of the Setting Sun*. London, 1902.

Jones, J. M. B. "Ibn Ishak Muhammad b. Ishak b. Yasar b. Khiyar (according to some sources, b. Khabbar, or Kuman, or Kutan)." *EI-O*.

Jones, Marsden. *See under* al-Wakidi, *Kitab* (1966).

Joseph b. Aknin. *Tib al-Nufus (The Healing of the Soul)*. In Bat Ye'or, *The Dhimmi* (1986): 224, 287.

Joseph b. Gorion. *Yosippon (History of the Jews)*. Mantua, 1474–[76].

————, and David Kyber. *Historia belli iudaici*. 1550.

————. *Sefer Yosifon: korot 'am Yisra'el bi-tejufat ha-Bayit ha-Sheni u-milhemet ha-Jehudim 'im ha-Roma'im*. Jerusalem, 1999.

Journal d'Egypte. [Nasser's speech of July 26, 1956]. July 27, 1956.

Judah b. Oved. *Ibn 'Attar, Zikkaron li-Bene Yisra'el*. In Vajda, *Un recueil de textes*: 87.

Julien, Charles A. *Histoire de l'Afrique du Nord: Tunisie, Algerie, Maroc.* Paris, 1931. Paris, 1951.

Jung, J. *Champions of Orthodoxy.* London, 1974.

Jung, Karl. "The Symbolic Life." *The Collected Works*, vol. 18. Princeton, NJ, 1939.

Juynboll, G. H. A., ed. *See under* al-Bukhari. *Sahih* (1862).

———. *The Authenticity of the Tradition Literature: Discussions in Modern Egypt.* Leyden, 1969.

Kamen, Henry. "The Mediterranean and the Expulsion of Spanish Jews in 1492." *Past and Present* 119 (May 1988): 30–55.

Kamil, Abdel Aziz. "Jewish Role in Aggression on the Islamic Base in Medina." In Al-Azhar, *Fourth Conference*: 399–414; extracts herein from Green, *Arab Theologians*: 26.

Kandel, S. *Genizai kezirato.* Budapest, 1909.

Kannoun, Abdullah. "Muslims and the Problem of Palestine." In Al-Azhar, *Fourth Conference*: 253–62; extracts herein from Green, *Arab Theologians*: 55–56.

Kaplan, Edward H., and Charles H. Small. "Anti-Israel Sentiment Predicts Antisemitism in Europe." *Journal of Conflict Resolution* 50 (2006): 548–61.

Kapsali, Eliyah, and Aryeh Shmuelevitz. *Seder Eliyahu zuta: History of the Ottomans and of Venice and that of the Jews in Turkey, Spain and Venice.* Jerusalem, 1975.

Karasso, D. "Masa' Teman." In Tobi, *The Jews of Yemen*: 121–90.

Karmers, J. H., and R. C. Repp. "Shaykh al-Islam." *EI-O*.

Karmon, Ely. "The Synagogue Bombings in Istanbul: Al-Qaeda's New Front?" *Policywatch* 806 (November 18, 2003).

Karsh, Efraim. *Arafat's War.* New York, 2003.

Kastalani. *See under* al-Bukhari, *Irsad as-sari* (1868).

Ibn Kathir. *Tafsir Ibn Kathir (abridged).* 10 vols. Riyadh, 2000.

Kattan, Naim. *Farewell Babylon.* Trans. from the Fr. by Sheila Fischman. New York, 1976.

Kaufmann Collection, David. [Geniza ms] XXI: "One and two thirds dinars." TS 16.272; TS 8 J 19. Budapest.

Kaufmann, David. "Zu den marokkanischen Piutim." *ZDMG* 50 (1896): 234–40.

Kayrawani, Ibn Abu Dinar. *See* Dinar.

Kayserling, Meyer. *See under* Gottheil, "Cordova"; "Ephraim B. Gershon."

Keatinge, M. *Travels in Europe and Africa. Comprising a Journey through France, Spain and Portugal to Morocco, also a Second through France in 1814.* London, 1816.

Kedourie, Elie, and Sylvia G. Haim, eds. *Zionism and Arabism in Palestine and Israel.* London, 1982.

———. *The Chatham House Version and Other Middle Eastern Studies.* Hanover, NH, 1984.

Kerem Hemer. See under Ankawa.

Ibn Khaldun. *Kitab al-'Ibar.* Bulaq, 1284 H.

Ibn Khaldun, and William MacGuckin Slane. *Histoire des Berères et des dynasties musulmanes de l'Afrique septentrionale (Kitab al-'Ibar).* 4 vols. Alger, 1852–56. 3 vols., Paris, 1925–34. 4 vols., Paris, 1968–69.

———. *The Muqaddima; An Introduction to History (Kitab al-'Ibar).* Trans. from the Ar. by F. Rosenthal. Bollingen Series 43. 3 vols. New York and London, 1958. Princeton, NJ, 1967. Abridged, 1 vol., with new introd., includes index, Princeton, NJ, 2005.

Khaled, Hassan. "Jihad in the Cause of Allah." In Al-Azhar, *Fourth Conference*: 127–48; extracts herein from Green, *Arab Theologians*: 66.

al-Khalidi, Salah. *Amrika min al-Dakhil bi-minzar Sayyid Qutb* [Inside America in the Eyes of Sayyid Qutb]. Jiddah, al-Saudiyah, and al-Mansurah, Egypt, 1986. Algeria and Dimashq, 2002.

———. *Haqa'iq Qur'aniyya al Qadiyya al-Filastinniya* [Qur'anic Facts regarding the Palestinian Issue]. N.p., 1991. London, 1994.

El-Khazen, Farid. *The Breakdown of the State in Lebanon—1967–1976.* Cambridge, 2000.

al-Khazraji, Ali b. al-Hasan. *al-'Uqud al-Lu'lu'iyyah Ta'rikh al-Dawlah al-Rasuliyyah.* Vol. A–B, ed. Muhammad al-Akwa' al-Hawali. San'a, Beirut, 1983.

Khomeini, Ruhollah. *Principes Politiques, Philosophiques, Sociaux et Religieux.* Trans. into Fr. and ed. by J.-M. Xaviere. Paris, 1979; Eng. trans. of excerpts herein from Bat Ye'or, *The Dhimmi* (1985): 396–97.

———. *A Clarification of Questions: An Unabridged Translation of Resaleh Towzih Al-Masael.* Boulder and London, 1984.

Khosrew, Molla. *Il Kitab Al-Gihad.* Italian trans. (*Trattato Sulla Guerra*) by Nicola Melis. Cagliari, 2002: 95–96. Herein, Eng. trans. by Ughetta Lubin.

Khoury, R. G. *See under* Levi Della-Vida, "Uthman b. 'Affan."

Kieser. *Der verpasste Friede.* Zürich, 2000.

Kiraly, Bela K., ed. *War and Society in East Central Europe.* Serial publication. Various places, 1979–.

Kister, M. J. "The Massacre of the Banū Qurayẓa: A Re-examination of a Tradition." *JSAI* 8 (1986): 61–96.

Klein, Aaron. "YMCA Warned to Vacate Hamas Town." *WorldNetDaily*, April 21, 2006.

———. "Abbas Urges: 'Raise Rifles against Israel.'" *WorldNetDaily*, January 11, 2007.

———. "Jews Flee Homes after Muslim Death Threats." *WorldNetDaily*, January 22, 2007.

Klein-Franke, Aviva. "The Orphans: Their Flight and Their Immigration to Eretz Israel: A Study of a Rescue Operation" (Heb.). In Gamliel et al., *Yemenite Paths* (1984): 85–111.

———. "Collecting the Djizya (Poll-Tax) in the Yemen." In Parfitt, *Israel* (2000): 175–206.

Kobak, Joseph, ed. *Jeschurun* 6 (1868): 1–34. Ibid., 8 (1873).

Ha-Kohen, Joseph. *Dibrei ha-Yamim.* Amsterdam, 1733.

Kohler, Kaufmann, and Isaac Broydé. "Solomon ben Jeroham." JewishEncyclopedia.com. http://www. jewishencyclopedia.com/view_friendly.jsp?artid =916 &letter=S (accessed October 1, 2007).

———, and M. Seligsohn. "Isaac Ben Samuel of Acre." JewishEncyclopedia.com. http://www.jewish encyclopedia.com/view.jsp?artid=239&letter=I (accessed October 1, 2007).

Kohut, George Alexander, ed. *Semitic Studies. In Memory of A. Kohut.* Berlin, 1897.

———. "Alfonsi, Petrus." In JewishEncyclopedia.com. http://www.jewishencyclopedia.com/view.jsp?artid =1195&letter=A&search=Alfonsi,%20Petrus (accessed November 19, 2007)

Komlos, O., ed. *Études orientales à la mémoire de Paul Hirschler.* Budapest, 1950.

Krauss, Samuel. *Das Leben Jesu nach jüdischen Quellen.* Berlin, 1902.

———. *Talmudische Archaeologie.* 3 vols. Leipzig, 1910–1912.

Krehl, ed. *See under* al-Bukhari. *Sahih.*

Krumenacker, Thomas. "Nazis Planned Holocaust for Palestine: Historians." *Boston Globe,* April 7, 2006.

Kuntzel, Matthias. "Iran's Obsession with the Jews." *Weekly Standard,* February 19, 2007.

Lachman, Shai. "Arab Rebellion and Terrorism in Palestine 1929–39. The Case of Sheikh Izz al-Din al Qassam and His Movement." In Kedourie and Haim, *Zionism and Arabism:* 52–99.

Lal, K. S. *The Legacy of Muslim Rule in India.* New Delhi, 1992.

Lammens, Henri. *Fatima et les filles de Mahomet: notes critiques pour l'étude de la sira.* Rome, 1912.

———. *L'Arabie occidentale à la veille de l'Hégire.* Beyrouth, 1928.

———. *Islam: Beliefs and Institutions.* New Delhi, 2002 (reprint).

Landau, Jacob M. *Jews in Nineteenth-Century Egypt (ha-Yehudim be-Mitsrayim ba-me'ah ha-tesha'-'esreh).* New York, 1969.

———. "Muslim Turkish Attitudes towards Jews, Zionism, and Israel." *Die Welt des Islams* 28 (1988): 291–300.

Landau, R. *Portrait of Tangier.* London, 1952.

———, and W. Swaan, *Morocco: Marrakesh, Fez, Rabat.* London, 1967.

Landshut, S. *Jewish Communities in the Muslim Countries of the Middle East.* Westport, CT, 1950.

Lane, Edward William. *An Account of the Customs of the Modern Egyptians.* Facsimile of the 1860 edition. Dover, New York, 1973.

———. *An Arabic-English Lexicon.* 6 vols. London, 1865.

Laoust, Henri. *Essai sur les doctrines sociales et politiques de Taki-d-Din Ahmad b. Taimiya, canoniste hanbalite, né à Harran en 661/1262, mort à Damas en 728/1328.* Dissertation, Paris. Cairo, 1939.

———. *Le Traité de Droit Public d'Ibn Taimiya (Slyasa Šar'iya).* Beirut, 1948.

Laskier, Michael M. "The Jews of Morocco and the Alliance Israélite Universelle: Selected Documents." In Schwarzfuchs, *East and Maghreb* 3 (1981): vii–xxiii.

———. "Aspects of Change and Modernization: The Jewish Communities of Morocco's Bled." In Abitbol, *Communautés juives* (1982): 329–64.

———. *The Alliance Israélite Universelle and the Jewish Communities of Morocco 1862–1962.* New York, 1983.

Lazarus-Yafeh, H. *Religious Thought and Practice in Islam* (Heb.). Tel Aviv, 1985.

Leard, A. *Marocco and the Moors, Being an Account of Travels, with a General Description of the Country and Its People.* 2nd ed., revised and ed. by R. Burton. London, 1891.

Lebel, Jennie. *Hajj Amin ve Berlin* [Hajj Amin and Berlin]. Tel Aviv, 1996.

Lecore-Carpentier, E. *L'Indicateur Tunisien—Annuaire des administrations de la régence de Tunis—Guide du commerce, de l'industrie de l'agriculture et des touristes.* Tunis, 1905.

Leder, S. "al-Wakidi, Muhammad b. 'Umar b. Wakidi." *EI-O.*

von Leers, Johann. "Judentum und Islam als Gegensatze [Judaism and Islam as Opposites]." *Die Judenfrage in Politik, Recht, and Wirtschaft* 6, no. 24 (December 24, 1942): 275–78. Herein, trans. by Steven Rendall.

Legget, Karby. *Wall Street Journal,* December 23, 2005: A1.

Lempriere, W. *A Tour through the Dominions of the Emperor of Morocco.* London, 1830.

Leo Africanus [Wazzan az-Zaiyati]. *Description de l'Afrique.* Trans. A. Epaulard. Paris, 1956.

Leszynsky, Rudolf. *Die Juden in Arabien z. Zeit Mohammeds.* Berlin, 1910.

Leven, Narcisse. *Cinquante ans d'histoire: l'Alliance Israélite Universelle (1860–1910).* 2 vols. Paris, 1911–1920.

Ha-Levi, Eliezer. *See* Loewe.

Levi Della-Vida, G., and R. G. Khoury. "Uthman b. 'Affan." *EI-O.*

Lévi-Provençal, Evariste. *Documents inédits d'histoire almohade; fragments manuscrits du "legajo" 1919 du fonds arabe de l'Escurial. Textes arabes relatifs à l'histoire de l'Occident musulman.* Paris, 1928, 1948.

———. *See under* Colin, *Un manuel hispanique de hisba* (1931).

———. *See under* Dozy, *Histoires* (1932).

———. *Un document sur la vie urbaine et les corps de métiers à Séville au XIIe siècle; Le Traité d'Ibn 'Abdun, publié avec une introduction et un glossaire* [A document about urban life and trade guilds in Seville in the 12th century; The Treaty of Ibn Abdun, published with an introduction and a glossary]. *Journal Asiatique* 224 (1934): 177–299.

———. "Les 'mémoires' de Abd Allah, dernier roi Ziride de Grenade." *al-Andalus* 3 (1935): 232–344; *ibid.* 4 (1936–39): 29–145; *ibid* 6 (1941): 1–63.

———. *Histoire de l'Espagne Musulmane*, vol. 1. Paris, 1950.

———. *Documents arabes inédits sur la vie sociale et économique en occident musulman au Moyen Age. Textes et traductions d'auteurs orientaux.* Cairo, 1955.

Levy, Moritz. *Die Sephardim in Bosnien* [The Sephardim in Bosnia: A Contribution to the History of the Jews in the Balkans]. Sarajevo, 1911. Citation trans. in Andric, *The Development*: 86, note 71.

Lewis, Bernard. "History-Writing and National Revival in Turkey." *Middle Eastern Affairs* 4 (1953): 225.

———. *The Emergence of Modern Turkey.* London, 1968.

———. "The Pro-Islamic Jews." *Judaism* 17, no. 4 (1968): 401.

———. *Race and Color in Islam.* New York, 1971.

———. *Islam in History.* New York, 1973.

———. *Islam, from the Prophet Muhammad to the Capture of Constantinople.* New York, 1974.

———, ed. *See under* Braude, *Christians and Jews in the Ottoman Empire* (1982).

———. *The Jews of Islam.* Princeton, NJ, 1984.

———. *Semites and Antisemites: An Inquiry into Conflict and Prejudice.* New York and London, 1986.

———. "The Arab World Discovers Antisemitism." *Commentary* (May 1986): 30–35.

———. *Die Juden in der islamischen Welt.* Munich, 1987.

———. "The New Antisemitism." *American Scholar* 75, no. 1 (2006): 25–36.

———. "Islamic Revival in Turkey." *International Affairs* 28: 48.

———, trans. *See under* Abd Allah of Granada, *Kitab al-Tibyan.*

Lewis, Geoffrey L., and Cecil Roth. "New Light on the Apostasy of Sabbatai Zevi." *JQR* 53 (1963): 219–25.

Lewis, N. "New Light on the Negev in Ancient Times." *Palestine Exploration Quarterly* 80 (1948): 116–17.

Lichtenstadter, Ilse. "And Become Ye Accursed Apes." *JSAI* 14 (1991): 159–75.

Lipman, Sonia L., and V. D. Lipman. *The Century of Moses Montefiore.* Oxford and New York, 1985.

Lipman, V. D. "Montagu." *EJ2* 12: 263.

Lisaan al-`Arab. See Manzur, *Lisan.*

Little, Donald P. "Communal Strife in Late Mamluk Jerusalem." *Islamic Law and Society* 6 (1999): 69–96.

Littman, David G., and Yehoshafat Harkabi. *See* Green, D. F. (pseud., 1971).

———. "Jews under Muslim Rule in the Late Nineteenth Century." *WLB* 28, nos. 35–36 (1975): 65–76.

———. "Jews under Muslim Rule—II: Morocco 1903–1912." *WLB* 29 (1976): 3–19.

———. "Jews under Muslim Rule: The Case of Persia." *WLB* 32 (1979): 7–8. http://www.dhimmitude.org/archive/littman_jews_under_muslims_case_of_persia .pdf (accessed October 1, 2007).

———. "Mission to Morocco (1863–64). " In Lipman, *The Century* (1985).

———, trans. *See under* Bat Ye'or, *The Dhimmi* (1985).

———, trans. *See under* Bat Ye'or, *The Decline* (1996).

———. "The Ancient Jewish Community of Iran and the Shiraz 'Show Trial.'" Written statement submitted to the UN Commission on Human Rights by Association for World Education, January 8, 2001. Listed as E/CN.4/2001/NGO/50 at http://ap.ohchr.org/documents/ alldocs.aspx?doc_id=2580 (accessed January 12, 2008). See also E/CN.4/2004/NGO/87, in chap. 34 in Spencer, *The Myth* (2005): 374–82 (2004 version).

———. "The Genocidal Hamas Charter." *National Review Online*, September, 26, 2002.

———, trans. *See under* Bat Ye'or, *Islam and Dhimmitude* (2003).

———. "Historical Facts and Figures: The Forgotten Jewish Refugees from Arab Countries."

———. "Human Rights and Human Wrongs at the United Nations." Part 5 of Spencer, ed., *The Myth* (2005): 305–472.

———, and Bat Ye'or. "Protected Peoples under Islam." In Spencer, *The Myth* (2005): 92–106.

Loeb, Isidore. "A Jewish Woman Martyred in Morocco (1834)." *Archives Israelite.* Vol. 41. Part 1 in no. 22 (1880): 181–82. Part 2 in no. 23: 187–88. Part 3 in no. 24: 196–97.

Loeb, Laurence. "The Jews in Southwest Iran: A Study of Cultural Persistence." PhD dissertation, Columbia, 1970.

———. *Outcaste—Jewish Life in Southern Iran.* New York, 1977.

———. "Dhimmi Status and Jewish Roles in Iranian Society." In *Ethnic Groups* 1: 89–105; and in Deshen, *Jews among Muslims* (1996): 249.

Loewe, Louis [Eliezer Ha-Levi]. In Stillman, *The Jews . . . Source Book*: 342–46.

———. *See in* Guenzburg, *Devir*: 12.

London Committee of Deputies of the British Jews. *Annual Reports:* 1877–1878; 1887; 1888.

London Times, April 15, 1893. *See in Jewish Chronicle*, April 28, 1893, p. 12.

Ibn Lutf, Babay. *Kitab-i Anusi. See under* Moreen, *An Introductory Study.*

Luncz, A. M. *Luah Eretz Yisrael: 5661 (Heb. Calendar).* Jerusalem, 1900–1901.

Lüttke, Moritz. *Aegyptiens neue Zeit. Ein Beitrag zur Culturgeschichte des gegenwartigen Jahrhunderts sowie zur Charakteristik des Orients unde des Islam,* 1. Leipzig, 1873: 97–99. Eng. trans. in J. B. Landau, *Jews*: 18–19.

Lynfield, Ben. "Palestinian Faction-Fighting Drifting into War." *Scotsman*, December 20, 2006. http://news .scotsman.com/topics.cfm?tid=1260&id=188622206 (accessed October 1, 2007).

Ma'atuf, S. *Habban (Hadramaut)* [Jewry in the Last Generations]. Tel Aviv, 1987.

Mackenzie, D. *The Khalifate of the West: Being a General Description of Morocco.* London, 1911.

Maçoudi. *Les prairies d'or.* Trans. by Barbier de Meynard. 9 vols. Paris, 1861–1917.

Madelung, W. "Imam Al-Qasim Ibn Ibrahim and Mu'tazilism." In Ehrensvärd, *On Both Sides*: 39–48.

Madhi, Ibrahim. Sermon held at Gaza City. Palestine Television, August 3, 2001.

al-Magili, Muhammad b. Abd al-Karim. "Ahkam ahl al-Dhimma." In Vajda, *Études* 2: 805–13.

Magoulis, Harry J. *See* Doukas.

al-Magribi, Samau'al. *Ifham al-Yahud* [Silencing the Jews]. Eng. trans. in Perlmann, *Proceedings*: 32.

Maharitz. "Letter of the 'Mahris' (Rabbi Yihye Salih) (Heb.)." In Qafih, *Tiklal Shivat Zion.*

al-Mahlawi, Uthman. "A Spearhead against Arab Nationalism." *Journal of Arab Nationalism* (January–March 1959). Quoted in Harkabi, *Arab Attitudes*: 130.

Mahmoud, Hassan. Inaugural speech. In Al-Azhar, *Fourth Conference*; extracts herein from Green, 15–16.

Maimonides, Moses [Rambam]. Epistle to Yemen (Iggeret Teiman). British Museum ms. f. 124a.

———. *Hilkot De'ot = Canones ethici* [Code of Laws]. Amsterdam, 1640.

———. *Iggerot,* Amsterdam, 1712.

———. *Iggeret Teiman.* Ed. by D. Holub. Vienna, 1874.

———, et al. *Kovets teshuvot ha-Rambam ve-igrotav.* Leipzig, 1859. Westmead, UK, 1969.

———. *Tahkemōni.* Warsaw, 1899.

———. *Moses Maimonides's Epistle to Yemen: The Arabic Original and the Three Hebrew Versions* (*Iggeret Teiman*). Ed. from manuscripts with introduction and notes by Abraham S. Halkin, and an Eng. transl. by Boaz Cohen. New York, 1952.

———. *Teshuvot ha-Rambam. . . .* Ed. by Joshua Blau. Jerusalem, 1934. 3 vols., 1957–61. 4 vols., 1986. Computer optical disc, 2002.

———. *Responsa.* Ed. by Alfred Freimann. Jerusalem, 1934.

———. *See also* Muntner, *Treatise on Asthma.*

Ibn Maja. *Sunan.* Cairo, 1313 H.

al-Majlisi, Muhammad. *Risala-yi Sawa'iq al-Yahud* [*The Treatise "Lightning Bolts against the Jews"*]. Trans. by V. B. Moreen in *Die Welt des Islams* 32 (1992): 187–93, reprod. in Bostom, *The Legacy*: 216–20.

Makki, Abu Talib Muhammad ibn Ali, and Richard Gramlich. *Die Nahrung der Herzen: Abu Talib al-Makkis Qut al-qulub.* Freiburger Islamstudien, Bd. 16. Stuttgart, 1992.

———, and Sa'id Nasib Makarim (ed.) *Qut al-qulub . . .* (Ar.). 2 vols. Beirut, 1995.

Makrizi. *Macrizi's Geschichte der Copten: Aus dem Handschriften zu Gotha und Wien mit Uebersetzung und Anmerkungen von Ferd Wüstenfeld.* Göttingen, 1845.

———. *See also* Quatremère, *Histoire des sultans mamlouks.*

Malachi, Eliezer Raphael ["A. R."]. "Under the Rule of Ibrahim Pasha." *Ha-Doar* 14 (1935): 28–31. Trans. by Anonymous from idem, *Studies in the History of the Old Yishuv*: 65–78

———. *Studies in the History of the Old Yishuv.* Ed. by G. Yardeni-Agmon and Shlomo Derech. Tel Aviv, 1971.

———. *Mi-Neged Tireh* [View the Land from a Distance]. Ed. by Elhanan Reiner and Haggai Ben-Shammai. Jerusalem, 2001.

Malcolm, Napier. *Five Years in a Persian Town.* New York, 1905.

Malik ibn Anas. *Sharh 'al-Zurqani 'ala Sahih 'al-Muwatta' li-'Imam 'al-'a'immah Malik ibn 'Anas.* With commentary by al-Zurkani. Cairo 1279–80 H (1862–63).

———. *Muwatta.* Trans. Aisha Abdarahman at-Tarjumana and Yaqub Johnson. http://www.usc.edu/dept/MSA/fundamentals/hadithsunnah/muwatta (accessed October 1, 2007).

al-Maliki, Abu Bakr Abd Allah. *Riyad an-Nufus.* See Idris, "Contributions" (1935).

Malka, E. *See under* Brunot.

Ibn Mammati. *Qawanin al-dawawin.* Cairo, 1943.

Mann, Jacob. "Moses b. Samuel, a Jewish Katib in Damascus, and His Pilgrimage to Medinah and Mekkah." *JRAS* (1919): 155–84. Reproduced in idem, *The Collected Articles.*

———. *The Jews in Egypt and in Palestine under the Fatimid Caliphs; a contribution to their political and communal history based chiefly on genizah material hitherto unpublished.* 2 vols. London, 1920–22. Republished, London, 1969; New York, 1970, with suppl. and Goitein's introd. added.

———. *Texts and Studies in Jewish History and Literature.* 2 vols. Philadelphia, 1931/1935.

———. *The Bible as read and preached in the old synagogue; a study in the cycles of the readings from Torah and Prophets, as well as from Psalms, and in the structure of the Midrashic homilies.* Cincinnati, 1940–66.

———. *The Collected Articles of Jacob Mann.* Gederah, 1971. New York, 1973.

du Mans, Raphael [Jacques Deutertre]. *Estat de la Perse en 1660.* Ed. by C. A. H. Schefer. Paris, 1890.

Mantsura, Shalom. Chronicle. In Ratzaby, "The Mawza' Exile."

Ibn Manzur, Muhammad ibn Mukarram. *Lisan al-'Arab.* Bulaq, Cairo, 1883.

Maoz, Moshe. "Changes in the Position of the Jewish Communities of Palestine and Syria in the Mid-Nineteenth Century." In idem, ed., *Studies on Palestine during the Ottoman Period.* Jerusalem, 1975: 156.

Maqqari, Ahmad ibn Muhammad. *Analectes sur l'histoire et la littérature des Arabes d'Espagne*. Tr. and ed. by Reinhart Dozy [et al.?]. 2 vols. Leyden, 1855–61. Repr. Amsterdam, 1967.

Marcais, Georges. *La Berberie musulmane et l'Orient au moyen-âge*. Paris, 1946.

———. *See under* al-Ahmar, *Rawdat*.

Marciano, E. R. *Ir ha-Kohanim Debdou*. Jerusalem, 1987.

Marcus, Itamar. "Palestinian TV, radio, newspapers and textbooks—in teaching the Islamic attitude toward Jews—have fueled an intense hatred for Israel and promoted violent jihad." July 21, 2001. http://www.aish.com/jewishissues/middleeast/Islams_War_Against_the_Jews_Quotes_from_the_Palestinian_Authority.asp (accessed October 1, 2007).

Marghinani, Ali ibn Abi Bakr. *[al-Hidayah] The Hedaya, or Guide—A Commentary on the Mussulman Laws*. 4 vols. Trans. by Charles Hamilton. N.p., 1791. [Reprinted New Delhi, 1982]. 1 vol., Lahore, 1982.

Margoliouth, D. S. *Mohammed and the Rise of Islam*. London, 1905. Reprinted New Delhi, 1985.

———. "Muhammad." In *Encyclopedia of Religion and Ethics* 8: 877–78.

del Marmol Carvajal, Luis, *L'Afrique*. Trans. by Ablancourt. 2 vols. Paris, 1661.

al-Marrakushi, Abdel Wahid, *The History of the Almohades*, ed. by R. Dozy. Leyden, 1881.

———. *Histoire des Almohades d'Abd el-Wah'id Merrakechi*. Alger, 1893.

Marx, A. "The Importance of the Geniza for Jewish History." *PAAJR* 16 (1947): 183.

Marx Jubilee Volume. New York, 1950.

Ibn Maryam, Muhammad ibn Muhammad. *El Bostan, ou, jardin des biographies des saints et savants de Tlemcen*. Ed. M. Ben Cheneb, trans. F. Provenzali. Alger, 1910.

Masha'al, Khalid. Video, February 2006. http://switch3.castup.net/cunet/gm.asp?ClipMediaID=123232&ak=null (accessed October 1, 2007).

———. Video-taped statement, March 17, 2006. http://switch3.castup.net/cunet/gm.asp?ClipMediaID=120176&ak=null (accessed October 1, 2007).

Mashash, J. H. *Otzar ha-Mikhtavim*. Jerusalem, 1968–1970.

Masriya, Yahudiya [Bat Ye'or]. *Les Juifs en Egypte*. Geneva, 1971. Herein, Eng. trans. by Susan Emanuel of the chapter: "The New Egyptian Jew Hatred—Local Elements and External Influences."

Massignon, Louis. *Le Maroc dans les premières années du XVIe siècle; tableau géographique d'après Léon l'Africain*. Alger, 1906. Frankfurt am Main, 1993.

———. "L'Interdit corporatif à l'encontre des Juifs islamisés de Fès du XVIe au XVIIe siècle." *Révue du Monde Musulman* 58 (1924): 221–24.

al-Mas'udi, et al. (eds). *Muruj al-dhahab wa-ma'adin al-jawhar*. Beirut, 1966.

di Matteo, I. "Le pretese contraddizioni della S. Scrittura secondo Ibn Hazm." *Bessarione* 27 (1923): 77–127.

al-Mawardi, *Les statuts gouvernementaux; ou, Règles de droit public et administratif*. Fr. trans. by E. Fagnan. Alger, 1915.

———. *Al-Ahkam as-Sultaniyyah = The Laws of Islamic Governance*. London, 1996.

Mawdudi, Sayyid Abul A'la. *Towards Understanding the Qur'an: English Version of Tafhim al Qur'an*. 3 vols. Leicester, UK, 1988–90.

Maxwell, G. *Lords of the Atlas: The Rise and Fall of the House of Glaova, 1839–1956*. London, 1966.

Mayer, Ann E. *Islam and Human Rights*. Boulder, CO, 1999.

Mayer, Léon Ary. *Mamluk Costume: A Survey*. Geneva, 1952.

———. "The Status of the Jews under the Mamluks (Heb.)." In Baer et al., *Magnes*: 161–67.

Mayer, Thomas. *Egypt and the Palestine Question—1936–1945*. Berlin, 1983.

McCheyne, R. M. *See under* Bonar.

McFarlane, Charles. *Constantinople in 1828*. London, 1829.

Meakin, Budgett J. E. "Jews of Morocco." *JQR* 4, no. 3 (1892): 369–96.

———. *The Moorish Empire, A Historical Epitome*. London and New York, 1899.

———. *The Land of the Moors; A Comprehensive Description*. London and New York, 1901.

———. *The Moors; A Comprehensive Description*. London and New York, 1902.

Megillat Teiman [The scroll of Yemen]. In Ratzaby, *Ha-Tsofeh le-Hokhmat Yisrael*: 7, 12.

Mélanges d'islamologie. See under Salmon.

Memorial Volume of the Rabbinical Seminary of Vienna. Jerusalem, 1946.

MEMRI (Middle East Media Research Institute) http://memri.org/archives.html (accessed October 1, 2007).

———. "The Meeting between the Sheik of Al-Azhar and the Chief Rabbi of Israel." *SR* 2 (February 8, 1998).

———. "Muslim-Christian Tensions in the Israeli-Arab Community." *SDS* 41 (August 2, 1999).

———. "A Friday Sermon on PA TV: . . . We Must Educate Our Children on the Love of Jihad." *SD* 240 (July 11, 2001).

———. "Former Iranian President Rafsanjani on Using a Nuclear Bomb against Israel." *SDS* 325 (January 3, 2002).

———. "Leading Egyptian Government Cleric Calls For: 'Martyrdom Attacks that Strike Horror into the Hearts of the Enemies of Allah.'" SDS 363 (April 7, 2002).

———. "The Damascus Blood Libel (1840) as Told by Syria's Minister of Defense, Mustafa Tlass." *Inquiry and Analysis Series* 99 (June 27, 2002).

———. "Friday Sermons in Saudi Mosques: Review and Analysis." *SR* 10 (September 26, 2002).

———. "Former Al-Azhar Fatwa Committee Head Sets Out the Jews' 20 Bad Traits as Described in the Qur'an." *SDS* 691 (April 6, 2004).

———. "Sheikh Yousef Al-Qaradhawi: 'There Is No Dialogue between Us and the Jews Except by the Sword and the Rifle.'" *SDS* 753 (July 27, 2004).

———. "Antisemitism in the Turkish Media (Part I)." *SDS* 900 (April 28, 2005).

———. "Antisemitism in the Turkish Media (Part II): Turkish Intellectuals against Antisemitism." *SDS* 904 (May 5, 2005).

———. "Antisemitism in the Turkish Media (Part III): Targeting Turkey's Jewish Citizens." *SDS* 916 (June 6, 2005).

———. "Iranian President at Tehran Conference." *SDS* 1013 (October 28, 2005).

———. "Iranian President Ahmadinejad on the 'Myth of the Holocaust.'" *SDS* 1091 (February 14, 2006).

———. "The Covenant of the Islamic Resistance Movement—Hamas." *SDS* 1092 (February 14, 2006).

———. "Sheik Yousef Al-Qaradhawi: Our War with the Jews Is in the Name of Islam." *TVM* 1052 (February 25, 2006).

———. "Leading Islamist Sheikh Yousef Al-Qaradhawi: We Are Fighting in the Name of Islam. . . . This Jihad Is an Individual Duty of the Entire Muslim Nation. . . . They Fight Us with the Torah. . . . We Should Fight Them with the Koran." *SDS* 1102 (February 28, 2006).

———. "Iran and Syria Beat the Drums of War." *SDS* 1225 (August 2, 2006).

———. "Sheik Yousef Al-Qaradhawi: The Jews of Today Bear Responsibility for Their Forefathers' Crime against Jesus." *TVM* 1249 (August 26, 2006).

———. "President Ahmadinejad: 'I Have a Connection with God, since God Said that the Infidels Will Have No Way to Harm the Believers . . .'" *SDS* 1328 (October 19, 2006).

Mendel, Menahem. *Korot ha-'Itim (Events of the Times)*. Vilna, 1840.

Meron, Ya'acov. "The Expulsion of the Jews from the Arab Countries: The Palestinians' Attitude towards It and Their Claims." In Shulewitz, *The Forgotten*: 84.

al-Meshad, Abd Allah. "Jews' Attitudes towards Islam and Muslims in the First Islamic Era." In Al-Azhar, *Fourth Conference*: 415–65; extracts herein from Green, *Arab Theologians*: 27–32.

Meyers, A. R. "Patronage and Protection: The Status of Jews in Precolonial Morocco." In Deshen, *Jewish Societies*: 85–104.

Michael the Syrian. *Chronique de Michel Le Syrien*. Ed. and trans. from the Syriac by Jean-Baptiste Chabot. Paris, 1899–1905. Extract herein, Eng. trans. in Bat Ye'or, *The Decline* (1996): 47.

Michael, Murad. *The Archives of Nahray b. Nissim, a Businessman in Eleventh-Century Egypt Jerusalem*.

Dissertation. http://links.jstor.org/sici?sici=0022-4995 (197304)16%3A1%3C15%3ATECMHO%3E2.0.CO %3B2-Q (accessed November 19, 2007).

Michael-Mallman, Klaus, and Martin Cuppers. "Elimination of the Jewish National Home in Palestine: The Einsatzkommando of the Panzer Army Africa, 1942." *Yad Vashem Studies* 35 (2007): 111–41.

Middle East Media Research Institute. *See* MEMRI.

Milano, A. *Storia degli Ebrei Italiani nel Levante*. Florence, 1949.

Miller, Judith. "The Istanbul Synagogue Massacre: An Investigation." *New York Times,* January 4, 1987.

Milson, Menachem. "What Is Arab Antisemitism?" MEMRI *SR* 26 (February 27, 2004).

Ministry of Education, Culture, and Guidance. *The Book of Palestine and the New Raids*. Baghdad, n.d.

Minorsky, V. *Tadhkirat al-Muluk. A Manual of Safavid Administration (circa 1137/1725)*. London, 1943.

Montagu, L. H. *Samuel Montagu, First Baron Swaythling: A Character Check*. London, 1913.

Morabia, Alfred. *Le Gihad dans l'Islam Médiéval, Le 'Combat Sacré' des origines au Xe siècle*. Paris, 1993.

Mordechai Hakohen. *Highid Mordekhai. See* Goldberg, Harvey E., *The Book of Mordechai*.

Moreen, Vera Basch. *An Introductory Study of the Kitab-I-Anusi by Babai Ibn Lutf*. Thesis, Harvard University, 1978.

———. *Iranian Jewry's Hour of Peril and Heroism—A Study of Babai Ibn Luft's Chronicle (1617–1662)*. New York and Jerusalem, 1987.

Moreno, Pedro C., ed. *Handbook on Religious Liberty around the World*. Charlottesville, VA, 1996.

Morier, James Justinian. *Second voyage en Perse, en Arménie et dans l'Asie-Mineure, fait de 1810 a 1816, avec le journal d'un voyage au golfe Persique par le Brésil et Bombay*. Paris, 1818.

———. *A Second Journey through Persia, Armenia and Asia Minor to Constantinople between the Years 1810 and 1816: With a Journal of the Voyage by the Brazils and Bombay to the Persian Gulf*. London, 1818.

Moses b. Samuel. Poems, in Oxford MS. Heb. F. 3 and 4.

Moubarac, Youakim. *L'islam et le dialogue islamo-chretien*. Beirut, 1972–73.

Mouette, G. *Histoire des conquestes de Mouley Archy*. Paris, 1683. Reprinted in de Castries, *Sources*.

Mounsey, Augustus Henry. *A Journey through the Caucasus and the Interior of Persia*. London, 1872. Elibron Classics replica ed. [US, 2005].

al-Mubarrad, Abu al-'Abbas [Muhammad ibn Yazid Mubarrad], W. Wright, and M. J. de Goeje (an.). *The Kamil of El-Mubarrad*. Issued in 12 parts as 2 vols. 1864. Repub. in 2 vols., Hildesheim, 1992.

Ibn Muftah. *Sharh al-Azhar*. In Zaydan, *Ahkam al-Dhimiyyin*: 350, n. 4

al-Muhasibi. *Ri'aya*. ms. Bodl. Hunter 611, 139 ff.

———. *Kitab al-ri'aya lihuquq Allah* [The Book of the

Patronage of the Law of Allah] (Ar.). Ed. by Margaret Smith. London, 1940.

Muhsin Khan, M. *See under* al-Bukhari (1987).

Muir, William. *The Life of Mahomet from Original Sources.* London, 1877. Kessinger Reprints, 2003.

Müller, August. *Der Islam im Morgen- und Abendlande.* 2 vols. Berlin, 1885–87.

Munk, Salomon. *Notice sur Joseph Ben-Jehouda, ou Aboul' Hadjadj Yousouf Ben Ya'hya al Sabti al-Maghrebi, disciple de Maimonide.* Paris, 1842.

Munro, Jane. "Dehodencq, Alfred." http://www.groveart .com/shared/views/article.html/section=art.021845 (accessed October 1, 2007).

Muntner, Suesmann, ed. *Treatise on Asthma* [by Maimonides]. Philadelphia, 1963.

Murphy, Brian. "Iran's Jews Caught Again in No Man's Land." *Associated Press*, July 30, 2006.

al-Murtada, Ahmad. *Kitab al-Azhar fi Fiqh al-A'immah al-Athar.* Beirut, 1972. Also published as: *Uyun al-Azhar.* Beirut, 1944.

———. *Tuhfat al-muluk fi al-siyar wa-al-suluk.* Beirut, 2001.

Muslim ibn al-Hajjaj. *Sahih.* Commentary of al-Nawawi. Cairo, 1866.

———. *Sahih.* Cairo, 1329–1333 H.

———. *Sahih Muslim* [Traditions]. Trans. by Abdul Hamid Siddiqui. www.usc.edu/dept/MSA/fundamentals/ hadithsunnah/muslim/ (accessed October 1, 2007).

Mustawfi Qazvini, Hamd Allah. *The Geographical Part of the Nuzhat-Al-Qúl-Ub.* Tr. and an. by G. Le Strange. "E. J. W. Gibb memorial" series, 2 vols. Leyden and London, 1915–19.

al-Muttaqi al-Hindi, Ali ibn Abd-al-Malik. *Kanz al 'ummal fi sunan al agwal wa al af'al* [Treasure of the Doers of Good Deeds]. 16 vols. Beirut, 1981.

Nacht, J. "Euphémismes sur la femme dans la littérature rabbinique." *REJ* 59: 36–41.

Nadaf, A. *Hoveret Seride Teman.* Jerusalem, 1938.

Nagel, T. *Das islamisches Recht.* Westhofen, 2001.

Nahum, Y. L. *Revelation of Yemenite Treasures* (Heb.). Holon, 1971.

———, and Y. Tobi. "Rabbi Yosef Shemen's Pamphlet, *Haye ha-Temanim*" [. . . on the distress of Yemenite Jewry in the twentieth century] (Heb.). In Yesha'yahu and Tobi, eds. *The Jews of Yemen* (1975): 95–113.

Nasafi. *See under* al-Baghawi.

al-Nasa'i. *Sunan.* Cairo, 1312 H.

al-Nasiri. *Kitab al-Istiqsa li-akhbar duwal al-Maghrib al-Aqsa.* 9 vols. Casablanca, 1954–56.

Nasrallah, Hassan. Speech, 1998. http://www.memri .org/bin/articles.cgi?Area=sr&ID=SR01102 (accessed November 19, 2007).

———. Speech, April 9, 2000. Excerpts in http:// www.mfa.gov.il/MFA/MFAArchive/2000_200/ 2000/4/Excerpts%20from%20Speech%20by%20Hiz bullah%20Secretary-General (accessed October 1, 2007).

Nasser, Gamel Abdel. Speech of July 26, 1956. *Journal d'Egypte*, July 27, 1956.

an-Nawawi, Yahya b. Saraf. *See under* Muslim, *Sahih* (1866).

———. *Minhadj at-Talibin: Le Guide des Zélés Croyants. Manuel de Jurisprudence musulmane selon le rite de Chafi'i.* Fr. trans. by L. W. C. van den Berg. 3 vols. Batavia, 1882–84.

———. *Sharh al-Nawawi 'ala Sahih Muslim.* Riyad, 2004.

Netanyahu, Benzion. *The Origins of the Inquisition.* New York, 1995.

———. *The Marranos of Spain.* Ithaca, NY, 1999.

Nettler, Ronald L. *Past Trials and Present Tribulations: A Muslim Fundamentalist's View of the Jews.* Oxford and New York, 1987.

———. "Islamic Archetypes of the Jews: Then and Now." In Wistrich, *Anti-Zionism* (1991): 66.

Netzer, A. "The Fate of the Jewish Community of Tabriz." In *Studies in Islamic History*: 419.

Neubauer, A., and A. E. Cowley. *Catalogue of the Hebrew manuscripts in the Bodleian Library and in the college libraries of Oxford.* 2 vols. Oxford, 1886–1906. Republ. in 1 vol., Oxford and New York, 1994.

———, ed. *Mediaeval Jewish Chronicles. Mediaeval Jewish Chronicles and Chronological Notes.* Parts 1–2. Oxford, 1887–95.

Neusner, Jacob, trans. *Mishnah.* New Haven, CT, 1988.

New York Sun. "Nasrallah's Nonsense." Editorial, March 11, 2005. http://www.nysun.com/article/10439 (accessed October 1, 2007).

New York Times. For archives 1851–1980, *see* http://query.nytimes.com/search/query?date_select =full&srchst=p (accessed November 19, 2007).

———. "Jews in Flight from Palestine." January 19, 1915. http://query.nytimes.com/gst/abstract.html?res =9F03E1DE1538E633A2575AC1A9679C946496D6 CF (accessed November 19, 2007).

———. "Turks and Germans Expelling Zionists." January 20, 1915. http://query.nytimes.com/mem/archive -free/pdf?res=9505EFDC1538E633A25751C2A9679 C946496D6CF (accessed November 19, 2007).

———. "Zionists in Peril of Turkish Attack." February 2, 1915.

———. "Threatens Massacre of Jews in Palestine." May 4, 1917.

———. "Cruel to Palestine Jews." May 8, 1917.

———. "Turks Killing Jews Who Resist Pillage." May 19, 1917.

———. "Twice Avert Eviction of Jerusalem Jews." May 30, 1917.

———. "Cruelties to Jews Deported in Jaffa." June 3, 1917.

———. "Nazis Reassure Arabs—Antisemitism Confined to Jews, Spokesman Explains." November 5, 1942.

———. "The Turkish Minorities." September 17, 1943.

———. "Jews in Morocco Frantic to Leave." March 12, 1956.

———. "500 Jews Leaving Tunisia in Month." March 25, 1956.

———. "Jews Show Drop in Arab Regions." July 4, 1959.

———. "Exodus Is Resumed by Moroccan Jews." February 8, 1962.

———. "Iran's New President Says Israel Must Be Wiped Off the Map." October 26, 2005. http://www.nytimes.com/2005/10/27/international/middleeast/27iran.html?_r=1&oref=slogin (accessed November 19, 2007).

Nicholls, William. *Christian Antisemitism. A History of Hate.* Northvale, NJ, and London, 1993.

Niebuhr, Carsten. *Travels through Arabia and Other Countries in the East.* Eng. trans. by Robert Hebron. Edinburgh, 1792.

Nilus, Sergei. *The Protocols of the Learned Elders of Zion.* Russia 1905. Eng. trans. by Victor E. Marsden. http://www.std.com/obi/Rants/Protocols/The_Protocols_of_The_Learned_Elders_of_Zion (accessed October 1, 2007).

Nini, Yehuda, *Yemen and Zion: The Jews of Yemen, 1800–1914* (Heb.). Jerusalem, 1982.

———. *The Jews of the Yemen, 1800–1914.* Trans. from the Heb. by H. Galai. Chur, 1990.

Noble Qur'an, The. Trans. by Al-Hilaalii, M. T. (Berlin), and M. M. Khan (al-Madina). Riyad, 1996. http://www.usc.edu/dept/MSA/quran/ (accessed October 1, 2007).

Nöldeke, Theodore. "The Koran." In *Encyclopedia Britannica*, 9th ed., vol. 16, 1891: 597. Reproduced in Ibn Warraq, *The Origins of the Koran.*

———, F. Schwally, and G. Tamer. *Tarikh al-Qur'an (Geschichte des Qorans).* Beirut, 2004.

Norris, H. T., and P. Chalmeta. "al-Murabitin." *EI-O.*

Nykl, A. R. *Hispano-Arabic Poetry.* Baltimore, 1946.

———, ed. *Selections from Hispano-Arabic Poetry.* Beirut, 1949.

Obadia, D. *The Community of Sefrou* (Heb.) 1–5. Jerusalem, 1975–1992.

———. *Fez and Its Sages* (Heb.) 2. Jerusalem, 1979.

O'Ballance, E. *War in Yemen.* London, 1971.

Ockley, S. *An Account of South West Barbary.* London, 1713.

Ökte, Faik. *The Tragedy of the Turkish Capital Tax.* Eng. trans. by Geoffrey Cox, with an intro. by David Brown. London, 1987.

Oren, Michael. *Six Days of War—June 1967 and the Making of the Modern Middle East.* Oxford, 2002.

Ovadia, A. *In the Paths of Yemen and Zion* (Heb.). Ed. by Y. Tobi. Tel Aviv, 1985.

Owadally, Mohamad Yasin. *Emergence of Dajjal. The Jewish King.* Delhi, 2001.

Own, Kamal Ahmad. "The Jews Are Enemies of Human Life as Is Evident from Their Holy Book." In Al-Azhar, *Fourth Conference*: 361–92; extracts herein from Green, *Arab Theologians*: 15, 19–20.

Palache, J. L. *De Sabbath-idee buiten het jodendom: Voordracht gehouden in der Vierde Jaarvergadering van het Genootschap voor de Joodsche Wetenschap in Nederland.* Amsterdam, 1925.

Palestine TV. Sermons, July 28, 2000; October 13, 2000; and June 8, 2001.

Palestinian Media Watch. December 12, 2005. http://www.pmw.org.il/Latest%20bulletins%20new.htm#b220106 (accessed October 1, 2007).

Papoulia, Vasiliki. "The Impact of Devshirme on Greek Society." In Kiraly, *War and Society* 2 (1982): 554–55.

Paquignon, Paul. "Quelques Documents sur la condition des Juifs au Maroc." *Revue du Monde Musulman* 9 (Paris, 1909): 112–19.

Pardoe, Julia. *The City of the Sultan and Domestic Manners of the Turks in 1836.* London, 1837.

Paret, Rudi. "Sure 2,256: la ikraha fi d-dini. Toleranz oder Resignation?" *Der Islam* 45 (1969): 299–300.

Parfitt, Tudor, *The Jews of Palestine.* Suffolk, UK, 1987.

———. *The Road to Redemption. The Jews of the Yemen 1900–1950.* Leyden, 1996.

———, ed. *Israel and Ishmael: Studies in Muslim Jewish Relations.* New York, 2000.

Parsons, F. V. *The Origins of the Moroccan Question 1880–1900.* London, 1976.

Pedersen, J. "Masdjid." *EI-S*: 331.

Pellat, Ch. "Maskh." *EI2*: 736–38.

Perdicaris, I. O. *American Claims and the Protection of Native Subjects in Morocco.* London, 1886.

Pérès, Henri. *La poésie andalouse en arabe classique au XIe siècle.* Paris, 1937.

Perlmann, Moshe. "A Late Muslim Jewish Disputation." *PAAJR* 12 (1942): 51.

———. *A Late Muslim Jewish Disputation.* New York, 1942.

———. "Eleventh-Century Andalusian Authors on the Jews of Granada." *PAAJR* 18 (1948–49): 269.

———, trans. *Judaism and Islam.* New York, 1970. For original pub., *see* Geiger, *Was hat Mohammad.*

———, ed., trans. *Ibn Kammuna's Examination of the Three Faiths; A Thirteenth-Century Essay in the Comparative Study of Religion.* Berkeley, CA, 1971.

———. "Notes on the Position of Jewish Physicians in Medieval Muslim Countries." *Israel Oriental Studies* 2 (1972): 316–17.

———, ed., trans. *Shaykh Damanhuri on the Churches of Cairo, 1739.* Berkeley, CA, 1975.

———, ed., trans. *The History of al-Tabari. Vol. 4, The Ancient Kingdoms.* Albany, NY, 1987.

———. "Samau'al al-Maghribi Ifh al-Yahud." *PAAJR* 32 (1964).

———. "The Medieval Polemics between Islam and Judaism." In Goitein, *Religion* (1974): 103–38.

———. "Dönme" *EI2.*

Pesikia Zutreta, We-zot haberakha. Venice, 1546.

Peters, Joan. *From Time Immemorial: The Origins of the Arab-Jewish Conflict over Palestine.* Chicago, 1984.

Peters, Rudolph. *Jihad in Classical and Modern Islam: A Reader.* Princeton, NJ, 1996.

Pew Research Center. "The Great Divide: How Westerners and Muslims View Each Other." *Pew Global Attitudes Project* (June 22, 2006).

Phares, Walid. *Lebanese Christian Nationalism, the Rise and Fall of an Ethnic Resistance.* Boulder, CO, and London, 1995.

Pickthall, Marmaduke William. *The Glorious Qur'an.* Elmhurst, NY, 2001.

Pires, Tome. *The Suma Oriental of Tome Pires, an Account of the East, from the Red Sea to Japan, Written in Malacca and India in 1512–1515, . . .* Vol. 1 of 2. London, 1944.

Pisa, Isaac. Letters (Casablanca, August 15 and 23, November 19, 1907) to AIU President, Paris. AIU Archives: MOROCCO II C 3.

———. Letters (February 9, 13, and 25, 1908) to AIU President, Paris. AIU Archives: MOROCCO I B 2.

Plat, V. *Alfred Dehodencq, 1822–1882.* Dissertation. Paris, 1977.

Poller, Nidra. "The Murder of Ilan Halimi." *Wall Street Journal,* February 26, 2006.

Porter, James. Correspondence to William Pitt, the Elder, London, dated February 3, 1758 (SP 97–40), and June 3, 1758 (SP 97–40). Reproduced in Bat Ye'or, *The Decline* (1996): 384–86.

Porush, Israel. *Peat ha-Shulhan* [The Corner of the Table]. Safed, 1836.

Proceedings of the American Academy for Jewish Research. Vol. 7, 1935–1936. Philadelphia, 1936.

Proceedings of the Seminar on Muslim-Jewish Relations in North Africa. Princeton, NJ, 1974.

Prusher, Ilene. "Turkish Jews Search for Answers." *Christian Science Monitor,* November 19, 2003.

Pryce-Jones, David. *The Closed Circle.* New York, 1989.

Pulsky, F. *The Tricolor on the Atlas.* London, 1886.

Al Qaeda. "Jihad against Jews and Crusaders." Fatwa, February 23, 1998. http://www.fas.org/irp/world/para/docs/980223-fatwa.htm (accessed October 1, 2007).

———. "Al Qaeda Training Manual." Discovered 2001. http://www.fas.org/irp/world/para/manualpart1.html (accessed October 1, 2007), and http://www.fas.org/irp/world/para/manualpart1_1.pdf (accessed October 1, 2007).

Qafih, J., ed. *Tiklal Shivat Zion.* Jerusalem, 1952.

———, ed. "The Book *Dofi Ha-Zeman* [The Chastisements of Time] of Rabbi Sa'id Sa'di: Events befalling the Jews of Yemen during the years 1717–1726 (Heb.)." *Sefunot* 1 (1956): 185–243.

———, ed. *See under* Hibshush, "Hayyim Hibshush" (1958).

———. "Keshareha shel Yahadut Teman Im Merkaze ha-Yahadut." *Yahudut Teman* (1976): 29–46.

———. *See under* Fayyumi, *Sefer Bustan al-'Uqul* (1984).

———. "Ketavim: Halakhah, Mahshavah, Divre Rishonim, Mishnat Ha-Rambam." *Yehude Teman* 1–2 (1989).

al-Qalqashandi. "The First Jews' Oath in Islam." In *Subh al-A'sha* [The morning of the blind], vol. 13 of 14, 266–67. Cairo, 1918. Eng. trans. in Stillman, *The Jews . . . Source Book*: 165–66.

Qaradawi, Yusuf. *The Lawful and the Prohibited in Islam (Al-Halal Wal-Haram Fil Islam).* Indianapolis, IN, 1980. *See also* http://www.witness-pioneer.org/vil/Books/Q_LP/ (accessed October 3, 2007).

———. *al-Islam—hadarat al-ghad* [Islam as the future civilization]. Cairo, 1995.

———. *The scholar and the tyrant: Sa'id ibn Jubayr & Hajjaj ibn Yusuf: an historical play.* Swansea, UK, and Milpitas, CA, 2002.

———. IslamOnline Web site at http://www.islamonline.net/english/index.shtml (accessed October 3, 2007).

al-Qasim, Yahya. *Ghayat al-Amani fi Akhbar al-Qutr al-Yamani.* Cairo, 1968.

al-Qassam, Faisal. Discussion transcript. *Al-Jazeera TV* (Qatar), May 15, 2001.

al-Qayrawani. *La Risala.* Fr. trans. from Ar. by Leon Bercher. 5th ed. Alger, 1960. Eng. trans. in Bat Ye'or, *The Dhimmi* (1985): 161; idem, *Islam and Dhimmitude* (2001): 99.

Qirqisani, Ya'qub ibn Ishaq. *Kitab al-Anwar Wal-Maraqib: Code of Islamic Law.* Ed. by Leon Nemoy. 7 vols. New York, 1939–1943.

Quatremère, Etienne Marc. *Histoire des sultans mamlouks de l'Egypte (Suluk li-ma'rifat Duwal al-muluk, al-Maqrisi).* 2 vols. Paris, 1837–45.

Qur'an. *See under* Ali; Arberry; Al-Azhar; Blachère; Dawood; *Noble Qur'an*; Pickthall; and Shakir.

Qurtubi, Muhammad ibn Ahmad, and Aisha Abdurrahman Bewley. *Tafsir Al-Qurtubi: Classical Commentary of the Holy Qur'an.* London, 2003.

Qutb, Sayyid. *'Adalah fi al-ijtimaiyah al-Islam.* Egypt, [1949]. Trans. as *Social Justice in Islam,* Washington, DC, 1953.

———. *Ma'rakatuna ma'a—al Yahud (Our Struggle with the Jews).* Commentary and Eng. trans. in Nettler, *Past Trials* (1987): 72–89.

———, M. A. Salahi, and A. A. Shamis, *In the Shade of the Qur'an = Fizilal al-Qur'an.* Vol. 1. Leicester, UK, 1999.

Raddatz, Hans-Peter. *Die Stellung und Bedeutung des Sufyan at-Tauri; ein Beitrag zur Geistesgeschichte d. frühen Islam* [The place and significance of the *Sufyan at-Tauri*—A contribution to the spiritual history of early Islam]. Dissertation, Bonn (May 31, 1967).

———. *Von Gott zu Allah?: Christentum und Islam in der liberalen Fortschrittsgesellschaft* [From God to Allah?—Christianity and Islam in liberal progressive society]. Munich, 2001.

————. *Von Allah zum Terror?: der Djihad und die Deformierung des Westens*. [From Allah to Terror?—Djihad and the Deformation of the West]. Munich, 2002.

————. *Allahs Schleier: die Frau im Kampf der Kulturen* [Allah's Veil—The Woman in the Clash of Civilizations]. Munich, 2004.

————. *Antisemitismus im (Gegenwarts-)Islam: Europa im Konflikt zwischen Toleranz und Ideologie (Antisemitism in [Contemporary] Islam: Europe in the Conflict between Tolerance and Ideology)*. Lecture held at Mannheim (July 14, 2006). Wetzlar, 2006. Herein, Eng. trans. by Michael J. Miller.

————. *Iran: persische Hochkultur und irrationale Macht* [Iran—Persian High Culture and Irrational Power]. Munich, 2006.

————. *Allah und die Juden: die islamische Renaissance des Antisemitismus* [Allah and the Jews—The Islamic Renaissance of Antisemitism]. Berlin, 2007.

Rafaeli, S. "Matzor Yerushalayim be-Yemei Ibrahim Pasha [The Siege of Jerusalem under Ibrahim Pasha: Chronicle of an English Family in Jerusalem]." In *Luah Eretz Yisrael: 5672* [Heb. Calendar], Jerusalem, 1911–12.

Raghib al-Isfahani. *al-Mufradat fi gharib al Qur'an*. Cairo, 1906.

Ranalli, Ralph. "Harvard to Return $2.5m Given by Arab President." *Boston Globe*, July 28, 2004.

Rantburg. "Al Qaeda Vows Reprisal for Israeli Attacks." *Associated Press*, July 27, 2006. http://rantburg.com/poparticle.php?ID=161005&D=2006-07-27&SO=&HC=1 (accessed October 1, 2007).

Ratzaby, Yehuda. "The Mawza' Exile (Heb.)." *Sefunot* 5 (1961): 383–90.

————, ed. *See under* al-Zaihri, *Sefer Hammusar* (1965).

————. "The Expulsion of Yemenite Jewry to Mawza' in 1679–80 in Light of Recently Discovered Sources (Heb.)" *Zion* 37 (1972): 197–215. Herein, Eng. trans. by Rivkah Fishman.

————. *The Yemenite Jews: Literature and Studies: Bibliography 1935–1975*. Jerusalem, 1976.

————. "Expulsion to the Desert—The Most Decisive Event in the History of the Jews of Yemen (Heb.)." *Et-Mol* 9, no. 3 [53] (January 1984): 16–18. Herein, Eng. trans. by Rivkah Fishman.

————. "Urban Jewish Life in Central Yemen (Heb.)." *Sefunot* 19 (1989): 123–64.

————. "Yemenite Jewry in Non-Jewish Courts: Eleven New Court Documents, 1864–1950 (Heb.)." In Toaff, *East and Maghreb* 6 (1995).

Raven, W. "Sira." *EI2*.

Reisser, Moshe. *Sha'arei Yerushalayim* [The Gates of Jerusalem]. Lwow, 1879.

"Report of the Iraqi Commission of Inquiry on the Farhud (1941)." In Stillman, *The Jews . . . Modern Times* (1991): 405–17.

Reports from Her Majesty's Consuls relating to the Condition of the Christians in Turkey. Vols. of 1860, 1867. Excerpts in Bat Ye'or, *The Decline (1996)*: 409–33.

Reuters. "Moslem Terror Chasing Out 1,000 Christian Arabs a Year." April 12, 2006. http://www.israelnationalnews.com/News/Flash.aspx/101940 (accessed October 3, 2007).

————. "Islamists Threaten Yemeni Jews for Selling Wine." January 29, 2007.

Ribbi, A. Letter (Tangier, March 10, 1908) to AIU President, Paris. AIU Archives: MOROCCO IV C II.

Rida, Rashid. *Tafsir al-Manar*. 12 vols. Cairo, 1906–1935. Republished as *Tafsir al-Qur'an al-Hakim al-Mustahir bi Tafsir al-Manar*, 12 vols., with indices. Cairo, 1954–1961.

Ridgeway, W. *Report on General Questions Connected with Morocco* (July 10, 1893). FO 99/302: 10–11.

Ibn ar-Rijal. *Al-Nusus al-Zahirah fi Ijlaa al-Yahud al-Fajirah, Dirasat Yamaniyyah* [The plain explanation of the expulsion of the wretched Jews]. Ed. by Abd al-Hadi al-Tazi. *Journal of Yemen Center for Studies and Research* 4. San'a, 1980.

Robson, James. "Tradition, the Second Foundation of Islam." *Muslim World* 41 (1951): 22.

————, trans. *See under* al-Baghawi. *Mishkat Al-Masabih* (1963).

————. "Hadith." *EI-O*.

Rodriguc, Aron, ed. *Ottoman and Turkish Jewry—Community and Leadership*. Bloomington, IN, 1992.

Rogge, O. John. *The Official German Report*. New York, 1961.

Rohlfs, F. G. *Adventures in Morocco and Journeys through the Oases of Draaand Tafilet*. London, 1874.

Romanelli, Samuel Aaron. *Massa' ba-'Arav* (Heb.). Cambridge, 1886. *See also* Schirman, *Ketavim*: 110.

————, Yedida Kalfon Stillman, and Norman A. Stillman. *Travail in an Arab Land*. Tuscaloosa, 1989.

Romero, Eugenio Maria. *El martirio de joven Hachuel o la heroina Hebrea*. Gibraltar, 1837.

————. *Jewish Heroine of the Nineteenth Century: A Tale Founded on Fact*. London, 1839.

Rondot, Pierre, and Paul Abela. *Les Chrétiens du Monde Arabe: Problématiques Actuelles et Enjeux*. Paris, 1989.

Rosen, Lawrence. "A Moroccan Jewish Community during the Middle Eastern Crisis." *American Scholar* 37 (Summer 1968): 435–51. Repr. in Sweet, *Peoples and Cultures* 2.

————. "Muslim-Jewish Relations in a Moroccan City." *IJMES* 3, no. 4 (October 1972): 435–49.

Rosenthal, Franz, trans. *See under* Khaldun, *Muqaddima*.

————. "Some Minor Problems in the Qur'an." In Starr, *Joshua Starr Memorial Volume*.

Roth, C. B. "Samuel Sumbal, Forgotten Jewish Statesman (Heb.)." *Studies and Activities* 3 (Ben Institute, Jerusalem, 1960): 13–17.

Roth, Cecil. *See under* Lewis, Geoffrey.

Rubin, Barry. *The Arab States and the Palestine Conflict*. Syracuse, NY, 1981.

Rubin, Michael. "Iran's Burgeoning WMD Programs." *Middle East Intelligence Bulletin* 4, no. 3 (March–April 2002). http://www.meib.org/articles/0203_irn1.htm (accessed October 1, 2007).

Rubin, Uri. "Apes, Pigs, and the Islamic Identity." *Israel Oriental Studies* 17 (1997): 89–93.

Rubinstein, E. "'The Protocols of the Elders of Zion' in the Arab-Jewish Conflict in Erez Israel in the Twenties (Heb.)." *Ha-Mizrah he-Hadash* 26 (1978): 37–42.

Runciman, Steven. *A History of the Crusades*. 3 vols. Cambridge, UK, 1951–55.

Russell, Jenna. "Harvard Is Pressured to Return $2.5m Gift." *Boston Globe*, May 11, 2003.

Rycaut, Paul. *The History of the Turkish Empire from the Year 1623 to the Year 1677*. London, 1680.

———. *The Present State of the Ottoman Empire*. London, 1686.

Sa'adia ben Joseph. *Kitab al-amanat wa'i-i'tiqadat*. Ed. by S. Landauer. Leyden, 1880.

———. *See under* Schechter (1903).

Sabari, Yihye. *Through the Paths of Yemen: The Memoirs of Yihye Sabari* (Heb.). Ed. by Y. Tobi, Tel Aviv, 1990.

Sabille, Jacques. *Les Juifs de Tunisie sous Vichy et L'occupation*. Paris, 1954.

Sabri, Ikrime. Sermon at Al-Aqsa Mosque, Jerusalem. *Voice of Palestine*, July 11, 1997.

Ibn Sa'd. *Biographien Muhammeds*. Ed. by E. Sachau et al. Leyden, 1904–15.

———. *Kitab Al-Tabaqat Al-Kabir*. 2 vols. Eng. trans. by S. Moinul Haq and H. K. Ghazanfar. New Delhi, 1993.

al-Sa'di, Abd Allah Muh. b. Hamzah b. Abu al-Najm, *Durar al-Ahadith al-Nabawiyya bi-al-Asanid al-Yahyawiyya li-al-Hadi Ila al-Haqq Yahya b. Husayn*. Ed. by Yahya 'Abd al-Karim al-Fudayl. Beirut, 1979.

al-Safir. "Nass al-Risala al-Maftuha wajahaha Hizballah ila-l-Mustad'afin fi Lubnan wa-l-Alam." Beirut, February 16, 1985. Abridged Eng. trans. as "The Hizballah 'Program'" at http://www.acsa2000.net/hizballah.htm (accessed October 1, 2007).

Safir, Jacob. *Even Sappir [Iben Safir]* (Heb.). Vol. 1, Lyck, 1866; vol. 2, Mainz, 1874.

Safran, J. M. "Identity and Differentiation in 9th-Century al-Andalus." *Speculum* 76 (2001): 582.

al-Sahuli, Yahya. *Fi Intiza' Atfal Ahl al-Dhimmah 'ind Mawt al-Aabawayni* [On Confiscating Children of the Protected Peoples upon the Death of Their Parents]. Manuscript. In Zabarah, *Nayl al-Watar*: 387.

Ibn Sa'id al-Andalusi. *Kitab Tabaqat al-umam*. Trans. R. Blachère. Beirut, 1912.

Said, Edward W. *Orientalism*. New York, 1978. Harmondsworth, 1995.

Salama, O. *See under* Cohen, A., *Jews in the Moslem Religious Court*.

Salmon, Pierre, ed. *Mélanges d'islamologie: Volume dédiée à la mémoire de Armand Abel*. Leyden, 1974.

Sambari, Joseph, and Shimon Shtober. *Sefer Divre Yosef*. Jerusalem, 1981. Ibid., 1994, with abstract in English.

Samhudi, Nur-ad-Din A. *Hulasat al-wafa' bi-ahbar dar al-mustafa*. Bulaq, 1868.

Samuel b. Ishaq Uceda. *Lehem dim'ah (The Bread of Tears)*. Venice, 1606. Eng. trans. in Bat Ye'or, *The Dhimmi* (1985): 354.

Samuel, S. M. *The History and Genealogy of the Jewish Families of Yates and Samuel of Liverpool, with Additions and Notes by L. Wolf*. London, 1901.

Sanasarian, Eliz. *Religious Minorities in Iran*. Cambridge, UK, 2000.

Santillana, M. *Proposal for a Tunisian Civil and Commercial Code*. Foreword by report author. Tunis, 1899.

Saphir, Jacob. *Igeret Teman ha-shenit 'al odot mashiah shav she-kam me-hadash be-Teman, shemo Yehudah Bar Shalom*. Vilna, 1872 or 1873.

Saqr, Atiyyah. "Jews as Depicted in the Qur'an." Online answer to the question: "What, according to the Qur'an, are the Jews' main characteristics and qualities?" IslamOnline.com, March 22, 2004. http://www.islamonline.com/news/newsfull.php?newid=449 (accessed November 20, 2007).

ha-Sarfati, Abner. *Yahas Fes*. Bibliothèque AIU: H84A. *See also* Semach, "Une chronique juive": 91.

Sassoon [Collection]. MS 1007.

Sassoon, David Solomon. *The Newly-Discovered Diwan of the Vizier Samuel Hannaghid*. Reprinted from the *Jewish Chronicle Supplement*, March 20, 1924. London, 1924.

———. "Le-Korot ha-Yehudim be-Teman." *Ha-Tsofeh le-Hokhmat Yisrael* 15 (1931): 1–26.

———, ed. *Diwan of Shemuel Hannaghid: According to a Unique Manuscript with an Introduction and Index of Poems*. Oxford, 1934.

———. *A History of the Jews in Baghdad*. Letchworth, 1949.

Satloff, Robert. *Among the Righteous: Lost Stories from the Holocaust's Long Reach into Arab Lands*. New York, 2006.

Saurin, Jules. *Manuel de l'émigrant en Tunisie*. Paris, 1894.

Sawirus ibn al-Muqaffa. *History of the Patriarchs of the Coptic Church of Alexandria*. 4 vols. Trans. B. T. A. Evetts. Paris, 1904–1914. See also *Patrologia Orientalis* 5 (Paris, 1907); repub. 1947; Turnhout, 2003.

El Sayed [al-Sayyid], Abdul Sattar. "The Jews in the Quran." In al-Azhar, *Fourth Conference*: 527–34; extracts in Green, *Arab Theologians*: 41–45.

Schacht, Joseph. "A Revaluation of Islamic Traditions." *JRAS* (1949): 143–54. Republished in Warraq, *The Quest*: 358–67.

———. *An Introduction to Islamic Law*. Oxford, UK, 1982.

Schauffler, William G. "Shabbaetai Zevi and His Followers." *JAOS* 2 (1851): 1–26.

Schechter, S. "A Geniza Ms." *A. Berliner Jubilee volume.* Berlin, 1903: Heb. Section, 108–12.

———, and Sa'adia ben Joseph. *Saadyana; Geniza fragments of writings of R. Saadya Gaon and others.* Cambridge, UK, 1903.

———. *See under* Hirsch, "Machpelah."

Schechtman, Joseph B. *On Wings of Eagles; The Plight, Exodus, and Homecoming of Oriental Jewry.* New York, 1961.

———. *The Mufti and the Fuehrer.* New York, 1965.

Scheiber, Alexander. "The Origins of 'Obadyah, the Norman Proselyte (A New Fragment in the Kaufmann Geniza Collection)." *Journal of Jewish Studies* 5 (London, 1954): 32–37.

———, ed. *See under* Goldziher, *Tagebuch* (1978).

———. *Geniza Studies.* Collectanea, 17. Hildesheim, 1981.

Schiff, Jacob H. "Jewish Restrictions in Morocco, Especially in the Interior." In *American Jewish Yearbook*, Philadelphia, 1906: 94–98.

Schleifer, Yigal. "One of the Kurds Leaders Is Jewish? So They Claim in Turkish Newspapers." *Jewish Telegraphic Agency*, April 7, 2003.

Schmitz, H. "Ka'b Al-Ahbar." *EI2* 4: 316–17.

Schoeps, Julius H. *See under* Faber, *Neu-alter Judenhass.*

Scholem, Gershom. Article in Hebrew concerning Gai Hizayon [The Spectacular Valley], written in Yemen, 1666/1667. *Kovets al Yad* 68, no. 4 (1946): 105–41.

———. *Sabbatai Zevi: The Mystical Messiah.* Princeton, NJ, 1973.

Schreiner, M. "Contribution à l'histoire des Juifs en Egypte." *REJ* 31 (1895): 9–10. Eng. trans. in Bat Ye'or, *The Dhimmi* (1985): 194–96.

———. In Kohut, *Semitic Studies* (1897): 495–513.

Schuster, Dan. "Roadblocks to Peace." *Michigan Daily,* April 6, 2005. http://www.michigandaily.com/home/index.cfm?event=displayArticlePrinterFriendly&uStory_id=373a012e-4fe2-4373-b917-6f8caeae027a (accessed October 1, 2007).

Schwab, W. M. *See under* Barnett, *The Sephardi Heritage.*

Schwarz, Jehoseph *Das Heilige Land* [The Holy Land]. Frankfurt, 1852.

———, *Tevuot ha-Aretz* [Crops of the Land]. Jerusalem, 1901.

Schwarzfuchs, S. *East and Maghreb: Researches in the History of the Jews in the Orient and North Africa,* vol. 3. Ramat Gan, Israel, 1981.

Seailles, G. *Alfred Dehodencq: L'Homme et l'artiste.* Paris, 1910.

Sedar, Irving, and Harold Greenberg. *Behind the Egyptian Sphinx.* Philadelphia, 1960.

Seligsohn, M. "Isaac Ben Samuel of Acre." *See under* Kohler.

———. "Machpelah." *See under* Hirsch.

———. "Michael Ben Shabbethai Cohen Balbo." *See under* Jacobs.

Sémach, Y. D. *Une Mission de l'Alliance au Yémen.*

Paris, 1910. Eng. trans. of extract herein from Bat Ye'or *The Dhimmi* (1985): 341–43.

———. "Une chronique juive de Fès: Le 'Yahas Fès' de Ribbi Abner Hassarfaty." *Hespéris* 19 (1934): 91–93.

Sen, Amartya. *Identity and Violence. The Illusion of Destiny.* New York, 2006.

Serels, M. Mitchell. *A History of the Jews of Tangier in the Nineteenth and Twentieth Centuries.* New York, 1991.

Serfaty, A. B. M. *The Jews of Gibraltar under British Rule.* Gibraltar, 1958.

Seri, S., and Y. Tobi. *New Poems of Rabbi Shalom Shabazi* (Heb.). Jerusalem, 1976.

Serjeant, Robert B. "A Judeo-Arab House-Deed from Habbán (with notes on the former Jewish communities of the Wahidi Sultanate)." *JRAS* 3–4 (October 1953): 117–31. Repr. in ibid., *Customary and Shariah Law in Arabian Society* 8. London, 1991: 113.

———. "A Judeo Arab House Deed from Habban." *JRAS* (1953)

———. "Hud and Other South Arabian Prophets." *Le Museon* 24 (1953): 121–79.

Shabazi, Shalom (Salem). Poems, in Hayyim, *Hafetz Hayyim.*

Shadegg, John. Floor Speech #2 in the Iraq Debate. February 13, 2007. http://johnshadegg.house.gov/News/DocumentSingle.aspx?DocumentID=58442 (accessed October 1, 2007).

Shakir, M. H., trans. *The Qur'an.* Elmhurst, NY, 1999.

Shaler, William. *Sketches of Algiers, Political, Historical, and Civil.* Boston, 1826.

al-Sharif, Kamil, and Mustaf'a Siba'i. *Ikhwan al-Muslimun fi Harb Filastin* (Ar.). Cairo, 1984.

Shaw, Stanford J. *Turkey and the Holocaust: Turkey's Role in Rescuing Turkish and European Jewry from Nazi Persecution, 1933–1945.* New York, 1993.

al-Shawkani, Muhammad. *Kitab al-Sayl al-Jarrar al-Mutadafiq 'ala Hada'iq al-Azhar* [The book of the abundant spring which flows from the flower gardens]. Vols. A–D. Beirut, 1985.

———. *Risalah fi Hukm Sibyan al-Dhimmiyyin idha Mat Abawahum* (On the law regarding children of protected peoples upon the death of their fathers). Manuscript. In Hibshi, *Thabt bi-Muallafat*: no. 163.

al-Shaybani. *The Islamic Law of Nations. Shaybani's Sitar.* Trans. with introduction, notes, and appendices by Majid Kadduri. Baltimore, 1966.

Shea, Nina, ed. *In the Lion's Den: A Shocking Account of Persecution and Martyrdom of Christians Today and How We Should Respond.* Nashville, 1997.

Shmuelevitz, Aryeh. *See under* Kapsali.

Shulewitz, Malka, ed. *The Forgotten Millions—The Modern Jewish Exodus from Arab Lands.* London, 1999.

Sick, Gary. "US Can Exploit Peaceful Iran Revolution." *Newsday*, June 11, 1997.

Silvestre de Sacy, Antoine Isaac. *Chrestomathie arabe,*

ou, Extraits de divers écrivains arabes, tant en prose qu'en vers, avec une traduction française et des notes. 3 vols., 2nd ed. Paris, 1826–27.

———. *Exposé de la religion des druzes, tiré des livres religieux de cette secte, et précédé d'une introduction et de la Vie du khalife Hakem-biamr-Allah.* 2 vols. Paris, 1838. Amsterdam, 1964.

Simon-Pikali, E. *See under* Cohen, A., *Jews in the Moslem Religious Court.*

Simon Wiesenthal Center. "Turkey—Demography." http://motlc.learningcenter.wiesenthal.org/text/x33/xm3316.html (accessed October 1, 2007).

Singer, Isidore, and Gotthard Deutsch. "Graetz, Heinrich." JewishEncyclopedia.com.

Sivan, Emmanuel. *L'Islam et La Croisade, idéologie et propagande dans les réactions musulmanes aux Croisades.* Paris, 1968.

———. *Islamic Fundamentalism and Antisemitism.* Lecture held February 18, 1985. Jerusalem, 1985.

———. *Interpretations of Islam, Past and Present.* Princeton, NJ, 1985.

———. "Islamic Fundamentalism, Antisemitism, and Anti-Zionism." In Wistrich, *Anti-Zionism* (1990): 82.

———. *Radical Islam: Medieval Theology and Modern Politics.* New Haven, CT, 1990.

———. "Palestine during the Crusades." In Avi-Yonah, *A History of the Holy Land* (2001): 244.

Skoglund, Elizabeth R. *A Quiet Courage: Per Anger, Wallenberg's Co-Liberator of Hungarian Jews.* Grand Rapids, MI, 1997.

Skrine, Francis Henry, and Edward Denison Ross. *The Heart of Asia. A History of Russian Turkestan and the Central Asian Khanates from the Earliest Times.* London, 1899.

Slouschz, N. "Études sur l'Histoire des Juifs au Maroc." Part 1: *Archives Marocaines* 4 (1905): 345. Part 2: ibid 6: 149.

———. "Israélites de Tripolitaine." *Bulletin AIU* (1906): 107–108. Eng. trans. reproduced from Bat Ye'or *The Dhimmi* (1985): 328–29.

———. *Travels in North Africa.* Philadelphia, 1927.

Smaja (Mardochée). *L'Extension de la juridiction et de la nationalité françaises en Tunisie.* Tunis, 1906.

Small, Charles H. *See under* Kaplan.

Smith, G. R., ed. *See under* Hamdani, *A Critical Edition.*

de Sola Pool. "The Levantine Jews in the United States." *American Jewish Yearbook* 15 (1913/1914): 208.

Solnick, Aluma. "Based on Koranic Verses, Interpretations, and Traditions, Muslim Clerics State: The Jews Are the Descendants of Apes, Pigs, and Other Animals." *SR* 11 (November 1, 2002) http://memri.org/bin/articles.cgi?Page=archives&Area=sr&ID=SR01102 (accessed October 1, 2007).

Soroudi, Sorour. "The Concept of Jewish Impurity and Its Reflection in Persian and Judeo-Persian Traditions." *Irano-Juduica* 3 (1994): 156.

Sourdel-Thomine, Janine, ed. *Ali of Heart.* Damascus, 1953.

Speer, Albert. *Inside the Third Reich.* New York, 1970.

Spencer, Robert, ed. *The Myth of Islamic Tolerance: How Islamic Law Treats Non-Muslims.* Amherst, NY, 2005.

———. *The Truth about Muhammad.* Washington, DC, 2006.

Sprenger, Aloys. *Das Leben und die Lehre des Mohammad.* 3 vols. Berlin, 1861–69. 1 vol., Hildesheim, Zurich, and New York, 2003.

Spyridon, S. N. "Annals of Palestine, 1821–1841." *Journal of the Palestine Oriental Society* 18 (1938): 114.

Staehelin, A. *In Algerien, Marokko, Palaestina und am Roten Meere Reiseskizzen.* Basel, 1891.

Stalinsky, Steven. "Palestinian Authority Sermons, 2000–2003." *SR* 24 (December 26, 2003) http://www.memri.org/bin/articles.cgi?Page=archives&Area=sr&ID=SR2403 (accessed October 1, 2007).

Starr, Joshua, and Conference on Jewish Relations (US). *The Joshua Starr Memorial Volume; Studies in History and Philology.* JSS 5 (1953).

Stein, E. *Alttestam. Bibelkritik i. D. späthellenist. Litt.* Lwow, 1935.

Steinschneider, Moritz. *Polemische und Apologetische Literatur in Arabischer Sprache Zwischen Muslimen, Christen, und Juden, in Abhandlungen für die Kunde des Morgenlandes.* Leipzig, 1877.

———. *Die arabische Literatur der Juden.* Frankfurt, 1902.

Stenhouse, Paul. "Muhammad, Qur'anic Texts, the Shari'a and Incitement to Violence." October 25, 2005: 2–3. http://www.jihadwatch.org/archives/008695.php (accessed October 1, 2007).

Stern, Henry A. *Dawnings of Light in the East.* London, 1854.

Stillman, Norman A. "Muslims and Jews in Morocco." *JQ* 5: 76–83.

———. "The Sefrou Remnant." *JSS* 35, nos. 3–4 (July–October 1973): 255.

———. "New Attitudes toward the Jew in the Arab World." *JSS* 37, nos. 3–4 (1975): 197.

———. "The Moroccan Experience—A Revisionist View." *Association for Jewish Studies, Newsletter* 18 (1976): 13–14

———. "The Moroccan Jewish Experience: A Revisionist View." *JQ* 9 (1978): 111–23.

———. *The Jews of Arab Lands. A History and Source Book.* Philadelphia, 1979.

———. *See under* Romanelli, *Travail in an Arab Land* (1989).

———. *The Jews of Arab Lands in Modern Times.* Philadelphia, 1991.

———. *Sephardi Religious Responses to Modernity.* Australia and Luxembourg, 1995.

Stookey, R. W. *Yemen: The Politics of the Yemen Arab Republic.* Boulder, CO, 1978.

Strauss, E. [E. Ashtor]. *Toldot ha'Yehudim be'Mizrahim Yisurehah (History of the Jews in Egypt and Syria under the Rule of the Mamluks)* Vol. 1 of 3. Jerusalem, 1944(–1970).

———. "The Methods of Islamic Polemics (Heb.)." In *Memorial Volume* (1946): 182–97.

———. "The Social Isolation of the Ahl ad-Dhimma." In Komlos, *Études* (1950): 73–94.

Stuart, Charles. *Journal of a Residence in Northern Persia and the Adjacent Provinces of Turkey.* London, 1854.

al-Suyuti, Jalal al-Din. *Tafsir al-Jalalayn.* Beirut, 1404 H (1984).

———. *Durr al-Manthur.* Vol. 3. Beirut, n.d. Quotes herein, in Eng. trans., reproduced from Bostom, *Legacy.*

Swaan, W. *See under* Landau, R.

Swedish Research Institute in Istanbul. *See* Ehrensvärd, *On Both Sides.*

Sweet, Louise Elizabeth. *Peoples and Cultures of the Middle East; An Anthropological Reader.* 2 vols. Garden City, NY, 1970.

Sykes, Percy Molesworth. *A History of Persia . . . with Maps and Illustrations.* 2 vols. London, 1930.

Syrian Arab News Agency. "Speech of President Bashar Al-Assad Welcoming His Holiness Pope John Paul II on His Arrival in Damascus." May 5, 2001.

Tabandeh, Sultanhussein. *A Muslim Commentary on the Universal Declaration of Human Rights.* Eng. trans. by F. J. Goulding. London, 1970.

al-Tabari. *Ta'rikh al-Rusul wa al-Muluk. Annales quos scripsit Abu Djafar Mohammed ibn Djarir al-Tabari.* 16 vols. Ed. by M. J. de Goeje. Leyden, 1879–1901. Reprinted Lugd. Bat, 1964–1965.

———. *Selections from the Annals of Tabari.* Ed. by M. J. de Goeje. Leyden, 1902.

———. *Kitab al-Jihad wa-Kitab al-jizyah wa-Ahkam al-muharibin min Kitab ikhtilaf al-fuqaha* [Book of the Holy War]. Ed. by Joseph Schacht. Leyden, 1933.

———. *A Renegade Jew as the Source of the Shi'ite "Heresy," and the "Conspiracy" to Destroy the Early Islamic Caliphate.* Eng. trans. in Nettler, "Islamic Archetypes of the Jews" (1990): 66.

———. *Jami` al-Bayān fii Tafsiir al-Qur'aan.* Ed. by Mahmud Shākir. 16 vols. Al-Qahirah, 1955–69; Beirut, 2001.

———. *The Commentary on the Qur'an; Being an Abridged Trans. of Jami' al-bayan 'an ta'wil ay al-Qur'an.* Introd. and notes by J. Cooper, ed. by W. F. Medlung and A. Jones. New York, 1987.

———. *The History of al-Tabari.* Volume 8. "The Victory of Islam." Eng. trans. by Michael Fishbein. Albany, NY, 1997.

———, and Yasir S. Ibrahim, trans. *Al-Tabari's Book of Jihad: A Translation from the Original Arabic.* Lewiston, NY, 2007.

Tabbara, Afiif 'Abd al-Fattah. *Al-Yahud fi al-Qur'an: tahlil 'ilmi li-nusus al-Qur'an fi al-yahud 'ala dau' al-ahdath al-hadira, ma'a qisas Ibrahim wa Yusuf wa*

Musa `alayhim al-salaam [The Jews in the Qur'an: Scientific Analysis of Qur'anic texts concerning the Jews in the Light of Modern Events Combined with the Stories of the Prophets Abraham, Joseph and Moses]. Beirut, 1965/66. 8th printing, 1980.

Taffiletta. *A Short and Strange Relation of Some Parts of the Life of Taffiletta.* London, 1669.

Taheri, Amir. "Press Release: Amir Taheri Addresses Queries about Dress Code Story." *Benador Associates,* May 22, 2006. http://www.benadorassociates .com/article/19508 (accessed October 1, 2007).

Ibn Taimiyya. *Slyasa Sar'iya. See under* Laoust, *Le Traité.*

Takacs, M. P. *A Blau Lajos Talmudtudomanyi Tarsulat: Evkonyve* (Hungarian). Budapest, 1935.

al-Tall, Abdallah. *Khatr al-Yahudiyya al-'Alamiyya 'Ala al-Islam wa-al-Mashiyya* [The Danger of World Jewry to Islam and Christianity]. Cairo, 1964.

Talmud: Tractate Baba Batra, section Hekerim [Abandoned Property], III, section 25. In *Majallat al-Mashriq* [*Orient Magazine*] 18: 770.

Tantawi, Muhammad Sayyid. *Das Volk Israels in Koran und Sunna.* Cairo, 1966.

———. *Banu Isra'il fi al-Qur'an wa al-Sunna* [The Children of Israel in the *Qur'an* and the *Traditions*]. PhD diss. pub. in 1968–69. Repub. Cairo. 1986; 3rd printing, 1407 H (1987).

———. *The Sons of Israel in the Koran and Muslim Tradition.* 2nd ed. Cairo, 2000.

al-Tarihi, al-Din bin Muhammad. *Majma' Al-Bahrain. See* http://www.islam4u.com/almojib/4/0/4.0.2.htm (accessed October 1, 2007).

Ta'riikh al-Khamiis. See under al-Diyarbakri, *Ta'rikh;* al-Tabari. *Ta'rikh* (1879).

Tavernier, Jean Baptiste, and François Bernier. *Collections of Travels through Turkey into Persia, and the East-Indies: Giving an Account of the Present State of Those Countries.* London, 1684.

Taylor-Schechter Collection. [Geniza mss] 11.3–9; 12.3 [trans. in Goitein, *Readings*], 192, 289, 290; 16.39, 272, 286, 296; 8 J 11, 19, 21, 26; 10 J 17, 18; 13 J 3, 4, 11, 14, 15, 22, 26, 28, 33, 36; 18 J 3; Box 25, f. 62 (N 118); J 17; K 25; NS J 3, 290. *See also* Cambridge University Library.

Teixeira, Pedro, et al. *The Travels of Pedro Teixeira: With His "Kings of Harmuz" and Extracts from His "Kings of Persia."* London, 1902. Reprint, Nendeln, Liechtenstein, 1967.

Terrasse, Henri. *Histoire du Maroc.* 2 vols. Paris, 1949.

de Thevenot, Jean, and Archibald Lovell. *The Travels of Monsieur de Thevenot into the Levant in Three Parts, Viz. into I. Turkey, II. Persia, III. the East-Indies.* London, 1687.

Tibi, Bassam. *Schatten Allahs.* Munich, 1996.

———. *Kreuzzug und Djihad.* Munich, 1999.

Tincq, Henri. *L'Etoile et la Croix. Jean-Paul II—Israël: l'explication.* Paris, 1993.

Tissot, C. *See under* Drummond-Hay.

Toaff, A., ed. *East and Maghreb: Researches in the History of the Jews in the Orient and North Africa 6.* Jerusalem, 1995.

Tobi, Yosef, ed. *See under* Yesha'yahu and Tobi, *The Jews of Yemen* (1975).

——, ed. *The Jews of Yemen in the Nineteenth Century* (Heb.). Tel Aviv, 1976.

——. *Legacy of the Jews of Yemen: Studies and Researches* (Heb.). Jerusalem, 1976.

——. *See under* Seri (1976).

——, ed. *The History of the Jews of Yosefemen from Their Own Chronicles* (Heb.). Jerusalem, 1979.

——, and Y. Tzur. *The Zaydi Sect and the Imams: The Foundations of Their Attitude to the Jews, Unit Two: The Jews of Yemen: Chapters in Their History and Culture* (Heb.). Tel Aviv, 1985.

——, ed. *See under* Ovadia, *In the Paths of Yemen and Zion* (1985).

——. *Studies in 'Megillat Teman': Community of San'a, Shabbateanism, Iraqi Family, Mahris* (Heb.). Jerusalem, 1986.

——. "The Attitude of Imam al-Hadi, the Founder of the Zaydi Kingdom to the Jews of Yemen." In Ben-Sasson, *The Culture* (1989): 53–82.

——, ed. *See under* Sabari, *Through the Paths of Yemen* (1990).

——. "Conversion to Islam among Yemenite Jews under Zaidi Rule: The Position of Zaidi Law, the Imam, and Muslim Society (Heb.)." *Pe'amim* 42 (1990): 105–26. Herein, Eng. trans. by Rivkah Fishman.

Toledano, Jacob M. *NerHa-Ma'arav: Hu Toledot Yisrael Be-Marokko.* Jerusalem, 1911.le Tourneau, Roger. "Notes sur les lettres latines de Nicolas Clénard, relatant son séjour dans le royaume de Fés (1540–1541)." *Hespéris* 19, nos. 1–2 (1934): 51.

——, and Louis Paye. "Les Cordonniers de Fès." *Hespéris* 22 (1936): 33.

——. *Fès avant le protectorat.* Casablanca, 1949.

——. *Fes in the Age of the Merinids.* Trans. from the Fr. (ibid) by B. A. Clement. The Centers of Civilization series 4. Norman, OK, 1961.

——. *Evolution politique de l'Afrique du Nord musulmane 1920–1961.* Paris, 1962.

Tritton, Arthur S. *The Caliphs and Their Non-Muslim Subjects: A Critical Study of the 'Umar Covenant.* London, 1930.

——. "Islam and the Protected Religions." *JRAS* 10 (1931): 34–38.

——. *Materials on Muslim Education in the Middle Ages.* London, 1957.

Twersky, Isadore, ed. *Studies in Medieval Jewish History and Literature.* Cambridge, MA, 1984.

Ubicini, M. A. *Letters on Turkey. Part 2. The Raiahs.* Trans. from the French by Lady Easthope. London, 1856.

Ufrani. *Nuzhat al-Hadi: Histoire de la dynastie Sa'dienne (1511–1670).* Ed. by O. Houdas. Paris, 1988.

US Department of State. *2001 Report on International Religious Freedom.* http://www.state.gov/g/drl/rls/irf/2001/ (accessed October 3, 2007).

Vacalopoulos, A. E. *Origins of the Greek Nation—The Byzantine Period.* New Brunswick, NJ, 1970.

Vajda, Georges S. "À propos de la situation des Juifs et des Chrétiens à Séville au début du XIIe siècle." *REJ* 99 (1935): 127–29. Herein, trans. by Michael J. Miller as "Concerning the Situation of Jews and Christians in Seville at the Beginning of the 12th Century."

——. "Juifs et musulmans selon le hadit." *Journal Asiatique* 229 (1937): 57–127. Herein, trans. by Susan Emanuel.

——. *Introduction à la pensée juive du Moyen Âge.* Paris, 1947.

——. *Répertoire des catalogues et inventaires de manuscrits arabes.* Paris, 1949.

——. *Judische Philosophie.* Bern, 1950.

——. "Notes de bibliographie maghrébine." *Hespéris* 7 (1950): 216.

——. "Un recueil de texts historiques judéomarocaines." *Hespéris* 12 (1951).

——. *Études d'Orientalisme dédiées à la mémoire de Lévi-Provençal.* 2 vols. Paris, 1962. See essay, in vol. 2, p. 811, "Un Traite Maghrebin 'Adversos Judaeos: Ahkam Ahl Al-Dimma Du Sayh Muhammad B. 'Abd Al-Karim Al-Magili.'"

——. "L'image du Juif dans le Tradition Islamique." *Les Nouveaux Cahiers* 13–14 (1968): 7. Eng. trans. in Littman, "Protected Peoples" (2005): 106.

Valadji, J. Annual report to the AIU Central Committee, Paris (Fez, September 1, 1903). AIU FRANCE: XIV F 25.

Vambery, Arminius. *Travels in Central Asia.* London, 1864.

Vatican Council (Second). "Declaration of the Relationship of the Church to Non-Christian Religions (Nostre Aetate)." October 28, 1965. http://www.vatican.va/archive/hist_councils/ii_vatican_council/documents/vat-ii_decl_19651028_nostra-aetate_en.html (accessed October 3, 2007).

Veccia Vaglieri, L. "Fadak." *EI2* 2: 725–27.

——. "Harra." *EI2* 3: 226–27.

Ibn Verga, Solomon, 'Azri'el Shohet, and Yitzhak Baer. *Sefer Shevet Yehudah.* Jerusalem, 1946.

Viré, F. "Kird." *EI2.*

Vryonis, Speros, Jr. "Seljuk Gulams and Ottoman Devshirmes." *Der Islam* 41 (1965).

——. "A Critical Analysis of Stanford J. Shaw's 'History of the Ottoman Empire and Modern Turkey.' Volume 1. Empire of the Gazis: The Rise and Decline of the Ottoman Empire, 1280–1808." *Balkan Studies.* 24 (1983): 57–62, 68 (off print). Reproduced in Bostom, *The Legacy*: 616–18.

————. "The Experience of Christians under Seljuk and Ottoman Domination, Eleventh to Sixteenth Century." In Gervers and Bikhazi, *Indigenous Christian Communities* (1990): 201.

————. *The Turkish State and History. Clio Meets the Grey Wolf.* New Rochelle, NY, 1991.

————. *The Mechanism of Catastrophe: The Turkish Pogrom of September 6–7, 1955 and the Destruction of the Greek Community of Istanbul.* New York, 2005.

al-Wakidi, Muhammad Ibn 'Umar. *Campaigns of Mohammad.* Ed. by A. von Kremer. Calcutta, 1855.

————. *Muhammed in Medina: das ist Vakidi's Kitab al-Maghazi, in verkürzter deutscher Wiedergabe.* Abridged German trans. by Julius Wellhausen. Berlin, 1882.

————. *The Kitab al-maghazi of al-Waqidi.* Ed. by Marsden Jones. Text in Ar., title-pages, preface and bibliography in Eng. 3 vols. London, 1966. Extracts trans. to Eng. and an. in Stillman, *The Jews . . . Source Book*: 129–36.

Ibn Walid, I. *Va-Yomer Yitzhak* (Heb.). Livorno (Leghorn), 1856.

Wanner, Jan. "Amin al-Husayni and Germany's Arab Policy in the Period 1939–1945." *Archiv Orientalni* 54 (1986): 244.

al-Wansharisi, Ahmad. *Al-Mi'yar al-mu'rib wa 'l-jami' al- mughrib 'an fatawi ahl Ifriqiya wa 'l-Andalus wa 'l-Maghrib.* 12 vols. Fez, 1314–1315 H (1896–1898). *See under* Idris, "Les tributaires." Selected extracts trans. herein by Michael J. Miller as "A Collection of Legal Opinions Demonstrating the Attitudes of Muslim Jurists and Citizens towards the Jews of Muslim Spain and North Africa, Ninth–Fifteenth Centuries." *See also* Amar, Emile, "La pierre de touche."

al-Waqidi. *See* al-Wakidi.

Ibn Warraq. *Why I Am Not a Muslim.* Amherst, NY, 1995.

————, ed. *The Origins of the Koran.* Amherst, NY, 1998.

————, ed. *The Quest for the Historical Muhammad.* Amherst, NY, 2000.

————. *Leaving Islam. Apostates Speak Out.* Amherst, NY, 2003.

————. Foreword in Bostom, *The Legacy of Jihad* (2005).

————. *Defending the West: A Critique of Edward Said's* Orientalism. Amherst, NY, 2007.

Washington Times. "Iran's Mushrooming Threat." June 15, 2004.

Washington, R. N. "Geographical Notice of the Empire of Morocco." *Journal of the Royal Geographical Society* 1 (1832): 123–55.

al-Wasi'i, Abd al-Wasi. *Ta'rikh al-Yaman [Ta'arikh Aliman].* Cairo, 1346 H [1928].

al-Wasiti, Ghazi. *Kitab Radd 'ala Ahl al-Dhimma,* Ed. by R. Gottheil, *JAOS* 41, 5 (1921): 396–97. Excerpted and an. in Norman Stillman, *The Jews . . . Source Book*: 275–76.

————. "An Answer to the Dhimmis." Treatise. Eng. trans. by Richard Gottheil. *JAOS* 41 (1921): 449.

Wasserstein, Bernard. Review of *Turkey and the Holocaust* (by Stanford Shaw). *Times Literary Supplement,* January 7, 1994: 4.

Waterbury, John, *The Commander of the Faithful: The Moroccan Political Elite: A Study in Segmented Politics.* New York, 1970.

Watson, R. S. *A Visit to Wazan: Sacred City of Morocco.* London, 1880.

Watt, W. Montgomery, trans. *The Faith and Practice of Al-Ghazali.* Oxford, UK, 1953.

————. "Al Ansar." *EI-O.*

————. "Hanif." *EI2* 3: 165.

————. "al-Hudaybiyya." *EI2* 3: 539.

Wattie, Chris. "Experts Say Report of Badges for Jews in Iran Is Untrue." *National Post,* May 19, 2006.

————. "Iran Eyes Badges for Jews—Law Would Require Non-Muslim Insignia." *National Post,* May 19, 2006.

Weber, Frank. *The Evasive Neutral.* Columbia, MO, 1979.

Webman, Esther. *Anti-Semitic Motifs in the Ideology of Hizballah and Hamas.* Tel Aviv, 1994.

Webster, D. E. *The Turkey of Atatürk.* Philadelphia, 1939.

Wegner, Gregory Paul. "A Propagandist of Extermination: Johann von Leers and the Antisemitic Formation of Children in Nazi Germany." *Paedagogica Historica* 43 (2007): 299–325.

Weil, Gustav. *Geschichte der Chalifen nach handschriftlichen, grösstentheils noch unbenützten Quellen bearbeitet* [History of the Califs]. 5 vols. Mannheim (1–3) and Stuttgart (4–5), 1846–62.

Wellhausen, Julius. *Muhammed in Medina: Das ist Vakidi's Kitab al-Maghazi in verkürzter deutscher Wiedergabe.* Berlin, 1882.

————. *Reste arabischen Heidentumes. Skizzen und Vorarbeiten* 3. Berlin, 1887.

————. *1. Medina vor dem Islam. 2. Muhammads Gemeindeordnung von Medina. 3. Seine Schreiben, und die Gesandtschaften an ihn. Skizzen und Vorarbeiten* 4. Berlin, 1889. No. 2 trans. by Wolfgang H. Behn as "Muhammad's Constitution of Medina" in Wensinck, *Muhammad*: 136–37.

————. *Die Ehe bei den Arabern.* Göttingen, 1893.

Wenner, M. *Modern Yemen, 1918–1966.* Baltimore, 1967.

Wensinck, Arent Jan. *Mohammed en de Joden te Medina.* Leyden, 1908.

————. *A Handbook of Early Muhammadan Tradition, Alphabetically Arranged.* Leyden, 1927. Repr. 1960, 1971.

————. *Concordance et indices de la tradition musulmane.* 7 vols. Leyden, 1936–69. 8 vols. in 4, 1992.

————, and J. H. Kramers. *Handwörterbuch des Islam.* Leyden, 1941.

————. *Muhammad and the Jews of Medina.* Trans. by Wolfgang H. Behn. Berlin, 1982.

————, and Å. S. Bazmee Ansari, "Baki' al-Gharkad." *EI2* 1: 957–58.

Wertheimer, J., ed. *The Modern Jewish Experience: A Reader's Guide.* New York, 1993.

Wiener, Justus Reid, et al. "Referral of Iranian President Ahmadinejad on the Charge of Incitement to Commit Genocide." *Jerusalem Center for Public Affairs.* Jerusalem, 2006.

Williams, A. Lukyn. *Adversus Judaeos.* Cambridge, 1935.

Wills, C. J. *Persia As It Is. Being Sketches of Modern Persian Life and Character.* London, 1887.

Wilson, Arnold T. "History of the Mission of the Fathers of the Society of Jesus, Established in Persia by the Reverend Father Alexander of Rhodes." *Bulletin of the School of Oriental Studies* 3 (1925): 695.

Wistrich, Robert S., ed. *Anti-Zionism and Antisemitism in the Contemporary World.* New York, 1990.

————. *Antisemitism—The Longest Hatred.* New York, 1991.

Wittek, Paul. *The Rise of the Ottoman Empire.* London, 1938. Richmond, 2001.

Wolfensohn, I. *Ka'b Al-Ahbar und seine Stellung im Hadith und in der islamischen Legendliteratur.* Gelnhausen, 1933.

Wolff, J. *Travels and Adventures of Joseph Wolff.* 2nd ed. London, 1861.

Wolfson, Israel [Abu Dhu'ayb, and Ben-Ze'ev, pseuds.]. *History of the Jews in Arab Countries during the Pre-Islamic Era.* N.d., n.p.

————. *See* Ben-Ze'ev.

World Jewish Congress. "Jews in Moslem Lands." Report to UNESCO, 1959.

Wortabet, Gregory. *Syria and the Syrians* 2. London, 1856.

Wright, Lawrence. *The Looming Tower. Al-Qaeda and the Road to 9/11.* New York, 2006.

Wright, W. *See under* al-Mubarrad, *Kamil.*

Wüstenfeld, Ferdinand. *See under* Yaqut, *Mu'jam* (1868); and idem, *Geographisches Wörterbuch* (1994).

————. *Die Geschichtschreiber der Araber und ihre Werke.* Göttingen, 1882.

————. *See under* Ibn Hisham, *Sirat Rasul Allah.*

Xinhua (Eng. version). "Hamas Leader Urges International Community to Respect Palestinian People's Choice." April 2, 2006. http://news.xinhuanet.com/english/2006-04/02/content_4373348.htm (accessed October 1, 2007).

Ya'ari, A. "Pinkas Shelihutam shel R. Yonah Moshe Navon u-R. Yona Saadia Navon (Heb.)." *Sinai* 25 (1949): 320–30.

————. *Sheluhei Eretz Yisrael* [Emissaries from the Land of Israel]. Jerusalem, 1951.

Yadlin, Rivka. *An Arrogant Oppressive Spirit. Anti-Zionism as Anti-Judaism in Egypt.* Oxford, 1989.

Yahia, Mohammed Taha. "The Attitude of the Jews toward Islam in the Early Days of Islam." In Al-Azhar, *Fourth Conference*: 393–97; extracts herein from Green, *Arab Theologians*: 25.

Ya'qub, Abu Yusuf. *Le Livre de l'impot foncier (Kitab al-Kharadj).* French trans. from Ar. and an. by E. Fagnan. Paris, 1921. Eng. trans. in Bat Ye'or, *The Dhimmi* (1985): 172–73.

Yaqut ibn Abd Allah al-Hamawi. *Mu'jam al-Buldan.* Vol. 3, ed. by F. Wüstenfeld. Leipzig, 1868.

————. *Yaqut's Geographisches Wörterbuch.* Trans. by F. Wüstenfeld. 6 vols. in 11. Frankfurt am Main, 1994.

Yavnieli, S. *Mas'a le-Teiman* [Voyage to Yemen]. Tel Aviv, 1873.

Yavuz, M. Hakun. *Islamic Political Identity in Turkey.* Oxford, 2003.

Yesha'yahu, Y., and S. Greidi, eds. *Mi-Teman le-Zion.* Tel Aviv, 1938. See "Pne Teman," 5–32.

————, and Y. Tobi, eds. *The Jews of Yemen: Studies and Researches* (Heb.). Jerusalem, 1975.

Yishai, Moshe. *Sir be-l'o to'ar: rishme selihut u-mas'a be-Paras.* Tel Aviv, 1950.

Yver, G. "Morocco." *EI1* 6: 579–606.

Zabarah al-San'ani, Muhammad. *Nayl al-Watar.* Cairo, 1350 H [1931].

Abu Zahra, Muhammad. "The Jihad: Striving." In Al-Azhar, *Fourth Conference*: 49–103; extracts herein from Green, *Arab Theologians*: 61.

al-Zaihri. *Sefer Hammusar* (Heb.). Ed. by Y. Ratzabi. Jerusalem, 1965.

az-Zaiyati, Wazzan. *See* Leo Africanus [pseud.].

Zakkar, Suhayl. *See under* al-Alwi, *Sirat al-Hadi.*

Zamakhshari. *Al-Kashshaaf `an Haqaa'iq GhawaamiD al-Tanziil wa-`Uyuun al-Aqaawiil fii Wujuuh alTa'wiil.* Ed. by M. H. Ahmad. Cairo, 1365 H [1946].

————. *Tafsir al-kashshaf an haqa'iq ghawamid at-tanzil wa-uyun al-aqawil fi wujuh at-ta'wil.* Cairo, 1953–1955. Beirut, 2001. Eng. trans. in Gatje. *The Qur'an*: 134.

Ibn Abi Zar. *Rawd al-Qirtas* [The Garden of Pages]. 1326. Fr. trans. in Beaumier, *Rawd al-Kirtas.*

al-Zarkashi, Muhammad ibn Abraham. *Ta'rikh al-dawlatayn al-Muwahhidiyah wa-al-Hafsiyah.* Tunis, 1872.

al-Zawahiri, Ayman. Videotape statement, cited in Rantburg, "Al Qaeda Vows Reprisal."

Ibn Abi Zayd al-Qayrawani. *See under* al-Qayrawani.

Zayd b. Ali. *Corpus iuris di Zayd ibn 'Ali, testo arabo . . . con introduzione . . . da eugenio griffini.* Milano, 1919.

————. *Majmu' al-Fiqh* [Anthology of Laws]. Algeria, 1941.

Zaydan, Abd al-Karim. *Ahkam al-Dhimiyyin wal-Musta'minin.* Baghdad, 1964.

Zeitlin, S. "Review: The Sabbatians and the Plague of Mysticism." *JQR* 49 (1958): 145–55.

Zenker, J.-Th. *Quarante questions addressées par les docteurs Juifs au prophète Mahomet (Qyrq Su'al).* Vienna, 1851.

Zenner, Walyer P. *See under* Deshen.

Zerkechi. *Ta'rikh ed-dasolateyn.* Ar. text (no. 1874 in *Catalogue of the Bibliothèque nationale*). MS no. 853. Tunis.

Zikier, M. [Zucker]. "Beirurim be-Toldot ha-Vikuhim ha-Datiyyim she-bein ha-Yahadut ve-ha-Islam (Heb.)." In *Festschrift Armand Kaminka zum Siebzigsten Geburtstage*. Vienna, 1937: 31–48.

Zir, Ali Muhammad. *Mu'tazilat al-Yaman: Dawlat al-Hadi wa-Fikruhu*. San'a-Beirut, 1981.

Zisser, Eyal. "The Return of Hizbullah." *Middle East Quarterly* 9, no. 4 (Fall 2002). http://www.meforum .org/article/499#_ftnref26 (accessed October 1, 2007).

Abu Zuhra. *Al-Imam Zayd*. Abidin, 1959.

Zunz, Leopold. *Namen der Juden. Eine geschichtliche Untersuchung*. Leipzig, 1837.

Zurkani. *See under* Malik ibn Anas, *Sharh 'al-Zurqani.*

Index of Places

Index of Persons, Peoples, Organizations, and Institutions

COMPILER'S REMARKS

Alphabetization ignores titles and common prefixes (e.g., al-, b., Abu, Ibn, Umm, de, and von), except "Abd" and "Ben-," also within names.

People are listed as they are usually named. Thus, most authors and modern names are by last name (e.g., Abbas, Mahmoud), whereas older names are often by first name (e.g., Abbas b. Bishr).

ABBREVIATIONS

b.	bin, ben
BF	biblical figure
Muh.	Muhammad